COLLINS COMPACT GERMAN DICTIONARY

GERMAN ▶ ENGLISH ENGLISH ▶ GERMAN

HarperCollins*Publishers*

First published in this edition 1993

© William Collins Sons & Co. Ltd. 1989

First reprint 1993

ISBN 0 00 470298 0

*A catalogue record for this book
is available from the British Library*

*Printed in Great Britain by
HarperCollins Manufacturing, Glasgow*

INTRODUCTION

This dictionary of German and English is designed to provide the user with wide-ranging and up-to-date coverage of the two languages, and is ideal for both school and reference use.

A special feature of Collins dictionaries is the comprehensive 'signposting' of meanings on both sides of the dictionary, guiding the user to the most appropriate translation for a given context. We hope you will find this dictionary easy and pleasant to consult for all your study and reference needs.

ABKÜRZUNGEN

ABBREVIATIONS

Adjektiv	**a**	adjective
Abkürzung	**abk, abbr**	abbreviation
Akkusativ	**acc**	accusative
Adverb	**ad**	adverb
Landwirtschaft	**AGR**	agriculture
Akkusativ	**akk**	accusative
Anatomie	**ANAT**	anatomy
Architektur	**ARCHIT**	architecture
Artikel	**art**	article
Astrologie	**ASTROL**	astrology
Astronomie	**ASTRON**	astronomy
attributiv	**attr**	attributive
Kraftfahrzeuge	**AUT**	automobiles
Hilfsverb	**aux**	auxiliary
Luftfahrt	**AVIAT**	aviation
besonders	**bes**	especially
Biologie	**BIOL**	biology
Botanik	**BOT**	botany
britisch	**Brit**	British
Chemie	**CHEM**	chemistry
Film	**CINE**	cinema
Konjunktion	**cj**	conjunction
umgangssprachlich (! vulgär)	**col(!)**	colloquial (! particularly offensive)
Handel	**COMM**	commerce
Komparativ	**comp**	comparative
Computer	**COMPUT**	computing
Kochen und Backen	**COOK**	cooking
zusammengesetztes Wort	**cpd**	compound
Dativ	**dat**	dative
kirchlich	**ECCL**	ecclesiastical
Eisenbahn	**EISENB**	railways
Elektrizität	**ELEK, ELEC**	electricity
besonders	**esp**	especially
und so weiter	**etc**	et cetera
etwas	**etw**	something
Euphemismus, Hüllwort	**euph**	euphemism
Femininum	**f**	feminine
übertragen	**fig**	figurative
Finanzwesen	**FIN**	finance
Genitiv	**gen**	genitive
Geographie	**GEOG**	geography
Geologie	**GEOL**	geology
Grammatik	**GRAM**	grammar
Geschichte	**HIST**	history
unpersönlich	**impers**	impersonal
unbestimmt	**indef**	indefinite
nicht getrennt gebraucht	**insep**	inseparable
Interjektion, Ausruf	**interj**	interjection
interrogativ, fragend	**interrog**	interrogative

ABKÜRZUNGEN

ABBREVIATIONS

unveränderlich	**inv**	invariable
unregelmäßig	**irreg**	irregular
jemand	**jd**	somebody
jemandem	**jdm**	(to) somebody
jemanden	**jdn**	somebody
jemandes	**jds**	somebody's
Rechtswesen	**JUR**	law
Konjunktion	**kj**	conjunction
Kochen und Backen	**KOCH**	cooking
Komparativ	**komp**	comparative
Sprachwissenschaft	**LING**	linguistics
wörtlich	**lit**	literal
literarisch	**liter**	literary
Literatur	**LITER**	of literature
Maskulinum	**m**	masculine
Mathematik	**MATH**	mathematics
Medizin	**MED**	medicine
Meteorologie	**MET**	meteorology
militärisch	**MIL**	military
Bergbau	**MIN**	mining
Musik	**MUS**	music
Substantiv, Hauptwort	**n**	noun
nautisch, Seefahrt	**NAUT**	nautical, naval
Nominativ	**nom**	nominative
Neutrum	**nt**	neuter
Zahlwort	**num**	numeral
Objekt	**obj**	object
oder	**od**	or
sich	**o.s.**	oneself
Parlament	**PARL**	parliament
abschätzig	**pej**	pejorative
Photographie	**PHOT**	photography
Physik	**PHYS**	physics
Plural	**pl**	plural
Politik	**POL**	politics
besitzanzeigend	**poss**	possessive
Partizip Perfekt	**pp**	past participle
Präfix, Vorsilbe	**präf, pref**	prefix
Präposition	**präp, prep**	preposition
Typographie	**PRINT**	printing
Pronomen, Fürwort	**pron**	pronoun
Psychologie	**PSYCH**	psychology
1. Vergangenheit, Imperfekt	**pt**	past tense
Radio	**RAD**	radio
Eisenbahn	**RAIL**	railways
Relativ-	**rel**	relative
Religion	**REL**	religion
jemand(-en, -em)	**sb**	someone, somebody
Schulwesen	**SCH**	school

ABKÜRZUNGEN

ABBREVIATIONS

Naturwissenschaft	SCI	science
schottisch	Scot	Scottish
Singular, Einzahl	sing	singular
etwas	sth	something
Suffix, Nachsilbe	suff	suffix
Superlativ	superl	superlative
Technik	TECH	technology
Nachrichtentechnik	TEL	telecommunications
Theater	THEAT	theatre
Fernsehen	TV	television
Typographie	TYP	printing
umgangssprachlich (! vulgär)	umg(!)	colloquial (! particularly offensive)
Hochschulwesen	UNIV	university
unpersönlich	unpers	impersonal
unregelmäßig	unreg	irregular
(nord)amerikanisch	US	(North) America
gewöhnlich	usu	usually
Verb	v	verb
intransitives Verb	vi	intransitive verb
reflexives Verb	vr	reflexive verb
transitives Verb	vt	transitive verb
Zoologie	ZOOL	zoology
zusammengesetztes Wort	zW	compound
zwischen zwei Sprechern	—	change of speaker
ungefähre Entsprechung	≃	cultural equivalent
eingetragenes Warenzeichen	®	registered trademark

REGULAR GERMAN NOUN ENDINGS

nom		*gen*	*pl*
-ant	*m*	-anten	-anten
-anz	*f*	-anz	-anzen
-ar	*m*	-ar(e)s	-are
-chen	*nt*	-chens	-chen
-ei	*f*	-ei	-eien
-elle	*f*	-elle	-ellen
-ent	*m*	-enten	-enten
-enz	*f*	-enz	-enzen
-ette	*f*	-ette	-etten
-eur	*m*	-eurs	-eure
-euse	*f*	-euse	-eusen
-heit	*f*	-heit	-heiten
-ie	*f*	-ie	-ien
-ik	*f*	-ik	-iken
-in	*f*	-in	-innen
-ine	*f*	-ine	-inen
-ion	*f*	-ion	-ionen
-ist	*m*	-isten	-isten
-ium	*nt*	-iums	-ien
-ius	*m*	-ius	-iusse
-ive	*f*	-ive	-iven
-keit	*f*	-keit	-keiten
-lein	*nt*	-leins	-lein
-ling	*m*	-lings	-linge
-ment	*nt*	-ments	-mente
-mus	*m*	-mus	-men
-schaft	*f*	-schaft	-schaften
-tät	*f*	-tät	-täten
-tor	*m*	-tors	-toren
-ung	*f*	-ung	-ungen
-ur	*f*	-ur	-uren

PHONETIC SYMBOLS / LAUTSCHRIFT

[ː] *length mark   Längezeichen* ['] *stress mark   Betonung*
['] *glottal stop   Knacklaut*

all vowel sounds are approximate only
alle Vokallaute sind nur ungefähre Entsprechungen

lie	[aɪ]	weit	day	[eɪ]	
now	[aʊ]	Haut	girl	[ɜː]	
above	[ə]	bitte	board	[ɔː]	
green	[iː]	viel	root	[uː]	Hut
pity	[ɪ]	Bischof	come	[ʌ]	Butler
rot	[ɒ,ɔ]	Post	salon	[ɔ̃]	Champignon
full	[ʊ]	Pult	avant (garde)	[ɑ̃]	Ensemble
			fair	[ɛə]	mehr
bet	[b]	Ball	beer	[ɪə]	Bier
dim	[d]	dann	toy	[ɔɪ]	Heu
face	[f]	Faß	pure	[ʊə]	
go	[g]	Gast	wine	[w]	
hit	[h]	Herr	thin	[θ]	
you	[j]	ja	this	[ð]	
cat	[k]	kalt			
lick	[l]	Last	Hast	[a]	mash
must	[m]	Mast	Ensemble	[ã]	avant (garde)
nut	[n]	Nuß	Metall	[e]	meths
bang	[ŋ]	lang	häßlich	[ɛ]	
pepper	[p]	Pakt	Cousin	[ɛ̃]	
sit	[s]	Rasse	vital	[i]	
shame	[ʃ]	Schal	Moral	[o]	
tell	[t]	Tal	Champignon	[õ]	salon
vine	[v]	was	ökonomisch	[ø]	
loch	[x]	Bach	gönnen	[œ]	
zero	[z]	Hase	Heu	[ɔy]	toy
leisure	[ʒ]	Genie	kulant	[u]	
			physisch	[y]	
bat	[æ]		Müll	[ʏ]	
farm	[ɑː]	Bahn	ich	[ç]	
set	[e]	Kette			

[⋆]   r can be pronounced before a vowel; Bindungs-R

DEUTSCH - ENGLISCH
GERMAN - ENGLISH

A

A, a [a:] *nt* A, a.

à [a] *präp* at.

Aal [a:l] *m* **-(e)s, -e** eel.

Aas [a:s] *nt* **-es, -e** *od* **Äser** carrion; **~geier** *m* vulture.

ab [ap] ◆*präp +dat* from; **Kinder ~ 12 Jahren** children from the age of 12; **~ morgen** from tomorrow; **~ sofort** as of now
◆*ad* **1** off; **links ~** to the left; **der Knopf ist ~** the button has come off; **~ nach Hause!** off you go home
2 (*zeitlich*): **von da ~** from then on; **von heute ~** from today, as of today
3 (*auf Fahrplänen*): **München ~ 12.20** leaving Munich 12.20
4 **~ und zu** *od* **an** now and then *od* again.

Abänderung ['ap'ɛndərʊŋ] *f* alteration.

Abart ['ap'a:rt] *f* (*BIOL*) variety; **a~ig** *a* abnormal.

Abbau ['apbaʊ] *m* **-(e)s** dismantling; (*Verminderung*) reduction (*gen* in); (*Verfall*) decline (*gen* in); (*MIN*) mining; quarrying; (*CHEM*) decomposition; **a~en** *vt* dismantle; (*MIN*) mine; quarry; (*verringern*) reduce; (*CHEM*) break down.

abbeißen ['apbaɪsən] *vt unreg* bite off.

Abberufung ['apbəru:fʊŋ] *f* recall.

abbestellen ['apbəʃtɛlən] *vt* cancel.

abbezahlen ['apbətsa:lən] *vt* pay off.

abbiegen ['apbi:gən] *unreg vi* turn off; (*Straße*) bend // *vt* bend; (*verhindern*) ward off.

Abbild ['apbɪlt] *nt* portrayal; (*einer Person*) image, likeness; **a~en** ['apbɪldən] *vt* portray; **~ung** *f* illustration.

Abbitte ['apbɪtə] *f*: **~ leisten** *od* **tun** make one's apologies (*bei* to).

abblenden ['apblɛndən] *vti* (*AUT*) dip (*Brit*), dim (*US*).

Abblendlicht *nt* dipped (*Brit*) *od* dimmed (*US*) headlights *pl*.

abbrechen ['apbrɛçən] *vti unreg* break off; (*Gebäude*) pull down; (*Zelt*) take down; (*aufhören*) stop; (*COMPUT*) abort.

abbrennen ['apbrɛnən] *unreg vt* burn off; (*Feuerwerk*) let off // *vi* (*aux sein*) burn down.

abbringen ['apbrɪŋən] *vt unreg*: **jdn von etw ~** dissuade sb from sth; **jdn vom Weg ~** divert sb.

abbröckeln ['apbrœkəln] *vti* crumble off *od* away.

Abbruch ['apbrʊx] *m* (*von Verhandlungen etc*) breaking off; (*von Haus*) demolition; **jdm/etw ~ tun** harm sb/sth; **a~reif** *a* only fit for demolition.

abbrühen ['apbry:ən] *vt* scald; **abgebrüht** (*umg*) hard-boiled.

abbuchen ['apbu:xən] *vt* debit.

abbürsten ['apbyrstən] *vt* brush off.

abdanken ['apdaŋkən] *vi* resign; (*König*) abdicate.

Abdankung *f* resignation; abdication.

abdecken ['apdɛkən] *vt* uncover; (*Tisch*) clear; (*Loch*) cover.

abdichten ['apdıçtən] *vt* seal; (*NAUT*) caulk.

abdrehen ['apdre:ən] *vt* (*Gas*) turn off; (*Licht*) switch off; (*Film*) shoot // *vi* (*Schiff*) change course.

Abdruck ['apdrʊk] *m* (*Nachdrucken*) reprinting; (*Gedrucktes*) reprint; (*Gips~, Wachs~*) impression; (*Finger~*) print; **a~en** *vt* print, publish.

abdrücken ['apdrykən] *vt* make an impression of; (*Waffe*) fire; (*Person*) hug, squeeze.

Abend ['a:bənt] *m* **-s, -e** evening; **guten ~** good evening; **zu ~ essen** have dinner *od* supper; **a~** *ad* evening; **~brot** *nt*, **~essen** *nt* supper; **~kasse** *f* box office; **~kurs** *m* evening classes *pl*; **~land** *nt* West; **a~lich** *a* evening; **~mahl** *nt* Holy Communion; **~rot** *nt* sunset; **abends** *ad* in the evening.

Abenteuer ['a:bəntɔʏər] *nt* **-s, -** adventure; **a~lich** *a* adventurous.

Abenteurer *m* **-s, -** adventurer; **~in** *f* adventuress.

aber ['a:bər] *kj* but; (*jedoch*) however; **das ist ~ schön** that's really nice; **nun ist ~ Schluß!** now that's enough!; **vielen Dank — ~ bitte!** thanks a lot — you're welcome // *ad*: **tausend und ~ tausend** thousands upon thousands; **A~glaube** *m* superstition; **~gläubisch** *a* superstitious.

aberkennen ['ap'ɛrkɛnən] *vt unreg*: **jdm etw ~** deprive sb of sth, take sth (away) from sb.

Aberkennung *f* taking away.

abermals ['a:bərma:ls] *ad* once again.

Abf. *abk* (= *Abfahrt*) dep.

abfahren ['apfa:rən] *unreg vi* leave, depart // *vt* take *od* cart away; (*Strecke*) drive; (*Reifen*) wear; (*Fahrkarte*) use.

Abfahrt ['apfa:rt] *f* departure; (*SKI*) descent; (*Piste*) run; **Abfahrtslauf** *m* (*SKI*) descent, run down; **Abfahrtszeit** *f* departure time.

Abfall ['apfal] *m* waste; (*von Speisen etc*) rubbish (*Brit*), garbage (*US*); (*Neigung*) slope; (*Verschlechterung*) decline; ~**eimer** *m* rubbish bin (*Brit*), garbage can (*US*); **a~en** *vi unreg* (*lit, fig*) fall *od* drop off; (*POL, vom Glauben*) break away; (*sich neigen*) fall *od* drop away.

abfällig ['apfɛlɪç] *a* disparaging, deprecatory.

abfangen ['apfaŋən] *vt unreg* intercept; (*Person*) catch; (*unter Kontrolle bringen*) check.

abfärben ['apfɛrbən] *vi* (*lit*) lose its colour; (*Wäsche*) run; (*fig*) rub off.

abfassen ['apfasən] *vt* write, draft.

abfertigen ['apfɛrtɪgən] *vt* prepare for dispatch, process; (*an der Grenze*) clear; (*Kundschaft*) attend to.

Abfertigung *f* preparing for dispatch, processing; clearance.

abfeuern ['apfɔʏərn] *vt* fire.

abfinden ['apfɪndən] *unreg vt* pay off // *vr* come to terms; **sich mit jdm** ~/**nicht** ~ put up with/not get on with sb.

Abfindung *f* (*von Gläubigern*) payment; (*Geld*) sum in settlement.

abflauen ['apflauən] *vi* (*Wind, Erregung*) die away, subside; (*Nachfrage, Geschäft*) fall *od* drop off.

abfliegen ['apfli:gən] *unreg vi* (*Flugzeug*) take off; (*Passagier auch*) fly // *vt* (*Gebiet*) fly over.

abfließen ['apfli:sən] *vi unreg* drain away.

Abflug ['apflu:k] *m* departure; (*Start*) take-off; ~**zeit** *f* departure time.

Abfluß ['apflʊs] *m* draining away; (*Öffnung*) outlet.

Abfuhr ['apfu:r] *f* -, -**en** removal; (*fig*) snub, rebuff.

abführen ['apfy:rən] *vt* lead away; (*Gelder, Steuern*) pay // *vi* (*MED*) have a laxative effect.

Abführmittel ['apfy:rmɪtəl] *nt* laxative, purgative.

abfüllen ['apfʏlən] *vt* draw off; (*in Flaschen*) bottle.

Abgabe ['apga:bə] *f* handing in; (*von Ball*) pass; (*Steuer*) tax; (*eines Amtes*) giving up; (*einer Erklärung*) giving.

Abgang ['apgaŋ] *m* (*von Schule*) leaving; (*THEAT*) exit; (*MED: Ausscheiden*) passing; (*Fehlgeburt*) miscarriage; (*Abfahrt*) departure; (*der*

Post, von Waren) dispatch.

Abgas ['apga:s] *nt* waste gas; (*AUT*) exhaust.

abgeben ['apge:bən] *unreg vt* (*Gegenstand*) hand *od* give in; (*Ball*) pass; (*Wärme*) give off; (*Amt*) hand over; (*Schuß*) fire; (*Erklärung, Urteil*) give; (*darstellen, sein*) make; **jdm etw** ~ (*überlassen*) let sb have sth // *vr*: **sich mit jdm/etw** ~ associate with sb/bother with sth.

abgehen ['apge:ən] *unreg vi* go away, leave; (*THEAT*) exit; (*Baby*) die; (*Knopf etc*) come off; (*abgezogen werden*) be taken off; (*Straße*) branch off; **etw geht jdm ab** (*fehlt*) sb lacks sth // *vt* (*Strecke*) go *od* walk along.

abgelegen ['apgəle:gən] *a* remote.

abgemacht ['apgəmaxt] *a* fixed; ~! done.

abgeneigt ['apgənaɪkt] *a* averse to, disinclined.

Abgeordnete(r) ['apgə'ɔrdnətə(r)] *mf* member of parliament; elected representative.

abgeschmackt ['apgəʃmakt] *a* tasteless.

abgesehen ['apgəze:ən] *a*: **es auf jdn/etw** ~ **haben** be after sb/sth; ~ **von** ... apart from ...

abgespannt ['apgəʃpant] *a* tired out.

abgestanden ['apgəʃtandən] *a* stale; (*Bier auch*) flat.

abgestorben ['apgəʃtɔrbən] *a* numb; (*BIOL, MED*) dead.

abgetragen ['apgətra:gən] *a* shabby, worn out.

abgewinnen ['apgəvɪnən] *vt unreg*: **einer Sache etw/Geschmack** ~ get sth/pleasure from sth.

abgewöhnen ['apgəvø:nən] *vt*: **jdm/sich etw** ~ cure sb of sth/give sth up.

abgleiten ['apglaɪtən] *vi unreg* slip, slide.

Abgott ['apgɔt] *m* idol.

abgöttisch ['apgœtɪʃ] *a*: ~ **lieben** idolize.

abgrenzen ['apgrɛntsən] *vt* (*lit, fig*) mark off; fence off.

Abgrund ['apgrʊnt] *m* (*lit, fig*) abyss.

abhacken ['aphakən] *vt* chop off.

abhalten ['aphaltən] *vt unreg* (*Versammlung*) hold; **jdn von etw** ~ (*fernhalten*) keep sb away from sth; (*hindern*) keep sb from sth.

abhanden [ap'handən] *a*: ~ **kommen** get lost.

Abhandlung ['aphandlʊŋ] *f* treatise, discourse.

Abhang ['aphaŋ] *m* slope.

abhängen ['aphɛŋən] *vt* (*Bild*) take down; (*Anhänger*) uncouple; (*Verfolger*) shake off // *vi unreg* (*Fleisch*) hang; **von jdm/etw** ~ depend on sb/

sth.

abhängig ['aphɛŋɪç] a dependent (von on); **A~keit** f dependence (von on).

abhärten ['aphɛrtən] vtr toughen (o.s.) up; **sich gegen etw ~** inure o.s. to sth.

abhauen ['aphaʊən] unreg vt cut off; (Baum) cut down // vi (umg) clear off od out.

abheben ['aphe:bən] unreg vt lift (up); (Karten) cut; (Masche) slip; (Geld) withdraw, take out // vi (Flugzeug) take off; (Rakete) lift off; (KARTEN) cut // vr stand out (von from), contrast (von with).

abhelfen ['aphɛlfən] vi unreg (+dat) remedy.

abhetzen ['aphɛtsən] vr wear od tire o.s. out.

Abhilfe ['aphɪlfə] f remedy; **~ schaffen** put things right.

abholen ['apho:lən] vt (Gegenstand) fetch, collect; (Person) call for; (am Bahnhof etc) pick up, meet.

abhören ['aphø:rən] vt (Vokabeln) test; (Telefongespräch) tap; (Tonband etc) listen to.

Abhörgerät nt bug.

Abitur [abi'tu:r] nt **-s, -e** German school leaving examination; **Abituri'ent(in** f) m candidate for school leaving certificate.

Abk. abk (= Abkürzung) abbr.

abkanzeln ['apkantsəln] vt (umg) bawl out.

abkapseln ['apkapsəln] vr shut od cut o.s. off.

abkaufen ['apkaʊfən] vt: **jdm etw ~** buy sth from sb.

abkehren ['apke:rən] vt (Blick) avert, turn away // vr turn away.

abklingen ['apklɪŋən] vi unreg die away; (Radio) fade out.

abknöpfen ['apknœpfən] vt unbutton; **jdm etw ~** (umg) get sth off sb.

abkochen ['apkɔxən] vt boil.

abkommen ['apkɔmən] vi unreg get away; **von der Straße/von einem Plan ~** leave the road/give up a plan; **A~** nt **-s, -** agreement.

abkömmlich ['apkœmlɪç] a available, free.

abkratzen ['apkratsən] vt scrape off // vi (umg) kick the bucket.

abkühlen ['apky:lən] vt cool down // vr (Mensch) cool down od off; (Wetter) get cool; (Zuneigung) cool.

abkürzen ['apkʏrtsən] vt shorten; (Wort auch) abbreviate; **den Weg ~** take a short cut.

Abkürzung f (Wort) abbreviation; (Weg) short cut.

abladen ['apla:dən] vt unreg unload.

Ablage ['apla:gə] f (für Akten) tray; (für Kleider) cloakroom.

ablassen ['aplasən] unreg vt (Wasser, Dampf) let off; (vom Preis) knock off // vi: **von etw ~** give sth up, abandon sth.

Ablauf ['aplaʊf] m (Abfluß) drain; (von Ereignissen) course; (einer Frist, Zeit) expiry (Brit), expiration (US); **a~en** unreg vi (abfließen) drain away; (Ereignisse) happen; (Frist, Zeit, Paß) expire // vt (Sohlen) wear (down od out).

ablegen ['aple:gən] vt put od lay down; (Kleider) take off; (Gewohnheit) get rid of; (Prüfung) take, sit; (Zeugnis) give.

Ableger m **-s, -** layer; (fig) branch, offshoot.

ablehnen ['aple:nən] vt reject; (Einladung) decline, refuse // vi decline, refuse.

Ablehnung f rejection; refusal.

ableiten ['aplaɪtən] vt (Wasser) divert; (deduzieren) deduce; (Wort) derive.

Ableitung f diversion; deduction; derivation; (Wort) derivative.

ablenken ['aplɛŋkən] vt turn away, deflect; (zerstreuen) distract // vi change the subject.

Ablenkung f distraction.

ablesen ['aple:zən] vt unreg read out; (Meßgeräte) read.

abliefern ['apli:fərn] vt deliver; **etw bei jdm/einer Dienststelle ~** hand sth over to sb/in at an office.

Ablieferung f delivery.

abliegen ['apli:gən] vi unreg be some distance away; (fig) be far removed.

ablösen ['aplø:zən] vt (abtrennen) take off, remove; (in Amt) take over from; (Wache) relieve.

Ablösung f removal; relieving.

abmachen ['apmaxən] vt take off; (vereinbaren) agree.

Abmachung f agreement.

abmagern ['apma:gərn] vi get thinner.

Abmagerungskur f diet; **eine ~ machen** go on a diet.

Abmarsch ['apmarʃ] m departure.

abmelden ['apmɛldən] vt (Zeitungen) cancel; (Auto) take off the road; **jdn bei der Polizei ~** register sb's departure with the police // vr give notice of one's departure; (im Hotel) check out.

abmessen ['apmɛsən] vt unreg measure.

Abmessung f measurement.

abmontieren ['apmɔnti:rən] vt take off.

abmühen ['apmy:ən] vr wear o.s. out.

Abnahme ['apna:mə] f **-, -n** removal; (COMM) buying; (Verringerung) decrease (gen in).

abnehmen ['apne:mən] unreg vt take

off, remove; (*Führerschein*) take away; (*Geld*) get (*jdm* out of sb); (*kaufen, umg: glauben*) buy (*jdm* from sb); (*Prüfung*) hold; (*Maschen*) decrease; **jdm Arbeit ~** take work off sb's shoulders // *vi* decrease; (*schlanker werden*) lose weight.

Abnehmer *m* **-s,** - purchaser, customer.

Abneigung ['apnaɪɡʊŋ] *f* aversion, dislike.

abnorm [ap'nɔrm] *a* abnormal.

abnutzen ['apnʊtsən] *vt* wear out.

Abnutzung *f* wear (and tear).

Abonnement [abɔn(ə)'maː] *nt* **-s, -s** subscription.

Abonnent(in *f*) [abɔ'nɛnt(ɪn)] *m* subscriber.

abonnieren [abɔ'niːrən] *vt* subscribe to.

Abordnung ['ap'ɔrdnʊŋ] *f* delegation.

Abort [a'bɔrt] *m* **-(e)s, -e** lavatory.

abpacken ['appakən] *vt* pack.

abpassen ['appasən] *vt* (*Person, Gelegenheit*) wait for; (*in Größe: Stoff etc*) adjust.

abpfeifen ['appfaɪfən] *vti unreg* (*SPORT*): (**das Spiel**) **~** blow the whistle (for the end of the game).

Abpfiff ['appfɪf] *m* final whistle.

abplagen ['applaːɡən] *vr* wear o.s. out.

Abprall ['appral] *m* rebound; (*von Kugel*) ricochet; **a~en** *vi* bounce off; ricochet.

abputzen ['apputsən] *vt* clean.

abraten ['apraːtən] *vi unreg* advise, warn (*jdm von etw* sb against sth).

abräumen ['aprɔymən] *vt* clear up *od* away.

abreagieren ['apreagiːrən] *vt* (*Zorn*) work off (*an +dat* on) // *vr* calm down.

abrechnen ['aprɛçnən] *vt* deduct, take off // *vi* (*lit*) settle up; (*fig*) get even.

Abrechnung *f* settlement; (*Rechnung*) bill.

Abrede ['apreːdə] *f*: **etw in ~ stellen** deny *od* dispute sth.

abregen ['apreːɡən] *vr* (*umg*) calm *od* cool down.

Abreise ['apraɪzə] *nf* departure; **a~n** *vi* leave, set off.

abreißen ['apraɪsən] *vt unreg* (*Haus*) tear down; (*Blatt*) tear off.

abrichten ['aprɪçtən] *vt* train.

abriegeln ['apriːɡəln] *vt* (*Tür*) bolt; (*Straße, Gebiet*) seal off.

Abriß ['aprɪs] *m* **-sses, -sse** (*Übersicht*) outline.

Abruf ['apruːf] *m*: **auf ~** on call; **a~en** *vt unreg* (*Mensch*) call away; (*COMM: Ware*) request delivery of.

abrunden ['aprʊndən] *vt* round off.

abrüsten ['apryːstən] *vi* disarm.

Abrüstung *f* disarmament.

abrutschen ['aprʊtʃən] *vi* slip; (*AVIAT*) sideslip.

Abs. *abk* (= *Absender*) sender, from.

Absage ['apzaːɡə] *f* **-, -n** refusal; **a~n** *vt* cancel, call off; (*Einladung*) turn down // *vi* cry off; (*ablehnen*) decline.

absägen ['apzɛːɡən] *vt* saw off.

Absatz ['apzats] *m* (*COMM*) sales *pl*; (*Bodensatz*) deposit; (*neuer Abschnitt*) paragraph; (*Treppen~*) landing; (*Schuh~*) heel; **~gebiet** *nt* (*COMM*) market.

abschaben ['apʃaːbən] *vt* scrape off; (*Möhren*) scrape.

abschaffen ['apʃafən] *vt* abolish, do away with.

Abschaffung *f* abolition.

abschalten ['apʃaltən] *vti* (*lit, umg*) switch off.

abschätzen ['apʃɛtsən] *vt* estimate; (*Lage*) assess; (*Person*) size up.

abschätzig ['apʃɛtsɪç] *a* disparaging, derogatory.

Abschaum ['apʃaʊm] *m* **-(e)s** scum.

Abscheu ['apʃɔy] *m* **-(e)s** loathing, repugnance; **a~erregend** *a* repulsive, loathsome; **a~lich** [ap'ʃɔylɪç] *a* abominable.

abschicken ['apʃɪkən] *vt* send off.

abschieben ['apʃiːbən] *vt unreg* push away; (*Person*) pack off.

Abschied ['apʃiːt] *m* **-(e)s, -e** parting; (*von Armee*) discharge; **~ nehmen** say good-bye (*von jdm* to sb), take one's leave (*von jdm* of sb); **seinen ~ nehmen** (*MIL*) apply for discharge; **Abschiedsbrief** *m* farewell letter.

abschießen ['apʃiːsən] *vt unreg* (*Flugzeug*) shoot down; (*Geschoß*) fire; (*umg: Minister*) get rid of.

abschirmen ['apʃɪrmən] *vt* screen.

abschlagen ['apʃlaːɡən] *vt unreg* (*abhacken, COMM*) knock off; (*ablehnen*) refuse; (*MIL*) repel.

abschlägig ['apʃlɛːɡɪç] *a* negative.

Abschlagszahlung *f* interim payment.

abschleifen ['apʃlaɪfən] *unreg vt* grind down; (*Rost*) polish off // *vr* wear off.

Abschlepp- ['apʃlɛp] *zW*: **~dienst** *m* (*AUT*) breakdown service (*Brit*), towing company (*US*); **a~en** *vt* (take in) tow; **~seil** *nt* towrope.

abschließen ['apʃliːsən] *unreg vt* (*Tür*) lock; (*beenden*) conclude, finish; (*Vertrag, Handel*) conclude // *vr* (*sich isolieren*) cut o.s. off.

Abschluß ['apʃlʊs] *m* (*Beendigung*) close, conclusion; (*COMM: Bilanz*) balancing; (*von Vertrag, Handel*) conclusion; **zum ~** in conclusion; **~prüfung** *f* final exam.

abschmieren ['apʃmiːrən] *vt* (*AUT*) grease, lubricate.

abschneiden ['apʃnaɪdən] *unreg vt* cut

off // vi do, come off.

Abschnitt ['apʃnɪt] m section; (MIL) sector; (Kontroll~) counterfoil; (MATH) segment; (Zeit~) period.

abschnüren ['apʃnyːrən] vt constrict.

abschöpfen ['apʃœpfən] vt skim off.

abschrauben ['apʃraubən] vt unscrew.

abschrecken ['apʃrekən] vt deter, put off; (mit kaltem Wasser) plunge in cold water; **~d** a deterrent; ~des Beispiel warning.

abschreiben ['apʃraibən] vt unreg copy; (verlorengeben) write off; (COMM) deduct.

Abschrift ['apʃrɪft] f copy.

Abschuß ['apʃus] m (eines Geschützes) firing; (Herunterschießen) shooting down; (Tötung) shooting.

abschüssig ['apʃʏsɪç] a steep.

abschütteln ['apʃʏtəln] vt shake off.

abschwächen ['apʃvɛçən] vt lessen; (Behauptung, Kritik) tone down // vr lessen.

abschweifen ['apʃvaifən] vi wander.

Abschweifung f digression.

abschwellen ['apʃvelən] vi unreg (Geschwulst) go down; (Lärm) die down.

abschwören ['apʃvøːrən] vi unreg (+dat) renounce.

abseh- ['apze:] zW: **~bar** a foreseeable; **in ~barer Zeit** in the foreseeable future; **das Ende ist ~bar** the end is in sight; **~en** unreg vt (Ende, Folgen) foresee // vi: **von etw ~en** refrain from sth; (nicht berücksichtigen) leave sth out of consideration.

abseits ['apzaits] ad out of the way // präp +gen away from; **A~** nt (SPORT) offside.

Absend- ['apzend] zW: **a~en** vt unreg send off, dispatch; **~er** m -s, - sender; **~ung** f dispatch.

absetz- ['apzets] zW: **~en** vt (niederstellen, aussteigen lassen) put down; (abnehmen) take off; (COMM: verkaufen) sell; (FIN: abziehen) deduct; (entlassen) dismiss; (König) depose; (streichen) drop; (hervorheben) pick out // vr (sich entfernen) clear off; (sich ablagern) be deposited; **A~ung** f (FIN: Abzug) deduction; (Entlassung) dismissal; (von König) deposing; (Streichung) dropping.

absichern ['apzɪçərn] vtr make safe; (schützen) safeguard.

Absicht ['apzɪçt] f intention; **mit ~** on purpose; **a~lich** a intentional, deliberate.

absinken ['apzɪŋkən] vi unreg sink; (Temperatur, Geschwindigkeit) decrease.

absitzen ['apzɪtsən] unreg vi dismount // vt (Strafe) serve.

absolut [apzo'lu:t] a absolute;

A~ismus [-'tɪsmʊs] m absolutism.

absolvieren [apzɔl'vi:rən] vt (SCH) complete.

absonder- ['apzɔndər] zW: **~lich** [ap'zɔndərlɪç] a odd, strange; **~n** vt separate; (ausscheiden) give off, secrete // vr cut o.s. off; **A~ung** f separation; (MED) secretion.

abspalten ['apʃpaltən] vt split off.

abspeisen ['apʃpaizən] vt (fig) fob off.

abspenstig ['apʃpenstɪç] a: **~ machen** lure away (jdm from sb).

absperren ['apʃperən] vt block od close off; (Tür) lock.

Absperrung f (Vorgang) blocking od closing off; (Sperre) barricade.

abspielen ['apʃpi:lən] vt (Platte, Tonband) play; (SPORT: Ball) pass // vr happen.

absplittern ['apʃplɪtərn] vt chip off.

Absprache ['apʃpra:xə] f arrangement.

absprechen ['apʃpreçən] vt unreg (vereinbaren) arrange; **jdm etw ~** deny sb sth.

abspringen ['apʃprɪŋən] vi unreg jump down/off; (Farbe, Lack) flake off; (AVIAT) bale out; (sich distanzieren) back out.

Absprung ['apʃprʊŋ] m jump.

abspülen ['apʃpy:lən] vt rinse; (Geschirr) wash up.

abstammen ['apʃtamən] vi be descended; (Wort) be derived.

Abstammung f descent; derivation.

Abstand ['apʃtant] m distance; (zeitlich) interval; **davon ~ nehmen, etw zu tun** refrain from doing sth; **~ halten** (AUT) keep one's distance; **mit ~ der beste** by far the best.

abstatten ['apʃtatən] vt (Dank) give; (Besuch) pay.

abstauben ['apʃtaubən] vti dust; (umg: stehlen) pinch.

Abstecher ['apʃteçər] m -s, - detour.

abstehen ['apʃte:ən] vi unreg (Ohren, Haare) stick out; (entfernt sein) stand away.

absteigen ['apʃtaigən] vi unreg (vom Rad etc) get off, dismount; (in Gasthof) put up (in +dat at); (SPORT) be relegated (in +akk to).

abstellen ['apʃtelən] vt (niederstellen) put down; (entfernt stellen) pull out; (hinstellen: Auto) park; (ausschalten) turn od switch off; (Mißstand, Unsitte) stop; (ausrichten) gear (auf +akk to).

Abstellgleis nt siding.

abstempeln ['apʃtempəln] vt stamp.

absterben ['apʃterbən] vi unreg die; (Körperteil) go numb.

Abstieg ['apʃti:k] m -(e)s, -e descent; (SPORT) relegation; (fig) decline.

abstimmen ['apʃtɪmən] vi vote // vt

(*Instrument*) tune (*auf* +*akk* to); (*Interessen*) match (*auf* +*akk* with); (*Termine, Ziele*) fit in (*auf* +*akk* with) // *vr* agree.

Abstimmung *f* vote.

Abstinenz [apsti'nɛnts] *f* abstinence; teetotalism; ~**ler(in** *f*) *m* -s, - teetotaller.

abstoßen ['apʃtoːsən] *vt unreg* push off *od* away; (*verkaufen*) unload; (*anekeln*) repel, repulse; ~**d** *a* repulsive.

abstrakt [ap'ʃtrakt] *a* abstract // *ad* abstractly, in the abstract.

abstreiten ['apʃtraitən] *vt unreg* deny.

Abstrich ['apʃtriç] *m* (*Abzug*) cut; (*MED*) smear; ~**e machen** lower one's sights.

abstufen ['apʃtuːfən] *vt* (*Hang*) terrace; (*Farben*) shade; (*Gehälter*) grade.

abstumpfen ['apʃtumpfən] *vt* (*lit, fig*) dull, blunt // *vi* (*lit, fig*) become dulled.

Absturz ['apʃturts] *m* fall; (*AVIAT*) crash.

abstürzen ['apʃtyrtsən] *vi* fall; (*AVIAT*) crash.

absuchen ['apzuːxən] *vt* scour, search.

absurd [ap'zurt] *a* absurd.

Abszeß [aps'tsɛs] *m* -**sses, -sse** abscess.

Abt [apt] *m* -**(e)s, ⁻e** abbot.

Abt. *abk* (= *Abteilung*) dept.

abtasten ['aptastən] *vt* feel, probe.

abtauen ['aptaʊən] *vti* thaw.

Abtei [ap'tai] *f* -, -**en** abbey.

Abteil [ap'tail] *nt* -**(e)s, -e** compartment; **a~en** *vt* divide up; (*abtrennen*) divide off; ~**ung** *f* (*in Firma, Kaufhaus*) department; (*in Krankenhaus*) section; (*MIL*) unit.

abtönen ['aptøːnən] *vt* (*PHOT*) tone down.

abtransportieren ['aptransportiːrən] *vt* take away, remove.

abtreiben ['aptraibən] *unreg vt* (*Boot, Flugzeug*) drive off course; (*Kind*) abort // *vi* be driven off course; abort.

Abtreibung *f* abortion.

abtrennen ['aptrɛnən] *vt* (*lostrennen*) detach; (*entfernen*) take off; (*abteilen*) separate off.

abtreten ['aptreːtən] *unreg vt* wear out; (*überlassen*) hand over, cede (*jdm* to sb) // *vi* go off; (*zurücktreten*) step down.

Abtritt ['aptrit] *m* resignation.

abtrocknen ['aptrɔknən] *vti* dry.

abtun ['aptuːn] *vt unreg* take off; (*fig*) dismiss.

abverlangen ['apfɛrlaŋən] *vt*: **jdm etw ~** demand sth from sb.

abwägen ['apvɛːgən] *vt unreg* weigh

up.

abwandeln ['apvandəln] *vt* adapt.

abwandern ['apvandərn] *vi* move away.

abwarten ['apvartən] *vt* wait for // *vi* wait.

abwärts ['apvɛrts] *ad* down.

Abwasch ['apvaʃ] *m* -**(e)s** washing-up; **a~en** *vt unreg* (*Schmutz*) wash off; (*Geschirr*) wash (up).

Abwasser ['apvasər] *nt* -**s, -wässer** sewage.

abwechseln ['apvɛksəln] *vir* alternate; (*Personen*) take turns; ~**d** *a* alternate.

Abwechslung *f* change.

Abweg ['apveːk] *m*: **auf ~e geraten/führen** go/lead astray; **a~ig** ['apvɛːgiç] *a* wrong.

Abwehr ['apveːr] *f* - defence; (*Schutz*) protection; (~*dienst*) counter intelligence (service); **a~en** *vt* ward off; (*Ball*) stop.

abweichen ['apvaiçən] *vi unreg* deviate; (*Meinung*) differ; ~**d** *a* deviant; differing.

abweisen ['apvaizən] *vt unreg* turn away; (*Antrag*) turn down; ~**d** *a* (*Haltung*) cold.

abwenden ['apvɛndən] *unreg vt* avert // *vr* turn away.

abwerfen ['apvɛrfən] *vt unreg* throw off; (*Profit*) yield; (*aus Flugzeug*) drop; (*Spielkarte*) discard.

abwerten ['apveːrtən] *vt* (*FIN*) devalue.

abwesend ['apveːzənt] *a* absent.

Abwesenheit ['apveːzənhait] *f* absence.

abwickeln ['apvikəln] *vt* unwind; (*Geschäft*) wind up.

abwiegen ['apviːgən] *vt unreg* weigh out.

abwischen ['apviʃən] *vt* wipe off *od* away; (*putzen*) wipe.

Abwurf ['apvurf] *m* throwing off; (*von Bomben etc*) dropping; (*von Reiter, SPORT*) throw.

abwürgen ['apvʏrgən] *vt* (*umg*) scotch; (*Motor*) stall.

abzahlen ['aptsaːlən] *vt* pay off.

abzählen ['aptsɛːlən] *vti* count (up).

Abzahlung *f* repayment; **auf ~ kaufen** buy on hire purchase.

abzapfen ['aptsapfən] *vt* draw off; **jdm Blut ~** take blood from sb.

abzäunen ['aptsɔʏnən] *vt* fence off.

Abzeichen ['aptsaiçən] *nt* badge; (*Orden*) decoration.

abzeichnen ['aptsaiçnən] *vt* draw, copy; (*Dokument*) initial // *vr* stand out; (*fig: bevorstehen*) loom.

Abziehbild *nt* transfer.

abziehen ['aptsiːən] *unreg vt* take off; (*Tier*) skin; (*Bett*) strip; (*Truppen*)

withdraw; (*subtrahieren*) take away, subtract; (*kopieren*) run off // *vi* go away; (*Truppen*) withdraw.
abzielen ['aptsi:lən] *vi* be aimed (*auf* +*akk* at).
Abzug ['aptsu:k] *m* departure; (*von Truppen*) withdrawal; (*Kopie*) copy; (*Subtraktion*) subtraction; (*Betrag*) deduction; (*Rauch~*) flue; (*von Waffen*) trigger.
abzüglich ['aptsy:klɪç] *präp* +*gen* less.
abzweigen ['aptsvaɪɡən] *vi* branch off // *vt* set aside.
Abzweigung *f* junction.
ach [ax] *interj* oh; ~ **ja!** (oh) yes; ~ **so!** I see; **mit A~ und Krach** by the skin of one's teeth.
Achse ['aksə] *f* -, -**n** axis; (*AUT*) axle.
Achsel ['aksəl] *f* -, -**n** shoulder; ~**höhle** *f* armpit; ~**zucken** *nt* shrug (of one's shoulders).
acht [axt] *num* eight; **sich in ~ nehmen** be careful (*vor* +*dat* of), watch out (*vor* +*dat* for); **etw außer ~ lassen** disregard sth; ~ **Tage** a week; ~**bar** *a* worthy; ~**e(r, s)** *a* eighth; ~**el** *num* eighth; ~**en** *vt* respect // *vi* pay attention (*auf* +*akk* to); **darauf ~en, daß ...** be careful that ...
ächten ['ɛçtən] *vt* outlaw, ban.
Achter- ['axtər] *zW*: ~**bahn** *f* roller coaster; ~**deck** *nt* (*NAUT*) afterdeck.
acht- *zW*: ~**fach** *a* eightfold; ~**geben** *vi unreg* take care (*auf* +*akk* of); ~**los** *a* careless; ~**mal** *ad* eight times; ~**sam** *a* attentive.
Achtung ['axtʊŋ] *f* attention; (*Ehrfurcht*) respect; **alle ~!** good for you/him *etc* // *interj* look out!; (*MIL*) attention!
achtzehn *num* eighteen.
achtzig *num* eighty.
ächzen ['ɛçtsən] *vi* groan (*vor* +*dat* with).
Acker ['akər] *m* -**s**, ⁔ field; ~**bau** *m* agriculture; **a~n** *vti* plough; (*umg*) slog away.
ADAC [a:de:'a:tse:] *abk* (= *Allgemeiner Deutscher Automobil-Club*) ≈ AA, RAC.
addieren [a'di:rən] *vt* add (up).
Addition [aditsi'o:n] *f* addition.
Adel ['a:dəl] *m* -**s** nobility; **a~ig, adlig** *a* noble.
Ader ['a:dər] *f* -, -**n** vein.
Adler ['a:dlər] *m* -**s**, - eagle.
Admiral [atmi'ra:l] *m* -**s**, -**e** admiral; **Admiralität** *f* admiralty.
adopt- *zW*: ~**ieren** [adɔp'ti:rən] *vt* adopt; **A~ion** [adɔptsi'o:n] *f* adoption; **A~iveltern** [adɔp'ti:f-] *pl* adoptive parents *pl*; **A~ivkind** *nt* adopted child.
Adress- *zW*: ~**ant** [adrɛ'sant] *m* send-

er; ~**at** [adrɛ'sa:t] *m* -**en**, -**en** addressee; ~**e** [a'drɛsə] *f* -, -**n** address; **a~ieren** [adrɛ'si:rən] *vt* address (*an* +*akk* to).
Adria ['a:dria] *f* - Adriatic.
Advent [at'vɛnt] *m* -(**e**)**s**, -**e** Advent; **Adventskranz** *m* Advent wreath.
aero- [aero] *präf* aero-.
Aerobic [ae'rɔbɪk] *nt* aerobics.
Affäre [a'fɛ:rə] *f* -, -**n** affair.
Affe ['afə] *m* -**n**, -**n** monkey.
affektiert [afɛk'ti:rt] *a* affected.
Affen- *zW*: **a~artig** *a* like a monkey; **mit a~artiger Geschwindigkeit** like a flash; ~**hitze** *f* (*umg*) incredible heat; ~**schande** *f* (*umg*) crying shame.
affig ['afɪç] *a* affected.
Afrika ['a:frika] *nt* -**s** Africa; ~**ner(in** *f*) [-'ka:nər(ɪn)] *m* -**s**, - African; **a~nisch** [-'ka:nɪʃ] *a* African.
After ['aftər] *m* -**s**, - anus.
AG [a:'ge:] *abk* (= *Aktiengesellschaft*) (*Brit*) (public) limited company, Ltd; (*US*) corporation, Inc.
ägäisch [ɛ'gɛ:ɪʃ] *a*: **~es Meer** Aegean.
Agent [a'gɛnt] *m* agent; **Agentur** [agɛn'tu:r] *f* agency.
Aggregat [agre'ga:t] *nt* -(**e**)**s**, -**e** aggregate; (*TECH*) unit; ~**zustand** *m* (*PHYS*) state.
Aggress- *zW*: ~**ion** [agresi'o:n] *f* aggression; **a~iv** [agrɛ'si:f] *a* aggressive; ~**ivität** [agresivi'tɛ:t] *f* aggressiveness.
Agitation [agitatsi'o:n] *f* agitation.
Agrar- [a'gra:r] *zW*: ~**politik** *f* agricultural policy; ~**staat** *m* agrarian state.
Ägypt- [ɛ'gʏpt] *zW*: ~**en** *nt* -**s** Egypt; ~**er(in** *f*) *m* -**s**, - Egyptian; **ä~isch** *a* Egyptian.
ah [a:] *interj* ah.
aha [a'ha:] *interj* aha.
Ahn [a:n] *m* -**en**, -**en** forebear.
ähneln ['ɛ:nəln] *vi* (+*dat*) be like, resemble // *vr* be alike *od* similar.
ahnen ['a:nən] *vt* suspect; (*Tod, Gefahr*) have a presentiment of.
ähnlich ['ɛ:nlɪç] *a* similar (*dat* to); **Ä~keit** *f* similarity.
Ahnung ['a:nʊŋ] *f* idea, suspicion; presentiment; **a~slos** *a* unsuspecting.
Ahorn ['a:hɔrn] *m* -**s**, -**e** maple.
Ähre ['ɛ:rə] *f* -, -**n** ear.
Aids [e:dz] *nt* AIDS.
Akademie [akade'mi:] *f* academy.
Akademiker(in *f*) [aka'de:mikər(ɪn)] *m* -**s**, - university graduate.
akademisch *a* academic.
akklimatisieren [aklimati'zi:rən] *vr* become acclimatized.
Akkord [a'kɔrt] *m* -(**e**)**s**, -**e** (*MUS*) chord; **im ~ arbeiten** do piecework; ~**arbeit** *f* piecework; **Akkordeon**

[a'kɔrdeɔn] *nt* **-s, -s** accordion.
Akrobat(in *f*) [akro'baːt(ɪn)] *m* **-en, -en** acrobat.
Akt [akt] *m* **-(e)s, -e** act; (*KUNST*) nude.
Akte ['aktə] *f* **-, -n** file; **aktenkundig** *a* on the files; **Aktenschrank** *m* filing cabinet; **Aktentasche** *f* briefcase.
Aktie ['aktsiə] *f* **-, -n** share.
Aktien- *zW*: **~emission** *f* share issue; **~gesellschaft** *f* joint-stock company; **~kurs** *m* share price.
Aktion [aktsi'oːn] *f* campaign; (*Polizei~, Such~*) action; **~är** [-'nɛːr] *m* **-s, -e** shareholder.
aktiv [ak'tiːf] *a* active; (*MIL*) regular; **~ieren** [-'viːrən] *vt* activate; **A~i'tät** *f* activity.
Aktualität [aktuali'tɛːt] *f* topicality; (*einer Mode*) up-to-dateness.
aktuell [aktu'ɛl] *a* topical; up-to-date.
Akustik [a'kʊstɪk] *f* acoustics *pl*.
akut [a'kuːt] *a* acute.
AKW [aːkaː'veː] *nt abk von* **Atomkraftwerk**.
Akzent [ak'tsɛnt] *m* accent; (*Betonung*) stress.
akzeptieren [aktsep'tiːrən] *vt* accept.
Alarm [a'larm] *m* **-(e)s, -e** alarm; **a~bereit** *a* standing by; **~bereitschaft** *f* stand-by; **a~ieren** [-'miːrən] *vt* alarm.
Alban- [al'baːn] *zW*: **~ien** *nt* **-s** - Albania; **~ier(in** *f*) *m* **-s,** - Albanian; **a~isch** *a* Albanian.
albern ['albərn] *a* silly.
Album ['albʊm] *nt* **-s, Alben** album.
Algebra ['algebra] *f* - algebra.
Alger- [al'geːr] *zW*: **~ien** *nt* **-s** Algeria; **~ier(in** *f*) *m* **-s,** - Algerian; **a~isch** *a* Algerian.
alias ['aːlias] *ad* alias.
Alibi ['aːlibi] *nt* **-s, -s** alibi.
Alimente [ali'mɛntə] *pl* alimony.
Alkohol ['alkohoːl] *m* **-s, -e** alcohol; **a~frei** *a* non-alcoholic; **~iker(in** *f*) [alko'hoːlikər(ɪn)] *m* **-s,** - alcoholic; **a~isch** *a* alcoholic; **~verbot** *nt* ban on alcohol.
All [al] *nt* **-s** universe; **a~'abendlich** *a* every evening; **'a~bekannt** *a* universally known.
alle(r, s) ['alə(r, s)] ◆ *a* **1** (*sämtliche*) all; **wir ~** all of us; **~ Kinder waren da** all the children were there; **~ Kinder mögen ... all** children like ...; **~ beide** both of us/them; **sie kamen ~** they all came; **~s Gute** all the best; **~s in ~m** all in all
2 (*mit Zeit- oder Maßangaben*) every; **~ vier Jahre** every four years; **~ fünf Meter** every five metres
◆ *pron* everything; **~s was er sagt** everything he says, all that he says

◆ *ad* (*zu Ende, aufgebraucht*) finished; **die Milch ist ~** the milk's all gone, there's no milk left; **etw ~ machen** finish sth up.
Allee [a'leː] *f* **-, -n** avenue.
allein [a'laɪn] *ad* alone; (*ohne Hilfe*) on one's own, by oneself; **nicht ~** (*nicht nur*) not only // *kj* but, only **A~erziehende(r)** *mf* single parent; **A~gang** *m*: **im A~gang** on one's own; **A~herrscher** *m* autocrat; **~stehend** *a* single.
allemal ['aləˈmaːl] *ad* (*jedesmal*) always; (*ohne weiteres*) with no bother; **ein für ~mal** once and for all.
allenfalls ['alənfals] *ad* at all events; (*höchstens*) at most.
aller- ['alər] *zW*: **~beste(r, s)** *a* very best; **~dings** *ad* (*zwar*) admittedly; (*gewiß*) certainly.
Allergie [aler'giː] *f* allergy; **allergisch** [a'lergɪʃ] *a* allergic.
aller- *zW*: **~hand** *a inv* (*umg*) all sorts of; **das ist doch ~hand!** that's a bit much; **~hand!** (*lobend*) good show!; **A~'heiligen** *nt* All Saints' Day; **~höchstens** *ad* at the very most; **~lei** *a inv* all sorts of; **~letzte(r, s)** *a* very last; **~seits** *ad* on all sides; **prost ~seits!** cheers everyone!; **~wenigste(r, s)** *a* very least.
alles *pron* everything; **~ in allem** all in all; **~ Gute!** all the best!
allgemein ['algəˈmaɪn] *a* general; **im ~en** in general; **~gültig** *a* generally accepted; **A~heit** *f* (*Menschen*) general public; (*pl: Redensarten*) general remarks *pl*.
Alliierte(r) [ali'iːrtə(r)] *m* ally.
all- *zW*: **~jährlich** *a* annual; **~mählich** *a* gradual; **A~tag** *m* everyday life; **~täglich** *a,ad* daily; (*gewöhnlich*) commonplace; **~tags** *ad* on weekdays; **~'wissend** *a* omniscient; **~zu** *ad* all too; **~zuoft** *ad* all too often; **~zuviel** *ad* too much.
Almosen ['almoːzən] *nt* **-s,** - alms *pl*.
Alpen ['alpən] *pl* Alps *pl*.
Alphabet [alfa'beːt] *nt* **-(e)s, -e** alphabet; **a~isch** *a* alphabetical.
Alptraum ['alptraʊm] *m* nightmare.
als [als] *kj* **1** (*zeitlich*) when; (*gleichzeitig*) as; **damals, ~ ...** (in the days) when ...; **gerade, ~ ...** just as ...
2 (*in der Eigenschaft*) as; **~ Antwort** as an answer; **~ Kind** as a child
3 (*bei Vergleichen*) than; **ich kam später ~ er** I came later than he (did) *od* later than him; **lieber ... ~** rather ... than; **nichts ~ Ärger** nothing but trouble
4: **~ ob/wenn** as if.
also ['alzoː] *kj* so; (*folglich*) therefore;

~ **gut** *od* **schön!** okay then; ~, **so was!** well really!; **na** ~! there you are then!

alt [alt] *a* old; **alles beim** ~**en lassen** leave everything as it was; **A**~ *m* **-s, -e** (*MUS*) alto; **Altar** [al'ta:r] *m* **-(e)s, -äre** altar; ~**bekannt** *a* long-known; **A**~'**eisen** *nt* scrap iron.

Alter ['altər] *nt* **-s,** - age; (*hohes*) old age; **im** ~ **von** at the age of; **a**~**n** *vi* grow old, age.

Alternativ- [alternati'ti:f] *in zW* alternative; ~**e** *f* alternative.

Alters- *zW*: ~**grenze** *f* age limit; ~**heim** *nt* old people's home; ~**versorgung** *f* old age pension.

Altertum *nt* antiquity.

alt- *zW*: **A**~**glascontainer** *m* bottle bank; ~'**hergebracht** *a* traditional; ~**klug** *a* precocious; ~**modisch** *a* old-fashioned; **A**~**papier** *nt* waste paper; **A**~**stadt** *f* old town.

Aluminium [alu'mi:niom] *nt* **-s** aluminium, aluminum (*US*); ~**folie** *f* tinfoil.

am [am] = **an dem**; ~ **Schlafen** (*umg*) sleeping; ~ **15. März** on March 15th; ~ **besten/schönsten** best/ most beautiful.

Amateur [ama'tø:r] *m* amateur.

Amboß ['ambɔs] *m* **-sses, -sse** anvil.

ambulant [ambu'lant] *a* outpatient.

Ambulanz [ambu'lants] *f* outpatients *sing.*

Ameise ['a:maizə] *f* **-, -n** ant.

Amerika [a'me:rika] *nt* **-s** America; ~**ner(in** *f*) [-'ka:nər(ın)] *m* **-s,** - American; **a**~**nisch** [-'ka:nıʃ] *a* American.

Ampel ['ampəl] *f* **-, -n** traffic lights *pl.*

amputieren [ampu'ti:rən] *vt* amputate.

Amsel ['amzəl] *f* **-, -n** blackbird.

Amt [amt] *nt* **-(e)s, -er** office; (*Pflicht*) duty; (*TEL*) exchange; **a**~**ieren** [am'ti:rən] *vi* hold office; **a**~**lich** *a* official.

Amts- *zW*: ~**person** *f* official; ~**richter** *m* district judge; ~**stunden** *pl* office hours *pl*; ~**zeit** *f* period of office.

amüsant [amy'zant] *a* amusing.

amüsieren [amy'zi:rən] *vt* amuse // *vr* enjoy o.s.

an [an] ◆ *präp* +*dat* **1** (*räumlich: wo?*) at; (*auf, bei*) on; (*nahe bei*) near; ~ **diesem Ort** at this place; ~ **der Wand** on the wall; **zu nahe** ~ **etw** too near to sth; **unten am Fluß** down by the river; **Köln liegt am Rhein** Cologne is on the Rhine.

2 (*zeitlich: wann?*) on; ~ **diesem Tag** on this day; ~ **Ostern** at Easter

3: **arm** ~ **Fett** low in fat; ~ **etw sterben** die of sth; ~ (**und für**) **sich** actually

◆ *präp* +*akk* **1** (*räumlich: wohin?*) to; **er ging** ~**s Fenster** he went (over) to the window; **etw** ~ **die Wand hängen/schreiben** hang/write sth on the wall

2 (*zeitlich: woran?*): ~ **etw denken** think of sth

3 (*gerichtet* ~) to; **ein Gruß/eine Frage** ~ **dich** greetings/a question to you

◆ *ad* **1** (*ungefähr*) about: ~ **die hundert** about a hundred

2 (*auf Fahrplänen*): **Frankfurt** ~ **18.30** arriving Frankfurt 18.30

3 (*ab*): **von dort/heute** ~ from there/ today onwards

4 (~*geschaltet,* ~*gezogen*) on; **das Licht ist** ~ the light is on; **ohne etwas** ~ with nothing on

◆ *siehe auch* **am**.

analog [ana'lo:k] *a* analogous; **A**~**ie** [-'gi:] *f* analogy.

Analyse [ana'ly:zə] *f* **-, -n** analysis.

analysieren [analy'zi:rən] *vt* analyse.

Ananas ['ananas] *f* **-,** - *od* **-se** pineapple.

Anarchie [anar'çi:] *f* anarchy.

Anatomie [anato'mi:] *f* anatomy.

anbahnen ['anba:nən] *vr* open up.

Anbau ['anbau] *m* (*AGR*) cultivation; (*Gebäude*) extension; **a**~**en** *vt* (*AGR*) cultivate; (*Gebäudeteil*) build on.

anbehalten ['anbəhaltən] *vt unreg* keep on.

anbei [an'bai] *ad* enclosed.

anbeißen ['anbaisən] *unreg vt* bite into // *vi* (*lit*) bite; (*fig*) swallow the bait; **zum A**~ (*umg*) good enough to eat.

anbelangen ['anbəlaŋən] *vt* concern; **was mich anbelangt** as far as I am concerned.

anbeten ['anbe:tən] *vt* worship.

Anbetracht ['anbətraxt] *m*: **in** ~ (+*gen*) in view of.

anbiedern ['anbi:dərn] *vr* make up (*bei* to).

anbieten ['anbi:tən] *unreg vt* offer // *vr* volunteer.

anbinden ['anbindən] *vt unreg* tie up; **kurz angebunden** (*fig*) curt.

Anblick ['anblık] *m* sight; **a**~**en** *vt* look at.

anbrechen ['anbrɛçən] *unreg vt* start; (*Vorräte*) break into // *vi* start; (*Tag*) break; (*Nacht*) fall.

anbrennen ['anbrɛnən] *vi unreg* catch fire; (*KOCH*) burn.

anbringen ['anbrıŋən] *vt unreg* bring; (*Ware*) sell; (*festmachen*) fasten.

Anbruch ['anbrux] *m* beginning; ~ **des Tages/der Nacht** dawn/ nightfall.

anbrüllen ['anbrylən] *vt* roar at.

Andacht ['andaxt] *f* **-, -en** devotion; (*Gottesdienst*) prayers *pl.*

andächtig ['andɛçtɪç] *a* devout.
andauern ['andaʊərn] *vi* last, go on; **~d** *a* continual.
Anden ['andən] *pl* Andes.
Andenken ['andɛŋkən] *nt* **-s**, - memory; souvenir.
andere(r, s) ['andərə(r,z)] *a* other; (*verschieden*) different; **ein ~s Mal** another time; **kein ~r** nobody else; **von etw ~m sprechen** talk about sth else; **andererseits** *ad* on the other hand.
ändern ['ɛndərn] *vt* alter, change // *vr* change.
andernfalls ['andərnfals] *ad* otherwise.
anders ['andərs] *ad* differently (*als* from); **wer ~?** who else?; **jd/ irgendwo ~** sb/somewhere else; **~ aussehen/klingen** look/sound different; **~artig** *a* different; **~farbig** *a* of a different colour; **~herum** *ad* the other way round; **~wo** *ad* somewhere else; **~woher** *ad* from somewhere else.
anderthalb ['andərt'halp] *a* one and a half.
Änderung ['ɛndərʊŋ] *f* alteration, change.
anderweitig ['andər'vaɪtɪç] *a* other // *ad* otherwise; (*anderswo*) elsewhere.
andeuten ['andɔʏtən] *vt* indicate; (*Wink geben*) hint at.
Andeutung *f* indication; hint.
Andrang ['andraŋ] *m* crush.
andrehen ['andre:ən] *vt* turn *od* switch on; (*umg*) **jdm etw ~** unload sth onto sb.
androhen ['andro:ən] *vt:* **jdm etw ~** threaten sb with sth.
aneignen ['an'aignən] *vt:* **sich** (*dat*) **etw ~** acquire sth; (*widerrechtlich*) appropriate sth.
aneinander [an'aɪ'nandər] *ad* at/on/to etc one another *od* each other; **~fügen** *vt* put together; **~geraten** *vi unreg* clash.
anekeln ['an'e:kəln] *vt* disgust.
Anemone [ane'mo:nə] *f* -, **-n** anemone.
anerkannt ['an'ɛrkant] *a* recognized, acknowledged.
anerkennen ['an'ɛrkɛnən] *vt unreg* recognize, acknowledge; (*würdigen*) appreciate; **~d** *a* appreciative; **anerkennenswert** *a* praiseworthy.
Anerkennung *f* recognition, acknowledgement; appreciation.
anfachen ['anfaxən] *vt* (*lit*) fan into flame; (*fig*) kindle.
anfahren ['anfa:rən] *unreg vt* deliver; (*fahren gegen*) hit; (*Hafen*) put into; (*fig*) bawl out // *vi* drive up; (*losfahren*) drive off.
Anfall ['anfal] *m* (*MED*) attack; **a~en** *unreg vt* attack; (*fig*) overcome // *vi* (*Arbeit*) come up; (*Produkt*) be ob-

tained.
anfällig ['anfɛlɪç] *a* delicate; **~ für etw** prone to sth.
Anfang ['anfaŋ] *m* **-(e)s, -fänge** beginning, start; **von ~ an** right from the beginning; **zu ~** at the beginning; **~ Mai** at the beginning of May; **a~en** *vti unreg* begin, start; (*machen*) do.
Anfänger(in *f*) ['anfɛŋər(ɪn)] *m* **-s**, - beginner.
anfänglich ['anfɛŋlɪç] *a* initial.
anfangs *ad* at first; **A~buchstabe** *m* initial *od* first letter; **A~stadium** *nt* initial stages *pl*.
anfassen ['anfasən] *vt* handle; (*berühren*) touch // *vi* lend a hand // *vr* feel.
anfechten ['anfɛçtən] *vt unreg* dispute; (*beunruhigen*) trouble.
anfertigen ['anfɛrtɪgən] *vt* make.
anfeuern ['anfɔʏərn] *vt* (*fig*) spur on.
anflehen ['anfle:ən] *vt* implore.
anfliegen ['anfli:gən] *vt unreg* fly to.
Anflug ['anflu:k] *m* (*AVIAT*) approach; (*Spur*) trace.
anfordern ['anfɔrdərn] *vt* demand; (*COMM*) requisition.
Anforderung *f* demand (*gen* for).
Anfrage ['anfra:gə] *f* inquiry; **a~n** *vi* inquire.
anfreunden ['anfrɔʏndən] *vr* make friends.
anfügen ['anfy:gən] *vt* add; (*beifügen*) enclose.
anfühlen ['anfy:lən] *vtr* feel.
anführen ['anfy:rən] *vt* lead; (*zitieren*) quote; (*umg: betrügen*) lead up the garden path.
Anführer *m* leader.
Anführung *f* leadership; (*Zitat*) quotation; **Anführungszeichen** *pl* quotation marks *pl*, inverted commas *pl*.
Angabe ['anga:bə] *f* statement; (*TECH*) specification; (*umg: Prahlerei*) boasting; (*SPORT*) service; **~n** *pl* (*Auskunft*) particulars *pl*.
angeben ['ange:bən] *unreg vt* give; (*anzeigen*) inform on; (*bestimmen*) set // *vi* (*umg*) boast; (*SPORT*) serve.
Angeber *m* **-s**, - (*umg*) show-off; **~ei** [-'raɪ] *f* (*umg*) showing off.
angeblich ['ange:plɪç] *a* alleged.
angeboren ['angəbo:rən] *a* inborn, innate (*jdm* in sb).
Angebot ['angəbo:t] *nt* offer; (*COMM*) supply (*an* +*dat* of).
angebracht ['angəbraxt] *a* appropriate, in order.
angegriffen ['angəgrɪfən] *a* exhausted.
angeheitert ['angəhaɪtərt] *a* tipsy.
angehen ['ange:ən] *unreg vt* concern; (*angreifen*) attack; (*bitten*) approach (*um* for) // *vi* (*Feuer*) light; (*umg: beginnen*) begin; **~d** *a* prospective.
angehören ['angəhø:rən] *vi* belong (*dat* to).

Angehörige(r) *mf* relative.

Angeklagte(r) ['angəkla:ktə(r)] *mf* accused.

Angel ['aŋəl] *f* -, -n fishing rod; (*Tür*-) hinge.

Angelegenheit ['angələ:gənhaɪt] *f* affair, matter.

Angel- *zW*: **~haken** *m* fish hook; **a~n** *vt* catch // *vi* fish; **~n** *nt* -s angling, fishing; **~rute** *f* fishing rod.

angemessen ['angəmɛsən] *a* appropriate, suitable.

angenehm ['angəne:m] *a* pleasant; **~**! (*bei Vorstellung*) pleased to meet you.

angenommen ['angənɔmən] *a* assumed; **~, wir ...** assuming we ...

angesehen ['angəze:ən] *a* respected.

angesichts ['angəzɪçts] *präp* +*gen* in view of, considering.

angespannt ['angəʃpant] *a* (*Aufmerksamkeit*) close; (*Arbeit*) hard.

Angestellte(r) ['angəʃtɛltə(r)] *mf* employee.

angetan ['angəta:n] *a*: **von jdm/etw ~ sein** be impressed by sb/sth; **es jdm ~ haben** appeal to sb.

angewiesen ['angəvi:zən] *a*: **auf jdn/ etw ~ sein** be dependent on sb/sth.

angewöhnen ['angəvø:nən] *vt*: **jdm/ sich etw ~** get sb/become accustomed to sth.

Angewohnheit ['angəvo:nhaɪt] *f* habit.

angleichen ['anglaɪçən] *vtr unreg* adjust (*dat* to).

Angler ['aŋlər] *m* -s, - angler.

angreifen ['angraɪfən] *vt unreg* attack; (*anfassen*) touch; (*Arbeit*) tackle; (*beschädigen*) damage.

Angreifer *m* -s, - attacker.

Angriff ['angrɪf] *m* attack; **etw in ~ nehmen** make a start on sth.

Angst [aŋst] *f* -, ¨e fear; **~ haben** be afraid *od* scared (*vor* +*dat* of); **~ haben um jdn/etw** be worried about sb/sth; **a~** *a*: **jdm ist a~** sb is afraid *od* scared; **jdm a~ machen** scare sb; **~hase** *m* (*umg*) chicken, scaredycat.

ängst- [ɛŋst] *zW*: **~igen** *vt* frighten // *vr* worry (o.s.) (*vor* +*dat*, *um* about); **~lich** *a* nervous; (*besorgt*) worried; **Ä~lichkeit** *f* nervousness.

anhaben ['anha:bən] *vt unreg* have on; **er kann mir nichts ~** he can't hurt me.

anhalt- ['anhalt] *zW*: **~en** *vt unreg* stop; (*gegen etw halten*) hold up (*jdm* against sb); **jdn zur Arbeit/ Höflichkeit ~en** make sb work/be polite // *vi* stop; (*andauern*) persist; **~end** *a* persistent; **A~er** *m* -s, - hitch-hiker; **per A~er fahren** hitchhike; **Anhaltspunkt** *m* clue.

anhand [an'hant] *präp* +*gen* with.

Anhang ['anhaŋ] *m* appendix; (*Leute*) family; supporters *pl*.

anhäng- ['anhɛŋ] *zW*: **~en** *vt unreg* hang up; (*Wagen*) couple up; (*Zusatz*) add (on); **A~er** *m* -s, - supporter; (*AUT*) trailer; (*am Koffer*) tag; (*Schmuck*) pendant; **A~erschaft** *f* supporters *pl*; **~lich** *a* devoted; **A~lichkeit** *f* devotion; **A~sel** *nt* -s, - appendage.

Anhäufung ['anhɔyfʊŋ] *f* accumulation.

anheben ['anhe:bən] *vt unreg* lift up; (*Preise*) raise.

Anhieb ['anhi:b] *m*: **auf ~** at the very first go; (*kurz entschlossen*) on the spur of the moment.

Anhöhe ['anhø:ə] *f* hill.

anhören ['anhø:rən] *vt* listen to; (*anmerken*) hear // *vr* sound.

animieren [ani'mi:rən] *vt* encourage, urge on.

Anis [a'ni:s] *m* -es, -e aniseed.

Ank. *abk* (= *Ankunft*) arr.

ankaufen ['ankaufən] *vt* purchase, buy.

Anker ['aŋkər] *m* -s, - anchor; **vor ~ gehen** drop anchor; **a~n** *vti* anchor; **~platz** *m* anchorage.

Anklage ['ankla:gə] *f* accusation; (*JUR*) charge; **~bank** *f* dock; **a~n** *vt* accuse; (*JUR*) charge (*gen* with).

Ankläger ['anklɛ:gər] *m* accuser.

Anklang ['anklaŋ] *m*: **bei jdm ~ finden** meet with sb's approval.

Ankleide- ['anklaɪdə] *zW*: **~kabine** *f* changing cubicle; **a~n** *vtr* dress.

anklopfen ['anklɔpfən] *vi* knock.

anknüpfen ['anknʏpfən] *vt* fasten *od* tie on; (*fig*) start // *vi* (*anschließen*) refer (*an* +*akk* to).

ankommen ['ankɔmən] *vi unreg* arrive; (*näherkommen*) approach; (*Anklang finden*) go down (*bei* with); **es kommt darauf an** it depends; (*wichtig sein*) that (is what) matters; **es darauf ~ lassen** let things take their course; **gegen jdn/etw ~** cope with sb/sth.

ankündigen ['ankʏndɪgən] *vt* announce.

Ankündigung *f* announcement.

Ankunft ['ankʊnft] *f* -, -künfte arrival.

Ankunftszeit *f* time of arrival.

ankurbeln ['ankʊrbəln] *vt* (*AUT*) crank; (*fig*) boost.

Anlage ['anla:gə] *f* disposition; (*Begabung*) talent; (*Park*) gardens *pl*; (*Beilage*) enclosure; (*TECH*) plant; (*FIN*) investment; (*Entwurf*) layout.

Anlaß ['anlas] *m* -sses, -lässe cause (*zu* for); (*Ereignis*) occasion; **aus ~** (+*gen*) on the occasion of; **~ zu etw geben** give rise to sth; **etw zum ~ nehmen** take the opportunity of sth.

anlassen *unreg vt* leave on; *(Motor)* start // *vr (umg)* start off.

Anlasser *m* -s, - *(AUT)* starter.

anläßlich ['anlɛslɪç] *präp* +*gen* on the occasion of.

Anlauf ['anlaʊf] *m* run-up; **a~en** *unreg vi* begin; *(Film)* show; *(SPORT)* run up; *(Fenster)* mist up; *(Metall)* tarnish; **rot a~en** colour; **angelaufen kommen** come running up // *vt* call at.

anlegen ['anle:gən] *vt* put *(an +akk* against/on); *(anziehen)* put on; *(gestalten)* lay out; *(Geld)* invest; *(Gewehr)* aim *(auf +akk* at); **es auf etw** *(akk)* ~ be out for sth/to do sth; **sich mit jdm** ~ *(umg)* quarrel with sb // *vi* call.

Anlegestelle *f*, landing place.

anlehnen ['anle:nən] *vt* lean *(an +akk* against); *(Tür)* leave ajar // *vr* lean *(an +akk* on).

anleiten ['anlaɪtən] *vt* instruct.

Anleitung *f* instructions *pl*.

anlernen ['anlɛrnən] *vt* teach, instruct.

anliegen ['anli:gən] *vi unreg (Kleidung)* cling; **A~** *nt* -s, - matter; *(Wunsch)* wish; **~d** *a* adjacent; *(beigefügt)* enclosed.

Anlieger *m* -s, - resident; '~ **frei**' 'residents only'.

anlügen ['anly:gən] *vt unreg* lie to.

anmachen ['anmaxən] *vt* attach; *(Elektrisches)* put on; *(Zigarette)* light; *(Salat)* dress.

anmaßen ['anma:sən] *vt*: **sich** *(dat)* **etw** ~ *(Recht)* lay claim to sth; **~d** *a* arrogant.

Anmaßung *f* presumption.

anmelden ['anmɛldən] *vt* announce // *vr (sich ankündigen)* make an appointment; *(polizeilich, für Kurs etc)* register.

Anmeldung *f* announcement; appointment; registration.

anmerken ['anmɛrkən] *vt* observe; *(anstreichen)* mark; **sich** *(dat)* **nichts** ~ **lassen** not give anything away.

Anmerkung *f* note.

Anmut ['anmu:t] *f* - grace; **a~en** *vt* give a feeling; **a~ig** *a* charming.

annähern ['annɛ:ərn] *vr* get closer; **~d** *a* approximate.

Annäherung *f* approach; **Annäherungsversuch** *m* advances *pl*.

Annahme ['anna:mə] *f* -, -n acceptance; *(Vermutung)* assumption.

annehm- ['anne:m] *zW*: **~bar** *a* acceptable; **~en** *unreg vt* accept; *(Namen)* take; *(Kind)* adopt; *(vermuten)* suppose, assume // *vr* take care *(gen* of); **A~lichkeit** *f* comfort.

Annonce [a'nõ:sə] *f* -, -n advertisement.

annoncieren [anõ'si:rən] *vti* advertise.

annullieren [anʊ'li:rən] *vt* annul.

anöden ['an'ø:dən] *vt (umg)* bore stiff.

anonym [ano'ny:m] *a* anonymous.

Anorak ['anorak] *m* -s, -s anorak.

anordnen ['an'ɔrdnən] *vt* arrange; *(befehlen)* order.

Anordnung *f* arrangement; order.

anpacken ['anpakən] *vt* grasp; *(fig)* tackle; **mit** ~ lend a hand.

anpassen ['anpasən] *vt* fit *(jdm sb)*; *(fig)* adapt *(dat* to) // *vr* adapt.

Anpassung *f* fitting; adaptation; **anpassungsfähig** *a* adaptable.

Anpfiff ['anpfɪf] *m (SPORT)* (starting) whistle; kick-off; *(umg)* rocket.

Anprall ['anpral] *m* collision *(gegen, an +akk* with).

anprangern ['anpraŋərn] *vt* denounce.

anpreisen ['anpraɪzən] *vt unreg* extol.

Anprobe ['anpro:bə] *f* trying on.

anprobieren ['anprobi:rən] *vt* try on.

anrechnen ['anrɛçnən] *vt* charge; *(fig)* count; **jdm etw hoch** ~ value sb's sth greatly.

Anrecht ['anrɛçt] *nt* right *(auf +akk* to).

Anrede ['anre:də] *f* form of address; **a~n** *vt* address; *(belästigen)* accost.

anregen ['anre:gən] *vt* stimulate; **angeregte Unterhaltung** lively discussion; **~d** *a* stimulating.

Anregung *f* stimulation; *(Vorschlag)* suggestion.

anreichern ['anraɪçərn] *vt* enrich.

Anreise ['anraɪzə] *f* journey; **a~n** *vi* arrive.

Anreiz ['anraɪts] *m* incentive.

Anrichte ['anrɪçtə] *f* -, -n sideboard; **a~n** *vt* serve up; **Unheil a~n** make mischief.

anrüchig ['anryçɪç] *a* dubious.

anrücken ['anrʏkən] *vi* approach; *(MIL)* advance.

Anruf ['anru:f] *m* call; **a~en** *vt unreg* call out to; *(bitten)* call on; *(TEL)* ring up, phone, call.

ans [ans] = **an das.**

Ansage ['anza:gə] *f* -, -n announcement; **a~n** *vt* announce // *vr* say one will come; **Ansager(in** *f)* *m* -s, - announcer.

Ansammlung *f* collection; *(Leute)* crowd.

ansässig ['anzɛsɪç] *a* resident.

Ansatz ['anzats] *m* start; *(Haar~)* hairline; *(Hals~)* base; *(Verlängerungsstück)* extension; *(Veranschlagung)* estimate; **~punkt** *m* starting point.

anschaffen ['anʃafən] *vt* buy, purchase.

Anschaffung *f* purchase.

anschalten ['anʃaltən] *vt* switch on.

anschau- ['anʃaʊ] *zW*: **~en** *vt* look at;

~lich a illustrative; **A~ung** f (Meinung) view; **aus eigener A~ung** from one's own experience.

Anschein ['anʃain] m appearance; **allem ~ nach** to all appearances; **den ~ haben** seem, appear; **a~end** a apparent.

Anschlag ['anʃlaːk] m notice; (Attentat) attack; (COMM) estimate; (auf Klavier) touch; (Schreibmaschine) character; **a~en** ['anʃlaːgən] unreg vt put up; (beschädigen) chip; (Akkord) strike; (Kosten) estimate // vi hit (an +akk against); (wirken) have an effect; (Glocke) ring; (Hund) bark.

anschließen ['anʃliːsən] unreg vt connect up; (Sender) link up // vir: (sich) an etw (akk) ~ adjoin sth; (zeitlich) follow sth // vr join (jdm/ etw sb/sth); (beipflichten) agree (jdm/etw with sb/sth); **~d** a adjacent; (zeitlich) subsequent // ad afterwards.

Anschluß ['anʃlus] m (ELEK, EISENB) connection; (von Wasser etc) supply; **im ~ an** (+akk) following; **~ finden** make friends.

anschmiegsam ['anʃmiːkzaːm] a affectionate.

anschnallen ['anʃnalən] vt buckle on // vr fasten one's seat belt.

anschneiden ['anʃnaidən] vt unreg cut into; (Thema) introduce.

anschreiben ['anʃraibən] vt unreg write (up); (COMM) charge up; (benachrichtigen) write to.

anschreien ['anʃraiən] vt unreg shout at.

Anschrift ['anʃrift] f address.

Anschuldigung ['anʃuldigʊŋ] f accusation.

anschwellen ['anʃvɛlən] vi unreg swell (up).

anschwemmen ['anʃvɛmən] vt wash ashore.

anschwindeln ['anʃvindəln] vt lie to.

ansehen ['anzeːən] vt unreg look at; **jdm etw ~** see sth (from sb's face); **jdn/etw als etw ~** look on sb/sth as sth; **~ für** consider; **A~** nt **-s** respect; (Ruf) reputation.

ansehnlich ['anzeːnlɪç] a fine-looking; (beträchtlich) considerable.

ansetzen ['anzɛtsən] vt (anfügen) fix on (an +akk to); (anlegen, an Mund etc) put (an +akk to); (festlegen) fix; (entwickeln) develop; (Fett) put on; (Blätter) grow; (zubereiten) prepare // vi (anfangen) start, begin; (Entwicklung) set in; (dick werden) put on weight // vr (Rost etc) start to develop.

Ansicht ['anzɪçt] f (Anblick) sight; (Meinung) view, opinion; **zur ~** on approval; **meiner ~ nach** in my opinion; **Ansichtskarte** f picture postcard; **Ansichtssache** f matter of opinion.

anspannen ['anʃpanən] vt harness; (Muskel) strain.

Anspannung f strain.

Anspiel ['anʃpiːl] nt (SPORT) start; **a~en** vi (SPORT) start play; **auf etw** (akk) **a~en** refer od allude to sth; **~ung** f reference, allusion (auf +akk to).

Ansporn ['anʃpɔrn] m **-(e)s** incentive.

Ansprache ['anʃpraːxə] f address.

ansprechen ['anʃprɛçən] unreg vt speak to (bitten, gefallen) appeal to; **jdn auf etw** (akk) (hin) **~** ask sb about sth // vi react (auf +akk to); **~d** a attractive.

anspringen ['anʃprɪŋən] unreg vi (AUT) start // vt jump at.

Anspruch ['anʃprux] m (Recht) claim (auf +akk to); **hohe Ansprüche stellen/haben** demand/expect a lot; **jdn/etw in ~ nehmen** occupy sb/take up sth; **anspruchslos** a undemanding; **anspruchsvoll** a demanding.

anstacheln ['anʃtaxəln] vt spur on.

Anstalt ['anʃtalt] f **-, -en** institution; **~en machen, etw zu tun** prepare to do sth.

Anstand ['anʃtant] m decency.

anständig ['anʃtɛndɪç] a decent; (umg) proper; (groß) considerable.

anstandslos ad without any ado.

anstarren ['anʃtarən] vt stare at.

anstatt [an'ʃtat] präp +gen instead of // kj: **~ etw zu tun** instead of doing sth.

Ansteck- ['anʃtɛk] zW: **a~en** vt pin on; (MED) infect; (Pfeife) light; (Haus) set fire to // vr: **ich habe mich bei ihm angesteckt** I caught it from him // vi (fig) be infectious; **a~end** a infectious; **~ung** f infection.

anstehen ['anʃteːən] vi unreg queue (up) (Brit), line up (US).

anstelle [an'ʃtɛlə] präp +gen in place of; **~n** [an'-] vt (einschalten) turn on; (Arbeit geben) employ; (machen) do // vr queue (up) (Brit), line up (US); (umg) act.

Anstellung f employment; (Posten) post, position.

Anstieg ['anʃtiːk] m **-(e)s, -e** climb; (fig: von Preisen etc) increase (gen in).

anstift- ['anʃtift] zW: **~en** vt (Unglück) cause; **jdn zu etw ~en** put sb up to sth; **A~er** m **-s, -** instigator.

anstimmen ['anʃtɪmən] vt (Lied) strike up with; (Geschrei) set up.

Anstoß ['anʃtoːs] m impetus; (Ärgernis) offence; (SPORT) kick-off; **der erste ~** the initiative; **~ nehmen an** (+dat) take offence at; **a~en** unreg *vt* push; (*mit Fuß*) kick // *vi* knock, bump; (*mit der Zunge*) lisp; (*mit Gläsern*) drink (a toast) (*auf +akk* to).

anstößig ['anʃtøːsɪç] *a* offensive, indecent; **A~keit** *f* indecency, offensiveness.

anstreichen ['anʃtraiçən] *vt unreg* paint.

Anstreicher *m* **-s,** - painter.

anstrengen ['anʃtrɛŋən] *vt* strain; (*JUR*) bring // *vr* make an effort; **angestrengt** *ad* as hard as one can; **~d** *a* tiring.

Anstrengung *f* effort.

Anstrich ['anʃtrɪç] *m* coat of paint.

Ansturm ['anʃtʊrm] *m* rush; (*MIL*) attack.

Antarktis [ant''arktɪs] *f* - Antarctic.

antasten ['antastən] *vt* touch; (*Recht*) infringe upon; (*Ehre*) question.

Anteil ['antail] *m* **-s, -e** share (*an +dat* in); (*Mitgefühl*) sympathy; **~ nehmen an** (*+dat*) share in; (*sich interessieren*) take an interest in; **~nahme** *f* - sympathy.

Antenne [an'tɛnə] *f* **-, -n** aerial.

Anti- ['anti] *in zW* anti; **~alko'holiker** *m* teetotaller; **a~autori'tär** *a* antiauthoritarian; **~biotikum** [anti-bi'oːtikʊm] *nt* **-s, -ka** antibiotic.

antik [an'tiːk] *a* antique; **A~e** *f* **-, -n** (*Zeitalter*) ancient world; (*Kunstgegenstand*) antique.

Antilope [anti'loːpə] *f* **-, -n** antelope.

Antipathie [antipa'tiː] *f* antipathy.

Antiquariat [antikvari'aːt] *nt* **-(e)s, -e** secondhand bookshop.

Antiquitäten [antikvi'tɛːtən] *pl* antiques *pl*; **~händler** *m* antique dealer.

Antrag ['antraːk] *m* **-(e)s, -träge** proposal; (*PARL*) motion; (*Gesuch*) application.

antreffen ['antrɛfən] *vt unreg* meet.

antreiben ['antraibən] *unreg vt* drive on; (*Motor*) drive; (*anschwemmen*) wash up // *vi* be washed up.

antreten ['antreːtən] *unreg vt* (*Amt*) take up; (*Erbschaft*) come into; (*Beweis*) offer; (*Reise*) start, begin // *vi* (*MIL*) fall in; (*SPORT*) line up; **gegen jdn ~** play/fight against sb.

Antrieb ['antriːp] *m* (*lit, fig*) drive; **aus eigenem ~** of one's own accord.

antrinken ['antrɪŋkən] *vt unreg* (*Flasche, Glas*) start to drink from; **sich** (*dat*) **Mut/einen Rausch ~** give oneself Dutch courage/get drunk; **angetrunken sein** be tipsy.

Antritt ['antrɪt] *m* beginning, commencement; (*eines Amts*) taking up.

antun ['antuːn] *vt unreg*: **jdm etw ~** do sth to sb; **sich** (*dat*) **Zwang ~** force o.s.; **sich** (*dat*) **etwas ~** (try to)

take one's own life.

Antwort ['antvɔrt] *f* **-, -en** answer, reply; **a~en** *vi* answer, reply.

anvertrauen ['anfɛrtrauən] *vt*: **jdm etw ~** entrust sb with sth; **sich jdm ~** confide in sb.

anwachsen ['anvaksən] *vi unreg* grow; (*Pflanze*) take root.

Anwalt ['anvalt] *m* **-(e)s, -wälte, Anwältin** ['anvɛltin] *f* solicitor; lawyer; (*fig*) champion.

Anwärter ['anvɛrtər] *m* candidate.

anweisen ['anvaizən] *vt unreg* instruct; (*zuteilen*) assign (*jdm etw* sth to sb).

Anweisung *f* instruction; (*COMM*) remittance; (*Post~, Zahlungs~*) money order.

anwend- ['anvɛnd] *zW*: **~bar** ['anvɛnt-] *a* practicable, applicable; **~en** *vt unreg* use, employ; (*Gesetz, Regel*) apply; **A~ung** *f* use; application.

Anwesen- ['anveːzən] *zW*: **a~d** *a* present; **die ~den** those present; **~heit** *f* presence.

anwidern ['anviːdərn] *vt* disgust.

Anzahl ['antsaːl] *f* number (*an +dat* of); **a~en** *vt* pay on account; **~ung** *f* deposit, payment on account.

Anzeichen ['antsaiçən] *nt* sign, indication.

Anzeige ['antsaigə] *f* **-, -n** (*Zeitungs~*) announcement; (*Werbung*) advertisement; (*bei Polizei*) report; **~ erstatten gegen jdn** report sb (to the police); **a~n** *vt* (*zu erkennen geben*) show; (*bekanntgeben*) announce; (*bei Polizei*) report; **~r** *m* indicator.

anziehen ['antsiːən] *unreg vt* attract; (*Kleidung*) put on; (*Mensch*) dress; (*Schraube, Seil*) pull tight; (*Knie*) draw up; (*Feuchtigkeit*) absorb // *vr* get dressed; **~d** *a* attractive.

Anziehung *f* (*Reiz*) attraction; **Anziehungskraft** *f* power of attraction; (*PHYS*) force of gravitation.

Anzug ['antsuːk] *m* suit; **im ~ sein** be approaching.

anzüglich ['antsyːklɪç] *a* personal; (*anstößig*) offensive; **A~keit** *f* offensiveness; (*Bemerkung*) personal remark.

anzünden ['antsyndən] *vt* light.

Anzünder *m* lighter.

anzweifeln ['antsvaifəln] *vt* doubt.

Apathie [apa'tiː] *f* apathy.

apathisch [a'paːtɪʃ] *a* apathetic.

Apfel ['apfəl] *m* **-s, ¨** apple; **~saft** *m* apple juice; **Apfelsine** [apfəl'ziːnə] *f* **-, -n** orange; **~wein** *m* cider.

Apostel [a'pɔstəl] *m* **-s,** - apostle.

Apostroph [apo'stroːf] *m* **-s, -e** apostrophe.

Apotheke [apo'teːkə] *f* **-, -n** chemist's

(shop), drugstore (US); **Apotheker(in** f) m -s, - chemist, druggist (US).

Apparat [apa'ra:t] m -(e)s, -e piece of apparatus; camera; telephone; (RAD. TV) set; **am ~!** speaking!; **~ur** [-'tu:r] f apparatus.

Appartement [apartə'mã:] nt -s, -s flat.

Appell [a'pɛl] m -s, -e (MIL) muster, parade; (fig) appeal; **a~ieren** [apɛ'li:rən] vi appeal (an +akk to).

Appetit [ape'ti:t] m -(e)s, -e appetite; **guten ~** enjoy your meal; **a~lich** a appetizing; **~losigkeit** f lack of appetite.

Applaus [ap'laus] m -es, -e applause.

Aprikose [apri'ko:zə] f -, -n apricot.

April [a'prɪl] m -(s), -e April.

Aquarell [akva'rɛl] nt -s, -e water-colour.

Aquarium [a'kva:riʊm] nt aquarium.

Äquator [ɛ'kva:tɔr] m -s equator.

Arab- ['arab] zW: **~er(in** f) m -s, - Arab; **~ien** [a'ra:biən] nt -s Arabia; **a~isch** [a'ra:bɪʃ] a Arabian.

Arbeit ['arbaɪt] f -, -en work (no art); (Stelle) job; (Erzeugnis) piece of work; (wissenschaftliche) dissertation; (Klassen~) test; **das war eine ~** that was a hard job; **a~en** vi work // vt work, make; **~er(in** f) m -s, - worker; (ungelernt) labourer; **~erschaft** f workers pl, labour force; **~geber** m -s, - employer; **~nehmer** m -s, - employee; **a~sam** a industrious.

Arbeits- in zW labour; **~amt** nt employment exchange; **a~fähig** a fit for work, able-bodied; **~gang** m operation; **~gericht** nt industrial tribunal; **~kräfte** pl workers pl, labour; **a~los** a unemployed, out-of-work; **~losigkeit** f unemployment; **~platz** m job; place of work; (Groß-raumbüro) workstation; **a~scheu** a work-shy; **~tag** m work(ing) day; **a~unfähig** a unfit for work; **~zeit** f working hours pl.

Archäologe [arçɛo'lo:gə] m -n, -n archaeologist.

Architekt(in f) [arçi'tɛkt(ɪn)] m -en, -en architect; **~ur** [-'tu:r] f architecture.

Archiv [ar'çi:f] nt -s, -e archive.

arg [ark] a bad, awful // ad awfully, very.

Argentin- [argen'ti:n] zW: **~ien** nt -s Argentina, the Argentine; **~ier(in** f) m -s, - Argentinian; **a~isch** a Argentinian.

Ärger ['ɛrgər] m -s (Wut) anger; (Un-annehmlichkeit) trouble; **ä~lich** a (zornig) angry; (lästig) annoying, aggravating; **ä~n** vt annoy // vr get annoyed; **~nis** nt -ses, -se annoyance.

arg- zW: **~listig** a cunning, insidious; **~los** a guileless, innocent; **A~losigkeit** f guilelessness, innocence; **Argument** [argu'mɛnt] nt argument; **A~wohn** m suspicion; **~wöhnisch** a suspicious.

Arie ['a:riə] f -, -n aria.

Aristokrat [arɪsto'kra:t] m -en, -en aristocrat; **~ie** [-'ti:] f aristocracy; **a~isch** a aristocratic.

Arktis ['arktɪs] f - Arctic.

arm [arm] a poor; **A~** m -(e)s, -e arm; (Fluß~) branch; **Arma'tur** f (ELEK) armature; **Arma'turenbrett** nt instrument panel; (AUT) dashboard; **A~band** nt bracelet; **A~banduhr** f (wrist) watch; **A~e(r)** mf poor man/woman; **die A~en** the poor; **Armee** [ar'me:] f -, -n army.

Ärmel ['ɛrməl] m -s, - sleeve; etw aus dem ~ schütteln (fig) produce sth just like that; **~kanal** m English Channel.

ärmlich ['ɛrmlɪç] a poor.

armselig a wretched, miserable.

Armut ['armu:t] f - poverty.

Aroma [a'ro:ma] nt -s, **Aromen** aroma; **aromatisch** [aro'ma:tɪʃ] a aromatic.

arrangieren [arã'ʒi:rən] vt arrange // vr come to an arrangement.

Arrest [a'rɛst] m -(e)s, -e detention.

arrogant [aro'gant] a arrogant.

Arroganz f arrogance.

Arsch [arʃ] m -es, -e (umg) arse, bum.

Art [a:rt] f -, -en (Weise) way; (Sorte) kind, sort; (BIOL) species; **eine ~ (von) Frucht** a kind of fruit; **Häuser aller ~** houses of all kinds; **es ist nicht seine ~, das zu tun** it's not like him to do that; **ich mache das auf meine ~** I do that my (own) way.

Arterie [ar'te:riə] f artery; **Arterien-verkalkung** f arteriosclerosis.

artig ['a:rtɪç] a good, well-behaved.

Artikel [ar'ti:kəl] m -s, - article.

Artillerie [artɪlə'ri:] f artillery.

Arznei [a:rts'naɪ] f medicine; **~mittel** nt medicine, medicament.

Arzt [a:rtst] m -es, -e, **Ärztin** ['ɛrtstɪn] f doctor.

ärztlich ['ɛ:rtstlɪç] a medical.

As [as] nt -ses, -se ace.

Asbest [as'bɛst] m -(e)s, -e asbestos.

Asche ['aʃə] f -, -n ash, cinder; **Aschenbahn** f cinder track; **Aschenbecher** m ashtray; **Aschermittwoch** m Ash Wednesday.

Asi- ['a:zi] zW: **~en** nt -s Asia; **~at(in** f) [azi'a:t(ɪn)] m -en, -en Asian; **a~atisch** [-'a:tɪʃ] a Asian.

asozial ['azotsia:l] a antisocial; (Familien) asocial.

Aspekt [as'pɛkt] m -(e)s, -e aspect.

Asphalt [as'falt] *m* **-(e)s, -e** asphalt; **a~ieren** [-'ti:rən] *vt* asphalt.

aß *v siehe* **essen**.

Assistent(in *f)* [asɪs'tɛnt(ɪn)] *m* assistant.

Assoziation [asotsiatsi'o:n] *f* association.

Ast [ast] *m* **-(e)s, ¨e** bough, branch; **~er** *f* **-, -n** aster.

ästhetisch [ɛs'te:tɪʃ] *a* aesthetic.

Asthma ['astma] *nt* **-s** asthma; **~tiker(in** *f)* [ast'ma:tikər(ɪn)] *m* **-s, -** asthmatic.

Astro- [astro] *zW:* **~'loge** *m* **-n, -n** astrologer; **~lo'gie** *f* astrology; **~'naut** *m* **-en, -en** astronaut; **~'nom** *m* **-en, -en** astronomer; **~no'mie** *f* astronomy.

Asyl [a'zy:l] *nt* **-s, -e** asylum; *(Heim)* home; *(Obdachlosen~)* shelter.

Atelier [atəli'e:] *nt* **-s, -s** studio.

Atem ['a:təm] *m* **-s** breath; **den ~ anhalten** hold one's breath; **außer ~** out of breath; **a~beraubend** *a* breathtaking; **a~los** *a* breathless; **~pause** *f* breather; **~zug** *m* breath.

Atheismus [ate'ɪsmʊs] *m* atheism.

Atheist *m* atheist; **a~isch** *a* atheistic.

Athen [a'te:n] *nt* **-s** Athens; **A~er(in** *f)* *m* **-s, -** Athenian; **a~isch** *a* Athenian.

Äther ['ɛ:tər] *m* **-s, -** ether.

Äthiop- [ɛti'o:p] *zW:* **~ien** *nt* **-s** Ethiopia; **~ier(in** *f)* *m* **-s, -** Ethiopian; **ä~isch** *a* Ethiopian.

Athlet [at'le:t] *m* **-en, -en** athlete.

Atlant- [at'lant] *zW:* **~ik** *m* **-s** Atlantic (Ocean); **a~isch** *a* Atlantic.

Atlas ['atlas] *m* **- od -ses, -se od At'lanten** atlas.

atmen ['a:tmən] *vti* breathe.

Atmosphäre [atmo'sfɛ:rə] *f* **-, -n** atmosphere.

atmosphärisch *a* atmospheric.

Atmung ['a:tmʊŋ] *f* respiration.

Atom [a'to:m] *nt* **-s, -e** atom; **a~ar** [ato'ma:r] *a* atomic; **~bombe** *f* atom bomb; **~energie** *f* atomic *od* nuclear energy; **~kraftgegner** *m* opponent of nuclear power; **~kraftwerk** *nt* nuclear power station; **~krieg** *m* nuclear *od* atomic war; **~macht** *f* atomic power; **~müll** *m* atomic waste; **~sperrvertrag** *m* (*POL*) nuclear non-proliferation treaty; **~strom** (electricity generated by) nuclear power; **~versuch** *m* atomic test; **~waffen** *pl* atomic weapons *pl*; **a~waffenfrei** *a* nuclear-free; **~zeitalter** *nt* atomic age.

Attentat ['atənta:t] *nt* **-(e)s, -e** (attempted) assassination (*auf +akk* of).

Attentäter ['atəntɛ:tər] *m* (would-be) assassin.

Attest [a'tɛst] *nt* **-(e)s, -e** certificate.

attraktiv [atrak'ti:f] *a* attractive.

Attrappe [a'trapə] *f* **-, -n** dummy.

Attribut [atri'bu:t] *nt* **-(e)s, -e** (*GRAM*) attribute.

ätzen ['ɛtsən] *vi* be caustic.

au [au] *interj* ouch!; **~ja!** oh yes!

auch [aux] *ad* **1** (*ebenfalls*) also, too, as well; **das ist ~ schön** that's nice too *od* as well; **er kommt — ich ~** he's coming — so am I, me too; **~ nicht** not ... either; **ich ~ nicht** nor I, me neither; **oder ~** or; **~ das noch!** not that as well!

2 (*selbst, sogar*) even; **~ wenn das Wetter schlecht ist** even if the weather is bad; **ohne ~ nur zu fragen** without even asking

3 (*wirklich*) really; **du siehst müde aus — bin ich ~** you look tired — (so) I am; **so sieht es ~ aus** it looks like it too

4 (**~ immer**): **wer ~** whoever; **was ~** whatever; **wie dem ~ sei** be that as it may; **wie sehr er sich ~ bemühte** however much he tried.

auf [auf] **♦** *präp + dat* (*wo?*) on; **~ dem Tisch** on the table; **~ der Reise** on the way; **~ der Post/dem Fest** at the post office/party; **~ der Straße** on the road; **~ dem Land/der ganzen Welt** in the country/the whole world

♦ *präp +akk* **1** (*wohin?*) on(to); **~ den Tisch** on(to) the table; **~ die Post gehen** go to the post office; **~ das Land** into the country; **etw ~ einen Zettel schreiben** write sth on a piece of paper

2: **~ deutsch** in German; **~ Lebenszeit** for my/his lifetime; **bis ~ ihn** except for him; **~ einmal** at once; **~ seinen Vorschlag (hin)** at his suggestion

♦ *ad* **1** (*offen*) open; **das Fenster ist ~** the window is open

2 (*hinauf*) up; **~ und ab** up and down; **~ und davon** up and away; **~!** (*los!*) come on!

3 (**~ gestanden**) up; **ist er schon ~?** is he up yet?

♦ *kj:* **~ daß** (so) that.

aufatmen ['aufʔa:tmən] *vi* heave a sigh of relief.

aufbahren ['aufba:rən] *vt* lay out.

Aufbau ['aufbau] *m* (*Bauen*) building, construction; (*Struktur*) structure; (*aufgebautes Teil*) superstructure; **a~en** *vt* erect, build (up); (*Existenz*) make; (*gestalten*) construct; (*gründen*) found, base (*auf +dat* on).

aufbauschen ['aufbauʃən] *vt* puff out; (*fig*) exaggerate.

aufbekommen ['aufbəkɔmən] *vt unreg* (*öffnen*) get open; (*Hausaufgaben*) be given.

aufbessern ['aufbɛsərn] *vt* (*Gehalt*) increase.

aufbewahren ['aʊfbəva:rən] *vt* keep; (*Gepäck*) put in the left-luggage office.

Aufbewahrung *f* (safe)keeping; (*Gepäck~*) left-luggage office (*Brit*), baggage check (*US*).

aufbieten ['aʊfbi:tən] *vt unreg* (*Kraft*) summon (up), exert; (*Armee, Polizei*) mobilize; (*Brautpaar*) publish the banns of.

aufblasen ['aʊfbla:zən] *unreg vt* blow up, inflate // *vr* (*umg*) become bigheaded.

aufbleiben ['aʊfblaɪbən] *vi unreg* (*Laden*) remain open; (*Person*) stay up.

aufblicken ['aʊfblɪkən] *vi* (*lit, fig*) look up (*zu* (*lit*) *at*, (*fig*) *to*).

aufblühen ['aʊfbly:ən] *vi* blossom, flourish.

aufbrauchen ['aʊfbraʊxən] *vt* use up.

aufbrausen ['aʊfbraʊzən] *vi* (*fig*) flare up; **~d** *a* hot-tempered.

aufbrechen ['aʊfbrɛçən] *unreg vt* break *od* prize (*Brit*) open // *vi* burst open; (*gehen*) start, set off.

aufbringen ['aʊfbrɪŋən] *vt unreg* (*öffnen*) open; (*in Mode*) bring into fashion; (*beschaffen*) procure; (*FIN*) raise; (*ärgern*) irritate; **Verständnis für etw ~** be able to understand sth.

Aufbruch ['aʊfbrʊx] *m* departure.

aufbrühen ['aʊfbry:ən] *vt* (*Tee*) make.

aufbürden ['aʊfbʏrdən] *vt* burden (*jdm etw* sb with sth).

aufdecken ['aʊfdɛkən] *vt* uncover.

aufdringlich ['aʊfdrɪŋlɪç] *a* pushy.

aufeinander [aʊfaɪ'nandər] *ad* on top of each other; (*schießen*) at each other; (*vertrauen*) each other; **~folgen** *vi* follow one another; **~folgend** *a* consecutive; **~legen** *vt* lay on top of one another; **~prallen** *vi* hit one another.

Aufenthalt ['aʊfɛnthalt] *m* stay; (*Verzögerung*) delay; (*EISENB: Halten*) stop; (*Ort*) haunt; **Aufenthaltsgenehmigung** *f* residence permit.

auferlegen ['aʊfɛrle:gən] *vt* impose (*jdm etw* sth upon sb).

Auferstehung ['aʊfɛrʃte:ʊŋ] *f* resurrection.

aufessen ['aʊfɛsən] *vt unreg* eat up.

auffahr- ['aʊffa:r] *zW*: **~en** *unreg vi* (*Auto*) run, crash (*auf +akk* into); (*herankommen*) draw up; (*hochfahren*) jump up; (*wütend werden*) flare up; (*in den Himmel*) ascend // *vt* (*Kanonen, Geschütz*) bring up; **~end** *a* hot-tempered; **A~t** *f* (*Haus~*) drive; (*Autobahn~*) slip road (*Brit*), (*freeway*) entrance (*US*); **A~unfall** *m* pile-up.

auffallen ['aʊffalən] *vi unreg* be noticeable; **jdm ~** strike sb; **~d** *a* strik-

ing.

auffällig ['aʊffɛlɪç] *a* conspicuous, striking.

auffangen ['aʊffaŋən] *vt unreg* catch; (*Funkspruch*) intercept; (*Preise*) peg.

auffassen ['aʊffasən] *vt* understand, comprehend; (*auslegen*) see, view.

Auffassung *f* (*Meinung*) opinion; (*Auslegung*) view, concept; (*also* **Auffassungsgabe**) grasp.

auffindbar ['aʊffɪntba:r] *a* to be found.

auffordern ['aʊffɔrdərn] *vt* (*befehlen*) call upon, order; (*bitten*) ask.

Aufforderung *f* (*Befehl*) order; (*Einladung*) invitation.

auffrischen ['aʊffrɪʃən] *vt* freshen up; (*Kenntnisse*) brush up; (*Erinnerungen*) reawaken // *vi* (*Wind*) freshen.

aufführen ['aʊffy:rən] *vt* (*THEAT*) perform; (*in einem Verzeichnis*) list, specify // *vr* (*sich benehmen*) behave.

Aufführung *f* (*THEAT*) performance; (*Liste*) specification.

Aufgabe ['aʊfga:bə] *f* -, **-n** task; (*SCH*) exercise; (*Haus~*) homework; (*Verzicht*) giving up; (*von Gepäck*) registration; (*von Post*) posting; (*von Inserat*) insertion.

Aufgang ['aʊfgaŋ] *m* ascent; (*Sonnen~*) rise; (*Treppe*) staircase.

aufgeben ['aʊfge:bən] *unreg vt* (*verzichten*) give up; (*Paket*) send, post; (*Gepäck*) register; (*Bestellung*) give; (*Inserat*) insert; (*Rätsel, Problem*) set // *vi* give up.

Aufgebot ['aʊfgəbo:t] *nt* supply; (*Ehe~*) banns *pl*.

aufgedunsen ['aʊfgedʊnzən] *a* swollen, puffed up.

aufgehen ['aʊfge:ən] *vi unreg* (*Sonne, Teig*) rise; (*sich öffnen*) open; (*klarwerden*) become clear (*jdm* to sb); (*MATH*) come out exactly; (*sich widmen*) be absorbed (*in +dat* in); **in Rauch/Flammen ~** go up in smoke/flames.

aufgelegt ['aʊfgəle:kt] *a*: **gut/ schlecht ~ sein** be in a good/bad mood; **zu etw ~ sein** be in the mood for sth.

aufgeregt ['aʊfgəre:kt] *a* excited.

aufgeschlossen ['aʊfgəʃlɔsən] *a* open, open-minded.

aufgeweckt ['aʊfgəvɛkt] *a* bright, intelligent.

aufgießen ['aʊfgi:sən] *vt unreg* (*Wasser*) pour over; (*Tee*) infuse.

aufgreifen ['aʊfgraɪfən] *vt unreg* (*Thema*) take up; (*Verdächtige*) pick up, seize.

aufgrund [aʊf'grʊnt] *präp +gen* on the basis of; (*wegen*) because of.

aufhaben ['aʊfha:bən] *vt unreg* have on; (*Arbeit*) have to do.

aufhalsen ['aʊfhalzən] *vt* (*umg*) **jdm**

etw ~ saddle *od* lumber sb with sth.

aufhalten ['aʊfhaltən] *unreg vt* (*Person*) detain; (*Entwicklung*) check; (*Tür, Hand*) hold open; (*Augen*) keep open // *vr* (*wohnen*) live; (*bleiben*) stay; **sich mit etw ~** waste time over.

aufhängen ['aʊfhɛŋən] *unreg vt* (*Wäsche*) hang up; (*Menschen*) hang // *vr* hang o.s.

Aufhänger *m* -s, - (*am Mantel*) hook; (*fig*) peg.

aufheben ['aʊfhe:bən] *unreg vt* (*hochheben*) raise, lift; (*Sitzung*) wind up; (*Urteil*) annul; (*Gesetz*) repeal, abolish; (*aufbewahren*) keep; **bei jdm gut aufgehoben sein** be well looked after at sb's // *vr* cancel itself out; **viel A~(s) machen** make a fuss (*von* about).

aufheitern ['aʊfhaɪtərn] *vtr* (*Himmel, Miene*) brighten; (*Mensch*) cheer up.

aufhellen ['aʊfhɛlən] *vtr* clear up; (*Farbe, Haare*) lighten.

aufhetzen ['aʊfhɛtsən] *vt* stir up (*gegen* against).

aufholen ['aʊfho:lən] *vt* make up // *vi* catch up.

aufhorchen ['aʊfhɔrçən] *vi* prick up one's ears.

aufhören ['aʊfhø:rən] *vi* stop; **~ etw zu tun** stop doing sth.

aufklappen ['aʊfklapən] *vt* open.

aufklären ['aʊfklɛ:rən] *vt* (*Geheimnis etc*) clear up; (*Person*) enlighten; (*sexuell*) tell the facts of life to; (*MIL*) reconnoitre // *vr* clear up.

Aufklärung *f* (*von Geheimnis*) clearing up; (*Unterrichtung, Zeitalter*) enlightenment; (*sexuell*) sex education; (*MIL, AVIAT*) reconnaissance.

aufkleben ['aʊfkle:bən] *vt* stick on.

Aufkleber *m* -s, - sticker.

aufknöpfen ['aʊfknœpfən] *vt* unbutton.

aufkommen ['aʊfkɔmən] *vi* *unreg* (*Wind*) come up; (*Zweifel, Mode*) arise; (*Mode*) start; **für jdn/etw ~** be liable *od* responsible for sb/sth.

aufladen ['aʊfla:dən] *vt* *unreg* load.

Auflage ['aʊfla:gə] *f* edition; (*Zeitung*) circulation; (*Bedingung*) condition; **jdm etw zur ~ machen** make sth a condition for sb.

auflassen ['aʊflasən] *vt* *unreg* (*offen*) leave open; (*aufgesetzt*) leave on.

auflauern ['aʊflaʊərn] *vi*: **jdm ~** lie in wait for sb.

Auflauf ['aʊflaʊf] *m* (*KOCH*) pudding; (*Menschen~*) crowd.

auflegen ['aʊfle:gən] *vt* put on; (*Telefon*) hang up; (*TYP*) print.

auflehnen ['aʊfle:nən] *vt* lean on // *vr* rebel (*gegen* against).

Auflehnung *f* rebellion.

auflesen ['aʊfle:zən] *vt* *unreg* pick up.

aufleuchten ['aʊflɔʏçtən] *vi* light up.

auflockern ['aʊflɔkərn] *vt* loosen; (*fig: Eintönigkeit etc*) liven up.

auflösen ['aʊflø:zən] *vtr* dissolve; (*Haare etc*) loosen; (*Mißverständnis*) sort out; (**in Tränen**) **aufgelöst sein** be in tears.

Auflösung *f* dissolving; (*fig*) solution.

aufmachen ['aʊfmaxən] *vt* open; (*Kleidung*) undo; (*zurechtmachen*) do up // *vr* set out.

Aufmachung *f* (*Kleidung*) outfit, getup; (*Gestaltung*) format.

aufmerksam ['aʊfmɛrkza:m] *a* attentive; **jdn auf etw** (*akk*) **~ machen** point sth out to sb; **A~keit** *f* attention, attentiveness.

aufmuntern ['aʊfmʊntərn] *vt* (*ermutigen*) encourage; (*erheitern*) cheer up.

Aufnahme ['aʊfna:mə] *f* -, -n reception; (*Beginn*) beginning; (*in Verein etc*) admission; (*in Liste etc*) inclusion; (*Notieren*) taking down; (*PHOT*) shot; (*auf Tonband etc*) recording; **a~fähig** *a* receptive; **~prüfung** *f* entrance test.

aufnehmen ['aʊfne:mən] *vt* *unreg* receive; (*hochheben*) pick up; (*beginnen*) take up; (*in Verein etc*) admit; (*in Liste etc*) include; (*fassen*) hold; (*notieren*) take down; (*fotografieren*) photograph; (*auf Tonband, Platte*) record; (*FIN: leihen*) take out; **es mit jdm ~ können** be able to compete with sb.

aufopfern ['aʊfɔpfərn] *vtr* sacrifice; **~d** *a* selfless.

aufpassen ['aʊfpasən] *vi* (*aufmerksam sein*) pay attention; **auf jdn/etw ~** look after *od* watch sb/sth; **aufgepaßt!** look out!

Aufprall ['aʊfpral] *m* -s, -e impact; **a~en** *vi* hit, strike.

Aufpreis ['aʊfpraɪs] *m* extra charge.

aufpumpen ['aʊfpʊmpən] *vt* pump up.

aufraffen ['aʊfrafən] *vr* rouse o.s.

aufräumen ['aʊfrɔʏmən] *vti* (*Dinge*) clear away; (*Zimmer*) tidy up.

aufrecht ['aʊfrɛçt] *a* (*lit, fig*) upright; **~erhalten** *vt* *unreg* maintain.

aufreg- ['aʊfre:g] *zW*: **~en** *vt* excite // *vr* get excited; **~end** *a* exciting; **A~ung** *f* excitement.

aufreibend ['aʊfraɪbənt] *a* strenuous.

aufreißen ['aʊfraɪsən] *vt* *unreg* (*Umschlag*) tear open; (*Augen*) open wide; (*Tür*) throw open; (*Straße*) take up.

aufreizen ['aʊfraɪtsən] *vt* incite, stir up; **~d** *a* exciting, stimulating.

aufrichten ['aʊfrɪçtən] *vt* put up, erect; (*moralisch*) console // *vr* rise; (*moralisch*) take heart (*an* +*dat* from).

aufrichtig ['aʊfrɪçtɪç] a sincere, honest; **A~keit** f sincerity.
aufrücken ['aʊfrʏkən] vi move up; (beruflich) be promoted.
Aufruf ['aʊfruːf] m summons; (zur Hilfe) call; (des Namens) calling out; **a~en** vt unreg (auffordern) call upon (zu for); (Namen) call out.
Aufruhr ['aʊfruːr] m -(e)s, -e uprising, revolt.
aufrührerisch ['aʊfryːrərɪʃ] a rebellious.
aufrunden ['aʊfrʊndən] vt (Summe) round up.
Aufrüstung ['aʊfrʏstʊŋ] f rearmament.
aufrütteln ['aʊfrʏtəln] vt (lit, fig) shake up.
aufs [aʊfs] = **auf das**.
aufsagen ['aʊfzaːgən] vt (Gedicht) recite.
aufsammeln ['aʊfzaməln] vt gather up.
aufsässig ['aʊfzɛsɪç] a rebellious.
Aufsatz ['aʊfzats] m (Geschriebenes) essay; (auf Schrank etc) top.
aufsaugen ['aʊfzaʊgən] vt unreg soak up.
aufschauen ['aʊfʃaʊən] vi look up.
aufscheuchen ['aʊfʃɔʏçən] vt scare od frighten away.
aufschieben ['aʊfʃiːbən] vt unreg push open; (verzögern) put off, postpone.
Aufschlag ['aʊfʃlaːk] m (Ärmel~) cuff; (Jacken~) lapel; (Hosen~) turn-up; (Aufprall) impact; (Preis~) surcharge; (Tennis) service; **a~en** [-gən] unreg vt (öffnen) open; (verwunden) cut; (hochschlagen) turn up; (aufbauen: Zelt, Lager) erect; (Wohnsitz) take up // vi (aufprallen) hit; (teurer werden) go up; (Tennis) serve.
aufschließen ['aʊfʃliːsən] unreg vt open up, unlock // vi (aufrücken) close up.
Aufschluß ['aʊfʃlʊs] m information; **a~reich** a informative, illuminating.
aufschnappen ['aʊfʃnapən] vt (umg) pick up // vi fly open.
aufschneiden ['aʊfʃnaɪdən] unreg vt (Geschwür) cut open; (Brot) cut up; (MED) lance // vi brag.
Aufschneider m -s, - boaster, braggart.
Aufschnitt ['aʊfʃnɪt] m (slices of) cold meat.
aufschrecken ['aʊfʃrɛkən] vt startle // vi unreg start up.
Aufschrei ['aʊfʃraɪ] m cry; **a~en** vi unreg cry out.
aufschreiben ['aʊfʃraɪbən] vt unreg write down.
Aufschrift ['aʊfʃrɪft] f (Inschrift) inscription; (auf Etikett) label.

Aufschub ['aʊfʃuːp] m -(e)s, -schübe delay, postponement.
Aufschwung ['aʊfʃvʊŋ] n (Elan) boost; (wirtschaftlich) upturn, boom; (SPORT) circle.
aufsehen ['aʊfzeːən] vi unreg (lit, fig) look up (zu lit) at, (fig) to); **A~** nt -s sensation, stir; **~erregend** a sensational.
Aufseher(in f) m -s, - guard; (im Betrieb) supervisor; (Museums~) attendant; (Park~) keeper.
aufsetzen ['aʊfzɛtsən] vt put on; (Flugzeug) put down; (Dokument) draw up // vr sit upright // vi (Flugzeug) touch down.
Aufsicht ['aʊfzɪçt] f supervision; **die ~ haben** be in charge.
aufsitzen ['aʊfzɪtsən] vi unreg (aufrecht hinsitzen) sit up; (aufs Pferd, Motorrad) mount, get on; (Schiff) run aground; **jdm ~** (umg) be taken in by sb.
aufsparen ['aʊfʃpaːrən] vt save (up).
aufsperren ['aʊfʃpɛrən] vt unlock; (Mund) open wide.
aufspielen ['aʊfʃpiːlən] vr show off.
aufspießen ['aʊfʃpiːsən] vt spear.
aufspringen ['aʊfʃprɪŋən] vi unreg jump (auf +akk onto); (hochspringen) jump up; (sich öffnen) spring open; (Hände, Lippen) become chapped.
aufspüren ['aʊfʃpyːrən] vt track down, trace.
aufstacheln ['aʊfʃtaxəln] vt incite.
Aufstand ['aʊfʃtant] m insurrection, rebellion.
aufständisch ['aʊfʃtɛndɪʃ] a rebellious, mutinous.
aufstecken ['aʊfʃtɛkən] vt stick on, pin up; (umg) give up.
aufstehen ['aʊfʃteːən] vi unreg get up; (Tür) be open.
aufsteigen ['aʊfʃtaɪgən] vi unreg (auf etw) get onto; (hochsteigen) climb; (Rauch) rise.
aufstellen ['aʊfʃtɛlən] vt (aufrecht stellen) put up; (aufreihen) line up; (nominieren) put up; (formulieren: Programm etc) draw up; (leisten: Rekord) set up.
Aufstellung f (SPORT) line-up; (Liste) list.
Aufstieg ['aʊfʃtiːk] m -(e)s, -e (auf Berg) ascent; (Fortschritt) rise; (beruflich, SPORT) promotion.
aufstoßen ['aʊfʃtoːsən] unreg vt push open // vi belch.
aufstützen ['aʊfʃtʏtsən] vr lean (auf +akk on) // vt (Körperteil) prop, lean; (Person) prop up.
aufsuchen ['aʊfzuːxən] vt (besuchen) visit; (konsultieren) consult.
Auftakt ['aʊftakt] m (MUS) upbeat;

(fig) prelude.

auftanken ['aʊftaŋkən] *vi* get petrol *(Brit)* od gas *(US)* // *vt* refuel.

auftauchen ['aʊftaʊxən] *vi* appear; *(aus Wasser etc)* emerge; *(U-Boot)* surface; *(Zweifel)* arise.

auftauen ['aʊftaʊən] *vti* thaw; *(fig)* relax.

aufteilen ['aʊftaɪlən] *vt* divide up; *(Raum)* partition.

Aufteilung *f* division; partition.

Auftrag ['aʊftraːk] *m* **-(e)s, -träge** order; *(Anweisung)* commission; *(Aufgabe)* mission; **im ~ von** on behalf of; **a~en** [-gən] *vt unreg (Essen)* serve; *(Farbe)* put on; *(Kleidung)* wear out; **jdm etw a~en** tell sb sth; **dick a~en** *(fig)* exaggerate; **~geber** *m* **-s, -** *(COMM)* purchaser, customer.

auftreiben ['aʊftraɪbən] *vt unreg (umg: beschaffen)* raise.

auftreten ['aʊftreːtən] *unreg vt* kick open // *vi* appear; *(mit Füßen)* tread; *(sich verhalten)* behave; **A~** *nt* **-s** *(Vorkommen)* appearance; *(Benehmen)* behaviour.

Auftrieb ['aʊftriːp] *m* *(PHYS)* buoyancy, lift; *(fig)* impetus.

Auftritt ['aʊftrɪt] *m* *(des Schauspielers)* entrance; *(lit, fig: Szene)* scene.

auftun ['aʊftuːn] *unreg vt* open // *vr* open up.

aufwachen ['aʊfvaxən] *vi* wake up.

aufwachsen ['aʊfvaksən] *vi unreg* grow up.

Aufwand ['aʊfvant] *m* **-(e)s** expenditure; *(Kosten auch)* expense; *(Luxus)* show.

aufwärmen ['aʊfvɛrmən] *vt* warm up; *(alte Geschichten)* rake up.

aufwärts ['aʊfvɛrts] *ad* upwards; **A~entwicklung** *f* upward trend.

aufwecken ['aʊfvɛkən] *vt* wake up, waken up.

aufweisen ['aʊfvaɪzən] *vt unreg* show.

aufwenden ['aʊfvɛndən] *vt unreg* expend; *(Geld)* spend; *(Sorgfalt)* devote.

aufwendig *a* costly.

aufwerfen ['aʊfvɛrfən] *vt unreg (Fenster etc)* throw open; *(Probleme)* throw up, raise.

aufwerten ['aʊfveːrtən] *vt* *(FIN)* revalue; *(fig)* raise in value.

aufwiegeln ['aʊfviːgəln] *vt* stir up, incite.

aufwiegen ['aʊfviːgən] *vt unreg* make up for.

Aufwind ['aʊfvɪnt] *m* up-current.

aufwirbeln ['aʊfvɪrbəln] *vt* whirl up; **Staub ~** *(fig)* create a stir.

aufwischen ['aʊfvɪʃən] *vt* wipe up.

aufzählen ['aʊftsɛːlən] *vt* list.

aufzeichnen ['aʊftsaɪçnən] *vt* sketch; *(schriftlich)* jot down; *(auf Band)* record.

Aufzeichnung *f* *(schriftlich)* note; *(Tonband~)* recording; *(Film~)* record.

aufzeigen ['aʊftsaɪgən] *vt* show, demonstrate.

aufziehen ['aʊftsiːən] *vt unreg (hochziehen)* raise, draw up; *(öffnen)* pull open; *(Uhr)* wind; *(umg: necken)* tease; *(großziehen: Kinder)* raise, bring up; *(Tiere)* rear.

Aufzug ['aʊftsuːk] *m* *(Fahrstuhl)* lift, elevator; *(Aufmarsch)* procession, parade; *(Kleidung)* get-up; *(THEAT)* act.

aufzwingen ['aʊftsvɪŋən] *vt unreg*: **jdm etw ~** force sth upon sb.

Aug- ['aʊg] *zW*: **~apfel** *m* eyeball; *(fig)* apple of one's eye; **~e** *nt* **-s, -n** eye; *(Fett~)* globule of fat; **unter vier ~en** in private; **~enblick** *m* moment; **im ~enblick** at the moment; **a~enblicklich** *a* *(sofort)* instantaneous; *(gegenwärtig)* present; **~enbraue** *f* eyebrow; **~enweide** *f* sight for sore eyes; **~enzeuge** *m* eye witness.

August [aʊˈgʊst] *m* **-(e)s** od **-, -e** August.

Auktion [aʊktsiˈoːn] *f* auction.

Aula ['aʊla] *f* **-, Aulen** od **-s** assembly hall.

aus [aʊs] ◆ *präp + dat* **1** *(räumlich)* out of; *(von ... her)* from; **er ist ~ Berlin** he's from Berlin; **~ dem Fenster** out of the window
2 *(gemacht/hergestellt ~)* made of; **ein Herz ~ Stein** a heart of stone
3 *(auf Ursache deutend)* out of; **~ Mitleid** out of sympathy; **~ Erfahrung** from experience; **~ Spaß** for fun
4: **~ ihr wird nie etwas** she'll never get anywhere
◆ *ad* **1** *(zu Ende)* finished, over; **~ und vorbei** over and done with
2 *(~geschaltet, ~gezogen)* out; *(Aufschrift an Geräten)* off; **Licht ~!** lights out!
3 *(in Verbindung mit von)*: **von Rom ~** from Rome; **vom Fenster ~** out of the window; **von sich ~** *(selbständig)* of one's own accord; **von ihm ~** as far as he's concerned.

ausarbeiten ['aʊsˈarbaɪtən] *vt* work out.

ausarten ['aʊsˈartən] *vi* degenerate; *(Kind)* become overexcited.

ausatmen ['aʊsˈaːtmən] *vi* breathe out.

ausbaden ['aʊsbaːdən] *vt*: **etw ~ müssen** *(umg)* carry the can for sth.

Ausbau ['aʊsbaʊ] *m* extension, expansion; removal; **a~en** *vt* extend, expand; *(herausnehmen)* take out, remove; **a~fähig** *a* *(fig)* worth develop-

ing.
ausbessern ['aʊsbɛsərn] vt mend, repair.
ausbeulen ['aʊsbɔʏlən] vt beat out.
Ausbeute ['aʊsbɔʏtə] f yield; (Fische) catch; **a~n** vt exploit; (MIN) work.
ausbild- ['aʊsbɪld] zW: **~en** vt educate; (Lehrling, Soldat) instruct, train; (Fähigkeiten) develop; (Geschmack) cultivate; **A~er** m **-s,** - instructor; **A~ung** f education; training, instruction; development, cultivation.
ausbleiben ['aʊsblaɪbən] vi unreg (Personen) stay away, not come; (Ereignisse) fail to happen, not happen.
Ausblick ['aʊsblɪk] m (lit, fig) prospect, outlook, view.
ausbrechen ['aʊsbrɛçən] unreg vi break out; **in Tränen/Gelächter ~** burst into tears/out laughing // vt break off.
ausbreiten ['aʊsbraɪtən] vt spread (out); (Arme) stretch out // vr spread; (über Thema) expand, enlarge (über +akk on).
ausbrennen ['aʊsbrɛnən] unreg vt scorch; (Wunde) cauterize // vi burn out.
Ausbruch ['aʊsbrʊx] m outbreak; (von Vulkan) eruption; (Gefühls~) outburst; (von Gefangenen) escape.
ausbrüten ['aʊsbryːtən] vt (lit, fig) hatch.
Ausdauer ['aʊsdaʊər] f perseverance, stamina; **ausdauernd** a persevering.
ausdehnen ['aʊsdeːnən] vtr (räumlich) expand; (Gummi) stretch; (Nebel) extend; (zeitlich) stretch; (fig: Macht) extend.
ausdenken ['aʊsdɛŋkən] vt unreg: **sich** (dat) **etw ~** think sth up.
Ausdruck ['aʊsdrʊk] m expression, phrase; (Kundgabe, Gesichts~) expression; (COMPUT) print-out, hard copy; **a~en** vt (COMPUT) print out.
ausdrücken ['aʊsdrʏkən] vt (auch vr: formulieren, zeigen) express; (Zigarette) put out; (Zitrone) squeeze.
ausdrücklich a express, explicit.
ausdrucks- zW: **~los** a expressionless, blank; **~voll** a expressive; **A~weise** f mode of expression.
auseinander [aʊs'aɪ'nandər] ad (getrennt) apart; **~ schreiben** write as separate words; **~bringen** vt unreg separate; **~fallen** vi unreg fall apart; **~gehen** vi unreg (Menschen) separate; (Meinungen) differ; (Gegenstand) fall apart; (umg: dick werden) put on weight; **~halten** vt unreg tell apart; **~nehmen** vt unreg take to pieces, dismantle; **~setzen** vt (erklären) set forth, explain // vr (sich

verständigen) come to terms, settle; (sich befassen) concern o.s.; **A~setzung** f argument.
auserlesen ['aʊs'ɛrleːzən] a select, choice.
Ausfahrt ['aʊsfaːrt] f (des Zuges etc) leaving, departure; (Autobahn~, Garagen~) exit, way out; (Spazierfahrt) drive, excursion.
Ausfall ['aʊsfal] m loss; (Nichtstattfinden) cancellation; (MIL) sortie; (Fechten) lunge; (radioaktiv) fallout; **a~en** vi unreg (Zähne, Haare) fall od come out; (nicht stattfinden) be cancelled; (wegbleiben) be omitted; (Person) drop out; (Lohn) be stopped; (nicht funktionieren) break down; (Resultat haben) turn out; **a~end** a impertinent; **~straße** f arterial road.
Ausfertigung ['aʊsfɛrtɪgʊŋ] f drawing up; making out; (Exemplar) copy.
ausfindig machen ['aʊsfɪndɪç maxən] vt discover.
ausflippen ['aʊsflɪpən] vi (umg) freak out.
Ausflucht ['aʊsflʊxt] f -, **-flüchte** excuse.
Ausflug ['aʊsfluːk] m excursion, outing.
Ausflügler ['aʊsflyːklər] m **-s,** - tripper.
Ausfluß ['aʊsflʊs] m outlet; (MED) discharge.
ausfragen ['aʊsfraːgən] vt interrogate, question.
ausfressen ['aʊsfrɛsən] vt unreg eat up; (aushöhlen) corrode; (umg: anstellen) be up to.
Ausfuhr ['aʊsfuːr] f -, **-en** export, exportation; in zW export.
ausführ- ['aʊsfyːr] zW: **~en** vt (verwirklichen) carry out; (Person) take out; (Hund) take for a walk; (COMM) export; (erklären) give details of; **~lich** a detailed // ad in detail; **A~lichkeit** f detail; **A~ung** f execution, performance; (Durchführung) completion; (Herstellungsart) version; (Erklärung) explanation.
ausfüllen ['aʊsfʏlən] vt fill up; (Fragebogen etc) fill in; (Beruf) be fulfilling for.
Ausgabe ['aʊsgaːbə] f (Geld) expenditure, outlay; (Aushändigung) giving out; (Gepäck~) left-luggage office; (Buch) edition; (Nummer) issue; (COMPUT) output.
Ausgang ['aʊsgaŋ] m way out, exit; (Ende) end; (Ausgangspunkt) starting point; (Ergebnis) result; (Ausgehtag) free time, time off; **kein ~** no exit.
Ausgangs- zW: **~basis** f, **~punkt** m starting point; **~sperre** f curfew.

ausgeben ['aʊsgeːbən] *unreg vt Geld* spend; *(austeilen)* issue, distribute // *vr: sich für etw/jdn* ~ pass o.s. off as sth/sb.

ausgedient ['aʊsgədiːnt] *a (Soldat)* discharged; *(verbraucht)* no longer in use; ~ **haben** have done good service.

ausgefallen ['aʊsgəfalən] *a (ungewöhnlich)* exceptional.

ausgeglichen ['aʊsgəglɪçən] *a* (well-) balanced; **A~heit** *f* balance; *(von Mensch)* even-temperedness.

Ausgeh- ['aʊsgeː] *zW*: **a~en** *vi unreg* go out; *(zu Ende gehen)* come to an end; *(Benzin)* run out; *(Haare, Zähne)* fall *od* come out; *(Feuer, Ofen, Licht)* go out; *(Strom)* go off; *(Resultat haben)* turn out; **mir ging das Benzin aus** I ran out of petrol *(Brit)* od gas *(US)*; **auf etw** *(akk)* **a~en** aim at sth; **von etw a~en** *(wegführen)* lead away from sth; *(herrühren)* come from sth; *(zugrunde legen)* proceed from sth; **wir können davon a~en, daß** ... we can take as our starting point that ...; **leer a~en** get nothing; **schlecht a~en** turn out badly; ~**verbot** *nt* curfew.

ausgelassen ['aʊsgəlasən] *a* boisterous, high-spirited; **A~heit** *f* boisterousness, high spirits *pl*, exuberance.

ausgelastet ['aʊsgəlastət] *a* fully occupied.

ausgelernt ['aʊsgəlɛrnt] *a* trained, qualified.

ausgemacht ['aʊsgəmaxt] *a (umg)* settled; *(Dummkopf etc)* out-and-out, downright; **es war eine ~e Sache, daß** ... it was a foregone conclusion that ...

ausgenommen ['aʊsgənɔmən] *präp +gen od dat, kj* except; **Anwesende sind** ~ present company excepted.

ausgeprägt ['aʊsgəprɛːkt] *a* prominent.

ausgerechnet ['aʊsgərɛçnət] *ad* just, precisely; ~ **du/heute** you of all people/today of all days.

ausgeschlossen ['aʊsgəʃlɔsən] *a (unmöglich)* impossible, out of the question.

ausgeschnitten ['aʊsgəʃnɪtən] *a (Kleid)* low-necked.

ausgesprochen ['aʊsgəʃprɔxən] *a (Faulheit, Lüge etc)* out-and-out; *(unverkennbar)* marked // *ad* decidedly.

ausgezeichnet ['aʊsgətsaɪçnət] *a* excellent.

ausgiebig ['aʊsgiːbɪç] *a (Gebrauch)* thorough, good; *(Essen)* generous, lavish; ~ **schlafen** have a good sleep.

Ausgleich ['aʊsglaɪç] *m* -(e)s balance; *(Vermittlung)* reconciliation; *(SPORT)* equalization; **zum** ~ *(+gen)*

in order to offset; **a~en** *unreg vt* balance *(out)*; reconcile; *(Höhe)* even up // *vi (SPORT)* equalize.

ausgraben ['aʊsgraːbən] *vt unreg* dig up; *(Leichen)* exhume; *(fig)* unearth.

Ausgrabung *f* excavation; *(Ausgraben auch)* digging up.

Ausguß ['aʊsgʊs] *m (Spüle)* sink; *(Abfluß)* outlet; *(Tülle)* spout.

aushalten ['aʊshaltən] *unreg vt* bear, stand; *(Geliebte)* keep // *vi* hold out; **das ist nicht zum A~** that is unbearable.

aushandeln ['aʊshandəln] *vt* negotiate.

aushändigen ['aʊshɛndɪgən] *vt*: **jdm etw** ~ hand sth over to sb.

Aushang ['aʊshaŋ] *m* notice.

aushängen ['aʊshɛŋən] *unreg vt (Meldung)* put up; *(Fenster)* take off its hinges // *vi* be displayed // *vr* hang out.

ausharren ['aʊsharən] *vi* hold out.

ausheben ['aʊsheːbən] *vt unreg (Erde)* lift out; *(Grube)* hollow out; *(Tür)* take off its hinges; *(Diebesnest)* clear out; *(MIL)* enlist.

aushelfen ['aʊshɛlfən] *vi unreg*: **jdm** ~ help sb out.

Aushilfe ['aʊshɪlfə] *f* help, assistance; *(Person)* (temporary) worker.

Aushilfskraft *f* temporary worker.

aushilfsweise *ad* temporarily, as a stopgap.

ausholen ['aʊshoːlən] *vi* swing one's arm back; *(zur Ohrfeige)* raise one's hand; *(beim Gehen)* take long strides; **weit** ~ *(fig)* be expansive.

aushorchen ['aʊshɔrçən] *vt* sound out, pump.

aushungern ['aʊshʊŋərn] *vt* starve out.

auskennen ['aʊskɛnən] *vr unreg* know thoroughly; *(an einem Ort)* know one's way about; *(in Fragen etc)* be knowledgeable.

Ausklang ['aʊsklaŋ] *m* end.

auskleiden ['aʊsklaɪdən] *vr* undress // *vt (Wand)* line.

ausklingen ['aʊsklɪŋən] *vi unreg (Ton, Lied)* die away; *(Fest)* peter out.

ausklopfen ['aʊsklɔpfən] *vt (Teppich)* beat; *(Pfeife)* knock out.

auskochen ['aʊskɔxən] *vt* boil; *(MED)* sterilize; **ausgekocht** *(fig)* out-and-out.

auskommen ['aʊskɔmən] *vi unreg*: **mit jdm** ~ get on with sb; **mit etw** ~ get by with sth; **A~** *nt* -**s**: **sein A~ haben** get by.

auskosten ['aʊskɔstən] *vt* enjoy to the full.

auskundschaften ['aʊskʊntʃaftən] *vt* spy out; *(Gebiet)* reconnoitre.

Auskunft ['aʊskʊnft] *f* -, **-künfte** information; *(nähere)* details *pl*, particulars *pl*; (*Stelle*) information office; (*TEL*) inquiries.

auslachen ['auslaxən] *vt* laugh at, mock.

ausladen ['ausla:dən] *vt unreg* unload; (*umg: Gäste*) cancel an invitation to.

Auslage ['ausla:gə] *f* shop window (display); ~**n** *pl* outlay, expenditure.

Ausland ['auslant] *nt* foreign countries *pl*; **im/ins** ~ abroad.

Ausländer(in *f*) ['auslɛndər(ın)] *m* -**s**, - foreigner.

ausländisch *a* foreign.

Auslands- *zW*: ~**gespräch** *nt* international call; ~**korrespondent(in** *f*) *m* foreign correspondent; ~**reise** *f* trip abroad.

auslassen ['auslasən] *unreg vt* leave out; (*Wort etc auch*) omit; (*Fett*) melt; (*Kleidungsstück*) let out; (*Wut, Ärger*) vent (*an* +*dat on*) // *vr*: **sich über etw** (*akk*) ~ speak one's mind about sth.

Auslassung *f* omission.

Auslauf ['auslauf] *m* (*für Tiere*) run; (*Ausfluß*) outflow, outlet; **a**~**en** *vi unreg* run out; (*Behälter*) leak; (*NAUT*) put out (to sea); (*langsam aufhören*) run down.

Ausläufer ['auslɔyfər] *m* (*von Gebirge*) spur; (*Pflanze*) runner; (*MET: von Hoch*) ridge; (*von Tief*) trough.

ausleeren ['ausle:rən] *vt* empty.

auslegen ['ausle:gən] *vt* (*Waren*) lay out; (*Köder*) put down; (*Geld*) lend; (*bedecken*) cover; (*Text etc*) interpret.

Auslegung *f* interpretation.

Ausleihe ['auslaiə] *f* -, -**n** issuing; (*Stelle*) issue desk; **a**~**n** *vt unreg* (*verleihen*) lend; **sich** (*dat*) **etw a**~**en** borrow sth.

Auslese ['ausle:zə] *f* -, -**n** selection; (*Elite*) elite; (*Wein*) choice wine; **a**~**n** *vt unreg* select; (*umg: zu Ende lesen*) finish.

ausliefern ['ausli:fərn] *vt* deliver (up), hand over; (*COMM*) deliver; **jdm/etw ausgeliefert sein** be at the mercy of sb/sth.

auslöschen ['auslœʃən] *vt* extinguish; (*fig*) wipe out, obliterate.

auslosen ['auslo:zən] *vt* draw lots for.

auslösen ['auslø:zən] *vt* (*Explosion, Schuß*) set off; (*hervorrufen*) cause, produce; (*Gefangene*) ransom; (*Pfand*) redeem.

Auslöser *m* -**s**, - (*PHOT*) release.

ausmachen ['ausmaxən] *vt* (*Licht, Radio*) turn off; (*Feuer*) put out; (*entdecken*) make out; (*vereinbaren*) agree; (*beilegen*) settle; (*Anteil darstellen, betragen*) represent; (*bedeuten*) matter; **macht es Ihnen etwas aus, wenn ...?** would you mind if ...?

ausmalen ['ausma:lən] *vt* paint; (*fig*) describe; **sich** (*dat*) **etw** ~ imagine sth.

Ausmaß ['ausma:s] *nt* dimension; (*fig auch*) scale.

ausmerzen ['ausmɛrtsən] *vt* eliminate.

ausmessen ['ausmɛsən] *vt unreg* measure.

Ausnahme ['ausna:mə] *f* -, -**n** exception; ~**fall** *m* exceptional case; ~**zustand** *m* state of emergency.

ausnahmslos *ad* without exception.

ausnahmsweise *ad* by way of exception, for once.

ausnehmen ['ausne:mən] *unreg vt* take out, remove; (*Tier*) gut; (*Nest*) rob; (*umg: Geld abnehmen*) clean out; (*ausschließen*) make an exception of // *vr* look, appear; ~**d** *a* exceptional.

ausnützen ['ausnytsən] *vt* (*Zeit, Gelegenheit*) use, turn to good account; (*Einfluß*) use; (*Mensch, Gutmütigkeit*) exploit.

auspacken ['auspakən] *vt* unpack.

auspfeifen ['auspfaifən] *vt unreg* hiss/boo at.

ausplaudern ['ausplaudərn] *vt* (*Geheimnis*) blab.

ausprobieren ['ausprobi:rən] *vt* try (out).

Auspuff ['auspuf] *m* -(**e**)**s**, -**e** (*TECH*) exhaust; ~**rohr** *nt* exhaust (pipe); ~**topf** *m* (*AUT*) silencer.

ausradieren ['ausradi:rən] *vt* erase, rub out; (*fig*) annihilate.

ausrangieren ['ausrãʒi:rən] *vt* (*umg*) chuck out.

ausrauben ['ausraubən] *vt* rob.

ausräumen ['ausrɔymən] *vt* (*Dinge*) clear away; (*Schrank, Zimmer*) empty; (*Bedenken*) put aside.

ausrechnen ['ausrɛçnən] *vt* calculate, reckon.

Ausrede ['ausre:də] *f* excuse; **a**~**n** *vi* have one's say // *vt*: **jdm etw a**~**n** talk sb out of sth.

ausreichen ['ausraiçən] *vi* suffice, be enough; ~**d** *a* sufficient, adequate; (*SCH*) adequate.

Ausreise ['ausraizə] *f* departure; **bei der** ~ when leaving the country; ~**erlaubnis** *f* exit visa; **a**~**n** *vi* leave the country.

ausreißen ['ausraisən] *unreg vt* tear *od* pull out // *vi* (*Riß bekommen*) tear; (*umg*) make off, scram.

ausrenken ['ausrɛŋkən] *vt* dislocate.

ausrichten ['ausrıçtən] *vt* (*Botschaft*) deliver; (*Gruß*) pass on; (*Hochzeit etc*) arrange; (*erreichen*) get anywhere (*bei* with); (*in gerade Linie bringen*) get in a straight line; (*angleichen*) bring into line; (*TYP*) justify; **ich werde es ihm** ~ I'll tell him.

ausrotten ['ausrɔtən] vt stamp out, exterminate.

ausrücken ['ausrʏkən] vi (MIL) move off; (Feuerwehr, Polizei) be called out; (umg: weglaufen) run away.

Ausruf ['ausru:f] m (Schrei) cry, exclamation; (Verkünden) proclamation; **a~en** vt unreg cry out, exclaim; call out; **Ausrufezeichen** nt exclamation mark.

ausruhen ['ausru:ən] vtr rest.

ausrüsten ['ausrʏstən] vt equip, fit out.

Ausrüstung f equipment.

ausrutschen ['ausrutʃən] vi slip.

Aussage ['ausza:gə] f -, -n (JUR) statement; **a~n** vt say, state // vi (JUR) give evidence.

ausschalten ['ausʃaltən] vt switch off; (fig) eliminate.

Ausschank ['ausʃaŋk] m -(e)s, -schänke dispensing, giving out; (COMM) selling; (Theke) bar.

Ausschau ['ausʃau] f: ~ halten look out, watch (nach for); **a~en** vi look out (nach for), be on the look-out.

ausscheiden ['ausʃaidən] unreg vt separate; (MED) give off, secrete // vi leave (aus etw sth); (SPORT) be eliminated od knocked out.

Ausscheidung f separation; secretion; (aus Amt) retiral; elimination.

ausschimpfen ['ausʃɪmpfən] vt scold, tell off.

ausschlafen ['ausʃla:fən] unreg vir have a long lie (in) // vt sleep off; **ich bin nicht ausgeschlafen** I didn't get enough sleep.

Ausschlag ['ausʃla:k] m (MED) rash; (Pendel~) swing; (Nadel) deflection; **den ~ geben** (fig) tip the balance; **a~en** [-gən] unreg vt knock out; (auskleiden) deck out; (verweigern) decline // vi (Pferd) kick out; (BOT) sprout; **a~gebend** a decisive.

ausschließen ['ausʃli:sən] vt unreg shut od lock out; (fig) exclude.

ausschließlich a, ad exclusive(ly) // präp +gen excluding, exclusive of.

Ausschluß ['ausʃlus] m exclusion.

ausschmücken ['ausʃmʏkən] vt decorate; (fig) embellish.

ausschneiden ['ausʃnaidən] vt unreg cut out; (Büsche) trim.

Ausschnitt ['ausʃnɪt] m (Teil) section; (von Kleid) neckline; (Zeitungs~) cutting; (aus Film etc) excerpt.

ausschreiben ['ausʃraibən] vt unreg (ganz schreiben) write out (in full); (ausstellen) write (out); (Stelle, Wettbewerb etc) announce, advertise.

Ausschreitung ['ausʃraituŋ] f excess.

Ausschuß ['ausʃus] m committee, board; (Abfall) waste, scraps pl; (COMM: auch ~ware f) reject.

ausschütten ['ausʃʏtən] vt pour out;

(Eimer) empty; (Geld) pay // vr shake (with laughter).

ausschweifend ['ausʃvaifənt] a (Leben) dissipated, debauched; (Phantasie) extravagant.

Ausschweifung f excess.

aussehen ['ausze:ən] vi unreg look; **es sieht nach Regen aus** it looks like rain; **es sieht schlecht aus** things look bad; **A~** nt -s appearance.

außen ['ausən] ad outside; (nach ~) outwards; ~ **ist es rot** it's red (on the) outside.

Außen- zW: ~**bordmotor** m outboard motor; ~**dienst** m: **im ~dienst sein** work outside the office; ~**handel** m foreign trade; ~**minister** m foreign minister; ~**ministerium** nt foreign office; ~**politik** f foreign policy; ~**seite** f outside; ~**seiter** m -s, - outsider; ~**welt** f outside world.

außer ['ausər] präp +dat (räumlich) out of; (abgesehen von) except; ~ **Gefahr** out of danger; ~ **Zweifel** beyond any doubt; ~ **Betrieb** out of order; ~ **sich** (dat) **sein/geraten** be beside o.s.; ~ **Dienst** retired; ~ **Landes** abroad // kj (ausgenommen) except; ~ **wenn** unless; ~ **daß** except; ~**dem** kj besides, in addition.

äußere(r, s) ['ɔysərə(r,z)] a outer, external.

außer- zW: ~**ehelich** a extramarital; ~**gewöhnlich** a unusual; ~**halb** präp +gen, ad outside.

äußerlich a, ad external.

äußern vt utter, express; (zeigen) show // vr give one's opinion; (sich zeigen) show itself.

außer- zW: ~**ordentlich** a extraordinary; ~**planmäßig** a unscheduled; ~'**stande** ad not in a position, unable.

äußerst ['ɔysərst] ad extremely, most; ~**e(r, s)** a utmost; (räumlich) farthest; (Termin) last possible; (Preis) highest.

aussetzen ['auszɛtsən] vt (Kind, Tier) abandon; (Boote) lower; (Belohnung) offer; (Urteil, Verfahren) postpone; **jdm/etw ausgesetzt sein** be exposed to sb/sth; **an jdm/etw etwas ~** find fault with sb/sth // vi (aufhören) stop; (Pause machen) drop out.

Aussicht ['auszɪçt] f view; (in Zukunft) prospect; **etw in ~ haben** have sth in view.

Aussichts- zW: **a~los** a hopeless; ~**punkt** m viewpoint; **a~reich** a promising; ~**turm** m observation tower.

aussöhnen ['ɔysøːnən] vt reconcile // vr reconcile o.s., become reconciled.

Aussöhnung f reconciliation.

aussondern ['auszɔndərn] vt separate, select.

aussortieren ['auszɔrtiːrən] vt sort out.

ausspannen ['aʊsʃpanən] vt spread od stretch out; (Pferd) unharness; (umg: Mädchen) steal (jdm from sb) // vi relax.

aussperren ['aʊsʃpɛrən] vt lock out.

Aussperrung f lock-out.

ausspielen ['aʊsʃpiːlən] vt (Karte) lead; (Geldprämie) offer as a prize; **jdn gegen jdn** ~ play sb off against sb // vi (KARTEN) lead; **ausgespielt haben** be finished.

Aussprache ['aʊsʃpraːxə] f pronunciation; (Unterredung) (frank) discussion.

aussprechen ['aʊsʃprɛçən] unreg vt pronounce; (äußern) say, express // vr (sich äußern) speak (über +akk about); (sich anvertrauen) unburden o.s.; (diskutieren) discuss // vi (zu Ende sprechen) finish speaking.

Ausspruch ['aʊsʃprʊx] m saying, remark.

ausspülen ['aʊsʃpyːlən] vt wash out; (Mund) rinse.

Ausstand ['aʊsʃtant] m strike; **in den** ~ **treten** go on strike.

ausstatten ['aʊsʃtatən] vt (Zimmer etc) furnish; **jdn mit etw** ~ equip sb od kit sb out with etw.

Ausstattung f (Ausstatten) provision; (Kleidung) outfit; (Aussteuer) dowry; (Aufmachung) make-up; (Einrichtung) furnishing.

ausstechen ['aʊsʃtɛçən] vt unreg (Augen, Rasen, Graben) dig out; (Kekse) cut out; (übertreffen) outshine.

ausstehen ['aʊsʃteːən] unreg vt stand, endure // vi (noch nicht dasein) be outstanding.

aussteigen ['aʊsʃtaɪgən] vi unreg get out, alight.

ausstellen ['aʊsʃtɛlən] vt exhibit, display; (umg: ausschalten) switch off; (Rechnung etc) make out; (Paß, Zeugnis) issue.

Ausstellung f exhibition; (FIN) drawing up; (einer Rechnung) making out; (eines Passes etc) issuing.

aussterben ['aʊsʃtɛrbən] vi unreg die out.

Aussteuer ['aʊsʃtɔʏər] f dowry.

Ausstieg ['aʊsʃtiːk] m -(e)s, -e exit.

ausstopfen ['aʊsʃtɔpfən] vt stuff.

ausstoßen ['aʊsʃtoːsən] vt unreg (Luft, Rauch) give off, emit; (aus Verein etc) expel, exclude; (Auge) poke out.

ausstrahlen ['aʊsʃtraːlən] vti radiate; (RAD) broadcast.

Ausstrahlung f radiation; (fig) charisma.

ausstrecken ['aʊsʃtrɛkən] vtr stretch out.

ausstreichen ['aʊsʃtraɪçən] vt unreg cross out; (glätten) smooth out.

ausströmen ['aʊsʃtrøːmən] vi (Gas) pour out, escape // vt give off; (fig) radiate.

aussuchen ['aʊszuːxən] vt select, pick out.

Austausch ['aʊstaʊʃ] m exchange; **a~bar** a exchangeable; **a~en** vt exchange, swop; **~motor** m reconditioned engine.

austeilen ['aʊstaɪlən] vt distribute, give out.

Auster ['aʊstər] f -, -n oyster.

austoben ['aʊstoːbən] vr (Kind) run wild; (Erwachsene) sow one's wild oats.

austragen ['aʊstraːgən] vt unreg (Post) deliver; (Streit etc) decide; (Wettkämpfe) hold.

Austral- [aʊs'traːl] zW: **~ien** nt -s Australia; **~ier(in** f) m -s, - Australian; **a~isch** a Australian.

austreiben ['aʊstraɪbən] vt unreg drive out, expel; (Geister) exorcize.

austreten ['aʊstreːtən] unreg vi (zur Toilette) be excused; **aus etw** ~ leave sth // vt (Feuer) tread out, trample; (Schuhe) wear out; (Treppe) wear down.

austrinken ['aʊstrɪŋkən] unreg vt (Glas) drain; (Getränk) drink up // vi finish one's drink, drink up.

Austritt ['aʊstrɪt] m emission; (aus Verein, Partei etc) retirement, withdrawal.

austrocknen ['aʊstrɔknən] vti dry up.

ausüben ['aʊsʔyːbən] vt (Beruf) practise, carry out; (Funktion) perform; (Einfluß) exert; (Reiz, Wirkung) exercise, have (auf jdn on sb).

Ausverkauf ['aʊsfɛrkaʊf] m sale; **a~en** vt sell out; (Geschäft) sell up; **a~t** a (Karten, Artikel) sold out; (THEAT: Haus) full.

Auswahl ['aʊsvaːl] f selection, choice (an +dat of).

auswählen ['aʊsvɛːlən] vt select, choose.

Auswander- ['aʊsvandər] zW: **~er** m emigrant; **a~n** vi emigrate; **~ung** f emigration.

auswärtig ['aʊsvɛrtɪç] a (nicht am/ vom Ort) out-of-town; (ausländisch) foreign.

auswärts ['aʊsvɛrts] ad outside; (nach außen) outwards; ~ **essen** eat out; **A~spiel** nt away game.

auswechseln ['aʊsvɛksəln] vt change, substitute.

Ausweg ['aʊsveːk] m way out; **a~los** a hopeless.

ausweichen ['aʊsvaɪçən] vi unreg: **jdm/etw** ~ (lit) move aside od make way for sb/sth; (fig) side-step sb/sth; **~d** a evasive.

ausweinen ['ausvainən] *vr* have a (good) cry.

Ausweis ['ausvais] *m* **-es, -e** identity card, passport; (*Mitglieds~, Bibliotheks~ etc*) card; **a~en** [-zən] *unreg vt* expel, banish // *vr* prove one's identity; **~papiere** *pl* identity papers *pl*; **~ung** *f* expulsion.

ausweiten ['ausvaitən] *vt* stretch.

auswendig ['ausvɛndiç] *ad* by heart; **~ lernen** *vt* learn by heart.

auswert- ['ausvɛrt] *zW:* **~en** *vt* evaluate; **A~ung** *f* evaluation, analysis; (*Nutzung*) utilization.

auswirk- ['ausvirk] *zW:* **~en** *vr* have an effect; **A~ung** *f* effect.

auswischen ['ausviʃən] *vt* wipe out; **jdm eins ~** (*umg*) put one over on sb.

Auswuchs ['ausvu:ks] *m* (out)growth; (*fig*) product.

auswuchten ['ausvuxtən] *vt* (*AUT*) balance.

auszahlen ['austsa:lən] *vt* (*Lohn, Summe*) pay out; (*Arbeiter*) pay off; (*Miterbe*) buy out // *vr* (*sich lohnen*) pay.

auszählen ['austsɛ:lən] *vt* (*Stimmen*) count; (*BOXEN*) count out.

auszeichnen ['austsaiçnən] *vt* honour; (*MIL*) decorate; (*COMM*) price // *vr* distinguish o.s.

Auszeichnung *f* distinction; (*COMM*) pricing; (*Ehrung*) awarding of decoration; (*Ehre*) honour; (*Orden*) decoration; **mit ~** with distinction.

ausziehen ['austsi:ən] *unreg vt* (*Kleidung*) take off; (*Haare, Zähne, Tisch etc*) pull out; (*nachmalen*) trace // *vr* undress // *vi* (*aufbrechen*) leave; (*aus Wohnung*) move out.

Auszug ['austsu:k] *m* (*aus Wohnung*) removal; (*aus Buch etc*) extract; (*Konto~*) statement; (*Ausmarsch*) departure.

Auto ['auto] *nt* **-s, -s** (motor-) car; **~ fahren** drive; **~bahn** *f* motorway; **~bahndreieck** *nt* motorway junction; **~bahnkreuz** *nt* motorway intersection; **~fähre** *f* car ferry; **~fahrer(in** *f*) *m* motorist, driver; **~fahrt** *f* drive; **autogen** [-'ge:n] *a* autogenous; **~'gramm** *nt* autograph; **Auto'mat** *m* **-en, -en** machine; **auto'matisch** *a* automatic; **autonom** [-'no:m] *a* autonomous.

Autor ['autɔr] *m* **-s, -en, Autorin** [au'to:rin] *f* author.

Auto- *zW:* **~radio** *nt* car radio; **~reifen** *m* car tyre; **~rennen** *nt* motor racing.

autoritär [autori'tɛ:r] *a* authoritarian.

Autorität *f* authority.

Auto- *zW:* **~stopp** *m:* per **~stopp fahren** hitch-hike; **~unfall** *m* car od motor accident; **~verleih** *m* car hire

(*Brit*) *od* rental (*US*); **~wäsche** *f* car wash.

Axt [akst] *f* **-, ̈-e** axe.

B

B, b [be:] *nt* B, b.

Baby ['be:bi] *nt* **-s, -s** baby; **~ausstattung** *f* layette; **~sitter** ['be:bizitər] *m* **-s, -** baby-sitter.

Bach [bax] *m* **-(e)s, ̈-e** stream, brook.

Back- [bak] *zW:* **~bord** *nt* **-(e)s, -e** (*NAUT*) port; **~e** *f* **-, -n** cheek; **b~en** *vti unreg* bake; **~enbart** *m* sideboards *pl*; **~enzahn** *m* molar.

Bäcker ['bɛkər] *m* **-s, -** baker; **~ei** [-'rai] *f* bakery; (**~laden**) baker's (shop).

Back- *zW:* **~obst** *nt* dried fruit; **~ofen** *m* oven; **~pflaume** *f* prune; **~pulver** *nt* baking powder; **~stein** *m* brick.

Bad [ba:t] *nt* **-(e)s, ̈-er** bath; (*Schwimmen*) bathe; (*Ort*) spa.

Bade- ['ba:də] *zW:* **~anstalt** *f* (swimming) baths *pl*; **~anzug** *m* bathing suit; **~hose** *f* bathing od swimming trunks *pl*; **~kappe** *f* bathing cap; **~mantel** *m* bath(ing) robe; **~meister** *m* baths attendant; **~mütze** *f* bathing cap; **b~n** *vi* bathe, have a bath // *vt* bath; **~ort** *m* spa; **~tuch** *nt* bath towel; **~wanne** *f* bath (tub); **~zimmer** *nt* bathroom.

Bagatelle [baga'tɛlə] *f* **-, -n** trifle.

Bagger ['bagər] *m* **-s, -** excavator; (*NAUT*) dredger; **b~n** *vti* excavate; (*NAUT*) dredge.

Bahn [ba:n] *f* **-, -en** railway, railroad (*US*); (*Weg*) road, way; (*Spur*) lane; (*Renn~*) track; (*ASTRON*) orbit; (*Stoff~*) length; **b~brechend** *a* pioneering; **~damm** *m* railway embankment; **b~en** *vt:* **sich/jdm einen Weg b~en** clear a way/a way for sb; **~fahrt** *f* railway journey; **~hof** *m* station; **auf dem ~hof** at the station; **~hofsvorsteher** *m* station-master; **~linie** *f* (railway) line; **~steig** *m* platform; **~steigkarte** *f* platform ticket; **~strecke** *f* (railway) line; **~übergang** *m* level crossing, grade crossing (*US*); **~wärter** *m* signalman.

Bahre ['ba:rə] *f* **-, -n** stretcher.

Bajonett [bajo'nɛt] *nt* **-(e)s, -e** bayonet.

Bakterien [bak'te:riən] *pl* bacteria *pl*.

Balance [ba'lã:sə] *f* **-, -n** balance, equilibrium.

balan'cieren *vti* balance.

bald [balt] *ad* (*zeitlich*) soon; (*beinahe*) almost; **~ig** ['baldiç] *a* early, speedy; **~möglichst** *ad* as soon as possible.

Baldrian ['baldria:n] *m* **-s, -e** valerian.

Balkan ['balka:n] *m*: der ~ the Balkans *pl*.

Balken ['balkən] *m* **-s, -** beam; (*Trag~*) girder; (*Stütz~*) prop.

Balkon [bal'kõ:] *m* **-s, -s** *od* **-e** balcony; (*THEAT*) (dress) circle.

Ball [bal] *m* **-(e)s, ̈s** ball; (*Tanz*) dance, ball.

Ballade [ba'la:də] *f* **-, -n** ballad.

Ballast ['balast] *m* **-(e)s, -e** ballast; (*fig*) weight, burden.

Ballen ['balən] *m* **-s, -** bale; (*ANAT*) ball; **b~** *vt* (*formen*) make into a ball; (*Faust*) clench // *vr* build up; (*Menschen*) gather.

Ballett [ba'lɛt] *nt* **-(e)s, -e** ballet.

Ballkleid *nt* evening dress.

Ballon [ba'lõ:] *m* **-s, -s** *od* **-e** balloon.

Ballspiel *nt* ball game.

Bambus ['bambus] *m* **-ses, -se** bamboo; **~rohr** *nt* bamboo cane.

banal [ba'na:l] *a* banal.

Banane [ba'na:nə] *f* **-, -n** banana.

band *etc v siehe* **binden**.

Band [bant] *m* **-(e)s, ̈e** (*Buch~*) volume // *nt* **-(e)s, ̈er** (*Stoff~*) ribbon, tape; (*Fließ~*) production line; (*Faß~*) hoop; (*Ton~*) tape; (*ANAT*) ligament; **etw auf ~ aufnehmen** tape sth; **am laufenden ~** (*umg*) non-stop // *nt* **-(e)s, -e** (*Freundschafts~ etc*) bond // [bɛnt] *f* **-, -s** band, group.

Bandage [ban'da:ʒə] *f* **-, -n** bandage.

bandagieren *vt* bandage.

Bande ['bandə] *f* **-, -n** band; (*Straßen~*) gang.

bändigen ['bɛndɪgən] *vt* (*Tier*) tame; (*Trieb, ·Leidenschaft*) control, restrain.

Bandit [ban'di:t] *m* **-en, -en** bandit.

Band- *zW*: **~maß** *nt* tape measure; **~scheibe** *f* (*ANAT*) disc; **~wurm** *m* tapeworm.

bange ['baŋə] *a* scared; (*besorgt*) anxious; **jdm wird es ~** sb is becoming scared; **jdm ~ machen** scare sb; **~n** *vi*: **um jdn/etw ~n** be anxious *od* worried about sb/sth.

Banjo ['banjo, 'bɛndʒo] *nt* **-s, -s** banjo.

Bank [baŋk] *f* **-, ̈e** (*Sitz~*) bench; (*Sand~ etc*) (sand)bank *od* -bar // *f* **-, -en** (*Geld~*) bank; **~anweisung** *f* banker's order; **~beamte(r)** *m* bank clerk.

Bankett [baŋ'kɛt] *nt* **-(e)s, -e** (*Essen*) banquet; (*Straßenrand*) verge (*Brit*), shoulder (*US*).

Bankier [baŋki'e:] *m* **-s, -s** banker.

Bank- *zW*: **~konto** *m* bank account; **~note** *f* banknote; **~raub** *m* bank robbery.

Bankrott [baŋ'krɔt] *m* **-(e)s, -e** bankruptcy; **~ machen** go bankrupt; **b~** *a* bankrupt.

Bann [ban] *m* **-(e)s, -e** (*HIST*) ban; (*Kirchen~*) excommunication; (*fig: Zauber*) spell; **b~en** *vt* (*Geister*) exorcise; (*Gefahr*) avert; (*bezaubern*) enchant; (*HIST*) banish; **~er** *nt* **-s, -** banner, flag.

bar [ba:r] *a* (*unbedeckt*) bare; (*frei von*) lacking (*gen* in); (*offenkundig*) utter, sheer; **~e(s)** **Geld** cash; **etw (in) ~ bezahlen** pay sth (in) cash; **etw für ~e Münze nehmen** (*fig*) take sth at its face value; **B~** *f* **-, -s** bar.

Bär [bɛ:r] *m* **-en, -en** bear.

Baracke [ba'rakə] *f* **-, -n** hut, barracks.

barbarisch [bar'ba:rɪʃ] *a* barbaric, barbarous.

Bar- *zW*: **b~fuß** *a* barefoot; **~geld** *nt* cash, ready money; **b~geldlos** *a* non-cash; **~hocker** *m* bar stool; **~kauf** *m* cash purchase; **~keeper** ['ba:rki:pər] *m* **-s, -** barman, bartender.

barmherzig [barm'hɛrtsɪç] *a* merciful, compassionate; **B~keit** *f* mercy, compassion.

Barometer [baro'me:tər] *nt* **-s, -** barometer.

Baron [ba'ro:n] *m* **-s, -e** baron; **~esse** [baro'nɛsə] *f* **-, -n,** **~in** *f* baroness.

Barren ['barən] *m* **-s, -** parallel bars *pl*; (*Gold~*) ingot.

Barriere [bari'ɛ:rə] *f* **-, -n** barrier.

Barrikade [bari'ka:də] *f* **-, -n** barricade.

Barsch [barʃ] *m* **-(e)s, -e** perch; **b~** *a* brusque, gruff.

Bar- *zW*: **~schaft** *f* ready money; **~scheck** *m* open *od* uncrossed cheque (*Brit*), open check (*US*).

Bart [ba:rt] *m* **-(e)s, ̈e** beard; (*Schlüssel~*) bit.

bärtig ['bɛ:rtɪç] *a* bearded.

Barzahlung *f* cash payment.

Base ['ba:zə] *f* **-, -n** (*CHEM*) base; (*Kusine*) cousin.

Basel ['ba:zəl] *nt* Basle.

BASIC ['be:sik] (*COMPUT*) BASIC.

basieren [ba'zi:rən] *vt* base // *vi* be based.

Basis ['ba:zɪs] *f* **-, Basen** basis.

Baß [bas] *m* **Basses, Bässe** bass; **~stimme** *f* bass voice.

Bassin [ba'sɛ̃:] *nt* **-s, -s** pool.

Bassist [ba'sɪst] *m* bass.

Bast [bast] *m* **-(e)s, -e** raffia.

basteln *vt* make // *vi* do handicrafts.

bat *etc v siehe* **bitten**.

Bataillon [batal'jo:n] *nt* **-s, -e** battalion.

Batist [ba'tɪst] *m* **-(e)s, -e** batiste.

Batterie [batə'ri:] *f* battery.

Bau [bau] *m* **-(e)s** (*Bauen*) building, construction; (*Aufbau*) structure; (*Körper~*) frame; (*Baustelle*) build-

ing site; *pl* ~**e** (*Tier*~) hole, burrow;
(*MIN*) working(s); *pl* ~**ten** (*Gebäude*) building; **sich im** ~ **befinden**
be under construction; ~**arbeiter** *m*
building worker.

Bauch [baux] *m* **-(e)s, Bäuche** belly;
(*ANAT auch*) stomach, abdomen;
~**fell** *nt* peritoneum; **b~ig** *a* bulging;
~**redner** *m* ventriloquist; ~**tanz**
m belly dance; belly dancing;
~**schmerzen** *pl*, ~**weh** *nt* stomachache.

bauen ['bauən] *vti* build; (*TECH*) construct; **auf jdn/etw** ~ depend *od* count
upon sb/sth.

Bauer ['bauər] *m* **-n** *od* **-s, -n** farmer;
(*Schach*) pawn // *nt od m* **-s, -** (*Vogel*~) cage.

Bäuerin ['bɔyərin] *f* farmer; (*Frau
des Bauers*) farmer's wife.

bäuerlich *a* rustic.

Bauern- *zW*: ~**fänge'rei** *f* deception;
~**haus** *nt* farmhouse; ~**hof** *m*
farm(yard).

Bau- *zW*: **b~fällig** *a* dilapidated;
~**fälligkeit** *f* dilapidation; ~**gelände** *f*
building site; ~**genehmigung** *f* building permit; ~**herr** *m* purchaser;
~**kasten** *m* box of bricks; ~**kosten**
pl construction costs *pl*; ~**land** *nt*
building land; **b~lich** *a* structural.

Baum [baum] *m* **-(e)s, Bäume** tree.

baumeln ['bauməln] *vi* dangle.

bäumen ['bɔymən] *vr* rear (up).

Baum- *zW*: ~**schule** *f* nursery;
~**stamm** *m* tree trunk; ~**stumpf** *m*
tree stump; ~**wolle** *f* cotton.

Bau- *zW*: ~**plan** *m* architect's plan;
~**platz** *m* building site; ~**sparkasse** *f*
building society; ~**stein** *m* building
stone, freestone; ~**stelle** *f* building
site; ~**teil** *nt* prefabricated part (of
building); ~**unternehmer** *m* contractor, builder; ~**weise** *f* (method of)
construction; ~**werk** *nt* building;
~**zaun** *m* hoarding.

Bayer(in *f*) ['baɪər(in)] *m* Bavarian.

Bayern ['baɪərn] *nt* Bavaria.

bayrisch ['baɪrɪʃ] *a* Bavarian.

Bazillus [ba'tsɪlus] *m* **-, Bazillen** bacil-
lus.

beabsichtigen [bə''apzɪçtɪgən] *vt* intend.

beachten [bə''axtən] *vt* take note of;
(*Vorschrift*) obey; (*Vorfahrt*) observe.

beachtlich *a* considerable.

Beachtung *f* notice, attention, observation.

Beamte(r) [bə''amtə(r)] *m* **-n, -n,
Beamtin** *f* official, civil servant;
(*Bank*~ *etc*) employee.

beängstigend [bə''ɛŋstɪgənt] *a* alarming.

beanspruchen [bə''anʃpruxən] *vt*

claim; (*Zeit, Platz*) take up, occupy;
(*Mensch*) take up sb's time.

beanstanden [bə''anʃtandən] *vt* complain about, object to.

Beanstandung *f* complaint.

beantragen [bə''antra:gən] *vt* apply
for, ask for.

beantworten [bə''antvɔrtən] *vt* answer.

Beantwortung *f* reply (*gen* to).

bearbeiten [bə''arbaɪtən] *vt* work;
(*Material*) work; (*Thema*) deal
with; (*Land*) cultivate; (*CHEM*) treat;
(*Buch*) revise; (*umg: beeinflussen
wollen*) work on.

Bearbeitung *f* processing; treatment;
cultivation; revision.

Beatmung [bə''a:tmuŋ] *f* respiration.

beaufsichtigen [bə''aufzɪçtɪgən] *vt*
supervise.

Beaufsichtigung *f* supervision.

beauftragen [bə''auftra:gən] *vt* instruct; **jdn mit etw** ~ entrust sb with
sth.

bebauen [bə'bauən] *vt* build on;
(*AGR*) cultivate.

beben ['be:bən] *vi* tremble, shake; **B~**
nt **-s, -** earthquake.

Becher ['bɛçər] *m* **-s, -** mug; (*ohne
Henkel*) tumbler.

Becken ['bɛkən] *nt* **-s, -** basin; (*MUS*)
cymbal; (*ANAT*) pelvis.

bedacht [bə'daxt] *a* thoughtful, careful; **auf etw** (*akk*) ~ **sein** be concerned about sth.

bedächtig [bə'dɛçtɪç] *a* (*umsichtig*)
thoughtful, reflective; (*langsam*)
slow, deliberate.

bedanken [bə'daŋkən] *vr* say thank
you (*bei jdm* to sb).

Bedarf [bə'darf] *m* **-(e)s** need, requirement; (*COMM*) demand; supply; **je
nach** ~ according to demand; **bei** ~
if necessary; ~ **an etw** (*dat*) **haben**
be in need of sth.

Bedarfs- *zW*: ~**artikel** *m* requisite;
~**fall** *m* case of need; ~**haltestelle** *f*
request stop.

bedauerlich [bə'dauərlɪç] *a* regret-
table.

bedauern [bə'dauərn] *vt* be sorry for;
(*bemitleiden*) pity; **B~** *nt* **-s** regret;
bedauernswert *a* (*Zustände*) regret-
table; (*Mensch*) pitiable, unfortunate.

bedecken [bə'dɛkən] *vt* cover.

bedeckt *a* covered; (*Himmel*) overcast.

bedenken [bə'dɛŋkən] *vt unreg* think
(over), consider; **B~** *nt* **-s, -** (*Überlegen*) process; (*Zweifel*) doubt;
(*Skrupel*) scruple.

bedenklich *a* doubtful; (*bedrohlich*)
dangerous, risky.

bedeuten [bə'dɔytən] *vt* mean; signify; (*wichtig sein*) be of impor-

tance; **~d** a important; (*beträchtlich*) considerable.

Bedeutung f meaning; significance; (*Wichtigkeit*) importance; **bedeutungslos** a insignificant, unimportant; **bedeutungsvoll** a momentous, significant.

bedienen [bə'di:nən] vt serve; (*Maschine*) work, operate // vr (*beim Essen*) help o.s.; (*gebrauchen*) make use (*gen* of).

Bedienung f service; (*Kellnerin*) waitress; (*Verkäuferin*) shop assistant; (*Zuschlag*) service (charge).

Bedingung f condition; (*Voraussetzung*) stipulation; **bedingungslos** a unconditional.

bedrängen [bə'drɛŋən] vt pester, harass.

bedrohen [bə'dro:ən] vt threaten.

bedrohlich a ominous, threatening.

Bedrohung f threat, menace.

bedrücken [bədrʏkən] vt oppress, trouble.

bedürf- [bə'dʏrf] zW: **~en** vi unreg +gen need, require; **B~nis** nt -ses, -se need; **B~nisanstalt** f public convenience, comfort station (*US*); **~tig** a in need (*gen* of), poor, needy.

beeilen [bə'aɪlən] vr hurry.

beeindrucken [bə''aɪndrʊkən] vt impress, make an impression on.

beeinflussen [bə''aɪnflʊsən] vt influence.

beeinträchtigen [bə''aɪntrɛçtɪgən] vt affect adversely; (*Freiheit*) infringe upon.

beend(ig)en [bə''ɛnd(ɪg)ən] vt end, finish, terminate.

beengen [bə''ɛŋən] vt cramp; (*fig*) hamper, oppress.

beerben [bə''ɛrbən] vt inherit from.

beerdigen [bə''e:rdɪgən] vt bury.

Beerdigung f funeral, burial; **Beerdigungsunternehmer** m undertaker.

Beere ['be:rə] f -, -n berry; (*Trauben~*) grape.

Beet [be:t] nt -(e)s, -e bed.

befähigen [bə'fɛ:ɪgən] vt enable.

befähigt a (*begabt*) talented; (*fähig*) capable (*für* of).

Befähigung f capability; (*Begabung*) talent, aptitude.

befahrbar [bə'fa:rba:r] a passable; (*NAUT*) navigable.

befahren [bə'fa:rən] vt unreg use, drive over; (*NAUT*) navigate // a used.

befallen [bə'falən] vt unreg come over.

befangen [bə'faŋən] a (*schüchtern*) shy, self-conscious; (*voreingenommen*) biased; **B~heit** f shyness; bias.

befassen [bə'fasən] vr concern o.s.

Befehl [bə'fe:l] m -(e)s, -e command, order; **b~en** unreg vt order; **jdm etw b~en** order sb to do sth // vi give orders; **Befehlshaber** m -s, - commanding officer; **Befehlsverweigerung** f insubordination.

befestigen [bə'fɛstɪgən] vt fasten (*an* +dat to); (*stärken*) strengthen; (*MIL*) fortify.

Befestigung f fastening; strengthening; (*MIL*) fortification.

befeuchten [bə'fɔʏçtən] vt damp(en), moisten.

befinden [bə'fɪndən] unreg vr be; (*sich fühlen*) feel // vt: **jdn/etw für od als etw ~** deem sb/sth to be sth // vi decide (*über* +akk on), adjudicate; **B~** nt -s health, condition; (*Meinung*) view, opinion.

befolgen [bə'fɔlgən] vt comply with, follow.

befördern [bə'fœrdərn] vt (*senden*) transport, send; (*beruflich*) promote.

Beförderung f transport, conveyance; promotion.

befragen [bə'fra:gən] vt question.

befreien [bə'fraɪən] vt set free; (*erlassen*) exempt.

Befreier m -s, - liberator.

Befreiung f liberation, release; (*Erlassen*) exemption.

befremden [bə'frɛmdən] vt surprise, disturb; **B~** nt -s surprise, astonishment.

befreunden [bə'frɔʏndən] vr make friends; (*mit Idee etc*) acquaint o.s.

befreundet a friendly.

befriedigen [bə'fri:dɪgən] vt satisfy; **~d** a satisfactory.

Befriedigung f satisfaction, gratification.

befristet [bə'frɪstət] a limited.

befruchten [bə'frʊxtən] vt fertilize; (*fig*) stimulate.

Befruchtung f: **künstliche ~** artificial insemination.

Befugnis [bə'fu:knɪs] f -, -se authorization, powers pl.

befugt a authorized, entitled.

Befund [bə'fʊnt] m -(e)s, -e findings pl; (*MED*) diagnosis.

befürchten [bə'fʏrçtən] vt fear.

Befürchtung f fear, apprehension.

befürwort- [bə'fy:rvɔrt] zW: **~en** vt support, speak in favour of; **B~er** m -s, - supporter, advocate.

begabt [bə'ga:pt] a gifted.

Begabung [bə'ga:bʊŋ] f talent, gift.

begann etc vt siehe **beginnen**.

begeben [bə'ge:bən] vr unreg (*gehen*) proceed (*zu, nach* to); (*geschehen*) occur; **B~heit** f occurrence.

begegnen [bə'ge:gnən] vi meet (*jdm* sb); meet with (*etw* (dat) sth); (*behandeln*) treat (*jdm* sb).

Begegnung f meeting.
begehen [bə'ge:ən] vt unreg (Straftat) commit; (abschreiten) cover; (Straße etc) use, negotiate; (Feier) celebrate.
begehren [bə'ge:rən] vt desire; **begehrenswert** a desirable.
begehrt a in demand; (Junggeselle) eligible.
begeistern [bə'gaɪstərn] vt fill with enthusiasm, inspire // vr: **sich für etw ~** get enthusiastic about sth.
begeistert a enthusiastic.
Begeisterung f enthusiasm.
Begierde [bə'gi:rdə] f -, -n desire, passion.
begierig [bə'gi:rɪç] a eager, keen.
begießen [bə'gi:sən] vt unreg water; (mit Alkohol) drink to.
Beginn [bə'gɪn] m -(e)s beginning; **zu ~** at the beginning; **b~en** vti unreg start, begin.
beglaubigen [bə'glaʊbɪgən] vt countersign.
Beglaubigung f countersignature.
begleichen [bə'glaɪçən] vt unreg settle, pay.
Begleit- [bə'glaɪt] zW: **b~en** vt accompany; (MIL) escort; **~er** m -s, - companion; (Freund) escort; (MUS) accompanist; **~erscheinung** f concomitant (occurrence); **~schreiben** nt covering letter; **~umstände** pl concomitant circumstances pl; **~ung** f company; (MIL) escort; (MUS) accompaniment.
beglücken [bə'glʏkən] vt make happy, delight.
beglückwünschen [bə'glʏkvʏnʃən] vt congratulate (zu on).
begnadigen [bə'gna:dɪgən] vt pardon.
Begnadigung f pardon, amnesty.
begnügen [bə'gny:gən] vr be satisfied, content o.s.
Begonie [bə'go:niə] f begonia.
begonnen v siehe **beginnen**.
begraben [bə'gra:bən] vt unreg bury.
Begräbnis [bə'grɛ:pnɪs] nt -ses, -se burial, funeral.
begreifen [bə'graɪfən] vt unreg understand, comprehend.
begreiflich [bə'graɪflɪç] a understandable.
Begrenztheit [bə'grɛntsthaɪt] f limitation, restriction; (fig) narrowness.
Begriff [bə'grɪf] m -(e)s, -e concept, idea; **im ~ sein, etw zu tun** to be about to do sth; **schwer von ~** (umg) slow, dense; **begriffsstutzig** a dense, slow.
begründ- [bə'grʏnd] zW: **~en** vt (Gründe geben) justify; **begründet** a well-founded, justified; **B~ung** f justification, reason.
begrüßen [bə'gry:sən] vt greet, welcome.

Begrüßung f greeting, welcome.
begünstigen [bə'gʏnstɪgən] vt (Person) favour; (Sache) further, promote.
begutachten [bə'gu:t'axtən] vt assess.
begütert [bə'gy:tərt] a wealthy, well-to-do.
behaart [bə'ha:rt] a hairy.
behäbig [bə'hɛ:bɪç] a (dick) portly, stout; (geruhsam) comfortable.
behagen [bə'ha:gən] vi: **das behagt ihm nicht** he does not like it; **B~** nt -s comfort, ease.
behaglich [bə'ha:klɪç] a comfortable, cosy; **B~keit** f comfort, cosiness.
behalten [bə'haltən] vt unreg keep, retain; (im Gedächtnis) remember.
Behälter [bə'hɛltər] m -s, - container, receptacle.
behandeln [bə'handəln] vt treat; (Thema) deal with; (Maschine) handle.
Behandlung f treatment; (von Maschine) handling.
beharren [bə'harən] vi: **auf etw (dat) ~** stick od keep to sth.
beharrlich [bə'harlɪç] a (ausdauernd) steadfast, unwavering; (hartnäckig) tenacious, dogged; **B~keit** f steadfastness; tenacity.
behaupten [bə'haʊptən] vt claim, assert, maintain; (sein Recht) defend // vr assert o.s.
Behauptung f claim, assertion.
beheizen [bə'haɪtsən] vt heat.
behelfen [bə'hɛlfən] vr unreg: **sich mit etw ~** make do with sth; **behelfsmäßig** a improvised, makeshift; (vorübergehend) temporary.
behelligen [bə'hɛlɪgən] vt trouble, bother.
beherbergen [bə'hɛrbɛrgən] vt put up, house.
beherrschen [bə'hɛrʃən] vt (Volk) rule, govern; (Situation) control; (Sprache, Gefühle) master // vr control o.s.
beherrscht a controlled.
Beherrschung f rule; control; mastery.
beherzigen [bə'hɛrtsɪgən] vt take to heart.
beherzt a spirited, brave.
behilflich [bə'hɪlflɪç] a helpful; **jdm ~ sein** help sb (bei with).
behindern [bə'hɪndərn] vt hinder, impede.
Behinderte(r) mf disabled person.
Behinderung f hindrance; (Körper~) handicap.
Behörde [bə'hø:rdə] f -, -n authorities pl.
behördlich [bə'hø:rtlɪç] a official.
behüten [bə'hy:tən] vt guard; **jdn vor etw (dat) ~** preserve sb from sth.

behutsam [bə'hu:tza:m] *a* cautious, careful; **B~keit** *f* caution, carefulness.

bei [baɪ] *präp + dat* **1** (*nahe ~*) near; (*zum Aufenthalt*) at, with; (*unter, zwischen*) among: **~ München** near Munich; **~ uns** at our place; **~ Friseur** at the hairdresser's; **~ seinen Eltern wohnen** live with one's parents; **~ einer Firma arbeiten** work for a firm; **etw ~ sich haben** have sth on one; **jdn ~ sich haben** have sb with one; **~ Goethe** in Goethe; **~m Militär** in the army **2** (*zeitlich*) at, on; (*während*) during; (*Zustand, Umstand*) in; **~ Nacht** at night; **~ Nebel** in fog; **~ Regen** if it rains; **~ solcher Hitze** in such heat; **~ meiner Ankunft** on my arrival; **~ der Arbeit** when I'm *etc* working; **~m Fahren** while driving.

beibehalten ['baɪbəhaltən] *vt unreg* keep, retain.

beibringen ['baɪbrɪŋən] *vt unreg* (*Beweis, Zeugen*) bring forward; (*Gründe*) adduce; **jdm etw ~** (*zufügen*) inflict sth on sb; (*zu verstehen geben*) make sb understand sth; (*lehren*) teach sb sth.

Beichte ['baɪçtə] *f* -, -**n** confession; **b~n** *vt* confess // *vi* go to confession.

Beichtstuhl *m* confessional.

beide(s) ['baɪdə(s)] *pron*, *a* both; **meine ~n Brüder** my two brothers, both my brothers; **die ersten ~n** the first two; **wir ~** we two; **einer von ~n** one of the two; **alles ~s** both (of them).

beider- ['baɪdər] *zW:* **~lei** *a inv* of both; **~seitig** *a* mutual, reciprocal; **~seits** *ad* mutually // *präp +gen* on both sides of.

beieinander [baɪ'aɪ'nandər] *ad* together.

Beifahrer ['baɪfa:rər] *m* passenger; **~sitz** *m* passenger seat.

Beifall ['baɪfal] *m* -(**e)s** applause; (*Zustimmung*) approval.

beifällig ['baɪfɛlɪç] *a* approving; (*Kommentar*) favourable.

beifügen ['baɪfy:gən] *vt* enclose.

beige ['be:ʒ] *a* beige, fawn.

beigeben ['baɪge:bən] *unreg vt* (*zufügen*) add; (*mitgeben*) give // *vi* (*nachgeben*) give in (*dat* to).

Beigeschmack ['baɪgəʃmak] *m* aftertaste.

Beihilfe ['baɪhɪlfə] *f* aid, assistance; (*Studien~*) grant; (*JUR*) aiding and abetting.

beikommen ['baɪkɔmən] *vi unreg* (+*dat*) get at; (*einem Problem*) deal with.

Beil [baɪl] *nt* -(**e)s**, -**e** axe, hatchet.

Beilage [baɪla:gə] *f* (*Buch~ etc*) sup-

plement; (*KOCH*) vegetables and potatoes *pl*.

beiläufig ['baɪlɔyfɪç] *a* casual, incidental // *ad* casually, by the way.

beilegen ['baɪle:gən] *vt* (*hinzufügen*) enclose, add; (*beimessen*) attribute, ascribe; (*Streit*) settle.

Beileid ['baɪlaɪt] *nt* condolence, sympathy; **herzliches ~** deepest sympathy.

beiliegend ['baɪli:gənt] *a* (*COMM*) enclosed.

beim [baɪm] = **bei dem**.

beimessen ['baɪmɛsən] *vt unreg* attribute, ascribe (*dat* to).

Bein [baɪn] *nt* -(**e)s**, -**e** leg; **~bruch** *m* fracture of the leg.

beinah(e) ['baɪna:(ə)] *ad* almost, nearly.

beinhalten [bə'ɪnhaltən] *vt* contain.

beipflichten ['baɪpflɪçtən] *vi:* **jdm/etw ~** agree with sb/sth.

beirren [bə'ɪrən] *vt* confuse, muddle; **sich nicht ~ lassen** not let o.s. be confused.

beisammen [baɪ'zamən] *ad* together; **B~sein** *nt* -**s** get-together.

Beischlaf ['baɪʃla:f] *m* sexual intercourse.

Beisein ['baɪzaɪn] *nt* -**s** presence.

beiseite [baɪ'zaɪtə] *ad* to one side, aside; (*stehen*) on one side, aside; **etw ~ legen** (*sparen*) put sth by; **jdn/etw ~ schaffen** put sb/get sth out of the way.

beisetzen ['baɪzɛtsən] *vt* bury.

Beisetzung *f* funeral.

Beisitzer ['baɪzɪtsər] *m* -**s**, - (*bei Prüfung*) assessor.

Beispiel ['baɪʃpi:l] *nt* -(**e)s**, -**e** example; **sich an jdm ein ~ nehmen** take sb as an example; **zum ~** for example; **b~haft** *a* exemplary; **b~los** *a* unprecedented, unexampled; **beispielsweise** *ad* for instance *od* example.

beißen ['baɪsən] *unreg vti* bite; (*stechen: Rauch, Säure*) burn // *vr* (*Farben*) clash; **~d** *a* biting, caustic; (*fig auch*) sarcastic.

Beistand ['baɪʃtant] *m* -(**e)s**, -̈**e** support, help; (*JUR*) adviser.

beistehen ['baɪʃte:ən] *vi unreg:* **jdm ~** stand by sb.

beisteuern ['baɪʃtɔyərn] *vt* contribute.

beistimmen ['baɪʃtɪmən] *vi* (+*dat*) agree with.

Beitrag ['baɪtra:k] *m* -(**e)s**, -̈**e** contribution; (*Zahlung*) fee, subscription; (*Versicherungs~*) premium; **b~en** ['baɪtra:gən] *vt unreg* contribute (*zu* to); (*mithelfen*) help (*zu* with).

beitreten ['baɪtre:tən] *vi unreg* join (*einem Verein* a club).

Beitritt ['baɪtrɪt] *m* joining, membership.

beiwohnen ['baɪvoːnən] *vi*: einer Sache (*dat*) ~ attend *od* be present at sth.

Beize ['baɪtsə] *f* -, -n (*Holz~*) stain; (*KOCH*) marinade.

beizeiten [baɪ'tsaɪtən] *ad* in time.

bejahen [bə'jaːən] *vt* (*Frage*) say yes to, answer in the affirmative; (*gutheißen*) agree with.

bejahrt [bə'jaːrt] *a* aged, elderly.

bekämpfen [bə'kɛmpfən] *vt* (*Gegner*) fight; (*Seuche*) combat // *vr* fight.

Bekämpfung *f* fight *od* struggle against.

bekannt [bə'kant] *a* (well-) known; (*nicht fremd*) familiar; mit jdm ~ sein know sb; jdn mit jdm ~ machen introduce sb to sb; das ist mir ~ I know that; es/sie kommt mir ~ vor it/she seems familiar; **B~e(r)** *mf* friend, acquaintance; **B~enkreis** *m* circle of friends; **B~gabe** *f* announcement; **~geben** *vt unreg* announce publicly; **~lich** *ad* as is well known, as you know; **~machen** *vt* announce; **B~machung** *f* publication; announcement; **B~schaft** *f* acquaintance.

bekehren [bə'keːrən] *vt* convert // *vr* become converted.

bekennen [bə'kɛnən] *vt unreg* confess; (*Glauben*) profess; Farbe ~ (*umg*) show where one stands.

Bekenntnis [bə'kɛntnɪs] *nt* -ses, -se admission, confession; (*Religion*) confession, denomination.

beklagen [bə'klaːgən] *vt* deplore, lament // *vr* complain; **beklagenswert** *a* lamentable, pathetic.

bekleiden [bə'klaɪdən] *vt* clothe; (*Amt*) occupy, fill.

Bekleidung *f* clothing.

beklemmen [bə'klɛmən] *vt* oppress.

beklommen [bə'klɔmən] *a* anxious, uneasy; **B~heit** *f* anxiety, uneasiness.

bekommen [bə'kɔmən] *unreg vt* get, receive; (*Kind*) have; (*Zug*) catch, get // *vi*: jdm ~ agree with sb.

bekömmlich [bə'kœmlɪç] *a* wholesome, easily digestible.

bekräftigen [bə'krɛftɪgən] *vt* confirm, corroborate.

Bekräftigung *f* corroboration.

bekreuzigen [bə'krɔʏtsɪgən] *vr* cross o.s.

bekümmern [bə'kʏmərn] *vt* worry, trouble.

bekunden [bə'kundən] *vt* (*sagen*) state; (*zeigen*) show.

belächeln [bə'lɛçəln] *vt* laugh at.

beladen [bə'laːdən] *vt unreg* load.

Belag [bə'laːk] *m* -(e)s, -e covering, coating; (*Brot~*) spread; (*Zahn~*) tartar; (*auf Zunge*) fur; (*Brems~*)

lining.

belagern [bə'laːgərn] *vt* besiege.

Belagerung *f* siege.

Belang [bə'laŋ] *m* -(e)s importance; **~e** *pl* interests *pl*, concerns *pl*; **b~en** *vt* (*JUR*) take to court; **b~los** *a* trivial, unimportant; **~losigkeit** *f* triviality.

belassen [bə'lasən] *vt unreg* (*in Zustand, Glauben*) leave; (*in Stellung*) retain.

belasten [bə'lastən] *vt* (*lit*) burden; (*fig: bedrücken*) trouble, worry; (*COMM: Konto*) debit; (*JUR*) incriminate // *vr* weigh o.s. down; (*JUR*) incriminate o.s.; **~d** *a* (*JUR*) incriminating.

belästigen [bə'lɛstɪgən] *vt* annoy, pester.

Belästigung *f* annoyance, pestering.

Belastung [bə'lastʊŋ] *f* (*lit*) load; (*fig: Sorge etc*) weight; (*COMM*) charge, debit(ing); (*JUR*) incriminatory evidence; **Belastungsprobe** *f* capacity test; (*fig*) test; **Belastungszeuge** *m* witness for prosecution.

belaufen [bə'laʊfən] *vr unreg* amount (*auf +akk* to).

belebt [bə'leːpt] *a* (*Straße*) crowded.

Beleg [bə'leːk] *m* -(e)s, -e (*COMM*) receipt; (*Beweis*) documentary evidence, proof; (*Beispiel*) example; **b~en** [bə'leːgən] *vt* cover; (*Kuchen, Brot*) spread; (*Platz*) reserve, book; (*Kurs, Vorlesung*) register for; (*beweisen*) verify, prove; (*MIL: mit Bomben*) bomb; **~schaft** *f* personnel, staff; **belegt** *a*: belegtes Brot open sandwich.

belehren [bə'leːrən] *vt* instruct, teach.

Belehrung *f* instruction.

beleibt [bə'laɪpt] *a* stout, corpulent.

beleidigen [bə'laɪdɪgən] *vt* insult, offend.

Beleidigung *f* insult; (*JUR*) slander, libel.

belesen [bə'leːzən] *a* well-read.

beleuchten [bə'lɔʏçtən] *vt* light, illuminate; (*fig*) throw light on.

Beleuchtung *f* lighting, illumination.

Belg- ['bɛlg] *zW*: **~ien** [-iən] *nt* Belgium; **~ier(in** *f)* *m* Belgian; **b~isch** *a* Belgian.

belichten [bə'lɪçtən] *vt* expose.

Belichtung *f* exposure; **Belichtungsmesser** *m* exposure meter.

Belieben [bə'liːbən] *nt*: (ganz) nach ~ (just) as you wish.

beliebig [bə'liːbɪç] *a* any you like, as you like; ~ viel as many as you like; ein ~es Thema any subject you like *od* want.

beliebt [bə'liːpt] *a* popular; sich bei jdm ~ machen make o.s. popular with sb; **B~heit** *f* popularity.

beliefern [bə'li:fərn] vt supply.
bellen ['belən] vi bark.
Belletristik [bele'trɪstɪk] f fiction and poetry.
belohnen [bə'lo:nən] vt reward.
Belohnung f reward.
belügen [bə'ly:gən] vt unreg lie to, deceive.
belustigen [bə'lʊstɪgən] vt amuse.
Belustigung f amusement.
bemalen [bə'ma:lən] vt paint.
bemängeln [bə'mɛŋəln] vt criticize.
bemannen [bə'manən] vt man.
bemerk- [bə'mɛrk] zW: **~bar** a perceptible, noticeable; **sich ~bar machen** (Person) make od get o.s. noticed; (Unruhe) become noticeable; **~en** vt (wahrnehmen) notice, observe; (sagen) say, mention; **~enswert** a remarkable, noteworthy; **B~ung** f remark; (schriftlich auch) note.
bemitleiden [bə'mɪtlaɪdən] vt pity.
bemühen [bə'my:ən] vr take trouble od pains.
Bemühung f trouble, pains pl, effort.
benachbart [bə'naxba:rt] a neighbouring.
benachrichtigen [bə'na:xrɪçtɪgən] vt inform.
Benachrichtigung f notification, information.
benachteiligen [bə'na:xtaɪlɪgən] vt disadvantage, victimize.
benehmen [bə'ne:mən] vr unreg behave; **B~** nt -s behaviour.
beneiden [bə'naɪdən] vt envy; **beneidenswert** a enviable.
benennen [bə'nɛnən] vt unreg name.
Bengel ['bɛŋəl] m -s, - (little) rascal od rogue.
benommen [bə'nɔmən] a dazed.
benötigen [bə'nø:tɪgən] vt need.
benutzen [bə'nʊtsən], **benützen** [bə'nʏtsən] vt use.
Benutzer m -s, - user; **b~freundlich** a user-friendly.
Benutzung f utilization, use.
Benzin [bɛnt'si:n] nt -s, -e (AUT) petrol (Brit), gas(oline) (US); **~kanister** m petrol can (Brit), gas can (US); **~tank** m petrol tank (Brit), gas tank (US); **~uhr** f petrol gauge (Brit), gas gauge (US).
beobacht- [bə'o:baxt] zW: **~en** vt observe; **B~er** m -s, - observer; (eines Unfalls) witness; (PRESSE, TV) correspondent; **B~ung** f observation.
bepacken [bə'pakən] vt load, pack.
bequem [bə'kve:m] a comfortable; (Ausrede) convenient; (Person) lazy, indolent; **~en** vr condescend (zu to); **B~lichkeit** f convenience, comfort; (Faulheit) laziness, indolence.
beraten [bə'ra:tən] unreg vt advise;

(besprechen) discuss, debate // vr consult; **gut/schlecht ~ sein** be well/ill advised; **sich ~ lassen** get advice.
Berater m -s, - adviser.
Beratung f advice, consultation; (Besprechung) consultation; **Beratungsstelle** f advice centre.
berauben [bə'raubən] vt rob.
berechenbar [bə'rɛçənba:r] a calculable.
berechnen [bə'rɛçnən] vt calculate; (COMM: anrechnen) charge; **~d** a (Mensch) calculating, scheming.
Berechnung f calculation; (COMM) charge.
berechtig- [bə'rɛçtɪg] zW: **~en** vt entitle, authorize; (fig) justify; **~t** [bə'rɛçtɪçt] a justifiable, justified; **B~ung** f authorization; (fig) justification.
bereden [bə're:dən] vtr (besprechen) discuss; (überreden) persuade.
Bereich [bə'raɪç] m -(e)s, -e (Bezirk) area; (PHYS) range; (Ressort, Gebiet) sphere.
bereichern [bə'raɪçərn] vt enrich // vr get rich.
bereinigen [bə'raɪnɪgən] vt settle.
bereit [bə'raɪt] a ready, prepared; **zu etw ~ sein** be ready for sth; **sich ~ erklären** declare o.s. willing; **~en** vt prepare, make ready; (Kummer, Freude) cause; **~halten** vt unreg keep in readiness; **~legen** vt lay out; **~machen** vtr prepare, get ready; **~s** ad already; **B~schaft** f readiness; (Polizei) alert; **B~schaftsdienst** m emergency service; **~stehen** vi unreg (Person) be prepared; (Ding) be ready; **~stellen** vt (Kisten, Pakete etc) put ready; (Geld etc) make available; (Truppen, Maschinen) put at the ready; **~willig** a willing, ready; **B~willigkeit** f willingness, readiness.
bereuen [bə'rɔyən] vt regret.
Berg [bɛrk] m -(e)s, -e mountain, hill; **b~ab** ad downhill; **b~auf** ad uphill; **~arbeiter** m miner; **~bahn** f mountain railway; **~bau** m mining; **b~en** ['bɛrgən] vt unreg (retten) rescue; (Ladung) salvage; (enthalten) contain; **~führer** m mountain guide; **b~ig** ['bɛrgɪç] a mountainous, hilly; **~kette** f mountain range; **~mann** m, pl **~leute** miner; **~rutsch** m landslide; **~steigen** nt mountaineering; **~steiger(in f)** m -s, - mountaineer, climber; **~ung** ['bɛrgʊŋ] f (von Menschen) rescue; (von Material) recovery; (NAUT) salvage; **~wacht** f mountain rescue service; **~werk** nt mine.
Bericht [bə'rɪçt] m -(e)s, -e report, account; **b~en** vti report; **~erstatter**

m **-s,** - reporter, (newspaper) correspondent.
berichtigen [bə'rɪçtɪgən] *vt* correct.
Berichtigung *f* correction.
Bernstein ['bɛrnʃtaɪn] *m* amber.
bersten ['bɛrstən] *vi unreg* burst, split.
berüchtigt [bə'rʏçtɪçt] *a* notorious, infamous.
berücksichtigen [bə'rʏkzɪçtɪgən] *vt* consider, bear in mind.
Berücksichtigung *f* consideration.
Beruf [bə'ru:f] *m* **-(e)s, -e** occupation, profession; (*Gewerbe*) trade; **b~en** *unreg vt* (*in Amt*) appoint (*in* +*akk* to; *zu* as) // *vr*: **sich auf jdn/etw b~en** refer *od* appeal to sb/sth; **b~en** *a* competent, qualified; **b~lich** *a* professional.
Berufs- *zW*: **~berater** *m* careers adviser; **~beratung** *f* vocational guidance; **~geheimnis** *nt* professional secret; **~leben** *nt* professional life; **b~mäßig** *a* professional; **~schule** *f* vocational *od* trade school; **~sportler** *m* professional (sportsman); **b~tätig** *a* employed; **~verkehr** *m* commuter traffic.
Berufung *f* vocation, calling; (*Ernennung*) appointment; (*JUR*) appeal; **~ einlegen** appeal.
beruhen [bə'ru:ən] *vi*: **auf etw** (*dat*) **~** be based on sth; **etw auf sich ~ lassen** leave sth at that.
beruhigen [bə'ru:ɪgən] *vt* calm, pacify, soothe // *vr* (*Mensch*) calm (o.s.) down; (*Situation*) calm down.
Beruhigung *f* reassurance; (*der Nerven*) calming; **zu jds ~** to reassure sb; **Beruhigungsmittel** *nt* sedative.
berühmt [bə'ry:mt] *a* famous; **B~heit** *f* (*Ruf*) fame; (*Mensch*) celebrity.
berühren [bə'ry:rən] *vt* touch; (*gefühlsmäßig bewegen*) affect; (*flüchtig erwähnen*) mention, touch on // *vr* meet, touch.
Berührung *f* contact.
besagen [bə'za:gən] *vt* mean.
besagt *a* (*Tag etc*) in question.
besänftig- [bə'zɛnftɪç] *zW*: **~en** *vt* soothe, calm; **~end** *a* soothing; **B~ung** *f* soothing, calming.
Besatz [bə'zats] *m* **-es, -e** trimming, edging; **~ung** *f* garrison; (*NAUT. AVIAT*) crew; **~ungsmacht** *f* occupying power.
beschädig- [bə'ʃɛ:dɪç] *zW*: **~en** *vt* damage; **B~ung** *f* damage; (*Stelle*) damaged spot.
beschaffen [bə'ʃafən] *vt* get, acquire // *a* constituted; **B~heit** *f* constitution, nature.
Beschaffung *f* acquisition.
beschäftigen [bə'ʃɛftɪgən] *vt* occupy; (*beruflich*) employ // *vr* occupy *od* concern o.s.

beschäftigt *a* busy, occupied.
Beschäftigung *f* (*Beruf*) employment; (*Tätigkeit*) occupation; (*Befassen*) concern.
beschämen [bə'ʃɛ:mən] *vt* put to shame; **~d** *a* shameful; (*Hilfsbereitschaft*) shaming.
beschämt *a* ashamed.
beschatten [bə'ʃatən] *vt* shade; (*Verdächtige*) shadow.
Bescheid [bə'ʃaɪt] *m* **-(e)s, -e** information; (*Weisung*) directions *pl*; **~ wissen** be well-informed (*über* +*akk* about); **ich weiß ~** I know; **jdm ~ geben** *od* **sagen** let sb know.
bescheiden [bə'ʃaɪdən] *vr unreg* content o.s. // *a* modest; **B~heit** *f* modesty.
bescheinen [bə'ʃaɪnən] *vt unreg* shine on.
bescheinigen [bə'ʃaɪnɪgən] *vt* certify; (*bestätigen*) acknowledge.
Bescheinigung *f* certificate; (*Quittung*) receipt.
bescheren [bə'ʃe:rən] *vt*: **jdm etw ~** give sb sth as a present; **jdn ~** give presents to sb.
Bescherung *f* giving of presents; (*umg*) mess.
beschildern [bə'ʃɪldərn] *vt* signpost.
beschimpfen [bə'ʃɪmpfən] *vt* abuse.
Beschimpfung *f* abuse, insult.
Beschlag [bə'ʃla:k] *m* **-(e)s, -e** (*Metallband*) fitting; (*auf Fenster*) condensation; (*auf Metall*) tarnish; finish; (*Hufeisen*) horseshoe; **jdn/etw in ~ nehmen** *od* **mit ~ belegen** monopolize sb/sth; **b~en** [bə'ʃla:gən] *unreg vt* cover; (*Pferd*) shoe; (*Fenster, Metall*) cover; **b~en sein** be well versed (*in od auf* +*dat* in) // *vir* (*Fenster etc*) mist over; **b~nahmen** *vt* seize, confiscate; requisition; **~nahmung** *f* confiscation, sequestration.
beschleunigen [bə'ʃlɔʏnɪgən] *vt* accelerate, speed up // *vi* (*AUT*) accelerate.
Beschleunigung *f* acceleration.
beschließen [bə'ʃli:sən] *vt unreg* decide on; (*beenden*) end, close.
Beschluß [bə'ʃlʊs] *m* **-sses, -schlüsse** decision, conclusion; (*Ende*) close, end.
beschmutzen [bə'ʃmʊtsən] *vt* dirty, soil.
beschönigen [bə'ʃø:nɪgən] *vt* gloss over.
beschränken [bə'ʃrɛŋkən] *vt* limit, restrict (*auf* +*akk* to) // *vr* restrict o.s.
beschränk- *zW*: **~t** *a* confined, narrow; (*Mensch*) limited, narrowminded; **Beschränktheit** *f* narrowness; **B~ung** *f* limitation.
beschreiben [bə'ʃraɪbən] *vt unreg* de-

scribe; (*Papier*) write on.
Beschreibung *f* description.
beschriften [bə'ʃrɪftən] *vt* mark, label.
Beschriftung *f* lettering.
beschuldigen [bə'ʃʊldɪgən] *vt* accuse.
Beschuldigung *f* accusation.
beschütz- [bə'ʃʏts] *zW:* **~en** *vt* protect (*vor* +*dat* from); **B~er** *m* **-s,** - protector.
Beschwerde [bə'ʃveːrdə] *f* **-, -n** complaint; (*Mühe*) hardship; (*pl: Leiden*) pain.
beschweren [bə'ʃveːrən] *vt* weight down; (*fig*) burden // *vr* complain.
beschwerlich *a* tiring, exhausting.
beschwichtigen [bə'ʃvɪçtɪgən] *vt* soothe, pacify.
beschwindeln [bə'ʃvɪndəln] *vt* (*betrügen*) cheat; (*belügen*) fib to.
beschwingt [bə'ʃvɪŋt] *a* cheery, in high spirits.
beschwören [bə'ʃvøːrən] *vt* unreg (*Aussage*) swear to; (*anflehen*) implore; (*Geister*) conjure up.
beseitigen [bə'zaɪtɪgən] *vt* remove.
Beseitigung *f* removal.
Besen ['beːzən] *m* **-s,** - broom; **~stiel** *m* broomstick.
besessen [bə'zɛsən] *a* possessed.
besetz- [bə'zɛts] *zW:* **~en** *vt* (*Haus, Land*) occupy; (*Platz*) take, fill; (*Posten*) fill; (*Rolle*) cast; (*mit Edelsteinen*) set; **~t** *a* full; (*TEL*) engaged, busy; (*Platz*) taken; (*WC*) engaged; **Besetzzeichen** *nt* engaged tone; **B~ung** *f* occupation; filling; (*von Rolle*) casting; (*die Schauspieler*) cast.
besichtigen [bə'zɪçtɪgən] *vt* visit, look at.
Besichtigung *f* visit.
Besied(e)lung [bə'ziːd(ə)lʊŋ] *f* population.
besiegen [bə'ziːgən] *vt* defeat, overcome.
besinnen [bə'zɪnən] *vr* unreg (*nachdenken*) think, reflect; (*erinnern*) remember; **sich anders ~** change one's mind.
besinnlich *a* contemplative.
Besinnung *f* consciousness; **zur ~ kommen** recover consciousness; (*fig*) come to one's senses; **besinnungslos** *a* unconscious.
Besitz [bə'zɪts] *m* **-es** possession; (*Eigentum*) property; **b~en** *vt* unreg possess, own; (*Eigenschaft*) have; **~er(in** *f*) *m* **-s,** - owner, proprietor; **~ergreifung** *f* occupation, seizure.
besoffen [bə'zɔfən] *a* (*umg*) drunk.
besohlen [bə'zoːlən] *vt* sole.
Besoldung [bə'zɔldʊŋ] *f* salary, pay.
besondere(r, s) [bə'zɔndərə(r,z)] *a* special; (*eigen*) particular; (*gesondert*) separate; (*eigentümlich*) pecu-

liar.
Besonderheit [bə'zɔndərhaɪt] *f* peculiarity.
besonders [bə'zɔndərs] *ad* especially, particularly; (*getrennt*) separately.
besonnen [bə'zɔnən] *a* sensible, level-headed; **B~heit** *f* prudence.
besorg- [bə'zɔrg] *zW:* **~en** *vt* (*beschaffen*) acquire; (*kaufen auch*) purchase; (*erledigen: Geschäfte*) deal with; (*sich kümmern um*) take care of; **B~nis** *f* **-, -se** anxiety, concern; **~t** [bə'zɔrçt] *a* anxious, worried; **Besorgtheit** *f* anxiety, worry; **B~ung** *f* acquisition; (*Kauf*) purchase.
bespielen [bə'ʃpiːlən] *vt* record.
bespitzeln [bə'ʃpɪtsəln] *vt* spy on.
besprechen [bə'ʃprɛçən] *unreg vt* discuss; (*Tonband etc*) record, speak onto; (*Buch*) review // *vr* discuss, consult.
Besprechung *f* meeting, discussion; (*von Buch*) review.
besser ['bɛsər] *a* better; **~n** *vt* make better, improve // *vr* improve; (*Menschen*) reform; **B~ung** *f* improvement; **gute B~ung!** get well soon; **B~wisser** *m* **-s,** - know-all.
Bestand [bə'ʃtant] *m* **-(e)s,** ⁻e (*Fortbestehen*) duration, stability; (*Kassen~*) amount, balance; (*Vorrat*) stock; **~ haben, von ~ sein** last long, endure.
beständig [bə'ʃtɛndɪç] *a* (*ausdauernd*) constant (*auch fig*); (*Wetter*) settled; (*Stoffe*) resistant; (*Klagen etc*) continual.
Bestandsaufnahme *f* stocktaking.
Bestandteil *m* part, component; (*Zutat*) ingredient.
bestärken [bə'ʃtɛrkən] *vt:* **jdn in etw** (*dat*) **~** strengthen *od* confirm sb in sth.
bestätigen [bə'ʃtɛːtɪgən] *vt* confirm; (*anerkennen, COMM*) acknowledge.
Bestätigung *f* confirmation; acknowledgement.
bestatt- [bə'ʃtat] *zW:* **~en** *vt* bury; **B~er** *m* **-s,** - undertaker; **B~ung** *f* funeral.
beste(r, s) ['bɛstə(r, s)] *a* best; **so ist es am ~n** it's best that way; **am ~n gehst du gleich** you'd better go at once; **jdn zum ~n haben** pull sb's leg; **etw zum ~n geben** tell a joke/ story *etc*; **aufs ~** in the best possible way; **zu jds B~n** for the benefit of sb.
bestechen [bə'ʃtɛçən] *vt* unreg bribe.
bestechlich *a* corruptible.
Bestechung *f* bribery, corruption.
Besteck [bə'ʃtɛk] *nt* **-(e)s, -e** knife, fork and spoon, cutlery; (*MED*) set of instruments.
bestehen [bə'ʃteːən] *unreg vi* be; ex-

ist; *(andauern)* last // *vt (Kampf, Probe, Prüfung)* pass; ~ **auf** (+*dat*) insist on; ~ **aus** consist of.

bestehlen [bə'ʃteːlən] *vt unreg* rob.

besteigen [bə'ʃtaigən] *vt unreg* climb, ascend; *(Pferd)* mount; *(Thron)* ascend.

Bestell- [bə'ʃtɛl] *zW:* **~buch** *nt* order book; **b~en** *vt* order; *(kommen lassen)* arrange to see; *(nominieren)* name; *(Acker)* cultivate; *(Grüße, Auftrag)* pass on; **~schein** *m* order coupon; **~ung** *f (COMM)* order; *(Bestellen)* ordering.

bestenfalls ['bɛstən'fals] *ad* at best.

bestens ['bɛstəns] *ad* very well.

Bestie ['bɛstiə] *f (lit, fig)* beast.

bestimm- [bə'ʃtɪm] *zW:* **~en** *vt (Regeln)* lay down; *(Tag, Ort)* fix; *(beherrschen)* characterize; *(ausersehen)* mean; *(ernennen)* appoint; *(definieren)* define; *(veranlassen)* induce; **~t** *a (entschlossen)* firm; *(gewiß)* certain, definite; *(Artikel)* definite; **suchen Sie etwas B~tes?** are you looking for something in particular? // *ad (gewiß)* definitely, for sure; **Bestimmtheit** *f* certainty; **B~ung** *f (Verordnung)* regulation; *(Festsetzen)* determining; *(Verwendungszweck)* purpose; *(Schicksal)* fate; *(Definition)* definition; **B~ungsort** *m* destination.

Bestleistung *f* best performance.

bestmöglich *a* best possible.

bestrafen [bə'ʃtraːfən] *vt* punish.

Bestrafung *f* punishment.

bestrahlen [bə'ʃtraːlən] *vt* shine on; *(MED)* treat with X-rays.

Bestrahlung *f (MED)* X-ray treatment, radiotherapy.

Bestreben [bə'ʃtreːbən] *nt* **-s** endeavour, effort.

bestreichen [bə'ʃtraiçən] *vt unreg (Brot)* spread.

bestreiten [bə'ʃtraitən] *vt unreg (abstreiten)* dispute; *(finanzieren)* pay for, finance.

bestreuen [bə'ʃtrɔyən] *vt* sprinkle, dust; *(Straße)* grit.

bestürmen [bə'ʃtʏrmən] *vt (mit Fragen, Bitten etc)* overwhelm, swamp.

bestürzt [bə'ʃtʏrtst] *a* dismayed.

Bestürzung *f* consternation.

Besuch [bə'zuːx] *m* **-(e)s, -e** visit; *(Person)* visitor; **einen ~ machen bei jdm** pay sb a visit *od* call; ~ **haben** have visitors; **bei jdm auf** *or* **zu ~ sein** be visiting sb; **b~en** *vt* visit; *(SCH etc)* attend; **gut ~t** well-attended; **~er(in** *f)* *m* **-s, -** visitor, guest; **Besuchszeit** *f* visiting hours *pl.*

betagt [bə'taːkt] *a* aged.

betätigen [bə'tɛːtɪgən] *vt (bedienen)* work, operate // *vr* involve o.s.; **sich als etw ~** work as sth.

Betätigung *f* activity; *(beruflich)* occupation; *(TECH)* operation.

betäuben [bə'tɔybən] *vt* stun; *(fig: Gewissen)* still; *(MED)* anaesthetize.

Betäubungsmittel *nt* anaesthetic.

Bete ['beːtə] *f* -, **-n:** **rote ~** beetroot *(Brit)*, beet *(US)*.

beteiligen [bə'tailɪgən] *vr (an +dat* in) take part, participate, share; *(an Geschäft: finanziell)* have a share // *vt:* **jdn ~** give sb a share *od* interest *(an +dat* in).

Beteiligung *f* participation; *(Anteil)* share, interest; *(Besucherzahl)* attendance.

beten ['beːtən] *vti* pray.

beteuern [bə'tɔyərn] *vt* assert; *(Unschuld)* protest.

Beteuerung *f* assertion, protest(ation), assurance.

Beton [be'tõ] *m* **-s, -s** concrete.

betonen [bə'toːnən] *vt* stress.

betonieren [beto'niːrən] *vt* concrete.

Betonung *f* stress, emphasis.

betören [bə'tøːrən] *vt* beguile.

Betr. *abk* (= *Betreff; betrifft)* re.

Betracht [bə'traxt] *m:* **in ~ kommen** be concerned *od* relevant; **etw in ~ ziehen** consider sth; **außer ~ bleiben** not be considered; **b~en** *vt* look at; *(fig auch)* consider; **~er(in** *f)* *m* **-s, -** onlooker.

beträchtlich [bə'trɛçtlɪç] *a* considerable.

Betrachtung *f (Ansehen)* examination; *(Erwägung)* consideration.

Betrag [bə'traːk] *m* **-(e)s, ̈e** amount; **b~en** [bə'traːgən] *unreg vt* amount to // *vr* behave; **~en** *nt* **-s** behaviour.

betreffen [bə'trɛfən] *vt unreg* concern, affect; **was mich betrifft** as for me; **~d** *a* relevant, in question.

betreffs [bə'trɛfs] *präp +gen* concerning, regarding.

betreiben [bə'traibən] *vt unreg (ausüben)* practise; *(Politik)* follow; *(Studien)* pursue; *(vorantreiben)* push ahead; *(TECH: antreiben)* drive.

betreten [bə'treːtən] *vt unreg* enter; *(Bühne etc)* step onto; **B~ verboten** keep off/out // *a* embarrassed.

Betrieb [bə'triːp] *m* **-(e)s, -e** *(Firma)* firm, concern; *(Anlage)* plant; *(Tätigkeit)* operation; *(Treiben)* traffic; **außer ~ sein** be out of order; **in ~ sein** be in operation.

Betriebs- *zW:* **b~fähig** *a* in working order; **~ferien** *pl* company holidays *pl (Brit)*, company vacation *(US)*; **~klima** *nt* (working) atmosphere; **~kosten** *pl* running costs *pl*; **~rat** *m* workers' council; **b~sicher** *a* safe, reliable; **~störung** f breakdown; **~unfall** m industrial accident; **~wirtschaft** f economics.

betrinken [bə'trɪŋkən] vr unreg get drunk.

betroffen [bə'trɔfən] a (bestürzt) amazed, perplexed; **von etw ~ werden** od **sein** be affected by sth.

betrüben [bə'try:bən] vt grieve.

betrübt [bə'try:pt] a sorrowful, grieved.

Betrug [bə'tru:k] m -(e)s deception; (JUR) fraud.

betrügen [bə'try:gən] unreg vt cheat; (JUR) defraud; (Ehepartner) be unfaithful to // vr deceive o.s.

Betrüger m -s, - cheat, deceiver; **b~isch** a deceitful; (JUR) fraudulent.

betrunken [bə'trʊŋkən] a drunk.

Bett [bɛt] nt -(e)s, -en bed; **ins** od **zu ~ gehen** go to bed; **~bezug** m duvet cover; **~decke** f blanket; (Daunen~) quilt; (Überwurf) bedspread.

Bettel- ['bɛtəl] zW: **b~arm** a very poor, destitute; **~ei** [bɛtə'laɪ] f begging; **b~n** vi beg.

bettlägerig ['bɛtlɛ:gərɪç] a bedridden.

Bettlaken nt sheet.

Bettler(in f) ['bɛtlər(ɪn)] m -s, - beggar.

Bett- zW: **~vorleger** m bedside rug; **~(t)uch** nt, **~wäsche** f, **~zeug** nt bedclothes pl, bedding.

beugen ['bɔygən] vt bend; (GRAM) inflect // vr (sich fügen) bow (dat to).

Beule ['bɔylə] f -, -n bump, swelling.

beunruhigen [bə'ʊnru:ɪgən] vt disturb, alarm // vr become worried.

Beunruhigung f worry, alarm.

beurlauben [bə'u:rlaubən] vt give leave od holiday to (Brit), grant vacation time to (US).

beurteilen [bə'ʊrtaɪlən] vt judge; (Buch etc) review.

Beurteilung f judgement; review; (Note) mark.

Beute ['bɔytə] f - booty, loot; **~l** m -s, - bag; (Geld~) purse; (Tabak~) pouch.

Bevölkerung [bə'fœlkərʊŋ] f population.

bevollmächtigen [bə'fɔlmɛçtɪgən] vt authorize.

Bevollmächtigte(r) mf authorized agent.

bevor [bə'fo:r] kj before; **~munden** vt insep dominate; **~stehen** vi unreg be in store (dat for); **~stehend** a imminent, approaching; **~zugen** vt insep prefer; **B~zugung** f preference.

bewachen [bə'vaxən] vt watch, guard.

Bewachung f (Bewachen) guarding; (Leute) guard, watch.

bewaffnen [bə'vafnən] vt arm.

Bewaffnung f (Vorgang) arming; (Ausrüstung) armament, arms pl.

bewahren [bə'va:rən] vt keep; **jdn vor jdm/etw ~** save sb from sb/sth.

bewähren [bə'vɛ:rən] vr prove o.s.; (Maschine) prove its worth.

bewahrheiten [bə'va:rhaɪtən] vr come true.

bewährt a reliable.

Bewährung f (JUR) probation; **Bewährungsfrist** f (period of) probation.

bewältigen [bə'vɛltɪgən] vt overcome; (Arbeit) finish; (Portion) manage.

bewandert [bə'vandərt] a expert, knowledgeable.

bewässern [bə'vɛsərn] vt irrigate.

Bewässerung f irrigation.

Beweg- [bə've:g] zW: **b~en** vtr move; **jdn zu etw b~en** induce sb to (do) sth; **~grund** [bə've:k-] m motive; **b~lich** a movable, mobile; (flink) quick; **b~t** a (Leben) eventful; (Meer) rough; (ergriffen) touched; **~ung** f movement, motion; (innere) emotion; (körperlich) exercise; **~ungsfreiheit** f freedom of movement od action; **b~ungslos** a motionless.

Beweis [bə'vaɪs] m -es, -e proof; (Zeichen) sign; **b~bar** [bə'vaɪz-] a provable; **b~en** vt unreg prove; (zeigen) show; **~mittel** nt evidence.

Bewerb- [bə'vɛrb] zW: **b~en** vr unreg apply (um for); **~er(in** f) m -s, - applicant; **~ung** f application.

bewerkstelligen [bə'vɛrkʃtɛlɪgən] vt manage, accomplish.

bewerten [bə've:rtən] vt assess.

bewilligen [bə'vɪlɪgən] vt grant, allow.

Bewilligung f granting.

bewirken [bə'vɪrkən] vt cause, bring about.

bewirten [bə'vɪrtən] vt entertain.

bewirtschaften [bə'vɪrtʃaftən] vt manage.

Bewirtung f hospitality.

bewog etc v siehe **bewegen**.

bewohn- [bə'vo:n] zW: **~bar** a inhabitable; **~en** vt inhabit, live in; **B~er(in** f) m -s, - inhabitant; (von Haus) resident.

bewölkt [bə'vœlkt] a cloudy, overcast.

Bewölkung f clouds pl.

Bewunder- [bə'vʊndər] zW: **~er** m -s, - admirer; **b~n** vt admire; **b~nswert** a admirable, wonderful; **~ung** f admiration.

bewußt [bə'vʊst] a conscious; (absichtlich) deliberate; **sich** (dat) **einer Sache ~ sein** be aware of sth; **~los** a unconscious; **B~losigkeit** f unconsciousness; **B~sein** nt consciousness; **bei B~sein** conscious.

bezahlen [bə'tsa:lən] vt pay (for).

Bezahlung f payment.

bezaubern [bə'tsaʊbərn] *vt* enchant, charm.

bezeichnen [bə'tsaɪçnən] *vt* (*kennzeichnen*) mark; (*nennen*) call; (*beschreiben*) describe; (*zeigen*) show, indicate; ~**d** *a* characteristic, typical (*für* of).

Bezeichnung *f* (*Zeichen*) mark, sign; (*Beschreibung*) description.

Bezichtigung [bə'tsɪçtɪgʊŋ] *f* accusation.

beziehen [bə'tsi:ən] *unreg vt* (*mit Überzug*) cover; (*Bett*) make; (*Haus, Position*) move into; (*Standpunkt*) take up; (*erhalten*) receive; (*Zeitung*) subscribe to, take; **etw auf jdn/etw** ~ relate sth to sb/sth // *vr* refer (*auf* +*akk* to); (*Himmel*) cloud over.

Beziehung *f* (*Verbindung*) connection; (*Zusammenhang*) relation; (*Verhältnis*) relationship; (*Hinsicht*) respect; ~**en haben** (*vorteilhaft*) have connections *od* contacts; **b~sweise** *ad* or; (*genauer gesagt auch*) that is, or rather.

Bezirk [bə'tsɪrk] *m* -**(e)s, -e** district.

Bezug [bə'tsu:k] *m* -**(e)s, ᵉe** (*Hülle*) covering; (*COMM*) ordering; (*Gehalt*) income, salary; (*Beziehung*) relationship (*zu* to); **in b~ auf** (+*akk*) with reference to; ~ **nehmen auf** (+*akk*) refer to.

bezüglich [bə'tsy:klɪç] *präp* +*gen* concerning, referring to // *a* concerning; (*GRAM*) relative.

bezwecken [bə'tsvɛkən] *vt* aim at.

bezweifeln [bə'tsvaɪfəln] *vt* doubt, query.

Bhf. *abk* (= *Bahnhof*) station.

Bibel ['bi:bəl] *f* -, -**n** Bible.

Biber ['bi:bər] *m* -**s, -** beaver.

Biblio- *zW*: ~**graphie** [bibliogra'fi:] *f* bibliography; ~**thek** [biblio'te:k] *f* -, -**en** library; ~**thekar(in** *f*) [bibliote'ka:r(ɪn)] *m* -**s, -e** librarian.

biblisch ['bi:blɪʃ] *a* biblical.

bieder ['bi:dər] *a* upright, worthy; (*Kleid etc*) plain.

bieg- [bi:g] *zW*: ~**en** *unreg vtr* bend // *vi* turn; ~**sam** ['bi:k-] *a* supple; **B~ung** *f* bend, curve.

Biene ['bi:nə] *f* -, -**n** bee.

Bienenhonig *m* honey.

Bier [bi:r] *nt* -**(e)s, -e** beer; ~**deckel** *m* beer mat; ~**krug** *m* beer mug.

bieten ['bi:tən] *unreg vt* offer; (*bei Versteigerung*) bid // *vr* (*Gelegenheit*) be open (*dat* to); **sich** (*dat*) **etw** ~ **lassen** put up with sth.

Bikini [bi'ki:ni] *m* -**s, -s** bikini.

Bilanz [bi'lants] *f* balance; (*fig*) outcome; ~ **ziehen** (*aus*) take stock (*aus* of).

Bild [bɪlt] *nt* -**(e)s, -er** (*lit, fig*) picture; photo; (*Spiegel~*) reflection; ~**bericht**

---

m pictorial report.

bilden ['bɪldən] *vt* form; (*erziehen*) educate; (*ausmachen*) constitute // *vr* arise; (*erziehen*) educate o.s.

Bilder- *zW*: ~**buch** *nt* picture book; ~**rahmen** *m* picture frame.

Bild- *zW*: ~**fläche** *f* screen; (*fig*) scene; ~**hauer** *m* -**s, -** sculptor; **b~hübsch** *a* lovely, pretty as a picture; **b~lich** *a* figurative; pictorial; ~**schirm** *m* television screen; (*COMPUT*) monitor; **b~schön** *a* lovely; ~**sichtgerät** *n* visual display unit, VDU; ~**ung** ['bɪldʊŋ] *f* formation; (*Wissen, Benehmen*) education; ~**ungslücke** *f* gap in one's education; ~**ungspolitik** *f* educational policy.

Billard ['bɪljart] *nt* -**s, -e** billiards; ~**kugel** *f* billiard ball.

billig ['bɪlɪç] *a* cheap; (*gerecht*) fair, reasonable; ~**en** ['bɪlɪgən] *vt* approve of; **B~laden** *m* (*umg*) discount store; **B~ung** *f* approval.

Billion [bɪli'o:n] *f* billion, trillion (*US*).

Binde ['bɪndə] *f* -, -**n** bandage; (*Arm~*) band; (*MED*) sanitary towel; ~**glied** *nt* connecting link; **b~n** *vt unreg* bind, tie; ~**strich** *m* hyphen; ~**wort** *nt* conjunction.

Bind- *zW*: ~**faden** *m* string; ~**ung** *f* bond, tie; (*Ski~*) binding.

binnen ['bɪnən] *präp* +*dat od gen* within; **B~hafen** *m* inland harbour; **B~handel** *m* internal trade.

Binse ['bɪnzə] *f* -, -**n** rush, reed; **Binsenwahrheit** *f* truism.

Bio- [bio] *zW* bio-; ~**graphie** [-gra'fi:] *f* biography; ~**loge** [-'lo:gə] *m* -**n, -n** biologist; ~**logie** [-lo'gi:] *f* biology; **b~logisch** [-'lo:gɪʃ] *a* biological.

Birke ['bɪrkə] *f* -, -**n** birch.

Birma ['bɪrma] *nt* Burma.

Birnbaum *m* pear tree.

Birne ['bɪrnə] *f* -, -**n** pear; (*ELEK*) (light) bulb.

bis [bɪs] ◆*präp* +*akk, ad* **1** (*zeitlich*) till, until; (~ *spätestens*) by; **Sie haben** ~ **Dienstag Zeit** you have until *od* till Tuesday; ~ **Dienstag muß es fertig sein** it must be ready by Tuesday; ~ **auf weiteres** until further notice; ~ **in die Nacht** into the night; ~ **bald/gleich** see you later/soon

2 (*räumlich*) (up) to; **ich fahre** ~ **Köln** I'm going to *od* I'm going as far as Cologne; ~ **an unser Grundstück** (right *od* up) to our plot; ~ **hierher** this far

3 (*bei Zahlen*) up to; ~ **zu** up to

4: ~ **auf etw** (*akk*) (*außer*) except sth; (*einschließlich*) including sth.

◆*kj* **1** (*mit Zahlen*) to; **10** ~ **20** 10 to 20

2 (*zeitlich*) till, until; ~ **es dunkel wird** till *od* until it gets dark; **von ...**

~ ... from ... to ...
Bischof ['bɪʃɔf] *m* -s, ⁻e bishop.
bischöflich ['bɪʃøːflɪç] *a* episcopal.
bisher [bɪs'heːr] *ad*, ~ig *a* till now, hitherto.
Biskuit [bɪs'kviːt] *m od nt* -(e)s, -s *od* -e biscuit; ~teig *m* sponge mixture.
biß *etc v siehe* **beißen.**
Biß [bɪs] *m* -sses, -sse bite.
bißchen ['bɪsçən] *a, ad* bit.
Bissen ['bɪsən] *m* -s, - bite, morsel.
bissig ['bɪsɪç] *a* (*Hund*) snappy; (*Bemerkung*) cutting, biting.
bist *v siehe* **sein.**
bisweilen [bɪs'vaɪlən] *ad* at times, occasionally.
Bit [bɪt] *nt* (*COMPUT*) bit.
Bitte ['bɪtə] *f* -, -n request; **b~** *interj* please; (*wie b~?*) (I beg your) pardon; (*als Antwort auf Dank*) you're welcome; **darf ich? — aber ~!** may I? — please do; **b~ schön!** it was a pleasure; **b~n** *vti unreg* ask (*um* for); **b~nd** *a* pleading, imploring.
bitter ['bɪtər] *a* bitter; ~böse *a* very angry; **B~keit** *f* bitterness; ~lich *a* bitter.
Blähungen ['blɛːʊŋən] *pl* (*MED*) wind.
blamabel [bla'maːbəl] *a* disgraceful.
Blamage [bla'maːʒə] *f* -, -n disgrace.
blamieren [bla'miːrən] *vr* make a fool of o.s., disgrace o.s. // *vt* let down, disgrace.
blank [blaŋk] *a* bright; (*unbedeckt*) bare; (*sauber*) clean, polished; (*umg: ohne Geld*) broke; (*offensichtlich*) blatant.
blanko ['blaŋko] *ad* blank; **B~scheck** *m* blank cheque.
Bläschen ['blɛːsçən] *nt* bubble; (*MED*) spot, blister.
Blase ['blaːzə] *f* -, -n bubble; (*MED*) blister; (*ANAT*) bladder; ~balg *m* -(e)s, -bälge bellows *pl*; **b~n** *vti unreg* blow.
Blas- ['blaːs] *zW:* ~instrument *nt* wind instrument; ~kapelle *f* brass band; ~musik *f* brass band music.
blaß [blas] *a* pale.
Blässe ['blɛsə] *f* - paleness, pallor.
Blatt [blat] *nt* -(e)s, ⁻er leaf; (*Zeitung*) newspaper; (*von Papier*) sheet; (*KARTEN*) hand.
blättern ['blɛtərn] *vi:* in etw (*dat*) ~ leaf through sth.
Blätterteig *m* flaky *od* puff pastry.
blau [blaʊ] *a* blue; (*umg*) drunk, stoned; (*KOCH*) boiled; (*Auge*) black; ~er Fleck bruise; Fahrt ins B~e mystery tour; ~äugig *a* blue-eyed; **B~licht** *nt* flashing blue light; ~machen *vi* (*umg*) skive off work.
Blech [blɛç] *nt* -(e)s, -e tin, sheet metal; (*Back~*) baking tray; ~büchse *f*, ~dose *f* tin, can; **b~en** *vti* (*umg*)

pay; ~schaden *m* (*AUT*) damage to bodywork.
Blei [blaɪ] *nt* -(e)s, -e lead.
Bleibe ['blaɪbə] *f* -, -n roof over one's head; **b~n** *vi unreg* stay, remain; **bleibenlassen** *vt unreg* leave (alone).
bleich [blaɪç] *a* faded, pale; ~en *vt* bleach.
Blei- *zW:* **b~ern** *a* leaden; **b~frei** *a* (*Benzin*) lead-free; ~stift *m* pencil; ~stiftspitzer *m* pencil sharpener.
Blende ['blɛndə] *f* -, -n (*PHOT*) aperture; **b~n** *vt* blind, dazzle; (*fig*) hoodwink; **b~nd** *a* (*umg*) grand; **b~nd aussehen** look smashing.
Blick [blɪk] *m* -(e)s, -e (*kurz*) glance, glimpse; (*Anschauen*) look, gaze; (*Aussicht*) view; **b~en** *vi* look; **sich b~en lassen** put in an appearance; ~fang *m* eye-catching object; ~feld *nt* range of vision (*auch fig*).
blieb *etc v siehe* **bleiben.**
blind [blɪnt] *a* blind; (*Glas etc*) dull; ~er Passagier stowaway; **B~darm** *m* appendix; **B~darmentzündung** *f* appendicitis; ~enschrift ['blɪndən-] *f* braille; **B~heit** *f* blindness; ~lings *ad* blindly; **B~schleiche** *f* slow worm.
blink- [blɪŋk] *zW:* ~en *vi* twinkle, sparkle; (*Licht*) flash, signal; (*AUT*) indicate // *vt* flash, signal; **B~er** *m* -s, - (*AUT*) indicator.
blinzeln ['blɪntsəln] *vi* blink, wink.
Blitz [blɪts] *m* -es, -e (flash of) lightning; ~ableiter *m* lightning conductor; **b~en** *vi* (*aufleuchten*) glint, shine; **es blitzt** (*MET*) there's a flash of lightning; ~licht *nt* flashlight; **b~schnell** *a, ad* as quick as a flash.
Block [blɔk] *m* -(e)s, ⁻e (*lit, fig*) block; (*von Papier*) pad; **Blockade** [blɔ'kaːdə] *f* -, -n blockade; ~flöte *f* recorder; **b~frei** *a* (*POL*) unaligned; **b~ieren** [blɔ'kiːrən] *vt* block // *vi* (*Räder*) jam; ~schrift *f* block letters *pl*.
blöd [bløːt] *a* silly, stupid; **B~sinn** *m* nonsense; ~sinnig *a* silly, idiotic.
blond [blɔnt] *a* blond, fair-haired.
bloß [bloːs] ◆*a* **1** (*unbedeckt*) bare; (*nackt*) naked; **mit der ~en Hand** with one's bare hand; **mit ~em Auge** with the naked eye
2 (*alleinig, nur*) mere; **der ~e Gedanke** the very thought; ~er Neid sheer envy
◆*ad* only, merely; **laß das ~!** just don't do that!; **wie ist das ~ passiert?** how on earth did that happen?
Blöße ['bløːsə] *f* -, -n bareness; nakedness; (*fig*) weakness.
bloß- *zW:* ~legen *vt* expose; ~stellen *vt* show up.
blühen ['blyːən] *vi* (*lit*) bloom, be in

bloom; (fig) flourish.
Blume ['bluːmə] f -, -n flower; (von Wein) bouquet; **Blumenkohl** m cauliflower; **Blumentopf** m flowerpot; **Blumenzwiebel** f bulb.
Bluse ['bluːzə] f -, -n blouse.
Blut [bluːt] nt -(e)s blood; **b~arm** a anaemic; (fig) penniless; **b~befleckt** a bloodstained; **~druck** m blood pressure.
Blüte ['blyːtə] f -, -n blossom; (fig) prime; **~zeit** f flowering period; (fig) prime.
Blutegel m leech.
bluten vi bleed.
Blütenstaub m pollen.
Blut- zW: **~er** m -s, - (MED) haemophiliac; **~erguß** m haemorrhage; (auf Haut) bruise; **~gruppe** f blood group; **b~ig** a bloody; **b~jung** a very young; **~probe** f blood test; **~spender** m blood donor; **~übertragung** f blood transfusion; **~ung** f bleeding, haemorrhage; **~vergiftung** f blood poisoning; **~wurst** f black pudding.
Bö(e) ['bøː(ə)] f -, -en squall.
Bock [bɔk] m -(e)s, ⁻e buck, ram; (Gestell) trestle, support; (SPORT) buck; **~wurst** f type of pork sausage.
Boden ['boːdən] m -s, ⁻ ground; (Fuß~) floor; (Meeres~, Faß~) bottom; (Speicher) attic; **~see** m: der **~see** Lake Constance; **b~los** a bottomless; (umg) incredible; **~schätze** pl mineral wealth; **~turnen** nt floor exercises pl.
Bogen ['boːgən] m -s, - (Biegung) curve; (ARCHIT) arch; (Waffe, MUS) bow; (Papier) sheet; **~gang** m arcade.
Bohle ['boːlə] f -, -n plank.
Bohne ['boːnə] f -, -n bean; **Bohnenkaffee** m pure coffee; **bohnern** vt wax, polish; **Bohnerwachs** nt floor polish.
Bohr- ['boːr] zW: **b~en** vt bore; **~er** m -s, - drill; **~insel** f oil rig; **~maschine** f drill; **~turm** m derrick.
Boje ['boːjə] f -, -n buoy.
Bolivien [boˈliːviən] nt Bolivia.
Bolzen ['bɔltsən] m -s, - bolt.
bombardieren [bɔmbarˈdiːrən] vt bombard; (aus der Luft) bomb.
Bombe ['bɔmbə] f -, -n bomb.
Bombenangriff m bombing raid.
Bombenerfolg m (umg) huge success.
Bonbon [bõˈbõː] m od nt -s, -s sweet.
Boot [boːt] nt -(e)s, -e boat.
Bord [bɔrt] m -(e)s, -e (AVIAT, NAUT) board; an ~ on board // nt (Brett) shelf; **Bordell** [bɔrˈdɛl] nt -s, -e brothel; **~stein** m kerb(stone).
borgen ['bɔrgən] vt borrow; jdm etw

~ lend sb sth.
borniert [bɔrˈniːrt] a narrow-minded.
Börse ['bœrzə] f -, -n stock exchange; (Geld~) purse.
Borste ['bɔrstə] f -, -n bristle.
Borte ['bɔrtə] f -, -n edging; (Band) trimming.
bös(e) [bøːs, 'bøːzə] a bad, evil; (zornig) angry.
bösartig ['bøːs-] a malicious.
Böschung ['bœʃʊŋ] f slope; (Ufer~ etc) embankment.
bos- ['boːs] zW: **~haft** a malicious, spiteful; **B~heit** f malice, spite.
böswillig ['bøːsvɪlɪç] a malicious.
bot etc v siehe **bieten**.
Botanik [boˈtaːnɪk] f botany.
botanisch [boˈtaːnɪʃ] a botanical.
Bot- ['boːt] zW: **~e** m -n, -n messenger; **~schaft** f message, news; (POL) embassy; **~schafter** m -s, - ambassador.
Bottich ['bɔtɪç] m -(e)s, -e vat, tub.
Bouillon [buˈljõː] f -, -s consommé.
Bowle ['boːlə] f -, -n punch.
Box- ['bɔks] zW: **b~en** vi box; **~er** m -s, - boxer; **~handschuh** m boxing glove; **~kampf** m boxing match.
boykottieren [bɔykɔˈtiːrən] vt boycott.
brach etc v siehe **brechen**.
brachte etc v siehe **bringen**.
Branche ['brãːʃə] f -, -n line of business; **Branchenverzeichnis** nt yellow pages pl.
Brand [brant] m -(e)s, ⁻e fire; (MED) gangrene; **b~en** [brandən] vi surge; (Meer) break; **b~marken** vt brand; (fig) stigmatize; **~salbe** f ointment for burns; **~stifter** m arsonist, fireraiser; **~stiftung** f arson; **~ung** f surf; **~wunde** f burn.
Branntwein ['brantvaɪn] m brandy.
Brasil- [braˈziːl] zW: **~ien** [-iən] nt Brazil; **~ianer(in** f) [-iˈaːnər(ɪn)] m Brazilian; **b~ianisch** a Brazilian.
Brat- [braːt] zW: **~apfel** m baked apple; **b~en** vt unreg roast, fry; **~en** m -s, - roast, joint; **~hähnchen** nt, **~huhn** nt roast chicken; **~kartoffeln** pl fried od roast potatoes pl; **~pfanne** f frying pan.
Bratsche ['braːtʃə] f -, -n viola.
Brat- zW: **~spieß** m spit; **~wurst** f grilled sausage.
Brauch [braʊx] m -(e)s, Bräuche custom; **b~bar** a usable, serviceable; (Person) capable; **b~en** vt (bedürfen) need; (müssen) have to; (verwenden) use.
Braue ['braʊə] f -, -n brow; **b~n** vt brew; **Braue'rei** f brewery.
braun [braʊn] a brown; ~ (von Sonne auch) tanned.
Bräune ['brɔynə] f - brownness; (Sonnen~) tan; **b~n** vt make brown;

(Sonne) tan.
braungebrannt *a* tanned.
Brause ['brauzə] *f* -, -n shower bath; *(von Gießkanne)* rose; *(Getränk)* lemonade; **b~n** *vi* roar; *(auch vr: duschen)* take a shower.
Braut [braut] *f* -, **Bräute** bride; *(Verlobte)* fiancée.
Bräutigam ['brɔʏtɪgam] *m* -s, -e bridegroom; fiancé.
Brautpaar *nt* bride and bridegroom, bridal pair.
brav [braːf] *a* *(artig)* good; *(ehrenhaft)* worthy, honest.
bravo ['braːvo] *interj* well done.
BRD ['beːr'deː] *f* *abk* *von* **Bundesrepublik Deutschland.**
Brech- ['brɛç] *zW:* **~eisen** *nt* crowbar; **b~en** *vti* *unreg* break; *(Licht)* refract; *(fig: Mensch)* crush; *(speien)* vomit; **~reiz** *m* nausea, retching.
Brei [braɪ] *m* -(e)s, -e *(Masse)* pulp; *(KOCH)* gruel; *(Hafer~)* porridge *(Brit)*, oat meal *(US)*.
breit [braɪt] *a* wide, broad; **B~e** *f* -, -n width; breadth; *(GEOG)* latitude; **~en** *vt:* etw über etw *(akk)* **~en** spread sth over sth; **B~engrad** *m* degree of latitude; **~machen** *vr* spread o.s. out; **~treten** *vt* *unreg* *(umg)* enlarge upon.
Brems- ['brɛms] *zW:* **~belag** *m* brake lining; **~e** [-zə] *f* -, -n brake; *(ZOOL)* horsefly; **b~en** [-zən] *vi* brake, apply the brakes // *vt* *(Auto)* brake; *(fig)* slow down; **~licht** *nt* brake light; **~pedal** *nt* brake pedal; **~spur** *f* tyre *(Brit)* *od* tire *(US)* marks *pl;* **~weg** *m* braking distance.
Brenn- [brɛn] *zW:* **b~bar** *a* inflammable; **b~en** *unreg* *vi* burn, be on fire; *(Licht, Kerze etc)* burn // *vt* *(Holz etc)* burn; *(Ziegel, Ton)* fire; *(Kaffee)* roast; darauf b~en, etw zu tun be dying to do sth; **~(n)essel** *f* nettle; **~spiritus** *m* methylated spirits; **~stoff** *m* liquid fuel.
brenzlig ['brɛntslɪç] *a* *(fig)* precarious.
Brett [brɛt] *nt* -(e)s, -er board, plank; *(Bord)* shelf; *(Spiel~)* board; **Schwarze(s)** ~ notice board; **~er** *pl* *(SKI)* skis *pl;* *(THEAT)* boards *pl;* **~erzaun** *m* wooden fence.
Brezel ['breːtsəl] *f* -, -n pretzel.
brichst *etc* *v* *siehe* **brechen.**
Brief [briːf] *m* -(e)s, -e letter; **~freund** *m* penfriend; **~kasten** *m* letterbox; **~kopf** *m* letterhead; **b~lich** *a,ad* by letter; **~marke** *f* postage stamp; **~öffner** *m* letter opener; **~papier** *nt* notepaper; **~tasche** *f* wallet; **~träger** *m* postman; **~umschlag** *m* envelope; **~wechsel** *m* correspondence.
briet *etc* *v* *siehe* **braten.**

Brikett [bri'kɛt] *nt* -s, -s briquette.
brillant [brɪl'jant] *a* *(fig)* sparkling, brilliant; **B~** *m* -en, -en brilliant, diamond.
Brille ['brɪlə] *f* -, -n spectacles *pl;* *(Schutz~)* goggles *pl;* *(Toiletten~)* (toilet) seat.
bringen ['brɪŋən] *vt* *unreg* bring; *(mitnehmen, begleiten)* take; *(einbringen: Profit)* bring in; *(veröffentlichen)* publish; *(THEAT, CINE)* show; *(RAD, TV)* broadcast; *(in einen Zustand versetzen)* get; *(umg: tun können)* manage; jdn dazu ~, etw zu tun make sb do sth; **jdn nach Hause** ~ take sb home; jdn um etw ~ make sb lose sth; **jdn auf eine Idee** ~ give sb an idea.
Brise ['briːzə] *f* -, -n breeze.
Brit- ['briːt] *zW:* **~e** *m,* **~in** *f* Briton; **b~isch** *a* British.
bröckelig ['brœkəlɪç] *a* crumbly.
Brocken ['brɔkən] *m* -s, - piece, bit; *(Fels~)* lump of rock.
brodeln ['broːdəln] *vi* bubble.
Brokat [bro'kaːt] *m* -(e)s, -e brocade.
Brombeere ['brɔmbeːrə] *f* blackberry, bramble *(Brit)*.
Bronchien ['brɔnçiən] *pl* bronchia(l tubes) *pl.*
Bronze ['brõːsə] *f* -, -n bronze.
Brosche ['brɔʃə] *f* -, -n brooch.
Broschüre [brɔ'ʃyːrə] *f* -, -n pamphlet.
Brot [broːt] *nt* -(e)s, -e bread; *(~laib)* loaf.
Brötchen ['brøːtçən] *nt* roll.
Bruch [brux] *m* -(e)s, ̈e breakage; *(zerbrochene Stelle)* break; *(fig)* split, breach; *(MED: Eingeweide~)* rupture, hernia; *(Bein~ etc)* fracture; *(MATH)* fraction.
brüchig ['brʏçɪç] *a* brittle, fragile; *(Haus)* dilapidated.
Bruch- *zW:* **~landung** *f* crash landing; **~strich** *m* *(MATH)* line; **~stück** *nt* fragment; **~teil** *m* fraction.
Brücke ['brʏkə] *f* -, -n bridge; *(Teppich)* rug.
Bruder ['bruːdər] *m* -s, ̈ brother.
brüderlich ['bryːdərlɪç] *a* brotherly.
Brühe ['bryːə] *f* -, -n broth, stock; *(pej)* muck.
brüllen ['brʏlən] *vi* bellow, scream.
brummen ['brumən] *vi* *(Bär, Mensch etc)* growl; *(Insekt, Radio)* buzz; *(Motoren)* roar; *(murren)* grumble // *vt* growl.
brünett [brʏ'nɛt] *a* brunette, dark-haired.
Brunnen ['brunən] *m* -s, - fountain; *(tief)* well; *(natürlich)* spring.
brüsk [brʏsk] *a* abrupt, brusque.
Brüssel ['brʏsəl] *nt* Brussels.
Brust [brust] *f* -, ̈e breast; *(Männer~)* chest.

brüsten ['brʏstən] vr boast.

Brust- zW: **~fellentzündung** f pleurisy; **~kasten** m chest; **~schwimmen** nt breast-stroke; **~warze** f nipple.

Brüstung ['brʏstʊŋ] f parapet.

Brut [bruːt] f -, -en brood; (Brüten) hatching; **brutal** [bruˈtaːl] a brutal; **Brutali'tät** f brutality; **~kasten** m incubator.

brüten ['bryːtən] vi hatch, brood (auch fig).

brutto ['brʊto] ad gross; **B~einkommen** nt, **B~gehalt** nt gross salary; **B~gewicht** nt gross weight; **B~lohn** m gross wages pl.

Bube ['buːbə] m -n, -n (Schurke) rogue; (KARTEN) jack.

Buch [buːx] nt -(e)s, -er (COMM) account book; **~binder** m bookbinder; **~drucker** m printer; **~e** f -, -n beech tree; **b~en** vt book; (Betrag) enter.

Bücher- ['byːçər] zW: **~brett** nt bookshelf; **~ei** [-'raɪ] f library; **~regal** nt bookshelves pl, bookcase; **~schrank** m bookcase.

Buch- zW: **~fink** m chaffinch; **~führung** f book-keeping, accounting; **~halter(in** f) m -s, - bookkeeper; **~handel** m book trade; **~händler(in** f) m bookseller; **~handlung** f bookshop.

Büchse ['bʏksə] f -, -n tin, can; (Holz~) box; (Gewehr) rifle; **Büchsenfleisch** nt tinned meat; **Büchsenöffner** m tin od can opener.

Buch- zW: **~stabe** m -ns, -n letter (of the alphabet); **b~stabieren** [buːxʃtaˈbiːrən] vt spell; **b~stäblich** ['buːxʃtɛːplɪç] a literal.

Bucht ['bʊxt] f -, -en bay.

Buchung ['buːxʊŋ] f booking; (COMM) entry.

Buckel ['bʊkəl] m -s, - hump.

bücken ['bʏkən] vr bend.

Bückling ['bʏklɪŋ] m (Fisch) kipper; (Verbeugung) bow.

Bude ['buːdə] f -, -n booth, stall; (umg) digs pl (Brit).

Büfett [bʏˈfeː] nt -s, -s (Anrichte) sideboard; (Geschirrschrank) dresser; kaltes ~ cold buffet.

Büffel ['bʏfəl] m -s, - buffalo.

Bug [buːk] m -(e)s, -e (NAUT) bow; (AVIAT) nose.

Bügel ['byːgəl] m -s, - (Kleider~) hanger; (Steig~) stirrup; (Brillen~) arm; **~brett** nt ironing board; **~eisen** nt iron; **~falte** f crease; **b~n** vti iron.

Bühne ['byːnə] f -, -n stage; **Bühnenbild** nt set, scenery.

Buhruf ['buːruːf] m boo.

buk etc v siehe **backen**.

Bulgarien [bʊlˈgaːriən] nt Bulgaria.

Bull- ['bʊl] zW: **~dogge** f bulldog; **~dozer** ['bʊldoːzər] m -s, - bulldozer; **~e** m -n, -n bull.

Bummel ['bʊməl] m -s, - stroll; (Schaufenster~) window-shopping; **~ant** [-'lant] m slowcoach; **~ei** [-'laɪ] f wandering; dawdling; skiving; **b~n** vi wander, stroll; (trödeln) dawdle; (faulenzen) skive, loaf around; **~streik** m go-slow; **~zug** m slow train.

Bund [bʊnt] m -(e)s, -e (Freundschafts~ etc) bond; (Organisation) union; (POL) confederacy; (Hosen~, Rock~) waistband // nt -(e)s, -e bunch; (Stroh~) bundle.

Bündel ['bʏndəl] nt -s, - bundle, bale; **b~n** vt bundle.

Bundes- ['bʊndəs] in zW Federal (bes West German); **~bahn** f Federal Railways pl; **~hauptstadt** f Federal capital; **~kanzler** m Federal Chancellor; **~land** nt Land; **~liga** f football league; **~präsident** m Federal President; **~rat** m upper house of West German Parliament; **~republik** f Federal Republic (of West Germany); **~staat** m Federal state; **~tag** m West German Parliament; **~verfassungsgericht** nt Federal Constitutional Court; **~wehr** f West German Armed Forces pl.

Bünd- zW: **b~ig** a (kurz) concise; **~nis** nt -ses, -se alliance.

Bunker ['bʊŋkər] m -s, - bunker.

bunt [bʊnt] a coloured; (gemischt) mixed; **jdm wird es zu ~** it's getting too much for sb; **B~stift** m coloured pencil, crayon.

Burg [bʊrk] f -, -en castle, fort.

Bürge ['bʏrgə] m -n, -n guarantor; **b~n** vi vouch (für for).

Bürger(in f) ['bʏrgər(ɪn)] m -s, - citizen; member of the middle class; **~krieg** m civil war; **b~lich** a (Rechte) civil; (Klasse) middleclass; (pej) bourgeois; **~meister** m mayor; **~recht** nt civil rights pl; **~schaft** f population, citizens pl; **~steig** m pavement; **~tum** nt citizens pl.

Bürgschaft f surety; **~ leisten** give security.

Büro [byˈroː] nt -s, -s office; **~angestellte(r)** mf office worker; **~automatisierung** f office automation, OA; **~klammer** f paper clip; **~krat** [byroˈkraːt] m -en, -en bureaucrat; **~kra'tie** f bureaucracy; **b~'kratisch** a bureaucratic; **~schluß** m office closing time.

Bursch(e) [bʊrʃ(ə)] m -en, -en lad, fellow; (Diener) servant.

Bürste ['bʏrstə] f -, -n brush; **b~n** vt brush.

Bus [bʊs] *m* **-ses, -se** bus.
Busch [bʊʃ] *m* **-(e)s, ̈e** bush, shrub.
Büschel ['byʃəl] *nt* **-s, -** tuft.
buschig *a* bushy.
Busen ['buːzən] *m* **-s, -** bosom; (*Meer~*) inlet, bay.
Buße ['buːsə] *f* **-, -n** atonement, penance; (*Geld*) fine.
büßen ['byːsən] *vti* do penance (for), atone (for).
Bußgeld ['buːsgelt] *nt* fine.
Büste ['bystə] *f* **-, -n** bust; **Büstenhalter** *m* bra.
Butter ['bʊtər] *f* **-** butter; **~blume** *f* buttercup; **~brot** *nt* (piece of) bread and butter; **~brotpapier** *nt* greaseproof paper; **~dose** *f* butter dish; **b~weich** *a* soft as butter; (*fig, umg*) soft.
b.w. *abk* (= *bitte wenden*) p.t.o.
Byte [baıt] *nt* **-s** byte.
bzgl. *abk* (= *bezüglich*) re.
bzw. *abk von* **beziehungsweise**.

C

(*siehe auch* **K, Z**;
für **CH** *siehe auch* **SCH**)

C, c [tseː] *nt* C, c.
ca. *abk* (= *circa*) approx.
Café [ka'feː] *nt* **-s, -s** café.
Cafeteria [kafete'riːa] *f* **-, -s** cafeteria.
Camp- [kɛmp] *zW:* **c~en** *vi* camp; **~er(in** *f*) *m* **-s, -** camper; **~ing** *nt* **-s** camping; **~ingkocher** *m* camping stove; **~ingplatz** *m* camp(ing) site.
CDU [tseːdeː'ʔuː] *f abk* (= *Christlich-Demokratische Union*) Christian Democratic Union.
Cellist [tʃe'lıst] *m* cellist.
Cello ['tʃɛlo] *nt* **-s, -s** *od* **Celli** cello.
Chamäleon [ka'mɛːleon] *nt* **-s, -s** chameleon.
Champagner [ʃam'panjər] *m* **-s, -** champagne.
Champignon ['ʃampınjõ] *m* **-s, -s** button mushroom.
Chance ['ʃãːs(ə)] *f* **-, -n** chance, opportunity.
Chaos ['kaːɔs] *nt* **-, -** chaos.
chaotisch [ka'oːtıʃ] *a* chaotic.
Charakter [ka'raktər] *m* **-s, -e** [karak'teːrə] character; **c~fest** *a* of firm character, strong; **c~i'sieren** *vt* characterize; **c~istisch** [karakte'rıstıʃ] *a* characteristic, typical (*für* of); **c~los** *a* unprincipled; **~losigkeit** *f* lack of principle; **~schwäche** *f* weakness of character; **~stärke** *f* strength of character; **~zug** *m* characteristic, trait.
charmant [ʃar'mant] *a* charming.
Charme [ʃarm] *m* **-s** charm.
Charterflug ['(t)ʃaːrtərfluːk] *m* charter flight.

Chassis [ʃa'siː] *nt* **-, -** chassis.
Chauffeur [ʃɔ'føːr] *m* chauffeur.
Chauvinist [ʃovi'nıst] *m* chauvinist, jingoist.
Chef [ʃɛf] *m* **-s, -s** head; (*umg*) boss; **~arzt** *m* head physician; **~in** *f* (*umg*) boss.
Chemie [çe'miː] *f* **-** chemistry; **~faser** *f* man-made fibre.
Chemikalie [çemi'kaːliə] *f* **-, -n** chemical.
Chemiker(in *f*) ['çeːmikər(ın)] *m* **-s, -** (industrial) chemist.
chemisch ['çeːmıʃ] *a* chemical; **~e Reinigung** dry cleaning.
Chiffre ['ʃıfrə] *f* **-, -n** (*Geheimzeichen*) cipher; (*in Zeitung*) box number.
Chile ['çiːle, 'tʃiːle] *nt* Chile; **~ne** [-'leːnə] *m*, **~nin** *f* Chilean; **c~nisch** *a* Chilean.
Chin- ['çiːn] *zW:* **~a** *nt* China; **~ese** [-'neːzə] *m*, **~esin** *f* Chinese; **c~esisch** *a* Chinese.
Chips [tʃıps] *pl* crisps *pl*, chips *pl* (*US*).
Chirurg [çi'rʊrk] *m* **-en, -en** surgeon; **~ie** [-'giː] *f* surgery; **c~isch** *a* surgical.
Chlor [kloːr] *nt* **-s** chlorine; **Chloro'form** *nt* **-s** chloroform.
Cholera ['koːlera] *f* **-** cholera.
cholerisch [ko'leːrıʃ] *a* choleric.
Chor [koːr] *m* **-(e)s, ̈e** choir; (*Musikstück, THEAT*) chorus; **~al** [ko'raːl] *m* **-s, -äle** chorale.
Choreograph [koreo'graːf] *m* **-en, -en** choreographer; **~ie** [-'fiː] *f* choreography.
Chorknabe *m* choirboy.
Christ ['krıst] *m* **-en, -en** Christian; **~baum** *m* Christmas tree; **~entum** *nt* Christianity; **~in** *f* Christian; **~kind** *nt* ≈ Father Christmas; (*Jesus*) baby Jesus; **c~lich** *a* Christian; **Christus** *m* **-** Christ.
Chrom [kroːm] *nt* **-s** (*CHEM*) chromium; chrome.
Chron- ['kroːn] *zW:* **~ik** *f* chronicle; **c~isch** *a* chronic; **c~ologisch** [-'loːgıʃ] *a* chronological.
Chrysantheme [kryzan'teːmə] *f* **-, -n** chrysanthemum.
circa ['tsırka] *ad* about, approximately.
Clown [klaʊn] *m* **-s, -s** clown.
cm *abk von* **Zentimeter**.
COBOL ['koːbɔl] (*COMPUT*) COBOL.
Cola ['koːla] *f* **-, -s** Coke ®.
Computer [kɔm'pjuːtər] *m* **-s, -** computer.
Conférencier [kõferãsi'eː] *m* **-s, -s** compère.
Coupé [ku'peː] *nt* **-s, -s** (*AUT*) coupé, sports version.
Coupon [ku'põ] *m* **-s, -s** coupon;

(*Stoff~*) length of cloth.

Cousin [ku'zɛ:] *m* **-s, -s** cousin; **~e** [ku'zi:nə] *f* **-, -n** cousin.

Creme [krɛ:m] *f* **-, -s** (*lit, fig*) cream; (*Schuh~*) polish; (*Zahn~*) paste; (*KOCH*) mousse; **c~farben** *a* cream(-coloured).

CSU [tse:'ɛs''u:] *f abk* (= *Christlich-Soziale Union*) Christian Social Union.

Curry(pulver *nt*) ['kœri(pulfər)] *m od nt* **-s** curry powder.

Cursor ['kœrsər] *m* cursor.

Cutter(in *f*) ['katər(ın)] *m* **-s, -** (*CINE*) editor.

D

D, d [de:] *nt* D, d.

da [da:] ♦*ad* **1** (*örtlich*) there; (*hier*) here; **~ draußen** out there; **~ bin ich** here I am; **~, wo** where; **ist noch Milch ~?** is there any milk left?

2 (*zeitlich*) then; (*folglich*) so

3: **~ haben wir Glück gehabt** we were lucky there; **~ kann man nichts machen** nothing can be done about it ♦*kj* (*weil*) as, since.

dabehalten *vt unreg* keep.

dabei [da'baı] *ad* (*räumlich*) close to it; (*noch dazu*) besides; (*zusammen mit*) with them; (*zeitlich*) during this; (*obwohl doch*) but, however; **was ist schon ~?** what of it?; **es ist doch nichts ~, wenn ...** it doesn't matter if ...; **bleiben wir ~** let's leave it at that; **es bleibt ~** that's settled; **das Dumme/Schwierige ~** the stupid/difficult part of it; **er war gerade ~, zu gehen** he was just leaving; **~sein** *vi unreg* (*anwesend*) be present; (*beteiligt*) be involved; **~stehen** *vi unreg* stand around.

Dach [dax] *nt* **-(e)s, ⁻er** roof; **~boden** *m* attic, loft; **~decker** *m* **-s, -** slater, tiler; **~fenster** *nt*, **~luke** *f* skylight; **~pappe** *f* roofing felt; **~rinne** *f* gutter; **~ziegel** *m* roof tile.

Dachs [daks] *m* **-es, -e** badger.

dachte *etc v siehe* **denken**.

Dackel ['dakəl] *m* **-s, -** dachshund.

dadurch [da'durç] *ad* (*räumlich*) through it; (*durch diesen Umstand*) thereby, in that way; (*deshalb*) because of that, for that reason // *kj*: **~, daß** because.

dafür [da'fy:r] *ad* for it; (*anstatt*) instead; **er kann nichts ~** he can't help it; **er ist bekannt ~** he is well-known for that; **was bekomme ich ~?** what will I get for it?

dagegen [da'ge:gən] *ad* against it; (*im Vergleich damit*) in comparison with it; (*bei Tausch*) to it; **ich habe**

nichts ~ I don't mind; **ich war ~** I was against it; **~ kann man nichts tun** one can't do anything about it // *kj* however; **~halten** *vt unreg* (*vergleichen*) compare with it; (*entgegnen*) object to it.

daheim [da'haım] *ad* at home; **D~** *nt* **-s** home.

daher [da'he:r] *ad* (*räumlich*) from there; (*Ursache*) from that // *kj* (*deshalb*) that's why.

dahin [da'hın] *ad* (*räumlich*) there; (*zeitlich*) then; (*vergangen*) gone; **~gegen** *kj* on the other hand; **~gehend** *ad* on this matter; **~gestellt** *ad*: **~gestellt bleiben** remain to be seen; **~gestellt sein lassen** leave sth open *od* undecided.

dahinten [da'hıntən] *ad* over there.

dahinter [da'hıntər] *ad* behind it; **~kommen** *vi unreg* get to the bottom of sth.

Dahlie ['da:liə] *f* **-, -n** dahlia.

dalli ['dali] *adv* (*umg*) chop chop.

damalig ['da:ma:lıç] *a* of that time, then.

damals ['da:ma:ls] *ad* at that time, then.

Damast [da'mast] *m* **-(e)s, -e** damask.

Dame ['da:mə] *f* **-, -n** lady; (*SCHACH, KARTEN*) queen; (*Spiel*) draughts; **damenhaft** *a* ladylike; **Damenwahl** *f* ladies' excuse-me.

damit [da'mıt] *ad* with it; (*begründend*) by that; **was meint er ~?** what does he mean by that?; **genug ~!** that's enough; **~ eilt es nicht** there's no hurry // *kj* in order that *od* to.

dämlich ['dɛ:mlıç] *a* (*umg*) silly, stupid.

Damm [dam] *m* **-(e)s, ⁻e** dyke; (*Stau~*) dam; (*Hafen~*) mole; (*Bahn~, Straßen~*) embankment.

Dämm- ['dɛm] *zW*: **d~en** *vt* (*Wasser*) dam up; (*Schmerzen*) keep back; **d~erig** *a* dim, faint; **d~ern** *vi* (*Tag*) dawn; (*Abend*) fall; **~erung** *f* twilight; (*Morgen~*) dawn; (*Abend~*) dusk.

dämonisch [dɛ'mo:nıʃ] *a* demoniacal.

Dampf [dampf] *m* **-(e)s, ⁻e** steam; (*Dunst*) vapour; **d~en** *vi* steam.

dämpfen ['dɛmpfən] *vt* (*KOCH*) steam; (*bügeln auch*) iron with a damp cloth; (*fig*) dampen, subdue.

Dampf- *zW*: **~er** *m* **-s, -** steamer; **~kochtopf** *m* pressure cooker; **~schiff** *nt* steamship; **~walze** *f* steamroller.

danach [da'na:x] *ad* after that; (*zeitlich auch*) afterwards; (*gemäß*) accordingly; according to which *od* that; **er sieht ~ aus** he looks it.

daneben [da'ne:bən] *ad* beside it; (*im Vergleich*) in comparison;

~benehmen *vr unreg* misbehave;
~gehen *vi unreg* miss; (*Plan*) fail.
Dän- ['dɛːn] *zW:* **~e** *m,* **~in** *f* Dane;
~emark *nt* Denmark; **d~isch** *a* Danish.

Dank [daŋk] *m* **-(e)s** thanks *pl;* vielen
od schönen **~** many thanks; jdm **~**
sagen thank sb; **d~** *präp* +*dat od
gen* thanks to; **d~bar** *a* grateful;
(*Aufgabe*) rewarding; **~barkeit** *f*
gratitude; **d~e** *interj* thank you,
thanks; **d~en** *vi* (+*dat*) thank;
d~enswert *a* (*Arbeit*) worthwhile;
rewarding; (*Bemühung*) kind;
d~sagen *vi* express one's thanks.

dann [dan] *ad* then; **~** und wann now
and then.

daran [da'ran] *ad* on it; (*stoßen*)
against it; es liegt **~,** daß ... the
cause of it is that ...; gut/schlecht **~**
sein be well-/badly off; das Beste/
Dümmste **~** the best/stupidest thing
about it; ich war nahe **~,** zu ... I was
on the point of ...; er ist **~** gestorben
he died from *od* of it; **~gehen** *vi
unreg* start; **~setzen** *vt* stake; er hat
alles **~gesetzt,** von Glasgow
wegzukommen he has done his utmost to get away from Glasgow.

darauf [da'rauf] *ad* (*räumlich*) on it;
(*zielgerichtet*) towards it; (*danach*)
afterwards; es kommt ganz **~** an, ob
... it depends whether ...; die Tage **~**
the days following *od* thereafter; am
Tag **~** the next day; **~folgend** *a*
(*Tag, Jahr*) next, following; **~legen**
vt lay *od* put on top.

daraus [da'raus] *ad* from it; was ist
~ geworden? what became of it?;
~ geht hervor, daß ... this means
that ...

Darbietung ['daːrbiːtʊŋ] *f* performance.

darf *etc* *v siehe* **dürfen**.

darin [da'rɪn] *ad* in (there), in it.

Dar- ['daːr] *zW:* **d~legen** *vt* explain,
expound, set forth; **~legung** *f* explanation; **~leh(e)n** *nt* **-s,** - loan.

Darm [darm] *m* **-(e)s,** ⸚e intestine;
(*Wurst~*) skin; **~saite** *f* gut string.

Darstell- ['daːrʃtɛl] *zW:* **d~en** *vt*
(*abbilden, bedeuten*) represent;
(*THEAT*) act; (*beschreiben*) describe
// *vr* appear to be; **~er(in** *f*) *m* **-s,** -
actor/actress; **~ung** *f* portrayal, depiction.

darüber [da'ryːbər] *ad* (*räumlich*)
over/above it; (*fahren*) over it;
(*mehr*) more; (*währenddessen*)
meanwhile; (*sprechen, streiten*)
about it; **~** geht nichts there's nothing like it.

darum [da'rum] *ad* (*räumlich*) round
it; er bittet **~** he is pleading for it; es
geht **~,** daß ... the thing is that ...;

er würde viel **~** geben, wenn ... he
would give a lot to ... // *kj* that's
why; ich tue es **~,** weil ... I am doing
it because ...

darunter [da'rʊntər] *ad* (*räumlich*) under it; (*dazwischen*) among them;
(*weniger*) less; ein Stockwerk **~** one
floor below (it); was verstehen Sie
~? what do you understand by that?.

das [das] *def art* the // *pron* that.

Dasein ['daːzain] *nt* **-s** (*Leben*) life;
(*Anwesenheit*) presence; (*Bestehen*)
existence; **d~** *vi unreg* be there.

daß [das] *kj* that.

dasselbe [das'zɛlbə] *art, pron* the
same.

dastehen ['daːʃteːən] *vi unreg* stand
there.

Datei [da'tai] *f* file.

Daten- ['daːtən] *zW:* **~bank** *f* data
base; **~sichtgerät** *nt* visual display
unit, VDU.

datieren [da'tiːrən] *vt* date.

Dattel ['datəl] *f* **-, -n** date.

Datum ['daːtʊm] *nt* **-s, Daten** date;
(*pl: Angaben*) data *pl.*

Dauer ['dauər] *f* **-, -n** duration;
(*gewisse Zeitspanne*) length; (*Bestand, Fortbestehen*) permanence; es
war nur von kurzer **~** it didn't last
long; auf die **~** in the long run; (*auf
längere Zeit*) indefinitely; **~auftrag**
m standing order; **d~haft** *a* lasting,
durable; **~karte** *f* season ticket;
~lauf *m* long-distance run; **d~n** *vi*
last; es hat sehr lang gedauert, bis er
... it took him a long time to ...;
dauernd *a* constant; **~welle** *f*
perm(anent wave); **~wurst** *f* German salami; **~zustand** *m* permanent
condition.

Daumen ['daumən] *m* **-s,** - thumb.

Daune ['daunə] *f* **-, -n** down;
Daunendecke *f* down duvet *od* quilt.

davon [da'fɔn] *ad* of it; (*räumlich*)
away; (*weg von*) from it; (*Grund*)
because of it; das kommt **~!** that's
what you get; **~** abgesehen apart
from that; **~** sprechen/wissen talk/
know of *od* about it; was habe ich **~**?
what's the point?; **~gehen** *vi unreg*
leave, go away; **~laufen** *vi unreg*
run away.

davor [da'foːr] *ad* (*räumlich*) in front
of it; (*zeitlich*) before (that); **~** warnen warn about it.

dazu [da'tsuː] *ad* (*legen, stellen*) by it;
(*essen, singen*) with it; und **~** noch
and in addition; ein Beispiel/seine
Gedanken **~** one example for/his
thoughts on this; wie komme ich
denn **~**? why should I?; **~** fähig sein
be capable of it; sich **~** äußern say
sth on it; **~gehören** *vi* belong to it;
~kommen *vi unreg* (*Ereignisse*)

happen too; (*an einen Ort*) come along.

dazwischen [da'tsvɪʃən] *ad* in between; (*räumlich auch*) between (them); (*zusammen mit*) among them; **der Unterschied ~** the difference between them; **~kommen** *vi unreg* (*hineingeraten*) get caught in it; **es ist etwas ~gekommen** something cropped up; **~reden** *vi* (*unterbrechen*) interrupt; (*sich einmischen*) interfere; **~treten** *vi unreg* intervene.

DB *abk* (= *Deutsche Bundesbahn*) Federal Railways.

DDR [de:de:'er] *f abk* (= *Deutsche Demokratische Republik*) GDR.

Debatte [de'batə] *f -, -n* debate.

Deck [dɛk] *nt -(e)s, -s od -e* deck; **an ~ gehen** go on deck; **~e** *f -, -n* cover; (*Bett~*) blanket; (*Tisch~*) tablecloth; (*Zimmer~*) ceiling; **unter einer ~e stecken** be hand in glove; **~el** *m -s, -* lid; **d~en** *vt* cover // *vr* coincide; **~ung** *f* (*Schützen*) covering; (*Schutz*) cover; (*SPORT*) defence; (*Übereinstimmen*) agreement; **d~ungsgleich** *a* congruent.

Defekt [de'fɛkt] *m -(e)s, -e* fault, defect; **d~** *a* faulty.

defensiv [defen'si:f] *a* defensive.

definieren [defi'ni:rən] *vt* define.

Definition [definitsi'o:n] *f* definition.

Defizit ['de:fitsɪt] *nt -s, -e* deficit.

deftig ['deftɪç] *a* (*Essen*) large; (*Witz*) coarse.

Degen ['de:gən] *m -s, -* sword.

degenerieren [degene'ri:rən] *vi* degenerate.

Dehn- ['de:n] *zW:* **d~bar** *a* elastic; (*fig: Begriff*) loose; **~barkeit** *f* elasticity; looseness; **d~en** *vtr* stretch.

Deich [daɪç] *m -(e)s, -e* dyke, dike.

Deichsel ['daɪksəl] *f -, -n* shaft; **d~n** *vt* (*fig, umg*) wangle.

dein [daɪn] *pron* your; (**D~** *in Briefen*) your; **~e(r, s)** yours; **~er** *pron gen of* **du** of you; **~erseits** *ad* on your part; **~esgleichen** *pron* people like you; **~etwegen**, **~etwillen** *ad* (*für dich*) for your sake; (*wegen dir*) on your account; **~ige** *pron:* **der/die/das ~ige** yours.

dekadent [deka'dɛnt] *a* decadent.

Dekadenz [deka'dɛnts] *f* decadence.

Deklination [deklinatsi'o:n] *f* declension.

deklinieren [dekli'ni:rən] *vt* decline.

Dekolleté [dekɔl'te:] *nt -s, -s* low neckline.

Deko- [deko] *zW:* **~rateur** [-ra'tø:r] *m* window dresser; **~ration** [-ratsi'o:n] *f* decoration; (*in Laden*) window dressing; **d~rativ** [-ra'ti:f] *a* decorative; **d~rieren** [-'ri:rən] *vt* decorate;

(*Schaufenster*) dress.

Delegation [delegatsi'o:n] *f* delegation.

delikat [deli'ka:t] *a* (*zart, heikel*) delicate; (*köstlich*) delicious.

Delikatesse [delika'tɛsə] *f -, -n* delicacy; (*pl: Feinkost*) delicatessen food; **Delikatessengeschäft** *nt* delicatessen.

Delikt [de'lɪkt] *nt -(e)s, -e* (*JUR*) offence.

Delle ['dɛlə] *f -, -n* (*umg*) dent.

Delphin [dɛl'fi:n] *m -s, -e* dolphin.

dem [de(:)m] *art dat von* **der**.

Demagoge [dema'go:gə] *m -n, -n* demagogue.

dementieren [demɛn'ti:rən] *vt* deny.

dem- *zW:* **~gemäß**, **~nach** *ad* accordingly; **~nächst** *ad* shortly.

Demokrat [demo'kra:t] *m -en, -en* democrat; **~ie** [-'ti:] *f* democracy; **d~isch** *a* democratic; **d~isieren** [-i'zi:rən] *vt* democratize.

demolieren [demo'li:rən] *vt* demolish.

Demon- [demo] *zW:* **~strant(in** *f)* [-'strant(ɪn)] *m* demonstrator; **~stration** [-stratsi'o:n] *f* demonstration; **d~strativ** [-stra'ti:f] *a* demonstrative; (*Protest*) pointed; **d~strieren** [-'stri:rən] *vti* demonstrate.

Demoskopie [demosko'pi:] *f* public opinion research.

Demut ['de:mu:t] *f -* humility.

demütig ['de:my:tɪç] *a* humble; **~en** ['de:my:tɪgən] *vt* humiliate; **D~ung** *f* humiliation.

demzufolge ['de:mtsu'fɔlgə] *ad* accordingly.

den [de(:)n] *art akk von* **der**.

denen ['de:nən] *pron dat pl von* **der**, **die**, **das**.

Denk- ['dɛŋk] *zW:* **d~bar** *a* conceivable; **d~en** *vti unreg* think; **~en** *nt -s* thinking; **~fähigkeit** *f* intelligence; **d~faul** *a* lazy; **~fehler** *m* logical error; **~mal** *nt -s, ̈-er* monument; **d~würdig** *a* memorable; **~zettel** *m:* **jdm einen ~zettel verpassen** teach sb a lesson.

denn [dɛn] *kj* for // *ad* then; (*nach Komparativ*) than; **warum ~?** why?

dennoch ['dɛnɔx] *kj* nevertheless.

Denunziant [denuntsi'ant] *m* informer.

deponieren [depo'ni:rən] *vt* (*COMM*) deposit.

Depot [de'po:] *nt -s, -s* warehouse; (*Bus~*, *EISENB*) depot; (*Bank~*) strongroom, safe (*US*).

Depression [depresi'o:n] *f* depression.

deprimieren [depri'mi:rən] *vt* depress.

der, die, das [de:r, di:, das] ◆ *def art* **gen des, der, des**, *dat* **dem, der, dem** *akk* **den, die, das,** *pl* **die**; **der Rhein** the Rhine; **der Klaus** (*umg*) Klaus; **die Frau** (*im allgemeinen*) women; **der Tod/das Leben** death/ life; **der Fuß des Berges** the foot of the hill; **gib es der Frau** give it to the woman; **er hat sich die Hand verletzt** he has hurt his hand

♦ *rel pron* (*bei Menschen*) who, that; (*bei Tieren, Sachen*) which, that; **der Mann, den ich gesehen habe** the man who *od* whom *od* that I saw

♦ *dem pron* he/she/it; (*jener, dieser*) that; *pl* those; **der/die war es** it was him/her; **der mit der Brille** the one with glasses; **ich will den (da)** I want that one.

derart ['dɛrˈʔaːrt] *ad* so; (*solcher Art*) such; **~ig** *a* such, this sort of.

derb [dɛrp] *a* sturdy; (*Kost*) solid; (*grob*) coarse; **D~heit** *f* sturdiness; solidity; coarseness.

der- *zW:* **'~'gleichen** *pron* such; **'~jenige** *pron* he; she; it; (*rel*) the one (who); that (which); **'~'maßen** *ad* to such an extent, so; **~'selbe** *art, pron* the same; **'~'weil(en)** *ad* in the meantime; **'~'zeitig** *a* present, current; (*damalig*) then.

des [dɛs] *art gen von* **der.**

desertieren [dezɛr'tiːrən] *vi* desert.

desgleichen ['dɛs'glaıçən] *pron* the same.

deshalb ['dɛs'halp] *ad* therefore, that's why.

Desinfektion [dezɪnfɛktsi'oːn] *f* disinfection; **Desinfektionsmittel** *nt* disinfectant.

desinfizieren [dezɪnfi'tsiːrən] *vt* disinfect.

dessen ['dɛsən] *pron gen von* **der, das;** **~'ungeachtet** *ad* nevertheless, regardless.

Dessert [dɛ'sɛːr] *nt* **-s, -s** dessert.

destillieren [dɛstɪ'liːrən] *vt* distil.

desto ['dɛsto] *ad* all *od* so much the; **~ besser** all the better.

deswegen ['dɛs'veːgən] *kj* therefore, hence.

Detail [de'taɪ] *nt* **-s, -s** detail.

Detektiv [detɛk'tiːf] *m* **-s, -e** detective.

deut- ['dɔʏt] *zW:* **~en** *vt* interpret, explain // *vi* point (*auf* +*akk* to *od* at); **~lich** *a* clear; (*Unterschied*) distinct; **D~lichkeit** *f* clarity; distinctness.

deutsch [dɔʏtʃ] *a* German; **auf ~** in German; **D~e Demokratische Republik** German Democratic Republic, East Germany; **~es Beefsteak** *nt* ≈ hamburger; **D~** *nt* German; **D~e** *f,* **D~er** *m* German; **ich bin D~er** I am German; **D~land** *nt* Germany.

Devise [de'viːzə] *f* **-, -n** motto, device; (*pl: FIN*) foreign currency *od* exchange.

Dezember [de'tsɛmbər] *m* **-(s), -** December.

dezent [de'tsɛnt] *a* discreet.

dezimal [detsi'maːl] *a* decimal; **D~bruch** *m* decimal (fraction); **D~system** *nt* decimal system.

d.h. *abk* (= *das heißt*) i.e.

Dia ['diːa] *nt* **-s, -s** (*PHOT*) slide, transparency.

Diabetes [dia'beːtɛs] *m* **-, -** (*MED*) diabetes.

Diagnose [dia'gnoːzə] *f* **-, -n** diagnosis.

diagonal [diago'naːl] *a* diagonal; **D~e** *f* **-, -n** diagonal.

Dialekt [dia'lɛkt] *m* **-(e)s, -e** dialect; **d~isch** *a* dialectal; (*Logik*) dialectical.

Dialog [dia'loːk] *m* **-(e)s, -e** dialogue.

Diamant [dia'mant] *m* diamond.

Diät [di'ɛːt] *f* **-** diet; **~en** *pl* (*POL*) allowance.

dich [dıç] *pron akk von* **du** you; yourself.

dicht [dıçt] *a* dense; (*Nebel*) thick; (*Gewebe*) close; (*undurchlässig*) (water)tight; (*fig*) concise // *ad*: **~ an/bei** close to; **~bevölkert** *a* densely *od* heavily populated; **D~e** *f* **-, -n** density; thickness; closeness; (water)tightness; (*fig*) conciseness; **~en** *vt* (*dicht machen*) make watertight; seal; (*NAUT*) caulk // *vti* (*LITER*) compose, write; **D~er(in** *f*) *m* **-s, -**, poet; (*Autor*) writer; **~erisch** *a* poetical; **~halten** *vi unreg* (*umg*) keep one's mouth shut; **D~ung** *f* (*TECH*) washer; (*AUT*) gasket; (*Gedichte*) poetry; (*Prosa*) (piece of) writing.

dick [dık] *a* thick; (*fett*) fat; **durch ~ und dünn** through thick and thin; **D~e** *f* **-, -n** thickness; fatness; **~flüssig** *a* viscous; **D~icht** *nt* **-s, -e** thicket; **D~kopf** *m* mule; **D~milch** *f* soured milk.

die [diː] *def art siehe* **der.**

Dieb(in *f*) [diːp/diːbɪn] *m* **-(e)s, -e** thief; **d~isch** *a* thieving; (*umg*) immense; **~stahl** *m* **-(e)s, -e** theft.

Diele ['diːlə] *f* **-, -n** (*Brett*) board; (*Flur*) hall, lobby.

dienen ['diːnən] *vi* serve (*jdm* sb).

Diener *m* **-s, -** servant; **~in** *f* (maid)servant; **~schaft** *f* servants *pl.*

Dienst [diːnst] *m* **-(e)s, -e** service; **außer ~** retired; **~ haben** be on duty.

Dienstag ['diːnstaːk] *m* Tuesday; **d~s** *ad* on Tuesdays.

Dienst- *zW:* **~geheimnis** *nt* professional secret; **~gespräch** *nt* business call; **d~habend** *a* (*Arzt*) on duty; **~leistungsgewerbe** *nt* service industries *pl;* **d~lich** *a* official; **~mädchen** *nt* domestic servant; **~reise** *f* business trip; **~stelle** *f* office; **~vorschrift** *f* service regulations *pl;* **~weg** *m* official channels *pl;* ~**zeit** *f* office hours *pl;* (*MIL*) period of service.

dies- [di:s] *zW:* ~**bezüglich** *a* (*Frage*) on this matter; ~**e(r, s)** [di:zə(r,z)] *pron* this (one); **dieselbe** [di:'zɛlbə] *pron, art* the same.

Dieselöl ['di:zəl'ø:l] *nt* diesel oil.

diesig ['di:zɪç] *a* drizzly.

dies- *zW:* ~**jährig** *a* this year's; ~**mal** *ad* this time; ~**seits** *präp* +*gen* on this side; **D**~**seits** *nt* - this life.

Dietrich ['di:trɪç] *m* -s, -e picklock.

differential [dɪferɛntsi'a:l] *a* differential; **D**~**getriebe** *nt* differential gear; **D**~**rechnung** *f* differential calculus.

differenzieren [dɪferɛn'tsi:rən] *vt* make differences in; **differenziert** complex.

Dikt- [dɪkt] *zW:* ~**aphon** [-a'fo:n] *nt* dictaphone; ~**at** [-'ta:t] *nt* -(e)s, -e dictation; ~**ator** [-'ta:tɔr] *m* dictator; **d**~**atorisch** [-a'to:rɪʃ] *a* dictatorial; ~**atur** [-a'tu:r] *f* dictatorship; **d**~**ieren** [-'ti:rən] *vt* dictate.

Dilemma [di'lɛma] *nt* -s, -s *od* -ta dilemma.

Dilettant [dile'tant] *m* dilettante, amateur; **d**~**isch** *a* amateurish, dilettante.

Dimension [dimɛnzi'o:n] *f* dimension.

Ding [dɪŋ] *nt* -(e)s, -e thing, object; **d**~**lich** *a* real, concrete; **Dings, Dingsbums** ['dɪŋksbums] *nt* - (*umg*) thingummybob.

Diözese [diø'tse:zə] *f* -, -n diocese.

Diphtherie [dɪfte'ri:] *f* diphtheria.

Diplom [di'plo:m] *nt* -(e)s, -e diploma, certificate; ~**at** [-'ma:t] *m* -en, -en diplomat; ~**atie** [-a'ti:] *f* diplomacy; **d**~**atisch** [-'matɪʃ] *a* diplomatic; ~**ingenieur** *m* qualified engineer.

dir [di:r] *pron dat von* **du** (to) you.

direkt [di'rɛkt] *a* direct; **D**~**or** *m* director; (*SCH*) principal, headmaster; **D**~**übertragung** *f* live broadcast.

Dirigent [diri'gɛnt] *m* conductor.

dirigieren [diri'gi:rən] *vt* direct; (*MUS*) conduct.

Dirne ['dɪrnə] *f* -, -n prostitute.

Diskette [dɪs'ketə] *f* diskette, floppy disk.

Diskont [dɪs'kɔnt] *m* -s, -e discount; ~**satz** *m* rate of discount.

Diskothek [dɪsko'te:k] *f* -, -en disco(theque).

diskret [dɪs'kre:t] *a* discreet; **D**~**ion** [-tsi'o:n] *f* discretion.

Diskussion [dɪskusi'o:n] *f* discussion; debate; **zur** ~ **stehen** be under discussion.

diskutabel [dɪsku'ta:bəl] *a* debatable.

diskutieren [dɪsku'ti:rən] *vti* discuss, debate.

Distanz [dɪs'tants] *f* distance.

Distel ['dɪstəl] *f* -, -n thistle.

Disziplin [dɪstsi'pli:n] *f* discipline.

Dividende [divi'dɛndə] *f* -, -n dividend.

dividieren [divi'di:rən] *vt* divide (*durch* by).

DM [de:'ʔɛm] *abk* (= *Deutsche Mark*) German Mark.

D-Mark ['de:mark] *f* D Mark, German Mark.

doch [dɔx] ♦ *ad* **1** (*dennoch*) after all; (*sowieso*) anyway; **er kam** ~ **noch** he came after all; **du weißt es ja** ~ **besser** you know better than I do anyway; **und** ~ ... and yet ...

2 (*als bejahende Antwort*) yes I do/it does *etc*; **das ist nicht wahr** — ~! that's not true — yes it is!

3 (*auffordernd*): **komm** ~ do come; **laß ihn** ~ just leave him; **nicht** ~! oh no!

4: **sie ist** ~ **noch so jung** but she's still so young; **Sie wissen** ~, **wie das ist** you know how it is(, don't you?); **wenn** ~ if only

♦ *kj* (*aber*) but; (*trotzdem*) all the same; **und** ~ **hat er es getan** but still he did it.

Docht [dɔxt] *m* -(e)s, -e wick.

Dogge ['dɔgə] *f* -, -n bulldog.

Dogma ['dɔgma] *nt* -s, -men dogma; **d**~**tisch** [dɔ'gmatɪʃ] *a* dogmatic.

Doktor ['dɔktɔr] *m* -s, -en [-'to:rən] doctor; **Doktorand** [-'rant] *m* -en, -en candidate for a doctorate; ~**arbeit** *f* doctoral thesis.

Dokument [doku'mɛnt] *nt* document.

Dokumentar- [dokumɛn'ta:r] *zW:* ~**bericht** [-'ta:rbərɪçt] *m* documentary; ~**film** *m* documentary (film); **d**~**isch** *a* documentary.

Dolch [dɔlç] *m* -(e)s, -e dagger.

dolmetschen ['dɔlmɛtʃən] *vti* interpret.

Dolmetscher(in *f*) *m* -s, - interpreter.

Dom [do:m] *m* -(e)s, -e cathedral.

dominieren [domi'ni:rən] *vt* dominate // *vi* predominate.

Dompfaff ['do:mpfaf] *m* bullfinch.

Donau ['do:nau] *f* Danube.

Donner ['dɔnər] *m* -s, - thunder; **d**~**n** *vi unpers* thunder.

Donnerstag ['dɔnərsta:k] *m* Thursday.

doof [do:f] *a* (*umg*) daft, stupid.

Doppel ['dɔpəl] *nt* -s, - duplicate; (*SPORT*) doubles; ~- *in zW* double; ~**bett** *nt* double bed; ~**fenster** *nt* double glazing; ~**gänger** *m* -s, - double; ~**haus** *nt* semi-detached house; ~**punkt** *m* colon; ~**stecker** *m* two-way adaptor; **d**~**t** *a* double; **in d**~**ter Ausführung** in duplicate; ~**zentner** *m* 100 kilograms; ~**zimmer** *nt* double room.

Dorf [dɔrf] *nt* -(e)s, ̈-er village; ~**bewohner** *m* villager.

Dorn [dɔrn] *m* -(e)s, -en (*BOT*) thorn;

pl **-e** (*Schnallen~*) tongue, pin; **d~ig** *a* thorny.
dörren ['dœrən] *vt* dry.
Dörrobst ['dœr'o:pst] *nt* dried fruit.
Dorsch [dɔrʃ] *m* **-(e)s, -e** cod.
dort [dɔrt] *ad* there; ~ **drüben** over there; ~**her** from there; ~**hin** (to) there; ~**ig** *a* of that place; in that town.
Dose ['do:zə] *f* **-, -n** box; (*Blech~*) tin, can; **Dosenöffner** *m* tin *od* can opener.
Dosis ['do:zɪs] *f* **-, Dosen** dose.
Dotter ['dɔtər] *m* **-s, -** egg yolk.
Dozent [do'tsɛnt] *m* university lecturer.
Drache [draxə] *m* **-n, -n** (*Tier*) dragon; ~**n** *m* **-s, -** kite.
Draht [dra:t] *m* **-(e)s, ⁻e** wire; auf ~ **sein** be on the ball; ~**gitter** *nt* wire grating; ~**seil** *nt* cable; ~**seilbahn** *f* cable railway, funicular; ~**zange** *f* pliers *pl.*
Drama ['dra:ma] *nt* **-s, Dramen** drama, play; ~**tiker** [-'ma:tikər] *m* **-s, -** dramatist; **d~tisch** [-'ma:tɪʃ] *a* dramatic.
dran [dran] *ad* (*umg*) jetzt bin ich ~! it's my turn now; *siehe* **daran.**
Drang [draŋ] *m* **-(e)s, ⁻e** (*Trieb*) impulse, urge, desire (*nach* for); (*Druck*) pressure.
drängeln ['drɛŋəln] *vti* push, jostle.
drängen ['drɛŋən] *vt* (*schieben*) push, press; (*antreiben*) urge // *vi* (*eilig sein*) be urgent; (*Zeit*) press; auf etw (*akk*) ~ press for sth.
drastisch ['drastɪʃ] *a* drastic.
drauf [drauf] *ad* (*umg*) *siehe* **darauf;** **D~gänger** *m* **-s, -** daredevil.
draußen ['drausən] *ad* outside, out-of-doors.
Dreck [drɛk] *m* **-(e)s** mud, dirt; **d~ig** *a* dirty, filthy.
Dreh- ['dre:] *zW:* ~**arbeiten** *pl* (*CINE*) shooting; ~**bank** *f* lathe; **d~bar** *a* revolving; ~**buch** *nt* (*CINE*) script; **d~en** *vti* turn, rotate; (*Zigaretten*) roll; (*Film*) shoot // *vr* turn; (*handeln von*) be (*um* about); ~**orgel** *f* barrel organ; ~**tür** *f* revolving door; ~**ung** *f* (*Rotation*) rotation; (*Um~, Wendung*) turn; ~**zahl** *f* rate of revolutions; ~**zahlmesser** *m* rev(olution) counter.
drei [drai] *num* three; **D~eck** *nt* triangle; ~**eckig** *a* triangular; ~**einhalb** *num* three and a half; ~**erlei** *a inv* of three kinds; ~**fach** *a,ad* triple, treble; ~**hundert** *num* three hundred; **D~königsfest** *nt* Epiphany; ~**mal** *ad* three times; ~**malig** *a* three times.
dreinreden ['drainre:dən] *vi:* jdm ~ (*dazwischenreden*) interrupt sb; (*sich einmischen*) interfere with sb.

dreißig ['draisɪç] *num* thirty.
dreist [draist] *a* bold, audacious; **D~igkeit** *f* boldness, audacity.
drei- *zW:* ~**viertel** *num* three-quarters; **D~viertelstunde** *f* three-quarters of an hour; ~**zehn** *num* thirteen.
dressieren [drɛ'si:rən] *vt* train.
Drill- ['drɪl] *zW:* ~**bohrer** *m* light drill; **d~en** *vt* (*bohren*) drill, bore; (*MIL*) drill; (*fig*) train; **Drilling** *m* triplet.
drin [drɪn] *ad* (*umg*) *siehe* **darin.**
dringen ['drɪŋən] *vi* unreg (*Wasser, Licht, Kälte*) penetrate (*durch* through; *in* +*akk* into); auf etw (*akk*) ~ insist on sth.
dringend ['drɪŋənt], **dringlich** ['drɪŋlɪç] *a* urgent.
Dringlichkeit *f* urgency.
drinnen ['drɪnən] *ad* inside, indoors.
dritte(r, s) ['drɪtə(r, s)] *a* third; ~ **Welt** Third World; **D~s Reich** Third Reich; **Drittel** *nt* **-s, -** third; **drittens** *ad* thirdly.
droben ['dro:bən] *ad* above, up there.
Droge ['dro:gə] *f* **-, -n** drug; **drogenabhängig** *a* addicted to drugs; **Drogenhändler** *m* drug pedlar, pusher; **Drogerie** [dro:gə-'ri:] *f* chemist's shop.
Drogist [dro'gɪst] *m* pharmacist, chemist.
drohen ['dro:ən] *vi* threaten (*jdm* sb).
dröhnen ['drø:nən] *vi* (*Motor*) roar; (*Stimme, Musik*) ring, resound.
Drohung ['dro:uŋ] *f* threat.
drollig ['drɔlɪç] *a* droll.
Drossel ['drɔsəl] *f* **-, -n** thrush.
drüben ['dry:bən] *ad* over there, on the other side.
drüber ['dry:bər] *ad* (*umg*) *siehe* **darüber.**
Druck [drʊk] *m* **-(e)s, -e** (*PHYS, Zwang*) pressure; (*TYP: Vorgang*) printing; (: *Produkt*) print; (*fig: Belastung*) burden, weight; ~**buchstabe** *m* block letter; ~**er** *m* printer.
Drück- ['drʏk] *zW:* **d~en** *vti* (*Knopf, Hand*) press; (*zu eng sein*) pinch; (*fig: Preise*) keep down; (*fig: belasten*) oppress, weigh down // *vr:* sich vor etw (*dat*) **d~en** get out of (doing) sth; **d~end** *a* oppressive; ~**er** *m* **-s, -** button; (*Tür~*) handle; (*Gewehr~*) trigger.
Druck- *zW:* ~**er** *m* **-s, -** printer; **Drucke'rei** *f* printing works, press; ~**erschwärze** *f* printer's ink; ~**fehler** *m* misprint; ~**knopf** *m* press stud, snap fastener; ~**sache** *f* printed matter; ~**schrift** *f* block *od* printed letters *pl.*
drum [drʊm] *ad* (*umg*) *siehe* **darum.**
drunten ['drʊntən] *ad* below, down there.

Drüse ['dry:zə] f -, -n gland.
Dschungel ['dʒʊŋəl] m -s, - jungle.
du [du:] pron (**D~** in Briefen) you; **D~** sagen siehe **duzen**.
ducken ['dʊkən] vt (Kopf, Person) duck; (fig) take down a peg or two // vr duck.
Duckmäuser ['dʊkmɔyzər] m -s, - yes-man.
Dudelsack ['du:dəlzak] m bagpipes pl.
Duell [du'ɛl] nt -s, -e duel.
Duett [du'ɛt] nt -(e)s, -e duet.
Duft [dʊft] m -(e)s, ⁻e scent, odour; **d~en** vi smell, be fragrant; **d~ig** a (Stoff, Kleid) delicate, diaphanous.
duld- ['dʊld] zW: **~en** vti suffer; (zulassen) tolerate; **~sam** a tolerant.
dumm [dʊm] a stupid; (ärgerlich) annoying; **der D~e** sein to be the loser; **~erweise** ad stupidly; **D~heit** f stupidity; (Tat) blunder, stupid mistake; **D~kopf** m blockhead.
dumpf [dʊmpf] a (Ton) hollow, dull; (Luft) close; (Erinnerung, Schmerz) vague; **~ig** a musty.
Düne ['dy:nə] f -, -n dune.
düngen ['dyŋən] vt manure.
Dünger m -s, - dung, manure; (künstlich) fertilizer.
dunkel ['dʊŋkəl] a dark; (Stimme) deep; (Ahnung) vague; (rätselhaft) obscure; (verdächtig) dubious, shady; im **~n tappen** (fig) grope in the dark.
Dunkel- zW: **~heit** f darkness; (fig) obscurity; **~kammer** f (PHOT) dark room; **d~n** vi unpers grow dark; **~ziffer** f estimated number of unreported cases.
dünn [dʏn] a thin; **~flüssig** a watery, thin.
Dunst [dʊnst] m -es, ⁻e vapour; (Wetter) haze.
dünsten ['dʏnstən] vt steam.
dunstig ['dʊnstɪç] a vaporous; (Wetter) hazy, misty.
Duplikat [dupli'ka:t] nt -(e)s, -e duplicate.
Dur [du:r] nt -, - (MUS) major.
durch [dʊrç] ◆präp +akk **1** (hin~) through; **~ den ganzen Urwald** through the jungle; **~ die ganze Welt reisen** travel all over the world
2 (mittels) through, by (means of); (aufgrund) due to, owing to; **Tod ~ Herzschlag/den Strang** death from a heart attack/by hanging; **~ die Post** by post; **~ seine Bemühungen** through his efforts
◆ad **1** (hin~) through; **die ganze Nacht ~** all through the night; **den Sommer ~** during the summer; **8 Uhr ~** past 8 o'clock; **~ und ~** completely **2** (~gebraten etc): **(gut) ~** well-done.

durch- zW: **~arbeiten** vti work through // vr work one's way through; **~'aus** ad completely; (unbedingt) definitely; **~aus nicht** absolutely not; **~blättern** vt leaf through.
Durchblick ['dʊrçblɪk] m view; (fig) comprehension; **d~en** vi look through; (umg: verstehen) understand (bei etw sth); **etw d~en lassen** (fig) hint at sth.
durchbrechen ['dʊrçbrɛçən] vti unreg break; [dʊrç'brɛçən] vt unreg insep (Schranken) break through; (Schallmauer) break; (Gewohnheit) break free from.
durchbrennen ['dʊrçbrɛnən] vi unreg (Draht, Sicherung) burn through; (umg) run away.
Durchbruch ['dʊrçbrʊx] m (Öffnung) opening; (MIL) breach; (von Gefühlen etc) eruption; (der Zähne) cutting; (fig) breakthrough; **zum ~ kommen** break through.
durch- zW: **~dacht** [dʊrç'daxt] a well thought-out; **~'denken** vt unreg insep think out; **'~drehen** vt (Fleisch) mince // vi (umg) crack up.
durcheinander [dʊrçʔaɪ'nandər] ad in a mess, in confusion; (umg: verwirrt) confused; **~ trinken** mix one's drinks; **D~** nt -s (Verwirrung) confusion; (Unordnung) mess; **~bringen** vt unreg mess up; (verwirren) confuse; **~reden** vi talk at the same time.
durch- zW: **D~fahrt** f transit; (Verkehr) thoroughfare; **D~fall** m (MED) diarrhoea; **~fallen** vi unreg fall through; (in Prüfung) fail; **~finden** vr unreg find one's way through; **~'forschen** vt insep explore; **~fragen** vr find one's way by asking.
durchführ- ['dʊrçfy:r] zW: **~bar** a feasible, practicable; **~en** vt carry out; **D~ung** f execution, performance.
Durchgang ['dʊrçgaŋ] m passage(way); (bei Produktion, Versuch) run; (SPORT) round; (bei Wahl) ballot; **~ verboten** no thoroughfare.
Durchgangs- zW: **~handel** m transit trade; **~lager** nt transit camp; **~verkehr** m through traffic.
durchgefroren ['dʊrçgəfro:rən] a (Mensch) frozen stiff.
durchgehen ['dʊrçge:ən] unreg vt (behandeln) go over // vi go through; (ausreißen: Pferd) break loose; (Mensch) run away; **mein Temperament ging mit mir durch** my temper got the better of me; **jdm etw ~ lassen** let sb get away with sth; **~d** a (Zug) through; (Öffnungszeiten) continuous.
durch- zW: **~greifen** vi unreg take

strong action; **~halten** *unreg vi* last out // *vt* keep up; **~kommen** *vi unreg* get through; (*überleben*) pull through.

durch'kreuzen *vt insep* thwart, frustrate.

durch- *zW*: **~lassen** *vt unreg* (*Person*) let through; (*Wasser*) let in; **~lässig** *a* leaky; **D~lauferhitzer** *m* **-s, -** (hot water) geyser.

durch- *zW*: **~leben** *vt insep* live *od* go through, experience; **'~lesen** *vt unreg* read through; **~leuchten** *vt insep* X-ray; **'~machen** *vt* go through; **die Nacht ~machen** make a night of it.

Durch- *zW*: **~marsch** *m* march through; **~messer** *m* **-s,** - diameter.

durch'nässen *vt insep* soak (through).

durch- *zW*: **~nehmen** *vt unreg* go over; **~numerieren** *vt* number consecutively.

durchqueren [dʊrçˈkveːrən] *vt insep* cross.

durch- *zW*: **D~reiche** *f* **-, -n** (serving) hatch; **D~reise** *f* transit; **auf der D~reise** passing through; (*Güter*) in transit; **~ringen** *vr unreg* reach after a long struggle; **~rosten** *vi* rust through.

durchs [dʊrçs] = **durch das.**

Durchsage [ˈdʊrçzaːgə] *f* **-, -n** intercom *od* radio announcement.

Durchsatz [ˈdʊrçzats] *m* throughput.

durchschauen [ˈdʊrçʃaʊən] *vi* (*lit*) look *od* see through // [dʊrçˈʃaʊən] *vt insep* (*Person, Lüge*) see through.

durchscheinen [ˈdʊrçʃaɪnən] *vi unreg* shine through; **~d** *a* translucent.

Durchschlag [ˈdʊrçʃlaːk] *m* (*Doppel*) carbon copy; (*Sieb*) strainer; **d~en** *unreg vt* (*entzweischlagen*) split (in two); (*sieben*) sieve // *vi* (*zum Vorschein kommen*) emerge, come out // *vr* get by; **d~end** *a* resounding.

durchschneiden [ˈdʊrçʃnaɪdən] *vt unreg* cut through.

Durchschnitt [ˈdʊrçʃnɪt] *m* (*Mittelwert*) average; **über/unter dem ~** above/below average; **im ~** on average; **d~lich** *a* average // *ad* on average.

Durchschnitts- *zW*: **~geschwindigkeit** *f* average speed; **~mensch** *m* average man, man in the street; **~wert** *m* average.

durch- *zW*: **D~schrift** *f* copy; **~sehen** *vt unreg* look through; **~setzen** *vt* enforce; **seinen Kopf ~setzen** get one's own way // *vr* (*Erfolg haben*) succeed; (*sich behaupten*) get one's way // [dʊrçˈzɛtsən] *vt insep* mix.

Durchsicht [ˈdʊrçzɪçt] *f* looking through, checking; **d~ig** *a* transpar-

ent; **~igkeit** *f* transparence.

durch- *zW*: '**~sprechen** *vt unreg* talk over; '**~stehen** *vt unreg* live through; '**~streichen** *vt unreg* cross out; **~'suchen** *vt insep* search; **D~'suchung** *f* search; **~trieben** [-ˈtriːbən] *a* cunning, wily; **~'wachsen** *a* (*lit: Speck*) streaky; (*fig: mittelmäßig*) so-so.

durch- *zW*: **~weg** *ad* throughout, completely; **~ziehen** *unreg vt* (*Faden*) draw through // *vi* pass through; **D~zug** *m* (*Luft*) draught; (*von Truppen, Vögeln*) passage.

dürfen [ˈdyrfən] *vi unreg* **1** (*Erlaubnis haben*) be allowed to; **ich darf das** I'm allowed to (do that); **darf ich?** may I?; **darf ich ins Kino?** can *od* may I go to the cinema?; **es darf geraucht werden** you may smoke **2** (*in Verneinungen*): **er darf das nicht** he's not allowed to (do that); **das darf nicht geschehen** that must not happen; **da darf sie sich nicht wundern** that shouldn't surprise her **3** (*in Höflichkeitsformeln*): **darf ich Sie bitten, das zu tun?** may *od* could I ask you to do that?; **was darf es sein?** what can I do for you? **4** (*können*): **das ~ Sie mir glauben** you can believe me **5** (*Möglichkeit*): **das dürfte genug sein** that should be enough; **es dürfte Ihnen bekannt sein, daß ...** as you will probably know ...

dürftig [ˈdyrftɪç] *a* (*ärmlich*) needy, poor; (*unzulänglich*) inadequate.

dürr [dyr] *a* dried-up; (*Land*) arid; (*mager*) skinny, gaunt; **D~e** *f* **-, -n** aridity; (*Zeit*) drought; (*Magerkeit*) skinniness.

Durst [dʊrst] *m* **-(e)s** thirst; **~ haben** be thirsty; **d~ig** *a* thirsty.

Dusche [ˈduːʃə] *f* **-, -n** shower; **d~n** *vir* have a shower.

Düse [ˈdyːzə] *f* **-, -n** nozzle; (*Flugzeug~*) jet.

Düsen- *zW*: **~antrieb** *m* jet propulsion; **~flugzeug** *nt* jet (plane); **~jäger** *m* jet fighter.

Dussel [ˈdʊsəl] *m* **-s,** - (*umg*) twit.

düster [ˈdyːstər] *a* dark; (*Gedanken, Zukunft*) gloomy.

Dutzend [ˈdʊtsənt] *nt* **-s, -e** dozen; **d~(e)mal** *ad* a dozen times; **d~weise** *ad* by the dozen.

duzen [ˈduːtsən] *vtr* use the familiar form of address *od* 'du' (*jdn* to *od* with sb).

Dynamik [dyˈnaːmɪk] *f* (*PHYS*) dynamics; (*fig: Schwung*) momentum; (*von Mensch*) dynamism.

dynamisch [dyˈnaːmɪʃ] *a* (*lit, fig*) dynamic.

Dynamit [dynaˈmiːt] *nt* **-s** dynamite.

Dynamo [dy'na:mo] *m* **-s, -s** dynamo.
D-Zug ['de:tsu:k] *m* through train.

E

E, e [e:] *nt* E, e.
Ebbe ['ɛbə] *f* -, **-n** low tide.
eben ['e:bən] *a* level; (*glatt*) smooth // *ad* just; (*bestätigend*) exactly; ~ **deswegen** just because of that; **ebenbürtig** *a*: jdm ebenbürtig sein to sb's peer; **E~e** *f* -, **-n** plain; **~falls** *ad* likewise; **~so** *ad* just as; **~sogut** *ad* just as well; **~sooft** *ad* just as often; **~soweit** *ad* just as far; **~sowenig** *ad* just as little.
Eber ['e:bər] *m* **-s,** - boar; **~esche** *f* mountain ash, rowan.
ebnen ['e:bnən] *vt* level.
Echo ['ɛço] *nt* **-s, -s** echo.
echt [ɛçt] *a* genuine; (*typisch*) typical; **E~heit** *f* genuineness.
Eck- ['ɛk] *zW:* **~ball** *m* corner (kick); **~e** *f* -, **-n** corner; (*MATH*) angle; **e~ig** *a* angular; **~zahn** *m* eye tooth.
edel ['e:dəl] *a* noble; **E~metall** *nt* rare metal; **E~stein** *m* precious stone.
EDV [e:de:'fau] *abk* (= *elektronische Datenverarbeitung*) electronic data processing.
Efeu ['e:fɔy] *m* **-s** ivy.
Effekten [ɛ'fɛktən] *pl* stocks *pl*.
effektiv [ɛfɛk'ti:f] *a* effective, actual.
EG ['e:'ge:] *abk* (= *Europäische Gemeinschaft*) European Community.
egal [e'ga:l] *a* all the same.
Ego- [e:go] *zW:* **~ismus** [-'ɪsmʊs] *m* selfishness, egoism; **~ist** [-'ɪst] *m* egoist; **e~istisch** *a* selfish, egoistic.
Ehe ['e:ə] *f* -, **-n** marriage; **e~** *kj* before; **~bruch** *m* adultery; **~frau** *f* married woman; wife; **~leute** *pl* married people *pl*; **e~lich** *a* matrimonial; (*Kind*) legitimate; **e~malig** *a* former; **e~mals** *ad* formerly; **~mann** *m* married man; husband; **~paar** *nt* married couple.
eher ['e:ər] *ad* (*früher*) sooner; (*lieber*) rather, sooner; (*mehr*) more.
eheste(r, s) ['e:əstə(r, s)] *a* (*früheste*) first, earliest; **am ~n** (*liebsten*) soonest; (*meist*) most; (*wahrscheinlichst*) most probably.
Ehr- ['e:r] *zW:* **e~bar** *a* honourable, respectable; **~e** *f* -, **-n** honour; **e~en** *vt* honour.
Ehren- ['e:rən] *zW:* **~gast** *m* guest of honour; **e~haft** *a* honourable; **~runde** *f* lap of honour; **~sache** *f* point of honour; **e~voll** *a* honourable; **~wort** *nt* word of honour.
Ehr- *zW:* **~furcht** *f* awe, deep respect; **~gefühl** *nt* sense of honour; **~geiz** *m* ambition; **e~geizig** *a* ambitious;

e~lich *a* honest; **~lichkeit** *f* honesty; **e~los** *a* dishonourable; **~ung** *f* honour(ing); **e~würdig** *a* venerable.
Ei [ai] *nt* **-(e)s, -er** egg; **e~** *interj* well, well.
Eich- ['aiç] *zW:* **~amt** *nt* Office of Weights and Measures; **~e** *f* -, **-n** oak (tree); **~el** *f* -, **-n** acorn; **e~en** *vt* standardize; **~hörnchen** *nt* squirrel; **~maß** *nt* standard.
Eid ['ait] *m* **-(e)s, -e** oath; **~echse** ['aidɛksə] *f* -, **-n** lizard; **e~esstattlich** *a*: e~esstattliche Erklärung affidavit; **~genosse** *m* Swiss.
Eidotter ['aidɔtər] *nt* egg yolk.
Eier- *zW:* **~becher** *m* eggcup; **~kuchen** *m* omelette; pancake; **~likör** *m* advocaat; **~schale** *f* eggshell; **~stock** *m* ovary; **~uhr** *f* egg timer.
Eifer ['aifər] *m* **-s** zeal, enthusiasm; **~sucht** *f* jealousy; **e~süchtig** *a* jealous (*auf +akk* of).
eifrig ['aifriç] *a* zealous, enthusiastic.
Eigelb ['aigɛlp] *nt* **-(e)s,** - egg yolk.
eigen ['aigən] *a* own; (*~artig*) peculiar; mit der/dem ihm **~en** ... with that ... peculiar to him; sich (*dat*) etw zu ~ **machen** make sth one's own; **E~art** *f* peculiarity; characteristic; **~artig** *a* peculiar; **~händig** *a* with one's own hand; **E~heim** *nt* owner-occupied house; **E~heit** *f* peculiarity; **~mächtig** *a* high-handed; **E~name** *m* proper name; **~s** *ad* expressly, on purpose; **E~schaft** *f* quality, property, attribute; **E~schaftswort** *nt* adjective; **E~sinn** *m* obstinacy; **~sinnig** *a* obstinate; **eigentlich** *a* actual, real // *ad* actually, really; **E~tor** *nt* own goal; **E~tum** *nt* property; **E~tümer(in** *f*) *m* **-s,** - owner, proprietor; **~tümlich** *a* peculiar; **E~tümlichkeit** *f* peculiarity; **E~tumswohnung** *f* freehold flat.
eignen ['aignən] *vr* be suited.
Eignung *f* suitability.
Eil- ['ail] *zW:* **~bote** *m* courier; **~brief** *m* express letter; **~e** *f* - haste; es hat keine **~e** there's no hurry; **e~en** *vi* (*Mensch*) hurry; (*dringend sein*) be urgent; **e~ends** *ad* hastily; **~gut** *nt* express goods *pl*, fast freight (*US*); **e~ig** *a* hasty, hurried; (*dringlich*) urgent; es **e~ig haben** be in a hurry; **~zug** *m* semi-fast train, limited stop train.
Eimer ['aimər] *m* **-s,** - bucket, pail.
ein(e) [ain(ə)] *num* one // *indef art* a, an // *ad*: nicht ~ noch aus wissen not know what to do; **~e(r, s)** *pron* one; (*jemand*) someone.
einander [ai'nandər] *pron* one another, each other.
einarbeiten ['ainarbaitən] *vr* familiar-

ize o.s. (*in* +*akk* with).

einatmen ['aɪnaːtmən] *vti* inhale, breathe in.

Einbahnstraße ['aɪnbaːnʃtraːsə] *f* one-way street.

Einband ['aɪnbant] *m* binding, cover.

einbau- ['aɪnbaʊ] *zW:* ~**en** *vt* build in; (*Motor*) install, fit; **E~möbel** *pl* built-in furniture.

einberufen ['aɪnbəruːfən] *vt unreg* convene; (*MIL*) call up.

einbeziehen ['aɪnbətsiːən] *vt unreg* include.

einbiegen ['aɪnbiːgən] *vi unreg* turn.

einbilden ['aɪnbɪldən] *vt:* **sich** (*dat*) etw ~ imagine sth.

Einbildung *f* imagination; (*Dünkel*) conceit; **Einbildungskraft** *f* imagination.

Einblick ['aɪnblɪk] *m* insight.

einbrechen ['aɪnbrɛçən] *vi unreg* (*in Haus*) break in; (*in Land etc*) invade; (*Nacht*) fall; (*Winter*) set in; (*durchbrechen*) break.

Einbrecher *m* **-s,** - burglar.

einbringen ['aɪnbrɪŋən] *vt unreg* bring in; (*Geld, Vorteil*) yield; (*mitbringen*) contribute.

Einbruch ['aɪnbrʊx] *m* (*Haus~*) break-in, burglary; (*Eindringen*) invasion; (*des Winters*) onset; (*Durchbrechen*) break; (*MET*) approach; (*MIL*) penetration; ~ **der Nacht** nightfall; **einbruchssicher** *a* burglar-proof.

einbürgern ['aɪnbyrgərn] *vt* naturalize // *vr* become adopted.

Einbürgerung *f* naturalization.

Einbuße ['aɪnbuːsə] *f* loss, forfeiture.

einbüßen ['aɪnbyːsən] *vt* lose, forfeit.

einchecken ['aɪntʃɛkən] *vti* check in.

eindecken ['aɪndɛkən] *vr* lay in stocks (*mit of*).

eindeutig ['aɪndɔʏtɪç] *a* unequivocal.

eindring- ['aɪndrɪŋ] *zW:* ~**en** *vi unreg* (*in* +*akk*) force one's way in(to); (*in Haus*) break in(to); (*in Land*) invade; (*Gas, Wasser*) penetrate; (*mit Bitten*) pester (*auf jdn* sb); ~**lich** *a* forcible, urgent; **E~ling** *m* intruder.

Eindruck ['aɪndrʊk] *m* impression; **eindrucksvoll** *a* impressive.

eindrücken ['aɪndrʏkən] *vt* press in.

eineiig ['aɪn'aɪɪç] *a* (*Zwillinge*) identical.

eineinhalb ['aɪn'aɪn'halp] *num* one and a half.

einengen ['aɪn'ɛŋən] *vt* confine, restrict.

einer- ['aɪnər] *zW:* '**E~'lei** *nt* **-s** sameness; '~'**lei** *a* (*gleichartig*) the same kind of; **es ist mir ~lei** it is all the same to me; ~**seits** *ad* on the one hand.

einfach ['aɪnfax] *a* simple; (*nicht mehrfach*) single // *ad* simply; **E~heit** *f* simplicity.

einfahren ['aɪnfaːrən] *unreg vt* bring in; (*Barriere*) knock down; (*Auto*) run in // *vi* drive in; (*Zug*) pull in; (*MIN*) go down.

Einfahrt *f* (*Vorgang*) driving in; pulling in; (*MIN*) descent; (*Ort*) entrance.

Einfall ['aɪnfal] *m* (*Idee*) idea, notion; (*Licht~*) incidence; (*MIL*) raid; **e~en** *vi unreg* (*Licht*) fall; (*MIL*) raid; (*einstimmen*) join in (*in* +*akk* with); (*einstürzen*) fall in, collapse; **etw fällt jdm ein** sth occurs to sb; **das fällt mir gar nicht ein** I wouldn't dream of it; **sich** (*dat*) **etwas e~en lassen** have a good idea.

einfältig ['aɪnfɛltɪç] *a* simple(-minded).

Einfamilienhaus [aɪnfaˈmiːliənhaʊs] *nt* detached house.

einfarbig ['aɪnfarbɪç] *a* all one colour; (*Stoff etc*) self-coloured.

einfetten ['aɪnfɛtən] *vt* grease.

einfinden ['aɪnfɪndən] *vr unreg* come, turn up.

einfließen ['aɪnfliːsən] *vi unreg* flow in.

einflößen ['aɪnfløːsən] *vt:* **jdm etw ~** (*lit*) give sb sth; (*fig*) instil sth in sb.

Einfluß ['aɪnflʊs] *m* influence; ~**bereich** *m* sphere of influence; **e~reich** *a* influential.

einförmig ['aɪnfœrmɪç] *a* uniform; **E~keit** *f* uniformity.

einfrieren ['aɪnfriːrən] *unreg vi* freeze (*in*) // *vt* freeze.

einfügen ['aɪnfyːgən] *vt* fit in; (*zusätzlich*) add.

Einfuhr ['aɪnfuːr] *f* **-** import; ~**artikel** *m* imported article.

einführ- ['aɪnfyːr] *zW:* ~**en** *vt* bring in; (*Mensch, Sitten*) introduce; (*Ware*) import; **E~ung** *f* introduction.

Eingabe ['aɪngaːbə] *f* petition; (*COMPUT*) input.

Eingang ['aɪngaŋ] *m* entrance; (*COMM: Ankunft*) arrival; (*Sendung*) post; **e~s** *ad, präp* +*gen* at the outset (*of*).

eingeben ['aɪngeːbən] *vt unreg* (*Arznei*) give; (*Daten etc*) enter; (*Gedanken*) inspire.

eingebildet ['aɪngəbɪldət] *a* imaginary; (*eitel*) conceited.

Eingeborene(r) ['aɪngəboːrənə(r)] *mf* native.

Eingebung *f* inspiration.

eingedenk ['aɪngədɛŋk] *präp* +*gen* bearing in mind.

eingefroren ['aɪngəfroːrən] *a* frozen.

eingehen ['aɪngeːən] *unreg vi* (*Aufnahme finden*) come in; (*verständlich sein*) be comprehensible (*jdm* to sb); (*Sendung, Geld*) be received;

(*Tier, Pflanze*) die; (*Firma*) fold; (*schrumpfen*) shrink; **auf etw** ~ go into sth; **auf jdn** ~ respond to sb // *vt* enter into; (*Wette*) make; ~**d** *a* exhaustive, thorough.

Eingemachte(s) ['aɪŋəmaxtə(s)] *nt* preserves *pl.*

eingenommen ['aɪŋənɔmən] *a* (*von*) fond (of), partial (to); (*gegen*) prejudiced.

eingeschrieben ['aɪŋəʃriːbən] *a* registered.

eingespielt ['aɪŋəʃpiːlt] *a:* **aufeinander** ~ **sein** be in tune with each other.

Eingeständnis ['aɪŋəʃtɛntnɪs] *nt* **-ses**, **-se** admission, confession.

eingestehen ['aɪŋəʃteːən] *vt unreg* confess.

eingetragen ['aɪŋətraːgən] *a* (*COMM*) registered.

Eingeweide ['aɪŋəvaɪdə] *nt* **-s**, - innards *pl*, intestines *pl.*

Eingeweihte(r) ['aɪŋəvaɪtə(r)] *mf* initiate.

eingleisig ['aɪŋglaɪzɪç] *a* single-track.

eingreifen ['aɪŋgraɪfən] *vi unreg* intervene, interfere; (*Zahnrad*) mesh.

Eingriff ['aɪŋgrɪf] *m* intervention, interference; (*Operation*) operation.

einhaken ['aɪnhaːkən] *vt* hook in // *vr:* **sich bei jdm** ~ link arms with sb // *vi* (*sich einmischen*) intervene.

Einhalt ['aɪnhalt] *m:* ~ **gebieten** (+*dat*) put a stop to; **e~en** *unreg vt* (*Regel*) keep // *vi* stop.

einhändigen ['aɪnhɛndɪgən] *vt* hand in.

einhängen ['aɪnhɛŋən] *vt* hang; (*Telefon: auch vi*) hang up; **sich bei jdm** ~ link arms with sb.

einheimisch ['aɪnhaɪmɪʃ] *a* native.

Einheit ['aɪnhaɪt] *f* unity; (*Maß, MIL*) unit; **e~lich** *a* uniform; **Einheitspreis** *m* uniform price.

einholen ['aɪnhoːlən] *vt* (*Tau*) haul in; (*Fahne, Segel*) lower; (*Vorsprung aufholen*) catch up with; (*Verspätung*) make up; (*Rat, Erlaubnis*) ask // *vi* (*einkaufen*) buy, shop.

Einhorn ['aɪnhɔrn] *nt* unicorn.

einhüllen ['aɪnhylən] *vt* wrap up.

einig ['aɪnɪç] *a* (*vereint*) united; **sich** (*dat*) ~ **sein** be in agreement; ~ **werden** agree; ~**e** ['aɪnɪgə] *pl* some; (*mehrere*) several; ~**e(r, s)** *a* some; **einigemal** *ad* a few times; ~**en** *vt* unite // *vr* agree (*auf* +*akk* on); ~**ermaßen** *ad* somewhat; (*leidlich*) reasonably; ~**es** *pron* something; ~**gehen** *vi unreg* agree; **E~keit** *f* unity; (*Übereinstimmung*) agreement; **E~ung** *f* agreement; (*Vereinigung*) unification.

einkalkulieren ['aɪnkalkuliːrən] *vt* take

into account, allow for.

Einkauf ['aɪnkaʊf] *m* purchase; **e~en** *vt* buy // *vi* go shopping.

Einkaufs- *zW:* ~**bummel** *m* shopping spree; ~**korb** *m* shopping basket; ~**netz** *nt* string bag; ~**wagen** *m* shopping trolley; ~**preis** *m* cost price; ~**zentrum** *nt* shopping centre.

einklammern ['aɪnklamərn] *vt* put in brackets, bracket.

Einklang ['aɪnklaŋ] *m* harmony.

einklemmen ['aɪnklɛmən] *vt* jam.

einkochen ['aɪnkɔxən] *vt* boil down; (*Obst*) preserve, bottle.

Einkommen ['aɪnkɔmən] *nt* **-s**, - income; ~**(s)steuer** *f* income tax.

Einkünfte ['aɪnkynftə] *pl* income, revenue.

einlad- ['aɪnlaːd] *zW:* ~**en** *vt unreg* (*Person*) invite; (*Gegenstände*) load; **jdn ins Kino** ~**en** take sb to the cinema; **E~ung** *f* invitation.

Einlage ['aɪnlaːgə] *f* (*Programm~*) interlude; (*Spar~*) deposit; (*Schuh~*) insole; (*Fußstütze*) support; (*Zahn~*) temporary filling; (*KOCH*) noodles *pl*, vegetables *pl etc* in soup.

einlagern *vt* store.

einlassen ['aɪnlasən] *unreg vt* let in; (*einsetzen*) set in // *vr:* **sich mit jdm/ auf etw** (*akk*) ~ get involved with sb/sth.

Einlauf ['aɪnlaʊf] *m* arrival; (*von Pferden*) finish; (*MED*) enema; **e~en** *unreg vi* arrive, come in; (*in Hafen*) enter; (*SPORT*) finish; (*Wasser*) run in; (*Stoff*) shrink // *vt* (*Schuhe*) break in; **jdm das Haus e~en** invade sb's house // *vr* (*SPORT*) warm up; (*Motor, Maschine*) run in.

einleben ['aɪnleːbən] *vr* settle down.

einlegen ['aɪnleːgən] *vt* (*einfügen:* *Blatt, Sohle*) insert; (*KOCH*) pickle; (*Pause*) have; (*Protest*) make; (*Veto*) use; (*Berufung*) lodge.

einleiten ['aɪnlaɪtən] *vt* introduce, start; (*Geburt*) induce.

Einleitung *f* introduction; induction.

einleuchten ['aɪnlɔʏçtən] *vi* be clear *od* evident (*jdm* to sb); ~**d** *a* clear.

einliefern ['aɪnliːfərn] *vt* take (*in* +*akk* into).

einlösen ['aɪnløːzən] *vt* (*Scheck*) cash; (*Schuldschein, Pfand*) redeem; (*Versprechen*) keep.

einmachen ['aɪnmaxən] *vt* preserve.

einmal ['aɪnmaːl] *ad* once; (*erstens*) first; (*zukünftig*) sometime; **nehmen wir** ~ **an** just let's suppose; **noch** ~ once more; **nicht** ~ not even; **auf** ~ all at once; **es war** ~ once upon a time there was/were; **E~eins** *nt* multiplication tables *pl*; ~**ig** *a* unique; (*einmal geschehend*) single; (*prima*) fantastic.

Einmannbetrieb [aɪn'manbətriːp] *m* one-man business.

Einmarsch ['aɪnmarʃ] *m* entry; (*MIL*) invasion; **e~ieren** *vi* march in.

einmischen ['aɪnmɪʃən] *vr* interfere (*in + akk* with).

einmütig ['aɪnmyːtɪç] *a* unanimous.

Einnahme ['aɪnnaːmə] *f* -, **-n** (*Geld*) takings *pl*, revenue; (*von Medizin*) taking; (*MIL*) capture, taking; **~quelle** *f* source of income.

einnehmen ['aɪnneːmən] *vt unreg* take; (*Stellung, Raum*) take up; **~ für/gegen** persuade in favour of/ against; **~d** *a* charming.

Einöde ['aɪnʔøːdə] *f* desert, wilderness.

einordnen ['aɪnʔɔrdnən] *vt* arrange, fit in // *vr* adapt; (*AUT*) get into lane.

einpacken ['aɪnpakən] *vt* pack (up).

einparken ['aɪnparkən] *vt* park.

einpendeln ['aɪnpɛndəln] *vr* even out.

einpflanzen ['aɪnpflantsən] *vt* plant; (*MED*) implant.

einplanen ['aɪnplaːnən] *vt* plan for.

einprägen ['aɪnprɛːgən] *vt* impress, imprint; (*beibringen*) impress (*jdm on sb*); **sich** (*dat*) **etw ~** memorize sth.

einrahmen ['aɪnraːmən] *vt* frame.

einräumen ['aɪnrɔʏmən] *vt* (*ordnend*) put away; (*überlassen: Platz*) give up; (*zugestehen*) admit, concede.

einreden ['aɪnreːdən] *vt*: **jdm/sich etw ~** talk sb/o.s. into believing sth.

einreiben ['aɪnraɪbən] *vt unreg* rub in.

einreichen ['aɪnraɪçən] *vt* hand in; (*Antrag*) submit.

Einreise ['aɪnraɪzə] *f* entry; **~bestimmungen** *pl* entry regulations *pl*; **~erlaubnis** *f*, **~genehmigung** *f* entry permit; **e~n** *vi* enter (*in ein Land a country*).

einrichten ['aɪnrɪçtən] *vt* (*Haus*) furnish; (*schaffen*) establish, set up; (*arrangieren*) arrange; (*möglich machen*) manage // *vr* (*in Haus*) furnish one's house; (*sich vorbereiten*) prepare o.s. (*auf +akk* for); (*sich anpassen*) adapt (*auf +akk* to).

Einrichtung *f* (*Wohnungs~*) furnishings *pl*; (*öffentliche Anstalt*) organization; (*Dienste*) service.

einrosten ['aɪnrɔstən] *vi* get rusty.

Eins [aɪns] *f* -, **-en** one; **e~** *num* one; **es ist mir alles e~** it's all one to me.

einsam ['aɪnzaːm] *a* lonely, solitary; **E~keit** *f* loneliness, solitude.

einsammeln ['aɪnzaməln] *vt* collect.

Einsatz ['aɪnzats] *m* (*Teil*) inset; (*an Kleid*) insertion; (*Verwendung*) use, employment; (*Spiel~*) stake; (*Risiko*) risk; (*MIL*) operation; (*MUS*) entry; **im ~** in action; **e~bereit** *a* ready for action.

einschalten ['aɪnʃaltən] *vt* (*einfügen*) insert; (*Pause*) make; (*ELEK*) switch on; (*AUT: Gang*) engage; (*Anwalt*) bring in // *vr* (*dazwischentreten*) intervene.

einschätzen ['aɪnʃɛtsən] *vt* estimate, assess // *vr* rate o.s.

einschenken ['aɪnʃɛŋkən] *vt* pour out.

einschicken ['aɪnʃɪkən] *vt* send in.

einschl. *abk* (= *einschließlich*) incl.

einschlafen ['aɪnʃlaːfən] *vi unreg* fall asleep, go to sleep.

einschläfernd ['aɪnʃlɛːfərnt] *a* (*MED*) soporific; (*langweilig*) boring; (*Stimme*) lulling.

Einschlag ['aɪnʃlaːk] *m* impact; (*fig: Beimischung*) touch, hint; **e~en** *unreg vt* knock in; (*Fenster*) smash, break; (*Zähne, Schädel*) smash in; (*Steuer*) turn; (*kürzer machen*) take up; (*Ware*) pack, wrap up; (*Weg, Richtung*) take // *vi* hit (*in etw (akk)* sth, *auf jdn* sb); (*sich einigen*) agree; (*Anklang finden*) work, succeed.

einschlägig ['aɪnʃlɛːgɪç] *a* relevant.

einschließen ['aɪnʃliːsən] *unreg vt* (*Kind*) lock in; (*Häftling*) lock up; (*Gegenstand*) lock away; (*Bergleute*) cut off; (*umgeben*) surround; (*MIL*) encircle; (*fig*) include, comprise // *vr* lock o.s. in.

einschließlich *ad* inclusive // *präp +gen* inclusive of, including.

einschmeicheln ['aɪnʃmaɪçəln] *vr* ingratiate o.s. (*bei* with).

einschnappen ['aɪnʃnapən] *vi* (*Tür*) click to; (*fig*) be touchy; **eingeschnappt sein** be in a huff.

einschneidend ['aɪnʃnaɪdənt] *a* incisive.

Einschnitt ['aɪnʃnɪt] *m* cutting; (*MED*) incision; (*Ereignis*) incident.

einschränken ['aɪnʃrɛŋkən] *vt* limit, restrict; (*Kosten*) cut down, reduce // *vr* cut down (on expenditure); **~d** *a* restrictive.

Einschränkung *f* restriction, limitation; reduction; (*von Behauptung*) qualification.

Einschreib- ['aɪnʃraɪb] *zW:* **~(e)brief** *m* recorded delivery letter; **e~en** *unreg vt* write in; (*Post*) send recorded delivery // *vr* register; (*UNIV*) enrol; **~en** *nt* recorded delivery letter.

einschreiten ['aɪnʃraɪtən] *vi unreg* step in, intervene; **~ gegen** take action against.

einschüchtern ['aɪnʃʏçtərn] *vt* intimidate.

einschweißen ['aɪnʃvaɪsən] *vt* shrinkwrap.

einsehen ['aɪnzeːən] *vt unreg* (*hineinsehen in*) realize; (*Akten*) have a look at; (*verstehen*) see; **E~** *nt* -s understanding; **ein E~ haben** show understanding.

einseitig ['aɪnzaɪtɪç] a one-sided.

Einsend- ['aɪnzɛnd] zW: **e~en** vt unreg send in; **~er m -s, -** sender, contributor; **~ung** f sending in.

einsetzen ['aɪnzɛtsən] vt put (in); (in Amt) appoint, install; (Geld) stake; (verwenden) use; (MIL) employ // vi (beginnen) set in; (MUS) enter, come in // vr work hard; **sich für jdn/etw ~** support sb/sth.

Einsicht ['aɪnzɪçt] f insight; (in Akten) look, inspection; **zu der ~ kommen, daß ...** come to the conclusion that ...; **e~ig** a (Mensch) judicious; **~nahme** f -, **-n** examination; **einsichtslos** a unreasonable; **einsichtsvoll** a understanding.

Einsiedler ['aɪnziːdlər] m hermit.

einsilbig ['aɪnzɪlbɪç] a (lit, fig) monosyllabic.

einsperren ['aɪnʃpɛrən] vt lock up.

einspielen ['aɪnʃpiːlən] vr (SPORT) warm up; **sich aufeinander ~** become attuned to each other // vt (Film: Geld) bring in; (Instrument) play in; **gut eingespielt** smoothly running.

einspringen ['aɪnʃprɪŋən] vi unreg (aushelfen) help out, step into the breach.

Einspritzmotor ['aɪnʃprɪtsmoːtɔr] m fuel injection engine.

Einspruch ['aɪnʃprʊx] m protest, objection; **Einspruchsrecht** nt veto.

einspurig ['aɪnʃpuːrɪç] a single-lane.

einst [aɪnst] ad once; (zukünftig) one od some day.

Einstand ['aɪnʃtant] m (TENNIS) deuce; (Antritt) entrance (to office).

einstecken ['aɪnʃtɛkən] vt stick in, insert; (Brief) post; (ELEK: Stecker) plug in; (Geld) pocket; (mitnehmen) take; (überlegen sein) put in the shade; (hinnehmen) swallow.

einstehen ['aɪnʃteːən] vi unreg guarantee (für jdn/etw sb/sth); (verantworten) answer (für for).

einsteigen ['aɪnʃtaɪgən] vi unreg get in od on; (in Schiff) go on board; (sich beteiligen) come in; (hineinklettern) climb in.

einstell- ['aɪnʃtɛl] zW: **~en** vti (aufhören) stop; (Geräte) adjust; (Kamera etc) focus; (Sender, Radio) tune in; (unterstellen) put; (in Firma) employ, take on // vr (anfangen) set in; (kommen) arrive; **sich auf jdn/etw ~en** adapt to sb/prepare o.s. for sth; **E~ung** f (Aufhören) suspension, cessation; (Justierung) adjustment; focusing; (von Arbeiter etc) appointment; (Haltung) attitude.

Einstieg ['aɪnʃtiːk] m -(e)s, -e entry; (fig) approach.

einstig ['aɪnstɪç] a former.

einstimmig ['aɪnʃtɪmɪç] a unanimous; (MUS) for one voice.

einst- ['aɪnst] zW: **~malig** a former; **~mals** ad once, formerly.

einstöckig ['aɪnʃtœkɪç] a single-storeyed.

Einsturz ['aɪnʃtʊrts] m collapse; **~gefahr** f danger of collapse.

einstürzen ['aɪnʃtʏrtsən] vi fall in, collapse.

einst- ['aɪnst] zW: **~weilen** ad meanwhile; (vorläufig) temporarily, for the time being; **~weilig** a temporary.

eintägig ['aɪntɛːgɪç] a one-day.

eintasten ['aɪntastən] vt key (in).

eintauschen ['aɪntaʊʃən] vt exchange.

eintausend ['aɪntaʊzənt] num one thousand.

einteil- ['aɪntaɪl] zW: **~en** vt (in Teile) divide (up); (Menschen) assign; **~ig** a one-piece.

eintönig ['aɪntøːnɪç] a monotonous; **E~keit** f monotony.

Eintopf(gericht nt) ['aɪntɔpf(gərɪçt)] m stew.

Eintracht ['aɪntraxt] f - concord, harmony.

einträchtig ['aɪntrɛçtɪç] a harmonious.

Eintrag ['aɪntraːk] m -(e)s, ̈-e entry; **amtlicher ~** entry in the register; **e~en** unreg vt (in Buch) enter; (Profit) yield; **jdm etw e~en** bring sb sth // vr put one's name down.

einträglich ['aɪntrɛːklɪç] a profitable.

eintreffen ['aɪntrɛfən] vi unreg happen; (ankommen) arrive.

eintreten ['aɪntreːtən] unreg vi occur; (hineingehen) enter (in etw (akk) sth); (sich einsetzen) intercede; (in Club, Partei) join (in etw (akk) sth); (in Stadium etc) enter // vt (Tür) kick open.

Eintritt ['aɪntrɪt] m (Betreten) entrance; (Anfang) commencement; (in Club etc) joining.

Eintritts- zW: **~geld** nt, **~preis** m charge for admission; **~karte** f (admission) ticket.

einüben ['aɪnʔyːbən] vt practise, drill.

Einvernehmen ['aɪnfɛrneːmən] nt -s, - agreement, understanding.

einverstanden ['aɪnfɛrʃtandən] interj agreed // a: **~ sein** agree, be agreed.

Einverständnis ['aɪnfɛrʃtɛntnɪs] nt understanding; (gleiche Meinung) agreement.

Einwand ['aɪnvant] m -(e)s, ̈-e objection.

Einwanderer ['aɪnvandərər] m immigrant.

einwandern vi immigrate.

Einwanderung f immigration.

einwandfrei a perfect // ad absolutely.

Einwegflasche ['aɪnveːgflaʃə] f no-deposit bottle.

einweichen ['aɪnvaɪçən] vt soak.

einweih- ['aɪnvaɪ] zW: **~en** vt (Kirche) consecrate; (Brücke) open; (Gebäude) inaugurate; (Person) initiate (in +akk in); **E~ung** f consecration; opening; inauguration; initiation.

einweisen ['aɪnvaɪzən] vt unreg (in Amt) install; (in Arbeit) introduce; (in Anstalt) send.

einwenden ['aɪnvɛndən] vt unreg object, oppose (gegen to).

einwerfen ['aɪnvɛrfən] vt unreg throw in; (Brief) post; (Geld) put in, insert; (Fenster) smash; (äußern) interpose.

einwickeln ['aɪnvɪkəln] vt wrap up; (fig umg) outsmart.

einwillig- ['aɪnvɪlɪg] zW: **~en** vi consent, agree (in +akk to); **E~ung** f consent.

einwirken ['aɪnvɪrkən] vi: **auf jdn/etw ~en** influence sb/sth.

Einwohner ['aɪnvoːnər] m -s, - inhabitant; **~'meldeamt** nt registration office; **~schaft** f population, inhabitants pl.

Einwurf ['aɪnvʊrf] m (Öffnung) slot; (Einwand) objection; (SPORT) throw-in.

Einzahl ['aɪntsaːl] f singular; **e~en** vt pay in; **~ung** f paying in.

einzäunen ['aɪntsɔynən] vt fence in.

Einzel ['aɪntsəl] nt -s, - (TENNIS) singles // in zW· individual; single; **~fall** m single instance, individual case; **~handel** m retail trade; **~handelspreis** m retail price; **~haft** f solitary confinement; **~heit** f particular, detail; **~karte** f single ticket; **e~n** a single; (vereinzelt) the odd // ad singly; **e~n angeben** specify; **der/die e~ne** the individual; **das e~ne** the particular; **ins e~ne gehen** go into detail(s); **~teil** nt component (part); **~zimmer** nt single room.

einziehen ['aɪntsiːən] unreg vt draw in, take in; (Kopf) duck; (Fühler, Antenne, Fahrgestell) retract; (Steuern, Erkundigungen) collect; (MIL) draft, call up; (aus dem Verkehr ziehen) withdraw; (konfiszieren) confiscate // vi move in(to); (Friede, Ruhe) come; (Flüssigkeit) penetrate.

einzig ['aɪntsɪç] a only; (ohnegleichen) unique; **das ~e** the only thing; **der/die ~e** the only one; **~artig** a unique.

Einzug ['aɪntsuːk] m entry, moving in.

Eis [aɪs] nt -es, - ice; (Speise~) ice cream; **~bahn** f ice od skating rink; **~bär** m polar bear; **~becher** m sundae; **~bein** nt pig's trotters pl;

~berg m iceberg; **~decke** f sheet of ice; **~diele** f ice-cream parlour.

Eisen ['aɪzən] nt -s, - iron; **~bahn** f railway, railroad (US); **~bahner** m -s, - railwayman, railway employee, railroader (US); **~bahnschaffner** m railway guard; **~bahnübergang** m level crossing, grade crossing (US); **~bahnwagen** m railway carriage; **~erz** nt iron ore; **e~haltig** a containing iron.

eisern ['aɪzərn] a iron; (Gesundheit) robust; (Energie) unrelenting; (Reserve) emergency.

Eis- zW: **e~frei** a clear of ice; **~hockey** nt ice hockey; **e~ig** ['aɪzɪç] a icy; **e~kalt** a icy cold; **~kunstlauf** m figure skating; **~laufen** nt ice skating; **~läufer(in** f) m ice-skater; **~pickel** m ice-axe; **~schießen** nt ≈ curling; **~schrank** m fridge, ice-box (US); **~zapfen** m icicle; **~zeit** f ice age.

eitel ['aɪtəl] a vain; **E~keit** f vanity.

Eiter ['aɪtər] m -s pus; **e~ig** a suppurating; **e~n** vi suppurate.

Ei- [aɪ] zW: **~weiß** nt -es, -e white of an egg; **~zelle** f ovum.

Ekel ['eːkəl] m -s nausea, disgust // nt -s, - (umg: Mensch) nauseating person; **e~erregend, e~haft, ek(e)lig** a nauseating, disgusting; **e~n** vt disgust; **es ekelt jdn** od **jdm** sb is disgusted // vr loathe, be disgusted (vor +dat at).

Ekstase [ɛk'staːzə] f -, -n ecstasy.

Ekzem [ɛk'tseːm] nt -s, -e (MED) eczema.

Elan [e'laːn] m -s elan.

elastisch [e'lastɪʃ] a elastic.

Elastizität [elastitsi'tɛːt] f elasticity.

Elch [ɛlç] m -(e)s, -e elk.

Elefant [ele'fant] m elephant.

elegant [ele'gant] a elegant.

Eleganz [ele'gants] f elegance.

Elek- [e'lɛk] zW: **~triker** [-trikər] m -s, - electrician; **e~trisch** [-trɪʃ] a electric; **e~trisieren** [-tri'ziːrən] vt (lit, fig) electrify; (Mensch) give an electric shock to // vr get an electric shock; **~trizität** [-tritsi'tɛːt] f electricity; **~trizitätswerk** nt electricity works, power plant.

Elektro- [e'lɛktro] zW: **~de** [elɛk'troːdə] f -, -n electrode; **~herd** m electric cooker; **~n** [-ɔn] nt -s, -en electron; **~nen(ge)hirn** [elɛk'troːnən-] nt electronic brain; **~nenrechner** m computer; **e~nisch** a electronic; **e~nische Post** electronic mail; **e~nischer Briefkasten** electronic mailbox; **~rasierer** m electric razor.

Element [ele'mɛnt] nt -s, -e element; (ELEK) cell, battery; **e~ar** [-'taːr] a elementary; (naturhaft) elemental.

Elend ['e:lɛnt] nt -(e)s misery; **e~** a miserable; **Elendsviertel** nt slum.

elf [ɛlf] num eleven; **E~** f -, -en (SPORT) eleven; **E~e** f -, -n elf; **E~enbein** nt ivory; **E~meter** m (SPORT) penalty (kick).

Elite [e'li:tə] f -, -n elite.

Elixier [eli'ksi:r] nt -s, -e elixir.

Ell- zW: **~e** ['ɛlə] f -, -n ell; (Maß) yard; **~(en)bogen** m elbow; **Ellipse** [ɛ'lɪpsə] f -, -n ellipse.

Elsaß ['ɛlzas] nt: das ~ Alsace.

Elster ['ɛlstər] f -, -n magpie.

elterlich ['ɛltərlɪç] a parental.

Eltern ['ɛltərn] pl parents pl; **~haus** nt home; **e~los** a parentless.

Email [e'ma:j] nt -s, -s enamel; **e~lieren** [ema'ji:rən] vt enamel.

Emanzipation [emantsipatsi'o:n] f emancipation.

emanzi'pieren vt emancipate.

Embryo ['ɛmbryo] m -s, -s od -nen embryo.

Emi- [emi] zW: **~gration** [-gratsi'o:n] f emigration; **e~grieren** [-'gri:rən] vi emigrate.

empfahl etc v siehe **empfehlen.**

Empfang [ɛm'pfaŋ] m -(e)s, ⁻e reception; (Erhalten) receipt; in ~ nehmen receive; **e~en** unreg vt receive // vi (schwanger werden) conceive.

Empfäng- [ɛm'pfɛŋ] zW: **~er** m -s, - receiver; (COMM) addressee, consignee; **e~lich** a receptive, susceptible; **~nis** f -, -se conception; **~nisverhütung** f contraception.

Empfangs- zW: **~bestätigung** f acknowledgement; **~dame** f receptionist; **~schein** m receipt; **~zimmer** nt reception room.

empfehlen [ɛm'pfe:lən] unreg vt recommend // vr take one's leave; **~swert** a recommendable.

Empfehlung f recommendation.

empfiehlst etc v siehe **empfehlen.**

empfind- [ɛm'pfɪnt] zW: **~en** [ɛm'pfɪndən] vt unreg feel; **~lich** a sensitive; (Stelle) sore; (reizbar) touchy; **~sam** a sentimental; **E~ung** f feeling, sentiment.

empfohlen v siehe **empfehlen.**

empor [ɛm'po:r] ad up, upwards.

empören [ɛm'pø:rən] vt make indignant; shock // vr become indignant; **~d** a outrageous.

Emporkömmling [ɛm'po:rkœmlɪŋ] m upstart, parvenu.

Empörung f indignation.

emsig ['ɛmzɪç] a diligent, busy.

End- ['ɛnd] in zW final; **~e** nt -s, -n end; am **~e** at the end; (schließlich) in the end; am **~e** sein be at the end of one's tether; **~e Dezember** at the end of December; **zu ~e sein** be finished; **e~en** vi end; **e~gültig** a final, definite; **Endivie** [ɛn'di:viə] f endive; **e~lich** a final; (MATH) finite // ad finally; **e~lich!** at last!; komm e~lich! come on!; **e~los** a endless, infinite; **~lospapier** nt continuous stationery; **~spiel** nt final(s); **~spurt** m (SPORT) final spurt; **~station** f terminus; **~ung** f ending.

Energie [enɛr'gi:] f energy; **~einsparung** f energy saving; **e~los** a lacking in energy, weak; **~wirtschaft** f energy industry.

energisch [e'nɛrgɪʃ] a energetic.

eng [ɛŋ] a narrow; (Kleidung) tight; (fig: Horizont auch) limited; (Freundschaft, Verhältnis) close; ~ an etw (dat) close to.

Engagement [ãgaʒə'mã:] nt -s, -s engagement; (Verpflichtung) commitment.

engagieren [ãga'ʒi:rən] vt engage; ein engagierter Schriftsteller a committed writer // vr commit o.s.

Enge ['ɛŋə] f -, -n (lit,fig) narrowness; (Land~) defile; (Meer~) straits pl; jdn in die ~ treiben drive sb into a corner.

Engel ['ɛŋəl] m -s, - angel; **e~haft** a angelic; **~macher(in f)** m -s, - (umg) backstreet abortionist.

eng- zW: **~herzig** a petty; **E~land** nt England; **E~länder** m Englishman; **E~länderin** f Englishwoman; **~lisch** a English; **E~paß** m defile, pass; (fig, Verkehr) bottleneck.

en gros [ã'gro:] ad wholesale.

engstirnig ['ɛŋʃtɪrnɪç] a narrow-minded.

Enkel ['ɛŋkəl] m -s, - grandson; **~in** f granddaughter.

enorm [e'nɔrm] a enormous.

Ensemble [ã'sãbəl] nt -s, -s company, ensemble.

entbehr- [ɛnt'be:r] zW: **~en** vt do without, dispense with; **~lich** a superfluous.

entbinden [ɛnt'bɪndən] unreg vt release (gen from); (MED) deliver // vi (MED) give birth.

Entbindung f release; (MED) confinement; **Entbindungsheim** nt maternity hospital.

entdeck- [ɛnt'dɛk] zW: **~en** vt discover. **E~er** m -s, - discoverer; **E~ung** f discovery.

Ente ['ɛntə] f -, -n duck; (fig) canard, false report.

enteignen [ɛnt'aignən] vt expropriate; (Besitzer) dispossess.

enteisen [ɛnt'aizən] vt de-ice, defrost.

enterben [ɛnt'ɛrbən] vt disinherit.

entfallen [ɛnt'falən] vi unreg drop, fall; (wegfallen) be dropped; jdm ~ (vergessen) slip sb's memory; **auf**

jdn ~ be allotted to sb.

entfalten [ɛntˈfaltən] vt unfold; (*Talente*) develop // vr open; (*Mensch*) develop one's potential.

Entfaltung f unfolding; (*von Talenten*) development.

entfern- [ɛntˈfɛrn] zW: **~en** vt remove; (*hinauswerfen*) expel // vr go away, withdraw; **~t** a distant; **weit davon ~t sein, etw zu tun be** far from doing sth; **E~ung** f distance; (*Wegschaffen*) removal; **E~ungsmesser** m **-s,** - (*PHOT*) rangefinder.

entfremd- [ɛntˈfrɛmd] zW: **~en** vt estrange, alienate; **E~ung** f alienation, estrangement.

entfrost- [ɛntˈfrɔst] zW: **~en** vt defrost; **E~er** m **-s,** - (*AUT*) defroster.

entführ- [ɛntˈfyːr] zW: **~en** vt carry off, abduct; kidnap; **E~er** m kidnapper; **E~ung** f abduction; kidnapping.

entgegen [ɛntˈgeːgən] präp +dat contrary to, against // ad towards; **~bringen** vt unreg bring; (*fig*) show (*jdm etw* sth); **~gehen** vi unreg (+dat) go to meet, go towards; **~gesetzt** a opposite; (*widersprechend*) opposed; **~halten** vt unreg (*fig*) object; **~kommen** vi unreg approach; meet (*jdm* sb); (*fig*) accommodate (*jdm* sb); **E~kommen** nt obligingness; **~kommend** a obliging; **~nehmen** vt unreg receive, accept; **~sehen** vi unreg (+dat) await; **~setzen** vt oppose (*dat* to); **~treten** vi unreg (+dat: *lit*) step up to; (*fig*) oppose, counter; **~wirken** vi (+dat) counteract.

entgegnen [ɛntˈgeːgnən] vt reply, retort.

entgehen [ɛntˈgeːən] vi unreg (*fig*) jdm ~ escape sb's notice; **sich** (*dat*) etw ~ lassen miss sth.

entgeistert [ɛntˈgaɪstərt] a thunderstruck.

Entgelt [ɛntˈgɛlt] nt **-(e)s, -e** compensation, remuneration.

entgleisen [ɛntˈglaɪzən] vi (*EISENB*) be derailed; (*fig: Person*) misbehave; ~ lassen derail.

entgräten [ɛntˈgrɛːtən] vt fillet, bone.

Enthaarungsmittel [ɛntˈhaːrʊŋsmɪtəl] nt depilatory.

enthalten [ɛntˈhaltən] unreg vt contain // vr abstain, refrain (*gen* from).

enthaltsam [ɛntˈhaltzaːm] a abstinent, abstemious; **E~keit** f abstinence.

enthemmen [ɛntˈhɛmən] vt: jdn ~ free sb from his inhibitions.

enthüllen [ɛntˈhylən] vt reveal, unveil.

Enthusiasmus [ɛntuziˈasmʊs] m enthusiasm.

entkommen [ɛntˈkɔmən] vi unreg get away, escape (*dat, aus* from).

entkräften [ɛntˈkrɛftən] vt weaken, exhaust; (*Argument*) refute.

entladen [ɛntˈlaːdən] unreg vt unload; (*ELEK*) discharge // vr (*ELEK, Gewehr*) discharge; (*Ärger etc*) vent itself.

entlang [ɛntˈlaŋ] präp +akk od dat, ad along; ~ **dem Fluß, den Fluß** ~ along the river; **~gehen** vi unreg walk along.

entlarven [ɛntˈlarfən] vt unmask, expose.

entlassen [ɛntˈlasən] vt unreg discharge; (*Arbeiter*) dismiss.

Entlassung f discharge; dismissal; **Entlassungsabfindung** f redundancy payment.

entlasten [ɛntˈlastən] vt relieve; (*Achse*) relieve the load on; (*Angeklagten*) exonerate; (*Konto*) clear.

Entlastung f relief; (*COMM*) crediting.

entlegen [ɛntˈleːgən] a remote.

entlocken [ɛntˈlɔkən] vt elicit (*jdm etw* sth from sb).

entmachten [ɛntˈmaxtən] vt deprive of power.

entmilitarisiert [ɛntmilitariˈziːrt] a demilitarized.

entmündigen [ɛntˈmyndigən] vt certify.

entmutigen [ɛntˈmuːtɪgən] vt discourage.

entnehmen [ɛntˈneːmən] vt unreg (+dat) take out (of), take (from); (*folgern*) infer (from).

entrahmen [ɛntˈraːmən] vt skim.

entreißen [ɛntˈraɪsən] vt unreg snatch (away) (*jdm etw* sth from sb).

entrichten [ɛntˈrɪçtən] vt pay.

entrosten [ɛntˈrɔstən] vt derust.

entrüst- [ɛntˈryst] zW: **~en** vt incense, outrage // vr be filled with indignation; **~et** a indignant, outraged; **E~ung** f indignation.

entschädigen [ɛntˈʃɛːdɪgən] vt compensate.

Entschädigung f compensation.

entschärfen [ɛntˈʃɛrfən] vt defuse; (*Kritik*) tone down.

Entscheid [ɛntˈʃaɪt] m **-(e)s, -e** decision; **e~en** vtir unreg decide; **e~end** a decisive; (*Stimme*) casting; **~ung** f decision.

entschieden [ɛntˈʃiːdən] a decided; (*entschlossen*) resolute; **E~heit** f firmness, determination.

entschließen [ɛntˈʃliːsən] vr unreg decide.

entschlossen [ɛntˈʃlɔsən] a determined, resolute; **E~heit** f determination.

Entschluß [ɛntˈʃlus] m decision; **e~freudig** a decisive; **~kraft** f determination, decisiveness.

entschuld- [ɛnt'ʃʊld] zW: **~igen** vt excuse // vr apologize; **E~igung** f apology; (Grund) excuse; **jdn um E~igung bitten** apologize to sb; **E~igung!** excuse me; (Verzeihung) sorry.

entsetz- [ɛnt'zɛts] zW: **~en** vt horrify; (MIL) relieve // vr be horrified od appalled; **E~en** nt -s horror, dismay; **~lich** a dreadful, appalling; **~t** a horrified.

entsinnen [ɛnt'zɪnən] vr unreg remember (gen sth).

entspannen [ɛnt'ʃpanən] vtr (Körper) relax; (POL: Lage) ease.

Entspannung f relaxation, rest, (POL) détente; **Entspannungspolitik** f policy of détente.

entsprechen [ɛnt'ʃprɛçən] vi unreg (+dat) correspond to; (Anforderungen, Wünschen) meet, comply with; **~d** a appropriate // ad accordingly.

entspringen [ɛnt'ʃprɪŋən] vi unreg spring (from).

entstehen [ɛnt'ʃteːən] vi unreg arise, result.

Entstehung f genesis, origin.

entstellen [ɛnt'ʃtɛlən] vt disfigure; (Wahrheit) distort.

entstören [ɛnt'ʃtøːrən] vt (RAD) eliminate interference from; (AUT) suppress.

enttäuschen [ɛnt'tɔyʃən] vt disappoint.

Enttäuschung f disappointment.

Entwarnung [ɛnt'varnʊŋ] f all clear (signal).

entwässern [ɛnt'vɛsərn] vt drain.

entweder ['ɛntveːdər] kj either.

entwenden [ɛnt'vɛndən] vt unreg purloin, steal.

entwerfen [ɛnt'vɛrfən] vt unreg (Zeichnung) sketch; (Modell) design; (Vortrag, Gesetz etc) draft.

entwerten [ɛnt'veːrtən] vt devalue; (stempeln) cancel.

Entwerter m -s, - ticket punching machine.

entwickeln [ɛnt'vɪkəln] vtr develop (auch PHOT); (Mut, Energie) show, display.

Entwickler m -s, - developer.

Entwicklung [ɛnt'vɪklʊŋ] f development; (PHOT) developing.

Entwicklungs- zW: **~hilfe** f aid for developing countries; **~jahre** pl adolescence sing; **~land** nt developing country.

entwöhnen [ɛnt'vøːnən] vt wean; (Süchtige) cure (dat, von of).

Entwöhnung f weaning; cure, curing.

entwürdigend [ɛnt'vʏrdɪgənt] a degrading.

Entwurf [ɛnt'vʊrf] m outline, design; (Vertrags~, Konzept) draft.

entziehen [ɛnt'tsiːən] unreg vt withdraw, take away (dat from); (Flüssigkeit) draw, extract // vr escape (dat from); (jds Kenntnis) be outside; (der Pflicht) shirk.

Entziehung f withdrawal.

Entziehungs- zW: **~anstalt** f drug addiction/alcoholism treatment centre; **~kur** f treatment for drug addiction/alcoholism.

entziffern [ɛnt'tsɪfərn] vt decipher; decode.

entzücken [ɛnt'tsʏkən] vt delight; **E~** nt -s delight; **~d** a delightful, charming.

entzünden [ɛnt'tsʏndən] vt light, set light to; (fig, MED) inflame; (Streit) spark off // vr (lit, fig) catch fire; (Streit) start; (MED) become inflamed.

Entzündung f (MED) inflammation.

entzwei [ɛnt'tsvaɪ] ad broken; in two; **~brechen** vti unreg break in two; **~en** vt set at odds // vr fall out; **~gehen** vi unreg break in two.

Enzian ['ɛntsiaːn] m -s, -e gentian.

Enzym [ɛn'tsyːm] nt -s, -e enzyme.

Epidemie [epide'miː] f epidemic.

Epilepsie [epile'psiː] f epilepsy.

Episode [epi'zoːdə] f -, -n episode.

Epoche [e'pɔxə] f -, -n epoch; **e~machend** a epoch-making.

Epos ['eːpɔs] nt -s, **Epen** epic (poem).

er [eːr] pron he; it.

erachten [ɛr''axtən] vt: **~ für** od **als** consider (to be); **meines E~s** in my opinion.

erarbeiten [ɛr''arbaɪtən] vt (auch sich (dat) **~**) work for, acquire; (Theorie) work out.

erbarmen [ɛr'barmən] vr have pity od mercy (über on); **E~** nt -s pity.

erbärmlich [ɛr'bɛrmlɪç] a wretched, pitiful; **E~keit** f wretchedness.

erbarmungslos [ɛr'barmʊŋsloːs] a pitiless, merciless.

erbau- [ɛr'bau] zW: **~en** vt build, erect; (fig) edify; **E~er** m -s, - builder; **~lich** a edifying; **E~ung** f construction; (fig) edification.

Erbe ['ɛrbə] m -n, -n heir // nt -s inheritance; (fig) heritage; **e~n** vt inherit.

erbeuten [ɛr'bɔytən] vt carry off; (MIL) capture.

Erb- [ɛrb] zW: **~faktor** m gene; **~folge** f (line of) succession; **~in** f heiress.

erbittern [ɛr'bɪtərn] vt embitter; (erzürnen) incense.

erbittert [ɛr'bɪtərt] a (Kampf) fierce, bitter.

erblassen [ɛr'blasən] vi, **erbleichen** [ɛr'blaɪçən] vi unreg (turn) pale.

conquest.

eröffnen [ɛr'œfnən] *vt* open; jdm etw ~ disclose sth to sb // *vr* present itself.

Eröffnung *f* opening.

erörtern [ɛr'œrtərn] *vt* discuss.

Erörterung *f* discussion.

Erotik [e'ro:tɪk] *f* eroticism.

erotisch *a* erotic.

erpress- [ɛr'prɛs] *zW*: ~en *vt* (*Geld etc*) extort; (*Mensch*) blackmail; **E~er** *m* **-s, -** blackmailer; **E~ung** *f* blackmail; extortion.

erraten [ɛr'ra:tən] *vt unreg* guess.

erreg- [ɛr're:g] *zW*: ~en *vt* excite; (*ärgern*) infuriate; (*hervorrufen*) arouse, provoke // *vr* get excited *od* worked up; **E~er** *m* **-s, -** causative agent; **E~ung** *f* excitement.

erreichbar *a* accessible, within reach.

erreichen [ɛr'raɪçən] *vt* reach; (*Zweck*) achieve; (*Zug*) catch.

errichten [ɛr'rɪçtən] *vt* erect, put up; (*gründen*) establish, set up.

erringen [ɛr'rɪŋən] *vt unreg* gain, win.

erröten [ɛr'rø:tən] *vi* blush, flush.

Errungenschaft [ɛr'rʊŋənʃaft] *f* achievement; (*umg: Anschaffung*) acquisition.

Ersatz [ɛr'zats] *m* **-es** substitute; replacement; (*Schaden~*) compensation; (*MIL*) reinforcements *pl*; ~**dienst** *m* (*MIL*) alternative service; ~**reifen** *m* (*AUT*) spare tyre; ~**teil** *nt* spare (part).

erschaffen [ɛr'ʃafən] *vt unreg* create.

erscheinen [ɛr'ʃaɪnən] *vi unreg* appear.

Erscheinung *f* appearance; (*Geist*) apparition; (*Gegebenheit*) phenomenon; (*Gestalt*) figure.

erschießen [ɛr'ʃi:sən] *vt unreg* shoot (dead).

erschlagen [ɛr'ʃla:gən] *vt unreg* strike dead.

erschöpf- [ɛr'ʃœpf] *zW*: ~en *vt* exhaust; ~end *a* exhaustive, thorough; ~t *a* exhausted; **E~ung** *f* exhaustion.

erschrecken [ɛr'ʃrɛkən] *vt* startle, frighten // *vi unreg* be frightened *od* startled; ~d *a* alarming, frightening.

erschrocken [ɛr'ʃrɔkən] *a* frightened, startled.

erschüttern [ɛr'ʃʏtərn] *vt* shake; (*ergreifen*) move deeply.

Erschütterung *f* shaking; shock.

erschweren [ɛr'ʃve:rən] *vt* complicate.

erschwingen [ɛr'ʃvɪŋən] *vt unreg* afford.

erschwinglich *a* within one's means.

ersehen [ɛr'ze:ən] *vt unreg*: aus etw ~, daß gather from sth that.

ersetzen [ɛr'zɛtsən] *vt* replace; jdm Unkosten *etc* ~ pay sb's expenses *etc*.

ersichtlich [ɛr'zɪçtlɪç] *a* evident, obvious.

ersparen [ɛr'ʃpa:rən] *vt* (*Ärger etc*) spare; (*Geld*) save.

Ersparnis *f* **-, -se** saving.

erst ['e:rst] *ad* **1** first; mach ~ mal die Arbeit fertig finish your work first; wenn du das ~ mal hinter dir hast once you've got that behind you **2** (*nicht früher als, nur*) only; (*nicht bis*) not till; ~ gestern only yesterday; ~ morgen not until tomorrow; ~ als only when, not until; wir fahren ~ später we're not going until later; er ist (gerade) ~ angekommen he's only just arrived **3**: wäre er doch ~ zurück! if only he were back!

erstatten [ɛr'ʃtatən] *vt* (*Kosten*) (re)pay; Anzeige *etc* ~ report sb; Bericht ~ make a report.

Erstaufführung ['e:rst'aʊffy:rʊŋ] *f* first performance.

erstaunen [ɛr'ʃtaʊnən] *vt* astonish // *vi* be astonished; **E~** *nt* **-s** astonishment.

erstaunlich *a* astonishing.

erst- ['e:rst] *zW*: **E~ausgabe** *f* first edition; ~**beste(r, s)** *a* first that comes along; ~**e(r, s)** *a* first.

erstechen [ɛr'ʃtɛçən] *vt unreg* stab (to death).

erstehen [ɛr'ʃte:ən] *vt unreg* buy // *vi* (a)rise.

erstens ['e:rstəns] *ad* firstly, in the first place.

ersticken [ɛr'ʃtɪkən] *vt* (*lit, fig*) stifle; (*Mensch*) suffocate; (*Flammen*) smother // *vi* (*Mensch*) suffocate; (*Feuer*) be smothered; in Arbeit ~ be snowed under with work.

erst- *zW*: ~**klassig** *a* first-class; **E~kommunion** *f* first communion; ~**malig** *a* first; ~**mals** *ad* for the first time.

erstrebenswert [ɛr'ʃtre:bənsve:rt] *a* desirable, worthwhile.

erstrecken [ɛr'ʃtrɛkən] *vr* extend, stretch.

ersuchen [ɛr'zu:xən] *vt* request.

ertappen [ɛr'tapən] *vt* catch, detect.

erteilen [ɛr'taɪlən] *vt* give.

Ertrag [ɛr'tra:k] *m* **-(e)s, ⁻e** yield; (*Gewinn*) proceeds *pl*; **e~en** *vt unreg* bear, stand.

erträglich [ɛr'trɛ:klɪç] *a* tolerable, bearable.

ertrinken [ɛr'trɪŋkən] *vi unreg* drown; **E~** *nt* **-s** drowning.

erübrigen [ɛr'y:brɪgən] *vt* spare // *vr* be unnecessary.

erwachen [ɛr'vaxən] *vi* awake.

erwachsen [ɛr'vaksən] *a* grown-up; **E~e(r)** *mf* adult; **E~enbildung** *f* adult education.

erwägen [ɛr'vɛːgən] *vt unreg* consider.

Erwägung *f* consideration.

erwähn- [ɛr'vɛːn] *zW:* **~en** *vt* mention; **~enswert** *a* worth mentioning; **E~ung** *f* mention.

erwärmen [ɛr'vɛrmən] *vt* warm, heat // *vr* get warm, warm up; **sich ~ für** warm to.

erwarten [ɛr'vartən] *vt* expect; *(warten auf)* wait for; **etw kaum ~ können** hardly be able to wait for sth.

Erwartung *f* expectation; **erwartungsgemäß** *ad* as expected; **erwartungsvoll** *a* expectant.

erwecken [ɛr'vɛkən] *vt* rouse, awake; **den Anschein ~** give the impression.

Erweis [ɛr'vais] *m* **-es, -e** proof; **e~en** *unreg vt* prove; *(Ehre, Dienst)* do *(jdm sb)* // *vr* prove *(als* to be).

Erwerb [ɛr'vɛrp] *m* **-(e)s, -e** acquisition; *(Beruf)* trade; **e~en** *vt unreg* acquire.

erwerbs- *zW:* **~los** *a* unemployed; **E~quelle** *f* source of income; **~tätig** *a* (gainfully) employed; **~unfähig** *a* unemployable.

erwidern [ɛr'viːdərn] *vt* reply; *(vergelten)* return.

erwiesen [ɛr'viːzən] *a* proven.

erwischen [ɛr'vɪʃən] *vt (umg)* catch, get.

erwünscht [ɛr'vʏnʃt] *a* desired.

erwürgen [ɛr'vʏrgən] *vt* strangle.

Erz [ɛːrts] *nt* **-es, -e** ore.

erzähl- [ɛr'tsɛːl] *zW:* **~en** *vt* tell // *vi:* sie kann gut **~en** she's a good storyteller; **E~er** *m* **-s, -** narrator; **E~ung** *f* story, tale.

Erz- *zW:* **~bischof** *m* archbishop; **~engel** *m* archangel.

erzeug- [ɛr'tsɔyg] *zW:* **~en** *vt* produce; *(Strom)* generate; **E~nis** *nt* **-ses, -se** product, produce; **E~ung** *f* production; generation.

erziehen [ɛr'tsiːən] *vt unreg* bring up; *(bilden)* educate, train.

Erziehung *f* bringing up; *(Bildung)* education.

Erziehungs- *zW:* **~beihilfe** *f* educational grant; **~berechtigte(r)** *f(m)* parent; guardian; **~heim** *nt* approved school.

erzielen [ɛr'tsiːlən] *vt* achieve, obtain; *(Tor)* score.

erzwingen [ɛr'tsvɪŋən] *vt unreg* force, obtain by force.

es [ɛs] *pron nom, akk* it.

Esche ['ɛʃə] *f* **-, -n** ash.

Esel ['eːzəl] *m* **-s, -** donkey, ass.

Eskalation [ɛskalatsi'oːn] *f* escalation.

eßbar ['ɛsbaːr] *a* eatable, edible.

essen ['ɛsən] *vti unreg* eat; **E~** *nt* **-s, -** meal; food; **Essenszeit** *f* mealtime; dinner time.

Essig ['ɛsɪç] *m* **-s, -e** vinegar; **~gurke** *f* gherkin.

Eß- ['ɛs] *zW:* **~kastanie** *f* sweet chestnut; **~löffel** *m* tablespoon; **~tisch** *m* dining table; **~waren** *pl* food stuffs *pl*, provisions *pl*; **~zimmer** *nt* dining room.

etablieren [eta'bliːrən] *vr* become established; set up in business.

Etage [e'taːʒə] *f* **-, -n** floor, storey; **Etagenbetten** *pl* bunk beds *pl*; **Etagenwohnung** *f* flat.

Etappe [e'tapə] *f* **-, -n** stage.

Etat [e'taː] *m* **-s, -s** budget.

etepetete [eːtəpe'teːtə] *a (umg)* fussy.

Ethik ['eːtɪk] *f* ethics *sing.*

ethisch ['eːtɪʃ] *a* ethical.

Etikett [eti'kɛt] *nt* **-(e)s, -e** label; tag; **~e** *f* etiquette, manners *pl*; **e~ieren** [-'tiːrən] *vt* label; tag.

etliche ['ɛtlɪçə] *pron pl* some, quite a few; **~s** a thing or two.

Etui [ɛt'viː] *nt* **-s, -s** case.

etwa ['ɛtva] *ad (ungefähr)* about; *(vielleicht)* perhaps; *(beispielsweise)* for instance; **nicht ~** by no means; **~ig** ['ɛtvaɪç] *a* possible; **etwas** *pron* something; anything; *(ein wenig)* a little // *ad* a little.

euch [ɔyç] *pron akk von* **ihr** you; yourselves // *dat von* **ihr** (to) you.

euer ['ɔyər] *pron gen von* **ihr** of you // *pron* your; **~e(r, s)** yours.

Eule ['ɔylə] *f* **-, -n** owl.

eure(r, s) ['ɔyrə(r, s)] *pron* your; yours; **eurerseits** *ad* on your part; **euresgleichen** *pron* people like you; **euretwegen, euretwillen** *ad (für euch)* for your sakes; *(wegen euch)* on your account.

eurige ['ɔyrɪgə] *pron:* **der/die/das ~** yours.

Euro- *zW:* **~pa** [ɔy'roːpa] *nt* Europe; **~päer(in)** [ɔyro'pɛːər(ɪn)] *mf* European; **e~päisch** *a* European; **~pameister** [ɔy'roːpa-] *m* European champion.

Euter ['ɔytər] *nt* **-s, -** udder.

ev. *abk von* **evangelisch**.

evakuieren [evaku'iːrən] *vt* evacuate.

evangelisch [evaŋ'geːlɪʃ] *a* Protestant.

Evangelium [evaŋ'geːliʊm] *nt* gospel.

eventuell [evɛntu'ɛl] *a* possible // *ad* possibly, perhaps.

evtl. *abk von* **eventuell**.

EWG [eːveː'geː] *f* - *abk* (= *Europäische Wirtschaftsgemeinschaft)* EEC, Common Market.

ewig ['eːvɪç] *a* eternal; **E~keit** *f* eternity.

Ex- [ɛks] *in zW* ex-.

exakt [ɛ'ksakt] *a* exact.

Examen [ɛ'ksaːmən] *nt* **-s, -** *od* **Examina** examination.

Exemplar [ɛksɛm'plaːr] *nt* **-s, -e** specimen; (*Buch~*) copy; **e~isch** *a* exemplary.

exerzieren [ɛksɛr'tsiːrən] *vi* drill.

Exil [ɛ'ksiːl] *nt* **-s, -e** exile.

Existenz [ɛksɪs'tɛnts] *f* existence; (*Unterhalt*) livelihood, living; (*pej: Mensch*) character; **~kampf** *m* struggle for existence; **~minimum** *nt* **-s** subsistence level.

existieren [ɛksɪs'tiːrən] *vi* exist.

exklusiv [ɛksklu'ziːf] *a* exclusive; **~e** [-'ziːvə] *ad, präp* +*gen* exclusive of, not including.

exotisch [ɛ'ksoːtɪʃ] *a* exotic.

Expedition [ɛkspeditsi'oːn] *f* expedition.

Experiment [ɛksperi'mɛnt] *nt* experiment; **e~ell** [-'tɛl] *a* experimental; **e~ieren** [-'tiːrən] *vi* experiment.

Experte [ɛks'pɛrtə] *m* **-n, -n, Expertin** *f* expert, specialist.

explo- [ɛksploː] *zW:* **~dieren** [-'diːrən] *vi* explode; **E~sion** [ɛksploziʹoːn] *f* explosion; **~siv** [-'ziːf] *a* explosive.

Export [ɛks'pɔrt] *m* **-(e)s, -e** export; **Exporteur** [-'tøːr] *m* exporter; **~handel** *m* export trade; **e~ieren** [-'tiːrən] *vt* export; **~land** *nt* exporting country.

Expreß- [ɛks'prɛs] *zW:* **~gut** *nt* express goods *pl od* freight; **~zug** *m* express (train).

extra ['ɛkstra] *a inv* (*umg: gesondert*) separate; (*besondere*) extra // *ad* (*gesondert*) separately; (*speziell*) specially; (*absichtlich*) on purpose; (*vor Adjektiven, zusätzlich*) extra; **E~** *nt* **-s, -s** extra; **E~ausgabe** *f*, **E~blatt** *nt* special edition.

Extrakt [ɛks'trakt] *m* **-(e)s, -e** extract.

extrem [ɛks'treːm] *a* extreme; **~istisch** [-'mɪstɪʃ] *a* (*POL*) extremist; **E~itäten** [-'tɛːtən] *pl* extremities *pl*.

exzentrisch [ɛks'tsɛntrɪʃ] *a* eccentric.

Exzeß [ɛks'tsɛs] *m* **-sses, -sse** excess.

F

F, f [ɛf] *nt* F, f.

Fa. *abk* (= *Firma*) firm; (*in Briefen*) Messrs.

Fabel ['faːbəl] *f* **-, -n** fable; **f~haft** *a* fabulous, marvellous.

Fabrik [fa'briːk] *f* factory; **~ant** [-'kant] *m* (*Hersteller*) manufacturer; (*Besitzer*) industrialist; **~arbeiter** *m* factory worker; **~at** [-'kaːt] *nt* **-(e)s, -e** manufacture, product; **~ation** [-atsi'oːn] *f* manufacture, production; **~gelände** *nt* factory premises *pl*.

Fach [fax] *nt* **-(e)s, -̈er** compartment; (*Sachgebiet*) subject; **ein Mann vom ~** an expert; **~arbeiter** *m* skilled worker; **~arzt** *m* (medical) specialist; **~ausdruck** *m* technical term.

Fächer ['fɛçər] *m* **-s, -** fan.

Fach- *zW:* **~hochschule** *f* ≈ technical college; **~kundig** *a* expert, specialist; **f~lich** *a* professional; expert; **~mann** *m, pl* **-leute** specialist; **f~männisch** *a* professional; **~schule** *f* technical college; **f~simpeln** *vi* talk shop; **~werk** *nt* timber frame.

Fackel ['fakəl] *f* **-, -n** torch.

fad(e) ['faːt, faːdə] *a* insipid; (*langweilig*) dull.

Faden ['faːdən] *m* **-s, -̈** thread; **f~scheinig** *a* (*lit, fig*) threadbare.

fähig ['fɛːɪç] *a* capable (*zu, gen* of); able; **F~keit** *f* ability.

fahnden ['faːndən] *vi:* **~ nach** search for.

Fahndung *f* search; **Fahndungsliste** *f* list of wanted criminals, wanted list.

Fahne ['faːnə] *f* **-, -n** flag, standard; **eine ~ haben** (*umg*) smell of drink; **Fahnenflucht** *f* desertion.

Fahr- ['faːr] *zW:* **~ausweis** *m* ticket; **~bahn** *f* carriageway (*Brit*), roadway.

Fähre ['fɛːrə] *f* **-, -n** ferry.

fahren ['faːrən] *unreg vt* drive; (*Rad*) ride; (*befördern*) drive, take; (*Rennen*) drive in // *vi* (*sich bewegen*) go; (*Schiff*) sail; (*abfahren*) leave; **mit dem Auto/Zug ~** go od travel by car/ train; **mit der Hand ~ über** (+*akk*) pass one's hand over.

Fahr- *zW:* **~er(in** *f*) *m* **-s, -** driver; **~erflucht** *f* hit-and-run; **~gast** *m* passenger; **~geld** *nt* fare; **~gestell** *nt* chassis; (*AVIAT*) undercarriage; **~karte** *f* ticket; **~kartenausgabe** *f*, **~kartenschalter** *m* ticket office; **f~lässig** *a* negligent; **f~lässige Tötung** manslaughter; **~lässigkeit** *f* negligence; **~lehrer** *m* driving instructor; **~plan** *m* timetable; **f~planmäßig** *a* (*EISENB*) scheduled; **~preis** *m* fare; **~prüfung** *f* driving test; **~rad** *nt* bicycle; **~schein** *m* ticket; **~schule** *f* driving school; **~stuhl** *m* lift (*Brit*), elevator (*US*).

Fahrt [faːrt] *f* **-, -en** journey; (*kurz*) trip; (*AUT*) drive; (*Geschwindigkeit*) speed; **gute ~!** have a good journey.

Fährte ['fɛːrtə] *f* **-, -n** track, trail.

Fahrtkosten *pl* travelling expenses *pl*.

Fahrtrichtung *f* course, direction.

Fahrzeug *nt* vehicle; **~halter** *m* **-s, -** owner of a vehicle.

Faksimile [fak'ziːmile] *nt* facsimile.

Faktor ['faktɔr] *m* factor.

Faktum ['faktʊm] *nt* **-s, -ten** fact.

Fakultät [fakul'tɛːt] *f* faculty.

Falke ['falkə] *m* **-n, -n** falcon.

Fall [fal] *m* **-(e)s, -̈e** (*Sturz*) fall; (*Sachverhalt, JUR, GRAM*) case; **auf jeden ~, auf alle -̈e** in any case; (*be-*

stimmt) definitely; **auf keinen ~!** no way!; **~e** *f* **-**, **-n** trap; **f~en** *vi unreg* fall; **etw f~en lassen** drop sth.

fällen ['fɛlən] *vt (Baum)* fell; *(Urteil)* pass.

fallenlassen *vt unreg (Bemerkung)* make; *(Plan)* abandon, drop.

fällig ['fɛlɪç] *a* due.

falls [fals] *ad* in case, if.

Fall- *zW:* **~schirm** *m* parachute; **~schirmjäger** *pl* paratroops *pl*; **~schirmspringer** *m* parachutist.

falsch [falʃ] *a* false; *(unrichtig)* wrong.

fälschen ['fɛlʃən] *vt* forge.

Falschgeld *nt* counterfeit money.

fälsch- *zW:* **~lich** *a* false; **~licherweise** *ad* mistakenly; **F~ung** *f* forgery.

Falte ['faltə] *f* **-**, **-n** *(Knick)* fold, crease; *(Haut~)* wrinkle; *(Rock~)* pleat; **f~n** *vt* fold; *(Stirn)* wrinkle.

familiär [famili'ɛːr] *a* familiar.

Familie [fa'miːliə] *f* family.

Familien- *zW:* **~kreis** *m* family circle; **~name** *m* surname; **~stand** *m* marital status.

Fanatiker [fa'naːtikər] *m* **-s**, **-** fanatic.

fanatisch *a* fanatical.

Fanatismus [fana'tɪsmʊs] *m* fanaticism.

fand *etc v siehe* **finden**.

Fang [faŋ] *m* **-(e)s**, **̈e** catch; *(Jagen)* hunting; *(Kralle)* talon, claw; **f~en** *unreg vt* catch // *vr* get caught; *(Flugzeug)* level out; *(Mensch: nicht fallen)* steady o.s.; *(fig)* compose o.s.; *(in Leistung)* get back on form.

Farb- ['farb] *zW:* **~aufnahme** *f* colour photograph; **~band** *m* typewriter ribbon; **~e** *f* **-**, **-n** colour; *(zum Malen etc)* paint; *(Stoff~)* dye; **f~echt** *a* colourfast.

färben ['fɛrbən] *vt* colour; *(Stoff, Haar)* dye.

farben- ['farbən] *zW:* **~blind** *a* colourblind; **~froh** *a* colourful, gay.

Farb- *zW:* **~fernsehen** *nt* colour television; **~film** *m* colour film; **~foto** *nt* colour photograph; **f~ig** *a* coloured; **~ige(r)** *mf* coloured; **~kasten** *m* paint-box; **f~los** *a* colourless; **~stift** *m* coloured pencil; **~stoff** *m* dye; **~ton** *m* hue, tone.

Färbung ['fɛrbʊŋ] *f* colouring; *(Tendenz)* bias.

Farn [farn] *m* **-(e)s**, **-e**, **~kraut** *nt* fern; bracken.

Fasan [fa'zaːn] *m* **-(e)s**, **-e(n)** pheasant.

Fasching ['faʃɪŋ] *m* **-s**, **-e** *od* **-s** carnival.

Faschismus [fa'ʃɪsmʊs] *m* fascism.

Faschist *m* fascist.

Faser ['faːzər] *f* **-**, **-n** fibre; **f~n** *vi* fray.

Faß [fas] *nt* **-sses**, **Fässer** vat, barrel; *(für Öl)* drum; **Bier vom ~** draught beer.

Fassade [fa'saːdə] *f* facade.

faßbar ['fasbaːr] *a* comprehensible.

fassen ['fasən] *vt (ergreifen)* grasp, take; *(inhaltlich)* hold; *(Entschluß etc)* take; *(verstehen)* understand; *(Ring etc)* set; *(formulieren)* formulate, phrase; **nicht zu ~** unbelievable // *vr* calm down.

Fassung ['fasʊŋ] *f (Umrahmung)* mounting; *(Lampen~)* socket; *(Wortlaut)* version; *(Beherrschung)* composure; **jdn aus der ~ bringen** upset sb; **fassungslos** *a* speechless.

fast [fast] *ad* almost, nearly.

fasten ['fastən] *vi* fast; **F~zeit** *f* Lent.

Fastnacht *f* Shrove Tuesday; carnival.

fatal [fa'taːl] *a* fatal; *(peinlich)* embarrassing.

faul [faʊl] *a* rotten; *(Person)* lazy; *(Ausreden)* lame; **daran ist etwas ~** there's sth fishy about it; **~en** *vi* rot; **faulenzen** *vi* idle; **Faulenzer** *m* **-s**, **-** idler, loafer; **F~heit** *f* laziness; **~ig** *a* putrid.

Fäulnis ['fɔylnɪs] *f* **-** decay, putrefaction.

Faust ['faʊst] *f* **-**, **Fäuste** fist; **auf eigene ~** off one's own bat; **~handschuh** *m* mitten.

Favorit [favo'riːt] *m* **-en**, **-en** favourite.

FDP [ɛfdeː'peː] *f abk* (= *Freie Demokratische Partei*) Free Democratic Party.

Februar ['feːbruaːr] *m* **-(s)**, **-e** February.

fechten ['fɛçtən] *vi unreg* fence.

Feder ['feːdər] *f* **-**, **-n** feather; *(Schreib~)* pen nib; *(TECH)* spring; **~ball** *m* shuttlecock; **~bett** *nt* continental quilt; **~halter** *m* penholder, pen; **f~leicht** *a* light as a feather; **f~n** *vi (nachgeben)* be springy; *(sich bewegen)* bounce // *vt* spring; **~ung** *f* suspension.

Fege- ['feːgə] *zW:* **~feuer** *nt* purgatory; **f~n** *vt* sweep.

fehl [feːl] *a:* **~ am Platz** *od* **Ort** out of place; **~en** *vi* be wanting *od* missing; *(abwesend sein)* be absent; **etw fehlt jdm** sb lacks sth; **du fehlst mir** I miss you; **was fehlt ihm?** what's wrong with him?; **F~er** *m* **-s**, **-** mistake, error; *(Mangel, Schwäche)* fault; **~erfrei** *a* faultless; without any mistakes; **~erhaft** *a* incorrect; faulty; **F~geburt** *f* miscarriage; **~gehen** *vi unreg* go astray; **F~griff** *m* blunder; **F~konstruktion** *f* badly designed thing; **F~schlag** *m* failure; **~schlagen** *vi unreg* fail; **F~start** *m*

(*SPORT*) false start; **F~zündung** *f*
(*AUT*) misfire, backfire.
Feier ['faɪər] *f* -, **-n** celebration;
~abend *m* time to stop work;
~abend machen stop, knock off; **jetzt
ist ~abend!** that's enough!; **f~lich** *a*
solemn; **~lichkeit** *f* solemnity;
~lichkeiten *pl* festivities *pl*; **f~n** *vti*
celebrate; **~tag** *m* holiday.
feig(e) ['faɪg(ə)] *a* cowardly; **F~e** *f* -,
-n fig; **F~heit** *f* cowardice; **F~ling** *m*
coward.
Feil- [faɪl] *zW:* **~e** *f* -, **-n** file; **f~schen**
vi haggle.
fein [faɪn] *a* fine; (*vornehm*) refined;
(*Gehör etc*) keen; **~!** great!
Feind [faɪnt] *m* **-(e)s, -e** enemy; **f~lich**
a hostile; **~schaft** *f* enmity; **f~selig**
a hostile; **~seligkeit** *f* hostility.
Fein- *zW:* **f~fühlend, f~fühlig** *a* sensitive; **~gefühl** *nt* delicacy, tact;
~heit *f* fineness; refinement; keen-
ness; **~kostgeschäft** *nt* delicatessen
(shop); **~schmecker** *m* **-s,** - gourmet.
Feld [fɛlt] *nt* **-(e)s, -er** field; (*SCHACH*)
square; (*SPORT*) pitch; **~herr** *m*
commander; **~stecher** *m* **-s,** - binoculars *pl*; **~webel** *m* **-s,** - sergeant;
~weg *m* path.
Felge ['fɛlgə] *f* -, **-n** (wheel) rim.
Fell [fɛl] *nt* **-(e)s, -e** fur; coat; (*von
Schaf*) fleece; (*von toten Tieren*)
skin.
Fels [fɛls] *m* **-en, -en, Felsen** ['fɛlzən]
m **-s,** - rock; (*Klippe*) cliff; **f~enfest**
a firm; **~ensprung** *m* ledge; **f~ig**
a rocky; **~spalte** *f* crevice.
feminin [femi'niːn] *a* feminine; (*pej*)
effeminate.
Fenster ['fɛnstər] *nt* **-s,** - window;
~brett *nt* windowsill; **~ platz** *m* window seat; **~putzer** *m* **-s,** - window
cleaner; **~scheibe** *f* windowpane;
~sims *m* windowsill.
Ferien ['feːriən] *pl* holidays *pl*, vacation (*US*); **~ haben** be on holiday;
~kurs *m* holiday course; **~reise** *f*
holiday; **~zeit** *f* holiday period.
Ferkel ['fɛrkəl] *nt* **-s,** - piglet.
fern [fɛrn] *a,ad* far-off, distant; **~ von
hier** a long way (away) from here;
der F~e Osten the Far East; **F~amt**
nt (*TEL*) exchange; **F~bedienung** *f*
remote control; **F~e** *f* -, **-n** distance;
~er *a,ad* further; (*weiterhin*) in future; **F~gespräch** *nt* trunk call;
F~glas *nt* binoculars *pl*; **~halten**
vtr unreg keep away; **F~lenkung** *f* remote control; **F~meldeamt** *nt* international exchange; **F~rohr** *nt* telescope; **F~schreiben** *nt* telex;
F~sehapparat *m* television set;
~sehen *vi unreg* watch television;
F~sehen *nt* **-s** television; **im**

F~sehen on television; **F~seher** *m*
television; **F~sehüberwachungsan-
lage** *f* closed-circuit television; **F~-
sprecher** *m* telephone; **F~sprechzelle**
f telephone box *od* booth (*US*).
Ferse ['fɛrzə] *f* -, **-n** heel.
fertig ['fɛrtɪç] *a* (*bereit*) ready; (*been-
det*) finished; (*gebrauchs~*) ready-
made; **F~bau** *m* prefab(ricated
house); **F~keit** *f* skill; **~machen** *vt*
(*beenden*) finish; (*umg: Person*)
finish; (: *körperlich*) exhaust; (:
moralisch) get down // *vr* get ready;
~stellen *vt* complete.
Fessel ['fɛsəl] *f* -, **-n** fetter; **f~n** *vt*
bind; (*mit Fesseln*) fetter; (*fig*) spell-
bind; **f~nd** *a* fascinating, captivat-
ing.
fest [fɛst] *a* firm; (*Nahrung*) solid;
(*Gehalt*) regular; **f~e Kosten** fixed
cost // *ad* (*schlafen*) soundly; **F~** *nt*
-(e)s, -e party; festival; **frohes ~!**
Happy Christmas!; **~angestellt** *a*
permanently employed; **~binden** *vt
unreg* tie, fasten; **~bleiben** *vi unreg*
stand firm; **F~essen** *nt* banquet;
~halten *unreg vt* seize, hold fast;
(*Ereignis*) record // *vr* hold on (*an
+dat* to); **~igen** *vt* strengthen;
F~igkeit *f* strength; **Festival**
['fɛstɪval] *nt* **-s, -s** festival; **F~land** *nt*
mainland; **~legen** *vt* fix // *vr* commit
o.s.; **~lich** *a* festive; **~machen** *vt*
fasten; (*Termin etc*) fix; **F~nahme** *f*
-, **-n** capture; **~nehmen** *vt unreg*
capture, arrest; **F~rede** *f* address;
~setzen *vt* fix, settle; **F~spiel** *nt*,
F~spiele *pl* festival; **~stehen** *vi
unreg* be certain; **~stellen** *vt* establish; (*sagen*) remark; **F~ung** *f* fortress; **F~wochen** *pl* festival.
Fett [fɛt] *nt* **-(e)s, -e** fat, grease; **f~** *a*
fat; (*Essen etc*) greasy; **f~arm** *a* low
fat; **f~en** *vt* grease; **f~ig** *a* greasy,
fatty; **~näpfchen** *nt:* **ins ~näpfchen
treten** put one's foot in it.
Fetzen ['fɛtsən] *m* **-s,** - scrap.
feucht [fɔʏçt] *a* damp; (*Luft*) humid;
F~igkeit *f* dampness; humidity.
Feuer ['fɔʏər] *nt* **-s,** - fire; (*zum
Rauchen*) a light; (*fig: Schwung*)
spirit; **~alarm** *m* fire alarm; **~eifer**
m zeal; **f~fest** *a* fireproof; **~gefahr** *f*
danger of fire; **f~gefährlich** *a* inflammable; **~leiter** *f* fire escape ladder;
~löscher *m* **-s,** - fire extinguisher;
~melder *m* **-s,** - fire alarm; **f~n** *vti*
(*lit, fig*) fire; **~stein** *m* flint; **~wehr**
f -, **-en** fire brigade; **~wehrwagen** *m*
fire engine; **~werk** *nt* fireworks *pl*;
~zeug *nt* (cigarette) lighter.
Fichte ['fɪçtə] *f* -, **-n** spruce, pine.
Fieber ['fiːbər] *nt* **-s,** - fever, temperature; **f~haft** *a* feverish; **~messer** *m*,
~thermometer *nt* thermometer.

fiel etc v siehe **fallen.**
fies [fiːs] a (umg) nasty.
Figur [fi'guːr] f -, -en figure; (Schach~) chessman, chess piece.
Filiale [fili'aːlə] f -, -n (COMM) branch.
Film [fɪlm] m -(e)s, -e film; ~**aufnahme** f shooting; **f~en** vti film; ~**kamera** f cine-camera.
Filter ['fɪltər] m -s, - filter; **f~n** vt filter; ~**papier** nt filter paper; ~**zigarette** f tipped cigarette.
Filz [fɪlts] m -es, -e felt; **f~en** vt (umg) frisk // vi (Wolle) mat; ~**stift** m felt-tip pen.
Finale [fi'naːlə] nt -s, -(s) finale; (SPORT) final(s).
Finanz [fi'nants] f finance; ~**amt** nt Inland Revenue Office; ~**beamte(r)** m revenue officer; **f~iell** [-tsi'ɛl] a financial; **f~ieren** [-'tsiːrən] vt finance; ~**minister** m Chancellor of the Exchequer (Brit), Minister of Finance.
Find- ['fɪnd] zW: **f~en** unreg vt find; (meinen) think // vr be (found); (sich fassen) compose o.s.; **ich finde nichts dabei, wenn ...** I don't see what's wrong if ...; **das wird sich f~en** things will work out; ~**er** m -s, - finder; **f~ig** a resourceful.
fing etc v siehe **fangen.**
Finger ['fɪŋər] m -s, - finger; ~**abdruck** m fingerprint; ~**hut** m thimble; (BOT) foxglove; ~**nagel** m fingernail; ~**spitze** f fingertip.
fingieren [fɪŋ'giːrən] vt feign.
fingiert a made-up, fictitious.
Fink ['fɪŋk] m -en, -en finch.
Finn- [fɪn] zW: ~**e** m, ~**in** f Finn; **f~isch** a Finnish; ~**land** nt Finland.
finster ['fɪnstər] a dark, gloomy; (verdächtig) dubious; (verdrossen) grim; (Gedanke) dark; **F~nis** f - darkness, gloom.
Finte ['fɪntə] f -, -n feint, trick.
Firma ['fɪrma] f -, -men firm.
Firmen- ['fɪrmən] zW: ~**inhaber** m owner of firm; ~**schild** nt (shop) sign; ~**zeichen** nt registered trademark.
Firnis ['fɪrnɪs] m -ses, -se varnish.
Fisch [fɪʃ] m -(e)s, -e fish // pl (ASTROL) Pisces; **f~en** vti fish; ~**er** m -s, - fisherman; ~**e'rei** f fishing, fishery; ~**fang** m fishing; ~**geschäft** nt fishmonger's (shop); ~**gräte** f fishbone.
fix [fɪks] a fixed; (Person) alert, smart; ~ **und fertig** finished; (erschöpft) done in; ~**ieren** [fi'ksiːrən] vt fix; (anstarren) stare at.
flach [flax] a flat; (Gefäß) shallow.
Fläche ['flɛçə] f -, -n area; (Ober~) surface; ~**inhalt** m surface area.
Flachland nt lowland.
flackern ['flakərn] vi flare, flicker.

Flagge ['flagə] f -, -n flag.
Flamme ['flamə] f -, -n flame.
Flanell [fla'nɛl] m -s, -e flannel.
Flanke ['flaŋkə] f -, -n flank; (SPORT: Seite) wing.
Flasche ['flaʃə] f -, -n bottle; (umg: Versager) wash-out.
Flaschen- zW: ~**bier** nt bottled beer; ~**öffner** m bottle opener; ~**zug** m pulley.
flatterhaft a flighty, fickle.
flattern ['flatərn] vi flutter.
flau [flau] a weak, listless; (Nachfrage) slack; **jdm ist ~** sb feels queasy.
Flaum [flaum] m -(e)s (Feder) down; (Haare) fluff.
flauschig ['flauʃɪç] a fluffy.
Flausen ['flauzən] pl silly ideas pl; (Ausflüchte) weak excuses pl.
Flaute ['flautə] f -, -n calm; (COMM) recession.
Flechte ['flɛçtə] f -, -n plait; (MED) dry scab; (BOT) lichen; **f~n** vt unreg plait; (Kranz) twine.
Fleck [flɛk] m -(e)s, -e, **Flecken** m -s, - spot; (Schmutz~) stain; (Stoff~) patch; (Makel) blemish; **nicht vom ~ kommen** (lit, fig) not get any further; **vom ~ weg** straight away; **f~enlos** a spotless; ~**enmittel** nt, ~**enwasser** nt stain remover; **f~ig** a spotted; stained.
Fledermaus ['fleːdərmaus] f bat.
Flegel ['fleːgəl] m -s, - (Mensch) lout; **f~haft** a loutish, unmannerly; ~**jahre** pl adolescence.
flehen ['fleːən] vi implore; **flehentlich** a imploring.
Fleisch ['flaɪʃ] nt -(e)s flesh; (Essen) meat; ~**brühe** f beef tea, stock; ~**er** m -s, - butcher; ~**e'rei** f butcher's (shop); ~**wolf** m mincer; ~**wunde** f flesh wound.
Fleiß ['flaɪs] m -es diligence, industry; **f~ig** a diligent, industrious.
fletschen ['flɛtʃən] vt (Zähne) show.
flexibel [flɛ'ksiːbəl] a flexible.
Flicken ['flɪkən] m -s, - patch; **f~** vt mend.
Flieder ['fliːdər] m -s, - lilac.
Fliege ['fliːgə] f -, -n fly; (Kleidung) bow tie; **f~n** vti unreg fly; **auf jdn/ etw f~en** (umg) be mad about sb/sth; **Fliegenpilz** m toadstool; ~**r** m -s, - flier, airman.
fliehen ['fliːən] vi unreg flee.
Fliese ['fliːzə] f -, -n tile.
Fließ- ['fliːs] zW: ~**band** nt production od assembly line; **f~en** vi unreg flow; **f~end** a flowing; (Rede, Deutsch) fluent; (Übergänge) smooth.
flimmern ['flɪmərn] vi glimmer.
flink [flɪŋk] a nimble, lively.

Flinte ['flɪntə] f -, -n rifle; shotgun.
Flitter ['flɪtər] m -s, - spangle, tinsel; **~wochen** pl honeymoon.
flitzen ['flɪtsən] vi flit.
Flocke ['flɔkə] f -, -n flake.
flog etc v siehe **fliegen**.
Floh [floː] m -(e)s, ̈e flea; **~markt** m flea market.
florieren [floˈriːrən] vi flourish.
Floskel ['flɔskəl] f -, -n empty phrase.
floß etc v siehe **fließen**.
Floß [floːs] nt -es, ̈e raft, float.
Flosse ['flɔsə] f -, -n fin.
Flöte ['fløːtə] f -, -n flute; (Block~) recorder.
Flötist(in f) [fløˈtɪst(ɪn)] m flautist.
flott [flɔt] a lively(; (elegant) smart; (NAUT) afloat; **F~e** f -, -n fleet, navy.
Fluch [fluːx] m -(e)s, ̈e curse; **f~en** vi curse, swear.
Flucht [fluxt] f -en flight; (Fenster~) row; (Reihe) range; (Zimmer~) suite; **f~artig** a hasty.
flücht- ['flʏçt] zW: **~en** vir flee, escape; **~ig** a fugitive; (vergänglich) transitory; (oberflächlich) superficial; (eilig) fleeting; **F~igkeit** f transitoriness; superficiality; **F~igkeitsfehler** m careless slip; **F~ling** m fugitive, refugee.
Flug [fluːk] m -(e)s, ̈e flight; **im ~** airborne, in flight; **~blatt** nt pamphlet.
Flügel ['flyːgəl] m -s, - wing; (MUS) grand piano.
Fluggast m airline passenger.
flügge ['flʏgə] a (fully-)fledged.
Flug- zW: **~geschwindigkeit** f flying od air speed; **~gesellschaft** f airline (company); **~hafen** m airport; **~höhe** f altitude (of flight); **~plan** m flight schedule; **~platz** m airport; (klein) airfield; **~schein** m plane ticket; **~verkehr** m air traffic; **~zeug** nt (aero)plane, airplane (US); **~zeugentführung** f hijacking of a plane; **~zeughalle** f hangar; **~zeugträger** m aircraft carrier.
Flunder ['flʊndər] f -, -n flounder.
flunkern ['flʊŋkərn] vi fib, tell stories.
Fluor ['fluːɔr] nt -s fluorine.
Flur [fluːr] m -(e)s, -e hall; (Treppen~) staircase.
Fluß [flʊs] m -sses, ̈sse river; (Fließen) flow; **im ~ sein** (fig) be in a state of flux.
flüssig ['flʏsɪç] a liquid; **F~keit** f liquid; (Zustand) liquidity; **~machen** vt (Geld) make available.
flüstern ['flʏstərn] vti whisper.
Flut [fluːt] f -, -en (lit, fig) flood; (Gezeiten) high tide; **f~en** vi flood; **~licht** nt floodlight.
Fohlen ['foːlən] nt -s, - foal.
Föhre ['føːrə] f -, -n Scots pine.
Folge ['fɔlgə] f -, -n series, sequence;

(Fortsetzung) instalment; (Auswirkung) result; **in rascher ~** in quick succession; **etw zur ~ haben** result in sth; **~n haben** have consequences; **einer Sache ~ leisten** comply with sth; **f~n** vi follow (jdm sb); (gehorchen) obey (jdm sb); **jdm f~n können** (fig) follow od understand sb; **f~nd** a following; **f~nde(r, s)** a following; **f~ndermaßen** ad as follows, in the following way; **f~nschwer** a momentous; **f~rn** vt conclude (aus +dat from); **~rung** f conclusion.
folglich ad consequently.
folgsam a obedient.
Folie ['foːliə] f -, -n foil.
Folter ['fɔltər] f -, -n torture; (Gerät) rack; **f~n** vt torture.
Fön ® [føːn] m -(e)s, -e hair-dryer; **f~en** vt (blow) dry.
Fontäne [fɔnˈtɛːnə] f -, -n fountain.
Förder- ['fœrdər] zW: **~band** nt conveyor belt; **~gebiet** nt development area; **~korb** m pit cage; **f~lich** a beneficial.
fordern ['fɔrdərn] vt demand.
Förder- zW: **f~n** vt promote; (unterstützen) help; (Kohle) extract; **~ung** f promotion; help; extraction.
Forderung ['fɔrdərʊŋ] f demand.
Forelle [foˈrɛlə] f trout.
Form [fɔrm] f -, -en shape; (Gestaltung) form; (Guß~) mould; (Back~) baking tin; **in ~ sein** be in good form od shape; **in ~ von** in the shape of; **~alität** f formality; **~at** [-ˈmaːt] nt -(e)s, -e format; (fig) distinction; **f~atieren** vt format; (unterteilen) set up; **f~bar** a malleable; **~el** f -, -n formula; **f~ell** [-ˈmɛl] a formal; **f~en** vt form, shape; **~fehler** m faux-pas, gaffe; (JUR) irregularity; **f~ieren** [-ˈmiːrən] vt form // vr form up.
förmlich ['fœrmlɪç] a formal; (umg) real; **F~keit** f formality.
Form- zW: **f~los** a shapeless; (Benehmen etc) informal; **~u'lar** nt -s, -e form; **f~u'lieren** vt formulate.
forsch [fɔrʃ] a energetic, vigorous; **~en** vi search (nach for) // vi (wissenschaftlich) (do) research; **~end** a searching; **F~er** m -s, - research scientist; (Natur~) explorer.
Forschung ['fɔrʃʊŋ] f research; **Forschungsreise** f scientific expedition.
Forst [fɔrst] m -(e)s, -e forest.
Förster ['fœrstər] m -s, - forester; (für Wild) gamekeeper.
fort [fɔrt] ad away; (verschwunden) gone; (vorwärts) on; **und so ~** and so on; **in einem ~** on and on; **~bestehen** vi unreg survive; **~bewegen** vtr move away; **~bilden** vr continue one's education;

~**bleiben** vi unreg stay away; F~**dauer** f continuance; ~**fahren** vi unreg depart; (fortsetzen) go on, continue; ~**führen** vt continue, carry on; ~**gehen** vi unreg go away; ~**geschritten** a advanced; ~**müssen** vi unreg have to go; ~**pflanzen** vr reproduce; F~**pflanzung** f reproduction; ~**schaffen** vt remove; ~**schreiten** vi unreg advance.

Forts. abk (= Fortsetzung) cont(d).

Fortschritt ['fɔrtʃrɪt] m advance; ~**e** machen make progress; f~**lich** a progressive.

fort- zW: ~**setzen** vt continue; F~**setzung** f continuation; (folgender Teil) instalment; F~**setzung folgt** to be continued; ~**während** a incessant, continual.

Foto ['fo:to] nt -s, -s photo(graph); ~**apparat** m camera; ~'**graf** m photographer; ~**gra'fie** f photography; (Bild) photograph; f~**gra'fieren** vt photograph // vi take photographs; ~**kopie** f photocopy; f~**kopieren** vt photocopy.

Foul [faul] nt -s, -s foul.

Fr. abk (= Frau) Mrs., Ms.

Fracht [fraxt] f -, -en freight; (NAUT) cargo; (Preis) carriage; ~ **zahlt** **Empfänger** (COMM) carriage forward; ~**er** m -s, - freighter, cargo boat; ~**gut** nt freight.

Frack [frak] m -(e)s, -e tails pl.

Frage ['fra:gə] f -, -n question; etw in ~ **stellen** question sth; jdm eine ~ **stellen** ask sb a question, put a question to sb; nicht in ~ **kommen** be out of the question; ~**bogen** m questionnaire; f~**n** vti ask; ~**zeichen** nt question mark.

fraglich a questionable, doubtful.

fraglos ad unquestionably.

Fragment [fra'gmɛnt] nt fragment.

fragwürdig ['fra:kvʏrdɪç] a questionable, dubious.

Fraktion [fraktsi'o:n] f parliamentary party.

frankieren [fraŋ'ki:rən] vt stamp, frank.

Frankiermaschine f franking machine.

franko ['fraŋko] ad post-paid; carriage paid.

Frankreich ['fraŋkraɪç] nt -s France.

Franse ['franzə] f -, -n fringe.

Franzose [fran'tso:zə] m Frenchman.

Französ- [fran'tsø:z] zW: ~**in** f Frenchwoman; f~**isch** a French.

fraß etc v siehe **fressen**.

Fratze ['fratsə] f -, -n grimace.

Frau [frau] f -, -en woman; (Ehe~) wife; (Anrede) Mrs., Ms.; ~ **Doktor** Doctor; ~**enarzt** m gynaecologist; ~**enbewegung** f feminist movement;

f~**enfeindlich** a anti-women; ~**enzimmer** nt female, broad (US).

Fräulein ['frɔʏlaɪn] nt young lady; (Anrede) Miss, Ms.

fraulich ['fraʊlɪç] a womanly.

frech [frɛç] a cheeky, impudent; F~**dachs** m cheeky monkey; F~**heit** f cheek, impudence.

Fregatte [fre'gatə] f frigate.

frei [fraɪ] a free; (Stelle, Sitzplatz auch) vacant; (Mitarbeiter) freelance; (unbekleidet) bare; sich (dat) einen Tag ~ **nehmen** take a day off; von etw ~ **sein** be free of sth; im F~**en** in the open air; ~ **sprechen** talk without notes; ~ **Haus** (COMM) carriage paid; ~**er** **Wettbewerb** (COMM) fair/open competition; F~**bad** nt open-air swimming pool; ~**bekommen** vt unreg: jdn/einen Tag ~**bekommen** get sb freed/get a day off; ~**gebig** a generous; ~**halten** vt unreg keep free; ~**händig** ad (fahren) with no hands; F~**heit** f freedom; ~**heitlich** a liberal; F~**heitsstrafe** f prison sentence; F~**karte** f free ticket; ~**lassen** vt unreg (set) free; ~**legen** vt expose; ~**lich** ad certainly, admittedly; ja ~**lich** yes of course; F~**lichtbühne** f open-air theatre; ~**machen** vt (Post) frank; **Tage** ~**machen** take days off // vr arrange to be free; (entkleiden) undress; ~**sprechen** vt unreg acquit (von of); F~**spruch** m acquittal; ~**stellen** vt: jdm etw ~**stellen** leave sth (up) to sb; F~**stoß** m free kick; F~**tag** m Friday; ~**tags** ad on Fridays; ~**willig** a voluntary; F~**zeit** f spare od free time; ~**zeitbeschäftigung** f leisure pursuit; ~**zügig** a liberal, broad-minded; (mit Geld) generous.

fremd [frɛmt] a (unvertraut) strange; (ausländisch) foreign; (nicht eigen) someone else's; etw ist jdm ~ sth is foreign to sb; ~**artig** a strange; F~**e(r)** ['frɛmdə(r)] mf stranger; (Ausländer) foreigner; F~**enführer** m (tourist) guide; F~**enlegion** f foreign legion; F~**enverkehr** m tourism; F~**enzimmer** nt guest room; F~**körper** m foreign body; ~**ländisch** a foreign; F~**ling** m stranger; F~**sprache** f foreign language; F~**wort** nt foreign od loan word.

Frequenz [fre'kvɛnts] f (RAD) frequency.

fressen ['frɛsən] vti unreg eat.

Freude ['frɔʏdə] f -, -n joy, delight.

freudig a joyful, happy.

freuen ['frɔʏən] vt unpers make happy od pleased; **freut mich!** pleased to meet you // vr be glad od happy; **sich auf etw** (akk) ~ look forward to sth;

sich über etw (akk) ~ be pleased about sth.

Freund [frɔynt] m -(e)s, -e friend; boyfriend; ~in [-dɪn] f friend; girl-friend; **f~lich** a kind, friendly; **f~licherweise** ad kindly; ~**lichkeit** f friendliness, kindness; ~**schaft** f friendship; **f~schaftlich** a friendly.

Frieden ['fri:dən] m -s, - peace; im ~ in peacetime.

Friedens- zW: ~**schluß** m peace agreement; ~**vertrag** m peace treaty; ~**zeit** f peacetime.

fried- ['fri:t] zW: ~**fertig** a peaceable; **F~hof** m cemetery; ~**lich** a peaceful.

frieren ['fri:rən] vti unreg freeze; **ich friere, es friert mich** I am freezing, I'm cold.

Fries [fri:s] m -es, -e (ARCHIT) frieze.

frigid(e) [fri'gi:t, fri'gi:də] a frigid.

Frikadelle [frika'dɛlə] f meatball.

frisch [frɪʃ] a fresh; (lebhaft) lively; ~ **gestrichen!** wet paint!; **sich ~ machen** freshen (o.s.) up; **F~e** f -freshness; liveliness.

Friseur [fri'zø:r] m, **Friseuse** [fri'zø:zə] f hairdresser.

Frisier- [fri'zi:r] zW: **f~en** vtr do (one's hair); (fig: Abrechnung) fiddle, doctor; ~**salon** m hairdressing salon; ~**tisch** m dressing table.

frißt etc v siehe **fressen**.

Frist [frɪst] f -, -en period; (Termin) deadline; **f~los** a (Entlassung) instant.

Frisur [fri'zu:r] f hairdo, hairstyle.

frivol [fri'vo:l] a frivolous.

froh [fro:] a happy, cheerful; **ich bin ~, daß** ... I'm glad that ...

fröhlich ['frø:lɪç] a merry, happy; **F~keit** f merriness, gaiety.

Frohsinn m cheerfulness.

fromm [frɔm] a pious, good; (Wunsch) idle.

Frömmigkeit ['frœmɪçkaɪt] f piety.

Fronleichnam [fro:n'laɪçna:m] m -(e)s Corpus Christi.

Front [frɔnt] f -, -en front; **f~al** [frɔn'ta:l] a frontal.

fror etc v siehe **frieren**.

Frosch [frɔʃ] m -(e)s, -e frog; (Feuerwerk) squib; ~**mann** m frogman; ~**schenkel** m frog's leg.

Frost [frɔst] m -(e)s, -e frost; ~**beule** f chilblain.

frösteln ['frœstəln] vi shiver.

Frost- zW: ~**gefahr** f icy conditions; **f~ig** a frosty; ~**schutzmittel** nt anti-freeze.

Frottee [frɔ'te:] nt od m -(s), -s towelling.

Frottier(hand)tuch [frɔ'ti:r(hant)tu:x] nt towel.

Frucht [fruxt] f -, -e (lit, fig) fruit; (Getreide) corn; **f~bar** a fruitful,

fertile; ~**barkeit** f fertility; **f~en** vi be of use; **f~los** a fruitless; ~**saft** m fruit juice.

früh [fry:] a,ad early; **heute ~** this morning; **F~aufsteher** m -s, - early riser; **F~e** f - early morning; ~**er** a earlier; (ehemalig) former // ad formerly; ~**er war das anders** that used to be different; ~**estens** ad at the earliest; **F~geburt** f premature birth/baby; **F~jahr** nt, **F~ling** m spring; ~**reif** a precocious; **F~stück** nt breakfast; ~**stücken** vi (have) breakfast; ~**zeitig** a early; (pej) untimely.

frustrieren [frus'tri:rən] vt frustrate.

Fuchs [fuks] m -es, -e fox; **f~en** (umg) vt rile, annoy; **f~teufelswild** a hopping mad.

Füchsin ['fyksɪn] f vixen.

fuchteln ['fuxtəln] vi gesticulate wildly.

Fuge ['fu:gə] f -, -n joint; (MUS) fugue.

fügen ['fy:gən] vt place, join // vr be obedient (in +akk to); (anpassen) adapt oneself (in +akk to) // vr unpers happen.

fügsam ['fy:kza:m] a obedient.

fühl- ['fy:l] zW: ~**bar** a perceptible, noticeable; ~**en** vtir feel; **F~er** m -s, - feeler.

fuhr etc v siehe **fahren**.

führen ['fy:rən] vt lead; (Geschäft) run; (Name) bear; (Buch) keep // vi lead // vr behave.

Führer ['fy:rər] m -s, - leader; (Fremden~) guide; ~**schein** m driving licence.

Führung ['fy:ruŋ] f leadership; (eines Unternehmens) management; (MIL) command; (Benehmen) conduct; (Museums~) conducted tour; **Führungskraft** f executive; **Führungszeugnis** nt certificate of good conduct.

Fülle ['fylə] f - wealth, abundance; **f~n** vtr fill; (KOCH) stuff; ~**n** nt -s, -foal; ~**r** m -s, -, **Füllfederhalter** m fountain pen.

Füllung f filling; (Holz~) panel.

fummeln ['fuməln] vi (umg) fumble.

Fund [funt] m -(e)s, -e find; ~**ament** [-da'mɛnt] nt foundation; **f~amental** a fundamental; ~**büro** nt lost property office, lost and found; ~**grube** f (fig) treasure trove; **f~ieren** [-'di:rən] vt back up; **f~iert** a sound.

fünf [fynf] num five; ~**hundert** num five hundred; **F~kampf** m pentathlon; ~**te(r, s)** a fifth; **F~tel** nt -s, -fifth; ~**zehn** num fifteen; ~**zig** num fifty.

Funk [fuŋk] m -s radio, wireless; ~**e(n)** m -ns, -n (lit, fig) spark;

f~eln vi sparkle; **~er** m -s, - radio operator; **~gerät** nt radio set; **~spruch** m radio signal; **~station** f radio station; **~streife** f police radio patrol.
Funktion [fʊŋktsi'oːn] f function; **f~ieren** [-'niːrən] vi work, function.
für [fyːr] präp +akk for; **was ~** what kind od sort of; **das F~ und Wider** the pros and cons pl; **Schritt ~ Schritt** step by step; **F~bitte** f intercession.
Furche ['fʊrçə] f -, -n furrow.
Furcht [fʊrçt] f - fear; **f~bar** a terrible, frightful.
fürcht- ['fʏrçt] zW: **~en** vt be afraid of, fear // vr be afraid (vor +dat of); **~erlich** a awful.
furchtlos a fearless.
furchtsam a timid.
füreinander [fyːr'aɪ'nandər] ad for each other.
Furnier [fʊr'niːr] nt -s, -e veneer.
fürs [fyːrs] = **für das.**
Fürsorge ['fyːrzɔrgə] f care; (Sozial~) welfare; **~r(in** f) m -s, - welfare worker; **~unterstützung** f social security, welfare benefit (US).
Fürsprache f recommendation; (um Gnade) intercession.
Fürsprecher m advocate.
Fürst [fʏrst] m -en, -en prince; **~entum** nt principality; **~in** f princess; **f~lich** a princely.
Fusion [fuzi'oːn] f merger.
Fuß [fuːs] m -es, "e foot; (von Glas, Säule etc) base; (von Möbel) leg; **zu ~** on foot; **~ball** m football; **~ballplatz** m football pitch; **~ballspiel** nt football match; **~ballspieler** m footballer; **~boden** m floor; **~bremse** f (AUT) footbrake; **~ende** nt foot; **~gänger(in** f) m -s, - pedestrian; **~gängerzone** f pedestrian precinct; **~note** f footnote; **~spur** f footprint; **~tritt** m kick; (Spur) footstep; **~weg** m footpath.
Futter ['fʊtər] nt -s, - fodder, feed; (Stoff) lining; **~al** [-'raːl] nt -s, -e case.
füttern ['fʏtərn] vt feed; (Kleidung) line.
Futur [fu'tuːr] nt -s, -e future.

G

G, g [geː] nt G, g.
g abk von **Gramm.**
gab etc v siehe **geben.**
Gabe ['gaːbə] f -, -n gift.
Gabel ['gaːbəl] f -, -n fork; **~ung** f fork.
gackern ['gakərn] vi cackle.
gaffen ['gafən] vi gape.

Gage ['gaːʒə] f -, -n fee; salary.
gähnen ['gɛːnən] vi yawn.
galant [ga'lant] a gallant, courteous.
Galerie [galə'riː] f gallery.
Galgen ['galgən] m -s, - gallows pl; **~frist** f respite; **~humor** m macabre humour.
Galle ['galə] f -, -n gall; (Organ) gallbladder.
Galopp [ga'lɔp] m -s, -s od -e gallop; **g~ieren** [-'piːrən] vi gallop.
Gamasche [ga'maʃə] f -, -n gaiter; (kurz) spat.
gammeln ['gaməln] vi (umg) bum around.
Gang [gaŋ] m -(e)s, "e walk; (Boten~) errand; (~art) gait; (Abschnitt eines Vorgangs) operation; (Essens~, Ablauf) course; (Flur etc) corridor; (Durch~) passage; (TECH) gear; **in ~ bringen** set up; (fig) get off the ground; **in ~ sein** be in operation; (fig) be underway; **g~** a: **g~ und gäbe** usual, normal.
gängig ['gɛŋɪç] a common, current; (Ware) in demand, selling well.
Ganove [ga'noːvə] m -n, -n (umg) crook.
Gans [gans] f -, "e goose.
Gänse- ['gɛnzə] zW: **~blümchen** nt daisy; **~braten** m roast goose; **~haut** f goose pimples pl; **~marsch** m: **im ~marsch** in single file; **Gänserich** m -s, -e gander.
ganz [gants] a whole; (vollständig) complete; **~ Europa** all Europe; **sein ~es Geld** all his money // ad quite; (völlig) completely; **~ und gar nicht** not at all; **es sieht ~ so aus** it really looks like it; **aufs G~e gehen** go for the lot.
gänzlich ['gɛntslɪç] a,ad complete(ly), entire(ly).
gar [gaːr] a cooked, done // ad quite; **~ nicht/nichts/keiner** not/nothing/nobody at all; **~ nicht schlecht** not bad at all.
Garage [ga'raːʒə] f -, -n garage.
Garantie [garan'tiː] f guarantee; **g~ren** vt guarantee; **er kommt garantiert** he's guaranteed to come.
Garbe ['garbə] f -, -n sheaf; (MIL) burst of fire.
Garderobe [gardə'roːbə] f -, -n wardrobe; (Abgabe) cloakroom; **Garderobenfrau** f cloakroom attendant; **Garderobenständer** m hallstand.
Gardine [gar'diːnə] f curtain.
gären ['gɛːrən] vi unreg ferment.
Garn [garn] nt -(e)s, -e thread; yarn (auch fig).
Garnele [gar'neːlə] f -, -n shrimp, prawn.
garnieren [gar'niːrən] vt decorate; (Speisen) garnish.

Garnitur [garni'tu:r] f (Satz) set; (Unterwäsche) set of (matching) underwear; (fig) **erste** ~ top rank; **zweite** ~ second rate.

garstig ['garstɪç] a nasty, horrid.

Garten ['gartən] m -s, ⸚ garden; ~**arbeit** f gardening; ~**gerät** nt gardening tool; ~**schere** f pruning shears pl; ~**tür** f garden gate.

Gärtner(in f) ['gɛrtnər(ɪn)] m -s, - gardener; ~**ei** [-'raɪ] f nursery; (Gemüse~) market garden (Brit), truck farm (US).

Gärung ['gɛ:rʊŋ] f fermentation.

Gas [ga:s] nt -es, -e gas; ~ **geben** (AUT) accelerate, step on the gas; ~**herd** m, ~**kocher** m gas cooker; ~**leitung** f gas pipeline; ~**maske** f gasmask; ~**pedal** nt accelerator, gas pedal.

Gasse ['gasə] f -, -n lane, alley; **Gassenjunge** m street urchin.

Gast [gast] m -es, ⸚e guest; (in Lokal) patron; **bei jdm zu** ~ **sein** be a guest at sb's place; ~**arbeiter(in** f) m foreign worker.

Gästebuch ['gɛstəbu:x] nt visitors' book, guest book.

Gast- zW: **g~freundlich** a hospitable; ~**geber** m -s, - host; ~**geberin** f hostess; ~**haus** nt, ~**hof** m hotel, inn; **g~ieren** [-'ti:rən] vi (THEAT) (appear as a) guest; **g~lich** a hospitable; ~**rolle** f guest role.

gastronomisch [gastro'no:mɪʃ] a gastronomic(al).

Gast- zW: ~**spiel** nt (THEAT) guest performance; ~**stätte** f restaurant; pub; ~**wirt** m innkeeper; ~**wirtschaft** f hotel, inn; ~**zimmer** nt (guest) room.

Gas- zW: ~**vergiftung** f gas poisoning; ~**werk** nt gasworks sing od pl; ~**zähler** m gas meter.

Gatte ['gatə] m -n, -n husband, spouse.

Gatter ['gatər] nt -s, - railing, grating; (Eingang) gate.

Gattin f wife, spouse.

Gattung ['gatʊŋ] f genus; kind.

Gaul [gaʊl] m -(e)s, **Gäule** horse; nag.

Gaumen ['gaʊmən] m -s, - palate.

Gauner ['gaʊnər] m -s, - rogue; ~**ei** [-'raɪ] f swindle.

Gaze ['ga:zə] f -, -n gauze.

geb. abk von **geboren**.

Gebäck [gə'bɛk] nt -(e)s, -e pastry.

gebacken [gə'bakən] a baked; (gebraten) fried.

Gebälk [gə'bɛlk] nt -(e)s timberwork.

Gebärde [gə'bɛ:rdə] f -, -n gesture; **g~n** vr behave.

gebären [gə'bɛ:rən] vt unreg give birth to, bear.

Gebärmutter f uterus, womb.

Gebäude [gə'bɔydə] nt -s, - building; ~**komplex** m (building) complex.

Gebell [gə'bɛl] nt -(e)s barking.

geben ['ge:bən] unreg vti (jdm etw) give (sb sth od sth to sb); (Karten) deal; **ein Wort gab das andere** one angry word led to another // v unpers **es gibt** there is/are; there will be; **was gibt's?** what's up?; **was gibt es im Kino?** what's on at the cinema?; **gegeben** given; **zu gegebener Zeit** in good time // vr (sich verhalten) behave, act; (aufhören) abate; **sich geschlagen** ~ admit defeat; **das wird sich schon** ~ that'll soon sort itself out.

Gebet [gə'be:t] nt -(e)s, -e prayer.

gebeten v siehe **bitten**.

Gebiet [gə'bi:t] nt -(e)s, -e area; (Hoheits~) territory; (fig) field; **g~en** vt unreg command, demand; **g~erisch** a imperious.

Gebilde [gə'bɪldə] nt -s, - object, structure; **g~t** a cultured, educated.

Gebirge [gə'bɪrgə] nt -s, - mountain chain.

Gebiß [gə'bɪs] nt -sses, -sse teeth pl; (künstlich) dentures pl.

gebissen v siehe **beißen**.

geblieben v siehe **bleiben**.

geboren [gə'bo:rən] a born; (Frau) née.

geborgen [gə'bɔrgən] a secure, safe.

Gebot [gə'bo:t] nt -(e)s, -e command(ment REL); (bei Auktion) bid.

geboten v siehe **bieten**.

Gebr. abk (= Gebrüder) Bros.

gebracht v siehe **bringen**.

gebraten [gə'bra:tən] a fried.

Gebrauch [gə'braʊx] m -(e)s, **Gebräuche** use; (Sitte) custom; **g~en** vt use.

gebräuchlich [gə'brɔyçlɪç] a usual, customary.

Gebrauchs- zW: ~**anweisung** f directions pl for use; ~**artikel** m article of everyday use; **g~fertig** a ready for use; ~**gegenstand** m commodity.

gebraucht [gə'braʊxt] a used; **G~wagen** m secondhand od used car.

gebrechlich [gə'brɛçlɪç] a frail.

gebrochen [gə'brɔxən] a broken.

Gebrüder [gə'bry:dər] pl brothers pl.

Gebrüll [gə'bryl] nt -(e)s roaring.

Gebühr [gə'by:r] f -, -en charge, fee; **nach** ~ fittingly; **über** ~ unduly; **g~en** vi: **jdm gebühren** be sb's due od due to sb // vr be fitting; **g~end** a,ad fitting(ly), appropriate(ly).

Gebühren- zW: ~**erlaß** m remission of fees; ~**ermäßigung** f reduction of fees; **g~frei** a free of charge; **g~pflichtig** a subject to charges.

gebunden v siehe **binden**.

Geburt [gə'buːrt] f -, -en birth.
Geburten- zW: ~**beschränkung** f, ~**kontrolle** f, ~**reglung** f birth control; ~**ziffer** f birth-rate.
gebürtig [gə'byrtɪç] a born in, native of; ~**e Schweizerin** native of Switzerland.
Geburts- zW: ~**anzeige** f birth notice; ~**datum** nt date of birth; ~**jahr** nt year of birth; ~**ort** m birthplace; ~**tag** m birthday; ~**urkunde** f birth certificate.
Gebüsch [gə'byʃ] nt -(e)s, -e bushes pl.
gedacht v siehe **denken**.
Gedächtnis [gə'dɛçtnɪs] nt -ses, -se memory; ~**feier** f commemoration.
Gedanke [gə'daŋkə] m -ns, -n thought; **sich über etw** (akk) ~**n machen** think about sth.
Gedanken- zW: ~**austausch** m exchange of ideas; **g~los** a thoughtless; ~**losigkeit** f thoughtlessness; ~**strich** m dash; ~**übertragung** f thought transference, telepathy; **g~voll** a thoughtful.
Gedeck [gə'dɛk] nt -(e)s, -e cover(ing); (Speisenfolge) menu; **ein** ~ **auflegen** lay a place.
gedeihen [gə'daɪən] vi unreg thrive, prosper.
gedenken [gə'dɛŋkən] vi unreg (sich erinnern: +gen) remember; (beabsichtigen) intend.
Gedenk- zW: ~**feier** f commemoration; ~**minute** f minute's silence; ~**tag** m remembrance day.
Gedicht [gə'dɪçt] nt -(e)s, -e poem.
gediegen [gə'diːgən] a (good) quality; (Mensch) reliable, honest.
Gedränge [gə'drɛŋə] nt -s crush, crowd; **ins** ~ **kommen** (fig) get into difficulties.
gedrängt a compressed; ~ **voll** packed.
gedrungen [gə'drʊŋən] a thickset, stocky.
Geduld [gə'dʊlt] f - patience; **g~en** [gə'dʊldən] vr be patient; **g~ig** a patient, forbearing; **Geduldsprobe** f trial of (one's) patience.
gedurft v siehe **dürfen**.
geehrt [gə'eːrt] a: **sehr** ~**e Frau X** dear Mrs X.
geeignet [gə'aɪgnət] a suitable.
Gefahr [gə'faːr] f -, -en danger; ~ **laufen, etw zu tun** run the risk of doing sth; **auf eigene** ~ at one's own risk.
gefährden [gə'fɛːrdən] vt endanger.
Gefahrenquelle f source of danger.
Gefahrenzulage f danger money.
gefährlich [gə'fɛːrlɪç] a dangerous.
Gefälle [gə'fɛlə] nt -s, - gradient, incline.

Gefallen [gə'falən] m -s, - favour // nt -s pleasure; **an etw** (dat) ~ **finden** derive pleasure from sth; **g~** vi unreg: **jdm g~** please sb; **er/es gefällt mir** I like him/it; **das gefällt mir an ihm** that's one thing I like about him; **sich** (dat) **etw g~ lassen** put up with sth // ptp von **fallen**.
gefällig [gə'fɛlɪç] a (hilfsbereit) obliging; (erfreulich) pleasant; **G~keit** f favour; helpfulness; **etw aus G~keit tun** do sth as a favour.
gefälligst ad kindly.
gefangen [gə'faŋən] a captured; (fig) captivated; **G~e(r)** m prisoner, captive; ~**halten** vt unreg keep prisoner; **G~nahme** f -, -n capture; ~**nehmen** vt unreg take prisoner; **G~schaft** f captivity.
Gefängnis [gə'fɛŋnɪs] nt -ses, -se prison; ~**strafe** f prison sentence; ~**wärter** m prison warder.
Gefäß [gə'fɛːs] nt -es, -e vessel (auch ANAT), container.
gefaßt [gə'fast] a composed, calm; **auf etw** (akk) ~ **sein** be prepared od ready for sth.
Gefecht [gə'fɛçt] nt -(e)s, -e fight; (MIL) engagement.
Gefieder [gə'fiːdər] nt -s, - plumage, feathers pl.
gefleckt [gə'flɛkt] a spotted, mottled.
geflogen v siehe **fliegen**.
geflossen v siehe **fließen**.
Geflügel [gə'flyːgəl] nt -s poultry.
Gefolge [gə'fɔlgə] nt -s, - retinue.
Gefolgschaft f following.
gefragt [gə'fraːkt] a in demand.
gefräßig [gə'frɛːsɪç] a voracious.
Gefreite(r) [gə'fraɪtə(r)] m -n, -n lance corporal; (NAUT) able seaman; (AVIAT) aircraftman.
gefrieren [gə'friːrən] vi unreg freeze.
Gefrier- zW: ~**fach** nt icebox; ~**fleisch** nt frozen meat; **g~getrocknet** a freeze-dried; ~**punkt** m freezing point; ~**schutzmittel** nt antifreeze; ~**truhe** f deep-freeze.
gefroren v siehe **frieren**.
gefügig [gə'fyːgɪç] a pliant; (Mensch) obedient.
Gefühl [gə'fyːl] nt -(e)s, -e feeling; **etw im** ~ **haben** have a feel for sth; **g~los** a unfeeling.
gefühls- zW: ~**betont** a emotional; **G~duselei** [-duːzə'laɪ] f emotionalism; ~**mäßig** a instinctive.
gefunden v siehe **finden**.
gegangen v siehe **gehen**.
gegebenenfalls [gə'geːbənənfals] ad if need be.
gegen ['geːgən] präp +akk 1 against; **nichts** ~ **jdn haben** have nothing against sb; **X** ~ **Y** (SPORT, JUR) X against Y

versus Y; **ein Mittel ~ Schnupfen** something for colds
2 (*in Richtung auf*) towards; **~ Osten** to(wards) the east; **~ Abend** towards evening; **~ einen Baum fahren** drive into a tree
3 (*ungefähr*) round about, around; **~ 3 Uhr** around 3 o'clock
4 (*gegenüber*) towards; **gerecht ~ alle** fair to all
5 (*im Austausch für*) for; **~ bar** for cash; **~ Quittung** against a receipt
6 (*verglichen mit*) compared with.
Gegenangriff *m* counter-attack.
Gegenbeweis *m* counter-evidence.
Gegend ['ge:gənt] *f* -, **-en** area, district.
Gegen- *zW:* **g~ei'nander** *ad* against one another; **~fahrbahn** *f* oncoming carriageway; **~frage** *f* counterquestion; **~gewicht** *nt* counterbalance; **~gift** *nt* antidote; **~leistung** *f* service in return; **~satz** *m* contrast; **~sätze überbrücken** overcome differences; **g~sätzlich** *a* contrary, opposite; (*widersprüchlich*) contradictory; **g~seitig** *a* mutual, reciprocal; **sich g~seitig helfen** help each other; **~seitigkeit** *f* reciprocity; **~spieler** *m* opponent; **~stand** *m* object; **g~ständlich** *a* objective, concrete; **~stimme** *f* vote against; **~stoß** *m* counterblow; **~stück** *nt* counterpart; **~teil** *nt* opposite; **im ~teil** on the contrary; **g~teilig** *a* opposite, contrary.
gegenüber [ge:gən''y:bər] *präp +dat* opposite; (*zu*) to(wards); (*angesichts*) in the face of // *ad* opposite; **G~** *nt* **-s**, - person opposite; **~liegen** *vr unreg* face each other; **~stehen** *vr unreg* be opposed (to each other); **~stellen** *vt* confront; (*fig*) contrast; **G~stellung** *f* confrontation; (*fig*) contrast; **~treten** *vi unreg* (*+dat*) face.
Gegen- *zW:* **~verkehr** *m* oncoming traffic; **~vorschlag** *m* counterproposal; **~wart** *f* present; **g~wärtig** *a* present; **das ist mir nicht g~wärtig** that has slipped my mind // *ad* at present; **~wert** *m* equivalent; **~wind** *m* headwind; **g~zeichnen** *vti* countersign.
gegessen *v siehe* **essen.**
Gegner ['ge:gnər] *m* **-s**, - opponent; **g~isch** *a* opposing; **~schaft** *f* opposition.
gegrillt [gə'grɪlt] *a* grilled.
Gehackte(s) [ge'haktə(s)] *nt* mince(d meat).
Gehalt [gə'halt] *m* **-(e)s, -e** content // *nt* **-(e)s, -er** salary.
Gehalts- *zW:* **~empfänger** *m* salary earner; **~erhöhung** *f* salary increase; **~zulage** *f* salary increment.

gehaltvoll *a* (*nahrhaft*) nutritious.
gehässig *a* spiteful, nasty; **G~keit** *f* spite(fulness).
Gehäuse [gə'hɔyzə] *nt* **-s**, - case; casing; (*von Apfel etc*) core.
geheim [gə'haɪm] *a* secret; **G~dienst** *m* secret service, intelligence service; **~halten** *vt unreg* keep secret; **G~nis** *nt* **-ses, -se** secret; mystery; **~nisvoll** *a* mysterious; **G~nummer** *f* (*TEL*) ex-directory (*Brit*) or unlisted (*US*) number; **G~polizei** *f* secret police.
gehen ['ge:ən] *unreg vti* go; (*zu Fuß ~*) walk; **~ nach** (*Fenster*) face // *v unpers:* **wie geht es** (**dir**)? how are you *od* things?; **mir/ihm geht es gut** I'm/he's (doing) fine; **geht das?** is that possible?; **geht's noch?** can you manage?; **es geht** not too bad, O.K.; **das geht nicht** that's not on; **es geht um etw** sth is concerned, it's about sth.
geheuer [gə'hɔyər] *a:* **nicht ~** eerie; (*fragwürdig*) dubious.
Gehilfe [gə'hɪlfə] *m* **-n**, **-n**, **Gehilfin** *f* assistant.
Gehirn [gə'hɪrn] *nt* **-(e)s, -e** brain; **~erschütterung** *f* concussion; **~wäsche** *f* brainwashing.
geholfen *v siehe* **helfen.**
Gehör [gə'hø:r] *nt* **-(e)s** hearing; **musikalisches ~** ear; **~ finden** gain a hearing; **jdm ~ schenken** give sb a hearing.
gehorchen [gə'hɔrçən] *vi* obey (*jdm sb*).
gehören [gə'hø:rən] *vi* belong // *vr unpers* be right *od* proper.
gehörig *a* proper; **~ zu** *od +dat* belonging to; part of.
gehorsam [gə'ho:rza:m] *a* obedient; **G~** *m* **-s** obedience.
Gehsteig ['ge:ʃtaɪk] *m*, **Gehweg** *m* ['ge:ve:k] pavement, sidewalk (*US*).
Geier ['gaɪər] *m* **-s**, - vulture.
Geige ['gaɪgə] *f* -, **-n** violin.
Geiger *m* **-s**, - violinist; **~zähler** *m* geiger counter.
geil [gaɪl] *a* randy (*Brit*), horny (*US*).
Geisel ['gaɪzəl] *f* -, **-n** hostage.
Geist [gaɪst] *m* **-(e)s, -er** spirit; (*Gespenst*) ghost; (*Verstand*) mind.
geisterhaft *a* ghostly.
Geistes- *zW:* **g~abwesend** *a* absentminded; **~blitz** *m* brainwave; **~gegenwart** *f* presence of mind; **g~krank** *a* mentally ill; **~kranke(r)** *mf* mentally ill person; **~krankheit** *f* mental illness; **~zustand** *m* state of mind.
geist- *zW:* **~ig** *a* intellectual; mental; (*Getränke*) alcoholic; **~ig behindert** mentally handicapped; **~lich** *a* spiritual, religious; clerical; **G~liche(r)**

m clergyman; **G~lichkeit** *f* clergy; **~los** *a* uninspired, dull; **~reich** *a* clever; witty; **~voll** *a* intellectual; (*weise*) wise.

Geiz [gaɪts] *m* **-es** miserliness, meanness; **g~en** *vi* be miserly; **~hals** *m*, **~kragen** *m* miser; **g~ig** *a* miserly, mean.

gekannt *v siehe* **kennen**.

geknickt [gə'knɪkt] *a* (*fig*) dejected.

gekocht [gə'kɔxt] *a* boiled.

gekonnt [gə'kɔnt] *a* skilful // *v siehe* **können**.

Gekritzel [gə'krɪtsəl] *nt* **-s** scrawl, scribble.

gekünstelt [ge'kynstəlt] *a* artificial, affected.

Gelächter [gə'lɛçtər] *nt* **-s**, **-** laughter.

geladen [ge'la:dən] *a* loaded; (*ELEK*) live; (*fig*) furious.

gelähmt [gə'lɛːmt] *a* paralysed.

Gelände [gə'lɛndə] *nt* **-s**, **-** land, terrain; (*von Fabrik, Sport~*) grounds *pl*; (*Bau~*) site; **~lauf** *m* cross-country race.

Geländer [gə'lɛndər] *nt* **-s**, **-** railing; (*Treppen~*) banister(s).

gelangen [gə'laŋən] *vi* (*an* +*akk so zu*) reach; (*erwerben*) attain; **in jds Besitz ~** come into sb's possession.

gelassen [gə'lasən] *a* calm, composed; **G~heit** *f* calmness, composure.

Gelatine [ʒela'ti:nə] *f* gelatine.

geläufig [gə'lɔyfɪç] *a* (*üblich*) common; **das ist mir nicht ~** I'm not familiar with that.

gelaunt [gə'laʊnt] *a*: **schlecht/gut ~** in a bad/good mood; **wie ist er ~?** what sort of mood is he in?

gelb [gɛlp] *a* yellow; (*Ampellicht*) amber; **~lich** *a* yellowish; **G~sucht** *f* jaundice.

Geld [gɛlt] *nt* **-(e)s**, **-er** money; **etw zu ~ machen** sell sth off; **~anlage** *f* investment; **~automat** *m* cash dispenser; **~beutel** *m*, **~börse** *f* purse; **~geber** *m* **-s**, **-** financial backer; **g~gierig** *a* avaricious; **~schein** *m* banknote; **~schrank** *m* safe, strongbox; **~strafe** *f* fine; **~stück** *nt* coin; **~wechsel** *m* exchange (of money).

Gelee [ʒe'le:] *nt od m* **-s**, **-s** jelly.

gelegen [gə'le:gən] *a* situated; (*passend*) convenient, opportune; **etw kommt jdm ~** sth is convenient for sb // *v siehe* **liegen**.

Gelegenheit [gə'le:gənhaɪt] *f* opportunity; (*Anlaß*) occasion; **bei jeder ~** at every opportunity.

Gelegenheits- *zW*: **~arbeit** *f* casual work; **~arbeiter** *m* casual worker; **~kauf** *m* bargain.

gelegentlich [gə'le:gəntlɪç] *a* occasional // *ad* occasionally; (*bei Gelegenheit*) some time (or other) // *präp*

+gen on the occasion of.

gelehrt [gə'le:rt] *a* learned; **G~e(r)** *mf* scholar; **G~heit** *f* scholarliness.

Geleise [gə'laɪzə] *nt* **-s**, **-** *siehe* **Gleis**.

Geleit [gə'laɪt] *nt* **-(e)s**, **-e** escort; **g~en** *vt* escort; **~schutz** *m* escort.

Gelenk [gə'lɛŋk] *nt* **-(e)s**, **-e** joint; **g~ig** *a* supple.

gelernt [gə'lɛrnt] *a* skilled.

Geliebte(r) [gə'li:ptə(r)] *mf* sweetheart, beloved.

geliehen *v siehe* **leihen**.

gelind(e) [gə'lɪnt, gə'lɪndə] *a* mild, light; (*fig: Wut*) fierce; **~e gesagt** to put it mildly.

gelingen [gə'lɪŋən] *vi unreg* succeed; **es ist mir gelungen, etw zu tun** I succeeded in doing sth.

gell [gɛl] *interj* isn't it?; aren't you? *etc*.

geloben [gə'lo:bən] *vt* vow, swear.

gelten ['gɛltən] *unreg vt* (*wert sein*) be worth; **jdm viel/wenig ~** mean a lot/not mean much to sb; **was gilt die Wette?** do you want to bet? // *vi* (*gültig sein*) be valid; (*erlaubt sein*) be allowed; **jdm ~** (*gemünzt sein auf*) be meant for *od* aimed at sb; **etw ~ lassen** accept sth; **als *od* für etw ~** be considered to be sth; **jdm *od* für jdn ~** (*betreffen*) apply to *od* for sb // *v unpers*: **es gilt, etw zu tun** it is necessary to do sth; **~d** a prevailing; **etw ~d machen** to assert sth; **sich ~d machen** make itself/o.s. felt.

Geltung ['gɛltʊŋ] *f*: **~ haben** have validity; **sich/etw** (*dat*) **verschaffen** establish oneself/sth; **etw zur ~ bringen** show sth to its best advantage; **zur ~ kommen** be seen/heard *etc* to its best advantage.

Geltungsbedürfnis *nt* desire for admiration.

Gelübde [gə'lypdə] *nt* **-s**, **-** vow.

gelungen [gə'lʊŋən] *a* successful.

gem. *abk von* **gemischt**.

gemächlich [gə'mɛːçlɪç] *a* leisurely.

Gemahl [gə'ma:l] *m* **-(e)s**, **-e** husband; **~in** *f* wife.

Gemälde [gə'mɛːldə] *nt* **-s**, **-** picture, painting.

gemäß [gə'mɛːs] *präp* +*dat* in accordance with // *a* appropriate (*dat* to).

gemäßigt *a* moderate; (*Klima*) temperate.

gemein [gə'maɪn] *a* common; (*niederträchtig*) mean; **etw ~ haben** (**mit**) have sth in common (with).

Gemeinde [gə'maɪndə] *f* **-**, **-n** district, community; (*Pfarr~*) parish; (*Kirchen~*) congregation; **~steuer** *f* local rates *pl*; **~verwaltung** *f* local administration; **~wahl** *f* local election.

Gemein- *zW:* **g~gefährlich** *a* dangerous to the public; **~heit** *f* commonness; mean thing to do/to say; **~platz** *m* commonplace, platitude; **g~sam** *a* joint, common (*auch MATH*); **g~same Sache mit jdm machen** be in cahoots with sb // *ad* together, jointly; **etw g~sam haben** have sth in common; **~samkeit** *f* community, having in common; **~schaft** *f* community; **in ~schaft mit** jointly *od* together with; **g~schaftlich** *a siehe* **g~sam; ~schaftsarbeit** *f* teamwork; team effort; **~sinn** *m* public spirit; **~wohl** *nt* common good.

Gemenge [gə'mɛŋə] *nt* **-s,** - mixture; (*Hand~*) scuffle.

gemessen [gə'mɛsən] *a* measured.

Gemetzel [gə'mɛtsəl] *nt* **-s,** - slaughter, carnage, butchery.

Gemisch [gə'mɪʃ] *nt* **-es, -e** mixture; **g~t** *a* mixed.

gemocht *v siehe* **mögen.**

Gemse ['gɛmzə] *f* -, -n chamois.

Gemunkel [gə'muŋkəl] *nt* **-s** gossip.

Gemurmel [gə'murməl] *nt* **-s** murmur(ing).

Gemüse [gə'myːzə] *nt* **-s,** - vegetables *pl;* **~garten** *m* vegetable garden; **~händler** *m* greengrocer.

gemußt *v siehe* **müssen.**

Gemüt [gə'myːt] *nt* **-(e)s, -er** disposition, nature; person; **sich** (*dat*) **etw zu ~e führen** (*umg*) indulge in sth; **die ~er erregen** arouse strong feelings; **g~lich** *a* comfortable, cosy; (*Person*) good-natured; **~lichkeit** *f* comfortableness, cosiness; amiability.

Gemüts- *zW:* **~mensch** *m* sentimental person; **~ruhe** *f* composure; **~szustand** *m* state of mind.

gemütvoll *a* warm, tender.

genannt *v siehe* **nennen.**

genau [gə'nau] *a,ad* exact(ly), precise(ly); **etw ~ nehmen** take sth seriously; **~genommen** *ad* strictly speaking; **G~igkeit** *f* exactness, accuracy; **~so** *ad* just the same; **~so gut** just as good.

genehm [gə'neːm] *a* agreeable, acceptable; **~igen** *vt* approve, authorize; **sich** (*dat*) **etw ~igen** indulge in sth; **G~igung** *f* approval, authorization; (*Schriftstück*) permit.

General [gene'raːl] *m* **-s, -e** *od* ⁼e general; **~direktor** *m* director general; **~konsulat** *nt* consulate general; **~probe** *f* dress rehearsal; **~streik** *m* general strike; **g~überholen** *vt* thoroughly overhaul.

Generation [generatsi'oːn] *f* generation.

Generator [gene'raːtɔr] *m* generator, dynamo.

generell [gene'rɛl] *a* general.

genesen [gə'neːzən] *vi unreg* convalesce, recover, get well.

Genesung *f* recovery, convalescence.

genetisch [ge'neːtɪʃ] *a* genetic.

Genf [gɛnf] *nt* Geneva; **~er See** Lake Geneva.

genial [geni'aːl] *a* brilliant; **G~i'tät** *f* brilliance, genius.

Genick [gə'nɪk] *nt* **-(e)s, -e** (back of the) neck; **~starre** *f* stiff neck.

Genie [ʒe'niː] *nt* **-s, -s** genius.

genieren [ʒe'niːrən] *vt* bother; **geniert es Sie, wenn ...?** do you mind if ...? // *vr* feel awkward *od* self-conscious.

genießbar *a* edible; drinkable.

genießen [gə'niːsən] *vt unreg* enjoy; eat; drink.

Genießer *m* **-s,** - epicure; pleasure lover; **g~isch** *a* appreciative // *ad* with relish.

genommen *v siehe* **nehmen.**

Genosse [gə'nɔsə] *m* **-n, -n, Genossin** *f* comrade (*bes POL*), companion; **Genossenschaft** *f* cooperative (association).

genug [gə'nuːk] *ad* enough.

Genüge [gə'nyːgə] *f* -: **jdm/etw ~ tun** *od* **leisten** satisfy sb/sth; **g~n** *vi* be enough (+*dat* for); **g~nd** *a* sufficient.

genügsam [gə'nyːkzaːm] *a* modest, easily satisfied; **G~keit** *f* moderation.

Genugtuung [gə'nuːktuːuŋ] *f* satisfaction.

Genuß [gə'nus] *m* **-sses, ⁼sse** pleasure; (*Zusichnehmen*) consumption; **in den ~ von etw kommen** receive the benefit of sth; **~mittel** *pl* (semi-) luxury items *pl.*

genüßlich [gə'nyslɪç] *ad* with relish.

geöffnet [gə'œfnət] *a* open.

Geograph [geo'graːf] *m* **-en, -en** geographer; **~ie** [-'fiː] *f* geography; **g~isch** *a* geographical.

Geologe [geo'loːgə] *m* **-n, -n** geologist; **Geolo'gie** *f* geology.

Geometrie [geome'triː] *f* geometry.

Gepäck [gə'pɛk] *nt* **-(e)s** luggage, baggage; **~abfertigung** *f*, **~annahme** *f*, **~aufgabe** *f*, **~ausgabe** *f* luggage office; **~aufbewahrung** *f* left-luggage office (*Brit*), baggage check (*US*); **~netz** *nt* luggage-rack; **~rückgabe** *f* luggage office; **~träger** *m* porter; (*Fahrrad*) carrier; **~wagen** *m* luggage van (*Brit*), baggage car (*US*).

gepflegt [gə'pfleːkt] *a* well-groomed; (*Park etc*) well looked after.

gerade [gə'raːdə] ♦ *a* straight; (*aufrecht*) upright; **eine ~ Zahl** an even number

♦ *ad* **1** (*genau*) just, exactly; (*speziell*) especially; **~ deshalb** that's just *od* exactly why; **das ist es ja ~!** that's just it!; **~ du** you especially;

warum ~ **ich?** why me (of all people)?; **jetzt** ~ **nicht!** not now!; ~ **neben** right next to

2 (*eben*, *soeben*) just; **er wollte** ~ **aufstehen** he was just about to get up; ~ **erst** only just; ~ **noch** (only) just.

Gerade *f* **-n, -n** straight line; **g~aus** *ad* straight ahead; **g~heraus** *ad* straight out, bluntly; **g~zu** *ad* (*beinahe*) virtually, almost.

gerannt *v siehe* **rennen**.

Gerät [gə'rɛ:t] *nt* **-(e)s, -e** device; (*Werkzeug*) tool; (*SPORT*) apparatus; (*Zubehör*) equipment *no pl*.

geraten [gə'ra:tən] *vi unreg* (*gelingen*) turn out well (*jdm* for sb); (*gedeihen*) thrive; **gut/schlecht** ~ turn out well/badly; **an jdn** ~ come across sb; **in etw** (*akk*) ~ get into sth; **in Angst** ~ get frightened; **nach jdm** ~ take after sb.

Geratewohl [gəra:tə'vo:l] *nt*: **aufs** ~ on the off chance; (*bei Wahl*) at random.

geräumig [gə'rɔymɪç] *a* roomy.

Geräusch [gə'rɔyʃ] *nt* **-(e)s, -e** sound, noise; **g~los** *a* silent.

gerben ['gɛrbən] *vt* tan.

gerecht [gə'rɛçt] *a* just, fair; **jdm/etw** ~ **werden** do justice to sb/sth; **G~igkeit** *f* justice, fairness.

Gerede [gə're:də] *nt* **-s** talk, gossip.

gereizt [gə'raɪtst] *a* irritable; **G~heit** *f* irritation.

Gericht [gə'rɪçt] *nt* **-(e)s, -e** court; (*Essen*) dish; **mit jdm ins** ~ **gehen** (*fig*) judge sb harshly; **das Jüngste** ~ the Last Judgement; **g~lich** *a,ad* judicial(ly), legal(ly).

Gerichts- *zW*: **~barkeit** *f* jurisdiction; **~hof** *m* court (of law); **~kosten** *pl* (legal) costs *pl*; **~saal** *m* courtroom; **~verfahren** *nt* legal proceedings *pl*; **~verhandlung** *f* court proceedings *pl*; **~svollzieher** *m* bailiff.

gerieben [gə'ri:bən] *a* grated; (*umg: schlau*) smart, wily // *v siehe* **reiben**.

gering [gə'rɪŋ] *a* slight, small; (*niedrig*) low; (*Zeit*) short; **~fügig** *a* slight, trivial; **~schätzig** *a* disparaging.

geringste(r, -s) *a* slightest, least; **~nfalls** *ad* at the very least.

gerinnen [gə'rɪnən] *vi unreg* congeal; (*Blut*) clot; (*Milch*) curdle.

Gerippe [gə'rɪpə] *nt* **-s, -** skeleton.

gerissen [gə'rɪsən] *a* wily, smart.

geritten *v siehe* **reiten**.

gern(e) ['gɛrn(ə)] *ad* willingly, gladly; ~ **haben**, ~ **mögen** like; **etwas** ~ **tun** like doing something; **ich möchte** ~ **...** I'd like ...; **ja,** ~ yes, please; yes, I'd like to; ~ **geschehen** it's a pleasure.

gerochen *v siehe* **riechen**.

Geröll [gə'rœl] *nt* **-(e)s, -e** scree.

Gerste ['gɛrstə] *f* **-, -n** barley; **Gerstenkorn** *nt* (*im Auge*) stye.

Geruch [gə'rʊx] *m* **-(e)s, ~e** smell, odour; **g~los** *a* odourless; **g~tilgend** *a* deodorant.

Gerücht [gə'rʏçt] *nt* **-(e)s, -e** rumour.

geruhen [gə'ru:ən] *vi* deign.

Gerümpel [gə'rʏmpəl] *nt* **-s** junk.

Gerüst [gə'rʏst] *nt* **-(e)s, -e** (*Bau~*) scaffold(ing); frame.

gesamt [gə'zamt] *a* whole, entire; (*Kosten*) total; (*Werke*) complete; **im ~en** all in all; **g~deutsch** *a* all-German; **G~eindruck** *m* general impression; **G~heit** *f* totality, whole; **G~schule** *f* ≈ comprehensive school.

gesandt *v siehe* **senden**.

Gesandte(r) [gə'zantə(r)] *m* envoy.

Gesandtschaft [gə'zantʃaft] *f* legation.

Gesang [gə'zaŋ] *m* **-(e)s, ~e** song; (*Singen*) singing; **~buch** *nt* (*REL*) hymn book.

Gesäß [gə'zɛ:s] *nt* **-es, -e** seat, bottom.

Geschäft [gə'ʃɛft] *nt* **-(e)s, -e** business; (*Laden*) shop; (*~sabschluß*) deal; **~emacher** *m* **-s,** wheeler-dealer; **g~ig** *a* active, busy; (*pej*) officious; **g~lich** *a* commercial // *ad* on business.

Geschäfts- *zW*: **~bericht** *m* financial report; **~essen** *nt* business lunch; **~führer** *m* manager; (*Klub*) secretary; **~geheimnis** *nt* trade secret; **~jahr** *nt* financial year; **~lage** *f* business conditions *pl*; **~mann** *m* businessman; **g~mäßig** *a* businesslike; **~reise** *f* business trip; **~schluß** *m* closing time; **~stelle** *f* office, place of business; **g~tüchtig** *a* efficient; **~viertel** *nt* business quarter; shopping centre; **~wagen** *m* company car; **~zeiten** *pl* business hours.

geschehen [gə'ʃe:ən] *vi unreg* happen; **es war um ihn** ~ that was the end of him.

gescheit [gə'ʃaɪt] *a* clever.

Geschenk [gə'ʃɛŋk] *nt* **-(e)s, -e** present, gift.

Geschichte [gə'ʃɪçtə] *f* **-, -n** story; (*Sache*) affair; (*Historie*) history.

geschichtlich *a* historical.

Geschick [gə'ʃɪk] *nt* **-(e)s, -e** aptitude; (*Schicksal*) fate; **~lichkeit** *f* skill, dexterity; **g~t** *a* skilful.

geschieden [gə'ʃi:dən] *a* divorced.

geschienen *v siehe* **scheinen**.

Geschirr [gə'ʃɪr] *nt* **-(e)s, -e** crockery; pots and pans *pl*; (*Pferd*) harness; **~spülmaschine** *f* dishwashing machine; **~tuch** *nt* dish cloth.

Geschlecht [gə'ʃlɛçt] *nt* **-(e)s, -er** sex; (*GRAM*) gender; (*KUNST*) species; family; **g~lich** *a* sexual.

Geschlechts- *zW:* **~krankheit** *f* venereal disease; **~teil** *nt* genitals *pl;* **~verkehr** *m* sexual intercourse.

geschlossen [gə'ʃlɔsən] *a* shut // *v siehe* **schließen.**

Geschmack [gə'ʃmak] *m* **-(e)s,** ⁻e taste; **nach jds** ~ to sb's taste; ~ **finden an etw** (*dat*) (come to) like sth; **g~los** *a* tasteless; (*fig*) in bad taste; **~(s)sache** *f* matter of taste; **~sinn** *m* sense of taste; **g~voll** *a* tasteful.

geschmeidig [gə'ʃmaɪdɪç] *a* supple; (*formbar*) malleable.

geschnitten *v siehe* **schneiden.**

Geschöpf [gə'ʃœpf] *nt* **-(e)s, -e** creature.

Geschoß [gə'ʃɔs] *nt* **-sses, -sse** (*MIL*) projectile, missile; (*Stockwerk*) floor.

geschossen *v siehe* **schießen.**

geschraubt [gə'ʃraʊpt] *a* stilted, artificial.

Geschrei [gə'ʃraɪ] *nt* **-s** cries *pl,* shouting; (*fig: Aufheben*) noise, fuss.

geschrieben *v siehe* **schreiben.**

Geschütz [gə'ʃʏts] *nt* **-es, -e** gun, cannon; **ein schweres ~ auffahren** (*fig*) bring out the big guns; **~feuer** *nt* artillery fire, gunfire; **g~t** *a* protected.

Geschwader [gə'ʃvaːdər] *nt* **-s, -** (*NAUT*) squadron; (*AVIAT*) group.

Geschwafel [gə'ʃvaːfəl] *nt* **-s** silly talk.

Geschwätz [gə'ʃvɛts] *nt* **-es** chatter, gossip; **g~ig** *a* talkative.

geschweige [gə'ʃvaɪgə] *ad:* ~ (**denn**) let alone, not to mention.

geschwind [gə'ʃvɪnt] *a* quick, swift; **G~igkeit** [-dɪçkaɪt] *f* speed, velocity; **G~igkeitsbegrenzung** *f* speed limit; **G~igkeitsüberschreitung** *f* exceeding the speed limit.

Geschwister [gə'ʃvɪstər] *pl* brothers and sisters *pl.*

geschwollen [gə'ʃvɔlən] *a* pompous.

geschwommen *v siehe* **schwimmen.**

Geschworene(r) [gə'ʃvoːrənə(r)] *mf* juror // *pl* jury.

Geschwulst [gə'ʃvʊlst] *f* **-, ⁻e** swelling; growth, tumour.

Geschwür [gə'ʃvyːr] *nt* **-(e)s, -e** ulcer.

Gesell- [gə'zɛl] *zW:* **~e** *m* **-n, -n** fellow; (*Handwerk~*) journeyman; **g~ig** *a* sociable; **~igkeit** *f* sociability; **~schaft** *f* society; (*Begleitung, COMM*) company; (*Abend~schaft etc*) party; **g~schaftlich** *a* social; **~schaftsordnung** *f* social structure; **~schaftsschicht** *f* social stratum.

gesessen *v siehe* **sitzen.**

Gesetz [gə'zɛts] *nt* **-es, -e** law; **~buch** *nt* statute book; **~entwurf** *m,* **~esvorlage** *f* bill; **g~gebend** *a* legislative; **~gebung** *f* legislation; **g~lich** *a* legal, lawful; **~lichkeit** *f* legality,

lawfulness; **g~los** *a* lawless; **g~mäßig** *a* lawful; **g~t** *a* (*Mensch*) sedate; **g~widrig** *a* illegal, unlawful.

ges. gesch. *abk* (= *gesetzlich geschützt*) registered.

Gesicht [gə'zɪçt] *nt* **-(e)s, -er** face; **das zweite ~** second sight; **das ist mir nie zu ~ gekommen** I've never laid eyes on that.

Gesichts- *zW:* **~ausdruck** *m* (facial) expression; **~farbe** *f* complexion; **~punkt** *m* point of view; **~züge** *pl* features *pl.*

Gesindel [gə'zɪndəl] *nt* **-s** rabble.

gesinnt [gə'zɪnt] *a* disposed, minded.

Gesinnung [gə'zɪnʊŋ] *f* disposition; (*Ansicht*) views *pl;* **Gesinnungswandel** *m* change of opinion, volteface.

gesittet [gə'zɪtət] *a* well-mannered.

Gespann [gə'ʃpan] *nt* **-(e)s, -e** team; (*umg*) couple; **g~t** *a* tense, strained; (*begierig*) eager; **ich bin g~t, ob I** wonder if *od* whether; **auf etw/jdn g~t sein** look forward to sth/meeting sb.

Gespenst [gə'ʃpɛnst] *nt* **-(e)s, -er** ghost, spectre; **g~erhaft** *a* ghostly.

gesperrt [gə'ʃpɛrt] *a* closed off.

Gespött [gə'ʃpœt] *nt* **-(e)s** mockery; **zum ~ werden** become a laughing stock.

Gespräch [gə'ʃprɛːç] *nt* **-(e)s, -e** conversation; discussion(s); (*Anruf*) call; **g~ig** *a* talkative; **~igkeit** *f* talkativeness; **Gesprächsthema** *nt* subject *od* topic (of conversation).

gesprochen *v siehe* **sprechen.**

gesprungen *v siehe* **springen.**

Gespür [gə'ʃpyːr] *nt* **-s** feeling.

Gestalt [gə'ʃtalt] *f* **-, -en** form, shape; (*Person*) figure; **in ~ von** in the form of; ~ **annehmen** take shape; **g~en** *vt* (*formen*) shape, form; (*organisieren*) arrange, organize // *vr* turn out (*zu* to be); **~ung** *f* formation; organization.

gestanden *v siehe* **stehen.**

Geständnis [gə'ʃtɛntnɪs] *nt* **-ses, -se** confession.

Gestank [gə'ʃtaŋk] *m* **-(e)s** stench.

gestatten [gə'ʃtatən] *vt* permit, allow; ~ **Sie?** may I?; **sich** (*dat*) ~, **etw zu tun** take the liberty of doing sth.

Geste ['gɛstə] *f* **-, -n** gesture.

gestehen [gə'ʃteːən] *vt* unreg confess.

Gestein [gə'ʃtaɪn] *nt* **-(e)s, -e** rock.

Gestell [gə'ʃtɛl] *nt* **-(e)s, -e** frame; (*Regal*) rack, stand.

gestern ['gɛstərn] *ad* yesterday; ~ **abend/morgen** yesterday evening/morning.

Gestirn [gə'ʃtɪrn] *nt* **-(e)s, -e** star; (*Sternbild*) constellation.

gestohlen *v siehe* **stehlen.**

gestorben *v siehe* **sterben.**

gestreift [gə'ʃtraift] a striped.

gestrichen [gə'ʃtriçən] a cancelled.

gestrig ['gɛstriç] a yesterday's.

Gestrüpp [gə'ʃtrʏp] nt -(e)s, -e undergrowth.

Gestüt [gə'ʃtyːt] nt -(e)s, -e stud farm.

Gesuch [gə'zuːx] nt -(e)s, -e petition; (Antrag) application; **g~t** a (COMM) in demand; wanted; (fig) contrived.

gesund [gə'zʊnt] a healthy; **wieder ~ werden** get better; **G~heit** f health(iness); **G~heit!** bless you!; **~heitlich** a,ad health attr, physical; **wie geht es Ihnen ~heitlich?** how's your health?; **~heitsschädlich** a unhealthy; **G~heitswesen** nt health service; **G~heitszustand** m state of health.

gesungen v siehe **singen**.

getan v siehe **tun**.

Getöse [gə'tøːzə] nt -s din, racket.

Getränk [gə'trɛŋk] nt -(e)s, -e drink; **Getränkekarte** f wine list.

getrauen [gə'trauən] vr dare, venture.

Getreide [gə'traidə] nt -s, - cereals pl, grain; **~speicher** m granary.

getrennt [gə'trɛnt] a separate.

Getriebe [gə'triːbə] nt -s, - (Leute) bustle; (AUT) gearbox.

getrieben v siehe **treiben**.

getroffen v siehe **treffen**.

getrost [gə'troːst] ad without any bother.

getrunken v siehe **trinken**.

Getue [gə'tuːə] nt -s fuss.

geübt [gə'yːpt] a experienced.

Gewächs [gə'vɛks] nt -es, -e growth; (Pflanze) plant.

gewachsen [gə'vaksən] a: **jdm/etw ~ sein** sb's equal/equal to sth.

Gewächshaus nt greenhouse.

gewagt [gə'vaːkt] a daring, risky.

gewählt [gə'vɛːlt] a (Sprache) refined, elegant.

Gewähr [gə'vɛːr] f - guarantee; **keine ~ übernehmen für** accept no responsibility for; **g~en** vt grant; (geben) provide; **g~leisten** vt guarantee.

Gewahrsam [gə'vaːrzaːm] m -s, -e safekeeping; (Polizei~) custody.

Gewährsmann m informant, source.

Gewährung f granting.

Gewalt [gə'valt] f -, -en power; (große Kraft) force; (~taten) violence; **mit aller ~** with all one's might; **~anwendung** f use of force; **g~ig** a tremendous; (Irrtum) huge; **~marsch** m forced march; **g~sam** a forcible; **g~tätig** a violent.

gewandt [gə'vant] a deft, skilful; (erfahren) experienced; **G~heit** f dexterity, skill.

gewann etc v siehe **gewinnen**.

Gewässer [gə'vɛsər] nt -s, - waters pl.

Gewebe [gə'veːbə] nt -s, - (Stoff) fabric; (BIOL) tissue.

Gewehr [gə'veːr] nt -(e)s, -e gun; rifle; **~lauf** m rifle barrel.

Geweih [gə'vai] nt -(e)s, -e antlers pl.

Gewerb- [gə'verb] zW: **~e** nt -s, - trade, occupation; **Handel und ~e** trade and industry; **~eschule** f technical school; **g~lich** a industrial; trade attr; **gewerbsmäßig** a professional; **Gewerbszweig** m line of trade.

Gewerkschaft [gə'vɛrkʃaft] f trade union; **~ler** m -s, - trade unionist; **Gewerkschaftsbund** m trade unions federation.

Gewicht [gə'viçt] nt -(e)s, -e weight; (fig) importance; **g~ig** a weighty.

gewieft [gə'viːft] a, **gewiegt** [gə'viːkt] a shrewd, cunning.

gewillt [gə'vɪlt] a willing, prepared.

Gewimmel [gə'vɪməl] nt -s swarm.

Gewinde [gə'vɪndə] nt -s, - (Kranz) wreath; (von Schraube) thread.

Gewinn [gə'vɪn] m -(e)s, -e profit; (bei Spiel) winnings pl; **etw mit ~ verkaufen** sell sth at a profit; **~- und Verlustrechnung** (COMM) profit and loss account; **~beteiligung** f profit-sharing; **g~bringend** a profitable; **g~en** unreg vt win; (erwerben) gain; (Kohle, Öl) extract // vi win; (profitieren) gain; **an etw** (dat) **g~en** gain in sth; **~er(in** f) m -s, - winner; **~spanne** f profit margin; **~(n)ummer** f winning number; **~ung** f winning; gaining; (von Kohle etc) extraction.

Gewirr [gə'vɪr] nt -(e)s, -e tangle; (von Straßen) maze.

gewiß [gə'vɪs] a,ad certain(ly).

Gewissen [gə'vɪsən] nt -s, - conscience; **g~haft** a conscientious; **~haftigkeit** f conscientiousness; **g~los** a unscrupulous.

Gewissens- zW: **~bisse** pl pangs of conscience pl, qualms pl; **~frage** f matter of conscience; **~freiheit** f freedom of conscience; **~konflikt** m moral conflict.

gewissermaßen [gəvɪsər'maːsən] ad more or less, in a way.

Gewißheit [gə'vɪshait] f certainty.

Gewitter [gə'vɪtər] nt -s, - thunderstorm; **g~n** vi unpers: **es gewittert** there's a thunderstorm.

gewitzt [gə'vɪtst] a shrewd, cunning.

gewogen [gə'voːgən] a well-disposed (+dat towards).

gewöhnen [gə'vøːnən] vt: **jdn an etw** (akk) **~** accustom sb to sth; (erziehen zu) teach sb sth // vr: **sich an etw** (akk) **~** get used od accustomed to sth.

Gewohnheit [gə'voːnhait] f habit; (Brauch) custom; **aus ~** from habit;

zur ~ werden become a habit.
Gewohnheits- *in* *zW* habitual;
~mensch *m* creature of habit;
~recht *nt* common law.
gewöhnlich [gə'vø:nlıç] *a* usual; ordinary; *(pej)* common; **wie ~** as usual.
gewohnt [gə'vo:nt] *a* usual; **etw ~ sein** be used to sth.
Gewöhnung *f* getting accustomed
(an +akk to).
Gewölbe [gə'vœlbə] *nt* **-s,** - vault.
gewonnen *v siehe* **gewinnen.**
geworden *v siehe* **werden.**
geworfen *v siehe* **werfen.**
Gewühl [gə'vy:l] *nt* **-(e)s** throng.
Gewürz [gə'vʏrts] *nt* **-es, -e** spice, seasoning; **~nelke** *f* clove; **~t** *a* spiced.
gewußt *v siehe* **wissen.**
Gezeiten [gə'tsaıtən] *pl* tides *pl.*
gezielt [gə'tsi:lt] *a* with a particular aim in mind, purposeful; *(Kritik)* pointed.
geziert [gə'tsi:rt] *a* affected.
gezogen *v siehe* **ziehen.**
Gezwitscher [gə'tsvıtʃər] *nt* **-s** twitter(ing), chirping.
gezwungen [gə'tsvʊŋən] *a* forced;
~ermaßen *ad* of necessity.
gibst *etc v siehe* **geben.**
Gicht ['gıçt] *f* - gout; **g~isch** *a* gouty.
Giebel ['gi:bəl] *m* **-s,** - gable; **~dach**
nt gable(d) roof; **~fenster** *nt* gable
window.
Gier [gi:r] *f* - greed; **g~ig** *a* greedy.
Gieß- ['gi:s] *zW:* **g~en** *vt unreg* pour;
(Blumen) water; *(Metall)* cast;
(Wachs) mould; **~kanne** *f* watering
can.
Gift [gıft] *nt* **-(e)s, -e** poison; **g~ig** *a*
poisonous; *(fig: boshaft)* venomous;
~zahn *m* fang.
ging *etc v siehe* **gehen.**
Ginster ['gınstər] *m* **-s,** - broom.
Gipfel ['gıpfəl] *m* **-s,** - summit, peak;
(fig) height; **g~n** *vi* culminate;
~treffen *nt* summit (meeting).
Gips [gıps] *m* **-es, -e** plaster; *(MED)*
plaster of Paris); **~abdruck** *m* plaster cast; **g~en** *vt* plaster; **~verband**
m plaster (cast).
Giraffe [gi'rafə] *f* -, **-n** giraffe.
Girlande [gır'landə] *f* -, **-n** garland.
Giro ['ʒi:ro] *nt* **-s, -s** giro; **~konto** *nt*
current account.
Gischt [gıʃt] *m* **-(e)s, -e** spray, foam.
Gitarre [gi'tarə] *f* -, **-n** guitar.
Gitter ['gıtər] *nt* **-s,** - grating, bars *pl;*
(für Pflanzen) trellis; *(Zaun)* railing(s); **~bett** *nt* cot; **~fenster** *nt*
barred window; **~zaun** *m* railing(s).
Glacéhandschuh [gla'se:hantʃu:] *m*
kid glove.
Gladiole [gladi'o:lə] *f* -, **-n** gladiolus.
Glanz [glants] *m* **-es** shine, lustre;
(fig) splendour.

glänzen ['glɛntsən] *vi* shine *(also fig)*,
gleam // *vt* polish; **~d** *a* shining;
(fig) brilliant.
Glanz- *zW:* **~leistung** *f* brilliant
achievement; **g~los** *a* dull; **~zeit** *f*
heyday.
Glas [gla:s] *nt* **-es, ̈er** glass; **~bläser**
m **-s,** - glass blower; **~er** *m* **-s,** -
glazier; **~faser** *f* fibreglass; **g~ieren**
[gla'zi:rən] *vt* glaze; **g~ig** *a* glassy;
~scheibe *f* pane; **~ur** [gla'zu:r] *f*
glaze; *(KOCH)* icing.
glatt [glat] *a* smooth; *(rutschig)* slippery; *(Absage)* flat; *(Lüge)* downright; **G~eis** *nt* (black) ice; **jdn aufs
G~eis führen** *(fig)* take sb for a ride.
Glätte ['glɛtə] *f* -, **-n** smoothness; slipperiness; **g~n** *vt* smooth out.
Glatze ['glatsə] *f* -, **-n** bald head; **eine
~ bekommen** go bald.
Glaube ['glaubə] *m* **-ns, -n** faith *(an
+akk* in); belief *(an +akk* in); **g~n**
vti believe *(an +akk* in, *jdm* sb);
think; **daran g~n müssen** *(umg)* be
for it; **Glaubensbekenntnis** *nt* creed.
glaubhaft ['glaubhaft] *a* credible.
gläubig ['glɔybıç] *a* *(REL)* devout;
(vertrauensvoll) trustful; **G~e(r)** *mf*
believer; **die G~en** the faithful; **G~er**
m **-s,** - creditor.
glaubwürdig ['glaubvʏrdıç] *a* credible; *(Mensch)* trustworthy; **G~keit** *f*
credibility; trustworthiness.
gleich [glaıç] *a* equal; *(identisch)*
(the) same, identical; **es ist mir ~**
it's all the same to me; **2 mal 2 ~ 4** 2
times 2 is *od* equals 4 // *ad* equally;
(sofort) straight away; *(bald)* in a
minute; **~ groß** the same size; **~
nach/an** right after/at; **~altrig** *a* of
the same age; **~artig** *a* similar;
~bedeutend *a* synonymous; **~berechtigt** *a* having equal rights;
G~berechtigung *f* equal rights *pl;*
~bleibend *a* constant; **~en** *unreg vi:*
jdm/etw ~en be like sb/sth // *vr* be
alike; **~falls** *ad* likewise; **danke
~falls!** the same to you; **G~-
förmigkeit** *f* uniformity; **~gesinnt**
a like-minded; **G~gewicht** *nt* equilibrium, balance; **~gültig** *a* indifferent; *(unbedeutend)* unimportant;
G~gültigkeit *f* indifference; **G~heit** *f*
equality; **~kommen** *vi unreg +dat*
be equal to; **~mäßig** *a* even, equal;
G~mut *m* equanimity; **G~nis** *nt*
-ses, -se parable; **~sam** *ad* as it
were; **G~strom** *m* *(ELEK)* direct
current; **~tun** *vi unreg:* **es jdm ~tun**
match sb; **G~ung** *f* equation; **~viel**
ad no matter; **~zeitig** *a* simultaneous.
Gleis [glaıs] *nt* **-es, -e** track, rails *pl;*
(Bahnsteig) platform.
gleiten ['glaıtən] *vi unreg* glide;

(*rutschen*) slide.
Gletscher ['glɛtʃər] *m* **-s**, - glacier;
~**spalte** *f* crevasse.
Glied [gliːt] *nt* **-(e)s, -er** member;
(*Arm, Bein*) limb; (*von Kette*) link;
(*MIL*) rank(s); **g~ern** *vt* organize,
structure; ~**erung** *f* structure, organization; ~**maßen** *pl* limbs *pl.*
glimmen ['glɪmən] *vi unreg* glow,
gleam.
glimpflich ['glɪmpflɪç] *a* mild, lenient;
~ davonkommen get off lightly.
glitzern ['glɪtsərn] *vi* glitter, twinkle.
Globus ['gloːbʊs] *m* - *od* **-ses, Globen**
od **-se** globe.
Glocke ['glɔkə] *f* -, **-n** bell; etw an die
große ~ hängen (*fig*) shout sth from
the rooftops.
Glocken- *zW:* ~**geläut** *nt* peal of
bells; ~**spiel** *nt* chime(s); (*MUS*)
glockenspiel; ~**turm** *m* bell tower.
Glosse ['glɔsə] *f* -, **-n** comment.
glotzen ['glɔtsən] *vi* (*umg*) stare.
Glück [glʏk] *nt* **-(e)s** luck, fortune;
(*Freude*) happiness; ~ haben be
lucky; viel ~ good luck; zum ~ fortunately; **g~en** *vi* succeed; es glückte
ihm, es zu bekommen he succeeded
in getting it.
gluckern ['glʊkərn] *vi* glug.
Glück- *zW:* **g~lich** *a* fortunate; (*froh*)
happy; **g~licherweise** *ad* fortunately; **Glücksbringer** *m* **-s**, - lucky
charm; **g~'selig** *a* blissful.
Glücks- *zW:* ~**fall** *m* stroke of luck;
~**kind** *nt* lucky person; ~**sache** *f*
matter of luck; ~**spiel** *nt* game of
chance.
Glückwunsch *m* congratulations *pl*,
best wishes *pl.*
Glüh- ['glyː] *zW:* ~**birne** *f* light bulb;
g~en *vi* glow; ~**wein** *m* mulled
wine; ~**würmchen** *nt* glow-worm.
Glut [gluːt] *f* -, **-en** (*Röte*) glow;
(*Feuers~*) fire; (*Hitze*) heat; (*fig*)
ardour.
GmbH ['geːˈɛmbeːˈhaː] *f abk* (=
*Gesellschaft mit beschränkter Haf-
tung*) (private) limited company,
Ltd. (*Brit*); corporation, inc. (*US*).
Gnade ['gnaːdə] *f* -, **-n** (*Gunst*) favour; (*Erbarmen*) mercy; (*Milde*)
clemency.
Gnaden- *zW:* ~**frist** *f* reprieve, respite; **g~los** *a* merciless; ~**stoß** *m*
coup de grâce.
gnädig ['gnɛːdɪç] *a* gracious; (*voll Erbarmen*) merciful.
Gold [gɔlt] *nt* **-(e)s** gold; **g~en** *a* gold-
en; ~**fisch** *m* goldfish; ~**grube** *f*
goldmine; ~**regen** *m* laburnum.
Golf [gɔlf] *m* **-(e)s, -e** gulf // *nt* **-s** golf;
~**platz** *m* golf course; ~**schläger** *m*
golf club; ~**spieler** *m* golfer; ~**strom**
m Gulf Stream.

Gondel ['gɔndəl] *f* -, **-n** gondola; (*Seilbahn*) cable-car.
gönnen ['gœnən] *vt:* jdm etw ~ not
begrudge sb sth; sich (*dat*) etw ~ allow oneself sth.
Gönner *m* **-s**, - patron; **g~haft** *a* pat-
ronizing.
Gosse ['gɔsə] *f* -, **-n** gutter.
Gott [gɔt] *m* **-es**, ¨**er** god; mein ~, um
~es Willen! for heaven's sake!; grüß
~! hello; ~ sei Dank! thank God!;
~**esdienst** *m* service; ~**eslästerung** *f*
blasphemy; ~**heit** *f* deity.
Gött- [gœt] *zW:* ~**in** *f* goddess; **g~lich**
a divine.
gottlos *a* godless.
Götze ['gœtsə] *m* **-n**, **-n** idol.
Grab [graːp] *nt* **-(e)s, ¨er** grave; **g~en**
['graːbən] *vt unreg* dig; ~**en** *m* **-s**, ¨
ditch; (*MIL*) trench; ~**stein** *m* grave-
stone.
Grad [graːt] *m* **-(e)s, -e** degree;
~**einteilung** *f* graduation.
Graf [graːf] *m* **-en, -en** count, earl;
~**schaft** *f* county.
Gräfin ['grɛːfɪn] *f* countess.
Gram [graːm] *m* **-(e)s** grief, sorrow.
grämen ['grɛːmən] *vr* grieve.
Gramm [gram] *nt* **-s, -e** gram(me).
Grammatik [gra'matɪk] *f* grammar.
grammatisch *a* grammatical.
Grammophon [gramo'foːn] *nt* **-s, -e**
gramophone.
Granat [gra'naːt] *m* **-(e)s, -e** (*Stein*)
garnet; ~**e** *f* -, **-n** (*MIL*) shell;
(*Hand~*) grenade.
Granit [gra'niːt] *m* **-s, -e** granite.
graphisch ['graːfɪʃ] *a* graphic.
Gras [graːs] *nt* **-es, ¨er** grass; **g~en** *vi*
graze; ~**halm** *m* blade of grass.
grassieren [gra'siːrən] *vi* be rampant,
rage.
gräßlich ['grɛslɪç] *a* horrible.
Grat [graːt] *m* **-(e)s, -e** ridge.
Gräte ['grɛːtə] *f* -, **-n** fishbone.
gratis ['graːtɪs] *a,ad* free (of charge);
G~probe *f* free sample.
Gratulation [gratulatsi'oːn] *f* congratu-
lation(s).
gratulieren [gratu'liːrən] *vi:* jdm ~ (zu
etw) congratulate sb (on sth); (**ich**)
gratuliere! congratulations!
grau [graʊ] *a* grey; ~**en** *vi unpers:* es
graut jdm vor etw sb dreads sth, sb
is afraid of sth // *vr:* sich ~en vor
dread, have a horror of; **G~en** *nt* **-s**
horror; ~**enhaft** *a* horrible; ~**haarig**
a grey-haired.
grausam ['graʊzaːm] *a* cruel; **G~keit**
f cruelty.
Grausen ['graʊzən] *nt* **-s** horror; **g~** *vi*
unpers, vr siehe **grauen**.
gravieren [gra'viːrən] *vt* engrave; ~**d**
a grave.
Grazie ['graːtsiə] *f* -, **-n** grace.

graziös [gratsi'ø:s] *a* graceful.

greif- [graɪf] *zW*: **~bar** *a* tangible, concrete; **in ~barer Nähe** within reach; **~en** *vt unreg* seize; grip; **nach etw ~en** reach for sth; **um sich ~en** *(fig)* spread; **zu etw ~en** *(fig)* turn to sth.

Greis [graɪs] *m* **-es, -e** old man; **~enalter** *nt* old age; **g~enhaft** *a* senile; **~in** *f* old woman.

grell [grɛl] *a* harsh.

Grenz- ['grɛnts] *zW*: **~beamte(r)** *m* frontier official; **~e** *f* -, **-n** boundary; *(Staats~)* frontier; *(Schranke)* limit; **g~en** *vi* border *(an +akk* on); **g~enlos** *a* boundless; **~fall** *m* borderline case; **~übergang** *m* frontier crossing.

Greuel ['grɔʏəl] *m* **-s, -** horror, revulsion; **etw ist jdm ein ~** sb loathes sth; **~tat** *f* atrocity.

greulich ['grɔʏlɪç] *a* horrible.

Griech- [gri:ç] *zW*: **~e** *m*, **~in** *f* Greek; **~enland** *nt* Greece; **g~isch** *a* Greek.

griesgrämig ['gri:sgrɛ:mɪç] *a* grumpy.

Grieß [gri:s] *m* **-es, -e** *(KOCH)* semolina.

Griff [grɪf] *m* **-(e)s, -e** grip; *(Vorrichtung)* handle; **g~bereit** *a* handy.

Grill [grɪl] *m* grill; **~e** *f* -, **-n** cricket; **g~en** *vt* grill.

Grimasse [grɪ'masə] *f* -, **-n** grimace.

grimmig ['grɪmɪç] *a* furious; *(heftig)* fierce, severe.

grinsen ['grɪnzən] *vi* grin.

Grippe ['grɪpə] *f* -, **-n** influenza, flu.

grob [grɔ:p] *a* coarse, gross; *(Fehler, Verstoß)* gross; **G~heit** *f* coarseness; coarse expression.

Groll [grɔl] *m* **-(e)s** resentment; **g~en** *vi* bear ill will *(+dat od mit* towards); *(Donner)* rumble.

Groschen ['grɔʃən] *m* 10 pfennig piece.

groß [gro:s] *a* big, large; *(hoch)* tall; *(fig)* great; **im ~en und ganzen on** the whole // *ad* greatly; **~artig** *a* great, splendid; **G~aufnahme** *f* *(CINE)* close-up; **G~britannien** *nt* Great Britain.

Größe ['grø:sə] *f* -, **-n** size; *(fig)* greatness; *(Länge)* height.

Groß- *zW*: **~einkauf** *m* bulk purchase; **~eltern** *pl* grandparents *pl*; **g~enteils** *ad* mostly.

Größenwahn ['grø:sənva:n] *m* megalomania.

Groß- *zW*: **~format** *nt* large size; **~handel** *m* wholesale trade; **~händler** *m* wholesaler; **~macht** *f* great power; **~maul** *m* braggart; **g~mütig** *a* magnanimous; **~mutter** *f* grandmother; **~rechner** *m* mainframe (computer); **g~spurig** *a* pompous; **~stadt** *f* city, large town.

größte(r, s) [grø:stə(r, s)] *a superl von* **groß**; **größtenteils** *ad* for the most part.

Groß- *zW*: **g~tun** *vi unreg* boast; **~vater** *m* grandfather; **g~ziehen** *vt unreg* raise; **g~zügig** *a* generous; *(Planung)* on a large scale.

grotesk [gro'tɛsk] *a* grotesque.

Grotte ['grɔtə] *f* -, **-n** grotto.

Grübchen ['gry:pçən] *nt* dimple.

Grube ['gru:bə] *f* -, **-n** pit; mine; **Grubenarbeiter** *m* miner.

grübeln ['gry:bəln] *vi* brood.

Gruft [gruft] *f* -, **⁻e** tomb, vault.

grün [gry:n] *a* green; **die G~en** *(POL)* the Greens; **G~anlage** *f* park.

Grund [grunt] *m* **-(e)s, ⁻e** ground; *(von See, Gefäß)* bottom; *(fig)* reason; **im ~e genommen** basically; **~ausbildung** *f* basic training; **~besitz** *m* land(ed property), real estate; **~buch** *nt* land register.

gründ- [grynd] *zW*: **~en** *vt* found; **~en auf** *(+akk)* base on // *vr* **g~en auf** *(+dat)* be based *(auf +dat* on); **G~er** *m* **-s, -** founder.

Grund- *zW*: **~gebühr** *f* basic charge; **~gesetz** *nt* constitution; **~lage** *f* foundation; **g~legend** *a* fundamental.

gründlich *a* thorough.

Grund- *zW*: **g~los** *a* groundless; **~regel** *f* basic rule; **~riß** *m* plan; *(fig)* outline; **~satz** *m* principle; **g~sätzlich** *a,ad* fundamental(ly); *(Frage)* of principle; *(prinzipiell)* on principle; **~schule** *f* elementary school; **~stein** *m* foundation stone; **~stück** *nt* estate; plot.

Gründung *f* foundation.

Grundzug *m* characteristic.

Grün- *zW*: **~kohl** *m* kale; **~schnabel** *m* greenhorn; **~span** *m* verdigris; **~streifen** *m* central reservation.

grunzen ['gruntsən] *vi* grunt.

Gruppe ['grupə] *f* -, **-n** group; **g~nweise** *ad* in groups.

gruppieren [gru'pi:rən] *vtr* group.

gruselig *a* creepy.

gruseln ['gru:zəln] *vi unpers*: **es gruselt jdm vor etw** sth gives sb the creeps // *vr* have the creeps.

Gruß [gru:s] *m* **-es, ⁻e** greeting; *(MIL)* salute; **viele ~e** best wishes; **mit freundlichen ~en** yours sincerely; **~e an** *(+akk)* regards to.

grüßen ['gry:sən] *vt* greet; *(MIL)* salute; **jdn von jdm ~** give sb sb's regards; **jdn ~ lassen** send sb one's regards.

gucken ['gukən] *vi* look.

Gulasch ['gu:laʃ] *nt* **-(e)s, -e** goulash.

gültig ['gyltɪç] *a* valid; **G~keit** *f* validity.

Gummi ['gumi] *nt od m* **-s, -s** rubber; *(~harze)* gum; **~band** *nt* rubber od

elastic band; (*Hosen~*) elastic;
~baum *m* rubber plant; **gummieren**
[gu'mi:rən] *vt* gum; **~knüppel** *m* rubber truncheon; **~strumpf** *m* elastic
stocking.
günstig ['gynstɪç] *a* convenient; (*Gelegenheit*) favourable; **das habe ich ~
bekommen** it was a bargain.
Gurgel ['gʊrgəl] *f* -, **-n** throat; **g~n** *vi*
gurgle; (*im Mund*) gargle.
Gurke ['gʊrkə] *f* -, **-n** cucumber; **saure
~** pickled cucumber, gherkin.
Gurt [gʊrt] *m* **-(e)s, -e** belt.
Gürtel ['gʏrtəl] *m* **-s, -** belt; (*GEOG*)
zone; **~reifen** *m* radial tyre.
Guß [gʊs] *m* **-sses, Güsse** casting;
(*Regen~*) downpour; (*KOCH*) glazing; **~eisen** *nt* cast iron.
gut [gu:t] ◆ *a* good; **alles G~e** all the
best; **also ~** all right then
◆ *ad* well; **~ schmecken** taste good;
~, aber ... ok, but ...; **(na) ~, ich
komme** all right, I'll come; **~ drei
Stunden** a good three hours; **das kann
~ sein** that may well be; **laß es ~
sein** that'll do.
Gut [gu:t] *nt* **-(e)s, ⁻er** (*Besitz*) possession; (*pl: Waren*) goods *pl*; **laß es g~
sein** that'll do; **~achten** *nt* **-s, -** (expert) opinion; **~achter** *m* **-s, -** expert; **g~artig** *a* good-natured; (*MED*)
benign; **g~bürgerlich** *a* (*Küche*)
(good) plain; **~dünken** *nt*: **nach
~dünken** at one's discretion.
Güte ['gy:tə] *f* - goodness, kindness;
(*Qualität*) quality.
Güter- *zW*: **~abfertigung** *f* (*EISENB*)
goods office; **~bahnhof** *m* goods station; **~wagen** *m* goods waggon
(*Brit*), freight car (*US*); **~zug** *m*
goods train (*Brit*), freight train (*US*).
Gut- *zW*: **g~gehen** *v unpers unreg*
work, come off; **es geht jdm g~** sb's
doing fine; **g~gemeint** *a* well meant;
g~gläubig *a* trusting; **~haben** *nt* **-s**
credit; **g~heißen** *vt unreg* approve
(of).
gütig ['gy:tɪç] *a* kind.
Gut- *zW*: **g~mütig** *a* good-natured;
~mütigkeit *f* good nature; **~schein**
m voucher; **g~schreiben** *vt unreg*
credit; **~schrift** *f* credit; **g~tun** *vi
unreg*: **jdm g~tun** do sb good;
g~willig *a* willing.
Gymnasium [gʏm'naːzɪʊm] *nt* grammar school (*Brit*), high school (*US*).
Gymnastik [gʏm'nastɪk] *f* exercises *pl*,
keep fit.

H

H, h [ha:] *nt* H, h.
Haag [ha:g] *m*: **Den ~** the Hague.
Haar [ha:r] *nt* **-(e)s, -e** hair; **um ein ~**
nearly; **an den ~en herbeigezogen**
(*umg: Vergleich*) very far-fetched;
~bürste *f* hairbrush; **h~en** *vir* lose
hair; **~esbreite** *f*: **um ~esbreite** by a
hair's-breadth; **h~genau** *ad* precisely; **h~ig** *a* hairy; (*fig*) nasty;
~klemme *f* hair grip; **~nadel** *f* hairpin; **h~scharf** *ad* (*beobachten*) very
sharply; (*daneben*) by a hair's
breadth; **~schnitt** *m* haircut;
~shampoo *nt* shampoo; **~spange** *f*
hair slide; **h~sträubend** *a* hairraising; **~teil** *nt* hairpiece;
~waschmittel *nt* shampoo.
Habe ['ha:bə] *f* - property.
haben ['ha:bən] *vt, v aux unreg* have;
Hunger/Angst ~ be hungry/afraid;
woher hast du das? where did you
get that from?; **was hast du denn?**
what's the matter (with you)?; **du
hast zu schweigen** you're to be quiet;
ich hätte gern I would like; **H~** *nt* **-s,
-** credit.
Habgier *f* avarice; **h~ig** *a* avaricious.
Habicht ['ha:bɪçt] *m* **-s, -e** hawk.
Habseligkeiten *pl* belongings *pl*.
Hachse ['haksə] *f* -, **-n** (*KOCH*)
knuckle.
Hacke ['hakə] *f* -, **-n** hoe; (*Ferse*)
heel; **h~n** *vt* hack, chop; (*Erde*) hoe.
Hackfleisch *nt* mince, minced meat.
Hafen ['ha:fən] *m* **-s, ⁻** harbour, port;
~arbeiter *m* docker; **~damm** *m* jetty, mole; **~stadt** *f* port.
Hafer ['ha:fər] *m* **-s, -** oats *pl*;
~flocken *pl* rolled oats *pl*; **~schleim**
m gruel.
Haft [haft] *f* - custody; **h~bar** *a* liable,
responsible; **~befehl** *m* warrant (of
arrest); **h~en** *vi* stick, cling; **h~en
für** be liable od responsible for;
h~enbleiben *vi unreg* stick (*an
+dat* to); **~pflicht** *f* liability;
~pflichtversicherung *f* third party insurance; **~schalen** *pl* contact lenses
pl; **~ung** *f* liability.
Hage- ['ha:gə] *zW*: **~butte** *f* -, **-n** rose
hip; **~dorn** *m* hawthorn.
Hagel ['ha:gəl] *m* **-s** hail; **h~n** *vi
unpers* hail.
hager ['ha:gər] *a* gaunt.
Hahn [ha:n] *m* **-s, ⁻e** cock; (*Wasser~*) tap, faucet (*US*).
Hähnchen ['hɛ:nçən] *nt* cockerel;
(*KOCH*) chicken.
Hai(fisch) ['haɪ(fɪʃ)] *m* **-(e)s, -e** shark.
Häkchen ['hɛ:kçən] *nt* small hook.
Häkel- ['hɛ:kəl] *zW*: **~arbeit** *f* crochet
work; **h~n** *vt* crochet; **~nadel** *f*
crochet hook.
Haken ['ha:kən] *m* **-s, -** hook; (*fig*)
catch; **~kreuz** *nt* swastika; **~nase** *f*
hooked nose.
halb [halp] *a* half; **~ eins** half past
twelve; **ein ~es Dutzend** half a doz-

en; **H~dunkel** nt semi-darkness.
halber ['halbər] präp +gen (wegen) on account of; (für) for the sake of.
Halb- zW: **~heit** f half-measure; **h~ieren** vt halve; **~insel** f peninsula; **h~jährlich** a half-yearly; **~kreis** m semicircle; **~kugel** f hemisphere; **~leiter** m semiconductor; **h~links** a (SPORT) inside left; **~mond** m halfmoon; (fig) crescent; **h~offen** a half-open; **~pension** f half-board; **h~rechts** a (SPORT) inside right; **~schuh** m shoe; **~tagsarbeit** f parttime work; **h~wegs** ad half-way; **h~wegs besser** more or less better; **~wertzeit** f half-life; **~wüchsige(r)** mf adolescent; **~zeit** f (SPORT) half; (Pause) half-time.
half etc v siehe **helfen**.
Hälfte ['hɛlftə] -, -n f half.
Halfter ['halftər] f -, -n, od nt -s, - halter; (Pistolen~) holster.
Halle ['halə] f -, -n hall; (AVIAT) hangar; **h~n** vi echo, resound; **Hallenbad** nt indoor swimming pool.
hallo [ha'lo:] interj hello.
Halluzination [halutsinatsi'o:n] f hallucination.
Halm [halm] m -(e)s, -e blade, stalk.
Hals [hals] m -es, ⸚e neck; (Kehle) throat; **~ über Kopf** in a rush; **~kette** f necklace; **~-Nasen-Ohren-Arzt** m ear nose and throat specialist; **~schlagader** f carotid artery; **~schmerzen** pl sore throat; **~tuch** nt scarf; **~wirbel** m cervical vertebra.
Halt [halt] m -(e)s, -e stop; (fester ~) hold; (innerer ~) stability; **h~** interj stop!, halt! // ad just; **h~bar** a durable; (Lebensmittel) non-perishable; (MIL, fig) tenable; **~barkeit** f durability; (non-)perishability.
halten ['haltən] unreg vt keep; (fest~) hold; **~ für** regard as; **~ von** think of // vi hold; (frisch bleiben) keep; (stoppen) stop; **an sich ~** restrain oneself // vr (frisch bleiben) keep; (sich behaupten) hold out; **sich rechts/links ~** keep to the right/left.
Haltestelle f stop.
Halteverbot nt: **hier ist ~** it's no waiting here.
Halt- zW: **h~los** a unstable; **h~machen** vi stop; **~ung** f posture; (fig) attitude; (Selbstbeherrschung) composure.
Halunke [ha'luŋkə] m -n, -n rascal.
hämisch ['hɛ:mɪʃ] a malicious.
Hammel ['haməl] m -s, ⸚ od - wether; **~fleisch** nt mutton.
Hammer ['hamər] m -s, ⸚ hammer.
hämmern ['hɛmərn] vti hammer.
Hämorrhoiden [hɛmɔro'i:dən] pl haemorrhoids.
Hampelmann ['hampəlman] m (lit,

fig) puppet.
Hamster ['hamstər] m -s, - hamster; **~ei** [-'raɪ] f hoarding; **h~n** vi hoard.
Hand [hant] f -, ⸚e hand; **~arbeit** f manual work; (Nadelarbeit) needlework; **~arbeiter** m manual worker; **~bremse** f handbrake; **~buch** nt handbook, manual.
Händedruck ['hɛndədruk] m handshake.
Handel ['handəl] m -s trade; (Geschäft) transaction.
handeln ['handəln] vi trade; act; **~ von** be about // vr unpers: **sich ~ um** be a question of, be about; **H~** nt -s action.
Handels- zW: **~bilanz** f balance of trade; **~kammer** f chamber of commerce; **~name** m trade name; **~reisende(r)** m commercial traveller; **~schule** f business school; **h~üblich** a customary; (Preis) going attr; **~vertreter** m sales representative.
Hand- zW: **~feger** m -s, - brush; **h~fest** a hefty; **h~gearbeitet** a handmade; **~gelenk** nt wrist; **~gemenge** nt scuffle; **~gepäck** nt hand-luggage; **h~greiflich** a palpable; **h~greiflich werden** become violent; **~griff** m flick of the wrist; **h~haben** vt insep handle.
Händler ['hɛndlər] m -s, - trader, dealer.
handlich ['hantlɪç] a handy.
Handlung ['handluŋ] f -, -en act(ion); (in Buch) plot; (Geschäft) shop; **Handlungsweise** f manner of dealing.
Hand- zW: **~pflege** f manicure; **~schelle** f handcuff; **~schlag** m handshake; **~schrift** f handwriting; (Text) manuscript; **~schuh** m glove; **~tasche** f handbag; **~tuch** nt towel; **~werk** nt trade, craft; **~werker** m -s, - craftsman, artisan; **~werkzeug** nt tools pl.
Hanf [hanf] m -(e)s hemp.
Hang [haŋ] m -(e)s, ⸚e inclination; (Ab~) slope.
Hänge- ['hɛŋə] in zW hanging; **~brücke** f suspension bridge; **~matte** f hammock.
hängen ['hɛŋən] vi unreg hang; **~ an** (fig) be attached to // vt hang (an +akk on(to)); **sich ~ an** (+akk) hang on to, cling to; **~bleiben** vi unreg be caught (an +dat on); (fig) remain, stick; **~lassen** vt unreg (vergessen) leave; **den Kopf ~lassen** get downhearted.
Hannover [ha'no:fər] nt -s Hanover.
hänseln ['hɛnzəln] vt tease.
hantieren [han'ti:rən] vi work, be busy; **mit etw ~** handle sth.

hapern ['haːpərn] *vi unpers*: **es hapert an etw** (*dat*) there is a lack of sth.
Happen ['hapən] *m* **-s**, - mouthful.
Hardware ['haːdwɛə] *f* hardware.
Harfe ['harfə] *f* -, **-n** harp.
Harke ['harkə] *f* -, **-n** rake; **h~n** *vti* rake.
harmlos ['harmloːs] *a* harmless; **H~igkeit** *f* harmlessness.
Harmonie [harmo'niː] *f* harmony; **h~ren** *vi* harmonize.
Harmonika [har'moːnika] *f* -, **-s** (*Zieh~*) concertina.
harmonisch [har'moːnɪʃ] *a* harmonious.
Harmonium [har'moːniʊm] *nt* **-s, -nien** *od* **-s** harmonium.
Harn [harn] *m* **-(e)s, -e** urine; **~blase** *f* bladder.
Harpune [har'puːnə] *f* -, **-n** harpoon.
harren ['harən] *vi* wait (*auf +akk* for).
hart [hart] *a* hard; (*fig*) harsh.
Härte ['hɛrtə] *f* -, **-n** hardness; (*fig*) harshness.
hart- *zW*: **~gekocht** *a* hard-boiled; **~herzig** *a* hard-hearted; **~näckig** *a* stubborn; **H~näckigkeit** *f* stubbornness; **H~platte** *f* hard disk.
Harz [haːrts] *nt* **-es, -e** resin.
Haschee [ha'ʃeː] *nt* **-s, -s** hash.
Haschisch ['haʃɪʃ] *nt* - hashish.
Hase ['haːzə] *m* **-n, -n** hare.
Haselnuß ['haːzəlnʊs] *f* hazelnut.
Hasenfuß *m* coward.
Hasenscharte *f* harelip.
Haß [has] *m* **-sses** hate, hatred.
hassen ['hasən] *vt* hate.
häßlich ['hɛslɪç] *a* ugly; (*gemein*) nasty; **H~keit** *f* ugliness; nastiness.
hast *v siehe* **haben**.
Hast [hast] *f* - haste; **h~en** *vi* rush; **h~ig** *a* hasty.
hat, hatte *etc v siehe* **haben**.
Haube ['haubə] *f* -, **-n** hood; (*Mütze*) cap; (*AUT*) bonnet, hood (*US*).
Hauch [haux] *m* **-(e)s, -e** breath; (*Luft~*) breeze; (*fig*) trace; **h~dünn** *a* very thin; **h~en** *vi* breathe.
Haue ['hauə] *f* -, **-n** hoe, pick; (*umg*) hiding; **h~n** *vt unreg* hew, cut; (*umg*) thrash.
Haufen ['haufən] *m* **-s**, - heap; (*Leute*) crowd; **ein ~ (x)** (*umg*) loads *od* a lot (of x); **auf einem ~** in one heap.
häufen ['hɔyfən] *vt* pile up // *vr* accumulate.
haufenweise *ad* in heaps; in droves; **etw ~ haben** have piles of sth.
häufig ['hɔyfɪç] *a,ad* frequent(ly); **H~keit** *f* frequency.
Haupt [haupt] *nt* **-(e)s, Häupter** head; (*Ober~*) chief; (*in zW*) main; **~bahnhof** *m* central station; **h~beruflich** *ad* as one's main occupation; **~darsteller(in** *f*) *m* leading

actor/actress; **~eingang** *m* main entrance; **~film** *m* main film.
Häuptling ['hɔyptlɪŋ] *m* chief, chieftain.
Haupt- *zW*: **~mann** *m, pl* **-leute** (*MIL*) captain; **~person** *f* central figure; **~quartier** *nt* headquarters *pl*; **~rolle** *f* leading part; **~sache** *f* main thing; **h~sächlich** *a,ad* chief(ly); **~satz** *m* main clause; **~schlagader** *f* aorta; **~schule** *f* ≈ secondary school; **~sendezeit** *f* (*TV*) prime time; **~stadt** *f* capital; **~straße** *f* main street; **~wort** *nt* noun.
Haus [haus] *nt* **-es, Häuser** house; **nach ~e** home; **zu ~e** at home; **~angestellte** *f* domestic servant; **~arbeit** *f* housework; (*SCH*) homework; **~arzt** *m* family doctor; **~aufgabe** *f* (*SCH*) homework; **~besitzer(in** *f*) *m*, **~eigentümer(in** *f*) *m* house-owner.
Häuser- ['hɔyzər-] *zW*: **~block** *m* block (of houses); **~makler** *m* estate agent (*Brit*), real estate agent (*US*).
Haus- *zW*: **~frau** *f* housewife; **h~gemacht** *a* home-made; **~halt** *m* household; (*POL*) budget; **h~halten** *vi unreg* (*sparen*) economize; **~hälterin** *f* housekeeper; **~haltsgeld** *nt* housekeeping (money); **~haltsgerät** *nt* domestic appliance; **~herr** *m* host; (*Vermieter*) landlord; **h~hoch** *ad*: **h~hoch verlieren** lose by a mile.
hausieren [hau'ziːrən] *vi* peddle.
Hausierer *m* **-s**, - peddlar.
häuslich ['hɔyslɪç] *a* domestic.
Haus- *zW*: **~meister** *m* caretaker; janitor; **~nummer** *f* street number; **~ordnung** *f* house rules *pl*; **~putz** *m* house cleaning; **~schlüssel** *m* frontdoor key; **~schuh** *m* slipper; **~suchung** *f* police raid; **~tier** *nt* domestic animal; **~wirt** *m* landlord; **~wirtschaft** *f* domestic science.
Haut [haut] *f* -, **Häute** skin; (*Tier~*) hide.
Haut- *zW*: **h~eng** *a* skin-tight; **~farbe** *f* complexion.
Haxe ['haksə] *f* -, **-n** *siehe* **Hachse**.
Hbf *abk von* **Hauptbahnhof**.
he [heː] *interj* hey.
Hebamme ['heːpˌamə] *f* -, **-n** midwife.
Hebel ['heːbəl] *m* **-s**, - lever.
heben ['heːbən] *vt unreg* raise, lift.
Hecht [hɛçt] *m* **-(e)s, -e** pike.
Heck [hɛk] *nt* **-(e)s, -e** stern; (*von Auto*) rear.
Hecke ['hɛkə] *f* -, **-n** hedge.
Heckenrose *f* dog rose.
Heckenschütze *m* sniper.
Heer [heːr] *nt* **-(e)s, -e** army.
Hefe ['heːfə] *f* -, **-n** yeast.
Heft [hɛft] *nt* **-(e)s, -e** exercise book; (*Zeitschrift*) number; (*von Messer*)

haft; **h~en** vt fasten (an +akk to); (nähen) tack; **~er** m -s, - folder.
heftig a fierce, violent; **H~keit** f fierceness, violence.
Heft- zW: **~klammer** f paper clip; **~maschine** f stapling machine; **~pflaster** nt sticking plaster; **~zwecke** f drawing pin.
Hehl [he:l] m od nt: **kein(en) ~ aus etw (dat) machen** make no secret of sth; **~er** m -s, - receiver (of stolen goods), fence.
Heide ['haɪdə] f -, -n heath, moor; (~kraut) heather // m -n, -n, **Heidin** f heathen, pagan; **~kraut** nt heather; **Heidelbeere** f bilberry; **Heidentum** nt paganism.
heikel ['haɪkəl] a awkward, thorny; (wählerisch) fussy.
Heil [haɪl] nt -(e)s well-being; (Seelen~) salvation; **h~** a in one piece, intact; **~and** m -(e)s, -e saviour; **h~bar** a curable; **h~en** vt cure // vi heal; **h~froh** a very relieved.
heilig ['haɪlɪç] a holy; **H~abend** m Christmas Eve; **H~e(r)** mf saint; **~en** vt sanctify, hallow; **H~enschein** m halo; **H~keit** f holiness; **~sprechen** vt unreg canonize; **H~tum** nt shrine; (Gegenstand) relic.
Heil- zW: **h~los** a unholy; **~mittel** nt remedy; **h~sam** a (fig) salutary; **Heilsarmee** f Salvation Army; **~ung** f cure.
Heim [haɪm] nt -(e)s, -e home; **h~** ad home.
Heimat ['haɪma:t] f -, -en home (town/country etc); **~land** nt homeland; **h~lich** a native, home attr; (Gefühle) nostalgic; **h~los** a homeless; **~ort** m home town/area; **~vertriebene(r)** mf displaced person.
Heim- zW: **~computer** m home computer; **h~fahren** vi unreg drive/go home; **~fahrt** f journey home; **h~gehen** vi unreg go home; (sterben) pass away; **h~isch** a (gebürtig) native; **sich h~isch fühlen** feel at home; **~kehr** f -, -en homecoming; **h~kehren** vi return home; **h~lich** a secret; **~lichkeit** f secrecy; **~reise** f journey home; **h~suchen** vt afflict; (Geist) haunt; **h~tückisch** a malicious; **~weg** m way home; **~weh** nt homesickness; **~weh haben** be homesick; **h~zahlen** vt: **jdm etw h~zahlen** pay back sb for sth.
Heirat ['haɪra:t] f -, -en marriage; **h~en** vti marry.
Heiratsantrag m proposal.
heiser ['haɪzər] a hoarse; **H~keit** f hoarseness.
heiß [haɪs] a hot; **~e(r) Draht** hot line; **~es Eisen** (umg) hot potato;

~blütig a hot-blooded.
heißen ['haɪsən] unreg vi be called; (bedeuten) mean; **das heißt** that is to say // vt command; (nennen) name // vi unpers it says; it is said.
Heißhunger m ravenous hunger.
heißlaufen vir unreg overheat.
heiter ['haɪtər] a cheerful; (Wetter) bright; **H~keit** f cheerfulness; (Belustigung) amusement.
Heiz- ['haɪts] zW: **h~bar** a heated; (Raum) with heating; **~decke** f electric blanket; **h~en** vt heat; **~er** m -s, - stoker; **~körper** m radiator; **~öl** nt fuel oil; **~sonne** f electric fire; **~ung** f heating; **~ungsanlage** f heating system.
hektisch ['hɛktɪʃ] a hectic.
Held [hɛlt] m -en, -en hero; **~in** f heroine.
helfen ['hɛlfən] unreg vi help (jdm sb, bei with); (nützen) be of use; **sich (dat) zu ~ wissen** be resourceful // v unpers: **es hilft nichts, du mußt ...** it's no use, you have to ...
Helfer m -s, - helper, assistant; **Helfershelfer** m accomplice.
hell [hɛl] a clear, bright; (Farbe, Bier) light; **~blau** a light blue; **~blond** a ash-blond; **H~e** f - clearness, brightness; **H~seher** m clairvoyant; **~wach** a wide-awake.
Helm [hɛlm] m -(e)s, -e (auf Kopf) helmet.
Hemd [hɛmt] nt -(e)s, -en shirt; (Unter~) vest; **~bluse** f blouse.
hemmen ['hɛmən] vt check, hold up; **gehemmt sein** be inhibited.
Hemmung f check; (PSYCH) inhibition; **hemmungslos** a unrestrained, without restraint.
Hengst [hɛŋst] m -es, -e stallion.
Henkel ['hɛŋkəl] m -s, - handle.
Henker m -s, - hangman.
Henne ['hɛnə] f -, -n hen.
her [he:r] ad **1** (Richtung) **komm ~ zu mir** come here (to me); **von England ~** from England; **von weit ~** from a long way away; **~ damit!** hand it over!; **wo hat er das ~?** where did he get that from?
2 (Blickpunkt): **von der Form ~** as far as the form is concerned
3 (zeitlich): **das ist 5 Jahre ~** that was 5 years ago; **wo bist du ~?** where do you come from? **ich kenne ihn von früher ~** I know him from before.
herab [hɛ'rap] ad down(ward(s)); **~hängen** vi unreg hang down; **~lassen** unreg vt let down // vr condescend; **~lassend** a condescending; **~setzen** vt lower, reduce; (fig) belittle, disparage; **~würdigen** vt belittle, disparage.

heran [hɛˈran] *ad:* näher ~! come up closer!; ~ zu mir! come up to me!; ~**bringen** *vt unreg* bring up (*an* +*akk* to); ~**fahren** *vi unreg* drive up (*an* +*akk* to); ~**kommen** *vi unreg* (*an* +*akk*) approach, come near; ~**machen** *vr:* sich an jdn ~**machen** make up to sb; ~**wachsen** *vi unreg* grow up; ~**ziehen** *vt unreg* pull nearer; (*aufziehen*) raise; (*ausbilden*) train; jdn zu etw ~**ziehen** call upon sb to help in sth.

herauf [hɛˈrauf] *ad* up(ward(s)), up here; ~**beschwören** *vt unreg* conjure up, evoke; ~**bringen** *vt unreg* bring up.

heraus [hɛˈraus] *ad* out; outside; from; ~**bekommen** *vt unreg* get out; (*fig*) find *od* figure out; ~**bringen** *vt unreg* bring out; (*Geheimnis*) elicit; ~**finden** *vt unreg* find out; ~**fordern** *vt* challenge; **H~forderung** *f* challenge; provocation; ~**geben** *vt unreg* give up, surrender; (*Geld*) give back; (*Buch*) edit; (*veröffentlichen*) publish; ~**geber** *m* -s, - editor; (*Verleger*) publisher; ~**halten** *vr unreg:* sich aus etw ~**halten** keep out of sth; ~**hängen** *vti unreg* hang out; ~**holen** *vt* get out (*aus* of); ~**kommen** *vi unreg* come out; dabei kommt nichts ~ nothing will come of it; ~**reißen** *vt unreg* tear out; pull out; ~**rücken** *vt* (*Geld*) fork out, hand over; mit etw ~**rücken** (*fig*) come out with sth; ~**stellen** *vr* turn out (*als* to be); ~**ziehen** *vt unreg* pull out, extract.

herb [hɛrp] *a* (slightly) bitter, acid; (*Wein*) dry; (*fig: schmerzlich*) bitter; (*: streng*) stern, austere.

herbei [hɛrˈbai] *ad* (over) here; ~**führen** *vt* bring about; ~**schaffen** *vt* procure.

herbemühen [ˈhɛːrbəmyːən] *vr* take the trouble to come.

Herberge [ˈhɛrbɛrgə] *f* -, -n shelter; hostel, inn.

Herbergsmutter *f*, **Herbergsvater** *m* warden.

her- *zW:* ~**bitten** *vt unreg* ask to come (here); ~**bringen** *vt unreg* bring here.

Herbst [hɛrpst] *m* -(e)s, -e autumn, fall (*US*); *h~lich a* autumnal.

Herd [hɛːrt] *m* -(e)s, -e cooker; (*fig, MED*) focus, centre.

Herde [ˈheːrdə] *f* -, -n herd; (*Schaf~*) flock.

herein [hɛˈrain] *ad* in (here), here; ~! come in!; ~**bitten** *vt unreg* ask in; ~**brechen** *vi unreg* set in; ~**bringen** *vt unreg* bring in; ~**dürfen** *vi unreg* have permission to enter; ~**fallen** *vi unreg* be caught, taken in; ~**fallen auf** (+*akk*) fall for; ~**kommen** *vi*

unreg come in; ~**lassen** *vt unreg* admit; ~**legen** *vt:* jdn ~**legen** take sb in.

Her- *zW:* ~**fahrt** *f* journey here; *h~fallen vi unreg:* h~fallen über fall upon; ~**gang** *m* course of events, circumstances *pl*; ~**geben** *vt unreg* give, hand (over); sich zu etw h~geben lend one's name to sth; *h~gehen vi unreg:* hinter jdm h~gehen follow sb; es geht hoch h~ there are a lot of goings-on; *h~halten vt unreg* hold out; h~halten müssen (*umg*) have to suffer; *h~hören vi* listen.

Hering [ˈheːrɪŋ] *m* -s, -e herring.

her- *zW:* ~**kommen** *vi unreg* come; komm mal ~! come here!; ~**kömmlich** *a* traditional; **H~kunft** *f* -, -künfte origin; ~**laufen** *vi unreg:* ~laufen hinter (+*dat*) run after.

Hermelin [hɛrməˈliːn] *m od nt* -s, -e ermine.

hermetisch [hɛrˈmeːtɪʃ] *a,ad* hermetic(ally).

her- [hɛr] *zW:* ~'**nach** *ad* afterwards; ~'**nieder** *ad* down.

Herr [hɛr] *m* -(e)n, -en master; (*Mann*) gentleman; (*REL*) Lord; (*vor Namen*) Mr.; mein ~! sir!; meine ~en! gentlemen!; ~**endoppel** *nt* men's doubles; ~**eneinzel** *nt* men's singles; ~**enhaus** *nt* mansion; ~**enkonfektion** *f* menswear; h~**enlos** *a* ownerless.

herrichten [ˈhɛrrɪçtən] *vt* prepare.

Herr- *zW:* ~**in** *f* mistress; ~**isch** *a* domineering; *h~lich a* marvellous, splendid; ~**lichkeit** *f* splendour, magnificence; ~**schaft** *f* power, rule; (*Herr und Herrin*) master and mistress; meine ~schaften! ladies and gentlemen!

herrschen [ˈhɛrʃən] *vi* rule; (*bestehen*) prevail, be.

Herrscher(in *f*) *m* -s, - ruler.

her- *zW:* ~**rühren** *vi* arise, originate; ~**sagen** *vt* recite; ~**stellen** *vt* make, manufacture; **H~steller** *m* -s, - manufacturer; **H~stellung** *f* manufacture.

herüber [hɛˈryːbər] *ad* over (here), across.

herum [hɛˈrum] *ad* about, (a)round; um etw ~ around sth; ~**führen** *vt* show around; ~**gehen** *vi unreg* walk *od* go round (um etw sth); walk about; ~**irren** *vi* wander about; ~**kriegen** *vt* (*umg*) bring *od* talk around; ~**sprechen** *vr unreg* get around, be spread; ~**treiben** *vir unreg* drift about; ~**ziehen** *vir unreg* wander about.

herunter [hɛˈruntər] *ad* downward(s), down (there); ~**gekommen** *a* run-down; **~hängen** vi unreg hang down; **~holen** vt bring down; **~kommen** vi unreg come down; (fig) come down in the world; **~machen** vt take down; (schimpfen) have a go at.

hervor [her'fo:r] ad out, forth; **~bringen** vt unreg produce; (Wort) utter; **~gehen** vi unreg emerge, result; **~heben** vt unreg stress; (als Kontrast) set off; **~ragend** a (fig) excellent; **~rufen** vt unreg cause, give rise to.

Herz [herts] nt -ens, -en heart; (KARTEN) hearts; **~anfall** m heart attack; **~enslust** f: nach ~enslust to one's heart's content; **~fehler** m heart defect; **h~haft** a hearty; **~infarkt** m heart attack; **~klopfen** nt palpitation; **h~lich** a cordial; **h~lichen Glückwunsch** congratulations pl; **h~liche Grüße** best wishes; **h~los** a heartless.

Herzog ['hertso:k] m -(e)s, ⸚e duke; **~in** f duchess; **h~lich** a ducal; **~tum** nt duchy.

Herzschlag m heartbeat; (MED) heart attack.

herzzerreißend a heartrending.

heterogen [hetero'ge:n] a heterogeneous.

Hetze ['hetsə] f -, -n (Eile) rush; **h~n** vt hunt; (verfolgen) chase; **jdn/etw auf jdn/etw h~n** set sb/sth on sb/sth // vi (eilen) rush; **h~n gegen** stir up feeling against; **h~n zu** agitate for; **Hetze'rei** f agitation; (Eile) rush.

Heu [hoy] nt -(e)s hay; **Geld wie ~** stacks of money; **~boden** m hayloft.

Heuchelei [hoyçə'lai] f hypocrisy.

heucheln ['hoyçəln] vt pretend, feign // vi be hypocritical.

Heuchler(in f**)** ['hoyçlər(ın)] m -s, - hypocrite; **h~isch** a hypocritical.

heulen ['hoylən] vi howl; cry; **das ~de Elend bekommen** get the blues.

Heuschnupfen m hay fever.

Heuschrecke ['hoyʃrekə] f grasshopper, locust.

heute ['hoytə] ad today; **~ abend/früh** this evening/morning.

heutig ['hoytıç] a today's.

heutzutage ['hoyttsuta:gə] ad nowadays.

Hexe ['heksə] f -, -n witch; **h~n** vi practise witchcraft; **ich kann doch nicht h~n** I can't work miracles; **Hexenkessel** m (lit, fig) cauldron; **Hexenschuß** m lumbago; **Hexe'rei** f witchcraft.

Hieb [hi:p] m -(e)s, -e blow; (Wunde) cut, gash; (Stichelei) cutting remark; **~e bekommen** get a thrashing.

hielt etc v siehe **halten**.

hier [hi:r] ad here; **~auf** ad thereupon; (danach) after that; **~be-**

halten vt unreg keep here; **~bei** ad herewith, enclosed; **~bleiben** vi unreg stay here; **~durch** ad by this means; (örtlich) through here; **~her** ad this way, here; **~hin** ad here; **~lassen** vt unreg leave here; **~mit** ad hereby; **~nach** ad hereafter; **~von** ad about this, hereof; **~zulande** ad in this country.

hiesig ['hi:zıç] a of this place, local.

hieß etc v siehe **heißen**.

Hilfe ['hilfə] f -, -n help; aid; **Erste ~** first aid; **~!** help!.

Hilf- zW: **h~los** a helpless; **~losigkeit** f helplessness; **h~reich** a helpful.

Hilfs- zW: **~arbeiter** m labourer; **h~bedürftig** a needy; **h~bereit** a ready to help; **~kraft** f assistant, helper; **~schule** f school for backward children.

hilfst etc v siehe **helfen**.

Himbeere ['hımbe:rə] f -, -n raspberry.

Himmel ['hıməl] m -s, - sky; (REL, liter) heaven; **h~blau** a sky-blue; **~fahrt** f Ascension; **h~schreiend** a outrageous; **Himmelsrichtung** f direction.

himmlisch ['hımlıʃ] a heavenly.

hin [hın] ad **1** (Richtung) **~ und zurück** there and back; **~ und her** to and fro; **bis zur Mauer ~** up to the wall; **wo ist er ~?** where has he gone?; **Geld ~, Geld her** money or no money **2** (auf ... ~): **auf meine Bitte ~** at my request; **auf seinen Rat ~** on the basis of his advice **3**: **mein Glück ist ~** my happiness has gone.

hinab [hı'nap] ad down; **~gehen** vi unreg go down; **~sehen** vi unreg look down.

hinauf [hı'nauf] ad up; **~arbeiten** vr work one's way up; **~steigen** vi unreg climb.

hinaus [hı'naus] ad out; **~gehen** vi unreg go out; **~gehen über** (+akk) exceed; **~laufen** vi unreg run out; **~laufen auf** (+akk) come to, amount to; **~lehnen** vr lean out; **~schieben** vt unreg put off, postpone; **~wollen** vi want to go out; **~wollen auf** (+akk) drive at, get at.

Hinblick ['hınblık] m: **in od im ~ auf** (+akk) in view of.

hinder- ['hındər] zW: **~lich** a awkward; **~n** vt hinder, hamper; **jdn an etw** (dat) **~n** prevent sb from doing sth; **H~nis** nt -ses, -se obstacle; **H~nisrennen** nt steeple chase.

hindeuten ['hındɔytən] vi point (auf +akk to).

hindurch [hın'durç] ad through; across; (zeitlich) over.

hinein [hı'naın] ad in; **~fallen** vi

unreg fall in; **~fallen in** (+*akk*) fall into; **~gehen** *vi unreg* go in; **~gehen in** (+*akk*) go into, enter; **~geraten** *vi unreg*: **~geraten in** (+*akk*) get into; **~passen** *vi* fit in; **~passen in** (+*akk*) fit into; **~steigern** *vr* get worked up; **~versetzen** *vr*: **sich ~versetzen in** (+*akk*) put oneself in the position of.

hin- ['hɪn] *zW*: **~fahren** *unreg vi* go; drive // *vt* take; drive; **H~fahrt** *f* journey there; **~fallen** *vi unreg* fall down; **~fällig** *a* frail, decrepit; (*Regel etc*) unnecessary, otiose; **H~gabe** *f* devotion; **~geben** *vr unreg* +*dat* give oneself up to, devote oneself to; **~gehen** *vi unreg* go; (*Zeit*) pass; **~halten** *vt unreg* hold out; (*warten lassen*) put off, stall.

hinken ['hɪŋkən] *vi* limp; (*Vergleich*) be unconvincing.

hin- ['hɪn] *zW*: **~legen** *vt* put down // *vr* lie down; **~nehmen** *vt unreg* (*fig*) put up with, take; **H~reise** *f* journey out; **~reißen** *vt unreg* carry away, enrapture; **sich ~reißen lassen, etw zu tun** get carried away and do sth; **~richten** *vt* execute; **H~richtung** *f* execution; **~setzen** *vt* put down // *vr* sit down; **~sichtlich** *präp* +*gen* with regard to; **H~spiel** *nt* (*SPORT*) first leg; **~stellen** *vt* put (down) // *vr* place o.s.

hintanstellen [hɪnt''anʃtɛlən] *vt* (*fig*) ignore.

hinten ['hɪntən] *ad* at the back; behind; **~herum** *ad* round the back; (*fig*) secretly.

hinter ['hɪntər] *präp* +*dat od akk* behind; (*nach*) after; **~ jdm hersein** be after sb; **H~achse** *f* rear axle; **H~bliebene(r)** *mf* surviving relative; **~e(r, s)** *a* rear, back; **~einander** *ad* one after the other; **H~gedanke** *m* ulterior motive; **~gehen** *vt unreg* deceive; **H~grund** *m* background; **H~halt** *m* ambush; **~hältig** *a* underhand, sneaky; **~her** *ad* afterwards, after; **H~hof** *m* backyard; **H~kopf** *m* back of one's head; **~'lassen** *vt unreg* leave; **~'legen** *vt* deposit; **H~list** *f* cunning, trickery; (*Handlung*) trick, dodge; **~listig** *a* cunning, crafty; **H~mann** *m, pl* **~männer** person behind; **H~rad** *nt* back wheel; **H~radantrieb** *m* (*AUT*) rear wheel drive; **~rücks** *ad* from behind; **H~tür** *f* back door; (*fig: Ausweg*) escape, loophole; **~'ziehen** *vt unreg* (*Steuern*) evade (paying).

hinüber [hɪ'ny:bər] *ad* across, over; **~gehen** *vi unreg* go over *od* across.

hinunter [hɪ'nʊntər] *ad* down; **~bringen** *vt unreg* take down; **~schlucken** *vt* (*lit, fig*) swallow; **~steigen** *vi unreg* descend.

Hinweg ['hɪnveːk] *m* journey out.

hinweg- [hɪn'vɛk] *zW*: **~helfen** *vi unreg*: **jdm über etw** (*akk*) **~helfen** help sb to get over sth; **~'setzen** *vr*: **sich ~setzen über** (+*akk*) disregard.

hin- ['hɪn] *zW*: **H~weis** *m* **-es, -e** (*Andeutung*) hint; (*Anweisung*) instruction; (*Verweis*) reference; **~weisen** *vi unreg* (*auf* +*akk*: *anzeigen*) point to; (*sagen*) point out, refer to; **~werfen** *vt unreg* throw down; **~ziehen** *vr unreg* (*fig*) drag on.

hinzu [hɪn'tsu:] *ad* in addition; **~fügen** *vt* add.

Hirn [hɪrn] *nt* **-(e)s, -e** brain(s); **~gespinst** *nt* **-(e)s, -e** fantasy; **h~verbrannt** *a* half-baked, crazy.

Hirsch [hɪrʃ] *m* **-(e)s, -e** stag.

Hirse ['hɪrzə] *f* **-, -n** millet.

Hirt ['hɪrt] *m* **-en, -en** herdsman; (*Schaf~, fig*) shepherd.

hissen ['hɪsən] *vt* hoist.

Historiker [hɪs'to:rikər] *m* **-s, -** historian.

historisch [hɪs'to:rɪʃ] *a* historical.

Hitze ['hɪtsə] *f* **-** heat; **h~beständig** *a* heat-resistant; **h~frei** *a*: **h~frei haben** have time off from school on account of excessively hot weather; **~welle** *f* heatwave.

hitzig ['hɪtsɪç] *a* hot-tempered; (*Debatte*) heated.

Hitz- *zW*: **~kopf** *m* hothead; **h~köpfig** *a* fiery, hotheaded; **~schlag** *m* heatstroke.

hm [(h)m] *interj* hm.

Hobby ['hɔbɪ] *nt* hobby.

Hobel ['ho:bəl] *m* **-s, -** plane; **~bank** *f* carpenter's bench; **h~n** *vti* plane; **~späne** *pl* wood shavings *pl*.

hoch [ho:x] *a* high; **H~** *nt* **-s, -s** (*Ruf*) cheer; (*MET*) anticyclone; **~achten** *vt* respect; **H~achtung** *f* respect, esteem; **~achtungsvoll** *ad* yours faithfully; **H~amt** *nt* high mass; **~begabt** *a* extremely gifted; **H~betrieb** *m* intense activity; (*COMM*) peak time; **H~burg** *f* stronghold; **~deutsch** *nt* High German; **~dotiert** *a* highly paid; **H~druck** *m* high pressure; **H~ebene** *f* plateau; **~erfreut** *a* highly delighted; **H~form** *f* top form; **~halten** *vt unreg* hold up; (*fig*) uphold, cherish; **H~haus** *nt* multistorey building; **~heben** *vt unreg* lift (up); **H~konjunktur** *f* boom; **H~land** *nt* highlands *pl*; **~leben** *vi*: **jdn ~leben lassen** give sb three cheers; **H~mut** *m* pride; **~mütig** *a* proud, haughty; **~näsig** *a* stuck-up, snooty; **H~ofen** *m* blast furnace; **~prozentig** *a* (*Alkohol*) strong; **H~rechnung** *f* projected result; **H~saison** *f* high season; **H~schätzung** *f* high esteem; **H~schule** *f* college; university;

H~sommer *m* middle of summer; **H~spannung** *f* high tension; **H~sprung** *m* high jump.
höchst [hø:çst] *ad* highly, extremely; **~e(r, s)** *a* highest; *(äußerste)* extreme.
Hochstapler ['ho:xstaplər] *m* **-s, -** swindler.
Höchst- *zW*: **h~ens** *ad* at the most; **~geschwindigkeit** *f* maximum speed; **h~persönlich** *ad* in person; **~preis** *m* maximum price; **h~wahrscheinlich** *ad* most probably.
Hoch- *zW*: **~verrat** *m* high treason; **~wasser** *nt* high water; *(Überschwemmung)* floods *pl*; **~würden** *m* Reverend; **~zahl** *f* (MATH) exponent.
Hochzeit ['hɔxtsait] *f* **-, -en** wedding; **Hochzeitsreise** *f* honeymoon.
hocken ['hɔkən] *vir* squat, crouch.
Hocker *m* **-s, -** stool.
Höcker ['hœkər] *m* **-s, -** hump.
Hoden ['ho:dən] *m* **-s, -** testicle.
Hof [ho:f] *m* **-(e)s, ̈e** *(Hinter~)* yard; *(Bauern~)* farm; *(Königs~)* court.
hoffen ['hɔfən] *vi* hope *(auf +akk* for).
hoffentlich ['hɔfəntliç] *ad* I hope, hopefully.
Hoffnung ['hɔfnuŋ] *f* hope.
Hoffnungs- *zW*: **h~los** *a* hopeless; **~losigkeit** *f* hopelessness; **~schimmer** *m* glimmer of hope; **h~voll** *a* hopeful.
höflich ['hø:fliç] *a* polite, courteous; **H~keit** *f* courtesy, politeness.
hohe(r, s) ['ho:ə(r, s)] *a siehe* **hoch**.
Höhe ['hø:ə] *f* **-, -n** height; *(An~)* hill.
Hoheit ['ho:hait] *f* (POL) sovereignty; *(Titel)* Highness.
Hoheitsgebiet *nt* sovereign territory.
Hoheitsgewässer *nt* territorial waters *pl*.
Höhen- ['hø:ən] *zW*: **~angabe** *f* altitude reading; *(auf Karte)* height marking; **~messer** *m* **-s, -** altimeter; **~sonne** *f* sun lamp; **~unterschied** *m* difference in altitude.
Höhepunkt *m* climax.
höher *a,ad* higher.
hohl [ho:l] *a* hollow.
Höhle ['hø:lə] *f* **-, -n** cave, hole; *(Mund~)* cavity; *(fig, ZOOL)* den.
Hohlheit *f* hollowness.
Hohlmaß *nt* measure of volume.
Hohn [ho:n] *m* **-(e)s** scorn.
höhnisch *a* scornful, taunting.
holen ['ho:lən] *vt* get, fetch; *(Atem)* take; **jdn/etw ~ lassen** send for sb/sth.
Holl- [hɔl] *zW*: **~and** *nt* Holland; **~änder** *m* Dutchman; **~änderin** *f* Dutchwoman; **h~ändisch** *a* Dutch.
Hölle ['hœlə] *f* **-, -n** hell.
höllisch ['hœliʃ] *a* hellish, infernal.
holperig ['hɔlpəriç] *a* rough, bumpy.

Holz [hɔlts] *nt* **-es, ̈er** wood.
hölzern ['hœltsərn] *a* (lit, fig) wooden.
Holz- *zW*: **~fäller** *m* **-s, -** lumberjack, woodcutter; **h~ig** *a* woody; **~kohle** *f* charcoal; **~scheit** *nt* log; **~schuh** *m* clog; **~weg** *m* (fig) wrong track; **~wolle** *f* fine wood shavings *pl*.
homosexuell [homozɛksu'ɛl] *a* homosexual.
Honig ['ho:niç] *m* **-s, -e** honey; **~wabe** *f* honeycomb.
Honorar [hono'ra:r] *nt* **-s, -e** fee.
honorieren [hono'ri:rən] *vt* remunerate; *(Scheck)* honour.
Hopfen ['hɔpfən] *m* **-s, -** hops *pl*.
hopsen ['hɔpsən] *vi* hop.
Hör- ['hø:r] *zW*: **~apparat** *m* hearing aid; **h~bar** *a* audible.
horch [hɔrç] *interj* listen; **~en** *vi* listen; *(pej)* eavesdrop.
Horde ['hɔrdə] *f* **-, -n** horde.
hören ['hø:rən] *vti* hear; **Musik/Radio ~** listen to music/the radio.
Hörer *m* **-s, -** hearer; *(RAD)* listener; *(UNIV)* student; *(Telefon~)* receiver.
Horizont [hori'tsɔnt] *m* **-(e)s, -e** horizon; **h~al** [-'ta:l] *a* horizontal.
Hormon [hɔr'mo:n] *nt* **-s, -e** hormone.
Hörmuschel *f* (TEL) earpiece.
Horn [hɔrn] *nt* **-(e)s, ̈er** horn; **~haut** *f* horny skin.
Hornisse [hɔr'nisə] *f* **-, -n** hornet.
Horoskop [horo'sko:p] *nt* **-s, -e** horoscope.
Hörsaal *m* lecture room.
horten ['hɔrtən] *vt* hoard.
Hose ['ho:zə] *f* **-, -n** trousers *pl*, pants *(US)* *pl*.
Hosen- *zW*: **~anzug** *m* trouser suit; **~rock** *m* culottes *pl*; **~tasche** *f* *(trouser)* pocket; **~träger** *m* braces *pl* (Brit), suspenders (US) *pl*.
Hostie ['hɔstiə] *f* (REL) host.
Hotel [ho'tɛl] *nt* **-s, -s** hotel.
Hotelier [hoteli'e:] *m* **-s, -s** hotelkeeper, hotelier.
Hubraum *m* (AUT) cubic capacity.
hübsch [hypʃ] *a* pretty, nice.
Hubschrauber ['hu:bʃraubər] *m* **-s, -** helicopter.
Huf ['hu:f] *m* **-(e)s, -e** hoof; **~eisen** *nt* horseshoe; **~nagel** *m* horseshoe nail.
Hüft- ['hyft] *zW*: **~e** *f* **-, -n** hip; **~gürtel** *m*, **~halter** *m* **-s, -** girdle.
Hügel ['hy:gəl] *m* **-s, -** hill; **h~ig** *a* hilly.
Huhn [hu:n] *nt* **-(e)s, ̈er** hen; *(KOCH)* chicken.
Hühner- ['hy:nər] *zW*: **~auge** *nt* corn; **~brühe** *f* chicken broth.
Hülle ['hylə] *f* **-, -n** cover(ing); wrapping; **in ~ und Fülle** galore; **h~n** *vt* cover, wrap *(in +akk* with).
Hülse ['hylzə] *f* **-, -n** husk, shell; **Hülsenfrucht** *f* pulse.

human [hu'ma:n] *a* humane; **~i'tär** *a* humanitarian; **H~i'tät** *f* humanity.
Hummel ['hʊməl] *f* -, **-n** bumblebee.
Hummer ['hʊmər] *m* **-s, -** lobster.
Humor [hu'mo:r] *m* **-s, -e** humour; **~ haben** have a sense of humour; **~ist** [-'rɪst] *m* humorist; **h~istisch** *a*, **h~voll** *a* humorous.
humpeln ['hʊmpəln] *vi* hobble.
Humpen ['hʊmpən] *m* **-s, -** tankard.
Hund [hʊnt] *m* **-(e)s, -e** dog.
Hunde- ['hʊndə] *zW:* **~hütte** *f* (dog) kennel; **~kuchen** *m* dog biscuit; **h~müde** *a* (*umg*) dog-tired.
hundert ['hʊndərt] *num* hundred; **H~'jahrfeier** *f* centenary; **~prozentig** *a,ad* one hundred per cent.
Hündin ['hʏndɪn] *f* bitch.
Hunger ['hʊŋər] *m* **-s** hunger; **~ haben** be hungry; **h~n** *vi* starve; **Hungersnot** *f* famine; **~streik** *m* hunger strike.
hungrig ['hʊŋrɪç] *a* hungry.
Hupe ['hu:pə] *f* -, **-n** horn; **h~n** *vi* hoot, sound one's horn.
hüpfen ['hʏpfən] *vi* hop, jump.
Hürde ['hʏrdə] *f* -, **-n** hurdle; (*für Schafe*) pen; **Hürdenlauf** *m* hurdling.
Hure ['hu:rə] *f* -, **-n** whore.
hurra [hu'ra:] *inter* hooray.
hurtig ['hʊrtɪç] *a,ad* brisk(ly), quick(ly).
huschen ['hʊʃən] *vi* flit, scurry.
Husten ['hu:stən] *m* **-s** cough; **h~** *vi* cough; **~anfall** *m* coughing fit; **~bonbon** *m od nt* cough drop; **~saft** *m* cough mixture.
Hut [hu:t] *m* **-(e)s, -̈e** hat // *f* - care; **auf der ~ sein** be on one's guard.
hüten ['hy:tən] *vt* guard // *vr* watch out; **sich ~, zu** take care not to; **sich ~ vor** beware of.
Hütte ['hʏtə] *f* -, **-n** hut, cottage; (*Eisen~*) forge.
Hyäne [hy'ɛ:nə] *f* -, **-n** hyena.
Hyazinthe [hya'tsɪntə] *f* -, **-n** hyacinth.
Hydrant [hy'drant] *m* hydrant.
hydraulisch [hy'draʊlɪʃ] *a* hydraulic.
Hygiene [hygi'e:nə] *f* - hygiene.
hygienisch [hygi'e:nɪʃ] *a* hygienic.
Hymne ['hʏmnə] *f* -, **-n** hymn, anthem.
hyper- ['hypɛr] *präf* hyper-.
Hypno- [hyp'no:] *zW:* **~se** *f* -, **-n** hypnosis; **h~tisch** *a* hypnotic; **~tiseur** [-ti'zø:r] *m* hypnotist; **h~ti'sieren** *vt* hypnotize.
Hypothek [hypo'te:k] *f* -, **-en** mortgage.
Hypothese [hypo'te:zə] *f* -, **-n** hypothesis.
hypothetisch [hypo'te:tɪʃ] *a* hypothetical.
Hysterie [hyste'ri:] *f* hysteria.
hysterisch [hys'te:rɪʃ] *a* hysterical.

I

I, i [i:] *nt* I, i.
i.A. *abk* (= *im Auftrag*) for; (*in Briefen auch*) pp.
ich [ɪç] *pron* I; **~ bin's!** it's me!; **I~** *nt* **-(s), -(s)** self; (*PSYCH*) ego.
Ideal [ide'a:l] *nt* **-s, -e** ideal; **i~** *a* ideal; **~ist** [-'lɪst] *m* idealist; **i~istisch** [-'lɪstɪʃ] *a* idealistic.
Idee [i'de:] *f* -, **-n** idea.
identifizieren [i'dɛntifi'tsi:rən] *vt* identify.
identisch [i'dɛntɪʃ] *a* identical.
Identität [identi'tɛ:t] *f* identity.
Ideo- [ideo] *zW:* **~loge** [-'lo:gə] *m* **-n, -n** ideologist; **~logie** [-lo'gi:] *f* ideology; **i~logisch** [-'lo:gɪʃ] *a* ideological.
Idiot [idi'o:t] *m* **-en, -en** idiot; **i~isch** *a* idiotic.
idyllisch [i'dʏlɪʃ] *a* idyllic.
Igel ['i:gəl] *m* **-s, -** hedgehog.
ignorieren [ɪgno'ri:rən] *vt* ignore.
ihm [i:m] *pron dat von* **er, es** (to) him, (to) it.
ihn [i:n] *pron akk von* **er** him; it; **~en** *pron dat von* **sie** *pl* (to) them; **I~en** *pron dat von* **Sie** (to) you.
ihr [i:r] ◆*pron* **1** *nom pl* you; **~ seid es** it's you
2 *dat von* **sie** *sing* to her; **gib es ~** give it to her; **er steht neben ~** he is standing beside her
◆*poss pron* **1** *sing* her; (*bei Tieren, Dingen*) its; **~ Mann** her husband
2 *pl* their; **die Bäume und ~e Blätter** the trees and their leaves
ihr(e) [i:r(ə)] *poss pron* your; **~e(r, s)** *poss pron sing* hers; its // *pl* theirs; **I~e(r, s)** *poss pron* yours; **~er** *pron gen von* **sie** *sing/pl* of her/them; **I~er** *pron gen von* **Sie** of you; **~erseits** *ad* for her/their part; **~esgleichen** *pron* people like her/them; (*von Dingen*) others like it; **~etwegen, ~etwillen** *ad* (*für sie*) for her/its/their sake; (*wegen ihr*) on her/its/their account; **~ige** *pron:* **der/die/das ~ige** hers; its; theirs.
illegal ['ɪlega:l] *a* illegal.
Illusion [ɪluzi'o:n] *f* illusion.
illusorisch [ɪlu'zo:rɪʃ] *a* illusory.
illustrieren [ɪlʊs'tri:rən] *vt* illustrate.
Illustrierte *f* **-n, -n** picture magazine.
Iltis ['ɪltɪs] *m* **-ses, -se** polecat.
im [ɪm] = **in dem**.
Imbiß ['ɪmbɪs] *m* **-sses, -sse** snack; **~halle** *f*, **~stube** *f* snack bar.
imitieren [ɪmi'ti:rən] *vt* imitate.
immatrikulieren [ɪmatriku'li:rən] *vir* register.
immer ['ɪmər] *ad* always; **~ wieder** again and again; **~ noch** still; **~ noch**

nicht still not; **für ~** forever; **~ wenn ich** ... everytime I ...; **~ schöner/trauriger** more and more beautiful/sadder and sadder; **was/wer (auch) ~** whatever/whoever; **~hin** *ad* all the same; **~zu** *ad* all the time.

Immobilien [ɪmo'bi:liən] *pl* real estate.

immun [ɪ'mu:n] *a* immune; **I~ität** [-i'tɛ:t] *f* immunity.

Imperfekt ['ɪmperfɛkt] *nt* **-s, -e** imperfect (tense).

Impf- ['ɪmpf] *zW*: **i~en** *vt* vaccinate; **~stoff** *m* vaccine, serum; **~ung** *f* vaccination; **~zwang** *m* compulsory vaccination.

imponieren [ɪmpo'ni:rən] *vi* impress (*jdm* sb).

Import [ɪm'pɔrt] *m* **-(e)s, -e** import; **i~ieren** [-'ti:rən] *vt* import.

impotent ['ɪmpotɛnt] *a* impotent.

imprägnieren [ɪmprɛ'gni:rən] *vt* (water)proof.

improvisieren [ɪmprovi'zi:rən] *vti* improvize.

Impuls [ɪm'pʊls] *m* **-es, -e** impulse; **i~iv** [-'zi:f] *a* impulsive.

imstande [ɪm'ʃtandə] *a*: **~ sein** in a position; (*fähig*) be able

in [ɪn] ♦ *präp +akk* **1** (*räumlich: wohin?*) in, into; **~ die Stadt** into town; **~ die Schule gehen** go to school **2** (*zeitlich*): **bis ~s 20. Jahrhundert** into *od* up to the 20th century ♦ *präp +dat* **1** (*räumlich: wo*) in; **~ der Stadt** in town; **~ der Schule sein** be at school **2** (*zeitlich: wann*): **~ diesem Jahr** this year; (**~ *jenem Jahr***) in that year; **heute ~ zwei Wochen** two weeks today.

Inanspruchnahme [ɪn''anʃpruxna:mə] *f* **-, -n** demands *pl* (*gen* on).

Inbegriff ['ɪnbəgrɪf] *m* embodiment, personification; **i~en** *ad* included.

indem [ɪn'de:m] *kj* while; **~ man etw macht** (*dadurch*) by doing sth.

Inder(in *f*) ['ɪndər(ɪn)] *m* Indian.

Indianer(in *f*) [ɪndi'a:nər(ɪn)] *m* **-s, -** Red Indian.

indianisch *a* Red Indian.

Indien ['ɪndiən] *nt* India.

indirekt ['ɪndɪrɛkt] *a* indirect.

indisch ['ɪndɪʃ] *a* Indian.

indiskret ['ɪndɪskre:t] *a* indiscreet.

indiskutabel ['ɪndɪskuta:bəl] *a* out of the question.

Individu- [ɪndividu] *zW*: **~alist** [-a'lɪst] *m* individualist; **~alität** [-ali'tɛ:t] *f* individuality; **i~ell** [-'ɛl] *a* individual; **~um** [ɪndi'vi:duʊm] *nt* **-s, -en** individual.

Indiz [ɪn'di:ts] *nt* **-es, -ien** sign (*für* of); (*JUR*) clue.

Indonesien [ɪndo'ne:ziən] *nt* Indo-nesia.

industrialisieren [ɪndʊstriali'zi:rən] *vt* industrialize.

Industrie [ɪndʊs'tri:] *f* industry; *in zW* industrial; **~gebiet** *nt* industrial area; **~gelände** *nt* industrial *od* trading estate; **industriell** [ɪndʊstri'ɛl] *a* industrial; **~zweig** *m* branch of industry.

ineinander [ɪn'aɪ'nandər] *ad* in(to) one another *od* each other.

Infarkt [ɪn'farkt] *m* **-(e)s, -e** coronary (thrombosis).

Infektion [ɪnfɛktsi'o:n] *f* infection; **Infektionskrankheit** *f* infectious disease.

Infinitiv ['ɪnfiniti:f] *m* **-s, -e** infinitive.

infizieren [ɪnfi'tsi:rən] *vt* infect // *vr* be infected (*bei* by).

Inflation [ɪnflatsi'o:n] *f* inflation.

inflationär [ɪnflatsio'nɛ:r] *a* inflationary.

infolge [ɪn'fɔlgə] *präp +gen* as a result of, owing to; **~dessen** [-'dɛsən] *ad* consequently.

Informatik [ɪnfɔr'ma:tɪk] *f* information studies *pl*.

Information [ɪnfɔrmatsi'o:n] *f* information *no pl*.

informieren [ɪnfɔr'mi:rən] *vt* inform // *vr* find out (*über +akk* about).

Infusion [ɪnfuzi'o:n] *f* infusion.

Ingenieur [ɪnʒeni'ø:r] *m* engineer; **~schule** *f* school of engineering.

Ingwer ['ɪŋvər] *m* **-s** ginger.

Inh. *abk* (= *Inhaber*) prop.; (= *Inhalt*) contents.

Inhaber(in *f*) ['ɪnha:bər(ɪn)] *m* **-s, -** owner; (*Haus~*) occupier; (*Lizenz~*) licensee, holder; (*FIN*) bearer.

inhalieren [ɪnha'li:rən] *vti* inhale.

Inhalt ['ɪnhalt] *m* **-(e)s, -e** contents *pl*; (*eines Buchs etc*) content; (*MATH*) area; volume; **i~lich** *a* as regards content.

Inhalts- *zW*: **~angabe** *f* summary; **i~los** *a* empty; **~sverzeichnis** *nt* table of contents.

inhuman ['ɪnhuma:n] *a* inhuman.

Initiative [initsia'ti:və] *f* initiative.

Injektion [ɪnjɛktsi'o:n] *f* injection.

inklusive [ɪnklu'zi:və] *präp, ad* inclusive (*gen* of).

inkognito [ɪn'kɔgnito] *ad* incognito.

Inkrafttreten [ɪn'krafttre:tən] *nt* **-s** coming into force.

Inland ['ɪnlant] *nt* **-(e)s** (*GEOG*) inland; (*POL, COMM*) home (country).

inmitten [ɪn'mɪtən] *präp +gen* in the middle of; **~ von** amongst.

innehaben ['ɪnəha:bən] *vt unreg* hold.

innen ['ɪnən] *ad* inside; **I~architekt** *m* interior designer; **I~einrichtung** *f* (interior) furnishings *pl*; **I~minister** *m* minister of the interior, Home Secretary (*Brit*); **I~politik** *f* domestic policy; **I~stadt** *f* town/city centre.

inner- ['ɪnər] *zW*: **~e(r, s)** *a* inner; (*im Körper, inländisch*) internal; **I~e(s)** *nt* inside; (*Mitte*) centre; (*fig*) heart; **Innereien** [-'raɪən] *pl* innards *pl*; **~halb** *ad, präp +gen* within; (*räumlich*) inside; **~lich** *a* internal; (*geistig*) inward; **I~ste(s)** *nt* heart; **~ste(r, s)** *a* innermost.

inoffiziell ['ɪn'ɔfitsiɛl] *a* unofficial.

ins [ɪns] = **in das.**

Insasse ['ɪnzasə] *m* **-n, -n** (*Anstalt*) inmate; (*AUT*) passenger.

insbesondere [ɪnsbə'zɔndərə] *ad* (e)specially.

Inschrift ['ɪnʃrɪft] *f* inscription.

Insekt [ɪn'zɛkt] *nt* **-(e)s, -en** insect.

Insel ['ɪnzəl] *f* **-, -n** island.

Inser- *zW*: **~at** [ɪnze'raːt] *nt* **-(e)s, -e** advertisement; **~ent** [ɪnze'rɛnt] *m* advertiser; **i~ieren** [ɪnze'riːrən] *vti* advertise.

insgeheim [ɪnsgə'haɪm] *ad* secretly.

insgesamt [ɪnsgə'zamt] *ad* altogether, all in all.

insofern ['ɪnzo'fɛrn], **insoweit** ['ɪnzo-'vaɪt] *ad* in this respect; **~ als** in so far as // *kj* if; (*deshalb*) (and) so.

Installateur [ɪnstala'tø:r] *m* electrician; plumber.

Instand- [ɪn'ʃtant] *zW*: **~haltung** *f* maintenance; **~setzung** *f* overhaul; (*eines Gebäudes*) restoration.

Instanz [ɪn'stants] *f* authority; (*JUR*) court; **~enweg** *m* official channels *pl*.

Instinkt [ɪn'stɪŋkt] *m* **-(e)s, -e** instinct; **i~iv** [-'tiːf] *a* instinctive.

Institut [ɪnsti'tuːt] *nt* **-(e)s, -e** institute.

Instrument [ɪnstru'mɛnt] *nt* instrument.

Intell- [ɪntɛl] *zW*: **i~ektuell** [-ɛktu'ɛl] *a* intellectual; **i~igent** [-i'gɛnt] *a* intelligent; **~igenz** [-i'gɛnts] *f* intelligence; (*Leute*) intelligentsia *pl*.

Intendant [ɪntɛn'dant] *m* director.

intensiv [ɪntɛn'ziːf] *a* intensive.

Interess- *zW*: **i~ant** [ɪntərɛ'sant] *a* interesting; **i~anterweise** *ad* interestingly enough; **~e** [ɪntə'resə] *nt* **-s, -n** interest; **~e haben be interested** (*an +dat* in); **~ent** [ɪntərɛ'sɛnt] *m* interested party; **i~ieren** [ɪntərɛ'siːrən] *vt* interest // *vr* be interested (*für* in).

Inter- [ɪntɛr] *zW*: **~nat** [-'naːt] *nt* **-(e)s, -e** boarding school; **i~national** [-natsio'naːl] *a* international; **i~pretieren** [-pre'tiːrən] *vt* interpret; **~vall** [-'val] *nt* **-s, -e** interval; **~view** ['vjuː] *nt* **-s, -s** interview; **i~viewen** [-'vjuːən] *vt* interview.

intim [ɪn'tiːm] *a* intimate; **I~ität** [ɪntimi'tɛːt] *f* intimacy.

intolerant ['ɪntolerant] *a* intolerant.

intransitiv ['ɪntranziti:f] *a* (*GRAM*) intransitive.

Intrige [ɪn'triːgə] *f* **-, -n** intrigue, plot.

Invasion [ɪnvazi'oːn] *f* invasion.

Inventar [ɪnvɛn'taːr] *nt* **-s, -e** inventory.

Inventur [ɪnvɛn'tuːr] *f* stocktaking; **~ machen** stocktake.

investieren [ɪnvɛs'tiːrən] *vt* invest.

Investition [ɪnvɛstitsi'oːn] *f* investment.

Investmentgesellschaft [ɪn'vɛstmɛntgəzɛlʃaft] *f* unit trust.

inwiefern [ɪnvi'fɛrn], **inwieweit** [ɪnvi-'vaɪt] *ad* how far, to what extent.

inzwischen [ɪn'tsvɪʃən] *ad* meanwhile.

Irak [i'raːk] *m* **-s:** **der ~** Iraq; **i~sch** *a* Iraqi.

Iran [i'raːn] *n* **-s:** **der ~** Iran; **i~isch** *a* Iranian.

irdisch ['ɪrdɪʃ] *a* earthly.

Ire ['iːrə] *m* **-n, -n** Irishman.

irgend ['ɪrgənt] *ad* at all; **wann/was/wer ~** whenever/whatever/whoever; **~ jemand/etwas** somebody/something; anybody/anything; **~ein(e,s)** some, any; **~einmal** *ad* someone or other; (*fragend*) ever; **~wann** *ad* sometime; **~wer** *ad* (*umg*) somebody; anybody; **~wie** *ad* somehow; **~wo** *ad* somewhere; anywhere; **~wohin** *ad* somewhere (or other).

Irin ['iːrɪn] *f* Irishwoman.

Irland ['ɪrlant] *nt* **-s** Ireland.

Ironie [iro'niː] *f* irony.

ironisch [i'roːnɪʃ] *a* ironic(al).

irre ['ɪrə] *a* crazy, mad; **I~(r)** *mf* lunatic; **~führen** *vt* mislead; **~machen** *vt* confuse; **~n** *vir* be mistaken; (*umher~*) wander, stray; **Irrenanstalt** *f* lunatic asylum.

irrig ['ɪrɪç] *a* incorrect, wrong.

Irr- *zW*: **i~sinnig** *a* mad, crazy; (*umg*) terrific; **~tum** *m* **-s, -tümer** mistake, error; **i~tümlich** *a* mistaken.

Island ['iːslant] *nt* **-s** Iceland.

Isolation [izolatsi'oːn] *f* isolation; (*ELEK*) insulation.

Isolator [izo'laːtɔr] *m* insulator.

Isolier- [izo'liːr] *zW*: **~band** *nt* insulating tape; **i~en** *vt* isolate; (*ELEK*) insulate; **~station** *f* (*MED*) isolation ward; **~ung** *f* isolation; (*ELEK*) insulation.

Israel ['ɪsraeːl] *nt* **-s** Israel; **~i** [-'eːli] *m* **-s, -s** Israeli; **~isch** *a* Israeli.

ißt *v siehe* **essen.**

ist *v siehe* **sein.**

Italien [i'taːliən] *nt* **-s** Italy; **~er(in** *f*) [-li'eːnər(ɪn)] *m* **-s** Italian; **i~isch** *a* Italian.

i.V. *abk von* **in Vertretung.**

J

J, j [jɔt] *nt* J, j.
ja [ja:] *adv* **1** yes; **haben Sie das gesehen? — ~ did you see it? —** yes(, I did); **ich glaube — (yes) I think so**
2 *(fragend)* really?; **ich habe gekündigt — ~?** I've quit — have you?; **du kommst, ~?** you're coming, aren't you?
3 sei ~ vorsichtig do be careful; **Sie wissen ~, daß** ... as you know, ...; **tu das ~ nicht!** don't do that!; **ich habe es ~ gewußt** I just knew it; **~, also,** ... well you see ...
Jacht [jaxt] *f* -, **-en** yacht.
Jacke ['jakə] *f* -, **-n** jacket; *(Woll~)* cardigan.
Jackett [ʒa'kɛt] *nt* **-s,** *od* **-e** jacket.
Jagd [ja:kt] *f* -, **-en** hunt; *(Jagen)* hunting; **~beute** *f* kill; **~flugzeug** *nt* fighter; **~gewehr** *nt* sporting gun.
jagen ['ja:gən] *vi* hunt; *(eilen)* race // *vt* hunt; *(weg~)* drive (off); *(verfolgen)* chase.
Jäger ['jɛ:gər] *m* **-s,** **-** hunter.
jäh [jɛ:] *a* sudden, abrupt; *(steil)* steep, precipitous.
Jahr [ja:r] *nt* **-(e)s,** **-e** year; **j~elang** *ad* for years.
Jahres- *zW:* **~abonnement** *nt* annual subscription; **~abschluß** *m* end of the year; *(COMM)* annual statement of account; **~bericht** *m* annual report; **~hauptversammlung** *f* annual general meeting, AGM; **~wechsel** *m* turn of the year; **~zahl** *f* date, year; **~zeit** *f* season.
Jahr- *zW:* **~gang** *m* age group; *(von Wein)* vintage; **~'hundert** *nt* **-s,** **-e** century; **~'hundertfeier** *f* centenary.
jährlich ['jɛ:rlıç] *a,ad* yearly.
Jahrmarkt *m* fair.
Jahr'zehnt *nt* decade.
Jähzorn ['jɛ:tsɔrn] *m* sudden anger; hot temper; **j~ig** *a* hot-tempered.
Jalousie [ʒalu'zi:] *f* venetian blind.
Jammer ['jamər] *m* **-s** misery; **es ist ein ~, daß** ... it is a crying shame that ...
jämmerlich ['jɛmərlıç] *a* wretched, pathetic.
jammern *vi* wail // *vt unpers:* **es jammert jdn** it makes sb feel sorry.
jammerschade *a:* **es ist ~** it is a crying shame.
Januar ['janua:r] *m* **-s,** **-e** January.
Japan ['ja:pan] *nt* **-s** Japan; **~er(in** *f)* [-'pa:nər(ın)] *m* **-s** Japanese; **j~isch** *a* Japanese.
Jargon [ʒar'gõ:] *m* **-s,** **-s** jargon.
jäten ['jɛ:tən] *vt:* **Unkraut ~** weed.

jauchzen ['jauxtsən] *vi* rejoice, shout (with joy).
jaulen ['jaulən] *vi* howl.
jawohl [ja'vo:l] *ad* yes (of course).
Jawort ['ja:vɔrt] *nt* consent.
Jazz [dʒɛs] *m* - Jazz.
je [je:] ◆ *ad* **1** *(jemals)* ever; **hast du so was ~ gesehen?** did you ever see anything like it?
2 *(jeweils)* every, each; **sie zahlten ~ 3 Mark** they paid 3 marks each
◆ *kj* **1:** **~ nach** depending on; **~ nachdem** it depends; **~ nachdem, ob** ... depending on whether ...
2: **~ eher, desto** *od* **um so besser** the sooner the better.
Jeans [dʒi:nz] *pl* jeans.
jede(r, s) ['je:də(r, s)] *a* every, each // *pron* everybody; *(~ einzelne)* each; **ohne ~ x** without any x.
jedenfalls *ad* in any case.
jedermann *pron* everyone.
jederzeit *ad* at any time.
jedesmal *ad* every time, each time.
jedoch [je'dɔx] *ad* however.
jemals ['je:ma:ls] *ad* ever.
jemand ['je:mant] *pron* somebody; anybody.
Jemen ['je:mən] *m* **-s:** **der ~** the Yemen.
jene(r, s) ['je:nə(r, s)] *a* that // *pron* that one.
jenseits ['je:nzaıts] *ad* on the other side // *präp +gen* on the other side of, beyond; **das J~** the hereafter, the beyond.
jetzig ['jɛtsıç] *a* present.
jetzt [jɛtst] *ad* now.
je- *zW:* **~weilig** *a* respective; **~weils** *ad:* **~weils zwei zusammen** two at a time; **zu ~weils 5 DM** at 5 marks each; **~weils das erste** the first each time.
Jh. *abk von* **Jahrhundert.**
Jockei ['dʒɔke] *m* **-s,** **-s** jockey.
Jod [jo:t] *nt* **-(e)s** iodine.
jodeln ['jo:dəln] *vi* yodel.
joggen ['dʒɔgən] *vi* jog.
Joghurt ['jo:gurt] *m* *od* *nt* **-s,** **-s** yogurt.
Johannisbeere [jo'hanısbe:rə] *f* redcurrant; **schwarze ~** blackcurrant.
johlen ['jo:lən] *vi* yell.
Jolle ['jɔlə] *f* -, **-n** dinghy.
jonglieren [ʒõ'gli:rən] *vt* juggle.
Jordanien [jɔr'da:nıən] *nt* **-s** Jordan.
Journal- [ʒurnal] *zW:* **~ismus** [-'lısmus] *m* journalism; **~ist(in** *f)* [-'lıst] *m* journalist; **j~istisch** *a* journalistic.
Jubel ['ju:bəl] *m* **-s** rejoicing; **j~n** *vi* rejoice.
Jubiläum [jubi'lɛ:um] *nt* **-s,** **Jubiläen** anniversary, jubilee.
jucken ['jukən] *vi* itch // *vt* **es juckt**

mich am Arm my arm is itching; das juckt mich that's itchy.

Juckreiz ['jʊkraɪts] m itch.

Jude ['juːdə] m -n, -n Jew.

Judentum nt - Judaism; Jewry.

Judenverfolgung f persecution of the Jews.

Jüd- ['jyːd] zW: ~**in** f Jewess; **j~isch** a Jewish.

Judo ['juːdo] nt -(s) judo.

Jugend ['juːgənt] f - youth; ~**club** m youth club; ~**herberge** f youth hostel; ~**kriminalität** f juvenile crime; **j~lich** a youthful; ~**liche(r)** mf teenager, young person.

Jugoslaw- [jugoˈslaːv] zW: ~**e** m, ~**in** f Yugoslavian; ~**ien** nt Yugoslavia; **j~isch** a Yugoslavian.

Juli ['juːli] m -(s), -s July.

jun. abk (= junior) jr.

jung [jʊŋ] a young; **J~e** m -n, -n boy, lad; **J~e(s)** nt young animal; (pl) young pl.

Jünger ['jyŋər] m -s, - disciple; **j~** a younger.

Jungfer ['jʊŋfər] f -, -n: alte ~ old maid.

Jungfernfahrt f maiden voyage.

Jung- zW: ~**frau** f virgin; (ASTROL) Virgo; ~**geselle** m bachelor; ~**gesellin** f unmarried woman.

jüngst [jyŋst] ad lately, recently; ~**e(r, s)** a youngest; (neueste) latest.

Juni ['juːni] m -(s), -s June.

Junior ['juːniɔr] m -s, -en [-ˈoːrən] junior.

Jurist [juˈrɪst] m jurist, lawyer; **j~isch** a legal.

Justiz [jʊsˈtiːts] f - justice; ~**beamte(r)** m judicial officer; ~**irrtum** m miscarriage of justice.

Juwel [juˈveːl] nt od m -s, -en jewel.

Juwelier [juveˈliːr] m -s, -e jeweller; ~**geschäft** nt jeweller's (shop).

Jux [jʊks] m -es, -e joke, lark.

K

K, k [kaː] nt K, k.

Kabarett [kabaˈrɛt] nt -s, -e od -s cabaret; ~**ist** [-ˈtɪst] m cabaret artiste.

Kabel ['kaːbəl] nt -s, - (ELEK) wire; (stark) cable; ~**fernsehen** nt cable television.

Kabeljau ['kaːbəljaʊ] m -s, -e od -s cod.

kabeln vti cable.

Kabine [kaˈbiːnə] f cabin; (Zelle) cubicle.

Kabinett [kabiˈnɛt] nt -s, -e (POL) cabinet.

Kachel ['kaxəl] f -, -n tile; **k~n** vt tile; ~**ofen** m tiled stove.

Käfer ['kɛːfər] m -s, - beetle.

Kaffee ['kafe] m -s, -s coffee; ~**kanne** f coffeepot; ~**klatsch** m, ~**kränzchen** nt hen party; coffee morning; ~**löffel** m coffee spoon; ~**satz** m coffee grounds pl.

Käfig ['kɛːfɪç] m -s, -e cage.

kahl [kaːl] a bald; ~**geschoren** a shaven, shorn; **K~heit** f baldness; ~**köpfig** a bald-headed.

Kahn [kaːn] m -(e)s, ˷e boat, barge.

Kai [kaɪ] m -s, -e od -s quay.

Kaiser ['kaɪzər] m -s, - emperor; ~**in** f empress; **k~lich** a imperial; ~**reich** nt empire; ~**schnitt** m (MED) Caesarian (section).

Kakao [kaˈkao] m -s, -s cocoa.

Kaktee [kakˈteː(ə)] f -, -n, **Kaktus** ['kaktʊs] m -, -se cactus.

Kalb [kalp] nt -(e)s, ˷er calf; **k~en** ['kalbən] vi calve; ~**fleisch** nt veal; **Kalbsleder** nt calf(skin).

Kalender [kaˈlɛndər] m -s, - calendar; (Taschen~) diary.

Kaliber [kaˈliːbər] nt -s, - (lit, fig) calibre.

Kalk [kalk] m -(e)s, -e lime; (BIOL) calcium; ~**stein** m limestone.

kalkulieren [kalkuˈliːrən] vt calculate.

Kalorie [kaloˈriː] f calorie.

kalt [kalt] a cold; mir ist (es) ~ I am cold; ~**bleiben** vi unreg be unmoved; ~**blütig** a cold-blooded; (ruhig) cool.

Kälte ['kɛltə] f - cold; coldness; ~**grad** m degree of frost od below zero; ~**welle** f cold spell.

kalt- zW: ~**herzig** a cold-hearted; ~**schnäuzig** a cold, unfeeling; ~**stellen** vt chill; (fig) leave out in the cold.

kam etc v siehe **kommen**.

Kamel [kaˈmeːl] nt -(e)s, -e camel.

Kamera ['kamera] f -, -s camera.

Kamerad [kaməˈraːt] m -en, -en comrade, friend; ~**schaft** f comradeship; **k~schaftlich** a comradely.

Kamille [kaˈmɪlə] f -, -n camomile; **Kamillentee** m camomile tea.

Kamin [kaˈmiːn] m -s, -e (außen) chimney; (innen) fireside, fireplace; ~**feger**, ~**kehrer** m -s, - chimney sweep.

Kamm [kam] m -(e)s, ˷e comb; (Berg~) ridge; (Hahnen~) crest.

kämmen ['kɛmən] vt comb // vr comb one's hair.

Kammer ['kamər] f -, -n chamber; small bedroom; ~**diener** m valet.

Kampagne [kamˈpanjə] f -, -n campaign.

Kampf [kampf] m -(e)s, ˷e fight, battle; (Wettbewerb) contest; (fig: Anstrengung) struggle; **k~bereit** a ready for action.

kämpfen ['kɛmpfən] vi fight.

Kämpfer m -s, - fighter, combatant.

Kampf- *zW:* **~handlung** *f* action; **k~los** *a* without a fight; **~richter** *m* (*SPORT*) referee; (*Tennis*) umpire.

Kanada ['kanada] *nt* **-s** Canada.

Kanadier(in *f)* [ka'na:diər(in)] *m* **-s, -** Canadian.

kanadisch [ka'na:dɪʃ] *a* Canadian.

Kanal [ka'na:l] *m* **-s, Kanäle** (*Fluß*) canal; (*Rinne, Ärmel~*) channel; (*für Abfluß*) drain; **~inseln** *pl* Channel Islands; **~isation** [-izatsi'o:n] *f* sewage system.

Kanarienvogel [ka'na:riənfo:gəl] *m* canary.

kanarisch [ka'na:rɪʃ] *a:* **K~e Inseln** Canary Islands, Canaries.

Kandi- [kandi] *zW:* **~dat** [-'da:t] *m* **-en, -en** candidate; **~datur** [-da'tu:r] *f* candidature, candidacy; **k~dieren** [-'di:rən] *vi* stand, run.

Kandis(zucker) ['kandɪs(tsʊkər] *m* **-** candy.

Känguruh ['kɛŋguru] *nt* **-s, -s** kangaroo.

Kaninchen [ka'ni:nçən] *nt* rabbit.

Kanister [ka'nɪstər] *m* **-s, -** can, canister.

Kännchen ['kɛnçən] *nt* pot.

Kanne ['kanə] *f* **-, -n** (*Krug*) jug; (*Kaffee~*) pot; (*Milch~*) churn; (*Gieß~*) can.

kannst *etc v siehe* **können**.

Kanon ['ka:nɔn] *m* **-s, -s** canon.

Kanone [ka'no:nə] *f* **-, -n** gun; (*HIST*) cannon; (*fig: Mensch*) ace.

Kantate [kan'ta:tə] *f* **-, -n** cantata.

Kante ['kantə] *f* **-, -n** edge.

Kantine [kan'ti:nə] *f* canteen.

Kanu ['ka:nu] *nt* **-s, -s** canoe.

Kanzel ['kantsəl] *f* **-, -n** pulpit.

Kanzler ['kantslər] *m* **-s, -** chancellor.

Kap [kap] *nt* **-s, -s** cape; **~ der Guten Hoffnung** Cape of Good Hope.

Kapazität [kapatsi'tɛ:t] *f* capacity; (*Fachmann*) authority.

Kapelle [ka'pɛlə] *f* (*Gebäude*) chapel; (*MUS*) band.

kapieren [ka'pi:rən] *vti* (*umg*) understand.

Kapital [kapi'ta:l] *nt* **-s, -e** *od* **-ien** capital; **~anlage** *f* investment; **~ismus** [-'lɪsmʊs] *m* capitalism; **~ist** [-'lɪst] *m* capitalist; **k~istisch** *a* capitalist.

Kapitän [kapi'tɛ:n] *m* **-s, -e** captain.

Kapitel [ka'pɪtəl] *nt* **-s, -** chapter.

Kapitulation [kapitulatsi'o:n] *f* capitulation.

kapitulieren [kapitu'li:rən] *vi* capitulate.

Kaplan [ka'pla:n] *m* **-s, Kapläne** chaplain.

Kappe ['kapə] *f* **-, -n** cap; (*Kapuze*) hood; **k~n** *vt* cut.

Kapsel ['kapsəl] *f* **-, -n** capsule.

Kapstadt ['kapʃtat] *nt* **-s** Cape Town.

kaputt [ka'pʊt] *a* (*umg*) kaput, broken; (*Person*) exhausted, finished; **am Auto ist etwas ~** there's something wrong with the car; **~gehen** *vi unreg* break; (*Schuhe*) fall apart; (*Firma*) go bust; (*Stoff*) wear out; (*sterben*) cop it; **~machen** *vt* break; (*Mensch*) exhaust, wear out.

Kapuze [ka'pu:tsə] *f* **-, -n** hood.

Karaffe [ka'rafə] *f* **-, -n** carafe; (*geschliffen*) decanter.

Karamel [kara'mɛl] *m* **-s** caramel; **~bonbon** *m od nt* toffee.

Karat [ka'ra:t] *nt* **-(e)s, -e** carat.

Karate [ka'ra:tə] *nt* **-s** karate.

Karawane [kara'va:nə] *f* **-, -n** caravan.

Kardinal [kardi'na:l] *m* **-s, Kardinäle** cardinal; **~zahl** *f* cardinal number.

Karfreitag [ka:r'fraita:k] *m* Good Friday.

kärglich ['kɛrklıç] *a* poor, scanty.

karibisch [ka'ri:bɪʃ] *a:* **K~e Inseln** Caribbean Islands.

kariert [ka'ri:rt] *a* (*Stoff*) checked; (*Papier*) squared.

Karies ['ka:riɛs] *f* -- caries.

Karikatur [karika'tu:r] *f* caricature; **~ist** [-'rɪst] *m* cartoonist.

Karneval ['karnəval] *m* **-s, -e** *od* **-s** carnival.

Karo ['ka:ro] *nt* **-s, -s** square; (*KARTEN*) diamonds; **~-As** *nt* ace of diamonds.

Karosserie [karɔsə'ri:] *f* (*AUT*) body(work).

Karotte [ka'rɔtə] *f* **-, -n** carrot.

Karpaten [kar'pa:tən] *pl* Carpathians.

Karpfen ['karpfən] *m* **-s, -** carp.

Karre ['karə] *f* **-, -n,** **~n** *m* **-s, -** cart, barrow.

Karriere [kari'ɛ:rə] *f* **-, -n** career; **~ machen** get on, get to the top; **~macher** *m* **-s, -** careerist.

Karte ['kartə] *f* **-, -n** card; (*Land~*) map; (*Speise~*) menu; (*Eintritts~, Fahr~*) ticket; **alles auf eine ~ setzen** put all one's eggs in one basket.

Kartei [kar'tai] *f* card index; **~karte** *f* index card.

Kartell [kar'tɛl] *nt* **-s, -e** cartel.

Kartenspiel *nt* card game; pack of cards.

Kartoffel [kar'tɔfəl] *f* **-, -n** potato; **~brei** *m,* **~mus** *nt,* **~püree** *nt* mashed potatoes *pl;* **~salat** *m* potato salad.

Karton [kar'tõ:] *m* **-s, -s** cardboard; (*Schachtel*) cardboard box; **k~iert** [karto'ni:rt] *a* hardback.

Karussell [karʊ'sɛl] *nt* **-s, -s** roundabout (*Brit*), merry-go-round.

Karwoche [ka:r'vɔxə] *f* Holy Week.

Käse ['kɛ:zə] *m* **-s, -** cheese; **~blatt** *nt* (*umg*) (local) rag; **~kuchen** *m* cheesecake.

Kaserne [ka'zɛrnə] f -, -n barracks pl; **Kasernenhof** m parade ground.

Kasino [ka'zi:no] nt -s, -s club; (MIL) officers' mess; (Spiel~) casino.

kaspisch ['kaspɪʃ] a: K~es Meer Caspian Sea.

Kasse ['kasə] f -, -n (Geldkasten) cashbox; (in Geschäft) till, cash register; (Kino~, Theater~ etc) box office; ticket office; (Kranken~) health insurance; (Spar~) savings bank; ~ machen count the money; getrennte ~ führen pay separately; an der ~ (in Geschäft) at the desk; gut bei ~ sein be in the money.

Kassen- zW: ~arzt m panel doctor (Brit); ~bestand m cash balance; ~patient m panel patient (Brit); ~prüfung f audit; ~sturz m: ~sturz machen check one's money; ~zettel m receipt.

Kassette [ka'sɛtə] f small box; (Tonband, PHOT) cassette; (Bücher~) case.

Kassettengerät nt, **Kassettenrecorder** m -s, - cassette recorder.

kassieren [ka'si:rən] vt take // vi: darf ich ~? would you like to pay now?

Kassierer [ka'si:rər] m -s, - cashier; (von Klub) treasurer.

Kastanie [kas'ta:niə] f chestnut; (Baum) chestnut tree.

Kasten ['kastən] m -s, ⁻ box (Sport auch), case; (Truhe) chest; ~wagen m van.

kastrieren [kas'tri:rən] vt castrate.

Katalog [kata'lo:k] m -(e)s, -e catalogue.

Katalysator [kataly'za:tɔr] m catalyst.

Katarrh [ka'tar] m -s, -e catarrh.

katastrophal [katastro'fa:l] a catastrophic.

Katastrophe [kata'stro:fə] f -, -n catastrophe, disaster.

Kat-Auto ['kat'auto] n car fitted with a device for purifying exhaust fumes.

Kategorie [katego'ri:] f category.

kategorisch [kate'go:rɪʃ] a categorical.

Kater ['ka:tər] m -s, - tomcat; (umg) hangover.

kath. abk (= katholisch) Cath.

Kathedrale [kate'dra:lə] f -, -n cathedral.

Kathode [ka'to:də] f -, -n cathode.

Katholik [kato'li:k] m -en, -en Catholic.

katholisch [ka'to:lɪʃ] a Catholic.

Kätzchen ['kɛtsçən] nt kitten.

Katze ['katsə] f -, -n cat; für die Katz (umg) in vain, for nothing.

Katzen- zW: ~auge nt cat's eye; (Fahrrad) rear light; ~jammer m (umg) hangover; ~sprung m (umg)

stone's throw; short journey.

Kauderwelsch ['kaudərvɛlʃ] nt -(s) jargon; (umg) double Dutch.

kauen ['kauən] vti chew.

Kauf [kauf] m -(e)s, Käufe purchase, buy; (Kaufen) buying; ein guter ~ a bargain; etw in ~ nehmen put up with sth; k~en vt buy.

Käufer(in f) ['kɔyfər(ɪn)] m -s, - buyer.

Kaufhaus nt department store.

Kaufkraft f purchasing power.

käuflich ['kɔyflɪç] a,ad purchasable, for sale; (pej) venal; ~ erwerben purchase.

Kauf- zW: k~lustig a interested in buying; ~mann m, pl -leute businessman; shopkeeper; k~männisch a commercial; ~männischer Angestellter office worker.

Kaugummi ['kaugumi] m chewing gum.

Kaulquappe ['kaulkvapə] f -, -n tadpole.

kaum [kaum] ad hardly, scarcely.

Kaution [kautsi'o:n] f deposit; (JUR) bail.

Kauz [kauts] m -es, Käuze owl; (fig) queer fellow.

Kavalier [kava'li:r] m -s, -e gentleman, cavalier; **Kavaliersdelikt** nt peccadillo.

Kaviar ['ka:viar] m caviar.

keck [kɛk] a daring, bold; K~heit f daring, boldness.

Kegel ['ke:gəl] m -s, - skittle; (MATH) cone; ~bahn f skittle alley; bowling alley; k~n vi play skittles.

Kehle ['ke:lə] f -, -n throat.

Kehlkopf m larynx.

Kehre ['ke:rə] f -, -n turn(ing), bend; k~n vti (wenden) turn; (mit Besen) sweep; sich an etw (dat) nicht k~n not heed sth.

Kehricht ['ke:rɪçt] m -s sweepings pl.

Kehrmaschine f sweeper.

Kehrseite f reverse, other side; wrong side; bad side.

kehrtmachen vi turn about, aboutturn.

keifen ['kaifən] vi scold, nag.

Keil ['kail] m -(e)s, -e wedge; (MIL) arrowhead; ~riemen m (AUT) fan belt.

Keim [kaim] m -(e)s, -e bud; (MED, fig) germ; k~en vi germinate; k~frei a sterile; ~zelle f (fig) nucleus.

kein [kain] a no, not ... any; ~e(r, s) pron no one, nobody; none.

keinesfalls ad on no account.

keineswegs ad by no means.

keinmal ad not once.

Keks [ke:ks] m od nt -es, -e biscuit.

Kelch [kɛlç] m -(e)s, -e cup, goblet, chalice.

Kelle ['kɛlə] *f* -, **-n** ladle; (*Maurer~*) trowel.

Keller ['kɛlər] *m* **-s**, - cellar; **~assel** *f* -, **-n** woodlouse.

Kellner ['kɛlnər] *m* **-s**, - waiter; **~in** *f* waitress.

keltern ['kɛltərn] *vt* press.

kennen ['kɛnən] *vt unreg* know; **~lernen** *vt* get to know; **sich ~lernen** get to know each other; (*zum erstenmal*) meet.

Kenner *m* **-s**, - connoisseur.

kenntlich *a* distinguishable, discernible; **etw ~ machen** mark sth.

Kenntnis *f* -, **-se** knowledge *no pl*; **etw zur ~ nehmen** note sth; **von etw ~ nehmen** take notice of sth; **jdn in ~ setzen** inform sb.

Kenn- *zW*: **~zeichen** *nt* mark, characteristic; **k~zeichnen** *vt insep* characterize; **~ziffer** *f* reference number.

kentern ['kɛntərn] *vi* capsize.

Keramik [ke'ra:mɪk] *f* -, **-en** ceramics *pl*, pottery.

Kerb- ['kɛrb] *zW*: **~e** *f* -, **-n** notch, groove; **k~en** *vt* notch; **~holz** *nt*: **etw auf dem ~holz haben** have done sth wrong.

Kerker ['kɛrkər] *m* **-s**, - prison.

Kerl [kɛrl] *m* **-s**, **-e** chap, bloke (*Brit*), guy; **sie ist ein netter ~** she's a good sort.

Kern [kɛrn] *m* **-(e)s**, **-e** (*Obst~*) pip, stone; (*Nuß~*) kernel; (*Atom~*) nucleus; (*fig*) heart, core; **~energie** *f* nuclear energy; **~forschung** *f* nuclear research; **~frage** *f* central issue; **k~gesund** *a* thoroughly healthy, fit as a fiddle; **k~ig** *a* robust; (*Ausspruch*) pithy; **~kraftwerk** *nt* nuclear power station; **k~los** *a* seedless, pipless; **~physik** *f* nuclear physics; **~reaktion** *f* nuclear reaction; **~schmelze** *f* meltdown; **~spaltung** *f* nuclear fission; **~waffen** *pl* nuclear weapons *pl*.

Kerze ['kɛrtsə] *f* -, **-n** candle; (*Zünd~*) plug; **kerzengerade** *a* straight as a die; **Kerzenständer** *m* candle holder.

keß [kɛs] *a* saucy.

Kessel ['kɛsəl] *m* **-s**, - kettle; (*von Lokomotive etc*) boiler; (*GEOG*) depression; (*MIL*) encirclement.

Kette ['kɛtə] *f* -, **-n** chain; **k~n** *vt* chain.

Ketten- *zW*: **~laden** *m* chain store; **~rauchen** *nt* chain smoking; **~reaktion** *f* chain reaction.

Ketzer ['kɛtsər] *m* **-s**, - heretic.

keuchen ['kɔʏçən] *vi* pant, gasp.

Keuchhusten *m* whooping cough.

Keule ['kɔʏlə] *f* -, **-n** club; (*KOCH*) leg.

keusch [kɔʏʃ] *a* chaste; **K~heit** *f* chastity.

kfm. *abk von* **kaufmännisch.**

Kfz [ka:'ɛf'tsɛt] *abk von* **Kraftfahrzeug.**

KG [ka:'ge:] *abk* (= *Kommanditgesellschaft*) limited partnership.

kg *abk von* **Kilogramm.**

kichern ['kɪçərn] *vi* giggle.

kidnappen ['kɪdnɛpən] *vt* kidnap.

Kiefer ['ki:fər] *m* **-s**, - jaw // *f* -, **-n** pine; **Kiefernzapfen** *m* pine cone.

Kiel [ki:l] *m* **-(e)s**, **-e** (*Feder~*) quill; (*NAUT*) keel.

Kieme ['ki:mə] *f* -, **-n** gill.

Kies [ki:s] *m* **-es**, **-e** gravel; **Kieselstein** ['ki:zəlʃtaɪn] *m* pebble.

Kilo ['ki:lo] kilo; **~gramm** [kilo'gram] *nt* **-s**, **-e** kilogram; **~meter** [kilo'me:tər] *m* kilometre; **~meterzähler** *m* ≈ milometer.

Kind [kɪnt] *nt* **-(e)s**, **-er** child; **von ~ auf** from childhood.

Kinder- ['kɪndər] *zW*: **~ei** *f* childishness; **~garten** *m* nursery school, playgroup; **~geld** *nt* family allowance; **~lähmung** *f* poliomyelitis; **k~leicht** *a* childishly easy; **k~los** *a* childless; **~mädchen** *nt* nursemaid; **k~reich** *a* with a lot of children; **~spiel** *nt* child's play; **~tagesstätte** *f* day-nursery; **~wagen** *m* pram, baby carriage (*US*).

Kind- *zW*: **~heit** *f* childhood; **k~isch** *a* childish; **k~lich** *a* childlike.

Kinn [kɪn] *nt* **-(e)s**, **-e** chin; **~haken** *m* (*Boxen*) uppercut; **~lade** *f* jaw.

Kino ['ki:no] *nt* **-s**, **-s** cinema; **~besucher** *m* cinema-goer; **~programm** *nt* film programme.

Kiosk ['ki:ɔsk] *m* **-(e)s**, **-e** kiosk.

Kipp- ['kɪp] *zW*: **~e** *f* -, **-n** cigarette end; (*umg*) fag; **auf der ~e stehen** (*fig*) be touch and go; **k~en** *vi* topple over, overturn // *vt* tilt.

Kirch- ['kɪrç] *zW*: **~e** *f* -, **-n** church; **~enlied** *nt* hymn; **~gänger** *m* **-s**, - churchgoer; **~hof** *m* churchyard; **k~lich** *a* ecclesiastical; **~turm** *m* church tower, steeple.

Kirmes ['kɪrmɛs] *f* -, **-sen** fair.

Kirsche ['kɪrʃə] *f* -, **-n** cherry.

Kissen ['kɪsən] *nt* **-s**, - cushion; (*Kopf~*) pillow; **~bezug** *m* pillowslip.

Kiste ['kɪstə] *f* -, **-n** box; chest.

Kitsch [kɪtʃ] *m* **-(e)s** trash; **k~ig** *a* trashy.

Kitt [kɪt] *m* **-(e)s**, **-e** putty; **Kittel** *m* **-s**, - overall, smock; **kitten** *vt* putty; (*fig: Ehe etc*) cement.

Kitz [kɪts] *nt* **-es**, **-e** kid; (*Reh~*) fawn.

kitzel- ['kɪtsəl] *zW*: **~ig** *a* (*lit*, *fig*) ticklish; **~n** *vt* tickle.

KKW [ka:ka:'ve:] *nt abk von* **Kernkraftwerk.**

kläffen ['klɛfən] *vi* yelp.

Klage ['kla:gə] *f* -, **-n** complaint; (*JUR*) action; **k~n** *vi* (*weh~*) lament, wail;

(*sich beschweren*) complain; (*JUR*) take legal action.

Kläger(in *f*) ['klɛːgər(ɪn)] *m* **-s,** - plaintiff.

kläglich ['klɛːklɪç] *a* wretched.

klamm [klam] *a* (*Finger*) numb; (*feucht*) damp.

Klammer ['klamər] *f* -, **-n** clamp; (*in Text*) bracket; (*Büro~*) clip; (*Wäsche~*) peg; (*Zahn~*) brace; **k~n** *vr* cling (*an* +*akk* to).

Klang [klaŋ] *m* **-(e)s,** ¨e sound; **k~voll** *a* sonorous.

Klappe ['klapə] *f* -, **-n** valve; (*Ofen~*) damper; (*umg: Mund*) trap; **k~n** *vi* (*Geräusch*) click // *vti* (*Sitz etc*) tip // *v unpers* work; **Klappentext** *m* blurb.

Klapper ['klapər] *f* -, **-n** rattle; **k~ig** *a* run-down, worn-out; **k~n** *vi* clatter, rattle; **~schlange** *f* rattlesnake; **~storch** *m* stork.

Klapp- *zW:* **~messer** *nt* jack-knife; **~rad** *nt* collapsible bicycle; **~stuhl** *m* folding chair; **~tisch** *m* folding table.

klar [klaːr] *a* clear; (*NAUT*) ready for sea; (*MIL*) ready for action; **sich** (*dat*) **im ~en sein über** (+*akk*) be clear about; **ins ~e kommen** get clear; **(na) ~!** of course.

Klär- ['klɛːr] *zW:* **~anlage** *f* purification plant; **k~en** *vt* (*Flüssigkeit*) purify; (*Probleme*) clarify // *vr* clear (*itself*) up.

Klarheit *f* clarity.

Klarinette [klari'nɛtə] *f* clarinet.

klar- *zW:* **~legen** *vt* clear up, explain; **~machen** *vt* (*Schiff*) get ready for sea; **jdm etw ~machen** make sth clear to sb; **~sehen** *vi unreg* see clearly; **K~sichtfolie** *f* transparent film; **~stellen** *vt* clarify.

Klärung ['klɛːrʊŋ] *f* purification; clarification.

Klasse ['klasə] *f* -, **-n** class; (*SCH auch*) form; **k~** *a* (*umg*) smashing.

Klassen- *zW:* **~arbeit** *f* test; **~bewußtsein** *nt* class consciousness; **~gesellschaft** *f* class society; **~kampf** *m* class conflict; **~lehrer** *m* form master; **k~los** *a* classless; **~sprecher(in** *f*) *m* form prefect; **~zimmer** *nt* classroom.

klassifizieren [klasifi'tsiːrən] *vt* classify.

Klassik ['klasɪk] *f* (*Zeit*) classical period; (*Stil*) classicism; **~er** *m* **-s,** - classic.

klassisch *a* (*lit, fig*) classical.

Klatsch [klatʃ] *m* **-(e)s, -e** smack, crack; (*Gerede*) gossip; **~base** *f* gossip, scandalmonger; **~e** *f* -, **-n** (*umg*) crib; **k~en** *vi* (*Geräusch*) clash; (*reden*) gossip; (*Beifall*) applaud, clap; **~mohn** *m* (corn) poppy; **k~naß** *a*

soaking wet.

Klaue ['klauə] *f* -, **-n** claw; (*umg: Schrift*) scrawl; **k~n** *vt* claw; (*umg*) pinch.

Klausel ['klauzəl] *f* -, **-n** clause.

Klausur [klau'zuːr] *f* seclusion; **~arbeit** *f* examination paper.

Klaviatur [klavia'tuːr] *f* keyboard.

Klavier [kla'viːr] *nt* **-s, -e** piano.

Kleb- ['klɛːb] *zW:* **k~en** *vt* stick (*an* +*akk* to); **k~rig** *a* sticky; **~stoff** *m* glue; **~streifen** *m* adhesive tape.

Klecks [klɛks] *m* **-es, -e** blot, stain; **k~en** *vi* blot; (*pej*) daub.

Klee [kleː] *m* **-s** clover; **~blatt** *nt* cloverleaf; (*fig*) trio.

Kleid [klaɪt] *nt* **-(e)s, -er** garment; (*Frauen~*) dress // *pl* clothes *pl*; **k~en** ['klaɪdən] *vt* clothe, dress; (*auch vi*) suit // *vr* dress.

Kleider- ['klaɪdər] *zW:* **~bügel** *m* coat hanger; **~bürste** *f* clothes brush; **~schrank** *m* wardrobe.

Kleid- *zW:* **~sam** *a* becoming; **~ung** *f* clothing; **~ungsstück** *nt* garment.

Kleie ['klaɪə] *f* -, **-n** bran.

klein [klaɪn] *a* little, small; **K~asien** *nt* Asia Minor; **K~e(r, s)** little one; **K~format** *nt* small size; **im K~format** small-scale; **K~geld** *nt* small change; **~hacken** *vt* chop up, mince; **K~igkeit** *f* trifle; **K~kind** *nt* infant; **K~kram** *m* details *pl*; **~laut** *a* dejected, quiet; **~lich** *a* petty, paltry; **Kleinod** ['klaɪnoːt] *nt* **-s, -odien** gem, jewel; treasure; **~schneiden** *vt* unreg chop up; **~städtisch** *a* provincial; **kleinstmöglich** *a* smallest possible.

Kleister ['klaɪstər] *m* **-s,** - paste; **k~n** *vt* paste.

Klemme ['klɛmə] *f* -, **-n** clip; (*MED*) clamp; (*fig*) jam; **k~n** *vt* (*festhalten*) jam; (*quetschen*) pinch, nip // *vr* catch o.s.; (*sich hineinzwängen*) squeeze o.s.; **sich hinter jdn/etw k~n** get on to sb/get down to sth // *vi* (*Tür*) stick, jam.

Klempner ['klɛmpnər] *m* **-s,** - plumber.

Kleptomanie [klɛptoma'niː] *f* kleptomania.

Klerus ['kleːrʊs] *m* - clergy.

Klette ['klɛtə] *f* -, **-n** burr.

Kletter- ['klɛtər] *zW:* **~er** *m* **-s,** - climber; **k~n** *vi* climb; **~pflanze** *f* creeper.

Klient(in *f*) [kli'ɛnt(ɪn)] *m* client.

Klima ['kliːma] *nt* **-s, -s** *od* **-te** [kli'maːtə] climate; **~anlage** *f* air conditioning; **~wechsel** *m* change of air.

Klinge ['klɪŋə] *f* -, **-n** blade, sword.

Klingel ['klɪŋəl] *f* -, **-n** bell; **~beutel** *m* collection bag; **k~n** *vi* ring.

klingen ['klɪŋən] *vi unreg* sound; *(Gläser)* clink.
Klinik ['kliːnɪk] *f* hospital, clinic.
Klinke ['klɪŋkə] *f* -, -n handle.
Klippe ['klɪpə] *f* -, -n cliff; *(im Meer)* reef; *(fig)* hurdle.
klipp und klar ['klɪp'ʊntklaːr] *a* clear and concise.
Klips [klɪps] *m* -es, -e clip; *(Ohr~)* earring.
klirren ['klɪrən] *vi* clank, jangle; *(Gläser)* clink; **~de Kälte** biting cold.
Klischee [klɪ'ʃeː] *nt* -s, -s *(Druckplatte)* plate, block; *(fig)* cliché; **~vorstellung** *f* stereotyped idea.
Klo [kloː] *nt* -s, -s *(umg)* loo *(Brit)*, john *(US)*.
Kloake [klo'aːkə] *f* -, -n sewer.
klobig ['kloːbɪç] *a* clumsy.
klopfen ['klɔpfən] *vti* knock; *(Herz)* thump; **es klopft** somebody's knocking; **jdm auf die Schulter ~** tap sb on the shoulder // *vt* beat.
Klopfer *m* -s, - *(Teppich~)* beater; *(Tür~)* knocker.
Klops [klɔps] *m* -es, -e meatball.
Klosett [klo'zɛt] *nt* -s, -e *od* -s lavatory, toilet; **~papier** *nt* toilet paper.
Kloß [kloːs] *m* -es, ⁻e *(Erd~)* clod; *(im Hals)* lump; *(KOCH)* dumpling.
Kloster ['kloːstər] *nt* -s, ⁻ *(Männer~)* monastery; *(Frauen~)* convent.
klösterlich ['kløːstərlɪç] *a* monastic; convent.
Klotz [klɔts] *m* -es, ⁻e log; *(Hack~)* block; **ein ~ am Bein** *(fig)* drag, millstone round sb's neck.
Klub [klʊp] *m* -s, -s club; **~sessel** *m* easy chair.
Kluft [klʊft] *f* -, ⁻e cleft, gap; *(GEOL)* gorge, chasm.
klug [kluːk] *a* clever, intelligent; **K~heit** *f* cleverness, intelligence.
Klumpen ['klʊmpən] *m* -s, - *(Erd~)* clod; *(Blut~)* lump, clot; *(Gold~)* nugget; *(KOCH)* lump; **k~** *vi* go lumpy, clot.
km *abk von* **Kilometer**.
km/h *abk* (= *Kilometer je Stunde*) kph, ≈ mph.
knabbern ['knabərn] *vti* nibble.
Knabe ['knaːbə] *m* -n, -n boy; **knabenhaft** *a* boyish.
Knäckebrot ['knɛkəbroːt] *nt* crispbread.
knacken ['knakən] *vti (lit, fig)* crack.
Knall [knal] *m* -(e)s, -e bang; *(Peitschen~)* crack; **~ und Fall** *(umg)* unexpectedly; **~bonbon** *nt* cracker; **k~en** *vi* bang; crack; **k~rot** *a* bright red.
knapp [knap] *a* tight; *(Geld)* scarce; *(Sprache)* concise; **eine ~e Stunde** just under an hour; **~ unter/neben** just under/by; **~halten** *vt unreg*

stint; **K~heit** *f* tightness; scarcity; conciseness.
knarren ['knarən] *vi* creak.
knattern ['knatərn] *vi* rattle; *(MG)* chatter.
Knäuel ['knɔʏəl] *m od nt* -s, - *(Woll~)* ball; *(Menschen~)* knot.
Knauf [knaʊf] *m* -(e)s, **Knäufe** knob; *(Schwert~)* pommel.
knautschen ['knaʊtʃən] *vti* crumple.
Knebel ['kneːbəl] *m* -s, - gag; **k~n** *vt* gag; *(NAUT)* fasten.
kneifen ['knaɪfən] *vti unreg* pinch; *(sich drücken)* back out; **vor etw ~** dodge sth.
Kneipe ['knaɪpə] *f* -, -n *(umg)* pub.
kneten ['kneːtən] *vt* knead; *(Wachs)* mould.
Knick [knɪk] *m* -(e)s, -e *(Sprung)* crack; *(Kurve)* bend; *(Falte)* fold; **k~en** *vti (springen)* crack; *(brechen)* break; *(Papier)* fold; **geknickt sein** be downcast.
Knicks [knɪks] *m* -es, -e curtsey; **k~en** *vi* curtsey.
Knie [kniː] *nt* -s, - knee; **~beuge** *f* -, -n knee bend; **~fall** *m* genuflection; **~gelenk** *nt* knee joint; **~kehle** *f* back of the knee; **k~n** *vi* kneel; **~scheibe** *f* kneecap; **~strumpf** *m* knee-length sock.
Kniff [knɪf] *m* -(e)s, -e *(fig)* trick, knack; **kniffelig** *a* tricky.
knipsen ['knɪpsən] *vti (Fahrkarte)* punch; *(PHOT)* take a snap (of), snap.
Knirps [knɪrps] *m* -es, -e little chap; ® *(Schirm)* telescopic umbrella.
knirschen ['knɪrʃən] *vi* crunch; **mit den Zähnen ~** grind one's teeth.
knistern ['knɪstərn] *vi* crackle.
Knitter- ['knɪtər] *zW:* **~falte** *f* crease; **k~frei** *a* non-crease; **k~n** *vi* crease.
Knoblauch ['knoːplaʊx] *m* -(e)s garlic.
Knöchel ['knœçəl] *m* -s, - knuckle; *(Fuß~)* ankle.
Knochen ['knɔxən] *m* -s, - bone; **~bau** *m* bone structure; **~bruch** *m* fracture; **~gerüst** *nt* skeleton.
knöchern ['knœçərn] *a* bone.
knochig ['knɔxɪç] *a* bony.
Knödel ['knøːdəl] *m* -s, - dumpling.
Knolle ['knɔlə] *f* -, -n bulb.
Knopf [knɔpf] *m* -(e)s, ⁻e button; *(Kragen~)* stud; **~loch** *nt* buttonhole.
knöpfen ['knœpfən] *vt* button.
Knorpel ['knɔrpəl] *m* -s, - cartilage, gristle; **k~ig** *a* gristly.
Knospe ['knɔspə] *f* -, -n bud.
Knoten ['knoːtən] *m* -s, - knot; *(BOT)* node; *(MED)* lump; **k~** *vt* knot; **~punkt** *m* junction.
Knüller ['knʏlər] *m* -s, - *(umg)* hit; *(Reportage)* scoop.

knüpfen ['knʏpfən] vt tie; (Teppich) knot; (Freundschaft) form.

Knüppel ['knʏpəl] m -s, - cudgel; (Polizei~) baton, truncheon; (AVIAT) (joy)stick; **~schaltung** f (AUT) floor-mounted gear change.

knurren ['knʊrən] vi (Hund) snarl, growl; (Magen) rumble; (Mensch) mutter.

knusperig ['knʊspərɪç] a crisp; (Keks) crunchy.

k.o. [ka:'o:] a (lit) knocked out; (fig) done in.

Koalition [koalitsi'o:n] f coalition.

Kobalt ['ko:balt] nt -s cobalt.

Kobold ['ko:bɔlt] m -(e)s, -e goblin, imp.

Kobra ['ko:bra] f -, -s cobra.

Koch [kɔx] m -(e)s, ⁻e cook; **~buch** nt cook(ery) book; **k~en** vti cook; (Wasser) boil; **~er** m -s, - stove, cooker.

Köcher ['kœçər] m -s, - quiver.

Kochgelegenheit ['kɔxgəle:gənhaɪt] f cooking facilities pl.

Köchin ['kœçɪn] f cook.

Koch- zW: **~löffel** m kitchen spoon; **~nische** f kitchenette; **~platte** f boiling ring, hotplate; **~salz** nt cooking salt; **~topf** m saucepan, pot.

Köder ['kø:dər] m -s, - bait, lure.

Koexistenz [koɛksɪs'tɛnts] f coexistence.

Koffein [kɔfe'i:n] nt -s caffeine; **k~frei** a decaffeinated.

Koffer ['kɔfər] m -s, - suitcase; (Schrank~) trunk; **~radio** nt portable radio; **~raum** m (AUT) boot (Brit), trunk (US).

Kognak ['kɔnjak] m -s, -s brandy, cognac.

Kohl [ko:l] m -(e)s, -e cabbage.

Kohle ['ko:lə] f -, -n coal; (Holz~) charcoal; (CHEM) carbon; **~hydrat** nt -(e)s, -e carbohydrate.

Kohlen- zW: **~dioxyd** nt -(e)s, -e carbon dioxide; **~händler** m coal merchant, coalman; **~säure** f carbon dioxide; **~stoff** m carbon.

Kohlepapier nt carbon paper.

kohlrübe f turnip.

Koje ['ko:jə] f -, -n cabin; (Bett) bunk.

Kokain [koka'i:n] nt -s cocaine.

kokett [ko'kɛt] a coquettish, flirtatious.

Kokosnuß ['ko:kɔsnʊs] f coconut.

Koks [ko:ks] m -es, -e coke.

Kolben ['kɔlbən] m -s, - (Gewehr~) rifle butt; (Keule) club; (CHEM) flask; (TECH) piston; (Mais~) cob.

Kolchose [kɔl'ço:zə] f -, -n collective farm.

Kolik ['ko:lɪk] f colic, gripe.

Kollaps [kɔ'laps] m -es, -e collapse.

Kolleg [kɔl'e:k] nt -s, -s od -ien lecture course; **~e** [kɔ'le:gə] m -n, -n, **~in** f colleague; **~ium** nt board; (SCH) staff.

Kollekte [kɔ'lɛktə] f -, -n (REL) collection.

kollektiv [kɔlɛk'ti:f] a collective.

Kollision [kɔlizi'o:n] f collision; (zeitlich) clash.

Köln [kœln] nt -s Cologne.

Kolonie [kolo'ni:] f colony.

kolonisieren [koloni'zi:rən] vt colonize.

Kolonne [ko'lɔnə] f -, -n column; (von Fahrzeugen) convoy.

Koloß [ko'lɔs] m -sses, -sse colossus.

kolossal [kolo'sa:l] a colossal.

Kombi- ['kɔmbi] zW: **~nation** [-natsi'o:n] f combination; (Vermutung) conjecture; (Hemdhose) combinations pl; **~nationsschloß** nt combination lock; **k~nieren** [-'ni:rən] vt combine // vi deduce, work out; (vermuten) guess; **~wagen** m station wagon; **~zange** f (pair of) pliers.

Komet [ko'me:t] m -en, -en comet.

Komfort [kɔm'fo:r] m -s luxury.

Komik ['ko:mɪk] f humour, comedy; **~er** m -s, - comedian.

komisch ['ko:mɪʃ] a funny.

Komitee [komi'te:] nt -s, -s committee.

Komma ['kɔma] nt -s, -s od -ta comma; 2 ~ 3 2 point 3.

Kommand- [kɔ'mand] zW: **~ant** [-'dant] m commander, commanding officer; **~eur** [-'dø:r] m commanding officer; **k~ieren** [-'di:rən] vti command; **Kommando** nt -s, -s command, order; (Truppe) detachment, squad; **auf Kommando** to order.

kommen ['kɔmən] vi unreg come; (näher~) approach; (passieren) happen; (gelangen, geraten) get; (Blumen, Zähne, Tränen etc) appear; (in die Schule, das Zuchthaus etc) go; ~ **lassen** send for (sth); **das kommt in den Schrank** that goes in the cupboard; **zu sich** ~ come round od to; **zu etw** ~ acquire sth; **um etw** ~ lose sth; **nichts auf jdn/etw** ~ **lassen** have nothing said against sb/sth; **jdm frech** ~ get cheeky with sb; **auf jeden vierten kommt ein Platz** there's one place for every fourth person; **wer kommt zuerst?** who's first?; **unter ein Auto** ~ be run over by a car; **wie hoch kommt das?** what does that cost?; **komm gut nach Hause!** safe journey (home); **~den Sonntag** next Sunday; **K~** nt -s coming.

Kommentar [kɔmɛn'ta:r] m commentary; **kein** ~ no comment; **k~los** a without comment.

Kommentator [kɔmɛn'ta:tɔr] m (TV) commentator.

kommentieren [kɔmɛn'tiːrən] *vt* comment on.

kommerziell [kɔmɛrtsi'ɛl] *a* commercial.

kommilitone [kɔmili'toːnə] *m* -n, -n fellow student.

Kommissar [kɔmɪ'saːr] *m* police inspector.

Kommission [kɔmɪsi'oːn] *f* (*COMM*) commission; (*Ausschuß*) committee.

Kommode [kɔ'moːdə] *f* -, -n (chest of) drawers.

Kommunalsteuer [kɔmuˈnaːlʃtɔyər] *f* rates *pl*.

Kommune [kɔ'muːnə] *f* -, -n commune.

Kommunikation [kɔmunikatsi'oːn] *f* communication.

Kommunion [kɔmuni'oːn] *f* communion.

Kommuniqué [kɔmyni'keː] *nt* -s, -s communiqué.

Kommunismus [kɔmu'nɪsmʊs] *m* communism.

Kommunist(in *f*) [kɔmu'nɪst(ɪn)] *m* communist; **k~isch** *a* communist.

kommunizieren [kɔmuni'tsiːrən] *vi* communicate; (*ECCL*) receive communion.

Komödie [ko'møːdiə] *f* comedy.

Kompagnon [kɔmpan'jõː] *m* -s, -s (*COMM*) partner.

kompakt [kɔm'pakt] *a* compact.

Kompanie [kɔmpa'niː] *f* company.

Kompaß ['kɔmpas] *m* -sses, -sse compass.

kompatibel [kɔmpa'tiːbəl] *a* compatible.

kompetent [kɔmpe'tɛnt] *a* competent.

Kompetenz *f* competence, authority.

komplett [kɔm'plɛt] *a* complete.

Komplikation [kɔmplikatsi'oːn] *f* complication.

Kompliment [kɔmpli'mɛnt] *nt* compliment.

Komplize [kɔm'pliːtsə] *m* -n, -n accomplice.

kompliziert [kɔmpli'tsiːrt] *a* complicated.

komponieren [kɔmpo'niːrən] *vt* compose.

Komponist [kɔmpo'nɪst] *m* composer.

Komposition [kɔmpozitsi'oːn] *f* composition.

Kompost [kɔm'pɔst] *m* -(e)s, -e compost.

Kompott [kɔm'pɔt] *nt* -(e)s, -e stewed fruit.

Kompromiß [kɔmpro'mɪs] *m* -sses, -sse compromise; **k~bereit** *a* willing to compromise; **~lösung** *f* compromise solution.

Kondens— [kɔn'dɛns] *zW*: **~ation** [kɔndɛnzatsi'oːn] *f* condensation; **~ator** [kɔndɛn'zaːtɔr] *m* condenser;

k~ieren [kɔndɛn'ziːrən] *vt* condense; **~milch** *f* condensed milk.

Konditionstraining [kɔnditsi'oːnstrɛːnɪŋ] *nt* fitness training.

Konditor [kɔn'diːtɔr] *m* pastrycook; **Konditorei** [kɔndito'raɪ] *f* café; cake shop.

Kondom [kɔn'doːm] *nt* -s, -e condom.

Konferenz [kɔnfe'rɛnts] *f* conference, meeting.

Konfession [kɔnfɛsi'oːn] *f* religion; (*christlich*) denomination; **k~ell** [-'nɛl] *a* denominational; **konfessionslos** *a* non-denominational.

Konfetti [kɔn'fɛti] *nt* -(s) confetti.

Konfirmand [kɔnfir'mant] *m* candidate for confirmation.

Konfirmation [kɔnfirmatsi'oːn] *f* (*ECCL*) confirmation.

konfirmieren [kɔnfir'miːrən] *vt* confirm.

konfiszieren [kɔnfis'tsiːrən] *vt* confiscate.

Konfitüre [kɔnfi'tyːrə] *f* -, -n jam.

Konflikt [kɔn'flɪkt] *m* -(e)s, -e conflict.

konfrontieren [kɔnfrɔn'tiːrən] *vt* confront.

konfus [kɔn'fuːs] *a* confused.

Kongreß [kɔn'grɛs] *m* -sses, -sse congress.

Kongruenz [kɔngru'ɛnts] *f* agreement, congruence.

König ['køːnɪç] *m* -(e)s, -e king; **~in** ['køːnɪgɪn] *f* queen; **k~lich** *a* royal; **~reich** *nt* kingdom; **~tum** *nt* -(e)s, -tümer kingship.

Konjugation [kɔnjugatsi'oːn] *f* conjugation.

konjugieren [kɔnju'giːrən] *vt* conjugate.

Konjunktion [kɔnjʊŋktsi'oːn] *f* conjunction.

Konjunktiv ['kɔnjʊŋktiːf] *m* -s, -e subjunctive.

Konjunktur [kɔnjʊŋk'tuːr] *f* economic situation; (*Hoch~*) boom.

konkav [kɔn'kaːf] *a* concave.

konkret [kɔn'kreːt] *a* concrete.

Konkurrent(in *f*) [kɔnku'rɛnt(ɪn)] *m* competitor.

Konkurrenz [kɔnku'rɛnts] *f* competition; **k~fähig** *a* competitive; **~kampf** *m* competition; (*umg*) rat race.

konkurrieren [kɔnku'riːrən] *vi* compete.

Konkurs [kɔn'kʊrs] *m* -es, -e bankruptcy.

können ['kœnən] *vti pt* **konnte**, *ptp* **gekonnt** *od* (*als Hilfsverb*) **können 1** be able to; **ich kann es machen** I can do it, I am able to do it; **ich kann es nicht machen** I can't do it, I'm not able to do it; **ich kann nicht ...** I can't ..., I cannot ...; **ich kann nicht**

mehr I can't go on
2 (*wissen, beherrschen*) know; ~ **Sie Deutsch?** can you speak German?; **er kann gut Englisch** he speaks English well; **sie kann keine Mathematik** she can't do mathematics
3 (*dürfen*) to be allowed to; **kann ich gehen?** can I go?; **könnte ich ...? could I ...?; kann ich mit?** (*umg*) can I come with you?
4 (*möglich sein*): **Sie könnten recht haben** you may be right; **das kann sein** that's possible; **kann sein** maybe.
Können ['kœnən] *nt* -s ability.
konnte etc *v siehe* **können**.
konsequent [kɔnze'kvɛnt] *a* consistent.
Konsequenz [kɔnze'kvɛnts] *f* consistency; (*Folgerung*) conclusion.
Konserv- [kɔn'zɛrv] *zW:* **k~ativ** [-a'ti:f] *a* conservative; ~**ative(r)** [-a'ti:və(r)] *mf* (*POL*) conservative; ~**e** *f* -, -**n** tinned food; ~**enbüchse** *f* tin, can; **k~ieren** [-'vi:rən] *vt* preserve; ~**ierung** *f* preservation; ~**ierungsmittel** *nt* preservative.
Konsonant [kɔnzo'nant] *m* consonant.
konstant [kɔn'stant] *a* constant.
konstruieren [kɔnstru'i:rən] *vt* construct.
Konstrukteur [kɔnstrʊk'tø:r] *m* engineer, designer.
Konstruktion [kɔnstrʊktsi'o:n] *f* construction.
konstruktiv [kɔnstrʊk'ti:f] *a* constructive.
Konsul ['kɔnzʊl] *m* -s, -n consul; ~**at** [-'la:t] *nt* consulate.
konsultieren [kɔnzʊl'ti:rən] *vt* consult.
Konsum [kɔn'zu:m] *m* -s consumption; ~**artikel** *m* consumer article; ~**ent** [-'mɛnt] *m* consumer; **k~ieren** [-'mi:rən] *vt* consume.
Kontakt [kɔn'takt] *m* -(e)s, -e contact; **k~arm** *a* unsociable; **k~freudig** *a* sociable; ~**linsen** *pl* contact lenses *pl*.
kontern ['kɔntərn] *vti* counter.
Kontinent ['kɔntinɛnt] *m* continent.
Kontingent [kɔntɪŋ'gɛnt] *nt* -(e)s, -e quota; (*Truppen~*) contingent.
kontinuierlich [kɔntinu'i:rlɪç] *a* continuous.
Konto ['kɔnto] *nt* -s, **Konten** account; ~**auszug** *m* statement (of account); ~**inhaber(in** *f)* *m* account holder; ~**stand** *m* balance.
Kontra ['kɔntra] *nt* -s, -s (*KARTEN*) double; **jdm** ~ **geben** (*fig*) contradict sb; ~**baß** *m* double bass; **Kontrahent** [-'hɛnt] *m* contracting party; ~**punkt** *m* counterpoint.
Kontrast [kɔn'trast] *m* -(e)s, -e contrast.
Kontroll- [kɔn'trɔl] *zW:* ~**e** *f* -, -n con-

trol, supervision; (*Paß~*) passport control; ~**eur** [-'lø:r] *m* inspector; **k~ieren** [-'li:rən] *vt* control, supervise; (*nachprüfen*) check.
Kontur [kɔn'tu:r] *f* contour.
Konvention [kɔnvɛntsi'o:n] *f* convention; **k~ell** [-'nɛl] *a* conventional.
Konversation [kɔnvɛrzatsi'o:n] *f* conversation; **Konversationslexikon** *nt* encyclopaedia.
konvex [kɔn'vɛks] *a* convex.
Konvoi ['kɔnvɔy] *m* -s, -s convoy.
Konzentration [kɔntsɛntratsi'o:n] *f* concentration.
konzentrieren [kɔntsɛn'tri:rən] *vtr* concentrate.
konzentriert *a* concentrated // *ad* (*zuhören, arbeiten*) intently.
Konzept [kɔn'tsɛpt] *nt* -(e)s, -e rough draft; **jdn aus dem** ~ **bringen** confuse sb.
Konzern [kɔn'tsɛrn] *m* -s, -e combine.
Konzert [kɔn'tsɛrt] *nt* -(e)s, -e concert; (*Stück*) concerto; ~**saal** *m* concert hall.
Konzession [kɔntsɛsi'o:n] *f* licence; (*Zugeständnis*) concession.
Konzil [kɔn'tsi:l] *nt* -s, -e *od* -ien council.
kooperativ [ko'opera'ti:f] *a* cooperative.
koordinieren [ko'ɔrdi'ni:rən] *vt* coordinate.
Kopf [kɔpf] *m* -(e)s, ¨e head; ~**bedeckung** *f* headgear; ~ **haut** *f* scalp; ~**hörer** *m* headphones *pl*; ~**kissen** *nt* pillow; **k~los** *a* panicstricken; **k~rechnen** *vi* do mental arithmetic; ~**salat** *m* lettuce; ~**schmerzen** *pl* headache; ~**sprung** *m* header, dive; ~**tuch** *nt* headscarf; ~**weh** *nt* headache; ~**zerbrechen** *nt*: **jdm** ~**zerbrechen machen** give sb a lot of headaches.
Kopie [ko'pi:] *f* copy; **k~ren** *vt* copy.
Koppel ['kɔpəl] *f* -, -n (*Weide*) enclosure // *nt* -s, - (*Gürtel*) belt; **k~n** *vt* couple; ~**ung** *f* coupling.
Koralle [ko'ralə] *f* -, -n coral; **Korallenriff** *nt* coral reef.
Korb [kɔrp] *m* -(e)s, ¨e basket; **jdm einen** ~ **geben** (*fig*) turn sb down; ~**ball** *m* basketball; ~**stuhl** *m* wicker chair.
Kord [kɔrt] *m* -(e)s, -e corduroy.
Kordel ['kɔrdəl] *f* -, -n cord, string.
Kork [kɔrk] *m* -(e)s, -e cork; ~**en** *m* -s, - stopper, cork; ~**enzieher** *m* -s, - corkscrew.
Korn [kɔrn] *nt* -(e)s, ¨er corn, grain; (*Gewehr*) sight; ~**blume** *f* cornflower.
Körper ['kœrpər] *m* -s, - body; ~**bau** *m* build; **k~behindert** *a* disabled; ~**gewicht** *nt* weight; ~**größe** *f*

height; **k~lich** a physical; **~pflege** f personal hygiene; **~schaft** f corporation; **~schaftssteuer** f corporation tax; **~teil** m part of the body.

korpulent [kɔrpu'lɛnt] a corpulent.

korrekt [kɔ'rɛkt] a correct; **K~or** m proofreader; **K~ur** [-'tu:r] f (eines Textes) proofreading; (Text) proof; (SCH) marking, correction.

Korrespond- [kɔrɛspɔnd] zW: **~ent(in** f) [-'dɛnt(ɪn)] m correspondent; **~enz** [-'dɛnts] f correspondence; **k~ieren** [-'di:rən] vi correspond.

Korridor ['kɔridoːr] m **-s, -e** corridor.

korrigieren [kɔri'giːrən] vt correct.

Korruption [kɔruptsi'oːn] f corruption.

Korsett [kɔr'zɛt] nt **-(e)s, -e** corset.

Kose- ['koːzə] zW: **~form** f pet form; **~name** m pet name; **~wort** nt term of endearment.

Kosmetik [kɔs'meːtɪk] f cosmetics pl; **~erin** f beautician.

kosmetisch a cosmetic; (Chirurgie) plastic.

kosmisch ['kɔsmɪʃ] a cosmic.

Kosmo- [kɔsmo] zW: **~naut** [-'naut] m **-en, -en** cosmonaut; **~polit** [-po'liːt] m **-en, -en** cosmopolitan; **k~politisch** [-po'liːtɪʃ] a cosmopolitan; **Kosmos** ['kɔsmɔs] m **-** cosmos.

Kost [kɔst] f **-** (Nahrung) food; (Verpflegung) board; **k~bar** a precious; (teuer) costly, expensive; **~barkeit** f preciousness; costliness, expensiveness; (Wertstück) valuable.

Kosten pl cost(s); (Ausgaben) expenses pl; **auf ~ von** at the expense of; **k~** vt cost **was kostet ...?** what does ... cost?, how much is ...? // vti (versuchen) taste; **~anschlag** m estimate; **k~los** a free (of charge).

köstlich ['kœstlɪç] a precious; (Einfall) delightful; (Essen) delicious; **sich ~ amüsieren** have a marvellous time.

Kost- zW: **~probe** f taste; (fig) sample; **k~spielig** a expensive.

Kostüm [kɔs'tyːm] nt **-s, -e** costume; (Damen~) suit; **~fest** nt fancy-dress party; **k~ieren** [kɔsty'miːrən] vtr dress up; **~verleih** m costume agency.

Kot [koːt] m **-(e)s** excrement.

Kotelett [kɔtə'lɛt] nt **-(e)s, -e** od **-s** cutlet, chop; **~en** pl sideboards pl.

Köter ['køːtər] m **-s, -** cur.

Kotflügel m (AUT) wing.

Krabbe ['krabə] f **-, -n** shrimp; **krabbeln** vi crawl.

Krach [krax] m **-(e)s, -s** od **-e** crash; (andauernd) noise; (umg: Streit) quarrel, argument; **k~en** vi crash; (beim Brechen) crack // vr (umg) argue, quarrel.

krächzen ['krɛçtsən] vi croak.

Kraft [kraft] f **-, ¨e** strength, power, force; (Arbeits~) worker; **in ~ treten** come into effect; **k~** präp +gen by virtue of; **~fahrer** m motor driver; **~fahrzeug** nt motor vehicle; **~fahrzeugbrief** m logbook; **~fahrzeugsteuer** f ≈ road tax.

kräftig ['krɛftɪç] a strong; **~en** [krɛftɪgən] vt strengthen.

Kraft- zW: **k~los** a weak; powerless; (JUR) invalid; **~probe** f trial of strength; **k~voll** a vigorous; **~wagen** m motor vehicle; **~werk** nt power station.

Kragen ['kraːgən] m **-s, -** collar; **~weite** f collar size.

Krähe ['krɛːə] f **-, -n** crow; **k~n** vi crow.

Kralle ['kralə] f **-, -n** claw; (Vogel~) talon; **k~n** vt clutch; (krampfhaft) claw.

Kram [kraːm] m **-(e)s** stuff, rubbish; **k~en** vi rummage; **~laden** m (pej) small shop.

Krampf [krampf] m **-(e)s, ¨e** cramp; (zuckend) spasm; **~ader** f varicose vein; **k~haft** a convulsive; (fig: Versuche) desperate.

Kran [kraːn] m **-(e)s, ¨e** crane; (Wasser~) tap.

Kranich ['kraːnɪç] m **-s, -e** (ZOOL) crane.

krank [krank] a ill, sick; **K~e(r)** mf sick person; invalid, patient.

kranken ['krankən] vi: **an etw** (dat) **~** (fig) suffer from sth.

kränken ['krɛnkən] vt hurt.

Kranken- zW: **~bericht** m medical report; **~geld** nt sick pay; **~haus** nt hospital; **~kasse** f health insurance; **~pfleger** m nursing orderly; **~schwester** f nurse; **~schein** m health insurance card; **~versicherung** f health insurance; **~wagen** m ambulance.

Krank- zW: **k~haft** a diseased; (Angst etc) morbid; **~heit** f illness, disease; **~heitserreger** m disease-carrying agent.

kränk- ['krɛnk] zW: **~lich** a sickly; **K~ung** f insult, offence.

Kranz [krants] m **-es, ¨e** wreath, garland.

kraß [kras] a crass.

Krater ['kraːtər] m **-s, -** crater.

Kratz- ['krats] zW: **~bürste** f (fig) crosspatch; **k~en** vti scratch; **~er** m **-s, -** scratch; (Werkzeug) scraper.

Kraul ['kraʊl] nt **-s** crawl; **~ schwimmen** do the crawl; **k~en** vi (schwimmen) do the crawl // vt (streicheln) tickle.

kraus [kraʊs] a crinkly; (Haar) frizzy; (Stirn) wrinkled; **K~e** ['kraʊzə] f **-, -n** frill, ruffle.

Kraut [kraʊt] *nt* -(e)s, **Kräuter** plant; (*Gewürz*) herb; (*Gemüse*) cabbage.
Krawall [kra'val] *m* -s, -e row, uproar.
Krawatte [kra'vatə] *f* -, -n tie.
Krebs [kreːps] *m* -es, -e crab; (*MED. ASTROL*) cancer.
Kredit [kre'diːt] *m* -(e)s, -e credit; ~**karte** *f* credit card.
Kreide ['kraɪdə] *f* -, -n chalk; **k~bleich** *a* as white as a sheet.
Kreis [kraɪs] *m* -es, -e circle; (*Stadt* *etc*) district; **im** ~ **gehen** (*lit, fig*) go round in circles.
kreischen ['kraɪʃən] *vi* shriek, screech.
Kreis- *zW*: ~**el** ['kraɪzəl] *m* -s, - top; (*Verkehrs~*) roundabout; **k~en** ['kraɪzən] *vi* spin; ~**lauf** *m* (*MED*) circulation; (*fig: der Natur etc*) cycle; ~**säge** *f* circular saw; ~**stadt** *f* county town; ~**verkehr** *m* roundabout traffic.
Kreißsaal ['kraɪs-zaːl] *m* delivery room.
Krematorium [krema'toːriʊm] *nt* crematorium.
Kreml ['krɛm(ə)l] *m* -s Kremlin.
krepieren [kre'piːrən] *vi* (*umg: sterben*) die, kick the bucket.
Krepp [krɛp] *m* -s, -s *od* -e crepe; ~**(p)apier** *nt* crepe paper; ~**sohle** *f* crepe sole.
Kresse ['krɛsə] *f* -, -n cress.
Kreta ['kreːta] *nt* -s Crete.
Kreuz [krɔʏts] *nt* -es, -e cross; (*ANAT*) small of the back; (*KARTEN*) clubs; **k~en** *vtr* cross // *vi* (*NAUT*) cruise; ~**er** *m* -s, - (*Schiff*) cruiser; ~**fahrt** *f* cruise; ~**gang** *m* cloisters *pl*; **k~igen** *vt* crucify; ~**igung** *f* crucifixion; ~**otter** *f* adder; ~**ung** *f* (*Verkehrs~*) crossing, junction; (*Züchten*) cross; ~**verhör** *nt* cross-examination; ~**weg** *m* crossroads; (*REL*) Way of the Cross; ~**worträtsel** *nt* crossword puzzle; ~**zug** *m* crusade.
Kriech- ['kriːç] *zW*: **k~en** *vi unreg* crawl, creep; (*pej*) grovel, crawl; ~**er** *m* -s, - crawler; ~**spur** *f* crawler lane; ~**tier** *nt* reptile.
Krieg [kriːk] *m* -(e)s, -e war.
kriegen ['kriːgən] *vt* (*umg*) get.
Kriegs- *zW*: ~**dienstverweigerer** *m* conscientious objector; ~**erklärung** *f* declaration of war; ~**fuß** *m*: **mit jdm/etw auf** ~**fuß stehen** be at loggerheads with sb/not get on with sth; ~**gefangene(r)** *m* prisoner of war; ~**gefangenschaft** *f* captivity; ~**gericht** *nt* court-martial; ~**schiff** *nt* warship; ~**verbrecher** *m* war criminal; ~**versehrte(r)** *m* person disabled in the war; ~**zustand** *m* state of war.
Krim [krɪm] *f* - Crimea.

Krimi ['kriːmi] *m* -s, -s (*umg*) thriller.
Kriminal- [krimi'naːl] *zW*: ~**beamte(r)** *m* detective; ~**i'tät** *f* criminality; ~**'polizei** *f* ≈ Criminal Investigation Department, CID (*Brit*), Federal Bureau of Investigation, FBI (*US*); ~**'roman** *m* detective story.
kriminell [krimi'nɛl] *a* criminal; **K~e(r)** *m* criminal.
Krippe ['krɪpə] *f* -, -n manger, crib; (*Kinder~*) crèche.
Krise ['kriːzə] *f* -, -n crisis; **k~ln** *vi*: **es kriselt** there's a crisis.
Kristall [krɪs'tal] *m* -s, -e crystal // *nt* -s (*Glas*) crystal.
Kriterium [kri'teːriʊm] *nt* criterion.
Kritik [kri'tiːk] *f* criticism; (*Zeitungs~*) review, write-up; ~**er** ['kriːtikər] *m* -s, - critic; **k~los** *a* uncritical.
kritisch ['kriːtɪʃ] *a* critical.
kritisieren [kriti'ziːrən] *vti* criticize.
kritzeln ['krɪtsəln] *vti* scribble, scrawl.
Krokodil [kroko'diːl] *nt* -s, -e crocodile.
Krokus ['kroːkʊs] *m* -, - *od* -se crocus.
Krone ['kroːnə] *f* -, -n crown; (*Baum~*) top.
krönen ['krøːnən] *vt* crown.
Kron- *zW*: ~**korken** *m* bottle top; ~**leuchter** *m* chandelier; ~**prinz** *m* crown prince.
Krönung ['krøːnʊŋ] *f* coronation.
Kropf [krɔpf] *m* -(e)s, -̈e (*MED*) goitre; (*von Vogel*) crop.
Kröte ['krøːtə] *f* -, -n toad.
Krücke ['krykə] *f* -, -n crutch.
Krug [kruːk] *m* -(e)s, -̈e jug; (*Bier~*) mug.
Krümel ['kryːməl] *m* -s, - crumb; **k~n** *vti* crumble.
krumm [krʊm] *a* (*lit, fig*) crooked; (*kurvig*) curved; ~**beinig** *a* bandylegged; ~**lachen** *vr* (*umg*) laugh o.s. silly; ~**nehmen** *vt unreg* (*umg*): **jdm etw** ~**nehmen** take sth amiss.
Krümmung ['krymʊŋ] *f* bend, curve.
Krüppel ['krypəl] *m* -s, - cripple.
Kruste ['krʊstə] *f* -, -n crust.
Kruzifix [krutsi'fɪks] *nt* -es, -e crucifix.
Kübel ['kyːbəl] *m* -s, - tub; (*Eimer*) pail.
Kubikmeter [ku'biːkmeːtər] *m* cubic metre.
Küche ['kyçə] *f* -, -n kitchen; (*Kochen*) cooking, cuisine.
Kuchen ['kuːxən] *m* -s, - cake; ~**form** *f* baking tin; ~**gabel** *f* pastry fork.
Küchen- *zW*: ~**herd** *m* range; (*Gas, ELEK*) cooker, stove; ~**schabe** *f* cockroach; ~**schrank** *m* kitchen cabinet.
Kuckuck ['kʊkʊk] *m* -s, -e cuckoo; **Kuckucksuhr** *f* cuckoo clock.
Kufe ['kuːfə] *f* -, -n (*Faß*) vat; (*Schlit-*

ten~) runner; (*AVIAT*) skid.

Kugel ['ku:gəl] *f* -, **-n** ball; (*MATH*) sphere; (*MIL*) bullet; (*Erd~*) globe; (*SPORT*) shot; **k~förmig** *a* spherical; **~kopf** *m* golf ball; **~lager** *nt* ball bearing; **k~rund** *a* (*Gegenstand*) round; (*umg: Person*) tubby; **~schreiber** *m* ball-point (pen), biro ®; **k~sicher** *a* bulletproof; **~stoßen** *nt* **-s** shot-put.

Kuh [ku:] *f* -, **-̈e** cow.

kühl [ky:l] *a* (*lit, fig*) cool; **K~anlage** *f* refrigerating plant; **K~e** *f* - coolness; **~en** *vt* cool; **K~er** *m* **-s**, - (*AUT*) radiator; **K~erhaube** *f* (*AUT*) bonnet (*Brit*), hood (*US*); **K~raum** *m* cold-storage chamber; **K~schrank** *m* refrigerator; **K~truhe** *f* freezer; **K~ung** *f* cooling; **K~wasser** *nt* cooling water.

kühn [ky:n] *a* bold, daring; **K~heit** *f* boldness.

Küken ['ky:kən] *nt* **-s**, - chicken.

kulant [ku'lant] *a* obliging.

Kuli ['ku:li] *m* **-s**, **-s** coolie; (*umg: Kugelschreiber*) biro ®.

Kulisse [ku'lisə] *f* -, **-n** scene.

kullern ['kulərn] *vi* roll.

Kult [kult] *m* **-(e)s**, **-e** worship, cult; **mit etw einen ~ treiben** make a cult out of sth; **k~ivieren** [-i'vi:rən] *vt* cultivate; **k~iviert** *a* cultivated, refined.

Kultur [kul'tu:r] *f* culture; civilization; (*des Bodens*) cultivation; **~banause** *m* (*umg*) philistine, low-brow; **k~ell** [-u'rɛl] *a* cultural.

Kümmel ['kyməl] *m* **-s**, - caraway seed; (*Branntwein*) kümmel.

Kummer ['kumər] *m* **-s** grief, sorrow.

kümmer- ['kymər] *zW*: **~lich** *a* miserable, wretched; **~n** *vr*: **sich um jdn ~n** look after sb; **sich um etw ~n** see to sth // *vt* concern; **das kümmert mich nicht** that doesn't worry me.

Kumpel ['kumpəl] *m* **-s**, - (*umg*) mate.

kündbar ['kyntba:r] *a* redeemable, recallable; (*Vertrag*) terminable.

Kunde ['kundə] *m* **-n**, **-n**, **Kundin** *f* customer // *f* -, **-n** (*Botschaft*) news; **Kundendienst** *m* after-sales service; **Kundenkonto** *nt* charge account.

Kund- *zW*: **~gabe** *f* announcement; **k~geben** *vt unreg* announce; **~gebung** *f* announcement; (*Versammlung*) rally.

Künd- *zW*: **k~igen** *vi* give in one's notice; **jdm k~igen** give sb his notice // *vt* cancel; (*jdm*) **die Stellung/Wohnung k~igen** give (sb) notice; **~igung** *f* notice; **~igungsfrist** *f* period of notice.

Kundschaft *f* customers *pl*, clientele.

künftig ['kynftıç] *a* future // *ad* in future.

Kunst [kunst] *f* -, **-̈e** art; (*Können*) skill; **das ist doch keine ~** it's easy; **~dünger** *m* artificial manure; **~faser** *f* synthetic fibre; **~fertigkeit** *f* skilfulness; **~geschichte** *f* history of art; **~gewerbe** *nt* arts and crafts *pl*; **~griff** *m* trick, knack; **~händler** *m* art dealer.

Künstler(in *f*) ['kynstlər(ın)] *m* **-s**, - artist; **k~isch** *a* artistic; **~name** *m* stagename; pseudonym.

künstlich ['kynstlıç] *a* artificial.

Kunst- *zW*: **~sammler** *m* **-s**, - art collector; **~seide** *f* artificial silk; **~stoff** *m* synthetic material; **~stück** *nt* trick; **~turnen** *nt* gymnastics; **k~voll** *a* ingenious, artistic; **~werk** *nt* work of art.

kunterbunt ['kuntərbunt] *a* higgledy-piggledy.

Kupfer ['kupfər] *nt* **-s**, - copper; **~geld** *nt* coppers *pl*; **k~n** *a* copper.

Kuppe ['kupə] *f* -, **-n** (*Berg~*) top; (*Finger~*) tip.

Kupp- ['kup] *zW*: **Kuppe'lei** *f* (*JUR*) procuring; **kuppeln** *vi* (*JUR*) procure; (*AUT*) declutch // *vt* join; **~lung** *f* coupling; (*AUT*) clutch.

Kur [ku:r] *f* -, **-en** cure, treatment.

Kür [ky:r] *f* -, **-en** (*SPORT*) free skating/exercises *pl*.

Kurbel ['kurbəl] *f* -, **-n** crank, winch; (*AUT*) starting handle; **~welle** *f* crankshaft.

Kürbis ['kyrbıs] *m* **-ses**, **-se** pumpkin; (*exotisch*) gourd.

Kur- ['ku:r] *zW*: **~gast** *m* visitor (to a health resort); **k~ieren** [ku'ri:rən] *vt* cure; **k~ios** [kuri'o:s] *a* curious, odd; **~iosi'tät** *f* curiosity; **~ort** *m* health resort; **~pfuscher** *m* quack.

Kurs [kurs] *m* **-es**, **-e** course; (*FIN*) rate; **~buch** *nt* timetable; **k~ieren** [kur'zi:rən] *vi* circulate; **k~iv** *ad* in italics; **~us** ['kurzus] *m* -, **Kurse** course; **~wagen** *m* (*EISENB*) through carriage.

Kurve ['kurvə] *f* -, **-n** curve; (*Straßen~ auch*) bend; **kurvenreich, kurvig** *a* (*Straße*) bendy.

kurz [kurts] *a* short; **~ gesagt** in short; **zu ~ kommen** come off badly; **den ~eren ziehen** get the worst of it; **K~arbeit** *f* short-time work; **~ärm(e)lig** *a* short-sleeved.

Kürze ['kyrtsə] *f* -, **-n** shortness, brevity; **k~n** *vt* cut short; (*in der Länge*) shorten; (*Gehalt*) reduce.

kurz- *zW*: **k~erhand** *ad* on the spot; **~fristig** *a* short-term; **K~geschichte** *f* short story; **~halten** *vt unreg* keep short; **~lebig** *a* short-lived.

kürzlich ['kyrtslıç] *ad* lately, recently.

Kurz- *zW*: **~schluß** *m* (*ELEK*) short circuit; **~schrift** *f* shorthand; **k~sichtig** *a* short-sighted; **~welle** *f* shortwave.

kuscheln ['kʊʃəln] vr snuggle up.

Kusine [ku'ziːnə] f cousin.

Kuß [kʊs] m **-sses, ꞏsse** kiss.

küssen ['kʏsən] vtr kiss.

Küste ['kʏstə] f **-, -n** coast, shore; **Küstenwache** f coastguard (station).

Küster ['kʏstər] m **-s, -** sexton, verger.

Kutsche ['kʊtʃə] f **-, -n** coach, carriage; **~r** m **-s, -** coachman.

Kutte ['kʊtə] f **-, -n** cowl.

Kuvert [ku'veːr] nt **-s, -e** od **-s** envelope; cover.

Kybernetik [kybɛr'neːtɪk] f cybernetics.

L

L, l [ɛl] nt L, l // **l.** abk von **Liter.**

Labor [la'boːr] nt **-s, -e** od **-s** lab; **~ant(in** f) [labo'rant(ɪn)] m lab(oratory) assistant; **~atorium** [labora'toːriʊm] nt laboratory.

Labyrinth [laby'rɪnt] nt **-s, -e** labyrinth.

lächeln ['lɛçəln] vi smile; **L~** nt **-s** smile.

lachen ['laxən] vi laugh.

lächerlich ['lɛçərlɪç] a ridiculous.

Lachgas nt laughing gas.

lachhaft a laughable.

Lachs [laks] m **-es, -e** salmon.

Lack [lak] m **-(e)s, -e** lacquer, varnish; (von Auto) paint; **l~ieren** [la'kiːrən] vt varnish; (Auto) spray; **~ierer** [la'kiːrər] m **-s, -** varnisher.

Lackmus ['lakmʊs] m od nt **-** litmus.

laden ['laːdən] vt unreg (Lasten) load; (JUR) summon; (einladen) invite.

Laden ['laːdən] m **-s, ꞏ** shop; (Fenster~) shutter; **~dieb** m shoplifter; **~diebstahl** m shoplifting; **~schluß** m closing time; **~tisch** m counter.

Ladung ['laːdʊŋ] f (Last) cargo, load; (Beladen) loading; (JUR) summons; (Einladung) invitation; (Spreng~) charge.

lag etc v siehe **liegen.**

Lage ['laːgə] f **-, -n** position, situation; (Schicht) layer; **in der ~ sein** be in a position.

Lager ['laːgər] nt **-s, -** camp; (COMM) warehouse; (Schlaf~) bed; (von Tier) lair; (TECH) bearing; **~bestand** m stocks pl; **~haus** nt warehouse, store.

lagern ['laːgərn] vi (Dinge) be stored; (Menschen) camp // vt store; (betten) lay down; (Maschine) bed.

Lagune [la'guːnə] f **-, -n** lagoon.

lahm [laːm] a lame; **~en** vi be lame, limp.

lähmen ['lɛːmən] vt paralyse.

lahmlegen vt paralyse.

Lähmung f paralysis.

Laib [laɪp] m **-s, -e** loaf.

Laie ['laɪə] m **-n, -n** layman; **laienhaft** a amateurish.

Laken ['laːkən] nt **-s, -** sheet.

Lakritze [la'krɪtsə] f **-, -n** liquorice.

lallen ['lalən] vti slur; (Baby) babble.

Lamelle [la'mɛlə] f lamella; (ELEK) lamina; (TECH) plate.

Lametta [la'mɛta] nt **-s** tinsel.

Lamm [lam] nt **-(e)s, ꞏer** lamb; **~fell** nt lambskin.

Lampe ['lampə] f **-, -n** lamp; **Lampenfieber** nt stage fright; **Lampenschirm** m lampshade.

Lampion [lampi'õː] m **-s, -s** Chinese lantern.

Land [lant] nt **-(e)s, ꞏer** land; (Nation, nicht Stadt) country; (Bundes~) state; **auf dem ~**(e) in the country; **~besitz** m landed property; **Landebahn** f runway; **l~en** ['landən] vti land.

Landes- ['landəs] zW: **~farben** pl national colours pl; **~innere(s)** nt inland region; **~sprache** f national language; **l~üblich** a customary; **~verrat** m high treason; **~währung** f national currency.

Land- zW: **~haus** nt country house; **~karte** f map; **~kreis** m administrative region; **l~läufig** a customary.

ländlich ['lɛntlɪç] a rural.

Land- zW: **~schaft** f countryside; (KUNST) landscape; **l~schaftlich** a scenic; regional; **~straße** f country road; **~streicher** m **-s, -** tramp; **~strich** m region; **~tag** m (POL) regional parliament.

Landung ['landʊŋ] f landing.

Landungs- zW: **~boot** nt landing craft; **~brücke** f jetty, pier; **~stelle** f landing place.

Land- zW: **~wirt** m farmer; **~wirtschaft** f agriculture; **~zunge** f spit.

lang [laŋ] a long; (Mensch) tall; **~atmig** a long-winded; **~e** ad for a long time; (dauern, brauchen) a long time.

Länge ['lɛŋə] f **-, -n** length; (GEOG) longitude.

langen ['laŋən] vi (ausreichen) do, suffice; (fassen) reach (nach for); **es langt mir** I've had enough.

Länge- zW: **Längengrad** m longitude; **Längenmaß** nt linear measure.

lang- zW: **L~eweile** f boredom; **~fristig** a long-term; **~lebig** a long-lived.

länglich a longish.

längs [lɛŋs] präp +gen od dat along // ad lengthwise.

lang- zW: **~sam** a slow; **L~samkeit** f

slowness; **L~schläfer(in** f) m late riser; **L~spielplatte** f long-playing record.

längst ['lɛŋst] ad: **das ist ~ fertig** that was finished a long time ago, that has been finished for a long time; **~e(r, s)** a longest.

lang- zW: **~weilen** vt bore // vr be bored; **~weilig** a boring, tedious; **L~welle** f long wave; **~wierig** a lengthy, long-drawn-out.

Lanze ['lantsə] f -, -n lance.

Lappalie [la'pa:liə] f trifle.

Lappen ['lapən] m -s, - cloth, rag; (ANAT) lobe.

läppisch ['lɛpɪʃ] a foolish.

Lappland ['laplant] nt -s Lapland.

Lapsus ['lapsʊs] m -, - slip.

Lärche ['lɛrçə] f -, -n larch.

Lärm [lɛrm] m -(e)s noise; **l~en** vi be noisy, make a noise.

Larve ['larfə] f -, -n (BIOL) larva.

las etc v siehe **lesen**.

lasch [laʃ] a slack.

Lasche ['laʃə] f -, -n (Schuh~) tongue.

Laser ['leɪzə] m -s, - laser.

lassen ['lasən] ♦vt pt **ließ**, ptp **gelassen 1** (unterlassen) stop; (momentan) leave; **laß das (sein)!** don't (do it)!; (hör auf) stop it!; **laß mich!** leave me alone; **~ wir das!** let's leave it; **er kann das Trinken nicht ~** he can't stop drinking
2 (zurücklassen) leave; **etw ~, wie es ist** leave sth (just) as it is
3 (überlassen): **jdm etw ~** let sb have sth
4 (zulassen): **jdn ins Haus ~** let sb into the house
♦vi: **laß mal, ich mache das schon** leave it, I'll do it
♦ (als Hilfsverb) pt **ließ**, ptp **lassen 1** (veranlassen): **etw machen ~** have od get sth done; **jdm etw schicken ~** have sth sent (to one)
2 (zulassen): **jdn etw wissen ~** let sb know sth; **das Licht brennen ~** leave the light on; **jdn warten ~** keep sb waiting; **das läßt sich machen** that can be done
3: **laß uns gehen** let's go.

lässig ['lɛsɪç] a casual; **L~keit** f casualness.

Last [last] f -, -en load, burden; (NAUT, AVIAT) cargo; (meist pl: Gebühr) charge; **jdm zur ~ fallen** be a burden to sb; **~auto** nt lorry, truck; **l~en** vi (auf +dat) weigh on.

Laster ['lastər] nt -s, - vice.

lästern ['lɛstərn] vti (Gott) blaspheme; (schlecht sprechen) mock.

Lästerung f jibe; (Gottes~) blasphemy.

lästig ['lɛstɪç] a troublesome, tiresome.

Last- zW: **~kahn** m barge; **~-**

kraftwagen m heavy goods vehicle; **~schrift** f debit; **~wagen** m lorry, truck.

Latein [la'taɪn] nt -s Latin; **~amerika** nt Latin America.

latent [la'tɛnt] a latent.

Laterne [la'tɛrnə] f -, -n lantern; (Straßen~) lamp, light; **Laternenpfahl** m lamppost.

latschen ['la:tʃən] vi (umg: gehen) wander, go; (lässig) slouch.

Latte ['latə] f -, -n lath; (SPORT) goalpost; (quer) crossbar.

Latzhose ['latsho:zə] f dungarees pl.

lau [lau] a (Nacht) balmy; (Wasser) lukewarm.

Laub [laup] nt -(e)s foliage; **~baum** m deciduous tree; **~frosch** m tree frog; **~säge** f fretsaw.

Lauch [laux] m -(e)s, -e leek.

Lauer ['lauər] f: **auf der ~ sein** od **liegen**, **l~n** vi lie in wait; (Gefahr) lurk.

Lauf [lauf] m -(e)s, **Läufe** run; (Wett~) race; (Entwicklung, ASTRON) course; (Gewehr) barrel; **einer Sache ihren ~ lassen** let sth take its course; **~bahn** f career.

laufen ['laufən] vti unreg run; (umg: gehen) walk; **~d** a running; (Monat, Ausgaben) current; **auf dem ~den sein/halten** be/keep up to date; **am ~den Band** (fig) continuously.

Läufer ['lɔyfər] m -s, - (Teppich, SPORT) runner; (Fußball) half-back; (Schach) bishop.

Lauf- zW: **~masche** f run, ladder (Brit); **~stall** m playpen; **~steg** m catwalk; **~werk** nt (COMPUT) disk drive; **~zettel** m circular.

Lauge ['laugə] f -, -n soapy water; (CHEM) alkaline solution.

Laune ['launə] f -, -n mood, humour; (Einfall) caprice; (schlechte) temper; **l~nhaft** a capricious, changeable.

launisch a moody; bad-tempered.

Laus [laus] f -, **Läuse** louse; **~bub** m rascal, imp.

lauschen ['lauʃən] vi eavesdrop, listen in.

lauschig ['lauʃɪç] a snug.

laut [laut] a loud // ad loudly; (lesen) aloud // präp +gen od dat according to; **L~** m -(e)s, -e sound.

Laute ['lautə] f -, -n lute.

lauten ['lautən] vi say; (Urteil) be.

läuten ['lɔytən] vti ring, sound.

lauter ['lautər] a (Wasser) clear, pure; (Wahrheit, Charakter) honest; inv (Freude, Dummheit etc) sheer; (mit pl) nothing but, only.

läutern ['lɔytərn] vt purify.

Läuterung f purification.

laut- zW: **~hals** ad at the top of one's

voice; **~los** a noiseless, silent; **L~schrift** f phonetics pl; **L~sprecher** m loudspeaker; **L~sprecherwagen** m loudspeaker van; **~stark** a vociferous; **L~stärke** f (RAD) volume.

lauwarm ['lauvarm] a (lit, fig) lukewarm.

Lava ['la:va] f -, **Laven** lava.

Lavendel [la'vɛndəl] m -s, - lavender.

Lawine [la'vi:nə] f avalanche; **Lawinengefahr** f danger of avalanches.

lax [laks] a lax.

Lazarett [latsa'rɛt] nt -(e)s, -e (MIL) hospital, infirmary.

leben ['le:bən] vti live; **L~** nt -s, - life; **~d** a living; **lebendig** [le'bɛndıç] a living, alive; (lebhaft) lively; **Lebendigkeit** f liveliness.

Lebens- zW: **~alter** nt age; **~art** f way of life; **~erwartung** f life expectancy; **l~fähig** a able to live; **~gefahr** f: **~gefahr!** danger!; **in ~gefahr** dangerously ill; **l~gefährlich** a dangerous; (Verletzung) critical; **~haltungskosten** pl cost of living sing; **~jahr** nt year of life; **~lauf** m curriculum vitae; **l~lustig** a cheerful, lively; **~mittel** pl food sing; **~mittelgeschäft** nt grocer's; **l~müde** a tired of life; **~retter** m lifesaver; **~standard** m standard of living; **~unterhalt** m livelihood; **~versicherung** f life insurance; **~wandel** m way of life; **~zeichen** nt sign of life.

Leber ['le:bər] f -, -n liver; **~fleck** m mole; **~tran** m cod-liver oil; **~wurst** f liver sausage.

Lebewesen nt creature.

Lebewohl nt farewell, goodbye.

leb- ['le:p] zW: **~haft** a lively, vivacious; **L~kuchen** m gingerbread; **~los** a lifeless.

leck [lɛk] a leaky, leaking; **L~** nt -(e)s, -e leak; **~en** vi (Loch haben) leak // vti (schlecken) lick.

lecker ['lɛkər] a delicious, tasty; **L~bissen** m dainty morsel.

led. abk von **ledig.**

Leder ['le:dər] nt -s, - leather; **l~n** a leather; **~waren** pl leather goods pl.

ledig ['le:dıç] a single; einer Sache ~ **sein** be free of sth; **~lich** ad merely, solely.

leer [le:r] a empty; vacant; ~ **machen** empty; **L~e** f - emptiness; **~en** vt empty // vr empty; **L~gewicht** nt weight when empty; **L~lauf** m neutral; **~stehend** a empty; **L~ung** f emptying; (Post) collection.

legal [le'ga:l] a legal, lawful; **~i'sieren** vt legalize; **L~i'tät** f legality.

legen ['le:gən] vt lay, put, place; (Ei) lay // vr lie down; (fig) subside.

Legende [le'gɛndə] f -, -n legend.

leger [le'ʒɛ:r] a casual.

legieren [le'gi:rən] vt alloy.

Legierung f alloy.

Legislative [legısla'ti:və] f legislature.

legitim [legi'ti:m] a legitimate; **L~ation** [-atsi'o:n] f legitimation; **~ieren** [-'mi:rən] vt legitimate // vr prove one's identity.

Lehm [le:m] m -(e)s, -e loam; **l~ig** a loamy.

Lehne ['le:nə] f -, -n arm; back; **l~n** vtr lean.

Lehnstuhl m armchair.

Lehr- zW: **~amt** nt teaching profession; **~brief** m indentures pl; **~buch** nt textbook.

Lehre ['le:rə] f -, -n teaching, doctrine; (beruflich) apprenticeship; (moralisch) lesson; (TECH) gauge; **l~n** vt teach; **~r(in** f) m -s, - teacher; **Lehrerzimmer** nt staff room.

Lehr- zW: **~gang** m course; **~jahre** pl apprenticeship; **~ling** m apprentice; **l~reich** a instructive; **~stelle** f apprenticeship; **~stuhl** m chair; **~zeit** f apprenticeship.

Leib [laıp] m -(e)s, -er body; halt ihn mir vom ~! keep him away from me; **l~haftig** a personified; (Teufel) incarnate; **l~lich** a bodily; (Vater etc) own; **~wache** f bodyguard.

Leiche ['laıçə] f -, -n corpse.

Leichen- zW: ~ **haus** nt mortuary; **~träger** m bearer; **~wagen** m hearse.

Leichnam ['laıçna:m] m -(e)s, -e corpse.

leicht [laıçt] a light; (einfach) easy; **L~athletik** f athletics sing; **~fallen** vi unreg: **jdm ~fallen** be easy for sb; **~fertig** a frivolous; **~gläubig** a gullible, credulous; **L~gläubigkeit** f gullibility, credulity; **~hin** ad lightly; **L~igkeit** f easiness; **mit L~igkeit** with ease; **~machen** vt: es sich (dat) **~machen** make things easy for oneself; **L~sinn** m carelessness; **~sinnig** a careless.

Leid [laıt] nt -(e)s grief, sorrow; **l~** a: etw l~ **haben** od **sein** be tired of sth; es tut mir/ihm l~ I am/he is sorry; er/das tut mir l~ I am sorry for him/it; **l~en** ['laıdən] unreg vt suffer; (erlauben) permit; **jdn/etw nicht l~en können** not be able to stand sb/sth // vi suffer; **~en** nt -s, - suffering; (Krankheit) complaint; **~enschaft** f passion; **l~enschaftlich** a passionate.

leider ['laıdər] ad unfortunately; ja, ~ yes, I'm afraid so; ~ **nicht** I'm afraid not.

Leidtragende(r) mf bereaved; (Benachteiligter) one who suffers.

Leidwesen nt: zu jds ~ to sb's dismay.

Leier ['laɪər] f -, -n lyre; (fig) old story; ~**kasten** m barrel organ.
Leihbibliothek f lending library.
leihen ['laɪən] vt unreg lend; **sich** (dat) etw ~ borrow sth.
Leih- zW: ~**gebühr** f hire charge; ~**haus** nt pawnshop; ~**schein** m pawn ticket; (Buch~ etc) borrowing slip; ~**wagen** m hired car.
Leim [laɪm] m -(e)s, -e glue; **l~en** vt glue.
Leine ['laɪnə] f -, -n line, cord; (Hunde~) leash, lead; ~**n** nt -s, - linen; **l~n** a linen.
Leintuch nt (Bett~) sheet; linen cloth.
Leinwand f (KUNST) canvas; (CINE) screen.
leise ['laɪzə] a quiet; (sanft) soft, gentle.
Leiste ['laɪstə] f -, -n ledge; (Zier~) strip; (ANAT) groin.
leisten ['laɪstən] vt (Arbeit) do; (Gesellschaft) keep; (Ersatz) supply; (vollbringen) achieve; **sich** (dat) etw ~ **können** be able to afford sth.
Leistung f performance; (gute) achievement.
Leistungs- zW: ~**druck** m pressure; **l~fähig** a efficient; ~**fähigkeit** f efficiency; ~**sport** m competitive sport; ~**zulage** f productivity bonus.
Leitartikel m leading article.
Leitbild nt model.
leiten ['laɪtən] vt lead; (Firma) manage; (in eine Richtung) direct; (ELEK) conduct.
Leiter ['laɪtər] m -s, - leader, head; (ELEK) conductor // f -, -n ladder.
Leit- zW: ~**faden** m guide; ~**motiv** nt leitmotiv; ~**planke** f crash barrier.
Leitung f (Führung) direction; (CINE, THEAT etc) production; (von Firma) management; directors pl; (Wasser~) pipe; (Kabel) cable; **eine lange** ~ **haben** be on the uptake.
Leitungs- zW: ~**draht** m wire; ~**rohr** nt pipe; ~**wasser** nt tap water.
Lektion [lɛktsi'oːn] f lesson.
Lektüre [lɛk'tyːrə] f -, -n (Lesen) reading; (Lesestoff) reading matter.
Lende ['lɛndə] f -, -n loin; **Lendenstück** nt fillet.
lenk- ['lɛŋk] zW: ~**bar** a (Fahrzeug) steerable; (Kind) manageable; ~**en** vt steer; (Kind) guide; (Blick, Aufmerksamkeit) direct (auf +akk at); **L~rad** nt steering wheel; **L~stange** f handlebars pl.
Leopard [leo'part] m -en, -en leopard.
Lepra ['leːpra] f - leprosy.
Lerche ['lɛrçə] f -, -n lark.
lern- ['lɛrn] zW: ~**begierig** a eager to learn; ~**en** vt learn.
lesbar ['leːsbaːr] a legible.

Lesbierin ['lɛsbiərɪn] f lesbian.
lesbisch ['lɛsbɪʃ] a lesbian.
Lese ['leːzə] f -, -n (Wein) harvest; ~**buch** nt reading book, reader; **l~n** vti unreg read; (ernten) gather, pick.
Leser(in f) m -s, - reader; ~**brief** m reader's letter; **l~lich** a legible.
Lesung ['leːzʊŋ] f (PARL) reading.
letzte(r, s) ['lɛtstə(r, s)] a last; (neueste) latest; **zum** ~**n Mal** ad for the last time; ~**ns** ad lately; ~**re(r, s)** a latter.
Leuchte ['lɔʏçtə] f -, -n lamp, light; **l~n** vi shine, gleam; ~**r** m -s, - candlestick.
Leucht- zW: ~**farbe** f fluorescent colour; ~**kugel** f, ~**rakete** f flare; ~**reklame** f neon sign; ~**röhre** f strip light; ~**turm** m lighthouse; ~**zifferblatt** nt luminous dial.
leugnen ['lɔʏgnən] vti deny.
Leugnung f denial.
Leukämie [lɔʏkɛ'miː] f leukaemia.
Leukoplast ® [lɔʏko'plast] nt -(e)s, -e elastoplast ®.
Leumund ['lɔʏmʊnt] m -(e)s, -e reputation.
Leumundszeugnis nt character reference.
Leute ['lɔʏtə] pl people pl.
Leutnant ['lɔʏtnant] m -s, -s od -e lieutenant.
Lexikon ['lɛksikɔn] nt -s, **Lexiken** od **Lexika** encyclopaedia.
libanesisch [liba'neːzɪʃ] a Lebanese.
Libanon ['liːbanɔn] m -s: (**der**) ~ the Lebanon.
Libelle [li'bɛlə] f -, -n dragonfly; (TECH) spirit level.
liberal [libe'raːl] a liberal; **L~e(r)** mf liberal; **L~ismus** [libera'lɪsmʊs] m liberalism.
Libero ['liːbero] m -s, -s (Fußball) sweeper.
Libyen ['liːbiən] nt -s Libya.
libysch ['liːbɪʃ] a Libyan.
Licht [lɪçt] nt -(e)s, -er light; ~**bild** nt photograph; (Dia) slide; ~**blick** m cheering prospect; **l~empfindlich** a sensitive to light; **l~en** vt clear; (Anker) weigh // vr clear up; (Haar) thin; ~**hupe** f flashing of headlights; ~**jahr** nt light year; ~**maschine** f dynamo; ~**schalter** m light switch.
Lichtung f clearing, glade.
Lid [liːt] nt -(e)s, -er eyelid; ~**schatten** m eyeshadow.
lieb [liːp] a dear; **das ist** ~ **von dir** that's kind of you; ~**äugeln** vi insep ogle (mit jdm/etw sb/sth).
Liebe ['liːbə] f -, -n love; **l~bedürftig** a: **l~bedürftig sein** need love; ~**lei** f flirtation; **l~n** vt love; like.
liebens- zW: ~**wert** a loveable; ~**würdig** a kind; ~**würdigerweise** ad

kindly; **L~würdigkeit** f kindness.
lieber ['liːbər] ad rather, preferably; **ich gehe ~ nicht** I'd rather not go // siehe **gern, lieb.**
Liebes- zW: **~brief** m love letter; **~kummer** m: **~kummer haben** be lovesick; **~paar** nt courting couple, lovers pl.
liebevoll a loving.
lieb- ['liːb] zW: **~gewinnen** vt unreg get fond of; **~haben** vt unreg be fond of; **L~haber** m -s, - lover; **L~habe'rei** f hobby; **~kosen** [liːp'koːzən] vt insep caress; **~lich** a lovely, charming; **L~ling** m darling; **L~lings-** in zW favourite; **~los** a unloving; **L~schaft** f love affair; **~ste(r, s)** a favourite; **etw am ~sten mögen** like sth best.
Lied [liːt] nt -(e)s, -er song; (ECCL) hymn; **~erbuch** nt songbook; hymn book.
liederlich ['liːdərlɪç] a slovenly; (Lebenswandel) loose, immoral; **L~keit** f slovenliness; immorality.
lief etc v siehe **laufen.**
Lieferant [liːfə'rant] m supplier.
liefern ['liːfərn] vt deliver; (versorgen mit) supply; (Beweis) produce.
Liefer- zW: **~schein** m delivery note; **~termin** m delivery date; **~ung** f delivery; supply; **~wagen** m van.
Liege ['liːgə] f -, -n bed.
liegen ['liːgən] vi unreg lie; (sich befinden) be; **mir liegt nichts/viel daran** it doesn't matter to me/it matters a lot to me; **es liegt bei Ihnen, ob ...** it's up to you whether ...; **Sprachen ~ mir nicht** languages are not my line; **woran liegt es?** what's the cause?; **~bleiben** vi unreg (Person) stay in bed; stay lying down; (Ding) be left (behind); **~lassen** vt unreg (vergessen) leave behind.
Liege- zW: **~sitz** m (AUT) reclining seat; **~stuhl** m deck chair; **~wagen** m (EISENB) couchette.
lieh etc v siehe **leihen.**
ließ etc v siehe **lassen.**
liest etc v siehe **lesen.**
Lift [lɪft] m -(e)s, -e od -s lift.
Likör [li'køːr] m -s, -e liqueur.
lila ['liːla] a inv purple, lilac; **L~** nt -s, -s (Farbe) purple, lilac.
Lilie ['liːliə] f lily.
Limonade [limo'naːdə] f lemonade.
Linde ['lɪndə] f -, -n lime tree, linden.
lindern ['lɪndərn] vt alleviate, soothe.
Linderung f alleviation.
Lineal [line'aːl] nt -s, -e ruler.
Linie ['liːniə] f line.
Linien- zW: **~blatt** nt ruled sheet; **~flug** m scheduled flight; **~richter** m linesman; **l~treu** a (POL) loyal to the party line.

linieren [lini'iːrən] vt line.
Linke ['lɪŋkə] f -, -n left side; left hand; (POL) left; **l~(r, s)** a left; **ein L~r** (POL) a left-winger; **l~ Masche** purl.
linkisch a awkward, gauche.
links [lɪŋks] ad to od on the left; **~ von mir** on od to my left; **L~außen** [lɪŋks''ausən] m -s, - (SPORT) outside left; **L~händer(in** f) m -s, - left-handed person; **L~kurve** f left-hand bend; **L~verkehr** m traffic on the left.
Linoleum [li'noːleum] nt -s lino(leum).
Linse ['lɪnzə] f -, -n lentil; (optisch) lens.
Lippe ['lɪpə] f -, -n lip; **Lippenstift** m lipstick.
lispeln ['lɪspəln] vi lisp.
Lissabon ['lɪsabɔn] nt -s Lisbon.
List [lɪst] f -, -en cunning; trick, ruse.
Liste ['lɪstə] f -, -n list.
listig ['lɪstɪç] a cunning, sly.
Litanei [lita'nai] f litany.
Liter ['liːtər] nt od m -s, - litre.
literarisch [lite'raːrɪʃ] a literary.
Literatur [litera'tuːr] f literature.
Litfaßsäule ['lɪtfasˌzɔylə] f advertising pillar.
Lithographie [litogra'fiː] f lithography.
Liturgie [litur'giː] f liturgy.
liturgisch [li'turgɪʃ] a liturgical.
Litze ['lɪtsə] f -, -n braid; (ELEK) flex.
live [laif] ad (RAD, TV) live.
Livree [li'vreː] f -, -n livery.
Lizenz [li'tsɛnts] f licence.
Lkw [ɛlkaː'veː] m abk von **Lastkraftwagen.**
Lob [loːp] nt -(e)s praise.
Lobby ['lɔbɪ] f lobby.
loben ['loːbən] vt praise; **lobenswert** a praiseworthy.
löblich ['løːplɪç] a praiseworthy, laudable.
Loch [lɔx] nt -(e)s, ⁻er hole; **l~en** vt punch holes in; **~er** m -s, - punch.
löcherig ['lœçərɪç] a full of holes.
Lochkarte f punch card.
Lochstreifen m punch tape.
Locke ['lɔkə] f -, -n lock, curl; **l~n** vt entice; (Haare) curl; **Lockenwickler** m -s, - curler.
locker ['lɔkər] a loose; **~lassen** vi unreg: **nicht ~lassen** not let up; **~n** vt loosen.
lockig ['lɔkɪç] a curly.
Lodenmantel ['loːdənmantəl] m thick woollen coat.
lodern ['loːdərn] vi blaze.
Löffel ['lœfəl] m -s, - spoon.
Logarithmus [loga'rɪtmus] m logarithm.
Loge ['loːʒə] f -, -n (THEAT) box; (Freimaurer) (masonic) lodge; (Pförtner~) office.

Logik ['lo:gɪk] f logic.
logisch ['lo:gɪʃ] a logical.
Lohn [lo:n] m -(e)s, -̈e reward; (Arbeits~) pay, wages pl; ~büro nt wages office; ~empfänger m wage earner.
lohnen ['lo:nən] vt (liter) reward (jdm etw sb for sth) // vr unpers be worth it; ~d a worthwhile.
Lohn- zW: ~steuer f income tax; ~streifen m pay slip; ~tüte f pay packet.
lokal [lo'ka:l] a local; **L~** nt -(e)s, -e pub(lic house); ~i'sieren vt localize.
Lokomotive [lokomo'ti:və] f -, -n locomotive.
Lokomotivführer m engine driver.
Lorbeer ['lɔrbe:r] m -s, -en (lit, fig) laurel; ~blatt nt (KOCH) bay leaf.
Lore ['lo:rə] f -, -n (MIN) truck.
Los [lo:s] nt -es, -e (Schicksal) lot, fate; (Lotterie~) lottery ticket.
los [lo:s] a (locker) loose; ~! go on!; etw ~ sein be rid of sth; was ist ~? what's the matter?; dort ist nichts/viel ~ there's nothing/a lot going on there; etw ~ haben (umg) be clever; ~binden vt unreg untie.
löschen ['lœʃən] vt (Feuer, Licht) put out, extinguish; (Durst) quench; (COMM) cancel; (COMPUT) delete; (Tonband) erase; (Fracht) unload // vi (Feuerwehr) put out a fire; (Papier) blot.
Lösch- zW: ~fahrzeug nt fire engine; fire boat; ~gerät nt fire extinguisher; ~papier nt blotting paper.
lose ['lo:zə] a loose.
Lösegeld nt ransom.
losen ['lo:zən] vi draw lots.
lösen ['lø:zən] vt loosen; (Rätsel etc) solve; (Verlobung) call off; (CHEM) dissolve; (Partnerschaft) break up; (Fahrkarte) buy // vr (aufgehen) come loose; (Zucker etc) dissolve; (Problem, Schwierigkeit) (re)solve itself.
los- zW: ~fahren vi unreg leave; ~gehen vi unreg set out; (anfangen) start; (Bombe) go off; auf jdn ~gehen go for sb; ~kaufen vt (Gefangene, Geißeln) pay ransom for; ~kommen vi unreg: von etw ~kommen get away from sth; ~lassen vt unreg (Seil) let go of; (Schimpfe) let loose; ~laufen vi unreg run off.
löslich ['lø:slɪç] a soluble; **L~keit** f solubility.
los- zW: ~lösen vtr free; ~machen vt loosen; (Boot) unmoor // vr get free; ~schrauben vt unscrew; ~sprechen vt unreg absolve.
Losung ['lo:zʊŋ] f watchword, slogan.
Lösung ['lø:zʊŋ] f (Lockermachen)

loosening; (eines Rätsels, CHEM) solution; **Lösungsmittel** nt solvent.
loswerden vt unreg get rid of.
Lot [lo:t] nt -(e)s, -e plummet; im ~ vertical; (fig) on an even keel.
löten ['lø:tən] vt solder.
Lothringen ['lo:trɪŋən] nt -s Lorraine.
Lötkolben m soldering iron.
Lotse ['lo:tsə] m -n, -n pilot; (AVIAT) air traffic controller; **l~n** vt pilot; (umg) lure.
Lotterie [lɔtə'ri:] f lottery.
Löwe ['lø:və] m -n, -n lion; (ASTROL) Leo; **Löwenanteil** m lion's share; **Löwenzahn** m dandelion.
loyal [loa'ja:l] a loyal.
lt. abk (= laut) according to.
Luchs ['lʊks] m -es, -e lynx.
Lücke ['lʏkə] f -, -n gap; **Lückenbüßer** m -s, - stopgap; **lückenlos** a complete.
Luder ['lu:dər] nt -s, - (pej: Frau) hussy; (bedauernswert) poor wretch.
Luft [lʊft] f -, -̈e air; (Atem) breath; in der ~ liegen be in the air; jdn wie ~ behandeln ignore sb; ~angriff m air raid; ~ballon m balloon; ~blase f air bubble; **l~dicht** a airtight; ~druck m atmospheric pressure.
lüften ['lʏftən] vti air; (Hut) lift, raise.
Luft- zW: ~fahrt f aviation; **l~gekühlt** a air-cooled; **l~ig** a (Ort) breezy; (Raum) airy; (Kleider) summery; ~kissenfahrzeug nt hovercraft; ~kurort m health resort; **l~leer** a: ~leerer Raum vacuum; ~linie f: in der ~linie as the crow flies; ~loch nt air-hole; (AVIAT) airpocket; ~matratze f lilo ® (Brit), air mattress; ~pirat m hijacker; ~post f airmail; ~röhre f (ANAT) wind pipe; ~schlange f streamer; ~schutzkeller m air-raid shelter.
Lüftung ['lʏftʊŋ] f ventilation.
Luft- zW: ~verkehr m air traffic; ~waffe f air force; ~zug m draught.
Lüge ['ly:gə] f -, -n lie; jdn/etw ~n strafen give the lie to sb/sth; **l~n** vi unreg lie.
Lügner(in f) m -s, - liar.
Luke ['lu:kə] f -, -n dormer window, hatch.
Lümmel ['lʏməl] m -s, - lout; **l~n** vr lounge (about).
Lump [lʊmp] m -en, -en scamp, rascal.
Lumpen ['lʊmpən] m -s, - rag; sich nicht l~ lassen not be mean.
lumpig ['lʊmpɪç] a shabby.
Lunge ['lʊŋə] f -, -n lung; **Lungenentzündung** f pneumonia; **lungenkrank** a consumptive.
lungern ['lʊŋərn] vi hang about.
Lupe ['lu:pə] f -, -n magnifying glass;

unter die ~ **nehmen** (*fig*) scrutinize.
Lupine [lu'pi:nə] *f* lupin.
Lust [lʊst] *f* -, ⁻e joy, delight; (*Neigung*) desire; ~ **haben zu** *od* **auf etw** (*akk*)/**etw zu tun** feel like sth/doing sth.
lüstern ['lʏstərn] *a* lustful, lecherous.
lustig ['lʊstɪç] *a* (*komisch*) amusing, funny; (*fröhlich*) cheerful.
Lüstling *m* lecher.
Lust- *zW:* **l~los** *a* unenthusiastic; **~mord** *m* sex(ual) murder; **~spiel** *nt* comedy.
lutschen ['lʊtʃən] *vti* suck; **am Daumen** ~ suck one's thumb.
Lutscher *m* -s, - lollipop.
Luxemburg ['lʊksəmbʊrk] *nt* -s Luxembourg.
luxuriös [lʊksuri'ø:s] *a* luxurious.
Luxus ['lʊksʊs] *m* - luxury; **~artikel** *pl* luxury goods *pl*; **~hotel** *nt* luxury hotel.
Lymphe ['lʏmfə] *f* -, -n lymph.
lynchen ['lʏnçən] *vt* lynch.
Lyrik ['ly:rɪk] *f* lyric poetry; **~er** *m* -s, - lyric poet.
lyrisch ['ly:rɪʃ] *a* lyrical.

M

M, m [ɛm] *nt* M, m // **m** *abk von* **Meter.**
Maas [maːs] *f* - Meuse.
Mach- [max] *zW:* **~art** *f* make; **m~bar** *a* feasible; **~e** *f* - (*umg*) show, sham.
machen ['maxən] ◆ *vt* **1** *do;* (*herstellen, zubereiten*) make; **was machst du da?** what are you doing (there)?; **das ist nicht zu** ~ that can't be done; **das Radio leiser** ~ turn the radio down; **aus Holz gemacht** made of wood
2 (*verursachen, bewirken*) make; **jdm Angst** ~ make sb afraid; **das macht die Kälte** it's the cold that does that
3 (*ausmachen*) matter; **das macht nichts** that doesn't matter; **die Kälte macht mir nichts** I don't mind the cold
4 (*kosten, ergeben*) be; **3 und 5 macht 8** 3 and 5 is *od* are 8; **was** *od* **wieviel macht das?** how much does that make?
5: **was macht die Arbeit?** how's the work going?; **was macht dein Bruder?** how is your brother doing?; **das Auto** ~ **lassen** have the car done; **mach's gut!** take care! (*viel Glück*) good luck!
◆ *vi*: **mach schnell** hurry up!; **Schluß** ~ finish (off); **mach schon!** come on!; **das macht müde** it makes you

tired; **in etw** (*dat*) ~ be *od* deal in sth
◆ *vr* come along (nicely); **sich an etw** (*akk*) ~ set about sth; **sich verständlich** ~ make oneself understood; **sich** (*dat*) **viel aus jdm/etw** ~ like sb/sth.
Macht [maxt] *f* -, ⁻e power; **~haber** *m* -s, - ruler.
mächtig ['mɛçtɪç] *a* powerful, mighty; (*umg: ungeheuer*) enormous.
Macht- *zW:* **m~los** *a* powerless; **~probe** *f* trial of strength; **~stellung** *f* position of power; **~wort** *nt*: **ein ~wort sprechen** lay down the law.
Machwerk *nt* work; (*schlechte Arbeit*) botched-up job.
Mädchen ['mɛːtçən] *nt* girl; **m~haft** *a* girlish; **~name** *m* maiden name.
Made ['maːdə] *f* -, -n maggot.
madig ['maːdɪç] *a* maggoty; **jdm etw** ~ **machen** spoil sth for sb.
mag *etc v siehe* **mögen.**
Magazin [maga'tsiːn] *nt* -s, -e magazine.
Magen ['maːgən] *m* -s, - *od* ⁼ stomach; **~schmerzen** *pl* stomachache.
mager ['maːgər] *a* lean; (*dünn*) thin; **M~keit** *f* leanness; thinness.
Magie [ma'giː] *f* magic.
Magier ['maːgiər] *m* -s, - magician.
magisch ['maːgɪʃ] *a* magical.
Magnet [ma'gneːt] *m* -s *od* -en, -en magnet; **~band** *nt* magnetic tape; **m~isch** *a* magnetic; **m~i'sieren** *vt* magnetize; **~nadel** *f* magnetic needle.
Mahagoni [maha'goːni] *nt* -s mahogany.
mähen ['mɛːən] *vti* mow.
Mahl [maːl] *nt* -(e)s, -e meal; **m~en** *vt unreg* grind; **~zeit** *f* meal // *interj* enjoy your meal.
Mahnbrief *m* reminder.
Mähne ['mɛːnə] *f* -, -n mane.
Mahn- ['maːn] *zW:* **m~en** *vt* remind; (*warnend*) warn; (*wegen Schuld*) demand payment from; **~ung** *f* reminder; admonition, warning.
Mähren ['mɛːrən] *nt* -s Moravia.
Mai [maɪ] *m* -(e)s, -e May; **~glöckchen** *nt* lily of the valley; **~käfer** *m* cockchafer; **~land** *nt* Milan; **m~ländisch** *a* Milanese.
Mais [maɪs] *m* -es, -e maize, corn (*US*); **~kolben** *m* corncob.
Majestät [majɛs'tɛːt] *f* majesty; **m~isch** *a* majestic.
Major [ma'joːr] *m* -s, -e (*MIL*) major; (*AVIAT*) squadron leader.
Majoran [majo'raːn] *m* -s, -e marjoram.
makaber [ma'kaːbər] *a* macabre.
Makel ['maːkəl] *m* -s, - blemish; (*moralisch*) stain; **m~los** *a* immaculate,

spotless.
mäkeln ['mɛːkəln] *vi* find fault.
Makkaroni [maka'roːni] *pl* macaroni *sing.*
Makler(in *f)* ['maːklər(ɪn)] *m* **-s,** - broker.
Makrele [ma'kreːlə] *f* -, **-n** mackerel.
Makrone [ma'kroːnə] *f* -, **-n** macaroon.
Mal [maːl] *nt* **-(e)s, -e** mark, sign; (*Zeitpunkt*) time; **m~** *ad* times; (*umg*) *siehe* **einmal; -m~** *suff* -times; **m~en** *vti* paint; **~er** *m* **-s,** - painter; **~e'rei** *f* painting; **m~erisch** *a* picturesque; **~kasten** *m* paintbox.
Mallorca [ma'lɔrka] *nt* **-s** Majorca.
malnehmen *vti unreg* multiply.
Malz [malts] *nt* **-es** malt; **~bonbon** *nt* cough drop; **~kaffee** *m* malt coffee.
Mama ['mama] *f* -, **-s, Mami** ['mami] *f* -, **-s** (*umg*) mum(my).
Mammut ['mamʊt] *nt* **-s, -e** *od* **-s** mammoth.
man [man] *pron* one, you; **~** **sagt, ...** they *od* people say ...; **wie schreibt ~ das?** how do you write it? how is it written?
manche(r, s) ['mançə(r, s)] *a* many a; (*pl*) a number of // *pron* some.
mancherlei *a inv* various // *pron* a variety of things.
manchmal *ad* sometimes.
Mandant(in *f)* [man'dant(ɪn)] *m* (*JUR*) client.
Mandarine [manda'riːnə] *f* mandarin, tangerine.
Mandat [man'daːt] *nt* **-(e)s, -e** mandate.
Mandel ['mandəl] *f* -, **-n** almond; (*ANAT*) tonsil.
Manege [ma'nɛːʒə] *f* -, **-n** ring, arena.
Mangel ['maŋəl] *f* -, **-n** mangle // *m* **-s,** ⁼ lack; (*Knappheit*) shortage (*an* +*dat* of); (*Fehler*) defect, fault; **~erscheinung** *f* deficiency symptom; **m~haft** *a* poor; (*fehlerhaft*) defective, faulty; **m~n** *vi unpers*: **es mangelt jdm an etw** (*dat*) sb lacks sth // *vt* (*Wäsche*) mangle; **m~s** *präp* +*gen* for lack of.
Manie [ma'niː] *f* mania.
Manier [ma'niːr] *f* - manner; style; (*pej*) mannerism; **~en** *pl* manners *pl*.
Manifest [mani'fɛst] *nt* **-es, -e** manifesto.
Maniküre [mani'kyːrə] *f* -, **-n** manicure; **m~n** *vt* manicure.
manipulieren [manipu'liːrən] *vt* manipulate.
Manko ['maŋko] *nt* **-s, -s** deficiency; (*COMM*) deficit.
Mann [man] *m* **-(e)s,** ⁼**er** man; (*Ehe~*) husband; (*NAUT*) hand; **seinen ~ stehen** hold one's own.
Männchen ['mɛnçən] *nt* little man;

(*Tier*) male.
Mannequin [manə'kɛː] *nt* **-s, -s** fashion model.
männlich ['mɛnlɪç] *a* (*BIOL*) male; (*fig, GRAM*) masculine.
Mannschaft *f* (*SPORT, fig*) team; (*NAUT, AVIAT*) crew; (*MIL*) other ranks *pl*.
Manöver [ma'nøːvər] *nt* **-s,** - manoeuvre.
manövrieren [manø'vriːrən] *vti* manoeuvre.
Mansarde [man'zardə] *f* -, **-n** attic.
Manschette [man'ʃɛtə] *f* cuff; (*TECH*) collar; sleeve; **Manschettenknopf** *m* cufflink.
Mantel ['mantəl] *m* **-s,** ⁼ coat; (*TECH*) casing, jacket.
Manuskript [manu'skrɪpt] *nt* **-(e)s, -e** manuscript.
Mappe ['mapə] *f* -, **-n** briefcase; (*Akten~*) folder.
Märchen ['mɛːrçən] *nt* fairy tale; **m~haft** *a* fabulous; **~prinz** *m* Prince Charming.
Marder ['mardər] *m* **-s,** - marten.
Margarine [marga'riːnə] *f* margarine.
Marienkäfer [ma'riːənkɛːfər] *m* ladybird.
Marine [ma'riːnə] *f* navy; **m~blau** *a* navy-blue.
marinieren [mari'niːrən] *vt* marinate.
Marionette [mario'nɛtə] *f* puppet.
Mark [mark] *f* -, - (*Münze*) mark // *nt* **-(e)s** (*Knochen~*) marrow; **durch ~ und Bein gehen** go right through sb; **m~ant** [mar'kant] *a* striking.
Marke ['markə] *f* -, **-n** mark; (*Warensorte*) brand; (*Fabrikat*) make; (*Rabatt~, Brief~*) stamp; (*Essens~*) ticket; (*aus Metall etc*) token, disc.
Mark- *zW*: **m~ieren** [mar'kiːrən] *vt* mark // *vti* (*umg*) act; **~ierung** *f* marking; **~ise** [mar'kiːzə] *f* -, **-n** awning; **~stück** *nt* one-mark piece.
Markt [markt] *m* **-(e)s,** ⁼**e** market; **~forschung** *f* market research; **m~gängig** *a* marketable; **~platz** *m* market place; **~wirtschaft** *f* market economy.
Marmelade [marmə'laːdə] *f* -, **-n** jam.
Marmor ['marmor] *m* **-s, -e** marble; **m~ieren** [-'riːrən] *vt* marble; **m~n** *a* marble.
Marokk- [ma'rɔk] *zW*: **~o** *nt* **-s** Morocco; **~aner(in** *f)* [marɔ'kaːnər(ɪn)] *m* **-s,** - Moroccan; **m~'anisch** *a* Moroccan.
Marone [ma'roːnə] *f* -, **-n** *od* **Maroni** chestnut.
Marotte [ma'rɔtə] *f* -, **-n** fad, quirk.
Marsch [marʃ] *m* **-(e)s,** ⁼**e** march; **m~** *interj* march // *f* -, **-en** marsh; **~befehl** *m* marching orders *pl*; **m~bereit** *a* ready to move; **m~ieren**

[mar'ʃiːrən] *vi* march.
Märtyrer(in *f)* ['mɛrtyrər(ɪn)] *m* **-s, -** martyr.
März [mɛrts] *m* **-(es), -e** March.
Marzipan [martsi'paːn] *nt* **-s, -e** marzipan.
Masche ['maʃə] *f* **-, -n** mesh; (*Strick~*) stitch; **das ist die neueste** ~ that's the latest thing; **Maschendraht** *m* wire mesh; **maschenfest** *a* runproof.
Maschine [ma'ʃiːnə] *f* machine; (*Motor*) engine; (*Schreib~*) typewriter; **maschinell** [maʃi'nɛl] *a* machine(-); mechanical.
Maschinen- *zW:* ~**bauer** *m* mechanical engineer; ~**gewehr** *nt* machine gun; ~**pistole** *f* submachine gun; ~**schaden** *m* mechanical fault; ~**schlosser** *m* fitter; ~**schrift** *f* typescript.
machineschreiben *vi unreg* type.
Maschinist [maʃi'nɪst] *m* engineer.
Maser ['maːzər] *f* **-, -n** grain; speckle; ~**n** *pl* (*MED*) measles *sing*; ~**ung** *f* grain(ing).
Maske ['maskə] *f* **-, -n** mask.
Maskenball *m* fancy-dress ball.
Maskerade [maskə'raːdə] *f* masquerade.
maskieren [mas'kiːrən] *vt* mask; (*verkleiden*) dress up // *vr* disguise o.s., dress up.
Maß [maːs] *nt* **-es, -e** measure; (*Mäßigung*) moderation; (*Grad*) degree, extent // *f* **, -(e)** litre of beer.
Massage [ma'saːʒə] *f* **-, -n** massage.
Maßanzug *m* made-to-measure suit.
Maßarbeit *f* (*fig*) neat piece of work.
Masse ['masə] *f* **-, -n** mass.
Massen- *zW:* ~**artikel** *m* mass-produced article; ~**grab** *nt* mass grave; **m~haft** *a* loads of; ~**medien** *pl* mass media *pl*; ~**veranstaltung** *f* mass meeting.
Masseur [ma'søːr] *m* masseur.
Masseuse [ma'søːzə] *f* masseuse.
maßgebend *a* authoritative.
maßhalten *vi unreg* exercise moderation.
massieren [ma'siːrən] *vt* massage; (*MIL*) mass.
massig ['masɪç] *a* massive; (*umg*) massive amount of.
mäßig ['mɛːsɪç] *a* moderate; ~**en** ['mɛːsɪgən] *vt* restrain, moderate; **M~keit** *f* moderation.
massiv [ma'siːf] *a* solid; (*fig*) heavy, rough; **M~** *nt* **-s, -e** massif.
Maß- *zW:* ~**krug** *m* tankard; **m~los** *a* extreme; ~**nahme** *f* **-, -n** measure, step; **m~regeln** *vt insep* reprimand; ~**stab** *m* rule, measure; (*fig*) standard; (*GEOG*) scale; **m~voll** *a* moderate.

Mast ['mast] *m* **-(e)s, -e(n)** mast; (*ELEK*) pylon.
mästen ['mɛstən] *vt* fatten.
Material [materi'aːl] *nt* **-s, -ien** material(s); ~**fehler** *m* material defect; ~**ismus** [-'lɪsmʊs] *m* materialism; ~**ist** [-'lɪst] *m* materialist; **m~istisch** [-'lɪstɪʃ] *a* materialistic.
Materie [ma'teːriə] *f* matter, substance.
materiell [materi'ɛl] *a* material.
Mathematik [matema'tiːk] *f* mathematics *sing*; ~**er(in** *f)* [mate-'maːtikər(ɪn)] *m* **-s, -** mathematician.
mathematisch [mate'maːtɪʃ] *a* mathematical.
Matratze [ma'tratsə] *f* **-, -n** mattress.
Matrixdrucker ['maːtrɪksdrʊkər] dot-matrix printer.
Matrize [ma'triːtsə] *f* **-, -n** matrix; (*zum Abziehen*) stencil.
Matrose [ma'troːzə] *m* **-n, -n** sailor.
Matsch [matʃ] *m* **-(e)s** mud; (*Schnee~*) slush; **m~ig** *a* muddy; slushy.
matt [mat] *a* weak; (*glanzlos*) dull; (*PHOT*) matt; (*Schach*) mate.
Matte ['matə] *f* **-, -n** mat.
Mattscheibe *f* (*TV*) screen; ~**haben** (*umg*) not be quite with it.
Mauer ['mauər] *f* **-, -n** wall; **m~n** *vti* build; lay bricks.
Maul [maul] *nt* **-(e)s, Mäuler** mouth; **m~en** *vi* (*umg*) grumble; ~**esel** *m* mule; ~**korb** *m* muzzle; ~**sperre** *f* lockjaw; ~**tier** *nt* mule; ~**wurf** *m* mole.
Maurer ['maurər] *m* **-s, -** bricklayer.
Maus [maus] *f* **-, Mäuse** (*auch COMPUT*) mouse.
Mause- [mauzə] *zW:* ~**falle** *f* mousetrap; **m~n** *vt* (*umg*) flinch // *vi* catch mice; **m~tot** *a* stone dead.
maximal [maksi'maːl] *a* maximum.
Maximum ['maksimʊm] *nt* maximum.
Maxi-Single ['maksi'sɪŋgl] *f* **-, -s** 12-inch single.
Mayonnaise [majo'nɛːzə] *f* **-, -n** mayonnaise.
m.E. *abk* (= *meines Erachtens*) in my opinion.
Mechan- [me'çaːn] *zW:* ~**ik** *f* mechanics *sing*; (*Getriebe*) mechanics *pl*; ~**iker** *m* **-s, -** mechanic, engineer; **m~isch** *a* mechanical; ~**ismus** [meça'nɪsmʊs] *m* mechanism.
meckern ['mɛkərn] *vi* bleat; (*umg*) moan.
Medaille [me'daljə] *f* **-, -n** medal.
Medaillon [medal'jõː] *nt* **-s, -s** (*Schmuck*) locket.
Medikament [medika'mɛnt] *nt* medicine.
meditieren [medi'tiːrən] *vi* meditate.
Medizin [medi'tsiːn] *f* **-, -en** medicine;

m~isch a medical.
Meer [me:r] nt -(e)s, -e sea; **~busen** m bay, gulf; **~enge** f straits pl; **Meeresspiegel** m sea level; **~rettich** m horseradish; **~schweinchen** nt guinea-pig.
Megaphon [mega'fo:n] nt -s, -e megaphone.
Mehl ['me:l] nt -(e)s, -e flour; **m~ig** a floury.
mehr [me:r] a,ad more; **~deutig** a ambiguous; **~ere** a several; **~eres** pron several things; **~fach** a multiple; (wiederholt) repeated; **M~heit** f majority; **~malig** a repeated; **~mals** ad repeatedly; **~stimmig** a for several voices; **~stimmig singen** harmonize; **M~wertsteuer** f value added tax, VAT; **M~zahl** f majority; (GRAM) plural.
meiden ['maidən] vt unreg avoid.
Meile ['mailə] f -, -n mile; **Meilenstein** m milestone; **meilenweit** a for miles.
mein [main] pron my; **~e(r, s)** mine.
Meineid ['main'ait] m perjury.
meinen ['mainən] vti think; (sagen) say; (sagen wollen) mean; **das will ich ~** I should think so.
mein- zW: **~erseits** ad for my part; **~esgleichen** pron people like me; **~etwegen** ad (für mich) for my sake; (wegen mir) on my account; (von mir aus) as far as I'm concerned; I don't care od mind.
Meinung ['mainuŋ] f opinion; **ganz meine ~** I quite agree; **jdm die ~ sagen** give sb a piece of one's mind.
Meinungs- zW: **~austausch** m exchange of views; **~umfrage** f opinion poll; **~verschiedenheit** f difference of opinion.
Meise ['maizə] f -, -n tit(mouse).
Meißel ['maisəl] m -s, - chisel; **m~n** vt chisel.
meist [maist] a,ad most(ly); **am ~en** the most; **~ens** ad generally, usually.
Meister ['maistər] m -s, - master; (SPORT) champion; **m~haft** a masterly; **~schaft** f mastery; (SPORT) championship; **~stück** nt, **~werk** nt masterpiece.
Melancholie [melaŋko'li:] f melancholy.
melancholisch [melaŋ'ko:liʃ] a melancholy.
Melde- ['mɛldə] zW: **~frist** f registration period; **m~n** vt report // vr report (bei to); (SCH) put one's hand up; (freiwillig) volunteer; (auf etw, am Telefon) answer; **sich zu Wort m~n** ask to speak; **~pflicht** f obligation to register with the police; **~stelle** f registration office.

Meldung ['mɛlduŋ] f announcement; (Bericht) report.
meliert [me'li:rt] a mottled, speckled.
melken ['mɛlkən] vt unreg milk.
Melodie [melo'di:] f melody, tune.
melodisch [me'lo:diʃ] a melodious, tuneful.
Melone [me'lo:nə] f -, -n melon; (Hut) bowler (hat).
Membran(e) [mem'bra:n(ə)] f -, -en (TECH) diaphragm.
Memoiren [memo'a:rən] pl memoirs pl.
Menge ['mɛŋə] f -, -n quantity; (Menschen~) crowd; (große Anzahl) lot (of); **m~n** vt mix // vr: **sich m~n in** (+akk) meddle with; **Mengenlehre** f (MATH) set theory; **Mengenrabatt** m bulk discount.
Mensch [mɛnʃ] m -en, -en human being, man; person; **kein ~** nobody // interj hey.
Menschen- zW: **~feind** m misanthrope; **m~freundlich** a philanthropical; **~kenner** m -s, - judge of human nature; **m~möglich** a humanly possible; **~recht** nt human rights pl; **m~unwürdig** a degrading; **~verstand** m: **gesunder ~enverstand** common sense.
Mensch- zW: **~heit** f humanity, mankind; **m~lich** a human; (human) humane; **~lichkeit** f humanity.
Menstruation [mɛnstruatsi'o:n] f menstruation.
Mentalität [mɛntali'tɛ:t] f mentality.
Menü [me'ny:] nt -s, -s (auch COMPUT) menu.
Merk- [mɛrk] zW: **~blatt** nt instruction sheet od leaflet; **m~en** vt notice; **sich** (dat) **etw m~en** remember sth; **m~lich** a noticeable; **~mal** nt sign, characteristic; **m~würdig** a odd.
meßbar ['mɛsba:r] a measurable.
Messe ['mɛsə] f -, -n fair; (ECCL) mass; **m~n** unreg vt measure // vr compete.
Messer nt -s, - knife; **~spitze** f knife point; (in Rezept) pinch.
Meßgerät nt measuring device, gauge.
Messing ['mɛsiŋ] nt -s brass.
Metall [me'tal] nt -s, -e metal; **m~en**, **m~isch** a metallic.
Meteor [mete'o:r] nt -s, -e meteor.
Meter ['me:tər] nt od m -s, - metre; **~maß** nt tape measure.
Methode [me'to:də] f -, -n method.
methodisch [me'to:diʃ] a methodical.
Metropole [metro'po:lə] f -, -n metropolis.
Metzger ['mɛtsgər] m -s, - butcher; **~ei** [-'rai] f butcher's (shop).
Meuchelmord ['mɔʏçəlmɔrt] m assassination.

Meute ['mɔʏtə] f -, -n pack; ~'**rei** f mutiny; ~**rn** vi mutiny.

miauen [mi'auən] vi miaow.

mich [mɪç] pron akk von **ich** me; myself.

Miene ['mi:nə] f -, -n look, expression.

mies [mi:s] a (umg) lousy.

Miet- ['mi:t] zW: ~**auto** nt hired car; ~**e** f -, -n rent; **zur** ~**e wohnen** live in rented accommodation; **m~en** vt rent; (Auto) hire; ~**er(in** f) m -s, - tenant; **Mietshaus** nt tenement, block of flats; ~**vertrag** m tenancy agreement.

Migräne [mi'grɛːnə] f -, -n migraine.

Mikro- ['mikro] zW: ~**computer** m microcomputer; ~**fon**, ~**phon** [-'foːn] nt -s, -e microphone; ~**skop** [-'skoːp] nt -s, -e microscope; **m~skopisch** a microscopic; ~**wellenherd** m microwave (oven).

Milch [mɪlç] f - milk; ~**glas** nt frosted glass; **m~ig** a milky; ~**kaffee** m white coffee; ~**pulver** nt powdered milk; ~**straße** f Milky Way; ~**zahn** m milk tooth.

mild [mɪlt] a mild; (Richter) lenient; (freundlich) kind, charitable; **M~e** ['mɪldə] f -, -n mildness; leniency; ~**ern** vt mitigate, soften; (Schmerz) alleviate; ~**ernde Umstände** extenuating circumstances.

Milieu [mili'øː] nt -s, -s background, environment; **m~geschädigt** a maladjusted.

Mili- [mili] zW: **m~tant** [-'tant] a militant; ~**tär** [-'tɛːr] nt -s military, army; ~**tärgericht** nt military court; **m~'tärisch** a military.

Milli- ['mɪli] zW: ~**ardär** [-ar'dɛːr] m multimillionaire; ~**arde** [-'ardə] f -, -n milliard; billion (bes US); ~**meter** m millimetre; ~**on** [-'oːn] f -, -en million; ~**onär** [-o'nɛːr] m millionaire.

Milz ['mɪlts] f -, -en spleen.

Mimik ['mi:mɪk] f mime.

Mimose [mi'moːzə] f -, -n mimosa; (fig) sensitive person.

minder ['mɪndər] a inferior // ad less; **M~heit** f minority; ~**jährig** a minor; **M~jährigkeit** f minority; ~**n** vtr decrease, diminish; **M~ung** f decrease; ~**wertig** a inferior; **M~wertigkeitskomplex** m inferiority complex.

Mindest- ['mɪndəst] zW: ~**alter** nt minimum age; ~**betrag** m minimum amount; **m~e(r, s)** a least; **m~ens**, **zum m~en** ad at least; ~**lohn** m minimum wage; ~**maß** nt minimum.

Mine ['mi:nə] f -, -n mine; (Bleistift~) lead; (Kugelschreiber~) refill; **Minenfeld** nt minefield.

Mineral [mine'raːl] nt -s, -e od -ien mineral; **m~isch** a mineral;

~**wasser** nt mineral water.

Miniatur [minia'tuːr] f miniature.

minimal [mini'maːl] a minimal.

Minimum ['minimʊm] nt minimum.

Minister [mi'nɪstər] m -s, - minister; **m~iell** [minɪste'riˈɛl] a ministerial; ~**ium** [minɪsˈteːrium] nt ministry; ~**präsident** m prime minister.

minus ['mi:nʊs] ad minus; **M~** nt -, - deficit; **M~pol** m negative pole; **M~zeichen** nt minus sign.

Minute [mi'nuːtə] f -, -n minute; **Minutenzeiger** m minute hand.

Mio. abk (= Million(en)) million(s).

mir [mi:r] pron dat von **ich** (to) me; ~ **nichts, dir nichts** just like that.

Misch- ['mɪʃ] zW: ~**ehe** f mixed marriage; **m~en** vt mix; ~**ling** m halfcaste; ~**ung** f mixture.

Miß- ['mɪs] zW: **m~'achten** vt insep disregard; ~'**achtung** f disregard; ~**behagen** nt discomfort, uneasiness; ~**bildung** f deformity; **m~'billigen** vt insep disapprove of; ~'**billigung** f disapproval; ~**brauch** m abuse; (falscher Gebrauch) misuse; **m~'brauchen** vt insep abuse; misuse (zu for); ~**erfolg** m failure; **m~'fallen** vi unreg insep displease (jdm sb); ~**fallen** nt -s displeasure; ~**geburt** f freak; (fig) abortion; ~**geschick** nt misfortune; **m~glücken** [mɪsˈglʏkən] vi insep fail; **jdm m~glückt etw** sb does not succeed with sth; ~**griff** m mistake; ~**gunst** f envy; **m~günstig** a envious; **m~'handeln** vt insep ill-treat; ~'**handlung** f ill-treatment.

Mission [mɪsiˈoːn] f mission; ~**ar** [mɪsio'naːr] m missionary.

Miß- zW: ~**klang** m discord; ~**kredit** m discredit; **m~lingen** [mɪsˈlɪŋən] vi unreg insep fail; ~**mut** m bad temper; **m~mutig** a cross; **m~'raten** vi (unreg insep) turn out badly // a illbred; ~**stand** m bad state of affairs; abuse; ~**stimmung** f ill-humour, discord; **m~'trauen** vi insep mistrust; ~**trauen** nt -s distrust, suspicion (of); ~**trauensantrag** m (POL) motion of no confidence; ~**trauensvotum** nt -s, -voten (POL) vote of no confidence; **m~trauisch** a distrustful, suspicious; ~**verhältnis** nt disproportion; ~**verständnis** nt misunderstanding; **m~verstehen** vt unreg insep misunderstand.

Mist [mɪst] m -(e)s dung; dirt; (umg) rubbish; ~**el** f -, -n mistletoe; ~**haufen** m dungheap.

mit [mɪt] präp +dat with; (mittels) by; ~ **der Bahn** by train; ~ **10 Jahren** at the age of 10 // ad along, too; **wollen Sie** ~? do you want to come along?

Mitarbeit ['mɪt'arbaɪt] f cooperation; **m~en** vi cooperate, collaborate; **~er(in** f) m collaborator; co-worker // pl staff.

Mit- zW: **~bestimmung** f participation in decision-making; **m~bringen** vt unreg bring along; **~bürger(in** f) m fellow citizen.

miteinander [mɪt'aɪ'nandər] ad together, with one another.

Mit- zW: **m~erleben** vt see, witness; **~esser** ['mɪt'esər] m -s, - blackhead; **m~geben** vt unreg give; **~gefühl** nt sympathy; **m~gehen** vi unreg go/come along; **m~genommen** a done in, in a bad way; **~gift** f dowry.

Mitglied ['mɪtgliːt] nt member; **Mitgliedsbeitrag** m membership fee; **~schaft** f membership.

Mit- zW: **m~halten** vi unreg keep up; **~hilfe** f help, assistance; **m~hören** vt listen in to; **m~kommen** vi unreg come along; (verstehen) keep up, follow; **~läufer** m hanger-on; (POL) fellow-traveller.

Mitleid nt sympathy; (Erbarmen) compassion; **~enschaft** f: in **~enschaft ziehen** affect; **m~ig** a sympathetic; **m~slos** a pitiless, merciless.

Mit- zW: **m~machen** vt join in, take part in; **~mensch** m fellow man; **m~nehmen** vt unreg take along/away; (anstrengen) wear out, exhaust; **zum M~nehmen** take away.

mitsamt [mɪt'zamt] präp +dat together with.

Mitschuld f complicity; **m~ig** a also guilty (an +dat of).

Mit- zW: **~schüler(in** f) m schoolmate; **m~spielen** vi join in, take part; **~spieler(in** f) m partner; **~spracherecht** ['mɪtʃpraːxərɛçt] nt voice, say.

Mittag ['mɪtaːk] m -(e)s, -e midday, lunchtime; (zu) **~ essen** have lunch; **m~** ad at lunchtime od noon; **~essen** nt lunch, dinner.

mittags ad at lunchtime od noon; **M~pause** f lunch break; **M~schlaf** m early afternoon nap, siesta.

Mittäter(in f) ['mɪttɛːtər(ɪn)] m accomplice.

Mitte ['mɪtə] f -, -n middle; (POL) centre; **aus unserer ~** from our midst.

mitteil- ['mɪttaɪl] zW: **~en** vt: **jdm etw ~en** inform sb of sth, communicate sth to sb; **M~ung** f communication.

Mittel ['mɪtəl] nt -s - means; method; (MATH) average; (MED) medicine; **ein ~ zum Zweck** a means to an end; **~alter** nt Middle Ages pl; **m~alterlich** a mediaeval; **~amerika**

nt Central America; **m~bar** a indirect; **~ding** nt cross; **~europa** nt Central Europe; **m~los** a without means; **m~mäßig** a mediocre, middling; **~mäßigkeit** f mediocrity; **~meer** nt Mediterranean; **~punkt** m centre; **m~s** präp +gen by means of; **~stand** m middle class; **~streckenrakete** f medium-range missile; **~streifen** m central reservation; **~stürmer** m centre-forward; **~weg** m middle course; **~welle** f (RAD) medium wave.

mitten ['mɪtən] ad in the middle; **~ auf der Straße/in der Nacht** in the middle of the street/night.

Mitternacht ['mɪtərnaxt] f midnight.

mittlere(r, s) ['mɪtlərə(r, s)] a middle; (durchschnittlich) medium, average.

mittlerweile ['mɪtlərvaɪlə] ad meanwhile.

Mittwoch ['mɪtvɔx] m -(e)s, -e Wednesday; **m~s** ad on Wednesdays.

mitunter [mɪt''untər] ad occasionally, sometimes.

Mit- zW: **m~verantwortlich** a also responsible; **m~wirken** vi contribute (bei to); (THEAT) take part (bei in); **~wirkung** f contribution; participation.

Möbel ['møːbəl] pl furniture; **~wagen** m furniture od removal van.

mobil [mo'biːl] a mobile; (MIL) mobilized; **M~iar** [mobili'aːr] nt -s, -e movable assets pl; **M~machung** f mobilization.

möblieren [mø'bliːrən] vt furnish; **möbliert wohnen** live in furnished accommodation.

möchte(n) ['møçtə(n)] v siehe **mögen**.

Mode ['moːdə] f -, -n fashion.

Modell [mo'dɛl] nt -s, -e model; **m~ieren** [-'liːrən] vt model.

Mode(n)schau f fashion show.

modern [mo'dɛrn] a modern; (modisch) fashionable; **modernisieren** vt modernize.

Mode- zW: **~schmuck** m fashion jewellery; **~schöpfer(in** f) m fashion designer; **~wort** nt fashionable word, buzz word.

modisch ['moːdɪʃ] a fashionable.

Mofa ['moːfa] nt -s, -s small moped.

mogeln ['moːgəln] vi (umg) cheat.

mögen ['møːgən] ◆vti pt **mochte**, ptp **gemocht** like; **magst du/mögen Sie ihn?** do you like him?; **ich möchte ...** I would like ..., I'd like ...; **er möchte in die Stadt** he'd like to go into town; **ich möchte nicht, daß du ...** I wouldn't like you to ...; **ich mag nicht mehr** I've had enough

◆(als Hilfsverb) pt **mochte**, ptp **mögen** like to; (wollen) want; **möchtest du etwas essen?** would you like something to eat?; **sie mag nicht bleiben** she doesn't want to stay; **das mag wohl sein** that may well be; **was mag das heißen?** what might that mean?; **Sie möchten zu Hause anrufen?** could you please call home?

möglich ['mø:klɪç] *a* possible; **~erweise** *ad* possibly; **M~keit** *f* possibility; **nach M~keit** if possible; **~st** *ad* as ... as possible.

Mohn [mo:n] *m* **-(e)s, -e** (*~blume*) poppy; (*~samen*) poppy seed.

Möhre ['mø:rə] *f* -, **-n, Mohrrübe** *f* carrot.

mokieren [mo'ki:rən] *vr* make fun (*über* +*akk* of).

Moldau ['mɔldau] *f* - Moldavia.

Mole ['mo:lə] *f* -, **-n** (harbour) mole.

Molekül [mole'ky:l] *nt* **-s, -e** molecule.

Molkerei [mɔlkə'rai] *f* dairy.

Moll [mɔl] *nt* -, - (*MUS*) minor (key); **m~ig** *a* cosy; (*dicklich*) plump.

Moment [mo'mɛnt] *m* **-(e)s, -e** moment; **im ~** at the moment; **~ (mal)!** just a moment // *nt* factor, element; **m~an** [-'ta:n] *a* momentary // *ad* at the moment.

Monarch [mo'narç] *m* **-en, -en** monarch; **~ie** [monar'çi:] *f* monarchy.

Monat ['mo:nat] *m* **-(e)s, -e** month; **m~elang** *ad* for months; **m~lich** *a* monthly; **~skarte** *f* monthly ticket.

Mönch ['mœnç] *m* **-(e)s, -e** monk.

Mond [mo:nt] *m* **-(e)s, -e** moon; **~finsternis** *f* eclipse of the moon; **m~hell** *a* moonlit; **~landung** *f* moon landing; **~schein** *m* moonlight; **~sonde** *f* moon probe.

Mono- [mono] *in zW* mono; **~log** [-'lo:k] *m* **-s, -e** monologue; **~pol** [-'po:l] *nt* **-s, -e** monopoly; **m~polisieren** [-poli'zi:rən] *vt* monopolize; **m~ton** [-'to:n] *a* monotonous; **~tonie** [-to'ni:] *f* monotony.

Monsun [mɔn'zu:n] *m* **-s, -e** monsoon.

Montag ['mo:nta:k] *m* **-(e)s, -e** Monday; **m~s** *ad* on Mondays.

Montage ['mɔn'ta:ʒə] *f* -, **-n** (*PHOT etc*) montage; (*TECH*) assembly; (*Einbauen*) fitting.

Monteur [mɔn'tø:r] *m* fitter.

montieren [mɔn'ti:rən] *vt* assemble.

Monument [monu'mɛnt] *nt* monument; **m~al** [-'ta:l] *a* monumental.

Moor [mo:r] *nt* **-(e)s, -e** moor.

Moos [mo:s] *nt* **-es, -e** moss.

Moped ['mo:pɛt] *nt* **-s, -s** moped.

Mops [mɔps] *m* **-es, -̈e** pug.

Moral [mo'ra:l] *f* -, **-en** morality; (*einer Geschichte*) moral; **m~isch** *a* moral.

Moräne [mo'rɛ:nə] *f* -, **-n** moraine.

Morast [mo'rast] *m* **-(e)s, -e** morass, mire; **m~ig** *a* boggy.

Mord [mɔrt] *m* **-(e)s, -e** murder; **~anschlag** *m* murder attempt.

Mörder ['mœrdər] *m* **-s, -** murderer; **~in** *f* murderess.

Mord- *zW*: **~kommission** *f* murder squad; **Mordsglück** *nt* (*umg*) amazing luck; **mordsmäßig** *a* (*umg*) terrific, enormous; **Mordsschreck** *m* (*umg*) terrible fright; **~verdacht** *m* suspicion of murder; **~waffe** *f* murder weapon.

morgen ['mɔrgən] *ad*, **M~** *nt* tomorrow; **~ früh** tomorrow morning; **M~** *m* **-s, -** morning; **M~mantel** *m*, **M~rock** *m* dressing gown; **M~röte** *f* dawn; **~s** *ad* in the morning.

morgig ['mɔrgɪç] *a* tomorrow's; **der ~e Tag** tomorrow.

Morphium ['mɔrfiʊm] *nt* morphine.

morsch [mɔrʃ] *a* rotten.

Morse- ['mɔrzə] *zW*: **~alphabet** *nt* Morse code; **m~n** *vi* send a message by Morse code.

Mörtel ['mœrtəl] *m* **-s, -** mortar.

Mosaik [moza'i:k] *nt* **-s, -en** *od* **-e** mosaic.

Moschee [mɔ'ʃe:] *f* -, **-n** [mɔ'ʃe:ən] mosque.

Moskau ['mɔskau] *nt* **-s** Moscow; **~er** *a* Muscovite.

Moskito [mɔs'ki:to] *m* **-s, -s** mosquito.

Most [mɔst] *m* **-(e)s, -e** (unfermented) fruit juice; (*Apfelwein*) cider.

Motel [mo'tɛl] *nt* **-s, -s** motel.

Motiv [mo'ti:f] *nt* **-s, -e** motive; (*MUS*) theme; **m~ieren** [moti'vi:rən] *vt* motivate; **~ierung** *f* motivation.

Motor ['mo:tɔr] *m* **-s, -en** [mo'to:rən] engine; (*bes ELEK*) motor; **~boot** *nt* motorboat; **~enöl** *nt* motor oil; **m~isieren** [motori'zi:rən] *vt* motorize; **~rad** *nt* motorcycle; **~schaden** *m* engine trouble *od* failure.

Motte ['mɔtə] *f* -, **-n** moth; **Mottenkugel** *f* mothball(s).

Motto ['mɔto] *nt* **-s, -s** motto.

Möwe ['mø:və] *f* -, **-n** seagull.

Mrd. *abk* (= *Milliarde(n)*) thousand millions, billion(s) (*US*).

Mücke ['mykə] *f* -, **-n** midge, gnat; **Mückenstich** *m* midge *od* gnat bite.

müde ['my:də] *a* tired.

Müdigkeit ['my:dɪçkait] *f* tiredness.

Muff [muf] *m* **-(e)s, -e** (*Handwärmer*) muff; **~el** *m* **-s, -** (*umg*) killjoy, sourpuss; **m~ig** *a* (*Luft*) musty.

Mühe ['my:ə] *f* -, **-n** trouble, pains *pl*; **mit Müh und Not** with great difficulty; **sich** (*dat*) **~ geben** go to a lot of trouble; **m~los** *a* without trouble, easy.

mühevoll *a* laborious, arduous.

Mühle ['my:lə] f -, -n mill; (*Kaffee~*) grinder.

Müh- zW: ~**sal** f -, -e hardship, tribulation; **m~sam** a arduous, troublesome; **m~selig** a arduous, laborious.

Mulde ['muldə] f -, -n hollow, depression.

Mull [mul] m -(e)s, -e thin muslin; ~**binde** f gauze bandage.

Müll [myl] m -(e)s refuse; ~**abfuhr** f rubbish disposal; (*Leute*) dustmen pl; ~**abladeplatz** m rubbish dump; ~**eimer** m dustbin, garbage can (*US*); ~**haufen** m rubbish heap; ~**schlucker** m -s, - garbage disposal unit; ~**verbrennungsanlage** f incinerator; ~**wagen** m dustcart, garbage truck (*US*).

mulmig ['mulmɪç] a rotten; (*umg*) dodgy; **jdm ist ~** sb feels funny.

multiplizieren [multipli'tsi:rən] vt multiply.

Mumie ['mu:miə] f mummy.

Mumm [mum] m -s (*umg*) gumption, nerve.

München ['mynçən] nt -s Munich.

Mund [munt] m -(e)s, ⁻er ['myndər] mouth; ~**art** f dialect.

Mündel ['myndəl] nt -s, - ward.

münden ['myndən] vi flow (*in +akk* into).

Mund- zW: **m~faul** a taciturn; ~**geruch** m bad breath; ~**harmonika** f mouth organ.

mündig ['myndɪç] a of age; **M~keit** f majority.

mündlich ['myntlɪç] a oral.

Mundstück nt mouthpiece; (*Zigaretten~*) tip.

Mündung ['myndun] f mouth; (*Gewehr*) muzzle.

Mund- zW: ~**wasser** nt mouthwash; ~**werk** nt: **ein großes ~werk haben** have a big mouth; ~**winkel** m corner of the mouth.

Munition [munitsi'o:n] f ammunition; **Munitionslager** nt ammunition dump.

munkeln ['munkəln] vi whisper, mutter.

Münster ['mynstər] nt -s, - minster.

munter ['muntər] a lively; **M~keit** f liveliness.

Münze ['myntsə] f -, -n coin; **m~n** vt coin, mint; **auf jdn gemünzt sein** be aimed at sb.

Münzfernsprecher ['myntsfernʃprɛçər] m callbox (*Brit*), pay phone.

mürb(e) ['myrb(ə)] a (*Gestein*) crumbly; (*Holz*) rotten; (*Gebäck*) crisp; **jdn ~ machen** wear sb down; **M~(e)teig** m shortcrust pastry.

murmeln ['murməln] vti murmer, mutter.

Murmeltier ['murməlti:r] nt marmot.

murren ['murən] vi grumble, grouse.

mürrisch ['myrɪʃ] a sullen.

Mus [mu:s] nt -es, -e purée.

Muschel ['muʃəl] f -, -n mussel; (*~schale*) shell; (*Telefon~*) receiver.

Muse ['mu:zə] f -, -n muse.

Museum [mu'ze:um] nt -s, **Museen** museum.

Musik [mu'zi:k] f music; (*Kapelle*) band; **m~alisch** [-'ka:lɪʃ] a musical; ~**box** f jukebox; ~**er** ['mu:zikər] m -s, - musician; ~**hochschule** f music school; ~**instrument** nt musical instrument; ~**truhe** f radiogram.

musizieren [muzi'tsi:rən] vi make music.

Muskat [mus'ka:t] m -(e)s, -e nutmeg.

Muskel ['muskəl] m⁻ -s, -n muscle; ~**kater** m: **einen ~kater haben** be stiff.

Muskulatur [muskula'tu:r] f muscular system.

muskulös [musku'lø:s] a muscular.

Muß [mus] nt - necessity, must.

Muße ['mu:sə] f - leisure.

müssen ['mysən] vi pt **mußte**, ptp **gemußt** od (*als Hilfsverb*) **müssen 1** (*Zwang*) must (*nur im Präsens*), have to; **ich muß es tun** I must do it, I have to do it; **ich mußte es tun** I had to do it; **er muß es nicht tun** he doesn't have to do it; **muß ich?** must I?, do I have to?; **wann müßt ihr zur Schule?** when do you have to go to school?; **er hat gehen ~** he (has) had to go; **muß das sein?** is that really necessary?; **ich muß mal** (*umg*) I need the toilet

2 (*sollen*): **das mußt du nicht tun!** you oughtn't to od shouldn't do that; **Sie hätten ihn fragen ~** you should have asked him

3 (*Vermutung*): **es muß geregnet haben** it must have rained; **es muß nicht wahr sein** it needn't be true.

müßig ['my:sɪç] a idle; **M~gang** m idleness.

Muster ['mustər] nt -s, - model; (*Dessin*) pattern; (*Probe*) sample; **m~gültig** a exemplary; **m~n** vt (*Tapete*) pattern; (*fig*, *MIL*) examine; (*Truppen*) inspect; ~**ung** f (*von Stoff*) pattern; (*MIL*) inspection.

Mut [mu:t] m courage; **nur ~!** cheer up!; **jdm ~ machen** encourage sb; **m~ig** a courageous; **m~los** a discouraged, despondent.

mutmaßlich ['mu:tma:slɪç] a presumed // ad probably.

Mutter ['mutər] f -, ⁻ mother; pl ~**n** (*Schrauben~*) nut; ~**gesellschaft** f parent company.

mütterlich ['mytərlɪç] a motherly; ~**erseits** ad on the mother's side.

Mutter- zW: ~**liebe** f motherly love; ~**mal** nt birthmark, mole; ~**schaft** f motherhood, maternity; **~schutz** *m* maternity regulations; **'m~'seelena'llein** *a* all alone; **~sprache** *f* native language; **~tag** *m* Mother's Day.

Mutti ['muti] *f* **-, -s** mum(my) (*Brit*), mom(my) (*US*).

mutwillig ['mu:tviliç] *a* malicious, deliberate.

Mütze ['mʏtsə] *f* **-, -n** cap.

MwSt *abk* (= *Mehrwertsteuer*) VAT.

mysteriös [mʏsteri'øːs] *a* mysterious.

Mythos ['myːtɔs] *m* **-, Mythen** myth.

N

N, n [ɛn] *nt* N, n.

na [na] *interj* well; **~ gut** okay then.

Nabel ['naːbəl] *m* **-s, -** navel; **~schnur** *f* umbilical cord.

nach [naːx] ◆ *präp +dat* **1** (*örtlich*) to; **~ Berlin** to Berlin; **~ links/rechts** (to the) left/right; **~ oben/hinten** up/back **2** (*zeitlich*) after; **einer ~ dem anderen** one after the other; **~ Ihnen!** after you!; **zehn (Minuten) ~ drei** ten (minutes) past three **3** (*gemäß*) according to; **~ dem Gesetz** according to the law; **dem Namen ~** judging by his/her name; **~ allem, was ich weiß** as far as I know ◆ *adv*: **ihm ~!** after him!; **~ und ~** gradually, little by little; **~ wie vor** still.

nachahmen ['naːxʔaːmən] *vt* imitate.

Nachahmung *f* imitation.

Nachbar(in *f*) ['naxbaːr(ɪn)] *m* **-s, -n** neighbour; **~haus** *nt*: **im ~haus** next door; **n~lich** *a* neighbourly; **~schaft** *f* neighbourhood; **~staat** *m* neighbouring state.

nach- *zW*: **~bestellen** *vt*: **50 Stück ~bestellen** order another 50; **N~bestellung** *f* (*COMM*) repeat order; **~bilden** *vt* copy; **N~bildung** *f* imitation, copy; **~blicken** *vi* gaze after; **~datieren** *vt* postdate.

nachdem [naːx'deːm] *kj* after; (*weil*) since; **je ~ (ob)** it depends (whether).

nach- *zW*: **~denken** *vi unreg* think (*über +akk* about); **N~denken** *nt* **-s** reflection, meditation; **~denklich** *a* thoughtful, pensive.

Nachdruck ['naːxdrʊk] *m* emphasis; (*TYP*) reprint, reproduction.

nachdrücklich ['naːxdrʏklıç] *a* emphatic.

nacheinander [naːxʔaɪ'nandər] *ad* one after the other.

nachempfinden ['naːxʔɛmpfɪndən] *vt unreg*: **jdm etw ~** feel sth with sb.

Nacherzählung ['naːxʔɛrtsɛːlʊŋ] *f* reproduction (of a story).

Nachfahr ['naːxfaːr] *m* **-s, -en** de-

scendant.

Nachfolge ['naːxfɔlgə] *f* succession; **n~n** *vi* (*lit*) follow (*jdm/etw* sb/sth); **~r(in** *f*) *m* **-s, -** successor.

nachforschen *vti* investigate.

Nachforschung *f* investigation.

Nachfrage ['naːxfraːgə] *f* inquiry; (*COMM*) demand; **n~n** *vi* inquire.

nach- *zW*: **~fühlen** *vt siehe* **~empfinden**; **~füllen** *vt* refill; **~geben** *vi unreg* give way, yield; **N~gebühr** *f* surcharge; (*Post*) excess postage; **N~geburt** *f* afterbirth.

nachgehen ['naːxgeːən] *vi unreg* follow (*jdm* sb); (*erforschen*) inquire (*einer Sache* into sth); (*Uhr*) be slow.

Nachgeschmack ['naːxgəʃmak] *m* aftertaste.

nachgiebig ['naːxgiːbıç] *a* soft, accommodating; **N~keit** *f* softness.

nachhaltig ['naːxhaltıç] *a* lasting; (*Widerstand*) persistent.

nachhelfen ['naːxhɛlfən] *vi unreg* assist, help (*jdm* sb).

nachher [naːx'heːr] *ad* afterwards.

Nachhilfeunterricht ['naːxhɪlfəʊntərrıçt] *m* extra tuition.

nachholen ['naːxhoːlən] *vt* catch up with; (*Versäumtes*) make up for.

Nachkomme ['naːxkɔmə] *m* **-, -n** descendant.

nachkommen *vi unreg* follow; (*einer Verpflichtung*) fulfil; **N~schaft** *f* descendants *pl*.

Nachkriegs- ['naːxkriːks] *in zW* postwar; **~zeit** *f* postwar period.

Nach- *zW*: **~laß** *m* **-lasses, -lässe** (*COMM*) discount, rebate; (*Erbe*) estate; **n~lassen** *unreg vt* (*Strafe*) remit; (*Summe*) take off; (*Schulden*) cancel // *vi* decrease, ease off; (*Sturm auch*) die down; (*schlechter werden*) deteriorate; **er hat n~gelassen** he has got worse; **n~lässig** *a* negligent, careless; **~lässigkeit** *f* negligence, carelessness.

nachlaufen ['naːxlaʊfən] *vi unreg* run after, chase (*jdm* sb).

nachmachen ['naːxmaxən] *vt* imitate, copy (*jdm etw* sth from sb); (*fälschen*) counterfeit.

Nachmittag ['naːxmıtaːk] *m* afternoon; **am ~, n~s** *ad* in the afternoon.

Nach- *zW*: **~nahme** *f* **-, -n** cash on delivery; **per ~nahme** C.O.D.; **~name** *m* surname; **~porto** *nt* excess postage.

nachprüfen ['naːxpryːfən] *vt* check, verify.

nachrechnen ['naːxrɛçnən] *vt* check.

Nachrede ['naːxreːdə] *f*: **üble ~** libel; slander.

Nachricht ['naːxrɪçt] f -, -en (piece of) news; (Mitteilung) message; ~en pl news; ~enagentur f news agency; ~endienst m (MIL) intelligence service; ~ensprecher(in f) m newsreader; ~entechnik f telecommunications sing.

Nachruf ['naːxruːf] m obituary.

nachsagen ['naːxzaːgən] vt repeat; jdm etw ~ say sth of sb.

nachschicken ['naːxʃɪkən] vt forward.

Nachschlag- ['naːxʃlaːg] zW: n~en vt unreg look up; **Nachschlagewerk** nt reference book.

Nach- zW: ~schlüssel m master key; ~schub m supplies pl; (Truppen) reinforcements pl.

nachsehen ['naːxzeːən] unreg vt (prüfen) check; jdm etw ~ forgive sb sth // vi (erforschen) look and see; das N~ haben come off worst.

nachsenden ['naːxzɛndən] vt unreg send on, forward.

Nachsicht ['naːxzɪçt] f - indulgence, leniency; n~ig a indulgent, lenient.

nachsitzen ['naːxzɪtsən] vi unreg: ~(müssen) (SCH) be kept in.

Nachspeise ['naːxʃpaɪzə] f dessert, sweet, pudding.

Nachspiel ['naːxʃpiːl] nt epilogue; (fig) sequel.

nachsprechen ['naːxʃprɛçən] vt unreg repeat (jdm after sb).

nächst [nɛːçst] präp +dat (räumlich) next to; (außer) apart from; ~beste(r, s) a first that comes along; (zweitbeste) next best; N~e(r) mf neighbour; ~e(r, s) a next; (nächstgelegen) nearest; N~enliebe f love for one's fellow men; ~ens ad shortly, soon; ~liegend a (lit) nearest; (fig) obvious; ~möglich a next possible.

nachsuchen ['naːxzuːxən] vi: um etw ~ ask od apply for sth.

Nacht [naxt] f -, -̈e night.

Nachteil ['naːxtaɪl] m disadvantage; n~ig a disadvantageous.

Nachthemd nt nightshirt; nightdress.

Nachtigall ['naxtɪgal] f -, -en nightingale.

Nachtisch ['naːxtɪʃ] m siehe **Nachspeise**.

Nachtklub m night club.

nächtlich ['nɛçtlɪç] a nightly.

Nachtlokal nt night club.

Nach- zW: ~trag m -(e)s, -̈räge supplement; n~tragen vt unreg carry (jdm after sb); (zufügen) add; jdm etw n~tragen hold sth against sb; n~trägllch a,ad later, subsequent(ly); additional(ly); n~trauern vi: jdm/etw n~trauern mourn the loss of sb/sth.

Nacht- zW: ~ruhe f sleep; n~s ad by night; ~schicht f nightshift; **nachtsüber** ad during the night; ~tarif m off-peak tariff; ~tisch m bedside table; ~wächter m night watchman.

Nach- zW: ~untersuchung f checkup; n~wachsen vi unreg grow again; ~wehen pl afterpains pl; (fig) aftereffects pl.

Nachweis ['naːxvaɪs] m -es, -e proof; n~bar a provable, demonstrable; n~en ['naːxvaɪzən] vt unreg prove; jdm etw n~en point sth out to sb; n~lich a evident, demonstrable.

nach- zW: ~wirken vi have aftereffects; **N~wirkung** f after-effect; **N~wort** nt appendix; **N~wuchs** m offspring; (beruflich etc) new recruits pl; ~zahlen vti pay extra; **N~zahlung** f additional payment; (zurückdatiert) back pay; ~zählen vt count again; **N~zügler** m -s, - straggler.

Nacken ['nakən] m -s, - nape of the neck.

nackt [nakt] a naked; (Tatsachen) plain, bare; **N~heit** f nakedness.

Nadel ['naːdəl] f -, -n needle; (Steck~) pin; ~kissen nt pincushion; ~öhr nt eye of a needle; ~wald m coniferous forest.

Nagel ['naːgəl] m -s, -̈ nail; ~feile f nailfile; ~haut f cuticle; ~lack m nail varnish; n~n vti nail; n~neu a brand-new; ~schere f nail scissors pl.

nagen ['naːgən] vti gnaw.

Nagetier ['naːgətiːr] nt rodent.

nah(e) ['naː(ə)] a,ad (räumlich) near(by); (Verwandte) near; (Freunde) close; (zeitlich) near, close; der N~e Osten the Near East // präp +dat near (to), close to; **N~aufnahme** f close-up.

Nähe ['nɛːə] f - nearness, proximity; (Umgebung) vicinity; in der ~ close by; at hand; aus der ~ from close to.

nahe- zW: ~bei ad nearby; ~gehen vi unreg grieve (jdm sb); ~kommen vi unreg get close (jdm to sb); ~legen vt: jdm etw ~legen suggest sth to sb; ~liegen vi unreg be obvious; ~liegend a obvious; ~n vir approach, draw near.

Näh- ['nɛː] zW: n~en vti sew; n~er a,ad nearer; (Erklärung, Erkundigung) more detailed; ~ere(s) nt details pl, particulars pl; ~erei f sewing, needlework; ~erin f seamstress; n~erkommen vir unreg get closer; n~ern vr approach.

nahe- zW: ~stehen vi unreg be close (jdm to sb); einer Sache ~stehen sympathize with sth; ~stehend a close; ~treten vi unreg: jdm (zu) ~treten offend sb; ~zu ad nearly.

Nähgarn *nt* thread.
nahm *etc v siehe* **nehmen**.
Näh- *zW:* **~maschine** *f* sewing machine; **~nadel** *f* needle.
nähren ['nɛːrən] *vtr* feed.
nahrhaft ['naːrhaft] *a* nourishing, nutritious.
Nahrung [naːrʊŋ] *f* food; (*fig auch*) sustenance.
Nahrungs- *zW:* **~mittel** *nt* foodstuffs *pl;* **~mittelindustrie** *f* food industry; **~suche** *f* search for food.
Nährwert *m* nutritional value.
Naht [naːt] *f* -, ⸚e seam; (*MED*) suture; (*TECH*) join; **n~los** *a* seamless; **n~los ineinander übergehen** follow without a gap.
Nah- *zW:* **~verkehr** *m* local traffic; **~verkehrszug** *m* local train; **~ziel** *nt* immediate objective.
naiv [naˈiːf] *a* naive; **N~ität** [naiviˈtɛːt] *f* naivety.
Name ['naːmə] *m* -ns, -n name; **im ~n von** on behalf of; **n~ns** *ad* by the name of; **~nstag** *m* name day, saint's day; **n~ntlich** *a* by name // *ad* particularly, especially.
namhaft ['naːmhaft] *a* (*berühmt*) famed, renowned; (*beträchtlich*) considerable; **~ machen** name.
nämlich ['nɛːmlɪç] *ad* that is to say, namely; (*denn*) since.
nannte *etc v siehe* **nennen**.
nanu [naˈnuː] *interj* well, well!
Napf [napf] *m* -(e)s, ⸚e bowl, dish.
Narbe ['narbə] *f* -, -n scar.
narbig ['narbɪç] *a* scarred.
Narkose [narˈkoːzə] *f* -, -n anaesthetic.
Narr [nar] *m* -en, -en fool; **n~en** *vt* fool; **~heit** *f* foolishness.
Närr- ['nɛr] *zW:* **~in** *f* fool; **n~isch** *a* foolish, crazy.
Narzisse [narˈtsɪsə] *f* -, -n narcissus, daffodil.
nasch- ['naʃ] *zW:* **~en** *vti* nibble; eat secretly; **~haft** *a* sweet-toothed.
Nase ['naːzə] *f* -, -n nose.
Nasen- *zW:* **~bluten** *nt* -s nosebleed; **~loch** *nt* nostril; **~tropfen** *pl* nose drops *pl.*
naseweis *a* pert, cheeky; (*neugierig*) nosey.
Nashorn ['naːshɔrn] *nt* rhinoceros.
naß [nas] *a* wet.
Nässe ['nɛsə] *f* - wetness; **n~n** *vt* wet.
naßkalt *a* wet and cold.
Naßrasur *f* wet shave.
Nation [natsiˈoːn] *f* nation.
national [natsioˈnaːl] *a* national; **N~hymne** *f* national anthem; **~isieren** [-iˈziːrən] *vt* nationalize; **N~i'sierung** *f* nationalization; **N~ismus** [-ˈlɪsmʊs] *m* nationalism; **~istisch** [-ˈlɪstɪʃ] *a* nationalistic; **N~i'tät** *f* nationality; **N~mannschaft** *f* national team; **N~sozialismus** *m* national socialism.
Natron ['naːtrɔn] *nt* -s soda.
Natter ['natər] *f* -, -n adder.
Natur [naˈtuːr] *f* nature; (*körperlich*) constitution; **~a'lismus** *m* naturalism; **~erscheinung** *f* natural phenomenon *od* event; **n~farben** *a* natural coloured; **n~gemäß** *a* natural; **~gesetz** *nt* law of nature; **~katastrophe** *f* natural disaster.
natürlich [naˈtyːrlɪç] *a* natural // *ad* naturally; **ja, ~!** yes, of course; **N~keit** *f* naturalness.
Natur- *zW:* **~produkt** *nt* natural product; **n~rein** *a* natural, pure; **~schutzgebiet** *nt* nature reserve; **~wissenschaft** *f* natural science; **~wissenschaftler(in** *f*) *m* scientist; **~zustand** *m* natural state.
nautisch ['naʊtɪʃ] *a* nautical.
Nazi ['naːtsi] *m* -s, -s Nazi.
n.Chr. *abk* (= *nach Christus*) AD.
Neapel [neˈaːpəl] *nt* -s Naples.
Nebel ['neːbəl] *m* -s, - fog, mist; **n~ig** *a* foggy, misty; **~scheinwerfer** *m* foglamp.
neben ['neːbən] *präp* +*akk od dat* next to; (*außer*) apart from, besides; **~an** [neːbənˈʔan] *ad* next door; **N~anschluß** *m* (*TEL*) extension; **~bei** [neːbənˈbaɪ] *ad* at the same time; (*außerdem*) additionally; (*beiläufig*) incidentally; **N~beschäftigung** *f* second job; **N~buhler(in** *f*) *m* -s, - rival; **~einander** [neːbənʔaɪˈnandər] *ad* side by side; **~einanderlegen** *vt* put next to each other; **N~eingang** *m* side entrance; **N~erscheinung** *f* side effect; **N~fach** *nt* subsidiary subject; **N~fluß** *m* tributary; **N~geräusch** *nt* (*RAD*) atmospherics *pl,* interference; **~her** [neːbənˈheːr] *ad* (*zusätzlich*) besides; (*gleichzeitig*) at the same time; (*daneben*) alongside; **~herfahren** *vi unreg* drive alongside; **N~kosten** *pl* extra charges *pl,* extras *pl;* **N~produkt** *nt* by-product; **N~rolle** *f* minor part; **N~sache** *f* trifle, side issue; **~sächlich** *a* minor, peripheral; **N~straße** *f* side street.
neblig ['neːblɪç] *a* = **nebelig**.
Necessaire [nesɛˈsɛːr] *nt* -s, -s (*Näh~*) needlework box; (*Nagel~*) manicure case.
neck- ['nɛk] *zW:* **~en** *vt* tease; **N~e'rei** *f* teasing; **~isch** *a* coy; (*Einfall, Lied*) amusing.
Neffe ['nɛfə] *m* -n, -n nephew.
negativ [negaˈtiːf] *a* negative; **N~** *nt* -s, -e (*PHOT*) negative.
Neger ['neːgər] *m* -s, - negro; **~in** *f* negress.
nehmen ['neːmən] *vt unreg* take; **jdn**

zu sich ~ take sb in; **sich ernst ~** take o.s. seriously; **nimm dir noch einmal** help yourself.

Neid [naɪt] *m* **-(e)s** envy; **~er** *m* **-s, -** envier; **n~isch** *a* envious, jealous.

neigen ['naɪgən] *vt* incline, lean; *(Kopf)* bow // *vi*: **zu etw ~** tend to sth.

Neigung *f* *(des Geländes)* slope; *(Tendenz)* tendency, inclination; *(Vorliebe)* liking; *(Zuneigung)* affection.

nein [naɪn] *ad* no.

Nelke ['nɛlkə] *f* **-, -n** carnation, pink; *(Gewürz)* clove.

Nenn- ['nɛn] *zW:* **n~en** *vt* *unreg* name; *(mit Namen)* call; **wie ~t man ...?** what do you call ...?; **n~enswert** *a* worth mentioning; **~er** *m* **-s, -** denominator; **~wert** *m* nominal value; *(COMM)* par.

Neon ['neːɔn] *nt* **-s** neon; **~licht** *nt* neon light; **~röhre** *f* neon tube.

Nerv [nɛrf] *m* **-s, -en** nerve; **jdm auf die ~en gehen** get on sb's nerves; **n~enaufreibend** *a* nerve-racking; **~enbündel** *nt* bundle of nerves; **~enheilanstalt** *f* mental home; **n~enkrank** *a* mentally ill; **~enschwäche** *f* neurasthenia; **~ensystem** *nt* nervous system; **~enzusammenbruch** *m* nervous breakdown; **n~ös** [nɛrˈvøːs] *a* nervous; **~osi'tät** *f* nervousness; **n~tötend** *a* nerve-racking; *(Arbeit)* soul-destroying.

Nerz [nɛrts] *m* **-es, -e** mink.

Nessel ['nɛsəl] *f* **-, -n** nettle.

Nest [nɛst] *nt* **-(e)s, -er** nest; *(umg: Ort)* dump.

nett [nɛt] *a* nice; *(freundlich auch)* kind; **~erweise** *ad* kindly.

netto ['nɛto] *ad* net.

Netz [nɛts] *nt* **-es, -e** net; *(Gepäck~)* rack; *(Einkaufs~)* string bag; *(Spinnen~)* web; *(System)* network; **jdm ins ~ gehen** *(fig)* fall into sb's trap; **~anschluß** *m* mains connection; **~haut** *f* retina.

neu [nɔy] *a* new; *(Sprache, Geschichte)* modern; **seit ~estem** (since) recently; **die ~esten Nachrichten** the latest news; **~ schreiben** rewrite, write again; **N~anschaffung** *f* new purchase *od* acquisition; **~artig** *a* a new kind of; **N~auflage** *f* new edition; **N~bau** *m* new building; **~erdings** *ad* *(kürzlich)* (since) recently; *(von neuem)* again; **N~erung** *f* innovation, new departure; **N~fundland** *nt* Newfoundland; **N~gier** *f* curiosity; **~gierig** *a* curious; **N~guinea** *nt* New Guinea; **N~heit** *f* newness, novelty; **N~igkeit** *f* news; **N~jahr** *nt* New Year; **~lich**

ad recently, the other day; **N~ling** *m* novice; **N~mond** *m* new moon.

neun [nɔyn] *num* nine; **~zehn** *num* nineteen; **~zig** *num* ninety.

neureich *a* nouveau riche; **N~e(r)** *mf* nouveau riche.

Neur- *zW:* **~ose** [nɔyˈroːzə] *f* **-, -n** neurosis; **~otiker** [nɔyˈroːtikər] *m* **-s, -** neurotic; **n~otisch** *a* neurotic.

Neusee- [nɔyˈzeː] *zW:* **~land** *nt* New Zealand; **~länder(in** *f)* *m* New Zealander; **n~ländisch** *a* New Zealand.

Neutr- *zW:* **n~al** [nɔyˈtraːl] *a* neutral; **n~ali'sieren** *vt* neutralize; **~ali'tät** *f* neutrality; **~on** ['nɔytrɔn] *nt* **-s, -en** neutron; **~um** ['nɔytrʊm] *nt* **-s, -a** *od* **-en** neuter.

Neu- *zW:* **~wert** *m* purchase price; **~zeit** *f* modern age; **n~zeitlich** *a* modern, recent.

nicht [nɪçt] *ad* **1** *(Verneinung)* not; **er ist es ~** it's not him, it isn't him; **er raucht ~** *(gerade)* he isn't smoking; *(gewöhnlich)* he doesn't smoke; **ich kann das ~ — ich auch ~** I can't do it — neither *od* nor can I; **es regnet ~ mehr** it's not raining any more

2 *(Bitte, Verbot):* **~!** don't!, no!; **~ berühren!** do not touch!; **~ doch!** don't!

3 *(rhetorisch):* **du bist müde, ~ (wahr)?** you're tired, aren't you?; **das ist schön, ~ (wahr)?** it's nice, isn't it?

4: **was du ~ sagst!** the things you say!

Nichtangriffspakt [nɪçtˈangrifspakt] *m* non-aggression pact.

Nichte ['nɪçtə] *f* **-, -n** niece.

nichtig ['nɪçtɪç] *a* *(ungültig)* null, void; *(wertlos)* futile; **N~keit** *f* nullity, invalidity; *(Sinnlosigkeit)* futility.

Nichtraucher(in *f)* *m* non-smoker.

nichtrostend *a* stainless.

nichts [nɪçts] *pron* nothing; **für ~ und wieder ~** for nothing at all; **N~** *nt* - nothingness; *(pej: Person)* nonentity; **~desto'weniger** *ad* nevertheless; **N~nutz** *m* **-es, -e** good-for-nothing; **~nutzig** *a* worthless, useless; **~sagend** *a* meaningless; **N~tun** *nt* **-s** idleness.

Nickel ['nɪkəl] *nt* **-s** nickel.

nicken ['nɪkən] *vi* nod.

Nickerchen ['nɪkərçən] *nt* nap.

nie [niː] *ad* never; **~ wieder** *od* **mehr** never again; **~ und nimmer** never ever.

nieder ['niːdər] *a* low; *(gering)* inferior // *ad* down; **N~gang** *m* decline; **~gehen** *vi* *unreg* descend; *(AVIAT)* come down; *(Regen)* fall; *(Boxer)* go down; **~geschlagen** *a* depressed, dejected; **N~geschlagenheit** *f* depression, dejection; **N~lage** *f* defeat;

N~lande *pl* Netherlands; **N~-länder(in** *f)* *m* Dutchman; Dutchwoman; **~ländisch** *a* Dutch; **~lassen** *vr unreg (sich setzen)* sit down; *(an Ort)* settle (down); *(Arzt, Rechtsanwalt)* set up a practice; **N~lassung** *f* settlement; *(COMM)* branch; **~legen** *vt* lay down; *(Arbeit)* stop; *(Amt)* resign; **N~rhein** *nt* Lower Rhine; **N~sachsen** *nt* Lower Saxony; **N~schlag** *m* *(MET)* precipitation; rainfall; **~schlagen** *unreg vt (Gegner)* beat down; *(Gegenstand)* knock down; *(Augen)* lower; *(Aufstand)* put down // *vr* *(CHEM)* precipitate; **N~schrift** *f* transcription; **~trächtig** *a* base, mean; **N~trächtigkeit** *f* meanness, baseness; outrage; **N~ung** *f* *(GEOG)* depression; flats *pl*.
niedlich ['ni:tlıç] *a* sweet, cute.
niedrig ['ni:drıç] *a* low; *(Stand)* lowly, humble; *(Gesinnung)* mean.
niemals ['ni:ma:ls] *ad* never.
niemand ['ni:mant] *pron* nobody, no one; **Niemandsland** *nt* no-man's land.
Niere ['ni:rə] *f* -, **-n** kidney; **Nierenentzündung** *f* kidney infection.
nieseln ['ni:zəln] *vi* drizzle.
niesen ['ni:zən] *vi* sneeze.
Niete ['ni:tə] *f* -, **-n** *(TECH)* rivet; *(Los)* blank; *(Reinfall)* flop; *(Mensch)* failure; **n~en** *vt* rivet.
Nikotin [niko'ti:n] *nt* -s nicotine.
Nil ['ni:l] *m* Nile; **~pferd** *nt* hippopotamus.
Nimmersatt ['nımərzat] *m* -(e)s, -e glutton.
nimmst *etc* *v siehe* **nehmen**.
nippen ['nıpən] *vti* sip.
nirgend- ['nırgənt] *zW:* **~s, ~wo** *ad* nowhere; **~wohin** *ad* nowhere.
Nische ['ni:ʃə] *f* -, **-n** niche.
nisten ['nıstən] *vi* nest.
Nitrat [ni'tra:t] *nt* -(e)s, -e nitrate.
Niveau [ni'vo:] *nt* -s, -e level.
Nixe ['nıksə] *f* -, **-n** water nymph.
noch [nox] ◆ *ad* **1** *(weiterhin)* still; ~ nicht not yet; ~ nie never (yet); ~ immer, immer ~ still; bleiben Sie doch ~ stay a bit longer
2 *(in Zukunft)* still, yet; das kann ~ passieren that might still happen; er wird ~ kommen he'll come (yet)
3 *(nicht später als):* ~ vor einer Woche only a week ago; ~ am selben Tag the very same day; ~ im 19. Jahrhundert as late as the 19th century; ~ heute today
4 *(zusätzlich):* wer war ~ da? who else was there?; ~ einmal once more, again; ~ dreimal three more times; ~ einer another one
5 *(bei Vergleichen):* ~ größer even bigger; das ist ~ besser that's better still; und wenn es ~ so schwer ist

however hard it is
6: Geld ~ und ~ heaps (and heaps) of money; sie hat ~ und ~ versucht, ... she tried again and again to ...
◆ *kj* weder **A** ~ **B** neither A nor B.
nochmal(s) ['nɔxma:l(s)] *ad* again, once more.
nochmalig ['nɔxma:lıç] *a* repeated.
Nominativ ['no:minati:f] *m* -s, -e nominative.
nominell [nomi'nɛl] *a* nominal.
Nonne ['nɔnə] *f* -, **-n** nun.
Nord(en) ['nɔrd(ən)] *m* -s north; **N~'irland** *nt* Northern Ireland; **n~isch** *a* northern.
nördlich ['nœrtlıç] *a* northerly, northern; ~ von, ~ *präp* +*gen* (to the) north of.
Nord- *zW:* **~pol** *m* North Pole; **~rhein-Westfalen** *nt* North Rhine-Westphalia; **~see** *f* North Sea; **n~wärts** *ad* northwards.
Nörg- ['nœrg] *zW:* **~e'lei** *f* grumbling; **n~eln** *vi* grumble; **~ler** *m* -s, - grumbler.
Norm [nɔrm] *f* -, **-en** norm; *(Größenvorschrift)* standard; **n~al** [nɔr'ma:l] *a* normal; **n~alerweise** *ad* normally; **n~ali'sieren** *vt* normalize // *vr* return to normal; **n~en** *vt* standardize.
Norweg- ['nɔrve:g] *zW:* **~en** *nt* Norway; **~er(in** *f)* *m* -s, - Norwegian; **n~isch** *a* Norwegian.
Not [no:t] *f* -, ¨e need; *(Mangel)* want; *(Mühe)* trouble; *(Zwang)* necessity; zur ~ if necessary; *(gerade noch)* just about.
Notar [no'ta:r] *m* -s, -e notary; **n~i'ell** *a* notarial.
Not- *zW:* **~ausgang** *m* emergency exit; **~behelf** *m* -s, -e makeshift; **~bremse** *f* emergency brake; **n~dürftig** *a* scanty; *(behelfsmäßig)* makeshift.
Note ['no:tə] *f* -, **-n** note; *(SCH)* mark *(Brit)*, grade *(US)*.
Noten- *zW:* **~blatt** *nt* sheet of music; **~schlüssel** *m* clef; **~ständer** *m* music stand.
Not- *zW:* **~fall** *m* (case of) emergency; **n~falls** *ad* if need be; **n~gedrungen** *a* necessary, unavoidable; etw n~gedrungen machen be forced to do sth.
notieren [no'ti:rən] *vt* note; *(COMM)* quote.
Notierung *f* *(COMM)* quotation.
nötig ['nø:tıç] *a* necessary; etw ~ haben need sth; **~en** *vt* compel, force; **~enfalls** *ad* if necessary.
Notiz [no'ti:ts] *f* -, **-en** note; *(Zeitungs~)* item; **~ nehmen** take notice; **~buch** *nt* notebook.
Not- *zW:* **~lage** *f* crisis, emergency;

n~landen vi make a forced od emergency landing; **n~leidend** a needy; **~lösung** f temporary solution; **~lüge** f white lie.

notorisch [no'to:rɪʃ] a notorious.

Not- zW: **~ruf** m emergency call; **~stand** m state of emergency; **~unterkunft** f emergency accommodation; **~verband** m emergency dressing; **~wehr** f - self-defence; **n~wendig** a necessary; **~wendigkeit** f necessity; **~zucht** f rape.

Novelle [no'vɛlə] f -, -n short story; (JUR) amendment.

November [no'vɛmbər] m -(s), - November.

Nr. abk (= Nummer) no.

Nu [nu:] m: **im ~** in an instant.

Nuance [ny'ã:sə] f -, -n nuance.

nüchtern ['nʏçtərn] a sober; (Magen) empty; (Urteil) prudent; **N~heit** f sobriety.

Nudel ['nu:dəl] f -, -n noodle; **~n** pasta; (in Suppe) noodles.

Null [nʊl] f -, -en nought, zero; (pej: Mensch) washout; **n~** num zero; (Fehler) no; **n~ Uhr** midnight; **n~ und nichtig** null and void; **~punkt** m zero; **auf dem ~punkt** at zero.

numerieren [nume'ri:rən] vt number.

numerisch [nu'me:rɪʃ] a numerical.

Nummer ['nʊmər] f -, -n number; (Größe) size; **Nummernschild** nt (AUT) number od license (US) plate.

nun [nu:n] ad now; das ist ~ mal so that's the way it is // interj well.

nur [nu:r] ad just, only; wo bleibt er ~? (just) where is he?.

Nürnberg ['nʏrnbɛrk] nt -s Nuremberg.

Nuß [nʊs] f -, **Nüsse** nut; **~baum** m walnut tree; hazelnut tree; **~knacker** m -s, - nutcracker.

Nüster ['ny:stər] f -, -n nostril.

Nutte ['nʊtə] f -, -n tart.

nutz [nʊts], **nütze** ['nʏtsə] a: zu nichts ~ sein be useless; **~en, nützen** vt use (zu etw for sth) // vi be of use; was nützt es? what's the use?, what use is it?; **N~en** m -s usefulness; profit; von N~en useful.

nützlich ['nʏtslɪç] a useful; **N~keit** f usefulness.

Nutz- zW: **n~los** a useless; **~losigkeit** f uselessness; **~nießer** m -s, - beneficiary.

Nylon ['naɪlɔn] nt nylon.

O

O, o [o:] nt O, o.

Oase [o'a:zə] f -, -n oasis.

ob [ɔp] kj if, whether; ~ das wohl wahr ist? can that be true?; und ~!

you bet!

Obdach ['ɔpdax] nt -(e)s shelter, lodging; **o~los** a homeless; **~lose(r)** mf homeless person.

Obduktion [ɔpdʊktsi'o:n] f postmortem.

obduzieren [ɔpdu'tsi:rən] vt do a post-mortem on.

O-Beine ['o:baɪnə] pl bow od bandy legs pl.

oben ['o:bən] ad above; (in Haus) upstairs; nach ~ up; von ~ down; ~ ohne topless; jdn von ~ bis unten ansehen look sb up and down; Befehl von ~ orders from above; **~an** ad at the top; **~auf** ad up above, on the top // a (munter) in form; **~drein** ad into the bargain; **~erwähnt, ~genannt** a above-mentioned.

Ober ['o:bər] m -s, - waiter; **~arm** m upper arm; **~arzt** m senior physician; **~aufsicht** f supervision; **~bayern** nt Upper Bavaria; **~befehl** m supreme command; **~befehlshaber** m commander-in-chief; **~bekleidung** f outer clothing; **~bürgermeister** m lord mayor; **~deck** nt upper od top deck; **o~e(r, s)** a upper; die ~en the bosses; (ECCL) the superiors; **~fläche** f surface; **o~flächlich** a superficial; **~geschoß** nt upper storey; **o~halb** ad, präp +gen above; **~haupt** nt head, chief; **~haus** nt upper house; House of Lords; **~hemd** nt shirt; **~herrschaft** f supremacy, sovereignty; **~in** f matron; (ECCL) Mother Superior; **~kellner** m head waiter; **~kiefer** m upper jaw; **~körper** m trunk, upper part of body; **~leitung** f direction; (ELEK) overhead cable; **~licht** nt skylight; **~lippe** f upper lip; **~schenkel** m thigh; **~schicht** f upper classes pl; **~schule** f grammar school (Brit), high school (US); **~schwester** f (MED) matron.

Oberst ['o:bərst] m -en od -s, -en od -e colonel; **o~e(r, s)** a very top, topmost.

Ober- zW: **~stufe** f upper school; **~teil** nt upper part; **~weite** f bust/chest measurement.

obgleich [ɔp'glaɪç] kj although.

Obhut ['ɔphu:t] f - care, protection; in jds ~ sein be in sb's care.

obig ['o:bɪç] a above.

Objekt [ɔp'jɛkt] nt -(e)s, -e object; **~iv** [-'ti:f] nt -s, -e lens; **o~iv** a objective; **~ivi'tät** f objectivity.

Oblate [o'bla:tə] f -, -n (Gebäck) wafer; (ECCL) host.

Obligation [ɔbligatsi'o:n] f bond.

obligatorisch [ɔbliga'to:rɪʃ] a compulsory, obligatory.

Oboe [o'bo:ə] f -, -n oboe.

Obrigkeit ['o:brɪçkaɪt] f (Behörden) authorities pl, administration; (Regierung) government.
obschon [ɔp'ʃo:n] kj although.
Observatorium [ɔpzɛrva'to:riʊm] nt observatory.
obskur [ɔps'ku:r] a obscure; (verdächtig) dubious.
Obst [o:pst] nt -(e)s fruit; **~baum** m fruit tree; **~garten** m orchard; **~händler** m fruiterer, fruit merchant; **~kuchen** m fruit tart.
obszön [ɔps'tsø:n] a obscene; **O~i'tät** f obscenity.
obwohl [ɔp'vo:l] kj although.
Ochse ['ɔksə] m -n, -n ox; (umg) cram, swot (Brit); **Ochsenschwanzsuppe** f oxtail soup; **Ochsenzunge** f oxtongue.
öd(e) ['ø:d(ə)] a (Land) waste, barren; (fig) dull; **O~e** f -, -n desert, waste(land); (fig) tedium.
oder ['o:dər] kj or; das stimmt, ~? that's right, isn't it?
Ofen ['o:fən] m -s, ∸ oven; (Heiz~) fire, heater; (Kohlen~) stove; (Hoch~) furnace; (Herd) cooker, stove; **~rohr** nt stovepipe.
offen ['ɔfən] a open; (aufrichtig) frank; (Stelle) vacant; ~ gesagt to be honest; **~bar** a obvious; **~baren** [ɔfən'ba:rən] vt reveal, manifest; **O~'barung** f (REL) revelation; **~bleiben** vi unreg (Fenster) stay open; (Frage, Entscheidung) remain open; **~halten** vt unreg keep open; **O~heit** f candour, frankness; **~herzig** a candid, frank; (Kleid) revealing; **~kundig** a well-known; (klar) evident; **~lassen** vt unreg leave open; **~sichtlich** a evident, obvious.
offensiv [ɔfɛn'zi:f] a offensive; **O~e** [-'zi:və] f -, -n defensive.
offenstehen vi unreg be open; (Rechnung) be unpaid; es steht Ihnen offen, es zu tun you are at liberty to do it.
öffentlich ['œfəntlɪç] a public; **Ö~keit** f (Leute) public; (einer Versammlung etc) public nature; in aller Ö~keit in public; an die Ö~keit dringen reach the public ear.
offiziell [ɔfitsi'ɛl] a official.
Offizier [ɔfi'tsi:r] m -s, -e officer; **Offizierskasino** nt officers' mess.
öffnen ['œfnən] vtr open; jdm die Tür ~ open the door for sb.
Öffner ['œfnər] m -s, - opener.
Öffnung ['œfnʊŋ] f opening; **Öffnungszeiten** pl opening times pl.
oft [ɔft] ad often.
öfter ['œftər] ad more often od frequently; **~s** ad often, frequently.
oftmals ad often, frequently.

oh [o:] interj oh; ~ je! oh dear.
OHG [o:ha:'ge:] abk (= Offene Handelsgesellschaft) general partnership.
ohne ['o:nə] präp +akk, kj without; das ist nicht ~ (umg) it's not bad; ~ weiteres without a second thought; ~ zu fragen without asking; ~ daß er es wußte without him knowing it; (sofort) immediately; **~dies** [o:nə'di:s] ad anyway; **~einander** [o:nə'ai'nandər] ad without each other; **~gleichen** [o:nə'glaiçən] a unsurpassed, without equal; **~hin** [o:nə'hɪn] ad anyway, in any case.
Ohnmacht ['o:nmaxt] f faint; (fig) impotence; in ~ fallen faint.
ohnmächtig ['o:nmɛçtɪç] a in a faint, unconscious; (fig) weak, impotent; sie ist ~ she has fainted.
Ohr [o:r] nt -(e)s, -en ear; (Gehör) hearing.
Öhr [ø:r] nt -(e)s, -e eye.
Ohren- zW: **~arzt** m ear specialist; **o~betäubend** a deafening; **~schmalz** nt earwax; **~schmerzen** pl earache; **~schützer** m -s, - earmuff.
Ohr- zW: **~feige** f slap on the face; box on the ears; **o~feigen** vt slap sb's face; box sb's ears; **~läppchen** nt ear lobe; **~ring** m earrings pl; **~wurm** m earwig; (MUS) catchy tune.
ökonomisch [øko'no:mɪʃ] a economical.
Oktave [ɔk'ta:və] f -, -n octave.
Oktober [ɔk'to:bər] m -(s), - October.
ökumenisch [øku'me:nɪʃ] a ecumenical.
Öl [ø:l] nt -(e)s, -e oil; **~baum** m olive tree; **ö~en** vt oil; (TECH) lubricate; **~farbe** f oil paint; **~feld** nt oilfield; **~film** m film of oil; **~heizung** f oil-fired central heating; **ö~ig** a oily.
oliv [o'li:f] a olive-green; **O~e** [o'li:və] f -, -n olive.
Öl- zW: **~meßstab** m dipstick; **~sardine** f sardine; **~standanzeiger** m (AUT) oil gauge; **~ung** f lubrication; oiling; (ECCL) anointment; die Letzte ~ung Extreme Unction; **~wechsel** m oil change; **~zeug** nt oilskins pl.
Olymp- [o'lɪmp] zW: **~iade** [-i'a:də] f Olympic Games pl; **~iasieger(in f)** [-iazi:gər(ɪn)] m (Sport) Olympic champion; **~iateilnehmer(in f)** m Olympic competitor; **o~isch** a Olympic.
Oma ['o:ma] f -, -s (umg) granny.
Omelett [ɔm(ə)'lɛt] nt -(e)s, -s omelet(te).
Omen ['o:mɛn] nt -s, - omen.
Omnibus ['ɔmnibʊs] m (omni)bus.
Onanie [ona'ni:] f masturbation; **o~ren** vi masturbate.
Onkel ['ɔŋkəl] m -s, - uncle.

Opa [ˈoːpa] *m* -s, -s (*umg*) grandpa.
Opal [oˈpaːl] *m* -s, -e opal.
Oper [ˈoːpər] *f* -, -n opera; opera house.
Operation [operatsiˈoːn] *f* operation; **Operationssaal** *m* operating theatre.
Operette [opeˈrɛtə] *f* operetta.
operieren [opeˈriːrən] *vti* operate.
Opern- *zW*: **~glas** *nt* opera glasses *pl*; **~haus** *nt* opera house; **~sänger(in** *f*) *m* operatic singer.
Opfer [ˈɔpfər] *nt* -s, - sacrifice; (*Mensch*) victim; **o~n** *vt* sacrifice; **~stock** *m* (*ECCL*) offertory box; **~ung** *f* sacrifice.
Opium [ˈoːpiʊm] *nt* -s opium.
opponieren [ɔpoˈniːrən] *vi* oppose (*gegen jdn/etw* sb/sth).
opportun [ɔpɔrˈtuːn] *a* opportune; **O~ist** [-ˈnɪst] *m* opportunist.
Opposition [ɔpozitsiˈoːn] *f* opposition; **o~ell** [-ˈnɛl] *a* opposing.
Optik [ˈɔptɪk] *f* optics *sing*; **~er** *m* -s, - optician.
optimal [ɔptiˈmaːl] *a* optimal, optimum.
Optimismus [ɔptiˈmɪsmʊs] *m* optimism.
Optimist [ɔptiˈmɪst] *m* optimist; **o~isch** *a* optimistic.
optisch [ˈɔptɪʃ] *a* optical.
Orakel [oˈraːkəl] *nt* -s, - oracle.
Orange [oˈrãːʒə] *f* -, -n orange; **o~** *a* orange; **Orangeade** [orãˈʒaːdə] *f* orangeade; **Orangeat** [orãˈʒaːt] *nt* -s, -e candied peel; **Orangensaft** *m* orange juice.
Orchester [ɔrˈkɛstər] *nt* -s, - orchestra.
Orchidee [ɔrçiˈdeːə] *f* -, -n orchid.
Orden [ˈɔrdən] *m* -s, - (*ECCL*) order; (*MIL*) decoration; **Ordensschwester** *f* nun.
ordentlich [ˈɔrdəntlɪç] *a* (*anständig*) decent, respectable; (*geordnet*) tidy, neat; (*umg*: *annehmbar*) not bad; (*umg*: *tüchtig*) real, proper; **~er Professor** (full) professor // *ad* properly; **O~keit** *f* respectability; tidiness, neatness.
ordinär [ɔrdiˈnɛːr] *a* common, vulgar.
ordnen [ˈɔrdnən] *vt* order, put in order.
Ordner *m* -s, - steward; (*COMM*) file.
Ordnung *f* order; (*Ordnen*) ordering; (*Geordnetsein*) tidiness; **~ machen** tidy up; **in ~**! okay.
Ordnungs- *zW*: **o~gemäß** *a* proper, according to the rules; **o~halber** *ad* as a matter of form; **~strafe** *f* fine; **o~widrig** *a* contrary to the rules, irregular; **~zahl** *f* ordinal number.
Organ [ɔrˈgaːn] *nt* -s, -e organ; (*Stimme*) voice; **~isation** [-izatsiˈoːn] *f* organisation; **~isator** [-iˈzaːtɔr] *m*

organizer; **o~isch** *a* organic; **o~isieren** [-iˈziːrən] *vt* organize, arrange; (*umg*: *beschaffen*) acquire // *vr* organize; **~ismus** [-ˈnɪsmʊs] *m* organism; **~ist** [-ˈnɪst] *m* organist.
Orgasmus [ɔrˈgasmʊs] *m* orgasm.
Orgel [ˈɔrgəl] *f* -, -n organ.
Orgie [ˈɔrgiə] *f* orgy.
Orient [ˈoːriɛnt] *m* -s Orient, east; **~ale** [-ˈtaːlə] *m* -n, -n Oriental; **o~alisch** [-ˈtaːlɪʃ] *a* oriental; **o~ieren** [-ˈtiːrən] *vt* (*örtlich*) locate; (*fig*) inform // *vr* find one's way *od* bearings; inform oneself; **~ierung** [-ˈtiːrʊŋ] *f* orientation; (*fig*) information; **~ierungssinn** *m* sense of direction.
original [origiˈnaːl] *a* original; **O~** *nt* -s, -e original; **O~fassung** *f* original version; **O~i'tät** *f* originality.
originell [origiˈnɛl] *a* original.
Orkan [ɔrˈkaːn] *m* -(e)s, -e hurricane.
Ornament [ɔrnaˈmɛnt] *nt* decoration, ornament; **o~al** [-ˈtaːl] *a* decorative, ornamental.
Ort [ɔrt] *m* -(e)s, -e *od* ̈er place; **an ~ und Stelle** on the spot; **o~en** *vt* locate.
ortho- [ɔrto] *zW*: **~dox** [-ˈdɔks] *a* orthodox; **O~graphie** [-graˈfiː] *f* spelling, orthography; **~'graphisch** *a* orthographic; **O~päde** [-ˈpɛːdə] *m* -n, -n orthopaedic specialist, orthopaedist; **O~pädie** [-pɛˈdiː] *f* orthopaedics *sing*; **~'pädisch** *a* orthopaedic.
örtlich [ˈœrtlɪç] *a* local; **Ö~keit** *f* locality.
Ortschaft *f* village, small town.
Orts- *zW*: **o~fremd** *a* non-local; **~gespräch** *nt* local (phone) call; **~name** *m* place-name; **~netz** *nt* (*TEL*) local telephone exchange area; **~zeit** *f* local time.
Ortung *f* locating.
Öse [ˈøːzə] *f* -, -n loop, eye.
Ost- [ɔst] *zW*: **~'asien** *nt* Eastern Asia; **~block** *m* (*POL*) Eastern bloc; **~en** *m* -s east; **~'ende** *nt* Ostend.
Oster- [ˈoːstər] *zW*: **~ei** *nt* Easter egg; **~fest** *nt* Easter; **~glocke** *f* daffodil; **~hase** *m* Easter bunny; **~montag** *m* Easter Monday; **~n** *nt* -s, - Easter.
Österreich [ˈøːstərraɪç] *nt* -s Austria; **~er(in** *f*) *m* -s, - Austrian; **ö~isch** *a* Austrian.
Ostersonntag *m* Easter Day *od* Sunday.
östlich [ˈœstlɪç] *a* eastern, easterly.
Ost- *zW*: **~see** *f* Baltic Sea; **o~wärts** *ad* eastwards; **~wind** *m* east wind.
Otter [ˈɔtər] *m* -s, - otter // *f* -, -n (*Schlange*) adder.
Ouvertüre [uvɛrˈtyːrə] *f* -, -n overture.
oval [oˈvaːl] *a* oval.
Ovation [ovatsiˈoːn] *f* ovation.

Ovulation [ovulatsi'o:n] f ovulation.
Oxyd [ɔ'ksy:t] nt -(e)s, -e oxide; **o~ieren** [ɔksy'di:rən] vti oxidize; **~ierung** f oxidization.
Ozean ['o:tsea:n] m -s, -e ocean; **~dampfer** m (ocean-going) liner.
Ozon [o'tso:n] nt -s ozone.

P

P, p [pe:] nt P, p.
Paar [pa:r] nt -(e)s, -e pair; (Ehe~) couple; **ein p~** a few; **p~en** vtr couple; (Tiere) mate; **~lauf** m pair skating; **p~mal** ad: **ein p~mal** a few times; **~ung** f combination; mating; **p~weise** ad in pairs; in couples.
Pacht [paxt] f -, -en lease; **p~en** vt lease.
Pächter ['pɛçtər] m -s, - leaseholder, tenant.
Pack [pak] m -(e)s, -e od ⁻e bundle, pack // nt -(e)s (pej) mob, rabble.
Päckchen ['pɛkçən] nt small package; (Zigaretten) packet; (Post~) small parcel.
Pack- zW: **p~en** vt pack; (fassen) grasp, seize; (umg: schaffen) manage; (fig: fesseln) grip; **~en m** -s, - bundle; (fig: Menge) heaps of; **~esel** m (lit, fig) packhorse; **~papier** nt brown paper, wrapping paper; **~ung** f packet; (Pralinen~) box; (MED) compress.
Pädagog- [pɛda'go:g] zW: **~e m** -n, -n teacher; **~ik** f education; **p~isch** a educational, pedagogical.
Paddel ['padəl] nt -s, - paddle; **~boot** nt canoe; **p~n** vi paddle.
Page ['pa:ʒə] m -n, -n page; **Pagenkopf** m pageboy.
Paket [pa'ke:t] nt -(e)s, -e packet; (Post~) parcel; **~karte** f dispatch note; **~post** f parcel post; **~schalter** m parcels counter.
Pakt [pakt] m -(e)s, -e pact.
Palast [pa'last] m -es, **Paläste** palace.
Palästin- [pales'ti:n] zW: **~a** nt -s Palestine; **~enser(in** f) [palesti-'nɛnzər(ɪn)] m -s, - Palestinian; **p~ensisch** a Palestinian.
Palme ['palmə] f -, -n palm (tree).
Palmsonntag m Palm Sunday.
Pampelmuse ['pampəlmu:zə] f -, -n grapefruit.
pampig ['pampɪç] a (umg: frech) fresh.
panieren [pa'ni:rən] vt (KOCH) bread.
Paniermehl [pa'ni:rme:l] nt breadcrumbs pl.
Panik ['pa:nɪk] f panic.
panisch ['pa:nɪʃ] a panic-stricken.
Panne ['panə] f -, -n (AUT etc) breakdown; (Mißgeschick) slip; **Pannen-**

hilfe f breakdown service.
panschen ['panʃən] vi splash about // vt water down.
Panther ['pantər] m -s, - panther.
Pantoffel [pan'tɔfəl] m -s, -n slipper; **~held** m (umg) henpecked husband.
Pantomime [panto'mi:mə] f -, -n mime.
Panzer ['pantsər] m -s, - armour; (Platte) armour plate; (Fahrzeug) tank; **~glas** nt bulletproof glass; **p~n** vtr armour; (fig) arm o.s.
Papa [pa'pa:] m -s, -s (umg) dad, daddy.
Papagei [papa'gai] m -s, -en parrot.
Papier [pa'pi:r] nt -s, -e paper; (Wert~) share; **~fabrik** f paper mill; **~geld** nt paper money; **~korb** m wastepaper basket; **~tüte** f paper bag.
Papp- [pap] zW: **~deckel** m, **~e** f -, -n cardboard; **Pappel** f -, -n poplar; **p~en** vti (umg) stick; **p~ig** a sticky; **~maché** [-ma'ʃe:] nt -s, -s papiermâché.
Paprika ['paprika] m -s, -s (Gewürz) paprika; (~schote) pepper.
Papst [pa:pst] m -(e)s, ⁻e pope.
päpstlich ['pɛ:pstlɪç] a papal.
Parabel [pa'ra:bəl] f -, -n parable; (MATH) parabola.
Parade [pa'ra:də] f (MIL) parade, review; (SPORT) parry; **~marsch** m march-past; **~schritt** m goose-step.
Paradies [para'di:s] nt -es, -e paradise; **p~isch** a heavenly.
paradox [para'dɔks] a paradoxical; **P~** nt -es, -e paradox.
Paragraph [para'gra:f] m -en, -en paragraph; (JUR) section.
parallel [para'le:l] a parallel; **P~e** f parallel.
Paranuß ['pa:ranus] f Brazil nut.
Parasit [para'zi:t] m -en, -en (lit, fig) parasite.
parat [pa'ra:t] a ready.
Pärchen ['pɛ:rçən] nt couple.
Parfüm [par'fy:m] nt -s, -s od -e perfume; **~erie** [-ə'ri:] f perfumery; **~flasche** f scent bottle; **p~ieren** [-'mi:rən] vt scent, perfume.
parieren [pa'ri:rən] vt parry // vi (umg) obey.
Paris [pa'ri:s] nt - Paris; **~er(in** f) m Parisian // a Parisian.
Park [park] m -s, -s park; **~anlage** f park; (um Gebäude) grounds pl; **p~en** vti park; **Parkett** [par'kɛt] nt -(e)s, -e parquet (floor); (THEAT) stalls pl; **~haus** nt multi-storey car park; **~lücke** f parking space; **~platz** m parking place; car park, parking lot (US); **~scheibe** f parking disc; **~uhr** f parking meter; **~verbot** nt no parking.

Parlament [parla'mɛnt] *nt* parliament; **~arier** [-'ta:riər] *m* -s, - parliamentarian; **p~arisch** [-'ta:rɪʃ] *a* parliamentary.

Parlaments- *zW*: **~beschluß** *m* vote of parliament; **~mitglied** *nt* member of parliament; **~sitzung** *f* sitting (of parliament).

Parodie [paro'di:] *f* parody; **p~ren** *vt* parody.

Parole [pa'ro:lə] *f* -, -n password; (*Wahlspruch*) motto.

Partei [par'tai] *f* party; **~ ergreifen für jdn** take sb's side; **p~isch** *a* partial, biased; **~nahme** *f* -, -n support, taking the part of; **~tag** *m* party conference.

Parterre [par'tɛr(ə)] *nt* -s, -s ground floor; (*THEAT*) stalls *pl.*

Partie [par'ti:] *f* part; (*Spiel*) game; (*Ausflug*) outing; (*Mann, Frau*) catch; (*COMM*) lot; **mit von der ~ sein** join in.

Partisan [parti'za:n] *m* -s *od* -en, -en partisan.

Partitur [parti'tu:r] *f* (*MUS*) score.

Partizip [parti'tsi:p] *nt* -s, -ien participle.

Partner(in *f*) ['partnər(ɪn)] *m* -s, - partner; **p~schaftlich** *a* as partners.

Party ['pa:rti] *f* -, -s *od* **Parties** party.

Paß [pas] *m* -sses, ¨sse pass; (*Ausweis*) passport.

Pass- *zW*: **p~abel** [pa'sa:bəl] *a* passable, reasonable; **~age** [pa'sa:ʒə] *f* -, -n passage; **~agier** [pasa'ʒi:r] *m* -s, -e passenger; **~agierflugzeug** *nt* airliner; **~ant** [pa'sant] *m* passer-by.

Paßamt *nt* passport office.

Paßbild *nt* passport photograph.

passen ['pasən] *vi* fit; (*Farbe*) go (*zu* with); (*auf Frage, KARTEN, SPORT*) pass; **das paßt mir nicht** that doesn't suit me; **er paßt nicht zu dir** he's not right for you; **~d** *a* suitable; (*zusammen~d*) matching; (*angebracht*) fitting; (*Zeit*) convenient.

passier- [pa'si:r] *zW*: **~bar** *a* passable; **~en** *vt* pass; (*durch Sieb*) strain // *vi* happen; **P~schein** *m* pass, permit.

Passion [pasi'o:n] *f* passion; **p~iert** [-'ni:rt] *a* enthusiastic, passionate; **Passionsspiel** *nt* Passion Play.

passiv ['pasi:f] *a* passive; **P~** *nt* -s, -e passive; **Passiva** *pl* (*COMM*) liabilities *pl*; **P~ität** *f* passiveness.

Paß- *zW*: **~kontrolle** *f* passport control; **~stelle** *f* passport office; **~straße** *f* (mountain) pass.

Paste ['pastə] *f* -, -n paste.

Pastell [pas'tɛl] *nt* -(e)s, -e pastel.

Pastete [pas'te:tə] *f* -, -n pie.

pasteurisieren [pastøri'zi:rən] *vt* pasteurize.

Pastor ['pastɔr] *m* vicar; pastor, minister.

Pate ['pa:tə] *m* -n, -n godfather; **Patenkind** *nt* godchild.

Patent [pa'tɛnt] *nt* -(e)s, -e patent; (*MIL*) commission; **p~** *a* clever; **~amt** *nt* patent office; **p~ieren** [-'ti:rən] *vt* patent; **~inhaber** *m* patentee.

Pater ['pa:tər] *m* -s, - *od* **Patres** (*ECCL*) Father.

pathetisch [pa'te:tɪʃ] *a* emotional; bombastic.

Pathologe [pato'lo:gə] *m* -n, -n pathologist.

pathologisch *a* pathological.

Pathos ['pa:tɔs] *nt* - emotiveness, emotionalism.

Patient(in *f*) [patsi'ɛnt(ɪn)] *m* patient.

Patin ['pa:tɪn] *f* godmother.

Patina ['pa:tina] *f* - patina.

Patriot [patri'o:t] *m* -en, -en patriot; **p~isch** *a* patriotic; **~ismus** [-'tɪsmʊs] *m* patriotism.

Patrone [pa'tro:nə] *f* -, -n cartridge.

patrouillieren [patrʊl'ji:rən] *vi* patrol.

patsch [patʃ] *interj* splash; **P~e** *f* -, -n (*umg: Bedrängnis*) mess, jam; **~en** *vti* smack, slap; (*im Wasser*) splash; **~naß** *a* soaking wet.

patzig ['patsɪç] *a* (*umg*) cheeky, saucy.

Pauke ['paʊkə] *f* -, -n kettledrum; **auf die ~ hauen** live it up.

pausbäckig ['paʊsbɛkɪç] *a* chubbycheeked.

pauschal [paʊ'ʃa:l] *a* (*Kosten*) inclusive; (*Urteil*) sweeping; **P~e** *f* -, -n, **P~gebühr** *f* flat rate; **P~preis** *m* all-in price; **P~reise** *f* package tour; **P~summe** *f* lump sum.

Pause ['paʊzə] *f* -, -n break; (*THEAT*) interval; (*Innehalten*) pause; (*Kopie*) tracing.

pausen *vt* trace; **~los** *a* non-stop; **P~zeichen** *nt* call sign; (*MUS*) rest.

Pauspapier ['paʊspapi:r] *nt* tracing paper.

Pavian ['pa:via:n] *m* -s, -e baboon.

Pazif- [pa'tsi:f] *zW*: **~ik** *m* ~s Pacific; **p~isch** *a*: **P~ischer Ozean** Pacific; **~ist** [patsi'fɪst] *m* pacifist; **p~istisch** *a* pacifist.

Pech ['pɛç] *nt* -s, -e pitch; (*fig*) bad luck; **~ haben** be unlucky; **p~schwarz** *a* pitch-black; **~strähne** *m* (*umg*) unlucky patch; **~vogel** *m* (*umg*) unlucky person.

Pedal [pe'da:l] *nt* -s, -e pedal.

Pedant [pe'dant] *m* pedant; **~e'rie** *f* pedantry; **p~isch** *a* pedantic.

Pegel ['pe:gəl] *m* -s, - water gauge; **~stand** *m* water level.

peilen ['pailən] *vt* get a fix on.

Pein [pain] *f* - agony, pain; **p~igen** *vt*

torture; (*plagen*) torment; **p~lich** *a* (*unangenehm*) embarrassing, awkward, painful; (*genau*) painstaking; **P~lichkeit** *f* painfulness, awkwardness; scrupulousness.

Peitsche ['paitʃə] *f* -, -n whip; **p~n** *vt* whip; (*Regen*) lash.

Pelikan ['pe:lika:n] *m* -s, -e pelican.

Pelle ['pɛlə] *f* -, -n skin; **p~n** *vt* skin, peel.

Pellkartoffeln *pl* jacket potatoes *pl*.

Pelz [pɛlts] *m* -es, -e fur.

Pendel ['pɛndəl] *nt* -s, - pendulum; **~verkehr** *m* shuttle traffic; (*für Pendler*) commuter traffic.

Pendler ['pɛndlər] *m* -s, - commuter.

penetrant [pene'trant] *a* sharp; (*Person*) pushing.

Penis ['pe:nɪs] *m* -, -se penis.

pennen ['pɛnən] *vi* (*umg*) kip.

Pension [penzi'o:n] *f* (*Geld*) pension; (*Ruhestand*) retirement; (*für Gäste*) boarding *od* guest-house; **~är(in** *f*) [-'nɛr(ɪn)] *m* -s, -e pensioner; **~at** [-'na:t] *nt* -(e)s, -e boarding school; **p~ieren** [-'ni:rən] *vt* pension (off); **p~iert** *a* retired; **~ierung** *f* retirement; **Pensionsgast** *m* boarder, paying guest.

Pensum ['pɛnzʊm] *nt* -s, **Pensen** quota; (*SCH*) curriculum.

per [pɛr] *präp* +*akk* by, per; (*pro*) per; (*bis*) by.

Perfekt ['pɛrfɛkt] *nt* -(e)s, -e perfect; **p~** [pɛr'fɛkt] *a* perfect; **~ionismus** [pɛrfɛktsio'nɪsmʊs] *m* perfectionism.

perforieren [pɛrfo'ri:rən] *vt* perforate.

Pergament [pɛrga'mɛnt] *nt* parchment; **~papier** *nt* greaseproof paper.

Periode [peri'o:də] *f* -, -n period;

periodisch [peri'o:dɪʃ] *a* periodic; (*dezimal*) recurring.

peripher [peri'fe:r] *a* peripheral; **~es** Gerät peripheral.

Perle ['pɛrlə] *f* -, -n (*lit, fig*) pearl; **p~n** *vi* sparkle; (*Tropfen*) trickle.

Perlmutt ['pɛrlmʊt] *nt* -s mother-of-pearl.

perplex [pɛr'plɛks] *a* dumbfounded.

Pers- ['pɛrz] *zW:* **~er(in** *f*) *m* **s-,** - Persian; **~i'aner** *m* -s, - Persian lamb; **~ien** [-iən] *nt* -s Persia; **p~isch** *a* Persian.

Person [pɛr'zo:n] *f* -, -en person; **ich für meine ~** personally I.

Personal [pɛrzo'na:l] *nt* -s personnel; (*Bedienung*) servants *pl*; **~ausweis** *m* identity card; **~computer** *m* personal computer, PC; **~ien** [iən] *pl* particulars *pl*; **~i'tät** *f* personality; **~mangel** *m* undermanning; **~pronomen** *nt* personal pronoun.

Personen- *zW:* **~aufzug** *m* lift, elevator (*US*); **~gesellschaft** *f* partnership; **~kraftwagen** *m* private motor-

car; **~schaden** *m* injury to persons; **~zug** *m* stopping train; passenger train.

personifizieren [pɛrzonifi'tsi:rən] *vt* personify.

persönlich [pɛr'zø:nlɪç] *a* personal // *ad* in person; personally; **P~keit** *f* personality.

Perspektive [pɛrspɛk'ti:və] *f* perspective.

Perücke [pe'rʏkə] *f* -, -n wig.

pervers [pɛr'vɛrs] *a* perverse; **P~i'tät** *f* perversity.

Pessimismus [pɛsi'mɪsmʊs] *m* pessimism.

Pessimist [pɛsi'mɪst] *m* pessimist; **p~isch** *a* pessimistic.

Pest [pɛst] *f* - plague.

Petersilie [petər'zi:liə] *f* parsley.

Petroleum [pe'tro:leʊm] *nt* -s paraffin, kerosene (*US*).

Pfad [pfa:t] *m* -(e)s, -e path; **~finder** *m* -s, - boy scout; **~finderin** *f* girl guide.

Pfahl [pfa:l] *m* -(e)s, ~e post, stake.

Pfand [pfant] *nt* -(e)s, ~er pledge, security; (*Flaschen~*) deposit; (*im Spiel*) forfeit; **~brief** *m* bond.

pfänden ['pfɛndən] *vt* seize, distrain.

Pfänderspiel *nt* game of forfeits.

Pfandhaus *nt* pawnshop.

Pfandschein *m* pawn ticket.

Pfändung ['pfɛndʊŋ] *f* seizure, distraint.

Pfanne ['pfanə] *f* -, -n (frying) pan.

Pfannkuchen *m* pancake; (*Berliner*) doughnut.

Pfarr- ['pfar] *zW:* **~ei** [-'rai] *f* parish; **~er** *m* -s, - priest; (*evangelisch*) vicar; minister; **~haus** *nt* vicarage; manse.

Pfau [pfaʊ] *m* -(e)s, -en peacock; **~enauge** *nt* peacock butterfly.

Pfeffer ['pfɛfər] *m* -s, - pepper; **~korn** *nt* peppercorn; **~kuchen** *m* gingerbread; **~minz** *nt* -es, -e peppermint; **~mühle** *f* pepper-mill; **p~n** *vt* pepper; (*umg: werfen*) fling; **gepfefferte Preise/Witze** steep prices/ spicy jokes.

Pfeife ['pfaifə] *f* -, -n whistle; (*Tabak~, Orgel~*) pipe; **p~n** *vti unreg* whistle; **~r** *m* -s, - piper.

Pfeil [pfail] *m* -(e)s, -e arrow.

Pfeiler ['pfailər] *m* -s, - pillar, prop; (*Brücken~*) pier.

Pfennig ['pfɛnɪç] *m* -(e)s, -e pfennig (*hundredth part of a mark*).

Pferd [pfe:rt] *nt* -(e)s, -e horse.

Pferde- ['pfe:rdə] *zW:* **~rennen** *nt* horse-race; horse-racing; **~schwanz** *m* (*Frisur*) ponytail; **~stall** *m* stable.

Pfiff [pfɪf] *m* -(e)s, -e whistle.

Pfifferling ['pfɪfərlɪŋ] *m* yellow chanterelle (*mushroom*); **keinen ~ wert**

not worth a thing.
pfiffig *a* sly, sharp.
Pfingsten ['pfɪŋstən] *nt* -, - Whitsun.
Pfingstrose ['pfɪŋstroːzə] *f* peony.
Pfirsich ['pfɪrzɪç] *m* -s, -e peach.
Pflanz- ['pflants] *zW:* **~e** *f* -, -n plant; **p~en** *vt* plant; **~enfett** *nt* vegetable fat; **p~lich** *a* vegetable; **~ung** *f* plantation.
Pflaster ['pflastər] *nt* -s, - plaster; (*Straße*) pavement; **p~n** *vt* pave; **~stein** *m* paving stone.
Pflaume ['pflaumə] *f* -, -n plum.
Pflege ['pfleːgə] *f* -, -n care; (*von Idee*) cultivation; (*Kranken~*) nursing; **in ~ sein** (*Kind*) be fostered out; **p~bedürftig** *a* needing care; **~eltern** *pl* foster parents *pl*; **~kind** *nt* foster child; **p~leicht** *a* easy-care; **~mutter** *f* foster mother; **p~n** *vt* look after; (*Kranke*) nurse; (*Beziehungen*) foster; **~r** *m* -s, - orderly; male nurse; **~rin** *f* nurse, attendant; **~vater** *m* foster father.
Pflicht [pflɪçt] *f* -, -en duty; (*SPORT*) compulsory section; **p~bewußt** *a* conscientious; **~fach** *nt* (*SCH*) compulsory subject; **~gefühl** *nt* sense of duty; **p~gemäß** *a* dutiful // *ad* as in duty bound; **~versicherung** *f* compulsory insurance.
pflücken ['pflʏkən] *vt* pick; (*Blumen auch*) pluck.
Pflug [pfluːk] *m* -(e)s, ⁻e plough.
pflügen ['pflyːgən] *vt* plough.
Pforte ['pfɔrtə] *f* -, -n gate; door.
Pförtner ['pfœrtnər] *m* -s, - porter, doorkeeper, doorman.
Pfosten ['pfɔstən] *m* -s, - post.
Pfote ['pfoːtə] *f* -, -n paw; (*umg: Schrift*) scrawl.
Pfropfen ['pfrɔpfən] *m* -s, - (*Flaschen~*) stopper; (*Blut~*) clot; **p~** *vt* (*stopfen*) cram; (*Baum*) graft.
pfui [pfʊi] *interj* ugh.
Pfund [pfʊnt] *nt* -(e)s, -e pound; **p~ig** *a* (*umg*) great.
pfuschen ['pfʊʃən] *vi* (*umg*) be sloppy; **jdm in etw** (*akk*) **~** interfere in sth.
Pfuscher ['pfʊʃər] *m* -s, - (*umg*) sloppy worker; (*Kur~*) quack; **~ei** [-'raɪ] *f* (*umg*) sloppy work; (*Kur~*) quackery.
Pfütze ['pfʏtsə] *f* -, -n puddle.
Phänomen [fɛno'meːn] *nt* -s, -e phenomenon; **p~al** [-'naːl] *a* phenomenal.
Phantasie [fanta'ziː] *f* imagination; **p~los** *a* unimaginative; **p~ren** *vi* fantasize; **p~voll** *a* imaginative.
phantastisch [fan'tastɪʃ] *a* fantastic.
Pharmazeut(in *f)* [farma'tsɔʏt(ɪn)] *m* -en, -en pharmacist.
Phase ['faːzə] *f* -, -n phase.
Philippinen [fɪlɪ'piːnən] *pl* Philippines.

Philologe [filo'loːgə] *m* -n, -n philologist.
Philologie [filolo'giː] *f* philology.
Philosoph [filo'zoːf] *m* -en, -en philosopher; **~ie** [-'fiː] *f* philosophy; **p~isch** *a* philosophical.
Phlegma ['flɛgma] *nt* -s lethargy; **p~tisch** [flɛ'gmaːtɪʃ] *a* lethargic.
Phonet- [fo'neːt] *zW:* **~ik** *f* phonetics *sing;* **p~isch** *a* phonetic.
Phosphor ['fɔsfor] *m* -s phosphorus.
Photo ['foːto] *nt* -s, -s *etc siehe* **Foto**.
Phrase ['fraːzə] *f* -, -n phrase; (*pej*) hollow phrase.
Physik [fy'ziːk] *f* physics *sing;* **p~alisch** [-'kaːlɪʃ] *a* of physics; **~er(in** *f)* ['fyːzikər(ɪn)] *m* -s, - physicist.
Physiologe [fyzio'loːgə] *m* -n, -n physiologist.
Physiologie [fyziolo'giː] *f* physiology.
physisch ['fyːzɪʃ] *a* physical.
Pianist(in *f)* [pia'nɪst(ɪn)] *m* pianist.
Pickel ['pɪkəl] *m* -s, - pimple; (*Werkzeug*) pickaxe; (*Berg~*) ice-axe; **p~ig** *a* pimply.
picken ['pɪkən] *vi* pick, peck.
Picknick ['pɪknɪk] *nt* -s, -e *od* -s picnic; **~ machen** have a picnic.
piepen ['piːpən], **piepsen** ['piːpsən] *vi* chirp.
Pietät [pie'tɛːt] *f* piety, reverence; **p~los** *a* impious, irreverent.
Pigment [pɪ'gmɛnt] *nt* pigment.
Pik [piːk] *nt* -s, -s (*KARTEN*) spades; **p~ant** [pi'kant] *a* spicy, piquant; (*anzüglich*) suggestive.
Pilger ['pɪlgər] *m* -s, - pilgrim; **~fahrt** *f* pilgrimage.
Pille ['pɪlə] *f* -, -n pill.
Pilot [pi'loːt] *m* -en, -en pilot.
Pils [pɪls] *nt* -, - lager.
Pilz [pɪlts] *m* -es, -e fungus; (*eßbar*) mushroom; (*giftig*) toadstool; **~krankheit** *f* fungal disease.
pingelig ['pɪŋəlɪç] *a* (*umg*) fussy.
Pinguin ['pɪŋguiːn] *m* -s, -e penguin.
Pinie ['piːniə] *f* pine.
pinkeln ['pɪŋkəln] *vi* (*umg*) pee.
Pinsel ['pɪnzəl] *m* -s, - paintbrush.
Pinzette [pɪn'tsɛtə] *f* tweezers *pl*.
Pionier [pio'niːr] *m* -s, -e pioneer; (*MIL*) sapper, engineer.
Pirat [pi'raːt] *m* -en, -en pirate; **~ensender** *m* pirate radio station.
Piste ['pɪstə] *f* -, -n (*SKI*) run, piste; (*AVIAT*) runway.
Pistole [pɪs'toːlə] *f* -, -n pistol.
Pizza ['pɪtsa] *f* -, -s pizza.
Pkw [peːkaː'veː] *m* -(s), -(s) *abk von* **Personenkraftwagen**.
plädieren [plɛ'diːrən] *vi* plead.
Plädoyer [plɛdoa'jeː] *nt* -s, -s speech for the defence; (*fig*) plea.
Plage ['plaːgə] *f* -, -n plague; (*Mühe*)

nuisance; **~geist** m pest, nuisance; **p~n** vt torment // vr toil, slave.

Plakat [pla'ka:t] nt -(e)s, -e placard; poster.

Plan [pla:n] -(e)s, ¨-e plan; (Karte) map; **~e** f -, -n tarpaulin; **p~en** vt plan; (Mord etc) plot; **~er** m -s, - planner; **Planet** [pla'ne:t] m -en -en planet; **p~gemäß** a according to schedule or plan; (EISENB) on time; **p~ieren** [pla'ni:rən] vt plane, level.

Planke ['plankə] f -, -n plank.

planlos a (Vorgehen) unsystematic; (Umherlaufen) aimless.

planmäßig a according to plan; systematic; (EISENB) scheduled.

Plansch- ['planʃ] zW: **~becken** nt paddling pool; **p~en** vi splash.

Plansoll nt -s output target.

Planstelle f post.

Plantage [plan'ta:ʒə] f -, -n plantation.

Planung f planning.

Planwirtschaft f planned economy.

plappern ['plapərn] vi chatter.

plärren ['plɛrən] vi (Mensch) cry, whine; (Radio) blare.

Plasma ['plasma] nt -s, **Plasmen** plasma.

Plastik ['plastık] f sculpture // nt -s (Kunststoff) plastic; **~folie** f plastic film.

plastisch ['plastıʃ] a plastic; stell dir das ~ vor! just picture it!

Platane [pla'ta:nə] f -, -n plane (tree).

Platin ['pla:tin] nt -s platinum.

Platitüde [plati'ty:də] f -, -n platitude.

platonisch [pla'to:nıʃ] a platonic.

platsch [platʃ] interj splash; **~en** vi splash; **~naß** a drenched.

plätschern ['plɛtʃərn] vi babble.

platt [plat] a flat; (umg: überrascht) flabbergasted; (fig: geistlos) flat, boring; **~deutsch** a low German; **P~e** f -, -n (Speisen~, PHOT, TECH) plate; (Stein~) flag; (Kachel) tile; (Schall~) record; **P~enspieler** m record player; **P~enteller** m turntable; **P~fuß** m flat foot.

Platz [plats] m -es, ¨-e place; (Sitz~) seat; (Raum) space, room; (in Stadt) square; (SPORT~) playing field; ~ nehmen take a seat; jdm ~ machen make room for sb; **~angst** f (MED) agoraphobia; (umg) claustrophobia; **~anweiser(in** f) m -s, - usher(ette).

Plätzchen ['plɛtsçən] nt spot; (Gebäck) biscuit.

Platz- zW: **p~en** vi burst; (Bombe) explode; vor Wut **p~en** (umg) be bursting with anger; **~karte** f seat reservation; **~mangel** m lack of space; **~patrone** f blank cartridge; **~regen** m downpour; **~wunde** f cut.

Plauderei [plaudə'raı] f chat, conversation; (RAD) talk.

plaudern ['plaudərn] vi chat, talk.

plausibel [plau'zi:bəl] a plausible.

plazieren [pla'tsi:rən] vt place // (SPORT) be placed; (Tennis) be seeded.

pleite ['plaıtə] a (umg) broke; **P~** f -, -n bankruptcy; (umg: Reinfall) flop; **P~ machen** go bust.

Plenum ['ple:num] nt -s plenum.

Plombe ['plombə] f -, -n lead seal; (Zahn~) filling.

plombieren [plom'bi:rən] vt seal; (Zahn) fill.

plötzlich ['plœtslıç] a sudden // ad suddenly.

plump [plump] a clumsy; (Hände) coarse; (Körper) shapeless; **~sen** vi (umg) plump down, fall.

Plunder ['plundər] m -s rubbish.

plündern ['plyndərn] vti plunder; (Stadt) sack.

Plünderung ['plyndəruŋ] f plundering, sack, pillage.

Plural ['plu:ra:l] m -s, -e plural; **p~istisch** [plura'lıstıʃ] a pluralistic.

Plus [plus] nt -, - plus; (FIN) profit; (Vorteil) advantage; **p~** ad plus.

Plüsch [ply:ʃ] m -(e)s, -e plush.

Plus- zW: **~pol** m (ELEK) positive pole; **~punkt** m point; (fig) point in sb's favour.

PLZ abk von **Postleitzahl**.

Po [po:] m -s, -s (umg) bottom, bum.

Pöbel ['pø:bəl] m -s mob, rabble; **~ei** [-'laı] f vulgarity; **p~haft** a low, vulgar.

pochen ['poxən] vi knock; (Herz) pound; auf etw (akk) ~ (fig) insist on sth.

Pocken ['pokən] pl smallpox.

Podium ['po:dium] nt podium; **Podiumsdiskussion** f panel discussion.

Poesie [poe'zi:] f poetry.

Poet [po'e:t] m -en, -en poet; **p~isch** a poetic.

Pointe [po'ɛ̃:tə] f -, -n point.

Pokal [po'ka:l] m -s, -e goblet; (SPORT) cup; **~spiel** nt cup-tie.

Pökel- ['pø:kəl] zW: **~fleisch** nt salt meat; **p~n** vt pickle, salt.

Pol [po:l] m -s, -e pole; **p~ar** [po'la:r] a polar; **~arkreis** m arctic circle; **~e** m -n, -n, **~in** f Pole; **~en** nt -s Poland.

polemisch [po'le:mıʃ] a polemical.

Police [po'li:s(ə)] f -, -n insurance policy.

Polier [po'li:r] m -s, -e foreman; **p~en** vt polish.

Poliklinik ['po:likli:nık] f outpatients.

Politik [poli'ti:k] f politics sing; (eine bestimmte) policy; **~er(in** f) [po'li:tikər(ın)] m -s, - politician.

politisch [po'li:tɪʃ] a political.
Politur [poli'tu:r] f polish.
Polizei [poli'tsai] f police; **~beamte(r)** m police officer; **p~lich** a police; **sich p~lich melden** register with the police; **~revier** nt police station; **~staat** m police state; **~streife** f police patrol; **~stunde** f closing time; **~wache** f = **~revier**.
Polizist [poli'tsɪst] m **-en, -en** policeman; **~in** f policewoman.
Pollen ['pɔlən] m **-s, -** pollen.
polnisch ['pɔlnɪʃ] a Polish.
Polster ['pɔlstər] nt **-s, -** cushion; (Polsterung) upholstery; (in Kleidung) padding; (fig: Geld) reserves pl; **~er** m **-s, -** upholsterer; **~möbel** pl upholstered furniture; **p~n** vt upholster; pad; **~ung** f upholstery.
Polter- ['pɔltər] zW: **~abend** m party on eve of wedding; **p~n** vi (Krach machen) crash; (schimpfen) rant.
Polyp [po'ly:p] m **-en -en** polyp; (pl: MED) adenoids pl; (umg) cop.
Pomade [po'ma:də] f pomade.
Pommes frites [pɔm'frɪt] pl chips pl, French fried potatoes pl.
Pomp [pɔmp] m **-(e)s** pomp.
Pony ['pɔni] m **-s, -s** (Frisur) fringe // nt **-s, -s** (Pferd) pony.
Popmusik ['pɔpmuzi:k] f pop music.
Popo [po'po:] m **-s, -s** bottom, bum.
populär [popu'lɛ:r] a popular.
Popularität [populari'tɛ:t] f popularity.
Pore ['po:rə] f **-, -n** pore.
Pornographie [pɔrnogra'fi:] f pornography.
porös [po'rø:s] a porous.
Porree ['pɔre] m **-s, -s** leek.
Portal [pɔr'ta:l] nt **-s, -e** portal.
Portefeuille [pɔrt'fø:j] nt (POL, FIN) portfolio.
Portemonnaie [pɔrtmɔ'nɛ:] nt **-s, -s** purse.
Portier [pɔrti'e:] m **-s, -s** porter.
Portion [pɔrtsi'o:n] f portion, helping; (umg: Anteil) amount.
Porto ['pɔrto] nt **-s, -s** postage; **p~frei** a post-free, (postage) prepaid.
Porträt [pɔr'trɛ:] nt **-s, -s** portrait; **p~ieren** [pɔrtrɛ'ti:rən] vt paint, portray.
Portug- ['pɔrtug] zW: **~al** nt **~s** Portugal; **~iese** [pɔrtu'gi:zə] m **-n, -n, ~iesin** f Portuguese; **p~'iesisch** a Portuguese.
Porzellan [pɔrtsɛ'la:n] nt **-s, -e** china, porcelain; (Geschirr) china.
Posaune [po'zaunə] f **-, -n** trombone.
Pose ['po:zə] f **-, -n** pose.
posieren [po'zi:rən] vi pose.
Position [pozitsi'o:n] f position.
positiv ['po:ziti:f] a positive; **P~** nt **-s, -e** (PHOT) positive.
possessiv ['pɔsɛsi:f] a possessive;

P~pronomen nt **-s, -e** possessive pronoun.
possierlich [pɔ'si:rlɪç] a funny.
Post [pɔst] f **-, -en** post (office); (Briefe) mail; **~amt** nt post office; **~anweisung** f postal order, money order; **~bote** m postman; **~en** m **-s, -** post, position; (COMM) item; (auf Liste) entry; (MIL) sentry; (Streik~) picket; **~er** nt **-s, -(s)** poster; **~fach** nt post-office box; **~karte** f postcard; **p~lagernd** ad poste restante; **~leitzahl** f postal code; **~scheckkonto** nt postal giro account; **~sparkasse** f post office savings bank; **~stempel** m postmark; **~wertzeichen** nt postage stamp.
potent [po'tɛnt] a potent.
Potential [potɛntsi'a:l] nt **-s, -e** potential.
potentiell [potɛntsi'ɛl] a potential.
Potenz [po'tɛnts] f power; (eines Mannes) potency.
Pracht [praxt] f **-** splendour, magnificence.
prächtig ['prɛçtɪç] a splendid.
Prachtstück nt showpiece.
prachtvoll a splendid, magnificent.
Prädikat [prɛdi'ka:t] nt **-(e)s, -e** title; (GRAM) predicate; (Zensur) distinction.
Prag [pra:k] nt **-s** Prague.
prägen ['prɛ:gən] vt stamp; (Münze) mint; (Ausdruck) coin; (Charakter) form.
prägnant [prɛ'gnant] a precise, terse.
Prägung ['prɛ:guŋ] f minting; forming; (Eigenart) character, stamp.
prahlen ['pra:lən] vi boast, brag.
Prahlerei [pra:lə'rai] f boasting.
Praktik ['praktɪk] f practice; **p~abel** [-'ka:bəl] a practicable; **~ant(in f)** [-'kant(ɪn)] m trainee; **~um** nt **-s, Praktika** od **Praktiken** practical training.
praktisch ['praktɪʃ] a practical, handy; **~er Arzt** general practitioner.
praktizieren [prakti'tsi:rən] vti practise.
Praline [pra'li:nə] f chocolate.
prall [pral] a firmly rounded; (Segel) taut; (Arme) plump; (Sonne) blazing; **~en** vi bounce, rebound; (Sonne) blaze.
Prämie ['prɛ:miə] f premium; (Belohnung) award, prize; **p~ren** [prɛ'mi:rən] vt give an award to.
Pranger ['praŋər] m **-s, -** (HIST) pillory; **jdn an den ~ stellen** (fig) pillory sb.
Präparat [prɛpa'ra:t] nt **-(e)s, -e** (BIOL) preparation; (MED) medicine.
Präposition [prɛpozitsi'o:n] f preposition.

Präsens ['prɛːzɛns] *nt* - present tense.
präsentieren [prɛzɛn'tiːrən] *vt* present.
Präservativ [prɛzɛrva'tiːf] *nt* **-s, -e** contraceptive.
Präsident(in *f)* [prɛzi'dɛnt(ın)] *m* president; **~schaft** *f* presidency.
Präsidium [prɛ'ziːdiʊm] *nt* presidency, chair(manship); (*Polizei~*) police headquarters *pl*.
prasseln ['prasəln] *vi* (*Feuer*) crackle; (*Hagel*) drum; (*Wörter*) rain down.
Praxis ['praksıs] *f* -, **Praxen** practice; (*Behandlungsraum*) surgery; (*von Anwalt*) office.
präzis [prɛ'tsiːs] *a* precise; **P~ion** [prɛtsizi'oːn] *f* precision.
predigen ['preːdıgən] *vti* preach.
Prediger *m* **-s, -** preacher.
Predigt ['preːdıçt] *f* -, **-en** sermon.
Preis [praıs] *m* **-es, -e** price; (*Sieges~*) prize; **um keinen ~** not at any price; **Preiselbeere** *f* cranberry; **p~en** [praızən] *vi unreg* praise; **p~geben** *vt unreg* abandon; (*opfern*) sacrifice; (*zeigen*) expose; **p~gekrönt** *a* prize-winning; **~gericht** *nt* jury; **p~günstig** *a* inexpensive; **~lage** *f* price range; **~träger(in** *f)* *m* prizewinner; **p~wert** *a* inexpensive.
prekär [preˈkɛːr] *a* precarious.
Prell- [prɛl] *zW:* **~bock** *m* buffers *pl*; **p~en** *vt* bump; (*fig*) cheat, swindle; **~ung** *f* bruise.
Premiere [prəmi'ɛːrə] *f* -, **-n** premiere.
Premierminister [prəmı'eːmınıstər] *m* prime minister, premier.
Presse ['prɛsə] *f* -, **-n** press; **~freiheit** *f* freedom of the press; **p~n** *vt* press; **~verlautbarung** *f* press release.
pressieren [prɛ'siːrən] *vi* (be in a) hurry.
Preßluft ['prɛsluft] *f* compressed air; **~bohrer** *m* pneumatic drill.
Prestige [prɛs'tiːʒə] *nt* **-s** prestige.
Preuß- [prɔys] *zW:* **~e** *m* **-n, -n, ~in** *f* Prussian; **~en** *nt* **-s** Prussia; **p~isch** *a* Prussian.
prickeln ['prıkəln] *vti* tingle, tickle.
Priester ['priːstər] *m* **-s, -** priest.
prima ['priːma] *a inv* first-class, excellent; **P~** *f* -, **Primen** sixth form, top class.
primär [pri'mɛːr] *a* primary.
Primel ['priːməl] *f* -, **-n** primrose.
primitiv [primi'tiːf] *a* primitive.
Prinz [prınts] *m* **-en, -en** prince; **Prinzessin** [prın'tsɛsın] *f* princess.
Prinzip [prın'tsiːp] *nt* **-s, -ien** principle; **p~iell** [-i'ɛl] *a,ad* on principle; **p~ienlos** *a* unprincipled.
Priorität [priori'tɛːt] *f* priority.
Prise ['priːzə] *f* -, **-n** pinch.
Prisma ['prısma] *nt* **-s, Prismen** prism.

privat [pri'vaːt] *a* private.
pro [proː] *präp +akk* per; **P~** *nt* - pro.
Probe ['proːbə] *f* -, **-n** test; (*Teststück*) sample; (*THEAT*) rehearsal; **jdn auf die ~ stellen** put sb to the test; **~exemplar** *nt* specimen copy; **~fahrt** *f* test drive; **p~n** *vt* try; (*THEAT*) rehearse; **p~weise** *ad* on approval; **~zeit** *f* probation period.
probieren [pro'biːrən] *vti* try; (*Wein, Speise*) taste, sample.
Problem [pro'bleːm] *nt* **-s, -e** problem; **~atik** [-'maːtık] *f* problem; **p~atisch** [-'maːtıʃ] *a* problematic; **p~los** *a* problem-free.
Produkt [pro'dʊkt] *nt* **-(e)s, -e** product; (*AGR*) produce *no pl*; **~ion** [prodʊktsi'oːn] *f* production; output; **p~iv** [-'tiːf] *a* productive; **~ivität** *f* productivity.
Produzent [produ'tsɛnt] *m* manufacturer; (*Film*) producer.
produzieren [produ'tsiːrən] *vt* produce.
Professor [pro'fɛsɔr] *m* professor.
Profi ['proːfi] *m* **-s, -s** (*umg, SPORT*) pro.
Profil [pro'fiːl] *nt* **-s, -e** profile; (*fig*) image; **p~ieren** [profi'liːrən] *vr* create an image for o.s.
Profit [pro'fiːt] *m* **-(e)s, -e** profit; **p~ieren** [profi'tiːrən] *vi* profit (*von* from).
Prognose [pro'gnoːzə] *f* -, **-n** prediction, prognosis.
Programm [pro'gram] *nt* **-s, -e** programme; (*COMPUT*) program; **p~ieren** [-'miːrən] *vt* programme; (*COMPUT*) program; **~ierer(in** *f)* *m* **-s, -** programmer.
progressiv [progrɛ'siːf] *a* progressive.
Projekt [pro'jɛkt] *nt* **-(e)s, -e** project; **~or** [pro'jɛktɔr] *m* projector.
proklamieren [prokla'miːrən] *vt* proclaim.
Prolet [pro'leːt] *m* **-en, -en** prole, pleb; **~ariat** [-ari'aːt] *nt* **-(e)s, -e** proletariat; **~arier** [-'taːriər] *m* **-s, -** proletarian.
Prolog [pro'loːk] *m* **-(e)s, -e** prologue.
Promenade [promə'naːdə] *f* promenade.
Promille [pro'mılə] *nt* **-(s), -** alcohol level.
prominent [promi'nɛnt] *a* prominent.
Prominenz [promi'nɛnts] *f* VIPs *pl*.
Promotion [promotsi'oːn] *f* doctorate, Ph.D.
promovieren [promo'viːrən] *vi* do a doctorate *od* Ph.D.
prompt [prɔmpt] *a* prompt.
Pronomen [pro'noːmɛn] *nt* **-s, -** pronoun.
Propaganda [propa'ganda] *f* - propaganda.

Propeller [pro'pɛlər] *m* **-s,** - propeller.
Prophet [pro'feːt] *m* **-en, -en** prophet.
prophezeien [profe'tsaɪən] *vt* prophesy.
Prophezeiung *f* prophecy.
Proportion [proportsi'oːn] *f* proportion; **p~al** *a* proportional.
Prosa ['proːza] *f* - prose; **p~isch** [pro'zaːɪʃ] *a* prosaic.
prosit ['proːzɪt] *interj* cheers.
Prospekt [pro'spɛkt] *m* **-(e)s, -e** leaflet, brochure.
prost [proːst] *interj* cheers.
Prostituierte [prostitu'iːrtə] *f* **-n, -n** prostitute.
Prostitution [prostitutsi'oːn] *f* prostitution.
Protest [pro'tɛst] *m* **-(e)s, -e** protest; **~ant(in** *f***)** [protɛs'tant] *m* Protestant; **p~antisch** [protɛs'tantɪʃ] *a* Protestant; **p~ieren** [protɛs'tiːrən] *vi* protest.
Prothese [pro'teːzə] *f* **-, -n** artificial limb; (*Zahn~*) dentures *pl*.
Protokoll [proto'kɔl] *nt* **-s, -e** register; (*von Sitzung*) minutes *pl*; (*diplomatisch*) protocol; (*Polizei~*) statement; **p~ieren** [-'liːrən] *vt* take down in the minutes.
protz- ['prots] *zW:* **~en** *vi* show off; **~ig** *a* ostentatious.
Proviant [provi'ant] *m* **-s, -e** provisions *pl*, supplies *pl*.
Provinz [pro'vɪnts] *f* **-, -en** province; **p~i'ell** *a* provincial.
Provision [provizi'oːn] *f* (*COMM*) commission.
provisorisch [provi'zoːrɪʃ] *a* provisional.
Provokation [provokatsi'oːn] *f* provocation.
provozieren [provo'tsiːrən] *vt* provoke.
Prozedur [protse'duːr] *f* procedure; (*pej*) carry-on.
Prozent [pro'tsɛnt] *nt* **-(e)s, -e** per cent, percentage; **~satz** *m* percentage; **p~ual** [-u'aːl] *a* percentage; as a percentage.
Prozeß [pro'tsɛs] *m* **-sses, -sse** trial, case.
Prozession [protsɛsi'oːn] *f* procession.
prüde ['pryːdə] *a* prudish; **P~rie** [-'riː] *f* prudery.
Prüf- ['pryːf] *zW:* **p~en** *vt* examine, test; (*nach~*) check; **~er** *m* **-s,** - examiner; **~ling** *m* examinee; **~ung** *f* examination; checking; **~ungsausschuß** *m* examining board.
Prügel ['pryːgəl] *m* **-s,** - cudgel // *pl* beating; **~ei** [-'laɪ] *f* fight; **~knabe** *m* scapegoat; **p~n** *vt* beat // *vr* fight; **~strafe** *f* corporal punishment.
Prunk [prʊŋk] *m* **-(e)s** pomp, show; **p~voll** *a* splendid, magnificent.
PS [peː'ɛs] *abk* (= *Pferdestärke*) horsepower, HP.

Psalm [psalm] *m* **-s, -en** psalm.
pseudo- ['psɔydo] *in zW* pseudo.
pst [pst] *interj* psst.
Psych- ['psyç] *zW:* **~iater** [-i'aːtər] *m* **-s, -** psychiatrist; **p~isch** *a* psychological; **~oanalyse** [-o'ana'lyːzə] *f* psychoanalysis; **~ologe** [-o'loːgə] *m* **-n, -n** psychologist; **~olo'gie** *f* psychology; **p~ologisch** *a* psychological.
Pubertät [puber'tɛːt] *f* puberty.
Publikum ['puːblikʊm] *nt* **-s** audience; (*SPORT*) crowd.
publizieren [publi'tsiːrən] *vt* publish, publicize.
Pudding ['pʊdɪŋ] *m* **-s, -e** *od* **-s** blancmange.
Pudel ['puːdəl] *m* **-s** poodle.
Puder ['puːdər] *m* **-s, -** powder; **~dose** *f* powder compact; **p~n** *vt* powder; **~zucker** *m* icing sugar.
Puff [pʊf] *m* **-s, -e** (*Wäsche~*) linen basket; (*Sitz~*) pouf; *pl* **-e** (*umg: Stoß*) push; *pl* **-s** (*umg: Bordell*) brothel; **~er** *m* **-s, -** buffer; **~erspeicher** *m* (*COMPUT*) buffer.
Pullover [pʊ'loːvər] *m* **-s, -** pullover, jumper.
Puls [pʊls] *m* **-es, -e** pulse; **~ader** *f* artery; **p~ieren** [pʊl'ziːrən] *vi* throb, pulsate.
Pult [pʊlt] *nt* **-(e)s, -e** desk.
Pulver ['pʊlfər] *nt* **-s, -** powder; **p~ig** *a* powdery; **~schnee** *m* powdery snow.
pummelig ['pʊməlɪç] *a* chubby.
Pumpe ['pʊmpə] *f* **-, -n** pump; **p~n** *vt* pump; (*umg*) lend; borrow.
Punkt [pʊŋkt] *m* **-(e)s, -e** point; (*bei Muster*) dot; (*Satzzeichen*) full stop; **p~ieren** [-'tiːrən] *vt* dot; (*MED*) aspirate.
pünktlich ['pʏŋktlɪç] *a* punctual; **P~keit** *f* punctuality.
Punktsieg *m* victory on points.
Punktzahl *f* score.
Punsch [pʊnʃ] *m* **-(e)s, -e** punch.
Pupille [pu'pɪlə] *f* **-, -n** pupil.
Puppe ['pʊpə] *f* **-, -n** doll; (*Marionette*) puppet; (*Insekten~*) pupa, chrysalis; **~nspieler** *m* puppeteer.
pur [puːr] *a* pure; (*völlig*) sheer; (*Whisky*) neat.
Püree [py're:] *nt* **-s, -s** mashed potatoes *pl*.
Purzel- ['pʊrtsəl] *zW:* **~baum** *m* somersault; **p~n** *vi* tumble.
Puste ['puːstə] *f* - (*umg*) puff; (*fig*) steam; **p~n** *vi* puff, blow.
Pute ['puːtə] *f* **-, -n** turkey-hen; **~r** *m* **-s, -** turkey-cock.
Putsch [pʊtʃ] *m* **-(e)s, -e** revolt, putsch.
Putz [pʊts] *m* **-es** (*Mörtel*) plaster, roughcast; **p~en** *vt* clean; (*Nase*)

wipe, blow // vr clean oneself; dress oneself up; **~frau** f charwoman; **p~ig** a quaint, funny; **~lappen** m cloth.

Puzzle ['pasəl] nt -s, -s jigsaw.

Pyjama [py'dʒa:ma] m -s, -s pyjamas pl.

Pyramide [pyra'mi:də] f -, -n pyramid.

Pyrenäen [pyre'nɛ:ən] pl Pyrenees pl.

Q

Q, q [ku:] nt Q, q.

Quacksalber ['kvakzalbər] m -s, - quack (doctor).

Quader ['kva:dər] m -s, - square stone; (MATH) cuboid.

Quadrat [kva'dra:t] nt -(e)s, -e square; **q~isch** a square; **~meter** m square metre.

quaken ['kva:kən] vi croak; (Ente) quack.

quäken ['kvɛ:kən] vi screech.

Qual [kva:l] f -, -en pain, agony; (seelisch) anguish.

Quäl- ['kvɛ:l] zW: **q~en** vt torment // vr struggle; (geistig) torment oneself; **~erei** [-ə'raɪ] f torture, torment; **~geist** m pest.

qualifizieren [kvalifi'tsi:rən] vtr qualify; (einstufen) label.

Qualität [kvali'tɛ:t] f quality; **Qualitätsware** f article of high quality.

Qualle ['kvalə] f -, -n jellyfish.

Qualm [kvalm] m -(e)s thick smoke; **q~en** vti smoke.

qualvoll ['kva:lfɔl] a excruciating, painful, agonizing.

Quant- ['kvant] zW: **~entheorie** f quantum theory; **~ität** [-i'tɛ:t] f quantity; **q~itativ** [-ita'ti:f] a quantitative; **~um** nt -s, **Quanten** quantity, amount.

Quarantäne [karan'tɛ:nə] f -, -n quarantine.

Quark [kvark] m -s curd cheese; (umg) rubbish.

Quarta ['kvarta] f -, **Quarten** third year of secondary school; **Quartal** [kvar'ta:l] nt -s, -e quarter (year).

Quartier [kvar'ti:r] nt -s, -e accommodation; (MIL) quarters pl; (Stadt~) district.

Quarz [kva:rts] m -es, -e quartz.

quasseln ['kvasəln] vi (umg) natter.

Quatsch [kvatʃ] m -es rubbish; **q~en** vi chat, natter.

Quecksilber ['kvɛkzilbər] nt mercury.

Quelle ['kvɛlə] f -, -n spring; (eines Flusses) source; **q~n** vi (hervor~) pour od gush forth; (schwellen) swell.

quer [kve:r] ad crossways, diagonally; (rechtwinklig) at right angles; ~ **auf** dem Bett across the bed; **Q~balken** m crossbeam; **~feldein** ad across country; **Q~flöte** f flute; **Q~schnitt** m cross-section; **~schnittsgelähmt** a paralysed below the waist; **Q~straße** f intersecting road.

quetschen ['kvɛtʃən] vt squash, crush; (MED) bruise.

Quetschung f bruise, contusion.

quieken ['kvi:kən] vi squeak.

quietschen ['kvi:tʃən] vi squeak.

Quint- ['kvint] zW: **~a** f -, -en second form in secondary school; **~essenz** [-'ɛsɛnts] f quintessence; **~ett** [-'tɛt] nt -(e)s, -e quintet.

Quirl [kvirl] m -(e)s, -e whisk.

quitt [kvit] a quits, even; **Q~e** f -, -n quince; **~ieren** [-'ti:rən] vt give a receipt for; (Dienst) leave; **Q~ung** f receipt.

Quiz [kvis] nt -, - quiz.

Quote ['kvo:tə] f -, -n number, rate.

R

R, r [ɛr] nt R, r.

Rabatt [ra'bat] m -(e)s, -e discount; **~e** f -, -n flowerbed, border; **~marke** f trading stamp.

Rabe ['ra:bə] m -n, -n raven.

rabiat [rabi'a:t] a furious.

Rache ['raxə] f - revenge, vengeance; **~n** m -s, - throat.

rächen ['rɛçən] vt avenge, revenge // vr take (one's) revenge; **das wird sich ~** you'll pay for that.

Rachitis [ra'xi:tɪs] f - rickets sing.

Rad [ra:t] nt -(e)s, -̈er wheel; (Fahr~) bike; **Radar** ['ra:da:r] m od nt -s radar; **Radarfalle** f speed trap; **Radarkontrolle** f radar-controlled speed trap; **Radau** [ra'dau] m -s (umg) row; **~dampfer** m paddle steamer; **radebrechen** vi insep: deutsch etc radebrechen speak broken German etc; **r~fahren** vi unreg cycle; **~fahrer(in** f) m cyclist; **~fahrweg** m cycle track od path.

Radier- [ra'di:r] zW: **r~en** vt rub out, erase; (ART) etch; **~gummi** m rubber, eraser; **~ung** f etching.

Radieschen [ra'di:sçən] nt radish.

radikal [radi'ka:l] a, **R~e(r)** mf radical.

Radio ['ra:dio] nt -s, -s radio, wireless; **r~ak'tiv** a radioactive; **~aktivi'tät** f radioactivity; **~apparat** m radio, wireless set.

Radius ['ra:diʊs] m -, **Radien** radius.

Rad- zW: **~kappe** f (AUT) hub cap; **~rennen** nt cycle race; cycle racing; **~sport** m cycling.

raff- [raf] zW: **~en** vt snatch, pick up; (Stoff) gather (up); (Geld) pile up, rake in; **R~inade** [-i'na:də] *f* refined sugar; **r~i'niert** *a* crafty, cunning.

ragen ['ra:gən] *vi* tower, rise.

Rahm [ra:m] *m* -s cream; **~en** *m* -s, - frame(work); **im ~en des Möglichen** within the bounds of possibility; **r~en** *vt* frame; **~enplan** *m* outline plan; **r~ig** *a* creamy.

Rakete [ra'ke:tə] *f* -, -n rocket; **Raketenstützpunkt** *m* missile base.

rammen ['ramən] *vt* ram.

Rampe ['rampə] *f* -, -n ramp; **Rampenlicht** *vt* (THEAT) footlights *pl*.

ramponieren [rampo'ni:rən] *vt* (umg) damage.

Ramsch [ramʃ] *m* -(e)s, -e junk.

ran [ran] *ad* (umg) = **heran**.

Rand [rant] *m* -(e)s, ̈er edge; (von Brille, Tasse etc) rim; (Hut~) brim; (auf Papier) margin; (Schmutz~, unter Augen) ring; (fig) verge, brink; **außer ~ und Band** wild; **am ~e bemerkt** mentioned in passing; **r~alieren** [randa'li:rən] *vi* (go on the) rampage.

Rang [raŋ] *m* -(e)s, ̈e rank; (Stand) standing; (Wert) quality; (THEAT) circle.

Rangier- [rãʒi:r] *zW:* **~bahnhof** *m* marshalling yard; **r~en** *vt* (EISENB) shunt, switch (US) // *vi* rank, be classed; **~gleis** *nt* siding.

Ranke ['raŋkə] *f* -, -n tendril, shoot.

rannte etc *v siehe* **rennen**.

ranzig ['rantsıç] *a* rancid.

Rappe ['rapə] *m* -n, -n black horse.

Rappen ['rapən] *m* (FIN) rappen, centime.

rar [ra:r] *a* rare; **sich ~ machen** (umg) keep oneself to oneself; **R~i'tät** *f* rarity; (Sammelobjekt) curio.

rasant [ra'zant] *a* quick, rapid.

rasch [raʃ] *a* quick; **~eln** *vi* rustle.

Rasen ['ra:zən] *m* -s, - lawn; grass; **r~** *vi* rave; (schnell) race; **r~d** *a* furious; **r~de Kopfschmerzen** a splitting headache; **~mäher** *m* -s, - *f* lawnmower; **~platz** *m* lawn.

Rasier- [ra'zi:r] *zW:* **~apparat** *m* shaver; **~creme** *f* shaving cream; **r~en** *vtr* shave; **~klinge** *f* razor blade; **~messer** *nt* razor; **~pinsel** *m* shaving brush; **~seife** *f* shaving soap *od* stick; **~wasser** *nt* shaving lotion.

Rasse ['rasə] *f* -, -n race; (Tier~) breed; **~hund** *m* thoroughbred dog; **Rassenhaß** *m* race *od* racial hatred; **Rassentrennung** *f* racial segregation.

Rassismus [ra'sısmʊs] *m* racism.

Rast [rast] *f* -, -en rest; **r~en** *vi* rest; **~haus** *nt*, **~hof** *m* (AUT) service station; **r~los** *a* tireless; (unruhig) restless; **~platz** *m* (AUT) layby; **~stätte**

f (AUT) service station.

Rasur [ra'zu:r] *f* shaving.

Rat [ra:t] *m* -(e)s, -schläge advice *no pl*; **ein ~** a piece of advice; **jdn zu ~e ziehen** consult sb; **keinen ~ wissen** not know what to do; **~e** *f* -, -n instalment; **r~en** *vti unreg* guess; (empfehlen) advise (jdm sb); **~enzahlung** *f* hire purchase; **~geber** *m* -s, - adviser; **~haus** *nt* town hall.

ratifizieren [ratifi'tsi:rən] *vt* ratify.

Ration [ratsi'o:n] *f* ration; **r~al** [-'na:l] *a* rational; **r~ali'sieren** *vt* rationalize; **r~ell** [-'nɛl] *a* efficient; **r~ieren** [-'ni:rən] *vt* ration.

Rat- *zW:* **r~los** *a* at a loss, helpless; **r~sam** *a* advisable; **~schlag** *m* (piece of) advice.

Rätsel ['rɛ:tsəl] *nt* -s, - puzzle; (Wort~) riddle; **r~haft** *a* mysterious; **es ist mir r~haft** it's a mystery to me.

Ratte ['ratə] *f* -, -n rat; **Rattenfänger** *m* -s, - ratcatcher.

rattern ['ratərn] *vi* rattle, clatter.

Raub [raʊp] *m* -(e)s robbery; (Beute) loot, booty; **~bau** *m* ruthless exploitation; **r~en** [raʊbən] *vt* rob; (Mensch) kidnap, abduct.

Räuber ['rɔybər] *m* -s, - robber.

Raub- *zW:* **~mord** *m* robbery with murder; **~tier** *nt* predator; **~überfall** *m* robbery with violence; **~vogel** *m* bird of prey.

Rauch ['raʊx] *m* -(e)s smoke; **r~en** *vti* smoke; **~er** *m* -s, - smoker; **~erabteil** *nt* (EISENB) smoker.

räuchern [rɔyçərn] *vt* smoke, cure.

Rauchfleisch *nt* smoked meat.

rauchig *a* smoky.

rauf [raʊf] *ad* (umg) = **herauf, hinauf**; **~en** *vt* (Haare) pull out // *vir* fight; **R~e'rei** *f* brawl, fight.

rauh [raʊ] *a* rough, coarse; (Wetter) harsh; **R~reif** *m* hoarfrost.

Raum [raʊm] *m* -(e)s, **Räume** space; (Zimmer, Platz) room; (Gebiet) area.

räumen ['rɔymən] *vt* clear; (Wohnung, Platz) vacate; (wegbringen) shift, move; (in Schrank etc) put away.

Raum- *zW:* **~fähre** *f* space shuttle; **~fahrt** *f* space travel; **~inhalt** *m* cubic capacity, volume.

räumlich ['rɔymlıç] *a* spatial; **R~keiten** *pl* premises *pl*.

Raum- *zW:* **~mangel** *m* lack of space; **~pflegerin** *f* cleaner; **~schiff** *nt* spaceship; **~schiffahrt** *f* space travel.

Räumung ['rɔymʊŋ] *f* vacating, evacuation; clearing (away); **Räumungsverkauf** *m* clearance sale; (bei Geschäftsaufgabe) closing down sale.

Raupe ['raupə] f -, -n caterpillar; (~nkette) (caterpillar) track; **Raupenschlepper** m caterpillar tractor.

raus [raus] ad (umg) = **heraus, hinaus.**

Rausch [rauʃ] m -(e)s, Räusche intoxication; **r~en** vi (Wasser) rush; (Baum) rustle; (Radio etc) hiss; (Mensch) sweep, sail; **r~end** a (Beifall) thunderous; (Fest) sumptuous; ~**gift** nt drug; ~**gifthandel** m drug traffic; ~**giftsüchtige(r)** mf drug addict.

räuspern ['rɔyspərn] vr clear one's throat.

Razzia ['ratsia] f -, **Razzien** raid.

Reagenzglas [rea'gɛntsglaːs] nt test tube.

reagieren [rea'giːrən] vi react (auf +akk to).

Reakt- zW: ~**ion** [reaktsi'oːn] f reaction; **r~io'när** a reactionary; ~**or** [re'aktɔr] m reactor.

real [re'aːl] a real, material; **R~ismus** [-'lɪsmus] m realism; ~**istisch** a realistic; **R~schule** f secondary school.

Rebe [re'bə] f -, -n vine.

Rebell [re'bɛl] m -en, -en rebel; ~**i'on** f rebellion; **r~isch** a rebellious.

Rechen ['rɛçən] m -s, - rake; **r~** vti rake; ~**fehler** m miscalculation; ~**maschine** f calculating machine; ~**schaft** f account; **für etw ~schaft ablegen** account for sth; ~**schieber** m slide rule.

Rech- ['rɛç] zW: **r~nen** vti calculate; **jdn/etw r~nen zu** count sb/sth among; **r~nen mit** reckon with; **r~nen auf** (+akk) count on; ~**nen** nt arithmetic; ~**ner** m -s, - calculator; (COMPUT) computer; ~**nung** f calculation(s); (COMM) bill, check (US); **jdm/etw ~nung tragen** take sb/sth into account; ~**nungsjahr** nt financial year; ~**nungsprüfer** m auditor.

recht [rɛçt] a, ad right; (vor Adjektiv) really, quite; **das ist mir ~** that suits me; **jetzt erst ~** now more than ever; **~ haben** be right; **jdm ~ geben** agree with sb; **R~** nt -(e)s, -e right; (JUR) law; **mit R~** rightly, justly; **von R~s wegen** by rights; **R~e** f -n, -n right (hand); (POL) Right; ~**e(r, s)** a right; (POL) right-wing; **ein R~r** m a right-winger; **R~e(s)** nt right thing; **etwas/nichts R~es** something/nothing proper; **R~eck** nt -s, -e rectangle; ~**eckig** a rectangular; ~**fertigen** vtr insep justify (o.s.); **R~fertigung** f justification; ~**mäßig** a legal, lawful.

rechts [rɛçts] ad on/to the right; **R~anwalt** m, **R~anwältin** f lawyer, barrister; **R~'außen** m -, - (SPORT) outside right.

rechtschaffen a upright.

Rechtschreibung f spelling.

Rechts- zW: ~**fall** m (law) case; ~**händer** m -s, - right-handed person; **r~kräftig** a valid, legal; ~**kurve** f right-hand bend; ~**streit** m law-suit; **r~verbindlich** a legally binding; ~**verkehr** m driving on the right; **r~widrig** a illegal; ~**wissenschaft** f jurisprudence.

rechtwinklig a right-angled.

rechtzeitig a timely // ad in time.

Reck [rɛk] nt -(e)s, -e horizontal bar; **r~en** vtr stretch.

Redakteur [redak'tøːr] m editor.

Redaktion [redaktsi'oːn] f editing; (Leute) editorial staff; (Büro) editorial office(s).

Rede ['reːdə] f -, -n speech; (Gespräch) talk; **jdn zur ~ stellen** take sb to task; ~**freiheit** f freedom of speech; **r~gewandt** a eloquent; **r~n** vi talk, speak // vt say; (Unsinn etc) talk; **Redensart** f set phrase; ~**wendung** f expression, idiom.

red- ['reːd] zW: ~**lich** a honest; **R~ner** m -s, - speaker, orator; ~**selig** a talkative, loquacious.

reduzieren [redu'tsiːrən] vt reduce.

Reede ['reːdə] f -, -n protected anchorage; ~**r** m -s, - shipowner; ~'**rei** f shipping line od firm.

reell [re'ɛl] a fair, honest; (MATH) real.

Refer- zW: ~**at** [refe'raːt] nt -(e)s, -e report; (Vortrag) paper; (Gebiet) section; ~**ent** [refe'rɛnt] m speaker; (Berichterstatter) reporter; (Sachbearbeiter) expert; ~**enz** [refe'rɛnts] f reference; **r~ieren** [refe'riːrən] vi: **r~ieren über** (+akk) speak od talk on.

Reflex [re'flɛks] m -es, -e reflex; ~**bewegung** f reflex action; **r~iv** [-'ksiːf] a (GRAM) reflexive.

Reform [re'fɔrm] f -, -en reform; ~**ati'on** f reformation; ~**haus** nt health food shop; **r~ieren** [-'miːrən] vt reform.

Regal [re'gaːl] nt -s, -e (book)shelves pl, bookcase; stand, rack.

Regel ['reːgəl] f -, -n rule; (MED) period; **r~mäßig** a regular; ~**mäßigkeit** f regularity; **r~n** vt regulate, control; (Angelegenheit) settle // vr: **sich von selbst r~n** take care of itself; **r~recht** a regular, proper, thorough; ~**ung** f regulation; settlement; **r~widrig** a irregular, against the rules.

Regen ['reːgən] m -s, - rain; **R~bogen** m rainbow; **R~bogenpresse** f tabloids pl; **R~mantel** m raincoat, mac(kintosh); **R~schauer** m shower (of rain); **R~schirm** m umbrella; ~**wurm** m earthworm.

Regie [re'ʒiː] *f* (*Film etc*) direction; (*THEAT*) production.

Regier- [re'giːr] *zW*: **r~en** *vti* govern, rule; **~ung** *f* government; (*Monarchie*) reign; **~ungswechsel** *m* change of government; **~ungszeit** *f* period in government; (*von König*) reign.

Regiment [regi'mɛnt] *nt* **-s, -er** regiment.

Region [regi'oːn] *f* region.

Regisseur [reʒɪ'søːr] *m* director; (*THEAT*) stage producer.

Register [re'gɪstər] *nt* **-s, -** register; (*in Buch*) table of contents, index.

registrieren [regɪs'triːrən] *vt* register.

reg- ['reːg] *zW*: **R~ler** *m* **-s, -** regulator, governor; **~los** ['reːkloːs] *a* motionless; **regnen** *vi unpers* rain; **regnerisch** *a* rainy.

regulär [regu'lɛːr] *a* regular.

regulieren [regu'liːrən] *vt* regulate; (*COMM*) settle.

Regung ['reːguŋ] *f* motion; (*Gefühl*) feeling, impulse; **regungslos** *a* motionless.

Reh [reː] *nt* **-(e)s, -e** deer, roe; **~bock** *m* roebuck; **~kalb** *nt*, **~kitz** *nt* fawn.

Reib- ['raɪb] *zW*: **~e** *f* **-, -n, ~eisen** *nt* grater; **r~en** *vt unreg* rub; (*KOCH*) grate; **~e'rei** *f* friction *no pl*; **~fläche** *f* rough surface; **~ung** *f* friction; **r~ungslos** *a* smooth.

reich [raɪç] *a* rich; **R~** *nt* **-(e)s, -e** empire, kingdom; (*fig*) realm; **das Dritte R~** the Third Reich; **~en** *vi* reach; (*genügen*) be enough *od* sufficient (*jdm* for sb) // *vt* hold out; (*geben*) pass, hand; (*anbieten*) offer; **~haltig** *a* ample, rich; **~lich** *a* ample, plenty of; **R~tum** *m* **-s, -tümer** wealth; **R~weite** *f* range.

reif [raɪf] *a* ripe; (*Mensch, Urteil*) mature; **R~** *m* **-(e)s** hoarfrost // **-(e)s, -e** (*Ring*) ring, hoop; **R~e** *f* - ripeness; maturity; **~en** *vi* mature; ripen; **R~en** *m* **-s, -** ring, hoop; (*Fahrzeug~*) tyre; **R~endruck** *m* tyre pressure; **R~enpanne** *f* puncture.

Reihe ['raɪə] *f* **-, -n** row; (*von Tagen etc, umg: Anzahl*) series *sing*; **der ~ nach** in turn; **er ist an der ~** it's his turn; **an die ~ kommen** have one's turn; **Reihenfolge** *f* sequence; **alphabetische Reihenfolge** alphabetical order; **~nhaus** *nt* terraced house.

Reim [raɪm] *m* **-(e)s, -e** rhyme; **r~en** *vt* rhyme.

rein [raɪn] *ad* (*umg*) = **herein, hinein** // *a, ad* pure(ly); (*sauber*) clean; **etw ins ~e schreiben** make a fair copy of sth; **etw ins ~e bringen** clear up sth; **R~fall** *m* (*umg*) let-down; **R~gewinn** *m* net profit; **R~heit** *f* purity; cleanness; **~igen** *vt* clean; (*Wasser*) puri-

fy; **R~igung** *f* cleaning; purification; (*Geschäft*) cleaners; **chemische R~igung** dry cleaning; dry cleaners; **~lich** *a* clean; **~rassig** *a* pedigree; **R~schrift** *f* fair copy.

Reis [raɪs] *m* **-es, -e** rice.

Reise ['raɪzə] *f* **-, -n** journey; (*Schiffs~*) voyage; **gute ~!** have a good journey; **~n** *pl* travels *pl*; **~andenken** *nt* souvenir; **~büro** *nt* travel agency; **r~fertig** *a* ready to start; **~führer** *m* guide(book); (*Mensch*) travel guide; **~gepäck** *nt* luggage; **~gesellschaft** *f* party of travellers; **~kosten** *pl* travelling expenses *pl*; **~leiter** *m* courier; **~lektüre** *f* reading matter for the journey; **r~n** *vi* travel; go (*nach* to); **Reisende(r)** *mf* traveller; **~paß** *m* passport; **~proviant** *m* food and drink for the journey; **~scheck** *m* traveller's cheque; **~ziel** *nt* destination.

Reiß- ['raɪs] *zW*: **r~en** *vti unreg* tear; (*ziehen*) pull, drag; (*Witz*) crack; **etw an sich r~en** snatch sth up; (*fig*) take over sth; **sich um etw r~en** scramble for sth; **~nagel** *m* drawing pin (*Brit*), thumbtack (*US*); **~verschluß** *m* zip(per), zip fastener; **~wolf** *m* shredder; **~zwecke** *f* = **~nagel**.

Reit- ['raɪt] *zW*: **r~en** *vti unreg* ride; **~er(in** *f*) *m* **-s, -** rider; (*MIL*) cavalryman, trooper; **~hose** *f* riding breeches *pl*; **~pferd** *nt* saddle horse; **~stiefel** *m* riding boot; **~zeug** *nt* riding outfit.

Reiz [raɪts] *m* **-es, -e** stimulus; (*angenehm*) charm; (*Verlockung*) attraction; **r~bar** *a* irritable; **~barkeit** *f* irritability; **r~en** *vt* stimulate; (*unangenehm*) irritate; (*verlocken*) appeal to, attract; **r~end** *a* charming; **r~voll** *a* attractive.

rekeln ['reːkəln] *vr* stretch out; (*lümmeln*) lounge *od* loll about.

Reklamation [reklamatsi'oːn] *f* complaint.

Reklame [re'klaːmə] *f* **-, -n** advertising; advertisement; **~ machen für etw** advertise sth.

rekonstruieren [rekɔnstru'iːrən] *vt* reconstruct.

Rekord [re'kɔrt] *m* **-(e)s, -e** record; **~leistung** *f* record performance.

Rektor ['rɛktɔr] *m* (*UNIV*) rector, vice-chancellor; (*SCH*) headteacher (*Brit*), principal (*US*); **~at** [-'raːt] *nt* **-(e)s, -e** rectorate, vice-chancellorship; headship; (*Zimmer*) rector's *etc* office.

Relais [rə'lɛː] *nt* **-, -** relay.

relativ [rela'tiːf] *a* relative; **R~ität** [relativi'tɛːt] *f* relativity.

relevant [rele'vant] *a* relevant.
Relief [reli'ɛf] *nt* **-s, -e** relief.
Religion [religi'oːn] *f* religion.
religiös [religi'øːs] *a* religious.
Reling ['reːlıŋ] *f* **-, -s** (*NAUT*) rail.
Remoulade [remu'laːdə] *f* remoulade.
Rendezvous [rãde'vuː] *nt* **-, -** rendezvous.
Renn- ['rɛn] *zW:* ~**bahn** *f* racecourse; (*AUT*) circuit, race track; **r~en** *vti unreg* run, race; ~**en** *nt* **-s, -** running; (*Wettbewerb*) race; ~**fahrer** *m* racing driver; ~**pferd** *nt* racehorse; ~**wagen** *m* racing car.
renovier- [reno'viːr] *zW:* ~**en** *vt* renovate; **R~ung** *f* renovation.
rentabel [rɛn'taːbəl] *a* profitable, lucrative.
Rentabilität [rɛntabili'tɛːt] *f* profitability.
Rente ['rɛntə] *f* **-, -n** pension; **rentendynamisch** *a* index-linked; **Rentenversicherung** *f* pension scheme.
Rentier ['rɛntiːr] *nt* reindeer.
rentieren [rɛn'tiːrən] *vr* pay, be profitable.
Rentner(in *f*) ['rɛntnər(ın)] *m* **-s, -** pensioner.
Reparatur [repara'tuːr] *f* repairing; repair; ~**werkstatt** *f* repair shop; (*AUT*) garage.
reparieren [repa'riːrən] *vt* repair.
Reportage [repɔr'taːʒə] *f* **-, -n** (on-the-spot) report; (*TV, RAD*) live commentary *od* coverage.
Reporter [rɛ'pɔrtər] *m* **-s, -** reporter, commentator.
Repressalien [reprɛ'saːliən] *pl* reprisals *pl*.
Reprivatisierung [reprivati'ziːruŋ] *f* denationalisation.
Reproduktion [reproduktsi'oːn] *f* reproduction.
reproduzieren [reprodu'tsiːrən] *vt* reproduce.
Reptil [rɛp'tiːl] *nt* **-s, -ien** reptile.
Republik [repu'bliːk] *f* republic; **r~anisch** [-'kaːnıʃ] *a* republican.
Reservat [rezɛr'vaːt] *nt* **-(e)s, -e** reservation.
Reserve [re'zɛrvə] *f* **-, -n** reserve; ~**rad** *nt* (*AUT*) spare wheel; ~**spieler** *m* reserve; ~**tank** *m* reserve tank.
reservieren [rezɛr'viːrən] *vt* reserve.
Reservoir [rezɛrvo'aːr] *nt* **-s, -e** reservoir.
Residenz [rezi'dɛnts] *f* residence, seat.
resignieren [rezı'gniːrən] *vi* resign.
resolut [rezo'luːt] *a* resolute.
Resonanz [rezo'nants] *f* (*lit*) resonance; (*fig*) response.
Resopal ® [rezo'paːl] *nt* **-s** Formica ®.
Resozialisierung [rezotsiali'ziːruŋ] *f* rehabilitation.

Respekt [re'spɛkt] *m* **-(e)s** respect; **r~ieren** [-'tiːrən] *vt* respect; **r~los** *a* disrespectful; **r~voll** *a* respectful.
Ressort [rɛ'soːr] *nt* **-s, -s** department.
Rest [rɛst] *m* **-(e)s, -e** remainder, rest; (*Über~*) remains *pl*.
Restaurant [rɛsto'rãː] *nt* **-s, -s** restaurant.
restaurieren [rɛstau'riːrən] *vt* restore.
Rest- *zW:* ~**betrag** *m* remainder, outstanding sum; **r~lich** *a* remaining; **r~los** *a* complete.
Resultat [rezul'taːt] *nt* **-(e)s, -e** result.
Retorte [re'tɔrtə] *f* **-, -n** retort.
Retouren [re'tuːrən] *pl* (*COMM*) returns *pl*.
retten ['rɛtən] *vt* save, rescue.
Rettich ['rɛtıç] *m* **-s, -e** radish.
Rettung *f* rescue; (*Hilfe*) help; seine letzte ~ his last hope.
Rettungs- *zW:* ~**boot** *nt* lifeboat; **r~los** *a* hopeless; ~**ring** *m* lifebelt, life preserver (*US*).
retuschieren [retu'ʃiːrən] *vt* (*PHOT*) retouch.
Reue ['rɔyə] *f* **-** remorse; (*Bedauern*) regret; **r~n** *vt:* es reut ihn he regrets (it) *od* is sorry (about it).
reuig ['rɔyıç] *a* penitent.
Revanche [re'vãːʃə] *f* **-, -n** revenge; (*SPORT*) return match.
revanchieren [revã'ʃiːrən] *vr* (*sich rächen*) get one's own back, have one's revenge; (*erwidern*) reciprocate, return the compliment.
Revier [re'viːr] *nt* **-s, -e** district; (*Jagd~*) preserve; police station/beat.
Revolte [re'vɔltə] *f* **-, -n** revolt.
Revolution [revolutsi'oːn] *f* revolution; ~**är** [-'nɛːr] *m* **-s, -e** revolutionary; **r~ieren** [-'niːrən] *vt* revolutionize.
Rezept [re'tsɛpt] *nt* **-(e)s, -e** recipe; (*MED*) prescription; ~**ion** [retsɛp-tsi'oːn] *f* reception; **r~pflichtig** *a* available only on prescription.
rezitieren [retsi'tiːrən] *vt* recite.
R-Gespräch ['ɛrgəʃprɛːç] *nt* reverse charge call (*Brit*), collect call (*US*).
Rhabarber [ra'barbər] *m* **-s** rhubarb.
Rhein [raın] *m* **-s** Rhine; **r~isch** *a* Rhenish.
Rhesusfaktor ['reːzusfaktɔr] *m* rhesus factor.
rhetorisch [re'toːrıʃ] *a* rhetorical.
Rheuma ['rɔyma] *nt* **-s, Rheumatismus** [rɔyma'tısmus] *m* rheumatism.
Rhinozeros [ri'noːtseros] *nt* **-** *od* **-ses, -se** rhinoceros.
rhyth- ['ryt] *zW:* ~**misch** *a* rhythmical; **R~mus** *m* rhythm.
Richt- ['rıçt] *zW:* **r~en** *vt* direct (*an +akk* at; (*fig*) to); (*Waffe*) aim (*auf +akk* at); (*einstellen*) adjust;

(instandsetzen) repair; *(zurechtmachen)* prepare; *(bestrafen)* pass judgement on // *vr:* **sich r~en nach** go by; **~er(in** *f)* *m* **-s, -** judge; **r~erlich** *a* judicial; **r~ig** *a* right, correct; *(echt)* proper; **bin ich hier r~ig?** am I in the right place? // *ad (umg: sehr)* really; **der/die ~ige** the right one/person; **das ~ige** the right thing; **~igkeit** *f* correctness; **~igstellung** *f* correction, rectification; **~preis** *m* recommended price; **~ung** *f* direction; tendency, orientation.

rieb *etc v siehe* **reiben.**

riechen ['riːçən] *vti unreg* smell *(an etw (dat)* sth; *nach* of); **ich kann das/ihn nicht ~** *(umg)* I can't stand it/him.

rief *etc v siehe* **rufen.**

Riegel ['riːgəl] *m* **-s, -** bolt, bar.

Riemen ['riːmən] *m* **-s, -** strap; *(Gürtel, TECH)* belt; *(NAUT)* oar.

Riese ['riːzə] *m* **-n, -n** giant; **rieseln** *vi* trickle; *(Schnee)* fall gently; **Riesenerfolg** *m* enormous success; **r~ngroß** *a* colossal, gigantic, huge.

riesig ['riːziç] *a* enormous, huge, vast.

riet *etc v siehe* **raten.**

Riff [rɪf] *nt* **-(e)s, -e** reef.

Rille ['rɪlə] *f* **-, -n** groove.

Rind [rɪnt] *nt* **-(e)s, -er** ox; cow; cattle *pl*; *(KOCH)* beef; **~e** *f* ['rɪndə] **-, -n** rind; *(Baum~)* bark; *(Brot~)* crust; **~fleisch** *nt* beef; **~vieh** *nt* cattle *pl*; *(umg)* blockhead, stupid oaf.

Ring [rɪŋ] *m* **-(e)s, -e** ring; **~buch** *nt* ring binder; **Ringelnatter** *f* grass snake; **r~en** *vi unreg* wrestle; **~en** *nt* **-s** wrestling; **~finger** *m* ring finger; **~kampf** *m* wrestling bout; **~richter** *m* referee; **rings um** *a* round; **ringsherum** *ad* round about; **~straße** *f* ring road; **ringsum(her)** *ad (rundherum)* round about; *(überall)* all round.

Rinn- ['rɪn] *zW:* **~e** *f* **-, -n** gutter, drain; **r~en** *vi unreg* run, trickle; **~stein** *m* gutter.

Rippchen ['rɪpçən] *nt* small rib; cutlet.

Rippe ['rɪpə] *f* **-, -n** rib; **Rippenfellentzündung** *f* pleurisy.

Risiko ['riːziko] *nt* **-s, -s** *od* **Risiken** risk.

riskant [rɪs'kant] *a* risky, hazardous.

riskieren [rɪs'kiːrən] *vt* risk.

Riß [rɪs] *m* **-sses, -sse** tear; *(in Mauer, Tasse etc)* crack; *(in Haut)* scratch; *(TECH)* design.

rissig ['rɪsiç] *a* torn; cracked; scratched.

ritt *etc v siehe* **reiten.**

Ritt [rɪt] *m* **-(e)s, -e** ride; **~er** *m* **-s, -** knight; **r~erlich** *a* chivalrous.

Ritze ['rɪtsə] *f* **-, -n** crack, chink.

Rivale [ri'vaːlə] *m* **-n, -n** rival.

Rivalität [rivali'tɛːt] *f* rivalry.

Rizinusöl ['riːtsinusøːl] *nt* castor oil.

Robbe ['rɔbə] *f* **-, -n** seal.

Roboter ['rɔbɔtər] *m* **-s, -** robot.

roch *etc v siehe* **riechen.**

Rock [rɔk] *m* **-(e)s, ̈e** skirt; *(Jackett)* jacket; *(Uniform~)* tunic.

Rodel ['roːdəl] *m* **-s, -** toboggan; **~bahn** *f* toboggan run; **r~n** *vi* toboggan.

roden ['roːdən] *vti* clear.

Rogen ['roːgən] *m* **-s, -** roe, spawn.

Roggen ['rɔgən] *m* **-s, -** rye.

roh [roː] *a* raw; *(Mensch)* coarse, crude; **R~bau** *m* shell of a building; **R~material** *nt* raw material; **R~öl** *nt* crude oil.

Rohr ['roːr] *nt* **-(e)s, -e** pipe, tube; *(BOT)* cane; *(Schilf)* reed; *(Gewehr~)* barrel; **~bruch** *m* burst pipe.

Röhre ['røːrə] *f* **-, -n** tube, pipe; *(RAD etc)* valve; *(Back~)* oven.

Rohr- *zW:* **~leitung** *f* pipeline; **~post** *f* pneumatic post; **~zucker** *m* cane sugar.

Rohstoff *m* raw material.

Rokoko ['rɔkoko] *nt* **-s** rococo.

Roll- ['rɔl] *zW:* **~(l)aden** *m* shutter; **~bahn** *f,* **~feld** *nt* *(AVIAT)* runway.

Rolle ['rɔlə] *f* **-, -n** roll; *(THEAT, soziologisch)* role; *(Garn~ etc)* reel, spool; *(Walze)* roller; *(Wäsche~)* mangle; **keine ~ spielen** not matter; **eine (wichtige) ~ spielen** be play a (major) part *od* role in; **r~n** *vti* roll; *(AVIAT)* taxi; **~r** *m* **-s, -** scooter; *(Welle)* roller.

Roll- *zW:* **~mops** *m* pickled herring; **~schuh** *m* roller skate; **~stuhl** *m* wheelchair; **~treppe** *f* escalator.

Rom [roːm] *nt* **-s** Rome.

Roman [ro'maːn] *m* **-s, -e** novel; **~tik** [ro'mantɪk] *f* romanticism; **~tiker** [ro'mantikər] *m* **-s, -** romanticist; **r~tisch** [ro'mantɪʃ] *a* romantic; **Romanze** [ro'mantsə] *f* **-, -n** romance.

Röm- ['røːm] *zW:* **~er** *m* **-s, -** wineglass; *(Mensch)* Roman; **r~isch** *a* Roman.

röntgen ['rœntgən] *vt* X-ray; **R~aufnahme** *f,* **R~bild** *nt* X-ray; **R~strahlen** *pl* X-rays *pl.*

rosa ['roːza] *a inv* pink, rose(-coloured).

Rose ['roːzə] *f* **-, -n** rose; **Rosenkohl** *m* Brussels sprouts *pl*; **Rosenkranz** *m* rosary.

rosig ['roːziç] *a* rosy.

Rosine [ro'ziːnə] *f* raisin, currant.

Roß [rɔs] *nt* **-sses, -sse** horse, steed; **~kastanie** *f* horse chestnut.

Rost [rɔst] *m* **-(e)s, -e** rust; *(Gitter)* grill, gridiron; *(Bett~)* springs *pl*;

~**braten** m roast(ed) meat, joint; r~**en** vi rust.

rösten ['rø:stən] vt roast; toast; grill.

Rost- zW: r~**frei** a rust-free; rust-proof; stainless; r~**ig** a rusty; ~**schutz** m rust-proofing.

rot [ro:t] a red; **in den ~en Zahlen** in the red; **das R~e Meer** the Red Sea.

Röte ['rø:tə] f - redness; **Röteln** pl German measles sing; r~**n** vtr redden.

rot- zW: ~**haarig** a red-haired; ~**ieren** [ro'ti:rən] vi rotate; **R~kehlchen** nt robin; **R~stift** m red pencil; **R~wein** m red wine.

Rouge [ru:ʒ] nt blusher.

Roulade [ru'la:də] f (KOCH) beef olive.

Route ['ru:tə] f -, -n route.

Routine [ru'ti:nə] f experience; routine.

Rübe ['ry:bə] f -, -n turnip; **gelbe ~** carrot; **rote ~** beetroot (Brit), beet (US).

rüber ['ry:bər] ad (umg) = **herüber, hinüber.**

Rubin [ru'bi:n] m -s, -e ruby.

Rubrik [ru'bri:k] f heading; (Spalte) column.

Ruck [ruk] m -(e)s, -e jerk, jolt.

Rück- ['rʏk] zW: ~**antwort** f reply, answer; r~**bezüglich** a reflexive; r~**blickend** a retrospective.

rücken ['rʏkən] vti move; **R~** m -s, - back; (Berg~) ridge; **R~mark** nt spinal cord; **R~schwimmen** nt backstroke; **R~wind** m following wind.

Rück- zW: ~**erstattung** f return, restitution; ~**fahrkarte** f return; ~**fahrt** f return journey; ~**fall** m relapse; r~**fällig** a relapsing; r~**fällig werden** relapse; ~**flug** m return flight; ~**frage** f question; ~**gabe** f return; ~**gang** m decline, fall; r~**gängig** a: **etw r~gängig machen** cancel sth; ~**grat** nt -(e)s, -e spine, backbone; ~**kehr** f -, -en return; ~**licht** nt back light; r~**lings** ad from behind; backwards; ~**nahme** f -, -n taking back; ~**porto** nt return postage; ~**reise** f return journey; (NAUT) home voyage; ~**ruf** m recall.

Rucksack ['rʊkzak] m rucksack.

Rück- zW: ~**schau** f reflection; ~**schluss** m conclusion; ~**schritt** m retrogression; r~**schrittlich** a reactionary; retrograde; ~**seite** f back; (von Münze etc) reverse; ~**sicht** f consideration; ~**sicht nehmen auf** (+akk) show consideration for; r~**sichtslos** a inconsiderate; (Fahren) reckless; (unbarmherzig) ruthless; r~**sichtsvoll** a considerate; ~**sitz** m back seat; ~**spiegel** m (AUT) rear-view mirror; ~**spiel** nt

return match; ~**sprache** f further discussion od talk; ~**stand** m arrears pl; r~**ständig** a backward, out-of-date; (Zahlungen) in arrears; ~**stoß** m recoil; ~**strahler** m -s, - rear reflector; ~**tritt** m resignation; ~**trittbremse** f pedal brake; ~**vergütung** f repayment; (COMM) refund; ~**versicherung** f reinsurance; r~**wärtig** a rear; r~**wärts** ad backward(s), back; ~**wärtsgang** m (AUT) reverse gear; ~**weg** m return journey, way back; r~**wirkend** a retroactive; ~**wirkung** f reaction; retrospective effect; ~**zahlung** f repayment; ~**zug** m retreat.

Rudel ['ru:dəl] nt -s, - pack; herd.

Ruder ['ru:dər] nt -s, - oar; (Steuer) rudder; ~**boot** nt rowing boat; r~**n** vti row.

Ruf [ru:f] m -(e)s, -e call, cry; (Ansehen) reputation; r~**en** vti unreg call; cry; ~**name** m usual (first) name; ~**nummer** f (tele)phone number; ~**zeichen** nt (RAD) call sign; (TEL) ringing tone.

Rüge ['ry:gə] f -, -n reprimand, rebuke.

Ruhe ['ru:ə] f - rest; (Ungestörtheit) peace, quiet; (Gelassenheit, Stille) calm; (Schweigen) silence; **jdn in ~ lassen** leave sb alone; **sich zur ~ setzen** retire; ~**!** be quiet!, silence!; r~**n** vi rest; ~**pause** f break; ~**platz** m resting place; ~**stand** m retirement; **letzte ~stätte** f final resting place; ~**störung** f breach of the peace; ~**tag** m closing day.

ruhig ['ru:ɪç] a quiet; (bewegungslos) still; (Hand) steady; (gelassen, friedlich) calm; (Gewissen) clear; **kommen Sie ~ herein** just come on in; **tu das ~** feel free to do that.

Ruhm [ru:m] m -(e)s fame, glory.

rühmen ['ry:mən] vt praise // vr boast.

Ruhr ['ru:r] f - dysentery.

Rühr- ['ry:r] zW: ~**ei** nt scrambled egg; r~**en** vtr (lit, fig) move, stir (auch KOCH) // vi: r~**en von** come od stem from; r~**en an** (+akk) touch; (fig) touch on; r~**end** a touching, moving; r~**ig** a active, lively; r~**selig** a sentimental, emotional; ~**ung** f emotion.

Ruin [ru'i:n] m -s, ~**e**, f -, -n ruin; r~**ieren** [rui'ni:rən] vt ruin.

rülpsen ['rʏlpsən] vi burp, belch.

rum [rʊm] ad (umg) = **herum.**

Rum [rʊm] m -s, -s rum.

Rumän- [ru'mɛ:n] zW: ~**e** m -n, -n, ~**in** f Ro(u)manian; ~**ien** nt -s Ro(u)mania; r~**isch** a Ro(u)manian.

Rummel ['rʊməl] m -s (umg) hubbub; (Jahrmarkt) fair; ~**platz** m fairground, fair.

Rumpf [rumpf] m **-(e)s, -̈e** trunk, torso; (AVIAT) fuselage; (NAUT) hull.
rümpfen ['rympfən] vt (Nase) turn up.
rund [runt] a round // ad (etwa) around; ~ **um etw** round sth; **R~brief** m circular; **R~e** ['rundə] f -, -n round; (in Rennen) lap; (Gesellschaft) circle; **R~fahrt** f (round) trip.
Rundfunk ['runtfuŋk] m **-(e)s** broadcasting; **im ~** on the radio; **~gerät** nt wireless set; **~sendung** f broadcast, radio programme.
Rund- zW: **r~heraus** ad straight out, bluntly; **r~herum** ad round about; all round; **r~lich** a plump, rounded; **~reise** f round trip; **~schreiben** nt (COMM) circular.
runter ['runtər] ad (umg) = **herunter, hinunter.**
Runzel ['runtsəl] f -, -n wrinkle; **r~ig** a wrinkled; **r~n** vt wrinkle; **die Stirn r~n** frown.
rupfen ['rupfən] vt pluck; **R~** m **-s, -** sackcloth.
ruppig ['rupıç] a rough, gruff.
Rüsche ['ry:ʃə] f -, -n frill.
Ruß [ru:s] m **-es** soot.
Russe ['rusə] m **-n, -n** Russian.
Rüssel ['rysəl] m **-s, -** snout; (Elefanten~) trunk.
rußig ['ru:sıç] a sooty.
Russ- [rus] zW: **~in** f Russian; **r~isch** a Russian.
Rußland ['ruslant] nt **-s** Russia.
rüsten ['rystən] vtri prepare; (MIL) arm.
rüstig ['rystıç] a sprightly, vigorous.
Rüstung ['rystuŋ] f preparation; arming; (Ritter~) armour; (Waffen etc) armaments pl; **Rüstungskontrolle** f arms control.
Rute ['ru:tə] f -, -n rod.
Rutsch [rutʃ] m **-(e)s, -e** slide; (Erd~) landslide; **~bahn** f slide; **r~en** vi slide; (ausr~en) slip; **r~ig** a slippery.
rütteln ['rytəln] vti shake, jolt.

S

S, s [ɛs] nt S, s.
S. abk (= Seite) p. // abk von **Schilling.**
s. abk (= siehe) see.
Saal [za:l] m **-(e)s, Säle** hall; room.
Saarland ['za:rlant] nt: **das ~** the Saar(land).
Saat [za:t] f -, **-en** seed; (Pflanzen) crop; (Säen) sowing.
Säbel ['zɛ:bəl] m **-s, -** sabre, sword.
Sabotage [zabo'ta:ʒə] f -, -n sabotage.
sabotieren [zabo'ti:rən] vt sabotage.
Sach- [zax] zW: **~bearbeiter** m specialist; **s~dienlich** a relevant, helpful; **~e** f -, -n thing; (Angelegenheit) affair, business; (Frage) matter; (Pflicht) task; **zur ~e** to the point; **s~kundig** a expert; **s~lich** a matter-of-fact, objective; (Irrtum, Angabe) factual.
sächlich ['zɛxlıç] a neuter.
Sachschaden m material damage.
Sachsen ['zaksən] nt **-s** Saxony.
sächsisch ['zɛksıʃ] a Saxon.
sacht(e) ['zaxt(ə)] ad softly, gently.
Sachverständige(r) mf expert.
Sack [zak] m **-(e)s, -̈e** sack; **~gasse** f cul-de-sac, dead-end street (US).
Sadismus [za'dısmus] m sadism.
Sadist [za'dıst] m sadist; **s~isch** a sadistic.
säen ['zɛ:ən] vti sow.
Saft [zaft] m **-(e)s, -̈e** juice; (BOT) sap; **s~ig** a juicy; **s~los** a dry.
Sage ['za:gə] f -, -n saga.
Säge ['zɛ:gə] f -, -n saw; **~mehl** nt sawdust; **s~n** vti saw.
sagen ['za:gən] vti say (jdm to sb); (mitteilen) tell (jdm sb); **~ Sie ihm, daß ...** tell him ...; **~haft** a legendary; (umg) great, smashing.
sah etc v siehe **sehen.**
Sahne ['za:nə] f - cream.
Saison [zɛ'zõ] f -, **-s** season; **~arbeiter** m seasonal worker.
Saite ['zaıtə] f -, -n string; **Saiteninstrument** nt string instrument.
Sakko [zako] m od nt **-s, -s** jacket.
Sakrament [zakra'mɛnt] nt sacrament.
Sakristei [zakrıs'taı] f sacristy.
Salat [za'la:t] m **-(e)s, -e** salad; (Kopfsalat) lettuce; **~soße** f salad dressing.
Salb- ['zalb] zW: **~e** f -, -n ointment; **~ei** [zal'baı] m od f **-s** od - sage; **s~en** vt anoint.
Saldo ['zaldo] m **-s, Salden** balance.
Salmiak [zalmi'ak] m **-s** sal ammoniac; **~geist** m liquid ammonia.
salopp [za'lɔp] a casual.
Salpeter [zal'pe:tər] m **-s** saltpetre; **~säure** f nitric acid.
Salve ['zalvə] f -, -n salvo.
Salz [zalts] nt **-es, -e** salt; **s~en** vt unreg salt; **s~ig** a salty; **~kartoffeln** pl boiled potatoes pl; **~säure** f hydrochloric acid.
Samen ['za:mən] m **-s, -** seed; (ANAT) sperm.
Sammel- ['zaməl] zW: **~band** m anthology; **s~n** vt collect // vr assemble, gather; (konzentrieren) concentrate.
Sammlung ['zamluŋ] f collection; assembly, gathering; concentration.
Samstag ['zamsta:k] m Saturday; **s~s** ad (on) Saturdays.
Samt [zamt] m **-(e)s, -e** velvet; **s~**

präp +*dat* (along) with, together with; s~ **und sonders** each and every one (of them).

sämtlich ['zɛmtlıç] *a* all (the), entire.

Sand [zant] *m* **-(e)s, -e** sand; **Sandale** [zan'da:lə] *f* **-, -n** sandal; ~**bank** *f* sandbank; **s~ig** ['zandıç] *a* sandy; ~**kasten** *m* sandpit; ~**kuchen** *m* Madeira cake; ~**papier** *nt* sandpaper; ~**stein** *m* sandstone; **s~strahlen** *vti insep* sandblast.

sandte *etc v siehe* **senden.**

Sanduhr *f* hourglass.

sanft [zanft] *a* soft, gentle; ~**mütig** *a* gentle, meek.

sang *etc v siehe* **singen.**

Sänger(in *f)* ['zɛŋər(ın)] *m* **-s, -** singer.

Sani- *zW:* **s~eren** [za'ni:rən] *vt* redevelop; *(Betrieb)* make financially sound // *vr* line one's pockets; become financially sound; **s~tär** [zani'tɛ:r] *a* sanitary; **s~täre Anlagen** sanitation; ~**täter** [zani'tɛ:tər] *m* **-s, -** first-aid attendant; *(MIL)* (medical) orderly.

sanktionieren [zaŋktsio'ni:rən] *vt* sanction.

Saphir ['za:fi:r] *m* **-s, -e** sapphire.

Sardelle [zar'dɛlə] *f* anchovy.

Sardin- [zar'di:n] *zW:* ~**e** *f* sardine; ~**ien** [-iən] *nt* **-s** Sardinia.

Sarg [zark] *m* **-(e)s, ⁻e** coffin.

Sarkasmus [zar'kasmʊs] *m* sarcasm.

sarkastisch [zar'kastıʃ] *a* sarcastic.

saß *etc v siehe* **sitzen.**

Satan ['za:tan] *m* **-s, -e** Satan; devil.

Satellit [zatɛ'li:t] *m* **-en, -en** satellite; ~**enfoto** *nt* satellite picture.

Satire [za'ti:rə] *f* **-, -n** satire.

satirisch [za'ti:rıʃ] *a* satirical.

satt [zat] *a* full; *(Farbe)* rich, deep; **jdn/etw ~ sein** *od* **haben** be fed up with sb/sth; **sich ~ hören/sehen an** (+*dat*) see/hear enough of; **sich ~ essen** eat one's fill; **~ machen** be filling.

Sattel ['zatəl] *m* **-s, ⁻** saddle; *(Berg)* ridge; **s~n** *vt* saddle; ~**schlepper** *m* articulated lorry.

sättigen ['zɛtıgən] *vt* satisfy; *(CHEM)* saturate.

Satz [zats] *m* **-es, ⁻e** *(GRAM)* sentence; *(Neben~, Adverbial~)* clause; *(Theorem)* theorem; *(MUS)* movement; *(TENNIS, Briefmarken etc)* set; *(Kaffee)* grounds *pl*; *(COMM)* rate; *(Sprung)* jump; ~**teil** *m* part of a sentence; ~**zeichen** *nt* punctuation mark.

Sau [zau] *f* **-, Säue** sow; *(umg)* dirty pig.

sauber ['zaubər] *a* clean; *(ironisch)* fine; ~**halten** *vt unreg* keep clean; **S~keit** *f* cleanness; *(einer Person)* cleanliness.

säuberlich ['zɔybərlıç] *ad* neatly.

saubermachen *vti* clean.

säubern *vt* clean; *(POL etc)* purge.

Säuberung *f* cleaning; purge.

Sauce ['zo:sə] *f* **-, -n** sauce, gravy.

sauer ['zauər] *a* sour; *(CHEM)* acid; *(umg)* cross; **Saurer Regen** acid rain.

Sauerei [zauə'rai] *f* *(umg)* rotten state of affairs, scandal; *(Schmutz etc)* mess; *(Unanständigkeit)* obscenity.

Sauer- *zW:* ~**milch** *f* sour milk; ~**stoff** *m* oxygen; ~**teig** *m* leaven.

saufen ['zaufən] *vti unreg* *(umg)* drink, booze.

Säufer ['zɔyfər] *m* **-s, -** *(umg)* boozer.

saugen ['zaugən] *vti unreg* suck.

Sauger [zaugər] *m* **-s, -** dummy, comforter *(US)*; *(auf Flasche)* teat; *(Staub~)* vacuum cleaner, hoover ®.

Säug- ['zɔyg] *zW:* **Säugetier** *nt* mammal; ~**ling** *m* infant, baby.

Säule ['zɔylə] *f* **-, -n** column, pillar.

Saum [zaum] *m* **-(e)s, Säume** hem; *(Naht)* seam.

säumen ['zɔymən] *vt* hem; seam // *vi* delay, hesitate.

Sauna ['zauna] *f* **-, -s** sauna.

Säure ['zɔyrə] *f* **-, -n** acid; *(Geschmack)* sourness, acidity.

sausen ['zauzən] *vi* blow; *(umg: eilen)* rush; *(Ohren)* buzz; **etw ~ lassen** *(umg)* not bother with sth.

Saustall ['zauʃtal] *m* *(umg)* pigsty.

Saxophon [zakso'fo:n] *nt* **-s, -e** saxophone.

SB *abk von* **Selbstbedienung.**

S-Bahn *abk* (= *Schnellbahn*) high speed railway; (= *Stadtbahn*) suburban railway.

schaben ['ʃa:bən] *vt* scrape.

schäbig ['ʃɛ:bıç] *a* shabby.

Schablone [ʃa'blo:nə] *f* **-, -n** stencil; *(Muster)* pattern; *(fig)* convention.

Schach [ʃax] *nt* **-s, -s** chess; *(Stellung)* check; ~**brett** *nt* chessboard; ~**figur** *f* chessman; **'s~'matt** *a* checkmate; ~**spiel** *nt* game of chess.

Schacht [ʃaxt] *m* **-(e)s, ⁻e** shaft.

Schachtel [ʃaxtəl] *f* **-, -n** box; *(pej: Frau)* bag, cow.

schade ['ʃa:də] *a* a pity *od* shame; **sich** (*dat*) **zu ~ sein für etw** consider oneself too good for sth // *interj*: **(wie)** ~! (what a) pity *od* shame.

Schädel ['ʃɛdəl] *m* **-s, -** skull; ~**bruch** *m* fractured skull.

Schaden ['ʃa:dən] *m* **-s, ⁻** damage; *(Verletzung)* injury; *(Nachteil)* disadvantage; **s~** *vi* (+*dat*) hurt; **einer Sache s~** damage sth; ~**ersatz** *m* compensation, damages *pl*; ~**freude** *f* malicious glee.

schadhaft ['ʃa:thaft] *a* faulty, damaged.

schäd- ['ʃɛ:t] *zW:* **~igen** ['ʃɛdɪgən] *vt* damage; (*Person*) do harm to, harm; **~lich** *a* harmful (*für* to); **S~lichkeit** *f* harmfulness; **S~ling** *m* pest.

Schadstoff ['ʃa:tʃtɔf] *m* harmful substance.

Schaf [ʃa:f] *nt* **-(e)s, -e** sheep; **~bock** *m* ram.

Schäfer ['ʃɛ:fər] *m* **-s, -** shepherd; **~hund** *m* Alsatian.

schaffen ['ʃafən] *vt unreg* create; (*Platz*) make; **sich** (*dat*) **etw ~** get o.s. sth // *vt* (*erreichen*) manage, do; (*erledigen*) finish; (*Prüfung*) pass; (*transportieren*) take // *vi* (*umg: arbeiten*) work; **sich an etw** (*dat*) **zu ~ machen** busy oneself with sth; **S~** *nt* **-s** (creative) activity.

Schaffner(in *f*) ['ʃafnər(ɪn)] *m* **-s, -** (*Bus~*) conductor/conductress; (*EISENB*) guard.

Schaft [ʃaft] *m* **-(e)s, ⁻e** shaft; (*von Gewehr*) stock; (*von Stiefel*) leg; (*BOT*) stalk; tree trunk; **~stiefel** *m* high boot.

Schakal [ʃa'ka:l] *m* **-s, -e** jackal.

schal [ʃa:l] *a* flat; (*fig*) insipid; **S~** *m* **-s, -e** *od* **-s** scarf.

Schälchen ['ʃɛ:lçən] *nt* cup, bowl.

Schale ['ʃa:lə] *f* **-, -n** skin; (*abgeschält*) peel; (*Nuß~, Muschel~, Ei~*) shell; (*Geschirr*) dish, bowl.

schälen ['ʃɛ:lən] *vt* peel; shell // *vr* peel.

Schall [ʃal] *m* **-(e)s, -e** sound; **~dämpfer** *m* **-s, -** (*AUT*) silencer; **s~dicht** *a* soundproof; **s~en** *vi* (re)sound; **s~end** *a* resounding, loud; **~mauer** *f* sound barrier; **~platte** *f* (gramophone) record.

Schalt- ['ʃalt] *zW:* **~bild** *nt* circuit diagram; **~brett** *nt* switchboard; **s~en** *vt* switch, turn // *vi* (*AUT*) change (gear); (*umg: begreifen*) catch on; **~er** *m* **-s, -** counter; (*an Gerät*) switch; **~erbeamte(r)** *m* counter clerk; **~hebel** *m* switch; (*AUT*) gear-lever; **~jahr** *nt* leap year; **~ung** *f* switching; (*ELEK*) circuit; (*AUT*) gear change.

Scham [ʃa:m] *f* **-** shame; (*~gefühl*) modesty; (*Organe*) private parts *pl*.

schämen ['ʃɛ:mən] *vr* be ashamed.

schamlos *a* shameless.

Schande ['ʃandə] *f* **-** disgrace.

schändlich ['ʃɛntlɪç] *a* disgraceful, shameful.

Schändung ['ʃɛndʊŋ] *f* violation, defilement.

Schank- ['ʃaŋk] *zW:* **~erlaubnis** *f* (publican's) licence; **~tisch** *m* bar.

Schanze ['ʃantsə] *f* **-, -n** (*Sprung~*) skijump.

Schar [ʃa:r] *f* **-, -en** band, company; (*Vögel*) flock; (*Menge*) crowd; **in ~en** in droves; **s~en** *vr* assemble, rally.

scharf [ʃarf] *a* sharp; (*Essen*) hot; (*Munition*) live; **~ nachdenken** think hard; **auf etw** (*acc*) **~ sein** (*umg*) be keen on sth.

Schärf- ['ʃɛrf] *zW:* **~e** *f* **-, -n** sharpness; (*Strenge*) rigour; **s~en** *vt* sharpen.

Scharf- *zW:* **s~machen** *vt* (*umg*) stir up; **~richter** *m* executioner; **~schütze** *m* marksman, sharpshooter; **~sinn** *nt* penetration, astuteness; **s~sinnig** *a* astute, shrewd.

Scharnier [ʃar'ni:r] *nt* **-s, -e** hinge.

Schärpe ['ʃɛrpə] *f* **-, -n** sash.

scharren ['ʃarən] *vti* scrape, scratch.

Schaschlik ['ʃaʃlɪk] *m od nt* **-s, -s** (shish) kebab.

Schatten ['ʃatən] *m* **-s, -** shadow; **~bild** *nt*, **~riß** *m* silhouette; **~seite** *f* shady side, dark side; **~wirtschaft** *f* black economy.

schattieren [ʃa'ti:rən] *vti* shade.

schattig ['ʃatɪç] *a* shady.

Schatulle [ʃa'tʊlə] *f* **-, -n** casket; (*Geld~*) coffer.

Schatz [ʃats] *m* **-es, ⁻e** treasure; (*Person*) darling.

schätz- ['ʃɛts] *zW:* **~bar** *a* assessable; **S~chen** *nt* darling, love; **~en** *vt* (*abschätzen*) estimate; (*Gegenstand*) value; (*würdigen*) value, esteem; (*vermuten*) reckon; **S~ung** *f* estimate; estimation; valuation; **nach meiner S~ung...** I reckon that...; **~ungsweise** *ad* approximately; it is thought.

Schau [ʃau] *f* **-** show; (*Ausstellung*) display, exhibition; **etw zur ~ stellen** make a show of sth, show sth off; **~bild** *nt* diagram.

Schauder ['ʃaudər] *m* **-s, -s** shudder; (*wegen Kälte*) shiver; **s~haft** *a* horrible; **s~n** *vi* shudder; shiver.

schauen ['ʃauən] *vi* look.

Schauer ['ʃauər] *m* **-s, -** (*Regen~*) shower; (*Schreck*) shudder; **~geschichte** *f* horror story; **s~lich** *a* horrific, spine-chilling.

Schaufel ['ʃaufəl] *f* **-, -n** shovel; (*NAUT*) paddle; (*TECH*) scoop; **s~n** *vt* shovel, scoop.

Schau- *zW:* **~fenster** *nt* shop window; **~fensterbummel** *m* window shopping (expedition); **~kasten** *m* showcase.

Schaukel ['ʃaukəl] *f* **-, -n** swing; **s~n** *vi* swing, rock; **~pferd** *nt* rocking horse; **~stuhl** *m* rocking chair.

Schaum [ʃaum] *m* **-(e)s, Schäume** foam; (*Seifen~*) lather.

schäumen ['ʃɔymən] *vi* foam.

Schaum- *zW:* **~gummi** *m* foam (rubber); **s~ig** *a* frothy, foamy; **~wein** *m* sparkling wine.

Schau- *zW:* **~platz** *m* scene; **s~rig** *a* horrific, dreadful; **~spiel** *nt* spectacle; (*THEAT*) play; **~spieler** *m* actor; **~spielerin** *f* actress; **s~spielern** *vi insep* act; **~spielhaus** *nt* theatre.

Scheck [ʃɛk] *m* **-s, -s** cheque; **~heft** *m* cheque book; **~karte** *f* cheque card.

scheffeln ['ʃɛfəln] *vt* amass.

Scheibe ['ʃaɪbə] *f* **-, -n** disc; (*Brot etc*) slice; (*Glas~*) pane; (*MIL*) target.

Scheiben- *zW:* **~bremse** *f* (*AUT*) disc brake; **~waschanlage** *f* (*AUT*) windscreen washers *pl*; **~wischer** *m* (*AUT*) windscreen wiper.

Scheich [ʃaɪç] *m* **-s, -e** *od* **-s** sheik(h).

Scheide ['ʃaɪdə] *f* **-, -n** sheath; (*Grenze*) boundary; (*ANAT*) vagina; **s~n** *unreg vt* separate; (*Ehe*) dissolve; sich **s~n lassen** get a divorce // *vi* (de)part.

Scheidung *f* (*Ehe~*) divorce.

Schein [ʃaɪn] *m* **-(e)s, -e** light; (*An~*) appearance; (*Geld*) (bank)note; (*Bescheinigung*) certificate; **zum ~** in pretence; **s~bar** *a* apparent; **s~en** *vi unreg* shine; (*Anschein haben*) seem; **s~heilig** *a* hypocritical; **~werfer** *m* **-s, -** floodlight; spotlight; (*Such~*) searchlight; (*AUT*) headlamp.

Scheiß- ['ʃaɪs] *in zW* (*umg*) bloody; **~e** *f* **-** (*umg*) shit.

Scheit [ʃaɪt] *nt* **-(e)s, -e** *od* **-er** log, billet.

Scheitel ['ʃaɪtəl] *m* **-s, -** top; (*Haar*) parting; **s~n** *vt* part.

scheitern ['ʃaɪtərn] *vi* fail.

Schelle ['ʃɛlə] *f* **-, -n** small bell; **s~n** *vi* ring.

Schellfisch ['ʃɛlfɪʃ] *m* haddock.

Schelm [ʃɛlm] *m* **-(e)s, -e** rogue; **s~isch** *a* mischievous, roguish.

Schelte ['ʃɛltə] *f* **-, -n** scolding; **s~n** *vt unreg* scold.

Schema ['ʃeːma] *nt* **-s, -s** *od* **-ta** scheme, plan; (*Darstellung*) schema; **nach ~** quite mechanically; **s~tisch** [ʃeˈmaːtɪʃ] *a* schematic; (*pej*) mechanical.

Schemel ['ʃeːməl] *m* **-s, -** (foot)stool.

Schenkel ['ʃɛŋkəl] *m* **-s, -** thigh.

schenken ['ʃɛŋkən] *vt* (*lit, fig*) give; (*Getränk*) pour; **sich** (*dat*) **etw ~** (*umg*) skip sth; **das ist geschenkt!** (*billig*) that's a giveaway!; (*nichts wert*) that's worthless!

Scherbe ['ʃɛrbə] *f* **-, -n** broken piece, fragment; (*archäologisch*) potsherd.

Schere ['ʃeːrə] *f* **-, -n** scissors *pl*; (*groß*) shears *pl*; **s~n** *vt unreg* cut; (*Schaf*) shear; (*kümmern*) bother // *vr* care; **scher dich zum Teufel!** get lost!; **~rei** *f* (*umg*) bother, trouble.

Scherz [ʃɛrts] *m* **-es, -e** joke; fun;

~frage *f* conundrum; **s~haft** *a* joking, jocular.

scheu [ʃɔy] *a* shy; **S~** *f* **-** shyness; (*Angst*) fear (*vor* +*dat* of); (*Ehrfurcht*) awe; **~en** *vr:* **sich ~en vor** (+*dat*) be afraid of, shrink from // *vt* shun // *vi* (*Pferd*) shy.

scheuern ['ʃɔyərn] *vt* scour, scrub.

Scheuklappe *f* blinker.

Scheune ['ʃɔynə] *f* **-, -n** barn.

Scheusal ['ʃɔyzaːl] *nt* **-s, -e** monster.

scheußlich ['ʃɔyslıç] *a* dreadful, frightful; **S~keit** *f* dreadfulness.

Schi [ʃiː] *m siehe* **Ski.**

Schicht [ʃıçt] *f* **-, -en** layer; (*Klasse*) class, level; (*in Fabrik etc*) shift; **~arbeit** *f* shift work; **s~en** *vt* layer, stack.

schick [ʃık] *a* stylish, chic; **~en** *vt* send // *vr* resign oneself (*in* +*akk* to) // *v unpers* (*anständig sein*) be fitting; **~lich** *a* proper, fitting; **S~sal** *nt* **-s, -e** fate; **S~salsschlag** *m* great misfortune, blow.

Schieb- ['ʃiːb] *zW:* **Schiebedach** *nt* (*AUT*) sun roof; **s~en** *vti unreg* (*auch Drogen*) push; (*Schuld*) put (*auf jdn* on sb); **Schiebetür** *f* sliding door; **~ung** *f* fiddle.

Schieds- ['ʃiːts] *zW:* **~gericht** *nt* court of arbitration; **~richter** *m* referee, umpire; (*Schlichter*) arbitrator; **~verfahren** *nt* arbitration.

schief [ʃiːf] *a* crooked; (*Ebene*) sloping; (*Turm*) leaning; (*Winkel*) oblique; (*Blick*) funny; (*Vergleich*) distorted // *ad* crooked(ly); (*ansehen*) askance; **etw ~ stellen** slope sth.

Schiefer ['ʃiːfər] *m* **-s, -** slate; **~dach** *nt* slate roof; **~tafel** *f* (child's) slate.

schiefgehen *vi unreg* (*umg*) go wrong.

schielen ['ʃiːlən] *vi* squint; **nach etw ~** (*fig*) eye sth.

schien *etc siehe* **scheinen.**

Schienbein *nt* shinbone.

Schiene ['ʃiːnə] *f* **-, -n** rail; (*MED*) splint; **s~n** *vt* put in splints.

schier [ʃiːr] *a* (*fig*) sheer // *ad* nearly, almost.

Schieß- ['ʃiːs] *zW:* **~bude** *f* shooting gallery; **s~en** *vti unreg* shoot (*auf* +*akk* at); (*Salat etc*) run to seed; (*Ball*) kick; (*Geschoß*) fire; **~e'rei** *f* shooting incident, shoot-up; **~pulver** *nt* gunpowder; **~scharte** *f* embrasure.

Schiff [ʃıf] *nt* **-(e)s, -e** ship, vessel; (*Kirchen~*) nave; **~bau** *m* shipbuilding; **~bruch** *m* shipwreck; **s~brüchig** *a* shipwrecked; **~chen** *nt* small boat; (*Weben*) shuttle; (*Mütze*) forage cap; **~er** *m* **-s, -** bargeman, boatman; **~(f)ahrt** *f* shipping;

(*Reise*) voyage; ~**(f)ahrtslinie** *f* shipping route.
Schikane [ʃi'ka:nə] *f* -, -n harassment; dirty trick; **mit allen** ~n with all the trimmings.
schikanieren [ʃika'ni:rən] *vt* harass, torment.
Schild [ʃilt] *m* -(e)s, -e shield; etw im ~e **führen** be up to sth // *nt* -(e)s, -er sign; nameplate; (*Etikett*) label; ~**drüse** *f* thyroid gland; **s~ern** ['ʃildərn] *vt* depict, portray; ~**erung** *f* description, portrayal; ~**kröte** *f* tortoise; (*Wasser~*) turtle.
Schilf [ʃilf] *nt* -(e)s, -e, ~**rohr** *nt* (*Pflanze*) reed; (*Material*) reeds *pl*, rushes *pl*.
schillern ['ʃilərn] *vi* shimmer; ~**d** *a* iridescent.
Schilling ['ʃiliŋ] *m* schilling.
Schimmel ['ʃiməl] *m* -s, - mould; (*Pferd*) white horse; **s~ig** *a* mouldy; **s~n** *vi* get mouldy.
schimmern ['ʃimərn] *vi* glimmer, shimmer.
Schimpanse [ʃim'panzə] *m* -n, -n chimpanzee.
Schimpf- [ʃimpf] *zW*: **s~en** *vti* scold // *vi* curse, complain; ~**wort** *nt* term of abuse.
Schind- ['ʃind] *zW*: **s~en** *unreg vt* maltreat, drive too hard; **Eindruck s~en** (*umg*) create an impression // *vr* sweat and strain, toil away (*mit* at); ~**e'rei** *f* grind, drudgery.
Schinken ['ʃiŋkən] *m* -s, - ham.
Schippe ['ʃipə] *f* -, -n shovel; **s~n** *vt* shovel.
Schirm [ʃirm] *m* -(e)s, -e (*Regen~*) umbrella; (*Sonnen~*) parasol, sunshade; (*Wand~*, *Bild~*) screen; (*Lampen~*) (lamp)shade; (*Mützen~*) peak; (*Pilz~*) cap; ~**mütze** *f* peaked cap; ~**ständer** *m* umbrella stand.
schizophren [ʃitso'fre:n] *a* schizophrenic.
Schlacht [ʃlaxt] *f* -, -en battle; **s~en** *vt* slaughter, kill; ~**enbummler** *m* football supporter; ~**er** *m* -s, - butcher; ~**feld** *nt* battlefield; ~**haus** *nt*, ~**hof** *m* slaughterhouse, abattoir; ~**schiff** *nt* battleship; ~**vieh** *nt* animals kept for meat; beef cattle.
Schlacke ['ʃlakə] *f* -, -n slag.
Schlaf [ʃla:f] *m* -(e)s sleep; ~**anzug** *m* pyjamas *pl*.
Schläfe ['ʃlɛ:fə] *f* -, -n temple.
schlafen ['ʃla:fən] *vi unreg* sleep; ~ **gehen** go to bed; **S~gehen** *nt* -s going to bed; **Schlafenszeit** *f* bedtime.
schlaff [ʃlaf] *a* slack; (*energielos*) limp; (*erschöpft*) exhausted.
Schlaf- *zW*: ~**gelegenheit** *f* sleeping accommodation; ~**lied** *nt* lullaby;

s~los *a* sleepless; ~**losigkeit** *f* sleeplessness, insomnia; ~**mittel** *nt* sleeping pill.
schläfrig ['ʃlɛ:friç] *a* sleepy.
Schlaf- *zW*: ~**saal** *m* dormitory; ~**sack** *m* sleeping bag; ~**tablette** *f* sleeping pill; ~**wagen** *m* sleeping car, sleeper; **s~wandeln** *vi insep* sleepwalk; ~**zimmer** *nt* bedroom.
Schlag [ʃla:k] *m* -(e)s, ⁼e (*lit*, *fig*) blow; stroke (*auch MED*); (*Puls~*, *Herz~*) beat; (*pl*: *Tracht Prügel*) beating; (*ELEK*) shock; (*Blitz~*) bolt, stroke; (*Autotür*) car door; (*umg*: *Portion*) helping; (*Art*) kind, type; **mit einem** ~ all at once; ~ **auf** ~ in rapid succession; ~**ader** *f* artery; ~**anfall** *m* stroke; **s~artig** *a* sudden, without warning; ~**baum** *m* barrier; **s~en** ['ʃla:gən] *unreg vti* strike, hit; (*wiederholt s~en*, *besiegen*) beat; (*Glocke*) ring; (*Stunde*) strike; (*Sahne*) whip; (*Schlacht*) fight; **nach jdm s~en** (*fig*) take after sb // *vr* fight; **sich gut s~en** (*fig*) do well; ~**er** ['ʃla:gər] *m* -s, - (*lit*, *fig*) hit; ~**ersänger(in** *f*) *m* pop singer.
Schläg- ['ʃlɛ:g] *zW*: ~**er** *m* -s, - brawler; (*SPORT*) bat; (*TENNIS etc*) racket; (*Golf*) club; hockey stick; (*Waffe*) rapier; ~**e'rei** *f* fight, punch-up.
Schlag- *zW*: **s~fertig** *a* quick-witted; ~**fertigkeit** *f* ready wit, quickness of repartee; ~**loch** *nt* pothole; ~**sahne** *f* (whipped) cream; ~**seite** *f* (*NAUT*) list; ~**wort** *nt* slogan, catch phrase; ~**zeile** *f* headline; ~**zeug** *nt* percussion; drums *pl*; ~**zeuger** *m* -s, - drummer.
Schlamassel [ʃla'masəl] *m* -s, - (*umg*) mess.
Schlamm [ʃlam] *m* -(e)s, -e mud; **s~ig** *a* muddy.
Schlamp- ['ʃlamp] *zW*: ~**e** *f* -, -n (*umg*) slut; **s~en** *vi* (*umg*) be sloppy; ~**e'rei** *f* (*umg*) disorder, untidiness; sloppy work.
Schlange ['ʃlaŋə] *f* -, -n snake; (*Menschen~*) queue (*Brit*), line-up (*US*); ~ **stehen** (form a) queue, line up.
Schlangen- *zW*: ~**biß** *m* snake bite; ~**gift** *nt* snake venom; ~**linie** *f* wavy line.
schlank [ʃlaŋk] *a* slim, slender; **S~heit** *f* slimness, slenderness; **S~heitskur** *f* diet.
schlapp [ʃlap] *a* limp; (*locker*) slack; **S~e** *f* -, -n (*umg*) setback.
Schlaraffenland [ʃla'rafənlant] *nt* land of milk and honey.
schlau [ʃlau] *a* crafty, cunning.
Schlauch [ʃlaux] *m* -(e)s, **Schläuche** hose; (*in Reifen*) inner tube; (*umg*:

Anstrengung) grind; **~boot** *nt* rubber dinghy; **~en** *vt* (*umg*) tell on, exhaust; **s~los** *a* (*Reifen*) tubeless.

Schlau- *zW:* **~heit** *f*, **Schläue** ['ʃlɔyə] *f* - cunning; **~kopf** *m* clever dick.

schlecht [ʃlɛçt] *a* bad; **es geht ihr ~** she's in a bad way; **~ gelaunt** in a bad mood; **~ und recht** after a fashion; **jdm ist ~** sb feels sick *od* bad; **~gehen** *vi unpers unreg:* **jdm geht es ~** sb is in a bad way; **S~igkeit** *f* badness; bad deed; **~machen** *vt* run down; **etw ~ machen** do sth badly.

schlecken ['ʃlɛkən] *vti* lick.

Schlegel ['ʃleːgəl] *m* **-s,** **-** (drum)stick; (*Hammer*) mallet, hammer; (*KOCH*) leg.

schleichen ['ʃlaɪçən] *vi unreg* creep, crawl; **~d** *a* gradual; creeping.

Schleier ['ʃlaɪər] *m* **-s,** **-** veil; **s~haft** *a* (*umg*): **jdm s~haft sein** be a mystery to sb.

Schleif- ['ʃlaɪf] *zW:* **~e** *f* -, **-n** loop; (*Band*) bow; **s~en** *vti drag // vi unreg* grind; (*Edelstein*) cut; (*MIL: Soldaten*) drill; **~stein** *m* grindstone.

Schleim [ʃlaɪm] *m* **-(e)s, -e** slime; (*MED*) mucus; (*KOCH*) gruel; **s~ig** *a* slimy.

Schlemm- ['ʃlɛm] *zW:* **s~en** *vi* feast; **~er** *m* **-s, -** gourmet; **~erei** *f* gluttony, feasting.

schlendern ['ʃlɛndərn] *vi* stroll.

schlenkern ['ʃlɛŋkərn] *vti* swing, dangle.

Schlepp- ['ʃlɛp] *zW:* **~e** *f* -, **-n** train; **s~en** *vt* drag; (*Auto, Schiff*) tow; (*tragen*) lug; **s~end** *a* dragging, slow; **~er** *m* **-s, -** tractor; (*Schiff*) tug.

Schleuder ['ʃlɔydər] *f* -, **-n** catapult; (*Wäsche~*) spin-drier; (*Butter~ etc*) centrifuge; **s~n** *vt* hurl; (*Wäsche*) spin-dry // *vi* (*AUT*) skid; **~preis** *m* give-away price; **~sitz** *m* (*AVIAT*) ejector seat; (*fig*) hot seat; **~ware** *f* cheap *od* cut-price goods *pl*.

schleunigst ['ʃlɔynɪçst] *ad* straight away.

Schleuse ['ʃlɔyzə] *f* -, **-n** lock; (*Schleusentor*) sluice.

schlicht [ʃlɪçt] *a* simple, plain; **~en** *vt* smooth, dress; (*Streit*) settle; **S~er** *m* **-s, -** mediator, arbitrator; **S~ung** *f* settlement; arbitration.

Schlick [ʃlɪk] *m* **-(e)s, -e** mud; (*Öl~*) slick.

schlief *etc v siehe* **schlafen.**

Schließ- ['ʃliːs] *zW:* **~e** *f* -, **-n** fastener; **s~en** *vtir unreg* close, shut; (*beenden*) close; (*Freundschaft, Bündnis, Ehe*) enter into; (*folgern*) infer (*aus +dat* from); **etw in sich s~en** include sth; **~fach** *nt* locker; **s~lich** *ad* finally; (*s~lich doch*) after

all.

Schliff [ʃlɪf] *m* **-(e)s, -e** cut(ting); (*fig*) polish.

schlimm [ʃlɪm] *a* bad; **~er** *a* worse; **~ste(r, s)** *a* worst; **~stenfalls** *ad* at (the) worst.

Schling- ['ʃlɪŋ] *zW:* **~e** *f* -, **-n** loop; (*des Henkers*) noose; (*Falle*) snare; (*MED*) sling; **~el** *m* **-s, -** rascal; **s~en** *unreg vt* wind; *vti* (*essen*) bolt (one's food), gobble; **s~ern** *vi* roll.

Schlips [ʃlɪps] *m* **-es, -e** tie.

Schlitten ['ʃlɪtən] *m* **-s, -** sledge, sleigh; **~bahn** *f* toboggan run; **~fahren** *nt* -s tobogganing.

schlittern ['ʃlɪtərn] *vi* slide.

Schlittschuh ['ʃlɪt-ʃuː] *m* skate; **~ laufen** skate; **~bahn** *f* skating rink; **~läufer(in** *f*) *m* skater.

Schlitz [ʃlɪts] *m* **-es, -e** slit; (*für Münze*) slot; (*Hosen~*) flies *pl*; **s~äugig** *a* slant-eyed; **s~en** *vt* slit.

schloß *etc v siehe* **schließen.**

Schloß [ʃlɔs] *nt* **-sses, ̈-sser** lock; (*an Schmuck etc*) clasp; (*Bau*) castle; chateau.

Schlosser ['ʃlɔsər] *m* **-s, -** (*Auto~*) fitter; (*für Schlüssel etc*) locksmith; **~ei** [-'raɪ] *f* metal (working) shop.

Schlot ['ʃloːt] *m* **-(e)s, -e** chimney; (*NAUT*) funnel.

schlottern ['ʃlɔtərn] *vi* shake, tremble; (*Kleidung*) be baggy.

Schlucht [ʃluxt] *f* -, **-en** gorge, ravine.

schluchzen ['ʃluxtsən] *vi* sob.

Schluck [ʃluk] *m* **-(e)s, -e** swallow; (*Menge*) drop; **~auf** *m* **-s, -s** hiccups *pl*; **s~en** *vti* swallow.

schludern ['ʃluːdərn] *vi* skimp, do sloppy work.

schlug *etc v siehe* **schlagen.**

Schlummer ['ʃlumər] *m* **-s** slumber; **s~n** *vi* slumber.

Schlund [ʃlunt] *m* **-(e)s, ̈-e** gullet; (*fig*) jaw.

schlüpfen ['ʃlypfən] *vi* slip; (*Vogel etc*) hatch (out).

Schlüpfer ['ʃlypfər] *m* **-s, -** panties *pl*, knickers *pl*.

schlüpfrig ['ʃlypfrɪç] *a* slippery; (*fig*) lewd; **S~keit** *f* slipperiness; (*fig*) lewdness.

schlurfen ['ʃlurfən] *vi* shuffle.

schlürfen ['ʃlyrfən] *vti* slurp.

Schluß [ʃlus] *m* **-sses, ̈-sse** end; (*~folgerung*) conclusion; **am ~** at the end; **~ machen mit** finish with.

Schlüssel ['ʃlysəl] *m* **-s, -** (*lit, fig*) key; (*Schraub~*) spanner, wrench; (*MUS*) clef; **~bein** *nt* collarbone; **~blume** *f* cowslip, primrose; **~bund** *m* bunch of keys; **~loch** *nt* keyhole; **~position** *f* key position; **~wort** *nt* keyword.

schlüssig ['ʃlʏsɪç] a conclusive.
Schluß- zW: **~licht** nt taillight; (fig) tailender; **~strich** m (fig) final stroke; **~verkauf** m clearance sale.
schmächtig ['ʃmɛçtɪç] a slight.
schmackhaft ['ʃmakhaft] a tasty.
schmal [ʃmaːl] a narrow; (Person, Buch etc) slender, slim; (karg) meagre.
schmälern ['ʃmɛːlərn] vt diminish; (fig) belittle.
Schmalfilm m cine film.
Schmalz [ʃmalts] nt **-es, -e** dripping, lard; (fig) sentiment, schmaltz; **s~ig** a (fig) schmaltzy.
schmarotzen [ʃmaˈrɔtsən] vi sponge; (BOT) be parasitic.
Schmarotzer m **-s, -** parasite; sponger.
Schmarren ['ʃmarən] m **-s, -** (Aus) small piece of pancake; (fig) rubbish, tripe.
schmatzen ['ʃmatsən] vi smack one's lips; eat noisily.
schmecken ['ʃmɛkən] vti taste; es schmeckt ihm he likes it.
Schmeichel- ['ʃmaɪçəl] zW: **~ei** [-'laɪ] f flattery; **s~haft** a flattering; **s~n** vi flatter.
schmeißen ['ʃmaɪsən] vt unreg (umg) throw, chuck.
Schmeißfliege f bluebottle.
Schmelz [ʃmɛlts] m **-es, -e** enamel; (Glasur) glaze; (von Stimme) melodiousness; **s~bar** a fusible; **s~en** vti unreg melt; (Erz) smelt; **~punkt** m melting point; **~wasser** nt melted snow.
Schmerz [ʃmɛrts] m **-es, -en** pain; (Trauer) grief; **s~empfindlich** a sensitive to pain; **s~en** vti hurt; **Schmerzensgeld** nt compensation; **s~haft, s~lich** a painful; **s~los** a painless; **s~stillend** a soothing; **~tablette** f painkiller.
Schmetterling ['ʃmɛtərlɪŋ] m butterfly.
Schmied [ʃmiːt] m **-(e)s, -e** blacksmith; **~e** ['ʃmaɪdə] f **-, -n** smithy, forge; **Schmiedeeisen** nt wrought iron; **s~en** vt forge; (Pläne) devise, concoct.
schmiegen ['ʃmiːgən] vt press, nestle // vr cling, nestle (up) (an +akk to).
Schmier- ['ʃmiːr] zW: **~e** f **-, -n** grease; (THEAT) greasepaint, makeup; **s~en** vt smear; (ölen) lubricate, grease; (bestechen) bribe // vti (schreiben) scrawl; **~fett** nt grease; **~fink** m messy person; **~geld** nt bribe; **s~ig** a greasy; **~seife** f soft soap.
Schminke ['ʃmɪŋkə] f **-, -n** make-up; **s~n** vtr make up.
schmirgel- ['ʃmɪrgəl] zW: **~n** vt sand

(down); **S~papier** nt emery paper.
schmollen ['ʃmɔlən] vi sulk, pout.
Schmor- ['ʃmoːr] zW: **~braten** m stewed od braised meat; **s~en** vt stew, braise.
Schmuck [ʃmʊk] m **-(e)s, -e** jewellery; (Verzierung) decoration.
schmücken ['ʃmʏkən] vt decorate.
Schmuck- zW: **s~los** a unadorned, plain; **~losigkeit** f simplicity; **~sachen** pl jewels pl, jewellery.
Schmuggel ['ʃmʊgəl] m **-s** smuggling; **s~n** vti smuggle.
Schmuggler m **-s, -** smuggler.
schmunzeln ['ʃmʊntsəln] vi smile benignly.
Schmutz [ʃmʊts] m **-es** dirt, filth; **~fink** m filthy creature; **~fleck** m stain; **s~ig** a dirty.
Schnabel ['ʃnaːbəl] m **-s, ⁻** beak, bill; (Ausguß) spout.
Schnake ['ʃnaːkə] f **-, -n** cranefly; (Stechmücke) gnat.
Schnalle ['ʃnalə] f **-, -n** buckle, clasp; **s~n** vt buckle.
Schnapp- ['ʃnap] zW: **s~en** vt grab, catch // vi snap; **~schloß** nt spring lock; **~schuß** m (PHOT) snapshot.
Schnaps [ʃnaps] m **-es, ⁻e** spirits pl; schnapps.
schnarchen ['ʃnarçən] vi snore.
schnauben ['ʃnaubən] vi snort // vr blow one's nose.
schnaufen ['ʃnaufən] vi puff, pant.
Schnauz- ['ʃnauts] zW: **~bart** m moustache; **~e** f **-, -n** snout, muzzle; (Ausguß) spout; (umg) gob.
Schnecke ['ʃnɛkə] f **-, -n** snail; **Schneckenhaus** nt snail's shell.
Schnee [ʃneː] m **-s** snow; (Ei~) beaten egg white; **~ball** m snowball; **~flocke** f snowflake; **~gestöber** nt snowstorm; **~glöckchen** nt snowdrop; **~kette** f (AUT) snow chain; **~pflug** m snowplough; **~schmelze** f **-, -** thaw; **~wehe** f snowdrift.
schneien ['ʃnaɪən] vi unpers snow.
Schneise ['ʃnaɪzə] f **-, -n** clearing.
schnell [ʃnɛl] a, ad quick(ly), fast; **S~hefter** m **-s, -** loose-leaf binder; **S~igkeit** f speed; **S~imbiß** m (Lokal) snack bar; **S~kochtopf** m (Dampfkochtopf) pressure cooker; **S~reinigung** f dry cleaner's; **~stens** ad as quickly as possible; **S~straße** f expressway; **S~zug** m fast od express train.
schneuzen ['ʃnɔytsən] vr blow one's

nose.

schnippisch ['ʃnɪpɪʃ] *a* sharp-tongued.

schnitt *etc v siehe* schneiden.

Schnitt [ʃnɪt] *m* **-(e)s, -e** cut(ting); (~*punkt*) intersection; (*Quer*~) (cross) section; (*Durch*~) average; (~*muster*) pattern; (*an Buch*) edge; (*umg: Gewinn*) profit; **~blumen** *pl* cut flowers *pl*; **~e** *f* **-, -n** slice; (*belegt*) sandwich; **~fläche** *f* section; **~lauch** *m* chive; **~muster** *nt* pattern; **~punkt** *m* (point of) intersection; **~stelle** *f* (*COMPUT*) interface; **~wunde** *f* cut.

Schnitz- ['ʃnɪts] *zW:* **~arbeit** *f* wood carving; **~el** *nt* **-s, -** chip; (*KOCH*) escalope; **s~en** *vt* carve; **~er** *m* **-s, -** carver; (*umg*) blunder; **~e'rei** *f* carving; carved woodwork.

schnoddrig ['ʃnɔdərɪç] *a* (*umg*) snotty.

Schnorchel ['ʃnɔrçəl] *m* **-s, -** snorkel.

Schnörkel ['ʃnœrkəl] *m* **-s, -** flourish; (*ARCHIT*) scroll.

schnorren ['ʃnɔrən] *vti* cadge.

schnüffeln ['ʃnʏfəln] *vi* sniff; **S~** *nt* (*umg: von Klebstoff etc*) glue-sniffing.

Schnüffler *m* **-s, -** snooper.

Schnuller ['ʃnʊlər] *m* **-s, -** dummy, comforter (*US*).

Schnupfen ['ʃnʊpfən] *m* **-s, -** cold.

schnuppern ['ʃnʊpərn] *vi* sniff.

Schnur [ʃnuːr] *f* **-, -̈e** string, cord; (*ELEK*) flex; **s~gerade** *a* straight (as a die).

schnüren ['ʃnyːrən] *vt* tie.

Schnurr- ['ʃnʊr] *zW:* **~bart** *m* moustache; **s~en** *vi* purr; (*Kreisel*) hum.

Schnür- ['ʃnyːr] *zW:* **~schuh** *m* lace-up (shoe); **~senkel** *m* shoelace.

schnurstracks *ad* straight (away).

Schock [ʃɔk] *m* **-(e)s, -e** shock; **s~ieren** [ʃɔ'kiːrən] *vt* shock, outrage.

Schöffe ['ʃœfə] *m* **-n, -n** lay magistrate.

Schokolade [ʃoko'laːdə] *f* **-, -n** chocolate.

Scholle ['ʃɔlə] *f* **-, -n** clod; (*Eis*~) ice floe; (*Fisch*) plaice.

schon [ʃoːn] *ad* **1** (*bereits*) already; er ist ~ da he's there already, he's already there; **ist er ~ da?** is he there yet?; **warst du ~ einmal da?** have you ever been there?; **ich war ~ einmal da** I've been there before; **das war ~ immer so** that has always been the case; **~ oft** often; **hast du ~ gehört?** have you heard?

2 (*bestimmt*) all right; **du wirst ~ sehen** you'll see (all right); **das wird ~ noch gut** that'll be OK

3 (*bloß*) just; **allein ~ das Gefühl** ... just the very feeling ...; **~ der Gedanke** the very thought; **wenn ich**

das ~ höre I only have to hear that

4 (*einschränkend*): **ja ~, aber** ... yes (well), but ...

5: **~ möglich** possible; **~ gut!** OK!; **du weißt ~** you know; **komm ~!** come on!

schön [ʃøːn] *a* beautiful; (*nett*) nice; **~e Grüße** best wishes; **~e Ferien** have a nice holiday; **~en Dank** (many) thanks.

schonen ['ʃoːnən] *vt* look after // *vr* take it easy; **~d** *a* careful, gentle.

Schön- *zW:* **~heit** *f* beauty; **~heitsfehler** *m* blemish, flaw; **~heitsoperation** *f* cosmetic plastic surgery; **s~machen** *vr* make oneself look nice.

Schon- *zW:* **~ung** *f* good care; (*Nachsicht*) consideration; (*Forst*) plantation of young trees; **s~ungslos** *a* unsparing, harsh; **~zeit** *f* close season.

Schöpf- ['ʃœpf] *zW:* **s~en** *vt* scoop, ladle; (*Mut*) summon up; (*Luft*) breathe in; **~er** *m* **-s, -** creator; **s~erisch** *a* creative; **~kelle** *f* ladle; **~löffel** *m* skimmer, scoop; **~ung** *f* creation.

Schorf [ʃɔrf] *m* **-(e)s, -e** scab.

Schornstein ['ʃɔrnʃtaɪn] *m* chimney; (*NAUT*) funnel; **~feger** *m* **-s, -** chimney sweep.

schoß *etc v siehe* schießen.

Schoß [ʃoːs] *m* **-es, -̈e** lap; (*Rock*~) coat tail; **~hund** *m* pet dog, lapdog.

Schote ['ʃoːtə] *f* **-, -n** pod.

Schotte ['ʃɔtə] *m* Scot, Scotsman.

Schotter ['ʃɔtər] *m* **-s, -** broken stone, road metal; (*EISENB*) ballast.

Schott- ['ʃɔt] *zW:* **~in** *f* Scotswoman; **s~isch** *a* Scottish, Scots; **~land** *nt* Scotland.

schraffieren [ʃra'fiːrən] *vt* hatch.

schräg [ʃrɛːk] *a* slanting, not straight; **etw ~ stellen** put sth at an angle; **~ gegenüber** diagonally opposite; **S~e** *f* **-, -n** slant; **S~strich** *m* oblique stroke.

Schramme ['ʃramə] *f* **-, -n** scratch; **s~n** *vt* scratch.

Schrank [ʃraŋk] *m* **-(e)s, -̈e** cupboard; (*Kleider*~) wardrobe; **~e** *f* **-, -n** barrier; **~enwärter** *m* (*EISENB*) level crossing attendant; **~koffer** *m* trunk.

Schraube ['ʃraubə] *f* **-, -n** screw.

schrauben *vt* screw; **S~schlüssel** *m* spanner; **S~zieher** *m* **-s, -** screwdriver.

Schraubstock ['ʃraubʃtɔk] *m* (*TECH*) vice.

Schreck [ʃrɛk] *m* **-(e)s, -e, ~en** *m* **-s, -** terror; fright; **s~en** *vt* frighten, scare; **~gespenst** *nt* spectre, nightmare; **s~haft** *a* jumpy, easily frightened; **s~lich** *a* terrible, dreadful.

Schrei [ʃraɪ] *m* **-(e)s, -e** scream; (*Ruf*) shout.

Schreib- ['ʃraɪb] *zW:* **~block** *m* writing pad; **~dichte** *f:* **einfache/doppelte ~dichte** (*Diskette*) single/double density; **s~en** *vti unreg* write; (*buchstabieren*) spell; **~en** *nt* **-s,** - letter, communication; **s~faul** *a* bad about writing letters; **~fehler** *m* spelling mistake; **~maschine** *f* typewriter; **~papier** *nt* notepaper; **~tisch** *m* desk; **~ung** *f* spelling; **~waren** *pl* stationery; **~warenhandlung** *f* stationer's; **~weise** *f* spelling; way of writing; **~zentrale** *f* typing pool; **~zeug** *nt* writing materials *pl.*

schreien ['ʃraɪən] *vti unreg* scream; (*rufen*) shout; **~d** *a* (*fig*) glaring; (*Farbe*) loud.

Schreiner ['ʃraɪnər] *m* **-s,** - joiner; (*Zimmermann*) carpenter; (*Möbel~*) cabinetmaker; **~ei** [-'raɪ] *f* joiner's workshop.

schreiten ['ʃraɪtən] *vi unreg* stride.

schrieb *etc v siehe* **schreiben.**

Schrift [ʃrɪft] *f* **-, -en** writing; handwriting; (*~art*) script; (*Gedrucktes*) pamphlet, work; **~deutsch** *nt* written German; **~führer** *m* secretary; **s~lich** *a* written // *ad* in writing; **~setzer** *m* compositor; **~sprache** *f* written language; **~steller(in** *f*) *m* **-s,** - writer; **~stück** *nt* document.

schrill [ʃrɪl] *a* shrill.

Schritt [ʃrɪt] *m* **-(e)s, -e** step; (*Gangart*) walk; (*Tempo*) pace; (*von Hose*) crutch; **~ fahren** drive at walking pace; **~macher** *m* **-s,** - pacemaker; **~(t)empo** *nt:* **im ~(t)empo** at a walking pace.

schroff [ʃrɔf] *a* steep; (*zackig*) jagged; (*fig*) brusque; (*ungeduldig*) abrupt.

schröpfen ['ʃrœpfən] *vt* (*fig*) fleece.

Schrot [ʃroːt] *m od nt* **-(e)s, -e** (*Blei*) (small) shot; (*Getreide*) coarsely ground grain, groats *pl;* **~flinte** *f* shotgun.

Schrott [ʃrɔt] *m* **-(e)s, -e** scrap metal; **~haufen** *m* scrap heap; **s~reif** *a* ready for the scrap heap.

schrubben ['ʃrʊbən] *vt* scrub.

Schrubber *m* **-s,** - scrubbing brush.

schrumpfen ['ʃrʊmpfən] *vi* shrink; (*Apfel*) shrivel.

Schub- ['ʃuːb] *zW:* **~fach** *nt* drawer; **~karren** *m* wheelbarrow; **~lade** *f* drawer.

schüchtern ['ʃʏçtərn] *a* shy; **S~heit** *f* shyness.

Schuft [ʃʊft] *m* **-(e)s, -e** scoundrel; **s~en** *vi* (*umg*) graft, slave away.

Schuh [ʃuː] *m* **-(e)s, -e** shoe; **~band** *nt* shoelace; **~creme** *f* shoe polish; **~löffel** *m* shoehorn; **~macher** *m* **-s,** -

shoemaker.

Schul- ['ʃuːl] *zW:* **~aufgaben** *pl* homework; **~besuch** *m* school attendance; **~buch** *nt* school book.

Schuld [ʃʊlt] *f* **-, -en** guilt; (*FIN*) debt; (*Verschulden*) fault; **s~** *a:* **s~ sein** *od* **haben** be to blame (*an +dat* for); **er ist** *od* **hat s~** it's his fault; **jdm s~ geben** blame sb; **s~en** ['ʃʊldən] *vt* owe; **s~enfrei** *a* free from debt; **~gefühl** *nt* feeling of guilt; **s~ig** *a* guilty (*an +dat* of); (*gebührend*) due; **jdm etw s~ig sein** owe sb sth; **jdm etw s~ig bleiben** not provide sb with sth; **s~los** *a* innocent, without guilt; **~ner** *m* **-s,** - debtor; **~schein** *m* promissory note, IOU; **~spruch** *m* verdict of guilty.

Schule [ʃuːlə] *f* **-, -n** school; **s~n** *vt* train, school.

Schüler(in *f*) ['ʃyːlər(ɪn)] *m* **-s,** - pupil; **~lotse** *m* pupil acting as road crossing warden.

Schul- ['ʃuːl] *zW:* **~ferien** *pl* school holidays *pl;* **s~frei** *a:* **s~freier Tag** holiday; **s~frei sein** be a holiday; **~hof** *m* playground; **~jahr** *nt* school year; **~junge** *m* schoolboy; **~mädchen** *nt* schoolgirl; **s~pflichtig** *a* of school age; **~schiff** *nt* (*NAUT*) training ship; **~stunde** *f* period, lesson; **~tasche** *f* school bag.

Schulter ['ʃʊltər] *f* **-, -n** shoulder; **~blatt** *nt* shoulder blade; **s~n** *vt* shoulder.

Schul- *zW:* **~ung** *f* education, schooling; **~zeugnis** *nt* school report.

Schund [ʃʊnt] *m* **-(e)s** trash, garbage; **~roman** *m* trashy novel.

Schuppe ['ʃʊpə] *f* **-, -n** scale; **~n** *pl* (*Haar~*) dandruff; **s~n** *vt* scale // *vr* peel; **~n** *m* **-s,** - shed.

schuppig ['ʃʊpɪç] *a* scaly.

Schur [ʃuːr] *f* **-,** -en shearing.

Schür- ['ʃyːr] *zW:* **s~en** *vt* rake; (*fig*) stir up; **schürfen** ['ʃʏrfən] *vti* scrape, scratch; (*MIN*) prospect, dig.

Schurke ['ʃʊrkə] *m* **-n, -n** rogue.

Schürze ['ʃʏrtsə] *f* **-, -n** apron.

Schuß [ʃʊs] *m* **-sses, -sse** shot; (*WEBEN*) woof; **~bereich** *m* effective range.

Schüssel ['ʃʏsəl] *f* **-, -n** bowl.

Schuß- *zW:* **~linie** *f* line of fire; **~verletzung** *f* bullet wound; **~waffe** *f* firearm; **~weite** *f* range (of fire).

Schuster ['ʃuːstər] *m* **-s,** - cobbler, shoemaker.

Schutt [ʃʊt] *m* **-(e)s** rubbish; (*Bau~*) rubble; **~abladeplatz** *m* refuse dump.

Schütt- ['ʃʏt] *zW:* **Schüttelfrost** *m* shivering; **s~eln** *vtr* shake; **s~en** *vt* pour; (*Zucker, Kies etc*) tip; (*ver~en*) spill // *vi unpers* pour (down).

Schutthalde f dump.

Schutthaufen m heap of rubble.

Schutz [ʃʊts] m -es protection; (Unterschlupf) shelter; **jdn in ~ nehmen** stand up for sb; **~anzug** m overalls pl; **~blech** nt mudguard; **~brille** f goggles pl.

Schütze ['ʃʏtsə] m -n, -n gunman; (Gewehr~) rifleman; (Scharf~, Sport~) marksman; (ASTROL) Sagittarius; **s~n** vt protect (vor +dat, gegen from); **Schützenfest** nt fair featuring shooting matches.

Schutz- zW: **~engel** m guardian angel; **~gebiet** nt protectorate; (Natur~) reserve; **~impfung** f immunisation; **s~los** a defenceless; **~mann** m, pl **-leute** od **-männer** policeman; **~patron** m patron saint.

Schwaben ['ʃvaːbən] nt Swabia.

schwäbisch ['ʃvɛːbiʃ] a Swabian.

schwach [ʃvax] a weak, feeble.

Schwäche ['ʃvɛçə] f -, -n weakness; **s~n** vt weaken.

Schwachheit f weakness.

schwächlich a weakly, delicate.

Schwächling m weakling.

Schwach- zW: **~sinn** m imbecility; **s~sinnig** a mentally deficient; (Idee) idiotic; **~strom** m weak current.

Schwächung ['ʃvɛçʊŋ] f weakening.

schwafeln ['ʃvaːfəln] vti drivel.

Schwager ['ʃvaːgər] m -s, ⁓ brother-in-law.

Schwägerin ['ʃvɛːgərin] f sister-in-law.

Schwalbe ['ʃvalbə] f -, -n swallow.

Schwall [ʃval] m -(e)s, -e surge; (Worte) flood, torrent.

schwamm etc v siehe **schwimmen**.

Schwamm [ʃvam] m -(e)s, ⁓e sponge; (Pilz) fungus; **s~ig** a spongy; (Gesicht) puffy.

Schwan [ʃvaːn] m -(e)s, ⁓e swan; **s~en** vi unpers: **jdm schwant etw** sb has a foreboding of sth.

schwanger ['ʃvaŋər] a pregnant.

schwängern ['ʃvɛŋərn] vt make pregnant.

Schwangerschaft f pregnancy.

Schwank [ʃvaŋk] m -(e)s, ⁓e funny story; **s~en** vi sway; (taumeln) stagger, reel; (Preise, Zahlen) fluctuate; (zögern) hesitate, vacillate; **~ung** f fluctuation.

Schwanz [ʃvants] m -es, ⁓e tail.

schwänzen ['ʃvɛntsən] (umg) vt skip, cut // vi play truant.

Schwarm [ʃvarm] m -(e)s, ⁓e swarm; (umg) heart-throb, idol.

schwärm- ['ʃvɛrm] zW: **~en** vi swarm; **~en für** be mad od wild about; **S~erei** f [-ə'raɪ] f enthusiasm; **~erisch** a impassioned, effusive.

Schwarte ['ʃvartə] f -, -n hard skin; (Speck~) rind.

schwarz [ʃvarts] a black; **~es Brett** notice board; **ins S~e treffen** (lit, fig) hit the bull's eye; **in den ~en Zahlen** in the black; **S~arbeit** f illicit work, moonlighting; **S~brot** nt black bread.

Schwärze ['ʃvɛrtsə] f -, -n blackness; (Farbe) blacking; (Drucker~) printer's ink; **s~n** vt blacken.

Schwarz- zW: **s~fahren** vi unreg travel without paying; drive without a licence; **~handel** m black-market (trade); **s~hören** vi listen to the radio without a licence; **~markt** m black market; **s~sehen** vi unreg (umg) see the gloomy side of things; (TV) watch TV without a licence; **~seher** m pessimist; (TV) viewer without a licence; **~wald** m Black Forest; **s~weiß** a black and white.

schwatzen ['ʃvatsən], **schwätzen** ['ʃvɛtsən] vi chatter.

Schwätzer ['ʃvɛtsər] m -s, - gasbag; **~in** f chatterbox, gossip.

schwatzhaft a talkative, gossipy.

Schwebe ['ʃveːbə] f: **in der ~** (fig) in abeyance; **~bahn** f overhead railway; **~balken** m (SPORT) beam; **s~n** vi drift, float; (hoch) soar.

Schwed- ['ʃveːd] zW: **~e** m Swede; **~en** nt Sweden; **~in** f Swede; **s~isch** a Swedish.

Schwefel ['ʃveːfəl] m -s sulphur; **s~ig** a sulphurous; **~säure** f sulphuric acid.

Schweig- ['ʃvaɪg] zW: **Schweigegeld** nt hush money; **s~en** vi unreg be silent; stop talking; **~en** nt -s silence; **s~sam** ['ʃvaɪkzaːm] a silent, taciturn; **~samkeit** f taciturnity, quietness.

Schwein [ʃvaɪn] nt -(e)s, -e pig; (umg) (good) luck.

Schweine- zW: **~fleisch** nt pork; **~rei** f mess; (Gemeinheit) dirty trick; **~stall** m pigsty.

schweinisch a filthy.

Schweinsleder nt pigskin.

Schweiß [ʃvaɪs] m -es sweat, perspiration; **s~en** vti weld; **~er** m -s, - welder; **~füße** pl sweaty feet pl; **~naht** f weld.

Schweiz [ʃvaɪts] f Switzerland; **~er(in** f) m Swiss; **s~erisch** a Swiss.

schwelgen ['ʃvɛlgən] vi indulge.

Schwelle ['ʃvɛlə] f -, -n threshold (auch fig); doorstep; (EISENB) sleeper; **s~n** vi unreg swell.

Schwellung f swelling.

Schwenk- ['ʃvɛŋk] zW: **s~bar** a swivel-mounted; **s~en** vt swing; (Fahne) wave; (abspülen) rinse // vi turn, swivel; (MIL) wheel; **~ung** f turn; wheel.

schwer [ʃveːr] a heavy; (schwierig) difficult, hard; (schlimm) serious, bad // ad (sehr) very (much) // (verletzt etc) seriously, badly; **S~arbeiter** m manual worker, labourer; **S~e** f -, -n weight, heaviness; (PHYS) gravity; **schwerelos** a weightless; (Kammer) zero-G; **~erziehbar** a difficult (to bring up); **~fallen** vi unreg: jdm **~fallen** be difficult for sb; **~fällig** a ponderous; **S~gewicht** nt heavyweight; (fig) emphasis; **~hörig** a hard of hearing; **S~industrie** f heavy industry; **S~kraft** f gravity; **S~kranke(r)** mf person who is seriously ill; **~lich** ad hardly; **~machen** vt: jdm/sich etw **~machen** make sth difficult for sb/o.s.; **~mütig** a melancholy; **~nehmen** vt unreg take to heart; **S~punkt** m centre of gravity; (fig) emphasis, crucial point.
Schwert [ʃveːrt] nt -(e)s, -er sword; **~lilie** f iris.
schwer- zW: **~tun** vi unreg: sich (dat od akk) **~tun** have difficulties; **S~verbrecher(in** f) m criminal, serious offender; **~verdaulich** a indigestible, heavy; **~verletzt** a badly injured; **~wiegend** a weighty, important.
Schwester [ʃvɛstər] f -, -n sister; (MED) nurse; **~lich** a sisterly.
Schwieger- [ʃviːgər] zW: **~eltern** pl parents-in-law pl; **~mutter** f mother-in-law; **~sohn** m son-in-law; **~tochter** f daughter-in-law; **~vater** m father-in-law.
Schwiele [ʃviːlə] f -, -n callus.
schwierig [ʃviːrɪç] a difficult, hard; **S~keit** f difficulty.
Schwimm- [ʃvɪm] zW: **~bad** nt swimming baths pl; **~becken** nt swimming pool; **s~en** vi unreg swim; (treiben, nicht sinken) float; (fig: unsicher sein) be all at sea; **~er** m -s, - swimmer; (Angeln) float; **~lehrer** m swimming instructor; **~weste** f life jacket.
Schwindel [ʃvɪndəl] m -s giddiness; dizzy spell; (Betrug) swindle, fraud; (Zeug) stuff; **s~frei** a; s~frei sein have a good head for heights; **s~n** vi (umg: lügen) fib; jdm schwindelt es sb feels dizzy.
schwinden [ʃvɪndən] vi unreg disappear; (sich verringern) decrease; (Kräfte) decline.
Schwind- [ʃvɪnd] zW: **~ler** m -s, - swindler; (Lügner) liar; **s~lig** a dizzy; mir ist s~lig I feel dizzy.
Schwing- [ʃvɪŋ] zW: **s~en** vti unreg swing; (Waffe etc) brandish; (vibrieren) vibrate; (klingen) sound; **~tür** f swing door(s); **~ung** f vibration; (PHYS) oscillation.

Schwips [ʃvɪps] m -es, -e: einen ~ haben be tipsy.
schwirren [ʃvɪrən] vi buzz.
schwitzen [ʃvɪtsən] vi sweat, perspire.
schwören [ʃvøːrən] vti unreg swear.
schwul [ʃvuːl] a (umg) gay, queer.
schwül [ʃvyːl] a sultry, close; **S~e** f - sultriness, closeness.
schwülstig [ʃvʏlstɪç] a pompous.
Schwung [ʃvʊŋ] m -(e)s, ̈e swing; (Triebkraft) momentum; (fig: Energie) verve, energy; (umg: Menge) batch; **s~haft** a brisk, lively; **s~voll** a vigorous.
Schwur [ʃvuːr] m -(e)s, ̈e oath; **~gericht** nt court with a jury.
sechs [zɛks] num six; **~hundert** num six hundred; **~te(r, s)** a sixth; **S~tel** nt -s - sixth.
sechzehn [zɛçtseːn] num sixteen.
sechzig [zɛçtsɪç] num sixty.
See [zeː] f -, -n sea // m -s, -n lake; **~bad** nt seaside resort; **~fahrt** f seafaring; (Reise) voyage; **~gang** m (motion of the sea); **~hund** m seal; **~igel** [zeːʔiːgəl] m sea urchin; **s~krank** a seasick; **~krankheit** f seasickness; **~lachs** m rock salmon.
Seele [zeːlə] f -, -n soul; **seelenruhig** ad calmly.
Seeleute [zeːlɔʏtə] pl seamen pl.
Seel- zW: **s~isch** a mental; **~sorge** f pastoral duties pl; **~sorger** m -s, - clergyman.
See- zW: **~macht** f naval power; **~mann** m, pl **~leute** seaman, sailor; **~meile** f nautical mile; **~not** f distress; **~pferd(chen)** nt sea horse; **~räuber** m pirate; **~rose** f water lily; **~stern** m starfish; **s~tüchtig** a seaworthy: **~weg** m sea route; auf dem **~weg** by sea; **~zunge** f sole.
Segel [zeːgəl] nt -s, - sail; **~boot** nt yacht; **~fliegen** nt -s gliding; **~flieger** m glider pilot; **~flugzeug** nt glider; **s~n** vti sail; **~schiff** nt sailing vessel; **~sport** m sailing; **~tuch** nt canvas.
Segen [zeːgən] m -s, - blessing; **segensreich** a beneficial.
Segler [zeːglər] m -s, - sailor, yachtsman.
segnen [zeːgnən] vt bless.
Seh- [zeː] zW: **s~en** vti unreg see; mal s~en(, ob ...) let's see (if ...); (in bestimmte Richtung) look; **s~enswert** a worth seeing; **~enswürdigkeiten** pl sights (of a town); **~er** m -s, - seer; **~fehler** m sight defect.
Sehn- [zeːn] zW: **~e** f -, -n sinew; (an Bogen) string; **s~en** vr long, yearn (nach for); **s~ig** a sinewy;

s~**lich** *a* ardent; ~**sucht** *f* longing;
s~**süchtig** *a* longing.
sehr [ze:r] *ad* very; (*mit Verben*) a
lot, (very) much; **zu ~** too much; **~
geehrte(r)** ... dear ....
seicht [zaɪçt] *a* (*lit, fig*) shallow.
Seide ['zaɪdə] *f* -, -n silk; **s~n** *a* silk;
Seidenpapier *nt* tissue paper.
seidig ['zaɪdɪç] *a* silky.
Seife ['zaɪfə] *f* -, -n soap.
Seifen- *zW*: ~**lauge** *f* soapsuds *pl*;
~**schale** *f* soap dish; ~**schaum** *m*
lather.
seihen ['zaɪən] *vt* strain, filter.
Seil [zaɪl] *nt* -(e)s, -e rope; cable;
~**bahn** *f* cable railway; ~**hüpfen** *nt*
-s, ~**springen** *nt* -s skipping;
~**tänzer(in** *f*) *m* tightrope walker.
sein [zaɪn] *vi pt* **war**, *ptp* **gewesen 1**
be; **ich bin** I am; **du bist** you are;
er/sie/es ist he/she/it is; **wir sind/ihr
seid/sie sind** we/you/they are; **wir
waren** we were; **wir sind gewesen** we
have been
2: seien Sie nicht böse don't be angry; **sei so gut und ...** be so kind as
to ...; **das wäre gut** that would *od*
that'd be a good thing; **wenn ich Sie
wäre** if I were *od* was you; **das wär's**
that's all, that's it; **morgen bin ich in
Rom** tomorrow I'll *od* I will *od* I shall
be in Rome; **waren Sie mal in Rom?**
have you ever been to Rome?
3: wie ist das zu verstehen? how is
that to be understood?; **er ist nicht zu
ersetzen** he cannot be replaced; **mit
ihr ist nicht zu reden** you can't talk
to her
4: mir ist kalt I'm cold; **was ist?**
what's the matter?, what is it?; **ist
was?** is something the matter?; **es
sei denn, daß ...** unless ...; **wie dem
auch sei** be that as it may; **wie wäre
es mit ...?** how *od* what about ...?;
laß das ~! stop that!
sein [zaɪn] *pron* his; its; ~**e(r, s)** his;
its; ~**er** *pron gen von* **er** of him;
~**erseits** *ad* for his part; ~**erzeit** *ad*
in those days, formerly; ~**esgleichen**
pron people like him; ~**etwegen**,
~**etwillen** *ad* (*für ihn*) for his sake;
(*wegen ihm*) on his account; (*von
ihm aus*) as far as he is concerned;
~**ige** *pron*: **der/die/das** ~**ige** his.
Seismograph [zaɪsmo'graːf] *m* -en,
-en seismograph.
seit [zaɪt] *präp*, *kj* since; **er ist ~** ei-
ner Woche hier he has been here for
a week; **~ langem** for a long time;
~**dem** [zaɪt'deːm] *ad, kj* since.
Seite ['zaɪtə] *f* -, -n side; (*Buch~*)
page; (*MIL*) flank.
Seiten- *zW*: ~**ansicht** *f* side view;
~**hieb** *m* (*fig*) passing shot, dig;
seitens *präp* (+*gen*) on the part of;

~**schiff** *nt* aisle; ~**sprung** *m* extramarital escapade; ~**stechen** *nt* (a)
stitch; ~**straße** *f* side road.
seit- *zW*: ~**her** [zaɪt'heːr] *ad, kj* since
(then); ~**lich** *a* on one *od* the side;
side; ~**wärts** *ad* sideways.
Sekretär [zekre'tɛːr] *m* secretary;
(*Möbel*) bureau; ~**in** *f* secretary.
Sekretariat [zekretari'aːt] *nt* -(e)s, -e
secretary's office, secretariat.
Sekt [zɛkt] *m* -(e)s, -e champagne.
Sekte ['zɛktə] *f* -, -n sect.
Sekunde [ze'kʊndə] *f* -, -n second.
selber ['zɛlbər] = **selbst**.
selbst [zɛlpst] ◆*pron* 1: **ich/er/wir ~** I
myself/he himself/we ourselves; **sie
ist die Tugend ~** she's virtue itself;
er braut sein Bier ~ he brews his
own beer; **wie geht's? — gut, und ~?**
how are things? — fine, and yourself?
2 (*ohne Hilfe*) alone, on my/his/one's
etc own; **von ~** by itself; **er kam von
~** he came of his own accord
◆*ad* even; ~ **wenn** even if; ~ **Gott**
even God (himself).
Selbst [zɛlpst] *nt* - self; ~**achtung**
f self-respect; **selbständig** ['zɛlp-
ʃtɛndɪç] *a* independent; **Selbständig-
keit** *f* independence; ~**auslöser** *m*
(*PHOT*) delayed-action shutter release; ~**bedienung** *f* self-service;
~**befriedigung** *f* masturbation;
~**beherrschung** *f* self-control; **s~be-
wußt** *a* (self-)confident; ~**bewußtsein** *nt* self-confidence; ~**erhaltung** *f*
self-preservation; ~**erkenntnis** *f* self-
knowledge; **s~gefällig** *a* smug, self-
satisfied; **s~gemacht** *a* home-made;
~**gespräch** *nt* conversation with oneself; ~**kostenpreis** *m* cost price;
s~los *a* unselfish, selfless; ~**mord** *m*
suicide; ~**mörder(in** *f*) *m* suicide;
s~mörderisch *a* suicidal; **s~sicher** *a*
self-assured; **s~tätig** *a* automatic;
s~verständlich *a* obvious // *ad* naturally; **ich halte das für
s~verständlich** I take that for
granted; ~**vertrauen** *nt* self-
confidence; ~**verwaltung** *f* autono-
my, self-government.
selig ['zeːlɪç] *a* happy, blissful; (*REL*)
blessed; (*tot*) late; **S~keit** *f* bliss.
Sellerie ['zɛləri] *m* -s, -(s) *od f* -, - celery.
selten ['zɛltən] *a* rare // *ad* seldom,
rarely; **S~heit** *f* rarity.
Selterswasser ['zɛltərsvasər] *nt* soda
water.
seltsam ['zɛltzaːm] *a* strange, curious;
~**erweise** *ad* curiously, strangely;
S~keit *f* strangeness.
Semester [ze'mɛstər] *nt* -s, - semester.
Semi- [zemi] *in zW* semi-; ~**kolon**
[-'koːlɔn] *nt* -s, -s semicolon; ~**nar**

[-'na:r] nt **-s, -e** seminary; (Kurs) seminar; (UNIV: Ort) department building.

Semmel ['zɛməl] f -, **-n** roll.

sen. abk (= senior) sen.

Senat [ze'na:t] m **-(e)s, -e** senate, council.

Sende- ['zɛndə] zW: **~bereich** m transmission range; **~folge** f (Serie) series; **s~n** vt unreg send // vti (RAD, TV) transmit, broadcast; **~r** m -s, - station; (Anlage) transmitter; **~reihe** f series (of broadcasts).

Sendung ['zɛndʊŋ] f consignment; (Aufgabe) mission; (RAD, TV) transmission; (Programm) programme.

Senf [zɛnf] m **-(e)s, -e** mustard.

Senk- ['zɛŋk] zW: **~blei** nt plumb; **~e** f -, **-n** depression; **s~en** vt lower // vr sink, drop gradually; **s~recht** a vertical, perpendicular; **~rechte** f **-n, -n** perpendicular; **~rechtstarter** m (AVIAT) vertical take-off plane; (fig) high-flyer.

Sensation [zɛnzatsi'o:n] f sensation; **s~ell** [-'nɛl] a sensational.

Sense ['zɛnzə] f -, **-n** scythe.

sensibel [zɛn'zi:bəl] a sensitive.

sentimental [zɛntimɛn'ta:l] a sentimental; **S~ität** f sentimentality.

separat [zepa'ra:t] a separate.

September [zɛp'tɛmbər] m **-(s)**, - September.

Serie ['ze:riə] f series; **serienweise** ad in series.

seriös [zeri'ø:s] a serious, bona fide.

Serum ['ze:rʊm] nt **-s, Seren** serum.

Service [zɛr'vi:s] nt **-(s)**, - set, service // ['sø:rvɪs] m -, **-s** service.

servieren [zɛr'vi:rən] vti serve.

Serviette [zɛrvi'ɛtə] f napkin, serviette.

Sessel ['zɛsəl] m **-s**, - armchair; **~lift** m chairlift.

seßhaft ['zɛshaft] a settled; (ansässig) resident.

setzen ['zɛtsən] vt put, set; (Baum etc) plant; (Segel, TYP) set // vr settle; (Person) sit down // vi (springen) leap; (wetten) bet.

Setz- [zɛts] zW: **~er** m **-s**, - (TYP) compositor; **~e'rei** f caseroom; **~ling** m young plant.

Seuche ['zɔʏçə] f -, **-n** epidemic; **Seuchengebiet** nt infected area.

seufzen ['zɔʏftsən] vti sigh.

Seufzer ['zɔʏftsər] m **-s**, - sigh.

Sex [zɛks] m **-(es)** sex; **~ualität** [-uali'tɛt] f sex, sexuality; **s~uell** [-u'ɛl] a sexual.

sezieren [ze'tsi:rən] vt dissect.

Shampoo [ʃam'pu:] nt shampoo.

Sibirien [zi'bi:riən] nt Siberia.

sibirisch [zi'bi:rɪʃ] a Siberian.

sich [zɪç] pron (mit Infinitiv) **1** (akk):

er/sie/es ... **~** he/she/it ... himself/herself/itself; **sie** (pl)/**man** ... **~** they/one ... themselves/oneself; **Sie** ... **~** you ... yourself/(pl) yourselves; **~ wiederholen** repeat oneself/itself

2 (dat): er/sie/es ... **~** he/she/it ... to himself/herself/itself; **sie** (pl)/**man** ... **~** they/one ... to themselves/oneself; **Sie** ... **~** you ... to yourself/(pl) yourselves; **sie hat ~ einen Pullover gekauft** she bought herself a jumper; **~ die Haare waschen** wash one's hair

3 (mit Präposition): **haben Sie Ihren Ausweis bei ~?** do you have your pass on you?; **er hat nichts bei ~** he's got nothing on him; **sie bleiben gern unter ~** they keep themselves to themselves

4 (einander) each other, one another; **sie bekämpfen ~** they fight each other/one another

5: dieses Auto fährt ~ gut this car drives well; **hier sitzt es ~ gut** it's good to sit here.

Sichel ['zɪçəl] f -, **-n** sickle; (Mond~) crescent.

sicher ['zɪçər] a safe (vor +dat from); (gewiß) certain (+gen of); (zuverlässig) secure, reliable; (selbst~) confident; **ich bin nicht ~** I'm not sure od certain; **~ nicht** surely not; **aber ~!** of course; **~gehen** vi unreg make sure.

Sicherheit ['zɪçərhaɪt] f safety; security (auch FIN); (Gewißheit) certainty; (Selbst~) confidence.

Sicherheits- zW: **~abstand** m safe distance; **~glas** nt safety glass; **~gurt** m safety belt; **s~halber** ad for safety; to be on the safe side; **~nadel** f safety pin; **~vorkehrung** f safety precaution.

sicher- zW: **~lich** ad certainly, surely; **~n** vt secure; (schützen) protect; (Waffe) put the safety catch on; **jdm/sich etw ~** secure sth for sb/for o.s.; **~stellen** vt impound; (COMPUT) save; **S~ung** f (Sichern) securing; (Vorrichtung) safety device; (an Waffen) safety catch; (ELEK) fuse; **S~ungskopie** f back-up copy.

Sicht [zɪçt] f - sight; (Aus~) view; **auf od nach ~** (FIN) at sight; **auf lange ~** on a long-term basis; **s~bar** a visible; **s~en** vt sight; (auswählen) sort out; **s~lich** a evident, obvious; **~verhältnisse** pl visibility; **~vermerk** m visa.

sickern ['zɪkərn] vi trickle, seep.

Sie [zi:] pron sing, pl, nom, akk you.

sie [zi:] pron sing nom she // akk her // pl nom they // akk them.

Sieb [zi:p] nt **-(e)s, -e** sieve; (KOCH) strainer; **s~en** ['zi:bən] vt sift; (Flüssigkeit) strain.

sieben ['ziːbən] *num* seven; **~hundert** *num* seven hundred; **S~sachen** *pl* belongings *pl*.

siebte(r, s) ['ziːptə(r,s)] *a* seventh; **Siebtel** *nt* -s, - seventh.

siebzehn ['ziːptseːn] *num* seventeen.

siebzig ['ziːptsɪç] *num* seventy.

sied- [ziːd] *zW:* **~en** *vti* boil, simmer; **Siedepunkt** *m* boiling point; **S~lung** *f* settlement; (*Häuser~lung*) housing estate.

Sieg [ziːk] *m* -(e)s, -e victory.

Siegel ['ziːgəl] *nt* -s, - seal; **~lack** *m* sealing wax; **~ring** *m* signet ring.

Sieg- *zW:* **s~en** *vi* be victorious; (*SPORT*) win; **~er** *m* -s, - victor; (*SPORT etc*) winner; **siegessicher** *a* sure of victory; **s~reich** *a* victorious.

siehe [ziːə] (*Imperativ*) see.

siehst *etc* *v* siehe **sehen**.

siezen ['ziːtsən] *vt* address as 'Sie'.

Signal [zɪ'gnaːl] *nt* -s, -e signal.

Silbe ['zɪlbə] *f* -, -n syllable.

Silber ['zɪlbər] *nt* -s silver; **s~n** *a* silver; **~papier** *nt* silver paper.

Silhouette [zilu'ɛtə] *f* silhouette.

Silo ['ziːlo] *nt* od *m* -s, -s silo.

Silvester(abend *m*) [zɪl'vɛstər(aːbənt)] *nt* -s, - New Year's Eve, Hogmanay (*Scot*).

simpel ['zɪmpəl] *a* simple.

Sims [zɪms] *nt* od *m* -es, -e (*Kamin~*) mantelpiece; (*Fenster~*) (window)-sill.

simulieren [zimu'liːrən] *vti* simulate; (*vortäuschen*) feign.

simultan [zimʊl'taːn] *a* simultaneous.

Sinfonie [zɪnfo'niː] *f* symphony.

singen ['zɪŋən] *vti unreg* sing.

Singular ['zɪŋgulaːr] *m* singular.

Singvogel ['zɪŋfoːgəl] *m* songbird.

sinken ['zɪŋkən] *vi unreg* sink; (*Preise etc*) fall, go down.

Sinn [zɪn] *m* -(e)s, -e mind; (*Wahrnehmungs~*) sense; (*Bedeutung*) sense, meaning; **~ für etw** sense of sth; **von ~en sein** be out of one's mind; **es hat keinen ~** there's no point; **~bild** *nt* symbol; **s~en** *vi unreg* ponder; **auf etw** (*akk*) **s~en** contemplate sth; **Sinnestäuschung** *f* illusion; **s~gemäß** *a* faithful; (*Wiedergabe*) in one's own words; **s~ig** *a* clever; **s~lich** *a* sensual, sensuous; (*Wahrnehmung*) sensory; **~lichkeit** *f* sensuality; **s~los** *a* senseless; meaningless; **~losigkeit** *f* senselessness; meaninglessness; **s~voll** *a* meaningful; (*vernünftig*) sensible.

Sintflut ['zɪntfluːt] *f* Flood.

Siphon [zi'fõː] *m* -s, -s siphon.

Sippe ['zɪpə] *f* -, -n clan, kin.

Sippschaft ['zɪpʃaft] *f* (*pej*) relations *pl*, tribe; (*Bande*) gang.

Sirene [zi'reːnə] *f* -, -n siren.

Sirup ['ziːrup] *m* -s syrup.

Sitt- [zɪt] *zW:* **~e** *f* -, -n custom // *pl* morals *pl*; **Sittenpolizei** *f* vice squad; **s~lich** *a* moral; **~lichkeit** *f* morality; **~lichkeitsverbrechen** *nt* sex offence; **s~sam** *a* modest, demure.

Situation [zituatsi'oːn] *f* situation.

Sitz [zɪts] *m* -es, -e seat; **der Anzug hat einen guten ~** the suit is a good fit; **s~en** *vi unreg* sit; (*Bemerkung, Schlag*) strike home, tell; (*Gelerntes*) have sunk in; **s~en bleiben** remain seated; **s~enbleiben** *vi unreg* (*SCH*) have to repeat a year; **auf etw** (*dat*) **s~enbleiben** be lumbered with sth; **s~end** *a* (*Tätigkeit*) sedentary; **s~enlassen** *vt unreg* (*SCH*) make (sb) repeat a year; (*Mädchen*) jilt; (*Wartenden*) stand up; **etw auf sich** (*dat*) **s~enlassen** take sth lying down; **~gelegenheit** *f* place to sit down; **~platz** *m* seat; **~streik** *m* sit-down strike; **~ung** *f* meeting.

Sizilien [zi'tsiːliən] *nt* Sicily.

Skala ['skaːla] *f* -, **Skalen** scale.

Skalpell [skal'pɛl] *nt* -s, -e scalpel.

Skandal [skan'daːl] *m* -s, -e scandal; **s~ös** [skanda'løːs] *a* scandalous.

Skandinav- [skandi'naːv] *zW:* **~ien** [-iən] *nt* Scandinavia; **~ier(in** *f*) *m* Scandinavian; **s~isch** *a* Scandinavian.

Skelett [ske'lɛt] *nt* -(e)s, -e skeleton.

Skepsis ['skɛpsɪs] *f* - scepticism.

skeptisch ['skɛptɪʃ] *a* sceptical.

Ski, Schi [ʃiː] *m* -s, -er ski; **~ laufen** *od* **fahren** ski; **~fahrer** *m*, **~läufer** *m* skier; **~lehrer** *m* ski instructor; **~lift** *m* ski-lift; **~springen** *nt* ski-jumping; **~stock** *m* ski-pole.

Skizze ['skɪtsə] *f* -, -n sketch.

skizzieren [skɪ'tsiːrən] *vti* sketch.

Sklave ['sklaːvə] *m* -n, -n, **Sklavin** *f* slave; **s~rei** *f* slavery.

Skonto ['skɔnto] *m* od *nt* -s, -s discount.

Skorpion [skɔrpi'oːn] *m* -s, -e scorpion; (*ASTROL*) Scorpio.

Skrupel ['skruːpəl] *m* -s, - scruple; **s~los** *a* unscrupulous.

Slalom ['slaːlɔm] *m* -s, -s slalom.

Smaragd [sma'rakt] *m* -(e)s, -e emerald.

Smoking ['smoːkɪŋ] *m* -s, -s dinner jacket.

s.o. *abk* = **siehe oben.**

so [zoː] ◆ *ad* **1** (*~sehr*) so; **~ groß/schön** *etc* so big/nice *etc*; **~ groß/schön wie ...** as big/nice as ...; **das hat ihn ~ geärgert, daß ...** that annoyed him so much that ...; **~ einer wie ich** somebody like me; **na ~ was!** well, well! **2** (*auf diese Weise*) like this; **mach es nicht ~** don't do it like that; **~**

oder ~ in one way or the other; **und ~ weiter** and so on; ... **oder ~ was** ... or something like that; **das ist gut ~** that's fine
3 (*umg: umsonst*): **ich habe es ~ bekommen** I got it for nothing
◆*kj*: ~ **daß** so that; ~ **wie es jetzt ist** as things are at the moment
◆*interj*: ~? really?; ~, **das wär's so**, that's it then.
sobald [zo'balt] *kj* as soon as.
Socke ['zɔkə] *f* -, -n sock.
Sockel ['zɔkəl] *m* -s, - pedestal, base.
Sodawasser ['zo:davasər] *nt* soda water.
Sodbrennen ['zo:tbrɛnən] *nt* -s, - heartburn.
soeben [zo''e:bən] *ad* just (now).
Sofa ['zo:fa] *nt* -s, -s sofa.
sofern [zo'fɛrn] *kj* if, provided (that).
sofort [zo'fɔrt] *ad* immediately, at once; ~**ig** *a* immediate.
Software ['sɔftwɛər] *f* software.
so- *zW*: ~**gar** [zo'ga:r] *ad* even; ~**genannt** ['zo:gənant] *a* so-called; ~**gleich** [zo'glaiç] *ad* straight away, at once.
Sohle ['zo:lə] *f* -, -n sole; (*Tal~ etc*) bottom; (*MIN*) level.
Sohn [zo:n] *m* -(e)s, -e son.
solang(e) [zo'laŋ(ə)] *kj* as *od* so long as.
solch [zɔlç] *pron* such; **ein ~e(r, s)...** such a...
Sold [zɔlt] *m* -(e)s, -e pay; **Soldat** [zɔl'da:t] *m* -en, -en soldier.
Söldner ['zœldnər] *m* -s, - mercenary.
solid(e) [zo'li:d(ə)] *a* solid; (*Leben, Person*) respectable; ~**arisch** [zoli'da:riʃ] *a* in/with solidarity; **sich ~arisch erklären** declare one's solidarity.
Solist(in f) [zo'list(in)] *m* soloist.
Soll [zɔl] *nt* -(s), -(s) (*FIN*) debit (side); (*Arbeitsmenge*) quota, target.
sollen ['zɔlən] ◆(*als Hilfsverb*) *pt* **sollte**, *ptp* **sollen 1** (*Pflicht, Befehl*) be supposed to; **du hättest nicht gehen ~** you shouldn't have gone, you oughtn't to have gone; **soll ich?** shall I?; **soll ich dir helfen?** shall I help you?; **sag ihm, er soll warten** tell him he's to wait; **was soll ich machen?** what should I do?
2 (*Vermutung*): **sie soll verheiratet sein** she's said to be married; **was soll das heißen?** what's that supposed to mean?; **man sollte glauben, daß ...** you would think that ...; **sollte das passieren, ...** if that should happen ...
◆*vti pt* **sollte**, *ptp* **gesollt**: **was soll das?** what's all this?; **das sollst du nicht** you shouldn't do that; **was soll's?** what the hell!

Solo ['zo:lo] *nt* -s, -s *od* **Soli** solo.
somit [zo'mit] *kj* and so, therefore.
Sommer ['zɔmər] *m* -s, - summer; **s~lich** *a* summery; summer; ~**schlußverkauf** *m* summer sale; ~**sprossen** *pl* freckles *pl*.
Sonate [zo'na:tə] *f* -, -n sonata.
Sonde ['zɔndə] *f* -, -n probe.
Sonder- ['zɔndər] *in zW* special; ~**angebot** *nt* special offer; **s~bar** *a* strange, odd; ~**fahrt** *f* special trip; ~**fall** *m* special case; **s~gleichen** *a inv* without parallel, unparalleled; **s~lich** *a* particular; (*außergewöhnlich*) remarkable; (*eigenartig*) peculiar; **s~n** *kj* but; **nicht nur ..., s~n** auch not only..., but also // *vt* separate; ~**preis** *m* special price; ~**zug** *m* special train.
Sonett [zo'nɛt] *nt* -(e)s, -e sonnet.
Sonnabend ['zɔn'a:bənt] *m* Saturday.
Sonne ['zɔnə] *f* -, -n sun; **s~n** *vr* sun oneself.
Sonnen- *zW*: ~**aufgang** *m* sunrise; **s~baden** *vi* sunbathe; ~**brand** *m* sunburn; ~**brille** *f* sunglasses *pl*; ~**creme** *f* suntan lotion; ~**energie** *f* solar energy; ~**finsternis** *f* solar eclipse; ~**schein** *m* sunshine; ~**schirm** *m* parasol, sunshade; ~**stich** *m* sunstroke; ~**uhr** *f* sundial; ~**untergang** *m* sunset; ~**wende** *f* solstice.
sonnig ['zɔniç] *a* sunny.
Sonntag ['zɔnta:k] *m* Sunday; **s~s** *ad* (on) Sundays.
sonst [zɔnst] *ad* otherwise (*auch kj*); (*mit pron, in Fragen*) else; (*zu anderer Zeit*) at other times, normally; ~ **noch etwas?** anything else?; ~ **nichts** nothing else; ~**ig** *a* other; ~**jemand** *pron* anybody (at all); ~**wo(hin)** *ad* somewhere else; ~**woher** *ad* from somewhere else.
sooft [zo''ɔft] *kj* whenever.
Sopran [zo'pra:n] *m* -s, -e soprano.
Sorge ['zɔrgə] *f* -, -n care, worry.
sorgen *vi*: **für jdn ~** look after sb; **für etw ~** take care of *od* see to sth // *vr* worry (*um* about); ~**frei** *a* carefree; **S~kind** *nt* problem child; ~**voll** *a* troubled, worried.
Sorgerecht *nt* custody (of a child).
Sorg- ['zɔrk] *zW*: ~**falt** *f* - care(fulness); **s~fältig** *a* careful; ~**los** *a* careless; (*ohne Sorgen*) carefree; **s~sam** *a* careful.
Sorte ['zɔrtə] *f* -, -n sort; (*Waren~*) brand; ~**n** *pl* (*FIN*) foreign currency.
sortieren [zɔr'ti:rən] *vt* sort (out).
Sortiment [zɔrti'mɛnt] *nt* assortment.
sosehr [zo'ze:r] *kj* as much as.
Soße ['zo:sə] *f* -, -n sauce; (*Braten~*) gravy.
Souffleur [zu'flø:r] *m*, **Souffleuse**

[zu'flø:zə] f prompter.
soufflieren [zu'fli:rən] vti prompt.
souverän [zuvə'rɛ:n] a sovereign; (*überlegen*) superior.
so- zW: ~**viel** [zo'fi:l] kj: ~**viel ich weiß** as far as I know // pron as much (*wie* as); **rede nicht** ~**viel** don't talk so much; ~**weit** [zo'vait] kj as far as // a: ~**weit sein** be ready; ~**weit wie** od **als möglich** as far as possible; **ich bin** ~**weit zufrieden** by and large I'm quite satisfied; ~**wenig** [zo've:nɪç] kj little as // pron as little (*wie* as); ~**wie** [zo'vi:] kj (*sobald*) as soon as; (*ebenso*) as well as; ~**wieso** [zovi'zo:] ad anyway.
Sowjet- [zɔ'vjɛt] zW: **s~isch** a Soviet; ~**union** f Soviet Union.
sowohl [zo'vo:l] kj: ~ ... **als** od **wie auch** both ... and.
sozial [zotsi'a:l] a social; **S~abgaben** pl national insurance contributions pl; **S~demokrat** m social democrat; ~**demokratisch** a social democratic; ~**i'sieren** vt socialize; **S~ismus** [-'lɪsmʊs] m socialism; **S~ist** [-'lɪst] m socialist; ~**istisch** a socialist; **S~politik** f social welfare policy; **S~produkt** nt (gross/net) national product; **S~staat** nt welfare state.
Sozio- [zotsio] zW: ~**loge** [-'lo:gə] m -n, -n sociologist; ~**logie** [-lo'gi:] f sociology; **s~logisch** [-'lo:gɪʃ] a sociological.
sozusagen [zotsu'za:gən] ad so to speak.
Spachtel ['ʃpaxtəl] m -s, - spatula.
spähen ['ʃpɛ:ən] vi peep, peek.
Spalier [ʃpa'li:r] nt -s, -e (*Gerüst*) trellis; (*Leute*) guard of honour.
Spalt [ʃpalt] m -(e)s, -e crack; (*Tür~*) chink; (*fig: Kluft*) split; ~**e** f -, -n crack, fissure; (*Gletscher~e*) crevasse; (*in Text*) column; **s~en** vtr (*lit, fig*) split; ~**ung** f splitting.
Span [ʃpa:n] m -(e)s, ⸚e shaving; ~**ferkel** nt sucking-pig; ~**ien** nt Spain; ~**ier(in** f) m Spaniard; **s~isch** a Spanish.
Spange ['ʃpaŋə] f -, -n clasp; (*Haar~*) hair slide; (*Schnalle*) buckle; (*Armreif*) bangle.
Spann- ['ʃpan] zW: ~**beton** m prestressed concrete; ~**e** f -, -n (*Zeit~e*) space; (*Differenz*) gap; **s~en** vt (*straffen*) tighten, tauten; (*befestigen*) brace // vi be tight; **s~end** a exciting, gripping; ~**ung** f tension; (*ELEK*) voltage; (*fig*) suspense; (*unangenehm*) tension.
Spar- ['ʃpa:r] zW: ~**buch** nt savings book; ~**büchse** f moneybox; **s~en** vti save; (*sich (dat) etw* save oneself sth; (*Bemerkung*) keep sth to oneself; **mit etw** (*dat*) **s~en** be spar-

ing with sth; **an etw** (*dat*) **s~en** economize on sth; ~**er** m -s, - saver.
Spargel ['ʃpargəl] m -s, - asparagus.
Spar- zW: ~**kasse** f savings bank; ~**konto** nt savings account.
spärlich ['ʃpɛ:rlɪç] a meagre; (*Bekleidung*) scanty.
Spar- zW: ~**maßnahme** f economy measure, cut; **s~sam** a economical, thrifty; ~**samkeit** f thrift, economizing; ~**schwein** nt piggy bank.
Sparte ['ʃpartə] f -, -n field; line of business; (*PRESSE*) column.
Spaß [ʃpa:s] m -es, ⸚e joke; (*Freude*) fun; **jdm** ~ **machen be** fun (for sb); **viel** ~! have fun!; **s~en** vi joke; **mit ihm ist nicht zu s~en** you can't take liberties with him; **s~haft, s~ig** a funny, droll; ~**verderber** m -s, - spoilsport.
spät [ʃpɛ:t] a, ad late; **wie** ~ **ist es?** what's the time?
Spaten ['ʃpa:tən] m -s, - spade.
spät- zW: ~**er** a, ad later; ~**estens** ad at the latest.
Spatz [ʃpats] m -en, -en sparrow.
spazier- [ʃpa'tsi:r] zW: ~**en** vi stroll, walk; ~**enfahren** vi unreg go for a drive; ~**engehen** vi unreg go for a walk; **S~gang** m walk; **S~stock** m walking stick; **S~weg** m path, walk.
SPD [ɛspe:'de:] f abk (= *Sozialdemokratische Partei Deutschlands*) Social Democratic Party.
Specht [ʃpɛçt] m -(e)s, -e woodpecker.
Speck [ʃpɛk] m -(e)s, -e bacon.
Spediteur [ʃpedi'tø:r] m carrier; (*Möbel~*) furniture remover.
Spedition [ʃpeditsi'o:n] f carriage; (~*sfirma*) road haulage contractor; removal firm.
Speer [ʃpe:r] m -(e)s, -e spear; (*SPORT*) javelin.
Speiche [ʃpaiçə] f -, -n spoke.
Speichel ['ʃpaiçəl] m -s saliva, spit(tle).
Speicher ['ʃpaiçər] m -s, - storehouse; (*Dach~*) attic, loft; (*Korn~*) granary; (*Wasser~*) tank; (*TECH*) store; (*COMPUT*) memory; **s~n** vt store; (*COMPUT*) save.
speien ['ʃpaiən] vti unreg spit; (*erbrechen*) vomit; (*Vulkan*) spew.
Speise ['ʃpaizə] f -, -n food; ~**eis** ['-ais] nt ice-cream; ~**kammer** f larder, pantry; ~**karte** f menu; **s~n** vt feed; eat // vi dine; ~**röhre** f gullet, oesophagus; ~**saal** m dining room; ~**wagen** m dining car.
Speku- [ʃpeku] zW: ~**lant** [-'lant] m speculator; ~**lation** [-latsi'o:n] f speculation; **s~lieren** [-'li:rən] vi (*fig*) speculate; **auf etw** (*akk*) **s~lieren** have hopes of sth.
Spelunke [ʃpe'lʊŋkə] f -, -n dive.

Spende ['ʃpɛndə] f -, -n donation; **s~n** vt donate, give; **~r** m -s, - donor, donator.

spendieren [ʃpɛn'diːrən] vt pay for, buy; **jdm etw ~** treat sb to sth, stand sb sth.

Sperling ['ʃpɛrlɪŋ] m sparrow.

Sperma ['ʃpɛrma] nt -s, **Spermen** sperm.

Sperr- ['ʃpɛr] zW: **~e** f -, -n barrier; (Verbot) ban; **s~en** vt block; (SPORT) suspend, bar; (vom Ball) obstruct; (einschließen) lock; (verbieten) ban // vr baulk, jib(e); **~gebiet** nt prohibited area; **~holz** nt plywood; **s~ig** a bulky; **~sitz** m (THEAT) stalls pl; **~stunde** f closing time.

Spesen ['ʃpeːzən] pl expenses pl; **~abrechnung** f expense account.

Spezial- [ʃpetsi'aːl] in zW special; **s~angefertigt** a custom-built; (Kleidung) tailor-made; **s~i'sieren** vr specialize; **~i'sierung** f specialization; **~ist** [-'lɪst] m specialist; **~i'tät** f speciality.

speziell [ʃpetsi'ɛl] a special.

spezifisch [ʃpe'tsiːfɪʃ] a specific.

Sphäre ['sfɛːrə] f -, -n sphere.

Spiegel ['ʃpiːgəl] m -s, - mirror; (Wasser~) level; (MIL) tab; **~bild** nt reflection; **s~bildlich** a reversed; **~ei** ['-'aɪ] nt fried egg; **s~n** vt mirror, reflect // vr be reflected // vi gleam; (wider~n) be reflective; **~schrift** f mirror-writing; **~ung** f reflection.

Spiel [ʃpiːl] nt -(e)s, -e game; (Schau~) play; (Tätigkeit) play(ing); (KARTEN) deck; (TECH) (free) play; **s~en** vti play; (um Geld) gamble; (THEAT) perform, act; **s~end** ad easily; **~er** m -s, - player; (um Geld) gambler; **~e'rei** f trifling pastime; **~feld** nt pitch, field; **~film** m feature film; **~plan** m (THEAT) programme; **~platz** m playground; **~raum** m room to manoeuvre, scope; **~regel** f rule; **~sachen** pl toys pl; **~verderber** m -s, - spoilsport; **~waren** pl, **~zeug** nt toys pl.

Spieß [ʃpiːs] m -es, -e spear; (Brat~) spit; **~bürger** m, **~er** m -s, - bourgeois; **~rutenlaufen** nt running the gauntlet.

Spikes [spaɪks] pl spikes pl; (AUT) studs pl.

Spinat [ʃpi'naːt] m -(e)s, -e spinach.

Spind [ʃpɪnt] m od nt -(e)s, -e locker.

Spinn- [ʃpɪn] zW: **~e** f -, -n spider; **s~en** vti unreg spin; (umg) talk rubbish; (verrückt) be crazy od mad; **~e'rei** f spinning mill; **~rad** nt spinning-wheel; **~webe** f cobweb.

Spion [ʃpi'oːn] m -s, -e spy; (in Tür) spyhole; **~age** [ʃpio'naːʒə] f -, -n espionage; **s~ieren** [ʃpio'niːrən] vi spy.

Spirale [ʃpi'raːlə] f -, -n spiral.

Spirituosen [ʃpiritu'oːzən] pl spirits pl.

Spiritus ['ʃpiːritus] m -, -se (methylated) spirit.

Spital [ʃpi'taːl] nt -s, -̈er hospital.

spitz [ʃpɪts] a pointed; (Winkel) acute; (fig: Zunge) sharp; (: Bemerkung) caustic; **S~bogen** m pointed arch; **S~bube** m rogue; **S~e** f -, -n point, tip; (Berg~) peak; (Bemerkung) taunt, dig; (erster Platz) lead, top; (meist pl: Gewebe) lace; **S~el** m -s, - police informer; **~en** vt sharpen.

Spitzen- zW: **~leistung** f top performance; **~lohn** m top wages pl; **~marke** f brand leader; **~sportler** m top-class sportsman.

spitzfindig a (over)subtle.

Spitzname m nickname.

Splitter ['ʃplɪtər] m -s, - splinter; **s~nackt** a stark naked.

sponsern ['sponzərn, 'ʃpɔnzərn] vt sponsor.

spontan [ʃpɔn'taːn] a spontaneous.

Sport [ʃpɔrt] m -(e)s, -e sport; (fig) hobby; **~lehrer(in** f) m games od P.E. teacher; **~ler(in** f) m -s, - sportsman/woman; **s~lich** a sporting; (Mensch) sporty; **~platz** m playing od sports field; **~verein** m sports club; **~wagen** m sports car.

Spott [ʃpɔt] m -(e)s mockery, ridicule; **s~billig** a dirt-cheap; **s~en** vi mock (über +akk at), ridicule.

spöttisch ['ʃpœtɪʃ] a mocking.

sprach etc v siehe **sprechen**.

Sprach- ['ʃpraːx] zW: **s~begabt** a good at languages; **~e** f -, -n language; **~fehler** m speech defect; **~führer** m phrasebook; **~gefühl** nt feeling for language; **~labor** nt language laboratory; **s~lich** a linguistic; **s~los** a speechless.

sprang etc v siehe **springen**.

Spray [spreː] m od nt -s, -s spray.

Sprech- ['ʃprɛç] zW: **~anlage** f intercom; **s~en** unreg vi speak, talk (mit to); **das spricht für ihn** that's a point in his favour // vt say; (Sprache) speak; (Person) speak to; **~er(in** f) m -s, - speaker; (für Gruppe) spokesman; (RAD, TV) announcer; **~stunde** f consultation (hour); (doctor's) surgery; **~stundenhilfe** f (doctor's) receptionist; **~zimmer** nt consulting room, surgery.

Spreng- ['ʃprɛŋ] zW: **~arbeiten** pl blasting operations pl; **s~en** vt sprinkle; (mit Sprengstoff) blow up; (Gestein) blast; (Versammlung) break up; **~kopf** m warhead; **~ladung** f explosive charge; **~stoff** m explosive(s).

Spreu [ʃprɔʏ] f - chaff.

sprichst etc v siehe **sprechen**.

Sprich- [ˈʃprɪç] zW: **~wort** nt proverb; **s~wörtlich** a proverbial.

Spring- [ˈʃprɪŋ] zW: **~brunnen** m fountain; **s~en** vi unreg jump; (Glas) crack; (mit Kopfsprung) dive; **~er** m -s, - jumper; (Schach) knight.

Spritz- [ˈʃprɪts] zW: **~e** f -, -n syringe; injection; (an Schlauch) nozzle; **s~en** vt spray; (MED) inject // vi splash; (heraus~en) spurt; (MED) give injections; **~pistole** f spray gun.

spröde [ˈʃprøːdə] a brittle; (Person) reserved, coy.

Sprosse [ˈʃprɔsə] f -, -n rung.

Spruch [ʃprʊx] m -(e)s, ⸚e saying, maxim; (JUR) judgement.

Sprudel [ˈʃpruːdəl] m -s, - mineral water; lemonade; **s~n** vi bubble.

Sprüh- [ˈʃpryː] zW: **~dose** f aerosol (can); **s~en** vti spray; (fig) sparkle; **~regen** m drizzle.

Sprung [ʃprʊŋ] m -(e)s, ⸚e jump; (Riß) crack; **~brett** nt springboard; **s~haft** a erratic; (Aufstieg) rapid; **~schanze** f skijump.

Spucke [ˈʃpʊkə] f - spit; **s~n** vti spit.

Spuk [ʃpuːk] m -(e)s, -e haunting; (fig) nightmare; **s~en** vi (Geist) walk; **hier spukt es** this place is haunted.

Spule [ˈʃpuːlə] f -, -n spool; (ELEK) coil.

Spül- [ˈʃpyːl] zW: **~e** f -, -n (kitchen) sink; **s~en** vti rinse; (Geschirr) wash up; (Toilette) flush; **~maschine** f dishwasher; **~mittel** nt washing-up liquid; **~stein** m sink; **~ung** f rinsing; flush; (MED) irrigation.

Spur [ʃpuːr] f -, -en trace; (Fuß~, Rad~, Tonband~) track; (Fährte) trail; (Fahr~) lane.

spür- [ˈʃpyːr] zW: **~bar** a noticeable, perceptible; **~en** vt feel.

spurlos ad without a trace.

Spurt [ʃpʊrt] m -(e)s, -s od -e spurt.

sputen [ˈʃpuːtən] vr make haste.

St. abk von **Stück** // abk (= Sankt) St.

Staat [ʃtaːt] m -(e)s, -en state; (Prunk) show; (Kleidung) finery; **mit etw ~ machen** show off od parade sth; **s~enlos** a stateless; **s~lich** a state(-); state-run.

Staats- zW: **~angehörigkeit** f nationality; **~anwalt** m public prosecutor; **~bürger** m citizen; **~dienst** m civil service; **s~feindlich** a subversive; **~mann**, pl **-männer** statesman; **~sekretär** m secretary of state.

Stab [ʃtaːp] m -(e)s, ⸚e rod; (Gitter~) bar; (Menschen) staff; **~hochsprung** m pole vault; **stabil** [ʃtaˈbiːl] a stable; (Möbel) sturdy; **stabili'sieren** vt stabilize.

Stachel [ˈʃtaxəl] m -s, -n spike; (von Tier) spine; (von Insekten) sting; **~beere** f gooseberry; **~draht** m barbed wire; **s~ig** a prickly; **~schwein** nt porcupine.

Stadion [ˈʃtaːdiɔn] nt -s, **Stadien** stadium.

Stadium [ˈʃtaːdiʊm] nt stage, phase.

Stadt [ʃtat] f -, ⸚e town.

Städt- [ˈʃtɛːt] zW: **~chen** nt small town; **Städtebau** m town planning; **~er(in** f) m -s, - town dweller; **s~isch** a municipal; (nicht ländlich) urban.

Stadt- zW: **~mauer** f city wall(s); **~mitte** f town centre; **~plan** m street map; **~rand** m outskirts pl; **~rundfahrt** f tour of a/the city; **~teil** m district, part of town; **~zentrum** nt town centre.

Staffel [ˈʃtafəl] f -, -n rung; (SPORT) relay (team); (AVIAT) squadron; **s~n** vt graduate.

stahl etc v siehe **stehlen**.

Stahl [ʃtaːl] m -(e)s, ⸚e steel.

stak etc v siehe **stecken**.

Stall [ʃtal] m -(e)s, ⸚e stable; (Kaninchen~) hutch; (Schweine~) sty; (Hühner~) henhouse.

Stamm [ʃtam] m -(e)s, ⸚e (Baum~) trunk; (Menschen~) tribe; (GRAM) stem; **~baum** m family tree; (von Tier) pedigree; **s~eln** vti stammer; **s~en** vi: **s~en von** od **aus** come from; **~gast** m regular (customer).

stämmig [ˈʃtɛmɪç] a sturdy; (Mensch) stocky.

Stammtisch [ˈʃtamtɪʃ] m table for the regulars.

stampfen [ˈʃtampfən] vti stamp; (stapfen) tramp; (mit Werkzeug) pound.

stand etc v siehe **stehen**.

Stand [ʃtant] m -(e)s, ⸚e position; (Wasser~, Benzin~ etc) level; (Stehen) standing position; (Zustand) state; (Spiel~) score; (Messe~ etc) stand; (Klasse) class; (Beruf) profession.

Standard [ˈʃtandart] m -s, -s standard.

Ständer [ˈʃtɛndər] m -s, - stand.

Standes- [ˈʃtandəs] zW: **~amt** nt registry office; **~beamte(r)** m registrar; **s~gemäß** a, ad according to one's social position; **~unterschied** m social difference.

Stand- zW: **s~haft** a steadfast; **~haftigkeit** f steadfastness; **s~halten** vi unreg stand firm (jdm/etw sb/sth), resist (jdm/etw sb/sth).

ständig ['ʃtɛndɪç] a permanent; (*un-unterbrochen*) constant, continual.

Stand- zW: **~licht** nt sidelights pl, parking lights pl (US); **~ort** m location; (MIL) garrison; **~punkt** m standpoint.

Stange ['ʃtaŋə] f -, -n stick; (*Stab*) pole, bar; rod; (*Zigaretten*) carton; **von der ~** (COMM) off the peg; **eine ~ Geld** quite a packet.

Stanniol [ʃtani'o:l] nt -s, -e tinfoil.

Stapel ['ʃta:pəl] m -s, - pile; (NAUT) stocks pl; **~lauf** m launch; **s~n** vt pile (up).

Star [ʃta:r] m -(e)s, -e starling; (MED) cataract // m -s, -s (*Film etc*) star.

starb etc v siehe **sterben.**

stark [ʃtark] a strong; (*heftig, groß*) heavy; (*Maßangabe*) thick.

Stärke ['ʃtɛrkə] f -, -n strength; heaviness; thickness; (KOCH, Wäsche~) starch; **s~n** vt strengthen; (*Wäsche*) starch.

Starkstrom m heavy current.

Stärkung ['ʃtɛrkuŋ] f strengthening; (*Essen*) refreshment.

starr [ʃtar] a stiff; (*unnachgiebig*) rigid; (*Blick*) staring; **~en** vi stare; **~en vor** od **von** be covered in; (*Waffen*) be bristling with; **S~heit** f rigidity; **~köpfig** a stubborn; **S~sinn** m obstinacy.

Start [ʃtart] m -(e)s, -e start; (AVIAT) takeoff; **~automatik** f (AUT) automatic choke; **~bahn** f runway; **s~en** vti start; take off; **~er** m -s, - starter; **~erlaubnis** f takeoff clearance.

Station [ʃtatsi'o:n] f station; hospital ward; **s~ieren** [-'ni:rən] vt station.

Statist [ʃta'tɪst] m extra, supernumerary; **~ik** f statistics; **~iker** m -s, - statistician; **s~isch** a statistical.

Stativ [ʃta'ti:f] nt -s, -e tripod.

statt [ʃtat] kj, präp +gen od dat instead of.

Stätte ['ʃtɛtə] f -, -n place.

statt- zW: **~finden** vi unreg take place; **~haft** a admissible; **~lich** a imposing, handsome.

Statue ['ʃta:tuə] f -, -n statue.

Status ['ʃta:tʊs] m -, - status; **~symbol** nt status symbol.

Statuten [ʃta'tu:tən] pl rules pl.

Stau [ʃtau] m -(e)s, -e blockage; (*Verkehrs~*) (traffic) jam.

Staub [ʃtaup] m -(e)s dust; **s~en** ['ʃtaubən] vi be dusty; **s~ig** a dusty; **~sauger** m vacuum cleaner; **~tuch** nt duster.

Staudamm m dam.

Staude ['ʃtaudə] f -, -n shrub.

stauen ['ʃtauən] vt (*Wasser*) dam up; (*Blut*) stop the flow of // vr (*Wasser*) become dammed up; (MED, Verkehr) become congested; (*Menschen*) collect together; (*Gefühle*) build up.

staunen ['ʃtaunən] vi be astonished; **S~** nt -s amazement.

Stauung ['ʃtauʊŋ] f (*von Wasser*) damming-up; (*von Blut, Verkehr*) congestion.

Std. abk (= Stunde) hr.

Steak [ste:k] nt steak.

Stech- ['ʃtɛç] zW: **s~en** vt unreg (*mit Nadel etc*) prick; (*mit Messer*) stab; (*mit Finger*) poke; (*Biene etc*) sting; (*Mücke*) bite; (*Sonne*) burn; (KARTEN) take; (ART) engrave; (*Torf, Spargel*) cut; **in See s~en** put to sea; **~en** nt -s, - (SPORT) play-off; jump-off; **s~end** a piercing, stabbing; (*Geruch*) pungent; **~palme** f holly; **~uhr** f time clock.

Steck- ['ʃtɛk] zW: **~brief** m 'wanted' poster; **~dose** f (wall) socket; **s~en** vt put, insert; (*Nadel*) stick; (*Pflanzen*) plant; (*beim Nähen*) pin // vi (*auch unreg*) be; (*festsitzen*) be stuck; (*Nadeln*) stick; **s~enbleiben** vi unreg get stuck; **s~enlassen** vt unreg leave in; **~enpferd** nt hobbyhorse; **~er** m -s, - plug; **~nadel** f pin; **~rübe** f turnip.

Steg [ʃte:k] m -(e)s, -e small bridge; (*Anlege~*) landing stage; **~reif** m: **aus dem ~reif** just like that.

stehen ['ʃte:ən] unreg vi stand (*zu* by); (*sich befinden*) be; (*in Zeitung*) say; (*still~*) have stopped; **jdm ~** suit sb // vi unpers: **es steht schlecht um** things are bad for; **wie steht's?** how are things?; (SPORT) what's the score?; **~ bleiben** remain standing; **~bleiben** vi unreg (*Uhr*) stop; (*Fehler*) stay as it is; **~lassen** vt unreg leave; (*Bart*) grow.

Stehlampe ['ʃte:lampə] f standard lamp.

stehlen ['ʃte:lən] vt unreg steal.

Stehplatz ['ʃte:plats] m standing place.

steif [ʃtaif] a stiff; **S~heit** f stiffness.

Steig- [ʃtaik] zW: **~bügel** m stirrup; **~eisen** nt crampon; **s~en** vi unreg rise; (*klettern*) climb; **s~en in** (+akk)/**auf** (+akk) get in/on; **s~ern** vt raise; (GRAM) compare // vi (*Auktion*) bid // vr increase; **~erung** f raising; (GRAM) comparison; **~ung** f incline, gradient, rise.

steil [ʃtail] a steep.

Stein [ʃtain] m -(e)s, -e stone; (*in Uhr*) jewel; **~bock** m (ASTROL) Capricorn; **~bruch** m quarry; **~butt** m -s, -e turbot; **s~ern** a (made of) stone; (*fig*) stony; **~gut** nt stoneware; **s~hart** a hard as stone; **s~ig** a stony; **s~igen** vt stone; **~kohle** f mineral coal.

Stelle ['ʃtɛlə] f -, -n place; (*Arbeit*) post, job; (*Amt*) office; **an Ihrer/ meiner** ~ in your/my place.

stellen vt put; (*Uhr etc*) set; (*zur Verfügung* ~) supply; (*fassen: Dieb*) apprehend // vr (*sich aufstellen*) stand; (*sich einfinden*) present oneself; (*bei Polizei*) give oneself up; (*vorgeben*) pretend (to be); **sich zu etw** ~ have an opinion of sth; **S~angebot** nt offer of a post; (*Zeitung*) vacancies; **S~gesuch** nt application for a post; **S~vermittlung** f employment agency.

Stell- zW: ~**ung** f position; (*MIL*) line; ~**ung nehmen zu** comment on; ~**ungnahme** f -, - comment; **s~vertretend** a deputy, acting; ~**vertreter** m deputy; ~**werk** nt (*EISENB*) signal box.

Stelze ['ʃtɛltsə] f -, -n stilt.

Stemm- ['ʃtɛm] zW: ~**bogen** m (*SKI*) stem turn; **s~en** vt lift (up); (*drücken*) press; **sich s~en gegen** (*fig*) resist, oppose.

Stempel ['ʃtɛmpəl] m -s, - stamp; (*BOT*) pistil; ~**kissen** nt inkpad; **s~n** vt stamp; (*Briefmarke*) cancel; **s~n gehen** (*umg*) be/go on the dole.

Stengel ['ʃtɛŋəl] m -s, - stalk.

Steno- [ʃteno] zW: ~**gramm** [-'gram] nt shorthand report; ~**graphie** [-gra'fiː] f shorthand; **s~graphieren** [-gra'fiːrən] vti write (in) shorthand; ~**typist(in** f) [-ty'pɪst(ɪn)] m shorthand typist.

Stepp- ['ʃtɛp] zW: ~**decke** f quilt; ~**e** f -, -n prairie; steppe; **s~en** vt stitch // vi tap-dance.

Sterb- ['ʃtɛrb] zW: **Sterbefall** m death; **s~en** vi unreg die; **s~lich** ['ʃtɛrplɪç] a mortal; ~**lichkeit** f mortality; ~**lichkeitsziffer** f death rate.

stereo- ['steːreo] in zW stereo(-); **S~anlage** f stereo (system); ~**typ** [ʃtereo'typ] a stereotype.

steril [ʃte'riːl] a sterile; ~**i'sieren** vt sterilize; **S~i'sierung** f sterilization.

Stern [ʃtɛrn] m -(e)s, -e star; ~**bild** nt constellation; ~**schnuppe** f -, -n meteor, falling star; ~**stunde** f historic moment.

stet [ʃteːt] a steady; ~**ig** a constant, continual; ~**s** ad continually, always.

Steuer ['ʃtɔyər] nt -s, - (*NAUT*) helm; (~**ruder**) rudder; (*AUT*) steering wheel // f -, -n tax; ~**erklärung** f tax return; ~**freibetrag** m tax allowance; ~**klasse** f tax group; ~**knüppel** m control column; (*AVIAT, COMPUT*) joystick; ~**mann** m, -pl -**männer** od -**leute** helmsman; **s~n** vti steer; (*Flugzeug*) pilot; (*Entwicklung, Tonstärke*) control; ~**paradies** nt tax haven; ~**rad** nt steering wheel; ~**ung** f

steering (*auch AUT*); piloting; control; (*Vorrichtung*) controls pl; ~**vergünstigung** f tax relief; ~**zahler** m -s, - taxpayer.

Steward ['stjuːərt] m -s, -s steward; **Stewardeß** ['stjuːərdɛs] f -, -**essen** stewardess; air hostess.

Stich [ʃtɪç] m -(e)s, -e (*Insekten*~) sting; (*Messer*~) stab; (*beim Nähen*) stitch; (*Färbung*) tinge; (*KARTEN*) trick; (*ART*) engraving; **jdn im** ~ **lassen** leave sb in the lurch; **s~eln** vi (*fig*) jibe; **s~haltig** a sound, tenable; ~**probe** f spot check; ~**wahl** f final ballot; ~**wort** nt cue; (*in Wörterbuch*) headword; (*für Vortrag*) note.

Stick- [ʃtɪk] zW: **s~en** vti embroider; ~**e'rei** f embroidery; **s~ig** a stuffy, close; ~**stoff** m nitrogen.

Stiefel ['ʃtiːfəl] m -s, - boot.

Stief- ['ʃtiːf] in zW step; ~**kind** nt stepchild; (*fig*) Cinderella; ~**mutter** f stepmother; ~**mütterchen** nt pansy.

Stiege ['ʃtiːgə] f -, -n staircase.

stiehlst etc v siehe **stehlen**.

Stiel [ʃtiːl] m -(e)s, -e handle; (*BOT*) stalk.

stier [ʃtiːr] a staring, fixed; **S~** m -(e)s, -e bull; (*ASTROL*) Taurus; ~**en** vi stare.

Stift [ʃtɪft] m -(e)s, -e peg; (*Nagel*) tack; (*Farb*~) crayon; (*Blei*~) pencil // nt -(e)s, -e (*charitable*) foundation; (*ECCL*) religious institution; **s~en** vt found; (*Unruhe*) cause; (*spenden*) contribute; ~**er(in** f) m -s, - founder; ~**ung** f donation; (*Organisation*) foundation; ~**zahn** m crown tooth.

Stil [ʃtiːl] m -(e)s, -e style.

still [ʃtɪl] a quiet; (*unbewegt*) still; (*heimlich*) secret; **S~er Ozean** Pacific; **S~e** f -, -n stillness, quietness; **in aller S~e** quietly; ~**en** vt stop; (*befriedigen*) satisfy; (*Säugling*) breast-feed; ~**halten** vi unreg keep still; ~**(l)egen** vt close down; **S~(l)egung** f shut-down; ~**schweigen** vi unreg be silent; **S~schweigen** nt silence; ~**schweigend** a, ad silent(ly); (*Einverständnis*) tacit(ly); **S~stand** m standstill; ~**stehen** vi unreg stand still.

Stimm- ['ʃtɪm] zW: ~**bänder** pl vocal chords pl; **s~berechtigt** a entitled to vote; ~**e** f -, -n voice; (*Wahl*~e) vote; **s~en** vt (*MUS*) tune; **das stimmte ihn traurig** that made him feel sad // vi be right; **s~en für/gegen** vote for/against; **stimmt so!** that's right; ~**enmehrheit** f majority (of votes); ~**enthaltung** f abstention; ~**gabel** f tuning fork; ~**recht** nt right to vote; ~**ung** f mood; atmosphere;

s~ungsvoll a enjoyable; full of atmosphere; **~zettel** m ballot paper.
stinken ['ʃtɪŋkən] vi unreg stink.
Stipendium [ʃti'pɛndiʊm] nt grant.
stirbst etc v siehe **sterben**.
Stirn [ʃtɪrn] f -, -en forehead, brow; (Frechheit) impudence; **~höhle** f sinus; **~runzeln** nt -s frown(ing).
stöbern ['ʃtøbərn] vi rummage.
stochern ['ʃtɔxərn] vi poke (about).
Stock [ʃtɔk] m -(e)s, ⸚e stick; (BOT) stock // pl **-werke** storey; **s~en** vi stop, pause; **s~end** a halting; **~ung** f stoppage; **~werk** nt storey, floor.
Stoff [ʃtɔf] m -(e)s, -e (Gewebe) material, cloth; (Materie) matter; (von Buch etc) subject (matter); **s~lich** a material; **~wechsel** m metabolism.
stöhnen ['ʃtøːnən] vi groan.
stoisch ['ʃtoːɪʃ] a stoical.
Stollen ['ʃtɔlən] m -s, - (MIN) gallery; (KOCH) cake eaten at Christmas; (von Schuhen) stud.
stolpern ['ʃtɔlpərn] vi stumble, trip.
Stolz [ʃtɔlts] m -es pride; **s~** a proud; **s~ieren** [ʃtɔl'tsiːrən] vi strut.
Stopf- ['ʃtɔpf] zW: **s~en** vt (hinein~en) stuff; (voll~en) fill (up); (nähen) darn // vi (MED) cause constipation; **~garn** nt darning thread.
Stoppel ['ʃtɔpəl] f -, -n stubble.
Stopp- ['ʃtɔp] zW: **s~en** vti stop; (mit Uhr) time; **~schild** nt stop sign; **~uhr** f stopwatch.
Stöpsel ['ʃtœpsəl] m -s, - plug; (für Flaschen) stopper.
Storch [ʃtɔrç] m -(e)s, ⸚e stork.
Stör- [ʃtøːr] zW: **s~en** vt disturb; (behindern, RAD) interfere with // vr sich an etw (dat) **s~en** let sth bother one; **s~end** a disturbing, annoying; **~enfried** m -(e)s, -e troublemaker.
störrisch ['ʃtœrɪʃ] a stubborn, perverse.
Störsender m jammer.
Störung f disturbance; interference.
Stoß [ʃtoːs] m -es, ⸚e (Schub) push; (Schlag) blow; knock; (mit Schwert) thrust; (mit Fuß) kick; (Erd~) shock; (Haufen) pile; **~dämpfer** m -s, - shock absorber; **s~en** unreg vt (mit Druck) shove, push; (mit Schlag) knock, bump; (mit Fuß) kick; (Schwert etc) thrust; (an~en: Kopf etc) bump; // vr get a knock; sich **s~en** an (+dat) (fig) take exception to // vi: **s~en** an od auf (+akk) bump into; (finden) come across; (angrenzen) be next to; **~stange** f (AUT) bumper.
stottern ['ʃtɔtərn] vti stutter.
Str. abk (= Straße) St.
Straf- ['ʃtraːf] zW: **~anstalt** f penal institution; **~arbeit** f (SCH) punishment; lines pl; **s~bar** a punishable;

~barkeit f criminal nature; **~e** f -, -n punishment; (JUR) penalty; (Gefängnis~e) sentence; (Geld~e) fine; **s~en** vt punish.
straff [ʃtraf] a tight; (streng) strict; (Stil etc) concise; (Haltung) erect; **~en** vt tighten, tauten.
Straf- zW: **~gefangene(r)** mf prisoner, convict; **~gesetzbuch** nt penal code.
Sträf- ['ʃtrɛːf] zW: **s~lich** a criminal; **~ling** m convict.
Straf- zW: **~porto** nt excess postage (charge); **~predigt** f telling-off; **~raum** m (SPORT) penalty area; **~recht** nt criminal law; **~stoß** m (SPORT) penalty (kick); **~tat** f punishable act; **~zettel** m ticket.
Strahl [ʃtraːl] m -s, -en ray, beam; (Wasser~) jet; **s~en** vi radiate; (fig) beam; **~entherapie** f radiotherapy; **~ung** f radiation.
Strähne ['ʃtrɛːnə] f -, -n strand.
stramm [ʃtram] a tight; (Haltung) erect; (Mensch) robust.
strampeln ['ʃtrampəln] vi kick (about), fidget.
Strand [ʃtrant] m -(e)s, ⸚e shore; (mit Sand) beach; **~bad** nt open-air swimming pool, lido; **s~en** ['ʃtrandən] vi run aground; (fig: Mensch) fail; **~gut** nt flotsam; **~korb** m beach chair.
Strang [ʃtraŋ] m -(e)s, ⸚e cord, rope; (Bündel) skein.
Strapaz- zW: **~e** [ʃtra'paːtsə] f -, -n strain, exertion; **s~ieren** [ʃtrapa'tsiːrən] vt (Material) treat roughly, punish; (Mensch, Kräfte) wear out, exhaust; **s~ierfähig** a hard-wearing; **s~iös** [ʃtrapatsi'øːs] a exhausting, tough.
Straße ['ʃtraːsə] f -, -n street, road.
Straßen- zW: **~bahn** f tram, streetcar (US); **~beleuchtung** f street lighting; **~feger** m, **~kehrer** m -s, - roadsweeper; **~sperre** f roadblock; **~verkehrsordnung** f highway code.
Strateg- [ʃtra'teːg] zW: **~e** m -n, -n strategist; **~ie** [ʃtrate'giː] f strategy; **s~isch** a strategic.
sträuben ['ʃtrɔʏbən] vt ruffle // vr bristle; (Mensch) resist (gegen etw sth).
Strauch [ʃtraʊx] m -(e)s, Sträucher bush, shrub.
Strauß [ʃtraʊs] m -es, Sträuße bunch; bouquet // pl -e ostrich.
Streb- ['ʃtreːb] zW: **s~en** vi strive (nach for), endeavour; **~er** m -s, - (pej) pusher, climber; (SCH) swot (Brit), bootlicker (US); **s~sam** a industrious.
Strecke ['ʃtrɛkə] f -, -n stretch; (Entfernung) distance; (EISENB)

line; (MATH) line; **s~n** vt stretch; (Waffen) lay down; (KOCH) eke out // vr stretch (oneself).

Streich [ʃtraiç] m -(e)s, -e trick, prank; (Hieb) blow; **s~eln** vt stroke; **s~en** unreg vt (berühren) stroke; (auftragen) spread; (anmalen) paint; (durch~en) delete; (nicht genehmigen) cancel // vi (berühren) brush; (schleichen) prowl; **~holz** nt match; **~instrument** nt string instrument.

Streif- ['ʃtraif] zW: **~e** f -, -n patrol; **s~en** vt (leicht berühren) brush against, graze; (Blick) skim over; (Thema, Problem) touch on; (ab~en) take off // vi (gehen) roam; **~en** m -s, - (Linie) stripe; (Stück) strip; (Film) film; **~endienst** m patrol duty; **~enwagen** m patrol car; **~schuß** m graze, grazing shot; **~zug** m scouting trip.

Streik [ʃtraik] m -(e)s, -s strike; **~brecher** m -s, - blackleg, strikebreaker; **s~en** vi strike; **~kasse** f strike fund; **~posten** m (strike) picket.

Streit [ʃtrait] m -(e)s, -e argument; dispute; **s~en** vir unreg argue; dispute; **~frage** f point at issue; **s~ig** a: jdm etw **s~ig machen** dispute sb's right to sth; **~igkeiten** pl quarrel, dispute; **~kräfte** pl (MIL) armed forces pl.

streng [ʃtrɛŋ] a severe; (Lehrer, Maßnahme) strict; (Geruch etc) sharp; **S~e** f -, severity; strictness; sharpness; **~genommen** ad strictly speaking; **~gläubig** a orthodox, strict; **~stens** ad strictly.

Streu [ʃtrɔy] f -, -en litter, bed of straw; **s~en** vt strew, scatter, spread; **~ung** f dispersion.

Strich [ʃtriç] m -(e)s, -e (Linie) line; (Feder~, Pinsel~) stroke; (von Geweben) nap; (von Fell) pile; **auf den ~ gehen** (umg) walk the streets; **jdm gegen den ~ gehen** (umg) rub sb up the wrong way; **einen ~ machen durch** (lit) cross out; (fig) foil; **~mädchen** nt streetwalker; **~punkt** m semicolon; **s~weise** ad here and there.

Strick [ʃtrik] m -(e)s, -e rope; **s~en** vti knit; **~jacke** f cardigan; **~leiter** f rope ladder; **~nadel** f knitting needle; **~waren** pl knitwear.

strikt [ʃtrikt] a strict.

strittig ['ʃtritiç] a disputed, in dispute.

Stroh [ʃtroː] nt -(e)s straw; **~blume** f everlasting flower; **~dach** nt thatched roof; **~halm** m (drinking) straw.

Strom [ʃtroːm] m -(e)s, -̈e river; (fig) stream; (ELEK) current; **s~abwärts** [-'apvɛrts] ad downstream; **s~aufwärts** [-'aufvɛrts] ad upstream.

strömen ['ʃtrøːmən] vi stream, pour.

Strom- zW: **~kreis** m circuit; **s~linienförmig** a streamlined; **~rechnung** f electricity bill; **~sperre** f power cut.

Strömung ['ʃtrøːmʊŋ] f current.

Strophe ['ʃtroːfə] f -, -n verse.

strotzen ['ʃtrɔtsən] vi: **vor** od **von** abound in, be full of.

Strudel ['ʃtruːdəl] m -s, - whirlpool, vortex; (KOCH) strudel.

Struktur [ʃtrʊk'tuːr] f structure.

Strumpf [ʃtrʊmpf] m -(e)s, -̈e stocking; **~band** nt garter; **~hose** f (pair of) tights.

Stube ['ʃtuːbə] f -, -n room.

Stuben- zW: **~arrest** m confinement to one's room; (MIL) confinement to quarters; **~hocker** m (umg) stay-at-home; **s~rein** a house-trained.

Stuck [ʃtʊk] m -(e)s stucco.

Stück [ʃtʏk] nt -(e)s, -e piece; (etwas) bit; (THEAT) play; **~chen** nt little piece; **~lohn** m piecework wages pl; **s~weise** ad bit by bit, piecemeal; (COMM) individually; **~werk** nt bits and pieces pl.

Student(in f) [ʃtu'dɛnt(ɪn)] m student; **s~isch** a student, academic.

Studie ['ʃtuːdiə] f study.

studieren [ʃtu'diːrən] vti study.

Studio ['ʃtuːdio] nt -s, -s studio.

Studium ['ʃtuːdiʊm] nt studies pl.

Stufe ['ʃtuːfə] f -, -n step; (Entwicklungs~) stage; **stufenweise** ad gradually.

Stuhl [ʃtuːl] m -(e)s, -̈e chair; **~gang** m bowel movement.

stülpen ['ʃtʏlpən] vt (umdrehen) turn upside down; (bedecken) put.

stumm [ʃtʊm] a silent; (MED) dumb; **Stummel** m -s, - stump; (Zigaretten~) stub; **S~film** m silent film; **S~heit** f silence; dumbness.

Stümper ['ʃtʏmpər] m -s, - incompetent, duffer; **s~haft** a bungling, incompetent; **s~n** vi (umg) bungle.

stumpf [ʃtʊmpf] a blunt; (teilnahmslos, glanzlos) dull; (Winkel) obtuse; **S~** m -(e)s, -̈e stump; **S~sinn** m tediousness; **~sinnig** a dull.

Stunde ['ʃtʊndə] f -, -n hour; (SCH) lesson.

stunden vt: **jdm etw ~** give sb time to pay sth; **S~geschwindigkeit** f average speed per hour; **S~kilometer** pl kilometres per hour; **~lang** a for hours; **S~lohn** m hourly wage; **S~plan** m timetable; **~weise** a by the hour; every hour.

stündlich ['ʃtʏntliç] a hourly.

Stups [ʃtʊps] m -es, -e (umg) push; **~nase** f snub nose.

stur [ʃtuːr] a obstinate, pigheaded.

Sturm [ʃtʊrm] m -(e)s, ⸚e storm, gale; (MIL etc) attack, assault.

stürm- [ʃtʏrm] zW: **~en** vi (Wind) blow hard, rage; (rennen) storm // vt (MIL, fig) storm // v unpers es ~t there's a gale blowing; **S~er** m -s, - (SPORT) forward, striker; **~isch** a stormy.

Sturmwarnung f gale warning.

Sturz [ʃtʊrts] m -es, ⸚e fall; (POL) overthrow.

stürzen [ʃtʏrtsən] vt (werfen) hurl; (POL) overthrow; (umkehren) overturn // vr rush; (hinein~) plunge // vi fall; (AVIAT) dive; (rennen) dash.

Sturz- zW: **~flug** m nose-dive; **~helm** m crash helmet.

Stute [ʃtuːtə] f -, -n mare.

Stütz- [ʃtʏts] zW: **~balken** m brace, joist; **~e** f -, -n support; help; **s~en** vt (lit, fig) support; (Ellbogen etc) prop up.

stutz- [ʃtʊts] zW: **~en** vt trim; (Ohr, Schwanz) dock; (Flügel) clip // vi hesitate; become suspicious; **~ig** a perplexed, puzzled; (mißtrauisch) suspicious.

Stützpunkt m point of support; (von Hebel) fulcrum; (MIL, fig) base.

Styropor ® [ʃtyroˈpoːr] nt -s polystyrene.

s.u. abk = siehe unten.

Subjekt [zʊpˈjɛkt] nt -(e)s, -e subject; **s~iv** [-ˈtiːf] a subjective; **~ivi'tät** f subjectivity.

Substantiv [ˈzʊpstantiːf] nt -s, -e noun.

Substanz [zʊpˈstants] f substance.

subtil [zʊpˈtiːl] a subtle.

subtrahieren [zʊptraˈhiːrən] vt subtract.

Subvention [zʊpvɛntsiˈoːn] f subsidy; **s~ieren** [-ˈniːrən] vt subsidize.

Such- [ˈzuːx] zW: **~aktion** f search; **~e** f -, -n search; **s~en** vti look (for), seek; (ver~en) try; **~er** m -s, - seeker, searcher; (PHOT) viewfinder.

Sucht [zʊxt] f -, ⸚e mania; (MED) addiction, craving.

süchtig [ˈzʏçtɪç] a addicted; **S~e(r)** mf addict.

Süd- [zyːt] zW: **~en** [ˈzyːdən] m -s south; **~früchte** pl Mediterranean fruit; **s~lich** a southern; **s~lich von** (to the) south of; **~pol** m South Pole; **s~wärts** ad southwards.

süffig [ˈzʏfɪç] a (Wein) pleasant to the taste.

süffisant [zʏfiˈzant] a smug.

suggerieren [zʊgeˈriːrən] vt suggest (jdm etw sth to sb).

Sühne [ˈzyːnə] f -, -n atonement, expiation; **s~n** vt atone for, expiate.

Sultan [ˈzʊltan] m -s, -e sultan; **~ine** [zʊltaˈniːnə] f sultana.

Sülze [ˈzʏltsə] f -, -n brawn.

Summ- [ˈzʊm] zW: **~e** f -, -n sum, total; **s~en** vti buzz; (Lied) hum.

Sumpf [zʊmpf] m -(e)s, ⸚e swamp, marsh; **s~ig** a marshy.

Sünde [ˈzʏndə] f -, -n sin; **Sündenbock** m (umg) scapegoat; **Sündenfall** m Fall (of man); **~r(in f)** m -s, - sinner.

Super [ˈzuːpər] nt -s (Benzin) four star (petrol); **Superlativ** [-latiːf] m -s, -e superlative; **~markt** m supermarket.

Suppe [ˈzʊpə] f -, -n soup.

süß [zyːs] a sweet; **S~e** f - sweetness; **~en** vt sweeten; **S~igkeit** f sweetness; (Bonbon etc) sweet (Brit), candy (US); **~lich** a sweetish; (fig) sugary; **S~speise** f pudding, sweet; **S~stoff** m sweetener; **S~wasser** nt fresh water.

Sylvester [zʏlˈvɛstər] nt -s, - siehe Silvester.

Symbol [zʏmˈboːl] nt -s, -e symbol; **s~isch** a symbolic(al).

Symmetrie [zʏmeˈtriː] f symmetry.

symmetrisch [zʏˈmeːtrɪʃ] a symmetrical.

Sympath- zW: **~ie** [zʏmpaˈtiː] f liking, sympathy; **s~isch** [zʏmˈpatɪʃ] a likeable; **er ist mir s~isch** I like him; **s~i'sieren** vi sympathize.

Symptom [zʏmpˈtoːm] nt -s, -e symptom; **s~atisch** [zʏmptoˈmatɪʃ] a symptomatic.

Synagoge [zynaˈgoːgə] f -, -n synagogue.

synchron [zʏnˈkroːn] a synchronous; **S~getriebe** nt synchromesh (gears pl); **~i'sieren** vt synchronize; (Film) dub.

Synonym [zynoˈnyːm] nt -s, -e synonym; **s~** a synonymous.

Synthese [zʏnˈteːzə] f -, -n synthesis.

synthetisch [zʏnˈteːtɪʃ] a synthetic.

Syphilis [ˈzyfilɪs] f - syphilis.

Syr- [ˈzyːr] zW: **~er(in f)** m Syrian; **~ien** nt Syria; **s~isch** a Syrian.

System [zʏsˈteːm] nt -s, -e system; **s~atisch** [zʏsteˈmatɪʃ] a systematic; **s~ati'sieren** vt systematize; **~platte** f system disk.

Szene [ˈstseːnə] f -, -n scene; **Szenerie** [stsenəˈriː] f scenery.

T

T, t [teː] T, t.

t abk (= Tonne) t.

Tabak [ˈtaːbak] m -s, -e tobacco.

Tabell- [taˈbɛl] zW: **t~arisch** [tabɛˈlaːrɪʃ] a tabular; **~e** f table; **Tabellenführer** m top of the table, league leader.

Tablett [taˈblɛt] *nt* tray; **~e** *f* tablet, pill.

Tabu [taˈbuː] *nt* taboo; **t~** *a* taboo.

Tachometer [taxoˈmeːtər] *m* **-s,** - (*AUT*) speedometer.

Tadel [ˈtaːdəl] *m* **-s,** - censure, scolding; (*Fehler*) fault, blemish; **t~los** *a* faultless, irreproachable; **t~n** *vt* scold; **t~nswert** *a* blameworthy.

Tafel [ˈtaːfəl] *f* **-,** **-n** table (*auch MATH*); (*Anschlag~*) board; (*Wand~*) blackboard; (*Schiefer~*) slate; (*Gedenk~*) plaque; (*Illustration*) plate; (*Schalt~*) panel; (*Schokolade etc*) bar.

Taft [taft] *m* **-(e)s** taffeta.

Tag [taːk] *m* **-(e)s, -e** day; daylight; **unter/über ~e** (*MIN*) underground/on the surface; **an den ~ kommen** come to light; **guten ~!** good morning/afternoon!; **t~aus, t~ein** *ad* day in, day out; **~dienst** *m* day duty.

Tage- [ˈtaːgə] *zW:* **~buch** [ˈtaːgəbuːx] *nt* diary, journal; **~geld** *nt* daily allowance; **t~lang** *ad* for days; **t~n** *vi* sit, meet // *v unpers:* **es tagt** dawn is breaking.

Tages- *zW:* **~ablauf** *m* course of the day; **~anbruch** *m* dawn; **~karte** *f* menu of the day; (*Fahrkarte*) day ticket; **~licht** *nt* daylight; **~ordnung** *f* agenda; **~zeit** *f* time of day; **~zeitung** *f* daily (paper).

täglich [ˈtɛːklɪç] *a, ad* daily.

tagsüber [ˈtaːksˈyːbər] *ad* during the day.

Tagung *f* conference.

Taille [ˈtaljə] *f* **-,** **-n** waist.

Takt [takt] *m* **-(e)s, -e** tact; (*MUS*) time; **~gefühl** *nt* tact; **~ik** *f* tactics *pl*; **t~isch** *a* tactical; **t~los** *a* tactless; **~losigkeit** *f* tactlessness; **~stock** *m* (conductor's) baton; **t~voll** *a* tactful.

Tal [taːl] *nt* **-(e)s, ̈er** valley.

Talent [taˈlɛnt] *nt* **-(e)s, -e** talent; **t~iert** [talɛnˈtiːrt] *a* talented, gifted.

Talisman [ˈtaːlɪsman] *m* **-s, -e** talisman.

Tal- *zW:* **~sohle** *f* bottom of a valley; **~sperre** *f* dam.

Tamburin [tambuˈriːn] *nt* **-s, -e** tambourine.

Tampon [ˈtampɔn] *m* **-s, -s** tampon.

Tang [taŋ] *m* **-(e)s, -e** seaweed.

Tangente [taŋˈgɛntə] *f* **-,** **-n** tangent.

tangieren [taŋˈgiːrən] *vt* (*lit*) touch; (*fig*) affect.

Tank [taŋk] *m* **-s, -s** tank; **t~en** *vi* fill up with petrol (*Brit*) *od* gas (*US*); (*AVIAT*) (re)fuel; **~er** *m* **-s, -,** **~schiff** *nt* tanker; **~stelle** *f* petrol (*Brit*) *od* gas (*US*) station; **~wart** *m* petrol pump (*Brit*) *od* gas station (*US*) attendant.

Tanne [ˈtanə] *f* **-,** **-n** fir; **Tannenbaum** *m* fir tree; **Tannenzapfen** *m* fir cone.

Tante [ˈtantə] *f* **-,** **-n** aunt.

Tanz [tants] *m* **-es, ̈e** dance; **t~en** *vti* dance.

Tänzer(in *f*) [ˈtɛntsər(ɪn)] *m* **-s, -** dancer.

Tanz- *zW:* **~fläche** *f* (dance) floor; **~schule** *f* dancing school.

Tapete [taˈpeːtə] *f* **-,** **-n** wallpaper; **Tapetenwechsel** *m* (*fig*) change of scenery.

tapezieren [tapeˈtsiːrən] *vt* (wall)paper.

Tapezierer [tapeˈtsiːrər] *m* **-s, -** (interior) decorator.

tapfer [ˈtapfər] *a* brave; **T~keit** *f* courage, bravery.

Tarif [taˈriːf] *m* **-s, -e** tariff, (scale of) fares/charges; **~lohn** *m* standard wage rate; **~verhandlungen** *pl* wage negotiations *pl*.

Tarn- [ˈtarn] *zW:* **t~en** *vt* camouflage; (*Person, Absicht*) disguise; **~farbe** *f* camouflage paint; **~ung** *f* camouflaging; disguising.

Tasche [ˈtaʃə] *f* **-,** **-n** pocket; handbag.

Taschen- *in zW* pocket; **~buch** *nt* paperback; **~dieb** *m* pickpocket; **~geld** *nt* pocket money; **~lampe** *f* (electric) torch, flashlight (*US*); **~messer** *nt* penknife; **~tuch** *nt* handkerchief.

Tasse [ˈtasə] *f* **-,** **-n** cup.

Tastatur [tastaˈtuːr] *f* keyboard.

Taste [ˈtastə] *f* **-,** **-n** push-button control; (*an Schreibmaschine*) key; **t~n** *vt* feel, touch // *vi* feel, grope // *vr* feel one's way.

tat *etc v siehe* **tun.**

Tat [taːt] *f* **-,** **-en** act, deed, action; **in der ~** indeed, as a matter of fact; **~bestand** *m* facts *pl* of the case; **t~enlos** *a* inactive.

Tät- [ˈtɛːt] *zW:* **~er(in** *f*) *m* **-s, -** perpetrator, culprit; **t~ig** *a* active; **in einer Firma t~ig sein** work for a firm; **~igkeit** *f* activity; (*Beruf*) occupation; **t~lich** *a* violent; **~lichkeit** *f* violence // *pl* blows *pl*.

tätowieren [tɛtoˈviːrən] *vt* tattoo.

Tat- *zW:* **~sache** *f* fact; **t~sächlich** *a* actual // *ad* really.

Tau [tau] *nt* **-(e)s, -e** rope // *m* **-(e)s** dew.

taub [taup] *a* deaf; (*Nuß*) hollow; **T~heit** *f* deafness; **~stumm** *a* deaf-and-dumb.

Taube [ˈtaubə] *f* **-,** **-n** dove; pigeon; **Taubenschlag** *m* dovecote; **hier geht es zu wie in einem Taubenschlag** it's a hive of activity here.

Tauch- [ˈtaux] *zW:* **t~en** *vt* dip // *vi* dive; (*NAUT*) submerge; **~er** *m* **-s, -** diver; **~eranzug** *m* diving suit; **~sieder** *m* **-s, -** immersion coil (*for* *boiling water*).

tauen ['tauən] *vti, v unpers* thaw.

Tauf- ['tauf] *zW:* ~**becken** *nt* font; ~**e** *f* -, -**n** baptism; **t~en** *vt* christen, baptize; ~**name** *m* Christian name; ~**pate** *m* godfather; ~**patin** *f* godmother; ~**schein** *m* certificate of baptism.

Taug- ['taug] *zW:* **t~en** *vi* be of use; **t~en für** do *od* be good for; **nicht t~en** be no good *od* useless; **Taugenichts** *m* -**es**, -**e** good-for-nothing; **t~lich** ['tauklıç] *a* suitable; (*MIL*) fit (for service).

Taumel ['tauməl] *m* -**s** dizziness; (*fig*) frenzy; **t~n** *vi* reel, stagger.

Tausch [tauʃ] *m* -**(e)s**, -**e** exchange; **t~en** *vt* exchange, swap; ~**handel** *m* barter.

täuschen ['tɔyʃən] *vt* deceive // *vi* be deceptive // *vr* be wrong; ~**d** *a* deceptive.

Täuschung *f* deception; (*optisch*) illusion.

tausend ['tauzənt] *num* (a) thousand; **T~füßler** *m* -**s**, - centipede; millipede.

Tauwetter *nt* thaw.

Taxi ['taksi] *nt* -**(s)**, -**(s)** taxi; ~**fahrer** *m* taxi driver; ~**stand** *m* taxi rank.

Tech- ['tɛç] *zW:* ~**nik** *f* technology; (*Methode, Kunstfertigkeit*) technique; ~**niker** *m* -**s**, - technician; **t~nisch** *a* technical; ~**nolo'gie** *f* technology; **t~no'logisch** *a* technological.

TEE [te:'e:''e:] *m abk* (= *Trans-Europ-Express*) Trans-European Express.

Tee [te:] *m* -**s**, -**s** tea; ~**kanne** *f* teapot; ~**löffel** *m* teaspoon.

Teer [te:r] *m* -**(e)s**, -**e** tar; **t~en** *vt* tar.

Teesieb *nt* tea strainer.

Teich [taıç] *m* -**(e)s**, -**e** pond.

Teig [taık] *m* -**(e)s**, -**e** dough; **t~ig** *a* doughy; ~**waren** *pl* pasta *sing.*

Teil [taıl] *m od nt* -**(e)s**, -**e** part; (*An~*) share; (*Bestand~*) component; **zum** ~ partly; **t~bar** *a* divisible; ~**betrag** *m* instalment; ~**chen** *nt* (atomic) particle; **t~en** *vtr* divide; (*mit jdm*) share; **t~haben** *vi unreg* share (*an* +*dat* in); ~**haber** *m* -**s**, - partner; ~**kaskoversicherung** *f* third party, fire and theft insurance; ~**nahme** *f* -, -**n** participation; (*Mitleid*) sympathy; **t~nahmslos** *a* disinterested, apathetic; **t~nehmen** *vi unreg* take part (*an* +*dat* in); ~**nehmer** *m* -**s**, - participant; **t~s** *ad* partly; ~**ung** *f* division; **t~weise** *ad* partially, in part; ~**zahlung** *f* payment by instalments.

Teint [tɛ̃:] *m* -**s**, -**s** complexion.

Telefax ['telefaks] *nt* fax.

Telefon [tele'fo:n] *nt* -**s**, -**e** telephone; ~**amt** *nt* telephone exchange; ~**anruf** *m*, ~**at** [telefo'na:t] *nt* -**(e)s**, -**e** (tele)phone call; ~**buch** *nt* telephone directory; ~**ieren** [telefo'ni:rən] *vi* telephone; **t~isch** [-ıʃ] *a* telephone; (*Benachrichtigung*) by telephone; ~**ist(in** *f*) [telefo'nıst(ın)] *m* telephonist; ~**nummer** *f* (tele)phone number; ~**verbindung** *f* telephone connection; ~**zelle** *f* telephone kiosk, callbox; ~**zentrale** *f* telephone exchange.

Telegraf [tele'gra:f] *m* -**en**, -**en** telegraph; ~**enleitung** *f* telegraph line; ~**enmast** *m* telegraph pole; ~**ie** [-'fi:] *f* telegraphy; **t~ieren** [-'fi:rən] *vti* telegraph, wire; **t~isch** *a* telegraphic.

Telegramm [tele'gram] *nt* -**s**, -**e** telegram, cable; ~**adresse** *f* telegraphic address.

Tele- *zW:* ~**objektiv** ['te:le'ɔpjɛkti:f] *nt* telephoto lens; ~**pathie** [telepa'ti:] *f* telepathy; **t~pathisch** [tele'pa:tıʃ] *a* telepathic; ~**skop** [tele'sko:p] *nt* -**e** telescope.

Telex ['tɛleks] *nt* -**es**, -**e** telex.

Teller ['tɛlər] *m* -**s**, - plate.

Tempel ['tɛmpəl] *m* -**s**, - temple.

Temperament [tɛmpera'mɛnt] *nt* temperament; (*Schwung*) vivacity, liveliness; **t~los** *a* spiritless; **t~voll** *a* high-spirited, lively.

Temperatur [tɛmpera'tu:r] *f* temperature.

Tempo ['tɛmpo] *nt* -**s**, -**s** speed, pace // *pl* **Tempi** (*MUS*) tempo; ~**!** get a move on!

Tendenz [tɛn'dɛnts] *f* tendency; (*Absicht*) intention; **t~iös** [-i'ø:s] *a* biased, tendentious.

tendieren [tɛn'di:rən] *vi* show a tendency, incline (*zu* to(wards)).

Tennis ['tɛnıs] *nt* - tennis; ~**platz** *m* tennis court; ~**schläger** *m* tennis racket; ~**spieler(in** *f*) *m* tennis player.

Tenor [te'no:r] *m* -**s**, **̈e** tenor.

Teppich ['tɛpıç] *m* -**s**, -**e** carpet; ~**boden** *m* wall-to-wall carpeting.

Termin [tɛr'mi:n] *m* -**s**, -**e** (*Zeitpunkt*) date; (*Frist*) time limit, deadline; (*Arzt~ etc*) appointment; ~**kalender** *m* diary, appointments book.

Termite [tɛr'mi:tə] *f* -, -**n** termite.

Terpentin [tɛrpɛn'ti:n] *nt* -**s**, -**e** turpentine, turps *sing.*

Terrasse [tɛ'rasə] *f* -, -**n** terrace.

Terrine [tɛ'ri:nə] *f* tureen.

territorial [tɛritori'a:l] *a* territorial.

Territorium [tɛri'to:rium] *nt* territory.

Terror ['tɛrɔr] *m* -**s** terror; reign of terror; **t~isieren** [tɛrori'zi:rən] *vt* terrorize; ~**ismus** [-'rısmus] *m* terror-

ism; **~ist** [-'rɪst] *m* terrorist.
Terz [tɛrts] *f* -, **-en** (*MUS*) third; **~ett**
[tɛr'tsɛt] *nt* -(e)s, -e trio.
Tesafilm ® ['te:zafɪlm] *m* sellotape
(*Brit*), Scotch tape ® (*US*).
Test [tɛst] *m* -s, -s test.
Testament [tɛsta'mɛnt] *nt* will, testa-
ment; (*REL*) Testament; **t~arisch**
[-'ta:rɪʃ] *a* testamentary; **Testamentsvollstrecker** *m* executor (of a
will).
Testbild *nt* (*TV*) test card.
testen *vt* test.
Tetanus ['te:tanʊs] *m* - tetanus;
~impfung *f* (anti-)tetanus injection.
teuer ['tɔyər] *a* dear, expensive;
T~ung *f* increase in prices;
T~ungszulage *f* cost of living bonus.
Teufel ['tɔyfəl] *m* -s, - devil.
teuflisch ['tɔyflɪʃ] *a* fiendish, diabolical.
Text [tɛkst] *m* -(e)s, -e text; (*Lieder~*)
words *pl*; **t~en** *vi* write the words.
textil [tɛks'ti:l] *a* textile; **T~ien** *pl* textiles *pl*; **T~industrie** *f* textile industry; **T~waren** *pl* textiles *pl*.
Theater [te'a:tər] *nt* -s, - theatre;
(*umg*) fuss; **~ spielen** (*lit, fig*) play-
act; **~besucher** *m* playgoer; **~kasse**
f box office; **~stück** *nt* (stage-)play.
Theke ['te:kə] *f* -, **-n** (*Schanktisch*)
bar; (*Ladentisch*) counter.
Thema ['te:ma] *nt* -s, **Themen** *od* -ta
theme, topic, subject.
Themse ['tɛmzə] *f* Thames.
Theo- [teo] *zW*: **~loge** [-'lo:gə] *m* -n,
-n theologian; **~logie** [-lo'gi:] *f* theology; **t~logisch** [-'lo:gɪʃ] *a* theologi-
cal; **~retiker** [-'re:tikər] *m* -s, - theo-
rist; **t~retisch** [-'re:tɪʃ] *a* theoretical;
~rie [-'ri:] *f* theory.
Thera- [tera] *zW*: **~peut** [-'pɔyt] *m*
-en, -en therapist; **t~peutisch**
[-'pɔytɪʃ] *a* therapeutic; **~pie** [-'pi:] *f*
therapy.
Therm- *zW*: **~albad** [tɛrm'a:lba:t] *nt*
thermal bath; thermal spa;
~odrucker ['tɛrmo-] *m* thermal
printer; **~ometer** [tɛrmo'me:tər] *nt* -
s, - thermometer; **~osflasche**
['tɛrmɔsflaʃə] *f* Thermos ® flask;
~ostat [tɛrmo'sta:t] *m* -(e)s *od* -en,
-e(n) thermostat.
These ['te:zə] *f* -, **-n** thesis.
Thrombose [trɔm'bo:zə] *f* -, **-n**
thrombosis.
Thron [tro:n] *m* -(e)s, **-e** throne;
~folge *f* succession (to the throne).
Thunfisch ['tu:nfɪʃ] *m* tuna.
Thymian ['ty:mia:n] *m* -s, **-e** thyme.
Tick [tɪk] *m* -(e)s, **-s** tic; (*Eigenart*)
quirk; (*Fimmel*) craze; **t~en** *vi* tick.
tief [ti:f] *a* deep; (*tiefsinnig*) profound;
(*Ausschnitt, Preis, Ton*) low; **T~** *nt*
-s, -s (*MET*) depression; **T~druck** *m*

low pressure; **T~e** *f* -, **-n** depth;
T~ebene *f* plain; **Tiefenpsychologie**
f depth psychology; **Tiefenschärfe** *f*
(*PHOT*) depth of focus; **T~garage** *f*
underground garage; **~gekühlt** *a* frozen; **~greifend** *a* far-reaching;
T~kühlfach *nt* deep-freeze compartment; **T~kühltruhe** *f* deep-freeze,
freezer; **T~land** *nt* lowlands *pl*;
T~punkt *m* low point; (*fig*) low ebb;
T~schlag *m* (*Boxen, fig*) blow below
the belt; **~schürfend** *a* profound;
T~see *f* deep sea; **~sinnig** *a* profound; melancholy; **T~stand** *m* low
level; **Tiefstwert** *m* minimum *od* lowest value.
Tier [ti:r] *nt* -(e)s, -e animal; **~arzt** *m*
vet(erinary surgeon); **~garten** *m*
zoo(logical gardens *pl*); **t~isch** *a* animal; (*lit, fig*) brutish; (*fig*: *Ernst
etc*) deadly; **~kreis** *m* zodiac;
~kunde *f* zoology; **t~liebend** *a* fond
of animals; **~quälerei** [-kvɛːlə'raɪ] *f*
cruelty to animals; **~schutzverein** *m*
society for the prevention of cruelty
to animals.
Tiger ['ti:gər] *m* -s, - tiger; **~in** *f* ti-
gress.
tilgen ['tɪlgən] *vt* erase; (*Sünden*) expiate; (*Schulden*) pay off.
Tinte ['tɪntə] *f* -, **-n** ink.
Tinten- *zW*: **~fisch** *m* cuttlefish;
~stift *m* copying *od* indelible pencil.
Tip [tɪp] *m* tip; **tippen** *vti* tap, touch;
(*umg*: *schreiben*) type; (*umg*: *raten*)
tip (*auf jdn* sb); (*im Lotto etc*) bet
(on).
Tipp- ['tɪp] *zW*: **~fehler** *m* (*umg*) typing error; **t~topp** *a* (*umg*) tip-top;
~zettel *m* (pools) coupon.
Tirol [ti'ro:l] *nt* the Tyrol; **~er(in** *f*) *m*
Tyrolean; **t~isch** *a* Tyrolean.
Tisch [tɪʃ] *m* -(e)s, -e table; **bei ~** at
table; **vor/nach ~** before/after eating;
unter den ~ fallen (*fig*) be dropped;
~decke *f* tablecloth; **~ler** *m* -s, -
carpenter, joiner; **~le'rei** *f* joiner's
workshop; (*Arbeit*) carpentry, join-
ery; **t~lern** *vi* do carpentry *etc*;
~rede *f* after-dinner speech; **~tennis**
nt table tennis.
Titel ['ti:təl] *m* -s, - title; **~anwärter**
m (*SPORT*) challenger; **~bild** *nt* cover (picture); (*von Buch*) frontis-
piece; **~geschichte** *f* main story;
~rolle *f* title role; **~seite** *f* cover;
(*Buch~*) title page; **~verteidiger** *m*
defending champion, title holder.
Toast [to:st] *m* -(e)s, -s *od* -e toast;
~er *m* -s, - toaster.
tob- ['to:b] *zW*: **~en** *vi* rage; (*Kinder*)
romp about; **T~sucht** *f* raving madness; **~süchtig** *a* maniacal.
Tochter ['tɔxtər] *f* -, ⁼ daughter;
~gesellschaft *f* subsidiary (compa-

ny).

Tod [to:t] *m* **-(e)s, -e** death; **t~ernst** *a* deadly serious // *ad* in dead earnest.

Todes- ['to:dəs] *zW:* **~angst** [-aŋst] *f* mortal fear; **~anzeige** *f* obituary (notice); **~fall** *m* death; **~strafe** *f* death penalty; **~ursache** *f* cause of death; **~urteil** *nt* death sentence; **~verachtung** *f* utter disgust.

todkrank *a* dangerously ill.

tödlich ['tø:tlɪç] *a* deadly, fatal.

tod- *zW:* **~müde** *a* dead tired; **~schick** *a* (*umg*) smart, classy; **~sicher** *a* (*umg*) absolutely od dead certain; **T~sünde** *f* deadly sin.

Toilette [toa'lɛtə] *f* toilet, lavatory; (*Frisiertisch*) dressing table; (*Kleidung*) outfit.

Toiletten- *zW:* **~artikel** *pl* toiletries *pl*, toilet articles *pl*; **~papier** *nt* toilet paper; **~tisch** *m* dressing table.

toi, toi, toi ['tɔy, 'tɔy, 'tɔy] *interj* touch wood.

tolerant [tole'rant] *a* tolerant.

Toleranz [tole'rants] *f* tolerance.

tolerieren [tole'ri:rən] *vt* tolerate.

toll [tɔl] *a* mad; (*Treiben*) wild; (*umg*) terrific; **~en** *vi* romp; **T~kirsche** *f* deadly nightshade; **~kühn** *a* daring; **T~wut** *f* rabies.

Tomate [to'ma:tə] *f* -, **-n** tomato; **Tomatenmark** *nt* tomato puree.

Ton [to:n] *m* **-(e)s, -e** (*Erde*) clay // *pl* **-e** (*Laut*) sound; (*MUS*) note; (*Redeweise*) tone; (*Farb~, Nuance*) shade; (*Betonung*) stress; **~abnehmer** *m* pick-up; **t~angebend** *a* leading; **~art** *f* (musical) key; **~band** *nt* tape; **~bandgerät** *nt* tape recorder.

tönen ['tø:nən] *vi* sound // *vt* shade; (*Haare*) tint.

tönern ['tø:nərn] *a* clay.

Ton- *zW:* **~fall** *m* intonation; **~film** *m* sound film; **~leiter** *f* (*MUS*) scale; **t~los** *a* soundless.

Tonne ['tɔnə] *f* -, **-n** barrel; (*Maß*) ton.

Ton- *zW:* **~spur** *f* soundtrack; **~taube** *f* clay pigeon; **~waren** *pl* pottery, earthenware.

Topf [tɔpf] *m* **-(e)s, -e** pot; **~blume** *f* pot plant.

Töpfer ['tœpfər] *m* -s, - potter; **~ei** [-'raɪ] *f* piece of pottery; potter's workshop; **~scheibe** *f* potter's wheel.

topographisch [topo'gra:fɪʃ] *a* topographic.

Tor [to:r] *m* **-en, -en** fool // *nt* **-(e)s, -e** gate; (*SPORT*) goal; **~bogen** *m* archway.

Torf [tɔrf] *m* **-(e)s** peat.

Tor- *zW:* **~heit** *f* foolishness; foolish deed; **~hüter** *m* -s, - goalkeeper.

töricht ['tø:rɪçt] *a* foolish.

torkeln ['tɔrkəln] *vi* stagger, reel.

Torpedo [tɔr'pe:do] *m* -s, -s torpedo.

Torte ['tɔrtə] *f* -, **-n** cake; (*Obst~*) flan, tart.

Tortur [tɔr'tu:r] *f* ordeal.

Torwart *m* **-(e)s, -e** goalkeeper.

tosen ['to:zən] *vi* roar.

tot [to:t] *a* dead.

total [to'ta:l] *a* total; **~itär** [totali'tɛ:r] *a* totalitarian; **T~schaden** *m* (*AUT*) complete write-off.

töten ['tø:tən] *vti* kill.

Toten- ['to:tən] *zW:* **~bett** *nt* death bed; **t~blaß** *a* deathly pale, white as a sheet; **~kopf** *m* skull; **~schein** *m* death certificate; **~stille** *f* deathly silence.

Tot- *zW:* **~e(r)** *mf* dead person; **t~fahren** *vt* *unreg* run over; **t~geboren** *a* stillborn; **t~lachen** *vr* (*umg*) laugh one's head off.

Toto ['to:to] *m* od *nt* -s, -s pools *pl*; **~schein** *m* pools coupon.

tot- *zW:* **~sagen** *vt:* jdn **~sagen** say that sb is dead; **T~schlag** *m* manslaughter; **~schlagen** *vt* *unreg* (*lit, fig*) kill; **~schweigen** *vt* *unreg* hush up; **~stellen** *vr* pretend to be dead.

Tötung ['tø:tʊŋ] *f* killing.

Toupet [tu'pe:] *nt* -s, -s toupee.

toupieren [tu'pi:rən] *vt* back-comb.

Tour [tu:r] *f* -, **-en** tour, trip; (*Umdrehung*) revolution; (*Verhaltensart*) way; in einer **~** incessantly; **Tourenzähler** *m* rev counter; **~ismus** [tu'rɪsmʊs] *m* tourism; **~ist** [tu'rɪst] *m* tourist; **~istenklasse** *f* tourist class; **Tournee** [tʊr'ne:] *f* -, **-n** (*THEAT etc*) tour; auf Tournee gehen go on tour.

Trab [tra:p] *m* **-(e)s** trot; **~ant** [tra'bant] *m* satellite; **~antenstadt** *f* satellite town; **t~en** *vi* trot.

Tracht [traxt] *f* -, **-en** (*Kleidung*) costume, dress; eine **~** Prügel a sound thrashing; **t~en** *vi* strive (*nach* for), endeavour; jdm nach dem Leben **t~en** seek to kill sb.

trächtig ['trɛçtɪç] *a* (*Tier*) pregnant.

Tradition [traditsi'o:n] *f* tradition; **t~ell** [-'nɛl] *a* traditional.

traf *etc v siehe* **treffen**.

Trag- ['tra:g] *zW:* **~bahre** *f* stretcher; **t~bar** *a* (*Gerät*) portable; (*Kleidung*) wearable; (*erträglich*) bearable.

träge ['trɛ:gə] *a* sluggish, slow; (*PHYS*) inert.

tragen ['tra:gən] *unreg vt* carry; (*Kleidung, Brille*) wear; (*Namen, Früchte*) bear; (*erdulden*) endure; sich mit einem Gedanken **~** have an idea in mind // *vi* (*schwanger sein*) be pregnant; (*Eis*) hold; zum **T~kommen** have an effect.

Träger ['trɛ:gər] *m* -s, - carrier; wearer; bearer; (*Ordens~*) holder; (*an*

Kleidung) (shoulder) strap; (*Körper-schaft etc*) sponsor; **~rakete** *f* launch vehicle; **~rock** *m* skirt with shoulder straps.

Trag- ['traːk] *zW:* **~fläche** *f* (*AVIAT*) wing; **~flügelboot** *nt* hydrofoil.

Trägheit ['trɛːkhait] *f* laziness; (*PHYS*) inertia.

Tragik ['traːgɪk] *f* tragedy.

tragisch ['traːgɪʃ] *a* tragic.

Tragödie [tra'gøːdiə] *f* tragedy.

Tragweite *f* range; (*fig*) scope.

Train- [trɛːn] *zW:* **~er** *m* **-s, -** (*SPORT*) trainer, coach; (*Fußball*) manager; **t~ieren** [trɛ'niːrən] *vti* train; (*Mensch auch*) coach; (*Übung*) practise; **~ing** *nt* **-s, -s** training; **~ingsanzug** *m* track suit.

Traktor ['traktɔr] *m* **-s, -en** tractor; (*von Drucker*) tractor feed.

trällern ['trɛlərn] *vti* trill, sing.

trampeln ['trampəln] *vti* trample, stamp.

trampen ['trɛmpən] *vi* hitch-hike.

Tran [traːn] *m* **-(e)s, -e** train oil, blubber.

Tranchierbesteck [trã'ʃiːrbəʃtɛk] *nt* (pair of) carvers.

tranchieren [trã'ʃiːrən] *vt* carve.

Träne ['trɛːnə] *f* **-, -n** tear; **t~n** *vi* water; **Tränengas** *nt* teargas.

trank *etc v siehe* **trinken.**

tränken ['trɛŋkən] *vt* (*Tiere*) water.

Trans- *zW:* **~formator** [transfɔr'maːtɔr] *m* transformer; **~istor** [tran'zistɔr] *m* transistor; **t~itiv** ['tranzitiːf] *a* transitive;

Transitverkehr *m* transit traffic; **Transitvisum** *nt* transit visa; **t~parent** [transpa'rɛnt] *a* transparent; **~parent** *nt* **-(e)s, -e** (*Bild*) transparency; (*Spruchband*) banner; **t~pirieren** [transpi'riːrən] *vi* perspire; **~plantation** [transplantatsi'oːn] *f* transplantation; (*Haut~plantation*) graft(ing).

Transport [trans'pɔrt] *m* **-(e)s, -e** transport; **t~ieren** [transpɔr'tiːrən] *vt* transport; **~kosten** *pl* transport charges *pl*, carriage; **~mittel** *nt* means of transportation; **~unternehmen** *nt* carrier.

Trapez [tra'peːts] *nt* **-es, -e** trapeze; (*MATH*) trapezium.

Traube ['traubə] *f* **-, -n** grape; bunch (of grapes); **Traubenzucker** *m* glucose.

trauen ['trauən] *vi:* **jdm/etw ~** trust sb/sth // *vr* dare // *vt* marry.

Trauer ['trauər] *f* **-** sorrow; (*für Verstorbenen*) mourning; **~fall** *m* death, bereavement; **~kleidung** *f* mourning; **t~n** *vi* mourn (*um* for); **~rand** *m* black border; **~spiel** *nt* tragedy.

traulich ['traulɪç] *a* cosy, intimate.

Traum [traum] *m* **-(e)s, Träume** dream; **Trauma** *nt* **-s, -men** trauma.

träum- ['trɔym] *zW:* **~en** *vti* dream; **T~er** *m* **-s, -** dreamer; **T~e'rei** *f* dreaming; **~erisch** *a* dreamy.

traumhaft *a* dreamlike; (*fig*) wonderful.

traurig ['trauriç] *a* sad; **T~keit** *f* sadness.

Trau- ['trau] *zW:* **~ring** *m* wedding ring; **~schein** *m* marriage certificate; **~ung** *f* wedding ceremony; **~zeuge** *m* witness (to a marriage).

treffen ['trɛfən] *unreg vti* strike, hit; (*Bemerkung*) hurt; (*begegnen*) meet; (*Entscheidung etc*) make; (*Maßnahmen*) take; **er hat es gut getroffen** he did well; **~ auf** (+*akk*) come across, meet with // *vr* meet; **es traf sich, daß...** it so happened that...; **es trifft sich gut** it's convenient; **wie es so trifft** as these things happen; **T~** *nt* **-s, -** meeting; **~d** *a* pertinent, apposite.

Treffer *m* **-s, -** hit; (*Tor*) goal; (*Los*) winner.

Treffpunkt *m* meeting place.

Treib- ['traib] *zW:* **~eis** *nt* drift ice; **t~en** *unreg vt* drive; (*Studien etc*) pursue; (*Sport*) do, go in for; **Unsinn t~en** fool around // *vi* (*Schiff etc*) drift; (*Pflanzen*) sprout; (*KOCH: aufgehen*) rise; (*Tee, Kaffee*) be diuretic; **~haus** *nt* greenhouse; **~stoff** *m* fuel.

Trend [trɛnt] *m* **-s, -s** trend; **~wende** *f* trend away (from sth).

trenn- ['trɛn] *zW:* **~bar** *a* separable; **~en** *vt* separate; (*teilen*) divide // *vr* separate; **sich ~en von** part with; **T~schärfe** *f* (*RAD*) selectivity; **T~ung** *f* separation; **T~wand** *f* partition (wall).

Trepp- [trɛp] *zW:* **t~ab** *ad* downstairs; **t~auf** *ad* upstairs; **~e** *f* **-, -n** stair(case); **Treppengeländer** *nt* banister; **Treppenhaus** *nt* staircase.

Tresor [tre'zoːr] *m* **-s, -e** safe.

treten ['treːtən] *unreg vi* step; (*Tränen, Schweiß*) appear; **~ nach** kick at; **~ in** (+*akk*) step in(to); **in Verbindung ~** get in contact; **in Erscheinung ~** appear // *vt* (*mit Fußtritt*) kick; (*nieder~*) tread, trample.

treu [trɔy] *a* faithful, true; **T~e** *f* **-** loyalty, faithfulness; **T~händer** *m* **-s, -** trustee; **T~handgesellschaft** *f* trust company; **~herzig** *a* innocent; **~los** *a* faithless.

Tribüne [tri'byːnə] *f* **-, -n** grandstand; (*Redner~*) platform.

Trichter ['trɪçtər] *m* **-s, -** funnel; (*in Boden*) crater.

Trick [trɪk] *m* **-s, -e** *od* **-s** trick; **~film**

m cartoon.

trieb *etc v siehe* **trieben.**

Trieb [tri:p] *m* -(e)s, -e urge, drive; *(Neigung)* inclination; *(an Baum etc)* shoot; ~**feder** *f (fig)* motivating force; ~**kraft** *f (fig)* drive; ~**täter** *m* sex offender; ~**werk** *nt* engine.

triefen ['tri:fən] *vi* drip.

triffst *etc v siehe* **treffen.**

triftig ['trɪftɪç] *a* good, convincing.

Trikot [tri'ko:] *nt* -s, -s vest; *(SPORT)* shirt.

Trimester [tri'mɛstər] *nt* -s, - term.

trimmen ['trɪmən] *vr* do keep fit exercises.

trink- ['trɪŋk] *zW:* ~**bar** *a* drinkable; ~**en** *vti unreg* drink; **T~er** *m* -s, - drinker; **T~geld** *nt* tip; **T~spruch** *m* toast; **T~wasser** *nt* drinking water.

Tripper ['trɪpər] *m* -s, - gonorrhoea.

Tritt [trɪt] *m* -(e)s, -e step; *(Fuß~)* kick; ~**brett** *nt (EISENB)* step; *(AUT)* running-board.

Triumph [tri'umf] *m* -(e)s, -e triumph; ~**bogen** *m* triumphal arch; **t~ieren** [-'fi:rən] *vi* triumph; *(jubeln)* exult.

trocken ['trɔkən] *a* dry; **T~element** *nt* dry cell; **T~haube** *f* hair-dryer; **T~heit** *f* dryness; ~**legen** *vt (Sumpf)* drain; *(Kind)* put a clean nappy on; **T~milch** *f* dried milk.

trocknen ['trɔknən] *vti* dry.

Trödel ['trø:dəl] *m* -s *(umg)* junk; ~**markt** *m* flea market; **t~n** *vi (umg)* dawdle.

Trog [tro:k] *m* -(e)s, ̈e trough.

Trommel ['trɔməl] *f* -, -n drum; ~**fell** *nt* eardrum; **t~n** *vti* drum.

Trommler ['trɔmlər] *m* -s, - drummer.

Trompete [trɔm'pe:tə] *f* -, -n trumpet; ~**r** *m* -s, - trumpeter.

Tropen ['tro:pən] *pl* tropics *pl;* ~**helm** *m* sun helmet.

tröpfeln ['trœpfəln] *vi* drop, trickle.

Tropfen ['trɔpfən] *m* -s, - drop; **t~** *vti* drip // *v unpers:* es tropft a few raindrops are falling; **t~weise** *ad* in drops.

Tropfsteinhöhle *f* stalactite cave.

tropisch ['tro:pɪʃ] *a* tropical.

Trost [tro:st] *m* -es consolation, comfort; **t~bedürftig** *a* in need of consolation.

tröst- ['trø:st] *zW:* ~**en** *vt* console, comfort; **T~er(in** *f)* *m* -s, - comfort(er); ~**lich** *a* comforting.

trost- *zW:* ~**los** *a* bleak; *(Verhältnisse)* wretched; **T~preis** *m* consolation prize; ~**reich** *a* comforting.

Trott [trɔt] *m* -(e)s, -e trot; *(Routine)* routine; **Trottel** *m* -s, - *(umg)* fool, dope; **t~en** *vi* trot; **Trottoir** [trɔto'a:r] *nt* -s, -s *od* -e pavement, sidewalk *(US).*

Trotz [trɔts] *m* -es pigheadedness; etw aus ~ tun do sth just to show them; jdm zum ~ in defiance of sb; **t~** *präp +gen od dat* in spite of; **t~dem** *ad* nevertheless, all the same // *kj* although; **t~ig** *a* defiant, pig-headed; ~**kopf** *m* obstinate child; ~**reaktion** *f* fit of pique.

trüb [try:p] *a* dull; *(Flüssigkeit, Glas)* cloudy; *(fig)* gloomy.

Trubel ['tru:bəl] *m* -s, - hurly-burly.

trüb- *zW:* ~**en** ['try:bən] *vt* cloud // *vr* become clouded; **T~heit** *f* dullness; cloudiness; gloom; **T~sal** *f* -, -e distress; ~**selig** *a* sad, melancholy; **T~sinn** *m* depression; ~**sinnig** *a* depressed, gloomy.

Trüffel ['tryfəl] *f* -, -n truffle.

trug *etc v siehe* **tragen.**

trüg- [try:g] *zW:* ~**en** *unreg vt* deceive // *vi* be deceptive; ~**erisch** *a* deceptive.

Trugschluß ['tru:gʃlʊs] *m* false conclusion.

Truhe ['tru:ə] *f* -, -n chest.

Trümmer ['trymər] *pl* wreckage; *(Bau~)* ruins *pl;* ~**haufen** *m* heap of rubble.

Trumpf [trʊmpf] *m* -(e)s, ̈e trump *(lit, fig)* trump; **t~en** *vti* trump.

Trunk [trʊŋk] *m* -(e)s, ̈e drink; **t~en** *a* intoxicated; ~**enheit** *f* intoxication; ~**enheit am Steuer** drunken driving; ~**sucht** *f* alcoholism.

Trupp [trʊp] *m* -s, -s troop; ~**e** *f* -, -n troop; *(Waffengattung)* force; *(Schauspiel~)* troupe; ~**en** *pl* troops *pl;* ~**enübungsplatz** *m* training area.

Truthahn ['tru:tha:n] *m* turkey.

Tschech- [tʃɛç] *zW:* ~**e** *m,* ~**in** *f,* ~**oslowake** [-oslo'va:kə] *m,* ~**oslowakin** *f* Czech, Czechoslovak(ian); **t~isch, t~oslowakisch** [-oslo'va:kɪʃ] *a* Czech, Czechoslovak(ian).

tschüs [tʃy:s] *interj* cheerio.

T-Shirt ['ti:ʃœrt] *nt* T-shirt.

Tube ['tu:bə] *f* -, -n tube.

Tuberkulose [tuberku'lo:zə] *f* -, -n tuberculosis.

Tuch [tu:x] *nt* -(e)s, ̈er cloth; *(Hals~)* scarf; *(Kopf~)* headscarf; *(Hand~)* towel.

tüchtig ['tyçtɪç] *a* efficient, (cap)able; *(umg: kräftig)* good, sound; **T~keit** *f* efficiency, ability.

Tücke ['tykə] *f* -, -n *(Arglist)* malice; *(Trick)* trick; *(Schwierigkeit)* difficulty, problem; **seine ~n haben** *a* temperamental.

tückisch ['tykɪʃ] *a* treacherous; *(böswillig)* malicious.

Tugend ['tu:gənt] *f* -, -en virtue; **t~haft** *a* virtuous.

Tüll [tyl] *m* -s, -e tulle; ~**e** *f* -, -n

spout.

Tulpe ['tʊlpə] f -, -n tulip.

Tumor ['tuːmɔr] m -s, -e tumour.

Tümpel ['tʏmpəl] m -s, - pool, pond.

Tumult [tu'mʊlt] m -(e)s, -e tumult.

tun [tuːn] *unreg vt* (*machen*) do; (*legen*) put; **jdm etw ~** (*antun*) do sth to sb; **etw tut es auch** sth will do; **das tut nichts** that doesn't matter; **das tut nichts zur Sache** that's neither here nor there // *vi* act; **so ~, als ob** act as if // *vr*: **es tut sich etwas/viel** something/a lot is happening.

tünchen ['tʏnçən] *vt* whitewash.

Tunesien [tu'neːziən] *nt* Tunisia.

Tunke ['tʊŋkə] f -, -n sauce; **t~n** *vt* dip, dunk.

tunlichst ['tuːnlɪçst] *ad* if at all possible; **~ bald** as soon as possible.

Tunnel ['tʊnəl] m -s, -s *od* - tunnel.

tupfen ['tʊpfən] *vti* dab; (*mit Farbe*) dot; **T~** m -s, - dot, spot.

Tür [tyːr] f -, -en door.

Turban ['tʊrbaːn] m -s, -e turban.

Turbine [tʊr'biːnə] f turbine.

Türk- [tʏrk] *zW*: **~e** m Turk; **~ei** [tʏr'kaɪ] f: **die ~ei** Turkey.

Türkis [tʏr'kiːs] m -es, -e turquoise; **t~** a turquoise.

türkisch ['tʏrkɪʃ] a Turkish.

Turm [tʊrm] m -(e)s, ̈e tower; (*Kirch~*) steeple; (*Sprung~*) diving platform; (*SCHACH*) castle, rook.

türmen ['tʏrmən] *vr* tower up // *vt* heap up // *vi* (*umg*) scarper, bolt.

Turn- ['tʊrn] *zW*: **t~en** *vi* do gymnastic exercises // *vt* perform; **~en** *nt* -s gymnastics; (*SCH*) physical education, P.E.; **~er(in f)** m -s, - gymnast; **~halle** f gym(nasium); **~hose** f gym shorts *pl*.

Turnier [tʊr'niːr] *nt* -s, -e tournament.

Turn- *zW*: **~verein** m gymnastics club; **~schuh** m gym shoe; **~zeug** *nt* gym things *pl*.

Tusche ['tʊʃə] f -, -n Indian ink.

tuscheln ['tʊʃəln] *vti* whisper.

Tuschkasten m paintbox.

Tüte ['tyːtə] f -, -n bag.

tuten ['tuːtən] *vi* (*AUT*) hoot (*Brit*), honk (*US*).

TÜV [tʏf] m *abk* (= *Technischer Überwachungsverein*) MOT.

Typ [tyːp] m -s, -en type; **~e** f -, -n (*TYP*) type; **Typenraddrucker** m daisy-wheel printer.

Typhus ['tyːfʊs] m - typhoid (fever).

typisch ['tyːpɪʃ] a typical (*für* of).

Tyrann [ty'ran] m -en, -en tyrant; **~ei** [-'naɪ] f tyranny; **t~isch** a tyrannical; **t~i'sieren** *vt* tyrannize.

U

U, u [uː] *nt* U, u.

u. *abk von* **und.**

u.a. *abk von* **unter anderem.**

U-Bahn ['uːbaːn] f underground, tube.

übel ['yːbəl] a bad; (*moralisch auch*) wicked; **jdm ist ~** sb feels sick; **Ü~ nt -s,** - evil; (*Krankheit*) disease; **~gelaunt** a bad-tempered; **Ü~keit** f nausea; **~nehmen** *vt unreg*: **jdm eine Bemerkung** *etc* **~nehmen** be offended at sb's remark *etc*.

üben ['yːbən] *vti* exercise, practise.

über ['yːbər] ◆ *präp +dat* **1** (*räumlich*) over, above; **zwei Grad ~ Null** two degrees above zero. **2** (*zeitlich*) over; **~ der Arbeit einschlafen** fall asleep over one's work ◆ *präp +akk* **1** (*räumlich*) over; (*hoch ~ auch*) above; (*quer ~ auch*) across. **2** (*zeitlich*) over; **~ Weihnachten** over Christmas; **~ kurz oder lang** sooner or later **3** (*mit Zahlen*): **Kinder ~ 12 Jahren** children over *od* above 12 years of age; **ein Scheck ~ 200 Mark** a cheque for 200 marks **4** (*auf dem Wege*) via; **nach Köln ~ Aachen** to Cologne via Aachen; **ich habe es ~ die Auskunft erfahren** I found out from information **5** (*betreffend*) about; **ein Buch ~ ...** a book about *od* on ...; **~ jdn/etw lachen** laugh about *od* at sb/sth **6**: **Macht ~ jdn haben** have power over sb; **sie liebt ihn ~ alles** she loves him more than everything ◆ *ad* over; **~ und ~** over and over; **den ganzen Tag ~** all day long; **jdm in etw** (*dat*) **~ sein** be superior to sb in sth.

überall [yːbər'al] *ad* everywhere; **~'hin** *ad* everywhere.

überanstrengen [yːbər'anʃtrɛŋən] *vtr insep* overexert (o.s.).

überarbeiten [yːbər'arbaɪtən] *vt insep* revise, rework // *vr* overwork (o.s.).

überaus ['yːbəraʊs] *ad* exceedingly.

überbelichten ['yːbərbəlɪçtən] *vt* (*PHOT*) overexpose.

über'bieten *vt unreg insep* outbid; (*übertreffen*) surpass; (*Rekord*) break.

Überbleibsel ['yːbərblaɪpsəl] *nt* -s, - residue, remainder.

Überblick ['yːbərblɪk] m view; (*fig: Darstellung*) survey, overview; (*Fähigkeit*) overall view, grasp (*über +akk* of); **ü~en** [-'blɪkən] *vt insep* survey.

überbring- [yːbər'brɪŋ] *zW*: **~en**

vt unreg insep deliver, hand over; **Ü~er** *m* **-s, -** bearer; **Ü~ung** *f* delivery.

überbrücken [y:bər'brʏkən] *vt insep* bridge (over).

über'dauern *vt insep* outlast.

über'denken *vt unreg insep* think over.

überdies [y:bər'di:s] *ad* besides.

überdimensional ['y:bərdimɛnziona:l] *a* oversize.

Überdruß ['y:bərdrʊs] *m* **-sses** weariness; **bis zum** ~ ad nauseam.

überdrüssig ['y:bərdrʏsɪç] *a* tired, sick (*gen* of).

übereifrig ['y:bəraifrɪç] *a* overkeen.

übereilt [y:bər''aılt] *a* (over)hasty, premature.

überein- [y:bər''aın] *zW:* **~ander** [y:bər'aı''nandər] *ad* one upon the other; (*sprechen*) about each other; **~kommen** *vi unreg* agree; **Ü~kunft** *f* **-, -künfte** agreement; **~stimmen** *vi* agree; **Ü~stimmung** *f* agreement.

überempfindlich ['y:bərɛmpfɪntlɪç] *a* hypersensitive.

überfahren [y:bər'fa:rən] *vt unreg insep* (*AUT*) run over; (*fig*) walk all over.

Überfahrt ['y:bərfa:rt] *f* crossing.

Überfall ['y:bərfal] *m* (*Bank~*, *MIL*) raid; (*auf jdn*) assault; **ü~en** *vt unreg insep* [-'falən] attack; (*Bank*) raid; (*besuchen*) surprise.

überfällig ['y:bərfɛlɪç] *a* overdue.

über'fliegen *vt unreg insep* fly over, overfly; (*Buch*) skim through.

Überfluß ['y:bərflʊs] *m* (super)-abundance, excess (*an +dat* of).

überflüssig ['y:bərflʏsɪç] *a* superfluous.

über'fordern *vt insep* demand too much of; (*Kräfte etc*) overtax.

über'führen *vt insep* (*Leiche etc*) transport; (*Täter*) have convicted (*gen* of).

Über'führung *f* transport; conviction; (*Brücke*) bridge, overpass.

Übergabe ['y:bərga:bə] *f* handing over; (*MIL*) surrender.

Übergang ['y:bərgaŋ] *m* crossing; (*Wandel, Überleitung*) transition.

Übergangs- *zW:* **~erscheinung** *f* transitory phenomenon; **~lösung** *f* provisional solution, stopgap; **~stadium** *nt* transitional stage; **~zeit** *f* transitional period.

über'geben *unreg insep vt* hand over; (*MIL*) surrender; **dem Verkehr ~** open to traffic // *vr* be sick.

übergehen [y:bər'ge:ən] *unreg vi* (*Besitz*) pass; (*zum Feind etc*) go over, defect; (*überleiten*) go on (*zu* to); (*sich verwandeln*) turn (*in +akk* into) // [-'ge:ən] *vt insep* pass over, omit.

Übergewicht ['y:bərgəvɪçt] *nt* excess weight; (*fig*) preponderance.

überglücklich ['y:bərglʏklɪç] *a* overjoyed.

übergroß ['y:bərgro:s] *a* outsize, huge.

überhandnehmen [y:bər'hantne:mən] *vi unreg* gain the ascendancy.

überhaupt [y:bər'haupt] *ad* at all; (*im allgemeinen*) in general; (*besonders*) especially; ~ **nicht/keine** not/none at all.

überheblich [y:bər'he:plɪç] *a* arrogant; **Ü~keit** *f* arrogance.

über'holen *vt insep* overtake; (*TECH*) overhaul.

überholt *a* out-of-date, obsolete.

über'hören *vt insep* not hear; (*absichtlich*) ignore.

überirdisch ['y:bər'ɪrdɪʃ] *a* supernatural, unearthly.

über'laden *vt unreg insep* overload // *a* (*fig*) cluttered.

über'lassen *unreg insep vt:* **jdm etw** ~ leave sth to sb // *vr:* **sich etw** (*dat*) ~ give o.s. over to sth.

über'lasten *vt insep* overload; (*Mensch*) overtax.

überlaufen ['y:bərlaufən] *unreg vi* (*Flüssigkeit*) flow over; (*zum Feind etc*) go over, defect // [-'laufən] *vt insep* (*Schauer etc*) come over; ~ **sein** be inundated *od* besieged.

Überläufer ['y:bərlɔʏfər] *m* deserter.

über'leben *vt insep* survive; **Ü~de(r)** *mf* survivor.

über'legen *vt insep* consider; **ich muß es mir** ~ I'll have to think about it // *a* superior; **Ü~heit** *f* superiority.

Überlegung *f* consideration, deliberation.

über'liefern *vt insep* hand down, transmit.

Überlieferung *f* tradition.

überlisten [y:bər'lɪstən] *vt insep* outwit.

überm ['y:bərm] = **über dem**.

Übermacht ['y:bərmaxt] *f* superior force, superiority.

übermächtig ['y:bərmɛçtɪç] *a* superior (in strength); (*Gefühl etc*) overwhelming.

übermannen [y:bər'manən] *vt insep* overcome.

Übermaß ['y:bərma:s] *nt* excess (*an +dat* of).

übermäßig ['y:bərmɛ:sɪç] *a* excessive.

Übermensch ['y:bərmɛnʃ] *m* superman; **ü~lich** *a* superhuman.

übermitteln [y:bər'mɪtəln] *vt insep* convey.

übermorgen ['y:bərmɔrgən] *ad* the day after tomorrow.

Übermüdung [y:bər'my:dʊŋ] *f* fatigue, overtiredness.

Übermut ['y:bərmu:t] *m* exuberance.

übermütig ['y:bərmy:tɪç] *a* exuberant, high-spirited; ~ **werden** get overconfident.

übernachten [y:bər'naxtən] *vi insep* spend the night (*bei jdm* at sb's place).

Übernachtung [y:bər'naxtʊŋ] *f* overnight stay.

Übernahme ['y:bərna:mə] *f* -, **-n** taking over *od* on, acceptance.

über'nehmen *unreg insep vt* take on, accept; (*Amt, Geschäft*) take over // *vr* take on too much.

über'prüfen *vt insep* examine, check.

Überprüfung *f* examination.

überqueren [y:bər'kve:rən] *vt insep* cross.

überragen [y:bər'ra:gən] *vt insep* tower above; (*fig*) surpass.

überraschen [y:bər'raʃən] *vt insep* surprise.

Überraschung *f* surprise.

überreden [y:bər're:dən] *vt insep* persuade.

überreichen [y:bər'raɪçən] *vt insep* present, hand over.

Überreste ['y:bərrɛstə] *pl* remains *pl*, remnants *pl*.

überrumpeln [y:bər'rʊmpəln] *vt insep* take by surprise.

überrunden [y:bər'rʊndən] *vt insep* lap.

übers ['y:bərs] = **über das**.

Überschall- ['y:bərʃal] *zW*: ~**flugzeug** *nt* supersonic jet; ~**geschwindigkeit** *f* supersonic speed.

über'schätzen *vtr insep* overestimate.

Überschlag ['y:bərʃla:k] *m* (*FIN*) estimate; (*SPORT*) somersault; **ü~en** [-'ʃla:gən] *unreg insep vt* (*berechnen*) estimate; (*auslassen: Seite*) omit // *vr* somersault; (*Stimme*) crack; (*AVIAT*) loop the loop // ['y:bərʃla:gən] *unreg vt* (*Beine*) cross // *vi* (*Wellen*) break over; (*Funken*) flash over.

überschnappen ['y:bərʃnapən] *vi* (*Stimme*) crack; (*umg: Mensch*) flip one's lid.

über'schneiden *vr unreg insep* (*lit, fig*) overlap; (*Linien*) intersect.

über'schreiben *vt unreg insep* provide with a heading; **jdm etw** ~ transfer *od* make over sth to sb.

über'schreiten *vt unreg insep* cross over; (*fig*) exceed; (*verletzen*) transgress.

Überschrift ['y:bərʃrɪft] *f* heading, title.

Überschuß ['y:bərʃʊs] *m* surplus (*an* +*dat* of).

überschüssig ['y:bərʃʏsɪç] *a* surplus, excess.

über'schütten *vt insep*: **jdn/etw mit** etw ~ (*lit*) pour sth over sb/sth; **jdn mit etw** ~ (*fig*) shower sb with sth.

überschwemmen [y:bər'ʃvɛmən] *vt insep* flood.

Überschwemmung *f* flood.

überschwenglich ['y:bərʃvɛŋlɪç] *a* effusive.

Übersee ['y:bərze:] *f*: **nach/in** ~ overseas; **ü~isch** *a* overseas.

über'sehen *vt unreg insep* look (out) over; (*fig: Folgen*) see, get an overall view of; (: *nicht beachten*) overlook.

über'senden *vt unreg insep* send, forward.

übersetz- *zW*: ~**en** [y:bər'zɛtsən] *vt insep* translate // ['y:bərzɛtsən] *vi* cross; **Ü~er(in** *f*) [-'zɛtsər(ɪn)] *m* -**s**, - translator; **Ü~ung** [-zɛtsʊŋ] *f* translation; (*TECH*) gear ratio.

Übersicht ['y:bərzɪçt] *f* overall view; (*Darstellung*) survey; **ü~lich** *a* clear; (*Gelände*) open; ~**lichkeit** *f* clarity, lucidity.

übersiedeln ['y:bərzi:dəln] *od* [y:bər'zi:dəln] *vi sep od insep* move.

über'spannen *vt insep* (*zu sehr spannen*) overstretch; (*überdecken*) cover.

über'spannt *a* eccentric; (*Idee*) wild, crazy; **Ü~heit** *f* eccentricity.

überspitzt [y:bər'ʃpɪtst] *a* exaggerated.

über'springen *vt unreg insep* jump over; (*fig*) skip.

überstehen [y:bər'ʃte:ən] *unreg vt insep* overcome, get over; (*Winter etc*) survive, get through // ['y:bərʃte:ən] *vi* project.

über'steigen *vt unreg insep* climb over; (*fig*) exceed.

über'stimmen *vt insep* outvote.

Überstunden ['y:bərʃtʊndən] *pl* overtime.

über'stürzen *insep vt* rush // *vr* follow (one another) in rapid succession.

überstürzt *a* (*over*)hasty.

über'tönen *vt insep* drown (out).

Übertrag ['y:bərtra:k] *m* -(**e**)**s**, **-träge** (*COMM*) amount brought forward; **ü~bar** [-'tra:kba:r] *a* transferable; (*MED*) infectious; **ü~en** [-'tra:gən] *unreg insep vt* transfer (*auf* +*akk* to); (*RAD*) broadcast; (*übersetzen*) render; (*Krankheit*) transmit; **jdm etw ü~en** assign sth to sb // *vr* spread (*auf* +*akk* to) // *a* figurative; ~**ung** [-'tra:gʊŋ] *f* transfer(ence); (*RAD*) broadcast; rendering; transmission.

über'treffen *vt unreg insep* surpass.

über'treiben *vt unreg insep* exaggerate.

Übertreibung *f* exaggeration.

übertreten [y:bər'tre:tən] *unreg vt*

insep cross; *(Gebot etc)* break // ['y:bərtre:tən] *vi (über Linie, Gebiet)* step (over); *(SPORT)* overstep; *(in andere Partei)* go over *(in +akk* to); *(zu anderem Glauben)* be converted.

Über'tretung *f* violation, transgression.

übertrieben [y:bər'tri:bən] *a* exaggerated, excessive.

übervölkert [y:bər'fœlkərt] *a* overpopulated.

übervoll ['y:bərfɔl] *a* overfull.

übervorteilen [y:bər'fɔrtailən] *vt insep* dupe, cheat.

über'wachen *vt insep* supervise; *(Verdächtigen)* keep under surveillance.

Überwachung *f* supervision; surveillance.

überwältigen [y:bər'vɛltigən] *vt insep* overpower; **~d** *a* overwhelming.

überweisen [y:bər'vaizən] *vt unreg insep* transfer.

Überweisung *f* transfer.

über'wiegen *vi unreg insep* predominate; **~d** *a* predominant.

über'winden *unreg insep vt* overcome // *vr* make an effort, bring oneself (to do sth).

Überwindung *f* effort, strength of mind.

Überzahl ['y:bərtsa:l] *f* superiority, superior numbers *pl*; **in der ~ sein** outnumber sb, be numerically superior.

überzählig ['y:bərtsɛ:liç] *a* surplus.

über'zeugen *vt insep* convince *(von etw* of sth) ; **~d** *a* convincing.

Überzeugung *f* conviction; **Überzeugungskraft** *f* power of persuasion.

überziehen ['y:bərtsi:ən] *unreg vt* put on // [-'tsi:ən] *vt insep* cover; *(Konto)* overdraw.

Überzug ['y:bərtsu:k] *m* cover; *(Belag)* coating.

üblich ['y:pliç] *a* usual.

U-Boot ['u:bo:t] *nt* submarine.

übrig ['y:briç] *a* remaining; **für jdn etwas ~ haben** *(umg)* be fond of sb; **die ~en** ['y:brigən] the others; **das ~e** the rest; **im ~en** besides; **~bleiben** *vi unreg* remain, be left (over); **übrigens** *ad* besides; *(nebenbei bemerkt)* by the way; **~lassen** *vt unreg* leave (over).

Übung ['y:buŋ] *f* practice; *(Turn~, Aufgabe etc)* exercise; **~ macht den Meister** practice makes perfect.

UdSSR [u:de:'ɛs'ɛs''ɛr] *f abk* (= *Union der Sozialistischen Sowjetrepubliken)* USSR.

Ufer ['u:fər] *nt* **-s, -** bank; *(Meeres~)* shore.

Uhr [u:r] *f* **-, -en** clock; *(Armband~)* watch; **wieviel ~ ist es?** what time is

it?; **1 ~** 1 o'clock; **20 ~** 8 o'clock, 20.00 (twenty hundred) hours; **~band** *nt* watch strap; **~kette** *f* watch chain; **~macher** *m* **-s, -** watchmaker; **~werk** *nt* clockwork; works of a watch; **~zeiger** *m* hand; **~zeigersinn** *m*: **im ~zeigersinn** clockwise; **entgegen dem ~zeigersinn** anticlockwise; **~zeit** *f* time (of day).

Uhu ['u:hu] *m* **-s, -s** eagle owl.

UKW [u:ka:'ve:] *abk* (= *Ultrakurzwelle)* VHF.

Ulk [ʊlk] *m* **-s, -e** lark; **u~ig** *a* funny.

Ulme ['ʊlmə] *f* **-, -n** elm.

Ultimatum [ʊlti'ma:tʊm] *nt* **-s, Ultimaten** ultimatum.

ultraviolett ['ʊltravio'lɛt] *a* ultraviolet.

um [ʊm] ◆ *präp +akk* **1** (*~ herum*) (a)round; **~ Weihnachten** around Christmas; **er schlug ~ sich** he hit about him

2 *(mit Zeitangabe)* at; **~ acht (Uhr)** at eight (o'clock)

3 *(mit Größenangabe)* by; **etw ~ 4 cm kürzen** shorten sth by 4 cm; **~ 10% teurer** 10% more expensive; **~ vieles besser** better by far; **~ nichts besser** not in the least bit better; **~ so besser** so much the better

4: **der Kampf ~ den Titel** the battle for the title; **~ Geld spielen** play for money; **Stunde ~ Stunde** hour after hour; **Auge ~ Auge** an eye for an eye ◆ *präp +gen*: **~ ... willen** for the sake of ...; **~ Gottes willen** for goodness *od (stärker)* God's sake

◆ *kj*: **~ ... zu** (in order) to; **zu klug, ~ zu ...** too clever to ...; **~ so besser/schlimmer** so much the better/worse

◆ *ad* **1** *(ungefähr)* about; **~ (die) Leute** about *od* around 30 people

2 *(vorbei)*: **die 2 Stunden sind ~** the two hours are up.

umänder- [ʊm'ɛndər] *zW*: **~n** *vt* alter; **U~ung** *f* alteration.

umarbeiten ['ʊm'arbaitən] *vt* remodel; *(Buch etc)* revise, rework.

umarmen [ʊm''armən] *vt insep* embrace.

Umbau ['ʊmbau] *m* **-(e)s, -e** *od* **-ten** reconstruction, alteration(s); **u~en** *vt* rebuild, reconstruct.

umbenennen ['ʊmbənɛnən] *vt unreg* rename.

umbilden ['ʊmbɪldən] *vt* reorganize; *(POL: Kabinett)* reshuffle.

umbinden ['ʊmbɪndən] *vt unreg* *(Krawatte etc)* put on.

umblättern ['ʊmblɛtərn] *vt* turn over.

umblicken ['ʊmblɪkən] *vr* look around.

umbringen ['ʊmbrɪŋən] *vt unreg* kill.

Umbruch ['ʊmbrux] *m* radical change; *(TYP)* make-up.

umbuchen ['ʊmbu:xən] *vti* change

one's reservation/flight *etc*.

umdenken ['ʊmdɛŋkən] *vi unreg* adjust one's views.

umdrehen ['ʊmdreːən] *vtr* turn (round); (*Hals*) wring.

Um'drehung *f* revolution; rotation.

umeinander [ʊmʔaɪ'nandər] *ad* round one another; (*füreinander*) for one another.

umfahren ['ʊmfaːrən] *vt unreg* run over // [-'faːrən] *insep* drive/sail round.

umfallen ['ʊmfalən] *vi unreg* fall down *od* over.

Umfang ['ʊmfaŋ] *m* extent; (*von Buch*) size; (*Reichweite*) range; (*Fläche*) area; (*MATH*) circumference; **u~reich** *a* extensive; (*Buch etc*) voluminous.

um'fassen *vt insep* embrace; (*umgeben*) surround; (*enthalten*) include; **~d** *a* comprehensive, extensive.

umform- ['ʊmfɔrm] *zW*: **~en** *vi* transform; **U~er** *m* **-s,** **-** (*ELEK*) transformer, converter.

Umfrage ['ʊmfraːgə] *f* poll.

umfüllen ['ʊmfʏlən] *vt* transfer; (*Wein*) decant.

umfunktionieren ['ʊmfʊŋktsioniːrən] *vt* convert, transform.

Umgang ['ʊmgaŋ] *m* company; (*mit jdm*) dealings *pl*; (*Behandlung*) way of behaving.

umgänglich ['ʊmgɛŋlɪç] *a* sociable.

Umgangs- *zW*: **~formen** *pl* manners *pl*; **~sprache** *f* colloquial language.

umgeb- [ʊm'geːb] *zW*: **~en** *vt unreg insep* surround; **U~ung** *f* surroundings *pl*; (*Milieu*) environment; (*Personen*) people in one's circle.

umgehen ['ʊmgeːən] *unreg vi* go (a)round; **im Schlosse ~** haunt the castle; **mit jdm grob** *etc* **~** treat sb roughly *etc*; **mit Geld sparsam ~** be careful with one's money // [-'geːən] *vt insep* bypass; (*MIL*) outflank; (*Gesetz etc*) circumvent; (*vermeiden*) avoid; **'~d** *a* immediate.

Um'gehung *f* bypassing; outflanking; circumvention; avoidance; **Umgehungsstraße** *f* bypass.

umgekehrt ['ʊmgəkeːrt] *a* reverse(d); (*gegenteilig*) opposite // *ad* the other way around; **und ~** and vice versa.

umgraben ['ʊmgraːbən] *vt unreg* dig up.

Umhang ['ʊmhaŋ] *m* wrap, cape.

umhauen ['ʊmhaʊən] *vt* fell; (*fig*) bowl over.

umher [ʊm'heːr] *ad* about, around; **~gehen** *vi unreg* walk about; **~ziehen** *vi unreg* wander from place to place.

umhinkönnen [ʊm'hɪnkœnən] *vi unreg*: **ich kann nicht umhin, das zu tun**

I can't help doing it.

umhören ['ʊmhøːrən] *vr* ask around.

Umkehr ['ʊmkeːr] *f* **-** turning back; (*Änderung*) change; **u~en** *vi* turn back // *vt* turn round, reverse; (*Tasche etc*) turn inside out; (*Gefäß etc*) turn upside down.

umkippen ['ʊmkɪpən] *vt* tip over // *vi* overturn; (*fig*: *Meinung ändern*) change one's mind; (*umg*: *Mensch*) keel over.

Umkleideraum ['ʊmklaɪdəraʊm] *m* changing- *od* dressing room.

umkommen ['ʊmkɔmən] *vi unreg* die, perish; (*Lebensmittel*) go bad.

Umkreis ['ʊmkraɪs] *m* neighbourhood; **im ~ von** within a radius of.

Umlage ['ʊmlaːgə] *f* share of the costs.

Umlauf ['ʊmlaʊf] *m* (*Geld~*) circulation; (*von Gestirn*) revolution; **~bahn** *f* orbit.

Umlaut ['ʊmlaʊt] *m* umlaut.

umlegen ['ʊmleːgən] *vt* put on; (*verlegen*) move, shift; (*Kosten*) share out; (*umkippen*) tip over; (*umg*: *töten*) bump off.

umleiten ['ʊmlaɪtən] *vt* divert.

Umleitung *f* diversion.

umliegend ['ʊmliːgənt] *a* surrounding.

um'rahmen *vt insep* frame.

um'randen *vt insep* border, edge.

umrechnen ['ʊmrɛçnən] *vt* convert.

Umrechnung *f* conversion; **Umrechnungskurs** *m* rate of exchange.

um'reißen *vt unreg insep* outline, sketch.

um'ringen *vt insep* surround.

Umriß ['ʊmrɪs] *m* outline.

umrühren ['ʊmryːrən] *vti* stir.

ums [ʊms] = **um das**.

Umsatz ['ʊmzats] *m* turnover.

umschalten ['ʊmʃaltən] *vt* switch.

Umschau ['ʊmʃaʊ] *f* look(ing) round; **~ halten nach** look around for; **u~en** *vr* look round.

Umschlag ['ʊmʃlaːk] *m* cover; (*Buch~ auch*) jacket; (*MED*) compress; (*Brief~*) envelope; (*Wechsel*) change; (*von Hose*) turn-up; **u~en** ['ʊmʃlaːgən] *unreg vi* change; (*NAUT*) capsize // *vt* knock over; (*Ärmel*) turn up; (*Seite*) turn over; (*Waren*) transfer; **~platz** *m* (*COMM*) distribution centre.

umschreiben *vt unreg* ['ʊmʃraɪbən] (*neu~*) rewrite; (*übertragen*) transfer (*auf* +*akk* to) // [-'ʃraɪbən] *insep* paraphrase; (*abgrenzen*) define.

umschulen ['ʊmʃuːlən] *vt* retrain; (*Kind*) send to another school.

Umschweife ['ʊmʃvaɪfə] *pl*: **ohne ~** without beating about the bush, straight out.

Umschwung ['ʊmʃvʊŋ] *m* change

(around), revolution.

umsehen ['ʊmzeːən] *vr unreg* look around *od* about; (*suchen*) look out (*nach* for).

umseitig ['ʊmzaɪtɪç] *ad* overleaf.

Umsicht ['ʊmzɪçt] *f* prudence, caution; **u~ig** *a* cautious, prudent.

umsonst [ʊm'zɔnst] *ad* in vain; (*gratis*) for nothing.

umspringen ['ʊmʃprɪŋən] *vi unreg* change; (*Wind auch*) veer; **mit jdm ~ treat sb badly.

Umstand ['ʊmʃtant] *m* circumstance; **Umstände** *pl* (*fig: Schwierigkeiten*) fuss; **in anderen Umständen sein** be pregnant; **Umstände machen** go to a lot of trouble; **unter Umständen** possibly.

umständlich ['ʊmʃtɛntlɪç] *a, ad* (*Methode*) cumbersome, complicated; (*Ausdrucksweise, Erklärung auch*) long-winded; (*Mensch*) ponderous.

Umstandskleid *nt* maternity dress.

Umstehende(n) ['ʊmʃteːəndə(n)] *pl* bystanders *pl*.

umsteigen ['ʊmʃtaɪgən] *vi unreg* (*EISENB*) change.

umstellen ['ʊmʃtɛlən] *vt* (*an anderen Ort*) change round, rearrange; (*TECH*) convert // *vr* adapt o.s. (*auf +akk* to) // [ʊm'ʃtɛlən] *vt insep* surround.

Umstellung ['ʊmʃtɛlʊŋ] *f* change; (*Umgewöhnung*) adjustment; (*TECH*) conversion.

umstimmen ['ʊmʃtɪmən] *vt* (*MUS*) retune; **jdn ~** make sb change his mind.

umstoßen ['ʊmʃtoːsən] *vt unreg* (*lit*) overturn; (*Plan etc*) change, upset.

umstritten [ʊm'ʃtrɪtən] *a* disputed.

Umsturz ['ʊmʃtʊrts] *m* overthrow.

umstürzen ['ʊmʃtʏrtsən] *vt* (*umwerfen*) overturn // *vi* collapse, fall down; (*Wagen*) overturn.

Umtausch ['ʊmtaʊʃ] *m* exchange; **u~en** *vt* exchange.

umwandeln ['ʊmvandəln] *vt* change, convert; (*ELEK*) transform.

umwechseln ['ʊmvɛksəln] *vt* change.

Umweg ['ʊmveːk] *m* detour, roundabout way.

Umwelt ['ʊmvɛlt] *f* environment; **u~freundlich** *a* not harmful to the environment; **u~feindlich** *a* ecologically harmful; **~schutz** *m* conservation; **~schützer** *m* environmentalist; **~verschmutzung** *f* environmental pollution.

umwenden ['ʊmvɛndən] *vtr unreg* turn (round).

um'werben *vt unreg insep* court, woo.

umwerfen ['ʊmvɛrfən] *vt unreg* (*lit*)

upset, overturn; (*Mantel*) throw on; (*fig: erschüttern*) upset, throw.

umziehen ['ʊmtsiːən] *unreg vtr* change // *vi* move.

umzingeln [ʊm'tsɪŋəln] *vt insep* surround, encircle.

Umzug ['ʊmtsuːk] *m* procession; (*Wohnungs~*) move, removal.

unab- ['ʊn'ap] *zW:* **~änderlich** *a* irreversible, unalterable; **~hängig** *a* independent; **U~hängigkeit** *f* independence; **~kömmlich** *a* indispensable; **zur Zeit ~kömmlich** not free at the moment; **~lässig** *a* incessant, constant; **~sehbar** *a* immeasurable; (*Folgen*) unforeseeable; (*Kosten*) incalculable; **~sichtlich** *a* unintentional; **~'wendbar** *a* inevitable.

unachtsam ['ʊn'axtzaːm] *a* careless; **U~keit** *f* carelessness.

unan- [ʊn'an] *zW:* **~fechtbar** *a* indisputable; **~gebracht** *a* uncalled-for; **~gemessen** *a* inadequate; **~genehm** *a* unpleasant; **~gepaßt** *a* nonconformist; **U~nehmlichkeit** *f* inconvenience // *pl* trouble; **~sehnlich** *a* unsightly; **~ständig** *a* indecent, improper.

unappetitlich ['ʊn'apetiːtlɪç] *a* unsavoury.

Unart ['ʊn'aːrt] *f* bad manners *pl*; (*Angewohnheit*) bad habit; **u~ig** *a* naughty, badly behaved.

unauf- ['ʊn'aʊf] *zW:* **~fällig** *a* unobtrusive; (*Kleidung*) inconspicuous; **~'findbar** *a* not to be found; **~gefordert** *a* unasked // *ad* spontaneously; **~haltsam** *a* irresistible; **~'hörlich** *a* incessant, continuous; **~merksam** *a* inattentive; **~richtig** *a* insincere.

unaus- ['ʊn'aʊs] *zW:* **~'bleiblich** *a* inevitable, unavoidable; **~geglichen** *a* unbalanced; **~'sprechlich** *a* inexpressible; **~'stehlich** *a* intolerable.

unbarmherzig ['ʊnbarmhɛrtsɪç] *a* pitiless, merciless.

unbeabsichtigt ['ʊnbə'apzɪçtɪçt] *a* unintentional.

unbeachtet ['ʊnbə'axtət] *a* unnoticed, ignored.

unbedenklich ['ʊnbə'dɛŋklɪç] *a* (*Plan*) unobjectionable // *ad* without hesitation.

unbedeutend ['ʊnbə'dɔytənt] *a* insignificant, unimportant; (*Fehler*) slight.

unbedingt ['ʊnbə'dɪŋt] *a* unconditional // *ad* absolutely; **mußt du ~ gehen?** do you really have to go?

unbefangen ['ʊnbə'faŋən] *a* impartial, unprejudiced; (*ohne Hemmungen*) uninhibited; **U~heit** *f* impartiality; uninhibitedness.

unbefriedig- ['ʊnbəfriːdɪg] *zW:* **~end**

a unsatisfactory; **~t** [-dıçt] *a* unsatisfied, dissatisfied.

unbefugt [ˈʊnbəfuːkt] *a* unauthorized.

unbegreiflich [ʊnbəˈgraıflıç] *a* inconceivable.

unbegrenzt [ˈʊnbəgrɛntst] *a* unlimited.

unbegründet [ˈʊnbəgryndət] *a* unfounded.

Unbehag- [ˈʊnbəhaːg] *zW:* **~en** *nt* discomfort; **u~lich** [-lıç] *a* uncomfortable; *(Gefühl)* uneasy.

unbeholfen [ˈʊnbəhɔlfən] *a* awkward, clumsy; **U~heit** *f* awkwardness, clumsiness.

unbeirrt [ˈʊnbəˈırt] *a* imperturbable.

unbekannt [ˈʊnbəkant] *a* unknown.

unbekümmert [ˈʊnbəkʏmərt] *a* unconcerned.

unbeliebt [ˈʊnbəliːpt] *a* unpopular.

unbequem [ˈʊnbəkveːm] *a* *(Stuhl)* uncomfortable; *(Mensch)* bothersome; *(Regelung)* inconvenient.

unberech- *zW:* **~enbar** [ʊnbəˈrɛçənbaːr] *a* incalculable; *(Mensch, Verhalten)* unpredictable; **~tigt** [ˈʊnbəreçtıçt] *a* unjustified; *(nicht erlaubt)* unauthorized.

unberührt [ˈʊnbərʏrt] *a* untouched, intact; **sie ist noch ~** she is still a virgin.

unbescheiden [ˈʊnbəʃaıdən] *a* presumptuous.

unbeschreiblich [ʊnbəˈʃraıplıç] *a* indescribable.

unbesonnen [ˈʊnbəzɔnən] *a* unwise, rash, imprudent.

unbeständig [ˈʊnbəʃtɛndıç] *a* *(Mensch)* inconstant; *(Wetter)* unsettled; *(Lage)* unstable.

unbestechlich [ʊnbəˈʃtɛçlıç] *a* incorruptible.

unbestimmt [ˈʊnbəʃtımt] *a* indefinite; *(Zukunft auch)* uncertain.

unbeteiligt [ˈʊnbətaılıçt] *a* unconcerned, indifferent.

unbewacht [ˈʊnbəvaxt] *a* unguarded, unwatched.

unbeweglich [ˈʊnbəveːklıç] *a* immovable.

unbewußt [ˈʊnbəvʊst] *a* unconscious.

unbrauchbar [ˈʊnbrauxbaːr] *a* *(Arbeit)* useless; *(Gerät auch)* unusable.

und [ʊnt] *kj* and; **~ so weiter** and so on.

Undank [ˈʊndaŋk] *m* ingratitude; **u~bar** *a* ungrateful; **~barkeit** *f* ingratitude.

undefinierbar [ʊndefiˈniːrbaːr] *a* indefinable.

undenkbar [ʊnˈdɛŋkbaːr] *a* inconceivable.

undeutlich [ˈʊndɔʏtlıç] *a* indistinct.

undicht [ˈʊndıçt] *a* leaky.

Unding [ˈʊndıŋ] *nt* absurdity.

undurch- [ˈʊndʊrç] *zW:* **~führbar** [-ˈfyːrbaːr] *a* impracticable; **~lässig** [-ˈlɛsıç] *a* waterproof, impermeable; **~sichtig** [-zıçtıç] *a* opaque; *(fig)* obscure.

uneben [ˈʊnˈeːbən] *a* uneven.

unehelich [ˈʊnˈeːəlıç] *a* illegitimate.

uneigennützig [ˈʊnˈaıgənnʏtsıç] *a* unselfish.

uneinig [ˈʊnˈaınıç] *a* divided; **~ sein** disagree; **U~keit** *f* discord, dissension.

uneins [ˈʊnˈaıns] *a* at variance, at odds.

unempfindlich [ˈʊnˈɛmpfıntlıç] *a* insensitive; *(Stoff)* practical.

unendlich [ʊnˈɛntlıç] *a* infinite; **U~keit** *f* infinity.

unent- [ˈʊnˈɛnt] *zW:* **~behrlich** [-ˈbeːrlıç] *a* indispensable; **~geltlich** [-gɛltlıç] *a* free (of charge); **~schieden** [-ˈʃiːdən] *a* undecided; **~schieden enden** *(SPORT)* end in a draw; **~schlossen** [-ˈʃlɔsən] *a* undecided; irresolute; **~wegt** [-ˈveːkt] *a* unswerving; *(unaufhörlich)* incessant.

uner- [ˈʊnˈɛr] *zW:* **~bittlich** [ˈbıtlıç] *a* unyielding, inexorable; **~fahren** [-ˈfaːrən] *a* inexperienced; **~freulich** [-ˈfrɔʏlıç] *a* unpleasant; **~gründlich** [-ˈgrʏntlıç] *a* unfathomable; **~heblich** [-ˈheːplıç] *a* unimportant; **~hört** [-ˈhøːrt] *a* unheard-of; *(Bitte)* outrageous; **~läßlich** [-ˈlɛslıç] *a* indispensable; **~laubt** [-laʊpt] *a* unauthorized; **~meßlich** [-ˈmɛslıç] *a* immeasurable, immense; **~müdlich** [-ˈmyːtlıç] *a* indefatigable; **~sättlich** [-ˈzɛtlıç] *a* insatiable; **~schöpflich** [-ˈʃœpflıç] *a* inexhaustible; **~schütterlich** [-ˈʃʏtərlıç] *a* unshakeable; **~schwinglich** [-ˈʃvıŋlıç] *a* *(Preis)* exorbitant; too expensive; **~träglich** [-ˈtreːklıç] *a* unbearable; *(Frechheit)* insufferable; **~wartet** [-vartət] *a* unexpected; **~wünscht** [-vʏnʃt] *a* undesirable, unwelcome.

unfähig [ˈʊnfɛːıç] *a* incapable *(zu of)*; incompetent; **U~keit** *f* incapacity; incompetence.

unfair [ˈʊnfɛːr] *a* unfair.

Unfall [ˈʊnfal] *m* accident; **~flucht** *f* hit-and-run (driving); **~stelle** *f* scene of the accident; **~versicherung** *f* accident insurance.

unfaßbar [ʊnˈfasbaːr] *a* inconceivable.

unfehlbar [ʊnˈfeːlbaːr] *a* infallible // *ad* inevitably; **U~keit** *f* infallibility.

unfit [ˈʊnfıt] *a* unfit.

unfrei [ˈʊnfraı] *a* not free, unfree; *(Paket)* unfranked; **~willig** *a* involuntary, against one's will.

unfreundlich [ˈʊnfrɔʏntlıç] *a* unfriendly; **U~keit** *f* unfriendliness.

Unfriede(n) [ˈʊnfriːdə(n)] *m* dissension, strife.

unfruchtbar [ˈʊnfrʊxtbaːr] *a* infertile;

(Gespräche) unfruitful; **U~keit** *f* infertility; unfruitfulness.

Unfug ['ʊnfuːk] *m* **-s** *(Benehmen)* mischief; *(Unsinn)* nonsense; **grober ~** *(JUR)* gross misconduct; malicious damage.

Ungar(in *f)* ['ʊŋgar(ɪn)] *m* Hungarian; **~n** *nt* Hungary; **u~isch** *a* Hungarian.

ungeachtet ['ʊŋgəˈaxtət] *präp* +*gen* notwithstanding.

ungeahnt ['ʊŋgəˈaːnt] *a* unsuspected, undreamt-of.

ungebeten ['ʊŋgəbeːtən] *a* uninvited.

ungebildet ['ʊŋgəbɪldət] *a* uneducated; uncultured.

ungedeckt ['ʊŋgədɛkt] *a* *(Scheck)* uncovered.

Ungeduld ['ʊŋgədʊlt] *f* impatience; **u~ig** [-dɪç] *a* impatient.

ungeeignet ['ʊŋgəˈaɪgnət] *a* unsuitable.

ungefähr ['ʊŋgəfɛːr] *a* rough, approximate; **das kommt nicht von ~** that's hardly surprising; **~lich** *a* not dangerous, harmless.

ungehalten ['ʊŋgəhaltən] *a* indignant.

ungeheuer ['ʊŋgəhɔʏər] *a* huge // *ad* *(umg)* enormously; **U~** *nt* **-s, -** monster; **~lich** [-'hɔʏərlɪç] *a* monstrous.

ungehobelt ['ʊŋgəhoːbəlt] *a* *(fig)* uncouth.

ungehörig ['ʊŋgəhøːrɪç] *a* impertinent, improper; **U~keit** *f* impertinence.

ungehorsam ['ʊŋgəhoːrzaːm] *a* disobedient; **U~** *m* disobedience.

ungeklärt ['ʊŋgəklɛːrt] *a* not cleared up; *(Rätsel)* unsolved.

ungeladen ['ʊŋgəlaːdən] *a* not loaded; *(Gast)* uninvited.

ungelegen ['ʊŋgəleːgən] *a* inconvenient.

ungelernt ['ʊŋgəlɛrnt] *a* unskilled.

ungelogen ['ʊŋgəloːgən] *ad* really, honestly.

ungemein ['ʊŋgəmaɪn] *a* uncommon.

ungemütlich ['ʊŋgəmyːtlɪç] *a* uncomfortable; *(Person)* disagreeable.

ungenau ['ʊŋgənaʊ] *a* inaccurate; **U~igkeit** *f* inaccuracy.

ungeniert ['ʊnʒeniːrt] *a* free and easy, unceremonious // *ad* without embarrassment, freely.

ungenießbar ['ʊŋgəniːsbaːr] *a* inedible; undrinkable; *(umg)* unbearable.

ungenügend ['ʊŋgənyːgənt] *a* insufficient, inadequate.

ungepflegt ['ʊŋgəpfleːkt] *a* *(Garten etc)* untended; *(Person)* unkempt; *(Hände)* neglected.

ungerade ['ʊŋgəraːdə] *a* uneven, odd.

ungerecht ['ʊŋgərɛçt] *a* unjust; **~fertigt** *a* unjustified; **U~igkeit** *f* injustice, unfairness.

ungern ['ʊŋgɛrn] *ad* unwillingly, reluctantly.

ungeschehen ['ʊŋgəʃeːən] *a*: **~ machen** undo.

Ungeschick- ['ʊŋgəʃɪk] *zW*: **~lichkeit** *f* clumsiness; **u~t** *a* awkward, clumsy.

ungeschminkt ['ʊŋgəʃmɪŋkt] *a* without make-up; *(fig)* unvarnished.

ungesetzlich ['ʊŋgəzɛtslɪç] *a* illegal.

ungestört ['ʊŋgəʃtøːrt] *a* undisturbed.

ungestraft ['ʊŋgəʃtraːft] *ad* with impunity.

ungestüm ['ʊŋgəʃtyːm] *a* impetuous; tempestuous; **U~** *nt* **-(e)s** impetuosity; passion.

ungesund ['ʊŋgəzʊnt] *a* unhealthy.

ungetrübt ['ʊŋgətryːpt] *a* clear; *(fig)* untroubled; *(Freude)* unalloyed.

Ungetüm ['ʊŋgətyːm] *nt* **-(e)s, -e** monster.

ungewiß ['ʊŋgəvɪs] *a* uncertain; **U~heit** *f* uncertainty.

ungewöhnlich ['ʊŋgəvøːnlɪç] *a* unusual.

ungewohnt ['ʊŋgəvoːnt] *a* unaccustomed.

Ungeziefer ['ʊŋgətsiːfər] *nt* **-s** vermin.

ungezogen ['ʊŋgətsoːgən] *a* rude, impertinent; **U~heit** *f* rudeness, impertinence.

ungezwungen ['ʊŋgətsvʊŋən] *a* natural, unconstrained.

ungläubig ['ʊŋglɔʏbɪç] *a* unbelieving; **die U~en** the infidel(s).

unglaublich [ʊn'glaʊplɪç] *a* incredible.

ungleich ['ʊŋglaɪç] *a* dissimilar; unequal // *ad* incomparably; **~artig** *a* different; **U~heit** *f* dissimilarity; inequality.

Unglück ['ʊŋglʏk] *nt* **-(e)s, -e** misfortune; *(Pech)* bad luck; *(~sfall)* calamity, disaster; *(Verkehrs~)* accident; **u~lich** *a* unhappy; *(erfolglos)* unlucky; *(unerfreulich)* unfortunate; **u~licherweise** [-'vaɪzə] *ad* unfortunately; **u~selig** *a* calamitous; *(Person)* unfortunate; **Unglücksfall** *m* accident, calamity.

ungültig ['ʊŋgʏltɪç] *a* invalid; **U~keit** *f* invalidity.

ungünstig ['ʊŋgʏnstɪç] *a* unfavourable.

ungut ['ʊŋguːt] *a* *(Gefühl)* uneasy; **nichts für ~** no offence.

unhaltbar ['ʊnhaltbaːr] *a* untenable.

Unheil ['ʊnhaɪl] *nt* evil; *(Unglück)* misfortune; **~ anrichten** cause mischief; **u~bar** *a* incurable; **u~bringend** *a* fatal, fateful; **u~voll** *a* disastrous.

unheimlich ['ʊnhaɪmlɪç] *a* weird, uncanny // *ad* *(umg)* tremendously.

unhöflich ['ʊnhøːflɪç] *a* impolite; **U~keit** *f* impoliteness.

unhygienisch ['ʊnhygiˈeːnɪʃ] *a* unhygienic.

Uni ['uni] f -, -s (umg) university; **u~**
|y'ni:| a self-coloured.

Uniform [uni'fɔrm] f uniform; **u~iert**
[-'mi:rt] a uniformed.

uninteressant ['ʊn'ınterɛsant] a unin-
teresting.

Universität [univerzı'tɛ:t] f university.

unkenntlich ['ʊnkɛntlıç] a unrecogniz-
able.

Unkenntnis ['ʊnkɛntnıs] f ignorance.

unklar ['ʊnklaːr] a unclear; **im ~en
sein über** (+akk) be in the dark
about; **U~heit** f unclarity; (Un-
entschiedenheit) uncertainty.

unklug ['ʊnkluːk] a unwise.

Unkosten ['ʊnkɔstən] pl expense(s).

Unkraut ['ʊnkraʊt] nt weed; weeds pl.

unlängst ['ʊnlɛŋst] ad not long ago.

unlauter ['ʊnlaʊtər] a unfair.

unleserlich ['ʊnleːzərlıç] a illegible.

unlogisch ['ʊnloːgıʃ] a illogical.

unlösbar [ʊn'løːsbar], **unlöslich**
[ʊn'løːslıç] a insoluble.

Unlust ['ʊnlʊst] f lack of enthusiasm;
u~ig a unenthusiastic.

unmäßig ['ʊnmɛːsıç] a immoderate.

Unmenge ['ʊnmɛŋə] f tremendous
number, hundreds pl.

Unmensch ['ʊnmɛnʃ] m ogre, brute;
u~lich a inhuman, brutal; (ungeheuer) awful.

unmerklich [ʊn'mɛrklıç] a imperceptible.

unmißverständlich ['ʊnmısfɛrʃtɛntlıç]
a unmistakable.

unmittelbar ['ʊnmıtəlbaːr] a immediate.

unmöbliert ['ʊnmøbliːrt] a unfur-
nished.

unmöglich ['ʊnmøːklıç] a impossible;
U~keit f impossibility.

unmoralisch ['ʊnmoraːlıʃ] a immoral.

Unmut ['ʊnmuːt] m ill humour.

unnachgiebig ['ʊnnaːxgiːbıç] a unyielding.

unnahbar [ʊn'naːbaːr] a unapproach-
able.

unnötig ['ʊnnøːtıç] a unnecessary.

unnütz ['ʊnnʏts] a useless.

unordentlich ['ʊn'ɔrdəntlıç] a untidy.

Unordnung ['ʊn'ɔrdnʊŋ] f disorder.

unparteiisch ['ʊnpartaııʃ] a impartial;
U~e(r) m umpire; (Fußball) referee.

unpassend ['ʊnpasənt] a inappropriate; (Zeit) inopportune.

unpäßlich ['ʊnpɛslıç] a unwell.

unpersönlich ['ʊnperzøːnlıç] a impersonal.

unpolitisch ['ʊnpoliːtıʃ] a apolitical.

unpraktisch ['ʊnpraktıʃ] a unpracti-
cal.

unpünktlich ['ʊnpʏnktlıç] a unpunc-
tual.

unrationell ['ʊnratsionɛl] a inefficient.

unrecht ['ʊnrɛçt] a wrong; **U~** nt

wrong; **zu U~** wrongly; **U~ haben**
wrong; **~mäßig** a unlawful, illegal.

unregelmäßig ['ʊnreːgəlmɛsıç] a irregular; **U~keit** f irregularity.

unreif ['ʊnraıf] a (Obst) unripe; (fig)
immature.

unrentabel ['ʊnrɛntaːbəl] a unprofit-
able.

unrichtig ['ʊnrıçtıç] a incorrect,
wrong.

Unruhe ['ʊnruːə] f -, -n unrest;
~stifter m troublemaker.

unruhig ['ʊnruːıç] a restless.

uns [ʊns] pron akk, dat von **wir** us;
ourselves.

unsachlich ['ʊnzaxlıç] a not to the
point, irrelevant.

unsagbar [ʊn'zaːkbaːr] a indescribable.

unsanft ['ʊnzanft] a rough.

unsauber ['ʊnzaʊbər] a unclean, dirty;
(fig) crooked; (MUS) fuzzy.

unschädlich ['ʊnʃɛːtlıç] a harmless;
jdn/etw ~ machen render sb/sth
harmless.

unscharf ['ʊnʃarf] a indistinct; (Bild
etc) out of focus, blurred.

unscheinbar ['ʊnʃaınbaːr] a insignificant; (Aussehen, Haus etc) unprepos-
sessing.

unschlagbar [ʊn'ʃlaːkbaːr] a invincible.

unschlüssig ['ʊnʃlʏsıç] a undecided.

Unschuld ['ʊnʃʊlt] f innocence; **u~ig**
[-dıç] a innocent.

unselbständig ['ʊnzɛlpʃtɛndıç] a dependent, over-reliant on others.

unser ['ʊnzər] pron our; **~e(r, s)** ours;
~einer, ~eins pron people like us;
unsererseits ad on our part;
unsertwegen, um unsertwillen ad
(für uns) for our sake; (wegen uns)
on our account.

unsicher ['ʊnzıçər] a uncertain;
(Mensch) insecure; **U~heit** f uncertainty; insecurity.

unsichtbar ['ʊnzıçtbaːr] a invisible.

Unsinn ['ʊnzın] m nonsense; **u~ig** a
nonsensical.

Unsitte ['ʊnzıtə] f deplorable habit.

unsittlich ['ʊnzıtlıç] a indecent.

unsportlich ['ʊnʃpɔrtlıç] a not sporty;
unfit; (Verhalten) unsporting.

unsre ['ʊnzrə] = **unsere**.

unsterblich ['ʊnʃtɛrplıç] a immortal;
U~keit f immortality.

Unstimmigkeit ['ʊnʃtımıçkaıt] f inconsistency; (Streit) disagreement.

unsympathisch ['ʊnzympaːtıʃ] a unpleasant; **er ist mir ~** I don't like
him.

untätig ['ʊntɛːtıç] a idle.

untauglich ['ʊntaʊklıç] a unsuitable;
(MIL) unfit.

unteilbar [ʊn'taılbaːr] a indivisible.

unten ['ʊntən] *ad* below; (*im Haus*) downstairs; (*an der Treppe etc*) at the bottom; **nach ~** down; **~ am Berg** *etc* at the bottom of the mountain *etc;* **ich bin bei ihm ~ durch** (*umg*) he's through with me.

unter [ʊntər] ◆*präp +dat* **1** (*räumlich, mit Zahlen*) under; (*drunter*) underneath, below; **~ 18 Jahren** under 18 years

2 (*zwischen*) among(st); **sie waren ~ sich** they were by themselves; **einer ~ ihnen** one of them; **~ anderem** among other things

◆*präp +akk* under, below.

Unterarm ['ʊntər'arm] *m* forearm.

unter *zW:* **~belichten** *vt* (*PHOT*) underexpose; **U~bewußtsein** *nt* subconscious; **~bezahlt** *a* underpaid.

unterbieten [ʊntər'biːtən] *vt unreg insep* (*COMM*) undercut; (*Rekord*) lower.

unterbinden [ʊntər'bɪndən] *vt unreg insep* stop, call a halt to.

unterbrech- [ʊntər'brɛç] *zW:* **~en** *vt unreg insep* interrupt; **U~ung** *f* interruption.

unterbringen ['ʊntərbrɪŋən] *vt unreg* (*in Koffer*) stow; (*in Zeitung*) place; (*Person: in Hotel etc*) accommodate, put up; (: *beruflich*) fix up (*auf, in* with).

unterdessen [ʊntər'dɛsən] *ad* meanwhile.

Unterdruck ['ʊntərdrʊk] *m* low pressure.

unterdrücken [ʊntər'drykən] *vt insep* suppress; (*Leute*) oppress.

untere(r, s) ['ʊntərə(r, s)] *a* lower.

untereinander [ʊntər'ai'nandər] *ad* with each other; among themselves *etc.*

unterentwickelt ['ʊntər'ɛntvɪkəlt] *a* underdeveloped.

unterernährt ['ʊntər'ɛrnɛːrt] *a* undernourished, underfed.

Unterernährung *f* malnutrition.

Unter'führung *f* subway, underpass.

Untergang ['ʊntərgaŋ] *m* (down)fall, decline; (*NAUT*) sinking; (*von Gestirn*) setting.

unter'geben *a* subordinate.

untergehen ['ʊntərgeːən] *vi unreg* go down; (*Sonne auch*) set; (*Staat*) fall; (*Volk*) perish; (*Welt*) come to an end; (*im Lärm*) be drowned.

Untergeschoß ['ʊntərgəʃɔs] *nt* basement.

unter'gliedern *vt insep* subdivide.

Untergrund ['ʊntərgrʊnt] *m* foundation; (*POL*) underground; **~bahn** *f* underground, tube, subway (*US*); **~bewegung** *f* underground (movement).

unterhalb ['ʊntərhalp] *präp +gen, ad* below; **~ von** below.

Unterhalt ['ʊntərhalt] *m* maintenance; **u~en** [ʊntər'haltən] *unreg insep vt* maintain; (*belustigen*) entertain // *vr* talk; (*sich belustigen*) enjoy o.s.; **~ung** *f* maintenance; (*Belustigung*) entertainment, amusement; (*Gespräch*) talk.

Unterhemd ['ʊntərhɛmt] *nt* vest, undershirt (*US*).

Unterhose ['ʊntərhoːzə] *f* underpants *pl.*

unterirdisch ['ʊntər'ɪrdɪʃ] *a* underground.

Unterkiefer ['ʊntərkiːfər] *m* lower jaw.

unterkommen ['ʊntərkɔmən] *vi unreg* find shelter; find work; **das ist mir noch nie untergekommen** I've never met with that.

Unterkunft ['ʊntərkʊnft] *f* -, -künfte accommodation.

Unterlage ['ʊntərlaːgə] *f* foundation; (*Beleg*) document; (*Schreib~ etc*) pad.

unter'lassen *vt unreg insep* (*versäumen*) fail (to do); (*sich enthalten*) refrain from.

unterlaufen [ʊntər'laufən] *vi unreg insep* happen // *a:* **mit Blut ~** suffused with blood; (*Augen*) bloodshot.

unterlegen ['ʊntərleːgən] *vt* lay *od* put under // [ʊntər'leːgən] *a* inferior (*dat* to); (*besiegt*) defeated.

Unterleib ['ʊntərlaip] *m* abdomen.

unter'liegen *vi unreg insep* be defeated *od* overcome (*jdm* by sb); (*unterworfen sein*) be subject to.

Untermiete ['ʊntərmiːtə] *f:* **zur ~ wohnen** be a subtenant *od* lodger; **~r(in** *f*) *m* subtenant, lodger.

unter'nehmen *vt unreg insep* undertake; **U~** *nt* **-s, -** undertaking, enterprise (*auch COMM*).

Unternehmer [ʊntər'neːmər] *m* **-s, -** entrepreneur, businessman.

Unterredung [ʊntər'reːdʊŋ] *f* discussion, talk.

Unterricht ['ʊntərrɪçt] *m* **-(e)s, -e** instruction, lessons *pl;* **u~en** [ʊntər'rɪçtən] *insep vt* instruct; (*SCH*) teach // *vr* inform o.s. (*über +akk* about).

Unterrock ['ʊntərrɔk] *m* petticoat, slip.

unter'sagen *vt insep* forbid (*jdm etw* sb to do sth).

unter'schätzen *vt insep* underestimate.

unter'scheiden *unreg insep vt* distinguish // *vr* differ.

Unter'scheidung *f* (*Unterschied*) distinction; (*Unterscheiden*) differentiation.

Unterschied ['ʊntərʃiːt] *m* **-(e)s, -e** difference, distinction; **im ~ zu** as distinct from; **u~lich** a varying, differing; (*diskriminierend*) discriminatory; **unterschiedslos** ad indiscriminately.

unter'schlagen vt unreg insep embezzle; (*verheimlichen*) suppress.

Unter'schlagung f embezzlement.

Unterschlupf ['untərʃlupf] m **-(e)s, -schlüpfe** refuge.

unter'schreiben vt unreg insep sign.

Unterschrift ['untərʃrift] f signature.

Unterseeboot ['untərze:bo:t] nt submarine.

Untersetzer ['untərzɛtsər] m tablemat; (*für Gläser*) coaster.

untersetzt [untər'zɛtst] a stocky.

unterste(r, s) ['untərstə(r, s)] a lowest, bottom.

unterstehen [untər'ʃte:ən] unreg vi insep be under (*jdm* sb) // vr dare // ['untərʃte:ən] vi shelter.

unterstellen [untər'ʃtələn] vt insep subordinate (*dat* to); (*fig*) impute (*jdm etw* sth to sb) // ['untərʃtələn] vt (*Auto*) garage, park // vr take shelter.

unter'streichen vt unreg insep (*lit, fig*) underline.

Unterstufe ['untərʃtu:fə] f lower grade.

unter'stützen vt insep support.

Unter'stützung f support, assistance.

unter'suchen vt insep (*MED*) examine; (*Polizei*) investigate.

Unter'suchung f examination, investigation, inquiry; **Untersuchungsausschuß** m committee of inquiry; **Untersuchungshaft** f imprisonment on remand.

Untertan ['untərta:n] m **-s, -en** subject.

untertänig ['untərtɛ:nɪç] a submissive, humble.

Untertasse ['untərtasə] f saucer.

untertauchen ['untərtauxən] vi dive; (*fig*) disappear, go underground.

Unterteil ['untərtail] nt od m lower part, bottom; **u~en** [untər'tailən] vt insep divide up.

Unterwäsche ['untərvɛʃə] f underwear.

unterwegs [untər've:ks] ad on the way.

unter'weisen vt unreg insep instruct.

unter'werfen unreg insep vt subject; (*Volk*) subjugate // vr submit (*dat* to).

unterwürfig ['untərvyrfıç] a obsequious, servile.

unter'zeichnen vt insep sign.

unter'ziehen unreg insep vt subject (*dat* to) // vr undergo (*etw* (*dat*) sth); (*einer Prüfung*) take.

untreu ['untrɔy] a unfaithful; **U~e** f unfaithfulness.

untröstlich [un'trø:stlıç] a inconsolable.

unüber- ['un'y:bər] zW: **~legt** [-le:kt] a ill-considered // ad without thinking; **~sehbar** [-'ze:ba:r] a incalculable.

unum- [un'um] zW: **~gänglich** [-'gɛŋlıç] a indispensable, vital; absolutely necessary; **~wunden** [-'vundən] a candid // ad straight out.

ununterbrochen [un'untərbrɔxən] a uninterrupted.

unver- [unfɛr] zW: **~änderlich** [-'ɛndərlıç] a unchangeable; **~antwortlich** [-'antvɔrtlıç] a irresponsible; (*unentschuldbar*) inexcusable; **~besserlich** [-'bɛsərlıç] a incorrigible; **~bindlich** [-'bıntlıç] a not binding; (*Antwort*) curt // ad (*COMM*) without obligation; **~blümt** [-'bly:mt] a, ad plain(ly), blunt(ly); **~daulich** ['-dauliç] a indigestible; **~dorben** ['-dɔrbən] a unspoilt; **~einbar** [-'ainba:r] a incompatible; **~fänglich** [-'fɛŋlıç] a harmless; **~froren** ['-fro:rən] a impudent; **~hofft** ['-hɔft] a unexpected; **~kennbar** [-'kɛnba:r] a unmistakable; **~meidlich** [-'maitlıç] a unavoidable; **~mutet** ['-mu:tət] a unexpected; **~nünftig** [-'nynftıç] a foolish; **~schämt** ['-ʃɛ:mt] a impudent; **U~schämtheit** f impudence, insolence; **~sehens** ['-ze:əns] ad all of a sudden; **~sehrt** ['-ze:rt] a uninjured; **~söhnlich** ['-zø:nlıç] a irreconcilable; **~ständlich** ['-ʃtɛntlıç] a unintelligible; **~träglich** ['-trɛ:klıç] a quarrelsome; (*Meinungen*, MED) incompatible; **~wüstlich** [-'vy:stlıç] a indestructible; (*Mensch*) irrepressible; **~zeihlich** [-'tsailıç] a unpardonable; **~züglich** [-'tsy:klıç] a immediate.

unvoll- ['unfɔl] zW: **~kommen** a imperfect; **~ständig** a incomplete.

unvor- ['unfo:r] zW: **~bereitet** a unprepared; **~eingenommen** a unbiased; **~hergesehen** [-'he:rgəzeːən] a unforeseen; **~sichtig** [-zıçtıç] a careless, imprudent; **~stellbar** [-'ʃtɛlba:r] a inconceivable; **~teilhaft** [-tailhaft] a disadvantageous.

unwahr ['unva:r] a untrue; **~scheinlich** a improbable, unlikely // ad (*umg*) incredibly.

unweigerlich [un'vaigərlıç] a unquestioning // ad without fail.

Unwesen ['unve:zən] nt nuisance; (*Unfug*) mischief; **sein ~ treiben** wreak havoc; **unwesentlich** a inessential, unimportant; **unwesentlich besser** marginally better.

Unwetter ['unvɛtər] nt thunderstorm.

unwichtig ['unvıçtıç] a unimportant.

unwider- [unvi:dər] zW: **~legbar** [-'le:kba:r] a irrefutable; **~ruflich**

[-'ru:flıç] *a* irrevocable; **~stehlich** [-'ſte:lıç] *a* irresistible.

unwill- ['ʊnvıl] *zW:* **U~e(n)** *m* indignation; **~ig** *a* indignant; *(widerwillig)* reluctant; **~kürlich** [-ky:rlıç] *a* involuntary // *ad* instinctively; *(lachen)* involuntarily.

unwirklich ['ʊnvırklıç] *a* unreal.

unwirsch ['ʊnvırʃ] *a* cross, surly.

unwirtschaftlich ['ʊnvırtʃaftlıç] *a* uneconomical.

unwissen- ['ʊnvısən] *zW:* **~d** *a* ignorant; **U~heit** *f* ignorance; **~schaftlich** *a* unscientific.

unwohl ['ʊnvo:l] *a* unwell, ill; **U~sein** *nt* **-s** indisposition.

unwürdig ['ʊnvvrdıç] *a* unworthy *(jds of sb).*

unzählig [ʊn'tsɛ:lıç] *a* innumerable, countless.

unzer- [ʊntsɛr] *zW:* **~brechlich** [-'brɛçlıç] *a* unbreakable; **~störbar** [-'ſtø:rba:r] *a* indestructible; **~trennlich** [-'trɛnlıç] *a* inseparable.

Unzucht ['ʊntsʊxt] *f* sexual offence.

unzüchtig ['ʊntsʏçtıç] *a* immoral; lewd.

unzu- ['ʊntsu] *zW:* **~frieden** *a* dissatisfied; **U~friedenheit** *f* discontent; **~länglich** ['ʊntsu:lɛŋlıç] *a* inadequate; **~lässig** ['ʊntsu:lɛsıç] *a* inadmissible; **~rechnungsfähig** ['ʊntsu:rɛçnʊŋsfɛ:ıç] *a* irresponsible; **~treffend** ['ʊntsu:-] *a* incorrect; **~verlässig** ['ʊntsu:-] *a* unreliable.

unzweideutig ['ʊntsvaıdɔʏtıç] *a* unambiguous.

üppig ['ʏpıç] *a* *(Frau)* curvaceous; *(Busen)* full, ample; *(Essen)* sumptuous; *(Vegetation)* luxuriant, lush.

uralt ['u:r'alt] *a* ancient, very old.

Uran [u'ra:n] *nt* **-s** uranium.

Ur- ['u:r] *in zW* original; **~aufführung** *f* first performance; **~einwohner** *m* original inhabitant; **~eltern** *pl* ancestors *pl;* **~enkel(in** *f)* *m* great-grandchild; **~großmutter** *f* great-grandmother; **~großvater** *m* great-grandfather; **~heber** *m* **-s,** - originator; *(Autor)* author.

Urin [u'ri:n] *m* **-s, -e** urine.

Urkunde ['u:rkʊndə] *f* **-, -n** document, deed.

Urlaub ['u:rlaʊp] *m* **-(e)s, -e** holiday(s *pl*) *(Brit),* vacation *(US); (MIL etc)* leave; **~er** [-laʊbər] *m* **-s,** - holidaymaker *(Brit),* vacationer *(US).*

Urne ['ʊrnə] *f* **-,** n urn.

Ursache ['u:rzaxə] *f* cause; **keine ~** that's all right.

Ursprung ['u:rʃprʊŋ] *m* origin, source; *(von Fluß)* source.

ursprünglich [u:r'ʃprʏŋlıç] *a, ad* original(ly).

Urteil ['ʊrtaıl] *nt* **-s, -e** opinion; *(JUR)*

sentence, judgement; **u~en** *vi* judge; **Urteilsspruch** *m* sentence, verdict.

Ur- *zW:* **~wald** *m* jungle; **~zeit** *f* prehistoric times *pl.*

USA [u:'ɛs''a:] *f abk* (= *Vereinigte Staaten von Amerika)* USA.

usw. [u:ɛsve:] *abk* (= *und so weiter)* etc.

Utensilien [utɛn'zi:liən] *pl* utensils *pl.*

Utopie [uto'pi:] *f* pipedream.

utopisch [u'to:pıʃ] *a* utopian.

u.U. *abk von* **unter Umständen.**

V

V, v [faʊ] *nt* V, v.

vag(e) [va:k, 'va:gə] *a* vague.

Vagina [va'gi:na] *f* -, **Vaginen** vagina.

Vakuum ['va:kuʊm] *nt* **-s, Vakua** *od* **Vakuen** vacuum.

Vanille [va'nıljə] *f* - vanilla.

Variation [variatsi'o:n] *f* variation.

variieren [vari'i:rən] *vti* vary.

Vase ['va:zə] *f* -, **-n** vase.

Vater ['fa:tər] *m* **-s,** ⁻ father; **~land** *nt* native country; Fatherland.

väterlich ['fɛ:tərlıç] *a* fatherly; **väterlicherseits** *ad* on the father's side.

Vater- *zW:* **~schaft** *f* paternity; **~unser** *nt* **-s,** - Lord's prayer.

Vati ['fa:ti] *m* daddy.

v.Chr. *abk* (= *vor Christus)* BC.

Vegetarier(in *f)* [vege'ta:riər(ın)] *m* **-s,** - vegetarian.

Veilchen ['faılçən] *nt* violet.

Vene ['ve:nə] *f* -, **-n** vein.

Venedig [ve'ne:dıç] *nt* Venice.

Ventil [vɛn'ti:l] *nt* **-s, -e** valve; **~ator** [vɛnti'la:tər] *m* ventilator.

verab- [fɛr'ap] *zW:* **~reden** *vt* agree, arrange; **sich jdm ~redet sein** have arranged to meet sb // *vr* arrange to meet *(mit jdm* sb); **V~redung** *f* arrangement; *(Treffen)* appointment; **~scheuen** *vt* detest, abhor; **~schieden** *vt* *(Gäste)* say goodbye to; *(entlassen)* discharge; *(Gesetz)* pass // *vr* take one's leave *(von* of); **V~schiedung** *f* leave-taking; discharge; passing.

ver- [fɛr] *zW:* **~achten** [-'axtən] *vt* despise; **~ächtlich** [-'ɛçtlıç] *a* contemptuous; *(verachtenswert)* contemptible; **jdn ~ächtlich machen** run sb down; **V~achtung** *f* contempt.

verallgemein- [fɛr'algəmaın] *zW:* **~ern** *vt* generalize; **V~erung** *f* generalization.

veralten [fɛr'altən] *vi* become obsolete *od* out-of-date.

Veranda [ve'randa] *f* -, **Veranden** veranda.

veränder- [fɛr'ɛndər] *zW:* **~lich** *a* changeable; **~n** *vtr* change, alter;

V~ung f change, alteration.
veran- [fɛr''an] zW: **~lagt** a with a ... nature; **V~lagung** f disposition; **~lassen** vt cause; **Maßnahmen ~lassen** take measures; **sich ~laßt sehen** feel prompted; **~schaulichen** vt illustrate; **~schlagen** vt estimate; **~stalten** vt organize, arrange; **V~stalter** m **-s,** - organizer; **V~staltung** f (Veranstalten) organizing; (Konzert etc) event, function.
verantwort- [fɛr''antvɔrt] zW: **~en** vt answer for // vr justify o.s.; **~lich** a responsible; **V~ung** f responsibility; **~ungsbewußt** a responsible; **~ungslos** a irresponsible.
verarbeiten [fɛr''arbaitən] vt process; (geistig) assimilate; **etw zu etw ~** make sth into sth.
Verarbeitung f processing; assimilation.
verärgern [fɛr''ɛrgərn] vt annoy.
verausgaben [fɛr''ausgɑːbən] vr run out of money; (fig) exhaust o.s.
veräußern [fɛr''ɔysərn] vt dispose of, sell.
Verb [vɛrp] nt **-s, -en** verb.
Verband [fɛr'bant] m **-(e)s, ⁻e** (MED) bandage, dressing; (Bund) association, society; (MIL) unit; **~kasten** m medicine chest, first-aid box; **~zeug** nt bandage.
verbannen [fɛr'banən] vt banish.
Verbannung f exile.
verbergen [fɛr'bɛrgən] vtr unreg hide (vor +dat from).
verbessern [fɛr'bɛsərn] vtr improve; (berichtigen) correct (o.s.).
Verbesserung f improvement; correction.
verbeugen [fɛr'bɔygən] vr bow.
Verbeugung f bow.
ver'biegen vi unreg bend.
ver'bieten vt unreg forbid (jdm etw sb to do sth).
verbilligt [fɛr'bilɪçt] a reduced.
ver'binden unreg vt connect; (kombinieren) combine; (MED) bandage; **jdm die Augen ~** blindfold sb // vr combine (auch CHEM), join.
verbindlich [fɛr'bɪntlɪç] a binding; (freundlich) friendly; **V~keit** f obligation; (Höflichkeit) civility.
Ver'bindung f connection; (Zusammensetzung) combination; (CHEM) compound; (UNIV) club.
ver'bitten vt unreg: **sich** (dat) **etw ~** not tolerate sth, not stand for sth.
verblassen [fɛr'blasən] vi fade.
Verbleib [fɛr'blaip] m **-(e)s** whereabouts; **v~en** [fɛr'blaibən] vi unreg remain.
verblüffen [fɛr'blʏfən] vt stagger, amaze.
Verblüffung f stupefaction.

ver'blühen vi wither, fade.
ver'bluten vi bleed to death.
verborgen [fɛr'bɔrgən] a hidden.
Verbot [fɛr'boːt] nt **-(e)s, -e** prohibition, ban; **v~en** a forbidden; **Rauchen v~en!** no smoking; **Verbotsschild** nt prohibitory sign.
Verbrauch [fɛr'braux] m **-(e)s** consumption; **v~en** vt use up; **~er** m **-s,** - consumer; **v~t** a used up, finished; (Luft) stale; (Mensch) worn-out.
Verbrechen [fɛr'brɛçən] nt **-s,** - crime; **v~** vt unreg perpetrate.
Verbrecher [fɛr'brɛçər] m **-s,** - criminal; **v~isch** a criminal.
ver'breiten vtr spread; **sich über etw** (akk) **~** expound on sth.
verbreitern [fɛr'braitərn] vt broaden.
Verbreitung f spread(ing), propagation.
verbrenn- [fɛr'brɛn] zW: **~bar** a combustible; **~en** unreg vt burn; (Leiche) cremate; **V~ung** f burning; (in Motor) combustion; (von Leiche) cremation; **V~ungsmotor** m internal combustion engine.
ver'bringen vt unreg spend.
verbrühen [fɛr'bryːən] vt scald.
verbuchen [fɛr'buːxən] vt (FIN) register; (Erfolg) enjoy; (Mißerfolg) suffer.
verbunden [fɛr'bundən] a connected; **jdm ~ sein** be obliged or indebted to sb; **falsch ~** (TEL) wrong number; **V~heit** f bond, relationship.
verbünden [fɛr'byndən] vr ally o.s.
Verbündete(r) [fɛr'byndətə(r)] mf ally.
ver'bürgen vr: **sich ~ für** vouch for.
ver'büßen vt: **eine Strafe ~** serve a sentence.
Verdacht [fɛr'daxt] m **-(e)s** suspicion.
verdächtig [fɛr'dɛçtɪç] a suspicious, suspect; **~en** [fɛr'dɛçtɪgən] vt suspect.
verdammen [fɛr'damən] vt damn, condemn; **verdammt!** damn!
ver'dampfen vi vaporize, evaporate.
ver'danken vt: **jdm etw ~** owe sb sth.
verdauen [fɛr'dauən] vt (lit, fig) digest.
verdaulich [fɛr'daulɪç] a digestible; **das ist schwer ~** that is hard to digest.
Verdauung f digestion.
Verdeck [fɛr'dɛk] nt **-(e)s, -e** (AUT) hood; (NAUT) deck; **v~en** vt cover (up); (verbergen) hide.
ver'denken vt unreg: **jdm etw ~** blame sb for sth, hold sth against sb.
Verderb- [fɛr'dɛrp] zW: **~en** [fɛr'dɛrbən] nt **-s** ruin; **v~en** unreg vt spoil; (schädigen) ruin; (moralisch) corrupt; **es mit jdm v~en** get into sb's bad books // vi (Essen) spoil,

rot; (*Mensch*) go to the bad; **v~lich** *a* (*Einfluß*) pernicious; (*Lebensmittel*) perishable.

verdeutlichen [fɛr'dɔɪtlɪçən] *vt* make clear.

ver'dichten *vtr* condense.

ver'dienen *vt* earn; (*moralisch*) deserve.

Ver'dienst *m* -**(e)s**, -**e** earnings *pl* // *nt* -**(e)s**, -**e** merit; (*Leistung*) service (*um* to).

verdient [fɛr'diːnt] *a* well-earned; (*Person*) deserving of esteem; **sich um etw ~ machen** do a lot for sth.

verdoppeln [fɛr'dɔpəln] *vt* double.

verdorben [fɛr'dɔrbən] *a* spoilt; (*geschädigt*) ruined; (*moralisch*) corrupt.

verdrängen [fɛr'drɛŋən] *vt* oust, displace (*auch PHYS*); (*PSYCH*) repress.

ver'drehen *vt* (*lit, fig*) twist; (*Augen*) roll; **jdm den Kopf ~** (*fig*) turn sb's head.

verdreifachen [fɛr'draɪfaxən] *vt* treble.

verdrießlich [fɛr'driːslɪç] *a* peevish, annoyed.

Verdruß [fɛr'drʊs] *m* -**sses**, -**sse** annoyance, worry.

verdummen [fɛr'dʊmən] *vt* make stupid // *vi* grow stupid.

verdunkeln [fɛr'dʊŋkəln] *vtr* darken; (*fig*) obscure.

Verdunk(e)lung *f* blackout; (*fig*) obscuring.

verdünnen [fɛr'dʏnən] *vt* dilute.

verdunsten [fɛr'dʊnstən] *vi* evaporate.

verdursten [fɛr'dʊrstən] *vi* die of thirst.

verdutzt [fɛr'dʊtst] *a* nonplussed, taken aback.

verehr- [fɛr'eːr] *zW:* **~en** *vt* venerate, worship (*auch REL*); **jdm etw ~en** present sb with sth; **V~er(in** *f*) *m* -**s**, - admirer, worshipper (*auch REL*); **~t** *a* esteemed; **V~ung** *f* respect; (*REL*) worship.

Verein [fɛr'aɪn] *m* -**(e)s**, -**e** club, association; **v~bar** *a* compatible; **v~baren** [-baːrən] *vt* agree upon; **~barung** *f* agreement; **v~fachen** [-faxən] *vt* simplify; **v~igen** [-ɪgən] *vtr* unite; **V~igte Staaten** *pl* United States; **~igung** *f* union; (*Verein*) association; **v~t** *a* united; **vereinzelt** *a* isolated.

vereiteln [fɛr'aɪtəln] *vt* frustrate.

ver'eitern *vi* suppurate, fester.

verengen [fɛr'ɛŋən] *vr* narrow.

vererb- [fɛr'ɛrb] *zW:* **~en** *vt* bequeath; (*BIOL*) transmit // *vr* be hereditary; **~lich** [fɛr'ɛrplɪç] *a* hereditary; **V~ung** *f* bequeathing; (*BIOL*) transmission; (*Lehre*) heredity.

verewigen [fɛr'eːvɪgən] *vt* immortalize // *vr* (*umg*) leave one's name.

ver'fahren *unreg vi* act; **~ mit** deal with // *vr* get lost // *a* tangled; **V~** *nt* -**s**, - procedure; (*TECH*) process; (*JUR*) proceedings *pl*.

Verfall [fɛr'fal] *m* -**(e)s** decline; (*von Haus*) dilapidation; (*FIN*) expiry; **v~en** *vi unreg* decline; (*Haus*) be falling down; (*FIN*) lapse; **v~en in** (+*acc*) lapse into; **v~en auf** (+*acc*) hit upon; **einem Laster v~en sein** be addicted to a vice.

ver'färben *vr* change colour.

Verfasser(in *f*) [fɛr'fasər(ɪn)] *m* -**s**, - author, writer.

Verfassung *f* constitution (*auch POL*).

Verfassungs- *zW:* **~gericht** *nt* constitutional court; **v~mäßig** *a* constitutional; **v~widrig** *a* unconstitutional.

ver'faulen *vi* rot.

ver'fehlen *vt* miss; **etw für verfehlt halten** regard sth as mistaken.

verfeinern [fɛr'faɪnərn] *vt* refine.

ver'filmen *vt* film.

ver'fluchen *vt* curse.

verfolg- [fɛr'fɔlg] *zW:* **~en** *vt* pursue; (*gerichtlich*) prosecute; (*grausam, bes POL*) persecute; **V~er** *m* -**s**, - pursuer; **V~ung** *f* pursuit; prosecution; persecution.

verfremden [fɛr'frɛmdən] *vt* alienate, distance.

verfrüht [fɛr'fryːt] *a* premature.

verfüg- [fɛr'fyːg] *zW:* **~bar** *a* available; **~en** *vt* direct, order // *vr* proceed // *vi:* **~en über** (+*akk*) have at one's disposal; **V~ung** *f* direction, order; **zur V~ung** at one's disposal; **jdm zur V~ung stehen** be available to sb.

verführ- [fɛr'fyːr] *zW:* **~en** *vt* tempt; (*sexuell*) seduce; **V~er** *m* tempter; seducer; **~erisch** *a* seductive; **V~ung** *f* seduction; (*Versuchung*) temptation.

ver'gammeln *vi* (*umg*) go to seed; (*Nahrung*) go off.

vergangen [fɛr'gaŋən] *a* past; **V~heit** *f* past.

vergänglich [fɛr'gɛŋlɪç] *a* transitory; **V~keit** *f* transitoriness, impermanence.

vergasen [fɛr'gaːzən] *vt* (*töten*) gas.

Vergaser *m* -**s**, - (*AUT*) carburettor.

vergaß *etc v siehe* **vergessen**.

vergeb- [fɛr'geːb] *zW:* **~en** *vt unreg* forgive (*jdm etw* sb for sth); (*weggeben*) give away; **~ens** *ad* in vain; **~lich** [fɛr'geːplɪç] *ad* in vain // *a* vain, futile; **V~ung** *f* forgiveness.

ver'gehen *unreg vi* pass by *od* away; **jdm vergeht etw** sb loses sth // *vr* commit an offence (*gegen etw* against sth); **sich an jdm ~** (*sexually*) assault sb; **V~** *nt* -**s**, - offence.

ver'gelten *vt unreg* pay back (*jdm*

etw sb for sth), repay.

Ver'geltung *f* retaliation, reprisal; **Vergeltungsschlag** *m* (MIL) reprisal.

vergessen [fɛr'gɛsən] *vt unreg* forget; **V~heit** *f* oblivion.

vergeßlich [fɛr'gɛslɪç] *a* forgetful; **V~keit** *f* forgetfulness.

vergeuden [fɛr'gɔydən] *vt* squander, waste.

vergewaltigen [fɛrgə'valtɪgən] *vt* rape; (*fig*) violate.

Vergewaltigung *f* rape.

vergewissern [fɛrgə'vɪsərn] *vr* make sure.

ver'gießen *vt unreg* shed.

vergiften [fɛr'gɪftən] *vt* poison.

Vergiftung *f* poisoning.

Vergißmeinnicht [fɛr'gɪsmaɪnnɪçt] *nt* -(e)s, -e forget-me-not.

vergißt *etc v siehe* **vergessen**.

Vergleich [fɛr'glaɪç] *m* -(e)s, -e comparison; (JUR) settlement; **im ~ mit** *od* **zu** compared with *od* to; **v~bar** *a* comparable; **v~en** *unreg vt* compare // *vr* reach a settlement.

vergnügen [fɛr'gny:gən] *vr* enjoy *od* amuse o.s.; **V~** *nt* -s, - pleasure; **viel V~!** enjoy yourself!

vergnügt [fɛr'gny:kt] *a* cheerful.

Vergnügung *f* pleasure, amusement; **Vergnügungspark** *m* amusement park; **vergnügungssüchtig** *a* pleasure-loving.

vergolden [fɛr'gɔldən] *vt* gild.

vergöttern [fɛr'gœtərn] *vt* idolize.

ver'graben *vt* bury.

ver'greifen *vr unreg*: **sich an jdm ~** lay hands on sb; **sich an etw ~** misappropriate sth; **sich im Ton ~** say the wrong thing.

vergriffen [fɛr'grɪfən] *a* (*Buch*) out of print, (*Ware*) out of stock.

vergrößern [fɛr'grø:sərn] *vt* enlarge; (*mengenmäßig*) increase; (*Lupe*) magnify.

Vergrößerung *f* enlargement; increase; magnification; **Vergrößerungsglas** *nt* magnifying glass.

Vergünstigung [fɛr'gynstɪgʊŋ] *f* concession, privilege.

vergüten [fɛr'gy:tən] *vt*: **jdm etw ~** compensate sb for sth.

Vergütung *f* compensation.

verhaften [fɛr'haftən] *vt* arrest.

Verhaftung *f* arrest.

ver'hallen *vi* die away.

ver'halten *unreg vr* be, stand; (*sich benehmen*) behave; (MATH) be in proportion to // *vt* hold *od* keep back; (*Schritt*) check; **V~** *nt* -s behaviour.

Verhältnis [fɛr'hɛltnɪs] *nt* -ses, -se relationship; (MATH) proportion, ratio // *pl* (*Umstände*) conditions *pl*; **über seine ~se leben** live beyond one's means; **v~mäßig** *a, ad* relative(ly),

comparative(ly).

verhandeln [fɛr'handəln] *vi* negotiate (*über etw* (*akk*) sth); (JUR) hold proceedings // *vt* discuss; (JUR) hear.

Verhandlung *f* negotiation; (JUR) proceedings *pl*; **Verhandlungspaket** *nt* package (of proposals).

ver'hängen *vt* (*fig*) impose, inflict.

Verhängnis [fɛr'hɛŋnɪs] *nt* -ses, -se fate, doom; **jdm zum ~ werden** be sb's undoing; **v~voll** *a* fatal, disastrous.

verharmlosen [fɛr'harmlo:zən] *vt* make light of, play down.

verhärten [fɛr'hɛrtən] *vr* harden.

verhaßt [fɛr'hast] *a* odious, hateful.

verheerend [fɛr'he:rənt] *a* disastrous, devastating.

verheimlichen [fɛr'haɪmlɪçən] *vt* keep secret (*jdm* from sb).

verheiratet [fɛr'haɪra:tət] *a* married.

ver'helfen *vi unreg*: **jdm ~ zu** help sb to get.

verherrlichen [fɛr'hɛrlɪçən] *vt* glorify.

ver'hexen *vt* bewitch; **es ist wie verhext** it's jinxed.

ver'hindern *vt* prevent; **verhindert sein** be unable to make it.

verhöhnen [fɛr'hø:nən] *vt* mock, sneer at.

Verhör [fɛr'hø:r] *nt* -(e)s, -e interrogation; (*gerichtlich*) (cross-)examination; **v~en** *vt* interrogate; (cross-)examine // *vr* misunderstand, mishear.

ver'hungern *vi* starve, die of hunger.

ver'hüten *vt* prevent, avert.

Ver'hütung *f* prevention; **Verhütungsmittel** *nt* contraceptive.

verirren [fɛr'ɪrən] *vr* go astray.

ver'jagen *vt* drive away *od* out.

verkalken [fɛr'kalkən] *vi* calcify; (*umg*) become senile.

verkannt [fɛr'kant] *a* unappreciated.

Verkauf [fɛr'kauf] *m* sale; **v~en** *vt* sell.

Verkäufer(in *f*) [fɛr'kɔyfər(ɪn)] *m* -s, - seller; salesman; (*in Laden*) shop assistant.

verkäuflich [fɛr'kɔyflɪç] *a* saleable.

Verkaufsbedingungen *pl* terms and conditions of sale.

Verkehr [fɛr'ke:r] *m* -s, -e traffic; (*Umgang, bes sexuell*) intercourse; (*Umlauf*) circulation; **v~en** *vi* (*Fahrzeug*) ply, run; (*besuchen*) visit regularly (*bei jdm* sb); **v~en mit** associate with // *vtr* turn, transform.

Verkehrs- *zW*: **~ampel** *f* traffic lights *pl*; **~amt** *nt* tourist office; **~delikt** *nt* traffic offence; **~stauung** *f*, **~stockung** *f* traffic jam, stoppage; **~teilnehmer** *m* road-user; **~unfall** *m* traffic accident; **~zeichen** *nt* traffic sign.

verkehrt a wrong; (*umgekehrt*) the wrong way round.
ver'kennen vt unreg misjudge, not appreciate.
ver'klagen vt take to court.
verkleiden [fɛr'klaɪdən] vtr disguise (o.s.), dress up.
Verkleidung f disguise; (*ARCHIT*) wainscoting.
verkleinern [fɛr'klaɪnərn] vt make smaller, reduce in size.
verklemmt [fɛr'klɛmt] a (*fig*) inhibited.
ver'klingen vi unreg die away.
ver'kneifen vt (*umg*): sich (*dat*) etw ~ (*Lachen*) stifle; (*Schmerz*) hide; (*sich versagen*) do without.
verknüpfen [fɛr'knʏpfən] vt tie (up), knot; (*fig*) connect.
ver'kommen vi unreg deteriorate, decay; (*Mensch*) go downhill, come down in the world // a (*moralisch*) dissolute, depraved.
verkörpern [fɛr'kœrpərn] vt embody, personify.
verkraften [fɛr'kraftən] vt cope with.
ver'kriechen vr unreg creep away, creep into a corner.
Verkrümmung f bend, warp; (*ANAT*) curvature.
verkrüppelt [fɛr'krʏpəlt] a crippled.
verkrustet [fɛr'krʊstət] a encrusted.
ver'kühlen vr get a chill.
ver'kümmern vi waste away.
ver'künden [fɛr'kʏndən] vt proclaim; (*Urteil*) pronounce.
verkürzen [fɛr'kʏrtsən] vt shorten; (*Wort*) abbreviate; sich (*dat*) die Zeit ~ while away the time.
Verkürzung f shortening; abbreviation.
Verlag [fɛr'la:k] m -(e)s, -e publishing firm.
verlangen [fɛr'laŋən] vt demand; desire; ~ Sie Herrn X ask for Mr X // vi: ~ nach ask for, desire; V~ nt -s, - desire (*nach* for); auf jds V~ (hin) at sb's request.
verlängern [fɛr'lɛŋərn] vt extend; (*länger machen*) lengthen.
Verlängerung f extension; (*SPORT*) extra time; **Verlängerungsschnur** f extension cable.
verlangsamen [fɛr'laŋza:mən] vtr decelerate, slow down.
Verlaß [fɛr'las] m: auf ihn/das ist kein ~ he/it cannot be relied upon.
ver'lassen unreg vt leave // vr depend (*auf* +*akk* on) // a desolate; (*Mensch*) abandoned; V~heit f loneliness.
verläßlich [fɛr'lɛslɪç] a reliable.
Verlauf [fɛr'laʊf] m course; v~en unreg vi (*zeitlich*) pass; (*Farben*) run // vr get lost; (*Menschenmenge*) disperse.

ver'lauten vi: etw ~ lassen disclose sth; new verlautet as reported.
ver'legen vt move; (*verlieren*) mislay; (*Buch*) publish // vr: sich auf etw (*akk*) ~ take up od to sth // a embarrassed; nicht ~ um never at a loss for; V~heit f embarrassment; (*Situation*) difficulty, scrape.
Verleger [fɛr'le:gər] m -s, - publisher.
Verleih [fɛr'laɪ] m -(e)s, -e hire service; v~en vt unreg lend; (*Kraft, Anschein*) confer, bestow; (*Preis, Medaille*) award; ~ung f lending; bestowal; award.
ver'leiten vt lead astray; ~ zu talk into, tempt into.
ver'lernen vt forget, unlearn.
ver'lesen unreg vt read out; (*aussondern*) sort out // vr make a mistake in reading.
verletz- [fɛr'lɛts] zW: ~en vt (*lit, fig*) injure, hurt; (*Gesetz etc*) violate; ~end a (*fig: Worte*) hurtful; ~lich a vulnerable, sensitive; ~te(r) mf injured person; V~ung f injury; (*Verstoß*) violation, infringement.
verleumd- [fɛr'lɔʏmd] zW: ~en vt slander; V~ung f slander, libel.
ver'lieben vr fall in love (*in jdn* with sb).
verliebt [fɛr'li:pt] a in love; V~heit f being in love.
verlieren [fɛr'li:rən] unreg vti lose // vr get lost.
verlob- [fɛr'lo:b] zW: ~en vr get engaged (*mit* to); V~te(r) [fɛr'lo:ptə(r)] mf fiancé(e); V~ung f engagement.
ver'locken vt entice, lure.
Ver'lockung f temptation, attraction.
verlogen [fɛr'lo:gən] a untruthful; V~heit f untruthfulness.
verlor etc v siehe **verlieren**.
verloren [fɛr'lo:rən] a lost; (*Eier*) poached; etw ~ geben give sth up for lost // v siehe **verlieren**; ~gehen vi unreg get lost.
verlosen [fɛr'lo:zən] vt raffle, draw lots for.
Verlosung f raffle, lottery.
verlottern [fɛr'lɔtərn], **verludern** [fɛr'lu:dərn] vi (*umg*) go to the dogs.
Verlust [fɛr'lʊst] m -(e)s, -e loss; (*MIL*) casualty.
ver'machen vt bequeath, leave.
Vermächtnis [fɛr'mɛçtnɪs] nt -ses, -se legacy.
Vermählung f wedding, marriage.
vermehren [fɛr'me:rən] vtr multiply; (*Menge*) increase.
Vermehrung f multiplying; increase.
ver'meiden vt unreg avoid.
vermeintlich [fɛr'maɪntlɪç] a supposed.
Vermerk [fɛr'mɛrk] m -(e)s, -e note; (*in Ausweis*) endorsement; v~en vt

note.

ver'messen *unreg vt* survey // *a* presumptuous, bold; **V~heit** *f* presumptuousness; recklessness.

Ver'messung *f* survey(ing).

ver'mieten *vt* let, rent (out); (*Auto*) hire out, rent.

Ver'mieter(in *f*) *m* **-s, -** landlord/landlady.

Ver'mietung *f* letting, renting (out); (*von Autos*) hiring (out).

vermindern [fɛr'mɪndərn] *vtr* lessen, decrease; (*Preise*) reduce.

Verminderung *f* reduction.

ver'mischen *vtr* mix, blend.

vermissen [fɛr'mɪsən] *vt* miss.

vermißt [fɛr'mɪst] *a* missing.

vermitteln [fɛr'mɪtəln] *vi* mediate // *vt* (*Gespräch*) connect; **jdm etw ~** help sb to obtain sth.

Vermittler [fɛr'mɪtlər] *m* **-s, -** (*Schlichter*) agent, mediator.

Vermittlung *f* procurement; (*Stellen~*) agency; (*TEL*) exchange; (*Schlichtung*) mediation.

ver'mögen *vt unreg* be capable of; **~ zu** be able to; **V~** *nt* **-s, -** wealth; (*Fähigkeit*) ability; **ein V~ kosten** cost a fortune; **~d** *a* wealthy.

vermuten [fɛr'muːtən] *vt* suppose, guess; (*argwöhnen*) suspect.

vermutlich *a* supposed, presumed // *ad* probably.

Vermutung *f* supposition; suspicion.

vernachlässigen [fɛr'naːxlɛsɪgən] *vt* neglect.

ver'nehmen *vt unreg* perceive, hear; (*erfahren*) learn; (*JUR*) (cross)-examine; **dem V~ nach** from what I/we *etc* hear.

vernehmlich [fɛr'neːmlɪç] *a* audible.

Vernehmung *f* (cross-)examination.

verneigen [fɛr'naɪgən] *vr* bow.

verneinen [fɛr'naɪnən] *vt* (*Frage*) answer in the negative; (*ablehnen*) deny; (*GRAM*) negate; **~d** *a* negative.

Verneinung *f* negation.

vernichten [fɛr'nɪçtən] *vt* annihilate, destroy; **~d** *a* (*fig*) crushing; (*Blick*) withering; (*Kritik*) scathing.

Vernichtung *f* destruction, annihilation.

verniedlichen [fɛr'niːtlɪçən] *vt* play down.

Vernunft [fɛr'nʊnft] *f* **-** reason, understanding.

vernünftig [fɛr'nʏnftɪç] *a* sensible, reasonable.

veröffentlichen [fɛr''œfəntlɪçən] *vt* publish.

Veröffentlichung *f* publication.

verordnen [fɛr''ɔrdnən] *vt* (*MED*) prescribe.

Verordnung *f* order, decree; (*MED*)

prescription.

ver'pachten *vt* lease (out).

ver'packen *vt* pack.

Ver'packung *f*, **Verpackungsmaterial** *nt* packing, wrapping.

ver'passen *vt* miss; **jdm eine Ohrfeige ~** (*umg*) give sb a clip round the ear.

ver'pflanzen *vt* transplant.

Ver'pflanzung *f* transplant(ing).

ver'pflegen *vt* feed, cater for.

Ver'pflegung *f* feeding, catering; (*Kost*) food; (*in Hotel*) board.

verpflichten [fɛr'pflɪçtən] *vt* oblige, bind; (*anstellen*) engage // *vr* undertake; (*MIL*) sign on // *vi* carry obligations; **jdm zu Dank verpflichtet sein** be obliged to sb.

Verpflichtung *f* obligation, duty.

verpönt [fɛr'pøːnt] *a* disapproved (of), taboo.

ver'prügeln *vt* (*umg*) beat up, do over.

Verputz [fɛr'pʊts] *m* plaster, roughcast; **v~en** *vt* plaster; (*umg: Essen*) put away.

Verrat [fɛr'raːt] *m* **-(e)s** treachery; (*POL*) treason; **v~en** *unreg vt* betray; (*Geheimnis*) divulge // *vr* give o.s. away.

Verräter [fɛr'rɛːtər] *m* **-s, -** traitor; **~in** *f* traitress; **v~isch** *a* treacherous.

ver'rechnen *vt*: **~ mit** set off against // *vr* miscalculate.

Verrechnungsscheck [fɛr'rɛçnʊŋsʃɛk] *m* crossed cheque.

verregnet [fɛr'reːgnət] *a* spoilt by rain, rainy.

ver'reisen *vi* go away (on a journey).

verrenken [fɛr'rɛŋkən] *vt* contort; (*MED*) dislocate; **sich** (*dat*) **den Knöchel ~** sprain one's ankle.

ver'richten *vt* do, perform.

verriegeln [fɛr'riːgəln] *vt* bolt up, lock.

verringern [fɛr'rɪŋərn] *vt* reduce // *vr* diminish.

Verringerung *f* reduction; lessening.

ver'rinnen *vi unreg* run out *od* away; (*Zeit*) elapse.

ver'rosten *vi* rust.

verrotten [fɛr'rɔtən] *vi* rot.

ver'rücken *vt* move, shift.

verrückt [fɛr'rʏkt] *a* crazy, mad; **V~e(r)** *mf* lunatic; **V~heit** *f* madness, lunacy.

Verruf [fɛr'ruːf] *m*: **in ~ geraten/bringen** fall/bring into disrepute; **v~en** *a* notorious, disreputable.

Vers [fɛrs] *m* **-es, -e** verse.

ver'sagen *vt*: **jdm/sich** (*dat*) **etw ~** deny sb/o.s. sth // *vi* fail; **V~** *nt* **-s** failure.

Versager [fɛr'zaːgər] *m* **-s, -** failure.

ver'salzen *vt unreg* put too much salt

in; (fig) spoil.

ver'sammeln vtr assemble, gather.

Ver'sammlung f meeting, gathering.

Versand [fɛr'zant] m -(e)s forwarding; dispatch; (~abteilung) dispatch department; ~haus nt mail-order firm.

versäumen [fɛr'zɔymən] vt miss; (unterlassen) neglect, fail.

ver'schaffen vt: jdm/sich etw ~ get od procure sth for sb/o.s.

verschämt [fɛr'ʃɛːmt] a bashful.

verschandeln [fɛr'ʃandəln] vt (umg) spoil.

verschärfen [fɛr'ʃɛrfən] vtr intensify; (Lage) aggravate.

ver'schätzen vr be out in one's reckoning.

ver'schenken vt give away.

ver'schicken vt send off.

ver'schieben vt unreg shift; (EISENB) shunt; (Termin) postpone.

verschieden [fɛr'ʃiːdən] a different; (pl: mehrere) various; sie sind ~ groß they are of different sizes; ~e pl various people/things pl; ~es pron various things pl; etwas V~es something different; V~heit f difference; **verschiedentlich** ad several times.

verschlafen [fɛr'ʃlaːfən] unreg vt sleep through; (fig: versäumen) miss // vir oversleep // a sleepy.

Verschlag [fɛr'ʃlaːk] m shed; **v~en** [fɛr'ʃlaːgən] vt unreg board up; **jdm den Atem v~en** take sb's breath away; **an einen Ort v~en werden** wind up in a place // a cunning.

verschlechtern [fɛr'ʃlɛçtərn] vt make worse // vr deteriorate, get worse.

Verschlechterung f deterioration.

Verschleiß [fɛr'ʃlais] m -es, -e wear and tear; **v~en** unreg vt wear out.

ver'schleppen vt carry off, abduct; (Krankheit) protract; (zeitlich) drag out.

ver'schleudern vt squander; (COMM) sell dirt-cheap.

verschließ- [fɛr'ʃliːs] zW: ~bar a lockable; ~en unreg vt close; lock // vr: sich einer Sache ~en close one's mind to sth.

verschlimmern [fɛr'ʃlɪmərn] vt make worse, aggravate // vr get worse, deteriorate.

verschlingen [fɛr'ʃlɪŋən] vt unreg devour, swallow up; (Fäden) twist.

verschlossen [fɛr'ʃlɔsən] a locked; (fig) reserved; **V~heit** f reserve.

ver'schlucken vt swallow // vr choke.

Verschluß [fɛr'ʃlʊs] m lock; (von Kleid etc) fastener; (PHOT) shutter; (Stöpsel) plug; **unter ~ halten** keep under lock and key.

verschlüsseln [fɛr'ʃlʏsəln] vt encode.

verschmähen [fɛr'ʃmɛːən] vt disdain, scorn.

verschmerzen [fɛr'ʃmɛrtsən] vt get over.

verschmutzen [fɛr'ʃmʊtsən] vt soil; (Umwelt) pollute.

verschneit [fɛr'ʃnait] a snowed up, covered in snow.

verschollen [fɛr'ʃɔlən] a lost, missing.

ver'schonen vt spare (jdn mit etw sb sth).

verschönern [fɛr'ʃøːnərn] vt decorate; (verbessern) improve.

ver'schreiben unreg vt (MED) prescribe // vr make a mistake (in writing); **sich einer Sache ~** devote oneself to sth.

verschroben [fɛr'ʃroːbən] a eccentric, odd.

verschrotten [fɛr'ʃrɔtən] vt scrap.

verschuld- [fɛr'ʃʊld] zW: ~en vt be guilty of; **V~en** nt -s fault, guilt; ~et a in debt; **V~ung** f fault; (Geld) debts pl.

ver'schütten vt spill; (zuschütten) fill; (unter Trümmer) bury.

ver'schweigen vt unreg keep secret; **jdm etw ~** keep sth from sb.

verschwend- [fɛr'ʃvɛnd] zW: ~en vt squander; **V~er** m -s, - spendthrift; ~erisch a wasteful, extravagant; **V~ung** f waste; extravagance.

verschwiegen [fɛr'ʃviːɡən] a discreet; (Ort) secluded; **V~heit** f discretion; seclusion.

ver'schwimmen vi unreg grow hazy, become blurred.

ver'schwinden vi unreg disappear, vanish; **V~** nt -s disappearance.

verschwommen [fɛr'ʃvɔmən] a hazy, vague.

verschwör- [fɛr'ʃvøːr] zW: ~en vr unreg plot, conspire; **V~er** m -s, - conspirator; **V~ung** f conspiracy, plot.

ver'sehen unreg vt supply, provide; (Pflicht) carry out; (Amt) fill; (Haushalt) keep // vr (fig) make a mistake; **ehe er (es) sich ~ hatte...** before he knew it...; **V~** nt -s, - oversight; **aus V~** by mistake; **versehentlich** ad by mistake.

Versehrte(r) [fɛr'zeːrtə(r)] mf disabled person.

ver'senden vt unreg forward, dispatch.

ver'senken vt sink // vr become engrossed (in +akk in).

versessen [fɛr'zɛsən] a: ~ auf (+akk) mad about.

ver'setzen vt transfer; (verpfänden) pawn; (umg) stand up; **jdm einen Tritt/Schlag ~** kick/hit sb; **etw mit etw ~** mix sth with sth; **jdn in gute Laune ~** put sb in a good mood // vr: **sich in jdn** od **in jds Lage ~** put o.s. in sb's place.

Ver'setzung f transfer.
verseuchen [fɛr'zɔyçən] vt contaminate.
versichern [fɛr'zɪçərn] vt assure; (mit Geld) insure.
Versicherung f assurance; insurance; **Versicherungsgesellschaft** f insurance company; **Versicherungspolice** f insurance policy.
ver'siegen vi dry up.
ver'sinken vi unreg sink.
versöhnen [fɛr'zø:nən] vt reconcile // vr become reconciled.
Versöhnung f reconciliation.
ver'sorgen vt provide, supply (mit with); (Familie etc) look after.
Ver'sorgung f provision; (Unterhalt) maintenance; (Alters~ etc) benefit, assistance.
verspäten [fɛr'ʃpɛ:tən] vr be late.
Verspätung f delay; ~ haben be late.
ver'sperren vt bar, obstruct.
ver'spotten vt ridicule, scoff at.
ver'sprechen vt unreg promise; sich (dat) etw von etw ~ expect sth from sth; **V~** nt -s, - promise.
verstaatlichen [fɛr'ʃta:tlɪçən] vt nationalize.
Verstand [fɛr'ʃtant] m intelligence; mind; den ~ verlieren go out of one's mind; über jds ~ gehen go beyond sb.
verständig [fɛr'ʃtɛndɪç] a sensible; ~en [fɛr'ʃtɛndɪgən] vt inform // vr communicate; (sich einigen) come to an understanding; **V~ung** f communication; (Benachrichtigung) informing; (Einigung) agreement.
verständ- [fɛr'ʃtɛnt] zW: ~lich a understandable, comprehensible; **V~lichkeit** f clarity, intelligibility; **V~nis** nt -ses, -se understanding; ~nislos a uncomprehending; ~nisvoll a understanding, sympathetic.
verstärk- [fɛr'ʃtɛrk] zW: ~en vt strengthen; (Ton) amplify; (erhöhen) intensify // vr intensify; **V~er** m -s, - amplifier; **V~ung** f strengthening; (Hilfe) reinforcements pl; (von Ton) amplification.
verstauchen [fɛr'ʃtauxən] vt sprain.
verstauen [fɛr'ʃtauən] vt stow away.
Versteck [fɛr'ʃtɛk] nt -(e)s, -e hiding (place); **v~en** vtr hide; **v~t** a hidden.
ver'stehen unreg vt understand // vr get on; das versteht sich (von selbst) that goes without saying.
versteigern [fɛr'ʃtaɪgərn] vt auction.
Versteigerung f auction.
verstell- [fɛr'ʃtɛl] zW: ~bar a adjustable, variable; ~en vt move, shift; (Uhr) adjust; (versperren) block; (fig) disguise // vr pretend, put

on an act; **V~ung** f pretence.
verstiegen [fɛr'ʃti:gən] a exaggerated.
verstimmt [fɛr'ʃtɪmt] a out of tune; (fig) cross, put out; (Magen) upset.
verstohlen [fɛr'ʃto:lən] a stealthy.
ver'stopfen vt block, stop up; (MED) constipate.
Ver'stopfung f obstruction; (MED) constipation.
verstorben [fɛr'ʃtɔrbən] a deceased, late.
verstört [fɛr'ʃtø:rt] a (Mensch) distraught.
Verstoß [fɛr'ʃto:s] m infringement, violation (gegen of); **v~en** unreg vt disown, reject // vi: **v~en gegen** offend against.
ver'streichen unreg vt spread // vi elapse.
ver'streuen vt scatter (about).
verstümmeln [fɛr'ʃtʏməln] vt maim, mutilate (auch fig).
verstummen [fɛr'ʃtumən] vi go silent; (Lärm) die away.
Versuch [fɛr'zu:x] m -(e)s, -e attempt; (SCI) experiment; **v~en** vt try; (verlocken) tempt // vr: sich an etw (dat) v~en try one's hand at sth; **Versuchskaninchen** nt guinea-pig; **versuchsweise** ad tentatively; ~ung f temptation.
versumpfen [fɛr'zumpfən] vi (fig umg) get into a booze-up.
versunken [fɛr'zuŋkən] a sunken; ~ sein in (+acc) be absorbed od engrossed in.
vertagen [fɛr'ta:gən] vti adjourn.
ver'tauschen vt exchange; (versehentlich) mix up.
verteidig- [fɛr'taɪdɪç] zW: ~en vt defend; **V~er** m -s, - defender; (JUR) defence counsel; **V~ung** f defence.
ver'teilen vt distribute; (Rollen) assign; (Salbe) spread.
Verteilung f distribution, allotment.
vertiefen [fɛr'ti:fən] vt deepen // vr: sich in etw (akk) ~ become engrossed od absorbed in sth.
Vertiefung f depression.
vertikal [vɛrti'ka:l] a vertical.
vertilgen [fɛr'tɪlgən] vt exterminate; (umg) eat up, consume.
vertonen [fɛr'to:nən] vt set to music.
Vertrag [fɛr'tra:k] m -(e)s, -̈e contract, agreement; (POL) treaty; **v~en** [fɛr'tra:gən] unreg vt tolerate, stand // vr get along; (sich aussöhnen) become reconciled; **v~lich** a contractual.
verträglich [fɛr'trɛ:klɪç] a good-natured, sociable; (Speisen) easily digested; (MED) easily tolerated; **V~keit** f sociability; good nature; digestibility.
Vertrags- zW: ~bruch m breach of

contract; **~partner** m party to a contract; **v~widrig** a contrary to contract.

vertrauen [fɛr'trauən] vi trust (jdm sb); **~ auf** (+akk) rely on; **V~** nt -s confidence; **~erweckend** a inspiring trust; **vertrauensvoll** a trustful; **vertrauenswürdig** a trustworthy.

vertraulich [fɛr'traulıç] a familiar; (geheim) confidential.

vertraut [fɛr'traut] a familiar; **V~heit** f familiarity.

ver'treiben vt unreg drive away; (aus Land) expel; (COMM) sell; (Zeit) pass.

vertret- [fɛr'tre:t] zW: **~en** vt unreg represent; (Ansicht) hold, advocate; **sich** (dat) **die Beine ~en** stretch one's legs; **V~er** m -s, - representative; (Verfechter) advocate; **V~ung** f representation; advocacy.

Vertrieb [fɛr'tri:p] m -(e)s, -e marketing.

ver'trocknen vi dry up.

ver'trösten vt put off.

vertun [fɛr'tu:n] unreg vt (umg) waste // vr make a mistake.

vertuschen [fɛr'tuʃən] vt hush od cover up.

verübeln [fɛr'y:bəln] vt: **jdm etw ~** be cross od offended with sb on account of sth.

verüben [fɛr'y:bən] vt commit.

verun- [fɛr'ʊn] zW: **~glimpfen** [-glımpfən] vt disparage; **~glücken** [-glʏkən] vi have an accident; **tödlich ~glücken** be killed in an accident; **~reinigen** vt soil; (Umwelt) pollute; **~sichern** vt rattle; (fig) unsettle; **~treuen** [-trɔyən] vt embezzle.

verur- [fɛr'u:r] zW: **~sachen** [-zaxən] vt cause; **~teilen** [-taılən] vt condemn; **V~teilung** f condemnation; (JUR) sentence.

verviel- [fɛr'fi:l] zW: **~fachen** [-faxən] vt multiply; **~fältigen** [-fɛltıgən] vt duplicate, copy; **V~fältigung** f duplication, copying.

vervoll- [fɛr'fɔl] zW: **~kommnen** [-kɔmnən] vt perfect; **~ständigen** [-ʃtɛndıgən] vt complete.

ver'wackeln vt (PHOTO) blur.

ver'wählen vr (TEL) dial the wrong number.

verwahr- [fɛr'va:r] **~en** vt keep, lock away // vr protest; **~losen** [-lo:zən] vi become neglected; (moralisch) go to the bad; **~lost** [-lo:st] a neglected; wayward.

verwalt- [fɛr'valt] zW: **~en** vt manage; administer; **V~er** m -s, - manager; (Vermögens~er) trustee; **V~ung** f administration; management; **V~ungsbezirk** m administrative district.

ver'wandeln vtr change, transform.

Ver'wandlung f change, transformation.

verwandt [fɛr'vant] a related (mit to); **V~e(r)** mf relative, relation; **V~schaft** f relationship; (Menschen) relations pl.

ver'warnen vt caution.

Ver'warnung f caution.

ver'wechseln vt confuse (mit with); mistake (mit for); **zum V~ ähnlich** as like as two peas.

Ver'wechslung f confusion, mixing up.

verwegen [fɛr've:gən] a daring, bold.

Verwehung [fɛr've:ʊŋ] f snow-/sanddrift.

verweichlicht [fɛr'vaıçlıçt] a effeminate, soft.

ver'weigern vt refuse (jdm etw sb sth); **den Gehorsam/die Aussage ~** refuse to obey/testify.

Ver'weigerung f refusal.

Verweis [fɛr'vaıs] m -es, -e reprimand, rebuke; (Hinweis) reference; **v~en** [fɛr'vaızən] vt unreg refer; **jdn von der Schule v~en** expel sb (from school); **jdn des Landes v~en** deport od expel sb.

ver'welken vi fade.

ver'wenden unreg vt use; (Mühe, Zeit, Arbeit) spend // vr intercede.

Ver'wendung f use.

ver'werfen vt unreg reject.

verwerflich [fɛr'vɛrflıç] a reprehensible.

ver'werten vt utilize.

Ver'wertung f utilization.

verwesen [fɛr've:zən] vi decay.

ver'wickeln vt tangle (up); (fig) involve (in +akk in) // vr get tangled (up); **sich ~ in** (+acc) (fig) get involved in.

verwildern [fɛr'vıldərn] vi run wild.

ver'winden vt unreg get over.

verwirklichen [fɛr'vırklıçən] vt realize, put into effect.

Verwirklichung f realization.

verwirren [fɛr'vırən] vt tangle (up); (fig) confuse.

Verwirrung f confusion.

verwittern [fɛr'vıtərn] vi weather.

verwitwet [fɛr'vıtvət] a widowed.

verwöhnen [fɛr'vø:nən] vt spoil.

verworfen [fɛr'vɔrfən] a depraved.

verworren [fɛr'vɔrən] a confused.

verwund- zW: **~bar** [fɛr'vuntba:r] a vulnerable; **~en** [fɛr'vundən] vt wound; **~erlich** [fɛr'vundərlıç] a surprising; **V~erung** [fɛr'vundəruŋ] f astonishment; **V~ete(r)** mf injured (person); **V~ung** f wound, injury.

ver'wünschen vt curse.

verwüsten [fɛr'vy:stən] vt devastate.

verzagen [fɛr'tsa:gən] vi despair.

ver'zählen vr miscount.

verzehren [fɛr'tseːrən] vt consume.

ver'zeichnen vt list; (Niederlage, Verlust) register.

Verzeichnis [fɛr'tsaɪçnɪs] nt -ses, -se list, catalogue; (in Buch) index.

verzeih- [fɛr'tsaɪ] zW: ~en vti unreg forgive (jdm etw sb for sth); ~lich a pardonable; **V~ung** f forgiveness, pardon; **V~ung!** sorry!, excuse me!

Verzicht [fɛr'tsɪçt] m -(e)s, -e renunciation (auf +akk of); **v~en** vi forgo, give up (auf etw (acc) sth).

ver'ziehen unreg vi move // vt put out of shape; (Kind) spoil; (Pflanzen) thin out; **das Gesicht ~** pull a face // vr go out of shape; (Gesicht) contort; (verschwinden) disappear.

verzieren [fɛr'tsiːrən] vt decorate, ornament.

verzinsen [fɛr'tsɪnzən] vt pay interest on.

ver'zögern vt delay.

Ver'zögerung f delay, time-lag; **Verzögerungstaktik** f delaying tactics pl.

verzollen [fɛr'tsɔlən] vt declare, pay duty on.

verzück- [fɛr'tsʏk] zW: ~t a enraptured; **V~ung** f ecstasy.

verzweif- [fɛr'tsvaɪf] zW: ~eln vi despair; ~elt a desperate; **V~lung** f despair.

verzwickt [fɛr'tsvɪkt] a (umg) awkward, complicated.

Vesuv [ve'zuːf] m Vesuvius.

Veto ['veːto] nt -s, -s veto.

Vetter ['fɛtər] m -s, -n cousin.

vgl. abk (= vergleiche) cf.

v.H. abk (= vom Hundert) pc.

vibrieren [vi'briːrən] vi vibrate.

Video ['viːdeo] nt video; ~gerät nt, ~recorder m video recorder.

Vieh [fiː] nt -(e)s cattle pl; **v~isch** a bestial.

viel [fiːl] a a lot of, much; ~e pl a lot of, many // ad a lot, much; ~ zuwenig much too little; ~erlei a a great variety of; ~es a a lot; ~fach a, ad many times; **auf ~fachen Wunsch** at the request of many people; **V~falt** f - variety; ~fältig a varied, many-sided.

vielleicht [fi'laɪçt] ad perhaps.

viel- zW: ~mal(s) ad many times; **danke ~mals** many thanks; ~mehr ad rather, on the contrary; ~sagend a significant; ~seitig a many-sided; ~versprechend a promising.

vier [fiːr] num four; **V~eck** nt -(e)s, -e four-sided figure; (gleichseitig) square; ~eckig a four-sided; square; **V~taktmotor** m four-stroke engine; ~te(r, s) ['fɪrtə(r,z)] a fourth; **V~tel** ['fɪrtəl] nt -s, - quarter; ~teljährlich a quarterly; **V~telnote** f crotchet;

V~telstunde [fɪrtəl'ʃtʊndə] f quarter of an hour; ~zehn ['fɪrtseːn] num fourteen; **in ~zehn Tagen** in a fortnight; ~zehntägig a fortnightly; ~zig ['fɪrtsɪç] num forty.

Villa ['vɪla] f -, Villen villa.

violett [vio'lɛt] a violet.

Violin- [vio'liːn] zW: ~e f -, -n violin; ~konzert nt violin concerto; ~schlüssel m treble clef.

Virus ['viːrʊs] m od nt -, Viren virus.

vis-à-vis [viza'viː] ad opposite.

Visier [vi'ziːr] nt -s, -e gunsight; (am Helm) visor.

Visite [vi'ziːtə] f -, -n (MED) visit; **Visitenkarte** f visiting card.

Visum ['viːzʊm] nt -s, Visa od Visen visa.

vital [vi'taːl] a lively, full of life, vital.

Vitamin [vita'miːn] nt -s, -e vitamin.

Vogel ['foːgəl] m -s, ⁺ bird; **einen ~ haben** (umg) have bats in the belfry; **jdm den ~ zeigen** (umg) tap one's forehead (to indicate that one thinks sb stupid); ~bauer nt birdcage; ~scheuche f -, - scarecrow.

Vogesen [vo'geːzən] pl Vosges pl.

Vokabel [vo'kaːbəl] f -, -n word.

Vokabular [vokabu'laːr] nt -s, -e vocabulary.

Vokal [vo'kaːl] m -s, -e vowel.

Volk [fɔlk] nt -(e)s, ⁺er people; nation.

Völker- ['fœlkər] zW: ~recht nt international law; **v~rechtlich** a according to international law; ~verständigung f international understanding.

Volks- zW: ~abstimmung f referendum; **v~eigen** a state-owned; ~fest nt fair; ~hochschule f adult education classes pl; ~lied nt folksong; ~republik f people's republic; **die ~republik China** the People's Republic of China; ~schule f elementary school; ~tanz m folk dance; **v~tümlich** ['fɔlkstyːmlɪç] a popular; ~wirtschaft f economics; ~zählung f (national) census.

voll [fɔl] a full; **etw ~ machen** fill sth up; **~ und ganz** completely; **jdn für ~ nehmen** (umg) take sb seriously; ~auf [fɔl''aʊf] ad amply; **V~bart** m full beard; ~'bringen vt unreg insep accomplish; ~'enden vt unreg finish, complete; **vollends** ['fɔlɛnts] ad completely; **V~'endung** f completion; ~er a fuller; (+gen) full of.

Volleyball ['vɔlibal] m volleyball.

Vollgas nt: **mit ~** at full throttle; **~ geben** step on it.

völlig ['fœlɪç] a, ad complete(ly).

voll- zW: ~jährig a of age; **V~kaskoversicherung** f fully comprehensive insurance; ~'kommen a perfect; **V~'kommenheit** f perfection; **V~kornbrot** nt wholemeal bread; **V~macht** f -, -en authority, full powers pl; **V~mond** m full moon; **V~pension** f full board; **~schlank** a: **Kleidung für V~schlanke** clothes for the fuller figure; **~ständig** a complete; **~'strecken** vt insep execute; **~tanken** vti fill up; **~zählig** a complete; in full number; **~'ziehen** vt unreg insep carry out // vr happen; **V~'zug** m execution.

Volt [vɔlt] nt - od -(e)s, - volt.

Volumen [vo'luːmən] nt -s, - od **Volumina** volume.

vom [fɔm] = **von dem**.

von [fɔn] präp +dat **1** (Ausgangspunkt) from; **~** ... bis from ... to; **~ morgens bis abends** from morning till night; **~** ... **nach** ... from ... to ...; **~** ... **aus** from ...; **~ dort aus** from there; **etw ~ sich aus tun** do sth of one's own accord; **~ mir aus** (umg) if you like, I don't mind; **~ wo/wann** ...? where/when ... from? **2** (Ursache, im Passiv) by; **ein Gedicht ~ Schiller** a poem by Schiller; **~ etw müde** tired from sth **3** (als Genitiv) of; **ein Freund ~ mir** a friend of mine; **nett ~ dir** nice of you; **jeweils zwei ~ zehn** two out of every ten **4** (über) about; **er erzählte vom Urlaub** he talked about his holiday **5**: **~ wegen!** (umg) no way!

vonei'nander [fɔnaɪ'nandər] ad from each other.

vonstatten [fɔn'ʃtatən] ad: **~ gehen** proceed, go.

vor [foːr] ◆präp +dat **1** (räumlich) in front of; **~ der Kirche links abbiegen** turn left before the church **2** (zeitlich) before; **ich war ~ ihm da** I was there before him; **~ 2 Tagen** 2 days ago; **5 (Minuten) ~ 4 5** (minutes) to 4; **~ kurzem** a little while ago **3** (Ursache) with; **~ Wut/Liebe** with rage/love; **~ Hunger sterben** die of hunger; **~ lauter Arbeit** because of work **4**: **~ allem, ~ allen Dingen** most of all ◆präp +akk (räumlich) in front of ◆ad: **~ und zurück** backwards and forwards.

Vorabend ['foːrʔaːbənt] m evening before, eve.

voran [fo'ran] ad before, ahead; **mach ~!** get on with it!; **~gehen** vi unreg go ahead; **einer Sache** (dat) **~gehen** precede sth; **~gehend** a previous; **~kommen** vi unreg come along, make progress.

Vor- ['foːr] zW: **~anschlag** m esti-

mate; **~arbeiter** m foreman.

voraus [fo'raus] ad ahead; (zeitlich) in advance; **jdm ~ sein** be ahead of sb; **im ~** in advance; **~gehen** vi unreg go (on) ahead; (fig) precede; **~haben** vt unreg: **jdm etw ~haben** have the edge on sb in sth; **V~sage** f -, -n prediction; **~sagen** vt predict; **~sehen** vt unreg foresee; **~setzen** vt assume; **~gesetzt, daß** ... provided that ...; **V~setzung** f requirement, prerequisite; **V~sicht** f foresight; **aller V~sicht nach** in all probability; **~sichtlich** ad probably.

Vorbehalt ['foːrbəhalt] m -(e)s, -e reservation, proviso; **v~en** vt unreg: **sich/jdm etw ~** reserve sth (for o.s.)/for sb; **v~los** a, ad unconditional(ly).

vorbei [foːr'baɪ] ad by, past; **das ist ~** that's over; **~gehen** vi unreg pass by, go past.

vorbe- zW: **~lastet** ['foːrbəlastət] a (fig) handicapped; **~reiten** ['foːrbəraɪtən] vt prepare; **V~reitung** f preparation; **~straft** ['foːrbəʃtraft] a previously convicted, with a record.

vorbeugen ['foːrbɔygən] vtr lean forward // vi prevent (einer Sache (dat) sth); **~d** a preventive.

Vorbeugung f prevention; **zur ~ gegen** for the prevention of.

Vorbild ['foːrbɪlt] nt model; **sich** (dat) **jdn zum ~ nehmen** model o.s. on sb; **v~lich** a model, ideal.

vorbringen ['foːrbrɪŋən] vt unreg advance, state.

Vorder- ['fɔrdər] zW: **~achse** f front axle; **~asien** nt the Near East; **v~e(r, s)** a front; **~grund** m foreground; **v~hand** ad for the present; **~mann** m, pl **-männer** man in front; **jdn auf ~mann bringen** (umg) get sb to shape up; **~seite** f front (side); **v~ste(r, s)** a front.

vordrängen ['foːrdrɛŋən] vr push to the front.

voreilig ['foːrʔaɪlɪç] a hasty, rash.

voreingenommen ['foːrʔaɪŋənɔmən] a biased; **V~heit** f bias.

vorenthalten ['foːrʔɛnthaltən] vt unreg: **jdm etw ~** withhold sth from sb.

vorerst ['foːrʔeːrst] ad for the moment od present.

Vorfahr ['foːrfaːr] m -en, -en ancestor; **v~en** vi unreg drive (on) ahead; (vors Haus etc) drive up.

Vorfahrt f (AUT) right of way; **~ achten!** give way!

Vorfahrts- zW: **~regel** f right of way; **~schild** nt give way sign; **~straße** f major road.

Vorfall ['foːrfal] m incident; **v~en** vi unreg occur.

vorfinden ['foːrfɪndən] vt unreg find.

vorführen ['fo:rfy:rən] *vt* show, display; **dem Gericht** ~ bring before the court.

Vorgabe ['fo:rga:bə] *f* (*SPORT*) start, handicap; **Vorgabe-** *in zW* (*COMPUT*) default.

Vorgang ['fo:rgaŋ] *m* course of events; (*bes SCI*) process.

Vorgänger(in *f*) ['fo:rgɛŋər(ɪn)] *m* **-s**, **-** predecessor.

vorgeben ['fo:rge:bən] *vt unreg* pretend, use as a pretext; (*SPORT*) give an advantage *od* a start of.

vorge- ['fo:rgə] *zW:* ~**faßt** [-fast] *a* preconceived; ~**fertigt** [-fɛrtɪçt] *a* prefabricated.

vorgehen ['fo:rge:ən] *vi unreg* (*voraus*) go (on) ahead; (*nach vorn*) go up front; (*handeln*) act, proceed; (*Uhr*) be fast; (*Vorrang haben*) take precedence; (*passieren*) go on; **V~** *nt* **-s** action.

Vorgeschmack ['fo:rgəʃmak] *m* foretaste.

Vorgesetzte(r) ['fo:rgəzɛtstə(r)] *mf* superior.

vorgestern ['fo:rgɛstərn] *ad* the day before yesterday.

vorhaben ['fo:rha:bən] *vt unreg* intend; **hast du schon was vor?** have you got anything on?; **V~** *nt* **-s**, **-** intention.

vorhalten ['fo:rhaltən] *unreg vt* hold *od* put up; (*fig*) reproach (*jdm etw sb* for sth) // *vi* last.

Vorhaltung *f* reproach.

vorhanden [fo:r'handən] *a* existing; (*erhältlich*) available.

Vorhang ['fo:rhaŋ] *m* curtain.

Vorhängeschloß ['fo:rhɛŋəʃlɔs] *nt* padlock.

vorher [fo:r'he:r] *ad* before(hand); ~**bestimmen** *vt* (*Schicksal*) preordain; ~**gehen** *vi unreg* precede; ~**ig** [fo:r'he:rɪç] *a* previous.

Vorherrschaft ['fo:rhɛrʃaft] *f* predominance, supremacy.

vorherrschen ['fo:rhɛrʃən] *vi* predominate.

vorher- [fo:r'he:r] *zW:* **V~sage** *f* **-**, **-n** forecast; ~**sagen** *vt* forecast, predict; ~**sehbar** *a* predictable; ~**sehen** *vt unreg* foresee.

vorhin [fo:r'hɪn] *ad* not long ago, just now; **vorhinein** ['fo:rhɪnaɪn] *ad:* **im vorhinein** beforehand.

vorig ['fo:rɪç] *a* previous, last.

Vorkaufsrecht ['fo:rkaʊfsrɛçt] *nt* option to buy.

Vorkehrung ['fo:rke:rʊŋ] *f* precaution.

vorkommen ['fo:rkɔmən] *vi unreg* come forward; (*geschehen, sich finden*) occur; (*scheinen*) seem (to be); **sich** (*dat*) **dumm** *etc* ~ feel stupid *etc*; **V~** *nt* **-s**, **-** occurrence.

Vorkriegs- ['fo:rkri:ks] *in zW* prewar.

Vorladung ['fo:rla:dʊŋ] *f* summons.

Vorlage ['fo:rla:gə] *f* model, pattern; (*Gesetzes~*) bill; (*SPORT*) pass.

vorlassen ['fo:rlasən] *vt unreg* admit; (*vorgehen lassen*) allow to go in front.

vorläufig ['fo:rlɔyfɪç] *a* temporary, provisional.

vorlaut ['fo:rlaʊt] *a* impertinent, cheeky.

vorlesen ['fo:rle:zən] *vt unreg* read (out).

Vorlesung *f* (*UNIV*) lecture.

vorletzte(r, s) ['fo:rlɛtstə(r, s)] *a* last but one.

Vorliebe ['fo:rli:bə] *f* preference, partiality.

vorliebnehmen [fo:r'li:pne:mən] *vi unreg:* ~ **mit** make do with.

vorliegen ['fo:rli:gən] *vi unreg* be (here); **etw liegt jdm vor** sb has sth; ~**d** *a* present, at issue.

vormachen ['fo:rmaxən] *vt:* **jdm etw** ~ show sb how to do sth; (*fig*) fool sb; have sb on.

Vormachtstellung ['fo:rmaxtʃtɛlʊŋ] *f* supremacy, hegemony.

Vormarsch ['fo:rmarʃ] *m* advance.

vormerken ['fo:rmɛrkən] *vt* book.

Vormittag ['fo:rmɪta:k] *m* morning; **v~s** *ad* in the morning, before noon.

Vormund ['fo:rmʊnt] *m* **-(e)s**, **-e** *od* **-münder** guardian.

vorn(e) ['fɔrn(ə)] *ad* in front; **von** ~ **anfangen** start at the beginning; **nach** ~ to the front.

Vorname ['fo:rna:mə] *m* first or Christian name.

vornehm ['fo:rne:m] *a* distinguished; refined; elegant; ~**en** *vt unreg* (*fig*) carry out; **sich** (*dat*) **etw** ~**en** start on sth; (*beschließen*) decide to do sth; **sich** (*dat*) **jdn** ~**en** tell sb off; ~**lich** *ad* chiefly, specially.

vornherein ['fɔrnhɛraɪn] *ad:* **von** ~ from the start.

Vorort ['fo:r'ɔrt] *m* suburb.

Vorrang ['fo:rraŋ] *m* precedence, priority; **v~ig** *a* of prime importance, primary.

Vorrat ['fo:rra:t] *m* stock, supply; **Vorratskammer** *f* pantry.

vorrätig ['fo:rrɛ:tɪç] *a* in stock.

Vorrecht ['fo:rrɛçt] *nt* privilege.

Vorrichtung ['fo:rrɪçtʊŋ] *f* device, contrivance.

vorrücken ['fo:rrʏkən] *vi* advance // *vt* move forward.

Vorsatz ['fo:rzats] *m* intention; (*JUR*) intent; **einen** ~ **fassen** make a resolution.

vorsätzlich ['fo:rzɛtslɪç] *a, ad* intentional(ly); (*JUR*) premeditated.

Vorschau ['fo:rʃaʊ] *f* (*RAD, TV*) (pro-

gramme) preview; (*Film*) trailer.
Vorschlag ['foːrʃlaːk] *m* suggestion, proposal; **v~en** *vt unreg* suggest, propose.
vorschnell ['foːrʃnɛl] *ad* hastily, too quickly.
vorschreiben ['foːrʃraibən] *vt unreg* prescribe, specify.
Vorschrift ['foːrʃrɪft] *f* regulation(s); rule(s); (*Anweisungen*) instruction(s); (*Dienst nach* ~ work-to-rule; **vorschriftsmäßig** *a* as per regulations/instructions.
Vorschuß ['foːrʃʊs] *m* advance.
vorsehen ['foːrzeːən] *unreg vt* provide for, plan // *vr* take care, be careful // *vi* be visible.
Vorsehung *f* providence.
vorsetzen ['foːrzɛtsən] *vt* move forward; (*vor etw*) put in front; (*anbieten*) offer.
Vorsicht ['foːrzɪçt] *f* caution, care; ~! look out!, take care!; (*auf Schildern*) caution!, danger!; ~, **Stufe!** mind the step!; **v~ig** *a* cautious, careful; **vorsichtshalber** *ad* just in case.
Vorsilbe ['foːrzɪlbə] *f* prefix.
Vorsitz ['foːrzɪts] *m* chair(manship); **~ende(r)** *mf* chairman/-woman.
Vorsorge ['foːrzɔrgə] *f* precaution(s), provision(s); **v~n** *vi*: **v~n für** make provision(s) for; **v~untersuchung** *f* check-up.
vorsorglich ['foːrzɔrklɪç] *ad* as a precaution.
Vorspeise ['foːrʃpaizə] *f* hors d'oeuvre, appetizer.
Vorspiel ['foːrʃpiːl] *nt* prelude.
vorsprechen ['foːrʃprɛçən] *unreg vt* say out loud, recite // *vi*: **bei jdm** ~ call on sb.
Vorsprung ['foːrʃprʊŋ] *m* projection, ledge; (*fig*) advantage, start.
Vorstadt ['foːrʃtat] *f* suburbs *pl*.
Vorstand ['foːrʃtant] *m* executive committee; (*COMM*) board (of directors); (*Person*) director, head.
vorstehen ['foːrʃteːən] *vi unreg* project; **etw** (*dat*) ~ (*fig*) be the head of sth.
vorstell- ['foːrʃtɛl] *zW*: **~bar** *a* conceivable; **~en** *vt* put forward; (*vor etw*) put in front; (*bekannt machen*) introduce; (*darstellen*) represent; **sich** (*dat*) **etw ~en** imagine sth; **V~ung** *f* (*Bekanntmachen*) introduction; (*THEAT etc*) performance; (*Gedanke*) idea, thought.
Vorstrafe ['foːrʃtraːfə] *f* previous conviction.
Vortag ['foːrtaːk] *m* day before (*einer Sache* sth).
vortäuschen ['foːrtɔyʃən] *vt* feign, pretend.
Vorteil ['fɔrtail] *m* **-s, -e** advantage

(*gegenüber* over); **im** ~ **sein** have the advantage; **v~haft** *a* advantageous.
Vortrag ['foːrtraːk] *m* **-(e)s, Vorträge** talk, lecture; **v~en** *vt unreg* carry forward; (*fig*) recite; (*Rede*) deliver; (*Lied*) perform; (*Meinung etc*) express.
vortrefflich [foːrtrɛflɪç] *a* excellent.
vortreten ['foːrtreːtən] *vi unreg* step forward; (*Augen etc*) protrude.
vorüber [fo'ryːbər] *ad* past, over; **~gehen** *vi unreg* pass (by); **~gehen an** (+*dat*) (*fig*) pass over; **~gehend** *a* temporary, passing.
Vorurteil ['foːr'ʊrtail] *nt* prejudice.
Vorverkauf ['foːrfɛrkaʊf] *m* advance booking.
Vorwahl ['foːrvaːl] *f* preliminary election; (*TEL*) dialling code.
Vorwand ['foːrvant] *m* **-(e)s, Vorwände** pretext.
vorwärts ['foːrvɛrts] *ad* forward; **V~gang** *m* (*AUT etc*) forward gear; **~gehen** *vi unreg* progress; **~kommen** *vi unreg* get on, make progress.
vorweg [foːr'vɛk] *ad* in advance; **V~nahme** *f* **-, -n** anticipation; **~nehmen** *vt unreg* anticipate.
vorweisen ['foːrvaizən] *vt unreg* show, produce.
vorwerfen ['foːrvɛrfən] *vt unreg*: **jdm etw** ~ reproach sb for sth, accuse sb of sth; **sich** (*dat*) **nichts vorzuwerfen haben** have nothing to reproach o.s. with.
vorwiegend ['foːrviːgənt] *a, ad* predominant(ly).
Vorwort ['foːrvɔrt] *nt* **-(e)s, -e** preface.
Vorwurf ['foːrvʊrf] *m* reproach; **jdm/ sich Vorwürfe machen** reproach sb/ o.s.; **vorwurfsvoll** *a* reproachful.
vorzeigen ['foːrtsaigən] *vt* show, produce.
vorzeitig ['ɪoːrtsaitɪç] *a* premature.
vorziehen ['foːrtsiːən] *vt unreg* pull forward; (*Gardinen*) draw; (*lieber haben*) prefer.
Vorzug ['foːrtsuːk] *m* preference; (*gute Eigenschaft*) merit, good quality; (*Vorteil*) advantage.
vorzüglich [foːr'tsyːklɪç] *a* excellent.
vulgär [vʊl'gɛːr] *a* vulgar.
Vulkan [vʊl'kaːn] *m* **-s, -e** volcano.

W

W, w [veː] *nt* W, w.
Waage ['vaːgə] *f* **-, -n** scales *pl*; (*ASTROL*) Libra; **w~recht** *a* horizontal.
Wabe ['vaːbə] *f* **-, -n** honeycomb.
wach [vax] *a* awake; (*fig*) alert; **W~e**

f -, **-n** guard, watch; **W~e halten** keep watch; **W~e stehen** stand guard; **~en** *vi* be awake; (*W~e halten*) guard.

Wacholder [va'xɔldər] *m* **-s,** - juniper.

Wachs [vaks] *nt* **-es, -e** wax.

wachsam ['vaxza:m] *a* watchful, vigilant, alert; **W~keit** *f* vigilance.

Wachs- *zW*: **w~en** *vi unreg* grow // *vt* (*Skier*) wax; **~tuch** *nt* oilcloth; **~tum** *nt* **-s** growth.

Wächter ['veçtər] *m* **-s,** - guard, warden, keeper; (*Parkplatz~*) attendant.

wackel- ['vakəl] *zW*: **~ig** *a* shaky, wobbly; **W~kontakt** *m* loose connection; **~n** *vi* shake; (*fig: Position*) be shaky.

wacker ['vakər] *a* valiant, stout // *ad* well, bravely.

Wade ['va:də] *f* -, **-n** (*ANAT*) calf.

Waffe ['vafə] *f* -, **-n** weapon.

Waffel *f* -, **-n** waffle; wafer.

Waffen- *zW*: **~schein** *m* gun licence; **~schieber** *m* gun-runner; **~stillstand** *m* armistice, truce.

Wagemut ['va:gəmu:t] *m* daring.

wagen ['va:gən] *vt* venture, dare.

Wagen ['va:gən] *m* **-s,** - vehicle; (*Auto*) car; (*EISENB*) carriage; (*Pferde~*) cart; **~heber** *m* **-s,** - jack.

Waggon [va'gõː] *m* **-s, -s** carriage; (*Güter~*) goods van, freight truck (*US*).

waghalsig ['va:khalzɪç] *a* foolhardy.

Wagnis ['va:knɪs] *nt* **-ses, -se** risk.

Wahl [va:l] *f* -, **-en** choice; (*POL*) election; **zweite ~** seconds *pl*.

wähl- ['vɛ:l] *zW*: **~bar** *a* eligible; **~en** *vti* choose; (*POL*) elect, vote (for); (*TEL*) dial; **W~er(in** *f*) *m* **-s,** - voter; **~erisch** *a* fastidious, particular.

Wahl- *zW*: **~fach** *nt* optional subject; **~gang** *m* ballot; **~kabine** *f* polling booth; **~kampf** *m* election campaign; **~kreis** *m* constituency; **~lokal** *nt* polling station; **w~los** *ad* at random; **~recht** *nt* franchise; **~spruch** *m* motto; **~urne** *f* ballot box.

Wahn [va:n] *m* **-(e)s** delusion; folly; **~sinn** *m* madness; **w~sinnig** *a* insane, mad // *ad* (*umg*) incredibly.

wahr [va:r] *a* true; **~en** *vt* maintain, keep.

während ['vɛ:rənd] *präp* +*gen* during // *kj* while; **~dessen** [vɛ:rənt'dɛsən] *ad* meanwhile.

wahr- *zW*: **~haben** *vt unreg*: etw nicht **~haben wollen** refuse to admit sth; **~haft** *ad* (*tatsächlich*) truly; **~haftig** [va:r'haftɪç] *a* true, real // *ad* really; **W~heit** *f* truth; **~nehmen** *vt unreg* perceive, observe; **W~nehmung** *f* perception; **~sagen** *vi* prophesy, tell fortunes; **W~sager(in** *f*) *m* **-s,** - fortune teller.

~scheinlich [va:r'ʃaɪnlɪç] *a* probable // *ad* probably; **W~'scheinlichkeit** *f* probability; **aller W~scheinlichkeit nach** in all probability; **W~zeichen** *nt* emblem.

Währung ['vɛ:rʊŋ] *f* currency.

Waise ['vaɪzə] *f* -, **-n** orphan; **Waisenhaus** *nt* orphanage.

Wald [valt] *m* **-(e)s,** ̈**er** wood(s); (*groß*) forest; **~sterben** *nt* dying of trees due to pollution.

Wal(fisch) ['va:l(fɪʃ)] *m* **-(e)s, -e** whale.

Wall [val] *m* **-(e)s,** ̈**e** embankment; (*Bollwerk*) rampart; **w~fahren** *vi unreg insep* go on a pilgrimage; **~fahrer(in** *f*) *m* pilgrim; **~fahrt** *f* pilgrimage.

Wal- *zW*: **~nuß** *f* walnut; **~roß** *nt* walrus.

Walze ['valtsə] *f* -, **-n** (*Gerät*) cylinder; (*Fahrzeug*) roller; **w~n** *vt* roll (out).

wälzen ['vɛltsən] *vt* roll (over); (*Bücher*) hunt through; (*Probleme*) deliberate on // *vr* wallow; (*vor Schmerzen*) roll about; (*im Bett*) toss and turn.

Walzer ['valtsər] *m* **-s,** - waltz.

Wand [vant] *f* -, ̈**e** wall; (*Trenn~*) partition; (*Berg~*) precipice.

Wandel ['vandəl] *m* **-s** change; **w~bar** *a* changeable, variable; **w~n** *vtr* change // *vi* (*gehen*) walk.

Wander- ['vandər] *zW*: **~er** *m* **-s,** - hiker, rambler; **w~n** *vi* hike; (*Blick*) wander; (*Gedanken*) stray; **~schaft** *f* travelling; **~ung** *f* walking tour, hike.

Wandlung *f* change, transformation.

Wange ['vaŋə] *f* -, **-n** cheek.

wankelmütig ['vaŋkəlmy:tɪç] *a* vacillating, inconstant.

wanken ['vankən] *vi* stagger; (*fig*) waver.

wann [van] *ad* when.

Wanne ['vanə] *f* -, **-n** tub.

Wanze ['vantsə] *f* -, **-n** bug.

Wappen ['vapən] *nt* **-s,** - coat of arms, crest; **~kunde** *f* heraldry.

war *etc v siehe* **sein**.

Ware ['va:rə] *f* -, **-n** ware.

Waren- *zW*: **~haus** *nt*: department store; **~lager** *nt* stock, store; **~probe** *f* sample; **~zeichen** *nt*: (eingetragenes) **~zeichen** (registered) trademark.

warf *etc v siehe* **werfen**.

warm [varm] *a* warm; (*Essen*) hot.

Wärm- ['vɛrm] *zW*: **~e** *f* -, **-n** warmth; **w~en** *vtr* warm, heat; **~flasche** *f* hot-water bottle.

warnen ['varnən] *vt* warn.

Warnung *f* warning.

Warschau ['varʃaʊ] *nt* Warsaw; **~er**

Pakt Warsaw Pact.

warten ['vartən] *vi* wait (*auf +akk* for); **auf sich ~ lassen** take a long time.

Wärter(in *f)* ['vɛrtər(ɪn)] *m* **-s, -** attendant.

Warte- ['vartə] *zW:* **~raum, ~saal** *m* (*EISENB*), **~zimmer** *nt* waiting room.

Wartung *f* servicing; service; **~ und Instandhaltung** maintenance.

warum [va'rʊm] *ad* why.

Warze ['vartsə] *f* **-, -n** wart.

was [vas] *pron* what; (*umg:* etwas) something; **~ für (ein)** ... what sort of ....

Wasch- ['vaʃ] *zW:* **w~bar** *a* washable; **~becken** *nt* washbasin; **w~echt** *a* colourfast; (*fig*) genuine.

Wäsche ['vɛʃə] *f* **-, -n** wash(ing); (*Bett~*) linen; (*Unter~*) underclothing; **~klammer** *f* clothes peg (*Brit*), clothespin (*US*); **~leine** *f* washing line (*Brit*), clothesline (*US*).

waschen ['vaʃən] *unreg vti* wash // *vr* (have a) wash; **sich** (*dat*) **die Hände ~** wash one's hands.

Wäsche'rei *f* laundry.

Wasch- *zW:* **~küche** *f* laundry room; **~lappen** *m* face flannel, washcloth (*US*); (*umg*) sissy; **~maschine** *f* washing machine; **~mittel** *nt*, **~pulver** *nt* detergent, washing powder; **~raum** *m* washroom.

Wasser ['vasər] *nt* **-s, -** water; **~ball** *m* water polo; **w~dicht** *a* waterproof; **~fall** *m* waterfall; **~farbe** *f* watercolour; **w~gekühlt** *a* (*AUT*) water-cooled; **~hahn** *m* tap, faucet (*US*); **~kraftwerk** *nt* hydroelectric power station; **~leitung** *f* water pipe; **~mann** *n* (*ASTROL*) Aquarius.

wässern ['vɛsərn] *vti* water.

Wasser- *zW:* **w~scheu** *a* afraid of the water; **~ski** *nt* water-skiing; **~stoff** *m* hydrogen; **~stoffbombe** *f* hydrogen bomb; **~waage** *f* spirit level; **~zeichen** *nt* watermark.

wäßrig ['vɛsriç] *a* watery.

waten ['va:tən] *vi* wade.

watscheln ['va:tʃəln] *vi* waddle.

Watt [vat] *nt* **-(e)s, -en** mud flats *pl* // *nt* **-s, -** (*ELEK*) watt; **~e** *f* **-, -n** cotton wool, absorbent cotton (*US*).

WC ['ve:'tse:] *nt abk* (= *water closet*) WC.

Web- ['ve:b] *zW:* **w~en** *vt unreg* weave; **~er** *m* **-s, -** weaver; **~e'rei** *f* (*Betrieb*) weaving mill; **~stuhl** *m* loom.

Wechsel ['vɛksəl] *m* **-s, -** change; (*COMM*) bill of exchange; **~beziehung** *f* correlation; **~geld** *nt* change; **w~haft** *a* (*Wetter*) variable; **~jahre** *pl* change of life; **~kurs** *m* rate of exchange; **w~n** *vt* change;

(*Blicke*) exchange // *vi* change; vary; (*Geld w~n*) have change; **~sprechanlage** two-way intercom; **~strom** *m* alternating current; **~stube** *f* bureau de change; **~wirkung** *f* interaction.

wecken ['vɛkən] *vt* wake (up); call.

Wecker ['vɛkər] *m* **-s, -** alarm clock.

wedeln ['ve:dəln] *vi* (*mit Schwanz*) wag; (*mit Fächer etc*) wave.

weder ['ve:dər] *kj* neither; **~ ... noch** ... neither ... nor ...

weg [vɛk] *ad* away, off; **über etw** (*akk*) **~ sein** be over sth; **er war schon ~** he had already left; **Finger ~!** hands off!; **W~** [ve:k] *m* **-(e)s, -e** way; (*Pfad*) path; (*Route*) route; **sich auf den W~ machen** be on one's way; **jdm aus dem W~ gehen** keep out of sb's way; **W~bereiter** *m* **-s, -** pioneer; **~bleiben** *vi unreg* stay away.

wegen ['ve:gən] *präp +gen od* (*umg*) *dat* because of.

weg- ['vɛk] *zW:* **~fahren** *vi unreg* drive away; leave; **~fallen** *vi unreg* be left out; (*Ferien, Bezahlung*) be cancelled; (*aufhören*) cease; **~gehen** *vi unreg* go away; leave; **~lassen** *vt unreg* leave out; **~laufen** *vi unreg* run away od off; **~legen** *vt* put aside; **~machen** *vt* (*umg*) get rid of; **~müssen** *vi unreg* (*umg*) have to go; **~nehmen** *vt unreg* take away; **~tun** *vt unreg* put away; **W~weiser** ['ve:gvaɪzər] *m* **-s, -** road sign, signpost; **~werfen** *vt unreg* throw away; **~werfend** *a* disparaging; **W~werfgesellschaft** *f* throw-away society.

weh [ve:] *a* sore; **~ tun** hurt, be sore; **jdm/sich ~ tun** hurt sb/o.s.; **~(e)** *interj:* **~(e),** wenn du... woe betide you if...; **o ~!** oh dear!; **~e!** just you dare!; **~en** *vti* blow; (*Fahnen*) flutter; **W~en** *pl* (*MED*) labour pains *pl*; **~leidig** *a* whiny, whining; **W~mut** *f* - melancholy; **~mütig** *a* melancholy.

Wehr [ve:r] *nt* **-(e)s, -e** weir // *f:* **sich zur ~ setzen** defend o.s.; **~dienst** *m* military service; **w~en** *vr* defend o.s.; **w~los** *a* defenceless; **~pflicht** *f* compulsory military service; **w~pflichtig** *a* liable for military service.

Weib [vaɪp] *nt* **-(e)s, -er** woman, female; wife; **~chen** *nt* female; **w~lich** *a* feminine.

weich [vaɪç] *a* soft; **W~e** *f* **-, -n** (*EISENB*) points *pl*; **~en** *vi unreg* yield, give way; **W~heit** *f* softness; **~lich** *a* soft, namby-pamby; **W~ling** *m* weakling.

Weide ['vaɪdə] *f* **-, -n** (*Baum*) willow; (*Gras*) pasture; **w~n** *vi* graze // *vr:* **sich an etw** (*dat*) **w~n** delight in sth.

weidlich ['vaɪtlɪç] *ad* thoroughly.
weigern ['vaɪgərn] *vr* refuse.
Weigerung ['vaɪgərʊŋ] *f* refusal.
Weih- ['vaɪ] *zW:* **~e** *f* -, **-n** consecration; (*Priester~*) ordination; **w~en** *vt* consecrate; ordain; **~er** *m* **-s,** - pond; **~nachten** *nt* -, - Christmas; **w~nachtlich** *a* Christmas; **~nachtsabend** *m* Christmas Eve; **~nachtslied** *nt* Christmas carol; **~nachtsmann** *m* Father Christmas, Santa Claus; **~nachtstag** *m* Christmas Day; **zweiter ~nachtstag** *m* Boxing Day; **~rauch** *m* incense; **~wasser** *nt* holy water.
weil [vaɪl] *kj* because.
Weile ['vaɪlə] *f* - while, short time.
Wein [vaɪn] *m* **-(e)s,** **-e** wine; (*Pflanze*) vine; **~bau** *m* cultivation of vines; **~beere** *f* grape; **~berg** *m* vineyard; **~bergschnecke** *f* snail; **~brand** *m* brandy; **w~en** *vti* cry; **das ist zum ~en** it's enough to make you cry *od* weep; **~karte** *f* wine list; **~lese** *f* vintage; **~rebe** *f* vine; **~stock** *m* vine; **~traube** *f* grape.
weise ['vaɪzə] *a* wise; **W~(r)** *mf* wise old man/woman, sage.
Weise ['vaɪzə] *f* -, **-n** manner, way; (*Lied*) tune; **auf diese ~** in this way; **w~n** *vt unreg* show.
Weisheit ['vaɪshaɪt] *f* wisdom; **Weisheitszahn** *m* wisdom tooth.
weiß [vaɪs] *a* white // *v siehe* **wissen**; **W~brot** *nt* white bread; **~en** *vt* whitewash; **W~glut** *f* (*TECH*) incandescence; **jdn bis zur W~glut bringen** (*fig*) make sb see red; **W~kohl** *m* (white) cabbage; **W~wein** *m* white wine.
weit [vaɪt] *a* wide; (*Begriff*) broad; (*Reise, Wurf*) long; **wie ~ ist es ...?** how far is it ...?; **in ~er Ferne** in the far distance; **das geht zu ~** that's going too far // *ad* far; **~aus** *ad* by far; **~blickend** *a* far-seeing; **W~e** *f* -, **-n** width; (*Raum*) space; (*von Entfernung*) distance; **~en** *vtr* widen.
weiter ['vaɪtər] *a* wider; broader; farther (away); (*zusätzlich*) further; **ohne ~es** without further ado; just like that // *ad* further; **~ nichts/ niemand** nothing/nobody else; **~arbeiten** *vi* go on working; **~empfehlen** *vt unreg* recommend (to others); **W~fahrt** *f* continuation of the journey; **~gehen** *vi unreg* go on; **~hin** *ad:* **etw ~hin tun** go on doing sth; **~leiten** *vt* pass on; **~machen** *vti* continue.
weit- *zW:* **~gehend** *a* considerable // *ad* largely; **~läufig** *a* (*Gebäude*) spacious; (*Erklärung*) lengthy; (*Verwandter*) distant; **~schweifig** *a* longwinded; **~sichtig** *a* (*MED*) long-

sighted; (*fig*) far-sighted; **W~sprung** *m* long jump; **~verbreitet** *a* widespread; **W~winkelobjektiv** *nt* (*PHOT*) wide-angle lens.
Weizen ['vaɪtsn] *m* **-s,** - wheat.
welche(r, s) ['vɛlçə(r, s)] ◆*interrog pron* which; **~r von beiden?** which (one) of the two?; **~n hast du genommen?** which (one) did you take?; **welch eine ... what a ...!;** **~ Freude!** what joy!
◆*indef pron* some; (*in Fragen*) any; **ich habe ~** I have some; **haben Sie ~?** do you have any?
◆*rel pron* (*bei Menschen*) who; (*bei Sachen*) which, that; **~(r, s) auch immer** whoever/whichever/whatever.
welk [vɛlk] *a* withered; **~en** *vi* wither.
Well- [vɛl] *zW:* **~blech** *nt* corrugated iron; **~e** *f* -, **-n** wave; (*TECH*) shaft.
Wellen- *zW:* **~bereich** *m* waveband; **~länge** *f* (*lit, fig*) wavelength; **~sittich** *m* budgerigar.
Welt [vɛlt] *f* -, **-en** world; **~all** *nt* universe; **~anschauung** *f* philosophy of life; **w~berühmt** *a* world-famous; **w~fremd** *a* unworldly; **~krieg** *m* world war; **w~lich** *a* worldly; (*nicht kirchlich*) secular; **~macht** *f* world power; **~meister** *m* world champion; **~meisterschaft** *f* world championships *pl;* **~raum** *m* space; **~reise** *f* trip round the world; **~stadt** *f* metropolis; **w~weit** *a* world-wide.
wem [ve:m] *pron* (*dat*) to whom.
wen [ve:n] *pron* (*akk*) who.
Wende ['vɛndə] *f* -, **-n** turn; (*Veränderung*) change; **~kreis** *m* (*GEOG*) tropic; (*AUT*) turning circle; **Wendeltreppe** *f* spiral staircase; **w~n** *vtir unreg* turn; **sich an jdn w~n** go/come to sb; **~punkt** *m* turning point.
Wendung *f* turn; (*Rede~*) idiom.
wenig ['ve:nɪç] *a, ad* little; **~e** ['ve:nɪgə] *pl* few *pl;* **~er** *a* less; (*mit pl*) fewer // *ad* less; **~ste(r, s)** *a* least; **am ~sten** least; **~stens** *ad* at least.
wenn [vɛn] *kj* **1** (*falls, bei Wünschen*) if; **~ auch ..., selbst ~ ...** even if ...; **~ ich doch ...** if only I ...
2 (*zeitlich*) when; **immer ~** whenever.
wennschon ['vɛnʃoːn] *ad:* **na ~** so what?; **~, dennschon!** in for a penny, in for a pound.
wer [ve:r] *pron* who.
Werbe- ['vɛrbə] *zW:* **~fernsehen** *nt* commercial television; **w~n** *unreg vt* win; (*Mitglied*) recruit // *vi* advertise; **um jdn/etw w~n** try to win sb/ sth; **für jdn/etw w~n** promote sb/sth; **~spot** *m* TV ad(vertisement).
Werbung *f* advertising; (*von Mitgliedern*) recruitment; (*um jdn/etw*) pro-

motion (um of).

werden ['ve:rdən] ◆vi pt **wurde**, ptp **geworden** become; **was ist aus ihm/ aus der Sache geworden?** what became of him/it?; **es ist nichts/gut geworden** it came to nothing/turned out well; **es wird Nacht/Tag** it's getting dark/light; **mir wird kalt** I'm getting cold; **mir wird schlecht** I feel ill; **Erster ~** come od be first; **das muß anders ~** that'll have to change; **rot/zu Eis ~** turn red/to ice; **was willst du (mal) ~?** what do you want to be?; **die Fotos sind gut geworden** the photos have come out nicely
◆ (als Hilfsverb) **1** (bei Futur): **er wird es tun** he will od he'll do it; **er wird das nicht tun** he will not od won't do it; **es wird gleich regnen** it's going to rain
2 (bei Konjunktiv): **ich würde ...** I would ...; **er würde gern ...** he would od he'd like to; **ich würde lieber ...** I would od I'd rather ...
3 (bei Vermutung): **sie wird in der Küche sein** she will be in the kitchen
4 (bei Passiv) ptp **worden**: **gebraucht ~** be used; **er ist erschossen worden** he has od he's been shot; **mir wurde gesagt, daß ...** I was told that ...

werfen ['vɛrfən] vt unreg throw.

Werft [vɛrft] f -, -en shipyard, dockyard.

Werk [vɛrk] nt -(e)s, -e work; (Tätigkeit) job; (Fabrik, Mechanismus) works pl; **ans ~ gehen** set to work; **~statt** f -, -stätten workshop; (AUT) garage; **~tag** m working day; **w~tags** ad on working days; **w~tätig** a working; **~zeug** nt tool.

Wermut ['ve:rmu:t] m -(e)s wormwood; (Wein) vermouth.

Wert [ve:rt] m -(e)s, -e worth; (FIN) value; **~ legen auf** (+akk) attach importance to; **es hat doch keinen ~** it's useless; **w~** a worth; (geschätzt) dear; worthy; **das ist nichts/viel w~** it's not worth anything/it's worth a lot; **das ist es/er mir w~** it's/he's worth that to me; **w~en** vt rate; **w~los** a worthless; **~papier** nt security; **w~voll** a valuable.

Wesen ['ve:zən] nt -s, - (Geschöpf) being; (Natur, Character) nature; **wesentlich** a significant; (beträchtlich) considerable.

weshalb [vɛs'halp] ad why.

Wespe ['vɛspə] f -, -n wasp.

wessen ['vɛsən] pron (gen) whose.

West- zW: **~deutschland** nt West Germany; **~e** f -, -n waistcoat, vest (US); (Woll~e) cardigan; **~en** m -s west; **~europa** nt Western Europe; **Westfalen** nt Westphalia;

~indien nt the West Indies; **w~lich** a western // ad to the west.

weswegen [vɛs've:gən] ad why.

wett [vɛt] a even; **W~bewerb** m competition; **W~e** f -, -n bet, wager; **~en** vti bet.

Wetter ['vɛtər] nt -s, - weather; **~bericht** m weather report; **~dienst** m meteorological service; **~lage** f (weather) situation; **~vorhersage** f weather forecast; **~warte** f -, -n weather station.

Wett- zW: **~kampf** m contest; **~lauf** m race; **w~machen** vt make good; **~streit** m contest.

wichtig ['vɪçtɪç] a important; **W~keit** f importance.

wickeln ['vɪkəln] vt wind; (Haare) set; (Kind) change; **jdn/etw in etw** (akk) ~ wrap sb/sth in sth.

Widder ['vɪdər] m -s, - ram; (ASTROL) Aries.

wider ['vi:dər] präp +akk against; **~'fahren** vi unreg happen (jdm to sb); **~'legen** vt refute.

widerlich ['vi:dərlɪç] a disgusting, repulsive.

wider- ['vi:dər] zW: **~rechtlich** a unlawful; **W~rede** f contradiction; **W~ruf** m retraction; countermanding; **w~'rufen** vt unreg insep retract; (Anordnung) revoke; (Befehl) countermand; **~setzen** vr insep oppose (jdm/etw sb/sth).

widerspenstig ['vi:dərʃpɛnstɪç] a wilful.

wider'sprechen vi unreg insep contradict (jdm sb).

Widerspruch ['vi:dərʃprʊx] m contradiction; **widerspruchslos** ad without arguing.

Widerstand ['vi:dərʃtant] m resistance.

Widerstands- zW: **~bewegung** f resistance (movement); **w~fähig** a resistant, tough; **w~los** a unresisting.

wider'stehen vi unreg insep withstand (jdm/etw sb/sth).

Wider- ['vi:dər] zW: **w~wärtig** a nasty, horrid; **~wille** m aversion (gegen to); **w~willig** a unwilling, reluctant.

widmen ['vɪtmən] vt dedicate // vtr devote (o.s.).

widrig ['vi:drɪç] a (Umstände) adverse.

wie [vi:] ◆ad how; **~ groß/schnell?** how big/fast?; **~ wär's?** how about it?; **~ ist er?** what's he like?; **~ gut du das kannst!** you're very good at it; **~ bitte?** (entrüstet) I beg your pardon!; **und ~!** and how!
◆kj **1** (bei Vergleichen): **so schön ~ ...** as beautiful as ...; **~ ich schon sagte** as I said; **~ du** like you; **singen**

~ **ein** ... sing like a ...; ~ **(zum Beispiel)** such as (for example)
2 (zeitlich): ~ **er das hörte, ging er** when he heard that he left; **er hörte, ~ der Regen fiel** he heard the rain falling.
wieder ['vi:dər] ad again; ~ **da sein** be back (again); **gehst du schon ~?** are you off again?; ~ **ein(e)**... another...; **W~aufbau** [-''aʊfbaʊ] m rebuilding; **~aufnehmen** vt unreg resume; **~bekommen** vt unreg get back; **~bringen** vt unreg bring back; **~erkennen** vt unreg recognize; **W~gabe** f reproduction; **~geben** vt unreg (zurückgeben) return; (Erzählung etc) repeat; (Gefühle etc) convey; **~gutmachen** [-'gu:tmaxən] vt make up for; (Fehler) put right; **W~'gutmachung** f reparation; **~'herstellen** vt restore; **~holen** vt insep repeat; **W~'holung** f repetition; **W~hören** nt: **auf W~hören** (TEL) goodbye; **W~kehr** f - return; (von Vorfall) repetition, recurrence; **~sehen** vt unreg see again; **auf W~sehen** goodbye; **~um** ad again; (andererseits) on the other hand; **W~wahl** f re-election.
Wiege ['vi:gə] f -, -n cradle; **w~n** vt (schaukeln) rock // vti unreg (Gewicht) weigh.
wiehern ['vi:ərn] vi neigh, whinny.
Wien [vi:n] nt Vienna; **~er** a Viennese; **~er(in** f) m Viennese; **~er Schnitzel** Wiener Schnitzel.
Wiese ['vi:zə] f -, -n meadow.
Wiesel ['vi:zəl] nt -s, - weasel.
wieso [vi:'zo:] ad why.
wieviel [vi:'fi:l] a how much; ~ **Menschen** how many people; **~mal** ad how often; **~te(r, s)** a: **zum ~ten Mal?** how many times?; **den W~ten haben wir?** what's the date?; **an ~ter Stelle?** in what place?; **der ~te Besucher war er?** how many visitors were there before him?
wieweit [vi:'vaɪt] ad to what extent.
wild [vɪlt] a wild; **W~** nt -(e)s game; **~ern** ['vɪldərn] vi poach; **~'fremd** a (umg) quite strange od unknown; **W~heit** f wildness; **W~leder** nt suede; **W~nis** f -, -se wilderness; **W~schwein** nt (wild) boar.
will etc v siehe **wollen**.
Wille ['vɪlə] m -ns, -n will; **w~n** präp +gen: **um... w~n** for the sake of...; **willensstark** a strong-willed.
will- zW: **~ig** a willing; **~kommen** [vɪl'kɔmən] a welcome; **jdn ~kommen heißen** welcome sb; **W~kommen** nt -s, - welcome; **~kürlich** a arbitrary; (Bewegung) voluntary.
wimmeln ['vɪməln] vi swarm (von with).

wimmern ['vɪmərn] vi whimper.
Wimper ['vɪmpər] f -, -n eyelash.
Wind [vɪnt] m -(e)s, -e wind; **~beutel** m cream puff; (fig) windbag; **~e** ['vɪndə] f -, -n (TECH) winch, windlass; (BOT) bindweed; **Windel** ['vɪndəl] f -, -n nappy, diaper (US); **w~en** ['vɪndən] vi unpers be windy // unreg vt wind; (Kranz) weave; (ent~en) twist // vr wind; (Person) writhe; **~hund** m greyhound; (Mensch) fly-by-night; **w~ig** ['vɪndɪç] a windy; (fig) dubious; **~mühle** f windmill; **~pocken** pl chickenpox; **~schutzscheibe** f (AUT) windscreen, windshield (US); **~stille** f calm; **~stoß** m gust of wind.
Wink [vɪŋk] m -(e)s, -e hint; (mit Kopf) nod; (mit Hand) wave.
Winkel ['vɪŋkəl] m -s, - (MATH) angle; (Gerät) set square; (in Raum) corner.
winken ['vɪŋkən] vti wave.
winseln ['vɪnzəln] vi whine.
Winter ['vɪntər] m -s, - winter; **w~lich** a wintry; **~sport** m winter sports pl.
Winzer ['vɪntsər] m -s, - vine grower.
winzig ['vɪntsɪç] a tiny.
Wipfel ['vɪpfəl] m -s, - treetop.
wir [vi:r] pron we; ~ **alle** all of us, we all.
Wirbel ['vɪrbəl] m -s, - whirl, swirl; (Trubel) hurly-burly; (Aufsehen) fuss; (ANAT) vertebra; **w~n** vi whirl, swirl; **~säule** f spine.
wird v siehe **werden**.
wirfst etc v siehe **werfen**.
wirken ['vɪrkən] vi have an effect; (erfolgreich sein) work; (scheinen) seem // vt (Wunder) work.
wirklich ['vɪrklɪç] a real // ad really; **W~keit** f reality.
wirksam ['vɪrkza:m] a effective; **W~keit** f effectiveness, efficacy.
Wirkung ['vɪrkʊŋ] f effect; **wirkungslos** a ineffective; **wirkungslos bleiben** have no effect; **wirkungsvoll** a effective.
wirr [vɪr] a confused, wild; **W~warr** [-var] m -s disorder, chaos.
Wirsing ['vɪrzɪŋ] m -s savoy cabbage.
wirst v siehe **werden**.
Wirt [vɪrt] m -(e)s, -e landlord; **~in** f landlady; **~schaft** f (Gaststätte) pub; (Haushalt) housekeeping; (eines Landes) economy; (umg: Durcheinander) mess; **w~schaftlich** a economical; (POL) economic.
Wirtschafts- zW: **~krise** f economic crisis; **~prüfer** m chartered accountant; **~wunder** nt economic miracle.
Wirtshaus nt inn.
Wisch [vɪʃ] m -(e)s, -e scrap of paper; **w~en** vt wipe; **~er** m -s, - (AUT)

wiper.

wispern ['vɪspərn] *vti* whisper.

Wißbegier(de) ['vɪsbəgiːr(də)] *f* thirst for knowledge; **w~ig** *a* inquisitive, eager for knowledge.

wissen ['vɪsən] *vt unreg* know; **was weiß ich!** I don't know!; **W~** *nt* **-s** knowledge; **W~schaft** *f* science; **W~schaftler(in** *f)* *m* **-s**, - scientist; **~schaftlich** *a* scientific; **wissenswert** *a* worth knowing; **wissentlich** *a* knowing.

wittern ['vɪtərn] *vt* scent; *(fig)* suspect.

Witterung *f* weather; *(Geruch)* scent.

Witwe ['vɪtvə] *f* -, -n widow; **~r** *m* -s, - widower.

Witz [vɪts] *m* -(e)s, -e joke; **~blatt** *nt* comic (paper); **~bold** *m* -(e)s, -e joker, wit; **w~ig** *a* funny.

wo [voː] *ad* where; *(umg: irgendwo)* somewhere; **im Augenblick, ~** ... the moment (that) ...; **die Zeit, ~** ... the time when ...; **~anders** [voː'?andərs] *ad* elsewhere; **~andershin** *ad* somewhere else; **~bei** [voː'baɪ] *ad (rel)* by/with which; *(interrog)* what ... in/ by/with.

Woche ['vɔxə] *f* -, -n week.

Wochen- *zW:* **~ende** *nt* weekend; **w~lang** *a, ad* for weeks; **~schau** *f* newsreel.

wöchentlich ['vœçəntlɪç] *a, ad* weekly.

wo- *zW:* **~durch** [voː'dʊrç] *ad (rel)* through which; *(interrog)* what ... through; **~für** [voː'fyːr] *ad (rel)* for which; *(interrog)* what ... for.

wog *etc* *v siehe* **wiegen**.

Woge ['voːgə] *f* -, -n wave.

wo- *zW:* **~gegen** [voː'geːgən] *ad (rel)* against which; *(interrog)* what ... against; **~her** [voː'heːr] *ad* where ... from; **~hin** [voː'hɪn] *ad* where ... to.

wohl [voːl] *ad* **1: sich ~ fühlen** *(zufrieden)* feel happy; *(gesundheitlich)* feel well; **~ oder übel** whether one likes it or not

2 *(wahrscheinlich)* probably; *(gewiß)* certainly; *(vielleicht)* perhaps; **sie ist ~ zu Hause** she's probably at home; **das ist doch ~ nicht dein Ernst!** surely you're not serious! **das mag ~ sein** that may well be; **ob das ~ stimmt?** I wonder if that's true; **er weiß das sehr ~** he knows that perfectly well.

Wohl [voːl] *nt* -(e)s welfare; **zum ~!** cheers!; **w~auf** [voːl'?aʊf] *ad* well; **~behagen** *nt* comfort; **~fahrt** *f* welfare; **~fahrtsstaat** *m* welfare state; **w~habend** *a* wealthy; **w~ig** *a* contented, comfortable; **w~schmeckend** *a* delicious; **~stand** *m* prosperity; **~standsgesellschaft** *f* affluent society; **~tat** *f* relief; act of charity;

~täter(in *f)* *m* benefactor; **w~tätig** *a* charitable; **w~tun** *vi unreg* do good *(jdm* sb); **w~verdient** *a* well-earned, well-deserved; **w~weislich** *ad* prudently; **~wollen** *nt* -s good will; **w~wollend** *a* benevolent.

wohn- ['voːn] *zW:* **~en** *vi* live; **W~gemeinschaft** *f* *(Menschen)* people sharing a flat; **~haft** *a* resident; **~lich** *a* comfortable; **W~ort** *m* domicile; **W~sitz** *m* place of residence; **W~ung** *f* house; *(Etagen~ung)* flat, apartment *(US)*; **W~wagen** *m* caravan; **W~zimmer** *nt* living room.

wölben ['vœlbən] *vtr* curve.

Wölbung *f* curve.

Wolf [vɔlf] *m* -(e)s, ̈-e wolf.

Wolke ['vɔlkə] *f* -, -n cloud; **Wolkenkratzer** *m* skyscraper.

wolkig ['vɔlkɪç] *a* cloudy.

Wolle ['vɔlə] *f* -, -n wool; **w~n** *a* woollen.

wollen ['vɔlən] ♦*vti* want; **ich will nach Hause** I want to go home; **er will nicht** he doesn't want to; **er wollte das nicht** he didn't want it; **wenn du willst** if you like; **ich will, daß du mir zuhörst** I want you to listen to me
♦ *(als Hilfsverb) ptp* **wollen**: **er will ein Haus kaufen** he wants to buy a house; **ich wollte, ich wäre** ... I wish I were ...; **etw gerade tun ~** be going to do sth.

wollüstig ['vɔlʏstɪç] *a* lusty, sensual.

wo- *zW:* **~mit** [voː'mɪt] *ad (rel)* with which; *(interrog)* what ... with; **~möglich** [voː'møːklɪç] *ad* probably, I suppose; **~nach** [voː'naːx] *ad (rel)* after/for which; *(interrog)* what ... for/after; **~ran** [voː'ran] *ad (rel)* on/at which; *(interrog)* what ... on/at; **~rauf** [voː'raʊf] *ad (rel)* on which; *(interrog)* what ... on; **~raus** [voː'raʊs] *ad (rel)* from/out of which; *(interrog)* what ... from/out of; **~rin** [voː'rɪn] *ad (rel)* in which; *(interrog)* what ... in.

Wort [vɔrt] *nt* -(e)s, ̈-er *od* -e word; **jdn beim ~ nehmen** take sb at his word; **mit anderen ~en** in other words; **w~brüchig** *a* not true to one's word.

Wörterbuch ['vœrtərbuːx] *nt* dictionary.

Wort- *zW:* **~führer** *m* spokesman; **w~karg** *a* taciturn; **~laut** *m* wording.

wörtlich ['vœrtlɪç] *a* literal.

Wort- *zW:* **~los** *a* mute; **w~reich** *a* wordy, verbose; **~schatz** *m* vocabulary; **~spiel** *nt* play on words, pun.

wo- *zW:* **~rüber** [voː'ryːbər] *ad (rel)* over/about which; *(interrog)* what ...

over/about; **~rum** [vo:'rum] *ad* (*rel*) about/round which; (*interrog*) what ... about/round; **~runter** [vo:'rontər] *ad* (*rel*) under which; (*interrog*) what ... under; **~von** [vo:'fɔn] *ad* (*rel*) from which; (*interrog*) what ... from; **~vor** [vo:'fo:r] *ad* (*rel*) in front of/before which; (*interrog*) in front of/before what; of what; **~zu** [vo:'tsu:] *ad* (*rel*) to/for which; (*interrog*) what ... for/to; (*warum*) why.

Wrack [vrak] *nt* **-(e)s, -s** wreck.

wringen ['vrɪŋgən] *vt unreg* wring.

Wucher ['vu:xər] *m* **-s** profiteering; **~er** *m* **-s, -** profiteer; **w~isch** *a* profiteering; **w~n** *vi* (*Pflanzen*) grow wild; **~ung** *f* (*MED*) growth, tumour.

Wuchs [vu:ks] *m* **-es** (*Wachstum*) growth; (*Statur*) build.

Wucht [vuxt] *f* **-** force.

wühlen ['vy:lən] *vi* scrabble; (*Tier*) root; (*Maulwurf*) burrow; (*umg: arbeiten*) slave away // *vt* dig.

Wulst [volst] *m* **-es, ̈e** bulge; (*an Wunde*) swelling.

wund [vont] *a* sore, raw; **W~e** ['vondə] *f* **-, -n** wound.

Wunder ['vondər] *nt* **-s, -** miracle; **es ist kein ~** it's no wonder; **w~bar** *a* wonderful, marvellous; **~kind** *nt* infant prodigy; **w~lich** *a* odd, peculiar; **w~n** *vr* be surprised (*über* +*akk* at) // *vt* surprise; **w~schön** *a* beautiful; **w~voll** *a* wonderful.

Wundstarrkrampf ['vontʃtarkrampf] *m* tetanus, lockjaw.

Wunsch [vonʃ] *m* **-(e)s, ̈e** wish.

wünschen ['vynʃən] *vt* wish; **sich** (*dat*) **etw ~** want sth, wish for sth; **wünschenswert** *a* desirable.

wurde *etc v siehe* **werden**.

Würde ['vyrdə] *f* **-, -n** dignity; (*Stellung*) honour; **w~voll** *a* dignified.

würdig ['vyrdɪç] *a* worthy; (*würdevoll*) dignified; **~en** ['vyrdɪgən] *vt* appreciate; **jdn keines Blickes ~en** not so much as look at sb.

Wurf [vorf] *m* **-s, ̈e** throw; (*Junge*) litter.

Würfel ['vyrfəl] *m* **-s, -** dice; (*MATH*) cube; **~becher** *m* (dice) cup; **w~n** *vi* play dice // *vt* dice; **~zucker** *m* lump sugar.

würgen ['vyrgən] *vti* choke.

Wurm [vorm] *m* **-(e)s, ̈er** worm; **w~en** *vt* (*umg*) rile, nettle; **~stichig** *a* worm-ridden.

Wurst [vorst] *f* **-, ̈e** sausage; **das ist mir ~** (*umg*) I don't care, I don't give a damn.

Würstchen ['vyrstçən] *nt* sausage.

Würze ['vyrtsə] *f* **-, -n** seasoning, spice.

Wurzel ['vortsəl] *f* **-, -n** root.

würz- ['vyrts] *zW*: **~en** *vt* season,

spice; **~ig** *a* spicy.

wusch *etc v siehe* **waschen**.

wußte *etc v siehe* **wissen**.

wüst [vy:st] *a* untidy, messy; (*ausschweifend*) wild; (*öde*) waste; (*umg: heftig*) terrible; **W~e** *f* **-, -n** desert.

Wut [vu:t] *f* **-** rage, fury; **~anfall** *m* fit of rage.

wüten ['vy:tən] *vi* rage; **~d** *a* furious, mad.

X

X, x [ɪks] *nt* X, x.

X-Beine ['ɪksbainə] *pl* knock-knees *pl*.

x-beliebig [ɪksbə'li:bɪç] *a* any (whatever).

xerokopieren [kseroko'pi:rən] *vt* xerox, photocopy.

x-mal ['ɪksma:l] *ad* any number of times, n times.

Xylophon [ksylo'fo:n] *nt* **-s, -e** xylophone.

Y

Y, y ['ʏpsilɔn] *nt* Y, y.

Ypsilon *nt* **-(s), -s** the letter Y.

Z

Z, z [tsɛt] *nt* Z, z.

Zacke ['tsakə] *f* **-, -n** point; (*Berg~*) jagged peak; (*Gabel~*) prong; (*Kamm~*) tooth.

zackig ['tsakɪç] *a* jagged; (*umg*) smart; (*Tempo*) brisk.

zaghaft ['tsa:khaft] *a* timid.

zäh [tsɛ:] *a* tough; (*Mensch*) tenacious; (*Flüssigkeit*) thick; (*schleppend*) sluggish; **Z~igkeit** *f* toughness; tenacity.

Zahl [tsa:l] *f* **-, -en** number; **z~bar** *a* payable; **z~en** *vti* pay; **z~en bitte!** the bill please!

zählen ['tsɛ:lən] *vti* count (*auf* +*akk* on); **~ zu** be numbered among.

Zähler ['tsɛ:lər] *m* **-s, -** (*TECH*) meter; (*MATH*) numerator.

Zahl- *zW*: **z~los** *a* countless; **z~reich** *a* numerous; **~tag** *m* payday; **~ung** *f* payment; **z~ungsfähig** *a* solvent; **~ungsrückstände** *pl* arrears *pl*; **~wort** *nt* numeral.

zahm [tsa:m] *a* tame.

zähmen ['tsɛ:mən] *vt* tame; (*fig*) curb.

Zahn [tsa:n] *m* **-(e)s, ̈e** tooth; **~arzt** *m* dentist; **~bürste** *f* toothbrush; **~creme** *f* toothpaste; **~fleisch** *nt* gums *pl*; **~pasta** *f* toothpaste; **~rad**

nt cog(wheel); **~schmerzen** pl tooth-ache; **~stein** m tartar; **~stocher** m **-s,** - toothpick.

Zange ['tsaŋə] f **-, -n** pliers pl; (Zucker~ etc) tongs pl; (Beiß~, ZOOL) pincers pl; (MED) forceps pl.

zanken ['tsaŋkən] vir quarrel.

zänkisch ['tseŋkɪʃ] a quarrelsome.

Zäpfchen ['tsɛpfçən] nt (ANAT) uvula; (MED) suppository.

Zapfen ['tsapfən] m **-s,** - plug; (BOT) cone; (Eis~) icicle; **z~** vt tap; **~streich** m (MIL) tattoo.

zappeln ['tsapəln] vi wriggle; fidget.

zart [tsart] a (weich, leise) soft; (Fleisch) tender; (fein, schwächlich) delicate; **Z~gefühl** nt tact; **Z~heit** f softness; tenderness; delicacy.

zärtlich ['tsɛːrtlɪç] a tender, affectionate; **Z~keit** f tenderness; **Z~keiten** pl caresses pl.

Zauber ['tsaubər] m **-s,** - magic; (~bann) spell; **~ei** [-'raɪ] f magic; **~er** m **-s,** - magician; conjuror; **z~haft** a magical, enchanting; **~künstler** m conjuror; **z~n** vi conjure, practise magic.

zaudern ['tsaudərn] vi hesitate.

Zaum [tsaum] m **-(e)s, Zäume** bridle; etw im ~ halten keep sth in check.

Zaun [tsaun] m **-(e)s, Zäune** fence; **~könig** m wren.

z.B. abk (= zum Beispiel) e.g.

Zebra ['tse:bra] nt zebra; **~streifen** m zebra crossing.

Zeche ['tsɛçə] f **-, -n** bill; (Bergbau) mine.

Zehe ['tse:ə] f **-, -n** toe; (Knoblauch~) clove.

zehn [tse:n] num ten; **~te(r, s)** a tenth; **Z~tel** nt **-s,** - tenth (part).

Zeich- ['tsaɪç] zW: **~en** nt **-s,** - sign; **z~nen** vti draw; (kenn~nen) mark; (unter~nen) sign; **~ner** m **-s,** - artist; **technischer ~ner** draughtsman; **~nung** f drawing; (Markierung) markings pl.

Zeige- ['tsaɪgə] zW: **~finger** m index finger; **z~n** vt show // vi point (auf +akk to, at) // vr show o.s.; **es wird sich z~n** time will tell; **es zeigte sich, daß ...** it turned out that ...; **~r** m **-s,** - pointer; (Uhr~r) hand.

Zeile ['tsaɪlə] f **-, -n** line; (Häuser~) row.

Zeit [tsaɪt] f **-, -en** time; (GRAM) tense; **zur ~** at the moment; **sich** (dat) **~ lassen** take one's time; **von ~ zu ~** from time to time; **~alter** nt age; **z~gemäß** a in keeping with the times; **~genosse** m contemporary; **z~ig** a early; **z~lich** a temporal; **~lupe** f slow motion; **z~raubend** a time-consuming; **~raum** m period; **~rechnung** f time, era; **nach/vor**

unserer ~rechnung A.D./B.C.; **~schrift** f periodical; **~ung** f newspaper; **~verschwendung** f waste of time; **~vertreib** m pastime, diversion; **z~weilig** a temporary; **z~weise** ad for a time; **~wort** nt verb; **~zünder** m time fuse.

Zell- ['tsɛl] zW: **~e** f **-, -n** cell; (Telefon~e) callbox; **~stoff** m cellulose.

Zelt [tsɛlt] nt **-(e)s, -e** tent; **z~en** vi camp.

Zement [tse'mɛnt] m **-(e)s, -e** cement; **z~ieren** [-'tiːrən] vt cement.

zensieren [tsɛn'ziːrən] vt censor; (SCH) mark.

Zensur [tsɛn'zuːr] f censorship; (SCH) mark.

Zentimeter [tsɛnti'meːtər] m od nt centimetre.

Zentner ['tsɛntnər] m **-s,** - hundredweight.

zentral [tsɛn'traːl] a central; **Z~e** f **-, -n** central office; (TEL) exchange; **Z~einheit** f central processing unit, CPU; **Z~heizung** f central heating.

Zentrum ['tsɛntrʊm] nt **-s, Zentren** centre.

zerbrech- [tsɛr'brɛç] zW: **~en** vti unreg break; **~lich** a fragile.

zerdrücken vt squash, crush; (Kartoffeln) mash.

Zeremonie [tseremo'niː] f ceremony.

Zerfall [tsɛr'fal] m decay; **z~en** vi unreg disintegrate, decay; (sich gliedern) fall (in +akk into).

zergehen vi unreg melt, dissolve.

zerkleinern [tsɛr'klaɪnərn] vt reduce to small pieces.

zerleg- [tsɛr'leːg] zW: **~bar** a able to be dismantled; **~en** vt take to pieces; (Fleisch) carve; (Satz) analyse.

zermürben [tsɛr'myrbən] vt wear down.

zerquetschen [tsɛr'kvɛtʃən] vt squash.

Zerrbild ['tsɛrbɪlt] nt caricature, distorted picture.

zer'reißen unreg vt tear to pieces // vi tear, rip.

zerren ['tsɛrən] vt drag // vi tug (an +dat at).

zer'rinnen vi unreg melt away.

zerrissen [tsɛr'rɪsən] a torn, tattered; **Z~heit** f tattered state; (POL) disunion, discord; (innere Z~heit) disintegration.

zerrütten [tsɛr'rʏtən] vt wreck, destroy.

zerrüttet a wrecked, shattered.

zer'schlagen unreg vt shatter, smash // vr fall through.

zer'schneiden vt unreg cut up.

zer'setzen vtr decompose, dissolve.

zer'springen vi unreg shatter, burst.

Zerstäuber [tsɛr'ʃtɔybər] m **-s,** - atomizer.

zerstör- [tsɛr'ʃtøːr] zW: **~en** vt destroy; **Z~ung** f destruction.

zerstreu- [tsɛr'ʃtrɔy] zW: **~en** vtr disperse, scatter; (unterhalten) divert; (Zweifel etc) dispel; **~t** a scattered; (Mensch) absent-minded; **Zerstreutheit** f absent-mindedness; **Z~ung** f dispersion; (Ablenkung) diversion.

zerstückeln [tsər'ʃtʏkəln] vt cut into pieces.

zer'teilen vt divide into parts.

Zertifikat [tsɛrtifi'kaːt] nt certificate.

zer'treten vt unreg crush underfoot.

zertrümmern [tsɛr'trʏmərn] vt shatter; (Gebäude etc) demolish.

zerzausen [tsɛr'tsauzən] vt (Haare) ruffle up, tousle.

zetern ['tseːtərn] vi shout, shriek.

Zettel ['tsetəl] m **-s**, - piece of paper, slip; (Notiz~) note; (Formular) form.

Zeug [tsɔyk] nt **-(e)s**, **-e** (umg) stuff; (Ausrüstung) gear; **dummes ~** (stupid) nonsense; **das ~ haben** zu have the makings of; **sich ins ~ legen** put one's shoulder to the wheel.

Zeuge ['tsɔygə] m **-n**, **-n**, **Zeugin** ['tsɔygɪn] f witness; **z~n** vi bear witness, testify; **es zeugt von ...** it testifies to ... // vt (Kind) father; **Zeugenaussage** f evidence.

Zeugnis ['tsɔygnɪs] nt **-ses**, **-se** certificate; (SCH) report; (Referenz) reference; (Aussage) evidence, testimony; **~ geben von** be evidence of, testify to.

z.H(d). abk (= zu Händen) attn.

Zickzack ['tsɪktsak] m **-(e)s**, **-e** zigzag.

Ziege ['tsiːgə] f **-**, **-n** goat; **Ziegenleder** nt kid.

Ziegel ['tsiːgəl] m **-s**, - brick; (Dach~) tile.

ziehen ['tsiːən] unreg vt draw; (zerren) pull; (SCHACH etc) move; (züchten) rear; **etw nach sich ~** lead to sth, entail sth // vi draw; (um~, wandern) move; (Rauch, Wolke etc) drift; (reißen) pull // v unpers: **es zieht** there is a draught, it's draughty // vr (Gummi) stretch; (Grenze etc) run; (Gespräche) be drawn out.

Ziehharmonika ['tsiːharmoˌnika] f concertina; accordion.

Ziehung ['tsiːʊŋ] f (Los~) drawing.

Ziel [tsiːl] nt **-(e)s**, **-e** (einer Reise) destination; (SPORT) finish; (MIL) target; (Absicht) goal, aim; **z~en** vi aim (auf +akk at); **z~los** a aimless; **~scheibe** f target; **z~strebig** a purposeful.

ziemlich ['tsiːmlɪç] a quite a; fair // ad rather; quite a bit.

Zierde ['tsiːrdə] f ornament.

zieren ['tsiːrən] vr act coy.

zierlich ['tsiːrlɪç] a dainty; **Z~keit** f daintiness.

Ziffer ['tsɪfər] f **-**, **-n** figure, digit; **~blatt** nt dial, clock-face.

zig [tsɪç] a (umg) umpteen.

Zigarette [tsigaˈrɛtə] f cigarette.

Zigaretten- zW: **~automat** m cigarette machine; **~schachtel** f cigarette packet; **~spitze** f cigarette holder.

Zigarillo [tsigaˈrɪlo] nt od m **-s**, **-s** cigarillo.

Zigarre [tsiˈgarə] f **-**, **-n** cigar.

Zigeuner(in f) [tsiˈgɔynər(ɪn)] m **-s**, - gipsy.

Zimmer ['tsɪmər] nt **-s**, - room; **~lautstärke** f reasonable volume; **~mädchen** nt chambermaid; **~mann** m carpenter; **z~n** vt make, carpenter; **~nachweis** m accommodation office; **~pflanze** f indoor plant.

zimperlich ['tsɪmpərlɪç] a squeamish; (pingelig) fussy, finicky.

Zimt [tsɪmt] m **-(e)s**, **-e** cinnamon.

Zink [tsɪŋk] nt **-(e)s** zinc.

Zinn [tsɪn] nt **-(e)s** (Element) tin; (in ~waren) pewter; **~soldat** m tin soldier.

Zins [tsɪns] m **-es**, **-en** interest; **Zinseszins** m compound interest; **~fuß** m, **~satz** m rate of interest; **z~los** a interest-free.

Zipfel ['tsɪpfəl] m **-s**, - corner; (spitz) tip; (Hemd~) tail; (Wurst~) end; **~mütze** f stocking cap; nightcap.

zirka ['tsɪrka] ad (round) about.

Zirkel ['tsɪrkəl] m **-s**, - circle; (MATH) pair of compasses.

Zirkus ['tsɪrkʊs] m **-**, **-se** circus.

zischen ['tsɪʃən] vi hiss.

Zitat [tsiˈtaːt] nt **-(e)s**, **-e** quotation, quote.

zitieren [tsiˈtiːrən] vt quote.

Zitronat [tsitroˈnaːt] nt **-(e)s**, **-e** candied lemon peel.

Zitrone [tsiˈtroːnə] f **-**, **-n** lemon; **Zitronenlimonade** f lemonade; **Zitronensaft** m lemon juice.

zittern ['tsɪtərn] vi tremble.

zivil [tsiˈviːl] a civil; (Preis) moderate; **Z~** nt **-s** plain clothes pl; (MIL) civilian clothing; **Z~bevölkerung** f civilian population; **Z~courage** f courage of one's convictions; **Z~dienstleistende(r)** f conscientious objector doing alternative service (in the community); **Z~isation** [tsivilizatsi'oːn] f civilization; **Z~isationskrankheit** f disease peculiar to civilization; **~isieren** vt civilize; **Z~ist** [tsiviˈlɪst] m civilian.

zog etc v siehe **ziehen**.

zögern ['tsøːgərn] vi hesitate.

Zoll [tsɔl] m **-(e)s**, **⁼e** customs pl; (Abgabe) duty; **~abfertigung** f customs clearance; **~amt** nt customs office;

~beamte(r) *m* customs official; **~erklärung** *f* customs declaration; **z~frei** *a* duty-free; **~kontrolle** *f* customs check; **z~pflichtig** *a* liable to duty, dutiable.

Zone ['tso:nə] *f* -, **-n** zone.

Zoo [tso:] *m* **-s**, **-s** zoo; **~loge** [tsoo'lo:gə] *m* **-n**, **-n** zoologist; **~lo'gie** *f* zoology; **z~'logisch** *a* zoological.

Zopf [tsɔpf] *m* **-(e)s**, **∸e** plait; pigtail; **alter ~** antiquated custom.

Zorn [tsɔrn] *m* **-(e)s** anger; **z~ig** *a* angry.

zottig ['tsɔtɪç] *a* shaggy.

z.T. *abk von* **zum Teil.**

zu [tsu:] ♦ *präp* +dat **1** (*örtlich*) to; **~m Bahnhof/Arzt gehen** go to the station/doctor; **~r Schule/Kirche gehen** go to school/church; **sollen wir ~ euch gehen?** shall we go to your place?; **sie sah ~ ihm hin** she looked towards him; **~m Fenster herein** through the window; **~ meiner Linken** to *od* on my left

2 (*zeitlich*) at; **~ Ostern** at Easter; **bis ~m 1. Mai** until May 1st; (*nicht später als*) by May 1st; **~ meiner Zeit** in my time

3 (*Zusatz*) with; **Wein ~m Essen trinken** drink wine with one's meal; **sich ~ jdm setzen** sit down beside sb; **setz dich doch ~ uns** (come and) sit with us; **Anmerkungen ~ etw** notes on sth

4 (*Zweck*) for; **Wasser ~m Waschen** water for washing; **Papier ~m Schreiben** paper to write on; **etw ~m Geburtstag bekommen** get sth for one's birthday

5 (*Veränderung*) into; **~ etw werden** turn into sth; **jdn ~ etw machen** make sb (into) sth; **~ Asche verbrennen** burn to ashes

6 (*mit Zahlen*): **3 ~ 2** (*SPORT*) 3-2; **das Stück ~ 2 Mark** at 2 marks each; **~m ersten Mal** for the first time

7: **~ meiner Freude** *etc* to my joy *etc*; **~m Glück** luckily; **~ Fuß** on foot; **es ist ~m Weinen** it's enough to make you cry

♦ *kj* to; **etw ~ essen** sth to eat; **um besser sehen ~ können** in order to see better; **ohne es ~ wissen** without knowing it; **noch ~ bezahlende Rechnungen** bills that are still to be paid

♦ *ad* **1** (*allzu*) too; **~ sehr** too much

2 (*örtlich*) toward(s); **er kam auf mich ~** he came up to me

3 (*geschlossen*) shut, closed; **die Geschäfte haben ~** the shops are closed; **'auf/~'** (*Wasserhahn etc*) 'on/off'

4 (*umg: los*): **nur ~!** just keep on!; **mach ~!** hurry up!

zualler- [tsu·'alər] *zW*: **~erst** *ad* first of all; **~letzt** *ad* last of all.

Zubehör ['tsu:bəhø:r] *nt* **-(e)s**, **-e** accessories *pl*.

zubereiten ['tsu:bərattən] *vt* prepare.

zubilligen ['tsu:bɪlɪgən] *vt* grant.

zubinden ['tsu:bɪndən] *vt unreg* tie up.

zubringen ['tsu:brɪŋən] *vt unreg* (*Zeit*) spend.

Zubringer *m* **-s**, - (*Straße*) approach *od* slip road.

Zucht [tsʊxt] *f* -, **-en** (*von Tieren*) breed(ing); (*von Pflanzen*) cultivation; (*Rasse*) breed; (*Erziehung*) raising; (*Disziplin*) discipline.

züchten ['tsʏçtən] *vt* (*Tiere*) breed; (*Pflanzen*) cultivate, grow.

Züchter *m* **-s**, - breeder; grower.

Zuchthaus *nt* prison, penitentiary (*US*).

züchtigen ['tsʏçtɪgən] *vt* chastise.

zucken ['tsʊkən] *vi* jerk, twitch; (*Strahl etc*) flicker // *vt* (*Schultern*) shrug.

Zucker ['tsʊkər] *m* **-s**, - sugar; (*MED*) diabetes; **~dose** *f* sugar bowl; **~guß** *m* icing; **z~krank** *a* diabetic; **z~n** *vt* sugar; **~rohr** *nt* sugar cane; **~rübe** *f* sugar beet.

Zuckung ['tsʊkʊŋ] *f* convulsion, spasm; (*leicht*) twitch.

zudecken ['tsu:dɛkən] *vt* cover (up).

zudem [tsu·'de:m] *ad* in addition (to this).

zudringlich ['tsu:drɪŋlɪç] *a* forward, pushing, obtrusive.

zudrücken ['tsu:drykən] *vt* close; **ein Auge ~** turn a blind eye.

zueinander [tsu·aɪ'nandər] *ad* to one other; (*in Verbverbindung*) together.

zuerkennen ['tsu:'ɛrkɛnən] *vt unreg* award (*jdm etw* sth to sb, sb sth).

zuerst [tsu·'e:rst] *ad* first; (*zu Anfang*) at first; **~ einmal** first of all.

Zufahrt ['tsu:fa:rt] *f* approach; **Zufahrtsstraße** *f* approach road; (*von Autobahn etc*) slip road.

Zufall ['tsu:fal] *m* chance; (*Ereignis*) coincidence; **durch ~** by accident; **so ein ~** what a coincidence; **z~en** *vi unreg* close, shut itself; (*Anteil, Aufgabe*) fall (*jdm* to sb).

zufällig ['tsu:fɛlɪç] *a* chance // *ad* by chance; (*in Frage*) by any chance.

Zuflucht ['tsu:flʊxt] *f* recourse; (*Ort*) refuge.

zufolge [tsu·'fɔlgə] *präp* +dat *od* gen judging by; (*laut*) according to.

zufrieden ['tsu:fri:dən] *a* content(ed), satisfied; **Z~heit** *f* satisfaction, contentedness; **~stellen** *vt* satisfy.

zufrieren ['tsu:fri:rən] *vi unreg* freeze up *od* over.

zufügen ['tsu:fy:gən] *vt* add (*dat* to); (*Leid etc*) cause (*jdm etw* sth to sb).

Zufuhr ['tsu:fu:r] f -, **-en** (Herbeibringen) supplying; (MET) influx.

Zug [tsu:k] m **-(e)s, -̈e** (EISENB) train; (Luft~) draught; (Ziehen) pull(ing); (Gesichts~) feature; (SCHACH etc) move; (Klingel~) pull; (Schrift~) stroke; (Atem~) breath; (Charakter~) trait; (an Zigarette) puff, pull, drag; (Schluck) gulp; (Menschengruppe) procession; (von Vögeln) flight; (MIL) platoon; **etw in vollen ~en genießen** enjoy sth to the full.

Zu- ['tsu:] zW: **~gabe** f extra; (in Konzert etc) encore; **~gang** m access, approach; **z~gänglich** a accessible; (Mensch) approachable.

zugeben ['tsu:ge:bən] vt unreg (beifügen) add, throw in; (zugestehen) admit; (erlauben) permit.

zugehen ['tsu:ge:ən] vi unreg (schließen) shut; **es geht dort seltsam zu** there are strange goings-on there; **auf jdn/etw ~** walk towards sb/sth; **dem Ende ~** be finishing.

Zugehörigkeit ['tsu:gəhø:rɪçkaɪt] f membership (zu of), belonging (zu to).

Zügel ['tsy:gəl] m **-s, -** rein(s); (fig auch) curb; **z~n** vt curb; (Pferd auch) rein in.

zuge- ['tsu:gə] zW: **Z~ständnis** nt **-ses, -se** concession; **~stehen** vt unreg admit; (Rechte) concede (jdm to sb); **~stiegen** a: **noch jemand ~gestiegen?** tickets please.

zugig ['tsu:gɪç] a draughty.

zügig ['tsy:gɪç] a speedy, swift.

zugreifen ['tsu:graɪfən] vi unreg seize od grab at; (helfen) help; (beim Essen) help o.s.

Zugriff ['tsu:grɪf] m (COMPUT) access.

zugrunde [tsu'grundə] ad: **~ gehen** collapse; (Mensch) perish; **einer Sache etw ~ legen** base sth on sth; **einer Sache ~ liegen** be based on sth; **~ richten** ruin, destroy.

zugunsten [tsu'gunstən] präp +gen od dat in favour of.

zugute [tsu'gu:tə] ad: **jdm etw ~ halten** concede sth; **jdm ~ kommen** be of assistance to sb.

Zugvogel m migratory bird.

Zuhälter ['tsu:hɛltər] m **-s, -** pimp.

Zuhause [tsu'hauzə] nt - home.

zuhören ['tsu:hø:rən] vi listen (dat to).

Zuhörer m **-s, -** listener; **~schaft** f audience.

zukleben ['tsu:kle:bən] vt paste up.

zukommen ['tsu:kɔmən] vi unreg come up (auf +akk to); (sich gehören) be fitting (jdm for sb); (Recht haben auf) be entitled to; **jdm etw ~ lassen** give sb sth; **etw auf sich ~ lassen** wait and see.

Zukunft ['tsu:kunft] f -, **Zukünfte** future.

zukünftig ['tsu:kynftɪç] a future; **mein ~er Mann** my husband to be // ad in future.

Zulage ['tsu:la:gə] f bonus, allowance.

zulassen ['tsu:lasən] vt unreg (hereinlassen) admit; (erlauben) permit; (Auto) license; (umg: nicht öffnen) keep shut.

zulässig ['tsu:lɛsɪç] a permissible, permitted.

zuleide [tsu'laɪdə] a: **jdm etw ~ tun** hurt od harm sb.

zuletzt [tsu'lɛtst] ad finally, at last.

zuliebe [tsu'li:bə] ad: **jdm ~** to please sb.

zum [tsum] = **zu dem**; **~ dritten Mal** for the third time; **~ Scherz** as a joke; **~ Trinken** for drinking.

zumachen ['tsu:maxən] vt shut; (Kleidung) do up, fasten // vi shut; (umg) hurry up.

zumal [tsu'ma:l] kj especially (as).

zumeist [tsu'maɪst] ad mostly.

zumindest [tsu'mɪndəst] ad at least.

zumut- zW: **~bar** ['tsu:mu:tba:r] a reasonable; **~e** ad: **wie ist ihm ~e?** how does he feel?; **~en** ['tsu:mu:tən] vt expect, ask (jdm of sb); **Z~ung** ['tsu:mu:tuŋ] f unreasonable expectation od demand, impertinence.

zunächst [tsu'nɛ:çst] ad first of all; **~ einmal** to start with.

Zunahme [tsu'na:mə] f -, **-n** increase.

Zuname ['tsu:na:mə] m surname.

Zünd- [tsynd] zW: **~en** vi (Feuer) light, ignite; (Motor) fire; (begeistern) fire (with enthusiasm) (bei jdm sb); **z~end** a fiery; **~er** m **-s, -** fuse; (MIL) detonator; **~holz** ['tsynt-] nt match; **~kerze** f (AUT) spark(ing) plug; **~schlüssel** m ignition key; **~schnur** f fuse wire; **~ung** f ignition.

zunehmen ['tsu:ne:mən] vi unreg increase, grow; (Mensch) put on weight.

Zuneigung f affection.

Zunft [tsunft] f -, **-̈e** guild.

zünftig ['tsynftɪç] a proper, real; (Handwerk) decent.

Zunge ['tsuŋə] f -, **-n** tongue.

zunichte [tsu'nɪçtə] ad: **~ machen** ruin, destroy; **~ werden** come to nothing.

zunutze [tsu'nutsə] ad: **sich (dat) etw ~ machen** make use of sth.

zuoberst [tsu'o:bərst] ad at the top.

zupfen ['tsupfən] vt pull, pick, pluck; (Gitarre) pluck.

zur [tsu:r] = **zu der**.

zurechnungsfähig ['tsu:rɛçnuŋsfɛ:ɪç] a responsible, accountable; **Z~keit** f responsibility, accountability.

zurecht- [tsu'rɛçt] zW: **~finden** vr

unreg find one's way (about);
~**kommen** *vi unreg* (be able to) deal
(*mit* with), manage; ~**legen** *vt* get
ready; (*Ausrede etc*) have ready;
~**machen** *vt* prepare // *vr* get ready;
~**weisen** *vt unreg* reprimand;
Z~**weisung** *f* reprimand, rebuff.

zureden ['tsuːreːdən] *vi* persuade,
urge (*jdm* sb).

zurück [tsuˈrʏk] *ad* back; ~**behalten**
vt unreg keep back; ~**bekommen** *vt*
unreg get back; ~**bleiben** *vi unreg*
(*Mensch*) remain behind; (*nicht
nachkommen*) fall behind, lag;
(*Schaden*) remain; ~**bringen** *vt
unreg* bring back; ~**fahren** *unreg vi*
travel back; (*vor Schreck*) recoil,
start // *vt* drive back; ~**finden** *vi
unreg* find one's way back; ~**fordern**
vt demand back; ~**führen** *vt* lead
back; etw auf etw (*akk*) ~**führen**
trace sth back to sth; ~**geben** *vt
unreg* give back; (*antworten*) retort
with; ~**geblieben** *a* retarded;
~**gehen** *vi unreg* go back; (*zeitlich*)
date back (*auf +akk* to); (*fallen*) go
down, fall; ~**gezogen** *a* retired, with-
drawn; ~**halten** *unreg vt* hold back;
(*Mensch*) restrain; (*hindern*) prevent
// *vr* (*reserviert sein*) be reserved;
(*im Essen*) hold back; ~**haltend** *a*
reserved; Z~**haltung** *f* reserve;
~**kehren** *vi* return; ~**kommen** *vi
unreg* come back; auf etw (*akk*)
~**kommen** return to sth; ~**lassen** *vt
unreg* leave behind; ~**legen** *vt* put
back; (*Geld*) put by; (*reservieren*)
keep back; (*Strecke*) cover;
~**nehmen** *vt unreg* take back;
~**schrecken** *vi* shrink (*vor +dat*
from); ~**stellen** *vt* put back, replace;
(*aufschieben*) put off, postpone;
(*MIL*) turn down; (*Interessen*) defer;
(*Ware*) keep; ~**treten** *vi unreg* step
back; (*vom Amt*) retire; gegenüber
od hinter etw ~**treten** diminish in importance in view of sth; ~**weisen** *vt
unreg* turn down; (*Mensch*) reject;
~**zahlen** *vt* repay, pay back;
~**ziehen** *unreg vt* pull back; (*Angebot*) withdraw // *vr* retire.

Zuruf ['tsuːruːf] *m* shout, cry.

Zusage ['tsuːzaːgə] *f* -, -n promise;
(*Annahme*) consent; **z~n** *vt* promise
// *vi* accept; jdm **z~n** (*gefallen*)
agree with *od* please sb.

zusammen [tsuˈzamən] *ad* together;
Z~**arbeit** *f* cooperation; ~**arbeiten** *vi*
cooperate; ~**beißen** *vt unreg*
(*Zähne*) clench; ~**bleiben** *vi unreg*
stay together; ~**brechen** *vi unreg*
collapse; (*Mensch auch*) break down;
~**bringen** *vt unreg* bring *od* get together; (*Geld*) get; (*Sätze*) put together; Z~**bruch** *m* collapse;

~**fassen** *vt* summarize; (*vereinigen*)
unite; Z~**fassung** *f* summary, résumé; ~**fügen** *vt* join (together),
unite; ~**halten** *vi unreg* stick together; Z~**hang** *m* connection; im/
aus dem Z~**hang** in/out of context;
~**hängen** *vi unreg* be connected *od*
linked; ~**kommen** *vi unreg* meet, assemble; (*sich ereignen*) occur at
once *od* together; ~**legen** *vt* put together; (*stapeln*) pile up; (*falten*)
fold; (*verbinden*) combine, unite;
(*Termine, Fest*) amalgamate; (*Geld*)
collect; ~**nehmen** *vt unreg* summon
up; alles ~**genommen** all in all // *vr*
pull o.s. together; ~**passen** *vi* go well
together, match; ~**schließen** *vtr
unreg* join (together); Z~**schluß** *m*
amalgamation; ~**schreiben** *vt unreg*
write as one word; (*Bericht*) put together; Z~**sein** *nt* -s get-together;
~**setzen** *vt* put together // *vr* (*Stoff*)
be composed of; (*Menschen*) get together; Z~**setzung** *f* composition;
~**stellen** *vt* put together; compile;
Z~**stoß** *m* collision; ~**stoßen** *vi
unreg* collide; ~**treffen** *vi unreg* coincide; (*Menschen*) meet; Z~**treffen** *nt*
meeting; coincidence; ~**zählen** *vt*
add up; ~**ziehen** *unreg vt* (*veren-
gern*) draw together; (*vereinigen*)
bring together; (*addieren*) add up //
vr shrink; (*sich bilden*) form, develop.

zusätzlich ['tsuːzɛtslɪç] *a* additional //
ad in addition.

zuschauen ['tsuːʃaʊən] *vi* watch, look
on.

Zuschauer(in *f*) *m* -s, - spectator // *pl*
(*THEAT*) audience.

zuschicken ['tsuːʃɪkən] *vt* send, forward (*jdm etw* sth to sb).

Zuschlag ['tsuːʃlaːk] *m* extra charge,
surcharge; **z~en** (*tsuːʃlaːgən*) *unreg
vt* (*Tür*) slam; (*Ball*) hit (*jdm* to
sb); (*bei Auktion*) knock down;
(*Steine etc*) knock into shape // *vi*
(*Fenster, Tür*) shut; (*Mensch*) hit,
punch; ~**karte** *f* (*EISENB*) surcharge
ticket; **z~pflichtig** *a* subject to
surcharge.

zuschneiden ['tsuːʃnaɪdən] *vt unreg*
cut out *od* to size.

zuschrauben ['tsuːʃraʊbən] *vt* screw
down *od* up.

zuschreiben ['tsuːʃraɪbən] *vt unreg*
(*fig*) ascribe, attribute; (*COMM*)
credit.

Zuschrift ['tsuːʃrɪft] *f* letter, reply.

zuschulden [tsuˈʃʊldən] *ad*: sich (*dat*)
etw ~ kommen lassen make o.s.
guilty of sth.

Zuschuß ['tsuːʃʊs] *m* subsidy, allowance.

zusehen ['tsuːzeːən] *vi unreg* watch

(*jdm/etw* sb/sth); (*dafür sorgen*) take care; **zusehends** *ad* visibly.

zusenden ['tsu:zɛndən] *vt unreg* forward, send on (*jdm etw* sth to sb).

zusichern ['tsu:zɪçərn] *vt* assure (*jdm etw* sb of sth).

zuspielen ['tsu:ʃpi:lən] *vti* pass (*jdm* to sb).

zuspitzen ['tsu:ʃpɪtsən] *vt* sharpen // *vr* (*Lage*) become critical.

zusprechen ['tsu:ʃprɛçən] *unreg vt* (*zuerkennen*) award (*jdm etw* sb sth, sth to sb); **jdm Trost ~** comfort sb // *vi* speak (*jdm* to sb); **dem Essen/ Alkohol ~** eat/drink a lot.

Zustand ['tsu:ʃtant] *m* state, condition; **z~e** [tsu:ʃtandə] *ad*: **z~e bringen** *vt unreg* bring about; **z~e kommen** *vi unreg* come about.

zuständig ['tsu:ʃtɛndɪç] *a* responsible; **Z~keit** *f* competence, responsibility.

zustehen ['tsu:ʃte:ən] *vi unreg*: **jdm ~** be sb's right.

zustellen ['tsu:ʃtɛlən] *vt* (*verstellen*) block; (*Post etc*) send.

zustimmen ['tsu:ʃtɪmən] *vi* agree (*dat* to).

Zustimmung *f* agreement, consent.

zustoßen ['tsu:ʃto:sən] *vi unreg* (*fig*) happen (*jdm* to sb).

zutage [tsu:ta:gə] *ad*: **~ bringen** bring to light; **~ treten** come to light.

Zutaten ['tsu:ta:tən] *pl* ingredients *pl*.

zutiefst [tsu:ti:fst] *ad* deeply.

zutragen ['tsu:tra:gən] *unreg vt* bring (*jdm etw* sth to sb); (*Klatsch*) tell // *vr* happen.

zutrau- ['tsu:trau] *zW*: **~en** *vt* credit (*jdm etw* sb with sth); **Z~en** *nt* **-s** trust (*zu* in); **~lich** *a* trusting, friendly; **Z~lichkeit** *f* trust.

zutreffen ['tsu:trɛfən] *vi unreg* be correct; apply; **Z~des bitte unterstreichen** please underline where applicable.

Zutritt ['tsu:trɪt] *m* access, admittance.

Zutun ['tsu:tu:n] *nt* **-s** assistance.

zuverlässig ['tsu:fɛrlɛsɪç] *a* reliable; **Z~keit** *f* reliability.

Zuversicht ['tsu:fɛrzɪçt] *f* - confidence; **z~lich** *a* confident.

zuviel [tsu:fi:l] *ad* too much.

zuvor [tsu:fo:r] *ad* before, previously; **~kommen** *vi unreg* anticipate (*jdm* sb), beat (sb) to it; **~kommend** *a* obliging, courteous.

Zuwachs ['tsu:vaks] *m* **-es** increase, growth; (*umg*) addition; **z~en** *vi unreg* become overgrown; (*Wunde*) heal (up).

zuwege [tsu:ve:gə] *ad*: **etw ~ bringen** accomplish sth.

zuweilen [tsu:vaɪlən] *ad* at times, now and then.

zuweisen ['tsu:vaɪzən] *vt unreg* assign, allocate (*jdm* to sb).

zuwenden ['tsu:vɛndən] *unreg vt* turn (*dat* towards); **jdm seine Aufmerksamkeit ~** give sb one's attention // *vr* devote o.s., turn (*dat* to).

zuwenig [tsu:ve:nɪç] *ad* too little.

zuwider [tsu:vi:dər] *ad*: **etw ist jdm ~** sb loathes sth, sb finds sth repugnant // *präp* +*dat* contrary to; **~handeln** *vi* act contrary (*dat* to); **einem Gesetz ~handeln** contravene a law.

zuziehen ['tsu:tsi:ən] *unreg vt* (*schließen: Vorhang*) draw, close; (*herbeirufen: Experten*) call in; **sich** (*dat*) **etw ~** (*Krankheit*) catch; (*Zorn*) incur // *vi* move in, come.

zuzüglich ['tsu:tsy:klɪç] *präp* +*gen* plus, with the addition of.

Zwang [tsvaŋ] *m* **-(e)s, ⁼e** compulsion, coercion.

zwängen ['tsvɛŋən] *vtr* squeeze.

zwanglos *a* informal.

Zwangs- *zW*: **~arbeit** *f* forced labour; (*Strafe*) hard labour; **~jacke** *f* straightjacket; **~lage** *f* predicament, tight corner; **z~läufig** *a* necessary, inevitable.

zwanzig ['tsvantsɪç] *num* twenty.

zwar [tsva:r] *ad* to be sure, indeed; **das ist ~ ..., aber** ... that may be ... but ...; **und ~ am Sonntag** on Sunday to be precise; **und ~ so schnell, daß** ... in fact so quickly that ...

Zweck ['tsvɛk] *m* **-(e)s, -e** purpose, aim; **es hat keinen ~** there's no point; **z~dienlich** *a* practical; expedient; **~e** *f* -, **-n** hobnail; (*Heft~e*) drawing pin, thumbtack (*US*); **z~los** *a* pointless; **z~mäßig** *a* suitable, appropriate; **zwecks** *präp* +*gen* for the purpose of.

zwei [tsvaɪ] *num* two; **~deutig** *a* ambiguous; (*unanständig*) suggestive; **~erlei** *a*: **~erlei Stoff** two different kinds of material; **~erlei Meinung** of differing opinions; **~fach** *a* double.

Zweifel ['tsvaɪfəl] *m* **-s, -** doubt; **z~haft** *a* doubtful, dubious; **z~los** *a* doubtless; **z~n** *vi* doubt (*an etw* (*dat*) sth).

Zweig [tsvaɪk] *m* **-(e)s, -e** branch; **~stelle** *f* branch (office).

zwei- *zW*: **~hundert** *num* two hundred; **Z~kampf** *m* duel; **~mal** *ad* twice; **~sprachig** *a* bilingual; **~spurig** *a* (*AUT*) two-lane; **~stimmig** *a* for two voices; **Z~taktmotor** *m* two-stroke engine.

zweit- [tsvaɪt] *ad*: **zu ~** together; (*bei mehreren Paaren*) in twos; **~beste(r, s)** *a* second best; **~e(r, s)** *a* second; **~ens** *ad* secondly; **~größte(r, s)** *a* second largest; **~klassig** *a* second-class; **~letzte(r, s)** *a* last but one, pe-

nultimate; **~rangig** a second-rate.
Zwerchfell ['tsvɛrçfɛl] nt diaphragm.
Zwerg [tsvɛrk] m -(e)s, -e dwarf.
Zwetsch(g)e ['tsvɛtʃ(g)ə] f -, -n plum.
Zwieback ['tsvi:bak] m -(e)s, -e rusk.
Zwiebel ['tsvi:bəl] f -, -n onion; (*Blumen~*) bulb.
Zwie- ['tsvi:] zW: **z~lichtig** a shady, dubious; **z~spältig** a (*Gefühle*) conflicting; (*Charakter*) contradictory; **~tracht** f discord, dissension.
Zwilling ['tsvɪlɪŋ] m -s, -e twin; **~e** pl (*ASTROL*) Gemini.
zwingen ['tsvɪŋən] vt unreg force; **~d** a (*Grund etc*) compelling.
zwinkern ['tsvɪŋkərn] vi blink; (*absichtlich*) wink.
Zwirn [tsvɪrn] m -(e)s, -e thread.
zwischen ['tsvɪʃən] präp +akk od dat between; **Z~bemerkung** f (incidental) remark; **Z~ding** nt cross; **~durch** [-'durç] ad in between; (*räumlich*) here and there; **Z~ergebnis** nt intermediate result;

Z~fall m incident; **Z~frage** f question; **Z~handel** m middlemen pl; middleman's trade; **Z~landung** f stop, intermediate landing; **~menschlich** a interpersonal; **Z~raum** m space; **Z~ruf** m interjection, **Z~station** f intermediate station; **Z~zeit** f interval; **in der Z~zeit** in the interim, meanwhile.
Zwist [tsvɪst] m -es, -e dispute, feud.
zwitschern ['tsvɪtʃərn] vti twitter, chirp.
zwo [tsvo:] num two.
zwölf [tsvœlf] num twelve.
Zyklus ['tsy:klus] m -, **Zyklen** cycle.
Zylinder [tsi'lɪndər] m -s, - cylinder; (*Hut*) top hat; **z~förmig** a cylindrical.
Zyniker ['tsy:nikər] m -s, - cynic.
zynisch ['tsy:nɪʃ] a cynical.
Zynismus [tsy'nɪsmus] m cynicism.
Zypern ['tsy:pərn] nt Cyprus.
Zyste ['tsystə] f -, -n cyst.
z.Z(t). abk von **zur Zeit.**

ENGLISH - GERMAN
ENGLISCH - DEUTSCH

A

A [eɪ] *n* (*MUS*) A *nt*; ~ **road** Hauptverkehrsstraße *f*.

a [eɪ, ə] *indef art* (*before vowel or silent h*: **an**) **1** ein; eine; ~ **woman** eine Frau; ~ **book** ein Buch; **an apple** ein Apfel; **she's** ~ **doctor** sie ist Ärztin

2 (*instead of the number 'one'*) ein; eine; ~ **year** ago vor einem Jahr; ~ **hundred/thousand** *etc* **pounds** (ein)hundert/(ein)tausend *etc* Pfund

3 (*in expressing ratios, prices etc*) pro; 3 ~ **day/week** 3 pro Tag/Woche, 3 am Tag/in der Woche; **10 km an hour** 10 km pro Stunde/in der Stunde.

A.A. *n abbr* = **Automobile Association** (*Brit*); **Alcoholics Anonymous.**

A.A.A. *n abbr* (*US*) = **American Automobile Association.**

aback [əˈbæk] *ad*: **to be taken** ~ verblüfft sein.

abandon [əˈbændən] *vt* (*give up*) aufgeben; (*desert*) verlassen // *n* Hingabe *f*.

abashed [əˈbæʃt] *a* verlegen.

abate [əˈbeɪt] *vi* nachlassen, sich legen.

abattoir [ˈæbətwɑː*] *n* (*Brit*) Schlachthaus *nt*.

abbey [ˈæbɪ] *n* Abtei *f*.

abbot [ˈæbət] *n* Abt *m*.

abbreviate [əˈbriːvɪeɪt] *vt* abkürzen.

abbreviation [əbriːvɪˈeɪʃən] *n* Abkürzung *f*.

abdicate [ˈæbdɪkeɪt] *vt* aufgeben // *vi* abdanken.

abdomen [ˈæbdəmən] *n* Unterleib *m*.

abduct [æbˈdʌkt] *vt* entführen.

aberration [æbəˈreɪʃən] *n* (geistige) Verwirrung *f*.

abet [əˈbet] *vt see* **aid.**

abeyance [əˈbeɪəns] *n*: **in** ~ in der Schwebe; (*disuse*) außer Kraft.

abhor [əbˈhɔː*] *vt* verabscheuen.

abide [əˈbaɪd] *vt* vertragen; leiden; ~ **by** *vt* sich halten an (+*acc*).

ability [əˈbɪlɪtɪ] *n* (*power*) Fähigkeit *f*; (*skill*) Geschicklichkeit *f*.

abject [ˈæbdʒekt] *a* (*liar*) übel; (*poverty*) größte(r, s); (*apology*) zerknirscht.

ablaze [əˈbleɪz] *a* in Flammen.

able [ˈeɪbl] *a* geschickt, fähig; **to be** ~ **to do sth** etw tun können; ~-**bodied** *a* kräftig; (*seaman*) Voll-.

ably [ˈeɪblɪ] *ad* geschickt.

abnormal [æbˈnɔːməl] *a* regelwidrig, abnorm.

aboard [əˈbɔːd] *ad*, *prep* an Bord (+*gen*).

abode [əˈbəʊd] *n*: **of no fixed** ~ ohne festen Wohnsitz.

abolish [əˈbɒlɪʃ] *vt* abschaffen.

abolition [æbəˈlɪʃən] *n* Abschaffung *f*.

abominable [əˈbɒmɪnəbl] *a* scheußlich.

aborigine [æbəˈrɪdʒɪniː] *n* Ureinwohner *m*.

abort [əˈbɔːt] *vt* abtreiben; fehlgebären; ~**ion** [əˈbɔːʃən] *n* Abtreibung *f*; (*miscarriage*) Fehlgeburt *f*; ~**ive** *a* mißlungen.

abound [əˈbaʊnd] *vi* im Überfluß vorhanden sein; **to** ~ **in** Überfluß haben an (+*dat*).

about [əˈbaʊt] ◆*ad* **1** (*approximately*) etwa, ungefähr; ~ **a hundred/thousand** *etc* etwa hundert/tausend *etc*; **at** ~ **2 o'clock** etwa um 2 Uhr; **I've just** ~ **finished** ich bin gerade fertig

2 (*referring to place*): herum, umher; **to leave things lying** ~ Sachen herumliegen lassen; **to run/walk** *etc* ~ herumrennen/gehen *etc*

3: **to be** ~ **to do sth** im Begriff sein, etw zu tun; **he was** ~ **to go to bed** er wollte gerade ins Bett gehen

◆*prep* **1** (*relating to*) über (+*acc*); **a book** ~ **London** ein Buch über London; **what is it** ~? worum geht es?; (*book etc*) wovon handelt es?; **we talked** ~ **it** wir haben darüber geredet; **what** *or* **how** ~ **doing this?** wollen wir das machen?

2 (*referring to place*) um (... herum); **to walk** ~ **the town** in der Stadt herumgehen; **her clothes were scattered** ~ **the room** ihre Kleider waren über das ganze Zimmer verstreut.

about-face [əˈbaʊtˈfeɪs] *n*, **about-turn** [əˈbaʊtˈtɜːn] *n* Kehrtwendung *f*.

above [əˈbʌv] *ad* oben // *prep* über; ~ **all** vor allem; ~ **board** *a* offen, ehrlich.

abrasive [əˈbreɪzɪv] *a* Abschleif-; (*personality*) zermürbend, aufreibend.

abreast [əˈbrest] *ad* nebeneinander; **to keep** ~ **of** Schritt halten mit.

abridge [əˈbrɪdʒ] *vt* (ab)kürzen.

abroad [əˈbrɔːd] *ad* (*be*) im Ausland; (*go*) ins Ausland.

abrupt [əˈbrʌpt] *a* (*sudden*) abrupt, jäh; (*curt*) schroff.

abscess [ˈæbsɪs] *n* Geschwür *nt*.

abscond [əbˈskɒnd] *vi* flüchten, sich davonmachen.

abseil [ˈæbsaɪl] *vi* (*also*: ~ **down**) sich abseilen.

absence ['æbsəns] n Abwesenheit f.

absent ['æbsənt] a abwesend, nicht da; (lost in thought) geistesabwesend; ~ee [æbsən'ti:] n Abwesende(r) m; ~eeism [æbsən'ti:ɪzəm] n Fehlen nt (am Arbeitsplatz/in der Schule); ~-minded a zerstreut.

absolute ['æbsəlu:t] a absolut; (power) unumschränkt; (rubbish) vollkommen, rein; ~ly [æbsə'lu:tlɪ] ad absolut, vollkommen; ~ly! ganz bestimmt!

absolve [əb'zɒlv] vt entbinden; freisprechen.

absorb [əb'zɔ:b] vt aufsaugen, absorbieren; (fig) ganz in Anspruch nehmen, fesseln; to be ~ed in a book in ein Buch vertieft sein; ~ent a absorbierend; ~ent cotton n (US) Verbandwatte f; ~ing a aufsaugend; (fig) packend.

abstain [əb'steɪn] vi (in vote) sich enthalten; to ~ from (keep from) sich enthalten (+gen).

abstemious [əb'sti:mɪəs] a enthaltsam.

abstention [əb'stenʃən] n (in vote) (Stimm)enthaltung f.

abstinence ['æbstɪnəns] n Enthaltsamkeit f.

abstract ['æbstrækt] a abstrakt.

absurd [əb'sɜ:d] a absurd.

abundance [ə'bʌndəns] n Überfluß m (of an +dat).

abundant [ə'bʌndənt] a reichlich.

abuse [ə'bju:s] n (rude language) Beschimpfung f; (ill usage) Mißbrauch m; (bad practice) (Amts)mißbrauch m // [ə'bju:z] vt (misuse) mißbrauchen.

abusive [ə'bju:sɪv] a beleidigend, Schimpf-.

abysmal [ə'bɪzməl] a scheußlich; (ignorance) bodenlos.

abyss [ə'bɪs] n Abgrund m.

AC abbr of **alternating current.**

academic [ækə'demɪk] a akademisch; (theoretical) theoretisch // n Akademiker(in f) m.

academy [ə'kædəmɪ] n (school) Hochschule f; (society) Akademie f.

accelerate [æk'seləreɪt] vi schneller werden; (AUT) Gas geben // vt beschleunigen.

acceleration [æksele'reɪʃən] n Beschleunigung f.

accelerator [ək'seləreɪtə*] n Gas(pedal) nt.

accent ['æksent] n Akzent m, Tonfall m; (mark) Akzent m; (stress) Betonung f.

accept [ək'sept] vt (take) annehmen; (agree to) akzeptieren; ~able a annehmbar; ~ance n Annahme f.

access ['ækses] n Zugang m; ~ible [æk'sesɪbl] a (easy to approach) zugänglich; (within reach) (leicht) erreichbar.

accessory [æk'sesərɪ] n Zubehörteil nt; **accessories** pl Zubehör nt; **toilet ac-**

cessories pl Toilettenartikel pl.

accident ['æksɪdənt] n Unfall m; (coincidence) Zufall m; by ~ zufällig; ~al [æksɪ'dentl] a unbeabsichtigt; ~ally [æksɪ'dentəlɪ] ad zufällig; ~-prone a: to be ~-prone zu Unfällen neigen.

acclaim [ə'kleɪm] vt zujubeln (+dat) // n Beifall m.

acclimatize [ə'klaɪmətaɪz], (US) **acclimate** [ə'klaɪmət] vt: to become ~d sich gewöhnen (to an +acc), sich akklimatisieren.

accolade ['ækəleɪd] n Auszeichnung f.

accommodate [ə'kɒmədeɪt] vt unterbringen; (hold) Platz haben für; (oblige) (aus)helfen (+dat).

accommodating [ə'kɒmədeɪtɪŋ] a entgegenkommend.

accommodation [ə'kɒmə'deɪʃən] n (US: ~s) Unterkunft f.

accompaniment [ə'kʌmpənɪmənt] n Begleitung f.

accompany [ə'kʌmpənɪ] vt begleiten.

accomplice [ə'kʌmplɪs] n Helfershelfer m, Komplize m.

accomplish [ə'kʌmplɪʃ] vt (fulfil) durchführen; (finish) vollenden; (aim) erreichen; ~ed a vollendet, ausgezeichnet; ~ment n (skill) Fähigkeit f; (completion) Vollendung f; (feat) Leistung f.

accord [ə'kɔ:d] n Übereinstimmung f; of one's own ~ freiwillig // vt gewähren; ~ance n: in ~ance with in Übereinstimmung mit; ~ing to prep nach, laut (+gen); ~ingly ad danach, dementsprechend.

accordion [ə'kɔ:dɪən] n Akkordeon nt.

accost [ə'kɒst] vt ansprechen.

account [ə'kaʊnt] n (bill) Rechnung f; (narrative) Bericht m; (report) Rechenschaftsbericht m; (in bank) Konto nt; (importance) Geltung f; ~s pl Bücher pl; on ~ auf Rechnung; of no ~ ohne Bedeutung; on no ~ keinesfalls; on ~ of wegen; to take into ~ berücksichtigen; ~ for vt (expenditure) Rechenschaft ablegen für; how do you ~ for that? wie erklären Sie (sich) das?; ~able a verantwortlich; ~ancy n Buchhaltung f; ~ant n Wirtschaftsprüfer(in f) m; ~ number n Kontonummer f.

accredited [ə'kredɪtɪd] a (offiziell) zugelassen.

accrue [ə'kru:] vi sich ansammeln.

accumulate [ə'kju:mjʊleɪt] vt ansammeln // vi sich ansammeln.

accuracy ['ækjʊrəsɪ] n Genauigkeit f.

accurate ['ækjʊrɪt] a genau; ~ly ad genau, richtig.

accusation [ækju:'zeɪʃən] n Anklage f, Beschuldigung f.

accuse [ə'kju:z] vt anklagen, beschuldigen; ~d n Angeklagte(r) mf.

accustom [ə'kʌstəm] vt gewöhnen (to

an (+*acc*); ~**ed** *a* gewohnt.

ace [eɪs] *n* As *nt*; (*col*) As *nt*, Kanone *f*.

ache [eɪk] *n* Schmerz *m* // *vi* (*be sore*) schmerzen, weh tun.

achieve [ə'tʃiːv] *vt* zustande bringen; (*aim*) erreichen; ~**ment** *n* Leistung *f*; (*act*) Erreichen *nt*.

acid ['æsɪd] *n* Säure *f* // *a* sauer, scharf; ~ **rain** *n* Saure(r) Regen *m*.

acknowledge [ək'nɒlɪdʒ] *vt* (*receipt*) bestätigen; (*admit*) zugeben; ~**ment** *n* Anerkennung *f*; (*letter*) Empfangsbestätigung *f*.

acne ['æknɪ] *n* Akne *f*.

acorn ['eɪkɔːn] *n* Eichel *f*.

acoustic [ə'kuːstɪk] *a* akustisch; ~**s** *npl* Akustik *f*.

acquaint [ə'kweɪnt] *vt* vertraut machen; **to be** ~**ed with sb** mit jdm bekannt sein; ~**ance** *n* (*person*) Bekannte(r) *mf*; (*knowledge*) Kenntnis *f*.

acquiesce [ækwɪ'es] *vi* sich abfinden (*in* mit).

acquire [ə'kwaɪə*] *vt* erwerben.

acquisition [ækwɪ'zɪʃən] *n* Errungenschaft *f*; (*act*) Erwerb *m*.

acquisitive [ə'kwɪzɪtɪv] *a* gewinnsüchtig.

acquit [ə'kwɪt] *vt* (*free*) freisprechen; **to** ~ **o.s. well** sich bewähren; ~**tal** *n* Freispruch *m*.

acre ['eɪkə*] *n* Morgen *m*.

acrid ['ækrɪd] *a* (*smell, taste*) bitter; (*smoke*) beißend.

acrimonious [ækrɪ'məʊnɪəs] *a* bitter.

acrobat ['ækrəbæt] *n* Akrobat *m*.

across [ə'krɒs] *prep* über (+ *acc*); **he lives** ~ **the river** er wohnt auf der anderen Seite des Flusses // *ad* hinüber, herüber; **ten metres** ~ zehn Meter breit; **he lives** ~ **from us** er wohnt uns gegenüber.

act [ækt] *n* (*deed*) Tat *f*; (*JUR*) Gesetz *nt*; (*THEAT*) Akt *m*; (*THEAT: turn*) Nummer *f* // *vi* (*take action*) handeln; (*behave*) sich verhalten; (*pretend*) vorgeben; (*THEAT*) spielen // *vt* (*in play*) spielen; **to** ~ **as** fungieren als; ~**ing** *a* stellvertretend // *n* Schauspielkunst *f*; (*performance*) Aufführung *f*.

action ['ækʃən] *n* (*deed*) Tat *f*; Handlung *f*; (*motion*) Bewegung *f*; (*way of working*) Funktionieren *nt*; (*battle*) Einsatz *m*, Gefecht *nt*; (*lawsuit*) Klage *f*, Prozeß *m*; **out of** ~ (*person*) nicht einsatzfähig; (*thing*) außer Betrieb; **to take** ~ etwas unternehmen; ~ **replay** *n* (*TV*) wiederholung *f*.

active ['æktɪv] *a* (*brisk*) rege, tatkräftig; (*working*) aktiv; (*GRAM*) aktiv, Tätigkeits-; ~**ly** *ad* aktiv; (*dislike*) offen.

activity [æk'tɪvɪtɪ] *n* Aktivität *f*; (*doings*) Unternehmungen *pl*; (*occupation*) Tätigkeit *f*.

actor ['æktə*] *n* Schauspieler *m*.

actress ['æktrɪs] *n* Schauspielerin *f*.

actual ['æktjʊəl] *a* wirklich; ~**ly** *ad* tatsächlich; ~**ly no** eigentlich nicht.

acumen ['ækjʊmen] *n* Scharfsinn *m*.

acute [ə'kjuːt] *a* (*severe*) heftig, akut; (*keen*) scharfsinnig.

ad [æd] *n abbr of* **advertisement**.

A.D. *ad abbr* (= *Anno Domini*) *n. Chr.*

Adam ['ædəm] *n* Adam *m*; ~'**s apple** *n* Adamsapfel *m*.

adamant ['ædəmənt] *a* eisern; hartnäckig.

adapt [ə'dæpt] *vt* anpassen // *vi* sich anpassen (*to* an +*acc*); ~**able** *a* anpassungsfähig; ~**ation** [ædæp'teɪʃən] *n* (*THEAT* etc) Bearbeitung *f*; (*adjustment*) Anpassung *f*; ~**er** *or* ~**or** *n* (*ELEC*) Zwischenstecker *m*.

add [æd] *vt* (*join*) hinzufügen; (*numbers: also:* ~ **up**) addieren; ~ **up** *vi* (*make sense*) stimmen; ~ **up to** *vt* ausmachen.

adder ['ædə*] *n* Kreuzotter *f*, Natter *f*.

addict ['ædɪkt] *n* Süchtige(r) *mf*; ~**ed** [ə'dɪktɪd] *a*: ~**ed to** -süchtig; ~**ion** [ə'dɪkʃən] *n* Sucht *f*; ~**ive** *a*: **to be** ~**ive** süchtig machen.

addition [ə'dɪʃən] *n* Anhang *m*, Addition *f*; (*MATH*) Addition *f*, Zusammenzählen *nt*; **in** ~ zusätzlich, außerdem; ~**al** *a* zusätzlich, weiter.

additive ['ædɪtɪv] *n* Zusatz *m*.

address [ə'dres] *n* Adresse *f*; (*speech*) Ansprache *f* // *vt* (*letter*) adressieren; (*speak to*) ansprechen; (*make speech to*) eine Ansprache halten an (+*acc*).

adept ['ædept] *a* geschickt; **to be** ~ **at** gut sein in (+*dat*).

adequate ['ædɪkwɪt] *a* angemessen.

adhere [əd'hɪə*] *vi*: ~ **to** (*lit*) haften an (+*dat*); (*fig*) festhalten an (+*dat*).

adhesive [əd'hiːzɪv] *a* klebend; Kleb(e)- // *n* Klebstoff *m*; ~ **tape** *n* (*Brit*) Klebestreifen *m*; (*US*) Heftpflaster *nt*.

ad hoc [æd'hɒk] *a* (*decision, committee*) Ad-hoc- // *ad* (*decide, appoint*) ad hoc.

adjacent [ə'dʒeɪsənt] *a* benachbart; ~ **to** angrenzend an (+*acc*).

adjective ['ædʒəktɪv] *n* Adjektiv *nt*, Eigenschaftswort *nt*.

adjoining [ə'dʒɔɪnɪŋ] *a* benachbart, Neben-.

adjourn [ə'dʒɜːn] *vt* vertagen // *vi* abbrechen.

adjudicate [ə'dʒuːdɪkeɪt] *vi* entscheiden, ein Urteil fällen.

adjust [ə'dʒʌst] *vt* (*alter*) anpassen; (*put right*) regulieren, richtig stellen // *vi* sich anpassen (*to* dat); ~**able** *a* verstellbar.

ad-lib [æd'lɪb] *vti* improvisieren; **ad lib** *ad* aus dem Stegreif.

administer [əd'mɪnɪstə*] *vt* (*manage*) verwalten; (*dispense*) ausüben; (*justice*) sprechen; (*medicine*) geben.

administration [ədmɪnɪs'treɪʃən] *n* Verwaltung *f*; (*POL*) Regierung *f*.
administrative [əd'mɪnɪstrətɪv] *a* Verwaltungs-.
administrator [əd'mɪnɪstreɪtə*] *n* Verwaltungsbeamte(r) *m*.
admiral ['ædmərəl] *n* Admiral *m*.
Admiralty ['ædmərəltɪ] *n* (*Brit*) Admiralität *f*.
admiration [ædmɪ'reɪʃən] *n* Bewunderung *f*.
admire [əd'maɪə*] *vt* (*respect*) bewundern; (*love*) verehren; **~r** *n* Bewunderer *m*.
admission [əd'mɪʃən] *n* (*entrance*) Einlaß, *f*; (*fee*) Eintritt(spreis) *m*; (*confession*) Geständnis *nt*.
admit [əd'mɪt] *vt* (*let in*) einlassen; (*confess*) gestehen; (*accept*) anerkennen; **~tance** *n* Zulassung *f*; **~tedly** *ad* zugegebenermaßen.
admonish [əd'mɒnɪʃ] *vt* ermahnen.
ad nauseam [æd'nɔ:sɪæm] *ad* (*repeat, talk*) endlos.
ado [ə'du:] *n*: **with more ~** ohne weitere Umstände.
adolescence [ædə'lesns] *n* Jugendalter *nt*.
adolescent [ædə'lesnt] *a* jugendlich // *n* Jugendliche(r) *mf*.
adopt [ə'dɒpt] *vt* (*child*) adoptieren; (*idea*) übernehmen; **~ion** [ə'dɒpʃən] *n* (*of child*) Adoption *f*; (*of idea*) Übernahme *f*.
adore [ə'dɔ:*] *vt* anbeten; verehren.
adorn [ə'dɔ:n] *vt* schmücken.
Adriatic [eɪdrɪ'ætɪk] *n*: **the ~** (Sea) die Adria.
adrift [ə'drɪft] *ad* Wind und Wellen preisgegeben.
adult ['ædʌlt] *n* Erwachsene(r) *mf*.
adultery [ə'dʌltərɪ] *n* Ehebruch *m*.
advance [əd'vɑ:ns] *n* (*progress*) Vorrücken *nt*; (*money*) Vorschuß *m* // *vt* (*move forward*) vorrücken; (*money*) vorschießen; (*argument*) vorbringen // *vi* vorwärtsgehen; **in ~** im voraus; **~d** *a* (*ahead*) vorgerückt; (*modern*) fortgeschritten; (*study*) für Fortgeschrittene; **~ment** *n* Förderung *f*; (*promotion*) Beförderung *f*.
advantage [əd'vɑ:ntɪdʒ] *n* Vorteil *m*; **to have an ~ over sb** jdm gegenüber im Vorteil sein; **to take ~ of** (*misuse*) ausnutzen; (*profit from*) Nutzen ziehen aus; **~ous** [ædvən'teɪdʒəs] *a* vorteilhaft.
advent ['ædvent] *n* Ankunft *f*; **A~** Advent *m*.
adventure [əd'ventʃə*] *n* Abenteuer *nt*.
adventurous [əd'ventʃərəs] *a* abenteuerlich, waghalsig.
adverb ['ædvɜ:b] *n* Adverb *nt*, Umstandswort *nt*.
adversary ['ædvəsərɪ] *n* Gegner *m*.
adverse ['ædvɜ:s] *a* widrig.

adversity [əd'vɜ:sɪtɪ] *n* Widrigkeit *f*, Mißgeschick *nt*.
advert ['ædvɜ:t] *n* Anzeige *f*.
advertise ['ædvətaɪz] *vt* werben für // *vi* annoncieren; **to ~ for sth** etw (per Anzeige) suchen.
advertisement [əd'vɜ:tɪsmənt] *n* Anzeige *f*, Inserat *nt*.
advertiser ['ædvətaɪzə*] *n* (*in newspaper etc*) Inserent *m*.
advertising ['ædvətaɪzɪŋ] *n* Werbung *f*.
advice [əd'vaɪs] *n* Rat(schlag) *m*; (*notification*) Benachrichtigung *f*.
advisable [əd'vaɪzəbl] *a* ratsam.
advise [əd'vaɪz] *vt* raten (+*dat*); **~r** *n* Berater *m*.
advisedly [əd'vaɪzədlɪ] *ad* (*deliberately*) bewußt.
advisory [əd'vaɪzərɪ] *a* beratend, Beratungs-.
advocate ['ædvəkeɪt] *vt* vertreten // *n* ['ædvəkət] Befürworter(in *f*) *m*.
Aegean [i:'dʒi:ən] *n*: **the ~** (Sea) die Ägäis.
aerial ['ɛərɪəl] *n* Antenne *f* // *a* Luft-.
aerobics [ɛər'əubɪks] *n* Aerobic *nt*.
aerodrome ['ɛərədrəum] *n* (*Brit*) Flugplatz *m*.
aerodynamic ['ɛərəudaɪ'næmɪks] *a* aerodynamisch.
aeroplane ['ɛərəpleɪn] *n* Flugzeug *nt*.
aerosol ['ɛərəsɒl] *n* Aerosol *nt*; Sprühdose *f*.
aesthetic [ɪs'θetɪk] *a* ästhetisch.
afar [ə'fɑ:*] *ad*: **from ~** aus der Ferne.
affable ['æfəbl] *a* umgänglich.
affair [ə'fɛə*] *n* (*concern*) Angelegenheit *f*; (*event*) Ereignis *nt*; (*love ~*) Verhältnis *nt*.
affect [ə'fekt] *vt* (*influence*) (ein-)wirken auf (+*acc*); (*move deeply*) bewegen; **this change doesn't ~ us** diese Änderung betrifft uns nicht; **~ed** *a* affektiert, gekünstelt.
affection [ə'fekʃən] *n* Zuneigung *f*; **~ate** [ə'fekʃənɪt] *a* liebevoll.
affiliated [ə'fɪlɪeɪtɪd] *a* angeschlossen (to *dat*).
affinity [ə'fɪnɪtɪ] *n* (*attraction*) gegenseitige Anziehung *f*; (*relationship*) Verwandtschaft *f*.
affirmation [æfə'meɪʃən] *n* Behauptung *f*.
affirmative [ə'fɜ:mətɪv] *a* bestätigend.
affix [ə'fɪks] *vt* aufkleben, anheften.
afflict [ə'flɪkt] *vt* quälen, heimsuchen.
affluence ['æfluəns] *n* (*wealth*) Wohlstand *m*.
affluent ['æfluənt] *a* wohlhabend, Wohlstands-.
afford [ə'fɔ:d] *vt* (sich) (*dat*) leisten; (*yield*) bieten, einbringen.
affront [ə'frʌnt] *n* Beleidigung *f*.
Afghanistan [æf'gænɪstɑ:n] *n* Afghanistan *nt*.

afield [ə'fiːld] *ad:* **far** ~ weit fort.

afloat [ə'fləʊt] *a:* **to be** ~ schwimmen.

afoot [ə'fʊt] *ad* im Gang.

afraid [ə'freɪd] *a* ängstlich; **to be** ~ **of** Angst haben vor (+*dat*); **to be** ~ **to** sich scheuen; **I am** ~ **I have ...** ich habe leider ...; **I'm** ~ **so/not** leider/leider nicht; **I am** ~ **that ...** ich fürchte, (daß) ...

afresh [ə'freʃ] *ad* von neuem.

Africa ['æfrɪkə] *n* Afrika *nt;* ~**n** *a* afrikanisch // *n* Afrikaner(in *f*) *m.*

aft [ɑːft] *ad* achtern.

after ['ɑːftə*] *prep* nach; (*following, seeking*) hinter ... (*dat*) ... her; (*in imitation*) nach, im Stil von // *ad:* **soon** ~ bald danach // *cj* nachdem; **what are you** ~? was wollen Sie?; ~ **he left** nachdem er gegangen war; ~ **you!** nach Ihnen!; ~ **all** letzten Endes; ~-**effects** *npl* Nachwirkungen *pl;* ~**life** *n* Leben *nt* nach dem Tode; ~**math** *n* Auswirkungen *pl;* ~**noon** *n* Nachmittag *m;* **good** ~**noon!** guten Tag!; ~**s** *n* (*col: dessert*) Nachtisch *m;* ~-**sales service** *n* (*Brit*) Kundendienst *m;* ~-**shave** (**lotion**) *n* Rasierwasser *nt;* ~**thought** *n* nachträgliche(r) Einfall *m;* ~**wards** *n* danach, nachher.

again [ə'gen] *ad* wieder, noch einmal; (*besides*) außerdem, ferner; ~ **and** ~ immer wieder.

against [ə'genst] *prep* gegen.

age [eɪdʒ] *n* (*of person*) Alter *nt;* (*in history*) Zeitalter *nt* // *vi* altern, alt werden // *vt* älter machen; **to come of** ~ mündig werden; **20 years of** ~ 20 Jahre alt; **it's been** ~**s since ...** es ist ewig her, seit ...; ~**d** *a* ... Jahre alt, -jährig; ['eɪdʒɪd] (*elderly*) betagt; **the** ~**d** die Alten *pl;* ~ **group** *n* Altersgruppe *f;* ~ **limit** *n* Altersgrenze *f.*

agency ['eɪdʒənsɪ] *n* Agentur *f;* Vermittlung *f;* (*CHEM*) Wirkung *f;* **through** *or* **by the** ~ **of ...** mit Hilfe von ...

agenda [ə'dʒendə] *n* Tagesordnung *f.*

agent ['eɪdʒənt] *n* (*COMM*) Vertreter *m;* (*spy*) Agent *m.*

aggravate ['ægrəveɪt] *vt* (*make worse*) verschlimmern; (*irritate*) reizen.

aggregate ['ægrɪgɪt] *n* Summe *f.*

aggression [ə'greʃən] *n* Aggression *f.*

aggressive *a* [ə'gresɪv] aggressiv.

aggrieved [ə'griːvd] *a* bedrückt, verletzt.

aghast [ə'gɑːst] *a* entsetzt.

agile ['ædʒaɪl] *a* flink; agil; (*mind*) rege.

agitate ['ædʒɪteɪt] *vt* rütteln; **to** ~ **for** sich starkmachen für.

ago [ə'gəʊ] *ad:* **two days** ~ vor zwei Tagen; **not long** ~ vor kurzem; **it's so long** ~ es ist schon so lange her.

agog [ə'gɒg] *a* gespannt.

agonizing ['ægənaɪzɪŋ] *a* quälend.

agony ['ægənɪ] *n* Qual *f;* **to be in** ~ Qualen leiden.

agree [ə'griː] *vt* (*date*) vereinbaren // *vi* (*have same opinion, correspond*) übereinstimmen (*with* mit); (*consent*) zustimmen; (*be in harmony*) sich vertragen; **to** ~ **to sth** einer Sache zustimmen; **to** ~ **that ...** (*admit*) zugeben; **daß ...;** **to** ~ **to do sth** sich bereit erklären, etw zu tun; **garlic doesn't** ~ **with me** Knoblauch vertrage ich nicht; **I** ~ einverstanden, ich stimme zu; **to** ~ **on sth** sich auf etw (*acc*) einigen; ~**able** *a* (*pleasing*) liebenswürdig; (*willing to consent*) einverstanden; ~**d** *a* vereinbart; ~**ment** *n* (*agreeing*) Übereinstimmung *f;* (*contract*) Vereinbarung *f,* Vertrag *m;* **to be in** ~**ment** übereinstimmen.

agricultural [ægrɪ'kʌltʃərəl] *a* landwirtschaftlich, Landwirtschafts-.

agriculture ['ægrɪkʌltʃə*] *n* Landwirtschaft *f.*

aground [ə'graʊnd] *ad:* **to run** ~ auf Grund laufen.

ahead [ə'hed] *ad* vorwärts; **to be** ~ voraus sein; ~ **of time** der Zeit voraus; **go right** *or* **straight** ~ gehen/fahren Sie geradeaus.

aid [eɪd] *n* (*assistance*) Hilfe *f,* Unterstützung *f;* (*person*) Hilfe *f;* (*thing*) Hilfsmittel *nt;* **in** ~ **of** zugunsten (+*gen*) // *vt* unterstützen, helfen (+*dat*); ~ **and abet** *vti* Beihilfe leisten (*sb* jdm).

aide [eɪd] *n* (*person*) Gehilfe *m;* (*MIL*) Adjutant *m.*

AIDS [eɪdz] *n abbr* (= *acquired immune deficiency syndrome*) Aids *nt.*

ailing ['eɪlɪŋ] *a* kränkelnd.

ailment ['eɪlmənt] *n* Leiden *nt.*

aim [eɪm] *vt* (*gun, camera*) richten auf (+*acc*) // *vi* (*with gun: also:* **take** ~) zielen; (*intend*) beabsichtigen // *n* (*intention*) Absicht *f,* Ziel *nt;* (*pointing*) Zielen *nt,* Richten *nt;* **to** ~ **at sth** etw anstreben; **to** ~ **to do** vorhaben, etw zu tun; ~**less** *a,* ~**lessly** *ad* ziellos.

ain't [eɪnt] (*col*) = **am not; are not; is not; has not; have not.**

air [ɛə*] *n* Luft *f;* (*manner*) Miene *f,* Anschein *m;* (*MUS*) Melodie *f* // *vt* lüften; (*fig*) an die Öffentlichkeit bringen // *cpd* Luft-; **by** ~ (*travel*) auf dem Luftwege; **to be on the** ~ (*RADIO, TV: programme*) gesendet werden; ~**bed** *n* (*Brit*) Luftmatratze *f;* ~-**borne** *a* in der Luft; ~-**conditioned** *a* mit Klimaanlage; ~-**conditioning** *n* Klimaanlage *f;* ~**craft** *n* Flugzeug *nt,* Maschine *f;* ~**craft carrier** *n* Flugzeugträger *m;* ~**field** *n* Flugplatz *m;* ~ **force** *n* Luftwaffe *f;* ~ **freshener** *n* Raumspray *nt;* ~**gun** *n* Luftgewehr *nt;* ~ **hostess** *n* (*Brit*) Stewardeß *f;* ~ **letter** *n* (*Brit*) Luftpostbrief *m;* ~**lift** *n* Luftbrücke *f;* ~**line** *n* Luftverkehrsgesellschaft *f;* ~**liner** *n*

Verkehrsflugzeug *nt*; ~**lock** *n* Luftblase *f*; ~**mail** *n*: by ~**mail** mit Luftpost; ~**plane** *n* (*US*) Flugzeug *nt*; ~**port** *n* Flughafen *m*, Flugplatz *m*; ~ **raid** *n* Luftangriff *m*; ~**sick** *a* luftkrank; ~**strip** *n* Landestreifen *m*; ~**terminal** *n* Terminal *m*; ~**tight** *a* luftdicht; ~ **traffic controller** *n* Fluglotse *m*; ~**y** *a* luftig; (*manner*) leichtfertig.

aisle [aɪl] *n* Gang *m*.

ajar [ə'dʒɑː*] *ad* angelehnt; einen Spalt offen.

akin [ə'kɪn] *a*: ~ **to** ähnlich (+*dat*).

alacrity [ə'lækrɪtɪ] *n* Bereitwilligkeit *f*.

alarm [ə'lɑːm] *n* (*warning*) Alarm *m*; (*bell etc*) Alarmanlage *f*; (*anxiety*) Sorge *f* // *vt* erschrecken; ~ **clock** *n* Wecker *m*.

alas [ə'læs] *interj* ach.

Albania [æl'beɪnɪə] *n* Albanien *nt*.

albeit [ɔːl'biːɪt] *cj* obgleich.

album [ælbəm] *n* Album *nt*.

alcohol ['ælkəhɒl] *n* Alkohol *m*; ~**ic** [ælkə'hɒlɪk] *a* (*drink*) alkoholisch // *n* Alkoholiker(in *f*) *m*; ~**ism** *n* Alkoholismus *m*.

alderman ['ɔːldəmən] *n*, *pl* -**men** Stadtrat *m*.

ale [eɪl] *n* Ale *nt*.

alert [ə'lɜːt] *a* wachsam // *n* Alarm *m* // *vt* alarmieren; to be on the ~ wachsam sein.

algebra ['ældʒɪbrə] *n* Algebra *f*.

Algeria [æl'dʒɪərɪə] *n* Algerien *nt*.

alias ['eɪlɪəs] *ad* alias // *n* Deckname *m*.

alibi ['ælɪbaɪ] *n* Alibi *nt*.

alien ['eɪlɪən] *n* Ausländer *m* // *a* (*foreign*) ausländisch; (*strange*) fremd; ~ **to** fremd (+*dat*); ~**ate** *vt* entfremden.

alight [ə'laɪt] *a* brennend; (*of building*) in Flammen // *vi* (*descend*) aussteigen; (*bird*) sich setzen.

align [ə'laɪn] *vt* ausrichten.

alike [ə'laɪk] *a* gleich, ähnlich // *ad* gleich, ebenso; to look ~ sich (*dat*) ähnlich sehen.

alimony ['ælɪmənɪ] *n* Unterhalt *m*, Alimente *pl*.

alive [ə'laɪv] *a* (*living*) lebend; (*lively*) lebendig, aufgeweckt; (*full of*) voll (*with* von), wimmelnd (*with* von).

all [ɔːl] *a* alle(r, s); ~ day/night den ganzen Tag/die ganze Nacht; ~ men are equal alle Menschen sind gleich; ~ five came alle fünf kamen; ~ the books/food die ganzen Bücher/das ganze Essen; ~ the time die ganze Zeit (über); ~ his life sein ganzes Leben (lang) ◆*pron* 1 alles; I ate it ~, I ate ~ of it ich habe alles gegessen; ~ of us/the boys went wir gingen alle/alle Jungen gingen; we ~ sat down wir setzten uns alle 2 (*in phrases*): above ~ vor allem; after ~ schließlich; at ~: not at ~ (*in answer to question*) überhaupt nicht; (*in answer*

to thanks) gern geschehen; I'm not at ~ tired ich bin überhaupt nicht müde; anything at ~ will do es ist egal, welche(r, s); ~ in ~ alles in allem ◆*ad* ganz; ~ **alone** ganz allein; it's not as hard as ~ that so schwer ist es nun auch wieder nicht; ~ the more/the better um so mehr/besser; ~ but fast; the score is 2 ~ es steht 2 zu 2.

allay [ə'leɪ] *vt* (*fears*) beschwichtigen.

all clear ['ɔːl'klɪə*] *n* Entwarnung *f*.

allegation [ælɪ'geɪʃən] *n* Behauptung *f*.

allege [ə'ledʒ] *vt* (*declare*) behaupten; (*falsely*) vorgeben; ~**dly** [ə'ledʒɪdlɪ] *ad* angeblich.

allegiance [ə'liːdʒəns] *n* Treue *f*.

allergic [ə'lɜːdʒɪk] *a* allergisch (*to* gegen).

allergy ['ælədʒɪ] *n* Allergie *f*.

alleviate [ə'liːvɪeɪt] *vt* lindern.

alley ['ælɪ] *n* Gasse *f*, Durchgang *m*.

alliance [ə'laɪəns] *n* Bund *m*, Allianz *f*.

allied ['ælaɪd] *a* vereinigt; (*powers*) alliiert; verwandt (*to* mit).

alligator ['ælɪgeɪtə*] *n* Alligator *m*.

all-in ['ɔːlɪn] *a*, *ad* (*Brit*: *charge*) alles inbegriffen, Gesamt-; ~ **wrestling** *n* Freistilringen *nt*.

all-night ['ɔːl'naɪt] *a* (*café, cinema*) die ganze Nacht geöffnet, Nacht-.

allocate ['æləkeɪt] *vt* zuteilen.

allot [ə'lɒt] *vt* zuteilen; ~**ment** *n* (*share*) Anteil *m*; (*plot*) Schrebergarten *m*.

all-out ['ɔːl'aʊt] *a* total; **all out** *ad* mit voller Kraft.

allow [ə'laʊ] *vt* (*permit*) erlauben, gestatten (*sb* jdm); (*grant*) bewilligen; (*deduct*) abziehen; (*concede*): to ~ that ... annehmen, daß ...; ~ **for** *vt* berücksichtigen, einplanen; ~**ance** *n* Beihilfe *f*; to make ~ances for berücksichtigen.

alloy ['ælɔɪ] *n* Metallegierung *f*.

all right *ad* (*well*) gut; (*correct*) richtig; (*as answer*) okay.

all-round ['ɔːl'raʊnd] *a* (*sportsman*) allseitig, Allround-; (*view*) Rundum-.

all-time ['ɔːl'taɪm] *a* (*record, high*) ... aller Zeiten, Höchst-.

allude [ə'luːd] *vi* hinweisen, anspielen (*to* auf +*acc*).

alluring [ə'ljʊərɪŋ] *a* verlockend.

allusion [ə'luːʒən] *n* Anspielung *f*.

ally ['ælaɪ] *n* Verbündete(r) *mf*; (*POL*) Alliierte(r) *m* // *vr* [ə'laɪ]: to ~ o.s. with sich verbünden mit.

almighty [ɔːl'maɪtɪ] *a* allmächtig.

almond ['ɑːmənd] *n* Mandel *f*.

almost ['ɔːlməʊst] *ad* fast, beinahe.

alms [ɑːmz] *npl* Almosen *nt*.

aloft [ə'lɒft] *ad* (*be*) in der Luft; (*throw*) in die Luft.

alone [ə'ləʊn] *a*, *ad* allein; to leave sth ~ etw sein lassen; let alone ... geschweige denn ...

along [ə'lɒŋ] *prep* entlang, längs // *ad* (*onward*) vorwärts, weiter; ~ **with** zusammen mit; **he was limping** ~ er humpelte einher; **all** ~ (*all the time*) die ganze Zeit; ~**side** *ad* (*walk*) nebenher; (*come*) nebendran; (*be*) daneben // *prep* (*walk, compared with*) neben (+*dat*); (*come*) neben (+*acc*); (*be*) entlang, neben (+*dat*); (*of ship*) längsseits (+*gen*).

aloof [ə'lu:f] *a* zurückhaltend // *ad* fern; **to stand** ~ abseits stehen.

aloud [ə'laud] *ad* laut.

alphabet ['ælfəbet] *n* Alphabet *nt*; ~**ical** [ælfə'betɪkl] *a* alphabetisch.

alpine ['ælpaɪn] *a* alpin, Alpen-.

Alps [ælps] *npl*: **the** ~ die Alpen.

already [ɔ:l'redɪ] *ad* schon, bereits.

alright ['ɔ:l'raɪt] *ad* (*Brit*) = **all right**.

Alsatian [æl'seɪʃən] *n* (*dog*) Schäferhund *m*.

also ['ɔ:lsəu] *ad* auch, außerdem.

altar ['ɔ:ltə*] *n* Altar *m*.

alter ['ɔ:ltə*] *vt* ändern; (*dress*) umändern; ~**ation** [ɒltə'reɪʃən] *n* Änderung *f*; Umänderung *f*; (*to building*) Umbau *m*.

alternate [ɒl'tɜ:nɪt] *a* abwechselnd // *vi* ['ɒltə:neɪt] abwechseln (*with* mit); **on** ~ **days** jeden zweiten Tag.

alternating ['ɒltɜ:neɪtɪŋ] *a*: ~ **current** Wechselstrom *m*.

alternative [ɒl'tɜ:nətɪv] *a* andere(r, s) // *n* Alternative *f*; ~**ly** *ad* im anderen Falle; ~**ly one could** ... oder man könnte ...

alternator ['ɒltɜ:neɪtə*] *n* (*AUT*) Lichtmaschine *f*.

although [ɔ:l'ðəu] *cj* obwohl.

altitude ['æltɪtju:d] *n* Höhe *f*.

alto ['æltəu] *n* Alt *m*.

altogether [ɔ:ltə'geðə*] *ad* (*on the whole*) im ganzen genómmen; (*entirely*) ganz und gar.

aluminium [ælju'mɪnɪəm], (*US*) **aluminum** [ə'lu:mɪnəm] *n* Aluminium *nt*.

always ['ɔ:lweɪz] *ad* immer.

am [æm] *see* **be**.

a.m. *ad abbr* (= *ante meridiem*) vormittags.

amalgamate [ə'mælgəmeɪt] *vi* (*combine*) sich vereinigen // *vt* (*mix*) amalgamieren.

amass [ə'mæs] *vt* anhäufen.

amateur ['æmətɜ:*] *n* Amateur *m*; (*pej*) Amateur *m*, Stümper *m*; ~**ish** *a* (*pej*) dilettantisch, stümperhaft.

amaze [ə'meɪz] *vt* erstaunen; **to be** ~**d** (**at**) erstaunt sein (über); ~**ment** *n* höchste(s) Erstaunen *nt*.

amazing [ə'meɪzɪŋ] *a* höchst erstaunlich.

Amazon ['æməzən] *n* (*GEOG*) Amazonas *m*.

ambassador [æm'bæsədə*] *n* Botschafter *m*.

amber ['æmbə*] *n* Bernstein *m*; **at** ~ (*Brit AUT*) (auf) gelb.

ambiguous [æm'bɪgjuəs] *a* zweideutig; (*not clear*) unklar.

ambition [æm'bɪʃən] *n* Ehrgeiz *m*.

ambitious [æm'bɪʃəs] *a* ehrgeizig.

ambivalent [æm'bɪvələnt] *n* (*attitude*) zwiespältig.

amble ['æmbl] *vi* (*usu:* ~ **along**) schlendern.

ambulance ['æmbjuləns] *n* Krankenwagen *m*; ~**man** *n* Sanitäter *m*.

ambush ['æmbuʃ] *n* Hinterhalt *m* // *vt* (aus dem Hinterhalt) überfallen.

amenable [ə'mi:nəbl] *a* gefügig; (*to reason*) zugänglich (*to dat*); (*to flattery*) empfänglich (*to für*); (*to law*) unterworfen (*to dat*).

amend [ə'mend] *vt* (*law etc*) abändern, ergänzen; **to make** ~**s** etw wiedergutmachen; ~**ment** *n* Abänderung *f*.

amenities [ə'mi:nɪtɪz] *npl* Einrichtungen *pl*.

America [ə'merɪkə] *n* Amerika *nt*; ~**n** *a* amerikanisch // *n* Amerikaner(in *f*) *m*.

amiable ['eɪmɪəbl] *a* liebenswürdig.

amicable ['æmɪkəbl] *a* freundschaftlich; (*settlement*) gütlich.

amid(st) [ə'mɪd(st)] *prep* mitten in *or* unter (+*dat*).

amiss [ə'mɪs] *ad*: **to take sth** ~ etw übelnehmen; **there's something** ~ da stimmt irgend etwas nicht.

ammunition [æmju'nɪʃən] *n* Munition *f*.

amnesia [æm'ni:zɪə] *n* Gedächtnisverlust *m*.

amnesty ['æmnɪstɪ] *n* Amnestie *f*.

among(st) [ə'mʌŋ(st)] *prep* unter.

amoral [æ'mɒrəl] *a* unmoralisch.

amorous ['æmərəs] *a* verliebt.

amount [ə'maunt] *n* (*of money*) Betrag *m*; (*of time, energy*) Aufwand *m* (*of an* +*dat*); (*of water, sand*) Menge *f* // *vi*: ~ **to** (*total*) sich belaufen auf (+*acc*); **this** ~**s to treachery** das kommt Verrat gleich; **it** ~**s to the same** es läuft aufs gleiche hinaus; **he won't** ~ **to much** aus ihm wird nie was.

amp(ère) ['æmp(eə*)] *n* Ampere *nt*.

amphibian [æm'fɪbɪən] *n* Amphibie *f*.

amphibious [æm'fɪbɪəs] *a* amphibisch, Amphibien-.

ample ['æmpl] *a* (*portion*) reichlich; (*dress*) weit, groß; ~ **time** genügend Zeit.

amplifier ['æmplɪfaɪə*] *n* Verstärker *m*.

amuse [ə'mju:z] *vt* (*entertain*) unterhalten; (*make smile*) belustigen; ~**ment** *n* (*feeling*) Unterhaltung *f*; (*recreation*) Zeitvertreib *m*; ~**ment arcade** *n* Spielhalle *f*.

an [æn, ən] *see* **a.**

anaemia [ə'ni:mɪə] *n* Anämie *f*.

anaemic [ə'niːmɪk] a blutarm.

anaesthetic [ænɪs'θetɪk] n Betäubungs-mittel nt; **under ~** unter Narkose.

anaesthetist [æ'niːsθɪtɪst] n Anästhe-sist(in f) m.

analgesic [ænæl'dʒiːsɪk] n schmerz-lindernde(s) Mittel nt.

analog(ue) ['ænəlɒg] a Analog-.

analogy [ə'nælədʒɪ] n Analogie f.

analyse ['ænəlaɪz] vt (Brit) analysieren.

analysis [ə'nælɪsɪs], pl **-ses** [-siːz] n Analyse f.

analyst ['ænəlɪst] n Analytiker(in f) m.

analytic(al) [ænə'lɪtɪk(əl)] a analytisch.

analyze ['ænəlaɪz] vt (US) = **analyse.**

anarchy ['ænəkɪ] n Anarchie f.

anathema [ə'næθɪmə] n (fig) Greuel nt.

anatomy [ə'nætəmɪ] n (structure) anatomische(r) Aufbau m; (study) Anatomie f.

ancestor ['ænsestə*] n Vorfahr m.

anchor ['æŋkə*] n Anker m // vi (also: **to drop ~**) ankern, vor Anker liegen // vt verankern; **to weigh ~** den Anker lichten; **~age** n Ankerplatz m.

anchovy ['æntʃəvɪ] n Sardelle f.

ancient ['eɪnʃənt] a alt; (car etc) uralt.

ancillary [æn'sɪlərɪ] a Hilfs-.

and [ænd] cj und; **~ so on** und so weiter; **try ~ come** versuche zu kommen; **better ~** better immer besser.

Andes ['ændiːz] npl: **the ~** die Anden pl.

anemia [ə'niːmɪə] n (US) = **anaemia.**

anesthetic [ænɪs'θetɪk] n (US) = **anaesthetic.**

anew [ə'njuː] ad von neuem.

angel ['eɪndʒəl] n Engel m.

anger ['æŋgə*] n Zorn m // vt ärgern.

angle ['æŋgl] n Winkel m; (point of view) Standpunkt m; **~r** n Angler m.

Anglican ['æŋglɪkən] a anglikanisch // n Anglikaner(in f) m.

angling ['æŋglɪŋ] n Angeln nt.

Anglo- ['æŋgləʊ] pref Anglo-.

angrily ['æŋgrɪlɪ] ad ärgerlich, böse.

angry ['æŋgrɪ] a ärgerlich, ungehalten, böse; (wound) entzündet; **to be ~ with sb** auf jdn böse sein; **to be ~ at sth** über etw (acc) verärgert sein.

anguish ['æŋgwɪʃ] n Qual f.

angular ['æŋgjʊlə*] a eckig, winkelförmig; (face) kantig.

animal ['ænɪməl] n Tier nt; (living creature) Lebewesen nt // a tierisch.

animate ['ænɪmeɪt] vt beleben // a ['ænɪmət] lebhaft; **~d** a lebendig; (film) Zeichentrick-.

animosity [ænɪ'mɒsɪtɪ] n Feindseligkeit f, Abneigung f.

aniseed ['ænɪsiːd] n Anis m.

ankle ['æŋkl] n (Fuß)knöchel m; **~ sock** n Söckchen nt.

annex ['æneks] n (also: Brit: **annexe**) Anbau m // vt [ə'neks] anfügen; (POL) annektieren, angliedern.

annihilate [ə'naɪəleɪt] vt vernichten.

anniversary [ænɪ'vɜːsərɪ] n Jahrestag m.

annotate ['ænəteɪt] vt kommentieren.

announce [ə'naʊns] vt ankündigen, an-zeigen; **~ment** n Ankündigung f; (official) Bekanntmachung f; **~r** n An-sager(in f) m.

annoy [ə'nɔɪ] vt ärgern; **don't get ~ed!** reg' dich nicht auf!; **~ance** n Ärgernis nt, Störung f; **~ing** a ärgerlich; (person) lästig.

annual ['ænjʊəl] a jährlich; (salary) Jahres- // n (plant) einjährige Pflanze f; (book) Jahrbuch nt; **~ly** ad jährlich.

annul [ə'nʌl] vt aufheben, annullieren; **~ment** n Aufhebung f, Annullierung f.

annum ['ænəm] n see **per.**

anomaly [ə'nɒməlɪ] n Abweichung f von der Regel.

anonymous [ə'nɒnɪməs] a anonym.

anorak ['ænəræk] n Anorak m, Windjacke f.

anorexia [ænə'reksɪə] n (MED) Magersucht f.

another [ə'nʌðə*] a, pron (different) ein(e) andere(r, s); (additional) noch eine(r, s); see also **one.**

answer ['ɑːnsə*] n Antwort f // vi ant-worten; (on phone) sich melden // vt (person) antworten (+dat); (letter, question) beantworten; (telephone) gehen an (+acc), abnehmen; (door) öffnen; **to ~ the phone** ans Telefon gehen; **in ~ to your letter** in Beantwortung Ihres Schreibens; **to ~ the bell** or **the door** auf-machen; **~ back** vi frech sein; **~ for** vt: **to ~ for sth** für etw verantwortlich sein; **~able** a: **to be ~ to sb for sth** jdm gegenüber für etw verantwortlich sein; **~ing machine** n Anrufbeantworter m.

ant [ænt] n Ameise f.

antagonism [æn'tægənɪzəm] n Ant-agonismus m.

antagonize [æn'tægənaɪz] vt reizen.

Antarctic [ænt'ɑːktɪk] a antarktisch // n: **the ~** die Antarktis.

antelope ['æntɪləʊp] n Antilope f.

antenatal [æntɪ'neɪtl] a vor der Geburt; **~ clinic** n Sprechstunde f für werdende Mütter.

antenna [æn'tenə], pl **~e** [-niː] n (BIOL) Fühler m; (RAD) Antenne f.

anthem ['ænθəm] n Hymne f; **national ~** Nationalhymne f.

anthology [æn'θɒlədʒɪ] n Gedichtsamm-lung f, Anthologie f.

anti- ['æntɪ] pref Gegen-, Anti-.

anti-aircraft ['æntɪ'eəkrɑːft] a Flugabwehr-.

antibiotic ['æntɪbaɪ'ɒtɪk] n Antibiotikum nt.

antibody ['æntɪbɒdɪ] n Antikörper m.

anticipate [æn'tɪsɪpeɪt] vt (expect: trouble, question) erwarten, rechnen mit;

(*look forward to*) sich freuen auf (+*acc*); (*do first*) vorwegnehmen; (*foresee*) ahnen, vorhersehen.

anticipation [æntɪsɪˈpeɪʃən] *n* Erwartung *f*; (*foreshadowing*) Vorwegnahme *f*.

anticlimax [ˈæntɪˈklaɪmæks] *n* Ernüchterung *f*.

anticlockwise [ˈæntɪˈklɒkwaɪz] *ad* entgegen dem Uhrzeigersinn.

antics [ˈæntɪks] *npl* Possen *pl*.

anticyclone [ˈæntɪˈsaɪkləʊn] *n* Hoch *nt*, Hochdruckgebiet *nt*.

antidote [ˈæntɪdəʊt] *n* Gegenmittel *nt*.

antifreeze [ˈæntɪfriːz] *n* Frostschutzmittel *nt*.

antihistamine [æntɪˈhɪstəmiːn] *n* Antihistamin *nt*.

antiquated [ˈæntɪkweɪtɪd] *a* antiquiert.

antique [ænˈtiːk] *n* Antiquität *f* // *a* antik; (*old-fashioned*) altmodisch; ~ **shop** *n* Antiquitätenladen *m*.

antiquity [ænˈtɪkwɪtɪ] *n* Altertum *nt*.

antiseptic [æntɪˈseptɪk] *n* Antiseptikum *nt* // *a* antiseptisch.

antisocial [æntɪˈsəʊʃl] *a* (*person*) ungesellig; (*law*) unsozial.

antlers [ˈæntləz] *npl* Geweih *nt*.

anus [ˈeɪnəs] *n* After *m*.

anvil [ˈænvɪl] *n* Amboß *m*.

anxiety [æŋˈzaɪətɪ] *n* Angst *f*; (*worry*) Sorge *f*.

anxious [ˈæŋkʃəs] *a* ängstlich; (*worried*) besorgt; **to be** ~ **to do sth** etw unbedingt tun wollen.

any [ˈenɪ] ◆ *a* **1** (*in questions etc*): **have you** ~ **butter?** haben Sie (etwas) Butter?; **have you** ~ **children?** haben Sie Kinder?; **if there are** ~ **tickets left** falls noch Karten da sind

2 (*with negative*): **I haven't** ~ **money/ books** ich habe kein Geld/keine Bücher

3 (*no matter which*) jede(r, s) (beliebige); ~ **colour (at all)** jede beliebige Farbe; **choose** ~ **book you like** nehmen Sie ein beliebiges Buch

4 (*in phrases*): **in** ~ **case** in jedem Fall; ~ **day now** jeden Tag; **at** ~ **moment** jeden Moment; **at** ~ **rate** auf jeden Fall

◆ *pron* **1** (*in questions etc*): **have you got** ~? haben Sie welche?; **can** ~ **of you sing?** kann (irgend)einer von euch singen?

2 (*with negative*): **I haven't** ~ (**of them**) ich habe keinen/keines (davon)

3 (*no matter which one(s)*): **take** ~ **of those books (you like)** nehmen Sie irgendeines dieser Bücher

◆ *ad* (*in questions etc*): **do you want** ~ **more soup/sandwiches?** möchten Sie noch Suppe/Brote?; **are you feeling** ~ **better?** fühlen Sie sich etwas besser?

2 (*with negative*): **I can't hear him** ~ **more** ich kann ihn nicht mehr hören.

anybody [ˈenɪbɒdɪ] *pron* (*no matter who*) jede(r); (*in questions etc*) (irgend)-

jemand, (irgend) eine(r); (*with negative*): **I can't see** ~ ich kann niemanden sehen.

anyhow [ˈenɪhaʊ] *ad* (*at any rate*): **I shall go** ~ ich gehe sowieso; (*haphazard*): **do it** ~ **you like** machen Sie es, wie Sie wollen.

anyone [ˈenɪwʌn] *pron* = **anybody**.

anything [ˈenɪθɪŋ] *pron* **1** (*in questions etc*) (irgend) etwas; **can you see** ~? können Sie etwas sehen?

2 (*with negative*): **I can't see** ~ ich kann nichts sehen

3 (*no matter what*): **you can say** ~ **you like** Sie können sagen, was Sie wollen; ~ **will do** wird irgend etwas, irgendeine(r, s); **he'll eat** ~ er ißt alles.

anyway [ˈenɪweɪ] *ad* (*at any rate*) auf jeden Fall; (*besides*): ~, **I couldn't come even if I wanted to** jedenfalls könnte ich nicht kommen, selbst wenn ich wollte; **why are you phoning,** ~? warum rufst du überhaupt an?

anywhere [ˈenɪwɛə*] *ad* (*in questions etc*) irgendwo; (: *with direction*) irgendwohin; (*no matter where*) überall; (: *with direction*) überallhin; (*with negative*): **I can't see him** ~ ich kann ihn nirgendwo *or* nirgends sehen; **can you see him** ~? siehst du ihn irgendwo?; **put the books down** ~ leg die Bücher irgendwohin.

apart [əˈpɑːt] *ad* (*parted*) auseinander; (*away*) beiseite, abseits; **10 miles** ~ 10 Meilen auseinander; **to take** ~ auseinandernehmen; ~ **from** *prep* außer.

apartheid [əˈpɑːteɪt] *n* Apartheid *f*.

apartment [əˈpɑːtmənt] *n* (*US*) Wohnung *f*; ~ **building** *n* (*US*) Wohnhaus *nt*.

apathy [ˈæpəθɪ] *n* Teilnahmslosigkeit *f*, Apathie *f*.

ape [eɪp] *n* (Menschen)affe *m* // *vt* nachahmen.

aperture [ˈæpətjʊə*] *n* Öffnung *f*; (*PHOT*) Blende *f*.

apex [ˈeɪpeks] *n* Spitze *f*.

apiece [əˈpiːs] *ad* pro Stück; (*per person*) pro Kopf.

apologetic [əpɒləˈdʒetɪk] *a* entschuldigend; **to be** ~ sich sehr entschuldigen.

apologize [əˈpɒlədʒaɪz] *vi* sich entschuldigen (*for sth to sb* für etw bei jdm).

apology [əˈpɒlədʒɪ] *n* Entschuldigung *f*.

apostle [əˈpɒsl] *n* Apostel *m*.

apostrophe [əˈpɒstrəfɪ] *n* Apostroph *m*.

appal [əˈpɔːl] *vt* erschrecken; ~**ling** *a* schrecklich.

apparatus [æpəˈreɪtəs] *n* Gerät *nt*.

apparel [əˈpærəl] *n* (*US*) Kleidung *f*.

apparent [əˈpærənt] *a* offenbar; ~**ly** *ad* anscheinend.

apparition [æpəˈrɪʃən] *n* (*ghost*) Erscheinung f, Geist m; (appearance) Erscheinen nt.

appeal [ə'pi:l] vi dringend ersuchen; dringend bitten (for um); sich wenden (to an +acc); (to public) appellieren (to an +acc); (JUR) Berufung einlegen // n Aufruf m; (JUR) Berufung f; it doesn't ~ to me es gefällt mir nicht; ~ing a ansprechend.

appear [ə'pɪə*] vi (come into sight) erscheinen; (be seen) auftauchen; (seem) scheinen; ~ance n (coming into sight) Erscheinen nt; (outward show) Äußere(s) nt; it would ~ that ... anscheinend ...

appease [ə'pi:z] vt beschwichtigen.

appendicitis [əpendɪ'saɪtɪs] n Blinddarmentzündung f.

appendix [ə'pendɪks], pl **-dices** [-dɪsi:z] n (in book) Anhang m; (MED) Blinddarm m.

appetite ['æpɪtaɪt] n Appetit m; (fig) Lust f.

appetizer ['æpətaɪzə*] n Appetitanreger m.

appetizing ['æpɪtaɪzɪŋ] a appetitanregend.

applaud [ə'plɔ:d] vti Beifall klatschen (+dat), applaudieren.

applause [ə'plɔ:z] n Beifall m, Applaus m.

apple ['æpl] n Apfel m; ~ **tree** n Apfelbaum m.

appliance [ə'plaɪəns] n Gerät nt.

applicable [ə'plɪkəbl] a anwendbar; (in forms) zutreffend.

applicant ['æplɪkənt] n Bewerber(in f) m.

application [æplɪ'keɪʃən] n (request) Antrag m; (for job) Bewerbung f; (putting into practice) Anwendung f; (hard work) Fleiß m; ~ **form** n Bewerbungsformular nt.

applied [ə'plaɪd] a angewandt.

apply [ə'plaɪ] vi (ask) sich wenden (to an +acc), sich melden; (be suitable) zutreffen // vt (place on) auflegen; (cream) auftragen; (put into practice) anwenden; to ~ for sth sich um etw bewerben; to ~ the brakes die Bremsen betätigen; to ~ o.s. to sth sich bei etw anstrengen.

appoint [ə'pɔɪnt] vt (to office) ernennen, berufen; (settle) festsetzen; ~ment n (meeting) Verabredung f; (at hairdresser etc) Bestellung f; (in business) Termin m; (choice for a position) Ernennung f; (UNIV) Berufung f.

appraisal [ə'preɪzl] n Beurteilung f.

appreciable [ə'pri:ʃəbl] a (perceptible) merklich; (able to be estimated) abschätzbar.

appreciate [ə'pri:ʃɪeɪt] vt (value) zu schätzen wissen; (understand) einsehen // vi (increase in value) im Wert steigen.

appreciation [əpri:ʃɪ'eɪʃən] n Wert-

schätzung f; (COMM) Wertzuwachs m.

appreciative [ə'pri:ʃɪətɪv] a (showing thanks) dankbar; (showing liking) anerkennend.

apprehend [æprɪ'hend] vt (arrest) festnehmen; (understand) erfassen.

apprehension [æprɪ'henʃən] n Angst f.

apprehensive [æprɪ'hensɪv] a furchtsam.

apprentice [ə'prentɪs] n Lehrling m; ~ship n Lehrzeit f.

approach [ə'prəutʃ] vi sich nähern // vt herantreten an (+acc); (problem) herangehen an (+acc) // n Annäherung f; (to problem) Ansatz m; (path) Zugang m, Zufahrt f; ~able a zugänglich.

appropriate [ə'prəuprɪət] a angemessen; (remark) angebracht // [ə'prəuprɪeɪt] vt (take for o.s.) sich aneignen; (set apart) bereitstellen.

approval [ə'pru:vəl] n (show of satisfaction) Beifall m; (permission) Billigung f; (COMM) on ~ bei Gefallen.

approve [ə'pru:v] vti billigen; I don't ~ of it/him ich halte nichts davon/von ihm; ~d **school** n (Brit) Erziehungsheim nt.

approximate [ə'prɒksɪmət] a annähernd, ungefähr // vt [ə'prɒksɪmeɪt] nahekommen (+dat); ~ly ad rund, ungefähr.

apricot ['eɪprɪkɒt] n Aprikose f.

April ['eɪprəl] n April m; ~ **Fools' Day** n der erste April.

apron ['eɪprən] n Schürze f.

apt [æpt] a (suitable) passend; (able) begabt; (likely): to be ~ to do sth dazu neigen, etw zu tun.

aptitude ['æptɪtju:d] n Begabung f.

aqualung ['ækwəlʌŋ] n Unterwasseratmungsgerät nt.

aquarium [ə'kwɛərɪəm] n Aquarium nt.

Aquarius [ə'kwɛərɪəs] n Wassermann m.

aquatic [ə'kwætɪk] a Wasser-.

Arab ['ærəb] n Araber(in f) m.

Arabia [ə'reɪbɪə] n Arabien nt.

Arabian [ə'reɪbɪən] a arabisch.

Arabic ['ærəbɪk] a arabisch // n Arabisch nt; ~ **numerals** arabische Ziffern.

arable ['ærəbl] a bebaubar, Kultur-.

arbitrary ['ɑ:bɪtrərɪ] a willkürlich.

arbitration [ɑ:bɪ'treɪʃən] n Schlichtung f.

arc [ɑ:k] n Bogen m.

arcade [ɑ:'keɪd] n Säulengang m.

arch [ɑ:tʃ] n Bogen m // vt überwölben; (back) krumm machen.

archaeologist [ɑ:kɪ'ɒlədʒɪst] n Archäologe m.

archaeology [ɑ:kɪ'ɒlədʒɪ] n Archäologie f.

archaic [ɑ:'keɪɪk] a altertümlich.

archbishop ['ɑ:tʃ'bɪʃəp] n Erzbischof m.

arch-enemy ['ɑ:tʃ'enəmɪ] n Erzfeind m.

archeology *etc* (*US*) = **archaelogy** *etc*.

archer ['ɑːtʃə*] *n* Bogenschütze *m*; **~y** *n* Bogenschießen *nt*.

archipelago [ɑːkɪ'pelɪgəʊ] *n* Archipel *m*; (*sea*) Inselmeer *nt*.

architect ['ɑːkɪtekt] *n* Architekt(in *f*) *m*; **~ural** [ɑːkɪ'tektʃərəl] *a* architektonisch; **~ure** *n* Architektur *f*.

archives ['ɑːkaɪvz] *npl* Archiv *nt*.

archway ['ɑːtʃweɪ] *n* Bogen *m*.

Arctic ['ɑːktɪk] *a* arktisch // *n*: **the ~** die Arktis.

ardent ['ɑːdənt] *a* glühend.

arduous ['ɑːdjuəs] *a* mühsam.

are [ɑː*] *see* **be**.

area ['ɛərɪə] *n* Fläche *f*; (*of land*) Gebiet *nt*; (*part of sth*) Teil *m*, Abschnitt *m*.

arena [ə'riːnə] *n* Arena *f*.

aren't [ɑːnt] = **are not**.

Argentina [ɑːdʒən'tiːnə] *n* Argentinien *nt*; **Argentinian** [ɑːdʒən'tɪnɪən] *a* argentinisch // *n* Argentinier(in *f*) *m*.

arguably ['ɑːgjʊəblɪ] *ad* wohl.

argue ['ɑːgjuː] *vi* diskutieren; (*angrily*) streiten.

argument ['ɑːgjʊmənt] *n* (*theory*) Argument *nt*; (*reasoning*) Argumentation *f*; (*row*) Auseinandersetzung *f*, Streit *m*; **to have an ~** sich streiten; **~ative** [ɑːgjʊ'mentətɪv] *a* streitlustig.

aria ['ɑːrɪə] *n* Arie *f*.

arid ['ærɪd] *a* trocken.

Aries ['ɛəriːz] *n* Widder *m*.

arise, *pt* **arose,** *pp* **arisen** [ə'raɪz, ə'rəʊz, ə'rɪzn] *vi* aufsteigen; (*get up*) aufstehen; (*difficulties etc*) entstehen; (*case*) vorkommen; **to ~ from sth** herrühren von etw.

aristocracy [ærɪs'tɒkrəsɪ] *n* Adel *m*, Aristokratie *f*.

aristocrat ['ærɪstəkræt] *n* Adlige(r) *mf*, Aristokrat(in *f*) *m*.

arithmetic [ə'rɪθmətɪk] *n* Rechnen *nt*, Arithmetik *f*.

ark [ɑːk] *n*: **Noah's A~** die Arche Noah.

arm [ɑːm] *n* Arm *m*; (*branch of military service*) Zweig *m* // *vt* bewaffnen.

armaments ['ɑːməmənts] *npl* Ausrüstung *f*.

arm: **~chair** *n* Lehnstuhl *m*; **~ed** *a* (*forces*) Streit-, bewaffnet; (*robbery*) bewaffnet.

armistice ['ɑːmɪstɪs] *n* Waffenstillstand *m*.

armour, (*US*) **armor** ['ɑːmə*] *n* (*knight's*) Rüstung *f*; (*MIL*) Panzerplatte *f*; **~ed car** *n* Panzerwagen *m*; **~y** *n* Waffenlager *nt*; (*factory*) Waffenfabrik *f*.

armpit ['ɑːmpɪt] *n* Achselhöhle *f*.

armrest ['ɑːmrest] *n* Armlehne *f*.

arms [ɑːmz] *npl* (*weapons*) Waffen *pl*; **~ race** *n* Wettrüsten *nt*.

army ['ɑːmɪ] *n* Armee *f*, Heer *nt*; (*host*) Heer *nt*.

aroma [ə'rəʊmə] *n* Duft *m*, Aroma *nt*; **~tic** [ærə'mætɪk] *a* aromatisch, würzig.

arose [ə'rəʊz] *pt of* **arise**.

around [ə'raʊnd] *ad* ringsherum; (*almost*) ungefähr // *prep* um ... herum; **is he ~?** ist er hier?

arouse [ə'raʊz] *vt* wecken.

arrange [ə'reɪndʒ] *vt* (*time, meeting*) festsetzen; (*holidays*) festlegen; (*flowers, hair, objects*) anordnen; **I ~d to meet him** ich habe mit ihm ausgemacht, ihn zu treffen; **it's all ~d** es ist alles arrangiert; **~ment** *n* (*order*) Reihenfolge *f*; (*agreement*) Vereinbarung *f*; **~ments** *npl* Pläne *pl*.

array [ə'reɪ] *n* (*collection*) Ansammlung *f*.

arrears [ə'rɪəz] *npl* (*of debts*) Rückstand *m*; (*of work*) Unerledigte(s) *nt*; **in ~** im Rückstand.

arrest [ə'rest] *vt* (*person*) verhaften; (*stop*) aufhalten // *n* Verhaftung *f*; **under ~** in Haft.

arrival [ə'raɪvəl] *n* Ankunft *f*.

arrive [ə'raɪv] *vi* ankommen (*at* in +*dat*, bei).

arrogance ['ærəgəns] *n* Überheblichkeit *f*, Arroganz *f*.

arrow ['ærəʊ] *n* Pfeil *m*.

arse [ɑːs] *n* (*col!*) Arsch *m* (!).

arsenal ['ɑːsɪnl] *n* Waffenlager *nt*, Zeughaus *nt*.

arsenic ['ɑːsnɪk] *n* Arsen *nt*.

arson ['ɑːsn] *n* Brandstiftung *f*.

art [ɑːt] *n* Kunst *f*; **A~s** *pl* Geisteswissenschaften *pl*.

artery ['ɑːtərɪ] *n* Schlagader *f*, Arterie *f*.

artful [ɑːtfʊl] *a* verschlagen.

art gallery *n* Kunstgalerie *f*.

arthritis [ɑː'θraɪtɪs] *n* Arthritis *f*.

artichoke ['ɑːtɪtʃəʊk] *n* Artischocke *f*; **Jerusalem ~** Erdartischocke *f*.

article ['ɑːtɪkl] *n* (*PRESS, GRAM*) Artikel *m*; (*thing*) Gegenstand *m*, Artikel *m*; (*clause*) Abschnitt *m*, Paragraph *m*; **to do one's ~s** (*JUR*) seine· Referendarzeit ableisten; **~ of clothing** Kleidungsstück *nt*.

articulate [ɑː'tɪkjʊlɪt] *a* (*able to express o.s.*) redegewandt; (*speaking clearly*) deutlich, verständlich; **to be ~** sich gut ausdrücken können // *vt* [ɑː'tɪkjʊleɪt] (*connect*) zusammenfügen, gliedern; **~d vehicle** *n* Sattelschlepper *m*.

artificial [ɑːtɪ'fɪʃəl] *a* künstlich, Kunst-; **~ respiration** *n* künstliche Atmung *f*.

artisan ['ɑːtɪzæn] *n* gelernte(r) Handwerker *m*.

artist ['ɑːtɪst] *n* Künstler(in *f*) *m*; **~ic** [ɑː'tɪstɪk] *a* künstlerisch; **~ry** *n* künstlerische(s) Können *nt*.

artless ['ɑːtlɪs] *a* ungekünstelt; (*character*) arglos.

art school *n* Kunsthochschule *f*.

as [æz] ◆ *cj* **1** (*referring to time*) als; ~

the years went by mit den Jahren; he came in ~ I was leaving als er hereinkam, ging ich gerade; ~ from tomorrow ab morgen

2 (in comparisons): ~ big ~ so groß wie; twice ~ big ~ zweimal so groß wie; ~ much/many ~ soviel/so viele wie; ~ soon ~ sobald

3 (since, because) da; he left early ~ he had to be home by 10 er ging früher, da er um 10 zu Hause sein mußte

4 (referring to manner, way) wie; do ~ you wish mach was du willst; ~ she said wie sie sagte

5 (concerning): ~ for or to that was das betrifft or angeht

6: ~ if or though als ob.

◆prep als; he works ~ a driver er arbeitet als Fahrer; he gave it to me ~ a present er hat es mir als Geschenk gegeben; see also long, such, well.

a.s.a.p. abbr of as soon as possible.

ascend [ə'send] vi aufsteigen // vt besteigen; ~ancy n Oberhand f.

ascent [ə'sent] n Aufstieg m; Besteigung f.

ascertain [æsə'teɪn] vt feststellen.

ascribe [əs'kraɪb] vt zuschreiben (to dat).

ash [æʃ] n Asche f; (tree) Esche f.

ashamed [ə'ʃeɪmd] a beschämt; to be ~ of sth sich für etw schämen.

ashen [æʃən] a (pale) aschfahl.

ashore [ə'ʃɔ:*] ad an Land.

ashtray ['æʃtreɪ] n Aschenbecher m.

Ash Wednesday n Aschermittwoch m.

Asia ['eɪʃə] n Asien nt; ~n, ~tic [eɪsɪ'ætɪk] a asiatisch // n Asiat(in f) m.

aside [ə'saɪd] ad beiseite // n beiseite gesprochene Worte pl.

ask [ɑ:sk] vt fragen; (permission) bitten um; ~ him his name frage ihn nach seinem Namen; he ~ed to see you er wollte dich sehen; to ~ sb to do sth jdn bitten, etw zu tun; to ~ sb about sth jdn nach etw fragen; to ~ (sb) a question jdn etwas fragen; to ~ sb out to dinner jdn zum Essen einladen; to ~ after sb nach jdm fragen; to ~ for sth um etw (acc) bitten.

askance [əs'kɑ:ns] ad: to look ~ at sb jdn schief ansehen.

askew [əs'kju:] ad schief.

asking price ['ɑ:skɪŋ-] n Verkaufspreis m.

asleep [ə'sli:p] a: to be ~ schlafen; to fall ~ einschlafen.

asparagus [əs'pærəgəs] n Spargel m.

aspect ['æspekt] n Aspekt m.

aspersions [əs'pɜ:ʃənz] npl: to cast ~ on sb/sth sich abfällig über jdn/etw äußern.

asphyxiation [əsfɪksɪ'eɪʃən] n Erstickung f.

aspirations [æspə'reɪʃənz] npl: to have

~ towards sth etw anstreben.

aspire [əs'paɪə*] vi streben (to nach).

aspirin ['æsprɪn] n Aspirin nt.

ass [æs] n (lit, fig) Esel m; (US col!) Arsch m (!).

assailant [ə'seɪlənt] n Angreifer m.

assassin [ə'sæsɪn] n Attentäter(in f) m; ~ate vt ermorden.

assault [ə'sɔ:lt] n Angriff m // vt überfallen; (woman) herfallen über (+acc).

assemble [ə'sembl] vt versammeln; (parts) zusammensetzen // vi sich versammeln.

assembly [ə'semblɪ] n (meeting) Versammlung f; (construction) Zusammensetzung f, Montage f; ~ line n Fließband nt.

assent [ə'sent] n Zustimmung f.

assert [ə'sɜ:t] vt erklären; ~ion [ə'sɜ:ʃən] n Behauptung f.

assess [ə'ses] vt schätzen; (tax) Bewertung f, Einschätzung f; ~ment n Bewertung f, Einschätzung f; ~or n Steuerberater m.

asset ['æset] n Vorteil m, Wert m; ~s pl Vermögen nt; (estate) Nachlaß m.

assiduous [ə'sɪdjʊəs] a fleißig, aufmerksam.

assign [ə'saɪn] vt zuweisen.

assignment [ə'saɪnmənt] n Aufgabe f, Auftrag m.

assimilate [ə'sɪmɪleɪt] vt sich aneignen, aufnehmen.

assist [ə'sɪst] vt beistehen (+dat); ~ance n Unterstützung f, Hilfe f; ~ant n Assistent(in f) m, Mitarbeiter(in f) m; (Brit: also: shop ~ant) Verkäufer(in f) m.

assizes [ə'saɪzɪz] npl Landgericht nt.

associate [ə'səʊʃɪɪt] n (partner) Kollege m, Teilhaber m; (member) außerordentliche(s) Mitglied nt // vt [ə'səʊʃɪeɪt] verbinden (with mit) // vi [ə'səʊʃɪeɪt] (keep company) verkehren (with mit).

association [əsəʊsɪ'eɪʃən] n Verband m, Verein m; (PSYCH) Assoziation f; (link) Verbindung f.

assorted [ə'sɔ:tɪd] a gemischt.

assortment [ə'sɔ:tmənt] n Sammlung f; (COMM) Sortiment nt (of von), Auswahl f (of an +dat).

assume [ə'sju:m] vt (take for granted) annehmen; (put on) annehmen, sich geben; ~d name n Deckname m.

assumption [ə'sʌmpʃən] n Annahme f.

assurance [ə'ʃʊərəns] n (firm statement) Versicherung f; (confidence) Selbstsicherheit f; (insurance) (Lebens)versicherung f.

assure [ə'ʃʊə*] vt (make sure) sicherstellen; (convince) versichern (+dat); (life) versichern.

asterisk ['æstərɪsk] n Sternchen nt.

astern [əs'tɜ:n] ad achtern.

asthma ['æsmə] n Asthma nt.

astonish [əs'tɒnɪʃ] vt erstaunen; ~ment n Erstaunen nt.

astound [əs'taʊnd] vt verblüffen.

astray [əs'treɪ] ad in die Irre; auf Abwege; to go ~ (go wrong) sich vertun; to lead ~ irreführen.

astride [əs'traɪd] ad rittlings // prep rittlings auf.

astrologer [əs'trɒlədʒə*] n Astrologe m, Astrologin f.

astrology [əs'trɒlədʒɪ] n Astrologie f.

astronaut ['æstrənɔːt] n Astronaut(in f) m.

astronomer [əs'trɒnəmə*] n Astronom m.

astronomical [æstrə'nɒmɪkəl] a astronomisch; (success) riesig.

astronomy [əs'trɒnəmɪ] n Astronomie f.

astute [əs'tjuːt] a scharfsinnig; schlau, gerissen.

asylum [ə'saɪləm] n (home) Heim nt; (refuge) Asyl nt.

at [æt, ət] prep **1** (referring to position, direction) an (+dat), bei (+dat); (with place) in (+dat); ~ the top an der Spitze; ~ home/school zu Hause/in der Schule; ~ the baker's beim Bäcker; to look ~ sth auf etw (acc) blicken; to throw sth ~ sb etw nach jdm werfen **2** (referring to time): ~ 4 o'clock um 4 Uhr; ~ night bei Nacht; ~ Christmas zu Weihnachten; ~ times manchmal **3** (referring to rates, speed etc): ~ £1 a kilo zu £1 pro Kilo; two ~ a time zwei auf einmal; ~ 50 km/h mit 50 km/h **4** (referring to manner): ~ a stroke mit einem Schlag; ~ peace in Frieden **5** (referring to activity): to be ~ work bei der Arbeit sein; to play ~ cowboys Cowboy spielen; to be good ~ sth gut in etw (dat) sein **6** (referring to cause): shocked/surprised/annoyed ~ sth schockiert/überrascht/verärgert über etw (acc); I went ~ his suggestion ich ging auf seinen Vorschlag hin.

ate [et, eɪt] pt of **eat**.

atheist ['eɪθɪɪst] n Atheist(in f) m.

Athens ['æθɪnz] n Athen nt.

athlete ['æθliːt] n Athlet m, Sportler m.

athletic [æθ'letɪk] a sportlich, athletisch; ~s n Leichtathletik f.

Atlantic [ət'læntɪk] a atlantisch // n: the ~ (Ocean) der Atlantik.

atlas ['ætləs] n Atlas m.

atmosphere ['ætməsfɪə*] n Atmosphäre f.

atom ['ætəm] n Atom nt; (fig) bißchen nt; ~ic [ə'tɒmɪk] a atomar, Atom-; ~(ic) bomb n Atombombe f; ~izer n Zerstäuber m.

atone [ə'təʊn] vi sühnen (for acc).

atrocious [ə'trəʊʃəs] a gräßlich.

atrocity [ə'trɒsɪtɪ] n Scheußlichkeit f; (deed) Greueltat f.

attach [ə'tætʃ] vt (fasten) befestigen; (importance etc) legen (to auf +acc), beimessen (to dat); to be ~ed to sb/sth an jdm/etw hängen.

attaché [ə'tæʃeɪ] n Attaché m; ~ case n Aktenkoffer m.

attachment [ə'tætʃmənt] n (tool) Zubehörteil nt; (love): ~ (to sb) Zuneigung f (zu jdm).

attack [ə'tæk] vt angreifen // n Angriff m; (MED) Anfall m; ~er n Angreifer(in f) m.

attain [ə'teɪn] vt erreichen; ~ments npl Kenntnisse pl.

attempt [ə'tempt] n Versuch m // vt versuchen; ~ed murder Mordversuch m.

attend [ə'tend] vt (go to) teilnehmen (an +dat); (lectures) besuchen; to ~ to (needs) nachkommen (+dat); (person) sich kümmern um; ~ance n (presence) Anwesenheit f; (people present) Besucherzahl f; good ~ance gute Teilnahme; ~ant n (companion) Begleiter(in f) m; Gesellschafter(in f) m; (in car park etc) Wächter(in f) m; (servant) Bedienstete(r) mf // a begleitend; (fig) damit verbunden.

attention [ə'tenʃən] n Aufmerksamkeit f; (care) Fürsorge f; (for machine etc) Pflege f // interj (MIL) Achtung!; for the ~ of ... zu Händen (von) ...

attentive [ə'tentɪv] a aufmerksam.

attest [ə'test] vi: to ~ to sich verbürgen für.

attic ['ætɪk] n Dachstube f, Mansarde f.

attitude ['ætɪtjuːd] n (mental) Einstellung f.

attorney [ə'tɜːnɪ] n (solicitor) Rechtsanwalt m; A~ General n Justizminister m.

attract [ə'trækt] vt anziehen; (attention) erregen; ~ion [ə'trækʃən] n Anziehungskraft f; (thing) Attraktion f; ~ive a attraktiv.

attribute ['ætrɪbjuːt] n Eigenschaft f, Attribut nt // vt [ə'trɪbjuːt] zuschreiben (to dat).

attrition [ə'trɪʃən] n: war of ~ Zermürbungskrieg m.

aubergine ['əʊbəʒiːn] n Aubergine f.

auburn ['ɔːbən] a kastanienbraun.

auction ['ɔːkʃən] n (also: sale by ~) Versteigerung f, Auktion f // vt versteigern; ~eer [ɔːkʃə'nɪə*] n Versteigerer m.

audacity [ɔː'dæsɪtɪ] n (boldness) Wagemut m; (impudence) Unverfrorenheit f.

audible ['ɔːdɪbl] a hörbar.

audience ['ɔːdɪəns] n Zuhörer pl, Zuschauer pl; (with king etc) Audienz f.

audio-typist ['ɔːdɪəʊ'taɪpɪst] n Phonotypistin f.

audio-visual ['ɔːdɪəʊ'vɪzjʊəl] a audiovisuell.

audit [ˈɔːdɪt] vt prüfen.
audition [ɔːˈdɪʃən] n Probe f.
auditorium [ɔːdɪˈtɔːrɪəm] n Zuschauerraum m.
augment [ɔːɡˈment] vt vermehren.
augur [ˈɔːɡə*] vi bedeuten, voraussagen; this ~s well das ist ein gutes Omen.
August [ˈɔːɡəst] n August m.
aunt [ɑːnt] n Tante f; ~y, ~ie n Tantchen nt.
au pair [ˈəʊˈpɛə*] n (also: ~ girl) Aupair-Mädchen nt.
aura [ˈɔːrə] n Nimbus m.
auspices [ˈɔːspɪsɪz] npl: under the ~ of unter der Schirmherrschaft von.
auspicious [ɔːsˈpɪʃəs] a günstig; verheißungsvoll.
austere [ɒsˈtɪə*] a streng; (room) nüchtern.
austerity [ɒsˈterɪtɪ] n Strenge f; (POL) wirtschaftliche Einschränkung f.
Australia [ɒsˈtreɪlɪə] n Australien nt; ~n a australisch; // n Australier(in f) m.
Austria [ˈɒstrɪə] n Österreich nt; ~n a österreichisch // n Österreicher(in f) m.
authentic [ɔːˈθentɪk] a echt, authentisch.
author [ˈɔːθə*] n Autor m, Schriftsteller m; (beginner) Urheber m, Schöpfer m.
authoritarian [ɔːθɒrɪˈtɛərɪən] a autoritär.
authoritative [ɔːˈθɒrɪtətɪv] a (account) maßgeblich; (manner) herrisch.
authority [ɔːˈθɒrɪtɪ] n (power) Autorität f; (expert) Autorität f, Fachmann m; the authorities pl die Behörden pl.
authorize [ˈɔːθəraɪz] vt bevollmächtigen; (permit) genehmigen.
auto [ˈɔːtəʊ] n (US) Auto nt, Wagen m.
autobiography [ɔːtəbaɪˈɒɡrəfɪ] n Autobiographie f.
autograph [ˈɔːtəɡrɑːf] n (of celebrity) Autogramm nt // vt mit Autogramm versehen.
automatic [ɔːtəˈmætɪk] a automatisch // n (gun) Selbstladepistole f; (car) Automatik m; ~ally ad automatisch.
automobile [ˈɔːtəməbiːl] n (US) Auto(mobil) nt.
autonomous [ɔːˈtɒnəməs] a autonom.
autumn [ˈɔːtəm] n Herbst m.
auxiliary [ɔːɡˈzɪlɪərɪ] a Hilfs-.
Av. abbr of **avenue**.
avail [əˈveɪl] vt: ~ o.s. of sth sich einer Sache bedienen // n: to no ~ nutzlos.
availability [əveɪləˈbɪlɪtɪ] n Erhältlichkeit f, Vorhandensein nt.
available [əˈveɪləbl] a erhältlich; zur Verfügung stehend; (person) erreichbar, abkömmlich.
avalanche [ˈævəlɑːnʃ] n Lawine f.
avarice [ˈævərɪs] n Habsucht f, Geiz m.
Ave. abbr of **avenue**.
avenge [əˈvendʒ] vt rächen, sühnen.

avenue [ˈævənjuː] n Allee f.
average [ˈævərɪdʒ] n Durchschnitt m // a durchschnittlich, Durchschnitts- // vt (figures) den Durchschnitt nehmen von; (perform) durchschnittlich leisten; (in car etc) im Schnitt fahren; on ~ durchschnittlich, im Durchschnitt; ~ out vi: to ~ out at im Durchschnitt betragen.
averse [əˈvɜːs] a: to be ~ to doing sth eine Abneigung dagegen haben, etw zu tun.
avert [əˈvɜːt] vt (turn away) abkehren; (prevent) abwehren.
aviary [ˈeɪvɪərɪ] n Vogelhaus nt.
aviation [eɪvɪˈeɪʃən] n Luftfahrt f, Flugwesen nt.
avid [ˈævɪd] a gierig (for auf +acc).
avocado [ævəˈkɑːdəʊ] n (also: Brit: ~ pear) Avocado(birne) f.
avoid [əˈvɔɪd] vt vermeiden; ~ance n Vermeidung f.
await [əˈweɪt] vt erwarten, entgegensehen (+dat).
awake [əˈweɪk] a wach // (v: pt awoke, pp awoken or awaked) vt (auf)wecken // vi aufwachen; to be ~ wach sein; ~ning n Erwachen nt.
award [əˈwɔːd] n (prize) Preis m // vt zuerkennen.
aware [əˈwɛə*] a bewußt; to be ~ sich bewußt sein (of gen); ~ness n Bewußtsein nt.
awash [əˈwɒʃ] a überflutet.
away [əˈweɪ] ad weg, fort; two hours ~ by car zwei Autostunden entfernt; the holiday was two weeks ~ es war noch zwei Wochen bis zum Urlaub; ~ match n (SPORT) Auswärtsspiel nt.
awe [ɔː] n Ehrfurcht f; ~-inspiring, ~some a ehrfurchtgebietend.
awful [ˈɔːful] a (very bad) furchtbar; ~ly ad furchtbar, sehr.
awkward [ˈɔːkwəd] a (clumsy) ungeschickt, linkisch; (embarrassing) peinlich.
awning [ˈɔːnɪŋ] n Markise f.
awoke [əˈwəʊk], **awoken** [əˈwəʊkən] pt, pp of **awake**.
awry [əˈraɪ] ad schief; to go ~ (person) fehlgehen; (plans) schiefgehen.
axe, (US) **ax** [æks] n Axt f, Beil nt // vt (end suddenly) streichen.
axis, pl **axes** [ˈæksɪs, -siːz] n Achse f.
axle [ˈæksl] n Achse f.
ay(e) [aɪ] interj (yes) ja; the ayes pl die Jastimmen pl.
azalea [əˈzeɪlɪə] n Azalee f.

B

B [biː] n (MUS) H nt.
B.A. n abbr of **Bachelor of Arts**.
babble [ˈbæbl] vi schwätzen; (stream)

murmeln.

baby ['beɪbɪ] n Baby nt, Säugling m; ~ **carriage** n (US) Kinderwagen m; ~-**sit** vi Kinder hüten, babysitten; ~-**sitter** n Babysitter m.

bachelor ['bætʃələ*] n Junggeselle m; **B~ of Arts/Science (B.A./B.Sc.)** Bakkalaureus m der philosophischen Fakultät/der Naturwissenschaften.

back [bæk] n (of person, horse) Rücken m; (of house) Rückseite f; (of train) Ende nt; (FOOTBALL) Verteidiger m // vt (support) unterstützen; (wager) wetten auf (+acc); (car) rückwärts fahren // vi (go backwards) rückwärts gehen or fahren // a hintere(r, s) // ad zurück; (to the rear) nach hinten; ~ **down** vi zurückstecken; ~ **out** vi sich zurückziehen; kneifen (col); ~ **up** vt (support) unterstützen; (car) zurücksetzen; (COMPUT) eine Sicherungskopie machen von; ~**bencher** n (Brit) Parlamentarier(in f) m; ~**bone** n Rückgrat nt; (support) Rückhalt m; ~**cloth** n Hintergrund m; ~**date** vt rückdatieren; ~**drop** n (THEAT) = ~**cloth**; (~ground) Hintergrund m; ~**fire** vi (plan) fehlschlagen; (TECH) fehlzünden; ~**ground** n Hintergrund m; (person's education) Vorbildung f; **family** ~**ground** Familienverhältnisse pl; ~**hand** n (TENNIS: also: ~hand stroke) Rückhand f; ~**handed** a (shot) Rückhand-; (compliment) zweifelhaft; ~**hander** n (Brit: bribe) Schmiergeld nt; ~**ing** n (support) Unterstützung f; ~**lash** n (fig) Gegenschlag m; ~**log** n (of work) Rückstand m; ~ **number** n (PRESS) alte Nummer f; ~**pack** n Rucksack m; ~ **pay** n (Gehalts- or Lohn)nachzahlung f; ~ **payments** pl Zahlungsrückstände pl; ~ **seat** n (AUT) Rücksitz m; ~**side** n (col) Hintern m; ~**stage** ad hinter den Kulissen; ~**stroke** n Rückenschwimmen nt; ~**up** a (train) Zusatz-; (plane) Sonder-; (COMPUT) Sicherungs- // n (see a) Zusatzzug m; Sondermaschine f; Sicherungskopie f; ~**ward** a (less developed) zurückgeblieben; (primitive) rückständig; ~**wards** ad rückwärts; ~**water** n (fig) Kaff nt; ~**yard** n Hinterhof m.

bacon ['beɪkən] n Schinkenspeck m.

bacteria [bæk'tɪərɪə] npl Bakterien pl.

bad [bæd] a schlecht, schlimm; to go ~ schlecht werden.

bade [bæd] pt of **bid**.

badge [bædʒ] n Abzeichen nt.

badger ['bædʒə*] n Dachs m.

badly ['bædlɪ] ad schlecht, schlimm; ~ **wounded** schwerverwundet; he needs it ~ er braucht es dringend; to be ~ **off** (for money) dringend Geld nötig haben.

badminton ['bædmɪntən] n Federball m, Badminton nt.

bad-tempered ['bæd'tempəd] a schlecht gelaunt.

baffle ['bæfl] vt (puzzle) verblüffen.

bag [bæg] n (sack) Beutel m; (paper) Tüte f; (hand~) Tasche f; (suitcase) Koffer m; (booty) Jagdbeute f; (col: old woman) alte Schachtel f // vt (put in sack) in einen Sack stecken; (hunting) erlegen; ~**s of** (col: lots of) eine Menge (+acc).

baggage ['bægɪdʒ] n Gepäck nt.

baggy ['bægɪ] a bauschig, sackartig.

bagpipes ['bægpaɪps] npl Dudelsack m.

Bahamas [bə'hɑːməz] npl: the ~ die Bahamas pl.

bail [beɪl] n (money) Kaution f // vt (prisoner: gen: **grant** ~ **to**) gegen Kaution freilassen; (boat: also: ~ **out**) ausschöpfen; **on** ~ (prisoner) gegen Kaution freigelassen; **to** ~ **sb out** die Kaution für jdn stellen; see also **bale**.

bailiff ['beɪlɪf] n Gerichtsvollzieher(in f) m.

bait [beɪt] n Köder m // vt mit einem Köder versehen; (fig) ködern.

bake [beɪk] vti backen; ~**d beans** gebackene Bohnen pl; ~**r** n Bäcker m; ~**ry** n Bäckerei f.

baking ['beɪkɪŋ] n Backen nt; ~ **powder** n Backpulver nt.

balance ['bæləns] n (scales) Waage f; (equilibrium) Gleichgewicht nt; (FIN: state of account) Saldo m; (difference) Bilanz f; (amount remaining) Restbetrag m // vt (weigh) wägen; (make equal) ausgleichen; ~ **of trade/payments** Handels-/Zahlungsbilanz f; ~**d** a ausgeglichen; ~ **sheet** n Bilanz f, Rechnungsabschluß m.

balcony ['bælkənɪ] n Balkon m.

bald [bɔːld] a kahl; (statement) knapp.

bale [beɪl] n Ballen m; **to** ~ or **bail out** (from a plane) abspringen.

baleful ['beɪlfʊl] a (sad) unglückselig; (evil) böse.

ball [bɔːl] n Ball m; ~ **bearing** n Kugellager nt.

ballet ['bæleɪ] n Ballett nt; ~ **dancer** n Ballettänzer(in f) m.

balloon [bə'luːn] n (Luft)ballon m.

ballot ['bælət] n (geheime) Abstimmung f.

ball-point (pen) ['bɔːlpɔɪnt('pen)] n Kugelschreiber m.

ballroom ['bɔːlrʊm] n Tanzsaal m.

balm [bɑːm] n Balsam m.

Baltic ['bɔːltɪk] n: the ~ (Sea) die Ostsee.

balustrade [bæləs'treɪd] n Brüstung f.

bamboo [bæm'buː] n Bambus m.

ban [bæn] n Verbot nt // vt verbieten.

banana [bə'nɑːnə] n Banane f.

band [bænd] n Band nt; (group) Gruppe f; (of criminals) Bande f; (MUS) Kapelle f, Band f // vi (+ together) sich zusammentun.

bandage ['bændɪdʒ] n Verband m; (elastic) Bandage f // vt (cut) verbinden; (broken limb) bandagieren.

bandaid ['bændeɪd] n (US) Heftpflaster nt.

bandwagon ['bændwægən] n: to jump on the ~ (fig) auf den fahrenden Zug aufspringen.

bandy ['bændɪ] vt wechseln; ~(-legged) a o-beinig.

bang [bæŋ] n (explosion) Knall m; (blow) Hieb m // vti knallen.

bangle ['bæŋgl] n Armspange f.

bangs [bæŋz] npl (US: fringe) Pony m.

banish ['bænɪʃ] vt verbannen.

banister(s) ['bænɪstə*(z)] n(pl) (Treppen)geländer nt.

bank [bæŋk] n (raised ground) Erdwall m; (of lake etc) Ufer nt; (FIN) Bank f // vt (tilt: AVIAT) in die Kurve bringen; (money) einzahlen; to ~ on sth mit etw rechnen; ~ account n Bankkonto nt; ~ card n Scheckkarte f; ~er n Bankier m; ~er's card n (Brit) = ~ card; B~ holiday n (Brit) gesetzliche(r) Feiertag m; ~ing n Bankwesen nt; ~note n Banknote f; ~ rate n Banksatz m.

bankrupt ['bæŋkrʌpt] a: to be ~ bankrott sein; to go ~ Pleite machen; ~cy n Bankrott m.

bank statement n Kontoauszug m.

banner ['bænə*] n Banner nt.

banns [bænz] npl Aufgebot nt.

baptism ['bæptɪzəm] n Taufe f.

baptize [bæp'taɪz] vt taufen.

bar [ba:*] n (rod) Stange f; (obstacle) Hindernis nt; (of chocolate) Tafel f; (of soap) Stück nt; (for food, drink) Buffet nt, Bar f; (pub) Wirtschaft f; (MUS) Takt(strich) m // vt (fasten) verriegeln; (hinder) versperren; (exclude) ausschließen; behind ~s hinter Gittern; the B~: to be called to the B~ als Anwalt zugelassen werden; ~ none ohne Ausnahme.

barbaric [ba:'bærɪk] a primitiv, unkultiviert.

barbecue ['ba:bɪkju:] n Barbecue nt.

barbed wire ['ba:bd'waɪə*] n Stacheldraht m.

barber ['ba:bə*] n Herrenfriseur m.

bar code n (on goods) Registrierkode f.

bare [bɛə*] a nackt; (trees, country) kahl; (mere) bloß // vt entblößen; ~back ad ungesattelt; ~faced a unverfroren; ~foot a, ad barfuß; ~ly ad kaum, knapp.

bargain ['ba:gɪn] n (sth cheap) günstiger Kauf; (agreement: written) Kaufvertrag m; (: oral) Geschäft nt; into the ~ obendrein; ~ for vt: he got more than he ~ed for er erlebte sein blaues Wunder.

barge [ba:dʒ] n Lastkahn m; ~ in vi

hereinplatzen; ~ into vt rennen gegen.

bark [ba:k] n (of tree) Rinde f; (of dog) Bellen nt // vi (dog) bellen.

barley ['ba:lɪ] n Gerste f; ~ sugar n Malzbonbon nt.

barmaid ['ba:meɪd] n Bardame f.

barman ['ba:mən] n Barkellner m.

barn [ba:n] n Scheune f.

barometer [bə'rɒmɪtə*] n Barometer nt.

baron ['bærən] n Baron m; ~ess n Baronin f.

barracks ['bærəks] npl Kaserne f.

barrage ['bæra:ʒ] n (gunfire) Sperrfeuer nt; (dam) Staudamm m; Talsperre f.

barrel ['bærəl] n Faß nt; (of gun) Lauf m.

barren ['bærən] a unfruchtbar.

barricade [bærɪ'keɪd] n Barrikade f // vt verbarrikadieren.

barrier ['bærɪə*] n (obstruction) Hindernis nt; (fence) Schranke f.

barrister ['bærɪstə*] n (Brit) Rechtsanwalt m.

barrow ['bærəʊ] n (cart) Schubkarren m.

bartender ['ba:tendə*] n (US) Barmann or -kellner m.

barter ['ba:tə*] vt: to ~ sth for sth um etw handeln.

base [beɪs] n (bottom) Boden m, Basis f; (MIL) Stützpunkt m // vt gründen; (opinion, theory): to be ~d on basieren auf (+dat) // a (low) gemein; ~ball n Baseball m; ~ment n Kellergeschoß nt.

bases ['beɪsi:z] npl of **basis**; ['beɪsɪz] npl of **base**.

bash [bæʃ] vt (col) (heftig) schlagen.

bashful ['bæʃful] a schüchtern.

basic ['beɪsɪk] a grundlegend; ~ally ad im Grunde.

basil ['bæzl] n Basilikum nt.

basin ['beɪsn] n (dish) Schüssel f; (for washing, also valley) Becken nt; (dock) (Trocken)becken nt.

basis ['beɪsɪs], pl -ses [-si:z] n Basis f, Grundlage f.

bask [ba:sk] vi: to ~ in the sun sich sonnen.

basket ['ba:skɪt] n Korb m; ~ball n Basketball m.

bass [beɪs] n (MUS, also instrument) Baß m; (voice) Baßstimme f.

bassoon [bə'su:n] n Fagott nt.

bastard ['ba:stəd] n Bastard m; (col!) Arschloch nt (!).

bastion ['bæstɪən] n (lit, fig) Bollwerk nt.

bat [bæt] n (SPORT) Schlagholz nt; Schläger m; (ZOOL) Fledermaus f // vt: he didn't ~ an eyelid er hat nicht mit der Wimper gezuckt.

batch [bætʃ] n (of letters) Stoß m; (of samples) Satz m.

bated ['beɪtɪd] a: with ~ breath mit angehaltenem Atem.

bath [bɑːθ] *n* Bad *nt*; (~ *tub*) Badewanne *f*; *see also* **baths** // *vt* baden; **to have a** ~ baden.

bathe [beɪð] *vti* baden; ~**r** *n* Badende(r) *mf*.

bathing ['beɪðɪŋ] *n* Baden *nt*; ~ **cap** *n* Badekappe *f*; ~ **costume**, (*US*) ~ **suit** *n* Badeanzug *m*; ~ **trunks** *npl* (*Brit*) Badehose *f*.

bathrobe ['bɑːθrəʊb] *n* Bademantel *m*.

bathroom ['bɑːθrʊm] *n* Bad(ezimmer) *nt*.

baths [bɑːðz] *npl* (Schwimm)bad *nt*.

bath towel *n* Badetuch *nt*.

batman ['bætmən] *n* (Offiziers)bursche *m*.

baton ['bætən] *n* (*of police*) Gummiknüppel *m*; (*MUS*) Taktstock *m*.

batter ['bætə*] *vt* verprügeln // *n* Schlagteig *m*; (*for cake*) Biskuitteig *m*; ~**ed** *a* (*hat, pan*) verbeult.

battery ['bætərɪ] *n* (*ELEC*) Batterie *f*; (*MIL*) Geschützbatterie *f*.

battle ['bætl] *n* Schlacht *f*; (*small*) Gefecht *nt* // *vi* kämpfen; ~**field** *n* Schlachtfeld *nt*; ~**ship** *n* Schlachtschiff *nt*.

bawdy ['bɔːdɪ] *a* unflätig.

bawl [bɔːl] *vi* brüllen.

bay [beɪ] *n* (*of sea*) Bucht *f* // *vi* bellen; **to keep at** ~ unter Kontrolle halten.

bay window *n* Erkerfenster *nt*.

bazaar [bə'zɑː*] *n* Basar *m*.

b. & b., B. & B. *abbr of* **bed and breakfast.**

BBC *n abbr* (= *British Broadcasting Corporation*) BBC.

B.C. *ad abbr* (= *before Christ*) v. Chr.

be, *pt* **was, were,** *pp* **been** [biː, wɒz, wɜː*, biːn] ◆*aux v* **1** (*with present participle: forming continuous tenses*): **what are you doing?** was machst du (gerade)?; **it is raining** es regnet; **I've been waiting for you for hours** ich warte schon seit Stunden auf dich

2 (*with pp: forming passives*): **to** ~ **killed** getötet werden; **the thief was nowhere to** ~ **seen** der Dieb war nirgendwo zu sehen

3 (*in tag questions*): **it was fun, wasn't it?** es hat Spaß gemacht, nicht wahr?

4 (*+ to +infinitive*): **the house is to** ~ **sold** das Haus soll verkauft werden; **he's not to open it** er darf es nicht öffnen

◆*v +complement* **1** (*gen*) sein; **I'm tired** ich bin müde; **I'm hot/cold** mir ist heiß/kalt; **he's a doctor** er ist Arzt; **2 and 2 are 4** 2 und 2 ist *or* sind 4; **she's tall/pretty** sie ist groß/hübsch; ~ **careful/quiet** sei vorsichtig/ruhig

2 (*of health*): **how are you?** wie geht es dir?; **he's very ill** er ist sehr krank; **I'm better now** jetzt geht es mir besser

3 (*of age*): **how old are you?** wie alt bist du? **I'm sixteen (years old)** ich bin sechzehn (Jahre alt)

4 (*cost*): **how much was the meal?** was *or* wieviel hat das Essen gekostet?; **that'll be £5.75, please** das macht £5.75, bitte

◆*vi* **1** (*exist, occur etc*) sein; **is there a God?** gibt es einen Gott?; ~ **that as it may** wie dem auch sei; **so** ~ **it** also gut

2 (*referring to place*) sein; **I won't** ~ **here tomorrow** ich werde morgen nicht hier sein

3 (*referring to movement*): **where have you been?** wo bist du gewesen?; **I've been in the garden** ich war im Garten

◆*impers v* **1** (*referring to time, distance, weather*) sein; **it's 5 o'clock** es ist 5 Uhr; **it's 10 km to the village** es sind 10 km bis zum Dorf; **it's too hot/cold** es ist zu heiß/kalt

2 (*emphatic*): **it's me** ich bin's; **it's the postman** es ist der Briefträger.

beach [biːtʃ] *n* Strand *m* // *vt* (*ship*) auf den Strand setzen.

beacon ['biːkən] *n* (*signal*) Leuchtfeuer *nt*; (*traffic* ~) Bake *f*.

bead [biːd] *n* Perle *f*; (*drop*) Tropfen *m*.

beak [biːk] *n* Schnabel *m*.

beaker ['biːkə*] *n* Becher *m*.

beam [biːm] *n* (*of wood*) Balken *m*; (*of light*) Strahl *m*; (*smile*) strahlende(s) Lächeln *nt* // *vi* strahlen.

bean [biːn] *n* Bohne *f*; ~ **sprouts** *npl* Sojasprossen *pl*.

bear [bɛə*] *n* Bär *m* // *v* (*pt* **bore,** *pp* **borne**) *vt* (*weight, crops*) tragen; (*tolerate*) ertragen; (*young*) gebären // *vi*: **to** ~ **right/left** sich rechts/links halten; ~ **out** *vt* (*suspicions etc*) bestätigen; ~ **up** *vi* sich halten.

beard [bɪəd] *n* Bart *m*; ~**ed** *a* bärtig.

bearer ['bɛərə*] *n* Träger *m*.

bearing ['bɛərɪŋ] *n* (*posture*) Haltung *f*; (*relevance*) Relevanz *f*; (*relation*) Bedeutung *f*; (*TECH*) Kugellager *nt*; ~**s** *pl* (*direction*) Orientierung *f*; (**ball**) ~**s** *pl* (Kugel)lager *nt*.

beast [biːst] *n* Tier *nt*, Vieh *nt*; (*person*) Bestie *f*; (*nasty person*) Biest *nt*; ~**ly** *a* viehisch; (*col*) scheußlich.

beat [biːt] *n* (*stroke*) Schlag *m*; (*pulsation*) (Herz)schlag *m*; (*police round*) Runde *f*; Revier *nt*; (*MUS*) Takt *m*; Beat *m* // *vti* (*pt* **beat,** *pp* **beaten**) schlagen; **to** ~ **it** abhauen; ~ **off** *vt* abschlagen; ~ **up** *vt* zusammenschlagen; ~**en** *a*: **off the** ~**en track** abgelegen; ~**ing** *n* Prügel *pl*.

beautiful ['bjuːtɪful] *a* schön; ~**ly** *ad* ausgezeichnet.

beauty ['bjuːtɪ] *n* Schönheit *f*; ~ **salon** *n* Schönheitssalon *m*; ~ **spot** *n* Schönheitsfleck *m*; (*Brit: TOURISM*) (besonders) schöne(r) Ort *m*.

beaver ['biːvə*] *n* Biber *m*.

became [bɪ'keɪm] pt of **become**.
because [bɪ'kɒz] cj weil // prep: ~ **of** wegen (+gen or (col) dat).
beck [bek] n: to be at the ~ **and call of sb** nach jds Pfeife tanzen.
beckon ['bekən] vt (also: ~ **to**) ein Zeichen geben (sb jdm).
become [bɪ'kʌm] (irreg: like **come**) vt werden; (clothes) stehen (+dat) // vi werden.
becoming [bɪ'kʌmɪŋ] a (suitable) schicklich; (clothes) kleidsam.
bed [bed] n Bett nt; (of river) Flußbett nt; (foundation) Schicht f; (in garden) Beet nt; to go to ~ zu Bett gehen; **single/double** ~ Einzel/Doppelbett nt; ~ **and breakfast** n Übernachtung f mit Frühstück; ~**clothes** npl Bettwäsche f; ~**ding** n Bettzeug nt.
bedlam ['bedləm] n (uproar) tolle(s) Durcheinander nt.
bedraggled [bɪ'dræɡld] a ramponiert.
bedridden ['bedrɪdn] a bettlägerig.
bedroom ['bedrʊm] n Schlafzimmer nt.
bedside ['bedsaɪd] n: at the ~ am Bett.
bed-sitter ['bed'sɪtə*] n (Brit) Einzimmerwohnung f, möblierte(s) Zimmer nt.
bedspread ['bedspred] n Tagesdecke f.
bedtime ['bedtaɪm] n Schlafenszeit f.
bee [biː] n Biene f.
beech [biːtʃ] n Buche f.
beef [biːf] n Rindfleisch nt; roast ~ Roastbeef nt; ~**burger** n Hamburger m.
beehive ['biːhaɪv] n Bienenstock m.
beeline ['biːlaɪn] n: to make a ~ **for** schnurstracks zugehen auf (+acc).
been [biːn] pp of **be**.
beer [bɪə*] n Bier nt.
beetle ['biːtl] n Käfer m.
beetroot ['biːtruːt] n (Brit) rote Bete f.
before [bɪ'fɔː*] prep vor // cj bevor // ad (of time) zuvor; früher; **the week** ~ die Woche zuvor or vorher; **I've done it** ~ das hab' ich schon mal getan; ~**hand** ad im voraus.
beg [beɡ] vti (implore) dringend bitten; (alms) betteln.
began [bɪ'ɡæn] pt of **begin**.
beggar ['beɡə*] n Bettler(in f) m.
begin [bɪ'ɡɪn] pt **began**, pp **begun** vti anfangen, beginnen; (found) gründen; to ~ **doing** or **to do sth** anfangen or beginnen, etw zu tun; to ~ **with** zunächst (einmal); ~**ner** n Anfänger m; ~**ning** n Anfang m.
begun [bɪ'ɡʌn] pp of **begin**.
behalf [bɪ'hɑːf] n: on ~ **of** im Namen (+gen); **on my** ~ für mich.
behave [bɪ'heɪv] vi sich benehmen.
behaviour, (US) **behavior** [bɪ'heɪvjə*] n Benehmen nt.
behead [bɪ'hed] vt enthaupten.
beheld [bɪ'held] pt, pp of **behold**.
behind [bɪ'haɪnd] prep hinter // ad (late)

im Rückstand; (in the rear) hinten // n (col) Hinterteil nt; ~ **the scenes** (fig) hinter den Kulissen.
behold [bɪ'həʊld] (irreg: like **hold**) vt (old) erblicken.
beige [beɪʒ] a beige.
being ['biːɪŋ] n (existence) (Da)sein nt; (person) Wesen nt; **to come into** ~ entstehen.
belated [bɪ'leɪtɪd] a verspätet.
belch [beltʃ] vi rülpsen // vt (smoke) ausspeien.
belfry ['belfrɪ] n Glockenturm m.
Belgian ['beldʒən] a belgisch // n Belgier(in f) m.
Belgium ['beldʒəm] n Belgien nt.
belie [bɪ'laɪ] vt Lügen strafen (+acc).
belief [bɪ'liːf] n Glaube m (in an +acc); (conviction) Überzeugung f.
believe [bɪ'liːv] vt glauben (+dat); (think) glauben, meinen, denken // vi (have faith) glauben; **to** ~ **in sth** an etw (acc) glauben; ~**r** n Gläubige(r) mf.
belittle [bɪ'lɪtl] vt herabsetzen.
bell [bel] n Glocke f.
belligerent [bɪ'lɪdʒərənt] a (person) streitsüchtig; (country) kriegsführend.
bellow ['beləʊ] vti brüllen.
bellows ['beləʊz] npl (TECH) Gebläse nt; (for fire) Blasebalg m.
belly ['belɪ] n Bauch m.
belong [bɪ'lɒŋ] vi gehören (to sb jdm); (to club) angehören (+dat); **it does not** ~ **here** es gehört nicht hierher; ~**ings** npl Habe f.
beloved [bɪ'lʌvɪd] a innig geliebt // n Geliebte(r) mf.
below [bɪ'ləʊ] prep unter // ad unten.
belt [belt] n (band) Riemen m; (round waist) Gürtel m // vt (fasten) mit Riemen befestigen; (col: beat) schlagen; ~**way** n (US AUT: ring road) Umgehungsstraße f.
bemused [bɪ'mjuːzd] a verwirrt.
bench [bentʃ] n (seat) Bank f; (workshop) Werkbank f; (judge's seat) Richterbank f; (judges) Richter pl.
bend [bend], pt, pp **bent** vt (curve) biegen; (stoop) beugen // vi sich biegen; sich beugen // n Biegung f; (Brit: in road) Kurve f; ~ **down** or **over** vi sich bücken.
beneath [bɪ'niːθ] prep unter // ad darunter.
benefactor ['benɪfæktə*] n Wohltäter(in f) m.
beneficial [benɪ'fɪʃl] a vorteilhaft; (to health) heilsam.
benefit ['benɪfɪt] n (advantage) Nutzen m // vt fördern // vi Nutzen ziehen (from aus).
Benelux ['benɪlʌks] n Beneluxstaaten pl.
benevolent [bɪ'nevələnt] a wohlwollend.
benign [bɪ'naɪn] a (person) gütig; (climate) mild.

bent [bent] *pt, pp of* **bend** // *n* (*inclination*) Neigung *f* // *a* (*col: dishonest*) unehrlich; **to be ~ on** versessen sein auf (*+acc*).

bequest [bɪ'kwest] *n* Vermächtnis *nt*.

bereaved [bɪ'riːvd] *npl:* **the ~** die Hinterbliebenen *pl*.

bereft [bɪ'reft] *a:* **~ of** bar (*+gen*).

beret ['berɪ] *n* Baskenmütze *f*.

Berlin [bɜː'lɪn] *n* Berlin *nt*.

berm [bɜːm] *n* (*US AUT*) Seitenstreifen *m*.

Bermuda [bɜː'mjuːdə] *n* Bermuda *nt*.

berry ['berɪ] *n* Beere *f*.

berserk [bə'sɜːk] *a:* **to go ~** wild werden.

berth [bɜːθ] *n* (*for ship*) Ankerplatz *m*; (*in ship*) Koje *f*; (*in train*) Bett *nt* // *vt* am Kai festmachen // *vi* anlegen.

beseech [bɪ'siːtʃ], *pt, pp* **besought** [-sɔːt] *vt* anflehen.

beset [bɪ'set], *pt, pp* **beset** *vt* bedrängen.

beside [bɪ'saɪd] *prep* neben, bei; (*except*) außer; **to be ~ o.s.** außer sich sein (*with* vor *+dat*); **that's ~ the point** das tut nichts zur Sache.

besides [bɪ'saɪdz] *prep* außer, neben // *ad* außerdem.

besiege [bɪ'siːdʒ] *vt* (*MIL*) belagern; (*surround*) umlagern, bedrängen.

best [best] *a* beste(r, s) // *ad* am besten; **the ~ part of** (*quantity*) das meiste (*+gen*); **at ~** höchstens; **to make the ~ of it** das Beste daraus machen; **to do one's ~** sein Bestes tun; **to the ~ of my knowledge** meines Wissens; **to the ~ of my ability** so gut ich kann; **for the ~** zum Besten; **~ man** *n* Trauzeuge *m*.

bestow [bɪ'stəu] *prep* verleihen.

bet [bet] *n* Wette *f* // *vti, pt, pp* **bet** *or* **betted** wetten.

betray [bɪ'treɪ] *vt* verraten.

better ['betə*] *a, ad* besser // *vt* verbessern // *n:* **to get the ~ of sb** jdn überwinden; **he thought ~ of it** er hat sich eines Besseren besonnen; **you had ~ leave** Sie gehen jetzt wohl besser; **to get ~** (*MED*) gesund werden; **~ off** *a* (*richer*) wohlhabender.

betting ['betɪŋ] *n* Wetten *nt*; **~ shop** *n* (*Brit*) Wettbüro *nt*.

between [bɪ'twiːn] *prep* zwischen; (*among*) unter // *ad* dazwischen.

beverage ['bevərɪdʒ] *n* Getränk *nt*.

bevy ['bevɪ] *n* Schar *f*.

beware [bɪ'weə*] *vti* sich hüten vor (*+dat*); **'~ of the dog'** 'Vorsicht, bissiger Hund!'

bewildered [bɪ'wɪldəd] *a* verwirrt.

bewitching [bɪ'wɪtʃɪŋ] *a* bestrickend.

beyond [bɪ'jɒnd] *prep* (*place*) jenseits (*+gen*); (*time*) über ... hinaus; (*out of reach*) außerhalb (*+gen*); // *ad* darüber hinaus; **~ doubt** ohne Zweifel; **~ repair**

nicht mehr zu reparieren.

bias ['baɪəs] *n* (*slant*) Neigung *f*; (*prejudice*) Vorurteil *nt*; **~(s)ed** *a* voreingenommen.

bib [bɪb] *n* Latz *m*.

Bible ['baɪbl] *n* Bibel *f*.

bicarbonate of soda [baɪ'kɑːbəneɪtəv'səudə] *n* Natron *nt*.

bicker ['bɪkə*] *vi* zanken.

bicycle ['baɪsɪkl] *n* Fahrrad *nt*.

bid [bɪd] *n* (*offer*) Gebot *nt*; (*attempt*) Versuch *m* // *vti, pt* **bade** [bæd] *or* **bid**, *pp* **bidden** ['bɪdn] *or* **bid** (*offer*) bieten; **to ~ farewell** Lebewohl sagen; **~der** *n* (*person*) Steigerer *m*; **the highest ~der** der Meistbietende; **~ding** *n* (*command*) Geheiß *nt*.

bide [baɪd] *vt:* **~ one's time** abwarten.

bifocals [baɪ'fəukəlz] *npl* Bifokalbrille *f*.

big [bɪg] *a* groß.

big dipper *n* Achterbahn *f*.

bigheaded ['bɪg'hedɪd] *a* eingebildet.

bigot ['bɪgət] *n* Frömmler *m*; **~ed** *a* bigott; **~ry** *n* Bigotterie *f*.

big top *n* Zirkuszelt *nt*.

bike [baɪk] *n* Rad *nt*.

bikini [bɪ'kiːnɪ] *n* Bikini *m*.

bile [baɪl] *n* (*BIOL*) Galle *f*.

bilingual [baɪ'lɪŋgwəl] *a* zweisprachig.

bill [bɪl] *n* (*account*) Rechnung *f*; (*POL*) Gesetzentwurf *m*; (*US FIN*) Geldschein *m*; **to fit** *or* **fill the ~** (*fig*) der/die/das richtige sein; **'post no ~s'** 'Plakate ankleben verboten'; **~board** *n* Reklameschild *nt*.

billet ['bɪlɪt] *n* Quartier *nt*.

billfold ['bɪlfəuld] *n* (*US*) Geldscheintasche *f*.

billion ['bɪlɪən] *n* Billion *f*; (*US*) Milliarde *f*.

bin [bɪn] *n* Kasten *m*; (*dust~*) (Abfall)eimer *m*; **litter ~** *n* Abfalleimer *m*.

bind [baɪnd], *pt, pp* **bound** *vt* (*tie*) binden; (*tie together*) zusammenbinden; (*oblige*) verpflichten; **~ing** *n* (Buch)einband *m* // *a* verbindlich.

binge [bɪndʒ] *n* (*col*) Sauferei *f*.

bingo ['bɪŋgəu] *n* Bingo *nt*.

binoculars [bɪ'nɒkjuləz] *npl* Fernglas *nt*.

biochemistry ['baɪəu'kemɪstrɪ] *n* Biochemie *f*.

biography [baɪ'ɒgrəfɪ] *n* Biographie *f*.

biological [baɪə'lɒdʒɪkəl] *a* biologisch.

biology [baɪ'ɒlədʒɪ] *n* Biologie *f*.

birch [bɜːtʃ] *n* Birke *f*.

bird [bɜːd] *n* Vogel *m*; (*Brit col: girl*) Mädchen *nt*; **~'s-eye view** *n* Vogelschau *f*; **~ watcher** *n* Vogelbeobachter(in *f*) *m*.

Biro ['baɪrəu] *n* ® Kugelschreiber *m*.

birth [bɜːθ] *n* Geburt *f*; **to give ~ to** zur Welt bringen; **~ certificate** *n*

Geburtsurkunde f; ~ **control** n Geburtenkontrolle f; ~**day** n Geburtstag m; ~**place** n Geburtsort m; ~ **rate** n Geburtenrate f.

biscuit ['bɪskɪt] n Keks m.

bisect [baɪ'sekt] vt halbieren.

bishop ['bɪʃəp] n Bischof m.

bit [bɪt] pt of **bite** // n bißchen, Stückchen nt; (horse's) Gebiß nt; (COMPUT) Bit nt; a ~ tired etwas müde.

bitch [bɪtʃ] n (dog) Hündin f; (unpleasant woman) Weibsstück nt.

bite [baɪt], pt **bit**, pp **bitten** vti beißen // n Biß m; (mouthful) Bissen m; let's have a ~ to eat laß uns etwas essen; to ~ one's nails Nägel kauen.

biting ['baɪtɪŋ] a beißend.

bitten ['bɪtn] pp of **bite**.

bitter ['bɪtə*] a bitter; (memory etc) schmerzlich; (person) verbittert // n (Brit: beer) dunkles Bier; ~**ness** n Bitterkeit f.

blab [blæb] vi klatschen // vt (also: ~ out) ausplaudern.

black [blæk] a schwarz; (night) finster // vt schwärzen; (shoes) wichsen; (eye) blau schlagen; (Brit INDUSTRY) boykottieren; to give sb a ~ eye jdm ein blaues Auge schlagen; in the ~ (bank account) in den schwarzen Zahlen; ~ **and blue** a grün und blau; ~**berry** n Brombeere f; ~**bird** n Amsel f; ~**board** n (Wand)tafel f; ~**currant** n schwarze Johannisbeere f; ~**en** vt schwärzen; (fig) verunglimpfen; ~**ice** n Glatteis nt; ~**jack** n (US) Siebzehn und Vier; ~**leg** n (Brit) Streikbrecher(in f) m; ~**list** n schwarze Liste f; ~**mail** n Erpressung f // vt erpressen; ~ **market** n Schwarzmarkt m; ~**out** n Verdunklung f; (MED): to have a ~**out** bewußtlos werden; the B~ **Sea** n das Schwarze Meer; ~ **sheep** n schwarzes Schaf nt; ~**smith** n Schmied m; ~ **spot** n (AUT) Gefahrenstelle f; (for unemployment etc) schwer betroffene(s) Gebiet nt.

bladder ['blædə*] n Blase f.

blade [bleɪd] n (of weapon) Klinge f; (of grass) Halm m; (of oar) Ruderblatt nt.

blame [bleɪm] n Tadel m, Schuld f // vt Vorwürfe machen (+dat); to ~ sb for sth jdm die Schuld an etw (dat) geben; he is to ~ er ist daran schuld.

bland [blænd] a mild.

blank [blæŋk] a leer, unbeschrieben; (look) verdutzt; (verse) Blank- // n (space) Lücke f; Zwischenraum m; (cartridge) Platzpatrone f; ~ **cheque** n Blankoscheck m; (fig) Freibrief m.

blanket ['blæŋkɪt] n (Woll)decke f.

blare [blɛə*] vi (radio) plärren; (horn) tuten; (MUS) schmettern.

blasé ['blɑːzeɪ] a blasiert.

blast [blɑːst] n Explosion f; (of wind) Windstoß m // vt (blow up) sprengen; ~!

(col) verflixt!; ~-**off** n (SPACE) (Raketen)abschuß m.

blatant ['bleɪtənt] a offenkundig.

blaze [bleɪz] n (fire) lodernde(s) Feuer nt // vi lodern // vt: ~ **a trail** Bahn brechen.

blazer ['bleɪzə*] n Blazer m.

bleach [bliːtʃ] n (also: household ~) Bleichmittel nt // vt bleichen.

bleachers ['bliːtʃəz] npl (US SPORT) unüberdachte Tribüne.

bleak [bliːk] a kahl, rauh; (future) trostlos.

bleary-eyed ['blɪərɪaɪd] a triefäugig; (on waking up) mit verschlafenen Augen.

bleat [bliːt] vi blöken; (fig: complain) meckern.

bleed [bliːd] v (pt, pp **bled** [bled]) vi bluten // vt (draw blood) zur Ader lassen; to ~ **to death** verbluten.

bleeper ['bliːpə*] n (of doctor etc) Funkrufempfänger m.

blemish ['blemɪʃ] n Makel m // vt verunstalten.

blend [blend] n Mischung f // vt mischen // vi sich mischen.

bless [bles], pt, pp **blessed** or **blest** [blest] vt segnen; (give thanks) preisen; (make happy) glücklich machen; ~ **you!** Gesundheit!; ~**ing** n Segen m; (at table) Tischgebet nt; (happiness) Wohltat f; Segen m; (good wish) Glück nt.

blew [bluː] pt of **blow**.

blight [blaɪt] vt zunichte machen.

blimey ['blaɪmɪ] interj (Brit col) verflucht.

blind [blaɪnd] a blind; (corner) unübersichtlich // n (for window) Rouleau nt // vt blenden; ~ **alley** n Sackgasse f; ~**fold** n Augenbinde f // a, ad mit verbundenen Augen // vt die Augen verbinden (sb jdm); ~**ly** ad blind; (fig) blindlings; ~**ness** n Blindheit f; ~ **spot** n (AUT) toter Winkel m; (fig) schwache(r) Punkt m.

blink [blɪŋk] vi blinzeln; ~**ers** npl Scheuklappen pl.

bliss [blɪs] n (Glück)seligkeit f.

blister ['blɪstə*] n Blase f // vi Blasen werfen.

blithe [blaɪð] a munter.

blitz [blɪts] n Luftkrieg m.

blizzard ['blɪzəd] n Schneesturm m.

bloated ['bləʊtɪd] a aufgedunsen; (col: full) nudelsatt.

blob [blɒb] n Klümpchen nt.

bloc [blɒk] n (POL) Block m.

block [blɒk] n (of wood) Block m, Klotz m; (of houses) Block m // vt hemmen; ~**ade** [blɒ'keɪd] n Blockade f // vt blockieren; ~**age** n Verstopfung f; ~**buster** n Knüller m; ~ **of flats** n (Brit) Häuserblock m; ~ **letters** pl Blockbuchstaben pl.

bloke [bləʊk] n (Brit col) Kerl m, Typ m.

blond(e) [blɒnd] a blond // n Blondine f.

blood [blʌd] n Blut nt; ~ **donor** n Blutspender m; ~ **group** n Blutgruppe f; ~ **pressure** n Blutdruck m; ~**shed** n Blutvergießen nt; ~**shot** n blutunterlaufen; ~**stained** a blutbefleckt; ~**stream** n Blut nt, Blutkreislauf m; ~ **test** n Blutprobe f; ~**thirsty** a blutrünstig; ~**y** a (Brit col!) verdammt; (lit) blutig; ~**y-minded** a (Brit col) stur.

bloom [bluːm] n Blüte f; (freshness) Glanz m // vi blühen.

blossom ['blɒsəm] n Blüte f // vi blühen.

blot [blɒt] n Klecks m // vt beklecksen; (ink) (ab)löschen; ~ **out** vt auslöschen.

blotchy ['blɒtʃɪ] a fleckig.

blotting paper ['blɒtɪŋpeɪpə*] n Löschpapier nt.

blouse [blaʊz] n Bluse f.

blow [bləʊ] n Schlag m // v (pt blew, pp blown [bləʊn]) vt blasen // vi (wind) wehen; to ~ one's nose sich (dat) die Nase putzen; ~ **away** vt wegblasen; ~ **down** vt unwehen; ~ **out** vi ausgehen; ~ **over** vi vorübergehen; ~ **up** vi explodieren // vt sprengen; ~**dry** n: to have a ~-dry sich fönen lassen // vt fönen; ~**lamp** n (Brit) Lötlampe f; ~-**out** n (AUT) geplatzte(r) Reifen m; ~**torch** n = ~lamp.

blue [bluː] a blau; (col: unhappy) niedergeschlagen; (obscene) pornographisch; (joke) anzüglich; out of the ~ (fig) aus heiterem Himmel; to have the ~s traurig sein; ~**bell** n Glockenblume f; ~**bottle** n Schmeißfliege f; ~ **film** n Pornofilm m; ~**print** n (fig) Entwurf m.

bluff [blʌf] vi bluffen, täuschen // n (deception) Bluff m; to call sb's ~ es darauf ankommen lassen.

blunder ['blʌndə*] n grobe(r) Fehler m, Schnitzer m // vi einen groben Fehler machen.

blunt [blʌnt] a (knife) stumpf; (talk) unverblümt // vt abstumpfen.

blur [blɜː*] n Fleck m // vt verschwommen machen.

blurb [blɜːb] n Waschzettel m.

blurt [blɜːt] vt: ~ **out** herausplatzen mit.

blush [blʌʃ] vi erröten // n (Scham)röte f.

blustery ['blʌstərɪ] a stürmisch.

boar [bɔː*] n Keiler m, Eber m.

board [bɔːd] n (of wood) Brett nt; (of card) Pappe f; (committee) Ausschuß m; (of firm) Aufsichtsrat m; (SCH) Direktorium nt; (NAUT, AVIAT): **on** ~ an Bord // vt (train) einsteigen in (+acc); (ship) an Bord gehen (+gen); ~ **and lodging** n Unterkunft f und Verpflegung; **full/half** ~ (Brit) Voll-/Halbpension f; **to go by the** ~ flachfallen, über Bord

gehen; ~ **up** vt mit Brettern vernageln; ~**er** n Kostgänger m; (SCH) Internatsschüler(in f) m; ~**ing card** n (AVIAT, NAUT) Bordkarte f; ~**ing house** n Pension f; ~**ing school** n Internat nt; ~ **room** n Sitzungszimmer nt.

boast [bəʊst] vi prahlen (about, of mit) // vt sich rühmen (+gen) // n Großtuerei f; Prahlerei f.

boat [bəʊt] n Boot nt; (ship) Schiff nt; ~**er** n (hat) Kreissäge f; ~**swain** ['bəʊsn] n = **bosun**.

bob [bɒb] vi sich auf und nieder bewegen; ~ **up** vi auftauchen // n (Brit col) = **shilling**.

bobbin ['bɒbɪn] n Spule f.

bobby ['bɒbɪ] n (Brit col) Bobby m.

bobsleigh ['bɒbsleɪ] n Bob m.

bode [bəʊd] vi: to ~ well/ill ein gutes/schlechtes Zeichen sein.

bodily ['bɒdɪlɪ] a, ad körperlich.

body ['bɒdɪ] n Körper m; (dead) Leiche f; (group) Mannschaft f; (AUT) Karosserie f; (trunk) Rumpf m; ~**guard** n Leibwache f; ~**work** n Karosserie f.

bog [bɒg] n Sumpf m // vt: to get ~ged down sich festfahren.

boggle ['bɒgl] vi stutzen; the mind ~s es ist kaum auszumalen.

bogus ['bəʊgəs] a unecht, Schein-.

boil [bɔɪl] vti kochen // n (MED) Geschwür nt; to come to the (Brit) or a (US) ~ zu kochen anfangen; to ~ **down** to (fig) hinauslaufen auf (+acc); ~ **over** vi überkochen; ~**ed potatoes** npl Salzkartoffeln pl; ~**er** n Boiler m; ~**er suit** n (Brit) Arbeitsanzug m; ~**ing point** n Siedepunkt m.

boisterous ['bɔɪstərəs] a ungestüm.

bold [bəʊld] a (fearless) unerschrocken; (handwriting) fest und klar.

bollard ['bɒləd] n (NAUT) Poller m; (Brit AUT) Pfosten m.

bolster ['bəʊlstə*] n Polster nt; ~ **up** vt unterstützen.

bolt [bəʊlt] n Bolzen m; (lock) Riegel m // ad: ~ **upright** kerzengerade // vt verriegeln; (swallow) verschlingen // vi (horse) durchgehen.

bomb [bɒm] n Bombe f // vt bombardieren; ~**ard** [bɒm'bɑːd] vt bombardieren; ~**ardment** [bɒm'bɑːdmənt] n Beschießung f; ~**shell** n (fig) Bombe f.

bona fide ['bəʊnə'faɪdɪ] a echt.

bond [bɒnd] n (link) Band nt; (FIN) Schuldverschreibung f.

bondage ['bɒndɪdʒ] n Sklaverei f.

bone [bəʊn] n Knochen m; (of fish) Gräte f; (piece of ~) Knochensplitter m // vt die Knochen herausnehmen (+dat); (fish) entgräten; ~ **idle** a stinkfaul.

bonfire ['bɒnfaɪə*] n Feuer nt im Freien.

bonnet ['bɒnɪt] n Haube f; (for baby) Häubchen nt; (Brit AUT) Motorhaube f.
bonus ['bəʊnəs] n Bonus m; (annual ~) Prämie f.
bony ['bəʊnɪ] a knochig, knochendürr.
boo [buː] vt auspfeifen.
booby trap ['buːbɪ-] n Falle f.
book [bʊk] n Buch nt; (COMM): ~s Bücher pl // vt (ticket etc) vorbestellen; (person) verwarnen; ~case n Bücherregal nt, Bücherschrank m; ~ing office n (Brit RAIL) Fahrkartenschalter m; (Brit THEAT) Vorverkaufsstelle f; ~-keeping n Buchhaltung f; ~let n Broschüre f; ~maker n Buchmacher m; ~seller n Buchhändler m; ~shop, ~ store n Buchhandlung f.
boom [buːm] n (noise) Dröhnen nt; (busy period) Hochkonjunktur f // vi dröhnen.
boon [buːn] n Wohltat f, Segen m.
boost [buːst] n Auftrieb m; (fig) Reklame f // vt Auftrieb geben; ~er n (MED) Wiederholungsimpfung f.
boot [buːt] n Stiefel m; (Brit AUT) Kofferraum m // vt (kick) einen Fußtritt geben; (COMPUT) laden; to ~ (in addition) obendrein.
booth [buːð] n (at fair) Bude f; (telephone ~) Zelle f; (voting ~) Kabine f.
booty ['buːtɪ] n Beute f.
booze [buːz] n (col) Alkohol m, Schnaps m // vi saufen.
border ['bɔːdə*] n Grenze f; (edge) Kante f; (in garden) (Blumen)rabatte f // a Grenz-; the B~s Grenzregion f zwischen England und Schottland; ~ on vt grenzen an (+acc); ~line n Grenze f.
bore [bɔː*] pt of **bear** // vt bohren; (weary) langweilen // n (person) langweilige(r) Mensch m; (thing) langweilige Sache f; (of gun) Kaliber nt; I am ~d ich langweile mich; ~dom n Langeweile f.
boring ['bɔːrɪŋ] a langweilig.
born [bɔːn] a: to be ~ geboren werden.
borne [bɔːn] pp of **bear**.
borough ['bʌrə] n Stadt(gemeinde) f, Stadtbezirk m.
borrow ['bɒrəʊ] vt borgen.
bosom ['bʊzəm] n Busen m.
boss [bɒs] n Chef m, Boß m // vt: ~ around herumkommandieren; ~y a herrisch.
bosun ['bəʊsn] n Bootsmann m.
botany ['bɒtənɪ] n Botanik f.
botch [bɒtʃ] vt (also: ~ up) verpfuschen.
both [bəʊθ] a beide(s); ~ (of) the books beide Bücher // pron beide(s) // ad: ~ X and Y sowohl X wie or als auch Y.
bother ['bɒðə*] vt (pester) quälen // vi (fuss) sich aufregen // n Mühe f, Umstand m; to ~ doing sth sich (dat) die Mühe machen, etw zu tun; what a ~!

wie ärgerlich!
bottle ['bɒtl] n Flasche f // vt (in Flaschen) abfüllen; ~ up vt aufstauen; ~neck n (lit, fig) Engpaß m; ~-opener n Flaschenöffner m.
bottom ['bɒtəm] n Boden m; (of person) Hintern m; (riverbed) Flußbett nt // a unterste(r, s).
bough [baʊ] n Zweig m, Ast m.
bought [bɔːt] pt, pp of **buy**.
boulder ['bəʊldə*] n Felsbrocken m.
bounce [baʊns] vi (ball) hochspringen; (person) herumhüpfen; (cheque) platzen // vt (auf)springen lassen // n (rebound) Aufprall m; ~r n Rausschmeißer m.
bound [baʊnd] pt, pp of **bind** // n Grenze f; (leap) Sprung m // vi (spring, leap) (auf)springen // a (obliged) gebunden, verpflichtet; out of ~s Zutritt verboten; to be ~ to do sth verpflichtet sein, etw zu tun, etw tun müssen; it's ~ to happen es muß so kommen; to be ~ for ... nach ... fahren.
boundary ['baʊndərɪ] n Grenze f.
bouquet [bʊ'keɪ] n Strauß m; (of wine) Blume f.
bourgeois ['bʊəʒwaː] a kleinbürgerlich, bourgeois // n Spießbürger(in f) m.
bout [baʊt] n (of illness) Anfall m; (contest) Kampf m.
bow n [bəʊ] (ribbon) Schleife f; (weapon, MUS) Bogen m; [baʊ] (with head, body) Verbeugung f; (of ship) Bug m // vi [baʊ] sich verbeugen; (submit) sich beugen (+dat).
bowels ['baʊəlz] npl Darm m; (centre) Innere nt.
bowl [bəʊl] n (basin) Schüssel f; (of pipe) (Pfeifen)kopf m; (wooden ball) (Holz)kugel f // vi (die Kugel) rollen; ~s n (game) Bowls-Spiel nt.
bow-legged ['bəʊlegɪd] a o-beinig.
bowler ['bəʊlə*] n Werfer m; (Brit: also: ~ hat) Melone f.
bowling ['bəʊlɪŋ] n Kegeln nt; ~ alley n Kegelbahn f; ~ green n Rasen m zum Bowling-Spiel.
bow tie ['bəʊ'taɪ] n Fliege f.
box [bɒks] n (also: cardboard ~) Schachtel f; (bigger) Kasten m; (THEAT) Loge f // vt einpacken // vi boxen; ~er n Boxer m; ~ing n (SPORT) Boxen nt; B~ing Day n (Brit) zweiter Weihnachtsfeiertag; ~ing gloves npl Boxhandschuhe pl; ~ing ring n Boxring m; ~ office n (Theater)kasse f; ~room n Rumpelkammer f.
boy [bɔɪ] n Junge m.
boycott ['bɔɪkɒt] n Boykott m // vt boykottieren.
boyfriend ['bɔɪfrend] n Freund m.
boyish ['bɔɪʃ] a jungenhaft.
B.R. n abbr of **British Rail**.
bra [braː] n BH m.

brace [breɪs] n (TECH) Stütze f; (MED) Klammer f // vt stützen; ~s pl (Brit) Hosenträger pl; to ~ o.s. for sth (fig) sich auf etw (acc) gefaßt machen.
bracelet ['breɪslɪt] n Armband nt.
bracing ['breɪsɪŋ] a kräftigend.
bracken ['brækən] n Farnkraut nt.
bracket ['brækɪt] n Halter m, Klammer f; (in punctuation) Klammer f; (group) Gruppe f // vt einklammern; (fig) in dieselbe Gruppe einordnen.
brag [bræg] vi sich rühmen.
braid [breɪd] n (hair) Flechte f; (trim) Borte f.
Braille [breɪl] n Blindenschrift f.
brain [breɪn] n (ANAT) Gehirn nt; (intellect) Intelligenz f, Verstand m; (person) kluge(r) Kopf m; ~s pl Verstand m; ~child n Erfindung f; ~wash vt eine Gehirnwäsche vornehmen bei; ~wave n Geistesblitz m; ~y a gescheit.
braise [breɪz] vt schmoren.
brake [breɪk] n Bremse f // vti bremsen; ~ fluid n Bremsflüssigkeit f; ~ light n Bremslicht nt.
bramble ['bræmbl] n Brombeere f.
bran [bræn] n Kleie f; (food) Frühstücksflocken pl.
branch [brɑːntʃ] n Ast m; (division) Zweig m // vi (also: ~ out) (road) sich verzweigen.
brand [brænd] n (COMM) Marke f, Sorte f; (on cattle) Brandmal nt // vt brandmarken; (COMM) ein Warenzeichen geben (+dat).
brandish ['brændɪʃ] vt (drohend) schwingen.
brand-new ['brænd'njuː] a funkelnagelneu.
brandy ['brændɪ] n Weinbrand m, Kognak m.
brash [bræʃ] a unverschämt.
brass [brɑːs] n Messing nt; the ~ (MUS) das Blech; ~ band n Blaskapelle f.
brassière ['bræsɪə*] n Büstenhalter m.
brat [bræt] n ungezogene(s) Kind nt, Gör nt.
bravado [brə'vɑːdəʊ] n Tollkühnheit f.
brave [breɪv] a tapfer // n indianische(r) Krieger m // vt die Stirn bieten (+dat).
bravery ['breɪvərɪ] n Tapferkeit f.
brawl [brɔːl] n Rauferei f.
brawn [brɔːn] n (ANAT) Muskeln pl; (strength) Muskelkraft f.
bray [breɪ] vi schreien.
brazen ['breɪzn] a (shameless) unverschämt // vt: ~ it out sich mit Lügen und Betrügen durchsetzen.
brazier ['breɪzɪə*] n (of workmen) offene(r) Kohlenofen m.
Brazil [brə'zɪl] n Brasilien nt; ~ian a brasilianisch // n Brasilianer(in f) m.
breach [briːtʃ] n (gap) Lücke f; (MIL) Durchbruch m; (of discipline) Verstoß m

(gegen die Disziplin); (of faith) Vertrauensbruch m // vt durchbrechen; ~ of contract Vertragsbruch m; ~ of the peace öffentliche Ruhestörung f.
bread [bred] n Brot nt; ~ and butter Butterbrot nt; ~bin, (US) ~box n Brotkasten m; ~crumbs npl Brotkrumen pl; (COOK) Paniermehl nt; ~line n: to be on the ~line sich gerade so durchschlagen.
breadth [bretθ] n Breite f.
breadwinner ['bredwɪnə*] n Ernährer m.
break [breɪk] v (pt broke, pp broken) vt (destroy) (ab- or zer)brechen; (promise) brechen, nicht einhalten // vi (fall apart) auseinanderbrechen; (collapse) zusammenbrechen; (of dawn) anbrechen // n (gap) Lücke f; (chance) Chance f, Gelegenheit f; (fracture) Bruch m; (rest) Pause f; ~ down vt (figures, data) aufschlüsseln; (undermine) überwinden // vi (car) eine Panne haben; (person) zusammenbrechen; ~ even vi die Kosten decken; ~ free or loose vi sich losreißen; ~ in vi (animal) abrichten; (horse) zureiten // vi (burglar) einbrechen; (interrupt) // in (+ acc); ~ off vi abbrechen; ~ open vt (door etc) aufbrechen; ~ out vi ausbrechen; to ~ out in spots Pickel bekommen; ~ up vi zerbrechen; (fig) sich zerstreuen; (SCH) in die Ferien gehen // vt brechen; ~age n Bruch m, Beschädigung f; ~down n (TECH) Panne f; (MED: also: nervous ~down) Zusammenbruch m; ~down van n (Brit) Abschleppwagen m; ~er n Brecher m.
breakfast ['brekfəst] n Frühstück nt.
break-in ['breɪkɪn] n Einbruch m.
breaking ['breɪkɪŋ] n: ~ and entering (JUR) Einbruch m.
breakthrough ['breɪkθruː] n Durchbruch m.
breakwater ['breɪkwɔːtə*] n Wellenbrecher m.
breast [brest] n Brust f; ~-feed vti (irreg: like feed) stillen; ~-stroke n Brustschwimmen nt.
breath [breθ] n Atem m; out of ~ außer Atem; under one's ~ flüsternd.
breathalyzer ['breθəlaɪzə*] n Röhrchen nt.
breathe [briːð] vti atmen; ~ in vti einatmen; ~ out vti ausatmen; ~r n Verschnaufpause f.
breathing ['briːðɪŋ] n Atmung f.
breathless ['breθlɪs] a atemlos.
breath-taking ['breθteɪkɪŋ] a atemberaubend.
breed [briːd] v (pt, pp bred [bred]) vi sich vermehren // vt züchten // n (race) Rasse f, Zucht f; ~er n (person) Züchter m; ~ing n Züchtung f; (up-

bringing) Erziehung f; *(education)* Bildung f.
breeze [bri:z] n Brise f.
breezy ['bri:zɪ] a windig; *(manner)* munter.
brevity ['brevɪtɪ] n Kürze f.
brew [bru:] vt brauen; *(plot)* anzetteln // vi *(storm)* sich zusammenziehen; **~ery** n Brauerei f.
bribe ['braɪb] n Bestechungsgeld nt or -geschenk nt // vt bestechen; **~ry** ['braɪbərɪ] n Bestechung f.
bric-a-brac ['brɪkəbræk] n Nippes pl.
brick [brɪk] n Backstein m; **~layer** n Maurer m; **~works** n Ziegelei f.
bridal ['braɪdl] a Braut-.
bride [braɪd] n Braut f; **~groom** n Bräutigam m; **bridesmaid** n Brautjungfer f.
bridge [brɪdʒ] n Brücke f; *(NAUT)* Kommandobrücke f; *(CARDS)* Bridge nt; *(ANAT)* Nasenrücken m // vt eine Brücke schlagen über (+acc); *(fig)* überbrücken.
bridle ['braɪdl] n Zaum m // vt *(fig)* zügeln; *(horse)* aufzäumen; **~ path** n Reitweg m.
brief [bri:f] a kurz // n *(JUR)* Akten pl // vt instruieren; **~s** pl Schlüpfer m, Slip m; **~case** n Aktentasche f; **~ing** n *(genaue)* Anweisung f; **~ly** ad kurz.
brigadier [brɪgə'dɪə*] n Brigadegeneral m.
bright [braɪt] a hell; *(cheerful)* heiter; *(idea)* klug; **~en (up)** vt aufhellen; *(person)* aufheitern // vi sich aufheitern.
brilliance ['brɪljəns] n Glanz m; *(of person)* Scharfsinn m.
brilliant ['brɪljənt] a glänzend.
brim [brɪm] n Rand m.
brine [braɪn] n Salzwasser nt.
bring [brɪŋ], pt, pp **brought** vt bringen; **~ about** vt zustande bringen; **~ back** vt zurückbringen; **~ down** vt *(price)* senken; **~ forward** vt *(meeting)* vorverlegen; *(COMM)* übertragen; **~ in** vt hereinbringen; *(harvest)* einbringen; **~ off** vt davontragen; *(success)* erzielen; **~ out** vt *(object)* herausbringen; **~ round** or **to** vt wieder zu sich bringen; **~ up** vt aufziehen; *(question)* zur Sprache bringen.
brink [brɪŋk] n Rand m.
brisk [brɪsk] a lebhaft.
brisket ['brɪskɪt] n Bruststück nt.
bristle ['brɪsl] n Borste f // vi sich sträuben; **bristling with** strotzend vor (+dat).
Britain ['brɪtən] n *(also:* **Great ~)** Großbritannien nt.
British ['brɪtɪʃ] a britisch; **the ~** pl die Briten pl; **the ~ Isles** pl die Britischen Inseln pl; **~ Rail** n die Britischen Eisenbahnen pl.
Briton ['brɪtən] n Brite m, Britin f.

brittle ['brɪtl] a spröde.
broach [brəʊtʃ] vt *(subject)* anschneiden.
broad [brɔ:d] a breit; *(hint)* deutlich; *(daylight)* hellicht; *(general)* allgemein; *(accent)* stark; **in ~ daylight** am hellichten Tag; **~cast** n Rundfunkübertragung f // vti, pt, pp **~cast** übertragen, senden; **~en** vt erweitern // vi sich erweitern; **~ly** ad allgemein gesagt; **~-minded** a tolerant.
broccoli ['brɒkəlɪ] n Brokkoli pl.
brochure ['brəʊʃʊə*] n Broschüre f.
broil [brɔɪl] vt *(grill)* grillen.
broke [brəʊk] pt of **break** // a *(col)* pleite.
broken ['brəʊkən] pp of **break** // a: ~ leg gebrochenes Bein; **in ~ English** in gebrochenen Englisch; **~-hearted** a untröstlich.
broker ['brəʊkə*] n Makler m.
brolly ['brɒlɪ] n *(Brit col)* Schirm m.
bronchitis [brɒŋ'kaɪtɪs] n Bronchitis f.
bronze [brɒnz] n Bronze f.
brooch [brəʊtʃ] n Brosche f.
brood [bru:d] n Brut f // vi brüten.
brook [brʊk] n Bach m.
broom [bru:m] n Besen m; **~stick** n Besenstiel m.
Bros. abbr of **Brothers**.
broth [brɒθ] n Suppe f, Fleischbrühe f.
brothel ['brɒθl] n Bordell nt.
brother ['brʌðə*] n Bruder m; **~-in-law** n Schwager m.
brought [brɔ:t] pt, pp of **bring**.
brow [braʊ] n *(eyebrow)* (Augen)braue f; *(forehead)* Stirn f; *(of hill)* Bergkuppe f.
brown [braʊn] a braun // n Braun nt // vt bräunen; **~ bread** n Mischbrot nt; **~ie** n Wichtel m; **~ paper** n Packpapier nt; **~ sugar** n braune(r) Zucker m.
browse [braʊz] vi *(in books)* blättern; *(in shop)* schmökern, herumschauen.
bruise [bru:z] n Bluterguß m, blaue(r) Fleck m // vt einen blauen Fleck geben/bekommen.
brunt [brʌnt] n volle Wucht f.
brush [brʌʃ] n Bürste f; *(for sweeping)* Handbesen m; *(for painting)* Pinsel m; *(fight)* kurze(r) Kampf m; *(MIL)* Scharmützel nt; *(fig)* Auseinandersetzung f // vt *(clean)* bürsten; *(sweep)* fegen; *(gen:* **~ past, ~ against)** streifen; **~ aside** vt abtun; **~ up** vt *(knowledge)* auffrischen; **~wood** n Gestrüpp nt.
brusque [bru:sk] a schroff.
Brussels sprouts ['brʌslz'spraʊts] npl Rosenkohl m.
brutal ['bru:tl] a brutal.
brute [bru:t] n *(person)* Scheusal nt // a: **by ~ force** mit roher Kraft.
B.Sc. n abbr of **Bachelor of Science**.
bubble ['bʌbl] n *(Luft)*blase f // vi sprudeln; *(with joy)* übersprudeln; ~

bath n Schaumbad nt; **~gum** n Kaugummi m or nt.

buck [bʌk] n Bock m; (US col) Dollar m // vi bocken; **to pass the ~ (to sb)** die Verantwortung (auf jdn) abschieben; **~ up** vi (col) sich zusammenreißen.

bucket ['bʌkɪt] n Eimer m.

buckle ['bʌkl] n Schnalle f // vt (an- or zusammen)schnallen // vi (bend) sich verziehen.

bud [bʌd] n Knospe f // vi knospen, keimen.

Buddhism ['budɪzəm] n Buddhismus m.

budding ['bʌdɪŋ] a angehend.

buddy ['bʌdɪ] n (col) Kumpel m.

budge [bʌdʒ] vti (sich) von der Stelle rühren.

budgerigar ['bʌdʒərɪgaː*] n Wellensittich m.

budget ['bʌdʒɪt] n Budget nt; (POL) Haushalt m // vi: to ~ for sth etw einplanen.

budgie ['bʌdʒɪ] n = **budgerigar**.

buff [bʌf] a (colour) lederfarben // n (enthusiast) Fan m.

buffalo ['bʌfələu], pl ~ or **~es** n (Brit) Büffel m; (US: bison) Bison m.

buffer ['bʌfə*] n Puffer m; (COMPUT) Pufferspeicher m.

buffet ['bʌfɪt] n (blow) Schlag m; ['bufeɪ] (Brit: bar) Imbißraum m, Erfrischungsraum m; (food) (kaltes) Büfett nt // vt ['bʌfɪt] (herum)stoßen; **~ car** n (Brit) Speisewagen m.

bug [bʌg] n (lit, fig) Wanze f // vt verwanzen.

bugle ['bjuːgl] n Jagd- or Bügelhorn nt.

build [bɪld] vt, pt, pp **built** bauen // n Körperbau m; **~ up** vt aufbauen; **~er** n Bauunternehmer m; **~ing** n Gebäude nt; **~ing society** n (Brit) Bausparkasse f.

built [bɪlt] pt, pp of **build** // a: **~-in** a (cupboard) eingebaut; **~-up area** n Wohngebiet nt.

bulb [bʌlb] n (BOT) (Blumen)zwiebel f; (ELEC) Glühlampe f, Birne f.

Bulgaria [bʌlˈgɛərɪə] n Bulgarien nt; **~n** a bulgarisch // n Bulgare m, Bulgarin f; (language) Bulgarisch nt.

bulge [bʌldʒ] n (Aus)bauchung f // vi sich (aus)bauchen.

bulk [bʌlk] n Größe f, Masse f; (greater part) Großteil m; **in ~** (COMM) en gros; **the ~ of** der größte Teil (+gen); **~head** n Schott nt; **~y** a (sehr) umfangreich; (goods) sperrig.

bull [bul] n (animal) Bulle m; (cattle) Stier m; (papal) Bulle f; **~dog** n Bulldogge f.

bulldozer ['buldəuzə*] n Planierraupe f.

bullet ['bulɪt] n Kugel f.

bulletin ['bulɪtɪn] n Bulletin nt, Bekanntmachung f.

bulletproof ['bulɪtpruːf] a kugelsicher.

bullfight ['bulfaɪt] n Stierkampf m; **~er** n Stierkämpfer m; **~ing** n Stierkampf m.

bullion ['buliən] n Barren m.

bullock ['bulək] n Ochse m.

bullring ['bulrɪŋ] n Stierkampfarena f.

bull's-eye ['bulzaɪ] n Zentrum nt.

bully ['bulɪ] n Raufbold m // vt einschüchtern.

bum [bʌm] n (col: backside) Hintern m; (tramp) Landstreicher m; (nasty person) fieser Kerl m.

bumblebee ['bʌmblbiː] n Hummel f.

bump [bʌmp] n (blow) Stoß m; (swelling) Beule f // vti stoßen, prallen; **~ into** vt stoßen gegen; (person) treffen; **~er** n (AUT) Stoßstange f // a (edition) dick; (harvest) Rekord-; **~er cars** npl (US: dodgems) Autoskooter pl.

bumptious ['bʌmpʃəs] a aufgeblasen.

bumpy ['bʌmpɪ] a holprig.

bun [bʌn] n Korinthenbrötchen nt.

bunch [bʌntʃ] n (of flowers) Strauß m; (of keys) Bund m; (of people) Haufen m.

bundle ['bʌndl] n Bündel nt // vt (also: **~ up**) bündeln.

bungalow ['bʌŋgələu] n einstöckige(s) Haus nt, Bungalow m.

bungle ['bʌŋgl] vt verpfuschen.

bunion ['bʌnjən] n entzündete(r) Fußballen m.

bunk [bʌŋk] n Schlafkoje f; **~ beds** npl Etagenbett nt.

bunker ['bʌŋkə*] n (coal store) Kohlenbunker m; (golf) Sandloch nt.

bunny ['bʌnɪ] n (also: **~ rabbit**) Häschen nt.

bunting ['bʌntɪŋ] n Fahnentuch nt.

buoy [bɔɪ] n Boje f; (lifebuoy) Rettungsboje f; **~ up** vt Auftrieb geben (+dat); **~ant** a (floating) schwimmend; (fig) heiter.

burden ['bɜːdn] n (weight) Ladung f, Last f; (fig) Bürde f // vt belasten.

bureau ['bjuərəu], pl **~x** [-z] n (Brit: writing desk) Sekretär m; (US: chest of drawers) Kommode f; (for information etc) Büro nt.

bureaucracy [bjuˈrɒkrəsɪ] n Bürokratie f.

bureaucrat ['bjuərəkræt] n Bürokrat(in f) m.

burglar ['bɜːglə*] n Einbrecher m; **~ alarm** n Einbruchssicherung f; **~y** n Einbruch m.

burial ['berɪəl] n Beerdigung f.

burly ['bɜːlɪ] a stämmig.

Burma ['bɜːmə] n Birma nt.

burn [bɜːn] v (pt, pp **burned** or **burnt**) vt verbrennen // vi brennen // n Brandwunde f; **~ down** vti abbrennen; **~er** n Brenner m; **~ing** a brennend.

burrow ['bʌrəu] n (of fox) Bau m; (of rabbit) Höhle f // vt eingraben.

bursar ['bɜːsə*] n Kassenverwalter m, Quästor m; ~**y** n (Brit) Stipendium nt.

burst [bɜːst] v (pt, pp **burst**) vt zerbrechen // vi platzen; (into tears) ausbrechen // n Explosion f; (outbreak) Ausbruch m; (in pipe) Bruch(stelle f) m; to ~ into flames in Flammen aufgehen; to ~ into tears in Tränen ausbrechen; to ~ out laughing in Gelächter ausbrechen; ~ **into** vt (room etc) platzen in (+acc); ~ **open** vi aufbrechen.

bury ['berɪ] vt vergraben; (in grave) beerdigen.

bus [bʌs] n (Auto)bus m, Omnibus m.

bush [buʃ] n Busch m; to **beat about the** ~ wie die Katze um den heißen Brei herumgehen.

bushy ['buʃɪ] a buschig.

busily ['bɪzɪlɪ] ad geschäftig.

business ['bɪznɪs] n Geschäft nt; (concern) Angelegenheit f; it's none of your ~ es geht dich nichts an; to mean ~ es ernst meinen; to be away on ~ geschäftlich verreist sein; it's my ~ to ... es ist meine Sache, zu ...; ~**like** a geschäftsmäßig; ~**man** n Geschäftsmann m; ~ **trip** n Geschäftsreise f; ~**woman** n Geschäftsfrau f.

busker ['bʌskə*] n (Brit) Straßenmusikant m.

bus-stop ['bʌsstɒp] n Bushaltestelle f.

bust [bʌst] n Büste f // a (broken) kaputt(gegangen); (business) pleite; to **go** ~ pleite machen.

bustle ['bʌsl] n Getriebe nt // vi hasten.

bustling ['bʌslɪŋ] a geschäftig.

busy ['bɪzɪ] a beschäftigt; (road) belebt // vt: to ~ o.s. sich beschäftigen; ~**body** n Übereifrige(r) mf; ~ **signal** n (US TEL) Besetztzeichen nt.

but [bʌt] ◆cj 1 (yet) aber; not X ~ Y nicht X sondern Y
2 (however): I'd love to come, ~ I'm busy ich würde gern kommen, bin aber beschäftigt
3 (showing disagreement, surprise etc): ~ that's fantastic! (aber) das ist ja fantastisch!
◆prep (apart from, except): nothing ~ trouble nichts als Ärger; no-one ~ him can do it niemand außer ihm kann es machen; ~ **for you/your help** ohne dich/deine Hilfe; **anything** ~ **that** alles, nur das nicht
◆ad (just, only): she's ~ **a child** sie ist noch ein Kind; **had I** ~ **known** wenn ich es nur gewußt hätte; **I can** ~ **try** ich kann es immerhin versuchen; **all** ~ **finished** so gut wie fertig.

butcher ['butʃə*] n Metzger m; (murderer) Schlächter m // vt schlachten; (kill) abschlachten; ~**'s (shop)** n Metzgerei f.

butler ['bʌtlə*] n Butler m.

butt [bʌt] n (cask) große(s) Faß nt; (Brit fig: target) Zielscheibe f; (thick end) dicke(s) Ende nt; (of gun) Kolben m; (of cigarette) Stummel m // vt (mit dem Kopf) stoßen; ~ **in** vi (interrupt) sich einmischen.

butter ['bʌtə*] n Butter f // vt buttern; ~ **bean** n Wachsbohne f; ~**cup** n Butterblume f.

butterfly ['bʌtəflaɪ] n Schmetterling m (SWIMMING: also: ~ stroke) Butterflystil m.

buttocks ['bʌtəks] npl Gesäß nt.

button ['bʌtn] n Knopf m // vti (also: ~ up) zuknöpfen.

buttress ['bʌtrɪs] n Strebepfeiler m; Stützbogen m.

buxom ['bʌksəm] a drall.

buy [baɪ] vt, pp **bought** vt kaufen // n Kauf m; to ~ **sb a drink** jdm einen Drink spendieren; ~**er** n Käufer(in f) m.

buzz [bʌz] n Summen nt // vi summen.

buzzer ['bʌzə*] n Summer m.

buzz word n Modewort nt.

by [baɪ] prep 1 (referring to cause, agent) von, durch; killed ~ **lightning** vom Blitz getötet; a painting ~ Picasso ein Gemälde von Picasso
2 (referring to method, manner, means): ~ bus/car/train mit dem Bus/Auto/Zug; to pay ~ cheque per Scheck bezahlen; ~ moonlight bei Mondschein; ~ saving hard, he ... indem er eisern sparte, ... er ...
3 (via, through) über (+acc); he came in ~ the back door er kam durch die Hintertür herein
4 (close to, past) bei, an (+dat); a holiday ~ the sea ein Urlaub am Meer; she rushed ~ me sie eilte an mir vorbei
5 (not later than): ~ 4 o'clock bis 4 Uhr; ~ this time tomorrow morgen um diese Zeit; ~ the time I got here it was too late als ich hier ankam, war es zu spät
6 (during): ~ day bei Tag
7 (amount): ~ the kilo/metre kiloweise/meterweise; paid ~ the hour stundenweise bezahlt
8 (MATH, measure): to divide ~ 3 durch 3 teilen; to multiply ~ 3 mit 3 malnehmen; a room 3 metres ~ 4 ein Zimmer 3 mal 4 Meter; it's broader ~ a metre es ist (um) einen Meter breiter
9 (according to) nach; it's all right ~ me von mir aus gern
10: (all) ~ oneself etc ganz allein
11: ~ the way übrigens
◆ad 1 see go, pass etc
2: ~ and ~ irgendwann; (with past tenses) nach einiger Zeit; ~ and large (on the whole) im großen und ganzen.

bye(-bye) ['baɪ('baɪ)] interj (auf) Wiedersehen.

by-election ['baɪɪˈlekʃən] n (Brit)

Nachwahl f.

bygone ['baɪgɒn] a vergangen // n: let ~s be ~s laß(t) das Vergangene vergangen sein.

by(e)-law ['baɪlɔ:] n Verordnung f.

bypass ['baɪpɑ:s] n Umgehungsstraße f // vt umgehen.

byproduct ['baɪprɒdʌkt] n Nebenprodukt nt.

bystander ['baɪstændə*] n Zuschauer m.

byte [baɪt] n (COMPUT) Byte nt.

byword ['baɪwɜ:d] n Inbegriff m.

C

C [si:] n (MUS): ~ **sharp/flat** Cis, cis nt/ Ces, ces nt.

C. abbr (= centigrade) C.

cab [kæb] n Taxi nt; (of train) Führerstand m; (of truck) Führersitz m.

cabaret ['kæbəreɪ] n Kabarett nt.

cabbage ['kæbɪdʒ] n Kohl(kopf) m.

cabin ['kæbɪn] n Hütte f; (NAUT) Kajüte f; (AVIAT) Kabine f; ~ **cruiser** n Motorjacht f.

cabinet ['kæbɪnɪt] n Schrank m; (for china) Vitrine f; (POL) Kabinett nt; ~-**maker** n Kunsttischler m.

cable ['keɪbl] n Drahtseil nt, Tau nt; (TEL) (Leitungs)kabel nt; (telegram) Kabel nt // vt kabeln, telegraphieren; ~-**car** n Seilbahn f; ~ **television** n Kabelfernsehen nt.

cache [kæʃ] n geheime(s) (Waffen-/ Proviant)lager nt.

cackle ['kækl] vi gacken.

cactus ['kæktəs], pl **cacti** [-taɪ] n Kaktus m, Kaktee f.

caddie, caddy ['kædɪ] n (GOLF) Golfjunge m.

cadet [kə'det] n Kadett m.

cadge [kædʒ] vt schmarotzen.

Caesarean [si:'zɛərɪən] a: ~ (**section**) n Kaiserschnitt m.

café ['kæfɪ] n Café nt, Restaurant nt.

cafeteria [kæfɪ'tɪərɪə] n Selbstbedienungsrestaurant nt.

caffein(e) ['kæfi:n] n Koffein nt.

cage [keɪdʒ] n Käfig m // vt einsperren.

cagey ['keɪdʒɪ] a geheimnistuerisch, zurückhaltend.

cagoule [kə'gu:l] n Windhemd nt.

cajole [kə'dʒəʊl] vt überreden.

cake [keɪk] n Kuchen m; (of soap) Stück nt; ~**d** a verkrustet.

Cairo ['kaɪərəʊ] n Kairo nt.

calamity [kə'læmɪtɪ] n Unglück nt, (Schicksals)schlag m.

calcium ['kælsɪəm] n Kalzium nt.

calculate ['kælkjʊleɪt] vt berechnen, kalkulieren; **calculating** a berechnend; **calculation** [-'leɪʃən] n Berechnung f; **calculator** n Rechner m.

calculus ['kælkjʊləs] n Rechenart f.

calendar ['kælɪndə*] n Kalender m; ~ **month** n Kalendermonat m.

calf [kɑ:f], pl **calves** n Kalb nt; (also: ~skin) Kalbsleder nt; (ANAT) Wade f.

calibre, (US) caliber ['kælɪbə*] n Kaliber nt.

call [kɔ:l] vt rufen; (name) nennen; (meeting) einberufen; (awaken) wecken; (TEL) anrufen // vi rufen; (visit: also: ~ **in**, ~ **round**) vorbeikommen // n (shout) Ruf m; (TEL) Anruf m; to be ~**ed** heißen; on ~ in Bereitschaft; ~ **back** vi (return) wiederkommen; (TEL) zurückrufen; ~ **for** vt (demand) erfordern, verlangen; (fetch) abholen; ~ **off** vt (cancel) absagen; ~ **on** vt (visit) besuchen; (turn to) bitten; ~ **out** vi rufen; ~ **up** vt (MIL) einberufen; ~**box** n (Brit) Telefonzelle f; ~**er** n Besucher(in f) m; (TEL) Anrufer m; ~ **girl** n Call-Girl nt; ~-**in** n (US: phone-in) Phone-in nt; ~**ing** n (vocation) Berufung f; ~**ing card** n (US) Visitenkarte f.

callous a ['kæləs] herzlos.

calm [kɑ:m] n Ruhe f; (NAUT) Flaute f // vt beruhigen // a ruhig; (person) gelassen; ~ **down** vi sich beruhigen // vt beruhigen.

Calor gas ['kælə'gæs] n ® Propangas nt.

calorie ['kælərɪ] n Kalorie f.

calve [kɑ:v] vi kalben.

calves [kɑ:vz] pl of **calf**.

camber ['kæmbə*] n Wölbung f.

Cambodia [kæm'bəʊdjə] n Kambodscha nt.

came [keɪm] pt of **come**.

camel ['kæməl] n Kamel nt.

cameo ['kæmɪəʊ] n Kamee f.

camera ['kæmərə] n Fotoapparat m; (CINE, TV) Kamera f; **in** ~ unter Ausschluß der Öffentlichkeit; ~**man** n Kameramann m.

camouflage ['kæmʊflɑ:ʒ] n Tarnung f // vt tarnen.

camp [kæmp] n Lager nt // vi zelten, campen // a affektiert.

campaign [kæm'peɪn] n Kampagne f; (MIL) Feldzug m // vi (MIL) Krieg führen; (fig) werben, Propaganda machen; (POL) den Wahlkampf führen.

campbed ['kæmp'bed] n (Brit) Campingbett nt.

camper ['kæmpə*] n Camper(in f) m; (vehicle) Camping-wagen m.

camping ['kæmpɪŋ] n: to go ~ zelten, Camping machen.

campsite ['kæmpsaɪt] n Campingplatz m.

campus ['kæmpəs] n Universitätsgelände nt, Campus m.

can [kæn] n Büchse f, Dose f; (for water) Kanne f // vt konservieren, in Büchsen einmachen.

can [kæn] *aux v* (*negative* **cannot, can't**; *conditional and pt* **could**) **1** (*be able to, know how to*) können; I ~ see you tomorrow, if you like ich könnte Sie morgen sehen, wenn Sie wollen; I ~ swim ich kann schwimmen; ~ you speak German? sprechen Sie Deutsch? **2** (*may*) können, dürfen; could I have a word with you? könnte ich Sie kurz sprechen?

Canada ['kænədə] *n* Kanada *nt*; **Canadian** [kə'neɪdɪən] *a* kanadisch // *n* Kanadier(in *f*) *m*.

canal [kə'næl] *n* Kanal *m*.

canary [kə'neərɪ] *n* Kanarienvogel *m*.

cancel ['kænsəl] *vt* absagen; (*delete*) durchstreichen; (*train*) streichen; **~lation** [kænsə'leɪʃən] *n* Absage *f*, Streichung *f*.

cancer ['kænsə*] *n* (*also ASTROL:* C~) Krebs *m*.

candid ['kændɪd] *a* offen, ehrlich.

candidate ['kændɪdeɪt] *n* Kandidat(in *f*) *m*.

candle ['kændl] *n* Kerze *f*; **~light** *n* Kerzenlicht *nt*; **~stick** *n* (*also:* ~ **holder**) Kerzenhalter *m*.

candour, (*US*) **candor** ['kændə*] *n* Offenheit *f*.

candy ['kændɪ] *n* Kandis(zucker) *m*; (*US*) Bonbons *pl*; **~-floss** *n* (*Brit*) Zuckerwatte *f*.

cane [keɪn] *n* (*BOT*) Rohr *nt*; (*stick*) Stock *m* // *vt* (*Brit SCH*) schlagen.

canine ['kænaɪn] *a* Hunde-.

canister ['kænɪstə*] *n* Blechdose *f*.

cannabis ['kænəbɪs] *n* Hanf *m*, Haschisch *nt*.

canned [kænd] *a* Büchsen-, eingemacht.

cannibal ['kænɪbəl] *n* Menschenfresser *m*.

cannon ['kænən] *pl* ~ *or* ~**s** *n* Kanone *f*.

cannot ['kænɒt] = **can not**.

canny ['kænɪ] *a* schlau.

canoe [kə'nuː] *n* Kanu *nt*.

canon ['kænən] *n* (*clergyman*) Domherr *m*; (*standard*) Grundsatz *m*.

canonize ['kænənaɪz] *vt* heiligsprechen.

can opener *n* Büchsenöffner *m*.

canopy ['kænəpɪ] *n* Baldachin *m*.

can't [kɑːnt] = **can not**.

cantankerous [kæn'tæŋkərəs] *a* zänkisch, mürrisch.

canteen [kæn'tiːn] *n* Kantine *f*; (*Brit: of cutlery*) Besteckkasten *m*; (*bottle*) Feldflasche *f*.

canter ['kæntə*] *n* Kanter *m* // *vi* in kurzem Galopp reiten.

canvas ['kænvəs] *n* Segeltuch *nt*; (*sail*) Segel *nt*; (*for painting*) Leinwand *f*; **under ~** (*camping*) in Zelten.

canvass ['kænvəs] *vi* um Stimmen werben.

canyon ['kænjən] *n* Felsenschlucht *f*.

cap [kæp] *n* Mütze *f*; (*of pen*) Kappe *f*; (*of bottle*) Deckel *m* // *vt* (*surpass*) übertreffen; (*in sport*) aufstellen.

capability [keɪpə'bɪlɪtɪ] *n* Fähigkeit *f*.

capable ['keɪpəbl] *a* fähig.

capacity [kə'pæsɪtɪ] *n* Fassungsvermögen *nt*; (*ability*) Fähigkeit *f*; (*position*) Eigenschaft *f*.

cape [keɪp] *n* (*garment*) Cape *nt*, Umhang *m*; (*GEOG*) Kap *nt*.

caper ['keɪpə*] *n* (*CULIN: gen:* ~s) Kaper *f*; (*prank*) Kapriole *f*.

capital ['kæpɪtl] *n* (~ *city*) Hauptstadt *f*; (*FIN*) Kapital *nt*; (~ *letter*) Großbuchstabe *m*; ~ **gains tax** *n* Kapitalertragssteuer *f*; **~ism** *n* Kapitalismus *m*; **~ist** *a* kapitalistisch // *n* Kapitalist(in *f*) *m*; **to ~ize on** *vt* Kapital schlagen aus; ~ **punishment** *n* Todesstrafe *f*.

capitulate [kə'pɪtjuleɪt] *vi* kapitulieren.

capricious [kə'prɪʃəs] *a* launisch.

Capricorn ['kæprɪkɔːn] *n* Steinbock *m*.

capsize [kæp'saɪz] *vti* kentern.

capsule ['kæpsjuːl] *n* Kapsel *f*.

captain ['kæptɪn] *n* Kapitän *m*; (*MIL*) Hauptmann *m* // *vt* anführen.

caption ['kæpʃən] *n* (*heading*) Überschrift *f*; (*to picture*) Unterschrift *f*.

captivate ['kæptɪveɪt] *vt* fesseln.

captive ['kæptɪv] *n* Gefangene(r) *mf* // *a* gefangen(gehalten).

captivity [kæp'tɪvɪtɪ] *n* Gefangenschaft *f*.

capture ['kæptʃə*] *vt* gefangennehmen; (*place*) erobern; (*attention*) erregen // *n* Gefangennahme *f*; (*data* ~) Erfassung *f*.

car [kɑː*] *n* Auto *nt*, Wagen *m*; (*RAIL*) Wagen *m*.

carafe [kə'ræf] *n* Karaffe *f*.

caramel ['kærəməl] *n* Karamelle *f*.

carat ['kærət] *n* Karat *nt*.

caravan ['kærəvæn] *n* (*Brit*) Wohnwagen *m*; (*in desert*) Karawane *f*; ~ **site** *n* (*Brit*) Campingplatz *m* für Wohnwagen.

carbohydrate [kɑːbəʊ'haɪdreɪt] *n* Kohlenhydrat *nt*.

carbon ['kɑːbən] *n* Kohlenstoff *m*; ~ **copy** *n* Durchschlag *m*; ~ **paper** *n* Kohlepapier *nt*.

carburettor, (*US*) **carburetor** ['kɑːbjʊretə*] *n* Vergaser *m*.

carcass ['kɑːkəs] *n* Kadaver *m*.

card [kɑːd] *n* Karte *f*; **~board** *n* Pappe *f*; ~ **game** *n* Kartenspiel *nt*.

cardiac ['kɑːdɪæk] *a* Herz-.

cardigan ['kɑːdɪgən] *n* Strickjacke *f*.

cardinal ['kɑːdɪnl] *a:* ~ **number** *n* Kardinalzahl *f* // *n* (*REL*) Kardinal *m*.

card index *n* Kartei *f*; (*in library*) Katalog *m*.

care [keə*] *n* (*of teeth, car etc*) Pflege *f*; (*of children*) Fürsorge *f*; (*carefulness*) Sorgfalt *f*; (*worry*) Sorge *f* // *vi:* **to ~ about** sich kümmern um; ~ **of** (c/o) bei; **in sb's ~** in jds Obhut; I don't ~ das ist mir egal; **I couldn't ~ less** es ist mir doch völlig egal; **to take ~** aufpassen; **to take ~ of** sorgen für; **to take ~ to do sth** sich bemühen, etw zu tun; **~ for** vt sorgen für; (like) mögen.

career [kə'rɪə*] n Karriere f, Laufbahn f // vi (also: **~ along**) rasen.

carefree ['kɛəfriː] a sorgenfrei.

careful ['kɛəfʊl] a sorgfältig; (**be**) **~!** pass auf!

careless a ['kɛəlɪs] nachlässig; **~ness** n Nachlässigkeit f.

caress [kə'rɛs] n Liebkosung f // vt liebkosen.

caretaker ['kɛəteɪkə*] n Hausmeister m.

car-ferry ['kɑːfɛrɪ] n Autofähre f.

cargo ['kɑːgəʊ], pl **~es** n Schiffsladung f.

car hire n Autovermietung f.

Caribbean [kærɪ'biːən] n: **the ~** (Sea) die Karibik.

caricature ['kærɪkətjʊə*] n Karikatur f.

caring ['kɛərɪŋ] a (society, organization) sozial eingestellt; (person) liebevoll.

carnage ['kɑːnɪdʒ] n Blutbad nt.

carnal ['kɑːnl] a fleischlich.

carnation [kɑː'neɪʃən] n Nelke f.

carnival ['kɑːnɪvəl] n Karneval m, Fasching m; (US: fun fair) Kirmes f.

carnivorous [kɑː'nɪvərəs] a fleischfressend.

carol ['kærl] n: (**Christmas**) **~** (Weihnachts)lied nt.

carp [kɑːp] n (fish) Karpfen m; **~ at** vt herumnörgeln an (+dat).

car park n (Brit) Parkplatz m; (covered) Parkhaus nt.

carpenter ['kɑːpɪntə*] n Zimmermann m.

carpentry ['kɑːpɪntrɪ] n Zimmerei f.

carpet ['kɑːpɪt] n Teppich m // vt mit einem Teppich auslegen; **~ slippers** npl Pantoffeln pl; **~ sweeper** n Teppichkehrer m.

carriage ['kærɪdʒ] n Kutsche f; (RAIL, of typewriter) Wagen m; (of goods) Beförderung f; (bearing) Haltung f; **~ return** n (on typewriter) Rücklauftaste f; **~way** n (Brit: part of road) Fahrbahn f.

carrier ['kærɪə*] n Träger(in f) m; (COMM) Spediteur m; **~ bag** n (Brit) Tragetasche m.

carrot ['kærət] n Möhre f, Karotte f.

carry ['kærɪ] vti tragen; **to get carried away** (fig) sich nicht mehr bremsen können; **~ on** vi (continue) weitermachen; (col: complain) Theater machen; **~ out** vt (orders) ausführen; (investigation) durchführen; **~cot** n (Brit) Babytragetasche f; **~-on** n (col: fuss) Theater nt.

cart [kɑːt] n Wagen m, Karren m // vt schleppen.

cartilage ['kɑːtɪlɪdʒ] n Knorpel m.

carton ['kɑːtən] n Karton m; (of milk) Tüte f.

cartoon [kɑː'tuːn] n (PRESS) Karikatur f; (comic strip) Comics pl; (CINE) (Zeichen)trickfilm m.

cartridge ['kɑːtrɪdʒ] n Patrone f.

carve [kɑːv] vt (wood) schnitzen; (stone) meißeln; (meat) (vor)schneiden; **~ up** vt aufschneiden.

carving ['kɑːvɪŋ] n Schnitzerei f; **~ knife** n Tranchiermesser nt.

car wash n Autowäsche f.

cascade [kæs'keɪd] n Wasserfall m // vi kaskadenartig herabfallen.

case [keɪs] n (box) Kasten m; (Brit: also: **suit~**) Koffer m; (JUR, matter) Fall m; **in ~ falls**, im Falle; **in any ~** jedenfalls, auf jeden Fall.

cash [kæʃ] n (Bar)geld nt // vt einlösen; **~ on delivery** (C.O.D.) per Nachnahme; **~ book** n Kassenbuch nt; **~ card** n Scheckkarte f; **~ desk** n (Brit) Kasse f; **~ dispenser** n Geldautomat m.

cashew [kæ'ʃuː] n (also: **~ nut**) Cashewnuß f.

cash flow n Cash-flow m.

cashier [kæ'ʃɪə*] n Kassierer(in f) m.

cashmere ['kæʃmɪə*] n Kaschmirwolle f.

cash register n Registrierkasse f.

casing ['keɪsɪŋ] n Gehäuse nt.

casino [kə'siːnəʊ] n Kasino nt.

cask [kɑːsk] n Faß nt.

casket ['kɑːskɪt] n Kästchen nt; (US: coffin) Sarg m.

casserole ['kæsərəʊl] n Kasserole f; (food) Auflauf m.

cassette [kæ'set] n Kassette f; **~ player** n Kassettengerät nt.

cast [kɑːst], pt, pp **cast** vt werfen; (horns) verlieren; (metal) gießen; (THEAT) besetzen; (vote) abgeben // n (THEAT) Besetzung f; (also: **plaster ~**) Gipsverband m; **~ off** vi (NAUT) losmachen.

castaway ['kɑːstəweɪ] n Schiffbrüchige(r) mf.

caste [kɑːst] n Kaste f.

casting vote ['kɑːstɪŋ-] n (Brit) entscheidende Stimme f.

cast iron n Gußeisen nt.

castle ['kɑːsl] n Burg f; Schloß nt; (chess) Turm m.

castor ['kɑːstə*] n (wheel) Laufrolle f; **~ oil** n Rizinusöl nt; **~ sugar** n (Brit) Streuzucker m.

castrate [kæs'treɪt] vt kastrieren.

casual ['kæʒjʊl] a (attitude) nachlässig; (dress) leger; (meeting) zufällig; (work) Gelegenheits-; **~ly** ad (dress) zwanglos, leger; (remark) beiläufig.

casualty ['kæʒjʊltɪ] n Verletzte(r) mf; (dead) Tote(r) mf; (also: **~ department**) Unfallstation f.

cat [kæt] n Katze f.

catalogue, (US) **catalog** ['kætəlɒg] n Katalog m // vt katalogisieren.

catalyst ['kætəlɪst] n Katalysator m.

cataract ['kætərækt] n (MED) graue(r) Star m.

catarrh [kə'tɑ:*] n Katarrh m.

catastrophe [kə'tæstrəfi] n Katastrophe f.

catch [kætʃ] v (pt, pp **caught**) vt fangen; (arrest) fassen; (train) erreichen; (person: by surprise) ertappen; (also: ~ up) einholen // vi (fire) in Gang kommen; (in branches etc) hängenbleiben // n (fish etc) Fang m; (trick) Haken m; (of lock) Sperrhaken m; to ~ an illness sich (dat) eine Krankheit holen; to ~ fire Feuer fangen; ~ on vi (understand) begreifen; (grow popular) ankommen; ~ up vi (fig) aufholen.

catching ['kætʃɪŋ] a ansteckend.

catchment area ['kætʃmənt-] n (Brit) Einzugsgebiet nt.

catch phrase ['kætʃfreɪz] n Slogan m.

catchy ['kætʃɪ] a (tune) eingängig.

catechism ['kætɪkɪzəm] n Katechismus m.

categoric(al) a [kætə'gɒrɪk(l)] kategorisch.

category ['kætɪgərɪ] n Kategorie f.

cater ['keɪtə*] vi versorgen; ~ for vt (Brit: party) ausrichten; (: needs) eingestellt sein auf (+acc); ~er n Lieferant(in f) m von Speisen und Getränken; ~ing n Gastronomie f.

caterpillar ['kætəpɪlə*] n Raupe f; ~ track n Gleiskette f.

cathedral [kə'θi:drəl] n Kathedrale f, Dom m.

Catholic ['kæθəlɪk] a (REL) katholisch; (tastes etc): c~ vielseitig // n Katholik(in f) m.

cat's-eye ['kætsaɪ] n (Brit AUT) Katzenauge nt.

cattle ['kætl] npl Vieh nt.

catty ['kætɪ] a gehässig.

caucus ['kɔ:kəs] n (POL) Gremium nt; (US: meeting) Sitzung f.

caught [kɔ:t] pt, pp of **catch**.

cauliflower ['kɒlɪflauə*] n Blumenkohl m.

cause [kɔ:z] n Ursache f; (purpose) Sache f // vt verursachen.

causeway ['kɔ:zweɪ] n Damm m.

caustic ['kɔ:stɪk] a ätzend; (fig) bissig.

caution ['kɔ:ʃən] n Vorsicht f; (warning) Verwarnung f // vt verwarnen.

cautious ['kɔ:ʃəs] a vorsichtig.

cavalier [kævə'lɪə*] a blasiert.

cavalry ['kævəlrɪ] n Kavallerie f.

cave [keɪv] n Höhle f; ~ in vi einstürzen; ~man n Höhlenmensch m.

cavern ['kævən] n Höhle f.

caviar(e) ['kævɪɑ:*] n Kaviar m.

cavity ['kævɪtɪ] n Loch nt.

cavort [kə'vɔ:t] vi umherspringen.

C.B. n abbr (= Citizens' Band (Radio)) CB.

C.B.I. n abbr (= Confederation of British Industry) ≈ BDI m.

cc n abbr (= cubic centimetres) cc; (= carbon copy) zk.

cease [si:s] vi aufhören // vt beenden; ~fire n Feuereinstellung f; ~less a unaufhörlich.

cedar ['si:də*] n Zeder f.

cede [si:d] vt abtreten.

ceiling ['si:lɪŋ] n Decke f; (fig) Höchstgrenze f.

celebrate ['selɪbreɪt] vti feiern; ~d a gefeiert.

celebration [selɪ'breɪʃən] n Feier f.

celebrity [sɪ'lebrɪtɪ] n gefeierte Persönlichkeit f.

celery ['selərɪ] n Sellerie m or f.

celestial [sɪ'lestɪəl] a himmlisch.

celibacy ['selɪbəsɪ] n Zölibat nt or m.

cell [sel] n Zelle f; (ELEC) Element nt.

cellar ['selə*] n Keller m.

'cello ['tʃeləu] n Cello nt.

cellophane ['seləfeɪn] n ® Cellophan nt ®.

cellular ['seljulə*] a zellular.

cellulose ['seljuləus] n Zellulose f.

Celt [kelt, selt] n Kelte m, Keltin f; ~ic a keltisch.

cement [sɪ'ment] n Zement m // vt zementieren; ~ mixer n Betonmischmaschine f.

cemetery ['semɪtrɪ] n Friedhof m.

cenotaph ['senətɑ:f] n Ehrenmal nt.

censor ['sensə*] n Zensor m // vt zensieren; ~ship n Zensur f.

censure ['senʃə*] vt rügen.

census ['sensəs] n Volkszählung f.

cent [sent] n (US: coin) Cent m; see also **per cent**.

centenary [sen'ti:nərɪ] n Jahrhundertfeier f.

center ['sentə*] n (US) = **centre**.

centi... ['sentɪ] pref: ~grade a Celsius; ~metre, (US) ~meter n Zentimeter nt; ~pede n Tausendfüßler m.

central ['sentrəl] a zentral; C~ America n Mittelamerika nt; ~ heating n Zentralheizung f; ~ize vt zentralisieren.

centre ['sentə*] n Zentrum nt // vt zentrieren; ~-forward n (SPORT) Mittelstürmer m; ~-half n (SPORT) Stopper m.

century ['sentjurɪ] n Jahrhundert nt.

ceramic [sɪ'ræmɪk] a keramisch; ~s npl Keramiken pl.

cereal ['sɪərɪəl] n (grain) Getreide nt; (at breakfast) Getreideflocken pl.

cerebral ['serɪbrəl] a zerebral; (intellectual) geistig.

ceremony ['serɪmənɪ] n; Zeremonie f; to stand on ~ förmlich sein.

certain ['sɜ:tən] a sicher; (particular) gewiß; for ~ ganz bestimmt; ~ly ad sicher, bestimmt; **~ty** n Gewißheit f.

certificate [sə'tɪfɪkɪt] n Bescheinigung f; (SCH etc) Zeugnis nt.

certified ['sɜːtɪfaɪd] a: **~ mail** n (US) Einschreiben nt; **~ public accountant** n (US) geprüfter Buchhalter.

certify ['sɜːtɪfaɪ] vt bescheinigen.

cervical ['sɜːvɪkl] a (smear, cancer) Gebärmutterhals-.

cervix ['sɜːvɪks] n Gebärmutterhals m.

cessation [se'seɪʃən] n Einstellung f, Ende nt.

cesspit ['sespɪt] n Senkgrube f.

c.f. abbr (= compare) vgl.

ch. abbr (= chapter) Kap.

chafe [tʃeɪf] vt scheuern.

chaffinch ['tʃæfɪntʃ] n Buchfink m.

chagrin ['ʃægrɪn] n Verdruß m.

chain [tʃeɪn] n Kette f // vt (also: ~ up) anketten; **~ reaction** n Kettenreaktion f; **~-smoke** vi kettenrauchen; **~ store** n Kettenladen m.

chair [tʃɛə*] n Stuhl m; (arm~) Sessel m; (UNIV) Lehrstuhl m // vt (meeting) den Vorsitz führen bei; **~lift** n Sessellift m; **~man** n Vorsitzende(r) m.

chalet ['ʃæleɪ] n Chalet nt.

chalice ['tʃælɪs] n Kelch m.

chalk ['tʃɔːk] n Kreide f.

challenge ['tʃælɪndʒ] n Herausforderung f // vt herausfordern; (contest) bestreiten.

challenging ['tʃælɪndʒɪŋ] a (tone) herausfordernd; (work) anspruchsvoll.

chamber ['tʃeɪmbə*] n Kammer f; **~ of commerce** n Handelskammer f; **~maid** n Zimmermädchen nt; **~ music** n Kammermusik f.

chamois ['ʃæmwɑː] n Gemse f.

champagne [ʃæm'peɪn] n Champagner m, Sekt m.

champion ['tʃæmpɪən] n (SPORT) Meister(in f) m; (of cause) Verfechter(in f) m; **~ship** n Meisterschaft f.

chance [tʃɑːns] n (luck) Zufall m; (possibility) Möglichkeit f; (opportunity) Gelegenheit f, Chance f; (risk) Risiko nt // a zufällig // vt: to ~ it es darauf ankommen lassen; **by** ~ zufällig; **to take a** ~ ein Risiko eingehen.

chancellor ['tʃɑːnsələ*] n Kanzler m; **C~ of the Exchequer** n (Brit) Schatzkanzler m.

chandelier [ʃændɪ'lɪə*] n Kronleuchter m.

change [tʃeɪndʒ] vt ändern; (replace, COMM: money) wechseln; (exchange) umtauschen; (transform) verwandeln // vi sich ändern; (~ trains) umsteigen; (~ clothes) sich umziehen; (be transformed): to ~ into sth sich in etw (acc) verwandeln // n Veränderung f; (money returned) Wechselgeld nt; (coins) Kleingeld nt; to ~ one's mind es sich (dat) anders überlegen; for a ~ zur

Abwechslung; **~able** a (weather) wechselhaft; ~ **machine** n Geldwechselautomat m; **~over** n Umstellung f.

changing ['tʃeɪndʒɪŋ] a veränderlich; **~ room** n (Brit) Umkleideraum m.

channel ['tʃænl] n (stream) Bachbett nt; (NAUT) Straße f; (TV) Kanal m; (fig) Weg m // vt (efforts) lenken; **the (English) C~** der Ärmelkanal; **the C~ Islands** npl die Kanalinseln pl.

chant [tʃɑːnt] n Gesang m; (of football fans etc) Sprechchor m // vt intonieren.

chaos ['keɪɒs] n Chaos nt.

chap [tʃæp] n (col) Kerl m.

chapel ['tʃæpəl] n Kapelle f.

chaperon ['ʃæpərəʊn] n Anstandsdame f.

chaplain ['tʃæplɪn] n Kaplan m.

chapped ['tʃæpt] a (skin, lips) spröde.

chapter ['tʃæptə*] n Kapitel nt.

char [tʃɑː*] vt (burn) verkohlen // n (Brit) = **charlady.**

character ['kærɪktə*] n Charakter m, Wesen nt; (in novel, film) Figur f; (in writing) Schriftzeichen nt; **~istic** [kærɪktə'rɪstɪk] a charakteristisch (of für) // n Kennzeichen nt; **~ize** vt charakterisieren, kennzeichnen.

charade [ʃə'rɑːd] n Scharade f.

charcoal ['tʃɑːkəʊl] n Holzkohle f.

charge [tʃɑːdʒ] n (cost) Preis m; (JUR) Anklage f; (explosive) Ladung f; (attack) Angriff m // vt (gun, battery) laden; (price) verlangen; (JUR) anklagen; (MIL) angreifen // vi (rush) (an)stürmen; **bank ~s** pl Bankgebühren pl; **free of** ~ kostenlos; **to reverse the ~s** (TEL) ein R-Gespräch führen; **to be in** ~ **of** verantwortlich sein für; **to take** ~ (der Verantwortung) übernehmen; **to ~ sth (up) to sb's account** jdm etw in Rechnung stellen; ~ **card** n Kundenkarte f.

charitable ['tʃærɪtəbl] a wohltätig; (lenient) nachsichtig.

charity ['tʃærɪtɪ] n (institution) Hilfswerk nt; (attitude) Nächstenliebe f.

charlady ['tʃɑːleɪdɪ] n (Brit) Putzfrau f.

charlatan ['ʃɑːlətən] n Scharlatan m.

charm [tʃɑːm] n Charme m; (spell) Bann m; (object) Talisman m // vt bezaubern; **~ing** a reizend.

chart [tʃɑːt] n Tabelle f; (NAUT) Seekarte f // vt (course) abstecken.

charter ['tʃɑːtə*] vt chartern // n Schutzbrief m; **~ed accountant** n Wirtschaftsprüfer(in f) m; ~ **flight** n Charterflug m.

charwoman ['tʃɑːwʊmən] n = **charlady.**

chase [tʃeɪs] vt jagen, verfolgen // n Jagd f.

chasm ['kæzəm] n Kluft f.

chassis ['ʃæsɪ] n Fahrgestell nt.

chastity ['tʃæstɪtɪ] n Keuschheit f.

chat [tʃæt] vi (also: **have a ~**) plaudern // n Plauderei f; **~ show** n (Brit) Talkshow f.
chatter ['tʃætə*] vi schwatzen; (teeth) klappern // n Geschwätz nt; **~box** n Quasselstrippe f.
chatty ['tʃæti] a geschwätzig.
chauffeur ['ʃəufə*] n Chauffeur m.
chauvinist ['ʃəuvinist] n (male ~) Chauvi m (col); (nationalist) Chauvinist(in f) m.
cheap [tʃiːp] a, ad billig; **~ly** ad billig.
cheat [tʃiːt] vti betrügen; (SCH) mogeln // n Betrüger(in f) m.
check [tʃek] vt (examine) prüfen; (make sure) nachsehen; (control) kontrollieren; (restrain) zügeln; (stop) anhalten // n (examination, restraint) Kontrolle f; (bill) Rechnung f; (pattern) Karo(muster) nt; (US) = **cheque**; ~ **in** vi (in hotel, airport) einchecken // vt (luggage) abfertigen lassen; ~ **out** vi (of hotel) abreisen; ~ **up** vi nachschauen; ~ **up on** vt kontrollieren; **~ered** a (US) = **chequered**; **~ers** n (US: draughts) Damespiel nt; **~-in (desk)** n Abfertigung f; **~ing account** n (US: current account) Girokonto nt; **~mate** n Schachmatt nt; **~out** n Kasse f; **~point** n Kontrollpunkt m; ~ **room** n (US: left-luggage office) Gepäckaufbewahrung f; **~up** n (Nach)prüfung f; (MED) (ärztliche) Untersuchung f.
cheek [tʃiːk] n Backe f; (fig) Frechheit f; **~bone** n Backenknochen m; **~y** a frech.
cheep [tʃiːp] vi piepsen.
cheer [tʃiə*] n Beifallsruf m; **~s** Hurrarufe pl; **~s!** Prost! // vt zujubeln; (encourage) aufmuntern // vi jauchzen; ~ **up** vi bessere Laune bekommen // vt aufmuntern; ~ **up!** nun lach doch mal!; **~ful** a fröhlich.
cheerio ['tʃiəri'əu] excl (Brit) tschüs!
cheese [tʃiːz] n Käse m; **~board** n (gemischte) Käseplatte f.
cheetah ['tʃiːtə] n Gepard m.
chef [ʃef] n Küchenchef m.
chemical ['kemikəl] a chemisch // n Chemikalie f.
chemist ['kemist] n (Brit: pharmacist) Apotheker m, Drogist m; (scientist) Chemiker m; **~ry** n Chemie f; **~'s (shop)** n (Brit) Apotheke f, Drogerie f.
cheque [tʃek] n (Brit) Scheck m; **~book** n Scheckbuch nt; ~ **card** n Scheckkarte f.
chequered ['tʃekəd] a (fig) bewegt.
cherish ['tʃeriʃ] vt (person) lieben; (hope) hegen.
cherry ['tʃeri] n Kirsche f.
chess [tʃes] n Schach nt; **~board** n Schachbrett nt; **~man** n Schachfigur f.
chest [tʃest] n (ANAT) Brust f; (box) Ki-

ste f; ~ **of drawers** n Kommode f.
chestnut ['tʃesnʌt] n Kastanie f; ~ **(tree)** n Kastanienbaum m.
chew [tʃuː] vti kauen; **~ing gum** n Kaugummi m.
chic [ʃiːk] a schick, elegant.
chick [tʃik] n Küken nt; (US col: girl) Biene f.
chicken ['tʃikin] n Huhn nt; (food) Hähnchen nt // ~ **out** vi (col) kneifen (col).
chickenpox ['tʃikinpɒks] n Windpocken pl.
chicory ['tʃikəri] n (in coffee) Zichorie f; (plant) Chicorée f.
chief [tʃiːf] n (of tribe) Häuptling m; (COMM) Chef m // a Haupt-; ~ **executive** n Geschäftsführer(in f) m; **~ly** ad hauptsächlich.
chiffon ['ʃifɒn] n Chiffon m.
chilblain ['tʃilblein] n Frostbeule f.
child [tʃaild], pl **~ren** ['tʃildrən] n Kind nt; **~birth** n Entbindung f; **~hood** n Kindheit f; **~ish** a kindisch; **~like** a kindlich; ~ **minder** n (Brit) Tagesmutter f.
Chile ['tʃili] n Chile nt; **~an** a chilenisch.
chill [tʃil] n Kühle f; (MED) Erkältung f // vt (CULIN) kühlen.
chilli ['tʃili] n Peperoni pl; (meal, spice) Chili m.
chilly ['tʃili] a kühl, frostig.
chime [tʃaim] n Geläut nt // vi ertönen.
chimney ['tʃimni] n Schornstein m; ~ **sweep** n Schornsteinfeger(in f) m.
chimpanzee [tʃimpæn'ziː] n Schimpanse m.
chin [tʃin] n Kinn m.
china ['tʃainə] n Porzellan nt.
China ['tʃainə] n China nt; **Chinese** [tʃai'niːz] a chinesisch // n, pl inv Chinese m, Chinesin f; (LING) Chinesisch.
chink [tʃiŋk] n (opening) Ritze f; (noise) Klirren nt.
chip [tʃip] n (of wood etc) Splitter m; (gen pl: CULIN) Pommes frites pl; (in poker etc; US: crisp) Chip m // vt absplittern; ~ **in** vi Zwischenbemerkungen machen.
chiropodist [ki'rɒpədist] n (Brit) Fußpfleger(in f) m.
chirp [tʃɜːp] vi zwitschern.
chisel ['tʃizl] n Meißel m.
chit [tʃit] n Notiz f.
chitchat ['tʃittʃæt] n Plauderei f.
chivalrous ['ʃivəlrəs] a ritterlich.
chivalry ['ʃivəlri] n Ritterlichkeit f.
chives [tʃaivz] npl Schnittlauch m.
chlorine ['klɔːriːn] n Chlor nt.
chock [tʃɒk]: **~-a-block**, **~-full** a vollgepfropft.
chocolate ['tʃɒklit] n Schokolade f.
choice [tʃɔis] n Wahl f; (of goods) Aus-

wahl f // a Qualitäts-.

choir ['kwaıə*] n Chor m; **~boy** n Chorknabe m.

choke [tʃəʊk] vi ersticken // vt erdrosseln; (block) (ab)drosseln // n (AUT) Starterklappe f.

cholera ['kɔlərə] n Cholera f.

cholesterol [kɒ'lestərəl] n Cholesterin nt.

choose [tʃuːz], pt chose, pp chosen vt wählen.

choosy ['tʃuːzı] a wählerisch.

chop [tʃɒp] vt (wood) spalten; (CULIN: also: ~ up) (zer)hacken // n Hieb m; (CULIN) Kotelett nt; **~s** pl (jaws) Lefzen pl.

chopper ['tʃɒpə*] n (helicopter) Hubschrauber m.

choppy ['tʃɒpı] a (sea) bewegt.

chopsticks ['tʃɒpstıks] npl (Eß)stäbchen pl.

choral ['kɔːrəl] a Chor-.

chord [kɔːd] n Akkord m.

chore [tʃɔː*] n Pflicht f; **~s** pl Hausarbeit f.

choreographer [kɒrı'ɒgrəfə*] n Choreograph(in f) m.

chorister ['kɒrıstə*] n Chorsänger(in f) m.

chortle ['tʃɔːtl] vi glucksen.

chorus ['kɔːrəs] n Chor m; (in song) Refrain m.

chose [tʃəʊz], **chosen** ['tʃəʊzn] pt, pp of **choose**.

Christ [kraıst] n Christus m.

christen ['krısn] vt taufen.

Christian ['krıstıən] a christlich // n Christ(in f) m; **~ity** [krıstı'ænıtı] n Christentum nt; **~ name** n Vorname m.

Christmas ['krısməs] n Weihnachten pl; **~ card** n Weihnachtskarte f; **~ Day** n der erste Weihnachtstag; **~ Eve** n Heiligabend m; **~ tree** n Weihnachtsbaum m.

chrome [krəʊm] n = **chromium plating**.

chromium ['krəʊmıəm] n Chrom nt; **~ plating** n Verchromung f.

chronic ['krɒnık] a chronisch.

chronicle ['krɒnıkl] n Chronik f.

chronological [krɒnə'lɒdʒıkəl] a chronologisch.

chubby ['tʃʌbı] a rundlich.

chuck [tʃʌk] vt werfen; **~ out** vt (person) rauswerfen; (old clothes etc) wegwerfen; **~ (up)** vt (Brit) hinwerfen.

chuckle ['tʃʌkl] vi in sich hineinlachen.

chug [tʃʌg] vi tuckern.

chum [tʃʌm] n Kumpel m.

chunk [tʃʌŋk] n Klumpen m; (of food) Brocken m.

church [tʃɜːtʃ] n Kirche f; **~yard** n Kirchhof m.

churlish ['tʃɜːlıʃ] a grob.

churn [tʃɜːn] n (for butter) Butterfaß nt;

(for milk) Milchkanne f; **~ out** vt (col) produzieren.

chute [ʃuːt] n Rutsche f; (rubbish ~) Müllschlucker m.

CIA n abbr (US: = Central Intelligence Agency) CIA m.

CID n abbr (Brit: = Criminal Investigation Department) Kripo f.

cider ['saıdə*] n Apfelwein m.

cigar [sı'gɑː*] n Zigarre f.

cigarette [sıgə'ret] n Zigarette f; **~ case** n Zigarettenetui nt; **~ end** n Zigarettenstummel m; **~ holder** n Zigarettenspitze f.

Cinderella [sındə'relə] n Aschenbrödel nt.

cinders ['sındəz] npl Asche f.

cine ['sını]: **~-camera** n (Brit) Filmkamera f; **~-film** n (Brit) Schmalfilm m.

cinema ['sınəmə] n Kino nt.

cinnamon ['sınəmən] n Zimt m.

cipher ['saıfə*] n (code) Chiffre f.

circle ['sɜːkl] n Kreis m; (in cinema) Rang m // vi kreisen // vt (surround) umgeben; (move round) kreisen um.

circuit ['sɜːkıt] n (track) Rennbahn f; (lap) Runde f; (ELEC) Stromkreis m; **~ous** [sə'kjuːıtəs] a weitschweifig.

circular ['sɜːkjʊlə*] a rund // n Rundschreiben nt.

circulate ['sɜːkjʊleıt] vi zirkulieren // vt in Umlauf setzen; **circulation** [-'leıʃən] n (of blood) Kreislauf m; (of newspaper) Auflage f; (of money) Umlauf m.

circumcise ['sɜːkəmsaız] vt beschneiden.

circumference [sə'kʌmfərəns] n (Kreis)umfang m.

circumspect ['sɜːkəmspekt] a umsichtig.

circumstances ['sɜːkəmstənsəz] npl Umstände pl; (financial condition) Verhältnisse pl.

circumvent [sɜːkəm'vent] vt umgehen.

circus ['sɜːkəs] n Zirkus m.

cistern ['sıstən] n Zisterne f; (of W.C.) Spülkasten m.

cite [saıt] vt zitieren, anführen.

citizen ['sıtızn] n Bürger(in f) m; **~ship** n Staatsbürgerschaft f.

citrus ['sıtrəs] a: **~ fruit** n Zitrusfrucht f.

city ['sıtı] n Großstadt f; **the C~** die City, das Finanzzentrum Londons.

civic ['sıvık] a (of town) städtisch; (of citizen) Bürger-; **~ centre** n Stadtverwaltung f.

civil ['sıvıl] a bürgerlich; (not military) zivil; (polite) höflich; **~ engineer** n Bauingenieur m; **~ian** [sı'vılıən] n Zivilperson f // a zivil, Zivil-.

civilization [sıvılaı'zeıʃən] n Zivilisation f.

civilized a zivilisiert.

civil: ~ **law** n Zivilrecht nt; ~ **servant** n Staatsbeamte(r) m; **C~ Service** n Staatsdienst m; ~ **war** n Bürgerkrieg m.

clad [klæd] a: ~ **in** gehüllt in (+acc).

claim [kleɪm] vt beanspruchen; (have opinion) behaupten // vi (for insurance) Ansprüche geltend machen // n (demand) Forderung f; (right) Anspruch m; (pretension) Behauptung f; ~**ant** n Antragsteller(in f) m.

clairvoyant [kleə'vɔɪənt] n Hellseher(in f) m.

clam [klæm] n Venusmuschel f.

clamber ['klæmbə*] vi kraxeln.

clammy ['klæmɪ] a klamm.

clamour ['klæmə*] vi: **to** ~ **for** nach etw verlangen.

clamp [klæmp] n Schraubzwinge f // vt einspannen; ~ **down on** vt Maßnahmen ergreifen gegen.

clan [klæn] n Clan m.

clandestine [klæn'destɪn] a geheim.

clang [klæŋ] vi scheppern.

clap [klæp] vi Klatschen // vt Beifall klatschen (+dat) // n (of hands) Klatschen nt; (of thunder) Donnerschlag m; ~**ping** n Klatschen nt.

claret ['klærɪt] n rote(r) Bordeaux(wein) m.

clarify ['klærɪfaɪ] vt klären, erklären.

clarinet [klærɪ'net] n Klarinette f.

clarity ['klærɪtɪ] n Klarheit f.

clash [klæʃ] n (fig) Konflikt m // vi zusammenprallen; (colours) sich beißen; (argue) sich streiten.

clasp [klɑːsp] n Griff m; (on jewels, bag) Verschluß m // vt umklammern.

class [klɑːs] n Klasse f // vt einordnen; ~**conscious** a klassenbewußt.

classic ['klæsɪk] n Klassiker m // a klassisch; ~**al** a klassisch.

classified ['klæsɪfaɪd] a (information) Geheim-; ~ **advertisement** n Kleinanzeige f.

classify ['klæsɪfaɪ] vt klassifizieren.

class: ~**mate** n Klassenkamerad(in f) m; ~**room** n Klassenzimmer nt.

clatter ['klætə*] vi klappern; (feet) trappeln.

clause [klɔːz] n (JUR) Klausel f; (GRAM) Satz m.

claustrophobia [klɔːstrə'fəʊbɪə] n Platzangst f.

claw [klɔː] n Kralle f // vt (zer)kratzen.

clay [kleɪ] n Lehm m; (for pots) Ton m.

clean [kliːn] a sauber // vt putzen; (clothes) reinigen; ~ **out** vt gründlich putzen; ~ **up** vt aufräumen; ~-**cut** a (person) adrett; (clear) klar; ~**er** n (person) Putzfrau f; ~**ing** n Putzen nt; (clothes) Reinigung f; ~**liness** ['klenlɪnɪs] n Reinlichkeit f.

cleanse [klenz] vt reinigen; ~**r** n (for face) Reinigungsmilch f.

clean-shaven ['kliːn'ʃeɪvn] a glattrasiert.

cleansing department ['klenzɪŋ-] n (Brit) Stadtreinigung f.

clear ['klɪə*] a klar; (road) frei // vt (road etc) freimachen; (obstacle) beseitigen; (JUR: suspect) freisprechen // vi klarwerden; (fog) sich lichten // ad: ~ **of** von ... entfernt; ~ **up** vt aufräumen; (solve) aufklären; ~**ance** ['klɪərns] n (removal) Räumung f; (free space) Lichtung f; (permission) Freigabe f; ~-**cut** a (case) eindeutig; ~**ing** n Lichtung f; ~**ing bank** n (Brit) Clearingbank f; ~**ly** ad klar; (obviously) eindeutig; ~**way** n (Brit) (Straße f mit) Halteverbot nt.

cleaver ['kliːvə*] n Hackbeil f.

clef [klef] n Notenschlüssel m.

cleft [kleft] n (in rock) Spalte f.

clemency ['klemənsɪ] n Milde f.

clench [klentʃ] vt (teeth) zusammenbeißen; (fist) ballen.

clergy ['klɜːdʒɪ] n Geistliche(n) pl; ~**man** n Geistliche(r) m.

clerical ['klerɪkəl] a (office) Schreib-, Büro-; (ECCL) geistlich.

clerk [klɑːk, (US) klɜːk] n (in office) Büroangestellte(r) mf; (US: sales person) Verkäufer(in f) m.

clever a ['klevə*] klug; (crafty) schlau.

cliché ['kliːʃeɪ] n Klischee nt.

click [klɪk] vt (heels) zusammenklappen; (tongue) schnalzen mit.

client ['klaɪənt] n Klient(in f) m; ~**ele** [kliːɑːn'tel] n Kundschaft f.

cliff [klɪf] n Klippe f.

climate ['klaɪmɪt] n Klima nt.

climax ['klaɪmæks] n Höhepunkt m.

climb [klaɪm] vt besteigen // vi steigen, klettern // n Aufstieg m; ~-**down** n Abstieg m; ~**er** n Bergsteiger(in f) m; ~**ing** n Bergsteigen nt.

clinch [klɪntʃ] vt (decide) entscheiden; (deal) festmachen.

cling [klɪŋ], pt, pp **clung** [klʌŋ] vi (clothes) eng anliegen; **to** ~ **to** sich festklammern an (dat).

clinic ['klɪnɪk] n Klinik f; ~**al** a klinisch.

clink [klɪŋk] vi klimpern.

clip [klɪp] n Spange f; (also: paper ~) Klammer f // vt (papers) heften; (hair, hedge) stutzen; ~**pers** pl (for hedge) Heckenschere f; (for hair) Haarschneidemaschine f; ~**ping** n Ausschnitt m.

cloak [kləʊk] n Umhang m // vt hüllen; ~**room** n (for coats) Garderobe f; (Brit: W.C.) Toilette f.

clock [klɒk] n Uhr f; ~ **in** or **on** vi stempeln; ~ **off** or **out** vi stempeln; ~**wise** ad im Uhrzeigersinn; ~**work** n Uhrwerk nt // a zum Aufziehen.

clog [klɒg] n Holzschuh m // vt verstopfen.

cloister ['klɔɪstə*] n Kreuzgang m.
clone [kləʊn] n Klon m.
close a, ad and derivatives [kləʊs] a (near) in der Nähe; (friend, connection, print) eng; (relative) nahe; (result) knapp; (examination) eingehend; (weather) schwül; (room) stickig // ad nahe, dicht; **to have a ~ shave** (fig) mit knapper Not davorkommen; **~ by, ~ at hand** a, ad in der Nähe // v and derivatives [kləʊz] vt (shut) schließen; (end) beenden // vi (shop etc) schließen; (door etc) sich schließen // n Ende nt; **~ down** vi schließen; **~d** a (shop etc) geschlossen; **~d shop** n Gewerkschaftszwang m; **~-knit** a eng zusammengewachsen; **~ly** ad eng; (carefully) genau.
closet ['klɒzɪt] n Schrank m.
close-up ['kləʊsʌp] n Nahaufnahme f.
closure ['kləʊʒə*] n Schließung f.
clot [klɒt] n (of blood) Blutgerinnsel nt; (fool) Blödmann m // vi gerinnen.
cloth [klɒθ] n (material) Tuch nt; (rag) Lappen m.
clothe [kləʊð] vt kleiden; **~s** npl Kleider pl; **~s brush** n Kleiderbürste f; **~s line** n Wäscheleine f; **~s peg, ~s pin** n (US) Wäscheklammer f.
clothing ['kləʊðɪŋ] n Kleidung f.
cloud [klaʊd] n Wolke f; **~burst** n Wolkenbruch m; **~y** a bewölkt; (liquid) trüb.
clout [klaʊt] vt hauen.
clove [kləʊv] n Gewürznelke f; **~ of garlic** n Knoblauchzehe f.
clover ['kləʊvə*] n Klee m.
clown [klaʊn] n Clown m // vi (also: **~ about, ~ around**) kaspern.
cloying ['klɔɪɪŋ] a (taste, smell) übersüß.
club [klʌb] n (weapon) Knüppel m; (society) Klub m; (also: **golf ~**) Golfschläger m // vt prügeln // vi: **to ~ together** zusammenlegen; **~s** npl (CARDS) Kreuz nt; **~ car** n (US RAIL) Speisewagen m; **~house** n Klubhaus nt.
cluck [klʌk] vi glucken.
clue [kluː] n Anhaltspunkt m; (in crosswords) Frage f; **I haven't a ~** (ich hab') keine Ahnung.
clump [klʌmp] n Gruppe f.
clumsy ['klʌmzɪ] a (person) unbeholfen; (shape) unförmig.
clung [klʌŋ] pt, pp of **cling**.
cluster ['klʌstə*] n (of trees etc) Gruppe f // vi sich drängen, sich scharen.
clutch [klʌtʃ] n Griff m; (AUT) Kupplung f // vt sich festklammern an (+dat).
clutter ['klʌtə*] vt vollpropfen; (desk) übersäen.
CM abbr (= centimetre) cm.
CND n abbr = Campaign for Nuclear Disarmament.

Co. abbr of **county; company**.
c/o abbr (= care of) c/o.
coach [kəʊtʃ] n (bus) Reisebus m; (old) Kutsche f; (RAIL) (Personen)wagen m; (trainer) Trainer m // vt (SCH) Nachhilfeunterricht geben (+dat); (SPORT) trainieren; **~ trip** n Busfahrt f.
coagulate [kəʊˈægjʊleɪt] vi gerinnen.
coal [kəʊl] n Kohle f; **~ face** n Streb m; **~ field** n Kohlengebiet nt.
coalition [kəʊəˈlɪʃən] n Koalition f.
coal: ~man, ~merchant n Kohlenhändler m; **~ mine** n Kohlenbergwerk nt.
coarse [kɔːs] a (lit) grob; (fig) ordinär.
coast [kəʊst] n Küste f // vi dahinrollen; (AUT) im Leerlauf fahren; **~al** a Küsten-; **~guard** n Küstenwache f; **~line** n Küste(nlinie) f.
coat [kəʊt] n Mantel m; (on animals) Fell m; (of paint) Schicht f // vt überstreichen; **~ of arms** n Wappen nt; **~hanger** n Kleiderbügel m; **~ing** n Überzug m; (of paint) Schicht f.
coax [kəʊks] vt beschwatzen.
cob [kɒb] n see **corn**.
cobbler ['kɒblə*] n Schuster m.
cobbles ['kɒblz], **cobblestones** ['kɒblstəʊnz] npl Pflastersteine pl.
cobweb ['kɒbweb] n Spinnennetz nt.
cocaine [kəˈkeɪn] n Kokain nt.
cock [kɒk] n Hahn m // vt (gun) entsichern; **~erel** n junge(r) Hahn m; **~-eyed** a (fig) verrückt.
cockle ['kɒkl] n Herzmuschel f.
cockney ['kɒknɪ] n echte(r) Londoner m.
cockpit ['kɒkpɪt] n (AVIAT) Pilotenkanzel f.
cockroach ['kɒkrəʊtʃ] n Küchenschabe f.
cocktail ['kɒkteɪl] n Cocktail m; **~ cabinet** n Hausbar f; **~ party** n Cocktailparty f.
cocoa ['kəʊkəʊ] n Kakao m.
coconut ['kəʊkənʌt] n Kokosnuß f.
cocoon [kəˈkuːn] n Kokon m.
cod [kɒd] n Kabeljau m.
C.O.D. abbr of **cash on delivery**.
code [kəʊd] n Kode m; (JUR) Kodex m.
cod-liver oil ['kɒdlɪvər-] n Lebertran m.
coercion [kəʊˈɜːʃən] n Zwang m.
coffee ['kɒfɪ] n Kaffee m; **~ bar** n (Brit) Café nt; **~ bean** n Kaffeebohne f; **~ break** n Kaffeepause f; **~ grounds** npl Kaffeesatz m; **~pot** n Kaffeekanne f; **~ table** n Couchtisch m.
coffin ['kɒfɪn] n Sarg m.
cog [kɒg] n (Rad)zahn m.
cogent ['kəʊdʒənt] a triftig, überzeugend, zwingend.
cognac ['kɒnjæk] n Kognak m.
coherent [kəʊˈhɪərənt] a zusammenhängend; (person) verständlich.
cohesion [kəʊˈhiːʒən] n Zusammenhang

m.

coil [kɔɪl] *n* Rolle *f*; (*ELEC*) Spule *f*; (*contraceptive*) Spirale *f* // *vt* aufwickeln.

coin [kɔɪn] *n* Münze *f* // *vt* prägen; **~age** *n* (*word*) Prägung *f*; **~-box** *n* (*Brit*) Münzfernsprecher *m.*

coincide [kəʊɪn'saɪd] *vi* (*happen together*) zusammenfallen; (*agree*) übereinstimmen; **~nce** [kəʊ'ɪnsɪdəns] *n* Zufall *m.*

coke [kəʊk] *n* Koks *m.*

Coke *n* ® (*drink*) Coca-Cola *f* ®.

colander ['kʌləndə*] *n* Durchschlag *m.*

cold [kəʊld] *a* kalt // *n* Kälte *f*; (*MED*) Erkältung *f*; I'm ~ mir ist kalt; **to catch** ~ sich erkälten; **in** ~ **blood** kaltblütig; **~ly** *ad* kalt; **~-shoulder** *vt* (jdm) die kalte Schulter zeigen; ~ **sore** *n* Erkältungsbläschen *nt.*

coleslaw ['kəʊlslɔː] *n* Krautsalat *m.*

colic ['kɒlɪk] *n* Kolik *f.*

collaborate [kə'læbəreɪt] *vi* zusammenarbeiten.

collaboration [kəlæbə'reɪʃən] *n* Zusammenarbeit *f*; (*POL*) Kollaboration *f.*

collapse [kə'læps] *vi* (*people*) zusammenbrechen; (*things*) einstürzen // *n* Zusammenbruch *m*, Einsturz *m.*

collapsible [kə'læpsəbl] *a* zusammenklappbar, Klapp-.

collar ['kɒlə*] *n* Kragen *m*; **~bone** *n* Schlüsselbein *nt.*

collateral [kɒ'lætərəl] *n* (zusätzliche) Sicherheit.

colleague ['kɒliːg] *n* Kollege *m*, Kollegin *f.*

collect [kə'lekt] *vt* sammeln; (*Brit: call and pick up*) abholen // *vi* sich sammeln // *ad*: **to call** ~ (*US TEL*) ein R-Gespräch führen; **~ion** [kə'lekʃən] *n* Sammlung *f*; (*ECCL*) Kollekte *f*; (*of post*) Leerung *f.*

collective [kə'lektɪv] *a* gemeinsam; (*POL*) kollektiv.

collector [kə'lektə*] *n* Sammler *m*; (*tax* ~) (Steuer)einnehmer *m.*

college ['kɒlɪdʒ] *n* (*UNIV*) College *nt*; (*TECH*) Fach-, Berufsschule *f.*

collide [kə'laɪd] *vi* zusammenstoßen.

colliery ['kɒlɪərɪ] *n* (*Brit*) Zeche *f.*

collision [kə'lɪʒən] *n* Zusammenstoß *m.*

colloquial [kə'ləʊkwɪəl] *a* umgangssprachlich.

collusion [kə'luːʒən] *n* geheime(s) Einverständnis *nt.*

colon ['kəʊlɒn] *n* Doppelpunkt *m*; (*MED*) Dickdarm *m.*

colonel ['kɜːnl] *n* Oberst *m.*

colonial [kə'ləʊnɪəl] *a* Kolonial-.

colonize ['kɒlənaɪz] *vt* kolonisieren.

colony ['kɒlənɪ] *n* Kolonie *f.*

colour, (*US*) **color** ['kʌlə*] *n* Farbe *f* // *vt* (*lit, fig*) färben // *vi* sich verfärben; **~s** *pl* (*of club*) Fahne *f*; ~ **bar** *n*

Rassenschranke *f*; **~-blind** *a* farbenblind; **~ed** *a* farbig; **~eds** *npl* Farbige *pl*; ~ **film** *n* Farbfilm *m*; **~ful** *a* bunt; (*personality*) schillernd; **~ing** *n* (*complexion*) Gesichtsfarbe *f*; (*substance*) Farbstoff *m*; ~ **scheme** *n* Farbgebung *f*; ~ **television** *n* Farbfernsehen *nt.*

colt [kəʊlt] *n* Fohlen *nt.*

column ['kɒləm] *n* Säule *f*; (*MIL*) Kolonne *f*; (*of print*) Spalte *f*; **~ist** ['kɒləmnɪst] *n* Kolumnist *m.*

coma ['kəʊmə] *n* Koma *nt.*

comb [kəʊm] *n* Kamm *m* // *vt* kämmen; (*search*) durchkämmen.

combat ['kɒmbæt] *n* Kampf *m* // *vt* bekämpfen.

combination [kɒmbɪ'neɪʃən] *n* Kombination *f.*

combine [kəm'baɪn] *vt* verbinden // *vi* sich vereinigen // *n* ['kɒmbaɪn] (*COMM*) Konzern *m*; ~ (**harvester**) *n* Mähdrescher *m.*

combustion [kəm'bʌstʃən] *n* Verbrennung *f.*

come [kʌm] *vi*, *pt* **came**, *pp* **come** kommen; ~ **to undone** aufgehen; ~ **about** *vi* geschehen; ~ **across** *vt* (*find*) stoßen auf (+*acc*); ~ **away** *vi* (*person*) weggehen; (*handle etc*) abgehen; ~ **back** *vi* zurückkommen; ~ **by** *vt* (*find*) zu etw kommen; ~ **down** *vi* (*price*) fallen; ~ **forward** *vi* (*volunteer*) sich melden; ~ **from** *vt* (*result*) kommen von; **where do you** ~ **from?** wo kommen Sie her?; **I** ~ **from London** ich komme aus London; ~ **in** *vi* hereinkommen; (*train*) einfahren; ~ **in for** *vt* abkriegen; ~ **into** *vt* (*inherit*) erben; ~ **off** *vi* (*handle*) abgehen; (*succeed*) klappen; ~ **on** *vi* (*progress*) vorankommen; ~ **on!** komm!; (*hurry*) beeil dich!; ~ **out** *vi* herauskommen; ~ **round** *vi* (*MED*) wieder zu sich kommen; ~ **to** *vi* (*MED*) wieder zu sich kommen; (*bill*) sich belaufen auf (+*acc*); ~ **up** *vi* hochkommen; (*sun*) aufgehen; (*problem*) auftauchen; ~ **up against** *vt* (*resistance, difficulties*) stoßen auf (+*acc*); ~ **upon** *vt* stoßen auf (+*acc*); ~ **up with** *vt* sich einfallen lassen.

comedian [kə'miːdɪən] *n* Komiker *m*; **comedienne** [-'en] *n* Komikerin *f.*

comedown ['kʌmdaʊn] *n* Abstieg *m.*

comedy ['kɒmədɪ] *n* Komödie *f.*

comet ['kɒmɪt] *n* Komet *m.*

comeuppance [kʌm'ʌpəns] *n*: **to get one's** ~ seine Quittung bekommen.

comfort ['kʌmfət] *n* Komfort *m*; (*consolation*) Trost *m* // *vt* trösten; **~able** *a* bequem; **~ably** *ad* (*sit etc*) bequem; (*live*) angenehm; ~ **station** *n* (*US*) öffentliche Toilette *f.*

comic ['kɒmɪk] *n* Comic(heft) *nt*; (*comedian*) Komiker *m* // *a* (*also:* **~al**) komisch.

coming ['kʌmɪŋ] n Kommen nt; **~(s) and going(s)** n(pl) Kommen und Gehen nt.

comma ['kɒmə] n Komma nt.

command [kə'mɑːnd] n Befehl m; (control) Führung f; (MIL) Kommando nt; (mastery) Beherrschung f // vt befehlen (+dat); (MIL) kommandieren; (be able to get) verfügen über (+acc); **~eer** [kɒmən'dɪə*] vt requirieren; **~er** n Kommandant m.

commandment [kə'mɑːndmənt] n (REL) Gebot nt.

commando [kə'mɑːndəʊ] n (Mitglied nt einer) Kommandotruppe f.

commemorate [kə'meməreɪt] vt gedenken (+gen).

commence [kə'mens] vti beginnen.

commend [kə'mend] vt (recommend) empfehlen; (praise) loben.

commensurate [kə'mensjʊrɪt] a entsprechend (with dat).

comment ['kɒment] n Bemerkung f // vi: to ~ (on) sich äußern (zu); **~ary** ['kɒməntrɪ] n Kommentar m; **~ator** ['kɒmənteɪtə*] n Kommentator m; (TV) Reporter(in f) m.

commerce ['kɒmɜːs] n Handel m.

commercial [kə'mɜːʃəl] a kommerziell, geschäftlich; (training) kaufmännisch // n (TV) Fernsehwerbung f; **~ break** n Werbespot m; **~ize** vt kommerzialisieren.

commiserate [kə'mɪzəreɪt] vi: to ~ with Mitleid haben mit.

commission [kə'mɪʃən] n (act) Auftrag m; (fee) Provision f; (body) Kommission f // vt beauftragen; (MIL) zum Offizier ernennen; (work of art) in Auftrag geben; **out of ~** außer Betrieb; **~aire** [kəmɪʃə'neə*] n (Brit) Portier m; **~er** n (POLICE) Polizeipräsident m.

commit [kə'mɪt] vt (crime) begehen; (entrust) anvertrauen; to ~ o.s. sich festlegen; **~ment** n Verpflichtung f.

committee [kə'mɪtɪ] n Ausschuß m.

commodity [kə'mɒdɪtɪ] n Ware f.

common ['kɒmən] a (cause) gemeinsam; (pej) gewöhnlich; (widespread) üblich, häufig // n Gemeindeland nt; **the C~s** npl (Brit) das Unterhaus; **~er** n Bürgerliche(r) mf; **~ law** n Gewohnheitsrecht nt; **~ly** ad gewöhnlich; **C~ Market** n Gemeinsame(r) Markt m; **~place** a alltäglich; **~room** n Gemeinschaftsraum m; **~ sense** n gesunde(r) Menschenverstand m; **the C~wealth** n das Commonwealth.

commotion [kə'məʊʃən] n Aufsehen nt.

communal ['kɒmjuːnl] a Gemeinde-; Gemeinschafts-.

commune ['kɒmjuːn] n Kommune f // vi sich mitteilen (with dat).

communicate [kə'mjuːnɪkeɪt] vt (transmit) übertragen // vi (be in touch) in Verbindung stehen; (make self understood) sich verständigen.

communication [kəmjuːnɪ'keɪʃən] n (message) Mitteilung f; (making understood) Kommunikation f; **~s** pl (transport etc) Verkehrswege pl; **~ cord** n (Brit) Notbremse f.

communion [kə'mjuːnɪən] n (also: Holy C~) Abendmahl nt, Kommunion f.

communism ['kɒmjʊnɪzəm] n Kommunismus m.

communist ['kɒmjʊnɪst] n Kommunist(in f) m // a kommunistisch.

community [kə'mjuːnɪtɪ] n Gemeinschaft f; **~ centre** n Gemeinschaftszentrum nt; **~ chest** n (US) Wohltätigkeitsfonds m.

commutation ticket [kɒmjʊ'teɪʃən'tɪkɪt] n (US) Zeitkarte f.

commute [kə'mjuːt] vi pendeln // vt umwandeln; **~r** n Pendler m.

compact [kəm'pækt] a kompakt // n ['kɒmpækt] (for make-up) Puderdose f; **~ disc** n Compact-disc f.

companion [kəm'pænɪən] n Begleiter(in f) m; **~ship** n Gesellschaft f.

company ['kʌmpənɪ] n Gesellschaft f; (COMM also) Firma f; to keep sb ~ jdm Gesellschaft leisten; **~ secretary** n (Brit) ≈ Prokurist(in f) m.

comparable ['kɒmpərəbl] a vergleichbar.

comparative [kəm'pærətɪv] a (relative) relativ; **~ly** ad verhältnismäßig.

compare [kəm'peə*] vt vergleichen // vi sich vergleichen lassen.

comparison [kəm'pærɪsn] n Vergleich m; **in ~ (with)** im Vergleich (mit or zu).

compartment [kəm'pɑːtmənt] n (RAIL) Abteil nt; (in drawer etc) Fach nt.

compass ['kʌmpəs] n Kompaß m; **~es** pl Zirkel m.

compassion [kəm'pæʃən] n Mitleid nt; **~ate** a mitfühlend.

compatible [kəm'pætɪbl] a vereinbar; (COMPUT) kompatibel.

compel [kəm'pel] vt zwingen.

compendium [kəm'pendɪəm] n Kompendium nt.

compensate ['kɒmpenseɪt] vt entschädigen // vi: to ~ for Ersatz leisten für.

compensation [kɒmpen'seɪʃən] n Entschädigung f.

compère ['kɒmpeə*] n Conférencier m.

compete [kəm'piːt] vi (take part) teilnehmen; (vie with) konkurrieren.

competence ['kɒmpɪtəns] n Fähigkeit f.

competent ['kɒmpɪtənt] a kompetent.

competition [kɒmpɪ'tɪʃən] n (contest) Wettbewerb m; (COMM, rivalry) Konkurrenz f.

competitive [kəm'petitiv] *a* Konkurrenz-; (*COMM*) konkurrenzfähig.

competitor [kəm'petitə*] *n* (*COMM*) Konkurrent(in *f*) *m*; (*participant*) Teilnehmer(in *f*) *m*.

compile [kəm'pail] *vt* zusammenstellen.

complacency [kəm'pleisnsi] *n* Selbstzufriedenheit *f*.

complacent [kəm'pleisnt] *a* selbstzufrieden.

complain [kəm'plein] *vi* sich beklagen; (*formally*) sich beschweren; **~t** *n* Klage *f*; (*formal* **~**) Beschwerde *f*; (*MED*) Leiden *nt*.

complement ['kɒmplimənt] *n* Ergänzung *f*; (*ship's crew etc*) Bemannung *f* // *vt* ['kɒmpliment] ergänzen; **~ary** [kɒmpli'mentəri] *a* (sich) ergänzend.

complete [kəm'pli:t] *a* (*full*) vollkommen, ganz; (*finished*) fertig // *vt* vervollständigen; (*finish*) beenden; (*fill in: form*) ausfüllen; **~ly** *ad* ganz.

completion [kəm'pli:ʃən] *n* Fertigstellung *f*; (*of contract etc*) Abschluß *m*.

complex ['kɒmpleks] *a* kompliziert.

complexion [kəm'plekʃən] *n* Gesichtsfarbe *f*; (*fig*) Aspekt *m*.

complexity [kəm'pleksiti] *n* Kompliziertheit *f*.

compliance [kəm'plaiəns] *n* Fügsamkeit *f*, Einwilligung *f*; **in ~ with sth** etw (*dat*) gemäß.

complicate ['kɒmplikeit] *vt* komplizieren; **~d** *a* kompliziert.

complication [kɒmpli'keiʃən] *n* Komplikation *f*.

complicity [kəm'plisiti] *n* Mittäterschaft *f* (*in* bei).

compliment ['kɒmplimənt] *n* Kompliment *nt* // *vt* jdm ein Kompliment machen (*sb* jdm); **~s** *pl* Grüße *pl*; **to pay sb a ~** jdm ein Kompliment machen; **~ary** [kɒmpli'mentəri] *a* schmeichelhaft; (*free*) Frei-, Gratis-.

comply [kəm'plai] *vi*: **to ~ with** erfüllen (+*acc*); entsprechen (+*dat*).

component [kəm'pəunənt] *a* Teil- // *n* Bestandteil *m*.

compose [kəm'pəuz] *vt* (*music*) komponieren; (*poetry*) verfassen; **to ~ o.s.** sich sammeln; **~d** *a* gefaßt; **~r** *n* Komponist(in *f*) *m*.

composite ['kɒmpəzit] *a* zusammengesetzt.

composition [kɒmpə'ziʃən] *n* (*MUS*) Komposition *f*; (*SCH*) Aufsatz *m*; (*structure*) Zusammensetzung *f*, Aufbau *m*.

compost ['kɒmpɒst] *n* Kompost *m*.

composure [kəm'pəuʒə*] *n* Fassung *f*.

compound ['kɒmpaund] *n* (*CHEM*) Verbindung *f*; (*enclosure*) Lager *nt*; (*LING*) Kompositum *nt* // *a* zusammengesetzt; (*fracture*) kompliziert; **~ interest** *n* Zinseszins *m*.

comprehend [kɒmpri'hend] *vt* begreifen.

comprehension [kɒmpri'henʃən] *n* Verständnis *nt*.

comprehensive [kɒmpri'hensiv] *a* umfassend; **~ insurance** *n* Vollkasko *nt*; **~ (school)** *n* (*Brit*) Gesamtschule *f*.

compress [kəm'pres] *vt* komprimieren // *n* ['kɒmpres] (*MED*) Kompresse *f*.

comprise [kəm'praiz] *vt* (*also*: **be ~d of**) umfassen, bestehen aus.

compromise ['kɒmprəmaiz] *n* Kompromiß *m* // *vt* kompromittieren // *vi* einen Kompromiß schließen.

compulsion [kəm'pʌlʃən] *n* Zwang *m*.

compulsive [kəm'pʌlsiv] *a* zwanghaft.

compulsory [kəm'pʌlsəri] *a* obligatorisch.

computer [kəm'pju:tə*] *n* Computer *m*, Rechner *m*; **~ize** *vt* (*information*) computerisieren; (*company, accounts*) auf Computer umstellen; **~ programmer** *n* Programmierer(in *f*) *m*; **~ programming** *n* Programmieren *nt*; **~ science** *n* Informatik *f*; **~ computing** *n* (*science*) Informatik *f*; (*work*) Computerei *f*.

comrade ['kɒmrid] *n* Kamerad *m*; (*POL*) Genosse *m*; **~ship** *n* Kameradschaft *f*.

con [kɒn] *vt* hereinlegen // *n* Schwindel *nt*.

concave ['kɒnkeiv] *a* konkav.

conceal [kən'si:l] *vt* (*secret*) verschweigen; (*hide*) verbergen.

concede [kən'si:d] *vt* (*grant*) gewähren; (*point*) zugeben // *vi* (*admit*) zugeben.

conceit [kən'si:t] *n* Einbildung *f*; **~ed** *a* eingebildet.

conceivable [kən'si:vəbl] *a* vorstellbar.

conceive [kən'si:v] *vt* (*idea*) ausdenken; (*imagine*) sich vorstellen // *vti* (*baby*) empfangen.

concentrate ['kɒnsəntreit] *vi* sich konzentrieren (*on* auf +*acc*) // *vt* konzentrieren.

concentration [kɒnsən'treiʃən] *n* Konzentration *f*; **~ camp** *n* Konzentrationslager *nt*, KZ *nt*.

concept ['kɒnsept] *n* Begriff *m*.

conception [kən'sepʃən] *n* (*idea*) Vorstellung *f*; (*BIOL*) Empfängnis *f*.

concern [kən'sɜ:n] *n* (*affair*) Angelegenheit *f*; (*COMM*) Unternehmen *nt*; (*worry*) Sorge *f* // *vt* (*interest*) angehen; (*be about*) handeln von; (*have connection with*) betreffen; **to be ~ed** (*about*) sich Sorgen machen (um); **~ing** *prep* hinsichtlich (+*gen*).

concert ['kɒnsət] *n* Konzert *nt*; **~ed** [kən'sɜ:tid] *a* gemeinsam; **~ hall** *n* Konzerthalle *f*.

concertina [kɒnsə'ti:nə] *n* Handharmonika *f*.

concerto [kən'tʃɜ:təu] *n* Konzert *nt*.

concession [kən'seʃən] n (*yielding*) Zugeständnis nt; **tax ~** Steuer-Konzession f.
conciliation [kənsɪlɪ'eɪʃən] n Versöhnung f; (*official*) Schlichtung f.
concise [kən'saɪs] a präzis.
conclude [kən'kluːd] vt (*end*) beenden; (*treaty*) (ab)schließen; (*decide*) schließen, folgern.
conclusion [kən'kluːʒən] n (Ab)schluß m; (*deduction*) Schluß m.
conclusive [kən'kluːsɪv] a schlüssig.
concoct [kən'kɒkt] vt zusammenbrauen; **~ion** n Gebräu nt.
concourse [kɒŋkɔːs] n (Bahnhofs)halle f, Vorplatz m.
concrete [kɒŋkriːt] n Beton m // a konkret.
concur [kən'kɜː*] vi übereinstimmen.
concurrently [kən'kʌrəntlɪ] ad gleichzeitig.
concussion [kɒn'kʌʃən] n (Gehirn)erschütterung f.
condemn [kən'dem] vt (JUR) verurteilen; (*building*) abbruchreif erklären.
condensation [kɒnden'seɪʃən] n Kondensation f.
condense [kən'dens] vi (CHEM) kondensieren // vt (*fig*) zusammendrängen; **~d milk** n Kondensmilch f.
condescending [kɒndɪ'sendɪŋ] a herablassend.
condition [kən'dɪʃən] n (*state*) Zustand m; (*presupposition*) Bedingung f // vt (*hair etc*) behandeln; (*accustom*) gewöhnen; **on ~ that ...** unter der Bedingung, daß ...; **~al** a bedingt; (GRAM) Bedingungs-; **~er** n (*for hair*) Spülung f; (*for fabrics*) Weichspüler m; **~s** pl (*circumstances*) Verhältnisse pl.
condolences [kən'dəʊlənsɪz] npl Beileid nt.
condom [kɒndəm] n Kondom nt or m.
condominium [kɒndə'mɪnɪəm] n (US) Eigentumswohnung f; (*block*) Eigentumsblock m.
condone [kən'dəʊn] vt gutheißen.
conducive [kən'djuːsɪv] a: **~ to** dienlich (dat).
conduct [kɒndʌkt] n (*behaviour*) Verhalten nt; (*management*) Führung f // vt [kən'dʌkt] führen; (MUS) dirigieren; **~ed tour** n Führung f; **~or** [kən'dʌktə*] n (*of orchestra*) Dirigent m; (*in bus, US: on train*) Schaffner m; (ELEC) Leiter m; **~ress** [kən'dʌktrɪs] n (*in bus*) Schaffnerin f.
cone [kəʊn] n (MATH) Kegel m; (*for ice cream*) (Waffel)tüte f; (*fir*) Tannenzapfen m.
confectioner [kən'fekʃənə*] n Konditor m; **~'s (shop)** n Konditorei f; **~y** n Süßigkeiten pl.
confederation [kənfedə'reɪʃən] n Bund m.

confer [kən'fɜː*] vt (*degree*) verleihen // vi (*discuss*) konferieren, verhandeln; **~ence** [kɒnfərəns] n Konferenz f.
confess [kən'fes] vti gestehen; (ECCL) beichten; **~ion** [kən'feʃən] n Geständnis nt; (ECCL) Beichte f; **~ional** [kən'feʃənl] n Beichtstuhl m.
confetti [kən'fetɪ] n Konfetti nt.
confide [kən'faɪd] vi: **to ~ in** (sich) anvertrauen (+dat).
confidence [kɒnfɪdəns] n Vertrauen nt; (*assurance*) Selbstvertrauen nt; (*secret*) Geheimnis nt; **in ~** (*speak, write*) vertraulich; **~ trick** n Schwindel m.
confident [kɒnfɪdənt] a (*sure*) überzeugt; (*self-assured*) selbstsicher; **~ial** [kɒnfɪ'denʃəl] a vertraulich.
confine [kən'faɪn] vt (*limit*) beschränken; (*lock up*) einsperren; **~s** [kɒnfaɪnz] npl Grenzen pl; **~d** a (*space*) eng; **~ment** n (*in prison*) Haft f; (MED) Wochenbett nt.
confirm [kən'fɜːm] vt bestätigen; **~ation** [kɒnfə'meɪʃən] n Bestätigung f; (REL) Konfirmation f; **~ed** a unverbesserlich; (*bachelor*) eingefleischt.
confiscate [kɒnfɪskeɪt] vt beschlagnahmen.
conflict [kɒnflɪkt] n Konflikt m // vi [kən'flɪkt] im Widerspruch stehen; **~ing** [kən'flɪktɪŋ] a widersprüchlich.
conform [kən'fɔːm] vi (*things*) entsprechen (to dat); (*people*) sich anpassen (to dat); (*to rules*) sich richten (to nach); **~ist** n Konformist(in f) m.
confound [kən'faʊnd] vt verblüffen; (*throw into confusion*) durcheinanderbringen.
confront [kən'frʌnt] vt (*enemy*) entgegentreten (+dat); (*problems*) sich stellen (+dat); **to ~ sb with sth** jdn mit etw konfrontieren; **~ation** [kɒnfrən-'teɪʃən] n Konfrontation f.
confuse [kən'fjuːz] vt verwirren; (sth with sth) verwechseln; **~d** a verwirrt; **confusing** a verwirrend; **confusion** [kən'fjuːʒən] n (*perplexity*) Verwirrung f; (*mixing up*) Verwechslung f; (*tumult*) Aufruhr m.
congeal [kən'dʒiːl] vi (*freeze*) gefrieren; (*clot*) gerinnen.
congenial [kən'dʒiːnɪəl] a angenehm.
congenital [kən'dʒenɪtəl] a angeboren.
congested [kən'dʒestɪd] a überfüllt.
congestion [kən'dʒestʃən] n Stau m.
conglomerate [kən'glɒmərət] n (COMM, GEOL) Konglomerat nt.
conglomeration [kənglɒmə'reɪʃən] n Anhäufung f.
congratulate [kən'grætjʊleɪt] vt beglückwünschen (on zu).
congratulations [kəngrætjʊ'leɪʃənz] npl Glückwünsche pl; **~!** gratuliere!,

herzlichen Glückwunsch!

congregate ['kɒŋgrɪgeɪt] *vi* sich versammeln.

congregation [kɒŋgrɪ'geɪʃən] *n* Gemeinde *f*.

congress ['kɒŋgres] *n* Kongreß *m*; **~man** *n* (*US*) Mitglied *nt* des amerikanischen Repräsentantenhauses.

conical ['kɒnɪkəl] *a* kegelförmig.

conifer ['kɒnɪfə*] *n* Nadelbaum *m*.

conjecture [kən'dʒektʃə*] *n* Vermutung *f*.

conjugal ['kɒndʒʊgəl] *a* ehelich.

conjugate ['kɒndʒʊgeɪt] *vt* konjugieren.

conjunction [kən'dʒʌŋkʃən] *n* Verbindung *f*; (*GRAM*) Konjunktion *f*.

conjunctivitis [kəndʒʌŋktɪ'vaɪtɪs] *n* Bindehautentzündung *f*.

conjure ['kʌndʒə*] *vi* zaubern; **~ up** *vt* heraufbeschwören; **~r** *n* Zauberkünstler(in *f*) *m*.

conk [kɒŋk]: **~ out** *vi* (*col*) den Geist aufgeben.

connect [kə'nekt] *vt* verbinden; (*ELEC*) anschließen; **to be ~ed with** ein Beziehung haben zu; (*be related to*) verwandt sein mit; **~ion** [kə'nekʃən] *n* Verbindung *f*; (*relation*) Zusammenhang *m*; (*ELEC, TEL, RAIL*) Anschluß *m*.

connive [kə'naɪv] *vi*: **to ~ at** stillschweigend dulden.

connoisseur [kɒnɪ'sɜː*] *n* Kenner *m*.

conquer ['kɒŋkə*] *vt* (*feelings*) überwinden; (*enemy*) besiegen; (*country*) erobern; **~or** *n* Eroberer *m*.

conquest ['kɒŋkwest] *n* Eroberung *f*.

cons [kɒnz] *npl see* **convenience, pro.**

conscience ['kɒnʃəns] *n* Gewissen *nt*.

conscientious [kɒnʃɪ'enʃəs] *a* gewissenhaft.

conscious ['kɒnʃəs] *a* bewußt; (*MED*) bei Bewußtsein; **~ness** *n* Bewußtsein *nt*.

conscript ['kɒnskrɪpt] *n* Wehrpflichtige(r) *m*; **~ion** [kən'skrɪpʃən] *n* Wehrpflicht *f*.

consecrate ['kɒnsɪkreɪt] *vt* weihen.

consecutive [kən'sekjʊtɪv] *a* aufeinanderfolgend.

consensus [kən'sensəs] *n* allgemeine Übereinstimmung *f*.

consent [kən'sent] *n* Zustimmung *f* // *vi* zustimmen (*to dat*).

consequence ['kɒnsɪkwəns] *n* (*importance*) Bedeutung *f*; (*effect*) Folge *f*.

consequently ['kɒnsɪkwəntlɪ] *ad* folglich.

conservation [kɒnsə'veɪʃən] *n* Erhaltung *f*; (*nature ~*) Umweltschutz *m*.

conservative [kən'sɜːvətɪv] *a* konservativ; **C~** *a* (*Brit*) konservativ // *n* Konservative(r) *mf*.

conservatory [kən'sɜːvətrɪ] *n* (*room*) Wintergarten *m*.

conserve [kən'sɜːv] *vt* erhalten.

consider [kən'sɪdə*] *vt* überlegen; (*take into account*) in Betracht ziehen; (*regard as*) halten für; **to ~ doing sth** denken daran, etw zu tun.

considerable [kən'sɪdərəbl] *a* beträchtlich.

considerably *ad* beträchtlich.

considerate [kən'sɪdərɪt] *a* rücksichtsvoll.

consideration [kənsɪdə'reɪʃən] *n* Rücksicht(nahme) *f*; (*thought*) Erwägung *f*; (*reward*) Entgelt *nt*.

considering [kən'sɪdərɪŋ] *prep* in Anbetracht (+*gen*).

consign [kən'saɪn] *vt* übergeben; **~ment** *n* Sendung *f*.

consist [kən'sɪst] *vi*: **to ~ of** bestehen aus.

consistency [kən'sɪstənsɪ] *n* (*of material*) Konsistenz *f*; (*of argument, person*) Konsequenz *f*.

consistent [kən'sɪstənt] *a* (*person*) konsequent; (*argument*) folgerichtig.

consolation [kɒnsə'leɪʃən] *n* Trost *m*.

console [kən'səʊl] *vt* trösten // ['kɒnsəʊl] Kontroll(pult) *nt*.

consolidate [kən'sɒlɪdeɪt] *vt* festigen.

consommé [kən'sɒmeɪ] *n* Fleischbrühe *f*.

consonant ['kɒnsənənt] *n* Konsonant *m*.

conspicuous [kən'spɪkjʊəs] *a* (*prominent*) auffällig; (*visible*) deutlich sichtbar.

conspiracy [kən'spɪrəsɪ] *n* Verschwörung *f*.

conspire [kən'spaɪə*] *vi* sich verschwören.

constable ['kʌnstəbl] *n* (*Brit*) Polizist(in *f*) *m*; **chief ~** Polizeipräsident *m*.

constabulary [kən'stæbjʊlərɪ] *n* Polizei *f*.

constant ['kɒnstənt] *a* (*continuous*) ständig; (*unchanging*) konstant; **~ly** *ad* ständig.

constellation [kɒnstə'leɪʃən] *n* Sternbild *nt*.

consternation [kɒnstə'neɪʃən] *n* Bestürzung *f*.

constipated ['kɒnstɪpeɪtəd] *a* verstopft.

constipation [kɒnstɪ'peɪʃən] *n* Verstopfung *f*.

constituency [kən'stɪtjʊənsɪ] *n* Wahlkreis *m*.

constituent [kən'stɪtjʊənt] *n* (*person*) Wähler *m*; (*part*) Bestandteil *m*.

constitute ['kɒnstɪtjuːt] *vt* (*make up*) bilden; (*amount to*) darstellen.

constitution [kɒnstɪ'tjuːʃən] *n* Verfassung *f*; **~al** *a* Verfassungs-.

constraint [kən'streɪnt] *n* Zwang *m*; (*shyness*) Befangenheit *f*.

construct [kən'strʌkt] *vt* bauen; **~ion** [kən'strʌkʃən] *n* Konstruktion *f*; (*building*) Bau *m*; **~ive** *a* konstruktiv.

construe [kən'struː] *vt* deuten.

consul ['kɒnsl] n Konsul m; ~ate ['kɒnsjʊlət] n Konsulat nt.

consult [kən'sʌlt] vt um Rat fragen; (doctor) konsultieren; (book) nachschlagen in (+dat); ~ant n (MED) Facharzt m; (other specialist) Gutachter m; ~ation [kɒnsəl'teɪʃən] n Beratung f; (MED) Konsultation f; ~ing room n Sprechzimmer nt.

consume [kən'sjuːm] vt verbrauchen; (food) konsumieren; ~r n Verbraucher m; ~r goods npl Konsumgüter pl; **consumerism** n Konsum m; ~r society n Konsumgesellschaft f.

consummate ['kɒnsʌmeɪt] vt (marriage) vollziehen.

consumption [kən'sʌmpʃən] n Verbrauch m; (of food) Konsum m.

cont. abbr (= continued) Forts.

contact ['kɒntækt] n (touch) Berührung f; (connection) Verbindung f; (person) Kontakt m // vt sich in Verbindung setzen mit; ~ lenses npl Kontaktlinsen pl.

contagious [kən'teɪdʒəs] a ansteckend.

contain [kən'teɪn] vt enthalten; to ~ o.s. sich zügeln; ~er n Behälter m; (transport) Container m.

contamination [kəntæmɪ'neɪʃən] n Verunreinigung f.

cont'd abbr (= continued) Forts.

contemplate ['kɒntəmpleɪt] vt (look at) (nachdenklich) betrachten; (think about) überdenken; (plan) vorhaben.

contemporary [kən'tempərərɪ] a zeitgenössisch // n Zeitgenosse m.

contempt [kən'tempt] n Verachtung f; ~ of court (JUR) Mißachtung f des Gerichts; ~ible a verachtenswert; ~uous a verächtlich.

contend [kən'tend] vt (argue) behaupten // vi kämpfen; ~er n (for post) Bewerber(in f) m; (SPORT) Wettkämpfer(in f) m.

content [kən'tent] a zufrieden // vt befriedigen // n ['kɒntent] (also: ~s) Inhalt m; ~ed a zufrieden.

contention [kən'tenʃən] n (dispute) Streit m; (argument) Behauptung f.

contentment [kən'tentmənt] n Zufriedenheit f.

contest ['kɒntest] n (Wett)kampf m // vt [kən'test] (dispute) bestreiten; (JUR) anfechten; (POL) kandidieren in (+dat); ~ant [kən'testənt] n Bewerber(in f) m.

context ['kɒntekst] n Zusammenhang m.

continent ['kɒntɪnənt] n Kontinent m; the C~ (Brit) das europäische Festland; ~al [kɒntɪ'nentl] a kontinental; ~al quilt n (Brit) Federbett nt.

contingency [kən'tɪndʒənsɪ] n Möglichkeit f.

contingent [kən'tɪndʒənt] n Kontingent nt.

continual [kən'tɪnjuəl] a (endless) fortwährend; (repeated) immer wiederkehrend; ~ly ad immer wieder.

continuation [kəntɪnju'eɪʃən] n Fortsetzung f.

continue [kən'tɪnjuː] vi (person) weitermachen; (thing) weitergehen // vt fortsetzen.

continuity [kɒntɪ'njuːɪtɪ] n Kontinuität f.

continuous [kən'tɪnjuəs] a ununterbrochen; ~ **stationery** n Endlospapier nt.

contort [kən'tɔːt] vt verdrehen; ~ion [kən'tɔːʃən] n Verzerrung f.

contour ['kɒntuə*] n Umriß m; (also: ~ line) Höhenlinie f.

contraband ['kɒntrəbænd] n Schmuggelware f.

contraception [kɒntrə'sepʃən] n Empfängnisverhütung f.

contraceptive [kɒntrə'septɪv] n empfängnisverhütende(s) Mittel nt // a empfängnisverhütend.

contract ['kɒntrækt] n Vertrag m // (vb: [kən'trækt]) vi (to do sth) sich vertraglich verpflichten; (muscle, metal) sich zusammenziehen // vt zusammenziehen; ~ion [kən'trækʃən] n (shortening) Verkürzung f; ~or [kən'træktə*] n Unternehmer m.

contradict [kɒntrə'dɪkt] vt widersprechen (+dat); ~ion [kɒntrə'dɪkʃən] n Widerspruch m; ~ory a widersprüchlich.

contraption [kən'træpʃən] n (col) Apparat m.

contrary ['kɒntrərɪ] a (opposite) entgegengesetzt; [kən'trɛərɪ] (obstinate) widerspenstig // n Gegenteil nt; on the ~ im Gegenteil.

contrast ['kɒntrɑːst] n Kontrast m // vt [kən'trɑːst] entgegensetzen; ~ing [kən'trɑːstɪŋ] a Kontrast-.

contravene [kɒntrə'viːn] vt verstoßen gegen.

contribute [kən'trɪbjuːt] vti: to ~ to beitragen zu.

contribution [kɒntrɪ'bjuːʃən] n Beitrag m.

contributor [kən'trɪbjutə*] n Beitragende(r) mf.

contrive [kən'traɪv] vt ersinnen // vi: to ~ to do sth es schaffen, etw zu tun.

control [kən'trəul] vt (direct, test) kontrollieren // n Kontrolle f; ~s pl (of vehicle) Steuerung f; (of engine) Schalttafel f; to be in ~ of (business, office) leiten; (group of children) beaufsichtigen; out of ~ außer Kontrolle; under ~ unter Kontrolle; ~ panel n Schalttafel f; ~ room n Kontrollraum m; ~ tower n (AVIAT) Kontrollturm m.

controversial [kɒntrə'vɜːʃəl] a umstritten.

controversy ['kɒntrəvɜːsɪ] n Kontroverse f.

conurbation [kɒnɜ:'beɪʃən] *n* Ballungsgebiet *nt*.

convalesce [kɒnvə'les] *vi* genesen; **~nce** *n* Genesung *f*.

convector [kən'vektə*] *n* Heizlüfter *m*.

convene [kən'vi:n] *vt* zusammenrufen // *vi* sich versammeln.

convenience [kən'vi:nɪəns] *n* Annehmlichkeit *f*; **all modern ~s**, (*Brit*) **all mod cons** mit allem Komfort; **at your ~** wann es Ihnen paßt.

convenient [kən'vi:nɪənt] *a* günstig.

convent ['kɒnvənt] *n* Kloster *nt*.

convention [kən'venʃən] *n* Versammlung *f*; (*custom*) Konvention *f*; **~al** *a* konventionell.

converge [kən'vɜ:dʒ] *vi* zusammenlaufen.

conversant [kən'vɜ:sənt] *a*: **to be ~ with** bewandert sein in (+*dat*).

conversation [kɒnvə'seɪʃən] *n* Gespräch *nt*; **~al** *a* Unterhaltungs-.

converse [kən'vɜ:s] *vi* sich unterhalten.

conversion [kən'vɜ:ʃən] *n* Umwandlung *f*; (*esp REL*) Bekehrung *f*.

convert [kən'vɜ:t] *vt* (*change*) umwandeln; (*REL*) bekehren // *n* ['kɒnvɜ:t] Bekehrte(r) *mf*; Konvertit(in *f*) *m*; **~ible** *n* (*AUT*) Kabriolett *nt* // *a* umwandelbar; (*FIN*) konvertierbar.

convex [kɒn'veks] *a* konvex.

convey [kən'veɪ] *vt* (*carry*) befördern; (*feelings*) vermitteln; **~or belt** *n* Fließband *nt*.

convict [kən'vɪkt] *vt* verurteilen // *n* ['kɒnvɪkt] Häftling *m*; **~ion** [kən'vɪkʃən] *n* (*verdict*) Verurteilung *f*; (*belief*) Überzeugung *f*.

convince [kən'vɪns] *vt* überzeugen; **~d** *a*: **~ that** überzeugt davon, daß; **convincing** *a* überzeugend.

convoluted [kɒnvə'lu:tɪd] *a* verwickelt; (*style*) gewunden.

convoy ['kɒnvɔɪ] *n* (*of vehicles*) Kolonne *f*; (*protected*) Konvoi *m*.

convulse [kən'vʌls] *vt* zusammenzucken lassen; **to be ~d with laughter** sich vor Lachen krümmen.

convulsion [kən'vʌlʃən] *n* (*esp MED*) Zuckung *f*, Krampf *m*.

coo [ku:] *vi* gurren.

cook [kuk] *vti* kochen // *n* Koch *m*, Köchin *f*; **~ book** *n* Kochbuch *nt*; **~er** *n* Herd *m*; **~ery** *n* Kochkunst *f*; **~ery book** (*Brit*) = **~ book**; **~ie** *n* (*US*) Plätzchen *nt*; **~ing** *n* Kochen *nt*.

cool [ku:l] *a* kühl // *vti* (ab)kühlen; **~ down** *vti* (*fig*) (sich) beruhigen; **~ness** *n* Kühle *f*; (*of temperament*) kühle(r) Kopf.

coop [ku:p] *n* Hühnerstall *m* // *vt*: **~ up** (*fig*) einpferchen.

cooperate [kəʊ'ɒpəreɪt] *vi* zusammenarbeiten; **cooperation** [-'reɪʃən] *n* Zusammenarbeit *f*.

cooperative [kəʊ'ɒpərətɪv] *a* hilfsbereit; (*COMM*) genossenschaftlich // *n* (*of farmers*) Genossenschaft *f*; (*~ store*) Konsumladen *m*.

coordinate [kəʊ'ɔ:dɪneɪt] *vt* koordinieren // *n* [kəʊ'ɔ:dɪnət] (*MATH*) Koordinate *f*; **~s** *pl* (*clothes*) Kombinationen *pl*.

coordination [kəʊɔ:dɪ'neɪʃən] *n* Koordination *f*.

cop [kɒp] *n* (*col*) Polyp *m*, Bulle *m*.

cope [kəʊp] *vi*: **to ~ with** fertig werden mit.

copious ['kəʊpɪəs] *a* reichhaltig.

copper ['kɒpə*] *n* (*metal*) Kupfer *nt*; (*col: policeman*) Polyp *m*, Bulle *m*; **~s** *pl* Kleingeld *nt*.

coppice ['kɒpɪs], **copse** [kɒps] *n* Unterholz *nt*.

copulate ['kɒpjʊleɪt] *vi* sich paaren.

copy ['kɒpɪ] *n* (*imitation*) Kopie *f*; (*of book etc*) Exemplar *nt*; (*of newspaper*) Nummer *f* // *vt* kopieren, abschreiben; **~right** *n* Copyright *nt*.

coral ['kɒrəl] *n* Koralle *f*; **~ reef** *n* Korallenriff *nt*.

cord [kɔ:d] *n* Schnur *f*; (*ELEC*) Kabel *nt*.

cordial ['kɔ:dɪəl] *a* herzlich // *n* Fruchtsaft *m*.

cordon ['kɔ:dn] *n* Absperrkette *f*; **~ off** *vt* abriegeln.

corduroy ['kɔ:dərɔɪ] *n* Kord(samt) *m*.

core [kɔ:*] *n* Kern *m* // *vt* entkernen.

cork [kɔ:k] *n* (*bark*) Korkrinde *f*; (*stopper*) Korken *m*; **~screw** *n* Korkenzieher *m*.

corn [kɔ:n] *n* (*Brit: wheat*) Getreide *nt*, Korn *nt*; (*US: maize*) Mais *m*; (*on foot*) Hühnerauge *nt*; **~ on the cob** Maiskolben *m*.

cornea ['kɔ:nɪə] *n* Hornhaut *f*.

corned beef ['kɔ:nd'bi:f] *n* Corned Beef *nt*.

corner ['kɔ:nə*] *n* Ecke *f*; (*on road*) Kurve *f* // *vt* in die Enge treiben; (*market*) monopolisieren // *vi* (*AUT*) in die Kurve gehen; **~stone** *n* Eckstein *m*.

cornet ['kɔ:nɪt] *n* (*MUS*) Kornett *nt*; (*Brit: of ice cream*) Eistüte *f*.

cornflakes ['kɔ:nfleɪks] *npl* Corn-flakes *pl* ®.

cornflour ['kɔ:nflaʊə*] *n* (*Brit*), **cornstarch** ['kɔ:nstɑ:tʃ] *n* (*US*) Maizena *nt* ®.

Cornwall ['kɔ:nwəl] *n* Cornwall *nt*.

corny ['kɔ:nɪ] *a* (*joke*) blöd(e).

corollary [kə'rɒlərɪ] *n* Folgesatz *m*.

coronary ['kɒrənərɪ] *n*: **~ (thrombosis)** *n* Herzinfarkt *m*.

coronation [kɒrə'neɪʃən] *n* Krönung *f*.

coroner ['kɒrənə*] *n* Untersuchungsrichter *m*.

coronet ['kɒrənɪt] *n* Adelskrone *f*.

corporal ['kɔ:pərəl] *n* Obergefreite(r) *m* // *a*: **~ punishment** Prügelstrafe *f*.

corporate ['kɔ:pərɪt] a gemeinschaftlich, korporativ.

corporation [kɔ:pə'reɪʃən] n (of town) Gemeinde f; (COMM) Körperschaft f, Aktiengesellschaft f.

corps [kɔ:*], pl **corps** [kɔ:z] n (Armee)korps nt.

corpse [kɔ:ps] n Leiche f.

corpuscle ['kɔ:pʌsl] n Blutkörperchen nt.

corral [kə'rɑ:l] n Pferch m, Korral m.

correct [kə'rekt] a (accurate) richtig; (proper) korrekt // vt korrigieren; ~ion [kə'rekʃən] n Berichtigung f.

correlation [kɔrɪ'leɪʃən] n Wechselbeziehung f.

correspond [kɔrɪs'pɔnd] vi (agree) übereinstimmen; (exchange letters) korrespondieren; ~ence n (similarity) Entsprechung f; (letters) Briefwechsel m, Korrespondenz f; ~ence course n Fernkurs m; ~ent n (PRESS) Berichterstatter m.

corridor ['kɔrɪdɔ:*] n Gang m.

corroborate [kə'rɔbəreɪt] vt bestätigen.

corrode [kə'rəʊd] vt zerfressen // vi rosten; **corrosion** [kə'rəʊʒən] n Korrosion f.

corrugated ['kɔrəgeɪtɪd] a gewellt; ~ **iron** n Wellblech nt.

corrupt [kə'rʌpt] a korrupt // vt verderben; (bribe) bestechen; ~ion [kə'rʌpʃən] n (of society) Verdorbenheit f; (bribery) Bestechung f.

corset ['kɔ:sɪt] n Korsett nt.

corsica ['kɔ:sɪkə] n Korsika nt.

cortège [kɔ:'tɛ:ʒ] n Zug m; (of funeral) Leichenzug m.

cosh [kɔʃ] n (Brit) Totschläger m.

cosmetic [kɔz'metɪk] n Kosmetikum nt.

cosmic ['kɔzmɪk] a kosmisch.

cosmonaut ['kɔzmənɔ:t] n Kosmonaut(in f) m.

cosmopolitan [kɔzmə'pɔlɪtən] a international; (city) Welt-.

cosmos ['kɔzmɔs] n Kosmos m.

cosset ['kɔsɪt] vt verwöhnen.

cost [kɔst] n Kosten pl, Preis m; ~s pl Kosten pl // vti, pp **cost** kosten; how much does it ~? wieviel kostet das?; at all ~s um jeden Preis.

co-star ['kəʊstɑ:*] n eine(r) der Hauptdarsteller.

cost-effective ['kɔstɪ'fektɪv] a rentabel.

costly ['kɔstlɪ] a kostspielig.

cost-of-living ['kɔstəv'lɪvɪŋ] a (allowance, index) Lebenshaltungskosten.

cost price ['kɔst'praɪs] n (Brit) Selbstkostenpreis m.

costume ['kɔstjuːm] n Kostüm nt; (fancy dress) Maskenkostüm nt; (Brit: also: **swimming** ~) Badeanzug m; ~ **jewellery** n Modeschmuck m.

cosy ['kəʊzɪ] a (Brit) behaglich; (: atmosphere) gemütlich.

cot [kɔt] n (Brit: child's) Kinderbett(chen) nt; (US: campbed) Feldbett nt.

cottage ['kɔtɪdʒ] n kleine(s) Haus nt; ~ **cheese** n Hüttenkäse m; ~ **industry** n Heimindustrie f; ~ **pie** n Auflauf mit Hackfleisch und Kartoffelbrei.

cotton ['kɔtn] n Baumwolle f; (thread) Garn nt; ~ **on to** vt (col) kapieren; ~ **candy** n (US) Zuckerwatte f; ~ **wool** n (Brit) Watte f.

couch [kaʊtʃ] n Couch f.

couchette [kuː'ʃet] n (on train, boat) Liegewagen(platz) m.

cough [kɔf] vi husten // n Husten m; ~ **drop** n Hustenbonbon nt.

could [kʊd] pt of **can**; ~**n't** = **could not**.

council ['kaʊnsl] n (of town) Stadtrat m; ~ **estate/house** n (Brit) Siedlung f/ Haus nt des sozialen Wohnungsbaus; ~**lor** ['kaʊnsɪlə*] n Stadtrat m/-rätin f.

counsel ['kaʊnsl] n (barrister) Anwalt m; (advice) Rat(schlag) m // vt beraten; ~**lor** n Berater m.

count [kaʊnt] vti zählen // n (reckoning) Abrechnung f; (nobleman) Graf m; ~ **on** vt zählen auf (+acc); ~**down** n Countdown m.

countenance ['kaʊntɪnəns] n (old) Antlitz nt // vt (tolerate) gutheißen.

counter ['kaʊntə*] n (in shop) Ladentisch m; (in café) Theke f; (in bank, post office) Schalter m // vt entgegnen; ~**act** [kaʊntə'rækt] vt entgegenwirken (+dat); ~-**espionage** n Spionageabwehr f.

counterfeit ['kaʊntəfɪt] n Fälschung f // vt fälschen // a gefälscht.

counterfoil ['kaʊntəfɔɪl] n (Kontroll)abschnitt m.

countermand ['kaʊntəmɑ:nd] vt rückgängig machen.

counterpart ['kaʊntəpɑ:t] n (object) Gegenstück nt; (person) Gegenüber nt.

counterproductive ['kaʊntəprə'dʌktɪv] a destruktiv.

countersign ['kaʊntəsaɪn] vt gegenzeichnen.

countess ['kaʊntɪs] n Gräfin f.

countless ['kaʊntlɪs] a zahllos, unzählig.

country ['kʌntrɪ] n Land nt; ~ **dancing** n (Brit) Volkstanz m; ~ **house** n Landhaus nt; ~**man** n (national) Landsmann m; (rural) Bauer m; ~**side** n Landschaft f.

county ['kaʊntɪ] n Landkreis m; (Brit) Grafschaft f.

coup [kuː], pl ~**s** [kuːz] n Coup m; (also: ~ **d'état**) n Staatsstreich m, Putsch m.

coupé [kuː'peɪ] n (AUT) Coupé nt.

couple ['kʌpl] n Paar nt; a ~ **of** ein paar // vt koppeln.

coupon ['kuːpɔn] n Gutschein m.

courage ['kʌrɪdʒ] n Mut m; **~ous** [kə'reɪdʒəs] a mutig.
courgette [kuə'ʒet] n (Brit) Zucchini f.
courier ['kurɪə*] n (for holiday) Reiseleiter m; (messenger) Kurier m.
course [kɔːs] n (race) Bahn f; (of stream) Lauf m; (golf ~) Platz m; (NAUT, SCH) Kurs m; (in meal) Gang m; **summer ~** n Sommerkurs m; **of ~** ad natürlich.
court [kɔːt] n (royal) Hof m; (JUR) Gericht nt // vt (woman) gehen mit; (danger) herausfordern; **to take to ~** vor Gericht bringen.
courteous ['kɜːtɪəs] a höflich.
courtesan [kɔːtɪ'zæn] n Kurtisane f.
courtesy ['kɜːtəsɪ] n Höflichkeit f.
court-house ['kɔːthaus] n (US) Gerichtsgebäude nt.
courtier ['kɔːtɪə*] n Höfling m.
court-martial ['kɔːt'mɑːʃəl], pl **courts-martial** ['kɔːts'mɑːʃəl] n Kriegsgericht nt // vt vor ein Kriegsgericht stellen.
courtroom ['kɔːtrum] n Gerichtssaal m.
courtyard ['kɔːtjɑːd] n Hof m.
cousin ['kʌzn] n Cousin m, Vetter m; Kusine f.
cove [kəuv] n kleine Bucht f.
covenant ['kʌvənənt] n (ECCL) Bund m; (JUR) Verpflichtung f.
cover ['kʌvə*] vt (spread over) bedecken; (shield) abschirmen; (include) sich erstrecken über (+acc); (protect) decken; (distance) zurücklegen; (report on) berichten über (+acc) // n (lid) Deckel m; (for bed) Decke f; (MIL) Bedeckung f; (of book) Einband m; (of magazine) Umschlag; (insurance) Versicherung f; **to take ~** (from rain) sich unterstellen; (MIL) in Deckung gehen; **under ~** (indoors) drinnen; **under ~ of** im Schutze (+ gen); **under separate ~** (COMM) mit getrennter Post; **to ~ up for sb** jdn decken; **~age** ['kʌvrɪdʒ] n (PRESS: reports) Berichterstattung f; (distribution) Verbreitung f; **~ charge** n Bedienungsgeld nt; **~ing** n Bedeckung f; **~ing letter**, (US) **~ letter** n Begleitbrief m; **~ note** n (INSURANCE) vorläufige(r) Versicherungsschein m.
covert ['kʌvət] a geheim.
cover-up ['kʌvərʌp] n Vertuschung f.
covet ['kʌvɪt] vt begehren.
cow [kau] n Kuh f // vt einschüchtern.
coward ['kauəd] n Feigling m; **~ice** ['kauədɪs] n Feigheit f; **~ly** a feige.
cowboy ['kaubɔɪ] n Cowboy m.
cower ['kauə*] vi kauern.
coxswain ['kɒksn] n (abbr: cox) Steuermann m.
coy [kɔɪ] a schüchtern.
coyote [kɔɪ'əutɪ] n Präriewolf m.
cozy ['kəuzɪ] a (US) = **cosy.**

CPA (US) abbr of **certified public accountant.**
crab [kræb] n Krebs m; **~ apple** n Holzapfel m.
crack [kræk] n Riß m, Sprung m; (noise) Knall m // vt (break) springen lassen; (joke) reißen; (nut, safe) knacken; (whip) knallen lassen // a erstklassig; (troops) Elite-; **~ down** vi: **to ~ down (on)** hart durchgreifen (bei); **~ up** vi (fig) zusammenbrechen; **~er** n (firework) Knallkörper m, Kracher m; (biscuit) Keks m; (Christmas ~) Knallbonbon nt.
crackle ['krækl] vi knistern; (fire) prasseln.
cradle ['kreɪdl] n Wiege f.
craft [krɑːft] n (skill) (Hand- or Kunst)fertigkeit f; (trade) Handwerk nt; (NAUT) Schiff nt; **~sman** n Handwerker m; **~smanship** n (quality) handwerkliche Ausführung f; (ability) handwerkliche(s) Können nt; **~y** a schlau.
crag [kræg] n Klippe f.
cram [kræm] vt vollstopfen (with mit) // vi (learn) pauken; **to ~ sth into** etw in (+acc) stopfen.
cramp [kræmp] n Krampf m // vt (limit) einengen; (hinder) hemmen; **~ed** a (position) verkrampft; (space) eng.
crampon ['kræmpən] n Steigeisen nt.
cranberry ['krænbərɪ] n Preiselbeere f.
crane [kreɪn] n (machine) Kran m; (bird) Kranich m.
crank [kræŋk] n (lever) Kurbel f; (person) Spinner m; **~shaft** n Kurbelwelle f.
cranny ['krænɪ] n see **nook.**
crash [kræʃ] n (noise) Krachen nt; (with cars) Zusammenstoß m; (with plane) Absturz m; (COMM) Zusammenbruch m // vt (plane) abstürzen mit // vi (cars) zusammenstoßen; (plane) abstürzen; (economy) zusammenbrechen; (noise) knallen; **~ course** n Schnellkurs m; **~ helmet** n Sturzhelm m; **~ landing** n Bruchlandung f.
crass [kræs] a kraß.
crate [kreɪt] n (lit, fig) Kiste f.
crater ['kreɪtə*] n Krater m.
cravat(e) [krə'væt] n Halstuch nt.
crave [kreɪv] vt verlangen nach.
crawl [krɔːl] vi kriechen; (baby) krabbeln // n Kriechen nt; (swim) Kraul nt.
crayfish ['kreɪfɪʃ] n, pl inv (freshwater) Krebs m; (saltwater) Languste f.
crayon ['kreɪən] n Buntstift m.
craze [kreɪz] n Fimmel m.
crazy ['kreɪzɪ] a verrückt; **~ paving** n Mosaikpflaster nt.
creak [kriːk] vi knarren.
cream [kriːm] n (from milk) Rahm m, Sahne f; (polish, cosmetic) Creme f;

(*fig: people*) Elite f // a cremfarbig; ~
cake n Sahnetorte f; ~ **cheese** n
Rahmquark m; **~y** a sahnig.
crease [kri:s] n Falte f // vt falten;
(*untidy*) zerknittern // vi (*wrinkle up*)
knittern.
create [kri'eit] vt erschaffen; (*cause*)
verursachen.
creation [kri'eiʃən] n Schöpfung f.
creative [kri'eitiv] a kreativ.
creator [kri'eitə*] n Schöpfer m.
creature ['kri:tʃə*] n Geschöpf nt.
crèche, creche [kreʃ] n Krippe f.
credence ['kri:dəns] n: to lend or give ~
to sth etw (dat) Glauben schenken.
credentials [kri'denʃəlz] npl Be-
glaubigungsschreiben nt.
credibility [kredi'biliti] n Glaubwürdig-
keit f.
credible ['kredibl] a (*person*)
glaubwürdig; (*story*) glaubhaft.
credit ['kredit] n (*COMM also*) Kredit m
// vt Glauben schenken (+dat); (*COMM*)
gutschreiben; **~s** pl (*of film*) die Mit-
wirkenden; **~able** a rühmlich; ~ **card**
n Kreditkarte f; **~or** n Gläubiger m.
creed [kri:d] n Glaubensbekenntnis nt.
creek [kri:k] n (*inlet*) kleine Bucht f;
(*US: river*) kleine(r) Wasserlauf m.
creep [kri:p], pt, pp **crept** vi kriechen;
~er n Kletterpflanze f; **~y** a
(*frightening*) gruselig.
cremation [kri'meiʃən] n Einäscherung
f.
crêpe [kreip] n Krepp m; ~ **bandage** n
(*Brit*) Elastikbinde f.
crept [krept] pt, pp of **creep**.
crescent ['kresnt] n (*of moon*)
Halbmond m.
cress [kres] n Kresse f.
crest [krest] n (*of cock*) Kamm m; (*of
wave*) Wellenkamm m; (*coat of arms*)
Wappen nt; **~fallen** a niedergeschlagen.
Crete [kri:t] n Kreta nt.
crevasse [kri'væs] n Gletscherspalte f.
crevice ['krevis] n Riß m.
crew [kru:] n Besatzung f, Mannschaft f;
~-cut n Bürstenschnitt m; **~-neck** n
runde(r) Ausschnitt m.
crib [krib] n (*bed*) Krippe f // vt spicken
(*col*).
crick [krik] n Muskelkrampf m.
cricket ['krikit] n (*insect*) Grille f;
(*game*) Kricket nt.
crime [kraim] n Verbrechen nt.
criminal ['kriminl] n Verbrecher m // a
kriminell; (*act*) strafbar.
crimson ['krimzn] a leuchtend rot.
cringe [krindʒ] vi sich ducken.
crinkle ['krinkl] vt zerknittern.
cripple ['kripl] n Krüppel m // vt
lahmlegen; (*MED*) verkrüppeln.
crisis ['kraisis], pl **-ses** ['kraisi:z] n
Krise f.
crisp [krisp] a knusprig; **~s** npl (*Brit*)

Chips pl.
criss-cross ['kriskrɒs] a gekreuzt,
Kreuz-.
criterion [krai'tiəriən], pl **-ria**
[krai'tiəriə] n Kriterium nt.
critic ['kritik] n Kritiker(in f) m; **~al** a
kritisch; **~ally** ad kritisch; (*ill*) gefährlich; **~ism** ['kritisizəm] n Kritik f;
~ize ['kritisaiz] vt kritisieren.
croak [krəuk] vi krächzen; (*frog*)
quaken.
crochet ['krəuʃei] n Häkelei f.
crockery ['krɒkəri] n Geschirr nt.
crocodile ['krɒkədail] n Krokodil nt.
crocus ['krəukəs] n Krokus m.
croft [krɒft] n (*Brit*) kleine(s) Pachtgut
nt.
crony ['krəuni] n (*col*) Kumpel m.
crook [kruk] n (*criminal*) Gauner m;
(*stick*) Hirtenstab m; **~ed** ['krukid] a
krumm.
crop [krɒp] n (*harvest*) Ernte f; (*riding
~*) Reitpeitsche f // vt ernten; ~ **up** vi
passieren.
croquet ['krəukei] n Krocket nt.
croquette [krə'ket] n Krokette f.
cross [krɒs] n Kreuz nt // vt (*road*) überqueren; (*legs*) übereinander legen;
kreuzen // a (*annoyed*) böse; ~ **out** vt
streichen; ~ **over** vi hinübergehen;
~bar n Querstange f; **~breed** n Kreuzung f; **~country (race)** n Geländelauf
m; **~-examine** vt ins Kreuzverhör
nehmen; **~-eyed** a: to be **~-eyed**
schielen; **~fire** n Kreuzfeuer nt; **~ing** n
(*crossroads*) (Straßen)kreuzung f; (*of
ship*) Überfahrt f; (*for pedestrians*)
Fußgängerüberweg m; **~ing guard** n
(*US*) Schülerlotse m; ~ **purposes** npl:
to be at ~ **purposes** aneinander vor-
beireden; **~reference** n Querverweis
m; **~roads** n Straßenkreuzung f; (*fig*)
Scheideweg m; ~ **section** n Querschnitt
m; **~walk** n (*US*) Fußgängerüberweg
m; **~wind** n Seitenwind m; **~word
(puzzle)** n Kreuzworträtsel nt.
crotch [krɒtʃ] n Zwickel m; (*ANAT*)
Unterleib nt.
crotchet ['krɒtʃit] n Viertelnote f.
crotchety ['krɒtʃiti] a launenhaft.
crouch [krautʃ] vi hocken.
croupier ['kru:piei] n Croupier m.
crow [krəu] n (*bird*) Krähe f; (*of cock*)
Krähen nt // vi krähen.
crowbar ['krəuba:*] n Stemmeisen nt.
crowd [kraud] n Menge f // vt (*fill*) über-
füllen // vi drängen; **~ed** a überfüllt.
crown [kraun] n Krone f; (*of head, hat*)
Kopf m // vt krönen; ~ **jewels** pl
Kronjuwelen pl; ~ **prince** n Kronprinz
m.
crow's-feet ['krəuzfi:t] npl Krähenfüße
pl.
crucial ['kru:ʃəl] a entscheidend.
crucifix ['kru:sifiks] n Kruzifix nt; **~ion**

[kruːsɪˈfɪkʃən] n Kreuzigung f.
crucify [ˈkruːsɪfaɪ] vt kreuzigen.
crude [kruːd] a (raw) roh; (humour, behaviour) grob; (basic) primitiv; ~ (oil) n Rohöl nt.
cruel [ˈkruəl] a grausam; ~ty n Grausamkeit f.
cruet [ˈkruːɪt] n Gewürzständer m.
cruise [kruːz] n Kreuzfahrt f // vi kreuzen; ~r n (MIL) Kreuzer m.
crumb [krʌm] n Krume f.
crumble [ˈkrʌmbl] vti zerbröckeln.
crumbly [ˈkrʌmblɪ] a krümelig.
crumpet [ˈkrʌmpɪt] n Tee(pfann)kuchen m.
crumple [ˈkrʌmpl] vt zerknittern.
crunch [krʌntʃ] n: the ~ (fig) der Knackpunkt // vt knirschen; ~y a knusprig.
crusade [kruːˈseɪd] n Kreuzzug m.
crush [krʌʃ] n Gedränge nt; (drink): lemon ~ Zitronensaft m // vt zerdrücken; (rebellion) unterdrücken.
crust [krʌst] n Kruste f.
crutch [krʌtʃ] n Krücke f.
crux [krʌks] n der springende Punkt.
cry [kraɪ] vi (shout) schreien; (weep) weinen // n (call) Schrei m; ~ off vi (plötzlich) absagen.
crypt [krɪpt] n Krypta f.
cryptic [ˈkrɪptɪk] a hintergründig.
crystal [ˈkrɪstl] n Kristall m; (glass) Kristallglas nt; (mineral) Bergkristall m; ~-clear a kristallklar; ~lize vti (lit) kristallisieren; (fig) klären.
cub [kʌb] n Junge(s) nt; (also: ~ scout) Wölfling m.
Cuba [ˈkjuːbə] n Kuba nt; ~n a kubanisch // n Kubaner(in f) m.
cubbyhole [ˈkʌbɪhəʊl] n Eckchen nt.
cube [kjuːb] n Würfel m // vt (MATH) hoch drei nehmen; ~ root n Kubikwurzel f.
cubic [ˈkjuːbɪk] a würfelförmig; (centimetre etc) Kubik-; ~ capacity n Fassungsvermögen nt.
cubicle [ˈkjuːbɪkl] n Kabine f.
cuckoo [ˈkukuː] n Kuckuck m; ~ clock n Kuckucksuhr f.
cucumber [ˈkjuːkʌmbə*] n Gurke f.
cuddle [ˈkʌdl] vti herzen, drücken (col).
cue [kjuː] n (THEAT) Stichwort nt; (snooker ~) Billardstock m.
cuff [kʌf] n (Brit: of shirt, coat etc) Manschette f; Aufschlag m; (US) = turn-up; off the ~ ad aus dem Handgelenk; ~link n Manschettenknopf m.
cuisine [kwɪˈziːn] n Kochkunst f, Küche f.
cul-de-sac [ˈkʌldəsæk] n Sackgasse f.
culinary [ˈkʌlɪnərɪ] a Koch-.
cull [kʌl] vt (flowers) pflücken; (select) auswählen.
culminate [ˈkʌlmɪneɪt] vi gipfeln.

culmination [kʌlmɪˈneɪʃən] n Höhepunkt m.
culottes [kjuːˈlɒts] npl Hosenrock m.
culpable [ˈkʌlpəbl] a schuldig.
culprit [ˈkʌlprɪt] n Täter m.
cult [kʌlt] n Kult m.
cultivate [ˈkʌltɪveɪt] vt (AGR) bebauen; (mind) bilden.
cultivation [kʌltɪˈveɪʃən] n (AGR) Bebauung f; (of person) Bildung f.
cultural [ˈkʌltʃərəl] a kulturell, Kultur-.
culture [ˈkʌltʃə*] n Kultur f; ~d a gebildet.
cumbersome [ˈkʌmbəsəm] a (object) sperrig.
cummerbund [ˈkʌməbʌnd] n Kummerbund m.
cumulative [ˈkjuːmjʊlətɪv] a gehäuft.
cunning [ˈkʌnɪŋ] n Verschlagenheit f // a schlau.
cup [kʌp] n Tasse f; (prize) Pokal m.
cupboard [ˈkʌbəd] n Schrank m.
Cupid [ˈkjuːpɪd] n Amor m.
cup-tie [ˈkʌptaɪ] n (Brit) Pokalspiel nt.
curate [ˈkjʊərɪt] n (Catholic) Kurat m; (Protestant) Vikar m.
curator [kjʊˈreɪtə*] n Kustos m.
curb [kɜːb] vt zügeln // n (on spending etc) Einschränkung f; (US) Bordstein m.
curdle [ˈkɜːdl] vi gerinnen.
cure [kjʊə*] n Heilmittel nt; (process) Heilverfahren nt // vt heilen.
curfew [ˈkɜːfjuː] n Ausgangssperre f; Sperrstunde f.
curiosity [kjʊərɪˈɒsɪtɪ] n Neugier f.
curious [ˈkjʊərɪəs] a neugierig; (strange) seltsam.
curl [kɜːl] n Locke f // vt locken // vi sich locken; ~ up vi sich zusammenrollen; (person) sich ankuscheln; ~er n Lockenwickler m; ~y a lockig.
currant [ˈkʌrənt] n Korinthe f.
currency [ˈkʌrənsɪ] n Währung f; to gain ~ an Popularität gewinnen.
current [ˈkʌrənt] n Strömung f // a (expression) gängig, üblich; (issue) neueste; ~ account n (Brit) Girokonto nt; ~ affairs npl Zeitgeschehen nt; ~ly ad zur Zeit.
curriculum [kəˈrɪkjʊləm], pl ~s or curricula [kəˈrɪkjʊlə] n Lehrplan m; ~ vitae (CV) n Lebenslauf m.
curry [ˈkʌrɪ] n Currygericht nt // vt: to ~ favour with sich einschmeicheln bei; ~ powder n Curry(pulver) nt.
curse [kɜːs] vi (swear) fluchen (at auf +acc) // vt (insult) verwünschen // n Fluch m.
cursor [ˈkɜːsə*] n (COMPUT) Cursor m.
cursory [ˈkɜːsərɪ] a flüchtig.
curt [kɜːt] a schroff.
curtail [kɜːˈteɪl] vt abkürzen; (rights) einschränken.
curtain [ˈkɜːtn] n Vorhang m.
curtsey [ˈkɜːtsɪ] n Knicks m // vi

knicksen.
curve [kɜːv] n Kurve f; (of body, vase etc) Rundung f // vi sich biegen; (hips, breasts) sich runden; (road) einen Bogen machen.
cushion ['kuʃən] n Kissen nt // vt dämpfen.
custard ['kʌstəd] n Vanillesoße f.
custodian [kʌs'təudɪən] n Kustos m, Verwalter(in f) m.
custody ['kʌstədɪ] n Aufsicht f; (police) Haft f; **to take into** ~ verhaften.
custom ['kʌstəm] n (tradition) Brauch m; (COMM) Kundschaft f; ~ary a üblich.
customer ['kʌstəmə*] n Kunde m, Kundin f.
customized ['kʌstəmaɪzd] a (car etc) mit Spezialausrüstung.
custom-made ['kʌstəm'meɪd] a speziell angefertigt.
customs ['kʌstəmz] npl Zoll m; ~ **officer** n Zollbeamte(r) m/f.
cut [kʌt], pt, pp **cut** vt schneiden; (wages) kürzen; (prices) heruntersetzen; // vi schneiden; (intersect) sich schneiden // n Schnitt m; (wound) Schnittwunde f; (in book, income etc) Kürzung f; (share) Anteil m; **to** ~ **a tooth** zahnen; ~ **down** vt (tree) fällen; (reduce) einschränken; ~ **off** vt (lit, fig) abschneiden; (allowance) sperren; ~ **out** vt (shape) ausschneiden; (delete) streichen; ~ **up** vt (meat) aufschneiden; ~**back** n Kürzung; (CINE) Rückblende.
cute [kjuːt] a niedlich.
cuticle ['kjuːtɪkl] n Nagelhaut f.
cutlery ['kʌtlərɪ] n Besteck nt.
cutlet ['kʌtlɪt] n (pork) Kotelett nt; (veal) Schnitzel nt.
cutout ['kʌtaut] n (cardboard ~) Ausschneidemodell nt.
cut-price ['kʌtpraɪs], (US) **cut-rate** ['kʌtreɪt] a verbilligt.
cut throat ['kʌtθrəut] n Verbrechertyp m // a mörderisch.
cutting ['kʌtɪŋ] a schneidend // n (Brit: PRESS) Ausschnitt m; (: RAIL) Durchstich m.
CV n abbr of curriculum vitae.
cwt abbr of hundredweight(s).
cyanide ['saɪənaɪd] n Zyankali nt.
cycle ['saɪkl] n Fahrrad nt; (series) Reihe f // vi radfahren; **cycling** ['saɪklɪŋ] n Radfahren nt; **cyclist** ['saɪklɪst] n Radfahrer(in f) m.
cyclone ['saɪkləun] n Zyklon m.
cygnet ['sɪgnɪt] n junge(r) Schwan m.
cylinder ['sɪlɪndə*] n Zylinder m; (TECH) Walze f; ~-**head gasket** n Zylinderkopfdichtung f.
cymbals ['sɪmbəlz] npl Becken nt.
cyn:c ['sɪnɪk] n Zyniker(in f) m; ~**al** a zynisch; ~**ism** ['sɪnɪsɪzəm] n Zynismus

m.
cypress ['saɪprɪs] n Zypresse f.
Cypriot ['sɪprɪət] a zypriotisch // n Zypriot(in f) m.
Cyprus ['saɪprəs] n Zypern nt.
cyst [sɪst] n Zyste f; ~**itis** n Blasenentzündung f.
czar [zɑː*] n Zar m.
Czech [tʃek] a tschechisch // n Tscheche m, Tschechin f.
Czechoslovakia [tʃekəslə'vækɪə] n die Tschechoslowakei; ~**n** a tschechoslowakisch // n Tschechoslowake m, Tschechoslowakin f.

D

D [diː] n (MUS): ~ **sharp/flat** Dis, dis nt/ Des, des nt.
dab [dæb] vt (wound, paint) betupfen // n (little bit) bißchen nt; (of paint) Tupfer m.
dabble ['dæbl] vi: **to** ~ **in sth** in etw (dat) machen.
dad [dæd], **daddy** ['dædɪ] n Papa m, Vati m; **daddy-long-legs** n Weberknecht m.
daffodil ['dæfədɪl] n Osterglocke f.
daft [dɑːft] a (col) blöd(e), doof.
dagger ['dægə*] n Dolch m.
daily ['deɪlɪ] a täglich // n (PRESS) Tageszeitung f; (woman) Haushaltshilfe f // ad täglich.
dainty ['deɪntɪ] a zierlich.
dairy ['deərɪ] n (Brit: shop) Milchgeschäft nt; (on farm) Molkerei f // a Milch-; ~ **farm** n Hof m mit Milchwirtschaft; ~ **produce** n Molkereiprodukte pl; ~ **store** n (US) Milchgeschäft nt.
dais ['deɪɪs] n Podium nt.
daisy ['deɪzɪ] n Gänseblümchen nt; ~ **wheel** n (on printer) Typenrad nt.
dale [deɪl] n Tal nt.
dam [dæm] n (Stau)damm m // vt stauen.
damage ['dæmɪdʒ] n Schaden m // vt beschädigen; ~**s** pl (JUR) Schaden(s)ersatz m.
damn [dæm] vt verdammen // n (col): **I don't give a** ~ das ist mir total egal // a (col: also: ~**ed**) verdammt; ~ **it!** verflucht!; ~**ing** a vernichtend.
damp [dæmp] a feucht // n Feuchtigkeit f // vt (also: ~**en**) befeuchten; (discourage) dämpfen.
damson ['dæmzən] n Damaszenerpflaume f.
dance [dɑːns] n Tanz m // vi tanzen; ~ **hall** n Tanzlokal nt; ~**r** n Tänzer m.
dancing ['dɑːnsɪŋ] n Tanzen nt.
dandelion ['dændɪlaɪən] n Löwenzahn m.
dandruff ['dændrəf] n (Kopf)schuppen pl.

Dane [deɪn] n Däne m, Dänin f.
danger ['deɪndʒə*] n Gefahr f; ~! (sign) Achtung!; **to be in ~ of doing sth** Gefahr laufen, etw zu tun; **~ous** a, **~ously** ad gefährlich.
dangle ['dæŋgl] vi baumeln // vt herabhängen lassen.
Danish ['deɪnɪʃ] a dänisch // n Dänisch nt.
dapper ['dæpə*] a elegant.
dare [dɛə*] vt herausfordern // vi: **to ~ (to) do sth** es wagen, etw zu tun; **I ~ say** ich würde sagen; **~-devil** n Draufgänger(in f) m.
daring ['dɛərɪŋ] a (audacious) verwegen; (bold) wagemutig; (dress) gewagt // n Mut m.
dark [dɑːk] a dunkel; (fig) düster, trübe; (deep colour) dunkel- // n Dunkelheit f; **to be left in the ~ about** im dunkeln sein über (+ acc); **after ~** nach Anbruch der Dunkelheit; **~en** vti verdunkeln; **~ glasses** npl Sonnenbrille f; **~ness** n Finsternis nt; **~room** n Dunkelkammer f.
darling ['dɑːlɪŋ] n Liebling m // a lieb.
darn [dɑːn] vt stopfen.
dart [dɑːt] n (weapon) Pfeil m; (in sewing) Abnäher m // vi sausen; **~s** pl (game) Pfeilwerfen nt; **~board** n Zielscheibe f.
dash [dæʃ] n Sprung m; (mark) (Gedanken)strich m; (small amount) bißchen nt // vt (hopes) zunichte machen // vi stürzen; **~ away** or **off** vi davonstürzen.
dashboard ['dæʃbɔːd] n Armaturenbrett nt.
dashing ['dæʃɪŋ] a schneidig.
data ['deɪtə] npl Einzelheiten pl, Daten pl; **~ base** n Datenbank f; **~ processing** n Datenverarbeitung f.
date [deɪt] n Datum nt; (for meeting etc) Termin m; (with person) Verabredung f; (fruit) Dattel f // vt (letter etc) datieren; (person) gehen mit; **~ of birth** Geburtsdatum nt; **to ~** ad bis heute; **out of ~** überholt; **up to ~** (clothes) modisch; (report) up-to-date; (with news) auf dem laufenden; **~d** a altmodisch.
daub [dɔːb] vt beschmieren; (paint) schmieren.
daughter ['dɔːtə*] n Tochter f; **~-in-law** n Schwiegertochter f.
daunting ['dɔːntɪŋ] a entmutigend.
dawdle ['dɔːdl] vi trödeln.
dawn [dɔːn] n Morgendämmerung f // vi dämmern; (fig): **it ~ed on him that ...** es dämmerte ihm, daß ...
day [deɪ] n Tag m; **the ~ before/after** am Tag zuvor/danach; **the ~ after tomorrow** übermorgen; **the ~ before yesterday** vorgestern; **by ~** am Tage; **~break** n Tagesanbruch m; **~dream** vi mit

offenen Augen träumen; **~light** n Tageslicht nt; **~ return** n (Brit) Tagesrückfahrkarte f; **~time** n Tageszeit f; **~-to-~** a alltäglich.
daze [deɪz] vt betäuben // n Betäubung f; **in a ~** benommen.
dazzle ['dæzl] vt blenden.
DC abbr (= direct current) Gleichstrom m.
D-day ['diːdeɪ] n (HIST) Tag der Invasion durch die Alliierten (6.6.44); (fig) der Tag X.
deacon ['diːkən] n Diakon m.
dead [ded] a tot; (without feeling) gefühllos; // ad ganz; (exactly) genau; **to shoot sb ~** jdn erschießen; **~ tired** todmüde; **to stop ~** abrupt stehenbleiben; **the ~** pl die Toten pl; **~en** vt (pain) abtöten; (sound) ersticken; **~ end** n Sackgasse f; **~ heat** n tote(s) Rennen nt; **~line** n Stichtag m; **~lock** n Stillstand m; **~ly** a tödlich; **~pan** a undurchdringlich; **the D~ Sea** n das Tote Meer.
deaf [def] a taub; **~en** vt taub machen; **~ness** n Taubheit f; **~-mute** n Taubstumme(r) m.
deal [diːl] n Geschäft nt // vt, pt, pp **dealt** [delt] austeilen; (CARDS) geben; **a great ~ of** sehr viel; **~ in** vt handeln mit; **~ with** vt (person) behandeln; (subject) sich befassen mit; (problem) in Angriff nehmen; **~er** n (COMM) Händler m; (CARDS) Kartengeber m; **~ings** npl (FIN) Geschäfte pl; (relations) Beziehungen pl.
dean [diːn] n (Protestant) Superintendent m; (Catholic) Dechant m; (UNIV) Dekan m.
dear [dɪə*] a lieb; (expensive) teuer // n Liebling m // interj: **~ me!** du liebe Zeit!; **D~ Sir** Sehr geehrter Herr!; **D~ John** Lieber John!; **~ly** ad (love) herzlich; (pay) teuer.
death [deθ] n Tod m; (statistic) Todesfall m; **~ certificate** n Totenschein m; **~ duties** npl (Brit) Erbschaftssteuer f; **~ly** a totenähnlich, Toten-; **~ penalty** n Todesstrafe f; **~ rate** n Sterblichkeitsziffer f.
debar [dɪˈbɑː*] vt ausschließen.
debase [dɪˈbeɪs] vt entwerten.
debatable [dɪˈbeɪtəbl] a anfechtbar.
debate [dɪˈbeɪt] n Debatte f // vt debattieren, diskutieren; (consider) überlegen.
debauchery [dɪˈbɔːtʃərɪ] n Ausschweifungen pl.
debilitating [dɪˈbɪlɪteɪtɪŋ] a schwächend.
debit ['debɪt] n Schuldposten m // vt belasten.
debris ['debriː] n Trümmer pl.
debt [det] n Schuld f; **to be in ~** verschuldet sein; **~or** n Schuldner m.

debunk [di:'bʌŋk] vt entlarven.
decade ['dekeɪd] n Jahrzehnt nt.
decaffeinated [di:'kæfɪneɪtɪd] a koffeinfrei.
decanter [dɪ'kæntə*] n Karaffe f.
decay [dɪ'keɪ] n Verfall m; (tooth ~) Karies m // vi verfallen; (teeth, meat etc) faulen; (leaves etc) verrotten.
deceased [dɪ'si:st] a verstorben.
deceit [dɪ'si:t] n Betrug m; ~**ful** a falsch.
deceive [dɪ'si:v] vt täuschen.
December [dɪ'sembə*] n Dezember m.
decency ['di:sənsɪ] n Anstand m.
decent [di:sənt] a (respectable) anständig; (pleasant) annehmbar.
deception [dɪ'sepʃən] n Betrug m.
deceptive [dɪ'septɪv] a irreführend.
decibel ['desɪbel] n Dezibel nt.
decide [dɪ'saɪd] vt entscheiden // vi sich entscheiden; to ~ on sth etw beschließen; ~**d** a entschieden; ~**dly** [-dɪdlɪ] ad entschieden.
deciduous [dɪ'sɪdjuəs] a Laub-.
decimal ['desɪməl] a dezimal // n Dezimalzahl f; ~ **point** n Komma nt.
decimate ['desɪmeɪt] vt dezimieren.
decipher [dɪ'saɪfə*] vt entziffern.
decision [dɪ'sɪʒən] n Entscheidung f, Entschluß m.
decisive [dɪ'saɪsɪv] a entscheidend; (person) entschlossen.
deck [dek] n (NAUT) Deck nt; (of cards) Pack m; ~**chair** n Liegestuhl m.
declaration [deklə'reɪʃən] n Erklärung f.
declare [dɪ'klɛə*] vt erklären; (CUSTOMS) verzollen.
decline [dɪ'klaɪn] n (decay) Verfall m; (lessening) Rückgang m // vt (invitation) ablehnen // vi (of strength) nachlassen; (say no) ablehnen.
declutch ['di:'klʌtʃ] vi auskuppeln.
decode ['di:'kəʊd] vt entschlüsseln.
decompose [di:kəm'pəʊz] vi (sich) zersetzen.
décor ['deɪkɔ:*] n Ausstattung f.
decorate ['dekəreɪt] vt (room: paper) tapezieren; (: paint) streichen; (adorn) (aus)schmücken; (cake) verzieren; (honour) auszeichnen.
decoration [dekə'reɪʃən] n (of house) (Wand)dekoration f; (medal) Orden m.
decorator ['dekəreɪtə*] n Maler m, Anstreicher m.
decorum [dɪ'kɔ:rəm] n Anstand m.
decoy ['di:kɔɪ] n Lockvogel m.
decrease ['di:kri:s] n Abnahme f // v [di:'kri:s] vermindern // vi abnehmen.
decree [dɪ'kri:] n Erlaß m; ~ **nisi** n vorläufiges Scheidungsurteil nt.
decrepit [dɪ'krepɪt] a hinfällig.
dedicate ['dedɪkeɪt] vt widmen.
dedication [dedɪ'keɪʃən] n (devotion) Ergebenheit; (in book) Widmung f.

deduce [dɪ'dju:s] vt ableiten, schließen (from aus).
deduct [dɪ'dʌkt] vt abziehen; ~**ion** [dɪ'dʌkʃən] n (of money) Abzug m; (conclusion) (Schluß)folgerung f.
deed [di:d] n Tat f; (document) Urkunde f.
deem [di:m] vt: to ~ sb/sth (to be) sth jdn/etw für etw halten.
deep [di:p] a tief // ad: the spectators stood 20 ~ die Zuschauer standen in 20 Reihen hintereinander; ~**en** vt vertiefen // vi (darkness) tiefer werden; ~**-freeze** n Tiefkühlung f; ~**-fry** vt fritieren; ~**ly** ad tief; ~**-sea diving** n Tiefseetauchen nt; ~**-seated** a tiefsitzend.
deer [dɪə*] n Reh nt; ~**skin** n Hirsch-/Rehleder nt.
deface [dɪ'feɪs] vt entstellen.
defamation [defə'meɪʃən] n Verleumdung f.
default [dɪ'fɔ:lt] n Versäumnis nt // vi versäumen // n (COMPUT) Standardwert m; by ~ durch Nichterscheinen nt.
defeat [dɪ'fi:t] n Niederlage f // vt schlagen; ~**ist** a defätistisch // n Defätist m.
defect ['di:fekt] n Fehler m // vi [dɪ'fekt] überlaufen; ~**ive** [dɪ'fektɪv] a fehlerhaft.
defence [dɪ'fens] n Verteidigung f; ~**less** a wehrlos.
defend [dɪ'fend] vt verteidigen; ~**ant** n Angeklagte(r) m; ~**er** n Verteidiger m.
defense [dɪ'fens] n (US) = **defence**.
defensive [dɪ'fensɪv] a defensiv // n: on the ~ in der Defensive.
defer [dɪ'fɜ:*] vt verschieben.
deference ['defərəns] n Rücksichtnahme f.
defiance [dɪ'faɪəns] n Trotz m, Unnachgiebigkeit f; in ~ of sth etw (dat) zum Trotz.
defiant [dɪ'faɪənt] a trotzig, unnachgiebig.
deficiency [dɪ'fɪʃənsɪ] n (lack) Mangel m; (weakness) Schwäche f.
deficient [dɪ'fɪʃənt] a mangelhaft.
deficit ['defɪsɪt] n Defizit nt.
defile [dɪ'faɪl] vt beschmutzen.
define [dɪ'faɪn] vt bestimmen; (explain) definieren.
definite ['defɪnɪt] a (fixed) definitiv; (clear) eindeutig; ~**ly** ad bestimmt.
definition [defɪ'nɪʃən] n Definition f; (PHOT) Schärfe f.
deflate [di:'fleɪt] vt die Luft ablassen aus.
deflect [dɪ'flekt] vt ablenken.
deform [dɪ'fɔ:m] vt deformieren; ~**ity** n Mißbildung f.
defraud [dɪ'frɔ:d] vt betrügen.
defray [dɪ'freɪ] vt (costs) übernehmen.
defrost [di:'frost] vt (fridge) abtauen; (food) auftauen; ~**er** n (US: demister)

Gebläse nt.
deft [deft] a geschickt.
defunct [dɪ'fʌŋkt] a verstorben.
defuse [diː'fjuːz] vt entschärfen.
defy [dɪ'faɪ] vt (disobey) sich widersetzen (+dat); (orders, death) trotzen (+dat); (challenge) herausfordern.
degenerate [dɪ'dʒenəreɪt] vi degenerieren // a [dɪ'dʒenərɪt] degeneriert.
degrading [dɪ'greɪdɪŋ] a erniedrigend.
degree [dɪ'griː] n Grad m; (UNIV) Universitätsabschluß m; by ~s allmählich; to some ~ zu einem gewissen Grad.
dehydrated [diːhaɪ'dreɪtɪd] a (person) ausgetrocknet; (food) Trocken-.
de-ice [diː'aɪs] vt enteisen.
deign [deɪn] vi sich herablassen.
deity ['diːɪtɪ] n Gottheit f.
dejected [dɪ'dʒektɪd] a niedergeschlagen.
delay [dɪ'leɪ] vt (hold back) aufschieben // vi (linger) sich aufhalten // n Aufschub m, Verzögerung f; (of train etc) Verspätung f; to be ~ed (train) Verspätung haben; without ~ unverzüglich.
delectable [dɪ'lektəbl] a köstlich; (fig) reizend.
delegate ['delɪgɪt] n Delegierte(r) mf // vt ['delɪgeɪt] delegieren.
delete [dɪ'liːt] vt (aus)streichen.
deliberate [dɪ'lɪbərɪt] a (intentional) absichtlich; (slow) bedächtig // vi [dɪ'lɪbəreɪt] (consider) überlegen; (debate) sich beraten; ~ly ad absichtlich.
delicacy ['delɪkəsɪ] n Zartheit f; (weakness) Anfälligkeit f; (food) Delikatesse f.
delicate ['delɪkɪt] a (fine) fein; (fragile) zart; (situation) heikel; (MED) empfindlich.
delicatessen [delɪkə'tesn] n Feinkostgeschäft nt.
delicious [dɪ'lɪʃəs] a lecker.
delight [dɪ'laɪt] n Wonne f // vt entzücken; to take ~ in sth Freude an etw (dat) haben; ~ed a: ~ed (at or with/to do) entzückt (über +acc/etw zu tun); ~ful a entzückend, herrlich.
delinquency [dɪ'lɪŋkwənsɪ] n Kriminalität f.
delinquent [dɪ'lɪŋkwənt] n Straffällige(r) mf // a straffällig.
delirious [dɪ'lɪrɪəs] a im Fieberwahn.
deliver [dɪ'lɪvə*] vt (goods) (ab)liefern; (letter) zustellen; (speech) halten; ~y n (Ab)lieferung f; (of letter) Zustellung f; (of speech) Vortragsweise f; (MED) Entbindung f; to take ~y of in Empfang nehmen.
delude [dɪ'luːd] vt täuschen.
deluge ['deljuːdʒ] n Überschwemmung f; (fig) Flut f // vt (fig) überfluten.
delusion [dɪ'luːʒən] n (Selbst)täuschung

f.
de luxe [dɪ'lʌks] a Luxus-.
delve [delv] vi: to ~ into sich vertiefen in (+acc).
demand [dɪ'mɑːnd] vt verlangen // n (request) Verlangen nt; (COMM) Nachfrage f; in ~ gefragt; on ~ auf Verlangen; ~ing a anspruchsvoll.
demarcation [diːmɑː'keɪʃən] n Abgrenzung f.
demean [dɪ'miːn] vt: to ~ o.s. sich erniedrigen.
demeanour, (US) **demeanor** [dɪ'miːnə*] n Benehmen nt.
demented [dɪ'mentɪd] a wahnsinnig.
demise [dɪ'maɪz] n Ableben nt.
demister [diː'mɪstə*] n (AUT) Gebläse nt.
demo ['deməʊ] n abbr (col: = demonstration) Demo f.
democracy [dɪ'mɒkrəsɪ] n Demokratie f.
democrat ['deməkræt] n Demokrat m; ~ic a [demə'krætɪk] demokratisch.
demolish [dɪ'mɒlɪʃ] vt (lit) abreißen; (fig) vernichten.
demolition [demə'lɪʃən] n Abbruch m.
demon ['diːmən] n Dämon m.
demonstrate ['demənstreɪt] vti demonstrieren.
demonstration [demən'streɪʃən] n Demonstration f.
demonstrator ['demənstreɪtə*] n (POL) Demonstrant(in f) m.
demote [dɪ'məʊt] vt degradieren.
demure [dɪ'mjʊə*] a ernst.
den [den] n (of animal) Höhle f; (study) Bude f.
denatured alcohol [diː'neɪtʃəd-] n (US) ungenießbar gemachte(r) Alkohol m.
denial [dɪ'naɪəl] n Leugnung f; official ~ Dementi nt.
denim ['denɪm] a Denim-; ~s npl Denim-Jeans pl.
Denmark ['denmɑːk] n Dänemark nt.
denomination [dɪnɒmɪ'neɪʃən] n (ECCL) Bekenntnis nt; (type) Klasse f; (FIN) Wert m.
denominator [dɪ'nɒmɪneɪtə*] n Nenner m.
denote [dɪ'nəʊt] vt bedeuten.
denounce [dɪ'naʊns] vt brandmarken.
dense [dens] a dicht; (stupid) schwer von Begriff; ~ly ad dicht.
density ['densɪtɪ] n Dichte f; single-/double-~ disk n Diskette f mit einfacher/doppelter Dichte.
dent [dent] n Delle f // vt (also: make a ~ in) einbeulen.
dental ['dentl] a Zahn-; ~ surgeon n = dentist.
dentist ['dentɪst] n Zahnarzt m/-ärztin f; ~ry n Zahnmedizin f.
dentures ['dentʃəz] npl Gebiß nt.

deny [dɪ'naɪ] *vt* leugnen; (*officially*) dementieren; (*help*) abschlagen.

deodorant [di:'əʊdərənt] *n* Deodorant *nt*.

depart [dɪ'pɑːt] *vi* abfahren; **to ~ from** (*fig: differ from*) abweichen von.

department [dɪ'pɑːtmənt] *n* (*COMM*) Abteilung *f*; (*UNIV*) Seminar *nt*; (*POL*) Ministerium *nt*; **~ store** *n* Warenhaus *nt*.

departure [dɪ'pɑːtʃə*] *n* (*of person*) Abreise *f*; (*of train*) Abfahrt *f*; (*of plane*) Abflug *m*; **new ~** Neuerung *f*; **~ lounge** *n* (*at airport*) Abflughalle *f*.

depend [dɪ'pend] *vi*: **to ~ on** abhängen von; (*rely on*) angewiesen sein auf (+*acc*); **it ~s** es kommt darauf an; **~ing on the result ...** abhängend vom Resultat ...; **~able** *a* zuverlässig; **~ant** *n* Angehörige(r) *mf*; **~ence** *n* Abhängigkeit *f*; **~ent** *a* abhängig (*on* von) // *n* = **~ant**.

depict [dɪ'pɪkt] *vt* schildern.

depleted [dɪ'pli:tɪd] *a* aufgebraucht.

deplorable [dɪ'plɔːrəbl] *a* bedauerlich.

deplore [dɪ'plɔː*] *vt* mißbilligen.

deploy [dɪ'plɔɪ] *vt* einsetzen.

depopulation ['di:pɒpjʊ'leɪʃən] *n* Entvölkerung *f*.

deport [dɪ'pɔːt] *vt* deportieren; **~ation** [diːpɔːˈteɪʃən] *n* Abschiebung *f*.

deportment [dɪ'pɔːtmənt] *n* Betragen *nt*.

depose [dɪ'pəʊz] *vt* absetzen.

deposit [dɪ'pɒzɪt] *n* (*in bank*) Guthaben *nt*; (*down payment*) Anzahlung *f*; (*security*) Kaution *f*; (*CHEM*) Niederschlag *m* // *vt* (*in bank*) deponieren; (*put down*) niederlegen; **~ account** *n* Sparkonto *nt*.

depot ['depəʊ] *n* Depot *nt*.

depraved [dɪ'preɪvd] *a* verkommen.

depreciate [dɪ'priːʃɪeɪt] *vi* im Wert sinken; **depreciation** [-'eɪʃən] *n* Wertminderung *f*.

depress [dɪ'pres] *vt* (*press down*) niederdrücken; (*in mood*) deprimieren; **~ed** *a* deprimiert; **~ing** *a* deprimierend; **~ion** [dɪ'preʃən] *n* (*mood*) Depression *f*; (*in trade*) Wirtschaftskrise *f*; (*hollow*) Vertiefung *f*; (*MET*) Tief (druckgebiet) *nt*.

deprivation [depri'veɪʃən] *n* Not *f*.

deprive [dɪ'praɪv] *vt*: **to ~ sb of sth** jdn etw (*gen*) berauben; **~d** *a* (*child*) sozial benachteiligt; (*area*) unterentwickelt.

depth [depθ] *n* Tiefe *f*; **in the ~s of** despair in tiefster Verzweiflung.

deputation [depju'teɪʃən] *n* Abordnung *f*.

deputize ['depjʊtaɪz] *vi* vertreten (*for acc*).

deputy ['depjʊtɪ] *a* stellvertretend // *n* (Stell)vertreter *m*.

derail [dɪ'reɪl] *vt*: **to be ~ed** entgleisen;

~ment *n* Entgleisung *f*.

deranged [dɪ'reɪndʒd] *a* verrückt.

derby ['dɑːbɪ] *n* (*US: bowler hat*) Melone *f*.

derelict ['derɪlɪkt] *a* verlassen.

deride [dɪ'raɪd] *vt* auslachen.

derisory [dɪ'raɪsərɪ] *a* spöttisch.

derivative [dɪ'rɪvətɪv] *n* Derivat *nt* // *a* abgeleitet.

derive [dɪ'raɪv] *vt* (*get*) gewinnen; (*deduce*) ableiten // *vi* (*come from*) abstammen.

dermatitis [dɜːmə'taɪtɪs] *n* Hautentzündung *f*.

derogatory [dɪ'rɒgətərɪ] *a* geringschätzig.

derrick ['derɪk] *n* Drehkran *m*.

derv [dɜːv] *n* (*Brit*) Dieselkraftstoff *m*.

descend [dɪ'send] *vti* hinuntersteigen; **to ~ from** abstammen von; **~ant** *n* Nachkomme *m*.

descent [dɪ'sent] *n* (*coming down*) Abstieg *m*; (*origin*) Abstammung *f*.

describe [dɪs'kraɪb] *vt* beschreiben.

description [dɪs'krɪpʃən] *n* Beschreibung *f*; (*sort*) Art *f*.

descriptive [dɪs'krɪptɪv] *a* beschreibend; (*word*) anschaulich.

desecrate ['desɪkreɪt] *vt* schänden.

desert ['dezət] *n* Wüste *f* // *v* [dɪ'zɜːt] *vt* verlassen; (*temporarily*) im Stich lassen // *vi* (*MIL*) desertieren; **~er** *n* Deserteur *m*; **~ion** [dɪ'zɜːʃən] *n* (*of wife*) Verlassen *nt*; (*MIL*) Fahnenflucht *f*; **~ island** *n* einsame Insel *f*; **~s** [dɪ'zɜːts] *pl*: **to get one's just ~s** seinen gerechten Lohn bekommen.

deserve [dɪ'zɜːv] *vt* verdienen.

deserving [dɪ'zɜːvɪŋ] *a* verdienstvoll.

design [dɪ'zaɪn] *n* (*plan*) Entwurf; (*planning*) Design *nt* // *vt* entwerfen.

designate ['dezɪgneɪt] *vt* bestimmen // *a* ['dezɪgnɪt] designiert.

designer [dɪ'zaɪnə*] *n* Designer(in *f*) *m*; (*TECH*) Konstrukteur(in *f*) *m*; (*fashion* ~) Modeschöpfer(in *f*) *m*.

desirable [dɪ'zaɪərəbl] *a* wünschenswert.

desire [dɪ'zaɪə*] *n* Wunsch *m*, Verlangen *nt* // *vt* (*lust*) begehren; (*ask for*) wollen.

desk [desk] *n* Schreibtisch *m*; (*Brit: in shop, restaurant*) Kasse *f*.

desolate ['desəlɪt] *a* öde; (*sad*) trostlos.

desolation [desə'leɪʃən] *n* Trostlosigkeit *f*.

despair [dɪs'peə*] *n* Verzweiflung *f* // *vi* verzweifeln (*of* an +*dat*).

despatch [dɪs'pætʃ] *n*, *vt* = **dispatch**.

desperate *a*, **~ly** *ad* ['despərɪt, -ɪtlɪ] verzweifelt.

desperation [despə'reɪʃən] *n* Verzweiflung *f*.

despicable [dɪs'pɪkəbl] *a* abscheulich.

despise [dɪs'paɪz] *vt* verachten.

despite [dɪs'paɪt] *prep* trotz (+*gen*).

despondent [dɪs'pɒndənt] *a* mutlos.

dessert [dɪˈzɜːt] n Nachtisch m; **~spoon** n Dessertlöffel m.
destination [destɪˈneɪʃən] n (of person) (Reise)ziel nt; (of goods) Bestimmungsort m.
destine [ˈdestɪn] vt (set apart) bestimmen.
destiny [ˈdestɪnɪ] n Schicksal nt.
destitute [ˈdestɪtjuːt] a notleidend.
destroy [dɪsˈtrɔɪ] vt zerstören; **~er** n (NAUT) Zerstörer m.
destruction [dɪsˈtrʌkʃən] n Zerstörung f.
destructive [dɪsˈtrʌktɪv] a zerstörend.
detach [dɪˈtætʃ] vt loslösen; **~able** a abtrennbar; **~ed** a (attitude) distanziert; (house) Einzel-; **~ment** n (MIL) Sonderkommando nt; (fig) Abstand m.
detail [ˈdiːteɪl] n Einzelheit f, Detail nt // vt (relate) ausführlich berichten; (appoint) abkommandieren; **in ~** im Detail; **~ed** a detailliert.
detain [dɪˈteɪn] vt aufhalten; (imprison) in Haft halten.
detect [dɪˈtekt] vt entdecken; **~ion** [dɪˈtekʃən] n Aufdeckung f; **~ive** n Detektiv m; **~ive story** n Kriminalgeschichte f) m; **~or** n Detektor m.
détente [ˈdeɪtɑːnt] n Entspannung f.
detention [dɪˈtenʃən] n Haft f; (SCH) Nachsitzen nt.
deter [dɪˈtɜː*] vt abschrecken.
detergent [dɪˈtɜːdʒənt] n Waschmittel nt.
deteriorate [dɪˈtɪərɪəreɪt] vi sich verschlechtern; **deterioration** [-ˈreɪʃən] n Verschlechterung f.
determination [dɪtɜːmɪˈneɪʃən] n Entschlossenheit f.
determine [dɪˈtɜːmɪn] vt bestimmen; **~d** a entschlossen.
deterrent [dɪˈterənt] n Abschreckungsmittel nt.
detest [dɪˈtest] vt verabscheuen.
detonate [ˈdetəneɪt] vt explodieren lassen // vi detonieren.
detour [ˈdiːtuə*] n Umweg m; (US AUT: diversion) Umleitung f // vt (US: traffic) umleiten.
detract [dɪˈtrækt] vi schmälern (from acc).
detriment [ˈdetrɪmənt] n: to the **~** of zum Schaden (+gen); **~al** [detrɪˈmentl] a schädlich.
devaluation [dɪvæljuˈeɪʃən] n Abwertung f.
devalue [ˈdiːˈvæljuː] vt abwerten.
devastate [ˈdevəsteɪt] vt verwüsten.
devastating [ˈdevəsteɪtɪŋ] a verheerend.
develop [dɪˈveləp] vt entwickeln; (resources) erschließen // vi sich entwickeln; **~ing country** n Entwick-

lungsland nt; **~ment** n Entwicklung f.
deviate [ˈdiːvɪeɪt] vi abweichen; **deviation** [-ˈeɪʃən] n Abweichung f.
device [dɪˈvaɪs] n Gerät nt.
devil [ˈdevl] n Teufel m; **~ish** a teuflisch.
devious [ˈdiːvɪəs] a (means) krumm; (person) verschlagen.
devise [dɪˈvaɪz] vt entwickeln.
devoid [dɪˈvɔɪd] a: **~ of** ohne.
devolution [diːvəˈluːʃən] n (POL) Dezentralisierung f.
devote [dɪˈvəʊt] vt widmen (to dat); **~d** a ergeben; **devotee** [devəʊˈtiː] n Anhänger(in f) m, Verehrer(in f) m.
devotion [dɪˈvəʊʃən] n (piety) Andacht f; (loyalty) Ergebenheit f, Hingabe f.
devour [dɪˈvaʊə*] vt verschlingen.
devout [dɪˈvaʊt] a andächtig.
dew [djuː] n Tau m.
dexterity [deksˈterɪtɪ] n Geschicklichkeit f.
DHSS n abbr (Brit) = Department of Health and Society Security.
diabetes [daɪəˈbiːtiːz] n Zuckerkrankheit f.
diabetic [daɪəˈbetɪk] a zuckerkrank; (food) Diabetiker- // n Diabetiker m.
diabolical [daɪəˈbɒlɪkl] a (col: weather, behaviour) saumäßig.
diagnose [ˈdaɪəgnəʊz] vt diagnostizieren.
diagnosis [daɪəgˈnəʊsɪs], pl **-ses** [-ˈnəʊsiːz] n Diagnose f.
diagonal [daɪˈægənl] a diagonal // n Diagonale f.
diagram [ˈdaɪəgræm] n Diagramm nt, Schaubild nt.
dial [ˈdaɪəl] n (TEL) Wählscheibe f; (of clock) Zifferblatt nt // vt wählen; **~ code** n (US) = **dialling code**; **~ tone** n (US) = **dialling tone**.
dialect [ˈdaɪəlekt] n Dialekt m.
dialling [ˈdaɪəlɪŋ]: **~ code** n Vorwahl f; **~ tone** n Amtszeichen nt.
dialogue [ˈdaɪəlɒg] n Dialog m.
diameter [daɪˈæmɪtə*] n Durchmesser m.
diamond [ˈdaɪəmənd] n Diamant m; **~s** pl (CARDS) Karo nt.
diaper [ˈdaɪəpə*] n (US) Windel f.
diaphragm [ˈdaɪəfræm] n Zwerchfell nt.
diarrhoea, (US) **diarrhea** [daɪəˈriːə] n Durchfall m.
diary [ˈdaɪərɪ] n Taschenkalender m; (account) Tagebuch nt.
dice [daɪs] n Würfel pl // vt in Würfel schneiden.
dichotomy [daɪˈkɒtəmɪ] n Kluft f.
dictate [dɪkˈteɪt] vt diktieren; **~s** [ˈdɪkteɪts] pl Gebote pl.
dictation [dɪkˈteɪʃən] n Diktat nt.
dictator [dɪkˈteɪtə*] n Diktator m.
dictatorship [dɪkˈteɪtəʃɪp] n Diktatur f.
diction [ˈdɪkʃən] n Ausdrucksweise f.

dictionary ['dɪkʃənrɪ] n Wörterbuch nt.
did [dɪd] pt of **do**.
didn't ['dɪdənt] = **did not**.
die [daɪ] vi sterben; **to be dying for sth/to do sth** etw unbedingt haben wollen/ darauf brennen, etw zu tun; **~ away** vi schwächer werden; **~ down** vi nachlassen; **~ out** vi aussterben.
diehard ['daɪhɑːd] n Dickkopf m; (POL) Reaktionär m.
diesel ['diːzəl]: **~ engine** n Dieselmotor m; **~ (oil)** n Diesel(kraftstoff) m.
diet ['daɪət] n Nahrung f; (special food) Diät f; (slimming) Abmagerungskur f // vi (also: **be on a ~**) eine Abmagerungskur machen.
differ ['dɪfə*] vi sich unterscheiden; (disagree) anderer Meinung sein; **~ence** n Unterschied m; **~ent** a anders; (two things) verschieden; **~ential** [dɪfə'renʃəl] n (in wages) Lohnstufe f; **~entiate** [dɪfə'renʃɪeɪt] vti unterscheiden; **~ently** ad anders; (from one another) unterschiedlich.
difficult ['dɪfɪkəlt] a schwierig; **~y** n Schwierigkeit f.
diffident ['dɪfɪdənt] a schüchtern.
diffuse [dɪ'fjuːs] a langatmig // vt [dɪ'fjuːz] vt verbreiten.
dig [dɪg] v (pt, pp **dug**) vt graben // n (prod) Stoß m; (remark) Spitze f; (archaeological) Ausgrabung f; **~ in** vi (MIL) sich eingraben; **~ into** vt (sb's past) wühlen in (+dat); (savings) angreifen; **~ up** vt ausgraben; (fig) aufgabeln.
digest [daɪ'dʒest] vt verdauen // n ['daɪdʒest] Auslese f; **~ion** n Verdauung f; **~ive** a (juices, system) Verdauungs-.
digit ['dɪdʒɪt] n Ziffer f; (ANAT) Finger m; **~al** a digital, Digital-.
dignified ['dɪgnɪfaɪd] a würdevoll.
dignity ['dɪgnɪtɪ] n Würde f.
digress [daɪ'gres] vi abschweifen.
digs [dɪgz] npl (Brit col) Bude f.
dilapidated [dɪ'læpɪdeɪtɪd] a baufällig.
dilate [daɪ'leɪt] vti (sich) weiten.
dilemma [daɪ'lemə] n Dilemma nt.
diligent ['dɪlɪdʒənt] a fleißig.
dilute [daɪ'luːt] vt verdünnen.
dim [dɪm] a trübe; (stupid) schwer von Begriff // vt verdunkeln; **to ~ one's headlights** (esp US) abblenden.
dime [daɪm] (US) Zehncentstück nt.
dimension [dɪ'menʃən] n Dimension f.
diminish [dɪ'mɪnɪʃ] vti verringern.
diminutive [dɪ'mɪnjʊtɪv] a winzig // n Verkleinerungsform f.
dimmer ['dɪmə*] n (US AUT) Abblendschalter m.
dimple ['dɪmpl] n Grübchen nt.
din [dɪn] n Getöse nt.
dine [daɪn] vi speisen; **~r** n Tischgast m; (RAIL) Speisewagen m.

dinghy ['dɪŋgɪ] n Dinghy nt; **rubber ~** Schlauchboot nt.
dingy ['dɪndʒɪ] a armselig.
dining car ['daɪnɪŋkɑː*] n (Brit) Speisewagen m.
dining room ['daɪnɪŋrʊm] n Eßzimmer nt; (in hotel) Speisezimmer nt.
dinner ['dɪnə*] n (lunch) Mittagessen nt; (evening) Abendessen nt; (public) Festessen nt; **~ jacket** n Smoking m; **~ party** n Tischgesellschaft f; **~ time** n Tischzeit f.
dinosaur ['daɪnəsɔː*] n Dinosaurier m.
dint [dɪnt] n: **by ~ of** durch.
diocese ['daɪəsɪs] n Diözese f.
dip [dɪp] n (hollow) Senkung f; (bathe) kurze(s) Bad(en) nt // vt eintauchen; (Brit AUT: lights) abblenden // vi (slope) sich senken, abfallen.
diploma [dɪ'pləʊmə] n Diplom nt.
diplomacy [dɪ'pləʊməsɪ] n Diplomatie f.
diplomat ['dɪpləmæt] n Diplomat(in f) m; **~ic** [dɪplə'mætɪk] a diplomatisch.
dipstick ['dɪpstɪk] n Ölmeßstab m.
dipswitch ['dɪpswɪtʃ] n (Brit AUT) Abblendschalter m.
dire [daɪə*] a schrecklich.
direct [daɪ'rekt] a direkt // vt leiten; (film) die Regie führen (+gen); (aim) richten; (order) anweisen; **can you ~ me to ...?** können Sie mir sagen, wie ich zu ... komme?
direction [dɪ'rekʃən] n Richtung f; (CINE) Regie f; Leitung f; **~s** (for use) Gebrauchsanleitung f; (orders) Anweisungen pl; **sense of ~** Orientierungssinn m.
directly [dɪ'rektlɪ] ad direkt; (at once) sofort.
director [dɪ'rektə*] n Direktor m; (of film) Regisseur m.
directory [dɪ'rektərɪ] n (TEL) Telefonbuch nt.
dirt [dɜːt] n Schmutz m, Dreck m; **~-cheap** a spottbillig; **~y** a schmutzig // vt beschmutzen; **~y trick** n gemeiner Trick.
disability [dɪsə'bɪlɪtɪ] n Körperbehinderung f.
disabled [dɪs'eɪbld] a körperbehindert.
disadvantage [dɪsəd'vɑːntɪdʒ] n Nachteil m.
disaffection [dɪsə'fekʃən] n Entfremdung f.
disagree [dɪsə'griː] vi nicht übereinstimmen; (quarrel) (sich) streiten; (food) nicht bekommen (with dat); **~able** a unangenehm; **~ment** n (between persons) Streit m; (between things) Widerspruch m.
disallow [dɪsə'laʊ] vt nicht zulassen.
disappear [dɪsə'pɪə*] vi verschwinden; **~ance** n Verschwinden nt.
disappoint [dɪsə'pɔɪnt] vt enttäuschen; **~ed** a enttäuscht; **~ing** a enttäu-

schend; ~**ment** n Enttäuschung f.
disapproval [dısə'pru:vəl] n Mißbilligung f.
disapprove [dısə'pru:v] vi mißbilligen (of acc).
disarm [dıs'a:m] vt entwaffnen; (POL) abrüsten; ~**ament** n Abrüstung f.
disarray ['dısə'reı] n: to be in ~ (army) in Auflösung (begriffen) sein; (clothes) in unordentlichem Zustand sein.
disaster [dı'za:stə*] n Katastrophe f.
disastrous [dı'za:strəs] a verhängnisvoll.
disband [dıs'bænd] vt auflösen // vi auseinandergehen.
disbelief ['dısbə'li:f] n Ungläubigkeit f.
disc [dısk] n Scheibe f; (record) (Schall)platte f; (COMPUT) = **disk**.
discard [dıs'ka:d] vt ablegen.
discern [dı'sз:n] vt erkennen; ~**ing** a scharfsinnig.
discharge [dıs'tʃa:dʒ] vt (ship) entladen; (duties) nachkommen (+dat); (dismiss) entlassen; (gun) abschießen; (JUR) freisprechen // n ['dıstʃa:dʒ] (of ship, ELEC) Entladung f; (dismissal) Entlassung f; (MED) Ausfluß m.
disciple [dı'saıpl] n Jünger m.
discipline ['dısıplın] n Disziplin f // vt (train) schulen; (punish) bestrafen.
disc jockey ['dıskdʒɒkı] n Diskjockey m.
disclaim [dıs'kleım] vt nicht anerkennen.
disclose [dıs'kləuz] vt enthüllen.
disclosure [dıs'kləuʒə*] n Enthüllung f.
disco ['dıskəu] n abbr of **discothèque**.
discoloured, (US) **discolored** [dıs'kʌləd] a verfärbt.
discomfort [dıs'kʌmfət] n Unbehagen nt.
disconcert [dıskən'sз:t] vt aus der Fassung bringen.
disconnect ['dıskə'nekt] vt abtrennen.
discontent ['dıskən'tent] n Unzufriedenheit f; ~**ed** a unzufrieden.
discontinue ['dıskən'tınju:] vt einstellen.
discord ['dısko:d] n Zwietracht f; (noise) Dissonanz f; ~**ant** [dıs'ko:dənt] a uneinig.
discothèque ['dıskəutek] n Diskothek f.
discount ['dıskaunt] n Rabatt m // vt [dıs'kaunt] außer acht lassen.
discourage [dıs'kʌrıdʒ] vt entmutigen; (prevent) abraten.
discouraging [dıs'kʌrıdʒıŋ] a entmutigend.
discourteous [dıs'kз:tıəs] a unhöflich.
discover [dıs'kʌvə*] vt entdecken; ~**y** n Entdeckung f.
discredit [dıs'kredıt] vt in Verruf bringen.
discreet a [dıs'kri:t] diskret.
discrepancy [dıs'krepənsı] n Dis-

krepanz f.
discriminate [dıs'krımıneıt] vi unterscheiden; to ~ **against** diskriminieren.
discriminating [dıs'krımıneıtıŋ] a anspruchsvoll.
discrimination [dıskrımı'neıʃən] n Urteilsvermögen nt; (pej) Diskriminierung f.
discuss [dıs'kʌs] vt diskutieren, besprechen; ~**ion** [dıs'kʌʃən] n Diskussion f, Besprechung f.
disdain [dıs'deın] vt verachten // n Verachtung f.
disease [dı'zi:z] n Krankheit f.
disembark [dısım'ba:k] vt aussteigen lassen // vi von Bord gehen.
disenchanted ['dısın'tʃa:ntıd] a desillusioniert.
disengage [dısın'geıdʒ] vt (AUT) auskuppeln.
disentangle ['dısın'tæŋgl] vt entwirren.
disfigure [dıs'fıgə*] vt entstellen.
disgrace [dıs'greıs] n Schande f // vt Schande bringen über (+acc); ~**ful** a unerhört.
disgruntled [dıs'grʌntld] a verärgert.
disguise [dıs'gaız] vt verkleiden; (feelings) verhehlen // n Verkleidung f; **in** ~ verkleidet, maskiert.
disgust [dıs'gʌst] n Abscheu f // vt anwidern; ~**ing** a widerlich.
dish [dıʃ] n Schüssel f; (food) Gericht nt; **to do** or **wash the ~es** abwaschen; ~ **up** vt auftischen; ~ **cloth** n Spüllappen m.
dishearten [dıs'ha:tn] vt entmutigen.
dishevelled [dı'ʃevəld] a (hair) zerzaust; (clothing) ungepflegt.
dishonest [dıs'ɒnıst] a unehrlich; ~**y** n Unehrlichkeit f.
dishonour, (US) **dishonor** [dıs'ɒnə*] n Unehre f; ~**able** a unehrenhaft.
dish towel n (US: tea towel) Geschirrtuch nt.
dishwasher ['dıʃwɒʃə*] n Geschirrspülmaschine f.
disillusion [dısı'lu:ʒən] vt enttäuschen, desillusionieren.
disincentive ['dısın'sentıv] n Entmutigung f.
disinfect [dısın'fekt] vt desinfizieren; ~**ant** n Desinfektionsmittel nt.
disintegrate [dıs'ıntıgreıt] vi sich auflösen.
disinterested [dıs'ıntrıstıd] a uneigennützig; (col) uninteressiert.
disjointed [dıs'dʒɒıntıd] a unzusammenhängend.
disk [dısk] n (COMPUT) Diskette f; **single-/double-sided** ~ einseitige/ beidseitige Diskette; ~ **drive** n Diskettenlaufwerk nt; ~**ette** n (US) = **disk**.
dislike [dıs'laık] n Abneigung f // vt nicht leiden können.

dislocate ['dɪsləʊkeɪt] vt auskugeln.
dislodge [dɪs'lɒdʒ] vt verschieben; (MIL) aus der Stellung werfen.
disloyal ['dɪs'lɔɪəl] a treulos.
dismal ['dɪzməl] a trostlos, trübe.
dismantle [dɪs'mæntl] vt demontieren.
dismay [dɪs'meɪ] n Bestürzung f // vt bestürzen.
dismiss [dɪs'mɪs] vt (employee) entlassen; (idea) von sich weisen; (send away) wegschicken; (JUR) abweisen; ~**al** n Entlassung f.
dismount [dɪs'maʊnt] vi absteigen.
disobedience [dɪsə'biːdɪəns] n Ungehorsam m.
disobedient [dɪsə'biːdɪənt] a ungehorsam.
disobey ['dɪsə'beɪ] vt nicht gehorchen (+dat).
disorder [dɪs'ɔːdə*] n (confusion) Verwirrung f; (commotion) Aufruhr m; (MED) Erkrankung f.
disorderly [dɪs'ɔːdəlɪ] a (untidy) unordentlich; (unruly) ordnungswidrig.
disorganized [dɪs'ɔːgənaɪzd] a unordentlich.
disown [dɪs'əʊn] vt (son) verstoßen.
disparaging [dɪs'pærɪdʒɪŋ] a geringschätzig.
disparity [dɪs'pærɪtɪ] n Verschiedenheit f.
dispassionate [dɪs'pæʃnɪt] a objektiv.
dispatch [dɪs'pætʃ] vt (goods) abschicken, abfertigen // n Absendung f; (esp MIL) Meldung f.
dispel [dɪs'pel] vt zerstreuen.
dispensary [dɪs'pensərɪ] n Apotheke f.
dispense [dɪs'pens]: ~ **with** vt verzichten auf (+acc); ~**r** n (container) Spender m.
dispensing [dɪs'pensɪŋ] a: ~ **chemist** (Brit) Apotheker m.
dispersal [dɪs'pɜːsəl] n Zerstreuung f.
disperse [dɪs'pɜːs] vt zerstreuen // vi sich verteilen.
dispirited [dɪs'pɪrɪtɪd] a niedergeschlagen.
displace [dɪs'pleɪs] vt verschieben; ~**d person** n Verschleppte(r) mf.
display [dɪs'pleɪ] n (of goods) Auslage f; (of feeling) Zurschaustellung f // vt zeigen; (ostentatiously) vorführen; (goods) ausstellen.
displease [dɪs'pliːz] vt mißfallen (+dat).
displeasure [dɪs'pleʒə*] n Mißfallen nt.
disposable [dɪs'pəʊzəbl] a Wegwerf-; ~ **nappy** n Papierwindel f.
disposal [dɪs'pəʊzəl] n (of property) Verkauf m; (throwing away) Beseitigung f; **to be at one's** ~ einem zur Verfügung stehen.
dispose [dɪs'pəʊz]: ~ **of** vt loswerden.
disposed [dɪs'pəʊzd] a geneigt.
disposition [dɪspə'zɪʃən] n Wesen nt.
disproportionate [dɪsprə'pɔːʃnɪt] a

unverhältnismäßig.
disprove [dɪs'pruːv] vt widerlegen.
dispute [dɪs'pjuːt] n Streit m; (also: **industrial** ~) Arbeitskampf m // vt bestreiten.
disqualify [dɪs'kwɒlɪfaɪ] vt disqualifizieren.
disquiet [dɪs'kwaɪət] n Unruhe f.
disregard [dɪsrɪ'gɑːd] vt nicht (be)achten.
disrepair ['dɪsrɪ'peə*] n: **to fall into** ~ verfallen.
disreputable [dɪs'repjʊtəbl] a verrufen.
disrespectful [dɪsrɪs'pektfʊl] a respektlos.
disrupt [dɪs'rʌpt] vt stören; (service) unterbrechen; ~**ion** [dɪs'rʌpʃən] n Störung f, Unterbrechung f.
dissatisfaction ['dɪssætɪs'fækʃən] n Unzufriedenheit f.
dissatisfied ['dɪs'sætɪsfaɪd] a unzufrieden.
dissect [dɪ'sekt] vt zerlegen, sezieren.
disseminate [dɪ'semɪneɪt] vt verbreiten.
dissent [dɪ'sent] n abweichende Meinung f.
dissertation [dɪsə'teɪʃən] n wissenschaftliche Arbeit f; (PhD) Doktorarbeit f.
disservice [dɪs'sɜːvɪs] n: **to do sb a** ~ jdm einen schlechten Dienst erweisen.
dissident ['dɪsɪdənt] a andersdenkend // n Dissident m.
dissimilar [dɪ'sɪmɪlə*] a unähnlich (to dat).
dissipate ['dɪsɪpeɪt] vt (waste) verschwenden; (scatter) zerstreuen.
dissociate [dɪ'səʊʃɪeɪt] vt trennen.
dissolute ['dɪsəluːt] a liederlich.
dissolution [dɪsə'luːʃən] n Auflösung f.
dissolve [dɪ'zɒlv] vt auflösen // vi sich auflösen.
dissuade [dɪ'sweɪd] vt: **to** ~ **sb from doing sth** jdn davon abbringen, etw zu tun.
distance ['dɪstəns] n Entfernung f; **in the** ~ in der Ferne.
distant ['dɪstənt] a entfernt, fern; (with time) fern; (formal) distanziert.
distaste [dɪs'teɪst] n Abneigung f; ~**ful** a widerlich.
distended [dɪs'tendɪd] a (stomach) aufgebläht.
distil [dɪs'tɪl] vt destillieren; ~**lery** n Brennerei f.
distinct [dɪs'tɪŋkt] a (separate) getrennt; (clear) klar, deutlich; **as** ~ **from** im Unterschied zu; ~**ion** [dɪs'tɪŋkʃən] n Unterscheidung f; (eminence) Auszeichnung f; ~**ive** a bezeichnend.
distinguish [dɪs'tɪŋgwɪʃ] vt unterscheiden; ~**ed** a (eminent) berühmt; ~**ing** a bezeichnend.
distort [dɪs'tɔːt] vt verdrehen; (mis-

represent) entstellen; **~ion** [dɪsˈtɔːʃən] *n* Verzerrung *f*.

distract [dɪsˈtrækt] *vt* ablenken; **~ing** *a* verwirrend; **~ion** [dɪsˈtrækʃən] *n* (*distress*) Raserei *f*; (*diversion*) Zerstreuung *f*.

distraught [dɪsˈtrɔːt] *a* bestürzt.

distress [dɪsˈtres] *n* Not *f*; (*suffering*) Qual *f* // *vt* quälen; **~ing** *a* erschütternd; **~ signal** *n* Notsignal *nt*.

distribute [dɪsˈtrɪbjuːt] *vt* verteilen.

distribution [dɪstrɪˈbjuːʃən] *n* Verteilung *f*.

distributor [dɪsˈtrɪbjutə*] *n* Verteiler *m*.

district [ˈdɪstrɪkt] *n* (*of country*) Kreis *m*; (*of town*) Bezirk *m*; **~ attorney** *n* (*US*) Oberstaatsanwalt *m*; **~ nurse** *n* (*Brit*) Kreiskrankenschwester *f*.

distrust [dɪsˈtrʌst] *n* Mißtrauen *nt* // *vt* mißtrauen (+*dat*).

disturb [dɪsˈtɜːb] *vt* stören; (*agitate*) erregen; **~ance** *n* Störung *f*; **~ed** *a* beunruhigt; **emotionally ~ed** emotional gestört; **~ing** *a* beunruhigend.

disuse [ˈdɪsˈjuːs] *n*: **to fall into ~** außer Gebrauch kommen.

disused [ˈdɪsˈjuːzd] *a* außer Gebrauch.

ditch [dɪtʃ] *n* Graben *m* // *vt* (*person*) loswerden; (*plan*) fallenlassen.

dither [ˈdɪðə*] *vi* verdattert sein.

ditto [ˈdɪtəʊ] *ad* dito, ebenfalls.

divan [dɪˈvæn] *n* Liegesofa *nt*.

dive [daɪv] *n* (*into water*) Kopfsprung *m*; (*AVIAT*) Sturzflug *m* // *vi* tauchen; **~r** *n* Taucher *m*.

diverge [daɪˈvɜːdʒ] *vi* auseinandergehen.

diverse [daɪˈvɜːs] *a* verschieden.

diversion [daɪˈvɜːʃən] *n* Ablenkung *f*; (*Brit AUT*) Umleitung *f*.

diversity [daɪˈvɜːsɪtɪ] *n* Vielfalt *f*.

divert [daɪˈvɜːt] *vt* ablenken; (*traffic*) umleiten.

divide [dɪˈvaɪd] *vt* teilen // *vi* sich teilen; **~d highway** *n* (*US*) Schnellstraße *f*.

dividend [ˈdɪvɪdend] *n* Dividende *f*.

divine [dɪˈvaɪn] *a* göttlich.

diving [ˈdaɪvɪŋ] *n* (*SPORT*) Turmspringen *nt*; (*underwater ~*) Tauchen *nt*; **~ board** *n* Sprungbrett *nt*.

divinity [dɪˈvɪnɪtɪ] *n* Gottheit *f*; (*subject*) Religion *f*.

division [dɪˈvɪʒən] *n* Teilung *f*; (*MIL*) Division *f*; (*part*) Abteilung *f*; (*in opinion*) Uneinigkeit *f*; (*Brit POL*) Abstimmung *f* durch Hammelsprung.

divorce [dɪˈvɔːs] *n* (Ehe)scheidung *f* // *vt* scheiden; **~d** *a* geschieden; **~e** [dɪvɔːˈsiː] *n* Geschiedene(r) *mf*.

divulge [daɪˈvʌldʒ] *vt* preisgeben.

D.I.Y. *n abbr* (*Brit*) *of* **do-it-yourself**.

dizzy [ˈdɪzɪ] *a* schwindlig.

DJ *n abbr of* **disc jockey**.

do [duː] *n* (*col: party etc*) Fete *f*
♦ *v* (*pt* **did**, *pp* **done**) *aux v* 1 (*in negative constructions and questions*): **I don't**

understand ich verstehe nicht; **didn't you know?** wußtest du das nicht?; **what ~ you think?** was meinen Sie?

2 (*for emphasis, in polite expressions*): **she does seem rather tired** sie scheint wirklich sehr müde zu sein; **~ sit down/help yourself** setzen Sie sich doch hin/greifen Sie doch zu

3 (*used to avoid repeating v*): **she swims better than I ~** sie schwimmt besser als ich; **she lives in Glasgow — so ~ I** sie wohnt in Glasgow — ich auch

4 (*in question tags*): **you like him, don't you?** du magst ihn doch, oder?

♦ *vt* 1 (*carry out, perform etc*) tun, machen; **what are you ~ing tonight?** was machst du heute abend?; **I've got nothing to ~** ich habe nichts zu tun; **to ~ one's hair/nails** sich die Haare/Nägel machen

2 (*AUT etc*) fahren

♦ *vi* 1 (*act, behave*): **~ as I ~** mach es wie ich

2 (*get on, fare*): **he's ~ing well/badly at school** er ist gut/schlecht in der Schule; **how ~ you ~?** guten Tag

3 (*be suitable*) gehen; (*be sufficient*) reichen; **to make ~ (with)** auskommen mit

do away with *vt* (*kill*) umbringen; (*abolish: law etc*) abschaffen

do up *vt* (*laces, dress, buttons*) zumachen; (*renovate: room, house*) renovieren

do with *vt* (*need*) brauchen; (*be connected*) zu tun haben mit

do without *vti* auskommen ohne.

docile [ˈdəʊsaɪl] *a* gefügig.

dock [dɒk] *n* Dock *nt*; (*JUR*) Anklagebank *f* // *vi* ins Dock gehen; **~s** *pl* Hafen *m*; **~er** *n* Hafenarbeiter *m*; **~yard** *n* Werft *f*.

doctor [ˈdɒktə*] *n* Arzt *m*, Arztin *f*; (*UNIV*) Doktor *m* // *vt* fälschen; (*drink etc*) etw beimischen (+*dat*); **D~ of Philosophy (Ph. D.)** *n* Doktor *m* der Philosophie (Dr. Phil.).

doctrine [ˈdɒktrɪn] *n* Doktrin *f*.

document [ˈdɒkjʊmənt] *n* Dokument *nt*; **~ary** [dɒkjuˈmentərɪ] *n* Dokumentarbericht *m*; (*film*) Dokumentarfilm *m* // *a* dokumentarisch; **~ation** [dɒkjumenˈteɪʃən] *n* dokumentarische(r) Nachweis *m*.

dodge [dɒdʒ] *n* Kniff *m* // *vt* ausweichen (+*dat*); **~ms** *npl* (*Brit*) Autoskooter *m*.

doe [dəʊ] *n* (*roe deer*) Ricke *f*; (*red deer*) Hirschkuh *f*; (*rabbit*) Weibchen *nt*.

does [dʌz] *v see* **do**; **~n't = ~ not**.

dog [dɒg] *n* Hund *m*; **~ collar** *n* Hundehalsband *m*; (*ECCL*) Kragen *m* des Geistlichen; **~-eared** *a* mit Eselsohren.

dogged [ˈdɒgɪd] *a* hartnäckig.

dogsbody [ˈdɒgzbɒdɪ] *n* Mädchen *nt* für

alles.

doings ['du:ɪŋz] *npl* (*activities*) Treiben *nt*.

do-it-yourself ['du:ɪtjə'self] *n* Do-it-yourself *nt*.

doldrums ['dɒldrəmz] *npl*: to be in the ~ (*business*) Flaute haben; (*person*) deprimiert sein.

dole [dəʊl] *n* (*Brit*) Stempelgeld *nt*; to be on the ~ stempeln gehen; ~ **out** *vt* ausgeben, austeilen.

doleful ['dəʊful] *a* traurig.

doll [dɒl] *n* Puppe *f* // *vt*: ~ o.s. up sich aufdonnern.

dollar ['dɒlə*] *n* Dollar *m*.

dolphin ['dɒlfɪn] *n* Delphin *m*.

domain [də'meɪn] *n* Domäne *f*.

dome [dəʊm] *n* Kuppel *f*.

domestic [də'mestɪk] *a* häuslich; (*within country*) Innen-, Binnen-; (*animal*) Haus-; ~**ated** *a* (*person*) häuslich; (*animal*) zahm.

dominant ['dɒmɪnənt] *a* vorherrschend.

dominate ['dɒmɪneɪt] *vt* beherrschen.

domineering [dɒmɪ'nɪərɪŋ] *a* herrisch.

dominion [də'mɪnɪən] *n* (*rule*) Regierungsgewalt *f*; (*land*) Staatsgebiet *nt* mit Selbstverwaltung.

domino ['dɒmɪnəʊ] *n*, *pl* ~**es** Dominostein *m*; ~**es** *n* (*game*) Domino(spiel) *nt*.

don [dɒn] *n* (*Brit*) akademische(r) Lehrer *m*.

donate [dəʊ'neɪt] *vt* (*blood, little money*) spenden; (*lot of money*) stiften.

donation [dəʊ'neɪʃən] *n* Spende *f*.

done [dʌn] *pp* of **do**.

donkey ['dɒŋkɪ] *n* Esel *m*.

donor ['dəʊnə*] *n* Spender *m*.

don't [dəʊnt] = **do not**.

doodle ['du:dl] *vi* kritzeln.

doom [du:m] *n* böse(s) Geschick *nt*; (*downfall*) Verderben *nt* // *vt*: to be ~ed zum Untergang verurteilt sein; ~**sday** *n* der Jüngste Tag.

door [dɔ:*] *n* Tür *f*; ~**bell** *n* Türklingel *f*; ~-**handle** *n* Türklinke *f*; ~**man** *n* Türsteher *m*; ~**mat** *n* Fußmatte *f*; ~**step** *n* Türstufe *f*; ~**way** *n* Türöffnung *f*.

dope [dəʊp] *n* (*drug*) Aufputschmittel *nt* // *vt* (*horse etc*) dopen.

dopey ['dəʊpɪ] *a* (*col*) bekloppt.

dormant ['dɔ:mənt] *a* latent.

dormitory ['dɔ:mɪtrɪ] *n* Schlafsaal *m*.

dormouse ['dɔ:maʊs], *pl* -**mice** [-maɪs] *n* Haselmaus *f*.

DOS [dɒs] *n abbr* (= disk operating system) DOS *nt*.

dosage ['dəʊsɪdʒ] *n* Dosierung *f*.

dose [dəʊs] *n* Dosis *f*.

doss house ['dɒs-] *n* (*Brit*) Bleibe *f*.

dot [dɒt] *n* Punkt *m*; ~**ted with** übersät mit; on the ~ pünktlich.

dote [dəʊt]: ~ **on** *vt* vernarrt sein in

(+acc).

dot-matrix printer [dɒt'meɪtrɪks-] *n* Matrixdrucker *m*.

double ['dʌbl] *a*, *ad* doppelt // *n* Doppelgänger *m* // *vt* verdoppeln // *vi* sich verdoppeln; on the ~, at the ~ (*Brit*) im Laufschritt; ~**s** *n* (*TENNIS*) Doppel *nt*; ~ **bass** *n* Kontrabaß *m*; ~ **bed** *n* Doppelbett *nt*; ~ **bend** *n* (*Brit*) S-Kurve *f*; ~-**breasted** *a* zweireihig; ~**cross** *vt* hintergehen; ~**decker** *n* Doppeldecker *m*; ~ **glazing** *n* (*Brit*) Doppelverglasung *f*; ~ **room** *n* Doppelzimmer *nt*.

doubly ['dʌblɪ] *ad* doppelt.

doubt [daʊt] *n* Zweifel *m* // *vt* bezweifeln; ~**ful** *a* zweifelhaft; ~**less** *ad* ohne Zweifel.

dough [dəʊ] *n* Teig *m*; ~**nut** *n* Berliner *m*.

douse [daʊz] *vt* (*drench*) mit Wasser begießen, durchtränken; (*extinguish*) ausmachen.

dove [dʌv] *n* Taube *f*; ~**tail** *vi* (*plans*) übereinstimmen.

dowdy ['daʊdɪ] *a* unmodern.

down [daʊn] *n* (*fluff*) Flaum *m*; (*hill*) Hügel *m* // *ad* unten; (*motion*) herunter; hinunter // *prep*: to go ~ the street die Straße hinuntergehen // *vt* niederschlagen; ~ with X! nieder mit X!; ~ under (*Brit col*) Australien *nt*; ~-**and-out** *n* Tramp *m*; ~-**at-heel** *a* schäbig; ~**cast** *a* niedergeschlagen; ~**fall** *n* Sturz *m*; ~**hearted** *a* niedergeschlagen; ~**hill** *ad* bergab; ~ **payment** *n* Anzahlung *f*; ~**pour** *n* Platzregen *m*; ~**right** *a* ausgesprochen; ~**stairs** *ad* unten; (*motion*) nach unten; ~**stream** *ad* flußabwärts; ~-**to-earth** *a* praktisch; ~**town** *ad* in die/der Innenstadt; ~**ward** *a*, *ad*, ~**wards** *ad* abwärts, nach unten.

dowry ['daʊrɪ] *n* Mitgift *f*.

doz. *abbr* (= dozen) Dtzd.

doze [dəʊz] *vi* dösen; ~ **off** *vi* einnicken.

dozen ['dʌzn] *n* Dutzend *nt*.

Dr. *abbr* of **doctor; drive**.

drab [dræb] *a* düster, eintönig.

draft [drɑ:ft] *n* Entwurf *m*; (*FIN*) Wechsel *m*; (*US MIL*) Einberufung *f* // *vt* skizzieren.

draftsman ['drɑ:ftsmən] *n* (*US*) = **draughtsman**.

drag [dræg] *vt* schleppen; (*river*) mit einem Schleppnetz absuchen // *vi* sich (dahin)schleppen // *n* (*bore*) etwas Blödes; in ~ als Tunte; ~ **on** *vi* sich in die Länge ziehen.

dragon ['drægən] *n* Drache *m*; ~**fly** *n* Libelle *f*.

drain [dreɪn] *n* (*lit*) Abfluß *m*; (*fig: burden*) Belastung *f* // *vt* ableiten; (*exhaust*) erschöpfen // *vi* (*of water*) abfließen; **~age** n Kanalisation f; **~ing board**, (US) **~board** n Ablaufbrett nt; **~pipe** n Abflußrohr nt.

drama ['drɑːmə] n Drama nt; **~tic** [drə'mætɪk] a dramatisch; **~tist** n Dramatiker m; **~tize** vt (events) dramatisieren; (adapt: for TV, cinema) bearbeiten.

drank [dræŋk] pt of **drink**.

drape [dreɪp] vt drapieren // npl: **~s** (US) Vorhänge pl; **~r** n (Brit) Tuchhändler m.

drastic ['dræstɪk] a drastisch.

draught, (US) **draft** [drɑːft] n Zug m; (NAUT) Tiefgang m; **~s** n (Brit) Damespiel nt; (beer): on **~** vom Faß; **~board** n (Brit) Zeichenbrett nt.

draughtsman ['drɑːftsmən] n technische(r) Zeichner m.

draw [drɔː], pt **drew**, pp **drawn** vt ziehen; (crowd) anlocken; (picture) zeichnen; (money) abheben; (water) schöpfen // vi (SPORT) unentschieden spielen // n (SPORT) Unentschieden nt; (lottery) Ziehung f; **~ near** vi näherrücken; **~ out** vi (train) ausfahren; (lengthen) sich hinziehen; **~ up** vi (stop) halten // vt (document) aufsetzen; **~back** n Nachteil m; **~bridge** n Zugbrücke f.

drawer [drɔː*] n Schublade f.

drawing ['drɔːɪŋ] n Zeichnung f; Zeichnen nt; **~ board** n Reißbrett nt; **~ pin** n (Brit) Reißzwecke f; **~ room** n Salon m.

drawl [drɔːl] n schleppende Sprechweise f.

drawn [drɔːn] pp of **draw**.

dread [dred] n Furcht f // vt fürchten; **~ful** a furchtbar.

dream [driːm] n Traum m // vti, pt, pp **dreamed** or **dreamt** [dremt] träumen (about von); **~er** n Träumer m; **~y** a verträumt.

dreary ['drɪərɪ] a trostlos, öde.

dredge [dredʒ] vt ausbaggern.

dregs [dregz] npl Bodensatz m; (fig) Abschaum m.

drench [drentʃ] vt durchnässen.

dress [dres] n Kleidung f; (garment) Kleid nt // vt anziehen; (MED) verbinden; to get **~ed** sich anziehen; **~ up** vi sich fein machen; **~ circle** n (Brit) erste(r) Rang m; **~er** n (furniture) Anrichte f; **~ing** n (MED) Verband m; (COOK) Soße f; **~ing gown** n (Brit) Morgenrock m; **~ing room** n (THEAT) Garderobe f; (SPORT) Umkleideraum m; **~ing table** n Toilettentisch m; **~maker** n Schneiderin f; **~making** n Schneidern nt; **~ rehearsal** n Generalprobe f; **~ shirt** n Frackhemd nt; **~y** a (col) schick.

dribble ['drɪbl] vi sabbern // vt (ball) dribbeln.

drew [druː] pt of **draw**.

dried [draɪd] a getrocknet; (fruit also) Dörr-; **~ milk** n Milchpulver nt.

drier ['draɪə*] n = **dryer**.

drift [drɪft] n Strömung f; (snow~) Schneewehe f; (fig) Richtung f // vi sich treiben lassen; **~wood** n Treibholz nt.

drill [drɪl] n Bohrer m; (MIL) Drill m // vt bohren; (MIL) ausbilden // vi bohren (for nach).

drink [drɪŋk] n Getränk nt; (spirits) Drink m // vti, pt **drank**, pp **drunk** trinken; **~er** n Trinker m; **~ing water** n Trinkwasser nt.

drip [drɪp] n Tropfen m // vi tropfen; **~-dry** a bügelfrei; **~ping** n Bratenfett nt.

drive [draɪv] n Fahrt f; (road) Einfahrt f; (campaign) Aktion f; (energy) Schwung m; (SPORT) Schlag m; (also: **disk ~**) Diskettenlaufwerk nt // v (pt **drove**, pp **driven** ['drɪvn]) vt (car) fahren; (animals) treiben; (power) antreiben; (force) treiben // vi fahren; to **~** sb mad jdn verrückt machen; **left-/right-hand ~** Links-/Rechtssteuerung f.

drivel ['drɪvl] n Faselei f.

driver ['draɪvə*] n Fahrer m; **~'s license** n (US) Führerschein m.

driveway ['draɪvweɪ] n Auffahrt f; (longer) Zufahrtsstraße f.

driving ['draɪvɪŋ] a (rain) stürmisch; **~ instructor** n Fahrlehrer m; **~ lesson** n Fahrstunde f; **~ licence** n (Brit) Führerschein m; **~ mirror** n Rückspiegel m; **~ school** n Fahrschule f; **~ test** n Fahrprüfung f.

drizzle ['drɪzl] n Nieselregen m // vi nieseln.

drone [drəʊn] n (sound) Brummen nt; (bee) Drohne f.

drool [druːl] vi sabbern.

droop [druːp] vi (schlaff) herabhängen.

drop [drɒp] n (of liquid) Tropfen m; (fall) Fall m // vt fallen lassen; (lower) senken; (abandon) fallenlassen // vi (fall) herunterfallen; **~s** pl (MED) Tropfen pl; **~ off** vi (sleep) einschlafen // vt (passenger) absetzen; **~ out** vi (withdraw) ausscheiden; **~-out** n Aussteiger m; **~per** n Pipette f; **~pings** npl Kot m.

drought [draʊt] n Dürre f.

drove [drəʊv] pt of **drive**.

drown [draʊn] vt ertränken; (sound) übertönen // vi ertrinken.

drowsy ['draʊzɪ] a schläfrig.

drudgery ['drʌdʒərɪ] n Plackerei f.

drug [drʌg] n (MED) Arznei f; (narcotic) Rauschgift nt // vt betäuben; **~ addict** n Rauschgiftsüchtige(r) mf; **~gist** n (US) Drogist(in) m(f); **~store** n (US) Drogerie f.

drum [drʌm] n Trommel f // vi trommeln; **~s** pl Schlagzeug nt; **~mer** n Trommler m.

drunk [drʌŋk] *pp of* **drink** // *a* betrunken // *n* (*also:* ~**ard**) Trinker(in *f*) *m*; ~**en** *a* betrunken.

dry [draɪ] *a* trocken // *vt* (ab)trocknen // *vi* trocknen; ~ **up** *vi* austrocknen // *vt* (*dishes*) abtrocknen; ~**-cleaning** *n* chemische Reinigung *f*; ~**er** *n* Trockner *m*; (*US: spin-drier*) (Wäsche)schleuder *f*; ~ **goods store** *n* (*US*) Kurzwarengeschäft *nt*; ~**ness** *n* Trockenheit *f*; ~ **rot** *n* Hausschwamm *m*.

dual ['djʊəl] *a* doppelt; ~ **carriageway** *n* (*Brit*) zweispurige Fahrbahn *f*; ~**control** *a* mit Doppelsteuerung; ~ **nationality** *n* doppelte Staatsangehörigkeit *f*; ~**-purpose** *a* Mehrzweck-.

dubbed [dʌbd] *a* (*film*) synchronisiert.

dubious ['dju:bɪəs] *a* zweifelhaft.

duchess [dʌtʃɪs] *n* Herzogin *f*.

duck [dʌk] *n* Ente *f* // *vi* sich ducken; ~**ling** *n* Entchen *nt*.

duct [dʌkt] *n* Röhre *f*.

dud [dʌd] *n* Niete *f* // *a* (*cheque*) ungedeckt.

due [dju:] *a* fällig; (*fitting*) angemessen // *n* Gebühr *f*; (*right*) Recht *nt* // *ad* (*south etc*) genau; ~**s** *pl* (*for club, union*) Beitrag *m*; (*in harbour*) Gebühren *pl*; ~ **to** wegen (+*gen*).

duel ['djʊəl] *n* Duell *nt*.

duet [dju:'et] *n* Duett *nt*.

duffel [dʌfl] *a*: ~ **bag** *n* Matchbeutel *m*, Matchsack *m*; ~ **coat** *n* Dufflecoat *m*.

dug [dʌg] *pt, pp of* **dig**.

duke [dju:k] *n* Herzog *m*.

dull [dʌl] *a* (*colour, weather*) trübe; (*stupid*) schwer von Begriff; (*boring*) langweilig // *vt* abstumpfen.

duly ['dju:lɪ] *ad* ordnungsgemäß.

dumb [dʌm] *a* (*lit*) stumm; (*col: stupid*) doof, blöde; ~**founded** [dʌm'faʊndɪd] *a* verblüfft.

dummy ['dʌmɪ] *n* Schneiderpuppe *f*; (*substitute*) Attrappe *f*; (*Brit: for baby*) Schnuller *m* // *a* Schein-.

dump [dʌmp] *n* Abfallhaufen *m*; (*MIL*) Stapelplatz *m*; (*col: place*) Nest *nt* // *vt* abladen, auskippen; ~**ing** *n* (*COMM*) Schleuderexport *m*; (*of rubbish*) Schuttabladen *nt*.

dumpling ['dʌmplɪŋ] *n* Kloß *m*, Knödel *m*.

dumpy ['dʌmpɪ] *a* pummelig.

dunce [dʌns] *n* Dummkopf *m*.

dune [dju:n] *n* Düne *f*.

dung [dʌŋ] *n* Dünger *m*.

dungarees [dʌŋgə'ri:z] *npl* Latzhose *f*.

dungeon ['dʌndʒən] *n* Kerker *m*.

dupe [dju:p] *n* Gefoppte(r) *m* // *vt* hintergehen, anführen.

duplex ['dju:pleks] *n* (*US*) zweistöckige Wohnung *f*.

duplicate ['dju:plɪkɪt] *n* Duplikat *nt* // *vt* ['dju:plɪkeɪt] verdoppeln; (*make copies*) kopieren; **in** ~ in doppelter Ausführung.

duplicity [dju:'plɪsɪtɪ] *n* Doppelspiel *nt*.

durable ['djʊərəbl] *a* haltbar.

duration [djʊə'reɪʃən] *n* Dauer *f*.

duress [djʊə'res] *n*: **under** ~ unter Zwang.

during ['djʊərɪŋ] *prep* während (+*gen*).

dusk [dʌsk] *n* Abenddämmerung *f*.

dust [dʌst] *n* Staub *m* // *vt* abstauben; (*sprinkle*) bestäuben; ~**bin** *n* (*Brit*) Mülleimer *m*; ~**er** *n* Staubtuch *nt*; ~ **jacket** *n* Schutzumschlag *m*; ~**man** *n* (*Brit*) Müllmann *m*; ~**y** *a* staubig.

Dutch [dʌtʃ] *a* holländisch, niederländisch // *n* (*LING*) Holländisch *nt*, Niederländisch *nt*; **the** ~ *pl* die Holländer, die Niederländer; **to go** ~ getrennte Kasse machen; ~**man/woman** *n* Holländer *m*, Niederländer *m*/ Holländerin *f*, Niederländerin *f*.

dutiful ['dju:tɪfʊl] *a* pflichtbewußt.

duty ['dju:tɪ] *n* Pflicht *f*; (*job*) Aufgabe *f*; (*tax*) Einfuhrzoll *m*; **on** ~ im Dienst; ~**-free** *a* zollfrei.

duvet ['du:veɪ] *n* (*Brit*) Daunendecke *nt*.

dwarf [dwɔ:f], *pl* **dwarves** [dwɔ:vz] *n* Zwerg *m* // *vt* überragen.

dwell [dwel], *pt, pp* **dwelt** [dwelt] *vi* wohnen; ~ **on** *vt* verweilen bei; ~**ing** *n* Wohnung *f*.

dwindle ['dwɪndl] *vi* schwinden.

dye [daɪ] *n* Farbstoff *m* // *vt* färben.

dying ['daɪɪŋ] *a* (*person*) sterbend; (*moments*) letzt.

dyke [daɪk] *n* (*Brit: channel*) Kanal *m*; (: *barrier*) Deich *m*, Damm *m*.

dynamic [daɪ'næmɪk] *a* dynamisch.

dynamite ['daɪnəmaɪt] *n* Dynamit *nt*.

dynamo ['daɪnəməʊ] *n* Dynamo *m*.

E

E [i:] *n* (*MUS*) E *nt*.

each [i:tʃ] *a* jeder/jede/jedes // *pron* (ein) jeder/(eine) jede/(ein) jedes; ~ **other** einander, sich.

eager *a* ['i:gə*] eifrig.

eagle ['i:gl] *n* Adler *m*.

ear [ɪə*] *n* Ohr *nt*; (*of corn*) Ähre *f*; ~**ache** *n* Ohrenschmerzen *pl*; ~**drum** *n* Trommelfell *nt*.

earl [ɜ:l] *n* Graf *m*.

early ['ɜ:lɪ] *a, ad* früh; ~ **retirement** *n* vorzeitige Pensionierung.

earmark ['ɪəmɑ:k] *vt* vorsehen.

earn [ɜ:n] *vt* verdienen.

earnest ['ɜ:nɪst] *a* ernst; **in** ~ *ad* im Ernst.

earnings ['ɜ:nɪŋz] *npl* Verdienst *m*.

earphones ['ɪəfəʊnz] *npl* Kopfhörer *pl*.

earring ['ɪərɪŋ] *n* Ohrring *m*.

earshot ['ɪəʃɒt] *n* Hörweite *f*.

earth [ɜ:θ] *n* Erde *f*; (*Brit ELEC*) Erdung *f* // *vt* erden; ~**enware** *n* Steingut nt; **~quake** n Erdbeben nt.

earthy ['ɜ:θɪ] a roh; (sensual) sinnlich.

earwig ['ɪəwɪg] n Ohrwurm m.

ease [i:z] n (simplicity) Leichtigkeit f; (social) Ungezwungenheit f // vt (pain) lindern; (burden) erleichtern; **at ~** ungezwungen; (MIL) rührt euch!; **~ off** or **up** vi nachlassen.

easel ['i:zl] n Staffelei f.

easily ['i:zɪlɪ] ad leicht.

east [i:st] n Osten m // a östlich // ad nach Osten.

Easter ['i:stə*] n Ostern nt; **~ egg** n Osterei nt.

easterly ['i:stəlɪ] a östlich, Ost-.

eastern ['i:stən] a östlich.

East Germany n die DDR.

eastward(s) ['i:stwəd(z)] ad ostwärts.

easy ['i:zɪ] a (task) einfach; (life) bequem; (manner) ungezwungen, natürlich // ad leicht; **~ chair** n Sessel m; **~-going** a gelassen; (lax) lässig.

eat [i:t], pt **ate**, pp **eaten** ['i:tn] vt essen; (animals) fressen; (destroy) (zer)fressen; **~ into**, **~ away** vt zerfressen.

eau de Cologne [əʊdəkə'ləʊn] n Kölnisch Wasser nt.

eaves [i:vz] npl Dachrand m.

eavesdrop ['i:vzdrɒp] vi lauschen; **to ~ on sb** jdn belauschen.

ebb [eb] n Ebbe f // vi (fig: also: **~ away**) (ab)ebben; **~ tide** n Ebbe f.

ebony ['ebənɪ] n Ebenholz nt.

ebullient [ɪ'bʌlɪənt] a sprudelnd, temperamentvoll.

eccentric [ɪk'sentrɪk] a exzentrisch // n Exzentriker(in f) m.

ecclesiastical [ɪkliːzɪ'æstɪkəl] a kirchlich.

echo ['ekəʊ], pl **~es** n Echo nt // vt zurückwerfen; (fig) nachbeten // vi widerhallen.

eclipse [ɪ'klɪps] n Finsternis f // vt verfinstern.

ecology [ɪ'kɒlədʒɪ] n Ökologie f.

economic [i:kə'nɒmɪk] a wirtschaftlich; **~al** a wirtschaftlich; (person) sparsam; **~s** n Volkswirtschaft f.

economist [ɪ'kɒnəmɪst] n Volkswirt(schaftler) m.

economize [ɪ'kɒnəmaɪz] vi sparen.

economy [ɪ'kɒnəmɪ] n (thrift) Sparsamkeit f; (of country) Wirtschaft f.

ecstasy ['ekstəsɪ] n Ekstase f.

ecstatic [eks'tætɪk] a hingerissen.

ecumenical [i:kjʊ'menɪkəl] a ökumenisch.

eczema ['eksɪmə] n Ekzem nt.

edge [edʒ] n Rand m; (of knife) Schneide f // vt (SEWING) einfassen; **on ~** (fig) = edgy; **to ~ away from** langsam abrücken von; **~ways** ad: **he couldn't get a word in ~ways** er kam überhaupt nicht zu Wort.

edgy ['edʒɪ] a nervös.

edible ['edɪbl] a eßbar.

edict ['i:dɪkt] n Erlaß m.

edifice ['edɪfɪs] n Gebäude nt.

edit ['edɪt] vt redigieren; **~ion** [ɪ'dɪʃən] n Ausgabe f; **~or** n (of newspaper) Redakteur m; (of book) Lektor m; **~orial** [edɪ'tɔ:rɪəl] a Redaktions- // n Leitartikel m.

educate ['edjʊkeɪt] vt erziehen, (aus)bilden.

education [edjʊ'keɪʃən] n (teaching) Unterricht m; (system) Schulwesen nt; (schooling) Erziehung f; Bildung f; **~al** a pädagogisch.

EEC n abbr (= European Economic Community) EG f.

eel [i:l] n Aal m.

eerie ['ɪərɪ] a unheimlich.

effect [ɪ'fekt] n Wirkung f // vt bewirken; **~s** pl (sound, visual) Effekte pl; **in ~** in der Tat; **to take ~** (law) in Kraft treten; (drug) wirken; **~ive** a, **~ly** ad wirksam, effektiv.

effeminate [ɪ'femɪnɪt] a weibisch.

effervescent [efə'vesnt] a (lit, fig) sprudelnd.

efficacy ['efɪkəsɪ] n Wirksamkeit f.

efficiency [ɪ'fɪʃənsɪ] n Leistungsfähigkeit f.

efficient [ɪ'fɪʃənt] a tüchtig; (TECH) leistungsfähig; (method) wirksam.

effigy ['efɪdʒɪ] n Abbild nt.

effort ['efət] n Anstrengung f; **~less** a mühelos.

effrontery [ɪ'frʌntərɪ] n Unverfrorenheit f.

effusive [ɪ'fju:sɪv] a überschwenglich.

e.g. ad abbr (= exempli gratia) z.B.

egalitarian [ɪgælɪ'tɛərɪən] a Gleichheits-, egalitär.

egg [eg] n Ei nt; **~ on** vt anstacheln; **~cup** n Eierbecher m; **~plant** n (esp US) Aubergine f; **~shell** n Eierschale f.

ego ['i:gəʊ] n Ich nt, Selbst nt.

egotism ['egəʊtɪzəm] n Ichbezogenheit f.

egotist ['egəʊtɪst] n Egozentriker m.

Egypt ['i:dʒɪpt] n Ägypten nt; **~ian** [ɪ'dʒɪpʃən] a ägyptisch // n Ägypter(in f) m.

eiderdown ['aɪdədaʊn] n Daunendecke f.

eight [eɪt] num acht; **~een** num achtzehn; **eighth** [eɪtθ] a achte(r, s) // n Achtel nt; **~y** num achtzig.

Eire ['ɛərə] n Irland nt.

either ['aɪðə*] cj: **~ ... or** entweder ... oder // pron: **~ of the two** eine(r, s) von beiden; **I don't want ~** ich will keins von beiden // a: **on ~ side** auf beiden Seiten // ad: **I don't ~** ich auch nicht.

eject [ɪ'dʒekt] vt ausstoßen, vertreiben.

eke [i:k]: **~ out** vt strecken.

elaborate [ɪ'læbərɪt] a sorgfältig aus-

gearbeitet, ausführlich // v [ɪ'læbəreɪt] vt
sorgfältig ausarbeiten // vi ausführlich
darstellen; ~**ly** ad genau, ausführlich.

elapse [ɪ'læps] vi vergehen.

elastic [ɪ'læstɪk] n Gummiband nt // a
elastisch; ~ **band** n (Brit) Gummiband
nt.

elated [ɪ'leɪtɪd] a froh.

elation [ɪ'leɪʃən] n gehobene Stimmung
f.

elbow ['elbəʊ] n Ellbogen m.

elder ['eldə*] a älter // n Ältere(r) mf;
~**ly** a ältere(r, s) // n: the ~**ly** die
Älteren.

eldest ['eldɪst] a älteste(r, s) // n Älte-
ste(r) mf.

elect [ɪ'lekt] vt wählen // a zukünftig;
~**ion** n Wahl f; ~**ioneering**
[ɪlekʃə'nɪərɪŋ] n Wahlpropaganda f;
~**or** n Wähler m; ~**oral** a Wahl-;
~**orate** n Wähler pl, Wählerschaft f.

electric [ɪ'lektrɪk] a elektrisch, Elektro-;
~**al** a elektrisch; ~ **blanket** n
Heizdecke f; ~ **chair** n elektrische(r)
Stuhl m; ~ **fire** n elektrische(r)
Heizofen m.

electrician [ɪlek'trɪʃən] n Elektriker m.

electricity [ɪlek'trɪsɪtɪ] n Elektrizität f.

electrify [ɪ'lektrɪfaɪ] vt elektrifizieren;
(fig) elektrisieren.

electrocute [ɪ'lektrəkjuːt] vt durch
elektrischen Strom töten.

electronic [ɪlek'trɒnɪk] a elektronisch,
Elektronen-; ~ **mail** n elektronische(r)
Briefkasten m; ~**s** n Elektronik f.

elegance ['elɪgəns] n Eleganz f.

elegant ['elɪgənt] a elegant.

element ['elɪmənt] n Element nt; ~**ary**
[elɪ'mentərɪ] a einfach; (primary)
Grund-.

elephant ['elɪfənt] n Elefant m.

elevate ['elɪveɪt] vt emporheben.

elevation [elɪ'veɪʃən] n (height) Erhebung f; (ARCHIT) (Quer)schnitt m.

elevator ['elɪveɪtə*] n (US) Fahrstuhl
m, Aufzug m.

eleven [ɪ'levn] num elf; ~**ses** npl (Brit)
zweite(s) Frühstück nt; ~**th** a elfte(r,
s).

elf [elf], pl **elves** [elvz] n Elfe f.

elicit [ɪ'lɪsɪt] vt herausbekommen.

eligible ['elɪdʒəbl] a wählbar; to be ~
for a pension pensionsberechtigt sein.

eliminate [ɪ'lɪmɪneɪt] vt ausschalten.

elimination [ɪlɪmɪ'neɪʃən] n Ausschal-
tung f.

elite [eɪ'liːt] n Elite f.

elm [elm] n Ulme f.

elocution [elə'kjuːʃən] n Sprecherzie-
hung f.

elongated ['iːlɒŋgeɪtɪd] a verlängert.

elope [ɪ'ləʊp] vi entlaufen; ~**ment** n
Entlaufen nt.

eloquence ['eləkwəns] n Beredsamkeit
f.

eloquent ['eləkwənt] a redegewandt.

else [els] ad sonst; who ~? wer sonst?;
sb ~ jd anders; or ~ sonst; ~**where** ad
anderswo, woanders.

elucidate [ɪ'luːsɪdeɪt] vt erläutern.

elude [ɪ'luːd] vt entgehen (+dat).

elusive [ɪ'luːsɪv] a schwer faßbar.

elves [elvz] npl of **elf**.

emaciated [ɪ'meɪsɪeɪtɪd] a abgezehrt.

emanate ['emaneɪt] vi ausströmen
(from aus).

emancipate [ɪ'mænsɪpeɪt] vt
emanzipieren; (slave) freilassen.

emancipation [ɪmænsɪ'peɪʃən] n
Emanzipation f; Freilassung f.

embankment [ɪm'bæŋkmənt] n (of
river) Uferböschung f; (of road)
Straßendamm m.

embargo [ɪm'bɑːgəʊ], pl ~**es** n
Embargo nt.

embark [ɪm'bɑːk] vi sich einschiffen; ~
on vt unternehmen; ~**ation**
[embɑː'keɪʃən] n Einschiffung f.

embarrass [ɪm'bærəs] vt in Verlegenheit
bringen; ~**ed** a verlegen; ~**ing** a peinlich; ~**ment** n Verlegenheit f.

embassy ['embəsɪ] n Botschaft f.

embed [ɪm'bed] vt einbetten.

embellish [ɪm'belɪʃ] vt verschönern.

embers ['embəz] npl Glut(asche) f.

embezzle [ɪm'bezl] vt unterschlagen;
~**ment** n Unterschlagung f.

embitter [ɪm'bɪtə*] vt verbittern.

embody [ɪm'bɒdɪ] vt (ideas) verkörpern; (new features) (in sich) vereinigen.

embossed [ɪm'bɒst] a geprägt.

embrace [ɪm'breɪs] vt umarmen;
(include) einschließen // vi sich umarmen // n Umarmung f.

embroider [ɪm'brɔɪdə*] vt (be)sticken;
(story) ausschmücken; ~**y** n Stickerei f.

emerald ['emərəld] n Smaragd m.

emerge [ɪ'mɜːdʒ] vi auftauchen; (truth)
herauskommen.

emergence [ɪ'mɜːdʒəns] n Erscheinen
nt.

emergency [ɪ'mɜːdʒənsɪ] n Notfall m;
~ **cord** n (US) Notbremse f; ~ **exit** n
Notausgang m; ~ **landing** n Notlandung
f; the ~ **services** npl die Notdienste pl.

emery board ['emərɪ-] n
Papiernagelfeile f.

emetic [ɪ'metɪk] n Brechmittel nt.

emigrant ['emɪgrənt] n Auswanderer m.

emigrate ['emɪgreɪt] vi auswandern.

emigration [emɪ'greɪʃən] n Auswande-
rung f.

eminence ['emɪnəns] n hohe(r) Rang
m.

eminent ['emɪnənt] a bedeutend.

emission [ɪ'mɪʃən] n Ausströmen nt.

emit [ɪ'mɪt] vt von sich (dat) geben.

emotion [ɪ'məʊʃən] n Emotion f, Gefühl
nt; ~**al** a (person) emotional; (scene)

ergreifend.

emotive [ɪ'məʊtɪv] a gefühlsbetont.

emperor ['empərə*] n Kaiser m.

emphasis ['emfəsɪs], pl **-ses** [-siːz] n (LING) Betonung f; (fig) Nachdruck m.

emphasize ['emfəsaɪz] vt betonen.

emphatic a, **~ally** ad [ɪm'fætɪk, -əlɪ] nachdrücklich.

empire ['empaɪə*] n Reich nt.

empirical [em'pɪrɪkəl] a empirisch.

employ [ɪm'plɔɪ] vt (hire) anstellen; (use) verwenden; **~ee** [emplɔɪ'iː] n Angestellte(r) mf; **~er** n Arbeitgeber(in f) m; **~ment** n Beschäftigung f; **~ment agency** n Stellenvermittlung f.

empower [ɪm'paʊə*] vt: to **~** sb to do sth jdn ermächtigen, etw zu tun.

empress ['emprɪs] n Kaiserin f.

emptiness ['emptɪnɪs] n Leere f.

empty ['emptɪ] a leer // n (bottle) Leergut nt // vt (contents) leeren; (container) ausleeren // vi (water) abfließen; (river) münden; (house) sich leeren; **~-handed** a mit leeren Händen.

emulate ['emjʊleɪt] vt nacheifern (+dat).

emulsion [ɪ'mʌlʃən] n Emulsion f.

enable [ɪ'neɪbl] vt: to **~** sb to do sth es jdm ermöglichen, etw zu tun.

enamel [ɪ'næməl] n Email nt; (of teeth) (Zahn)schmelz m.

enact [ɪn'ækt] vt (law) erlassen; (play) aufführen; (role) spielen.

encased [ɪn'keɪst] a: **~** in (enclosed) eingeschlossen in (+dat); (covered) verkleidet mit.

enchant [ɪn'tʃɑːnt] vt bezaubern; **~ing** a entzückend.

encircle [ɪn'sɜːkl] vt umringen.

encl. abbr (= enclosed) Anl.

enclose [ɪn'kləʊz] vt einschließen; (in letter) beilegen (in, with dat); **~d** (in letter) beiliegend, anbei.

enclosure [ɪn'kləʊʒə*] n Einfriedung f; (in letter) Anlage f.

encompass [ɪn'kʌmpəs] vt (include) umfassen.

encore ['ɒŋkɔː*] n Zugabe f.

encounter [ɪn'kaʊntə*] n Begegnung f; (MIL) Zusammenstoß m // vt treffen; (resistance) stoßen auf (+acc).

encourage [ɪn'kʌrɪdʒ] vt ermutigen; **~ment** n Ermutigung f, Förderung f.

encouraging [ɪn'kʌrɪdʒɪŋ] a ermutigend, vielversprechend.

encroach [ɪn'krəʊtʃ] vi: to **~** (up)on eindringen in (+acc); (time) in Anspruch nehmen.

encrusted [ɪn'krʌstɪd] a: **~** with besetzt mit.

encumber [ɪn'kʌmbə*] vt: to be **~ed** with (parcels) beladen sein mit; (debts) belastet sein mit.

encyclop(a)edia [ensaɪkləʊ'piːdɪə] n Konversationslexikon nt.

end [end] n Ende nt, Schluß m; (purpose) Zweck m // vt (also: **bring to an ~**, **put an ~ to**) beenden // vi zu Ende gehen; **in the ~** zum Schluß; (object) hochkant; **to stand on ~** (hair) zu Berge stehen; **for hours on ~** stundenlang; **~ up** vi landen.

endanger [ɪn'deɪndʒə*] vt gefährden.

endearing [ɪn'dɪərɪŋ] a gewinnend.

endeavour, (US) **endeavor** [ɪn'devə*] n Bestrebung f // vi sich bemühen.

ending ['endɪŋ] n Ende nt.

endless ['endlɪs] a endlos.

endorse [ɪn'dɔːs] vt unterzeichnen; (approve) unterstützen; **~ment** n (on licence) Eintrag m.

endow [ɪn'daʊ] vt: **~** sb with sth jdm etw verleihen; (with money) jdm etw stiften.

endurance [ɪn'djʊərəns] n Ausdauer f.

endure [ɪn'djʊə*] vt ertragen // vi (last) (fort)dauern.

enemy ['enɪmɪ] n Feind m // a feindlich.

energetic [enə'dʒetɪk] a tatkräftig.

energy ['enədʒɪ] n Energie f.

enforce [ɪn'fɔːs] vt durchsetzen.

engage [ɪn'geɪdʒ] vt (employ) einstellen; (in conversation) verwickeln; (TECH) einschalten // vi (TECH) ineinandergreifen; (clutch) fassen; **to ~ in** sich beteiligen an (+dat); **~d** a verlobt; (Brit: TEL, toil) besetzt; (: busy) beschäftigt; **to get ~d** sich verloben; **~d tone** n (Brit TEL) Besetztzeichen nt; **~ment** n (appointment) Verabredung f; (to marry) Verlobung f; (MIL) Gefecht nt; **~ment ring** n Verlobungsring m.

engaging [ɪn'geɪdʒɪŋ] a gewinnend.

engender [ɪn'dʒendə*] vt hervorrufen.

engine ['endʒɪn] n (AUT) Motor m; (RAIL) Lokomotive f; **~ driver** n Lokführer(in f) m.

engineer [endʒɪ'nɪə*] n Ingenieur m; (US RAIL) Lokomotivführer m.

engineering [endʒɪ'nɪərɪŋ] n Technik f.

England ['ɪŋglənd] n England nt.

English ['ɪŋglɪʃ] a englisch // n (LING) Englisch nt; **the ~** pl die Engländer; **the ~ Channel** n der Ärmelkanal m; **~man/woman** n Engländer m/ Engländerin f.

engraving [ɪn'greɪvɪŋ] n Stich m.

engrossed [ɪn'grəʊst] a vertieft.

engulf [ɪn'gʌlf] vt verschlingen.

enhance [ɪn'hɑːns] vt steigern, heben.

enigma [ɪ'nɪgmə] n Rätsel nt; **~tic** [enɪg'mætɪk] a rätselhaft.

enjoy [ɪn'dʒɔɪ] vt genießen; (privilege) besitzen; **to ~ o.s.** sich amüsieren; **~able** a erfreulich; **~ment** n Genuß m, Freude f.

enlarge [ɪn'lɑːdʒ] vt erweitern; (PHOT) vergrößern // vi: to **~** on sth etw weiter ausführen; **~ment** n Vergrößerung f.

enlighten [ɪn'laɪtn] vt aufklären; **the**

E~ment n (HIST) die Aufklärung.
enlist [ɪn'lɪst] vt gewinnen // vi (MIL) sich melden.
enmity ['enmɪtɪ] n Feindschaft f.
enormity [ɪ'nɔːmɪtɪ] n Ungeheuerlichkeit f.
enormous [ɪ'nɔːməs] a ungeheuer.
enough [ɪ'nʌf] a, ad genug; **funnily ~** komischerweise.
enquire [ɪn'kwaɪə*] vti = **inquire**.
enrage [ɪn'reɪdʒ] vt wütend machen.
enrich [ɪn'rɪtʃ] vt bereichern.
enrol [ɪn'rəʊl] vt einschreiben // vi (register) sich anmelden; **~ment** n (for course) Anmeldung f.
en route [ãːn'ruːt] ad unterwegs.
ensign ['ensaɪn] n (NAUT) Flagge f; (MIL) Fähnrich m.
enslave [ɪn'sleɪv] vt versklaven.
ensue [ɪn'sjuː] vi folgen, sich ergeben.
ensure [ɪn'ʃʊə*] vt garantieren.
entail [ɪn'teɪl] vt mit sich bringen.
entangle [ɪn'tæŋgl] vt verwirren, verstricken.
enter ['entə*] vt eintreten in (+dat), betreten; (club) beitreten (+dat); (in book) eintragen // vi hereinkommen, hineingehen; **~ for** vt sich beteiligen an (+dat); **~ into** vt (agreement) eingehen; (plans) eine Rolle spielen bei; **~ (up)on** vt beginnen.
enteritis [entə'raɪtɪs] n Dünndarmentzündung f.
enterprise ['entəpraɪz] n (in person) Initiative f; (COMM) Unternehmen nt.
enterprising ['entəpraɪzɪŋ] a unternehmungslustig.
entertain [entə'teɪn] vt (guest) bewirten; (amuse) unterhalten; **~er** n Unterhaltungskünstler(in f) m; **~ing** a unterhaltsam; **~ment** n Unterhaltung f.
enthralled [ɪn'θrɔːld] a gefesselt.
enthusiasm [ɪn'θuːzɪæzəm] n Begeisterung f.
enthusiast [ɪn'θuːzɪæst] n Enthusiast m; **~ic** [ɪnθuːzɪ'æstɪk] a begeistert.
entice [ɪn'taɪs] vt verleiten, locken.
entire [ɪn'taɪə*] a ganz; **~ly** ad ganz, völlig; **~ty** [ɪn'taɪərətɪ] n: **in its ~ty** in seiner Gesamtheit.
entitle [ɪn'taɪtl] vt (allow) berechtigen; (name) betiteln; **~d** a (book) mit dem Titel.
entity ['entɪtɪ] n Ding nt, Wesen nt.
entourage [ɒntʊ'rɑːʒ] n Gefolge nt.
entrails ['entreɪlz] npl Eingeweide pl.
entrance ['entrəns] n Eingang m; (entering) Eintritt m // vt [ɪn'trɑːns] hinreißen; **~ examination** n Aufnahmeprüfung f; **~ fee** n Eintrittsgeld nt; **~ ramp** n (US AUT) Einfahrt f.
entrant ['entrənt] n (for exam) Kandidat m; (in race) Teilnehmer m.
entreat [ɪn'triːt] vt anflehen.
entrenched [ɪn'trentʃt] a (fig) verwurzelt.

entrepreneur [ɒntrəprə'nɜː*] n Unternehmer(in f) m.
entrust [ɪn'trʌst] vt anvertrauen (sb with sth jdm etw).
entry ['entrɪ] n Eingang m; (THEAT) Auftritt m; (in account) Eintragung f; (in dictionary) Eintrag m; **'no ~'** 'Eintritt verboten'; (for cars) 'Einfahrt verboten'; **~ form** n Anmeldeformular nt; **~ phone** n Sprechanlage f.
enumerate [ɪ'njuːməreɪt] vt aufzählen.
enunciate [ɪ'nʌnsɪeɪt] vt aussprechen.
envelop [ɪn'veləp] vt einhüllen.
envelope ['envələʊp] n Umschlag m.
enviable ['envɪəbl] a beneidenswert.
envious ['envɪəs] a neidisch.
environment [ɪn'vaɪərənmənt] n Umgebung f; (ecology) Umwelt f; **~al** [ɪnvaɪərən'mentl] a Umwelt-.
envisage [ɪn'vɪzɪdʒ] vt sich (dat) vorstellen.
envoy ['envɔɪ] n Gesandte(r) mf.
envy ['envɪ] n Neid m // vt: **to ~ sb sth** jdn um etw beneiden.
enzyme ['enzaɪm] n Enzym nt.
ephemeral [ɪ'femərəl] a flüchtig.
epic ['epɪk] n Epos nt // a episch.
epidemic [epɪ'demɪk] n Epidemie f.
epilepsy ['epɪlepsɪ] n Epilepsie f.
epileptic [epɪ'leptɪk] a epileptisch // n Epileptiker(in f) m.
episode ['epɪsəʊd] n (incident) Vorfall m; (story) Episode f.
epistle [ɪ'pɪsl] n Brief m.
epitaph ['epɪtɑːf] n Grab(in)schrift f.
epithet ['epɪθət] n Beiname m.
epitome [ɪ'pɪtəmɪ] n Inbegriff m.
epitomize [ɪ'pɪtəmaɪz] vt verkörpern.
equable ['ekwəbl] a ausgeglichen.
equal ['iːkwl] a gleich // n Gleichgestellte(r) mf // vt gleichkommen (+dat); **~ to the task** der Aufgabe gewachsen; **~ity** [ɪ'kwɒlɪtɪ] n Gleichheit f; (equal rights) Gleichberechtigung f; **~ize** vt gleichmachen // vi (SPORT) ausgleichen; **~izer** n (SPORT) Ausgleich(streffer) m; **~ly** ad gleich.
equanimity [ekwə'nɪmɪtɪ] n Gleichmut m.
equate [ɪ'kweɪt] vt gleichsetzen.
equation [ɪ'kweɪʒən] n Gleichung f.
equator [ɪ'kweɪtə*] n Äquator m.
equestrian [ɪ'kwestrɪən] a Reit-.
equilibrium [iːkwɪ'lɪbrɪəm] n Gleichgewicht nt.
equinox ['iːkwɪnɒks] n Tag- und Nachtgleiche f.
equip [ɪ'kwɪp] vt ausrüsten; **~ment** n Ausrüstung f; (TECH) Gerät nt.
equitable ['ekwɪtəbl] a gerecht, billig.
equities ['ekwɪtɪz] npl (Brit COMM) Stammaktien pl.
equivalent [ɪ'kwɪvələnt] a gleichwertig (to dat), entsprechend (to dat) // n

Äquivalent *nt*; (*in money*) Gegenwert *m*.

equivocal [ɪ'kwɪvəkəl] *a* zweideutig.

era ['ɪərə] *n* Epoche *f*, Ära *f*.

eradicate [ɪ'rædɪkeɪt] *vt* ausrotten.

erase [ɪ'reɪz] *vt* ausradieren; (*tape*) löschen; **~r** *n* Radiergummi *m*.

erect [ɪ'rekt] *a* aufrecht // *vt* errichten.

erection [ɪ'rekʃən] *n* Errichtung *f*; (*ANAT*) Erektion *f*.

ermine ['ɜːmɪn] *n* Hermelin(pelz) *m*.

erode [ɪ'rəʊd] *vt* zerfressen; (*land*) auswaschen.

erotic [ɪ'rɒtɪk] *a* erotisch; **~ism** [ɪ'rɒtɪsɪzəm] *n* Erotik *f*.

err [ɜː*] *vi* sich irren.

errand ['erənd] *n* Besorgung *f*; **~ boy** *n* Laufbursche *m*.

erratic [ɪ'rætɪk] *a* unberechenbar.

erroneous [ɪ'rəʊnɪəs] *a* irrig.

error ['erə*] *n* Fehler *m*.

erudite ['erʊdaɪt] *a* gelehrt.

erupt [ɪ'rʌpt] *vi* ausbrechen; **~ion** *n* Ausbruch *m*.

escalate ['eskəleɪt] *vi* sich steigern.

escalator ['eskəleɪtə*] *n* Rolltreppe *f*.

escape [ɪs'keɪp] *n* Flucht *f*; (*of gas*) Entweichen *nt* // *vti* entkommen (+*dat*); (*prisoners*) fliehen; (*leak*) entweichen.

escapism [ɪs'keɪpɪzəm] *n* Flucht *f* (vor der Wirklichkeit).

escort ['eskɔːt] *n* (*person accompanying*) Begleiter *m*; (*guard*) Eskorte *f* // *vt* [ɪs'kɔːt] (*lady*) begleiten; (*MIL*) eskortieren.

Eskimo ['eskɪməʊ] *n* Eskimo *m*.

especially [ɪs'peʃəlɪ] *ad* besonders.

espionage ['espɪənɑːʒ] *n* Spionage *f*.

esplanade ['espləneɪd] *n* Promenade *f*.

espouse [ɪ'spaʊz] *vt* Partei ergreifen für.

Esquire [ɪs'kwaɪə*] *n* (*abbr* Esq.) J. Brown ~ Herrn J. Brown.

essay ['eseɪ] *n* Aufsatz *m*; (*LITER*) Essay *m*.

essence ['esəns] *n* (*quality*) Wesen *nt*; (*extract*) Essenz *f*.

essential [ɪ'senʃəl] *a* (*necessary*) unentbehrlich; (*basic*) wesentlich // *n* Allernötigste(s) *nt*; **~ly** *ad* eigentlich.

establish [ɪs'tæblɪʃ] *vt* (*set up*) gründen; (*prove*) nachweisen; **~ed** *a* anerkannt; (*belief, laws etc*) herrschend; **~ment** *n* (*setting up*) Einrichtung *f*; the E~ment das Establishment.

estate [ɪs'teɪt] *n* Gut *nt*; (*Brit: housing* ~) Siedlung *f*; (*will*) Nachlaß *m*; **~ agent** *n* (*Brit*) Grundstücksmakler *m*; **~ car** *n* (*Brit*) Kombiwagen *m*.

esteem [ɪs'tiːm] *n* Wertschätzung *f*.

esthetic [es'θetɪk] *a* (*US*) = **aesthetic**.

estimate ['estɪmət] *n* Schätzung *f*; (*of price*) (Kosten)voranschlag *m* // *vt* ['estɪmeɪt] schätzen.

estimation [estɪ'meɪʃən] *n* Einschätzung *f*; (*esteem*) Achtung *f*.

estranged [ɪ'streɪndʒd] *a* entfremdet.

estuary ['estjʊərɪ] *n* Mündung *f*.

etc *abbr* (= *et cetera*) etc.

etching ['etʃɪŋ] *n* Kupferstich *m*.

eternal [ɪ'tɜːnl] *a* ewig.

eternity [ɪ'tɜːnɪtɪ] *n* Ewigkeit *f*.

ether ['iːθə*] *n* (*MED*) Äther *m*.

ethical ['eθɪkəl] *a* ethisch.

ethics ['eθɪks] *n* Ethik *f* // *npl* Moral *f*.

Ethiopia [iːθɪ'əʊpɪə] *n* Äthiopien *nt*.

ethnic ['eθnɪk] *a* Volks-, ethnisch.

etiquette ['etɪket] *n* Etikette *f*.

euphemism ['juːfɪmɪzəm] *n* Euphemismus *m*.

Eurocheque ['jʊərəʊ'tʃek] *n* Euroscheck *m*.

Europe ['jʊərəp] *n* Europa *nt*; **~an** [-'piːən] *a* europäisch // *n* Europäer(in *f*) *m*.

evacuate [ɪ'vækjʊeɪt] *vt* (*place*) räumen; (*people*) evakuieren.

evacuation [ɪvækjʊ'eɪʃən] *n* Räumung *f*; Evakuierung *f*.

evade [ɪ'veɪd] *vt* (*escape*) entkommen (+*dat*); (*avoid*) meiden; (*duty*) sich entziehen (+*dat*).

evaluate [ɪ'væljʊeɪt] *vt* bewerten; (*information*) auswerten.

evaporate [ɪ'væpəreɪt] *vi* verdampfen // *vt* verdampfen lassen; **~d milk** *n* Kondensmilch *f*.

evasion [ɪ'veɪʒən] *n* Umgehung *f*.

evasive [ɪ'veɪzɪv] *a* ausweichend.

eve [iːv] *n*: on the ~ of am Vorabend (+*gen*).

even ['iːvən] *a* eben; gleichmäßig; (*score etc*) unentschieden; (*number*) gerade // *ad*: ~ **you** sogar du; ~ if selbst wenn; ~ so dennoch; to get ~ with sb jdm heimzahlen; ~ **out** *vi* sich ausgleichen.

evening ['iːvnɪŋ] *n* Abend *m*; in the ~ abends, am Abend; ~ **class** *n* Abendschule *f*; ~ **dress** *n* (*man's*) Gesellschaftsanzug *m*; (*woman's*) Abendkleid *nt*.

event [ɪ'vent] *n* (*happening*) Ereignis *nt*; (*SPORT*) Disziplin *f*; in the ~ of im Falle (+*gen*); **~ful** *a* ereignisreich.

eventual [ɪ'ventʃʊəl] *a* (*final*) schließlich; **~ity** [ɪventʃʊ'ælɪtɪ] *n* Möglichkeit *f*; **~ly** *ad* (*at last*) am Ende; (*given time*) schließlich.

ever ['evə*] *ad* (*always*) immer; (*at any time*) je(mals); ~ **since** *ad* seitdem // *cj* seit; **~green** *n* Immergrün *nt*; **~lasting** *a* immerwährend.

every ['evrɪ] *a* jede(r, s); ~ **other/third day** jeden zweiten/dritten Tag; ~ **one of** them alle; I have ~ **confidence** in him ich habe uneingeschränktes Vertrauen in ihn; we wish you ~ **success** wir wünschen Ihnen viel Erfolg; he's ~ **bit** as clever as his brother er ist genauso klug wie sein Bruder; ~ **now and then** ab und zu; **~body** *pron* = **~one; ~day** *a* (*daily*) täglich; (*commonplace*) alltäglich, Alltags-; **~one** *pron* jeder, alle *pl*; **~thing** *pron* alles; **~where** *ad* überall(hin); (*wherever*) wohin; **~where you** go wohin du auch gehst.

evict [ɪ'vɪkt] *vt* ausweisen; **~ion** *n* Ausweisung *f*.

evidence ['evɪdəns] *n* (*sign*) Spur *f*; (*proof*) Beweis *m*; (*testimony*) Aussage *f*.

evident ['evɪdənt] *a* augenscheinlich; **~ly** *ad* offensichtlich.

evil ['iːvl] *a* böse // *n* Böse *nt*.

evocative [ɪ'vɒkətɪv] *a*: to be ~ of sth an etw (*acc*) erinnern.

evoke [ɪ'vəʊk] *vt* hervorrufen.

evolution [iːvə'luːʃən] *n* Entwicklung *f*; (*of life*) Evolution *f*.

evolve [ɪ'vɒlv] *vt* entwickeln // *vi* sich entwickeln.

ewe [juː] *n* Mutterschaf *nt*.

ex- [eks] *pref* Ex-, Alt-, ehemalig.

exacerbate [ek'sæsəbeɪt] *vt* verschlimmern.

exact [ɪg'zækt] *a* genau // *vt* (*demand*) verlangen; **~ing** *a* anspruchsvoll; **~itude** *n* Genauigkeit *f*.

exaggerate [ɪg'zædʒəreɪt] *vti* übertreiben.

exaggeration [ɪgzædʒə'reɪʃən] *n* Übertreibung *f*.

exalted [ɪg'zɔːltɪd] *a* (*position, style*) hoch; (*person*) exaltiert.

exam [ɪg'zæm] *n abbr of* **examination.**

examination [ɪgzæmɪ'neɪʃən] *n* Untersuchung *f*; (*SCH*) Prüfung *f*, Examen *nt*; (*customs*) Kontrolle *f*.

examine [ɪg'zæmɪn] *vt* untersuchen; (*SCH*) prüfen; (*consider*) erwägen; **~r** *n* Prüfer *m*.

example [ɪg'zɑːmpl] *n* Beispiel *nt*; for ~ zum Beispiel.

exasperate [ɪg'zɑːspəreɪt] *vt* zum Verzweifeln bringen.

exasperating [ɪg'zɑːspəreɪtɪŋ] *a* ärgerlich, zum Verzweifeln bringend.

exasperation [ɪgzɑːspə'reɪʃən] *n* Verzweiflung *f*.

excavate ['ekskəveɪt] *vt* ausgraben.

excavation [ekskə'veɪʃən] *n* Ausgrabung *f*.

exceed [ɪk'siːd] *vt* überschreiten; (*hopes*) übertreffen.

excel [ɪk'sel] *vi* sich auszeichnen.

excellence ['eksələns] *n* Vortrefflichkeit *f*.

excellency ['eksələnsɪ] *n*: His E~ Seine Exzellenz *f*.

excellent ['eksələnt] *a* ausgezeichnet.

except [ɪk'sept] *prep* (*also*: ~ for, ~ing) außer (+*dat*) // *vt* ausnehmen; **~ion** [ɪk'sepʃən] *n* Ausnahme *f*; to take ~ion to Anstoß nehmen an (+*dat*); **~ional** [ɪk'sepʃənl] *a* außergewöhnlich.

excerpt ['eksɜːpt] *n* Auszug *m*.

excess [ɪk'ses] *n* Übermaß *nt* (*of* an +*dat*); Exzeß *m*; ~ **baggage** *n* Mehrgepäck *nt*; ~ **fare** *n* Nachlösegebühr *f*; **~ive** *a* übermäßig.

exchange [ɪks'tʃeɪndʒ] *n* Austausch *m*; (*also*: **telephone ~**) Zentrale *f* // *vt* (*goods*) tauschen; (*greetings*) austauschen; (*money, blows*) wechseln; ~ **rate** *n* Wechselkurs *m*.

Exchequer [ɪks'tʃekə*] *n*: the ~ (*Brit*) das Schatzamt.

excise ['eksaɪz] *n* Verbrauchssteuer *f* // *vt* [ek'saɪz] (*MED*) herausschneiden.

excite [ɪk'saɪt] *vt* erregen; to get **~d** sich aufregen; **~ment** *n* Aufregung *f*.

exciting [ɪk'saɪtɪŋ] *a* spannend.

exclaim [ɪks'kleɪm] *vi* ausrufen.

exclamation [eksklə'meɪʃən] *n* Ausruf *m*; ~ **mark** *n* Ausrufezeichen *nt*.

exclude [ɪks'kluːd] *vt* ausschließen.

exclusion [ɪks'kluːʒən] *n* Ausschluß *m*.

exclusive [ɪks'kluːsɪv] *a* (*select*) exklusiv; (*sole*) ausschließlich, Allein-; ~ **of** exklusive (+*gen*); **~ly** *ad* nur, ausschließlich.

excommunicate [ekskə'mjuːnɪkeɪt] *vt* exkommunizieren.

excrement ['ekskrɪmənt] *n* Kot *m*.

excruciating [ɪks'kruːʃɪeɪtɪŋ] *a* qualvoll.

excursion [ɪks'kɜːʃən] *n* Ausflug *m*.

excusable [ɪks'kjuːzəbl] *a* entschuldbar.

excuse [ɪks'kjuːs] *n* Entschuldigung *f* // *vt* [ɪks'kjuːz] entschuldigen; ~ **me!** entschuldigen Sie!

ex-directory ['eksdaɪ'rektərɪ] *a* (*Brit*): to be ~ nicht im Telefonbuch stehen.

execute ['eksɪkjuːt] *vt* (*carry out*) ausführen; (*kill*) hinrichten.

execution [eksɪ'kjuːʃən] *n* Ausführung *f*; (*killing*) Hinrichtung *f*; **~er** *n* Scharfrichter *m*.

executive [ɪg'zekjutɪv] *n* (*COMM*) Geschäftsführer *m*; (*POL*) Exekutive *f* // *a* Exekutiv-, ausführend.

executor [ɪg'zekjutə*] *n* Testamentsvollstrecker *m*.

exemplary [ɪg'zemplərɪ] *a* musterhaft.

exemplify [ɪg'zemplɪfaɪ] *vt* veranschaulichen.

exempt [ɪg'zempt] *a* befreit // *vt* befreien; **~ion** [ɪg'zempʃən] *n* Befreiung *f*.

exercise ['eksəsaɪz] *n* Übung *f* // *vt* (*power*) ausüben; (*muscle, patience*) üben; (*dog*) ausführen // *vi* Sport treiben; ~ **book** *n* (Schul)heft *nt*.

exert [ɪg'zɜːt] *vt* (*influence*) ausüben; ~ **o.s.** sich anstrengen; **~ion** [-ʃən] *n* Anstrengung *f*.

exhale [eks'heɪl] *vti* ausatmen.

exhaust [ɪg'zɔːst] *n* (*fumes*) Abgase *pl*; (*pipe*) Auspuffrohr *nt* // *vt* erschöpfen; **~ed** *a* erschöpft; **~ion** *n* Erschöpfung *f*; **~ive** *a* erschöpfend.

exhibit 66 **extinguish**

exhibit [ɪgˈzɪbɪt] n (ART) Ausstellungsstück nt // vt ausstellen; (of temper etc) zur Schaustellung f; ~ion [eksɪˈbɪʃən] n (ART) Ausstellung f; (of temper etc) Zurschaustellung f; ~ionist [eksɪˈbɪʃənɪst] n Exhibitionist m.

exhilarating [ɪgˈzɪləreɪtɪŋ] a erhebend.

exhort [ɪgˈzɔːt] vt ermahnen.

exile [ˈeksaɪl] n Exil nt; (person) Verbannte(r) mf // vt verbannen.

exist [ɪgˈzɪst] vi existieren; ~ence n Existenz f; ~ing a bestehend.

exit [ˈeksɪt] n Ausgang m; (THEAT) Abgang m // vi (THEAT) abtreten; (COMPUT) aus einem Programm herausgehen; ~ ramp n (US AUT) Ausfahrt f.

exonerate [ɪgˈzɒnəreɪt] vt entlasten.

exorbitant [ɪgˈzɔːbɪtənt] a übermäßig; (price) Phantasie-.

exotic [ɪgˈzɒtɪk] a exotisch.

expand [ɪksˈpænd] vt ausdehnen // vi sich ausdehnen.

expanse [ɪksˈpæns] n Fläche f.

expansion [ɪksˈpænʃən] n Erweiterung f.

expatriate [eksˈpætrɪɪt] n Ausländer(in f) m.

expect [ɪksˈpekt] vt erwarten; (suppose) annehmen // vi: to be ~ing ein Kind erwarten; ~ancy n Erwartung f; ~ant mother n werdende Mutter f; ~ation [ekspekˈteɪʃən] n Hoffnung f.

expedience [ɪksˈpiːdɪəns], **expediency** [ɪksˈpiːdɪənsɪ] n Zweckdienlichkeit f.

expedient [ɪksˈpiːdɪənt] a zweckdienlich // n (Hilfs)mittel nt.

expedition [ekspɪˈdɪʃən] n Expedition f.

expel [ɪksˈpel] vt ausweisen; (student) (ver)weisen.

expend [ɪksˈpend] vt (effort) aufwenden; ~iture n Ausgaben pl.

expense [ɪksˈpens] n Kosten pl; ~s pl Spesen pl; at the ~ of auf Kosten von; ~ account n Spesenkonto nt.

expensive [ɪksˈpensɪv] a teuer.

experience [ɪksˈpɪərɪəns] n (incident) Erlebnis nt; (practice) Erfahrung f // vt erleben; ~d a erfahren.

experiment [ɪksˈperɪmənt] n Versuch m, Experiment nt // vi [ɪksˈperɪment] experimentieren; ~al [ɪksperɪˈmentl] a experimentell.

expert [ˈekspɜːt] n Fachmann m; (official) Sachverständige(r) m // a erfahren; ~ise [ekspəˈtiːz] n Sachkenntnis f.

expire [ɪksˈpaɪə*] vi (end) ablaufen; (die) sterben; (ticket) verfallen.

expiry [ɪksˈpaɪərɪ] n Ablauf m.

explain [ɪksˈpleɪn] vt erklären.

explanation [ekspləˈneɪʃən] n Erklärung f.

explanatory [ɪksˈplænətərɪ] a erklärend.

explicit [ɪksˈplɪsɪt] a ausdrücklich.

explode [ɪksˈpləud] vi explodieren // vt (bomb) sprengen; (theory) platzen lassen.

exploit [ˈeksplɔɪt] n (Helden)tat f // vt [ɪksˈplɔɪt] ausbeuten; ~ation [eksplɔɪˈteɪʃən] n Ausbeutung f.

exploration [eksplɔːˈreɪʃən] n Erforschung f.

exploratory [eksˈplɒrətərɪ] a Probe-.

explore [ɪksˈplɔː*] vt (travel) erforschen; (search) untersuchen; ~r n Erforscher(in f) m.

explosion [ɪksˈpləuʒən] n (lit) Explosion f; (fig) Ausbruch m.

explosive [ɪksˈpləuzɪv] a explosiv, Spreng- // n Sprengstoff m.

exponent [eksˈpəunənt] n Exponent m.

export [eksˈpɔːt] vt exportieren // n [ˈekspɔːt] Export m // cpd (trade) Export-; ~er n Exporteur m.

expose [ɪksˈpəuz] vt (to danger etc) aussetzen (to dat); (imposter) entlarven.

exposed [ɪksˈpəuzd] a (position) exponiert.

exposure [ɪksˈpəuʒə*] n (MED) Unterkühlung f; (PHOT) Belichtung f; ~ meter n Belichtungsmesser m.

expound [ɪksˈpaund] vt entwickeln.

express [ɪksˈpres] a ausdrücklich; (speedy) Expreß-, Eil- // n (RAIL) Zug m // ad (send) per Expreß // vt ausdrücken; to ~ o.s. sich ausdrücken; ~ion [ɪksˈpreʃən] n Ausdruck m; ~ive a ausdrucksvoll; ~ly ad ausdrücklich; ~way n (US: urban motorway) Schnellstraße f.

expulsion [ɪksˈpʌlʃən] n Ausweisung f.

expurgate [ˈekspɜːgeɪt] vt zensieren.

exquisite [eksˈkwɪzɪt] a erlesen.

extend [ɪksˈtend] vt (visit etc) verlängern; (building) ausbauen; (hand) ausstrecken; (welcome) bieten // vi (land) sich erstrecken.

extension [ɪksˈtenʃən] n Erweiterung f; (of building) Anbau m; (TEL) Apparat m.

extensive [ɪksˈtensɪv] a (knowledge) umfassend; (use) weitgehend.

extent [ɪksˈtent] n Ausdehnung f; (fig) Ausmaß nt; to a certain ~ bis zu einem gewissen Grade; to such an ~ that ... dermaßen, daß ...; to what ~? inwieweit?

extenuating [eksˈtenjueɪtɪŋ] a mildernd.

exterior [eksˈtɪərɪə*] a äußere(r, s), Außen- // n Äußere(s) nt.

exterminate [eksˈtɜːmɪneɪt] vt ausrotten.

extermination [ekstɜːmɪˈneɪʃən] n Ausrottung f.

external [eksˈtɜːnl] a äußere(r, s), Außen-.

extinct [ɪksˈtɪŋkt] a ausgestorben; ~ion [ɪksˈtɪŋkʃən] n Aussterben nt.

extinguish [ɪksˈtɪŋgwɪʃ] vt

(aus)löschen; ~**er** n Löschgerät nt.

extort [ɪks'tɔːt] vt erpressen (sth from sb jdn um etw); ~**ion** [ɪks'tɔːʃən] n Erpressung f; ~**ionate** [ɪks'tɔːʃənɪt] a überhöht, erpresserisch.

extra ['ekstrə] a zusätzlich // ad besonders // n (for car etc) Extra nt; (charge) Zuschlag m; (THEAT) Statist m.

extra... [ekstrə] pref außer...

extract [ɪks'trækt] vt (heraus)ziehen // n ['ekstrækt] (from book etc) Auszug m; (COOK) Extrakt m.

extracurricular ['ekstrəkə'rɪkjʊlə*] a außerhalb des Stundenplans.

extradite ['ekstrədaɪt] vt ausliefern.

extramarital [ekstrə'mærɪtl] a außerehelich.

extramural [ekstrə'mjʊərl] a (course) Volkshochschul-.

extraordinary [ɪks'trɔːdnrɪ] a außerordentlich; (amazing) erstaunlich.

extravagance [ɪks'trævəgəns] n Verschwendung f; (lack of restraint) Zügellosigkeit f; (an ~) Extravaganz f.

extravagant [ɪks'trævəgənt] a extravagant.

extreme [ɪks'triːm] a (edge) äußerste(r, s), hinterste(r, s); (cold) äußerste(r, s); (behaviour) außergewöhnlich, übertrieben // n Extrem nt; ~**ly** ad äußerst, höchst.

extremity [ɪks'tremɪtɪ] n (end) Spitze f, äußerste(s) Ende nt; (hardship) bitterste Not f; (ANAT) Hand f; Fuß m.

extricate ['ekstrɪkeɪt] vt losmachen, befreien.

extrovert ['ekstrəʊvɜːt] n extrovertierte(r) Mensch m.

exuberant [ɪg'zuːbərənt] a ausgelassen.

exude [ɪg'zjuːd] vt absondern.

exult [ɪg'zʌlt] vi frohlocken.

eye [aɪ] n Auge nt; (of needle) Öhr nt // vt betrachten; (up and down) mustern; to keep an ~ on aufpassen auf (+acc); ~**ball** n Augapfel m; ~**bath** n Augenbad nt; ~**brow** n Augenbraue f; ~**brow pencil** n Augenbrauenstift m; ~**drops** npl Augentropfen pl; ~**lash** n Augenwimper f; ~**lid** n Augenlid nt; ~**liner** n Eyeliner nt; ~**opener** n that was an ~-opener das hat mir die Augen geöffnet; ~**shadow** n Lidschatten m; ~**sight** n Sehkraft f; ~**sore** n Schandfleck m; ~ **witness** n Augenzeuge m.

F

F [ef] n (MUS) F nt.

F. abbr (= Fahrenheit) F.

fable ['feɪbl] n Fabel f.

fabric ['fæbrɪk] n Stoff m; (fig) Gefüge nt.

fabrication [fæbrɪ'keɪʃən] n Erfindung f.

fabulous ['fæbjʊləs] a sagenhaft.

face [feɪs] n Gesicht nt; (surface) Oberfläche f; (of clock) Zifferblatt nt // vt (point towards) liegen nach; (situation, difficulty) sich stellen (+dat); ~ **down** (person) mit dem Gesicht nach unten; (card) mit der Vorderseite nach unten; to make or pull a ~ das Gesicht verziehen; in the ~ of angesichts (+gen); on the ~ of it so, wie es aussieht; ~ to ~ Auge in Auge; to ~ up to sth einer Sache ins Auge sehen; ~ **cloth** n (Brit) Waschlappen m; ~ **cream** n Gesichtscreme f; ~ **lift** n Facelifting nt; ~ **powder** n (Gesichts)puder m.

facet ['fæsɪt] n Aspekt m; (of gem) Facette f.

facetious [fə'siːʃəs] a witzig.

face value n Nennwert m; (fig) to take sth at its ~ etw für bare Münze nehmen.

facial ['feɪʃəl] a Gesichts-.

facile ['fæsaɪl] a oberflächlich; (US: easy) leicht.

facilitate [fə'sɪlɪteɪt] vt erleichtern.

facilities [fə'sɪlɪtɪz] npl Einrichtungen pl; credit ~ Kreditmöglichkeiten pl.

facing ['feɪsɪŋ] a zugekehrt // prep gegenüber.

fact [fækt] n Tatsache f; in ~ in der Tat.

faction ['fækʃən] n Splittergruppe f.

factor ['fæktə*] n Faktor m.

factory ['fæktərɪ] n Fabrik f.

factual ['fæktjʊəl] a sachlich.

faculty ['fækəltɪ] n Fähigkeit f; (UNIV) Fakultät f; (US: teaching staff) Lehrpersonal nt.

fad [fæd] n Tick m; (fashion) Masche f.

fade [feɪd] vi (lose colour) verblassen; (grow dim) nachlassen; (sound, memory) schwächer werden; (wither) verwelken.

fag [fæg] n (col: cigarette) Kippe f.

fail [feɪl] vt (exam) nicht bestehen; (student) durchfallen lassen; (courage) verlassen; (memory) im Stich lassen // vi (supplies) zu Ende gehen; (student) durchfallen; (eyesight) nachlassen; (light) schwächer werden; (crop) fehlschlagen; (remedy) nicht wirken; ~ **to** do sth (neglect) es unterlassen, etw zu tun; (be unable) es nicht schaffen, etw zu tun; without ~ unbedingt; ~**ing** n Schwäche f // prep mangels (+gen); ~**ure** n (person) Versager m; (act) Versagen nt; (TECH) Defekt m.

faint [feɪnt] a schwach // n Ohnmacht f // vi ohnmächtig werden.

fair [feə*] a schön; (hair) blond; (skin) hell; (just) gerecht, fair; (not very good) mittelmäßig; (sizeable) ansehnlich // ad (play) fair // n (COMM) Messe f; (Brit: fun~) Jahrmarkt m; ~**ly** ad (honestly) gerecht, fair; (rather) ziemlich; ~**ness** n Fairneß f.

fairy ['fɛərɪ] n Fee f; ~ **tale** n Märchen nt.

faith [feɪθ] n Glaube m; (trust) Vertrauen nt; (sect) Bekenntnis nt; ~**ful** a treu; **yours** ~**fully** (Brit) hochachtungsvoll.

fake [feɪk] n (thing) Fälschung f; (person) Schwindler m // a vorgetäuscht // vt fälschen.

falcon ['fɔːlkən] n Falke m.

fall [fɔːl] n Fall m, Sturz m; (decrease) Fallen nt; (of snow) (Schnee)fall m; (US: autumn) Herbst m // vi, pt **fell**, pp **fallen** ['fɔːlən] (lit, fig) fallen; (night) hereinbrechen; ~**s** pl (waterfall) Fälle pl; ~ **back** vi zurückweichen; ~ **back on** vt zurückgreifen auf (+ acc); ~ **behind** vi zurückbleiben; ~ **down** vi (person) hinfallen; (building) einstürzen; ~ **flat** vi (lit) platt hinfallen; (joke) nicht ankommen; ~ **for** vt (trick) hereinfallen auf (+acc); (person) sich verknallen in (+acc); ~ **in** vi (roof) einstürzen; ~ **off** vi herunterfallen (von); (diminish) sich vermindern; ~ **out** vi sich streiten; (MIL) wegtreten; ~ **through** vi (plan) ins Wasser fallen.

fallacy ['fæləsɪ] n Trugschluß m.

fallen ['fɔːlən] pp of **fall**.

fallible ['fæləbl] a fehlbar.

fallout ['fɔːlaʊt] n radioaktive(r) Niederschlag m; ~ **shelter** n Atombunker m.

fallow ['fæləʊ] a brach(liegend).

false [fɔːls] a falsch; (artificial) künstlich; **under** ~ **pretences** unter Vorspiegelung falscher Tatsachen; ~ **alarm** n Fehlalarm m; ~ **teeth** npl (Brit) Gebiß nt.

falter ['fɔːltə*] vi schwanken; (in speech) stocken.

fame [feɪm] n Ruhm m.

familiar [fə'mɪlɪə*] a bekannt; (intimate) familiär; **to be** ~ **with** vertraut sein mit; ~**ize** vt vertraut machen.

family ['fæmɪlɪ] n Familie f; (relations) Verwandtschaft f; ~ **business** n Familienunternehmen nt; ~ **doctor** n Hausarzt m.

famine ['fæmɪn] n Hungersnot f.

famished ['fæmɪʃt] a ausgehungert.

famous ['feɪməs] a berühmt; ~**ly** ad (get on) prächtig.

fan [fæn] n (folding) Fächer m; (ELEC) Ventilator m; (admirer) Fan m // vt fächeln; ~ **out** vi sich (fächerförmig) ausbreiten.

fanatic [fə'nætɪk] n Fanatiker(in f) m.

fan belt n Keilriemen m.

fanciful ['fænsɪfʊl] a (odd) seltsam; (imaginative) phantasievoll.

fancy ['fænsɪ] n (liking) Neigung f; (imagination) Einbildung f // a schick // vt (like) gern haben; wollen; (imagine) sich einbilden; **he fancies her** er mag

sie; ~ **dress** n Maskenkostüm nt; ~-**dress ball** n Maskenball m.

fang [fæŋ] n Fangzahn m; (snake's) Giftzahn m.

fantastic [fæn'tæstɪk] a phantastisch.

fantasy ['fæntəzɪ] n Phantasie f.

far [fɑː*] a weit // ad weit entfernt; (very much) weitaus, by ~ bei weitem; so ~ soweit; bis jetzt; **go as** ~ **as the farm** gehen Sie bis zum Bauernhof; **as** ~ **as I know** soweit or soviel ich weiß; ~**away** a weit entfernt.

farce [fɑːs] n Farce f.

farcical ['fɑːsɪkəl] a lächerlich.

fare [fɛə*] n Fahrpreis m; Fahrgeld nt; (food) Kost f.

Far East n: **the** ~ der Ferne Osten.

farewell [fɛə'wel] n Abschied(sgruß m) m // interj lebe wohl!

farm [fɑːm] n Bauernhof m, Farm f // vt bewirtschaften; ~**er** n Bauer m, Landwirt m; ~**hand** n Landarbeiter m; ~**house** n Bauernhaus nt; ~**ing** n Landwirtschaft f; ~**land** n Ackerland nt; ~**yard** n Hof m.

fart [fɑːt] (col!) n Furz m // vi furzen.

farther ['fɑːðə*] ad weiter.

farthest ['fɑːðɪst] a fernste(r, s) // ad am weitesten.

fascinate ['fæsɪneɪt] vt faszinieren.

fascination [fæsɪ'neɪʃən] n Faszination f.

fascist ['fæʃɪst] n Faschist m // a faschistisch.

fashion ['fæʃən] n (of clothes) Mode f; (manner) Art f (und Weise f) // vt machen; **in** ~ in Mode; **out of** ~ unmodisch; ~**able** a (clothes) modisch; (place) elegant; ~ **show** n Mode(n)schau f.

fast [fɑːst] a schnell; (firm) fest // ad schnell; (firmly) fest // n Fasten nt // vi fasten; **to be** ~ (clock) vorgehen.

fasten ['fɑːsn] vt (attach) befestigen; (seat belt) festmachen; (with rope) zuschnüren // vi sich schließen lassen; ~**er**, ~**ing** n Verschluß m.

fastidious [fæs'tɪdɪəs] a wählerisch.

fat [fæt] a dick // n Fett nt.

fatal ['feɪtl] a tödlich; (disastrous) verhängnisvoll; ~**ity** [fə'tælɪtɪ] n (road death etc) Todesopfer nt; ~**ly** ad tödlich.

fate [feɪt] n Schicksal nt; ~**ful** a (prophetic) schicksalsschwer; (important) schicksalhaft.

father ['fɑːðə*] n Vater m; (REL) Pater m; ~-**in-law** n Schwiegervater m; ~**ly** a väterlich.

fathom ['fæðəm] n Klafter m // vt ausloten; (fig) ergründen.

fatigue [fə'tiːg] n Ermüdung f.

fatten ['fætn] vt dick machen; (animals) mästen // vi dick werden.

fatty ['fætɪ] a fettig // n (col) Dickerchen nt.

fatuous ['fætjʊəs] a albern, affig.
faucet ['fɔːsɪt] n (US) Wasserhahn m.
fault [fɔːlt] n (defect) Defekt m; (ELEC)
Störung f; (blame) Schuld f; (GEOG)
Verwerfung f; it's your ~ du bist daran
schuld; at ~ im Unrecht // vt: to ~ sth
etwas an etw (dat) auszusetzen haben;
~less a tadellos; **~y** a fehlerhaft,
defekt.
favour, (US) **favor** ['feɪvə*] n (approval) Wohlwollen nt; (kindness)
Gefallen m // vt (prefer) vorziehen; in ~
of für; zugunsten (+gen); to find ~ with
sb bei jdm Anklang finden; **~able** a
günstig; **~ite** ['feɪvərɪt] a Lieblings- // n
(child) Liebling m; (SPORT) Favorit m;
~itism n (SCH) Bevorzugung f.
fawn [fɔːn] n rehbraun // n (colour) Rehbraun nt; (animal) (Reh)kitz nt // vi: to
~ (up)on (fig) katzbuckeln vor (+dat).
fax [fæks] n (document) Fax nt; (machine) Telefax nt // vt per Fax schicken.
FBI ['efbiː'aɪ] n abbr (US: = Federal
Bureau of Investigation) FBI nt.
fear [fɪə*] n Furcht f // vt fürchten; **~ful**
a (timid) furchtsam; (terrible) fürchterlich; **~less** a furchtlos.
feasible ['fiːzəbl] a durchführbar.
feast [fiːst] n Festmahl nt; (REL: also:
~ day) Feiertag m // vi sich gütlich tun
(on an +dat).
feat [fiːt] n Leistung f.
feather ['feðə*] n Feder f.
feature ['fiːtʃə*] n (Gesichts)zug m;
(important part) Grundzug m; (CINE,
PRESS) Feature nt // vt darstellen; (advertising etc) groß herausbringen // vi
vorkommen; featuring X mit X; ~ film
n Spielfilm m.
February ['februərɪ] n Februar m.
fed [fed] pt, pp of **feed**.
federal ['fedərəl] a Bundes-.
federation [fedə'reɪʃən] n (society) Verband m; (of states) Staatenbund m.
fed-up [fed'ʌp] a: to be ~ with sth etw
satt haben; I'm ~ ich habe die Nase
voll.
fee [fiː] n Gebühr f.
feeble ['fiːbl] a (person) schwach;
(excuse) lahm.
feed [fiːd] n (for baby) Essen nt; (for animals) Futter nt // vt, pt, pp, **fed**
füttern; (support) ernähren; (data) eingeben; to ~ on fressen; **~back** n
(information) Feedback nt; **~ing bottle**
n (Brit) Flasche f.
feel [fiːl] n: it has a soft ~ es fühlt sich
weich an; to get the ~ of sth sich an etw
(acc) gewöhnen // v (pt, pp **felt**) vt
(sense) fühlen; (touch) anfassen; (think)
meinen // vi (person) sich fühlen; (thing)
sich anfühlen; I ~ cold mir ist kalt; I ~
like a cup of tea ich habe Lust auf eine
Tasse Tee; ~ about or around vi her-
umsuchen; **~er** n Fühler m; **~ing** n
Gefühl nt; (opinion) Meinung f.
feet [fiːt] pl of **foot**.
feign [feɪn] vt vortäuschen.
feline ['fiːlaɪn] a katzenartig.
fell [fel] pt of **fall** // vt (tree) fällen.
fellow ['feləʊ] n (man) Kerl m; ~ **citizen** n Mitbürger(in f) m; ~ **country-
man** n Landsmann m; ~ **men** npl Mit-
menschen pl; **~ship** n (group) Körper-
schaft f; (friendliness) Kameradschaft f;
(scholarship) Forschungsstipendium nt;
~ **student** n Kommilitone m,
Kommilitonin f.
felony ['felənɪ] n schwere(s) Verbrechen
nt.
felt [felt] pt, pp of **feel** // n Filz m; **~-tip
pen** n Filzstift m.
female ['fiːmeɪl] n (of animals) Weibchen nt // a weiblich.
feminine ['femɪnɪn] a (GRAM) weiblich;
(qualities) fraulich.
feminist ['femɪnɪst] n Feminist(in f) m.
fence [fens] n Zaun m // vt (also: ~ in)
einzäunen // vi fechten.
fencing ['fensɪŋ] n Zaun m; (SPORT)
Fechten nt.
fend [fend] vi: ~ for o.s. sich (allein)
durchschlagen; ~ **off** vt abwehren.
fender ['fendə*] n Kaminvorsetzer m;
(US AUT) Kotflügel m.
ferment [fə'ment] vi (CHEM) gären //
['fɜːment] n (excitement) Unruhe f.
fern [fɜːn] n Farn m.
ferocious [fə'rəʊʃəs] a wild, grausam.
ferret ['ferɪt] n Frettchen nt // vt: to ~
out aufspüren.
ferry ['ferɪ] n Fähre f // vt übersetzen.
fertile ['fɜːtaɪl] a fruchtbar.
fertilize ['fɜːtɪlaɪz] vt (AGR) düngen;
(BIOL) befruchten; **~r** n (Kunst)dünger
m.
fervent ['fɜːvənt] a (admirer) glühend;
(hope) innig.
fervour, (US) **fervor** ['fɜːvə*] n Leidenschaft f.
fester ['festə*] vi eitern.
festival ['festɪvəl] n (REL etc) Fest nt;
(ART, MUS) Festspiele pl.
festive ['festɪv] a festlich; the ~ **season**
(Christmas) die Festzeit f.
festivity [fes'tɪvɪtɪ] n Festlichkeit f.
festoon [fes'tuːn] vt: to ~ **with**
schmücken mit.
fetch [fetʃ] vt holen; (in sale) einbringen.
fetching ['fetʃɪŋ] a reizend.
fête [feɪt] n Fest nt.
fetus ['fiːtəs] n (US) = **foetus**.
feud [fjuːd] n Fehde f; **~al** a Feudal-.
fever ['fiːvə*] n Fieber nt; **~ish** a
(MED) fiebrig; (fig) fieberhaft.
few [fjuː] a wenig; **a ~** a, pron einige;
~er a weniger; **~est** a wenigste(r, s).
fiancé [fɪ'ɑːnseɪ] n Verlobte(r) m; **~e** n
Verlobte f.

fib [fɪb] n Flunkerei f // vi flunkern.
fibre, (US) **fiber** ['faɪbə*] n Faser f; ~-**glass** n Glaswolle f.
fickle ['fɪkl] a unbeständig.
fiction ['fɪkʃən] n (novels) Romanliteratur f; (story) Erdichtung f; ~**al** a erfunden.
fictitious [fɪk'tɪʃəs] a erfunden, fingiert.
fiddle ['fɪdl] n Geige f; (trick) Schwindelei f // vt (Brit: accounts) frisieren; ~ **with** vi herumfummeln an (+dat).
fidelity [fɪ'delɪtɪ] n Treue f.
fidget ['fɪdʒɪt] vi zappeln.
field [fiːld] n Feld nt; (range) Gebiet nt; ~ **marshal** n Feldmarschall m; ~**work** n (UNIV) Feldforschung f.
fiend [fiːnd] n Teufel m; ~**ish** a teuflisch.
fierce [fɪəs] a wild.
fiery ['faɪərɪ] a (hot-tempered) hitzig.
fifteen [fɪf'tiːn] num fünfzehn.
fifth [fɪfθ] a fünfte(r, s) // n Fünftel nt.
fifty ['fɪftɪ] num fünfzig; ~-~ a halbe halbe, fifty fifty (col).
fig [fɪg] n Feige f.
fight [faɪt] n Kampf m; (brawl) Schlägerei f; (argument) Streit m // v (pt, pp **fought**) vt kämpfen gegen; sich schlagen mit; (fig) bekämpfen // vi kämpfen; sich schlagen; streiten; ~**er** n Kämpfer(in f) m; (plane) Jagdflugzeug nt; ~**ing** n Kämpfen nt; (war) Kampfhandlungen pl.
figment ['fɪgmənt] n: ~ **of the imagination** reine Einbildung f.
figurative ['fɪgərətɪv] a bildlich.
figure ['fɪgə*] n (of person) Figur f; (person) Gestalt f; (number) Ziffer f // vt (US: imagine) glauben // vi (appear) erscheinen; ~ **out** vt herausbekommen; ~**head** n (NAUT, fig) Galionsfigur f; ~ **of speech** n Redensart f.
filament ['fɪləmənt] n Faden m; (ELEC) Glühfaden m.
filch [fɪltʃ] vt (col) filzen.
file [faɪl] n (tool) Feile f; (dossier) Akte f; (folder) Aktenordner m; (COMPUT) Datei f; (row) Reihe f // vt (metal, nails) feilen; (papers) abheften; (claim) einreichen // vi: to ~ **in/out** hintereinander hereinkommen/hinausgehen; to ~ **past** vorbeimarschieren.
filing ['faɪlɪŋ] n Ablage f; ~ **cabinet** n Aktenschrank m.
fill [fɪl] vt füllen; (occupy) ausfüllen; (satisfy) sättigen // n: to eat one's ~ sich richtig satt essen; ~ **in** vt (hole) (auf)füllen; (form) ausfüllen; ~ **up** vt (container) auffüllen; (form) ausfüllen // vi (AUT) tanken.
fillet ['fɪlɪt] n Filet nt; ~ **steak** n Filetsteak nt.
filling ['fɪlɪŋ] n (COOK) Füllung f; (for tooth) (Zahn)plombe f; ~ **station** n

Tankstelle f.
film [fɪlm] n Film m // vt (scene) filmen; ~ **star** n Filmstar m; ~**strip** n Filmstreifen m.
filter ['fɪltə*] n Filter m // vt filtern; ~ **lane** n (Brit) Abbiegespur f; ~-**tipped** a Filter-.
filth [fɪlθ] n Dreck m; ~**y** a dreckig; (weather) scheußlich.
fin [fɪn] n Flosse f.
final ['faɪnl] a letzte(r, s); End-; (conclusive) endgültig // n (FOOTBALL etc) Endspiel nt; ~**s** pl (UNIV) Abschlußexamen nt; (SPORT) Schlußrunde f; ~**e** [fɪ'nɑːlɪ] n (MUS) Finale nt; ~**ist** n (SPORT) Schlußrundenteilnehmer m; ~**ize** vt endgültige Form geben (+dat); abschließen; ~**ly** ad (lastly) zuletzt; (eventually) endlich; (irrevocably) endgültig.
finance [faɪ'næns] n Finanzwesen nt; ~**s** pl Finanzen pl // vt finanzieren.
financial [faɪ'nænʃəl] a Finanz-; finanziell.
find [faɪnd], pt, pp **found** vt finden // n Fund m; to ~ **sb guilty** jdn für schuldig erklären; ~ **out** vt herausfinden; ~**ings** npl (JUR) Ermittlungsergebnis nt; (of report) Befund m.
fine [faɪn] a fein; (good) gut; (weather) schön // ad (well) gut; (small) klein // n (JUR) Geldstrafe f // vt (JUR) mit einer Geldstrafe belegen; ~ **arts** npl die schönen Künste pl.
finery ['faɪnərɪ] n Putz m.
finger ['fɪŋgə*] n Finger m // vt befühlen; ~**nail** n Fingernagel m; ~**print** n Fingerabdruck m; ~**tip** n Fingerspitze f.
finicky ['fɪnɪkɪ] a pingelig.
finish ['fɪnɪʃ] n Ende nt; (SPORT) Ziel nt; (of object) Verarbeitung f; (of paint) Oberflächenwirkung f // vt beenden; (book) zu Ende lesen // vi aufhören; (SPORT) ans Ziel kommen; to be ~**ed with sth** fertig sein mit etw; ~**ing line** n Ziellinie f; ~**ing school** n Mädchenpensionat nt.
finite ['faɪnaɪt] a endlich, begrenzt.
Finland ['fɪnlənd] n Finnland nt.
Finn [fɪn] n Finne m, Finnin f; ~**ish** a finnisch // n (LING) Finnisch nt.
fir [fɜː*] n Tanne f.
fire [faɪə*] n Feuer nt; (in house etc) Brand m // vt (gun) abfeuern; (imagination) entzünden; (dismiss) hinauswerfen // vi (AUT) zünden; to be on ~ brennen; ~ **alarm** n Feueralarm m; ~**arm** n Schußwaffe f; ~ **brigade** (Brit), ~ **department** (US) n Feuerwehr f; ~ **engine** n Feuerwehrauto nt; ~ **escape** n Feuerleiter f; ~ **extinguisher** n Löschgerät nt; ~**man** n Feuerwehrmann m; ~**place** n Kamin

m; **~side** n Kamin m; **~station** n
Feuerwehrwache f; **~works** npl
Feuerwerk nt.
firing ['faɪərɪŋ] n Schießen nt; **~ squad**
n Exekutionskommando nt.
firm [fɜːm] a fest // n Firma f.
first [fɜːst] a erste(r, s) // ad zuerst;
(arrive) als erste(r); (happen) zum erstenmal // n (person: in race) Erste(r)
mf; (UNIV) Eins f; (AUT) erste(r) Gang
m; **at ~** zuerst; **~ of all** zu allererst; **~
aid** n Erste Hilfe f; **~-aid kit** n Ver-
bandskasten m; **~-class** a erstklassig;
(travel) erster Klasse; **~-hand** a aus
erster Hand; **~ly** ad erstens; **~ name**
n Vorname m; **~-rate** a erstklassig.
fiscal ['fɪskəl] a Finanz-.
fish [fɪʃ] n, pl inv Fisch m // vi fischen;
angeln; **to go ~ing** angeln gehen; (in
sea) fischen gehen; **~erman** n Fischer
m; **~ farm** n Fischzucht f; **~ fingers**
npl (Brit) Fischstäbchen; **~ing boat** n
Fischerboot nt; **~ing line** n Angel-
schnur f; **~ing rod** n Angel(rute) f;
~monger's (shop) n Fischhändler m;
~ slice n Fischvorleger m; **~ sticks**
npl (US) = **~ fingers**; **~y** a (col:
suspicious) faul.
fission ['fɪʃən] n Spaltung f.
fissure ['fɪʃə*] n Riß m.
fist [fɪst] n Faust f.
fit [fɪt] a (MED) gesund; (SPORT) in
Form, fit; (suitable) geeignet // vt
passen (+dat); (insert, attach) einsetzen
// vi (correspond) passen (zu); (clothes)
passen; (in space, gap) hineinpassen // n
(of clothes) Sitz m; (MED, of anger) Anfall m; (of laughter) Krampf m; **by ~s
and starts** (move) ruckweise; (work)
unregelmäßig; **~ in** vi hineinpassen;
(fig: person) passen; **~ out** vi (also: **~
up**) ausstatten; **~ful** a (sleep) unruhig;
~ment n Einrichtungsgegenstand m;
~ness n (suitability) Eignung f; (MED)
Gesundheit f; (SPORT) Fitneß f; **~ted
carpet** n Teppichboden m; **~ted
kitchen** n Einbauküche f; **~ter** n
(TECH) Monteur m; **~ting** a passend //
n (of dress) Anprobe f; (piece of
equipment) (Ersatz)teil nt; **~ting room**
n Anproberaum m; **~tings** npl Zubehör
nt.
five [faɪv] num fünf; **~r** n (col: Brit)
Fünf-Pfund-Note f; (: US) Fünf-Dollar-
Note f.
fix [fɪks] vt befestigen; (settle) festsetzen; (repair) reparieren // n: **in a ~**
in der Klemme; **~ up** vt (meeting)
arrangieren; **to ~ sb up with sth** jdm
etw (acc) verschaffen; **~ation** n Fixie-
rung f; **~ed** a fest; **~ture** ['fɪkstʃə*] n
Installationsteil m; (SPORT) Spiel nt.
fizz [fɪz] vi sprudeln.
fizzle ['fɪzl] vi: **to ~ out** verpuffen.
fizzy ['fɪzɪ] a Sprudel-, sprudelnd.

flabbergasted ['flæbəgɑːstɪd] a (col)
platt.
flabby ['flæbɪ] a wabbelig.
flag [flæg] n Fahne f // vi (strength)
nachlassen; (spirit) erlahmen; **~ down**
vt anhalten.
flagpole ['flægpəʊl] n Fahnenstange f.
flagrant ['fleɪgrənt] a kraß.
flair [flɛə*] n Talent nt.
flak [flæk] n Flakfeuer nt.
flake [fleɪk] n (of snow) Flocke f; (of
rust) Schuppe f // vi (also: **~ off**) abblättern.
flamboyant [flæm'bɔɪənt] a extravagant.
flame [fleɪm] n Flamme f.
flamingo [flə'mɪŋgəʊ] n Flamingo m.
flammable ['flæməbl] a brennbar.
flan [flæn] n (Brit) Obsttorte f.
flank [flæŋk] n Flanke f // vt flankieren.
flannel ['flænl] n Flanell m; (Brit: also:
face **~**) Waschlappen m; (Brit col) Geschwafel nt; **~s** pl Flanellhose f.
flap [flæp] n Klappe f; (col: crisis)
(helle) Aufregung f // vt (wings)
schlagen mit // vi flattern.
flare [flɛə*] n (signal) Leuchtsignal nt;
(in skirt etc) Weite f; **~ up** vi auf-
flammen; (fig) aufbrausen; (revolt)
(plötzlich) ausbrechen.
flash [flæʃ] n Blitz m; (also: **news ~**)
Kurzmeldung f; (PHOT) Blitzlicht nt //
vt aufleuchten lassen // vi aufleuchten; **in
a ~** im Nu; **~ by or past** vi vor-
beirasen; **~back** n Rückblende f;
~bulb n Blitzlichtbirne f; **~ cube** n
Blitzwürfel m; **~light** n Blitzlicht nt.
flashy ['flæʃɪ] a (pej) knallig.
flask [flɑːsk] n (CHEM) Kolben m; (also:
vacuum **~**) Thermosflasche f.
flat [flæt] a flach; (dull) matt; (MUS)
erniedrigt; (beer) schal; (tyre) platt // n
(Brit: rooms) Wohnung f; (MUS) b nt;
(AUT) Platte(r) m; **to work ~ out** auf
Hochtouren arbeiten; **~ly** ad glatt;
~ten vt (also: **~ten out**) ebnen.
flatter ['flætə*] vt schmeicheln (+dat);
~ing a schmeichelhaft; **~y** n Schmei-
chelei f.
flatulence ['flætjʊləns] n Blähungen pl.
flaunt [flɔːnt] vt prunken mit.
flavour, (US) **flavor** ['fleɪvə*] n
Geschmack m // vt würzen;
strawberry-~ed a mit Erdbeerge-
schmack; **~ing** n Würze f.
flaw [flɔː] n Fehler m; **~less** a einwandfrei.
flax [flæks] n Flachs m; **~en** a
flachsfarben.
flea [fliː] n Floh m.
fleck [flek] n (mark) Fleck m; (pattern)
Tupfen m.
flee [fliː], pt, pp **fled** [fled] vi fliehen // vt
fliehen vor (+dat); (country) fliehen aus.
fleece [fliːs] n Vlies nt // vt (col)

schröpfen.
fleet [fliːt] n Flotte f.
fleeting ['fliːtɪŋ] a flüchtig.
Flemish ['flemɪʃ] a flämisch.
flesh [fleʃ] n Fleisch nt; ~ **wound** n Fleischwunde f.
flew [fluː] pt of **fly**.
flex [fleks] n Kabel nt // vt beugen; ~**ibility** [fleksɪ'bɪlɪtɪ] n Biegsamkeit f; (fig) Flexibilität f; ~**ible** a biegsam; (plans) flexibel.
flick [flɪk] n leichte(r) Schlag m // vt leicht schlagen; ~ **through** vt durchblättern.
flicker ['flɪkə*] n Flackern nt // vi flackern.
flier ['flaɪə*] n Flieger m.
flight [flaɪt] n Flug m; (fleeing) Flucht f; (also: ~ of steps) Treppe f; to take ~ die Flucht ergreifen; to put to ~ in die Flucht schlagen; ~ **attendant** n (US) Steward(eß f) m; ~ **deck** n Flugdeck nt.
flimsy ['flɪmzɪ] a (thin) hauchdünn; (excuse) fadenscheinig.
flinch [flɪntʃ] vi zurückschrecken (away from vor +dat).
fling [flɪŋ], pt, pp **flung** vt schleudern.
flint [flɪnt] n Feuerstein m.
flip [flɪp] vt werfen.
flippant ['flɪpənt] a schnippisch.
flipper ['flɪpə*] n Flosse f.
flirt [flɜːt] vi flirten // n: he/she is a ~ er/sie flirtet gern; ~**ation** [flɜː'teɪʃən] n Flirt m.
flit [flɪt] vi flitzen.
float [fləut] n (FISHING) Schwimmer m; (esp in procession) Plattformwagen m // vi schwimmen; (in air) schweben // vt (COMM) gründen; (currency) floaten.
flock [flɒk] n (of sheep, REL) Herde f; (of birds) Schwarm m; (of people) Schar f.
flog [flɒg] vt prügeln; (col: sell) verkaufen.
flood [flʌd] n Überschwemmung f; (fig) Flut f // vt überschwemmen; ~**ing** n Überschwemmung f; ~**light** n Flutlicht nt.
floor [flɔː*] n (Fuß)boden m; (storey) Stock m // vt (person) zu Boden schlagen; **ground** ~ (Brit), **first** ~ (US) n Erdgeschoß nt; **first** ~ (Brit), **second** ~ (US) n erste(r) Stock m; ~**board** n Diele f; ~ **show** n Kabarettvorstellung f.
flop [flɒp] n Plumps m; (failure) Reinfall m // vi (fail) durchfallen.
floppy ['flɒpɪ] a hängend; ~ **(disk)** n (COMPUT) Diskette f.
flora ['flɔːrə] n Flora f; ~**l** a Blumen-.
florid ['flɒrɪd] a (style) blumig.
florist ['flɒrɪst] n Blumenhändler(in f) m; ~**'s (shop)** n Blumengeschäft nt.
flounce [flaʊns] vi: to ~ **out** hinausstürmen.
flounder ['flaʊndə*] vi (fig) ins Schleudern kommen // n (ZOOL) Flunder f.
flour ['flaʊə*] n Mehl nt.
flourish ['flʌrɪʃ] vi blühen; gedeihen // n (waving) Schwingen nt; (of trumpets) Tusch m, Fanfare f; ~**ing** a blühend.
flout [flaʊt] vt mißachten.
flow [fləu] n Fließen nt; (of sea) Flut f // vi fließen; ~ **chart** n Flußdiagramm nt.
flower ['flaʊə*] n Blume f // vi blühen; ~ **bed** n Blumenbeet nt; ~**pot** n Blumentopf m; ~**y** a (style) blumenreich.
flown [fləun] pp of **fly**.
flu [fluː] n Grippe f.
fluctuate ['flʌktjʊeɪt] vi schwanken.
fluctuation [flʌktjʊ'eɪʃən] n Schwankung f.
fluent a, ~**ly** ad ['fluːənt, -lɪ] fließend.
fluff [flʌf] n Fussel f; ~**y** a flaumig.
fluid ['fluːɪd] n Flüssigkeit f // a (lit) flüssig; (fig: plans) veränderbar.
fluke [fluːk] n (col) Dusel m.
flung [flʌŋ] pt, pp of **fling**.
fluoride ['fluərɪd] n Fluorid nt.
flurry ['flʌrɪ] n (of activity) Aufregung f; (of snow) Gestöber nt.
flush [flʌʃ] n Erröten nt; (of excitement) Glühen nt // vt (aus)spülen // vi erröten // a glatt; ~ **out** vt aufstöbern; ~**ed** a rot.
flustered ['flʌstəd] a verwirrt.
flute [fluːt] n Querflöte f.
flutter ['flʌtə*] n Flattern nt // vi flattern.
flux [flʌks] n: in a state of ~ im Fluß.
fly [flaɪ] n (insect) Fliege f; (on trousers: also: **flies**) (Hosen)schlitz m // v (pt **flew**, pp **flown**) vt fliegen // vi fliegen; (flee) fliehen; (flag) wehen; ~ **away** or **off** vi (bird, insect) wegfliegen; ~**ing** n Fliegen nt // a: with ~**ing colours** mit fliegenden Fahnen; ~**ing start** gute(r) Start m; ~**ing visit** Stippvisite f; ~**ing saucer** n fliegende Untertasse f; ~**over** n (Brit) Überführung f; ~**past** n Luftparade f; ~**sheet** n (for tent) Regendach nt.
foal [fəul] n Fohlen nt.
foam [fəum] n Schaum m // vi schäumen; ~ **rubber** n Schaumgummi m.
fob [fɒb] vt: to ~ **off** andrehen (sb sth jdm etw); (with promise) abspeisen.
focal ['fəukəl] a Brenn-.
focus ['fəukəs] n, pl ~**es** Brennpunkt m // vt (attention) konzentrieren; (camera) scharf einstellen // vi sich konzentrieren (on auf +acc); **in** ~ scharf eingestellt; **out of** ~ unscharf.
fodder ['fɒdə*] n Futter nt.
foe [fəu] n (liter) Feind m.
foetus ['fiːtəs] n Fötus m.
fog [fɒg] n Nebel m; ~ **lamp** n (AUT)

Nebellampe *f*; **~gy** *a* neblig.
foil [fɔɪl] *vt* vereiteln // *n* (*metal, also fig*) Folie *f*; (*fencing*) Florett *nt*.
fold [fəʊld] *n* (*bend, crease*) Falte *f*; (*AGR*) Pferch *m* // *vt* falten; ~ **up** *vt* (*map etc*) zusammenfalten // *vi* (*business*) eingehen; **~er** *n* Schnellhefter *m*; **~ing** *a* (*chair etc*) Klapp-.
foliage ['fəʊlɪɪdʒ] *n* Laubwerk *nt*.
folk [fəʊk] *npl* Volk *nt* // *a* Volks-; **~s** *pl* Leute *pl*; **~lore** ['fəʊklɔ:*] *n* (*study*) Volkskunde *f*; (*tradition*) Folklore *f*; **~ song** *n* Volkslied *nt*; (*modern*) Folksong *m*.
follow ['fɒləʊ] *vt* folgen (+*dat*); (*fashion*) mitmachen // *vi* folgen; ~ **up** *vt* verfolgen; **~er** *n* Anhänger(in *f*) *m*; **~ing** *a* folgend // *n* (*people*) Gefolgschaft *f*.
folly ['fɒlɪ] *n* Torheit *f*.
fond [fɒnd] *a*: to be ~ of gern haben.
fondle ['fɒndl] *vt* streicheln.
font [fɒnt] *n* Taufbecken *nt*.
food [fu:d] *n* Essen *nt*; (*for animals*) Futter *nt*; ~ **mixer** *n* Küchenmixer *m*; ~ **poisoning** *n* Lebensmittelvergiftung *f*; ~ **processor** *n* Küchenmaschine *f*; **~stuffs** *npl* Lebensmittel *pl*.
fool [fu:l] *n* Narr *m*, Närrin *f* // *vt* (*deceive*) hereinlegen // *vi* (*also*: ~ **around**) (herum)albern; **~hardy** *a* tollkühn; **~ish** *a* albern; **~proof** *a* idiotensicher.
foot [fʊt] *n, pl* feet Fuß *m* // *vt* (*bill*) bezahlen; on ~ zu Fuß; **~age** *n* (*CINE*) Filmmaterial *nt*; **~ball** *n* Fußball *m*; (*game: Brit*) Fußball *m*; (: *US*) Football *m*; **~ball player** *n* (*Brit: also*: **~baller**) Fußball(spiel)er *m*; (*US*) Footballer *m*; **~brake** *n* Fußbremse *f*; **~bridge** *n* Fußgängerbrücke *f*; **~hills** *npl* Ausläufer *pl*; **~hold** *n* Halt *m*; **~ing** *n* (*lit*) Halt *m*; (*fig*) Verhältnis *nt*; **~lights** *npl* Rampenlicht *nt*; **~man** *n* Bediensteter(r) *m*; **~note** *n* Fußnote *f*; **~path** *n* Fußweg *m*; **~print** *n* Fußabdruck *m*; **~sore** *a* fußkrank; **~step** *n* Schritt *m*; **~wear** *n* Schuhzeug *nt*.
for [fɔ:*] ◆*prep* **1** für; is this ~ me? ist das für mich?; the train ~ London der Zug nach London; he went ~ the paper er ging die Zeitung holen; give it to me — what ~? gib es mir — warum?
2 (*because of*) wegen; ~ this reason aus diesem Grunde
3 (*referring to distance*): there are roadworks ~ 5 km die Baustelle ist 5 km lang; we walked ~ miles wir sind meilenweit gegangen
4 (*referring to time*) seit; (: *with future sense*) für; he was away ~ 2 years er war zwei Jahre lang weg
5 (*with infinitive clauses*): it is not ~ me to decide das kann ich nicht ent-

scheiden; ~ this to be possible ... damit dies möglich wird/wurde ...
6 (*in spite of*) trotz (+*gen or col*) +dat); ~ all his complaints obwohl er sich ständig beschwert
◆*cj* denn.
forage ['fɒrɪdʒ] *n* (Vieh)futter *nt*.
foray ['fɒreɪ] *n* Raubzug *m*.
forbid [fə'bɪd], *pt* **forbad(e)** [fə'bæd], *pp* **forbidden** [fə'bɪdn] *vt* verbieten; **~ding** *a* einschüchternd.
force [fɔ:s] *n* Kraft *f*; (*compulsion*) Zwang *m* // *vt* zwingen; (*lock*) aufbrechen; **in** ~ (*rule*) gültig; (*group*) in großer Stärke; **the F~s** *pl* (*Brit*) die Streitkräfte; **~d** [fɔ:st] *a* (*smile*) gezwungen; (*landing*) Not-; **~feed** *vt* zwangsernähren; **~ful** *a* (*speech*) kraftvoll; (*personality*) resolut.
forceps ['fɔ:seps] *npl* Zange *f*.
forcibly ['fɔ:səblɪ] *ad* zwangsweise.
ford [fɔ:d] *n* Furt *f* // *vt* durchwaten.
fore [fɔ:*] *n*: to the ~ in den Vordergrund.
forearm ['fɔ:rɑ:m] *n* Unterarm *m*.
foreboding [fɔ:'bəʊdɪŋ] *n* Vorahnung *f*.
forecast ['fɔ:kɑ:st] *n* Vorhersage *f* // (*irreg: like* cast) voraussagen.
forecourt ['fɔ:kɔ:t] *n* (*of garage*) Vorplatz *m*.
forefathers ['fɔ:fɑ:ðəz] *npl* Vorfahren *pl*.
forefinger ['fɔ:fɪŋgə*] *n* Zeigefinger *m*.
forefront ['fɔ:frʌnt] *n* Spitze *f*.
forego [fɔ:'gəʊ] (*irreg: like* go) *vt* verzichten auf (+*acc*).
foreground ['fɔ:graʊnd] *n* Vordergrund *m*.
forehead ['fɒrɪd] *n* Stirn *f*.
foreign ['fɒrɪn] *a* Auslands-; (*accent*) ausländisch; (*trade*) Außen-; (*body*) Fremd-; **~er** *n* Ausländer(in *f*) *m*; ~ **exchange** *n* Devisen *pl*; **F~ Minister** *n* (*Brit*) Außenminister *m*; **F~ Office** *n* Außenministerium *nt*.
foreleg ['fɔ:leg] *n* Vorderbein *nt*.
foreman ['fɔ:mən] *n* Vorarbeiter *m*.
foremost ['fɔ:məʊst] *a* erste(r, s) // *ad*: first and ~ vor allem.
forensic [fə'rensɪk] *a* gerichtsmedizinisch.
forerunner ['fɔ:rʌnə*] *n* Vorläufer *m*.
foresee [fɔ:'si:] (*irreg: like* see) *vt* vorhersehen; **~able** *a* absehbar.
foreshadow [fɔ:'ʃædəʊ] *vt* andeuten.
foresight ['fɔ:saɪt] *n* Voraussicht *f*.
forest ['fɒrɪst] *n* Wald *m*.
forestall [fɔ:'stɔ:l] *vt* zuvorkommen (+*dat*).
forestry ['fɒrɪstrɪ] *n* Forstwirtschaft *f*.
foretaste ['fɔ:teɪst] *n* Vorgeschmack *m*.
foretell [fɔ:'tel] (*irreg: like* tell) *vt* vorhersagen.
forever [fə'revə*] *ad* für immer.
foreword ['fɔ:wɜ:d] *n* Vorwort *nt*.

forfeit ['fɔːfɪt] n Einbuße f // vt verwirken.

forgave [fə'geɪv] pt of **forgive**.

forge [fɔːdʒ] n Schmiede f // vt fälschen; (iron) schmieden; ~ **ahead** vi Fortschritte machen; ~r n Fälscher m; ~**ry** n Fälschung f.

forget [fə'get], pt **forgot**, pp **forgotten** vti vergessen; ~**ful** a vergeßlich; ~**me-not** n Vergißmeinnicht nt.

forgive [fə'gɪv], pt **forgave**, pp **forgiven** vt verzeihen (sb for sth jdm etw).

forgiveness [fə'gɪvnəs] n Verzeihung f.

forgo [fɔː'gəʊ] see **forego**.

forgot [fə'gɒt] pt of **forget**.

forgotten [fə'gɒtn] pp of **forget**.

fork [fɔːk] n Gabel f; (in road) Gabelung f // vi (road) sich gabeln; ~ **out** vt (col: pay) blechen; ~**lift truck** n Gabelstapler m.

forlorn [fə'lɔːn] a (person) verlassen; (hope) vergeblich.

form [fɔːm] n Form f; (type) Art f; (figure) Gestalt f; (SCH) Klasse f; (bench) (Schul)bank f; (document) Formular nt // vt formen; (be part of) bilden.

formal ['fɔːməl] a formell; (occasion) offiziell; ~**ity** [fɔː'mælɪtɪ] n Förmlichkeit f; ~**ities** pl Formalitäten pl; ~**ly** ad (ceremoniously) formell; (officially) offiziell.

format ['fɔːmæt] n Format nt // vt (COMPUT) formatieren.

formation [fɔː'meɪʃən] n Bildung f; (AVIAT) Formation f.

formative ['fɔːmətɪv] a (years) formend.

former ['fɔːmə*] a früher; (opposite of latter) erstere(r, s); ~**ly** ad früher.

formidable ['fɔːmɪdəbl] a furchtbar.

formula ['fɔːmjʊlə] n Formel f; ~**te** ['fɔːmjʊleɪt] vt formulieren.

forsake [fə'seɪk], pt **forsook** [fə'sʊk], pp **forsaken** [fə'seɪkən] vt verlassen.

fort [fɔːt] n Feste f, Fort nt.

forte ['fɔːtɪ] n Stärke f, starke Seite f.

forth [fɔːθ] ad: **and so** ~ und so weiter; ~**coming** a kommend; (character) entgegenkommend; ~**right** a offen; ~**with** ad umgehend.

fortification [fɔːtɪfɪ'keɪʃən] n Befestigung f.

fortify ['fɔːtɪfaɪ] vt (ver)stärken; (protect) befestigen.

fortitude ['fɔːtɪtjuːd] n Seelenstärke f.

fortnight ['fɔːtnaɪt] n vierzehn Tage pl; ~**ly** a zweiwöchentlich // ad alle vierzehn Tage.

fortress ['fɔːtrɪs] n Festung f.

fortuitous [fɔː'tjuːɪtəs] a zufällig.

fortunate ['fɔːtʃənɪt] a glücklich; ~**ly** ad glücklicherweise, zum Glück.

fortune ['fɔːtʃən] n Glück nt; (money) Vermögen nt; ~**-teller** n Wahrsager(in

f) m.

forty ['fɔːtɪ] num vierzig.

forum ['fɔːrəm] n Forum nt.

forward ['fɔːwəd] a vordere(r, s); (movement) vorwärts; (person) vorlaut; (planning) Voraus- // ad vorwärts // n (SPORT) Stürmer m // vt (send) schicken; (help) fördern; ~**(s)** ad vorwärts.

forwent [fɔː'went] pt of **forgo**.

fossil ['fɒsl] n Fossil nt, Versteinerung f.

foster ['fɒstə*] vt (talent) fördern; ~ **child** n Pflegekind nt; ~ **mother** n Pflegemutter f.

fought [fɔːt] pt, pp of **fight**.

foul [faʊl] a schmutzig; (language) gemein; (weather) schlecht // n (SPORT) Foul nt // vt (mechanism) blockieren; (SPORT) foulen; ~ **play** n (SPORT) Foulspiel nt; (LAW) Verbrechen nt.

found [faʊnd] pt, pp of **find** // vt gründen; ~**ation** [faʊn'deɪʃən] n (act) Gründung f; (fig) Fundament nt; (also: ~**ation cream**) Grundierungscreme f; ~**ations** pl Fundament nt.

founder ['faʊndə*] n Gründer(in f) m // vi sinken.

foundry ['faʊndrɪ] n Gießerei f.

fountain ['faʊntɪn] n (Spring)brunnen m; ~ **pen** n Füllfederhalter m.

four [fɔː*] num vier; **on all** ~s auf allen vieren; ~**-poster** n Himmelbett nt; ~**some** n Quartett nt; ~**teen** num vierzehn; ~**teenth** a vierzehnte(r, s) ~**th** a vierte(r, s).

fowl [faʊl] n Huhn nt; (food) Geflügel nt.

fox [fɒks] n Fuchs m // vt täuschen; ~**trot** n Foxtrott m.

foyer ['fɔɪeɪ] n Foyer nt, Vorhalle f.

fraction ['frækʃən] n (MATH) Bruch m; (part) Bruchteil m.

fracture ['fræktʃə*] n (MED) Bruch m // vt brechen.

fragile ['frædʒaɪl] a zerbrechlich.

fragment ['frægmənt] n Bruchstück nt; (small part) Splitter m.

fragrance ['freɪgrəns] n Duft m.

fragrant ['freɪgrənt] a duftend.

frail [freɪl] a schwach, gebrechlich.

frame [freɪm] n Rahmen m; (of spectacles: also: ~s) Gestell nt; (body) Gestalt f // vt einrahmen; (col: incriminate): **to** ~ **sb** jdm etw anhängen; ~ **of mind** n Verfassung f; ~**work** n Rahmen m; (of society) Gefüge nt.

France [frɑːns] n Frankreich nt.

franchise ['fræntʃaɪz] n (POL) (aktives) Wahlrecht nt; (COMM) Lizenz f.

frank [fræŋk] a offen // vt (letter) frankieren; ~**ly** ad offen gesagt; ~**ness** n Offenheit f.

frantic ['fræntɪk] a verzweifelt.

fraternal [frə'tɜːnl] a brüderlich.

fraternity [frə'tɜːnɪtɪ] n (club) Vereini-

gung f; (spirit) Brüderlichkeit f; (US SCH) Studentenverbindung f.
fraternize ['frætənaiz] vi fraternisieren.
fraud [fro:d] n (trickery) Betrug m; (person) Schwindler(in f) m.
fraudulent ['fro:djulənt] a betrügerisch.
fraught [fro:t] a voller (with gen).
fray [frei] n Rauferei f // vti ausfransen; tempers were ~ed die Gemüter waren erhitzt.
freak [fri:k] n Monstrosität f; (storm etc) Ausnahmeerscheinung f.
freckle ['frekl] n Sommersprosse f.
free [fri:] a frei; (loose) lose; (liberal) freigebig // vt (set free) befreien; (unblock) freimachen; ~ (of charge), for ~ ad gratis, umsonst; ~dom n Freiheit f; ~-for-all n (fight) allgemeine(s) Handgemenge nt; ~ gift n Geschenk nt; ~hold property n (freie(r)) Grundbesitz m; ~ kick n Freistoß m; ~lance a frei; (artist) freischaffend; ~ly ad frei; (admit) offen; ~mason n Freimaurer m; ~post n ≈ Gebühr zahlt Empfänger; ~-range a (hen) Farmhof-; (eggs) Land-; ~ trade n Freihandel m; ~way n (US) Autobahn f; ~wheel vt im Freilauf fahren; ~ will n: of one's own ~ will aus freien Stücken.
freeze [fri:z] v (pt froze, pp frozen) vi gefrieren; (feel cold) frieren // vt (lit, fig) einfrieren // n (fig, FIN) Stopp m; ~r n Tiefkühltruhe f; (in fridge) Gefrierfach nt.
freezing ['fri:zɪŋ] a eisig; (~ cold) eiskalt; ~ point n Gefrierpunkt m.
freight [freit] n Fracht f; ~ train n Güterzug m.
French [frentʃ] a französisch // n (LING) Französisch nt; the ~ pl die Franzosen; ~ bean n grüne Bohne f; ~ fried (potatoes) (Brit), ~ fries (US) npl Pommes frites pl; ~man/woman n Franzose m/Französin f; ~ window n Verandatür f.
frenzy ['frenzi] n Raserei f.
frequency ['fri:kwənsi] n Häufigkeit f; (PHYS) Frequenz f.
frequent ['fri:kwənt] a häufig // [fri'kwent] vt (regelmäßig) besuchen.
fresco ['freskəu] n Fresko nt.
fresh [freʃ] a frisch; ~en vi (also: ~en up) (sich) auffrischen; (person) sich frisch machen; ~er n (Brit UNIV: col) Erstsemester nt; ~ly ad gerade; ~man n (US) = ~er; ~ness n Frische f; ~water a (US) Süßwasser-.
fret [fret] vi sich (dat) Sorgen machen.
friar ['fraiə*] n Klosterbruder m.
friction ['frɪkʃən] n (lit, fig) Reibung f.
Friday ['fraidei] n Freitag m.
fridge [frɪdʒ] n (Brit) Kühlschrank m.
fried [fraid] a gebraten.
friend [frend] n Freund(in f) m; ~liness n Freundlichkeit f; ~ly a

freundlich; (relations) freundschaftlich; ~ship n Freundschaft f.
frieze [fri:z] n Fries m.
frigate ['frigit] n Fregatte f.
fright [frait] n Schrecken m; to take ~ es mit der Angst zu tun bekommen; ~en vt erschrecken; to be ~ened Angst haben; ~ening a schrecklich; ~ful a, ~fully ad (col) furchtbar.
frigid ['frɪdʒɪd] a (woman) frigide.
frill [fril] n Rüsche f.
fringe [frɪndʒ] n Besatz m; (Brit: of hair) Pony m; (fig) Peripherie f; ~ benefits npl zusätzliche Leistungen pl.
frisk [frisk] vt durchsuchen.
frisky ['friski] a lebendig, ausgelassen.
fritter ['fritə*] vt: to ~ away vergeuden.
frivolous ['frivələs] a frivol.
frizzy ['frizi] a kraus.
fro [frəu] see to.
frock [frok] n Kleid nt.
frog [frog] n Frosch m; ~man n Froschmann m.
frolic ['frolik] vi ausgelassen sein.
from [from] prep 1 (indicating starting place) von; (indicating origin etc) aus (+dat); a letter/telephone call ~ my sister ein Brief/Anruf von meiner Schwester; where do you come ~? woher kommen Sie?; to drink ~ the bottle aus der Flasche trinken
2 (indicating time) von ... an; (: past) seit; ~ one o'clock to or until or till two von ein Uhr bis zwei; ~ January (on) ab Januar
3 (indicating distance) von ... (entfernt)
4 (indicating price, number etc) ab (+dat); ~ £10 ab £10; there were ~ 20 to 30 people there es waren zwischen 20 und 30 Leute da
5 (indicating difference): he can't tell red ~ green er kann nicht zwischen rot und grün unterscheiden; to be different ~ sb/sth anders sein als jd/etw
6 (because of, on the basis of): ~ what he says aus dem, was er sagt; weak ~ hunger schwach vor Hunger.
front [frʌnt] n Vorderseite f; (of house) Fassade f; (promenade: also: sea ~) Strandpromenade f; (MIL, POL, MET) Front f; (fig: appearances) Fassade f // a (forward) vordere(r, s), Vorder-; (first) vorderste(r, s); in ~ ad vorne; in ~ of vor; ~age n Vorderfront f; ~al a frontal, Vorder-; ~ier ['frʌntɪə*] n Grenze f; ~ door n Haustür f; ~ page n Titelseite f; ~ room n (Brit) Wohnzimmer nt; ~-wheel drive n Vorderradantrieb m.
frost [frost] n Frost m; ~bite n Erfrierung f; ~ed a (glass) Milch-; ~y a frostig.
froth [frɒθ] n Schaum m.
frown [fraun] n Stirnrunzeln nt // vi die Stirn runzeln.

froze [frəuz] *pt of* **freeze**.

frozen ['frəuzn] *pp of* **freeze**.

frugal ['fru:gəl] *a* sparsam, bescheiden.

fruit [fru:t] *n, pl inv* (*as collective*) Obst *nt*; (*particular*) Frucht *f*; **~erer** *n* Obsthändler *m*; **~erer's (shop)** *n* Obsthandlung *f*; **~ful** *a* fruchtbar; **~ion** [fru:'ɪʃən] *n*: **to come to ~ion** in Erfüllung gehen; **~ juice** *n* Fruchtsaft *m*; **~ machine** *n* (*Brit*) Spielautomat *m*; **~ salad** *n* Obstsalat *m*.

frustrate [frʌs'treɪt] *vt* vereiteln; **~d** *a* gehemmt; (*PSYCH*) frustriert.

fry [fraɪ], *pt, pp* **fried** *vt* braten; **small ~** *pl* kleine Fische *pl*; **~ing pan** *n* Bratpfanne *f*.

ft. *abbr of* **foot, feet**.

fuddy-duddy ['fʌdɪdʌdɪ] *n* altmodische(r) Kauz *m*.

fudge [fʌdʒ] *n* Karamellen *pl*.

fuel [fjuəl] *n* Treibstoff *m*; (*for heating*) Brennstoff *m*; (*for lighter*) Benzin *nt*; **~ oil** *n* (*diesel fuel*) Heizöl *nt*; **~ tank** *n* Tank *m*.

fugitive ['fju:dʒɪtɪv] *n* Flüchtling *m*.

fulfil [ful'fɪl] *vt* (*duty*) erfüllen; (*promise*) einhalten; **~ment** *n* Erfüllung *f*.

full [ful] *a* (*box, bottle, price*) voll; (*person: satisfied*) satt; (*member, power, employment, moon*) Voll-; (*complete*) vollständig, Voll-; (*speed*) höchste(r, s); (*skirt*) weit // *ad*: **~ well** wohl; **in ~** vollständig; **~-length** *a* (*portrait*) lebensgroß; **~ moon** *n* Vollmond *m*; **~-scale** (*attack*) General-; (*drawing*) in Originalgröße; **~ stop** *n* Punkt *m*; **~-time** *a* (*job*) Ganztags- // *ad* (*work*) ganztags // *n* (*SPORT*) Spielschluß *nt*; **~y** *ad* völlig; **~y-fledged** *a* (*lit, fig*) flügge.

fulsome ['fulsəm] *a* übertrieben.

fumble ['fʌmbl] *vi* herumfummeln (*with* an +*dat*).

fume [fju:m] *vi* qualmen; (*fig*) kochen (*col*); **~s** *pl* Abgase *pl*.

fumigate ['fju:mɪgeɪt] *vt* ausräuchern.

fun [fʌn] *n* Spaß *m*; **to make ~ of** sich lustig machen über (+*acc*).

function ['fʌŋkʃən] *n* Funktion *f*; (*occasion*) Veranstaltung *f* // *vi* funktionieren; **~al** *a* funktionell.

fund [fʌnd] *n* (*money*) Geldmittel *pl*, Fonds *m*; (*store*) Vorrat *m*; **~s** *pl* Mittel *pl*.

fundamental [fʌndə'mentl] *a* fundamental, grundlegend.

funeral ['fju:nərəl] *n* Beerdigung *f*; **~ parlour** *n* Leichenhalle *f*; **~ service** *n* Trauergottesdienst *m*.

funfair ['fʌnfeə*] *n* (*Brit*) Jahrmarkt *m*.

fungus ['fʌŋgəs], *pl* **-gi** ['fʌŋgaɪ] *n* Pilz *m*.

funnel ['fʌnl] *n* Trichter *m*; (*NAUT*) Schornstein *m*.

funny ['fʌnɪ] *a* komisch.

fur [fɜ:*] *n* Pelz *m*; **~ coat** *n* Pelzmantel *m*.

furious ['fjuərɪəs] *a* wütend; (*attempt*) heftig.

furlong ['fɜ:lɒŋ] *n* = 220 yards.

furlough ['fɜ:ləu] *n* (*US MIL*) Urlaub *m*.

furnace ['fɜ:nɪs] *n* (Brenn)ofen *m*.

furnish ['fɜ:nɪʃ] *vt* einrichten; (*supply*) versehen; **~ings** *npl* Einrichtung *f*.

furniture ['fɜ:nɪtʃə*] *n* Möbel *pl*; **piece of ~** Möbelstück *nt*.

furrow ['fʌrəu] *n* Furche *f*.

furry ['fɜ:rɪ] *a* (*tongue*) pelzig; (*animal*) Pelz-.

further ['fɜ:ðə*] *a* weitere(r, s) // *ad* weiter // *vt* fördern; **~ education** *n* Weiterbildung *f*; Erwachsenenbildung *f*; **~more** *ad* ferner.

furthest ['fɜ:ðɪst] *superl of* **far**.

furtive ['fɜ:tɪv] *a* verstohlen.

fury ['fjuərɪ] *n* Wut *f*, Zorn *m*.

fuse [fju:z] *n* (*ELEC*) Sicherung *f*; (*of bomb*) Zünder *m* // *vt* verschmelzen // *vi* (*Brit ELEC*) durchbrennen; **~ box** *n* Sicherungskasten *m*.

fuselage ['fju:zəlɑ:ʒ] *n* Flugzeugrumpf *m*.

fusion ['fju:ʒən] *n* Verschmelzung *f*.

fuss [fʌs] *n* Theater *nt*; **~y** *a* kleinlich.

futile ['fju:taɪl] *a* zwecklos, sinnlos.

futility [fju:'tɪlɪtɪ] *n* Zwecklosigkeit *f*.

future ['fju:tʃə*] *a* zukünftig // *n* Zukunft *f*; **in (the) ~** in Zukunft.

fuze [fju:z] (*US*) = **fuse**.

fuzzy ['fʌzɪ] *a* (*indistinct*) verschwommen; (*hair*) kraus.

G

G [dʒi:] *n* (*MUS*) G *nt*.

gabble ['gæbl] *vi* plappern.

gable ['geɪbl] *n* Giebel *m*.

gadget ['gædʒɪt] *n* Vorrichtung *f*.

Gaelic ['geɪlɪk] *a* gälisch // *n* (*LING*) Gälisch *nt*.

gaffe [gæf] *n* Fauxpas *m*.

gag [gæg] *n* Knebel *m*; (*THEAT*) Gag *m* // *vt* knebeln.

gaily ['geɪlɪ] *ad* lustig, fröhlich.

gain [geɪn] *vt* (*obtain*) erhalten; (*win*) gewinnen // *vi* (*improve*) gewinnen (*in* an +*dat*); (*clock*) vorgehen // *n* Gewinn *m*; **to ~ on sb** jdn einholen.

gait [geɪt] *n* Gang *m*.

gal. *abbr of* **gallon**.

gala ['gɑːlə] *n* Fest *nt*.

galaxy ['gæləksɪ] *n* Sternsystem *nt*.

gale [geɪl] *n* Sturm *m*.

gallant ['gælənt] *a* tapfer; (*polite*) galant; **~ry** *n* Tapferkeit *f*; Galanterie *f*.

gallbladder ['gɔ:lblædə*] *n* Gallenblase *f*.

gallery ['gælərɪ] *n* (*also: art ~*) Galerie

f.

galley ['gælɪ] *n* (*ship's kitchen*) Kombüse *f*; (*ship*) Galeere *f*.

gallon ['gælən] *n* Gallone *f*.

gallop ['gæləp] *n* Galopp *m* // *vi* galoppieren.

gallows ['gæləʊz] *n* Galgen *m*.

gallstone ['gɔːlstəʊn] *n* Gallenstein *m*.

galore [gə'lɔː*] *ad* in Hülle und Fülle.

galvanize ['gælvənaɪz] *vt* (*metal*) galvanisieren; (*fig*) elektrisieren.

gamble ['gæmbl] *vi* (um Geld) spielen // *vt* (*risk*) aufs Spiel setzen // *n* Risiko *nt*; **~r** *n* Spieler(in *f*) *m*.

gambling ['gæmblɪŋ] *n* Glücksspiel *nt*.

game [geɪm] *n* Spiel *nt*; (*hunting*) Wild *nt* // *a* bereit (*for* zu); **~keeper** *n* Wildhüter *m*.

gammon ['gæmən] *n* geräucherte(r) Schinken *m*.

gamut ['gæmət] *n* Tonskala *f*.

gang [gæŋ] *n* (*of criminals, youths*) Bande *f*; (*of workmen*) Kolonne *f* // *vi*: **to ~ up** on sb sich gegen jdn verschwören.

gangrene ['gæŋgriːn] *n* Brand *m*.

gangster ['gæŋstə*] *n* Gangster *m*.

gangway ['gæŋweɪ] *n* (*NAUT*) Laufplanke *f*; (*aisle*) Gang *m*.

gaol [dʒeɪl] (*Brit*) = **jail**.

gap [gæp] *n* Lücke *f*.

gape [geɪp] *vi* glotzen.

gaping ['geɪpɪŋ] *a* (*wound*) klaffend; (*hole*) gähnend.

garage ['gærɑːʒ] *n* Garage *f*; (*for repair*) (Auto)reparaturwerkstatt *f*; (*for petrol*) Tankstelle *f*.

garbage ['gɑːbɪdʒ] *n* Abfall *m*; **~ can** *n* (*US*) Mülltonne *f*.

garbled ['gɑːbld] *a* (*story*) verdreht.

garden ['gɑːdn] *n* Garten *m*; **~er** *n* Gärtner(in *f*) *m*; **~ing** *n* Gärtnern *nt*.

gargle ['gɑːgl] *vi* gurgeln.

gargoyle ['gɑːgɔɪl] *n* Wasserspeier *m*.

garish ['gεərɪʃ] *a* grell.

garland ['gɑːlənd] *n* Girlande *f*.

garlic ['gɑːlɪk] *n* Knoblauch *m*.

garment ['gɑːmənt] *n* Kleidungsstück *nt*.

garnish ['gɑːnɪʃ] *vt* (*food*) garnieren.

garrison ['gærɪsən] *n* Garnison *f*.

garrulous ['gærʊləs] *a* geschwätzig.

garter ['gɑːtə*] *n* (*US*) Strumpfband *nt*.

gas [gæs] *n* Gas *nt*; (*esp US: petrol*) Benzin *nt* // *vt* vergasen; **~ cooker** *n* (*Brit*) Gasherd *m*; **~ cylinder** *n* Gasflasche *f*; **~ fire** *n* Gasofen *m*.

gash [gæʃ] *n* klaffende Wunde *f* // *vt* tief verwunden.

gasket ['gæskɪt] *n* Dichtungsring *m*.

gas: **~mask** *n* Gasmaske *f*; **~ meter** *n* Gaszähler *m*.

gasoline ['gæsəliːn] *n* (*US*) Benzin *nt*.

gasp [gɑːsp] *vi* keuchen; (*in astonishment*) tief Luft holen // *n* Keu-

chen *nt*.

gas: **~ ring** *n* Gasring *m*; **~sy** *a* (*drink*) sprudelnd; **~ tap** *n* Gashahn *m*.

gastric ['gæstrɪk] *a* Magen-.

gate [geɪt] *n*; (*barrier*) Schranke *f*; **~crash** *vt* (*Brit: party*) platzen in (+*acc*); **~way** *n* Toreingang *m*.

gather ['gæðə*] *vt* (*people*) versammeln; (*things*) sammeln // *vi* (*understand*) annehmen; (*deduce*) schließen (*from* aus); (*assemble*) sich versammeln; **to ~ speed** schneller werden; **~ing** *n* Versammlung *f*.

gauche [gəʊʃ] *a* linkisch.

gaudy ['gɔːdɪ] *a* schreiend.

gauge [geɪdʒ] *n* (*instrument*) Meßgerät *nt*; (*RAIL*) Spurweite *f*; (*dial*) Anzeiger *m*; (*measure*) Maß *nt* // *vt* (*lit*) (ab)messen; (*fig*) abschätzen.

gaunt [gɔːnt] *a* hager.

gauntlet ['gɔːntlɪt] *n* (*knight's*) (Fehde)handschuh *m*.

gauze [gɔːz] *n* Gaze *f*.

gave [geɪv] *pt of* **give**.

gay [geɪ] *a* (*homosexual*) schwul; (*lively*) lustig.

gaze [geɪz] *n* Blick *m* // *vi* (an)blicken (*at acc*).

gazelle [gə'zel] *n* Gazelle *f*.

gazetteer [gæzɪ'tɪə*] *n* geographische(s) Lexikon *nt*.

gazumping [gə'zʌmpɪŋ] *n* (*Brit*) Verkauf eines Hauses an einen zweiten Bieter trotz Zusage an den ersten.

GB *n abbr* (= *Great Britain*) GB.

GCE *n abbr* (*Brit*) of **General Certificate of Education**.

GCSE *n abbr* (*Brit:* = *General Certificate of Secondary Education*) ≈ Hauptschulabschluß *m*.

gear [gɪə*] *n* Getriebe *nt*; (*equipment*) Ausrüstung *f*; (*AUT*) Gang *m* // *vt* (*fig: adapt*): **to be ~ed** ausgerichtet sein (*to* auf +*acc*); **top** *or* (*US*) **high/low** ~ höchste(r)/niedrige(r) Gang *m*; **in** ~ eingekuppelt; **~ box** *n* Getriebe(gehäuse) *nt*; **~ lever**, **~ shift** (*US*) *n* Schalthebel *m*.

geese [giːs] *npl of* **goose**.

gel [dʒel] *n* Gel *nt*.

gelatin(e) ['dʒelətiːn] *n* Gelatine *f*.

gelignite ['dʒelɪgnaɪt] *n* Plastiksprengstoff *m*.

gem [dʒem] *n* Edelstein *m*; (*fig*) Juwel *nt*.

Gemini ['dʒemɪniː] *n* Zwillinge *pl*.

gender ['dʒendə*] *n* (*GRAM*) Geschlecht *nt*.

gene [dʒiːn] *n* Gen *nt*.

general ['dʒenərəl] *n* General *m* // *a* allgemein; **~ delivery** *n* (*US*) Ausgabe(schalter *m*) *f* postlagernder Sendungen; **~ election** *n* allgemeine Wahlen *pl*; **~ization** [-aɪ'zeɪʃən] *n* Verallgemeinerung *f*; **~ize** *vi* verallgemeinern; **~ly** *ad* allgemein, im allgemeinen; **~ practitioner (G.P.)** *n* praktische(r) Arzt *m*, praktische Ärztin *f*.

generate ['dʒenəreɪt] *vt* erzeugen.

generation [dʒenə'reɪʃən] *n* Generation *f*; (*act*) Erzeugung *f*.

generator ['dʒenəreɪtə*] *n* Generator *m*.

generosity [dʒenə'rɒsɪtɪ] *n* Großzügigkeit *f*.

generous ['dʒenərəs] *a* großzügig.

genetics [dʒɪ'netɪks] *n* Genetik *f*.

Geneva [dʒɪ'niːvə] *n* Genf *nt*.

genial ['dʒiːnɪəl] *a* freundlich, jovial.

genitals ['dʒenɪtlz] *npl* Genitalien *pl*.

genius ['dʒiːnɪəs] *n* Genie *nt*.

genocide ['dʒenəʊsaɪd] *n* Völkermord *m*.

gent [dʒent] *n abbr of* **gentleman**.

genteel [dʒen'tiːl] *a* (*polite*) wohlanständig; (*affected*) affektiert.

gentle ['dʒentl] *a* sanft, zart.

gentleman ['dʒentlmən] *n* Herr *m*; (*polite*) Gentleman *m*.

gentleness ['dʒentlnɪs] *n* Zartheit *f*, Milde *f*.

gently ['dʒentlɪ] *ad* zart, sanft.

gentry ['dʒentrɪ] *n* Landadel *m*.

gents [dʒents] *n*: G~ (*lavatory*) Herren.

genuine ['dʒenjʊɪn] *a* echt.

geographic(al) [dʒɪə'græfɪk(əl)] *a* geographisch.

geography [dʒɪ'ɒɡrəfɪ] *n* Geographie *f*.

geological [dʒɪəʊ'lɒdʒɪkəl] *a* geologisch.

geologist [dʒɪ'ɒlədʒɪst] *n* Geologe *m*, Geologin *f*.

geology [dʒɪ'ɒlədʒɪ] *n* Geologie *f*.

geometry [dʒɪ'ɒmɪtrɪ] *n* Geometrie *f*.

geranium [dʒɪ'reɪnɪəm] *n* Geranie *f*.

geriatric [dʒerɪ'ætrɪk] *a* Alten- // *n* Greis(in *f*) *m*.

germ [dʒɜːm] *n* Keim *m*; (*MED*) Bazillus *m*.

German ['dʒɜːmən] *a* deutsch // *n* Deutsche(r) *mf*; (*LING*) Deutsch *nt*; **~ measles** *n* Röteln *pl*.

Germany ['dʒɜːmənɪ] *n* Deutschland *nt*.

germination [dʒɜːmɪ'neɪʃən] *n* Keimen *nt*.

gesticulate [dʒes'tɪkjʊleɪt] *vi* gestikulieren.

gesture ['dʒestʃə*] *n* Geste *f*.

get [get], *pt, pp* **got**, *pp* **gotten** (*US*) ♦*vi* **1** (*become, be*) werden; to ~ old/tired alt/müde werden; to ~ **married** heiraten

2 (*go*) (an)kommen, gehen

3 (*begin*): to ~ to know sb jdn kennenlernen; let's ~ going *or* started fangen wir an!

4 (*modal aux v*): you've got to do it du mußt es tun

♦*vt* **1**: to ~ sth done (*do*) etw machen;

(*have done*) etw machen lassen; to ~ sth going *or* to go etw in Gang bringen *or* bekommen; to ~ sb to do sth jdn dazu bringen, etw zu tun

2 (*obtain*: *money, permission, results*) erhalten; (*find*: *job, flat*) finden; (*fetch*: *person, doctor, object*) holen; to ~ sth for sb jdm etw besorgen; ~ **me Mr Jones, please** (*TEL*) verbinden Sie mich bitte mit Mr Jones

3 (*receive*: *present, letter*) bekommen, kriegen; (*acquire*: *reputation etc*) erwerben

4 (*catch*) bekommen, kriegen; (*hit*: *target etc*) treffen, erwischen; ~ **him!** (*to dog*) faß!

5 (*take, move*) bringen; to ~ sth to sb jdm etw bringen

6 (*understand*) verstehen; (*hear*) mitbekommen; **I've got it!** ich hab's!

7 (*have, possess*): to **have got** etw haben.

get about *vi* herumkommen; (*news*) sich verbreiten

get along *vi* (*people*) (gut) zurechtkommen; (*depart*) sich (*acc*) auf den Weg machen

get at *vt* (*facts*) herausbekommen; to ~ at sb (*nag*) an jdm herumnörgeln

get away *vi* (*leave*) sich (*acc*) davonmachen; (*escape*) entkommen (*from dat*); to ~ away with sth mit etw davon kommen

get back *vi* (*return*) zurückkommen // *vt* zurückbekommen

get by *vi* (*pass*) vorbeikommen; (*manage*) zurechtkommen

get down *vi* (her)untergehen // *vt* (*depress*) fertigmachen; to ~ down to in Angriff nehmen; (*find time to do*) kommen zu

get in *vi* (*train*) ankommen; (*arrive home*) heimkommen

get into *vt* (*enter*) hinein-/hereinkommen in (+*acc*); (: *car train etc*) einsteigen in (+*acc*); (*clothes*) anziehen

get off *vi* (*from train etc*) aussteigen; (*from horse*) absteigen // *vt* aussteigen aus; absteigen von

get on *vi* (*progress*) vorankommen; (*be friends*) auskommen; (*age*) alt werden; (*onto train etc*) einsteigen; (*onto horse*) aufsteigen // *vt* einsteigen in (+*acc*); aufsteigen auf (+*acc*)

get out *vi* (*of house*) herauskommen; (*of vehicle*) aussteigen // *vt* (*take out*) herausholen

get out of *vt* (*duty etc*) herumkommen um

get over *vt* (*illness*) sich (*acc*) erholen von; (*surprise*) verkraften; (*news*) fassen; (*loss*) sich abfinden mit

get round *vt* herumkommen; (*fig*: *person*) herumkriegen

get through to vt (TEL) durchkommen zu

get together vi zusammenkommen

get up vi aufstehen // vt hinaufbringen; (go up) hinaufgehen; (organize) auf die Beine stellen

get up to vt (reach) erreichen; (prank etc) anstellen.

getaway ['getəweɪ] n Flucht f.

geyser ['giːzə*] n Geiser m; (heater) Durchlauferhitzer m.

ghastly ['gɑːstlɪ] a (horrible) gräßlich.

gherkin ['gɜːkɪn] n Gewürzgurke f.

ghetto ['getəu] n G(h)etto nt.

ghost [gəust] n Gespenst nt; ~**ly** a gespenstisch.

giant ['dʒaɪənt] n Riese m // a riesig, Riesen-.

gibberish ['dʒɪbərɪʃ] n dumme(s) Geschwätz nt.

gibe [dʒaɪb] n spöttische Bemerkung f.

giblets ['dʒɪblɪts] npl Geflügelinnereien pl.

giddiness ['gɪdɪnəs] n Schwindelgefühl nt.

giddy ['gɪdɪ] a schwindlig.

gift [gɪft] n Geschenk nt; (ability) Begabung f; ~**ed** a begabt; ~ **token** or **voucher** n Geschenkgutschein m.

gigantic [dʒaɪ'gæntɪk] a riesenhaft.

giggle ['gɪgl] vi kichern // n Gekicher nt.

gild [gɪld] vt vergolden.

gill [dʒɪl] n (1/4 pint) Viertelpinte f // n [gɪl] (of fish) Kieme f.

gilt [gɪlt] n Vergoldung f // a vergoldet; ~**-edged** a mündelsicher.

gimmick ['gɪmɪk] n Gag m.

gin [dʒɪn] n Gin m.

ginger ['dʒɪndʒə*] n Ingwer m; ~ **ale** n, ~ **beer** n Ingwerbier nt; ~**bread** n Pfefferkuchen m; ~**-haired** a rothaarig.

gingerly ['dʒɪndʒəlɪ] ad behutsam.

gipsy ['dʒɪpsɪ] n Zigeuner(in f) m.

giraffe [dʒɪ'rɑːf] n Giraffe f.

girder ['gɜːdə*] n Eisenträger m.

girdle ['gɜːdl] n Hüftgürtel m.

girl [gɜːl] n Mädchen nt; ~**friend** n Freundin f; ~**ish** a mädchenhaft.

giro ['dʒaɪrəu] n (bauk ~) Giro nt; (post office ~) Postscheckverkehr m.

girth [gɜːθ] n (measure) Umfang m; (strap) Sattelgurt m.

gist [dʒɪst] n Wesentliche(s) nt.

give [gɪv], pt **gave**, pp **given** vt geben // vi (break) nachgeben; ~ **away** vt (give free) verschenken; (betray) verraten; ~ **back** vt zurückgeben; ~ **in** vi nachgeben // vt (hand in) abgeben; ~ **off** vt abgeben; ~ **out** vt verteilen; (announce) bekanntgeben; ~ **up** vti aufgeben; **to** ~ **o.s. up** sich stellen; (after siege) sich ergeben; ~ **way** vi (Brit: traffic) Vorfahrt lassen; (to feelings) nachgeben (+dat).

glacier ['glæsɪə*] n Gletscher m.

glad [glæd] a froh.

gladioli [glædɪ'əulaɪ] npl Gladiolen pl.

gladly ['glædlɪ] ad gern(e).

glamorous ['glæmərəs] a reizvoll.

glamour ['glæmə*] n Glanz m.

glance [glɑːns] n Blick m // vi (hin)blicken (at auf +acc); ~ **off** vi (fly off) abprallen von.

glancing ['glɑːnsɪŋ] a (blow) Streif-.

gland [glænd] n Drüse f.

glare [glɛə*] n (light) grelle(s) Licht nt; (stare) wilde(r) Blick m // vi grell scheinen; (angrily) böse ansehen (at acc).

glaring ['glɛərɪŋ] a (injustice) schreiend; (mistake) kraß.

glass [glɑːs] n Glas nt; (mirror: also: looking ~) Spiegel m; ~**es** pl Brille f; ~**house** n Gewächshaus nt; ~**ware** n Glaswaren pl; ~**y** a glasig.

glaze [gleɪz] vt verglasen; (finish with a ~) glasieren // n Glasur f; ~**d** a (eye) glasig; (pottery) glasiert.

glazier ['gleɪzɪə*] n Glaser m.

gleam [gliːm] n Schimmer m // vi schimmern; ~**ing** a schimmernd.

glean [gliːn] vt (fig) ausfindig machen.

glee [gliː] n Frohsinn m.

glen [glen] n Bergtal nt.

glib [glɪb] a oberflächlich.

glide [glaɪd] vi gleiten; ~**r** n (AVIAT) Segelflugzeug nt.

gliding ['glaɪdɪŋ] n Segelfliegen nt.

glimmer ['glɪmə*] n Schimmer m.

glimpse [glɪmps] n flüchtige(r) Blick m // vt flüchtig erblicken.

glint [glɪnt] n Glitzern nt // vi glitzern.

glisten ['glɪsn] vi glänzen.

glitter ['glɪtə*] vi funkeln // n Funkeln nt.

gloat ['gləut] vi: to ~ **over** sich weiden an (+dat).

global ['gləubl] a global.

globe [gləub] n Erdball m; (sphere) Globus m.

gloom [gluːm] n (darkness) Dunkel nt; (depression) düstere Stimmung f; ~**y** a düster.

glorify ['glɔːrɪfaɪ] vt verherrlichen.

glorious ['glɔːrɪəs] a glorreich.

glory ['glɔːrɪ] n Ruhm m.

gloss [glɒs] n (shine) Glanz m; ~ **over** vt übertünchen.

glossary ['glɒsərɪ] n Glossar nt.

glossy ['glɒsɪ] a (surface) glänzend.

glove [glʌv] n Handschuh m; ~ **compartment** n (AUT) Handschuhfach nt.

glow [gləu] vi glühen // n Glühen nt.

glower ['glauə*] vi: to ~ **at** finster anblicken.

glucose ['gluːkəus] n Traubenzucker m.

glue [gluː] n Klebstoff m // vt kleben.

glum [glʌm] a bedrückt.

glut [glʌt] n Überfluß m.

glutton ['glʌtn] n Vielfraß m; a ~ **for work** ein Arbeitstier nt; ~**y** n Völlerei f.

glycerin(e) ['glɪsəriːn] n Glyzerin nt.
gnarled [nɑːld] a knorrig.
gnat [næt] n Stechmücke f.
gnaw [nɔː] vt nagen an (+dat).
gnome [nəʊm] n Gnom m.
go [gəʊ], pt **went**, pp **gone** vi gehen; (travel) reisen, fahren; (depart: train) (ab)fahren; (be sold) verkauft werden; (work) gehen, funktionieren; (fit, suit) passen (with zu); (become) werden; (break etc) nachgeben // n (pl **~es**) (energy) Schwung m; (attempt) Versuch m; he's going to do it er wird es tun; to ~ **for a walk** spazieren gehen; to ~ **dancing** tanzen gehen; how did it ~? wie war's?; to have a ~ **at sth** etw versuchen; to be on the ~ auf Trab sein; whose ~ is it? wer ist dran?; ~ **about** vi (rumour) umgehen // vt: how do I ~ about this? wie packe ich das an?; ~ **ahead** vi (proceed) weitergehen; ~ **along** vi dahingehen, dahinfahren // vt entlanggehen, entlangfahren; to ~ along with (agree to support) zustimmen (+dat); ~ **away** vi (depart) weggehen; ~ **back** vi (return) zurückgehen; ~ **back on** vt (promise) nicht halten; ~ **by** vi (years, time) vergehen // vt sich richten nach; ~ **down** vi (sun) untergehen // vt hinuntergehen, hinunterfahren; ~ **for** vt (fetch) holen (gehen); (like) mögen; (attack) sich stürzen auf (+acc); ~ **in** vi hineingehen; ~ **in for** vt (competition) teilnehmen an; ~ **into** vt (enter) hineingehen in (+acc); (study) sich befassen mit; ~ **off** vi (depart) weggehen; (lights) ausgehen; (milk etc) sauer werden; (explode) losgehen // vt (dislike) nicht mehr mögen; ~ **on** vi (continue) weitergehen; (col: complain) meckern; (lights) angehen; ~ **on with** sth mit etw weitermachen; ~ **out** vi (fire, light) ausgehen; (of house) hinausgehen; ~ **over** vi (ship) kentern // vt (examine, check) durchgehen; ~ **through** vt (town etc) durchgehen, durchfahren; ~ **up** vi (price) steigen; ~ **without** vt sich behelfen ohne; (food) entbehren.
goad [gəʊd] vt anstacheln.
go-ahead ['gəʊəhed] a zielstrebig; (progressive) fortschrittlich // n grüne(s) Licht nt.
goal [gəʊl] n Ziel nt; (SPORT) Tor nt; ~**keeper** n Torwart m; ~-**post** n Torpfosten m.
goat [gəʊt] n Ziege f.
gobble ['gɒbl] vt (also: ~ down, ~ up) hinunterschlingen.
go-between ['gəʊbɪtwiːn] n Mittelsmann n.
goblet ['gɒblɪt] n Kelch(glas nt) m.
god [gɒd] n Gott m; **G~** n Gott m; ~**child** n Patenkind nt; ~**daughter** n

Patentochter f; ~**dess** n Göttin f; ~**father** n Pate m; ~-**forsaken** a gottverlassen; ~**mother** n Patin f; ~**send** n Geschenk nt des Himmels; ~**son** n Patensohn m.
goggles ['gɒglz] npl Schutzbrille f.
going ['gəʊɪŋ] n (horse-racing) Bahn f // a (rate) gängig; (concern) gutgehend; it's hard ~ es ist schwierig.
gold [gəʊld] n Gold nt // a golden; ~**en** a golden, Gold-; ~**fish** n Goldfisch m; ~**mine** n Goldgrube f; ~-**plated** a vergoldet; ~**smith** n Goldschmied(in f) m.
golf [gɒlf] n Golf nt; ~**ball** n (also on typewriter) Golfball m; ~ **club** n (society) Golfklub m; (stick) Golfschläger m; ~ **course** n Golfplatz m; ~**er** n Golfspieler(in f) m.
gondola ['gɒndələ] n Gondel f.
gone [gɒn] pp of **go**.
gong [gɒŋ] n Gong m.
good [gʊd] n (benefit) Wohl nt; (moral excellence) Güte f // a gut; ~**s** pl Waren pl, Güter pl; a ~ **deal** (of) ziemlich viel; a ~ **many** ziemlich viele; ~**bye!** interj auf Wiedersehen!; **G~ Friday** n Karfreitag m; ~-**looking** a gutaussehend; ~ **morning!** interj guten Morgen!; ~-**natured** a gutmütig; (joke) harmlos; ~**ness** n Güte f; (virtue) Tugend f; ~**s train** n (Brit) Güterzug; ~**will** n (favour) Wohlwollen nt; (COMM) Firmenansehen nt.
goose [guːs], pl **geese** n Gans f.
gooseberry ['guzbərɪ] n Stachelbeere f.
gooseflesh ['guːsfleʃ] n, **goose pimples** npl Gänsehaut f.
gore [gɔː*] vt aufspießen // n Blut nt.
gorge [gɔːdʒ] n Schlucht f // vr: to ~ o.s. (sich voll)fressen.
gorgeous ['gɔːdʒəs] a prächtig.
gorilla [gə'rɪlə] n Gorilla m.
gorse [gɔːs] n Stechginster m.
gory ['gɔːrɪ] a blutig.
go-slow ['gəʊ'sləʊ] n (Brit) Bummelstreik m.
gospel ['gɒspəl] n Evangelium nt.
gossip ['gɒsɪp] n Klatsch m; (person) Klatschbase f // vi klatschen.
got [gɒt] pt, pp of **get**; ~**ten** (US) pp of **get**.
gout [gaʊt] n Gicht f.
govern ['gʌvən] vt regieren; verwalten.
governess ['gʌvənɪs] n Gouvernante f.
government ['gʌvnmənt] n Regierung f.
governor ['gʌvənə*] n Gouverneur m.
gown [gaʊn] n Gewand nt; (UNIV) Robe f.
G.P. n abbr of **general practitioner**.
grab [græb] vt packen.
grace [greɪs] n Anmut f; (blessing) Gnade f; (prayer) Tischgebet nt // vt (adorn) zieren; (honour) auszeichnen; 5 days' ~ 5 Tage Aufschub m; ~**ful** a an-

mutig.

gracious ['greɪʃəs] a gnädig; (kind) freundlich.

grade [greɪd] n Grad m; (slope) Gefälle nt // v (classify) einstufen; **~ crossing** n (US) Bahnübergang m; **~ school** n (US) Grundschule f.

gradient ['greɪdɪənt] n Steigung f; Gefälle nt.

gradual ['grædjʊəl] a allmählich.

graduate ['grædjʊɪt] n: to be a ~ das Staatsexamen haben // vi ['grædjʊeɪt] das Staatsexamen machen.

graduation [grædjʊ'eɪʃən] n Erlangung f eines akademischen Grades.

graffiti [grə'fiːtɪ] npl Graffiti pl.

graft [grɑːft] n (hard work) Schufterei f; (MED) Verpflanzung f // vt propfen; (fig) aufpropfen; (MED) verpflanzen.

grain [greɪn] n Korn nt; (in wood) Maserung f.

gram [græm] n Gramm nt.

grammar ['græmə*] n Grammatik f; **~ school** n (Brit) Gymnasium nt.

gramme [græm] n = **gram.**

granary ['grænərɪ] n Kornspeicher m.

grand [grænd] a großartig; **~children** npl Enkel pl; **~dad** n Opa m; **~daughter** n Enkelin f; **~eur** ['grændjə*] n Erhabenheit f; **~father** n Großvater m; **~iose** ['grændɪəʊs] a (imposing) großartig; (pompous) schwülstig; **~ma** n Oma f; **~mother** n Großmutter f; **~pa** n = **~dad**; **~parents** npl Großeltern pl; **~ piano** n Flügel m; **~son** n Enkel m; **~stand** n Haupttribüne f.

granite ['grænɪt] n Granit m.

granny ['grænɪ] n Oma f.

grant [grɑːnt] vt gewähren // n Unterstützung f; (UNIV) Stipendium nt; to take sth for **~ed** etw als selbstverständlich (an)nehmen.

granulated sugar ['grænjʊleɪtɪd-] n Zuckerraffinade f.

granule ['grænjuːl] n Körnchen nt.

grape [greɪp] n (Wein)traube f.

grapefruit ['greɪpfruːt] n Pampelmuse f, Grapefruit f.

graph [grɑːf] n Schaubild nt; **~ic** ['græfɪk] a (descriptive) anschaulich; (drawing) graphisch; **~ics** ['græfɪks] npl Grafik f.

grapple ['græpl] vi: to ~ with kämpfen mit.

grasp [grɑːsp] vt ergreifen; (understand) begreifen // n Griff m; (of subject) Beherrschung f; **~ing** a habgierig.

grass [grɑːs] n Gras nt; **~hopper** n Heuschrecke f; **~land** n Weideland nt; **~-roots** a an der Basis; ~ **snake** n Ringelnatter f.

grate [greɪt] n Kamin m // vi (sound) knirschen; (on nerves) zerren (on an +dat) // vt (cheese) reiben.

grateful ['greɪtfʊl] a dankbar.

grater ['greɪtə*] n Reibe f.

gratify ['grætɪfaɪ] vt befriedigen.

gratifying ['grætɪfaɪɪŋ] a erfreulich.

grating ['greɪtɪŋ] n (iron bars) Gitter nt // a (noise) knirschend.

gratitude ['grætɪtjuːd] n Dankbarkeit f.

gratuity [grə'tjuːɪtɪ] n Gratifikation f.

grave [greɪv] n Grab nt // a (serious) ernst.

gravel ['grævəl] n Kies m.

grave: ~ **stone** n Grabstein m; **~yard** n Friedhof m.

gravity ['grævɪtɪ] n Schwerkraft f; (seriousness) Schwere f.

gravy ['greɪvɪ] n (Braten)soße f.

gray [greɪ] a = **grey.**

graze [greɪz] vi grasen // vt (touch) streifen; (MED) abschürfen // n (MED) Abschürfung f.

grease [griːs] n (fat) Fett nt; (lubricant) Schmiere f // vt (ab)schmieren; **~proof** a (Brit: paper) Butterbrot-.

greasy ['griːsɪ] a fettig.

great [greɪt] a groß; (col: good) prima; **~-grandfather/mother** n Urgroßvater m/mutter f; **~ly** ad sehr; **~ness** n Größe f.

Greece [griːs] n Griechenland nt.

greed [griːd] n (also: **~iness**) Gier f (for nach); (meanness) Geiz m; **~y** a gierig.

Greek [griːk] a griechisch // n Grieche m, Griechin f; (LING) Griechisch nt.

green [griːn] a grün // n (village ~) Dorfwiese f; **~ belt** n Grüngürtel m; **~ card** n (AUT) grüne Versicherungskarte f; **~ery** n Grün nt; grüne(s) Laub nt; **~gage** n Reineclaude f; **~grocer** n (Brit) Obst- und Gemüsehändler m; **~house** n Gewächshaus nt; **~ish** a grünlich.

Greenland ['griːnlənd] n Grönland nt.

greet [griːt] vt grüßen; **~ing** n Gruß m; **~ing(s) card** n Glückwunschkarte f.

gregarious [grɪ'gɛərɪəs] a gesellig.

grenade [grɪ'neɪd] n Granate f.

grew [gruː] pt of **grow.**

grey [greɪ] a grau; **~-haired** a grauhaarig; **~hound** n Windhund m; **~ish** a gräulich.

grid [grɪd] n Gitter nt; (ELEC) Leitungsnetz nt; (on map) Gitternetz nt.

grief [griːf] n Gram m, Kummer m.

grievance ['griːvəns] n Beschwerde f.

grieve [griːv] vi sich grämen // vt betrüben.

grievous ['griːvəs] a: ~ **bodily harm** (JUR) schwere Körperverletzung f.

grill [grɪl] n Grill m // vt (Brit) grillen; (question) in die Mangel nehmen.

grille [grɪl] n (on car etc) (Kühler)gitter nt.

grim [grɪm] a grimmig; (situation) düster.

grimace [grɪ'meɪs] n Grimasse f // vi

Grimassen schneiden.

grime [graɪm] n Schmutz m.

grimy ['graɪmɪ] a schmutzig.

grin [grɪn] n Grinsen nt // vi grinsen.

grind [graɪnd] vt, pt, pp **ground** mahlen; (US: meat) durch den Fleischwolf drehen; (sharpen) schleifen; (teeth) knirschen mit // n (bore) Plackerei f.

grip [grɪp] n Griff m; (suitcase) Handkoffer m // vt packen; **~ping** a (exciting) spannend.

grisly ['grɪzlɪ] a gräßlich.

gristle ['grɪsl] n Knorpel m.

grit [grɪt] n Splitt m; (courage) Mut m // vt (teeth) knirschen mit; (road) (mit Splitt (be)streuen.

groan [grəʊn] n Stöhnen nt // vi stöhnen.

grocer ['grəʊsə*] n Lebensmittelhändler m; **~ies** pl Lebensmittel pl; **~'s (shop)** n Lebensmittelgeschäft nt.

groggy ['grɒgɪ] a benommen.

groin [grɔɪn] n Leistengegend f.

groom [gru:m] n (also: bride~) Bräutigam m; (for horses) Pferdeknecht m // vt (horse) striegeln; (well-)~ed gepflegt.

groove [gru:v] n Rille f, Furche f.

grope [grəʊp] vi tasten; ~ **for** vt suchen nach.

gross [grəʊs] a (coarse) dick, plump; (bad) grob, schwer; (COMM) brutto; **~ly** ad höchst.

grotesque [grəʊ'tesk] a grotesk.

grotto ['grɒtəʊ] n Grotte f.

ground [graʊnd] pt, pp of **grind** // n Boden m; (land) Grundbesitz m; (reason) Grund m; (US: also: ~ wire) Endleitung f; **~s** pl (dregs) Bodensatz m; (around house) (Garten)anlagen pl // vi (run ashore) stranden, auflaufen; on the ~ am Boden; to the ~ zu Boden; to gain/lose ~ Boden gewinnen/verlieren; ~ **cloth** n (US) = ~ **sheet**; **~ing** n (instruction) Anfangsunterricht m; **~less** a grundlos; **~sheet** n (Brit) Zeltboden m; ~ **staff** n Bodenpersonal nt; ~ **swell** n (of sea) Dünung; (fig) Zurnahme f; **~work** n Grundlage f.

group [gru:p] n Gruppe f // vti (also: ~ **together**) (sich) gruppieren.

grouse [graʊs] n, pl inv (bird) schottische(s) Moorhuhn nt // vi (complain) meckern.

grove [grəʊv] n Gehölz nt, Hain m.

grovel ['grɒvl] vi (fig) kriechen.

grow [grəʊ], pt **grew**, pp **grown** vi wachsen; (become) werden // vt (raise) anbauen; ~ **up** vi aufwachsen; **~er** n Züchter m; **~ing** a zunehmend.

growl [graʊl] vi knurren.

grown [grəʊn] pp of **grow**; **~-up** n Erwachsene(r) mf.

growth [grəʊθ] n Wachstum nt; (increase) Zunahme f; (of beard etc)

Wuchs m.

grub [grʌb] n Made f, Larve f; (col: food) Futter nt; **~by** a schmutzig.

grudge [grʌdʒ] n Groll m // vt misgönnen (sb sth jdm etw); **to bear sb a** ~ einen Groll gegen jdn hegen.

gruelling ['grʊəlɪŋ] a (climb, race) mörderisch.

gruesome ['gru:səm] a grauenhaft.

gruff [grʌf] a barsch.

grumble ['grʌmbl] vi murren.

grumpy ['grʌmpɪ] a verdrießlich.

grunt [grʌnt] vi grunzen // n Grunzen nt.

G-string ['dʒi:-] n Minislip m.

guarantee [gærən'ti:] n Garantie f // vt garantieren.

guard [ga:d] n (sentry) Wache f; (Brit: RAIL) Zugbegleiter m // vt bewachen; **~ed** a vorsichtig; **~ian** n Vormund m; (keeper) Hüter m; **~'s van** n (Brit RAIL) Dienstwagen m.

guerrilla [gə'rɪlə] n Guerilla(kämpfer) m; ~ **warfare** n Guerillakrieg m.

guess [ges] vti (er)raten, schätzen // n Vermutung f; **~work** n Raterei f.

guest [gest] n Gast m; **~-house** n Pension f; ~ **room** n Gastzimmer nt.

guffaw [gʌ'fɔ:] vi schallend lachen.

guidance ['gaɪdəns] n (control) Leitung f; (advice) Beratung f.

guide [gaɪd] n Führer m // vt führen; **(girl)** ~ n Pfadfinderin f; **~book** n Reiseführer m; ~ **dog** n Blindenhund m; **~lines** npl Richtlinien pl.

guild [gɪld] n (HIST) Gilde f; **~hall** n (Brit) Stadthalle f.

guile [gaɪl] n Arglist f.

guillotine [gɪlə'ti:n] n Guillotine f.

guilt [gɪlt] n Schuld f; **~y** a schuldig.

guinea pig ['gɪnɪ-] n Meerschweinchen nt; (fig) Versuchskaninchen nt.

guise [gaɪz] n: **in the** ~ **of** in der Form (+gen).

guitar [gɪ'tɑ:*] n Gitarre f.

gulf [gʌlf] n Golf m; (fig) Abgrund m.

gull [gʌl] n Möwe f.

gullet ['gʌlɪt] n Schlund m.

gullible ['gʌlɪbl] a leichtgläubig.

gully ['gʌlɪ] n (Wasser)rinne f.

gulp [gʌlp] vt (also: ~ **down**) hinunterschlucken // vi (gasp) schlucken.

gum [gʌm] n (around teeth) Zahnfleisch nt; (glue) Klebstoff m; (also: chewing-~) Kaugummi m // vt gummieren; **~boots** npl (Brit) Gummistiefel pl.

gumption ['gʌmpʃən] n (col) Mumm m.

gun [gʌn] n Schußwaffe f; (large) Kanonenboot nt; **~fire** n Geschützfeuer nt; **~man** n bewaffnete(r) Verbrecher m; **~ner** n Kanonier m, Artillerist m; **~point** n: at **~point** mit Waffengewalt; **~powder** n Schießpulver nt; **~shot** n Schuß m; **~smith** n Büchsenmacher(in f) m.

gurgle ['gɜ:gl] vi gluckern.

guru ['goru:] n Guru m.

gush [gʌʃ] vi (rush out) hervorströmen; (fig) schwärmen.

gusset ['gʌsɪt] n Keil m, Zwickel m.

gust [gʌst] n Windstoß m, Bö f.

gusto ['gʌstəʊ] n Genuß m, Lust f.

gut [gʌt] n (ANAT) Gedärme pl; (string) Darm m; **~s** pl (fig) Schneid m.

gutter ['gʌtə*] n Dachrinne f; (in street) Gosse f.

guttural ['gʌtərəl] a guttural, Kehl-.

guy [gaɪ] n (also: ~rope) Halteseil nt; (man) Typ m, Kerl m.

guzzle ['gʌzl] vti (drink) saufen; (eat) fressen.

gym [dʒɪm] n (also: **gymnasium**) Turnhalle f; (also: **gymnastics**) Turnen nt; **~nast** ['dʒɪmnæst] n Turner(in f) m; **~nastics** [dʒɪm'næstɪks] n Turnen nt, Gymnastik f; **~ shoes** npl Turnschuhe pl; **~ slip** n (Brit) Schulträgerrock m.

gynaecologist, (US) **gynecologist** [gaɪnɪ'kɒlədʒɪst] n Frauenarzt m/-ärztin f.

gynaecology, (US) **gynecology** [gaɪnɪ'kɒlədʒɪ] n Gynäkologie f, Frauenheilkunde f.

gypsy ['dʒɪpsɪ] n = **gipsy.**

gyrate [dʒaɪ'reɪt] vi kreisen.

H

haberdashery [hæbə'dæʃərɪ] n (Brit) Kurzwaren pl.

habit ['hæbɪt] n (An)gewohnheit f; (monk's) Habit nt or m.

habitable ['hæbɪtəbl] a bewohnbar.

habitat ['hæbɪtæt] n Lebensraum m.

habitual [hə'bɪtjʊəl] a gewohnheitsmäßig; **~ly** ad gewöhnlich.

hack [hæk] vt hacken // n Hieb m; (writer) Schreiberling m.

hackneyed ['hæknɪd] a abgedroschen.

had [hæd] pt, pp of **have.**

haddock ['hædək], pl **~** or **~s** n Schellfisch m.

hadn't ['hædnt] = **had not.**

haemorrhage, (US) **hemorrhage** ['hemərɪdʒ] n Blutung f.

haemorrhoids, (US) **hemorrhoids** ['hemərɔɪdz] npl Hämorrhoiden pl.

haggard ['hægəd] a abgekämpft.

haggle ['hægl] vi feilschen.

Hague [heɪg] n: **The ~** Den Haag nt.

hail [heɪl] n Hagel m // vt umjubeln // vi hageln; **~stone** n Hagelkorn nt.

hair [hɛə*] n Haar nt, Haare pl; (one ~) Haar nt; **~brush** n Haarbürste f; **~cut** n Haarschnitt m; **to get a ~cut** sich (dat) die Haare schneiden lassen; **~do** n Frisur f; **~dresser** n Friseur m, Friseuse f; **~dresser's** n Friseursalon m; **~ dryer** n Trockenhaube f; (hand) Fön m; **~grip** n Klemme f; **~net** n Haarnetz nt; **~pin** n Haarnadel f; **~pin bend,** (US) **~pin curve** n Haarnadelkurve f; **~raising** a haarsträubend; **~ remover** n Enthaarungsmittel nt; **~ spray** n Haarspray nt; **~style** n Frisur f; **~y** a haarig.

hake [heɪk] n Seehecht m.

half [hɑ:f], pl **halves** n Hälfte f // a halb // ad halb, zur Hälfte; **~-an-hour** eine halbe Stunde; **two and a ~** zweieinhalb; **to cut sth in ~** etw halbieren; **~-back** n (SPORT) Läufer m; **~-breed** n, **~-caste** n Mischling m; **~-hearted** a lustlos; **~-hour** n halbe Stunde f; **~-penny** ['heɪpnɪ] n (Brit) halbe(r) Penny m; **(at) ~-price** zum halben Preis; **~ term** n (Brit SCH) Ferien pl an der Mitte des Trimesters; **~-time** n Halbzeit f; **~way** ad halbwegs, auf halbem Wege.

hall [hɔ:l] n Saal m; (entrance ~) Hausflur m; (building) Halle f; **~ of residence** n (Brit) Studentenwohnheim nt.

hallmark ['hɔ:lmɑ:k] n Stempel m.

hallo [hʌ'ləʊ] see **hello.**

Hallowe'en ['hæləʊ'i:n] n Tag m vor Allerheiligen.

hallucination [həlu:sɪ'neɪʃən] n Halluzination f.

hallway ['hɔ:lweɪ] n Korridor m.

halo ['heɪləʊ] n Heiligenschein m.

halt [hɔ:lt] n Halt m // vti anhalten.

halve [hɑ:v] vt halbieren.

halves [hɑ:vz] pl of **half.**

ham [hæm] n Schinken m.

hamburger ['hæmbɜ:gə*] n Hamburger m.

hamlet ['hæmlɪt] n Weiler m.

hammer ['hæmə*] n Hammer m // vt hämmern.

hammock ['hæmək] n Hängematte f.

hamper ['hæmpə*] vt (be)hindern // n Picknickkorb m.

hamster ['hæmstə*] n Hamster m.

hand [hænd] n Hand f; (of clock) (Uhr)zeiger m; (worker) Arbeiter m // vt (pass) geben; **to give sb a ~** jdm helfen; **at ~** nahe; **to ~** zur Hand; **in ~** (under control) unter Kontrolle; (being done) im Gange; (extra) übrig; **on ~** zur Verfügung; **on the one ~ ..., on the other ~ ...** einerseits ..., andererseits ...; **~ in** vt abgeben; (forms) einreichen; **~ out** vt austeilen; **~ over** vt (deliver) übergeben; (surrender) abgeben; (: prisoner) ausliefern; **~bag** n Handtasche f; **~book** n Handbuch nt; **~brake** n Handbremse f; **~cuffs** npl Handschellen pl; **~ful** n Handvoll f; (col: person) Plage f.

handicap ['hændɪkæp] n Handikap nt // vt benachteiligen; **mentally/physically ~ped** geistig/körperlich behindert.

handicraft ['hændɪkrɑ:ft] n Kunsthandwerk *nt*.

handiwork ['hændɪwɜːk] *n* Arbeit *f*; (*fig*) Werk *nt*.

handkerchief ['hæŋkətʃɪf] *n* Taschentuch *nt*.

handle ['hændl] *n* (*of door etc*) Klinke *f*; (*of cup etc*) Henkel *m*; (*for winding*) Kurbel *f* // *vt* (*touch*) anfassen; (*deal with: things*) sich befassen mit; (: *people*) umgehen mit; ~**bar(s)** *n(pl)* Lenkstange *f*.

hand: ~ **luggage** *n* Handgepäck *nt*; ~**made** *a* handgefertigt; ~**out** *n* (*distribution*) Verteilung *f*; (*charity*) Geldzuwendung *f*; (*leaflet*) Flugblatt *nt*; ~**rail** *n* Geländer *nt*; (*on ship*) Reling *f*; ~**shake** *n* Händedruck *f*.

handsome ['hænsəm] *a* gutaussehend.

handwriting ['hændraɪtɪŋ] *n* Handschrift *f*.

handy ['hændɪ] *a* praktisch; (*shops*) leicht erreichbar.

handyman ['hændɪmən] *n* Bastler *m*.

hang [hæŋ] *v* (*pt, pp* hung) *vt* aufhängen; (*criminal: pt, pp* hanged) hängen // *vi* hängen // *n*: to get the ~ of sth (*col*) den richtigen Dreh bei etw herauskriegen; ~ **about** *vi* sich herumtreiben; ~ **on** *vi* (*wait*) warten; ~ **up** *vi* (*TEL*) auflegen.

hanger ['hæŋə*] *n* Kleiderbügel *m*.

hanger-on ['hæŋər'ɒn] *n* Anhänger(in *f*) *m*.

hang-gliding ['hæŋglaɪdɪŋ] *n* Drachenfliegen *nt*.

hangover ['hæŋəʊvə*] *n* Kater *m*.

hang-up ['hæŋʌp] *n* Komplex *m*.

hanker ['hæŋkə*] *vi* sich sehnen (*for, after* nach).

hankie, hanky ['hæŋkɪ] *n abbr of* handkerchief.

haphazard ['hæp'hæzəd] *a* zufällig.

happen ['hæpən] *vi* sich ereignen, passieren; as it ~s I'm going there today zufällig(erweise) gehe ich heute (dort)hin; ~**ing** *n* Ereignis *nt*.

happily ['hæpɪlɪ] *ad* glücklich; (*fortunately*) glücklicherweise.

happiness ['hæpɪnɪs] *n* Glück *nt*.

happy ['hæpɪ] *a* glücklich; ~ **birthday!** alles Gute zum Geburtstag!; ~**-go-lucky** *a* sorglos.

harass ['hærəs] *vt* plagen; ~**ment** *n* Belästigung *f*.

harbour, (*US*) **harbor** ['hɑːbə*] *n* Hafen *m* // *vt* (*hope etc*) hegen; (*criminal etc*) Unterschlupf gewähren.

hard [hɑːd] *a* (*firm*) hart; (*difficult*) schwer; (*harsh*) hart(herzig) // *ad* (*work*) hart; (*try*) sehr; (*push, hit*) fest; no ~ **feelings** ich nehme es dir nicht übel; ~ **of hearing** schwerhörig; to be ~ done by übel dran sein; ~**back** *n* kartonierte Ausgabe *f*; ~ **cash** *n* Bargeld *nt*; ~ **disk** *n* (*COMPUT*) Fest-

platte *f*; ~**en** *vt* erhärten; (*fig*) verhärten // *vi* hart werden; (*fig*) sich verhärten; ~**-headed** *a* nüchtern; ~ **labour** *n* Zwangsarbeit *f*.

hardly ['hɑːdlɪ] *ad* kaum.

hard: ~**ness** *n* Härte *f*; (*difficulty*) Schwierigkeit *f*; ~**ship** *n* Not *f*; ~**-up** *a* knapp bei Kasse; ~**ware** *n* Eisenwaren *pl*; (*COMPUT*) Hardware *f*; ~**ware shop** *n* Eisenwarenhandlung *f*; ~**wearing** *a* strapazierfähig; ~**-working** *a* fleißig.

hardy ['hɑːdɪ] *a* widerstandsfähig.

hare [hɛə*] *n* Hase *m*; ~**-brained** *a* schwachsinnig.

harm [hɑːm] *n* Schaden *m* // *vt* schaden (+*dat*); **out of** ~'s **way** in Sicherheit; ~**ful** *a* schädlich; ~**less** *a* harmlos.

harmonica [hɑː'mɒnɪkə] *n* Mundharmonika *f*.

harmonious [hɑː'məʊnɪəs] *a* harmonisch.

harmonize ['hɑːmənaɪz] *vt* abstimmen // *vi* harmonieren.

harmony ['hɑːmənɪ] *n* Harmonie *f*.

harness ['hɑːnɪs] *n* Geschirr *nt* // *vt* (*horse*) anschirren; (*fig*) nutzbar machen.

harp [hɑːp] *n* Harfe *f* // *vi*: to ~ **on about** sth sich auf etw (*dat*) herumreiten.

harpoon [hɑː'puːn] *n* Harpune *f*.

harrowing ['hærəʊɪŋ] *a* nervenaufreibend.

harsh [hɑːʃ] *a* (*rough*) rauh; (*severe*) streng; ~**ness** *n* Härte *f*.

harvest ['hɑːvɪst] *n* Ernte *f* // *vti* ernten.

harvester ['hɑːvɪstə*] *n* Mähbinder *m*.

has [hæz] *v see* have.

hash [hæʃ] *vt* kleinhacken // *n* (*mess*) Kuddelmuddel *m*; (*meat*) Haschee *nt*.

hashish ['hæʃɪʃ] *n* Haschisch *nt*.

hasn't ['hæznt] = **has not**.

hassle ['hæsl] *n* (*col*) Theater *nt*.

haste [heɪst] *n* Eile *f*; ~**n** ['heɪsn] *vt* beschleunigen // *vi* eilen.

hasty ['heɪstɪ] *a* hastig; (*rash*) vorschnell.

hat [hæt] *n* Hut *m*.

hatch [hætʃ] *n* (*NAUT: also*: ~**-way**) Luke *f*; (*in house*) Durchreiche *f* // *vi* (*young*) ausschlüpfen // *vt* (*brood*) ausbrüten; (*plot*) aushecken.

hatchback ['hætʃbæk] *n* (*AUT*) (Auto *m* mit) Heckklappe *f*.

hatchet ['hætʃɪt] *n* Beil *nt*.

hate [heɪt] *vt* hassen // *n* Haß *m*; ~**ful** *a* verhaßt.

hatred ['heɪtrɪd] *n* Haß *m*.

haughty ['hɔːtɪ] *a* hochnäsig, überheblich.

haul [hɔːl] *vt* ziehen // *n* (*catch*) Fang *m*; ~**age** *n* Spedition *f*; ~**ier**, (*US*) ~**er** *n* Spediteur *m*.

haunch [hɔːntʃ] *n* Lende *f*.

haunt [hɔːnt] *vt* (*ghost*) spuken in

(+*dat*); (*memory*) verfolgen; (*pub*) häufig besuchen // *n* Lieblingsplatz *m*; **the castle is ~ed** in dem Schloß spukt es.

have, *pt, pp* **had** [hæv, hæd] ◆*aux v* **1** haben; (*esp with vs of motion*) sein; to **~ arrived/slept** angekommen sein/ geschlafen haben; **to ~ been** gewesen sein; **having eaten** *or* **when he had eaten,** he left nachdem er gegessen hatte, ging er

2 (*in tag questions*): **you've done it, ~n't you?** du hast es doch gemacht, oder nicht?

3 (*in short answers and questions*): **you've made a mistake — no I ~n't/so I ~** du hast einen Fehler gemacht — nein(, hab ich nicht)/ja, stimmt; **we ~n't paid — yes we ~!** wir haben nicht bezahlt — doch; **I've been there before, ~ you?** ich war schon einmal da, du auch?

◆*modal aux v* (*be obliged*): **to ~ (got) to do sth** etw tun müssen; **you ~n't to tell her** du darfst es ihr nicht erzählen

◆*vt* **1** (*possess*) haben; **he has (got) blue eyes** er hat blaue Augen; **I ~ (got) an idea** ich habe eine Idee

2 (*referring to meals etc*): **to ~ breakfast/a cigarette** frühstücken/eine Zigarette rauchen

3 (*receive, obtain etc*) haben; **may I ~ your address?** kann ich Ihre Adresse haben?; **to ~ a baby** ein Kind bekommen

4 (*maintain, allow*): **he will ~ it that he is right** er besteht darauf, daß er recht hat; **I won't ~ it** das lasse ich mir nicht bieten

5: **to ~ sth done** etw machen lassen; **to ~ sb do sth** jdn etw machen lassen; **he soon had them all laughing** er brachte sie alle zum Lachen

6 (*experience, suffer*): **she had her bag stolen** man hat ihr die Tasche gestohlen; **he had his arm broken** er hat sich den Arm gebrochen

7 (+ *noun: take, hold etc*): **to ~ a walk/ rest** spazierengehen/sich ausruhen; **to ~ a meeting/party** eine Besprechung/Party haben

have out *vt*: **to ~ it out with sb** (*settle a problem etc*) etw mit jdm bereden.

haven ['heɪvn] *n* Zufluchtsort *m*.

haven't ['hævnt] = **have not**.

haversack ['hævəsæk] *n* Rucksack *m*.

havoc ['hævək] *n* Verwüstung *f*.

Hawaii [hə'waɪiː] *n* Hawaii *nt*.

hawk [hɔːk] *n* Habicht *m*.

hay [heɪ] *n* Heu *nt*; **~ fever** *n* Heu- schnupfen *m*; **~stack** *n* Heuschober *m*.

haywire ['heɪwaɪə*] *a* (*col*) durch- einander.

hazard ['hæzəd] *n* Risiko *nt* // *vt* aufs Spiel setzen; **~ous** *a* gefährlich; **~ (warning) lights** *npl* (*AUT*) Warnblink- licht *nt*.

haze [heɪz] *n* Dunst *m*.

hazelnut ['heɪzlnʌt] *n* Haselnuß *f*.

hazy ['heɪzɪ] *a* (*misty*) dunstig; (*vague*) verschwommen.

he [hiː] *pron* er.

head [hed] *n* Kopf *m*; (*leader*) Leiter *m* // *vt* (an)führen, leiten; (*ball*) köpfen; **~s (or tails)** kopf (oder Zahl); **~ first** mit dem Kopf nach unten; **~ over heels** kopf- über; **~ for** *vt* zugehen auf (+*acc*); **~ache** *n* Kopfschmerzen *pl*; **~dress** *n* Kopfschmuck *m*; **~ing** *n* Überschrift *f*; **~lamp** *n* (*Brit*) Scheinwerfer *m*; **~land** *n* Landspitze *f*; **~light** *n* = **~lamp**; **~line** *n* Schlagzeile *f*; **~long** *ad* kopf- über; **~master** *n* (*of primary school*) Rektor *m*; (*of secondary school*) Direktor *m*; **~mistress** *n* Rektorin *f*; Direktorin *f*; **~ office** *n* Zentrale *f*; **~- on** *a* Frontal-; **~phones** *npl* Kopfhörer *pl*; **~quarters (HQ)** *npl* Zentrale *f*; (*MIL*) Hauptquartier *nt*; **~rest** *n* Kopf- stütze *f*; **~room** *n* (*of bridges etc*) lichte Höhe *f*; **~scarf** *n* Kopftuch *nt*; **~strong** *a* eigenwillig; **~ waiter** *n* Oberkellner *m*; **~way** *n* Fortschritte *pl*; **~wind** *n* Gegenwind *m*; **~y** *a* berau- schend.

heal [hiːl] *vt* heilen // *vi* verheilen.

health [helθ] *n* Gesundheit *f*; **your ~!** prost!; **~ food** *n* Reformkost *f*; **the H~ Service** *n* (*Brit*) das Gesundheitswesen *nt*; **~y** *a* gesund.

heap [hiːp] *n* Haufen *m* // *vt* häufen.

hear [hɪə*] *v* (*pt, pp* **heard** [hɜːd]) *vt* hören; (*listen to*) anhören // *vi* hören; **~ing** *n* Gehör *nt*; (*JUR*) Verhandlung *f*; **~ing aid** *n* Hörapparat *m*; **~say** *n* Hörensagen *nt*.

hearse [hɜːs] *n* Leichenwagen *m*.

heart [hɑːt] *n* Herz *nt*; **~s** *pl* (*CARDS*) Herz *nt*; **by ~** auswendig; **~ attack** *n* Herzanfall *m*; **~beat** *n* Herzschlag *m*; **~breaking** *a* herzzerbrechend; **~broken** *a* (ganz)gebrochen; **~burn** *n* Sodbrennen *nt*; **~ failure** *n* Herzschlag *m*; **~felt** *a* aufrichtig.

hearth [hɑːθ] *n* Herd *m*.

heartily ['hɑːtɪlɪ] *ad* herzlich; (*eat*) herz- haft.

heartless ['hɑːtlɪs] *a* herzlos.

hearty ['hɑːtɪ] *a* kräftig; (*friendly*) freundlich.

heat [hiːt] *n* Hitze *f*; (*of food, water etc*) Wärme *f*; (*SPORT*: *also*: **qualifying ~**) Ausscheidungsrunde *f* // *vt* (*house*) heizen; (*substance*) heiß machen, erhitzen; **~ up** *vi* warm werden // *vt* aufwärmen; **~ed** *a* erhitzt; (*fig*) hitzig; **~er** *n* (Heiz)ofen *m*.

heath [hiːθ] *n* (*Brit*) Heide *f*.

heathen ['hiːðən] *n* Heide *m* // *a* heidnisch, Heiden-.

heather ['heðə*] *n* Heidekraut *nt*.

heating ['hiːtɪŋ] *n* Heizung *f*.

heatstroke ['hi:tstrəʊk] n Hitzschlag m.
heatwave ['hi:tweɪv] n Hitzewelle f.
heave [hi:v] vt hochheben; (sigh) ausstoßen // vi wogen; (breast) sich heben // n Heben nt.
heaven ['hevn] n Himmel m; ~ly a himmlisch.
heavily ['hevɪlɪ] ad schwer.
heavy ['hevɪ] a schwer; ~ **goods vehicle (HGV)** n Lastkraftwagen (LKW) m; ~**weight** n (SPORT) Schwergewicht nt.
Hebrew ['hi:bru:] a hebräisch // n (LING) Hebräisch nt.
heckle ['hekl] vt unterbrechen.
hectic ['hektɪk] a hektisch.
he'd [hi:d] = **he had; he would**.
hedge [hedʒ] n Hecke f // vt einzäunen // vi (fig) ausweichen; to ~ one's bets sich absichern.
hedgehog ['hedʒhɒg] n Igel m.
heed [hi:d] vt (also: take ~ of) beachten // n Beachtung f; ~**less** a achtlos.
heel [hi:l] n Ferse f; (of shoe) Absatz m // vt (shoes) mit Absätzen versehen.
hefty ['heftɪ] a (person) stämmig; (portion) reichlich.
heifer ['hefə*] n Färse f.
height [haɪt] n (of person) Größe f; (of object) Höhe f; ~**en** vt erhöhen.
heir [ɛə*] n Erbe m; ~**ess** ['ɛərɪs] n Erbin f; ~**loom** n Erbstück nt.
helicopter ['helɪkɒptə*] n Hubschrauber m.
heliport ['helɪpɔ:t] n Hubschrauberlandeplatz m.
hell [hel] n Hölle f // interj verdammt!
he'll [hi:l] = **he will, he shall**.
hellish ['helɪʃ] a höllisch, verteufelt.
hello [hʌ'ləʊ] interj Hallo.
helm [helm] n Ruder nt, Steuer nt.
helmet ['helmɪt] n Helm m.
helmsman ['helmzmən] n Steuermann m.
help [help] n Hilfe f // vt helfen (+dat); I can't ~ it ich kann nichts dafür; ~ yourself bedienen Sie sich; ~**er** n Helfer m; ~**ful** a hilfreich; ~**ing** n Portion f; ~**less** a hilflos.
hem [hem] n Saum m // vt säumen; ~ **in** vt einengen.
he-man ['hi:mæn] n (col) Macho m.
hemorrhage ['hemərɪdʒ] n (US) = **haemorrhage**.
hemorrhoids ['hemərɔɪdz] npl (US) = **haemorrhoids**.
hen [hen] n Henne f.
hence [hens] ad von jetzt an; (therefore) daher; ~**forth** ad von nun an; (from then on) von da an.
henchman ['hentʃmən] n Gefolgsmann m.
henpecked ['henpekt] a: to be ~ unter dem Pantoffel stehen; ~ **husband** n Pantoffelheld m.
her [hɜ:*] pron (acc) sie; (dat) ihr //

poss a ihr; see also **me, my**.
herald ['herəld] n (Vor)bote m // vt verkünden.
heraldry ['herəldrɪ] n Wappenkunde f.
herb [hɜ:b] n Kraut nt.
herd [hɜ:d] n Herde f.
here [hɪə*] ad hier; (to this place) hierher; ~**after** ad hernach, künftig // n Jenseits nt; ~**by** ad hiermit.
hereditary [hɪ'redɪtərɪ] a erblich.
heredity [hɪ'redɪtɪ] n Vererbung f.
heresy ['herəsɪ] n Ketzerei f.
heretic ['herətɪk] n Ketzer m.
heritage ['herɪtɪdʒ] n Erbe nt.
hermetically [hɜ:'metɪkəlɪ] ad: ~ sealed hermetisch verschlossen.
hermit ['hɜ:mɪt] n Einsiedler m.
hernia ['hɜ:nɪə] n Bruch m.
hero ['hɪərəʊ], pl ~**es** n Held m; ~**ic** [hɪ'rəʊɪk] a heroisch.
heroin ['herəʊɪn] n Heroin nt.
heroine ['herəʊɪn] n Heldin f.
heroism ['herəʊɪzəm] n Heldentum nt.
heron ['herən] n Reiher m.
herring ['herɪŋ] n Hering m.
hers [hɜ:z] pron ihre(r, s); see also **mine**.
herself [hɜ:'self] pron sich (selbst); (emphatic) selbst; see also **oneself**.
he's [hi:z] = **he is, he has**.
hesitant ['hezɪtənt] a zögernd.
hesitate ['hezɪteɪt] vi zögern.
hesitation [hezɪ'teɪʃən] n Zögern nt.
hew [hju:], pt **hewed**, pp **hewn** vt hauen, hacken.
hexagon ['heksəgən] n Sechseck nt; ~**al** [hek'sægənəl] a sechseckig.
heyday ['heɪdeɪ] n Blüte f, Höhepunkt m.
HGV n abbr of **heavy goods vehicle**.
hi [haɪ] interj he, hallo.
hiatus [haɪ'eɪtəs] n (gap) Lücke f.
hibernation [haɪbə'neɪʃən] n Winterschlaf m.
hiccough, hiccup ['hɪkʌp] vi den Schluckauf haben; ~**s** pl Schluckauf m.
hide [haɪd] n (skin) Haut f, Fell nt // v (pt, **hid** [hɪd], pp **hidden** ['hɪdn]) vt verstecken // vi sich verstecken; ~**-and-seek** n Versteckspiel nt; ~**away** n Versteck nt.
hideous ['hɪdɪəs] a abscheulich.
hiding ['haɪdɪŋ] n (beating) Tracht f Prügel; to be in ~ (concealed) sich versteckt halten; ~ **place** n Versteck nt.
hi-fi ['haɪfaɪ] n Hi-Fi f // a Hi-Fi-.
high [haɪ] a hoch; (wind) stark // ad hoch; ~**boy** n (US: tallboy) hochbeinige Kommode f; ~**brow** a (betont) intellektuell; ~**chair** n Hochstuhl m; ~**er education** n Hochschulbildung f; ~**-handed** a eigenmächtig; ~**-heeled** a hochhackig; ~**jack** vt = **hijack**; ~**jump** n (SPORT) Hochsprung m; the **H~lands** npl das schottische Hochland;

~light n (fig) Höhepunkt m // vt hervorheben; **~ly** ad höchst; **~ly strung** a überempfindlich; **~ness** n Höhe f; **H~ness** n Hoheit f; **~-pitched** a hoch; **~-rise block** n Hochhaus nt; **~ school** n (US) Oberschule f; **~ season** n (Brit) Hochsaison f; **~ street** n (Brit) Hauptstraße f.

highway ['haɪweɪ] n Landstraße f; **H~ Code** n (Brit) Straßenverkehrsordnung f.

hijack ['haɪdʒæk] vt entführen; **~er** n Entführer(in f) m.

hike [haɪk] vi wandern // n Wanderung f; **~r** n Wanderer m.

hilarious [hɪ'lɛərɪəs] a lustig.

hill [hɪl] n Berg m; **~side** n (Berg)hang m; **~y** a hügelig.

hilt [hɪlt] n Heft nt; **up to the ~** ganz und gar.

him [hɪm] pron (acc) ihn; (dat) ihm; see also **me**.

himself [hɪm'self] pron sich (selbst); (emphatic) selbst; see also **oneself**.

hind [haɪnd] a hinter, Hinter-.

hinder ['hɪndə*] vt (stop) hindern; (delay) behindern.

hindrance ['hɪndrəns] n (delay) Behinderung f; (obstacle) Hindernis nt.

hindsight ['haɪndsaɪt] n: **with ~** im nachhinein.

Hindu ['hɪnduː] n Hindu m.

hinge [hɪndʒ] n Scharnier nt; (on door) Türangel f // vi (fig) abhängen (on von).

hint [hɪnt] n Tip m; (trace) Anflug m // vt: **to ~ that** andeuten, daß // vi andeuten (at acc).

hip [hɪp] n Hüfte f.

hippopotamus [hɪpə'pɒtəməs], pl **~es** or **-mi** [-maɪ] n Nilpferd m.

hire ['haɪə*] vt (worker) anstellen; (Brit: car) mieten // n Miete f; **for ~** (taxi) frei; **~ purchase (H.P.)** n (Brit) Teilzahlungskauf m.

his [hɪz] poss a sein // poss pron seine(r, s); see also **my, mine**.

hiss [hɪs] vi zischen // n Zischen nt.

historian [hɪs'tɔːrɪən] n Historiker m.

historic [hɪs'tɒrɪk] a historisch.

historical [hɪs'tɒrɪkəl] a historisch, geschichtlich.

history ['hɪstərɪ] n Geschichte f.

hit [hɪt] vt, pt, pp **hit** schlagen; (injure) treffen // n (blow) Schlag m; (success) Erfolg m (MUS) Hit m; **to ~ it off with sb** prima mit jdm auskommen; **~-and-run driver** n jd, der Fahrerflucht begeht.

hitch [hɪtʃ] vt festbinden; (also: **~ up**) hochziehen // n (difficulty) Haken m; **to ~ a lift** trampen.

hitch-hike ['hɪtʃhaɪk] vi trampen, **~r** n Tramper m.

hitherto ['hɪðə'tuː] ad bislang.

hive [haɪv] n Bienenkorb m // vt: **to ~ off** ausgliedern.

HMS abbr = His(Her) Majesty's Ship.

hoard [hɔːd] n Schatz m // vt horten, hamstern.

hoarding ['hɔːdɪŋ] n Bretterzaun m; (Brit: for advertising) Reklamewand f.

hoarfrost ['hɔː'frɒst] n (Rauh)reif m.

hoarse [hɔːs] a heiser, rauh.

hoax [həʊks] n Streich m.

hob [hɒb] n Kochmulde f.

hobble ['hɒbl] vi humpeln.

hobby ['hɒbɪ] n Hobby nt; **~-horse** n (fig) Steckenpferd nt.

hobo ['həʊbəʊ] n (US) Tippelbruder m.

hock [hɒk] n (wine) weiße(r) Rheinwein m.

hockey ['hɒkɪ] n Hockey nt.

hoe [həʊ] n Hacke f // vt hacken.

hog [hɒg] n Schlachtschwein nt // vt mit Beschlag belegen; **to go the whole ~** aufs Ganze gehen.

hoist [hɔɪst] n Winde f // vt hochziehen.

hold [həʊld] v (pt, pp **held**) vt halten; (contain) enthalten; (be able to contain) fassen; (breath) anhalten; (meeting) abhalten // vi (withstand pressure) aushalten // n (grasp) Halt m; (NAUT) Schiffsraum m; **~ the line!** (TEL) bleiben Sie am Apparat!; **to ~ one's own** sich behaupten; **~ back** vt zurückhalten; **~ down** vt niederhalten; (job) behalten; **~ off** vt (enemy) abwehren; **~ on** vi sich fasthalten; (resist) durchhalten; (wait) warten; **~ on to** vt an etw (dat) festhalten; (keep) behalten; **~ out** vt hinhalten // vi aushalten; **~ up** vt (delay) aufhalten; (rob) überfallen; **~all** n (Brit) Reisetasche f; **~er** n Behälter m; **~ing** n (share) (Aktien)anteil m; **~up** n (Brit: in traffic) Stockung f; (robbery) Überfall m.

hole [həʊl] n Loch nt // vt durchlöchern.

holiday ['hɒlədɪ] n (day) Feiertag m; freie(r) Tag m; (vacation) Urlaub m; (SCH) Ferien pl; **~ camp** n Ferienlager nt; **~-maker** n (Brit) Urlauber(in f) m; **~ resort** n Ferienort m.

holiness ['həʊlɪnɪs] n Heiligkeit f.

Holland ['hɒlənd] n Holland nt.

hollow ['hɒləʊ] a hohl; (fig) leer // n Vertiefung f; **~ out** vt aushöhlen.

holly ['hɒlɪ] n Stechpalme f.

holocaust ['hɒləkɔːst] n Inferno nt.

holster ['həʊlstə*] n Pistolenhalfter m.

holy ['həʊlɪ] a heilig; **the H~ Ghost** or **Spirit** n der Heilige Geist.

homage ['hɒmɪdʒ] n Huldigung f; **to pay ~ to** huldigen (+dat).

home [həʊm] n Zuhause nt; (institution) Heim nt, Anstalt f // a einheimisch; (POL) inner // ad heim, nach Hause; **at ~** zu Hause; **~ address** n Heimatadresse f; **~coming** n Heimkehr f; **~ computer** n Heimcomputer m; **~land**

n Heimat(land *nt*) *f*; ~**less** *a* obdachlos; ~**ly** *a* häuslich; (*US: ugly*) unscheinbar; ~-**made** *a* selbstgemacht; **H~ Office** *n* (*Brit*) Innenministerium *nt*; ~ **rule** *n* Selbstverwaltung *f*; **H~ Secretary** *n* (*Brit*) Innenminister(in *f*) *m*; ~**sick** *a*: **to be ~sick** Heimweh haben; ~ **town** *n* Heimatstadt *f*; ~**ward** *a* heimwärts; ~**work** *n* Hausaufgaben *pl*.

homicide ['hɒmɪsaɪd] *n* (*US*) Totschlag *m*.

homoeopathy [həʊmɪ'ɒpəθɪ] *n* Homöopathie *f*.

homogeneous [hɒmə'dʒiːnɪəs] *a* homogen.

homosexual ['hɒməʊ'seksjʊəl] *a* homosexuell // *n* Homosexuelle(r) *mf*.

honest ['ɒnɪst] *a* ehrlich; ~**ly** *ad* ehrlich; ~**y** *n* Ehrlichkeit *f*.

honey ['hʌnɪ] *n* Honig *m*; ~**comb** *n* Honigwabe *f*; ~**moon** *n* Flitterwochen *pl*, Hochzeitsreise *f*; ~**suckle** *n* Geißblatt *nt*.

honk [hɒŋk] *vi* hupen.

honorary ['ɒnərərɪ] *a* Ehren-.

honour, (*US*) **honor** ['ɒnə*] *vt* ehren; (*cheque*) einlösen // *n* Ehre *f*; ~**able** *a* ehrenwert; (*intention*) ehrenhaft; ~**s degree** *n* (*SCH*) akademischer Grad mit Prüfung im Spezialfach.

hood [hʊd] *n* Kapuze *f*; (*Brit AUT*) Verdeck *nt*; (*US AUT*) Kühlerhaube *f*.

hoodlum ['huːdləm] *n* Rowdy *m*; (*member of gang*) Gangster *m*.

hoodwink ['hʊdwɪŋk] *vt* reinlegen.

hoof [huːf], *pl* **hooves** *n* Huf *m*.

hook [hʊk] *n* Haken *m* // *vt* einhaken.

hooligan ['huːlɪgən] *n* Rowdy *m*.

hoop [huːp] *n* Reifen *m*.

hoot [huːt] *vi* (*AUT*) hupen; ~**er** *n* (*NAUT*) Dampfpfeife *f*; (*Brit AUT*) (Auto)hupe *f*.

hoover ['huːvə*] ® (*Brit*) *n* Staubsauger *m* // *vt* staubsaugen.

hooves [huːvz] *pl of* **hoof**.

hop [hɒp] *vi* hüpfen, hopsen // *n* (*jump*) Hopser *m*.

hope [həʊp] *vti* hoffen // *n* Hoffnung *f*; **I hope so/not** hoffentlich/hoffentlich nicht; ~**ful** *a* hoffnungsvoll; (*promising*) vielversprechend; ~**fully** *ad* hoffentlich; ~**less** *a* hoffnungslos.

hops [hɒps] *npl* Hopfen *pl*.

horizon [hə'raɪzn] *n* Horizont *m*; ~**tal** [hɒrɪ'zɒntl] *a* horizontal.

hormone ['hɔːməʊn] *n* Hormon *nt*.

horn [hɔːn] *n* Horn *nt*; (*AUT*) Hupe *f*.

hornet ['hɔːnɪt] *n* Hornisse *f*.

horny ['hɔːnɪ] *a* schwielig; (*US col*) scharf.

horoscope ['hɒrəskəʊp] *n* Horoskop *nt*.

horrible ['hɒrɪbl] *a* fürchterlich.

horrid ['hɒrɪd] *a* scheußlich.

horrify ['hɒrɪfaɪ] *vt* entsetzen.

horror ['hɒrə*] *n* Schrecken *m*; ~ **film**

n Horrorfilm *m*.

hors d'oeuvre [ɔː'dɜːvr] *n* Vorspeise *f*.

horse [hɔːs] *n* Pferd *nt*; **on ~back** berittten; ~ **chestnut** *n* Roßkastanie *f*; ~**man/woman** *n* Reiter *m*/Reiterin *f*; ~**power (h.p.)** *n* Pferdestärke *f*, PS *nt*; ~-**racing** *n* Pferderennen *nt*; ~**radish** *n* Meerrettich *m*; ~**shoe** *n* Hufeisen *nt*.

horticulture ['hɔːtɪkʌltʃə*] *n* Gartenbau *m*.

hose(pipe) ['həʊz(paɪp)] *n* Schlauch *m*.

hosiery ['həʊzɪərɪ] *n* Strumpfwaren *pl*.

hospitable [hɒs'pɪtəbl] *a* gastfreundlich.

hospital ['hɒspɪtl] *n* Krankenhaus *nt*.

hospitality [hɒspɪ'tælɪtɪ] *n* Gastfreundschaft *f*.

host [həʊst] *n* Gastgeber *m*; (*innkeeper*) (Gast)wirt *m*; (*large number*) Heerschar *f*; (*ECCL*) Hostie *f*.

hostage ['hɒstɪdʒ] *n* Geisel *f*.

hostel ['hɒstəl] *n* Herberge *f*; **(youth)** ~ *n* Jugendherberge *f*.

hostess ['həʊstes] *n* Gastgeberin *f*.

hostile ['hɒstaɪl] *a* feindlich.

hostility [hɒs'tɪlɪtɪ] *n* Feindschaft *f*; **hostilities** *pl* Feindseligkeiten *pl*.

hot [hɒt] *a* heiß; (*drink, food, water*) warm; (*spiced*) scharf; **I'm ~** mir ist heiß; ~**bed** *n* (*fig*) Nährboden *m*; ~**dog** *n* heiße(s) Würstchen *nt*.

hotel [həʊ'tel] *n* Hotel *nt*; ~**ier** *n* Hotelier *m*.

hot: ~**headed** *a* hitzig; ~**house** *n* Treibhaus *nt*; ~ **line** *n* (*POL*) heiße(r) Draht *m*; ~**ly** *ad* (*argue*) hitzig; ~**plate** *n* Kochplatte *f*; ~-**water bottle** *n* Wärmflasche *f*.

hound [haʊnd] *n* Jagdhund *m* // *vt* hetzen.

hour ['aʊə*] *n* Stunde *f*; (*time of day*) (Tages)zeit *f*; ~**ly** *a*, *ad* stündlich.

house [haʊs] *n* Haus *nt* // *vt* [haʊz] unterbringen; **on the ~** auf Kosten des Hauses; ~**boat** *n* Hausboot *nt*; ~**breaking** *n* Einbruch *m*; ~-**coat** *n* Morgenmantel *m*; ~**hold** *n* Haushalt *m*; ~**keeper** *n* Haushälterin *f*; ~**keeping** *n* Haushaltung *f*; ~-**warming party** *n* Einweihungsparty *f*; ~**wife** *n* Hausfrau *f*; ~**work** *n* Hausarbeit *f*.

housing ['haʊzɪŋ] *n* (*act*) Unterbringung *f*; (*houses*) Wohnungen *pl*; (*POL*) Wohnungsbau *m*; (*covering*) Gehäuse *nt*; ~ **development**, (*Brit*) ~ **estate** *n* (Wohn)siedlung *f*.

hovel ['hɒvəl] *n* elende Hütte *f*.

hover ['hɒvə*] *vi* (*bird*) schweben; (*person*) herumstehen; ~**craft** *n* Luftkissenfahrzeug *nt*.

how [haʊ] *ad* wie; ~ **are you?** wie geht es Ihnen?; ~ **much milk?** wieviel Milch?; ~ **many people?** wie viele Leute?

however [haʊ'evə*] *ad* (*but*) (je)doch, aber; ~ **you phrase it** wie Sie es auch ausdrücken.

howl [haul] n Heulen nt // vi heulen.

h.p., H.P. abbr of **hire purchase; horse power.**

H.Q. abbr of **headquarters.**

hub [hʌb] n Radnabe f.

hubbub ['hʌbʌb] n Tumult m.

hubcap ['hʌbkæp] n Radkappe f.

huddle ['hʌdl] vi: to ~ **together** sich zusammendrängen.

hue [hju:] n Färbung f; ~ **and cry** n Zetergeschrei nt.

huff [hʌf] n: to go into a ~ einschnappen.

hug [hʌg] vt umarmen // n Umarmung f.

huge [hju:dʒ] a groß, riesig.

hulk [hʌlk] n (ship) abgetakelte(s) Schiff nt; (person) Koloß m.

hull [hʌl] n Schiffsrumpf m.

hullo [hʌ'ləu] see **hello.**

hum [hʌm] vti summen.

human ['hju:mən] a menschlich // n (also: ~ **being**) Mensch m.

humane [hju:'meɪn] a human.

humanity [hju:'mænɪtɪ] n Menschheit f; (kindliness) Menschlichkeit f.

humble ['hʌmbl] a demütig; (modest) bescheiden // vt demütigen.

humbug ['hʌmbʌg] n Humbug m; (Brit: sweet) Pfefferminzbonbon nt.

humdrum ['hʌmdrʌm] a stumpfsinnig.

humid ['hju:mɪd] a feucht; ~**ity** [hju:'mɪdɪtɪ] n Feuchtigkeit f.

humiliate [hju:'mɪlɪeɪt] vt demütigen.

humiliation [hju:mɪlɪ'eɪʃən] n Demütigung f.

humility [hju:'mɪlɪtɪ] n Demut f.

humorous ['hju:mərəs] a humorvoll.

humour, ** (US) **humor ['hju:mə*] n (fun) Humor m; (mood) Stimmung f // vt bei Stimmung halten.

hump [hʌmp] n Buckel m.

hunch [hʌntʃ] n (Vor)ahnung f; ~**back** n Bucklige(r) mf; ~**ed** a gekrümmt.

hundred ['hʌndrɪd] num hundert; ~**weight** n Zentner m (Brit) = 50.8 kg; (US) = 45.3 kg.

hung [hʌŋ] pt, pp of **hang.**

Hungarian [hʌŋ'gɛərɪən] a ungarisch // n Ungar(in f) m; (LING) Ungarisch nt.

Hungary ['hʌŋgərɪ] n Ungarn nt.

hunger ['hʌŋgə*] n Hunger m // vi hungern; ~ **strike** n Hungerstreik m.

hungry ['hʌŋgrɪ] a hungrig; to be ~ Hunger haben.

hunk [hʌŋk] n (of bread) Stück nt.

hunt [hʌnt] vt jagen; (search) suchen (for acc) // vi jagen // n Jagd f; ~**er** n Jäger m; ~**ing** n Jagd f.

hurdle ['hɜ:dl] n (lit, fig) Hürde f.

hurl [hɜ:l] vt schleudern.

hurrah [hu'rɑ:], **hurray** [hu'reɪ] n Hurra nt.

hurricane ['hʌrɪkən] n Orkan m.

hurried ['hʌrɪd] a eilig; (hasty) übereilt; ~**ly** ad übereilt, hastig.

hurry ['hʌrɪ] n Eile f // vi sich beeilen // vt (an)treiben; (job) übereilen; to be in a ~ es eilig haben; ~ **up** vi sich beeilen // vt (person) zur Eile antreiben; (work) vorantreiben.

hurt [hɜ:t], pt, pp **hurt** vt weh tun (+dat); (injure, fig) verletzen // vi weh tun; ~**ful** a schädlich; (remark) verletzend.

hurtle ['hɜ:tl] vi sausen.

husband ['hʌzbənd] n (Ehe)mann m.

hush [hʌʃ] n Stille f // vt zur Ruhe bringen // interj pst, still.

husk [hʌsk] n Spelze f.

husky ['hʌskɪ] a (voice) rauh; (figure) stämmig // n Eskimohund m.

hustle ['hʌsl] vt (push) stoßen; (hurry) antreiben // n: ~ **and bustle** Geschäftigkeit f.

hut [hʌt] n Hütte f.

hutch [hʌtʃ] n (Kaninchen)stall m.

hyacinth ['haɪəsɪnθ] n Hyazinthe f.

hybrid ['haɪbrɪd] n Kreuzung f // a Misch-.

hydrant ['haɪdrənt] n (also: fire ~) Hydrant m.

hydraulic [haɪ'drɒlɪk] a hydraulisch.

hydrofoil ['haɪdrəufɔɪl] n Tragflügelboot nt.

hydrogen ['haɪdrɪdʒən] n Wasserstoff m.

hygiene ['haɪdʒi:n] n Hygiene f.

hygienic [haɪ'dʒi:nɪk] a hygienisch.

hymn [hɪm] n Kirchenlied nt.

hype [haɪp] n (col) Publicity f.

hypermarket ['haɪpə'mɑ:kɪt] n (Brit) Hypermarket m.

hyphen ['haɪfən] n Bindestrich m.

hypnosis [hɪp'nəusɪs] n Hypnose f.

hypnotic [hɪp'nɒtɪk] a hypnotisierend.

hypnotize ['hɪpnətaɪz] vt hypnotisieren.

hypocrisy [hɪ'pɒkrɪsɪ] n Heuchelei f.

hypocrite ['hɪpəkrɪt] n Heuchler m.

hypocritical [hɪpə'krɪtɪkəl] a scheinheilig, heuchlerisch.

hypothermia ['haɪpəu'θɜ:mɪə] n Unterkühlung f.

hypothetic(al) [haɪpəu'θetɪk(əl)] a hypothetisch.

hysterical [hɪs'terɪkəl] a hysterisch.

hysterics [hɪs'terɪks] npl hysterische(r) Anfall m.

I

I [aɪ] pron ich.

ice [aɪs] n Eis nt // vt (COOK) mit Zuckerguß überziehen // vi (also: ~ **up**) vereisen; ~ **axe** n Eispickel m; ~**berg** n Eisberg m; ~**box** n (US) Kühlschrank m; ~ **cream** n Eis nt; ~ **cube** n Eiswürfel m; ~ **hockey** n Eishockey nt.

Iceland ['aɪslənd] n Island nt.

ice: ~ **lolly** n (Brit) Eis nt am Stiel; ~

rink n (Kunst)eisbahn f; ~ **skating** n Schlittschuhlaufen nt.

icicle ['aɪsɪkl] n Eiszapfen m.

icing ['aɪsɪŋ] n (on cake) Zuckerguß m; (on window) Vereisung f; ~ **sugar** n (Brit) Puderzucker m.

icon ['aɪkɒn] n Ikone f.

icy ['aɪsɪ] a (slippery) vereist; (cold) eisig.

I'd [aɪd] = I would; I had.

idea [aɪ'dɪə] n Idee f.

ideal [aɪ'dɪəl] n Ideal nt // a ideal; ~ist n Idealist m.

identical [aɪ'dentɪkəl] a identisch; (twins) eineiig.

identification [aɪdentɪfɪ'keɪʃən] n Identifizierung f; **means of** ~ Ausweispapiere pl.

identify [aɪ'dentɪfaɪ] vt identifizieren; (regard as the same) gleichsetzen.

identikit picture [aɪ'dentɪkɪt-] n Phantombild nt.

identity [aɪ'dentɪtɪ] n Identität f; ~ **card** n Personalausweis m.

ideology [aɪdɪ'ɒlədʒɪ] n Ideologie f.

idiom ['ɪdɪəm] n (expression) Redewendung f; (dialect) Idiom nt; ~atic [-'mætɪk] a idiomatisch.

idiosyncrasy [ɪdɪə'sɪŋkrəsɪ] n Eigenart f.

idiot ['ɪdɪət] n Idiot(in f) m; ~ic [ɪdɪ'ɒtɪk] a idiotisch.

idle ['aɪdl] a (doing nothing) untätig; (lazy) faul; (useless) nutzlos; (machine) still(stehend); (threat, talk) leer // vi (machine) leerlaufen // vt: to ~ away the time die Zeit vertrödeln; ~ness n Müßiggang m; Faulheit f.

idol ['aɪdl] n Idol nt; ~ize vt vergöttern.

i.e. abbr (= that is) d.h.

if [ɪf] cj 1 wenn; (in case also) falls; ~ I were you wenn ich Sie wäre
2 (although): (even) ~ (selbst or auch) wenn
3 (whether) ob
4: ~ so/not wenn ja/nicht; ~ only ... wenn ... doch nur ...; ~ only I could wenn ich doch nur könnte; see also **as**.

ignite [ɪg'naɪt] vt (an)zünden // vi sich entzünden.

ignition [ɪg'nɪʃən] n Zündung f; **to switch on/off the** ~ den Motor anlassen/abstellen; ~ **key** n (AUT) Zündschlüssel m.

ignorance ['ɪgnərəns] n Unwissenheit f.

ignorant ['ɪgnərənt] a unwissend; **to be** ~ **of** nicht wissen.

ignore [ɪg'nɔː*] vt ignorieren.

I'll [aɪl] = I will, I shall.

ill [ɪl] a krank // n Übel nt // ad schlecht; **to take** or **be taken** ~ krank werden; ~-**advised** a unklug; ~-**at-ease** a unbehaglich.

illegal a [ɪ'liːgəl] illegal.

illegible [ɪ'ledʒəbl] a unleserlich.

illegitimate [ɪlɪ'dʒɪtɪmət] a unehelich.

ill: ~-**fated** a unselig; ~ **feeling** n Verstimmung f.

illicit [ɪ'lɪsɪt] a verboten.

illiterate [ɪ'lɪtərət] a ungebildet.

ill-mannered [ɪl'mænəd] a ungehobelt.

illness ['ɪlnəs] n Krankheit f.

illogical [ɪ'lɒdʒɪkəl] a unlogisch.

ill-treat ['ɪl'triːt] vt mißhandeln.

illuminate [ɪ'luːmɪneɪt] vt beleuchten.

illumination [ɪluːmɪ'neɪʃən] n Beleuchtung f; ~s pl festliche Beleuchtung f.

illusion [ɪ'luːʒən] n Illusion f; **to be under the** ~ **that** ... sich (dat) einbilden, daß ...

illusory [ɪ'luːsərɪ] a trügerisch.

illustrate ['ɪləstreɪt] vt (book) illustrieren; (explain) veranschaulichen.

illustration [ɪləs'treɪʃən] n Illustration f; (explanation) Veranschaulichung f.

illustrious [ɪ'lʌstrɪəs] a berühmt.

ill will ['ɪl'wɪl] n Groll m.

I'm [aɪm] = I am.

image ['ɪmɪdʒ] n Bild nt; (public ~) Image nt; ~ry n Symbolik f.

imaginary [ɪ'mædʒɪnərɪ] a eingebildet; (world) Phantasie-.

imagination [ɪmædʒɪ'neɪʃən] n Einbildung f; (creative) Phantasie f.

imaginative [ɪ'mædʒɪnətɪv] a phantasiereich, einfallsreich.

imagine [ɪ'mædʒɪn] vt sich vorstellen; (wrongly) sich einbilden.

imbalance [ɪm'bæləns] n Unausgeglichenheit f.

imbecile ['ɪmbəsiːl] n Schwachsinnige(r) mf.

imbue [ɪm'bjuː] vt: to ~ sth with etw erfüllen mit.

imitate ['ɪmɪteɪt] vt imitieren.

imitation [ɪmɪ'teɪʃən] n Imitation f.

immaculate [ɪ'mækjulɪt] a makellos; (dress) tadellos; (ECCL) unbefleckt.

immaterial [ɪmə'tɪərɪəl] a unwesentlich; **it is** ~ **whether** ... es ist unwichtig, ob ...

immature [ɪmə'tjuə*] a unreif.

immediate [ɪ'miːdɪət] a (instant) sofortig; (near) unmittelbar; (relatives) nächste(r, s); (needs) dringlich; ~ly ad sofort; ~ly **next to** direkt neben.

immense [ɪ'mens] a unermeßlich.

immerse [ɪ'mɜːs] vt eintauchen; **to be** ~d **in** (fig) vertieft sein in (+acc).

immersion heater [ɪ'mɜːʃənhiːtə*] n (Brit) Boiler m.

immigrant ['ɪmɪgrənt] n Einwanderer m.

immigrate ['ɪmɪgreɪt] vi einwandern.

immigration [ɪmɪ'greɪʃən] n Einwanderung f.

imminent ['ɪmɪnənt] a bevorstehend.

immobile [ɪ'məubaɪl] a unbeweglich.

immobilize [ɪ'məubɪlaɪz] vt lähmen.

immoral [ɪ'mɒrəl] a unmoralisch; ~ity [ɪmə'rælɪtɪ] n Unsittlichkeit f.

immortal [ɪ'mɔːtl] *a* unsterblich; **~ize** *vt* unsterblich machen.

immune [ɪ'mjuːn] *a* (*secure*) sicher (*from* vor +*dat*); (*MED*) immun.

immunity [ɪ'mjuːnɪtɪ] *n* (*MED, JUR*) Immunität *f*; (*fig*) Freiheit *f*.

immunize ['ɪmjʊnaɪz] *vt* immunisieren.

imp [ɪmp] *n* Kobold *m*.

impact ['ɪmpækt] *n* (*lit*) Aufprall *m*; (*fig*) Wirkung *f*.

impair [ɪm'pɛə*] *vt* beeinträchtigen.

impale [ɪm'peɪl] *vt* aufspießen.

impart [ɪm'pɑːt] *vt* mitteilen; (*knowledge*) vermitteln; (*exude*) abgeben.

impartial [ɪm'pɑːʃəl] *a* unparteiisch.

impassable [ɪm'pɑːsəbl] *a* unpassierbar.

impasse [æm'pɑːs] *n* Sackgasse *f*.

impassive [ɪm'pæsɪv] *a* gelassen.

impatience [ɪm'peɪʃəns] *n* Ungeduld *f*.

impatient *a* [ɪm'peɪʃənt] ungeduldig.

impeccable [ɪm'pekəbl] *a* tadellos.

impede [ɪm'piːd] *vt* (be)hindern.

impediment [ɪm'pedɪmənt] *n* Hindernis *nt*; (*in speech*) Sprachfehler *m*.

impending [ɪm'pendɪŋ] *a* bevorstehend.

impenetrable [ɪm'penɪtrəbl] *a* (*lit, fig*) undurchdringlich.

imperative [ɪm'perətɪv] *a* (*necessary*) unbedingt erforderlich // *n* (*GRAM*) Imperativ *m*, Befehlsform *f*.

imperceptible [ɪmpə'septəbl] *a* nicht wahrnehmbar.

imperfect [ɪm'pɜːfɪkt] *a* (*faulty*) fehlerhaft; **~ion** [-'fekʃən] *n* Unvollkommenheit *f*; (*fault*) Fehler *m*.

imperial [ɪm'pɪərɪəl] *a* kaiserlich; **~ism** *n* Imperialismus *m*.

impersonal [ɪm'pɜːsnl] *a* unpersönlich.

impersonate [ɪm'pɜːsəneɪt] *vt* sich ausgeben als; (*for amusement*) imitieren.

impertinent [ɪm'pɜːtɪnənt] *a* unverschämt, frech.

impervious [ɪm'pɜːvɪəs] *a* (*fig*) unempfänglich (*to* für).

impetuous [ɪm'petjʊəs] *a* ungestüm.

impetus ['ɪmpɪtəs] *n* Triebkraft *f*; (*fig*) Auftrieb *m*.

impinge [ɪm'pɪndʒ]: **~ on** *vt* beeinträchtigen.

implacable [ɪm'plækəbl] *a* unerbittlich.

implement ['ɪmplɪmənt] *n* Werkzeug *nt* // ['ɪmplɪment] *vt* ausführen.

implicate ['ɪmplɪkeɪt] *vt* verwickeln.

implication [ɪmplɪ'keɪʃən] *n* (*effect*) Auswirkung *f*; (*in crime*) Verwicklung *f*.

implicit [ɪm'plɪsɪt] *a* (*suggested*) unausgesprochen; (*utter*) vorbehaltlos.

implore [ɪm'plɔː*] *vt* anflehen.

imply [ɪm'plaɪ] *vt* (*hint*) andeuten; (*be evidence for*) schließen lassen auf (+*acc*).

impolite [ɪmpə'laɪt] *a* unhöflich.

import [ɪm'pɔːt] *vt* einführen // *n*
['ɪmpɔːt] Einfuhr *f*; (*meaning*) Bedeutung *f*.

importance [ɪm'pɔːtəns] *n* Bedeutung *f*.

important [ɪm'pɔːtənt] *a* wichtig; **it's not ~** es ist unwichtig.

importer [ɪm'pɔːtə*] *n* Importeur *m*.

impose [ɪm'pəʊz] *vti* auferlegen (*on dat*); (*penalty, sanctions*) verhängen (*on gegen*); **to ~ (o.s.) on sb** sich jdm aufdrängen.

imposing [ɪm'pəʊzɪŋ] *a* eindrucksvoll.

imposition [ɪmpə'zɪʃən] *n* (*of burden, fine*) Auferlegung *f*; (*SCH*) Strafarbeit *f*; **to be an ~** (*on person*) eine Zumutung sein.

impossible *a* [ɪm'pɒsəbl] unmöglich.

impostor [ɪm'pɒstə*] *n* Hochstapler *m*.

impotence ['ɪmpətəns] Impotenz *f*.

impotent ['ɪmpətənt] *a* machtlos; (*sexually*) impotent.

impound [ɪm'paʊnd] *vt* beschlagnahmen.

impoverished [ɪm'pɒvərɪʃt] *a* verarmt.

impracticable [ɪm'præktɪkəbl] *a* undurchführbar.

impractical [ɪm'præktɪkəl] *a* unpraktisch.

imprecise [ɪmprə'saɪs] *a* ungenau.

impregnable [ɪm'pregnəbl] *a* (*castle*) uneinnehmbar.

impregnate ['ɪmpregneɪt] *vt* (*saturate*) sättigen; (*fertilize*) befruchten.

impress [ɪm'pres] *vt* (*influence*) beeindrucken; (*imprint*) (auf)drücken; **to ~ sth on sb** jdm etw einschärfen.

impression [ɪm'preʃən] *n* Eindruck *m*; (*on wax, footprint*) Abdruck *m*; (*of book*) Auflage *f*; (*take-off*) Nachahmung *f*; **I was under the ~** ich hatte den Eindruck; **~able** *a* leicht zu beeindrucken; **~ist** *n* Impressionist *m*.

impressive [ɪm'presɪv] *a* eindrucksvoll.

imprint ['ɪmprɪnt] *n* Abdruck *m*.

imprison [ɪm'prɪzn] *vt* ins Gefängnis schicken; **~ment** *n* Inhaftierung *f*.

improbable [ɪm'prɒbəbl] *a* unwahrscheinlich.

impromptu [ɪm'prɒmptjuː] *a, ad* aus dem Stegreif, improvisiert.

improper [ɪm'prɒpə*] *a* (*indecent*) unanständig; (*unsuitable*) unpassend.

improve [ɪm'pruːv] *vt* verbessern // *vi* besser werden; **~ment** *n* (Ver)-besserung *f*.

improvise ['ɪmprəvaɪz] *vti* improvisieren.

imprudent [ɪm'pruːdənt] *a* unklug.

impudent ['ɪmpjʊdənt] *a* unverschämt.

impulse ['ɪmpʌls] *n* Impuls *m*; **to act on ~** spontan handeln.

impulsive [ɪm'pʌlsɪv] *a* impulsiv.

impunity [ɪm'pjuːnɪtɪ] *n* Straflosigkeit *f*.

impure [ɪm'pjʊə*] *a* (*dirty*) verunreinigt; (*bad*) unsauber.

impurity [ɪm'pjʊərɪtɪ] *n* Unreinheit *f*;

(TECH) Verunreinigung *f*.

in [ɪn] ◆*prep* **1** *(indicating place, position)* in (+ *dat*); *(with motion)* in (+ *acc*); ~ **here/there** hier/dort; ~ **London** in London; ~ **the United States** in den Vereinigten Staaten

2 *(indicating time: during)* in (+ *dat*); ~ **summer** im Sommer; ~ **1988** in Jahre) 1988; ~ **the afternoon** nachmittags, am Nachmittag

3 *(indicating time: in the space of)* innerhalb von; **I'll see you ~ 2 weeks** *or* ~ **2 weeks' time** ich sehe Sie in zwei Wochen

4 *(indicating manner, circumstances, state etc)* in (+ *dat*); ~ **the sun/rain** in der Sonne/im Regen; ~ **English/French** auf Englisch/Französisch; ~ **a loud/soft voice** mit lauter/leiser Stimme

5 *(with ratios, numbers)*: **1 ~ 10** jeder zehnte; **20 pence ~ the pound** 20 Pence pro Pfund; **they lined up ~ twos** sie stellten sich in Zweierreihe auf

6 *(referring to people, works)*: **the disease is common ~ children** die Krankheit ist bei Kindern häufig; ~ **Dickens** bei Dickens; **we have a loyal friend ~ him** er ist uns ein treuer Freund

7 *(indicating profession etc)*: **to be ~ teaching/the army** Lehrer(in)/beim Militär sein; **to be ~ publishing** im Verlagswesen arbeiten

8 *(with present participle)*: ~ **saying this, I** ... wenn ich das sage, ... ich; ~ **accepting this view, he** ... weil er diese Meinung akzeptierte, ... er

◆*ad*: **to be ~** *(person: at home, work)* dasein; *(train, ship, plane)* angekommen sein; *(in fashion)* in sein; **to ask sb ~** jdn hereinbitten; **to run/limp** *etc* ~ hereingerannt/-gehumpelt *etc* kommen

◆*n*: **the ~s and outs** *(of proposal, situation etc)* die Feinheiten.

in., ins *abbr of* **inch(es)**.

inability [ɪnəˈbɪlɪtɪ] *n* Unfähigkeit *f*.

inaccessible [ɪnækˈsesəbl] *a* unzugänglich.

inaccurate [ɪnˈækjʊrɪt] *a* ungenau; *(wrong)* unrichtig.

inactivity [ɪnækˈtɪvɪtɪ] *n* Untätigkeit *f*.

inadequate [ɪnˈædɪkwət] *a* unzulänglich.

inadvertently [ɪnədˈvɜːtəntlɪ] *ad* unabsichtlich.

inadvisable [ɪnədˈvaɪzəbl] *a* nicht ratsam.

inane [ɪˈneɪn] *a* dumm, albern.

inanimate [ɪnˈænɪmət] *a* leblos.

inappropriate [ɪnəˈprəʊprɪət] *a* *(clothing)* ungeeignet; *(remark)* unangebracht.

inarticulate [ɪnɑːˈtɪkjʊlət] *a* unklar.

inasmuch as [ɪnəzˈmʌtʃəz] *ad* da; *(in so far as)* soweit.

inaudible [ɪnˈɔːdəbl] *a* unhörbar.

inaugural [ɪˈnɔːgjʊrəl] *a* Eröffnungs-.

inaugurate [ɪˈnɔːgjʊreɪt] *vt (open)* einweihen; *(admit to office)* (feierlich) einführen.

inauguration [ɪnɔːgjʊˈreɪʃən] *n* Eröffnung *f*; (feierliche) Amtseinführung *f*.

in-between [ɪnbɪˈtwiːn] *a* Zwischen-.

inborn [ˈɪnˈbɔːn] *a* angeboren.

inbred [ˈɪnˈbred] *a* angeboren.

Inc. *abbr (US) of* **incorporated**.

incalculable [ɪnˈkælkjʊləbl] *a (consequences)* unabsehbar.

incapable [ɪnˈkeɪpəbl] *a* unfähig *(of doing sth* etw zu tun).

incapacitate [ɪnkəˈpæsɪteɪt] *vt* untauglich machen.

incapacity [ɪnkəˈpæsɪtɪ] *n* Unfähigkeit *f*.

incarcerate [ɪnˈkɑːsəreɪt] *vt* einkerkern.

incarnation [ɪnkɑːˈneɪʃən] *n (ECCL)* Menschwerdung *f*; *(fig)* Inbegriff *m*.

incendiary [ɪnˈsendɪərɪ] *a* Brand-.

incense [ˈɪnsens] *n* Weihrauch *m* // *vt* [ɪnˈsens] erzürnen.

incentive [ɪnˈsentɪv] *n* Anreiz *m*.

incessant *a*, **~ly** *ad* [ɪnˈsesnt, -lɪ] unaufhörlich.

incest [ˈɪnsest] *n* Inzest *m*.

inch [ɪntʃ] *n* Zoll *m*; **to be within an ~ of** kurz davor sein; **he didn't give an ~** er gab keinen Zentimeter nach; **to ~ forward** *vi* sich Stückchen für Stückchen vorwärts bewegen.

incidence [ˈɪnsɪdəns] *n* Auftreten *nt*; *(of crime)* Quote *f*.

incident [ˈɪnsɪdənt] *n* Vorfall *m*; *(disturbance)* Zwischenfall *m*.

incidental [ɪnsɪˈdentl] *a (music)* Begleit-; *(unimportant)* nebensächlich; *(remark)* beiläufig; **~ly** [-ˈdentəlɪ] *a* übrigens.

incinerator [ɪnˈsɪnəreɪtə*] *n* Verbrennungsofen *m*.

incipient [ɪnˈsɪpɪənt] *a* beginnend.

incision [ɪnˈsɪʒən] *n* Einschnitt *m*.

incisive [ɪnˈsaɪsɪv] *a (style)* treffend; *(person)* scharfsinnig.

incite [ɪnˈsaɪt] *vt* anstacheln.

inclination [ɪnklɪˈneɪʃən] *n* Neigung *f*.

incline [ˈɪnklaɪn] *n* Abhang *m* // [ɪnˈklaɪn] *vt* neigen; *(fig)* veranlassen // *vi* sich neigen; **to be ~d to** do sth dazu neigen, etw zu tun.

include [ɪnˈkluːd] *vt* einschließen; *(on list, in group)* aufnehmen.

including [ɪnˈkluːdɪŋ] *prep*: ~ X X inbegriffen.

inclusion [ɪnˈkluːʒən] *n* Aufnahme *f*.

inclusive [ɪnˈkluːsɪv] *a* inklusive; *(COMM)* inklusive; ~ **of** einschließlich (+ *gen*).

incoherent [ɪnkəʊˈhɪərənt] *a* zusammenhanglos.

income [ˈɪnkʌm] *n* Einkommen *nt*; *(from business)* Einkünfte *pl*; ~ **tax** Lohnsteuer *f*; *(of self-employed)* Ein-

kommenssteuer f.
incoming ['ɪnkʌmɪŋ] a: ~ **flight** ein-
treffende Maschine f.
incomparable [ɪn'kɒmpərəbl] a unver-
gleichlich.
incompatible [ɪnkəm'pætəbl] a
unvereinbar; (people) unverträglich.
incompetence [ɪn'kɒmpɪtəns] n
Unfähigkeit f.
incompetent [ɪn'kɒmpɪtənt] a unfähig.
incomplete [ɪnkəm'pliːt] a unvoll-
ständig.
incomprehensible [ɪnkɒmprɪ'hensəbl]
a unverständlich.
inconceivable [ɪnkən'siːvəbl] a unvorstellbar.
incongruous [ɪn'kɒŋgruəs] a seltsam;
(remark) unangebracht.
inconsiderate [ɪnkən'sɪdərət] a
rücksichtslos.
inconsistency [ɪnkən'sɪstənsɪ] n Wider-
sprüchlichkeit f; (state) Unbeständigkeit
f.
inconsistent [ɪnkən'sɪstənt] a (action,
speech) widersprüchlich; (person, work)
unbeständig; ~ **with** nicht überein-
stimmend mit.
inconspicuous [ɪnkən'spɪkjuəs] a
unauffällig.
incontinent [ɪn'kɒntɪnənt] a (MED)
nicht fähig, Stuhl und Harn
zurückzuhalten.
inconvenience [ɪnkən'viːnɪəns] n
Unbequemlichkeit f; (trouble to others)
Unannehmlichkeiten pl.
inconvenient [ɪnkən'viːnɪənt] a ungelegen; (journey) unbequem.
incorporate [ɪn'kɔːpəreɪt] vt (include)
aufnehmen; (contain) enthalten.
incorporated [ɪn'kɔːpəreɪtɪd] a: ~**d
company** (US: abbr Inc.) eingetragene
Aktiengesellschaft f.
incorrect [ɪnkə'rekt] a unrichtig.
incorrigible [ɪn'kɒrɪdʒəbl] a unverbesserlich.
incorruptible [ɪnkə'rʌptəbl] a unzer-
störbar; (person) unbestechlich.
increase ['ɪnkriːs] n Zunahme f; (pay ~)
Gehaltserhöhung f; (in size) Vergrößerung f // vt [ɪn'kriːs] erhöhen; (wealth,
rage) vermehren; (business) erweitern //
vi zunehmen; (prices) steigen; (in size)
größer werden; (in number) sich vermehren.
increasing [ɪn'kriːsɪŋ] a (number)
steigend.
increasingly [ɪn'kriːsɪŋlɪ] ad
zunehmend.
incredible [ɪn'kredəbl] a unglaublich.
incredulous [ɪn'kredjʊləs] a ungläubig.
increment ['ɪnkrɪmənt] n Zulage f.
incriminate [ɪn'krɪmɪneɪt] vt belasten.
incubation [ɪnkjʊ'beɪʃən] n Ausbrüten
nt.
incubator ['ɪnkjʊbeɪtə*] n Brutkasten

m.
incumbent [ɪn'kʌmbənt] n Amtsin-
haber(in f) m // a: it is ~ **on** him **to** ... es
obliegt ihm, ...
incur [ɪn'kɜː*] vt sich zuziehen; (debts)
machen.
incurable [ɪn'kjʊərəbl] a unheilbar;
(fig) unverbesserlich.
incursion [ɪn'kɜːʃən] n Einfall m.
indebted [ɪn'detɪd] a (obliged) verpflichtet (to sb jdm).
indecent [ɪn'diːsnt] a unanständig; ~
assault n (Brit) Notzucht f; ~ **exposure** n Exhibitionismus m.
indecisive [ɪndɪ'saɪsɪv] a (battle) nicht
entscheidend; (person) unentschlossen.
indeed [ɪn'diːd] ad tatsächlich, in der
Tat; **yes** ~! Allerdings!
indefinite [ɪn'defɪnɪt] a unbestimmt;
~**ly** ad auf unbestimmte Zeit; (wait)
unbegrenzt lange.
indelible [ɪn'deləbl] a unauslöschlich.
indemnify [ɪn'demnɪfaɪ] vt entschädigen; (safeguard) versichern.
indemnity [ɪn'demnɪtɪ] n (insurance)
Versicherung f; (compensation)
Schadenersatz m.
independence [ɪndɪ'pendəns] n
Unabhängigkeit f.
independent [ɪndɪ'pendənt] a
unabhängig.
indestructible [ˌɪndɪs'trʌktəbl] a unzer-
störbar.
indeterminate [ˌɪndɪ'tɜːmɪnɪt] a unbestimmt.
index ['ɪndeks] n Index m; ~ **card** n
Karteikarte f; ~ **finger** n Zeigefinger
m; ~**-linked**, (US) ~**ed** a (salaries)
der Inflationsrate (dat) angeglichen;
(pensions) dynamisch.
India ['ɪndɪə] n Indien nt; ~**n** a indisch //
n Inder(in f) m; **Red** ~**n** Indianer(in f)
m; **the** ~**n Ocean** n der Indische Ozean.
indicate ['ɪndɪkeɪt] vt anzeigen; (hint)
andeuten.
indication [ɪndɪ'keɪʃən] n Anzeichen nt;
(information) Angabe f.
indicative [ɪn'dɪkətɪv] a: ~ **of**
bezeichnend für // n (GRAM) Indikativ
m.
indicator ['ɪndɪkeɪtə*] n (sign)
(An)zeichen nt; (AUT) Richtungs-
anzeiger m.
indices ['ɪndɪsiːz] pl of **index**.
indict [ɪn'daɪt] vt anklagen; ~**ment** n
Anklage f.
indifference [ɪn'dɪfrəns] n Gleichgültig-
keit f; Unwichtigkeit f.
indifferent [ɪn'dɪfrənt] a gleichgültig;
(mediocre) mäßig.
indigenous [ɪn'dɪdʒɪnəs] a einheimisch.
indigestion [ɪndɪ'dʒestʃən] n Ver-
dauungsstörung f.
indignant [ɪn'dɪgnənt] a: to be ~ **about**

sth über etw (acc) empört sein.

indignation [ɪndɪgˈneɪʃən] n Entrüstung f.

indignity [ɪnˈdɪgnɪtɪ] n Demütigung f.

indirect a, **~ly** ad [ɪndɪˈrekt, -lɪ] indirekt.

indiscreet [ɪndɪsˈkriːt] a (insensitive) taktlos; (telling secrets) indiskret.

indiscretion [ɪndɪsˈkreʃən] n Taktlosigkeit f; Indiskretion f.

indiscriminate [ɪndɪsˈkrɪmɪnət] a wahllos; kritiklos.

indispensable [ɪndɪsˈpensəbl] a unentbehrlich.

indisposed [ɪndɪsˈpəuzd] a unpäßlich.

indisputable [ɪndɪsˈpjuːtəbl] a unbestreitbar; (evidence) unanfechtbar.

indistinct [ɪndɪsˈtɪŋkt] a undeutlich.

individual [ɪndɪˈvɪdjuəl] n Individuum nt // a individuell; (case) Einzel-; (of, for one person) eigen, individuell; (characteristic) eigentümlich; **~ly** ad einzeln, individuell.

indivisible [ɪndɪˈvɪzəbl] a unteilbar.

indoctrinate [ɪnˈdɒktrɪneɪt] vt indoktrinieren.

Indonesia [ɪndəuˈniːzɪə] n Indonesien nt.

indoor [ˈɪndɔː*] a Haus-; Zimmer-; Innen-; (SPORT) Hallen-; **~s** [ɪnˈdɔːz] ad drinnen, im Haus.

induce [ɪnˈdjuːs] vt dazu bewegen; (reaction) herbeiführen; **~ment** n Veranlassung f; (incentive) Anreiz m.

induction [ɪnˈdʌkʃən] n (MED: of birth) Einleitung f; **~ course** n (Brit) Einführungskurs m.

indulge [ɪnˈdʌldʒ] vt (give way) nachgeben (+dat); (gratify) frönen (+dat) // vi frönen (in dat); **~nce** n Nachsicht f; (enjoyment) Genuß m; **~nt** a nachsichtig; (pej) nachgiebig.

industrial [ɪnˈdʌstrɪəl] a Industrie-, industriell; (dispute, injury) Arbeits-; **~ action** n Arbeitskampfmaßnahmen pl; **~ estate** n (Brit) Industriegebiet nt; **~ist** n Industrielle(r) mf; **~ize** vt industrialisieren; **~ park** n (US) = **~ estate**.

industrious [ɪnˈdʌstrɪəs] a fleißig.

industry [ˈɪndəstrɪ] n Industrie f; (diligence) Fleiß m.

inebriated [ɪˈniːbrɪeɪtɪd] a betrunken.

inedible [ɪnˈedɪbl] a ungenießbar.

ineffective [ɪnɪˈfektɪv], **ineffectual** [ɪnɪˈfektjuəl] a unwirksam; (person) untauglich.

inefficiency [ɪnɪˈfɪʃənsɪ] n Ineffizienz f.

inefficient [ɪnɪˈfɪʃənt] a ineffizient; (ineffective) unwirksam.

inept [ɪˈnept] a (remark) unpassend; (person) ungeeignet.

inequality [ɪnɪˈkwɒlɪtɪ] n Ungleichheit f.

inert [ɪˈnɜːt] a träge; (CHEM) inaktiv; (motionless) unbeweglich.

inertia [ɪˈnɜːʃə] n Trägheit f.

inescapable [ɪnɪsˈkeɪpəbl] a unvermeidbar.

inevitable [ɪnˈevɪtəbl] a unvermeidlich.

inexcusable [ɪnɪksˈkjuːzəbl] a unverzeihlich.

inexhaustible [ɪnɪgˈzɔːstəbl] a unerschöpflich.

inexorable [ɪnˈeksərəbl] a unerbittlich.

inexpensive [ɪnɪksˈpensɪv] a preiswert.

inexperience [ɪnɪksˈpɪərɪəns] n Unerfahrenheit f; **~d** a unerfahren.

inexplicable [ɪnɪksˈplɪkəbl] a unerklärlich.

inextricably [ɪnɪksˈtrɪkəblɪ] ad untrennbar.

infallible [ɪnˈfæləbl] a unfehlbar.

infamous [ˈɪnfəməs] a (place) verrufen; (deed) schändlich; (person) niederträchtig.

infamy [ˈɪnfəmɪ] n Verrufenheit f; Niedertracht f; (disgrace) Schande f.

infancy [ˈɪnfənsɪ] n frühe Kindheit f; (fig) Anfangsstadium nt.

infant [ˈɪnfənt] n kleine(s) Kind nt, Säugling m; **~ile** a kindisch, infantil; **~ school** n (Brit) Grundschule f (für die ersten beiden Jahrgänge).

infantry [ˈɪnfəntrɪ] n Infanterie f.

infatuated [ɪnˈfætjueɪtɪd] a vernarrt; to become **~** with sich vernarren in (+acc).

infatuation [ɪnfætjuˈeɪʃən] n Vernarrtheit f (with in +acc).

infect [ɪnˈfekt] vt anstecken (also fig); **~ed with** (illness) infiziert mit; **~ion** n Infektion f; **~ious** [ɪnˈfekʃəs] a ansteckend.

infer [ɪnˈfɜː*] vt schließen; **~ence** [ˈɪnfərəns] n Schlußfolgerung f.

inferior [ɪnˈfɪərɪə*] a (rank) untergeordnet; (quality) minderwertig // n Untergebene(r) m; **~ity** [ɪnfɪərɪˈɒrɪtɪ] n Minderwertigkeit f; (in rank) untergeordnete Stellung f; **~ity complex** n Minderwertigkeitskomplex m.

infernal [ɪnˈfɜːnl] a höllisch.

infertile [ɪnˈfɜːtaɪl] a unfruchtbar.

infertility [ɪnfɜːˈtɪlɪtɪ] n Unfruchtbarkeit f.

infested [ɪnˈfestɪd] a: to be **~** with wimmeln von.

infidelity [ɪnfɪˈdelɪtɪ] n Untreue f.

in-fighting [ˈɪnfaɪtɪŋ] n Nahkampf m.

infiltrate [ˈɪnfɪltreɪt] vt infiltrieren; (spies) einschleusen // vi (MIL, liquid) einsickern; (POL) unterwandern (into acc).

infinite [ˈɪnfɪnɪt] a unendlich.

infinitive [ɪnˈfɪnɪtɪv] n Infinitiv m.

infinity [ɪnˈfɪnɪtɪ] n Unendlichkeit f.

infirm [ɪnˈfɜːm] a gebrechlich.

infirmary [ɪnˈfɜːmərɪ] n Krankenhaus nt.

infirmity [ɪnˈfɜːmɪtɪ] n Schwäche f, Gebrechlichkeit f.

inflamed [ɪnˈfleɪmd] a entzündet.

inflammable [ɪnˈflæməbl] *a* (*Brit*) feuergefährlich.

inflammation [ɪnfləˈmeɪʃən] *n* Entzündung *f*.

inflatable [ɪnˈfleɪtəbl] *a* aufblasbar.

inflate [ɪnˈfleɪt] *vt* aufblasen; (*tyre*) aufpumpen; (*prices*) hochtreiben.

inflation [ɪnˈfleɪʃən] *n* Inflation *f*; **~ary** *a* (*increase*) inflationistisch; (*situation*) inflationär.

inflexible [ɪnˈfleksəbl] *a* (*person*) nicht flexibel; (*opinion*) starr; (*thing*) unbiegsam.

inflict [ɪnˈflɪkt] *vt* zufügen (*sth on sb* jdm etw); (*wound*) beibringen (*on dat*).

influence [ˈɪnfluəns] *n* Einfluß *m* // *vt* beeinflussen.

influential [ɪnfluˈenʃəl] *a* einflußreich.

influenza [ɪnfluˈenzə] *n* Grippe *f*.

influx [ˈɪnflʌks] *n* (*of people*) Zustrom *m*; (*of ideas*) Eindringen *nt*.

inform [ɪnˈfɔːm] *vt* informieren; **to keep sb ~ed** jdn auf dem laufenden halten // *vi*: **to ~ on sb** jdn denunzieren.

informal [ɪnˈfɔːməl] *a* zwanglos; **~ity** [ɪnfɔːˈmælɪtɪ] *n* Zwangloseheit *f*.

informant [ɪnˈfɔːmənt] *n* Informant(in *f*) *m*.

information [ɪnfəˈmeɪʃən] *n* Auskunft *f*, Information *f*; **a piece of ~** eine Auskunft, eine Information; **~ office** *n* Informationsbüro *nt*.

informative [ɪnˈfɔːmətɪv] *a* informativ; (*person*) mitteilsam.

informer [ɪnˈfɔːmə*] *n* Denunziant(in *f*) *m*.

infra-red [ˈɪnfrəˈred] *a* infrarot.

infrequent [ɪnˈfriːkwənt] *a* selten.

infringe [ɪnˈfrɪndʒ] *vt* (*law*) verstoßen gegen; **~ upon** *vt* verletzen; **~ment** *n* Verstoß *m*, Verletzung *f*.

infuriating [ɪnˈfjuərɪeɪtɪŋ] *a* ärgerlich.

infusion [ɪnˈfjuːʒən] *n* (*tea etc*) Aufguß *m*.

ingenious [ɪnˈdʒiːnɪəs] *a* genial.

ingenuity [ɪndʒɪˈnjuːɪtɪ] *n* Genialität *f*.

ingenuous [ɪnˈdʒenjuəs] *a* aufrichtig; (*naive*) naiv.

ingot [ˈɪŋgət] *n* Barren *m*.

ingrained [ɪnˈgreɪnd] *a* tiefsitzend (*attr*).

ingratiate [ɪnˈgreɪʃɪeɪt] *vt* einschmeicheln (*o.s. with sb* sich bei jdm).

ingratitude [ɪnˈgrætɪtjuːd] *n* Undankbarkeit *f*.

ingredient [ɪnˈgriːdɪənt] *n* Bestandteil *m*; (*COOK*) Zutat *f*.

inhabit [ɪnˈhæbɪt] *vt* bewohnen; **~ant** *n* Bewohner(in *f*) *m*; (*of island, town*) Einwohner(in *f*) *m*.

inhale [ɪnˈheɪl] *vt* einatmen; (*MED, cigarettes*) inhalieren.

inherent [ɪnˈhɪərənt] *a* innewohnend (*in dat*).

inherit [ɪnˈherɪt] *vt* erben; **~ance** *n*

Erbe *nt*, Erbschaft *f*.

inhibit [ɪnˈhɪbɪt] *vt* hemmen; **to ~ sb from doing sth** jdn daran hindern, etw zu tun; **~ion** [ɪnhɪˈbɪʃən] *n* Hemmung *f*.

inhospitable [ɪnhosˈpɪtəbl] *a* (*person*) ungastlich; (*country*) unwirtlich.

inhuman [ɪnˈhjuːmən] *a* unmenschlich.

inimitable [ɪˈnɪmɪtəbl] *a* unnachahmlich.

iniquity [ɪˈnɪkwɪtɪ] *n* Ungerechtigkeit *f*.

initial [ɪˈnɪʃəl] *a* anfänglich, Anfangs- // *n* Initiale *f* // *vt* abzeichnen; (*POL*) paraphieren; **~s** *pl* Initialen *pl*; **~ly** *ad* anfangs.

initiate [ɪˈnɪʃɪeɪt] *vt* einführen; (*negotiations*) einleiten; **to ~ sb into a secret** jdn in ein Geheimnis einweihen; **to ~ proceedings against sb** (*JUR*) gerichtliche Schritte gegen jdn einleiten.

initiation [ɪnɪʃɪˈeɪʃən] *n* Einführung *f*; Einleitung *f*.

initiative [ɪˈnɪʃətɪv] *n* Initiative *f*.

inject [ɪnˈdʒekt] *vt* einspritzen; (*fig*) einflößen; **~ion** *n* Spritze *f*.

injunction [ɪnˈdʒʌŋkʃən] *n* Verfügung *f*.

injure [ˈɪndʒə*] *vt* verletzen; **~d** *a* (*person, arm*) verletzt.

injury [ˈɪndʒərɪ] *n* Verletzung *f*; **to play ~ time** (*SPORT*) nachspielen.

injustice [ɪnˈdʒʌstɪs] *n* Ungerechtigkeit *f*.

ink [ɪŋk] *n* Tinte *f*.

inkling [ˈɪŋklɪŋ] *n* (dunkle) Ahnung *f*.

inlaid [ˈɪnleɪd] *a* eingelegt, Einlege-.

inland [ˈɪnlænd] *a* Binnen-; (*domestic*) Inlands- // *ad* landeinwärts; **~ revenue** *n* (*Brit*) Fiskus *m*.

in-laws [ˈɪnlɔːz] *npl* (*parents-in-law*) Schwiegereltern *pl*; (*others*) angeheiratete Verwandte *pl*.

inlet [ˈɪnlet] *n* Einlaß *m*; (*bay*) kleine Bucht *f*.

inmate [ˈɪnmeɪt] *n* Insasse *m*.

inn [ɪn] *n* Gasthaus *nt*, Wirtshaus *nt*.

innate [ɪˈneɪt] *a* angeboren.

inner [ˈɪnə*] *a* inner, Innen-; (*fig*) verborgen; **~ city** *n* Innenstadt *f*; **~ tube** *n* (*of tyre*) Schlauch *m*.

innings [ˈɪnɪŋz] *n* (*CRICKET*) Innenrunde *f*.

innocence [ˈɪnəsns] *n* Unschuld *f*; (*ignorance*) Unkenntnis *f*.

innocent [ˈɪnəsnt] *a* unschuldig.

innocuous [ɪˈnɒkjuəs] *a* harmlos.

innovation [ɪnəʊˈveɪʃən] *n* Neuerung *f*.

innuendo [ɪnjuˈendəʊ] *n* (versteckte) Anspielung *f*.

innumerable [ɪˈnjuːmərəbl] *a* unzählig.

inoculation [ɪnɒkjuˈleɪʃən] *n* Impfung *f*.

inopportune [ɪnˈɒpətjuːn] *a* (*remark*) unangebracht; (*visit*) ungelegen.

inordinately [ɪˈnɔːdɪnɪtlɪ] *ad* unmäßig.

in-patient [ˈɪnpeɪʃənt] *n* stationäre(r) Patient(in *f*) *m*.

input [ˈɪnput] *n* (*COMPUT*) Eingabe *f*;

(*power* ~) Energiezufuhr *f*; (*of energy, work*) Aufwand *m*.

inquest ['ɪnkwest] *n* gerichtliche Untersuchung *f*.

inquire [ɪn'kwaɪə*] *vi* sich erkundigen // *vt (price)* sich erkundigen nach; ~ **into** *vt* untersuchen.

inquiry [ɪn'kwaɪərɪ] *n* (*question*) Erkundigung *f*; (*investigation*) Untersuchung *f*; ~ **office** *n* (*Brit*) Auskunft(sbüro *nt*) *f*.

inquisitive [ɪn'kwɪzɪtɪv] *a* neugierig.

inroad ['ɪnrəʊd] *n* (*MIL*) Einfall *m*; (*fig*) Eingriff *m*.

insane [ɪn'seɪn] *a* wahnsinnig; (*MED*) geisteskrank.

insanity [ɪn'sænɪtɪ] *n* Wahnsinn *m*.

insatiable [ɪn'seɪʃəbl] *a* unersättlich.

inscribe [ɪn'skraɪb] *vt* eingravieren; (*book etc*): to ~ (**to sb**) (jdm) widmen.

inscription [ɪn'skrɪpʃən] *n* (*on stone*) Inschrift *f*; (*in book*) Widmung *f*.

inscrutable [ɪn'skru:təbl] *a* unergründlich.

insect ['ɪnsekt] *n* Insekt *nt*; ~**icide** [ɪn'sektɪsaɪd] *n* Insektenvertilgungsmittel *nt*.

insecure [ɪnsɪ'kjʊə*] *a* (*person*) unsicher; (*thing*) nicht fest *or* sicher.

insecurity [ɪnsɪ'kjʊərɪtɪ] *n* Unsicherheit *f*.

insemination [ɪnsemɪ'neɪʃən] *n*: artificial ~ künstliche Befruchtung *f*.

insensible [ɪn'sensɪbl] *a* (*unconscious*) bewußtlos.

insensitive [ɪn'sensɪtɪv] *a* (*to pain*) unempfindlich; (*without feelings*) gefühllos.

inseparable [ɪn'sepərəbl] *a* (*people*) unzertrennlich; (*word*) untrennbar.

insert [ɪn'sɜːt] *vt* einfügen; (*coin*) einwerfen; (*stick into*) hineinstecken; (*advert*) aufgeben // *n* ['ɪnsɜːt] (*in book*) Einlage *f*; (*in magazine*) Beilage *f*; ~**ion** *n* Einfügung *f*; (*PRESS*) Inserat *nt*.

in-service ['ɪn'sɜːvɪs] *a* (*training*) berufsbegleitend.

inshore ['ɪn'ʃɔː*] *a* Küsten- // *ad* ['ɪn'ʃɔː*] an der Küste.

inside ['ɪn'saɪd] *n* Innenseite *f*, Innere(s) *nt* // *a* innere(r, s), Innen- // *ad* (*place*) innen; (*direction*) nach innen, hinein // *prep* (*place*) in (+*dat*); (*direction*) in (+*acc*) ... hinein; (*time*) innerhalb (+*gen*); ~ **10 minutes** unter 10 Minuten; ~**s** *pl* (*col*) Eingeweide *nt*; ~ **forward** *n* (*SPORT*) Halbstürmer *m*; ~ **lane** *n* (*AUT: in Britain*) linke Spur; ~ **out** *ad* linksherum; (*know*) in- und auswendig.

insidious [ɪn'sɪdɪəs] *a* heimtückisch.

insight ['ɪnsaɪt] *n* Einsicht *f*; Einblick *m* (*into* in +*acc*).

insignificant [ɪnsɪg'nɪfɪkənt] *a* unbedeutend.

insincere [ɪnsɪn'sɪə*] *a* unaufrichtig.

insinuate [ɪn'sɪnjʊeɪt] *vt* (*hint*) andeuten.

insipid [ɪn'sɪpɪd] *a* fad(e).

insist [ɪn'sɪst] *vi* bestehen (*on* auf +*acc*); ~**ence** *n* Bestehen *nt*; ~**ent** *a* hartnäckig; (*urgent*) dringend.

insole ['ɪnsəʊl] *n* Einlegesohle *f*.

insolence ['ɪnsələns] *n* Frechheit *f*.

insolent ['ɪnsələnt] *a* frech.

insoluble [ɪn'sɒljʊbl] *a* unlösbar; (*CHEM*) unlöslich.

insolvent [ɪn'sɒlvənt] *a* zahlungsunfähig.

insomnia [ɪn'sɒmnɪə] *n* Schlaflosigkeit *f*.

inspect [ɪn'spekt] *vt* prüfen; (*officially*) inspizieren; ~**ion** *n* Inspektion *f*; ~**or** *n* (*official*) Inspektor *m*; (*police*) Polizeikommissar *m*; (*Brit: on buses, trains*) Kontrolleur *m*.

inspiration [ɪnspɪ'reɪʃən] *n* Inspiration *f*.

inspire [ɪn'spaɪə*] *vt* (*respect*) einflößen (*in dat*); (*hope*) wecken (*in* in +*dat*); (*person*) inspirieren.

instability [ɪnstə'bɪlɪtɪ] *n* Unbeständigkeit *f*, Labilität *f*.

install [ɪn'stɔːl] *vt* (*put in*) installieren; (*telephone*) anschließen; (*establish*) einsetzen; ~**ation** [ɪnstə'leɪʃən] *n* (*of person*) (Amts)einsetzung *f*; (*of machinery*) Installierung *f*; (*machines etc*) Anlage *f*.

instalment, (*US*) **installment** [ɪn'stɔːlmənt] *n* Rate *f*; (*of story*) Fortsetzung *f*; to pay in ~s auf Raten zahlen.

instance ['ɪnstəns] *n* Fall *m*; (*example*) Beispiel *nt*; for ~ zum Beispiel; in the first ~ zunächst.

instant ['ɪnstənt] *n* Augenblick *m* // *a* augenblicklich, sofortig; ~ **coffee** *n* Pulverkaffee *m*.

instantaneous [ɪnstən'teɪnɪəs] *a* unmittelbar.

instantly ['ɪnstəntlɪ] *ad* sofort.

instead [ɪn'sted] *ad* statt dessen; ~ **of** *prep* anstatt (+*gen*).

instep ['ɪnstep] *n* Spann *m*; (*of shoe*) Blatt *nt*.

instigation [ɪnstɪ'geɪʃən] *n* Veranlassung *f*; (*of crime etc*) Anstiftung *f*.

instil [ɪn'stɪl] *vt* (*fig*) beibringen (*in sb* jdm).

instinct ['ɪnstɪŋkt] *n* Instinkt *m*; ~**ive** [ɪn'stɪŋktɪv] *a* instinktiv.

institute ['ɪnstɪtju:t] *n* Institut *nt* // *vt* einführen; (*search*) einleiten.

institution [ɪnstɪ'tju:ʃən] *n* Institution *f*; (*home*) Anstalt *f*.

instruct [ɪn'strʌkt] *vt* anweisen; (*officially*) instruieren; ~**ion** [ɪn'strʌkʃən] *n* Unterricht *m*; ~**ions** *pl* Anweisungen *pl*; (*for use*) Gebrauchsanweisung *f*; ~**ive** *a* lehrreich; ~**or** *n* Lehrer *m*; (*MIL*) Ausbilder *m*.

instrument ['ɪnstrʊmənt] n Instrument nt; ~al [ɪnstrʊ'mentl] a (MUS) Instrumental-; (helpful) behilflich (in bei); ~ panel n Armaturenbrett nt.

insubordinate [ɪnsə'bɔːdənət] a aufsässig, widersetzlich.

insubordination ['ɪnsəbɔːdɪ'neɪʃən] n Gehorsamsverweigerung f.

insufferable [ɪn'sʌfərəbl] a unerträglich.

insufficient [ɪnsə'fɪʃənt] a ungenügend.

insular ['ɪnsjələ*] a (fig) engstirnig.

insulate ['ɪnsjʊleɪt] vt (ELEC) isolieren; (fig) abschirmen (from vor +dat).

insulating tape n Isolierband nt.

insulation [ɪnsjʊ'leɪʃən] n Isolierung f.

insulin ['ɪnsjʊlɪn] n Insulin nt.

insult ['ɪnsʌlt] n Beleidigung f // [ɪn'sʌlt] vt beleidigen; ~ing [ɪn'sʌltɪŋ] a beleidigend.

insuperable [ɪn'suːpərəbl] a unüberwindlich.

insurance [ɪn'ʃʊərəns] n Versicherung f; fire/life ~ Feuer-/Lebensversicherung; ~ agent n Versicherungsvertreter m; ~ policy n Versicherungspolice f.

insure [ɪn'ʃʊə*] vt versichern.

insurrection [ɪnsə'rekʃən] n Aufstand m.

intact [ɪn'tækt] a unversehrt.

intake ['ɪnteɪk] n (place) Einlaßöffnung f; (act) Aufnahme f; (Brit SCH): an ~ of 200 a year ein Neuzugang von 200 im Jahr.

intangible [ɪn'tændʒəbl] a nicht greifbar.

integral ['ɪntɪɡrəl] a (essential) wesentlich; (complete) vollständig; (MATH) Integral-.

integrate ['ɪntɪɡreɪt] vt integrieren // vi sich integrieren.

integrity [ɪn'teɡrɪtɪ] n (honesty) Redlichkeit f, Integrität f.

intellect ['ɪntɪlekt] n Intellekt m; ~ual [ɪntɪ'lektjʊəl] a geistig, intellektuell // n Intellektuelle(r) mf.

intelligence [ɪn'telɪdʒəns] n (understanding) Intelligenz f; (news) Information f; (MIL) Geheimdienst m.

intelligent [ɪn'telɪdʒənt] a intelligent; ~ly ad klug; (write, speak) verständlich.

intelligentsia [ɪntelɪ'dʒentsɪə] n Intelligenz f.

intelligible [ɪn'telɪdʒəbl] a verständlich.

intend [ɪn'tend] vt beabsichtigen; that was ~ed for you das war für dich gedacht.

intense [ɪn'tens] a stark, intensiv; (person) ernsthaft; ~ly ad äußerst; (study) intensiv.

intensify [ɪn'tensɪfaɪ] vt verstärken, intensivieren.

intensity [ɪn'tensɪtɪ] n Intensität f.

intensive [ɪn'tensɪv] a intensiv; ~ care

unit n Intensivstation f.

intent [ɪn'tent] n Absicht f; to all ~s and purposes praktisch; to be ~ on doing sth fest entschlossen sein, etw zu tun.

intention [ɪn'tenʃən] n Absicht f.

intentional a, ~ly ad [ɪn'tenʃənl, -nəlɪ] absichtlich.

intently [ɪn'tentlɪ] ad konzentriert.

inter [ɪn'tɜː*] vt beerdigen.

interact [ɪntər'ækt] vi aufeinander einwirken; ~ion n Wechselwirkung f.

intercede [ɪntə'siːd] vi sich verwenden.

intercept [ɪntə'sept] vt abfangen.

interchange ['ɪntətʃeɪndʒ] n (exchange) Austausch m; (on roads) Verkehrskreuz nt // [ɪntə'tʃeɪndʒ] vt austauschen; ~able [ɪntə'tʃeɪndʒəbl] a austauschbar.

intercom ['ɪntəkɒm] n (Gegen-)sprechanlage f.

intercourse ['ɪntəkɔːs] n (exchange) Beziehungen pl; (sexual) Geschlechtsverkehr m.

interest ['ɪntrest] n Interesse nt; (FIN) Zinsen pl; (COMM: share) Anteil m; (group) Interessengruppe f // vt interessieren; ~ed a (having claims) beteiligt; (attentive) interessiert; to be ~ed in sich interessieren für; ~ing a interessant; ~ rate n Zinssatz m.

interface ['ɪntəfeɪs] n (COMPUT) Schnittstelle f, Interface nt.

interfere [ɪntə'fɪə*] vi (meddle) sich einmischen (with in +acc); (disrupt) stören (with acc).

interference [ɪntə'fɪərəns] n Einmischung f; (TV) Störung f.

interim ['ɪntərɪm] n: in the ~ inzwischen.

interior [ɪn'tɪərɪə*] n Innere(s) nt // a innere(r, s), Innen-; ~ designer n Innenarchitekt(in f) m.

interjection [ɪntə'dʒekʃən] n Ausruf m.

interlock [ɪntə'lɒk] vi ineinandergreifen.

interloper ['ɪntələʊpə*] n Eindringling m.

interlude ['ɪntəluːd] n Pause f.

intermarry [ɪntə'mærɪ] vi untereinander heiraten.

intermediary [ɪntə'miːdɪərɪ] n Vermittler m.

intermediate [ɪntə'miːdɪət] a Zwischen-, Mittel-.

interminable [ɪn'tɜːmɪnəbl] a endlos.

intermission [ɪntə'mɪʃən] n Pause f.

intermittent [ɪntə'mɪtənt] a periodisch, stoßweise.

intern [ɪn'tɜːn] vt internieren // ['ɪntɜːn] n (US) Assistenzarzt m/ -ärztin f.

internal [ɪn'tɜːnl] a (inside) innere(r, s); (domestic) Inlands-; ~ly ad innen; (MED) innerlich; 'not to be taken ~ly' 'nur zur äußerlichen Anwendung'; I~ Revenue Service (IRS) n (US) Finanzamt nt.

international [ɪntə'næʃnəl] *a* international // *n* (SPORT) Nationalspieler(in *f*) *m*; (: *match*) internationale(s) Spiel *nt*.

interplay ['ɪntəpleɪ] *n* Wechselspiel *nt*.

interpret [ɪn'tɜːprɪt] *vt* (*explain*) auslegen, interpretieren; (*translate*) dolmetschen; **~ation** ['teɪʃən] *n* Interpretation *f*; **~er** *n* Dolmetscher(in *f*) *m*.

interrelated [ɪntərɪ'leɪtɪd] *a* untereinander zusammenhängend.

interrogate [ɪn'terəɡeɪt] *vt* verhören.

interrogation [ɪntərə'ɡeɪʃən] *n* Verhör *nt*.

interrogative [ɪntə'rɒɡətɪv] *a* Frage-.

interrupt [ɪntə'rʌpt] *vt* unterbrechen; **~ion** *n* Unterbrechung *f*.

intersect [ɪntə'sekt] *vt* (durch) schneiden // *vi* sich schneiden; **~ion** *n* (*of roads*) Kreuzung *f*; (*of lines*) Schnittpunkt *m*.

intersperse [ɪntə'spɜːs] *vt*: to **~** sth with sth etw mit etw durchsetzen.

intertwine [ɪntə'twaɪn] *vti* (sich) verflechten.

interval ['ɪntəvəl] *n* Abstand *m*; (*Brit*: SCH, THEAT, SPORT) Pause *f*; at **~**s in Abständen.

intervene [ɪntə'viːn] *vi* dazwischenliegen; (*act*) einschreiten (*in* gegen).

intervention [ɪntə'venʃən] *n* Eingreifen *nt*, Intervention *f*.

interview ['ɪntəvjuː] *n* (PRESS etc) Interview *nt*; (*for job*) Vorstellungsgespräch *nt* // *vt* interviewen; **~er** *n* Interviewer *m*.

intestine [ɪn'testɪn] *n*: large/small **~** Dick-/Dünndarm *m*.

intimacy ['ɪntɪməsɪ] *n* Intimität *f*.

intimate ['ɪntɪmət] *a* (*inmost*) innerste(r, s); (*knowledge*) eingehend; (*familiar*) vertraut; (*friends*) eng // ['ɪntɪmeɪt] *vt* andeuten.

intimidate [ɪn'tɪmɪdeɪt] *vt* einschüchtern.

intimidation [ɪntɪmɪ'deɪʃən] *n* Einschüchterung *f*.

into ['ɪntʊ] *prep* (*motion*) in (+acc) ... hinein; 5 **~** 25 25 durch 5.

intolerable [ɪn'tɒlərəbl] *a* unerträglich.

intolerant [ɪn'tɒlərənt] *a*: **~** of unduldsam gegen(über).

intoxicate [ɪn'tɒksɪkeɪt] *vt* berauschen; **~d** *a* betrunken.

intoxication [ɪntɒksɪ'keɪʃən] *n* Rausch *m*.

intractable [ɪn'træktəbl] *a* schwer zu handhaben; (*problem*) schwer lösbar.

intransigent [ɪn'trænsɪdʒənt] *a* unnachgiebig.

intravenous [ɪntrə'viːnəs] *a* intravenös.

in-tray ['ɪntreɪ] *n* Eingangskorb *m*.

intrepid [ɪn'trepɪd] *a* unerschrocken.

intricate ['ɪntrɪkət] *a* kompliziert.

intrigue [ɪn'triːɡ] *n* Intrige *f* // *vt* faszinieren // *vi* intrigieren.

intriguing [ɪn'triːɡɪŋ] *a* faszinierend.

intrinsic [ɪn'trɪnsɪk] *a* innere(r, s); (*difference*) wesentlich.

introduce [ɪntrə'djuːs] *vt* (*person*) vorstellen (*to sb* jdm); (*sth new*) einführen; (*subject*) anschneiden; to **~** sb to sth jdn in etw (*acc*) einführen.

introduction [ɪntrə'dʌkʃən] *n* Einführung *f*; (*to book*) Einleitung *f*.

introductory [ɪntrə'dʌktərɪ] *a* Einführungs-, Vor-.

introspective [ɪntrəʊ'spektɪv] *a* nach innen gekehrt.

introvert ['ɪntrəʊvɜːt] *n* Introvertierte(r) *mf* // *a* introvertiert.

intrude [ɪn'truːd] *vi* stören (*on acc*); **~r** *n* Eindringling *m*.

intrusion [ɪn'truːʒən] *n* Störung *f*.

intrusive [ɪn'truːsɪv] *a* aufdringlich.

intuition [ɪntjuː'ɪʃən] *n* Intuition *f*.

inundate ['ɪnʌndeɪt] *vt* (*lit, fig*) überschwemmen.

invade [ɪn'veɪd] *vt* einfallen in (+acc); **~r** *n* Eindringling *m*.

invalid ['ɪnvəlɪd] *n* (*disabled*) Invalide *m* // *a* (*ill*) krank; (*disabled*) invalide; [ɪn'vælɪd] (*not valid*) ungültig.

invaluable [ɪn'væljʊəbl] *a* unschätzbar.

invariable [ɪn'vɛərɪəbl] *a* unveränderlich.

invariably [ɪn'vɛərɪəblɪ] *ad* ausnahmslos.

invasion [ɪn'veɪʒən] *n* Invasion *f*.

invent [ɪn'vent] *vt* erfinden; **~ion** [ɪn'venʃən] *n* Erfindung *f*; **~ive** *a* erfinderisch; **~or** *n* Erfinder *m*.

inventory ['ɪnvəntrɪ] *n* Inventar *nt*.

inverse ['ɪnvɜːs] *n* Umkehrung *f* // *a* umgekehrt.

invert [ɪn'vɜːt] *vt* umdrehen; **~ed commas** *npl* (*Brit*) Anführungsstriche *pl*.

invertebrate [ɪn'vɜːtɪbrət] *n* wirbellose(s) Tier *nt*.

invest [ɪn'vest] *vt* investieren.

investigate [ɪn'vestɪɡeɪt] *vt* untersuchen.

investigation [ɪnvestɪ'ɡeɪʃən] *n* Untersuchung *f*.

investigator [ɪn'vestɪɡeɪtə*] *n* Untersuchungsbeamte(r) *m*.

investiture [ɪn'vestɪtʃə*] *n* Amtseinsetzung *f*.

investment [ɪn'vestmənt] *n* Investition *f*.

investor [ɪn'vestə*] *n* (Geld)anleger *m*.

inveterate [ɪn'vetərət] *a* unverbesserlich.

invidious [ɪn'vɪdɪəs] *a* unangenehm; (*distinctions, remark*) ungerecht.

invigilate [ɪn'vɪdʒɪleɪt] *vti* (*in exam*) Aufsicht führen (*über*).

invigorating [ɪn'vɪɡəreɪtɪŋ] *a* stärkend.

invincible [ɪn'vɪnsəbl] *a* unbesiegbar.

inviolate [ɪn'vaɪələt] *a* unverletzt.
invisible [ɪn'vɪzəbl] *a* unsichtbar; ~ **ink** *n* Geheimtinte *f*.
invitation [ɪnvɪ'teɪʃən] *n* Einladung *f*.
invite [ɪn'vaɪt] *vt* einladen.
inviting [ɪn'vaɪtɪŋ] *a* einladend.
invoice ['ɪnvɔɪs] *n* Rechnung *f* // *vt* (*goods*) in Rechnung stellen (*sth for sb* jdm etw *acc*).
invoke [ɪn'vəuk] *vt* anrufen.
involuntary [ɪn'vɒləntərɪ] *a* unabsichtlich.
involve [ɪn'vɒlv] *vt* (*entangle*) verwickeln; (*entail*) mit sich bringen; ~**d** *a* verwickelt; ~**ment** *n* Verwicklung *f*.
inward ['ɪnwəd] *a* innere(r, s); (*curve*) Innen-; ~(**s**) *ad* nach innen; ~**ly** *ad* im Innern.
I/O *abbr* (= *input/output*) I/O.
iodine ['aɪədiːn] *n* Jod *nt*.
iota [aɪ'əutə] *n* (*fig*) bißchen *nt*.
IOU *n abbr of* **I owe you.**
IQ *n abbr* (= *intelligence quotient*) IQ *m*.
IRA *n abbr* (= *Irish Republican Army*) IRA *f*.
Iran [ɪ'rɑːn] *n* Iran *nt*; ~**ian** [ɪ'reɪnɪən] *a* iranisch // *n* Iraner(in *f*) *m*; (*LING*) Iranisch *nt*.
Iraq [ɪ'rɑːk] *n* Irak; ~**i** *a* irakisch // *n* Iraker(in *f*) *m*; (*LING*) Irakisch *nt*.
irascible [ɪ'ræsɪbl] *a* reizbar.
irate [aɪ'reɪt] *a* zornig.
Ireland ['aɪələnd] *n* Irland *nt*.
irksome ['ɜːksəm] *a* lästig.
iron ['aɪən] *n* Eisen *nt*; (*for ironing*) Bügeleisen *nt* // *a* eisern // *vt* bügeln; ~ **out** *vt* (*lit, fig*) ausbügeln; **I~ Curtain** *n* Eiserne(r) Vorhang *m*.
ironic(al) [aɪ'rɒnɪk(əl)] *a* ironisch; (*coincidence etc*) witzig.
ironing ['aɪənɪŋ] *n* Bügeln *nt*; (*laundry*) Bügelwäsche *f*; ~ **board** *n* Bügelbrett *nt*.
ironmonger ['aɪənmʌŋgə*] *n* (*Brit*) Eisenwarenhändler *m*; ~**'s** (**shop**) *n* Eisenwarenhandlung *f*.
iron ore ['aɪənɔː*] *n* Eisenerz *nt*.
irony ['aɪərənɪ] *n* Ironie *f*.
irrational [ɪ'ræʃənl] *a* irrational.
irreconcilable [ɪrekən'saɪləbl] *a* unvereinbar.
irrefutable [ɪrɪ'fjuːtəbl] *a* unwiderlegbar.
irregular [ɪ'regjulə*] *a* unregelmäßig; (*shape*) ungleich(mäßig); (*fig*) unüblich; (*behaviour*) ungehörig; ~**ity** [ɪregju'lærɪtɪ] *n* Unregelmäßigkeit *f*; Ungleichmäßigkeit *f*; (*fig*) Vergehen *nt*.
irrelevant [ɪ'reləvənt] *a* belanglos, irrelevant.
irreparable [ɪ'repərəbl] *a* nicht wiedergutzumachen.
irreplaceable [ɪrɪ'pleɪsəbl] *a* unersetzlich.
irrepressible [ɪrɪ'presəbl] *a* nicht zu

unterdrücken; (*joy*) unbändig.
irresistible [ɪrɪ'zɪstəbl] *a* unwiderstehlich.
irresolute [ɪ'rezəluːt] *a* unentschlossen.
irrespective [ɪrɪ'spektɪv]: ~ **of** *prep* ungeachtet (+*gen*).
irresponsible [ɪrɪ'spɒnsəbl] *a* verantwortungslos.
irreverent [ɪ'revərənt] *a* respektlos.
irrevocable [ɪ'revəkəbl] *a* unwiderrufbar.
irrigate ['ɪrɪgeɪt] *vt* bewässern.
irrigation [ɪrɪ'geɪʃən] *n* Bewässerung *f*.
irritable ['ɪrɪtəbl] *a* reizbar.
irritate ['ɪrɪteɪt] *vt* irritieren, reizen (*also MED*).
irritation [ɪrɪ'teɪʃən] *n* (*anger*) Ärger *m*; (*MED*) Reizung *f*.
IRS *n abbr of* **Internal Revenue Service.**
is [ɪz] *v see* **be.**
Islam ['ɪzlɑːm] *n* Islam *m*.
island ['aɪlənd] *n* Insel *f*; ~**er** *n* Inselbewohner(in *f*) *m*.
isle [aɪl] *n* (kleine) Insel *f*.
isn't ['ɪznt] = **is not.**
isolate ['aɪsəuleɪt] *vt* isolieren; ~**d** *a* isoliert; (*case*) Einzel-.
isolation [aɪsəu'leɪʃən] *n* Isolierung *f*.
Israel ['ɪzreɪəl] *n* Israel *nt*; ~**i** [ɪz'reɪlɪ] *a* israelisch // *n* Israeli *mf*.
issue ['ɪʃuː] *n* (*matter*) Frage *f*; (*outcome*) Ausgang *m*; (*of newspaper, shares*) Ausgabe *f*; (*offspring*) Nachkommenschaft *f* // *vt* ausgeben; (*warrant*) erlassen; (*documents*) ausstellen; (*orders*) erteilen; (*books*) herausgeben; (*verdict*) ausgeben; **to be at** ~ zur Debatte stehen; **to take** ~ **with sb over sth** jdm in etw (*dat*) widersprechen.
isthmus ['ɪsməs] *n* Landenge *f*.
it [ɪt] *pron* **1** (*specific:* subject) er/sie/es; (*: direct object*) ihn/sie/es; (*: indirect object*) ihm/ihr/ihm; **about/from/in/of** ~ darüber/davon/darin/davon
2 (*impersonal*) es; ~**'s raining** es regnet; **it's Friday tomorrow** morgen ist Freitag; **who is** ~? — ~**'s me** wer ist da? — ich (bin's).
Italian [ɪ'tæljən] *a* italienisch // *n* Italiener(in *f*) *m*; (*LING*) Italienisch *nt*.
italic [ɪ'tælɪk] *a* kursiv; ~**s** *npl* Kursivschrift *f*.
Italy ['ɪtəlɪ] *n* Italien *nt*.
itch [ɪtʃ] *n* Juckreiz *m*; (*fig*) Lust *f* // *vi* jucken; **to be** ~**ing to do sth** darauf brennen, etw zu tun; ~**y** *a* juckend.
it'd ['ɪtd] = **it would; it had.**
item ['aɪtəm] *n* Gegenstand *m*; (*on list*) Posten *m*; (*in programme*) Nummer *f*; (*in agenda*) (Programm)punkt *m*; (*in newspaper*) (Zeitungs)notiz *f*; ~**ize** *vt* verzeichnen.
itinerant [ɪ'tɪnərənt] *a* (*person*) um-

herreisend.

itinerary [aɪ'tɪnərərɪ] n Reiseroute f.

it'll ['ɪtl] = **it will, it shall**.

its [ɪts] poss a (masculine, neuter) sein; (feminine) ihr.

it's [ɪts] = **it is; it has**.

itself [ɪt'self] pron sich (selbst); (emphatic) selbst.

ITV n abbr (Brit) of **Independent Television**.

I.U.D. n abbr (= intra-uterine device) Pessar nt.

I've [aɪv] = **I have**.

ivory ['aɪvərɪ] n Elfenbein nt; ~ **tower** n (fig) Elfenbeinturm m.

ivy ['aɪvɪ] n Efeu nt.

J

jab [dʒæb] vti (hinein)stechen // n Stich m, Stoß m; (col) Spritze f.

jabber ['dʒæbə*] vi plappern.

jack [dʒæk] n (AUT) (Wagen)heber m; (CARDS) Bube m; ~ **up** vt aufbocken.

jackal ['dʒækəl] n (ZOOL) Schakal m.

jackdaw ['dʒækdɔ:] n Dohle f.

jacket ['dʒækɪt] n Jacke f; (of book) Schutzumschlag m; (TECH) Ummantelung f.

jack-knife ['dʒæknaɪf] vi (truck) sich zusammenschieben.

jack plug n (ELEC) Buchsenstecker m.

jackpot ['dʒækpɒt] n Haupttreffer m.

jade [dʒeɪd] n (stone) Jade m.

jaded ['dʒeɪdɪd] a ermattet.

jagged ['dʒægɪd] a zackig.

jail [dʒeɪl] n Gefängnis nt // vt einsperren; ~**er** n Gefängniswärter m.

jam [dʒæm] n Marmelade f; (also: traffic ~) (Verkehrs)stau m; (col: trouble) Klemme f // vt (wedge) einklemmen; (cram) hineinzwängen; (obstruct) blockieren // vi sich verklemmen; to ~ sth into sth etw in etw (acc) hineinstopfen.

Jamaica [dʒə'meɪkə] n Jamaika nt.

jangle ['dʒæŋgl] vti klimpern.

janitor ['dʒænɪtə*] n Hausmeister m.

January ['dʒænjʊərɪ] n Januar m.

Japan [dʒə'pæn] n Japan nt; ~**ese** [dʒæpə'ni:z] a japanisch // n, pl inv Japaner(in f) m; (LING) Japanisch nt.

jar [dʒɑ:*] n Glas nt // vi kreischen; (colours spiel) nicht harmonieren.

jargon ['dʒɑ:gən] n Fachsprache f, Jargon m.

jaundice ['dʒɔ:ndɪs] n Gelbsucht f; ~**d** a (fig) mißgünstig.

jaunt [dʒɔ:nt] n Spritztour f; ~**y** a (lively) munter; (brisk) flott.

javelin ['dʒævlɪn] n Speer m.

jaw [dʒɔ:*] n Kiefer m.

jay [dʒeɪ] n (ZOOL) Eichelhäher m.

jaywalker ['dʒeɪwɔ:kə*] n unvorsicht-

ige(r) Fußgänger m.

jazz [dʒæz] n Jazz m; ~ **up** vt (MUS) verjazzen; (enliven) aufpolieren; ~**y** a (colour) schreiend, auffallend.

jealous ['dʒeləs] a (envious) mißgünstig; (husband) eifersüchtig; ~**y** n Mißgunst f; Eifersucht f.

jeans [dʒi:nz] npl Jeans pl.

jeep [dʒi:p] n Jeep m.

jeer [dʒɪə*] vi höhnisch lachen (at über +acc), verspotten (at sb jdn).

jelly ['dʒelɪ] n Gelee nt; (dessert) Grütze f; ~**fish** n Qualle f.

jeopardize ['dʒepədaɪz] vt gefährden.

jeopardy ['dʒepədɪ] n: to be in ~ in Gefahr sein.

jerk [dʒɜ:k] n Ruck m; (col: idiot) Trottel m // vt ruckartig bewegen // vi sich ruckartig bewegen.

jerkin ['dʒɜ:kɪn] n Wams nt.

jerky ['dʒɜ:kɪ] a (movement) ruckartig; (ride) rüttelnd.

jersey ['dʒɜ:zɪ] n Pullover m.

jest [dʒest] n Scherz m; in ~ im Spaß // vi spaßen.

Jesus ['dʒi:zəs] n Jesus m.

jet [dʒet] n (stream: of water etc) Strahl m; (spout) Düse f; (AVIAT) Düsenflugzeug nt; ~-**black** a rabenschwarz; ~ **engine** n Düsenmotor m; ~-**lag** n Jet-lag m.

jettison ['dʒetɪsn] vt über Bord werfen.

jetty ['dʒetɪ] n Landesteg m, Mole f.

Jew [dʒu:] n Jude m.

jewel ['dʒu:əl] n (lit, fig) Juwel nt; ~(**l)er** n Juwelier m; ~(**l)er's (shop)** n Juwelier m; ~(**le)ry** n Schmuck m.

Jewess ['dʒu:ɪs] n Jüdin f.

Jewish ['dʒu:ɪʃ] a jüdisch.

jibe [dʒaɪb] n spöttische Bemerkung f.

jiffy ['dʒɪfɪ] n (col): in a ~ sofort.

jigsaw (puzzle) ['dʒɪgsɔ:(pʌzl)] n Puzzle(spiel) nt.

jilt [dʒɪlt] vt den Laufpaß geben (+dat).

jingle ['dʒɪŋgl] n (advertisement) Werbesong m // vti klimpern; (bells) bimmeln.

jinx [dʒɪŋks] n: there's a ~ on it es ist verhext.

jitters ['dʒɪtəz] npl (col): to get the ~ einen Bammel kriegen.

job [dʒɒb] n (piece of work) Arbeit f; (position) Stellung f; (duty) Aufgabe f; (difficulty) Mühe f; it's a good ~ he ... es ist ein Glück, daß er ...; just the ~ genau das Richtige; ~**centre** n (Brit) Arbeitsamt nt; ~**less** a arbeitslos.

jockey ['dʒɒkɪ] n Jockei m // vi: to ~ for position sich in eine gute Position drängeln.

jocular ['dʒɒkjʊlə*] a scherzhaft.

jog [dʒɒg] vt (an)stoßen // vi (run) joggen; to ~ **along** vor sich (acc) hinwursteln; (work) seinen Gang gehen; ~**ging** n Jogging nt.

join [dʒɔɪn] *vt* (*put together*) verbinden (*to* mit); (*club*) beitreten (+*dat*); (*person*) sich anschließen (+*dat*) // *vi* (*unite*) sich vereinigen // *n* Verbindungsstelle *f*, Naht *f*; ~ **in** *vti* mitmachen (*sth* bei etw); ~ **up** *vi* (*MIL*) zur Armee gehen.

joiner ['dʒɔɪnə*] *n* Schreiner *m*; ~**y** *n* Schreinerei *f*.

joint [dʒɔɪnt] *n* (*TECH*) Fuge *f*; (*of bones*) Gelenk *nt*; (*of meat*) Braten *m*; (*col: place*) Lokal *nt* // *a* gemeinsam; ~ **account** *n* (*with bank etc*) gemeinsame(s) Konto *nt*; ~**ly** *ad* gemeinsam.

joist [dʒɔɪst] *n* Träger *m*.

joke [dʒəʊk] *n* Witz *m* // *vi* Witze machen; **to play a** ~ **on sb** jdm einen Streich spielen; ~**r** *n* Witzbold *m*; (*CARDS*) Joker *m*.

jolly ['dʒɒlɪ] *a* lustig // *ad* (col) ganz schön.

jolt [dʒəʊlt] *n* (*shock*) Schock *m*; (*jerk*) Stoß *m* // *vt* (*push*) stoßen; (*shake*) durchschütteln; (*fig*) aufrütteln // *vi* holpern.

Jordan ['dʒɔːdən] *n* Jordanien *nt*; (*river*) Jordan *m*.

jostle ['dʒɒsl] *vt* anrempeln.

jot [dʒɒt] *n*: **not one** ~ kein Jota *nt*; ~ **down** *vt* notieren; ~**ter** *n* (*Brit*) Notizblock *m*.

journal ['dʒɜːnl] *n* (*diary*) Tagebuch *nt*; (*magazine*) Zeitschrift *f*; ~**ese** ['dʒɜːnə'liːz] *n* Zeitungsstil *m*; ~**ism** *n* Journalismus *m*; ~**ist** *n* Journalist(in *f*) *m*.

journey ['dʒɜːnɪ] *n* Reise *f*.

jovial ['dʒəʊvɪəl] *a* jovial.

joy [dʒɔɪ] *n* Freude *f*; ~**ful**, ~**ous** *a* freudig; ~ **ride** *n* Schwarzfahrt *f*; ~**stick** *n* Steuerknüppel *m*; (*COMPUT*) Joystick *m*.

J.P. *n abbr of* **Justice of the Peace.**

Jr *abbr of* **junior.**

jubilant ['dʒuːbɪlənt] *a* triumphierend.

jubilee ['dʒuːbɪliː] *n* Jubiläum *nt*.

judge [dʒʌdʒ] *n* Richter *m*; (*fig*) Kenner *m* // *vt* (*JUR: person*) die Verhandlung führen über (+*acc*); (*case*) verhandeln; (*assess*) beurteilen; (*estimate*) einschätzen; ~**ment** *n* (*JUR*) Urteil *nt*; (*ECCL*) Gericht *nt*; (*ability*) Urteilsvermögen *nt*.

judicial [dʒuː'dɪʃəl] *a* gerichtlich, Justiz-.

judiciary [dʒuː'dɪʃɪərɪ] *n* Gerichtsbehörden *pl*; (*judges*) Richterstand *m*.

judicious [dʒuː'dɪʃəs] *a* weis(e).

judo ['dʒuːdəʊ] *n* Judo *nt*.

jug [dʒʌg] *n* Krug *m*.

juggernaut ['dʒʌgənɔːt] *n* (*Brit: huge truck*) Schwertransporter *m*.

juggle ['dʒʌgl] *vti* jonglieren; ~**r** *n* Jongleur *m*.

Jugoslav ['juːgəʊ'slɑːv] *etc* = **Yugoslav** *etc*.

juice [dʒuːs] *n* Saft *m*.

juicy ['dʒuːsɪ] *a* (*lit, fig*) saftig.

jukebox ['dʒuːkbɒks] *n* Musikautomat *m*.

July [dʒuː'laɪ] *n* Juli *m*.

jumble ['dʒʌmbl] *n* Durcheinander *nt* // *vt* (*also:* ~ **up**) durcheinanderwerfen; (*facts*) durcheinanderbringen; ~ **sale** *n* (*Brit*) Basar *m*, Flohmarkt *m*.

jumbo (jet) ['dʒʌmbəʊ-] *n* Jumbo(-Jet) *m*.

jump [dʒʌmp] *vi* springen; (*nervously*) zusammenzucken // *vt* überspringen // *n* Sprung *m*; **to** ~ **the queue** (*Brit*) sich vordrängeln.

jumper ['dʒʌmpə*] *n* (*Brit: pullover*) Pullover *m*; (*US: dress*) Trägerkleid *nt*; ~ **cables** *npl* (*US*) = **jump leads.**

jump leads *npl* (*Brit*) Überbrückungskabel *nt*.

jumpy ['dʒʌmpɪ] *a* nervös.

Jun *abbr of* **junior.**

junction ['dʒʌŋkʃən] *n* (*Brit: of roads*) (Straßen)kreuzung *f*; (*RAIL*) Knotenpunkt *m*.

juncture ['dʒʌŋktʃə*] *n*: **at this** ~ in diesem Augenblick.

June [dʒuːn] *n* Juni *m*.

jungle ['dʒʌŋgl] *n* Dschungel *m*.

junior ['dʒuːnɪə*] *a* (*younger*) jünger; (*after name*) junior; (*SPORT*) Junioren-; (*lower position*) untergeordnet; (*for young people*) Junioren- // *n* Jüngere(r) *mf*; ~ **school** *n* (*Brit*) Grundschule *f*.

junk [dʒʌŋk] *n* (*rubbish*) Plunder *m*; (*ship*) Dschunke *f*; ~ **food** *n* Plastikessen *nt*; ~**shop** *n* Ramschladen *m*.

Junr *abbr of* **junior.**

jurisdiction [dʒʊərɪs'dɪkʃən] *n* Gerichtsbarkeit *f*; (*range of authority*) Zuständigkeit(sbereich *m*) *f*.

juror ['dʒʊərə*] *n* Geschworene(r) *mf*; (*in competition*) Preisrichter *m*.

jury ['dʒʊərɪ] *n* (*court*) Geschworene *pl*; (*in competition*) Jury *f*.

just [dʒʌst] *a* gerecht // *ad* (*recently, now*) gerade, eben; (*barely*) gerade noch; (*exactly*) genau, gerade; (*only*) nur, bloß; (*a small distance*) gleich; (*absolutely*) einfach; ~ **as I arrived** gerade als ich ankam; ~ **as nice** genauso nett; ~ **as well** um so besser; ~ **now** soeben, gerade; ~ **try** versuch es mal.

justice ['dʒʌstɪs] *n* (*fairness*) Gerechtigkeit *f*; ~ **of the peace** *n* Friedensrichter *m*.

justifiable ['dʒʌstɪfaɪəbl] *a* berechtigt.

justification [dʒʌstɪfɪ'keɪʃən] *n* Rechtfertigung *f*.

justify ['dʒʌstɪfaɪ] *vt* rechtfertigen; (*text*) justieren.

justly ['dʒʌstlɪ] *ad* (*say*) mit Recht;

(condemn) gerecht.

jut [dʒʌt] *vi (also: ~ out)* herausragen, vorstehen.

juvenile ['dʒuːvənaɪl] *a (young)* jugendlich; *(for the young)* Jugend- // *n* Jugendliche(r) *mf.*

juxtapose ['dʒʌkstəpəʊz] *vt* nebeneinanderstellen.

K

K *abbr* (= *one thousand*) Tsd.; (= *Kilobyte*) K.

kangaroo [kæŋgəˈruː] *n* Känguruh *nt.*

karate [kəˈrɑːtɪ] *n* Karate *nt.*

kebab [kəˈbæb] *n* Kebab *m.*

keel [kiːl] *n* Kiel *m*; **on an even ~** *(fig)* im Lot.

keen [kiːn] *a* begeistert; *(intelligence, wind, blade)* scharf; *(sight, hearing)* gut; **to be ~ to do** or **on doing** etw unbedingt tun wollen; **to be ~ on sth/sb** scharf auf etw/jdn sein.

keep [kiːp], *pt, pp* **kept** *vt (retain)* behalten; *(have)* haben; *(animals, one's word)* halten; *(support)* versorgen; *(maintain in state)* halten; *(preserve)* aufbewahren; *(restrain)* abhalten // *vi (continue in direction)* sich halten; *(food)* sich halten; *(remain: quiet etc)* bleiben // *n* Unterhalt *m*; *(tower)* Burgfried *m*; *(col):* **for ~s** für immer; **to ~ sth to o.s.** etw für sich behalten; **it ~s happening** es passiert immer wieder; **~ back** *vt* fernhalten; *(secret)* verschweigen; **~ on** *vi:* **~ on doing sth** etw immer weiter tun; **~ out** *vt* nicht hereinlassen; '**~ out**' 'Eintritt verboten!'; **~ up** *vi* Schritt halten // *vt* aufrechterhalten; *(continue)* weitermachen; **to ~ up with** Schritt halten mit; **~er** *n* Wärter(in *f*) *m*; **(goal~)** Torhüter(in *f*) *m*; **~-fit** *n* keep-fit *m*; **~ing** *n (care)* Obhut *f*; **in ~ing with** in Übereinstimmung mit; **~sake** *n* Andenken *nt.*

keg [keg] *n* Faß *nt.*

kennel ['kenl] *n* Hundehütte *f*; **~s** *pl:* **to put a dog in ~s** einen Hund in Pflege geben.

Kenya ['kenjə] *n* Kenia *nt*; **~n** *a* kenianisch // *n* Kenianer(in *f*) *m.*

kept [kept] *pt, pp of* **keep.**

kerb ['kɜːb] *n (Brit)* Bordstein *m.*

kernel ['kɜːnl] *n* Kern *m.*

kerosene ['kerəsiːn] *n* Kerosin *nt.*

ketchup ['ketʃəp] *n* Ketchup *nt or m.*

kettle ['ketl] *n* Kessel *m*; **~drum** *n* Pauke *f.*

key [kiː] *n* Schlüssel *m*; *(of piano, typewriter)* Taste *f*; *(MUS)* Tonart *f* // *vt (also: ~ in)* eingeben; **~board** *n* Tastatur *f*; **~ed up** *a (person)* überdreht; **~hole** *n* Schlüsselloch *nt*; **~note** *n* Grundton *m*; **~ ring** *n* Schlüsselring *m.*

khaki ['kɑːkɪ] *n* K(h)aki *nt* // *a* k(h)aki(farben).

kibbutz [kɪˈbʊts] *n* Kibbutz *m.*

kick [kɪk] *vt* einen Fußtritt geben (+*dat*), treten // *vi* treten; *(baby)* strampeln; *(horse)* ausschlagen // *n* (Fuß)tritt *m*; *(thrill)* Spaß *m*; **he does it for ~s** er macht das aus Jux; **~ off** *vi (SPORT)* anstoßen; **~-off** *n (SPORT)* Anstoß *m.*

kid [kɪd] *n (col: child)* Kind *nt*; *(goat)* Zicklein *nt*; *(leather)* Glacéleder *m* // *vi (col)* Witze machen.

kidnap ['kɪdnæp] *vt* entführen; **~per** *n* Entführer *m*; **~ping** *n* Entführung *f.*

kidney ['kɪdnɪ] *n* Niere *f.*

kill [kɪl] *vt* töten, umbringen // *vi* töten // *n* Tötung *f*; *(hunting)* (Jagd)beute *f*; **~er** *n* Mörder(in *f*) *m*; **~ing** *n* Mord *m*; **~joy** *n* Spaßverderber(in *f*) *m.*

kiln [kɪln] *n* Brennofen *m.*

kilo ['kiːləʊ] *n* Kilo *nt*; **~byte** *n (COMPUT)* Kilobyte *nt*; **~gram(me)** *n* Kilogramm *nt*; **~metre**, *(US)* **~meter** *n* Kilometer *m*; **~watt** *n* Kilowatt *nt.*

kilt [kɪlt] *n* Schottenrock *m.*

kin [kɪn] *n* Verwandtschaft *f.*

kind [kaɪnd] *a* freundlich // *n* Art *f*; **a ~ of** eine Art von; **(two) of a ~** (zwei) von der gleichen Art; **in ~** auf dieselbe Art; *(in goods)* in Naturalien.

kindergarten ['kɪndəgɑːtn] *n* Kindergarten *m.*

kind-hearted ['kaɪnd'hɑːtɪd] *a* gutherzig.

kindle ['kɪndl] *vt (set on fire)* anzünden; *(rouse)* reizen, (er)wecken.

kindly ['kaɪndlɪ] *a* freundlich // *ad* liebenswürdig(erweise); **would you ~ ...?** wären Sie so freundlich und ...?

kindness ['kaɪndnəs] *n* Freundlichkeit *f.*

kindred ['kɪndrɪd] *n* Verwandtschaft *f* // *a:* **~ spirit** *n* Gleichgesinnte(r) *mf.*

king [kɪŋ] *n* König *m*; **~dom** *n* Königreich *nt*; **~fisher** *n* Eisvogel *m*; **~-size** *a (cigarette)* Kingsize.

kinky ['kɪŋkɪ] *a (col) (person, ideas)* verrückt; *(sexual)* abartig.

kiosk ['kiːɒsk] *n (Brit TEL)* Telefonhäuschen *nt.*

kipper ['kɪpə*] *n* Räucherhering *m.*

kiss [kɪs] *n* Kuß *m* // *vt* küssen // *vi:* **they ~ed** sie küßten sich.

kit [kɪt] *n* Ausrüstung *f*; *(tools)* Werkzeug *nt.*

kitchen ['kɪtʃɪn] *n* Küche *f*; **~ sink** *n* Spülbecken *nt.*

kite [kaɪt] *n* Drachen *m.*

kith [kɪθ] *n:* **~ and kin** Blutsverwandte *pl.*

kitten ['kɪtn] *n* Kätzchen *nt.*

kitty ['kɪtɪ] *n (money)* Kasse *f.*

km *abbr* (= *kilometre*) km.

knack [næk] *n* Dreh *m*, Trick *m.*

knapsack ['næpsæk] *n* Rucksack *m*; *(MIL)* Tornister *m.*

knead [ni:d] vt kneten.
knee [ni:] n Knie nt; **~cap** n Kniescheibe f.
kneel [ni:l], pt, pp **knelt** vi (also: ~ **down**) knien.
knell [nel] n Grabgeläute nt.
knelt [nelt] pt, pp of **kneel**.
knew [nju:] pt of **know**.
knickers ['nıkəz] npl (Brit) Schlüpfer m.
knife [naıf], pl **knives** n Messer nt // vt erstechen.
knight [naıt] n Ritter m; (chess) Springer m; **~hood** n (title): **to get a ~hood** zum Ritter geschlagen werden.
knit [nıt] vti stricken // vi (bones) zusammenwachsen; **~ting** n (occupation) Stricken nt; (work) Strickzeug nt; **~ting machine** n Strickmaschine f; **~ting needle** n Stricknadel f; **~wear** n Strickwaren pl.
knives [naıvz] pl of **knife**.
knob [nɒb] n Knauf m; (on instrument) Knopf m; (Brit: of butter etc) kleine(s) Stück nt.
knock [nɒk] vt schlagen; (criticize) heruntermachen // n Schlag m; (on door) Klopfen nt; **to ~ at** or **on the door** an die Tür klopfen; **~ down** vt umwerfen; (with car) anfahren; **~ off** vt (do quickly) hinhauen; (col: steal) klauen // vi (finish) Feierabend machen; **~ out** vt ausschlagen; (BOXING) k.o. schlagen; **~ over** vt (person, object) umwerfen; (with car) anfahren; **~er** n (on door) Türklopfer m; **~-kneed** a x-beinig; **~out** n (lit) K.o.-Schlag m; (fig) Sensation f.
knot [nɒt] n Knoten m // vt (ver)knoten.
knotty ['nɒtı] a (fig) kompliziert.
know [nəʊ], pt **knew** pp **known** vt wissen; (be able to) können; (be acquainted with) kennen; (recognize) erkennen; **to ~ how to do sth** wissen, wie man etw macht, etw tun können; **to ~ about** or **of sth/sb** etw/jdn kennen; **~-all** n Alleswisser m; **~-how** n Kenntnis f, Know-how nt; **~ing** a (look, smile) wissend; **~ingly** ad wissend; (intentionally) wissentlich.
knowledge ['nɒlıdʒ] n Wissen nt, Kenntnis f; **~able** a informiert.
known [nəʊn] pp of **know**.
knuckle ['nʌkl] n Fingerknöchel m.
K.O. n abbr of **Knockout**.
Korea [kə'rıə] n Korea nt.
kosher ['kəʊʃə*] a koscher.

L

l. abbr of **litre**.
lab [læb] n (col) Labor nt.
label ['leıbl] n Etikett nt // vt etikettieren.
laboratory [lə'bɒrətərı] n Laboratorium nt.
laborious [lə'bɔ:rıəs] a mühsam.
labour, (US) **labor** ['leıbə*] n Arbeit f; (workmen) Arbeitskräfte pl; (MED) Wehen pl // vi: **to ~ (at)** sich abmühen (mit) // vt breittreten (col); **in ~** (MED) in den Wehen; **L~, the L~ party** (Brit) die Labour Party; **hard ~** Zwangsarbeit f; **~ed** a (movement) gequält; (style) schwerfällig; **~er** n Arbeiter m.
lace [leıs] n (fabric) Spitze f; (of shoe) Schnürsenkel m; (braid) Litze f // vt (also ~ **up**) (zu)schnüren.
lack [læk] n Mangel m // vt nicht haben; **sb ~s sth** jdm fehlt etw (nom); **to be ~ing** fehlen; **sb is ~ing in sth** es fehlt jdm an etw (dat); **through** or **for ~ of** aus Mangel an (+dat).
lackadaisical [lækə'deızıkəl] a lasch.
lacquer ['lækə*] n Lack m.
lad [læd] n Junge m.
ladder ['lædə*] n Leiter f; (Brit: in tights) Laufmasche f // vt (Brit: tights) Laufmaschen bekommen in (+dat).
laden ['leıdn] a beladen, voll.
ladle ['leıdl] n Schöpfkelle f.
lady ['leıdı] n Dame f; (title) Lady f; **young ~** junge Dame; **the ladies' (room)** die Damentoilette; **~bird** m, (US) **~bug** n Marienkäfer m; **~-in-waiting** n Hofdame f; **~like** a damenhaft, vornehm; **~ship** n: **your ~ship** Ihre Ladyschaft.
lag [læg] vi (also: ~ **behind**) zurückbleiben // vt (pipes) verkleiden.
lager ['lɑ:gə*] n helle(s) Bier nt.
lagging ['lægıŋ] n Isolierung f.
laid [leıd] pt, pp of **lay**; **~ back** a (col) cool.
lain [leın] pp of **lie**.
lair [lɛə*] n Lager nt.
laity ['leııtı] n Laien pl.
lake [leık] n See m.
lamb [læm] n Lamm nt; (meat) Lammfleisch nt; **~ chop** n Lammkotelett nt; **lambswool** n Lammwolle f.
lame [leım] a lahm; (excuse) faul.
lament [lə'ment] n Klage f // vt beklagen.
laminated ['læmıneıtıd] a beschichtet.
lamp [læmp] n Lampe f; (in street) Straßenlaterne f.
lampoon [læm'pu:n] vt verspotten.
lamp: ~post n (Brit) Laternenpfahl m; **~shade** n Lampenschirm m.
lance [lɑ:ns] n Lanze f // vt (MED) aufschneiden; **~ corporal** n (Brit) Obergefreite(r) m.
land [lænd] n Land nt // vi (from ship) an Land gehen; (AVIAT, end up) landen // vt (obtain) kriegen; (passengers) absetzen; (goods) abladen; (troops, space probe) landen; **~ing** n Landung f; (on stairs) (Treppen)absatz m; **~ing**

gear n Fahrgestell nt; **~ing stage** n (Brit) Landesteg m; **~ing strip** n Landebahn f; **~lady** n (Haus)wirtin f; **~locked** a landumschlossen, Binnen-; **~lord** n (of house) Hauswirt m, Besitzer m; (of pub) Gastwirt m; (of land) Grundbesitzer m; **~mark** n Wahrzeichen nt; (fig) Meilenstein m; **~owner** n Grundbesitzer m.

landscape ['lændskeɪp] n Landschaft f.

landslide ['lændslaɪd] n (GEOG) Erdrutsch m; (POL) überwältigende(r) Sieg m.

lane [leɪn] n (in town) Gasse f; (in country) Weg m; (of motorway) Fahrbahn f, Spur f; (SPORT) Bahn f.

language ['læŋgwɪdʒ] n Sprache f; bad ~ unanständige Ausdrücke; **~ laboratory** n Sprachlabor nt.

languid ['læŋgwɪd] a schlaff, matt.

languish ['læŋgwɪʃ] vi schmachten.

lank [læŋk] a dürr.

lanky ['læŋkɪ] a schlaksig.

lantern ['læntən] n Laterne f.

lap [læp] n Schoß m; (SPORT) Runde f // vt (also: ~ up) auflecken // vi (water) plätschern.

lapel [lə'pel] n Revers nt or m.

lapse [læps] n (moral) Fehltritt m // vi (decline) nachlassen; (expire) ablaufen; (claims) erlöschen; to ~ into bad habits sich schlechte Gewohnheiten angewöhnen.

larceny ['lɑːsənɪ] n Diebstahl m.

lard [lɑːd] n Schweineschmalz m.

larder ['lɑːdə*] n Speisekammer f.

large [lɑːdʒ] a groß; at ~ auf freiem Fuß; **~ly** ad zum größten Teil; **~-scale** a groß angelegt, Groß-.

largesse [lɑː'ʒes] n Freigebigkeit f.

lark [lɑːk] n (bird) Lerche f; (joke) Jux m; **~ about** vi (col) herumalbern.

laryngitis [lærɪn'dʒaɪtɪs] n Kehlkopfentzündung f.

larynx ['lærɪŋks] n Kehlkopf m.

lascivious [lə'sɪvɪəs] a wollüstig.

laser ['leɪzə*] n Laser m; **~ printer** n Laserdrucker m.

lash [læʃ] n Peitschenhieb m; (eye~) Wimper f // vt (rain) schlagen gegen; (whip) peitschen; (bind) festbinden; **~ out** vi (with fists) um sich schlagen; (spend money) sich in Unkosten stürzen // vt (money etc) springen lassen.

lass [læs] n Mädchen nt.

lasso [læ'suː] n Lasso nt.

last [lɑːst] a letzte(r, s) // ad zuletzt; (last time) das letztemal // vi (continue) dauern; (remain good) sich halten; (money) ausreichen; at ~ endlich; ~ night gestern abend; ~ week letzte Woche; ~ but one vorletzte(r, s); **~-ditch** a (attempt) in letzter Minute; **~ing** a dauerhaft; (shame etc) andauernd; **~ly** ad schließlich; **~-minute** a in letzter

Minute.

latch [lætʃ] n Riegel m.

late [leɪt] a spät; (dead) verstorben // ad spät; (after proper time) zu spät; to be ~ zu spät kommen; of ~ in letzter Zeit; in ~ May Ende Mai; **~comer** n Nachzügler(in f) m; **~ly** ad in letzter Zeit.

lateness ['leɪtnəs] n (of person) Zuspätkommen nt; (of train) Verspätung f; ~ of the hour die vorgerückte Stunde.

later ['leɪtə*] a (date etc) später; (version etc) neuer // ad später.

lateral ['lætərəl] a seitlich.

latest ['leɪtɪst] a (fashion) neueste(r, s) // n (news) Neu(e)ste(s) nt; at the ~ spätestens.

lathe [leɪð] n Drehbank f.

lather ['lɑːðə*] n (Seifen)schaum m; vt einschäumen // vi schäumen.

Latin ['lætɪn] n Latein nt // a lateinisch; (Roman) römisch; **~ America** n Lateinamerika nt; **~-American** a lateinamerikanisch.

latitude ['lætɪtjuːd] n (GEOG) Breite f; (freedom) Spielraum m.

latter ['lætə*] a (second of two) letztere (coming at end) letzte(r, s), später // n: the ~ der/die/das letztere, die letzteren; **~ly** ad in letzter Zeit.

lattice ['lætɪs] n Gitter nt.

laudable ['lɔːdəbl] a löblich.

laugh [lɑːf] n Lachen nt // vi lachen; ~ at vt lachen über (+acc); ~ off vt lachend abtun; **~able** a lachhaft; **~ing stock** n Zielscheibe f des Spottes; **~ter** n Gelächter nt.

launch [lɔːntʃ] n (of ship) Stapellauf m; (of rocket) Abschuß m; (boat) Barkasse f; (of product) Einführung f // vt (set afloat) vom Stapel lassen; (rocket) (ab)schießen; (product) auf den Markt bringen; **~ing** n Stapellauf m; **~(ing) pad** n Abschußrampe f.

launder ['lɔːndə*] vt waschen.

launderette [lɔːn'dret], (US) **laundromat** ['lɔːndrəmæt] n Waschsalon m.

laundry ['lɔːndrɪ] n (place) Wäscherei f; (clothes) Wäsche f; to do the ~ waschen.

laureate ['lɔːrɪət] a see **poet**.

laurel ['lɔrəl] n Lorbeer m.

lavatory ['lævətrɪ] n Toilette f.

lavender ['lævɪndə*] n Lavendel m.

lavish ['lævɪʃ] a (extravagant) verschwenderisch; (generous) großzügig // vt (money) verschwenden (on auf +acc); (attentions, gifts) überschütten mit (on sb jdn).

law [lɔː] n Gesetz nt; (system) Recht nt; (as studies) Jura no art; **~-abiding** a gesetzestreu; ~ **and order** n Recht nt und Ordnung f; ~ **court** n Gerichtshof m; **~ful** a gesetzlich; **~less** a gesetzlos.

lawn [lɔːn] n Rasen m; **~mower** n Rasenmäher m; ~ **tennis** n

Rasentennis m.

law school n Rechtsakademie f.

lawsuit ['lɔːsuːt] n Prozeß m.

lawyer ['lɔːjə*] n Rechtsanwalt m, Rechtsanwältin f.

laxative ['læksətɪv] n Abführmittel nt.

laxity ['læksɪtɪ] n Laxheit f.

lay [leɪ] pt of **lie** // a Laien- // vt, pt, pp **laid** (place) legen; (table) dekken; (egg) legen; (trap) stellen; (money) wetten; ~ **aside** vt zurücklegen; ~ **by** vt (set aside) beiseite legen; ~ **down** vt hinlegen; (rules) vorschreiben; (arms) strecken; **to ~ down the law** Vorschriften machen; ~ **off** vt (workers) (vorübergehend) entlassen; ~ **on** vt (water, gas) anschließen; (concert etc) veranstalten; ~ **out** vt (her)auslegen; (money) ausgeben; (corpse) aufbahren; ~ **up** vt (subj: illness) ans Bett fesseln; (supplies) anlegen; ~**about** n Faulenzer m; ~**by** n (Brit) Parkbucht f; (bigger) Rastplatz m.

layer ['leɪə*] n Schicht f.

layette [leɪ'et] n Babyausstattung f.

layman ['leɪmən] n Laie m.

layout ['leɪaʊt] n Anlage f; (ART) Layout nt.

laze [leɪz] vi faulenzen.

laziness ['leɪzɪnəs] n Faulheit f.

lazy ['leɪzɪ] a faul; (slow-moving) träge.

lb. abbr of **pound** (weight).

lead [liːd] n (front position) Führung f; (distance, time ahead) Vorsprung f; (example) Vorbild nt; (clue) Tip m; (of police) Spur f; (THEAT) Hauptrolle f; (dog's) Leine f; (led) (chemical) Blei nt; (of pencil) (Bleistift)mine f // a [led] bleiern, Blei- // v [liːd] (pt, pp **led**) vt (guide) führen; (group etc) leiten // vi (be first) führen; **in the ~** (SPORT, fig) in Führung; ~ **astray** vt irreführen; ~ **away** vt wegführen; (prisoner) abführen; ~ **back** vi zurückführen; ~ **on** vt anführen; ~ **on to** vt (induce) dazu bringen; ~ **to** vt (street) (hin)führen nach; (result in) führen zu; ~ **up to** vt (drive) führen zu; (speaker etc) hinführen auf (+acc).

leaden ['lednj] a (sky, sea) bleiern; (heavy: footsteps) bleischwer.

leader ['liːdə*] n Führer m, Leiter m; (of party) Vorsitzende(r) m; (PRESS) Leitartikel m; ~**ship** n (office) Leitung f; (quality) Führerschaft f.

leading ['liːdɪŋ] a führend; ~ **lady** n (THEAT) Hauptdarstellerin f; ~ **light** n (person) führende(r) Geist m.

leaf [liːf], pl **leaves** n Blatt nt // vi: **to ~ through** durchblättern; **to turn over a new ~** einen neuen Anfang nachen.

leaflet ['liːflɪt] n (advertisement) Prospekt m; (pamphlet) Flugblatt nt; (for information) Merkblatt nt.

league [liːg] n (union) Bund m; (SPORT) Liga f; **to be in ~ with** unter einer Decke stecken mit.

leak [liːk] n undichte Stelle f; (in ship) Leck nt // vt (liquid etc) durchlassen // vi (pipe etc) undicht sein; (liquid etc) auslaufen; **the information was ~ed to the enemy** die Information wurde dem Feind zugespielt; ~ **out** vi (liquid etc) auslaufen; (information) durchsickern.

leaky ['liːkɪ] a undicht.

lean [liːn] a mager // n (v: pt, pp **leaned** or **leant** [lent]) vi sich neigen // vt (an)lehnen; **to ~ against** sich an etw (dat) angelehnt sein; sich an etw (acc) anlehnen; ~ **back** vi sich zurücklehnen; ~ **forward** vi sich vorbeugen; ~ **on** vi sich stützen auf (+acc); ~ **out** vi sich hinauslehnen; ~ **over** vi sich hinüberbeugen; ~**ing** n Neigung f // a schief; ~**-to** n Anbau m.

leap [liːp] n Sprung m // vi, pt, pp **leaped** or **leapt** [lept] springen; ~**frog** n Bockspringen nt; ~ **year** n Schaltjahr nt.

learn [lɜːn], pt, pp **learned** or **learnt** vti lernen; (find out) erfahren; **to ~ how to do sth** etw (er)lernen; ~**ed** ['lɜːnɪd] a gelehrt; ~**er** n Anfänger(in f) m; (AUT) (Brit: also ~ **driver**) Fahrschüler(in f) m; ~**ing** n Gelehrsamkeit f.

lease [liːs] n (of property) Mietvertrag m // vt pachten.

leash [liːʃ] n Leine f.

least [liːst] a geringste(r, s) // ad am wenigsten // n Mindeste(s) nt; **the ~** possible effort möglichst geringer Aufwand; **at ~** zumindest; **not in the ~!** durchaus nicht!

leather ['leðə*] n Leder nt.

leave [liːv], pt, pp **left** vt verlassen; (~ behind) zurücklassen; (forget) vergessen; (allow to remain) lassen; (after death) hinterlassen; (entrust) überlassen (to sb jdm) // vi weggehen, wegfahren; (for journey) abreisen; (bus, train) abfahren // n Erlaubnis f; (MIL) Urlaub m; **to be left** (remain) übrigbleiben; **there's some milk left** es ist noch etwas Milch übrig; **on ~** auf Urlaub; ~ **behind** vt (person, object) dalassen; (: forget) liegenlassen, stehenlassen; ~ **out** vt auslassen; ~ **of absence** n Urlaub.

leaves [liːvz] pl of **leaf**.

Lebanon ['lebənən] n Libanon m.

lecherous ['letʃərəs] a lüstern.

lecture ['lektʃə*] n Vortrag m; (UNIV) Vorlesung f // vi einen Vortrag halten; (UNIV) lesen // vt (scold) abkanzeln; **to give a ~ on sth** einen Vortrag über etwas halten; ~**r** n Vortragende(r) mf; (Brit: UNIV) Dozent(in f) m.

led [led] pt, pp of **lead**.

ledge [ledʒ] n Leiste f; (window ~) Sims m or nt; (of mountain) (Fels)vorsprung *m.*

ledger ['ledʒə*] *n* Hauptbuch *nt.*

lee [li:] *n* Windschatten *m*; (*NAUT*) Lee *f.*

leech [li:tʃ] *n* Blutegel *m.*

leek [li:k] *n* Lauch *m.*

leer [lɪə*] *vi* schielen (*at* nach).

leeway ['li:weɪ] *n* (*fig*): to have some ~ etwas Spielraum haben.

left [left] *pt, pp of* **leave** // *a* linke(r, s) // *n* (*side*) linke Seite *f* // *ad* links; **on the ~** links; **to the ~** nach links; **the L~** (*POL*) die Linke *f*; **~-handed** *a* linkshändig; **~-hand side** *n* linke Seite *f*; **~-luggage (office)** *n* (*Brit*) Gepäckaufbewahrung *f*; **~-overs** *pl* Reste *pl*; **~-wing** *a* linke(r, s).

leg [leg] *n* Bein *nt*; (*of meat*) Keule *f*; (*stage*) Etappe *f*; **1st/2nd ~** (*SPORT*) 1./2. Etappe.

legacy ['legəsɪ] *n* Erbe *nt*, Erbschaft *f.*

legal ['li:gəl] *a* gesetzlich; (*allowed*) legal; **~ holiday** *n* (*US*) gesetzlicher Feiertag; **~ize** *vt* legalisieren; **~ly** *ad* gesetzlich; legal; **~ tender** *n* gesetzliche(s) Zahlungsmittel *nt.*

legend ['ledʒənd] *n* Legende *f*; **~ary** *a* legendär.

legible ['ledʒəbl] *a* leserlich.

legislation [ledʒɪs'leɪʃən] *n* Gesetzgebung *f.*

legislative ['ledʒɪslətɪv] *a* gesetzgebend.

legislature ['ledʒɪslətʃə*] *n* Legislative *f.*

legitimate [lɪ'dʒɪtɪmət] *a* rechtmäßig, legitim; (*child*) ehelich.

legroom ['legrʊm] *n* Platz *m* für die Beine.

leisure ['leʒə*] *n* Freizeit *f*; **to be at ~** Zeit haben; **~ly** *a* gemächlich.

lemon ['lemən] *n* Zitrone *f*; (*colour*) Zitronengelb *nt*; **~ade** [lemə'neɪd] *n* Limonade *f.*

lend [lend], *pt, pp* **lent** *vt* leihen; **to ~ sb sth** jdm etw leihen; **~ing library** *n* Leihbibliothek *f.*

length [leŋθ] *n* Länge *f*; (*section of road, pipe etc*) Strecke *f*; (*of material*) Stück *nt*; **at ~** (*lengthily*) ausführlich; (*at last*) schließlich; **~en** *vt* verlängern // *vi* länger werden; **~ways** *ad* längs; **~y** *a* sehr lang, langatmig.

lenient ['li:nɪənt] *a* nachsichtig.

lens [lenz] *n* Linse *f*; (*PHOT*) Objektiv *nt.*

lent [lent] *pt, pp of* **lend.**

Lent [lent] *n* Fastenzeit *f.*

lentil ['lentl] *n* Linse *f.*

Leo ['li:əʊ] *n* Löwe *m.*

leotard ['li:əta:d] *n* Trikot *nt*, Gymnastikanzug *m.*

leper ['lepə*] *n* Leprakranke(r) *mf.*

leprosy ['leprəsɪ] *n* Lepra *f.*

lesbian ['lezbɪən] *a* lesbisch // *n* Lesbierin *f.*

less [les] *a, ad, pron* weniger; **~ than half** weniger als die Hälfte; **~ than ever** weniger denn je; **~ and ~** immer weniger; **the ~ he works** je weniger er arbeitet.

lessen ['lesn] *vi* abnehmen // *vt* verringern, verkleinern.

lesser ['lesə*] *a* kleiner, geringer; **to a ~ extent** in geringerem Maße.

lesson ['lesn] *n* (*SCH*) Stunde *f*; (*unit of study*) Lektion *f*; (*fig*) Lehre *f*; (*ECCL*) Lesung *f*; **a maths ~** eine Mathestunde.

lest [lest] *cj*: **~ it happen** damit es nicht passiert.

let [let] *vt, pt, pp* **let** lassen; (*Brit: lease*) vermieten; **to ~ sb do sth** jdn etw tun lassen; **to ~ sb know sth** jdn etw wissen lassen; **~'s go!** gehen wir!; **~ him come** soll er doch kommen; **~ down** *vt* hinunterlassen; (*disappoint*) enttäuschen; **~ go** *vi* loslassen // *vt* (*things*) loslassen; (*person*) gehen lassen; **~ in** *vt* hereinlassen; (*water*) durchlassen; **~ off** *vt* (*gun*) abfeuern; (*steam*) ablassen; (*forgive*) laufen lassen; **~ on** *vi* durchblicken lassen; (*pretend*) vorgeben; **~ out** *vt* herauslassen; (*scream*) fahren lassen; **~ up** *vi* nachlassen; (*stop*) aufhören.

lethal ['li:θəl] *a* tödlich.

letter ['letə*] *n* (*of alphabet*) Buchstabe *m*; (*message*) Brief *m*; **~ bomb** *n* Briefbombe *f*; **~box** *n* (*Brit*) Briefkasten *m*; **~ of credit** *n* Akkreditiv *m*; **~ing** *n* Beschriftung *f.*

lettuce ['letɪs] *n* (Kopf)salat *m.*

let-up ['letʌp] *n* (*col*) Nachlassen *nt.*

leukaemia, (*US*) **leukemia** [lu:'ki:mɪə] *n* Leukämie *f.*

level ['levl] *a* (*ground*) eben; (*at same height*) auf gleicher Höhe; (*equal*) gleich gut; (*head*) kühl // *ad* auf gleicher Höhe // *n* (*instrument*) Wasserwaage *f*; (*altitude*) Höhe *f*; (*flat place*) ebene Fläche *f*; (*position on scale*) Niveau *nt*; (*amount, degree*) Grad *m*; // *vt* (*ground*) einebnen; (*blow*) versetzen (*at sb* jdm); (*remark*) richten (*at* gegen); **to draw ~ with** gleichziehen mit; **to be ~ with** auf einer Höhe sein mit; **'A' ~s** *npl* (*Brit*) ≈ Abitur *nt*; **'O' ~s** *npl* (*Brit*) ≈ mittlere Reife; **on the ~** (*fig: honest*) ehrlich; **~ off** *or* **out** *vi* flach *or* eben werden; (*fig*) sich ausgleichen; (*plane*) horizontal fliegen // *vt* (*ground*) planieren; (*differences*) ausgleichen; **~ crossing** *n* (*Brit*) Bahnübergang *m*; **~-headed** *a* vernünftig.

lever ['li:və*] *n* Hebel *m*; (*fig*) Druckmittel *nt* // *vt* (hoch)stemmen; **~age** *n* Hebelkraft *f*; (*fig*) Einfluß *m.*

levity ['levɪtɪ] *n* Leichtfertigkeit *f.*

levy ['levɪ] *n* (*of taxes*) Erhebung *f*; (*tax*) Abgaben *pl*; (*MIL*) Aushebung *f* // *vt* erheben; (*MIL*) ausheben.

lewd [lu:d] *a* unzüchtig, unanständig.
liability [laɪə'bɪlɪtɪ] *n* (*burden*) Belastung *f*; (*duty*) Pflicht *f*; (*debt*) Verpflichtung *f*; (*proneness*) Anfälligkeit *f*; (*responsibility*) Haftung *f*.
liable ['laɪəbl] *a* (*responsible*) haftbar; (*prone*) anfällig; **to be ~** für etw (*dat*) unterliegen; **it's ~ to happen** es kann leicht vorkommen.
liaise [li:'eɪz] *vi* zusammenarbeiten (*with* mit).
liaison [li:'eɪzɒn] *n* Verbindung *f*.
liar ['laɪə*] *n* Lügner *m*.
libel ['laɪbəl] *n* Verleumdung *f* // *vt* verleumden.
liberal ['lɪbərəl] *a* (*generous*) großzügig; (*open-minded*) aufgeschlossen; (*POL*) liberal.
liberate ['lɪbəreɪt] *vt* befreien.
liberation [lɪbə'reɪʃən] *n* Befreiung *f*.
liberty ['lɪbətɪ] *n* Freiheit *f*; (*permission*) Erlaubnis *f*; **to be at ~ to do sth** etw tun dürfen; **to take the ~ of doing sth** sich (*dat*) erlauben, etw zu tun.
Libra ['li:brə] *n* Waage *f*.
librarian [laɪbrɛərɪən] *n* Bibliothekar(in *f*) *m*.
library ['laɪbrərɪ] *n* Bibliothek *f*; (*lending* ~) Bücherei *f*.
Libya ['lɪbɪə] *n* Libyen *nt*; **~n** *a* libysch // *n* Libyer(in *f*) *m*.
lice [laɪs] *npl* of **louse**.
licence, (*US*) **license** ['laɪsəns] *n* (*permit*) Erlaubnis *f*; (*also*: **driving ~**, (*US*) **driver's ~**) Führerschein *m*; (*excess*) Zügellosigkeit *f*; **~ number** *n* (Kraftfahrzeug)kennzeichen *nt*; **~ plate** *n* (*US AUT*) Nummernschild *nt*.
license ['laɪsəns] *n* (*US*) = **licence** // *vt* genehmigen, konzessionieren; **~d** *a* (*for alcohol*) konzessioniert (*für den Ausschank von Alkohol*).
licentious [laɪ'senʃəs] *a* ausschweifend.
lichen ['laɪkən] *n* Flechte *f*.
lick [lɪk] *vt* lecken // *n* Lecken *nt*; **a ~ of paint** ein bißchen Farbe.
licorice ['lɪkərɪs] *n* = **liquorice**.
lid [lɪd] *n* Deckel *m*; (*eye~*) Lid *nt*.
lido ['li:dəʊ] *n* (*Brit*) Freibad *nt*.
lie [laɪ] *n* Lüge *f* // *vi* lügen // *vi, pt* **lay**, *pp* **lain** (*rest, be situated*) liegen; (*put o.s. in position*) sich legen; **to ~ low** (*fig*) untertauchen; **~ about** *vi* (*things*) herumliegen; (*people*) faulenzen; **~-down** *n*: **to have a ~-down** (*Brit*) ein Nickerchen machen; **~-in** *n*: **to have a ~-in** (*Brit*) sich ausschlafen.
lieu [lu:] *n*: **in ~ of** anstatt (+*gen*).
lieutenant [lef'tenənt] *n* Leutnant *m*.
life [laɪf], *pl* **lives** *n* Leben *nt*; **~ assurance** (*Brit*) *n* Lebensversicherung *f*; **~belt** (*Brit*) *n* Rettungsring *m*; **~boat** *n* Rettungsboot *nt*; **~guard** *n* Rettungsschwimmer *m*; **~ insurance** *n* = **~ as-**

surance; **~ jacket** *n* Schwimmweste *f*; **~less** *a* (*dead*) leblos; (*dull*) langweilig; **~like** *a* lebenswahr, naturgetreu; **~line** *n* (*lit*) Rettungsleine *f*; (*fig*) Rettungsanker *m*; **~long** *a* lebenslang; **~ preserver** *n* (*US*) = **~belt**; **~saver** *n* Lebensretter(in *f*) *m*; **~ sentence** *n* lebenslängliche Freiheitsstrafe; **~-sized** *a* in Lebensgröße; **~ span** *n* Lebensspanne *f*; **~style** *n* Lebensstil *m*; **~ support system** *n* (*MED*) Lebenserhaltungssystem *nt*; **~time** *n*: **in his ~time** während er lebte; **once in a ~time** einmal im Leben.
lift [lɪft] *vt* hochheben // *vi* sich heben // *n* (*Brit*: *elevator*) Aufzug *m*, Lift *m*; **to give sb a ~** (*Brit*) jdn mitnehmen; **~-off** *n* Abheben *nt* (vom Boden).
ligament ['lɪgəmənt] *n* Band *nt*.
light [laɪt] *n* Licht *nt*; (*for cigarette etc*): **have you got a ~?** haben Sie Feuer?; **~s** *pl* (*AUT*) Beleuchtung *f* // *vt, pt, pp* **lighted** *or* **lit** beleuchten; (*lamp*) anmachen; (*fire, cigarette*) anzünden // *a* (*bright*) hell; (*pale*) hell-; (*not heavy, easy*) leicht; (*punishment*) milde; (*touch*) leicht; **~ up** *vi* (*lamp*) angehen; (*face*) aufleuchten // *vt* (*illuminate*) beleuchten; (*lights*) anmachen; **~ bulb** *n* Glühbirne *f*; **~en** *vi* (*brighten*) hell werden; (*lightning*) blitzen // *vt* (*give light to*) erhellen; (*hair*) aufhellen; (*gloom*) aufheitern; (*make less heavy*) leichter machen; (*fig*) erleichtern; **~er** *n* Feuerzeug *nt*; **~-headed** *a* (*thoughtless*) leichtsinnig; (*giddy*) schwindlig; **~-hearted** *a* leichtherzig, fröhlich; **~house** *n* Leuchtturm *m*; **~ing** *n* Beleuchtung *f*; **~ly** *ad* leicht; (*irresponsibly*) leichtfertig; **to get off ~ly** mit einem blauen Auge davonkommen; **~ness** *n* (*of weight*) Leichtigkeit *f*; (*of colour*) Helle *f*.
lightning ['laɪtnɪŋ] *n* Blitz *m*; **~ conductor**, (*US*) **~ rod** *n* Blitzableiter *m*.
light: **~ pen** *n* Lichtstift *m*; **~weight** *a* (*suit*) leicht; **~weight boxer** *n* Leichtgewichtler *m*; **~ year** *n* Lichtjahr *nt*.
like [laɪk] *vt* mögen, gernhaben // *prep* wie // *a* (*similar*) ähnlich; (*equal*) gleich // *n*: **the ~** dergleichen; **his ~s and dislikes** was er mag und was er nicht mag; **I would ~, I'd ~** ich möchte gern; **would you ~ a coffee?** möchten Sie einen Kaffee?; **to be** *or* **look ~ sb/sth** jdm/etw ähneln; **that's just ~ him** das ist typisch für ihn; **do it ~ this** mach es so; **it is nothing ~ ...** es ist nicht zu vergleichen mit ...; **~able** *a* sympathisch.
likelihood ['laɪklɪhʊd] *n* Wahrscheinlichkeit *f*.
likely ['laɪklɪ] *a* wahrscheinlich; **he's ~ to leave** er geht möglicherweise; **not ~!**

wohl kaum.

likeness ['laiknis] n Ähnlichkeit f; (portrait) Bild nt.

likewise ['laikwaiz] ad ebenso.

liking ['laikiŋ] n Zuneigung f; (taste for) Vorliebe f.

lilac ['lailək] n Flieder m // a (colour) fliederfarben.

lily ['lili] n Lilie f; ~ **of the valley** n Maiglöckchen nt.

limb [lim] n Glied nt.

limber ['limbə*]: ~ **up** vi sich auflockern; (fig) sich vorbereiten.

limbo ['limbəʊ] n: to **be in** ~ (fig) in der Schwebe sein.

lime [laim] n (tree) Linde f; (fruit) Limone f; (substance) Kalk m.

limelight ['laimlait] n: to **be in the** ~ (fig) im Rampenlicht stehen.

limestone ['laimstəʊn] n Kalkstein m.

limit ['limit] n Grenze f; (col) Höhe f // vt begrenzen, einschränken; ~**ation** n Einschränkung f; ~**ed** a beschränkt; to **be** ~**ed to** sich beschränken auf (acc); ~**ed (liability) company (Ltd)** n (Brit) Gesellschaft f mit beschränkter Haftung, GmbH f.

limp [limp] n Hinken nt // vi hinken // a schlaff.

limpet ['limpit] n (fig) Klette f.

limpid ['limpid] a klar.

line [lain] n Linie f; (rope) Leine f; (on face) Falte f; (row) Reihe f; (of hills) Kette f; (US: queue) Schlange f; (company) Linie f, Gesellschaft f; (RAIL) Strecke f; (pl) Geleise pl; (TEL) Leitung f; (written) Zeile f; (direction) Richtung f; (fig: business) Branche f; (range of items) Kollektion f // vt (coat) füttern; (border) säumen; **in** ~ **with** in Übereinstimmung mit; ~ **up** vi sich aufstellen // vt aufstellen; (prepare) sorgen für; (support) mobilisieren; (surprise) planen.

linear ['liniə*] a gerade; (measure) Längen-.

lined [laind] a (face) faltig; (paper) liniert.

linen ['linin] n Leinen nt; (sheets etc) Wäsche f.

liner ['lainə*] n Überseedampfer m.

linesman ['lainzmən] n (SPORT) Linienrichter m.

line-up ['lainʌp] n Aufstellung f.

linger ['liŋgə*] vi (remain long) verweilen; (taste) (zurück)bleiben; (delay) zögern, verharren.

lingerie ['lænʒəri:] n Damenunterwäsche f.

lingering ['liŋgəriŋ] a (doubt) zurückbleibend; (disease) langwierig; (taste) nachhaltend; (look) lang.

lingo ['liŋgəʊ], pl ~**es** n (col) Sprache f.

linguist ['liŋgwist] n Sprachkundige(r) mf; (UNIV) Sprachwissenschaftler(in f)

m.

linguistic [liŋ'gwistik] a sprachlich; sprachwissenschaftlich; ~**s** n Sprachwissenschaft f, Linguistik f.

lining ['lainiŋ] n (of clothes) Futter nt.

link [liŋk] n Glied nt; (connection) Verbindung f; ~**s** pl (GOLF) Golfplatz m // vt verbinden; ~ **up** vt verbinden // vi zusammenkommen; (companies) sich zusammenschließen; ~-**up** (TEL) Verbindung f; (of spaceships) Kopplung f.

lino ['lainəʊ] n, **linoleum** [li'nəʊliəm] n Linoleum nt.

linseed oil ['linsi:d'ɔil] n Leinöl nt.

lion ['laiən] n Löwe m; ~**ess** n Löwin f.

lip [lip] n Lippe f; (of jug) Schnabel m; ~**read** vi irreg von den Lippen ablesen; ~ **salve** n Lippenbalsam m; to **pay** ~ **service (to)** ein Lippenbekenntnis ablegen (zu); ~**stick** n Lippenstift m.

liqueur [li'kjʊə*] n Likör m.

liquid ['likwid] n Flüßigkeit f // a flüssig.

liquidate ['likwideit] vt liquidieren.

liquidation [likwi'deifən] n Liquidation f.

liquidize ['likwidaiz] vt (CULIN) (im Mixer) pürieren.

liquidizer ['likwidaizə*] n Mixgerät nt.

liquor ['likə*] n Alkohol m.

liquorice ['likəris] n Lakritze f.

liquor store n (US) Spirituosengeschäft nt.

Lisbon ['lizbən] n Lissabon nt.

lisp [lisp] n Lispeln nt // vti lispeln.

list [list] n Liste f, Verzeichnis nt; (of ship) Schlagseite f // vt (write down) eine Liste machen von; (verbally) aufzählen // vi (ship) Schlagseite haben.

listen ['lisn] vi hören; ~ **to** vt zuhören (+dat); ~**er** n (Zu)hörer(in f) m.

listless ['listləs] a lustlos.

lit [lit] pt, pp of **light**.

literacy ['litərəsi] n Fähigkeit f zu lesen und zu schreiben.

literal ['litərəl] a buchstäblich; (translation) wortwörtlich; ~**ly** ad wörtlich; buchstäblich.

literary ['litərəri] a literarisch.

literate ['litərət] a des Lesens und Schreibens kundig.

literature ['litrətʃə*] n Literatur f.

lithe [laið] a geschmeidig.

litigation [liti'geifən] n Prozeß m.

litre, (US) **liter** ['li:tə*] n Liter m.

litter ['litə*] n (rubbish) Abfall m; (of animals) Wurf m // vt in Unordnung bringen; to **be** ~**ed with** übersät sein mit; ~ **bin** n (Brit) Abfalleimer m.

little ['litl] a klein // ad, n wenig; **a** ~ ein bißchen; ~ **by** ~ nach und nach.

live [liv] vi leben; (dwell) wohnen // vt (life) führen // a [laiv] lebendig; (MIL) scharf; (ELEC) geladen; (broadcast) live; ~ **down** vt: I'll never ~ it down das wird man mir nie vergessen; ~ **on**

vi weiterleben; **to ~ on** sth von etw leben; **to ~ together** *vi* zusammenleben; *(share a flat)* zusammenwohnen; **~ up to** *vt (standards)* gerecht werden (+*dat*); *(principles)* anstreben; *(hopes)* entsprechen (+*dat*).

livelihood ['laivlihud] *n* Lebensunterhalt *m*.

lively ['laivli] *a* lebhaft, lebendig.

liven up [laivn-] *vt* beleben.

liver ['livə*] *n* (ANAT) Leber *f*.

livery ['livəri] *n* Livree *f*.

lives [laivz] *pl of* **life**.

livestock ['laivstɒk] *n* Vieh *nt*.

livid ['livid] *a* (*lit*) bläulich; *(furious)* fuchsteufelswild.

living ['liviŋ] *n* (Lebens)unterhalt *m* // *a* lebendig; *(language etc)* lebend; **to earn or make a ~** sich (*dat*) seinen Lebensunterhalt verdienen; **~ conditions** *npl* Wohnverhältnisse *pl*; **~ room** *n* Wohnzimmer *nt*; **~ standards** *npl* Lebensstandard *m*; **~ wage** *n* ausreichender Lohn *m*.

lizard ['lizəd] *n* Eidechse *f*.

load [ləud] *n* (*burden*) Last *f*; *(amount)* Ladung *f* // *vt* *(also:* **~ up**): **~ (with)** (be)laden (mit); *(COMPUT)* laden; *(camera)* Film einlegen in (+*acc*); *(gun)* laden; **a ~ of, ~s of** (*fig*) jede Menge; **~ed** *a* beladen; *(dice)* präpariert; *(question)* Fang-; *(col: rich)* steinreich; **~ing bay** *n* Ladeplatz *m*.

loaf [ləuf] *n* Brot *nt* // *vi* *(also:* **~ about, ~ around**) herumlungern, faulenzen.

loan [ləun] *n* Leihgabe *f*; *(FIN)* Darlehen *nt* // *vt* leihen; **on ~** geliehen.

loath [ləuθ] *a*: **to be ~** to do sth etw ungern tun.

loathe [ləuð] *vt* verabscheuen.

loathing ['ləuðiŋ] *n* Abscheu *f*.

loaves [ləuvz] *pl of* **loaf**.

lobby ['lɒbi] *n* Vorhalle *f*; *(POL)* Lobby *f* // *vt* politisch beeinflussen (wollen).

lobe [ləub] *n* Ohrläppchen *nt*.

lobster ['lɒbstə*] *n* Hummer *m*.

local ['ləukəl] *a* ortsansässig, Orts- // *n* *(pub)* Stammwirtschaft *f*; **the ~s** *pl* die Ortsansässigen *pl*; **~ anaesthetic** *n* (MED) örtliche Betäubung *f*; **~ authority** *n* städtische Behörden *pl*; **~ call** *n* (TEL) Ortsgespräch *nt*; **~ government** *n* Gemeinde-/Kreisverwaltung *f*; **~ity** [ləu'kæliti] *n* Ort *m*; **~ly** *ad* örtlich, am Ort.

locate [ləu'keit] *vt* ausfindig machen; *(establish)* errichten.

location [ləu'keiʃən] *n* Platz *m*, Lage *f*; **on ~** (CINE) auf Außenaufnahme.

loch [lɒx] *n* (Scot) See *m*.

lock [lɒk] *n* Schloß *nt*; (NAUT) Schleuse *f*; *(of hair)* Locke *f* // *vt* *(fasten)* (ver)schließen *nt* // *vi* *(door etc)* sich schließen (lassen); *(wheels)* blockieren.

locker ['lɒkə*] *n* Spind *m*.

locket ['lɒkit] *n* Medaillon *nt*.

lockout ['lɒkaut] *n* Aussperrung *f*.

locksmith ['lɒksmiθ] *n* Schlosser(in *f*) *m*.

lock-up ['lɒkʌp] *n* Gefängnis *nt*.

locum ['ləukəm] *n* (MED) Vertreter(in *f*) *m*.

locust ['ləukəst] *n* Heuschrecke *f*.

lodge [lɒdʒ] *n* *(gatehouse)* Pförtnerhaus *nt*; *(freemasons')* Loge *f* // *vi* (in Untermiete) wohnen *(with* bei); *(get stuck)* stecken(bleiben) // *vt* *(protest)* einreichen; **~r** *n* (Unter)mieter *m*.

lodgings ['lɒdʒiŋz] *n* (Miet)wohnung *f*.

loft [lɒft] *n* (Dach)boden *m*.

lofty ['lɒfti] *a* hoch(ragend); *(proud)* hochmütig.

log [lɒg] *n* Klotz *m*; *(book)* = **logbook**.

logbook ['lɒgbuk] *n* Bordbuch *nt*; *(for lorry)* Fahrtenschreiber *m*; *(AUT)* Kraftfahrzeugbrief *m*.

loggerheads ['lɒgəhedz] *npl*: **to be at ~** sich in den Haaren liegen.

logic ['lɒdʒik] *n* Logik *f*; **~al** *a* logisch.

logistics [lɒ'dʒistiks] *npl* Logistik *f*.

logo ['ləugəu] *n* Firmenzeichen *nt*.

loin [lɔin] *n* Lende *f*.

loiter ['lɔitə*] *vi* herumstehen.

loll [lɒl] *vi* *(also:* **~ about**) sich rekeln.

lollipop ['lɒlipɒp] *n* (Dauer)lutscher *m*; **~ man/lady** *n* (Brit) ≈ Schülerlotse *m*.

London ['lʌndən] *n* London *nt*; **~er** *n* Londoner(in *f*) *m*.

lone [ləun] *a* einsam.

loneliness ['ləunlinəs] *n* Einsamkeit *f*.

lonely ['ləunli] *a* einsam.

loner ['ləunə*] *n* Einzelgänger(in *f*) *m*.

long [lɒŋ] *a* lang; *(distance)* weit // *ad* lange // *vi* sich sehnen *(for* nach); **before ~** bald; **as ~ as** solange; **in the ~ run** auf die Dauer; **don't be ~!** beeil dich!; **how ~ is the street?** wie lang ist die Straße?; **how ~ is the lesson?** wie lange dauert die Stunde; **6 metres ~** 6 Meter lang; **6 months ~** 6 Monate lang; **all night ~** die ganze Nacht; **he no ~er comes** er kommt nicht mehr; **~ ago** vor langer zeit; **before ~** lange vorher; **at ~ last** endlich; **~-distance** *a* Fern-.

longevity [lɒn'dʒeviti] *n* Langlebigkeit *f*.

long: ~-haired *a* langhaarig; **~-hand** *n* Langschrift *f*; **~ing** *n* Sehnsucht *f* // *a* sehnsüchtig.

longitude ['lɒŋgitju:d] *n* Längengrad *m*.

long: ~ jump *n* Weitsprung *m*; **~-lost** *a* längst verloren geglaubt; **~-playing record** *n* Langspielplatte *f*; **~-range** *a* Langstrecken-, Fern-; **~-sighted** *a* weitsichtig; **~-standing** *a* alt, seit langer Zeit bestehend; **~-suffering** *a* schwer geprüft; **~-term** *a* langfristig; **~ wave** *n* Langwelle *f*; **~-winded** *a* langatmig.

loo [luː] n (Brit col) Klo nt.

look [lʊk] vi schauen; (seem) aussehen; (building etc): **to ~ on to the sea** aufs Meer gehen; // n Blick m; **~s** pl Aussehen nt; **~ after** vt (care for) sorgen für; (watch) aufpassen auf (+acc); **~ at** vt ansehen; (consider) sich überlegen; **~ back** vi sich umsehen; (fig) zurückblicken; **~ down on** vt (fig) herabsehen auf (+acc); **~ for** vt (seek) suchen; **~ forward to** vt sich freuen auf (+acc); (in letters): **we ~ forward to hearing from you** wir hoffen, bald von Ihnen zu hören; **~ into** vt untersuchen; **~ on** vi zusehen; **~ out** vi hinaussehen; (take care) aufpassen; **~ out for** vt Ausschau halten nach; (be careful) achtgeben auf (+acc); **~ round** vi sich umsehen; **~ to** vt (take care of) achtgeben auf (+acc); (rely on) sich verlassen auf (+acc); **~ up** vi aufblicken; (improve) sich bessern // vt (word) nachschlagen; (person) besuchen; **~ up to** vt aufsehen zu; **~-out** n (watch) Ausschau f; (person) Wachposten m; (place) Ausguck m; (prospect) Aussichten pl; **to be on the ~-out for sth** nach etw Ausschau halten.

loom [luːm] n Webstuhl m // vi sich abzeichnen.

loony ['luːnɪ] n (col) Verrückte(r) mf.

loop [luːp] n Schlaufe f; **~hole** n (fig) Hintertürchen nt.

loose [luːs] a lose, locker; (free) frei; (inexact) unpräzise // vt lösen, losbinden; **~ change** n Kleingeld nt; **~ chippings** npl (on road) Rollsplit m; **~ end** n: **to be at a ~ end** (Brit) or **at ~ ends** (US) nicht wissen, was man tun soll; **~ly** ad locker, lose; **~n** vt lockern, losmachen.

loot [luːt] n Beute f // vt plündern; **~ing** n Plünderung f.

lop [lɒp]: **~ off** vt abhacken.

lop-sided ['lɒp'saɪdɪd] a schief.

lord [lɔːd] n (ruler) Herr m; (Brit, title) Lord m; **the L~** (Gott) der Herr m; **the (House of) L~s** das Oberhaus; **~ship** n: **your L~ship** Eure Lordschaft.

lore [lɔː*] n Überlieferung f.

lorry ['lɒrɪ] n (Brit) Lastwagen m; **~ driver** n (Brit) Lastwagenfahrer(in f) m.

lose [luːz] pt, pp **lost** vt verlieren; (chance) verpassen // vi verlieren; **to ~** (time) (clock) nachgehen; **~r** n Verlierer m.

loss [lɒs] n Verlust m; **at a ~** (COMM) mit Verlust; (unable) außerstande.

lost [lɒst] pt, pp of **lose** // a verloren; **~ property**, (US) **~ and found** n Fundsachen pl.

lot [lɒt] n (quantity) Menge f; (fate, at auction) Los nt; (col: people, things) Haufen m; **the ~** alles; (people) alle; **a ~ of** sing viel // pl viele; **~s of** massenhaft, viel(e); **I read a ~** ich lese viel; **to draw ~s for sth** etw verlosen.

lotion ['ləʊʃən] n Lotion f.

lottery ['lɒtərɪ] n Lotterie f.

loud [laʊd] a laut; (showy) schreiend // ad laut; **~hailer** n (Brit) Megaphon nt; **~ly** ad laut; **~speaker** n Lautsprecher m.

lounge [laʊndʒ] n (in hotel) Gesellschaftsraum m; (in house) Wohnzimmer nt // vi sich herumlümmeln; **~ suit** n (Brit) Straßenanzug m.

louse [laʊs], pl **lice** n Laus f.

lousy ['laʊzɪ] a (fig) miserabel.

lout [laʊt] n Lümmel m.

louvre, (US) louver ['luːvə*] a (door, window) Jalousie-.

lovable ['lʌvəbl] a liebenswert.

love [lʌv] n Liebe f; (person) Liebling m; (SPORT) null // vt (person) lieben; (activity) gerne mögen; **to ~ to do sth** etw (sehr) gerne tun; **to be in ~ with sb** in jdn verliebt sein; **to make ~** sich lieben; **for the ~ of** aus Liebe zu; **'15 ~'** (TENNIS) 15 null; **~ affair** n (Liebes)verhältnis nt; **~ letter** n Liebesbrief m; **~ life** n Liebesleben nt.

lovely ['lʌvlɪ] a schön.

lover ['lʌvə*] n Liebhaber(in f) m.

loving ['lʌvɪŋ] a liebend, liebevoll.

low [ləʊ] a niedrig; (rank) niedere(r, s); (level, note, neckline) tief; (intelligence, density) gering; (vulgar) ordinär; (not loud) leise; (depressed) gedrückt // ad (not high) niedrig; (not loudly) leise // n (low point) Tiefstand m; (MET) Tief nt; **to feel ~** sich mies fühlen; **turn (down) ~** vt leiser stellen; **~-cut** a (dress) tiefausgeschnitten.

lower ['ləʊə*] vt herunterlassen; (eyes, gun) senken; (reduce) herabsetzen, senken // vr: **to ~ o.s. (to)** (fig) sich herablassen zu.

low: ~-fat a fettarm, Mager-; **~ lands** npl (GEO) Flachland nt; **~ly** a bescheiden; **~-lying** a tiefgelegen.

loyal ['lɔɪəl] a treu; **~ty** n Treue f.

lozenge ['lɒzɪndʒ] n Pastille f.

L.P. n abbr of **long-playing record**.

L-plates ['elpleɪts] npl (Brit) L-Schild nt (für Fahrschüler).

Ltd abbr of **limited company**.

lubricant ['luːbrɪkənt] n Schmiermittel nt.

lubricate ['luːbrɪkeɪt] vt schmieren.

lucid ['luːsɪd] a klar; (sane) bei klarem Verstand; (moment) licht.

luck [lʌk] n Glück nt; **bad ~** Pech nt; **good ~!** viel Glück!; **~ily** ad glücklicherweise, zum Glück; **~y** a Glücks-; **to be ~y** Glück haben.

lucrative ['luːkrətɪv] a einträglich.

ludicrous ['luːdɪkrəs] a grotesk.

lug [lʌg] vt schleppen.

luggage ['lʌgɪdʒ] n Gepäck nt; ~ **rack** n Gepäcknetz nt.
lugubrious [lu:'gu:brɪəs] a traurig.
lukewarm ['lu:kwɔ:m] a lauwarm; (indifferent) lau.
lull [lʌl] n Flaute f // vt einlullen; (calm) beruhigen.
lullaby ['lʌləbaɪ] n Schlaflied nt.
lumbago [lʌm'beɪgəʊ] n Hexenschuß m.
lumber ['lʌmbə*] n Plunder m; (wood) Holz nt; ~**jack** n Holzfäller m.
luminous ['lu:mɪnəs] a Leucht-.
lump [lʌmp] n Klumpen m; (MED) Schwellung f; (in breast) Knoten m; (of sugar) Stück nt // vt (also: ~ **together**) zusammentun; (judge together) in einen Topf werfen; ~ **sum** n Pauschalsumme f; ~**y** a klumpig.
lunacy ['lu:nəsɪ] n Irrsinn m.
lunar ['lu:nə*] a Mond-.
lunatic ['lu:nətɪk] n Wahnsinnige(r) mf // a wahnsinnig, irr; ~ **asylum** n Irrenanstalt f.
lunch [lʌntʃ] n (also ~**eon** [-ən]) Mittagessen nt; ~**time** n Mittagszeit f; ~**eon meat** n Frühstücksfleisch nt; ~**eon voucher** n Essensmarke f.
lung [lʌŋ] n Lunge f.
lunge [lʌndʒ] vi (also: ~ **forward**) (los)stürzen; **to** ~ **at** sich stürzen auf (+acc).
lurch [lɜ:tʃ] vi taumeln; (NAUT) schlingern // n Ruck m; (NAUT) Schlingern nt; **to leave sb in the** ~ jdn im Stich lassen.
lure [ljʊə*] n Köder m; (fig) Lockung f // vt (ver)locken.
lurid ['ljʊərɪd] a (shocking) grausig, widerlich; (colour) grell.
lurk [lɜ:k] vi lauern.
luscious ['lʌʃəs] a köstlich.
lush [lʌʃ] a satt; (vegetation) üppig.
lust [lʌst] n (sensation) Wollust f; (greed) Gier f // vi gieren (after nach).
lustre, (US) **luster** ['lʌstə*] n Glanz m.
lusty ['lʌstɪ] a gesund und munter.
Luxembourg ['lʌksəmbɔ:g] n Luxemburg nt.
luxuriant [lʌg'zjʊərɪənt] a üppig.
luxurious [lʌg'zjʊərɪəs] a luxuriös, Luxus-.
luxury ['lʌkʃərɪ] n Luxus m // cpd Luxus-.
lying ['laɪɪŋ] n Lügen nt // a verlogen.
lynx [lɪŋks] n Luchs m.
lyric ['lɪrɪk] n Lyrik f; (pl: words for song) (Lied)text m // a lyrisch; ~**al** a lyrisch, gefühlvoll.

M

M. abbr of **metre; mile; million.**
M.A. abbr of **Master of Arts.**

mac [mæk] n (Brit col) Regenmantel m.
macaroni [mækə'rəʊnɪ] n Makkaroni pl.
mace [meɪs] n Amtsstab m; (spice) Muskat m.
machine [mə'ʃi:n] n Maschine f // vt (dress etc) mit der Maschine nähen; ~ **gun** n Maschinengewehr nt; ~ **language** n (COMPUT) Maschinensprache f; ~**ry** [mə'ʃi:nərɪ] n Maschinerie f.
macho ['mætʃəʊ] a macho.
mackerel ['mækrəl] n Makrele f.
mackintosh ['mækɪntɒʃ] n (Brit) Regenmantel m.
mad [mæd] a verrückt; (dog) tollwütig; (angry) wütend; ~ **about** (fond of) verrückt nach, versessen auf (+acc).
madam ['mædəm] n gnädige Frau f.
madden ['mædn] vt verrückt machen; (make angry) ärgern.
made [meɪd] pt, pp of **make.**
Madeira [mə'dɪərə] n (GEOG) Madeira nt; (wine) Madeira m.
made-to-measure ['meɪdtə'meʒə*] a (Brit) Maß-.
madly ['mædlɪ] ad wahnsinnig.
madman ['mædmən] n Verrückte(r) m, Irre(r) m.
madness ['mædnəs] n Wahnsinn m.
Madrid [mə'drɪd] n Madrid nt.
Mafia ['mæfɪə] n Mafia f.
magazine ['mægəzi:n] n Zeitschrift f; (in gun) Magazin nt.
maggot ['mægət] n Made f.
magic ['mædʒɪk] n Zauberei f, Magie f; (fig) Zauber m // a magisch, Zauber-; ~**al** a magisch; ~**ian** [mə'dʒɪʃən] n Zauberer m.
magistrate ['mædʒɪstreɪt] n (Friedens)richter m.
magnanimous [mæg'nænɪməs] a großmütig.
magnesium [mæg'ni:zɪəm] n Magnesium nt.
magnet ['mægnɪt] n Magnet m; ~**ic** [mæg'netɪk] a magnetisch; ~**ic tape** n Magnetband nt; ~**ism** n Magnetismus m; (fig) Ausstrahlungskraft f.
magnificence [mæg'nɪfɪsəns] n Großartigkeit f.
magnificent [mæg'nɪfɪsənt] a großartig.
magnify ['mægnɪfaɪ] vt vergrößern; ~**ing glass** n Lupe f.
magnitude ['mægnɪtju:d] n (size) Größe f; (importance) Ausmaß nt.
magpie ['mægpaɪ] n Elster f.
mahogany [mə'hɒgənɪ] n Mahagoni nt // cpd Mahagoni-.
maid [meɪd] n Dienstmädchen nt; **old** ~ n alte Jungfer f.
maiden ['meɪdn] n (liter) Maid f // a (flight, speech) Jungfern-; ~ **name** n Mädchenname m.
mail [meɪl] n Post f // vt aufgeben; ~ **box** n (US) Briefkasten m; ~**ing list** n Anschreibeliste f; ~ **order** n Bestellung

f durch die Post; **~ order firm** n Versandhaus nt.

maim [meɪm] vt verstümmeln.

main [meɪn] a hauptsächlich, Haupt // n (pipe) Hauptleitung f; **the ~s** (ELEC) das Stromnetz nt; **in the ~** im großen und ganzen; **~frame** n (COMPUT) Großrechner m; **~land** n Festland nt; **~ road** n Hauptstraße f; **~stay** n (fig) Hauptstütze f; **~stream** n Hauptrichtung f.

maintain [meɪn'teɪn] vt (machine, roads) instand halten; (support) unterhalten; (keep up) aufrechterhalten; (claim) behaupten; (innocence) beteuern.

maintenance ['meɪntənəns] n (TECH) Wartung f; (of family) Unterhalt m.

maize [meɪz] n Mais m.

majestic [mə'dʒestɪk] a majestätisch.

majesty ['mædʒɪstɪ] n Majestät f.

major ['meɪdʒə*] n Major m // a (MUS) Dur; (more important) Haupt-; (bigger) größer.

Majorca [mə'jɔːkə] n Mallorca nt.

majority [mə'dʒɒrɪtɪ] n Mehrheit f; (JUR) Volljährigkeit f.

make [meɪk] vt, pt, pp **made** machen; (appoint) ernennen (zu); (cause to do sth) veranlassen; (reach) erreichen; (in time) schaffen; (earn) verdienen // n Marke f; **to ~ sth happen** etw geschehen lassen; **to ~** it es schaffen; **what time do you ~** it? wie spät hast du es? **to ~ do with** auskommen mit; **~ for** vi gehen/ fahren nach; **~ out** vt (write out) ausstellen; (understand) verstehen; (write: cheque) ausstellen; **~ up** vt (make) machen; (face) schminken; (quarrel) beilegen; (story etc) erfinden // vi sich versöhnen; **~ up for** vt wiedergutmachen; (COMM) vergüten; **~-believe** n Phantasie f; **~r** n (COMM) Hersteller m; **~shift** a behelfsmäßig, Not-; **~-up** n Schminke f, Make-up nt; **~-up remover** n Make-up-Entferner m.

making ['meɪkɪŋ] n: **in the ~** im Entstehen; **to have the ~s of** das Zeug haben zu.

malaise [mæ'leɪz] n Unbehagen nt.

Malaya [mə'leɪə] n Malaya nt.

Malaysia [mə'leɪzɪə] n Malaysia nt.

male [meɪl] n Mann m; (animal) Männchen nt // a männlich.

malevolent [mə'levələnt] a übelwollend.

malfunction [mæl'fʌŋkʃən] n (MED) Funktionsstörung f; (of machine) Defekt m.

malice ['mælɪs] n Bosheit f.

malicious [mə'lɪʃəs] a böswillig, gehässig.

malign [mə'laɪn] vt verleumden // a böse.

malignant [mə'lɪgnənt] a bösartig.

mall [mɔːl] n (also: **shopping ~**) Ein-

kaufszentrum nt.

malleable ['mælɪəbl] a formbar.

mallet ['mælɪt] n Holzhammer m.

malnutrition ['mælnjuː'trɪʃən] n Unterernährung f.

malpractice ['mæl'præktɪs] n Amtsvergehen nt.

malt [mɔːlt] n Malz nt.

Malta ['mɔːltə] n Malta nt; **Maltese** [-'tiːz] a maltesisch // n, pl inv Malteser(in f) m.

maltreat [mæl'triːt] vt mißhandeln.

mammal ['mæməl] n Säugetier nt.

mammoth ['mæməθ] n Mammut nt // a Mammut-.

man [mæn], pl **men** n Mann m; (human race) der Mensch, die Menschen pl // vt bemannen.

manage ['mænɪdʒ] vi zurechtkommen // vt (control) führen, leiten; (cope with) fertigwerden mit; **~able** a (person, animal) fügsam; (object) handlich; **~ment** n (control) Führung f, Leitung f; (directors) Management nt; **~r** n Geschäftsführer m; **~ress** ['mænɪdʒə'res] n Geschäftsführerin f; **~rial** [mænə'dʒɪərɪəl] a (post) leitend; (problem etc) Management-.

managing ['mænɪdʒɪŋ] a: **~ director** n Betriebsleiter m.

mandarin ['mændərɪn] n (fruit) Mandarine f.

mandatory ['mændətərɪ] a obligatorisch.

mane [meɪn] n Mähne f.

maneuver [mə'nuːvə*] (US) = **manoeuvre**.

manfully ['mænfʊlɪ] ad mannhaft.

mangle ['mæŋgl] vt verstümmeln // n Mangel f.

mango ['mæŋgəʊ], pl **~es** n Mango(pflaume) f.

mangy ['meɪndʒɪ] a (dog) räudig.

manhandle ['mænhændl] vt grob behandeln.

manhole ['mænhəʊl] n (Straßen)schacht m.

manhood ['mænhʊd] n Mannesalter nt; (manliness) Männlichkeit f.

man-hour ['mæn'aʊə*] n Arbeitsstunde f.

manhunt ['mænhʌnt] n Fahndung f.

mania ['meɪnɪə] n Manie f; **~c** ['meɪnɪæk] n Wahnsinnige(r) mf.

manic ['mænɪk] a (behaviour, activity) hektisch; **~-depressive** n Manisch-Depressive(r) mf.

manicure ['mænɪkjʊə*] n Maniküre f; **~ set** n Necessaire nt.

manifest ['mænɪfest] vt offenbaren // a offenkundig; **~ation** n (sign) Anzeichen nt.

manifesto [mænɪ'festəʊ] n Manifest nt.

manipulate [mə'nɪpjʊleɪt] vt handhaben; (fig) manipulieren.

mankind [mæn'kaɪnd] n Menschheit f.
manly ['mænlɪ] a männlich; mannhaft.
man-made ['mæn'meɪd] a (fibre) künstlich.
manner ['mænə*] n Art f, Weise f; **in a ~ of speaking** sozusagen; **~s** pl Manieren pl; **~ism** n (of person) Angewohnheit f; (of style) Maniertheit f.
manoeuvre, (US) **maneuver** [mə'nuːvə*] vti manövrieren // n (MIL) Feldzug m; (general) Manöver nt, Schachzug m.
manor ['mænə*] n Landgut nt; **~ house** n Herrenhaus nt.
manpower ['mænpaʊə*] n Arbeitskräfte pl.
mansion ['mænʃən] n Villa f.
manslaughter ['mænslɔːtə*] n Totschlag m.
mantelpiece ['mæntlpiːs] n Kaminsims m.
mantle ['mæntl] n (cloak) lange(r) Umhang m.
manual ['mænjʊəl] a manuell, Hand- // n Handbuch nt.
manufacture [mænjʊ'fæktʃə*] vt herstellen // n Herstellung f; **~r** n Hersteller m.
manure [mə'njʊə*] n Dünger m.
manuscript ['mænjʊskrɪpt] n Manuskript nt.
Manx [mæŋks] a der Insel Man.
many ['menɪ] a, pron viele; **a great ~** sehr viele; **~ a time** oft.
map [mæp] n (Land)karte f; (of town) Stadtplan m // vt eine Karte machen von; **~ out** vt (fig) ausarbeiten.
maple ['meɪpl] n Ahorn m.
mar [mɑː*] vt verderben.
marathon ['mærəθən] n (SPORT) Marathonlauf m; (fig) Marathon m.
marauder [mə'rɔːdə*] n Plünderer m.
marble ['mɑːbl] n Marmor m; (for game) Murmel f.
March [mɑːtʃ] n März m.
march [mɑːtʃ] vi marschieren // n Marsch m; **~-past** n Vorbeimarsch m.
mare [mɛə*] n Stute f.
margarine [mɑːdʒə'riːn] n Margarine f.
margin ['mɑːdʒɪn] n Rand m; (extra amount) Spielraum m; (COMM) Spanne f; **~al** a (note) Rand-; (difference) geringfügig; **~ al (seat)** n (POL) Wahlkreis, der nur mit knapper Mehrheit gehalten wird.
marigold ['mærɪɡəʊld] n Ringelblume f.
marina [mə'riːnə] n Yachthafen m.
marinate ['mærɪneɪt] vt marinieren.
marine [mə'riːn] a Meeres-, See- // n (MIL) Marineinfanterist m.
marital ['mærɪtl] a ehelich, Ehe-; **~ status** n Familienstand m.
maritime ['mærɪtaɪm] a See-.
mark [mɑːk] n (coin) Mark f; (spot) Fleck m; (scar) Kratzer m; (sign) Zeichen nt; (target) Ziel nt; (SCH) Note f // vt (make mark) Flecken/Kratzer machen auf (+acc); (indicate) markieren; (exam) korrigieren; **to ~ time** (lit, fig) auf der Stelle treten; **~ out** vt bestimmen; (area) abstecken; **~ed** a deutlich; **~er** n (in book) (Lese)zeichen nt; (on road) Schild nt.
market ['mɑːkɪt] n Markt m; (stock ~) Börse f // vt (COMM: new product) auf den Markt bringen; (sell) vertreiben; **~ garden** n (Brit) Handelsgärtnerei f; **~ing** n Marketing nt; **~ place** n Marktplatz m **~ research** n Marktforschung f; **~ value** n Marktwert m.
marksman ['mɑːksmən] n Scharfschütze m.
marmalade ['mɑːməleɪd] n Orangenmarmelade f.
maroon [mə'ruːn] vt aussetzen // a (colour) kastanienbraun.
marquee [mɑː'kiː] n große(s) Zelt nt.
marriage ['mærɪdʒ] n Ehe f; (wedding) Heirat f; **~ bureau** n Heiratsinstitut nt; **~ certificate** n Heiratsurkunde f.
married ['mærɪd] a (person) verheiratet; (couple, life) Ehe-.
marrow ['mærəʊ] n (Knochen)mark nt; (vegetable) Kürbis m.
marry ['mærɪ] vt (join) trauen; (take as husband, wife) heiraten // vi (also: get married) heiraten.
Mars [mɑːz] n (planet) Mars m.
marsh [mɑːʃ] n Sumpf m.
marshal ['mɑːʃəl] n (US) Bezirkspolizeichef m // vt (an)ordnen, arrangieren.
marshy ['mɑːʃɪ] a sumpfig.
martial ['mɑːʃəl] a kriegerisch; **~ law** n Kriegsrecht nt.
martyr ['mɑːtə*] n (lit, fig) Märtyrer(in f) m // vt zum Märtyrer machen; **~dom** n Martyrium nt.
marvel ['mɑːvəl] n Wunder nt // vi sich wundern (at über +acc); **~lous**, (US) **~ous** a wunderbar.
Marxist ['mɑːksɪst] n Marxist(in f) m.
marzipan [mɑːzɪ'pæn] n Marzipan nt.
mascara [mæs'kɑːrə] n Wimperntusche f.
mascot ['mæskət] n Maskottchen nt.
masculine ['mæskjʊlɪn] a männlich.
mash [mæʃ] n Brei m; **~ed potatoes** npl Kartoffelbrei m or -püree nt.
mask [mɑːsk] n (lit, fig) Maske f // vt maskieren, verdecken.
mason ['meɪsn] n (stone~) Steinmetz m; (free~) Freimaurer m; **~ic** [mə'sɒnɪk] a Freimaurer-; **~ry** n Mauerwerk nt.
masquerade [mæskə'reɪd] n Maskerade f // vi: **to ~ as** sich ausgeben als.
mass [mæs] n Masse f; (greater part) Mehrheit f; (REL) Messe f // vi sich sammeln; **the ~es** npl die Masse(n) f(pl).

massacre ['mæsəkə*] n Blutbad nt // vt niedermetzeln, massakrieren.

massage ['mæsɑ:ʒ] n Massage f // vt massieren.

massive ['mæsɪv] a gewaltig, massiv.

mass media ['mæs'mi:dɪə] npl Massenmedien pl.

mass production n Massenproduktion f.

mast [mɑ:st] n Mast m.

master ['mɑ:stə*] n Herr m; (NAUT) Kapitän m; (teacher) Lehrer m; (artist) Meister m // vt meistern; (language etc) beherrschen; **M~ of Arts/Science (M.A./M.Sc.)** n Magister m der philosophischen/naturwissenschaftlichen Fakultät; ~ **key** n Hauptschlüssel m; ~**ly** a meisterhaft; ~**mind** n Kapazität f // vt geschickt lenken; ~**piece** n Meisterwerk nt; ~ **plan** n kluge(r) Plan m; ~**y** n Können nt.

masturbate ['mæstəbeɪt] vi masturbieren, onanieren.

mat [mæt] n Matte f; (for table) Untersetzer m // a = **mat(t)**.

match [mætʃ] n Streichholz nt; (sth corresponding) Pendant nt; (SPORT) Wettkampf m; (ball games) Spiel nt // vt (be alike, suit) passen zu; (equal) gleichkommen (+dat) // vi zusammenpassen; it's a good ~ es paßt gut (for sa); ~**box** n Streichholzschachtel f; ~**ing** a passend.

mate [meɪt] n (companion) Kamerad m; (spouse) Lebensgefährte m, (of animal) Weibchen nt/Männchen nt; (NAUT) Schiffsoffizier m // vi (animals) sich paaren // vt (animals) paaren.

material [mə'tɪərɪəl] n Material nt; (for book, cloth) Stoff m // a (important) wesentlich; (damage) Sach-; (comforts etc) materiell; ~**s** pl Materialien pl; ~**istic** a materialistisch; ~**ize** vi sich verwirklichen, zustande kommen.

maternal [mə'tɜ:nl] a mütterlich, Mutter-.

maternity [mə'tɜ:nɪtɪ] a (dress) Umstands-; (benefit) Wochen-; ~ **hospital** n Entbindungsheim nt.

math [mæθ] n (US) = **maths**.

mathematics [mæθə'mætɪks] n Mathematik f.

maths [mæθs], (US) **math** [mæθ] n Mathe f.

matinée ['mætɪneɪ] n Matinee f.

mating ['meɪtɪŋ] n Paarung f; ~ **call** n Lockruf m.

matrices ['meɪtrɪsi:z] pl of **matrix**.

matriculation [mətrɪkju'leɪʃən] n Immatrikulation f.

matrimonial [mætrɪ'məʊnɪəl] a ehelich, Ehe-.

matrimony ['mætrɪmənɪ] n Ehestand m.

matrix ['meɪtrɪks], pl **matrices** n Matrize f; (GEOL etc) Matrix f.

matron ['meɪtrən] n (MED) Oberin f; (SCH) Hausmutter f; ~**ly** a matronenhaft.

mat(t) [mæt] a (paint) matt.

matted ['mætɪd] a verfilzt.

matter ['mætə*] n (substance) Materie f; (affair) Angelegenheit f // vi darauf ankommen; it doesn't ~ es macht nichts; no ~ how/what egal wie/was; what is the ~? was ist los?; as a ~ of course selbstverständlich; as a ~ of fact eigentlich; ~**-of-fact** a sachlich, nüchtern.

mattress ['mætrəs] n Matratze f.

mature [mə'tjuə*] a reif // vi reif werden.

maturity [mə'tjuərɪtɪ] n Reife f.

maudlin ['mɔ:dlɪn] a gefühlsduselig.

maul [mɔ:l] vt übel zurichten.

mauve [məʊv] a mauve.

maximum ['mæksɪməm] a Höchst-, Maximal- // n, pl **maxima** ['mæksɪmə] Maximum nt.

May [meɪ] n Mai m.

may [meɪ] vi (be possible) können; (have permission) dürfen; he ~ come er kommt vielleicht.

maybe ['meɪbi:] ad vielleicht.

Mayday ['meɪdeɪ] n (message) SOS nt.

mayhem ['meɪhem] n Chaos nt; (US) Körperverletzung f.

mayonnaise [meɪə'neɪz] n Mayonnaise f.

mayor [mɛə*] n Bürgermeister m; ~**ess** (wife) (die) Frau f Bürgermeister; (lady ~) Bürgermeisterin f.

maypole ['meɪpəʊl] n Maibaum m.

maze [meɪz] n (lit) Irrgarten m; (fig) Wirrwarr nt.

M.D. abbr of **Doctor of Medicine.**

me [mi:] pron 1 (direct) mich; it's ~ ich bin's
2 (indirect) mir; give them to ~ gib sie mir
3 (after prep: +acc) mich; (: +dat) mir; with/without ~ mit mir/ohne mich.

meadow ['medəʊ] n Wiese f.

meagre, (US) **meager** ['mi:gə*] a dürftig, spärlich.

meal [mi:l] n Essen nt, Mahlzeit f; (grain) Schrotmehl nt; to have a ~ essen (gehen); ~**time** n Essenszeit f.

mean [mi:n] a (stingy) geizig; (spiteful) gemein; (average) durchschnittlich, Durchschnitts- // vt, pt, pp **meant** (signify) bedeuten; (intend) vorhaben, beabsichtigen // n (average) Durchschnitt m; ~**s** pl Mittel pl; (wealth) Vermögen nt; by ~s of durch; by all ~s selbstverständlich; by no ~s keineswegs; do you ~ me? meinst du mich?; do you ~ it? meinst du das ernst?; what do you ~? was willst du damit sagen?; to be meant for sb/sth für jdn/etw bestimmt sein.

meander [mɪˈændə*] *vi* sich schlängeln.

meaning [ˈmiːnɪŋ] *n* Bedeutung *f*; *(of life)* Sinn *m*; **~ful** *a* bedeutungsvoll; *(life)* sinnvoll; **~less** *a* sinnlos.

meanness [ˈmiːnnəs] *n (stinginess)* Geiz *m*; *(spitefulness)* Gemeinheit *f*.

meant [ment] *pt, pp of* **mean**.

meantime [ˈmiːnˈtaɪm], **meanwhile** [ˈmiːnˈwaɪl] *ad* inzwischen.

measles [ˈmiːzlz] *n* Masern *pl*.

measly [ˈmiːzlɪ] *a (col)* poplig.

measure [ˈmeʒə*] *vti* messen // *n* Maß *nt*; *(step)* Maßnahme *f*; **~d** *a (slow)* gemessen; **~ments** *npl* Maße *pl*.

meat [miːt] *n* Fleisch *nt*; **cold ~** *n* Aufschnitt *m*; **~ ball** *n* Fleischkloß *m*; **~ pie** *n* Fleischpastete *f*; **~y** *a (lit)* fleischig; *(fig)* gehaltvoll.

Mecca [ˈmekə] *n* Mekka *nt (also fig)*.

mechanic [mɪˈkænɪk] *n* Mechaniker *m*; **~s** *n* Mechanik *f* // *npl* Technik *f*; **~al** *a* mechanisch.

mechanism [ˈmekənɪzəm] *n* Mechanismus *m*.

mechanize [ˈmekənaɪz] *vt* mechanisieren.

medal [ˈmedl] *n* Medaille *f*; *(decoration)* Orden *m*; **~list**, *(US)* **~ist** *n* Medaillengewinner(in *f*) *m*.

meddle [ˈmedl] *vi* sich einmischen *(in* in +*acc)*; **to ~ with sth** sich an etw *(dat)* zu schaffen machen.

media [ˈmiːdɪə] *npl* Medien *pl*.

mediaeval [medɪˈiːvəl] *a* = **medieval**.

median [ˈmiːdɪən] *n (US: also: ~ strip)* Mittelstreifen *m*.

mediate [ˈmiːdɪeɪt] *vi* vermitteln.

mediation [miːdɪˈeɪʃən] *n* Vermittlung *f*.

mediator [ˈmiːdɪeɪtə*] *n* Vermittler *m*.

Medicaid [ˈmedɪkeɪd] *n (US) medizinisches Versorgungsprogramm für Sozialschwache.*

medical [ˈmedɪkəl] *a* medizinisch; Medizin-; ärztlich // *n* (ärztliche) Untersuchung *f*.

Medicare [ˈmedɪkeə*] *n (US) staatliche Krankenversicherung besonders für Ältere.*

medicated [ˈmedɪkeɪtɪd] *a* medizinisch.

medication [medɪˈkeɪʃən] *n (drugs etc)* Medikamente *pl*.

medicinal [meˈdɪsɪnl] *a* medizinisch, Heil-.

medicine [ˈmedsɪn] *n* Medizin *f*; *(drugs)* Arznei *f*.

medieval [medɪˈiːvəl] *a* mittelalterlich.

mediocre [miːdɪˈəʊkə*] *a* mittelmäßig.

mediocrity [miːdɪˈɒkrɪtɪ] *n* Mittelmäßigkeit *f*.

meditate [ˈmedɪteɪt] *vi* nachdenken *(on* über +*acc)*; meditieren.

meditation [medɪˈteɪʃən] *n* Nachsinnen *nt*; Meditation *f*.

Mediterranean [medɪtəˈreɪnɪən] *a*

Mittelmeer-; *(person)* südländisch; **the ~** (Sea) das Mittelmeer.

medium [ˈmiːdɪəm] *a* mittlere(r, s), Mittel-, mittel- // *n* Mitte *f*; *(means)* Mittel *nt*; *(person)* Medium *nt*; **happy ~** goldener Mittelweg; **~ wave** *n* Mittelwelle *f*.

medley [ˈmedlɪ] *n* Gemisch *nt*.

meek [miːk] *a* sanft(mütig); *(pej)* duckmäuserisch.

meet [miːt], *pt, pp* **met** *vt (encounter)* treffen, begegnen (+*dat*); *(by arrangement)* sich treffen mit; *(difficulties)* stoßen auf (+*acc*); *(become acquainted with)* kennenlernen; *(fetch)* abholen; *(join)* zusammentreffen mit; *(satisfy)* entsprechen (+*dat*) // *vi* sich treffen; *(become acquainted)* sich kennenlernen; **~ with** *vt (problems)* stoßen auf (+*acc*); *(US: people)* zusammentreffen mit; **~ing** *n* Treffen *nt*; *(business ~)* Besprechung *f*; *(of committee)* Sitzung *f*; *(assembly)* Versammlung *f*.

megabyte [ˈmegəbaɪt] *n (COMPUT)* Megabyte *nt*.

melancholy [ˈmelənkəlɪ] *a (person)* melancholisch; *(sight, event)* traurig.

mellow [ˈmeləʊ] *a* mild, weich; *(fruit)* reif; *(fig)* gesetzt // *vi* reif werden.

melodious [mɪˈləʊdɪəs] *a* wohlklingend.

melody [ˈmelədɪ] *n* Melodie *f*.

melon [ˈmelən] *n* Melone *f*.

melt [melt] *vi* schmelzen; *(anger)* verfliegen // *vt* schmelzen; **~ away** *vi* dahinschmelzen; **~ down** *vt* einschmelzen; **~down** *n (in nuclear reactor)* Kernschmelze *f*; **~ing point** *n* Schmelzpunkt *m*; **~ing pot** *n (fig)* Schmelztiegel *m*.

member [ˈmembə*] *n* Mitglied *nt*; *(of tribe, species)* Angehörige(r) *m*; *(ANAT)* Glied *nt*; **M~ of Parliament (MP)** *n (Brit)* Parlamentsmitglied *nt*; **M~ of the European Parliament (MEP)** *n (Brit)* Mitglied *nt* des Europäischen Parlaments; **~ship** *n* Mitgliedschaft *f*; **to seek ~ship of** einen Antrag auf Mitgliedschaft stellen; **~ship card** *n* Mitgliedskarte *f*.

memento [məˈmentəʊ] *n* Andenken *nt*.

memo [ˈmeməʊ] *n* Mitteilung *f*.

memoirs [ˈmemwɑːz] *npl* Memoiren *pl*.

memorable [ˈmemərəbl] *a* denkwürdig.

memorandum [meməˈrændəm], *pl* **-da** [-də] *n* Mitteilung *f*.

memorial [mɪˈmɔːrɪəl] *n* Denkmal *nt* // *a* Gedenk-.

memorize [ˈmeməraɪz] *vt* sich einprägen.

memory [ˈmemərɪ] *n* Gedächtnis *nt*; *(of computer)* Speicher *m*; *(sth recalled)* Erinnerung *f*.

men [men] *pl of* **man**.

menace [ˈmenɪs] *n* Drohung *f*; Gefahr *f*

// vt bedrohen.
menacing ['menisiŋ] a drohend.
menagerie [mɪ'nædʒərɪ] n Tierschau f.
mend [mend] vt reparieren, flicken // vi (ver)heilen // n ausgebesserte Stelle f; on the ~ auf dem Wege der Besserung; ~ing n (articles) Flickarbeit f.
menial ['mi:nɪəl] a niedrig.
meningitis [menɪn'dʒaɪtɪs] n Hirnhautentzündung f, Meningitis f.
menopause ['menəupɔ:z] n Wechseljahre pl, Menopause f.
menstruation [menstru'eɪʃən] n Menstruation f.
mental ['mentl] a geistig, Geistes-; (arithmetic) Kopf-; (hospital) Nerven-; (cruelty) seelisch; (col: abnormal) verrückt; ~ity [men'tælɪtɪ] n Mentalität f.
menthol ['menθəl] n Menthol nt.
mention ['menʃən] n Erwähnung f // vt erwähnen; don't ~ it! bitte (sehr), gern geschehen.
mentor ['mentɔ:*] n Mentor m.
menu ['menju:] n Speisekarte f.
MEP n abbr of **Member of the European Parliament.**
mercenary ['mɜ:sɪnərɪ] a (person) geldgierig; (MIL) Söldner- // n Söldner m.
merchandise ['mɜ:tʃəndaɪz] n (Handels)ware f.
merchant ['mɜ:tʃənt] n Kaufmann m; ~ navy, (US) ~ marine n Handelsmarine f.
merciful ['mɜ:sɪful] a gnädig.
merciless ['mɜ:sɪləs] a erbarmungslos.
mercury ['mɜ:kjʊrɪ] n Quecksilber nt.
mercy ['mɜ:sɪ] n Erbarmen nt; Gnade f; at the ~ of ausgeliefert (+dat).
mere a, ~ly ad [mɪə*, 'mɪəlɪ] bloß.
merge [mɜ:dʒ] vt verbinden; (COMM) fusionieren // vi verschmelzen; (roads) zusammenlaufen; (COMM) fusionieren; ~r n (COMM) Fusion f.
meringue [mə'ræŋ] n Baiser nt.
merit ['merɪt] n Verdienst nt; (advantage) Vorzug m // vt verdienen.
mermaid ['mɜ:meɪd] n Wassernixe f.
merry ['merɪ] a fröhlich; ~-go-round n Karussell nt.
mesh [meʃ] n Masche f // vi (gears) ineinandergreifen.
mesmerize ['mezməraɪz] vt hypnotisieren; (fig) faszinieren.
mess [mes] n Unordnung f; (dirt) Schmutz m; (trouble) Schwierigkeiten pl; (MIL) Messe f; ~ about or around vi (tinker with) herummurksen (with an +dat); (play the fool) herumalbern; (do nothing in particular) herumgammeln; ~ up vt verpfuschen; (make untidy) in Unordnung bringen.
message ['mesɪdʒ] n Mitteilung f; to get the ~ kapieren.
messenger ['mesɪndʒə*] n Bote m.

Messrs ['mesəz] abbr (on letters) die Herren.
messy ['mesɪ] a schmutzig; (untidy) unordentlich.
met [met] pt, pp of **meet.**
metabolism [me'tæbəlɪzəm] n Stoffwechsel m.
metal ['metl] n Metall nt.
metaphor ['metəfɔ:*] n Metapher f.
mete [mi:t]: **to ~ out** vt austeilen.
meteorology [mi:tɪə'rɒlədʒɪ] n Meteorologie f.
meter ['mi:tə*] n Zähler m; (US) = **metre.**
method ['meθəd] n Methode f; ~ical [mɪ'θɒdɪkəl] a methodisch; **M~ist** ['meθədɪst] a methodistisch // n Methodist(in f) m; ~ology [meθə'dɒlədʒɪ] n Methodik f.
meths [meθs], **methylated spirit** ['meθɪleɪtɪd'spɪrɪt] n (Brit) (Brenn)-spiritus m.
meticulous [mɪ'tɪkjʊləs] a (über)genau.
metre, (US) **meter** ['mi:tə*] n Meter m or nt.
metric ['metrɪk] a (also: ~al) metrisch.
metropolitan [metrə'pɒlɪtən] a der Großstadt; **the M~ Police** n (Brit) die Londoner Polizei.
mettle ['metl] n Mut m.
mew [mju:] vi (cat) miauen.
mews [mju:z] n: ~ **cottage** n (Brit) ehemaliges Kutscherhäuschen.
Mexican ['meksɪkən] a mexikanisch // n Mexikaner(in f) m.
Mexico ['meksɪkəʊ] n Mexiko nt; ~ **City** n Mexiko City f.
miaow [mi:'aʊ] vi miauen.
mice [maɪs] pl of **mouse.**
microchip ['maɪkrəʊtʃɪp] n Mikrochip m.
micro(computer) ['maɪkrəʊ(kəm'pju:tə*)] n Mikrocomputer m.
microcosm ['maɪkrəʊkɒzəm] n Mikrokosmos m.
microfilm ['maɪkrəʊfɪlm] n Mikrofilm f // vt auf Mikrofilm aufnehmen.
microphone ['maɪkrəfəʊn] n Mikrophon nt.
microprocessor ['maɪkrəʊ'prəʊsesə*] n Mikroprozessor m.
microscope ['maɪkrəskəʊp] n Mikroskop nt.
microwave ['maɪkrəʊweɪv] n (also: ~ oven) Mikrowelle(nherd nt) f.
mid [mɪd] a: **in ~ afternoon** am Nachmittag; **in ~ air** in der Luft; **in ~ May** Mitte Mai.
midday ['mɪd'deɪ] n Mittag m.
middle ['mɪdl] n Mitte f; (waist) Taille f // a mittlere(r, s), Mittel-; **in the ~ of** mitten in (+dat); ~-**aged** a mittleren Alters; **the M~ Ages** npl das Mittelalter; ~-**class** a Mittelstands-; **the**

M~ East n der Nahe Osten; **~man** n (COMM) Zwischenhändler m; **~ name** n zweiter Vorname m; **~ weight** n (BOXING) Mittelgewicht nt.
middling ['mɪdlɪŋ] a mittelmäßig.
midge [mɪdʒ] n Mücke f.
midget ['mɪdʒɪt] n Liliputaner(in f) m.
Midlands ['mɪdləndz] npl die Midlands pl.
midnight ['mɪdnaɪt] n Mitternacht f.
midriff ['mɪdrɪf] n Taille f.
midst [mɪdst] n: in the ~ of (persons) mitten unter (+dat); (things) mitten in (+dat).
midsummer ['mɪd'sʌmə*] n Hochsommer m.
midway ['mɪd'weɪ] ad auf halbem Wege // a Mittel-.
midweek ['mɪd'wi:k] ad in der Mitte der Woche.
midwife ['mɪdwaɪf], pl **-wives** [-waɪvz] n Hebamme f; **~ry** ['mɪdwɪfərɪ] n Geburtshilfe f.
midwinter ['mɪd'wɪntə*] n tiefste(r) Winter m.
might [maɪt] v pt of **may** // n Macht f, Kraft f; I ~ come ich komme vielleicht; I ~ as well go ich könnte genauso gut gehen; you ~ like to try du könntest vielleicht versuchen; **~y** a, ad mächtig.
migraine ['mi:greɪn] n Migräne f.
migrant ['maɪgrənt] a Wander-; (bird) Zug-.
migrate [maɪ'greɪt] vi (ab)wandern; (birds) (fort)ziehen.
migration [maɪ'greɪʃən] n Wanderung f, Zug m.
mike [maɪk] n = **microphone**.
Milan [mɪ'læn] n Mailand nt.
mild [maɪld] a mild; (medicine, interest) leicht; (person) sanft.
mildew ['mɪldju:] n (on plants) Mehltau m; (on food) Schimmel m.
mildly ['maɪldlɪ] ad leicht; **to put it ~** gelinde gesagt.
mile [maɪl] n Meile f; **~age** n Meilenzahl f; **~stone** n (lit, fig) Meilenstein m.
military ['mɪlɪtərɪ] a militärisch, Militär-, Wehr-.
militate ['mɪlɪteɪt] vi entgegenwirken (against dat).
militia [mɪ'lɪʃə] n Miliz f.
milk [mɪlk] n Milch f // vt (lit, fig) melken; **~ chocolate** n Milchschokolade f; **~man** n Milchmann m; **~ shake** n Milchmixgetränk nt; **~y** a milchig; **M~y Way** n Milchstraße f.
mill [mɪl] n Mühle f; (factory) Fabrik f // vt mahlen // vi (move around) umherlaufen.
millennium [mɪ'lenɪəm], pl **~s** or **-ia** [-nɪə] n Jahrtausend nt.
miller ['mɪlə*] n Müller m.
millet ['mɪlɪt] n Hirse f.

milligram(me) ['mɪlɪgræm] n Milligramm nt.
millimetre, (US) **millimeter** ['mɪlɪmi:tə*] n Millimeter m.
milliner ['mɪlɪnə*] n Hutmacher(in f) m; **~y** n (hats) Hüte pl.
million ['mɪljən] n Million f; **a ~ times** tausendmal; **~aire** [mɪljə'nɛə*] n Millionär(in f) m.
millstone ['mɪlstəʊn] n Mühlstein m.
milometer [maɪ'lɒmɪtə*] n Kilometerzähler m.
mime [maɪm] n Pantomime f // vti mimen.
mimic ['mɪmɪk] n Mimiker m // vti nachahmen; **~ry** ['mɪmɪkrɪ] n Nachahmung f; (BIOL) Mimikry f.
min. abbr (= minute(s); minimum) min.
minaret [mɪnə'ret] n Minarett nt.
mince [mɪns] vt (zer)hacken // vi (walk) trippeln // n (meat) Hackfleisch nt; **~meat** n süße Pastetenfüllung f; **~ pie** n gefüllte (süße) Pastete f; **mincer** n Fleischwolf m.
mind [maɪnd] n Verstand m, Geist m; (opinion) Meinung f // vt aufpassen auf (+acc); (object to) etwas haben gegen; **on my ~** auf dem Herzen; **to my ~** meiner Meinung nach; **to be out of one's ~** wahnsinnig sein; **to bear** or **keep in ~** bedenken; **to change one's ~** es sich (dat) anders überlegen; **to make up one's ~** sich entschließen; **I don't ~** das macht mir nichts aus; **~ you,** allerdings ...; **never ~!** macht nichts!; **'~ the step'** 'Vorsicht Stufe'; **~ your own business** kümmern Sie sich um Ihre eigenen Angelegenheiten; **minder** n Aufpasser(in f) m; **~ful** a achtsam (of auf +acc); **~less** a sinnlos.
mine [maɪn] n (coal~) Bergwerk nt; (MIL) Mine f // vt abbauen; (MIL) verminen.
mine [maɪn] pron meine(r, s); **that book is ~** das Buch gehört mir; **a friend of ~** ein Freund von mir.
minefield ['maɪnfi:ld] n Minenfeld nt.
miner ['maɪnə*] n Bergarbeiter m.
mineral ['mɪnərəl] a mineralisch, Mineral- // n Mineral nt; **~s** pl (Brit: soft drinks) alkoholfreie Getränke pl; **~ water** n Mineralwasser nt.
minesweeper ['maɪnswi:pə*] n Minensuchboot nt.
mingle ['mɪŋgl] vi sich mischen (with unter +acc).
miniature ['mɪnɪtʃə*] a Miniatur- // n Miniatur f.
minibus ['mɪnɪbʌs] n Kleinbus m.
minim ['mɪnɪm] n halbe Note f.
minimal ['mɪnɪml] a minimal.
minimize ['mɪnɪmaɪz] vt auf das Mindestmaß beschränken.
minimum ['mɪnɪməm] n, pl **minima**

['mɪnɪmə] Minimum nt // a Mindest-.
mining ['maɪnɪŋ] n Bergbau m // a Bergbau-, Berg-.
miniskirt ['mɪnɪskɜːt] n Minirock m.
minister ['mɪnɪstə*] n (Brit POL) Minister m; (ECCL) Pfarrer m // vi: **to ~ to sb** sich um jdn kümmern; **~ial** [mɪnɪs'tɪərɪəl] a ministeriell, Minister-.
ministry ['mɪnɪstrɪ] n (Brit POL) Ministerium nt; (ECCL: office) geistliche(s) Amt nt.
mink [mɪŋk] n Nerz m; **~ coat** n Nerzmantel m.
minnow ['mɪnəʊ] n Elritze f.
minor ['maɪnə*] a kleiner; (operation) leicht; (problem, poet) unbedeutend; (MUS) Moll // n (Brit: under 18) Minderjährige(r) mf.
minority [maɪ'nɒrɪtɪ] n Minderheit f.
mint [mɪnt] n Minze f; (sweet) Pfefferminzbonbon nt // vt (coins) prägen; **the (Royal) M~**, (US) **the (US) M~** die Münzanstalt; **in ~ condition** in tadellosem Zustand.
minus ['maɪnəs] n Minuszeichen nt; (amount) Minusbetrag m // prep minus, weniger.
minuscule ['mɪnəskjuːl] a winzig.
minute [maɪ'njuːt] a winzig; (detailed) minuziös // n ['mɪnɪt] Minute f; (moment) Augenblick m; **~s** pl Protokoll nt.
miracle ['mɪrəkl] n Wunder nt.
miraculous [mɪ'rækjʊləs] a wunderbar.
mirage ['mɪrɑːʒ] n Fata Morgana f.
mire ['maɪə*] n Morast m.
mirror ['mɪrə*] n Spiegel m // vt (wider)spiegeln.
mirth [mɜːθ] n Heiterkeit f.
misadventure [mɪsəd'ventʃə*] n Mißgeschick nt, Unfall m.
misanthropist [mɪ'zænθrəpɪst] n Menschenfeind m.
misapprehension ['mɪsæprɪ'henʃən] n Mißverständnis nt.
misbehave ['mɪsbɪ'heɪv] vi sich schlecht benehmen.
miscalculate ['mɪs'kælkjʊleɪt] vt falsch berechnen.
miscarriage ['mɪskærɪdʒ] n (MED) Fehlgeburt f; **~ of justice** n Fehlurteil nt.
miscellaneous [mɪsɪ'leɪnɪəs] a verschieden.
mischance [mɪs'tʃɑːns] n Mißgeschick nt.
mischief ['mɪstʃɪf] n Unfug m.
mischievous ['mɪstʃɪvəs] a (person) durchtrieben; (glance) verschmitzt; (rumour) bösartig.
misconception ['mɪskən'sepʃən] n fälschliche Annahme f.
misconduct [mɪs'kɒndʌkt] n Vergehen nt; **professional ~** Berufsvergehen nt.
misconstrue ['mɪskən'struː] vt mißverstehen.

misdeed [mɪs'diːd] n Untat f.
misdemeanour, (US) **misdemeanor** [mɪsdɪ'miːnə*] n Vergehen nt.
miser ['maɪzə*] n Geizhals m.
miserable ['mɪzərəbl] a (unhappy) unglücklich; (headache, weather) fürchterlich; (poor) elend; (contemptible) erbärmlich.
miserly ['maɪzəlɪ] a geizig.
misery ['mɪzərɪ] n Elend nt, Qual f.
misfire ['mɪs'faɪə*] vi (gun) versagen; (engine) fehlzünden; (plan) fehlgehen.
misfit ['mɪsfɪt] n Außenseiter m.
misfortune [mɪs'fɔːtʃən] n Unglück nt.
misgiving(s) [mɪs'gɪvɪŋ(z)] n(pl) Bedenken pl.
misguided ['mɪs'gaɪdɪd] a fehlgeleitet; (opinions) irrig.
mishandle ['mɪs'hændl] vt falsch handhaben.
mishap ['mɪshæp] n Mißgeschick nt.
misinform ['mɪsɪn'fɔːm] vt falsch unterrichten.
misinterpret ['mɪsɪn'tɜːprɪt] vt falsch auffassen.
misjudge ['mɪs'dʒʌdʒ] vt falsch beurteilen.
mislay [mɪs'leɪ] (irreg: like lay) vt verlegen.
mislead [mɪs'liːd] (irreg: like lead) vt (deceive) irreführen; **~ing** a irreführend.
mismanage ['mɪs'mænɪdʒ] vt schlecht verwalten.
misnomer ['mɪs'nəʊmə*] n falsche Bezeichnung f.
misogynist [mɪ'sɒdʒɪnɪst] n Weiberfeind m.
misplace ['mɪs'pleɪs] vt verlegen.
misprint ['mɪsprɪnt] n Druckfehler m.
Miss [mɪs] n Fräulein nt.
miss [mɪs] vt (fail to hit, catch) verfehlen; (not notice) verpassen; (be too late) versäumen, verpassen; (omit) auslassen; (regret the absence of) vermissen // vi fehlen // n (shot) Fehlschuß m; (failure) Fehlschlag m; **that was a near ~** das war sehr knapp; **I ~ you** du fehlst mir; **~ out** vt auslassen.
missal ['mɪsəl] n Meßbuch f.
misshapen ['mɪs'ʃeɪpən] a mißgestaltet.
missile ['mɪsaɪl] n Rakete f.
missing ['mɪsɪŋ] a (person) vermißt; (thing) fehlend; **to be ~** fehlen.
mission ['mɪʃən] n (work) Auftrag m; (people) Delegation f; (REL) Mission f; **~ary** n Missionar(in f) m.
misspell ['mɪs'spel] (irreg: like spell) vt falsch schreiben.
misspent ['mɪs'spent] a (youth) vergeudet.
mist [mɪst] n Dunst m, Nebel m // vi (also: **~ over**, **~ up**) sich trüben; (: Brit: windows) sich beschlagen.

mistake [mɪs'teɪk] n Fehler m // vt (irreg: like **take**) (misunderstand) mißverstehen; (mix up) verwechseln (for mit); to make a ~ einen Fehler machen; by ~ aus Versehen; to ~ A for B A mit B verwechseln; ~n a (idea) falsch; to be ~n sich irren.

mister ['mɪstə*] n (col) Herr m; see **Mr.**

mistletoe ['mɪsltəʊ] n Mistel f.

mistook [mɪs'tʊk] pt of **mistake.**

mistress ['mɪstrɪs] n (teacher) Lehrerin f; (in house) Herrin f; (lover) Geliebte f; see **Mrs.**

mistrust ['mɪs'trʌst] vt mißtrauen (+dat).

misty ['mɪstɪ] a neblig.

misunderstand ['mɪsʌndə'stænd] (irreg: like **understand**) vti mißverstehen, falsch verstehen; ~ing n Mißverständnis nt; (disagreement) Meinungsverschiedenheit f.

misuse ['mɪs'juːs] n falsche(r) Gebrauch m // ['mɪs'juːz] vt falsch gebrauchen.

mitigate ['mɪtɪgeɪt] vt mildern.

mitt(en) ['mɪt(n)] n Fausthandschuh m.

mix [mɪks] vt (blend) (ver)mischen // vi (liquids) sich (ver)mischen lassen; (people: get on) sich vertragen; (: associate) Kontakt haben // n (mixture) Mischung f; ~ up (mix) zusammenmischen; (confuse) verwechseln; ~ed a gemischt; ~ed-up a durcheinander; ~er n (for food) Mixer m; ~ture n Mischung f; ~-up n Durcheinander nt

mm abbr (= millimetre) mm.

moan [məʊn] n Stöhnen nt; (complaint) Klage f // vi stöhnen: (complain) maulen.

moat [məʊt] n (Burg)graben m.

mob [mɒb] n Mob m; (the masses) Pöbel m // vt (star) herfallen über (+acc).

mobile ['məʊbaɪl] a beweglich; (library etc) fahrbar // n (decoration) Mobile nt; ~ **home** n Wohnwagen m.

mobility [məʊ'bɪlɪtɪ] n Beweglichkeit f.

mobilize ['məʊbɪlaɪz] vt mobilisieren.

moccasin ['mɒkəsɪn] n Mokassin m.

mock [mɒk] vt verspotten; (defy) trotzen (+dat) // a Schein-; ~ery n Spott m; (person) Gespött nt.

mod [mɒd] a see **convenience.**

mode [məʊd] n (Art f und) Weise f.

model ['mɒdl] n Modell nt; (example) Vorbild nt; (in fashion) Mannequin nt // a (railway) Modell-; (perfect) Muster-; vorbildlich // vt (make) bilden; (clothes) vorführen // vi als Mannequin arbeiten.

modem ['məʊdem] n Modem nt.

moderate ['mɒdərət] a gemäßigt // n (POL) Gemäßigte(r) mf // ['mɒdəreɪt] vi sich mäßigen // vt mäßigen.

moderation [mɒdə'reɪʃən] n Mäßigung f; **in ~** mit Maßen.

modern ['mɒdən] a modern; (history, languages) neuere(r, s); (Greek etc) Neu-; ~ize vt modernisieren.

modest ['mɒdɪst] a bescheiden; ~y n Bescheidenheit f.

modicum ['mɒdɪkəm] n bißchen nt.

modification [mɒdɪfɪ'keɪʃən] n (Ab)änderung f.

modify ['mɒdɪfaɪ] vt abändern.

module ['mɒdjʊl] n (component) (Bau)element nt; (SPACE) (Raum)kapsel f.

mogul ['məʊgəl] n (fig) Mogul m.

mohair ['məʊhɛə*] n Mohair m.

moist [mɔɪst] a feucht; ~en ['mɔɪsn] vt befeuchten; ~ure n Feuchtigkeit f; ~urizer n Feuchtigkeitscreme f.

molar ['məʊlə*] n Backenzahn m.

molasses [mə'læsɪz] npl Melasse f.

mold [məʊld], n, vt (US) = **mould.**

mole [məʊl] n (spot) Leberfleck m; (animal) Maulwurf m; (pier) Mole f.

molest [məʊ'lest] vt belästigen.

mollycoddle ['mɒlɪkɒdl] vt verhätscheln.

molt [məʊlt] vi (US) = **moult.**

molten ['məʊltən] a geschmolzen.

mom [mɒm] n (US) = **mum.**

moment ['məʊmənt] n Moment m, Augenblick m; (importance) Tragweite f; at the ~ im Augenblick; ~ary a kurz; ~ous [məʊ'mentəs] a folgenschwer.

momentum [məʊ'mentəm] n Schwung m; to gather ~ in Fahrt kommen.

mommy ['mɒmɪ] n (US) = **mummy.**

Monaco ['mɒnəkəʊ] n Monaco nt.

monarch ['mɒnək] n Herrscher(in f) m; ~y n Monarchie f.

monastery ['mɒnəstrɪ] n Kloster nt.

monastic [mə'næstɪk] a klösterlich, Kloster-.

Monday ['mʌndeɪ] n Montag m.

monetary ['mʌnɪtərɪ] a Geld-; (of currency) Währungs-.

money ['mʌnɪ] n Geld nt; to make ~ Geld verdienen; ~lender n Geldverleiher m; ~ order n Postanweisung f; ~-spinner n (col) Verkaufsschlager m (col).

mongol ['mɒŋgəl] n (MED) mongoloide(s) Kind nt // a mongolisch; (MED) mongoloid.

mongrel ['mʌŋgrəl] n Promenadenmischung f.

monitor ['mɒnɪtə*] n (SCH) Klassenordner m; (television ~) Monitor m // vt (broadcasts) abhören; (control) überwachen.

monk [mʌŋk] n Mönch m.

monkey ['mʌŋkɪ] n Affe m; ~ nut n (Brit) Erdnuß f; ~ wrench n (TECH) Engländer m, Franzose m.

mono- ['mɒnəʊ] pref Mono-.

monochrome ['mɒnəkrəʊm] a schwarz-weiß.

monopolize [mə'nɒpəlaɪz] vt beherrschen.

monopoly [məˈnɒpəlɪ] *n* Monopol *nt*.

monosyllable [ˈmɒnəsɪləbl] *n* ein-silbige(s) Wort *nt*.

monotone [ˈmɒnətəʊn] *n* gleich-bleibende(r) Ton(fall) *m*; **to speak in a** ~ monoton sprechen.

monotonous [məˈnɒtənəs] *a* eintönig.

monotony [məˈnɒtənɪ] *n* Eintönigkeit *f*, Monotonie *f*.

monster [ˈmɒnstə*] *n* Ungeheuer *nt*; (*person*) Scheusal *nt*.

monstrosity [mɒnsˈtrɒsɪtɪ] *n* Unge-heuerlichkeit *f*; (*thing*) Monstrosität *f*.

monstrous [ˈmɒnstrəs] *a* (*shocking*) gräßlich, ungeheuerlich; (*huge*) riesig.

month [mʌnθ] *n* Monat *m*; ~**ly** *a* monatlich, Monats- // *ad* einmal im Monat // *n* (*magazine-*) Monatsschrift *f*.

monument [ˈmɒnjʊmənt] *n* Denkmal *nt*; ~**al** [mɒnjʊˈmentl] *a* (*huge*) gewaltig; (*ignorance*) ungeheuer.

moo [muː] *vi* muhen.

mood [muːd] *n* Stimmung *f*, Laune *f*; **to be in a good/bad** ~ gute/schlechte Laune haben; ~**y** *a* launisch.

moon [muːn] *n* Mond *m*; ~**light** *n* Mondlicht *nt*; ~**lighting** *n* Schwarzarbeit *f*; ~**lit** *a* mondhell.

moor [mʊə*] *n* Heide *f*, Hochmoor *nt* // *vt* (*ship*) festmachen, verankern // *vi* anlegen; ~**ings** *npl* Liegeplatz *m*.

moorland [ˈmʊələnd] *n* Heidemoor *nt*.

moose [muːs] *n* Elch *m*.

mop [mɒp] *n* Mop *m* // *vt* (auf)wischen; ~ **up** *vt* aufwischen.

mope [məʊp] *vi* Trübsal blasen.

moped [ˈməʊped] *n* Moped *nt*.

moral [ˈmɒrəl] *a* moralisch; (*values*) sittlich; (*virtuous*) tugendhaft // *n* Moral *f*; ~**s** *pl* Moral *f*; ~**e** [mɒˈrɑːl] *n* Moral *f*; ~**ity** [məˈrælɪtɪ] *n* Sittlichkeit *f*.

morass [məˈræs] *n* Sumpf *m*.

morbid [ˈmɔːbɪd] *a* krankhaft; (*jokes*) makaber.

more [mɔː*] ♦ *a* (*greater in number etc*) mehr; (*additional*) noch mehr; **do you want (some)** ~ **tea?** möchten Sie noch etwas Tee?; **I have no** *or* **I don't have any** ~ **money** ich habe kein Geld mehr ♦ *pron* (*greater amount*) mehr; (*further or additional amount*) noch mehr; **is there any** ~? gibt es noch mehr?; (*left over*) ist noch etwas da?; **there's no** ~ es ist nichts mehr da ♦ *ad* mehr; ~ **dangerous/easily etc (than)** gefährlicher/einfacher *etc* (als); ~ **and** ~ immer mehr; ~ **and more ex-cited** immer aufgeregter; ~ **or less** mehr oder weniger; ~ **than ever** mehr denn je; ~ **beautiful than ever** schöner denn je.

moreover [mɔːˈrəʊvə*] *ad* überdies.

morgue [mɔːg] *n* Leichenschauhaus *nt*.

moribund [ˈmɒrɪbʌnd] *a* aussterbend.

Mormon [ˈmɔːmən] *n* Mormone *m*, Mormonin *f*.

morning [ˈmɔːnɪŋ] *n* Morgen; *m* **in the** ~ am Morgen; **7 o'clock in the** ~ 7 Uhr morgens.

Morocco [məˈrɒkəʊ] *n* Marokko *nt*.

moron [ˈmɔːrɒn] *n* Schwachsinnige(r) *mf*.

morose [məˈrəʊs] *a* mürrisch.

morphine [ˈmɔːfiːn] *n* Morphium *nt*.

Morse [mɔːs] *n* (*also:* ~ **code**) Morseal-phabet *nt*.

morsel [ˈmɔːsl] *n* Bissen *m*.

mortal [ˈmɔːtl] *a* sterblich; (*deadly*) töd-lich; (*very great*) Todes- // *n* (*human being*) Sterbliche(r) *mf*; ~**ity** [mɔːˈtælɪtɪ] *n* Sterblichkeit *f*; (*death rate*) Sterblichkeitsziffer *f*.

mortar [ˈmɔːtə*] *n* (*for building*) Mörtel *m*; (*bowl*) Mörser *m*; (*MIL*) Granatwerfer *m*.

mortgage [ˈmɔːgɪdʒ] *n* Hypothek *f* // *vt* eine Hypothek aufnehmen (+*acc*); ~ **company** (*US*) ≈ Bausparkasse *f*.

mortify [ˈmɔːtɪfaɪ] *vt* beschämen.

mortuary [ˈmɔːtjʊərɪ] *n* Leichenhalle *f*.

Moscow [ˈmɒskəʊ] *n* Moskau *nt*.

Moslem [ˈmɒzləm] *a*, *n* = **Muslim**.

mosque [mɒsk] *n* Moschee *f*.

mosquito [mɒsˈkiːtəʊ], *pl* ~**es** *n* Moskito *m*.

moss [mɒs] *n* Moos *nt*.

most [məʊst] *a* meiste(r, s) // *ad* am meisten; (*very*) höchst // *n* das meiste, der größte Teil; (*people*) die meisten; ~ **men** die meisten Männer; **at the (very)** ~ allerhöchstens; **to make the** ~ **of** das Beste machen aus; **a** ~ **interesting book** ein höchst interessantes Buch; ~**ly** *ad* größtenteils.

MOT *n abbr* (*Brit*) (= *Ministry of Transport*): **the** ~ **(test)** ≈ der TÜV.

motel [məʊˈtel] *n* Motel *nt*.

moth [mɒθ] *n* Nachtfalter *m*; (*wool-eating*) Motte *f*; ~**ball** *n* Mottenkugel *f*.

mother [ˈmʌðə*] *n* Mutter *f* // *vt* bemuttern; ~**hood** *n* Mutterschaft *f*; ~**-in-law** *n* Schwiegermutter *f*; ~**ly** *a* mütterlich; ~**-to-be** *n* werdende Mutter *f*; ~ **tongue** *n* Muttersprache *f*.

motif [məʊˈtiːf] *n* Motiv *nt*.

motion [ˈməʊʃən] *n* Bewegung *f*; (*in meeting*) Antrag *m* // *vti* winken (+*dat*), zu verstehen geben (+*dat*); ~**less** *a* regungslos; ~ **picture** *n* Film *m*.

motivated [ˈməʊtɪveɪtɪd] *a* motiviert.

motivation [məʊtɪˈveɪʃən] *n* Motivie-rung *f*.

motive [ˈməʊtɪv] *n* Motiv *nt*, Beweg-grund *m* // *a* treibend.

motley [ˈmɒtlɪ] *a* bunt.

motor [ˈməʊtə*] *n* Motor *m*; (*Brit col: vehicle*) Auto *nt* // *a* Motor-; ~**bike** *n* Motorrad *nt*; ~**boat** *n* Motorboot *nt*; ~**car** *n* (*Brit*) Auto *nt*; ~**cycle** *n*

Motorrad nt; **~cycle racing** n Motorradrennen nt; **~cyclist** n Motorradfahrer(in f) m; **~ing** n (Brit) Autofahren nt // a Auto-; **~ist** ['məʊtərɪst] n Autofahrer(in f) m; **~ racing** n (Brit) Autorennen nt; **~ scooter** n Motorroller m; **~ vehicle** n Kraftfahrzeug nt; **~way** n (Brit) Autobahn f.

mottled ['mɒtld] a gesprenkelt.

motto ['mɒtəʊ], pl **~es** n Motto nt.

mould, (US) **mold** [məʊld] n Form f; (mildew) Schimmel m // vt (lit, fig) formen; **~er** vi (decay) vermodern; **~y** a schimmelig.

moult, (US) **molt** [məʊlt] vi sich mausern.

mound [maʊnd] n (Erd)hügel m.

mount [maʊnt] n (liter: hill) Berg m; (horse) Pferd nt; (for jewel etc) Fassung f // vt (horse) steigen auf (+acc); (put in setting) fassen; (exhibition) veranstalten; (attack) unternehmen // vi (also: ~ up) sich häufen; (on horse) aufsitzen.

mountain ['maʊntɪn] n Berg m // cpd Berg-; **~eer** [maʊntɪˈnɪə*] n Bergsteiger(in f) m; **~eering** n Bergsteigen nt; **~ous** a bergig; **~ rescue team** n Bergwacht f; **~side** n Berg(ab)hang m.

mourn [mɔːn] vt betrauern, beklagen // vi trauern (for um); **~er** n Trauernde(r) mf; **~ful** a traurig; **~ing** n (grief) Trauer f // cpd (dress) Trauer-; in **~ing** (period etc) in Trauer; (dress) in Trauerkleidung f.

mouse [maʊs], pl **mice** n Maus f; **~trap** n Mausefalle f.

mousse [muːs] n (CULIN) Creme f; (cosmetic) Schaumfestiger m.

moustache [məsˈtɑːʃ] n Schnurrbart m.

mousy ['maʊsɪ] a (colour) mausgrau; (person) schüchtern.

mouth [maʊθ], pl **~s** [maʊðz] n Mund m; (general) Öffnung f; (of river) Mündung f; **~ful** n Mundvoll m; **~ organ** n Mundharmonika f; **~piece** n (lit) Mundstück nt; (fig) Sprachrohr nt; **~wash** n Mundwasser nt; **~watering** a lecker, appetitlich.

movable ['muːvəbl] a beweglich.

move [muːv] n (movement) Bewegung f; (in game) Zug m; (step) Schritt m; (of house) Umzug m // vt bewegen; (people) transportieren; (in job) versetzen; (emotionally) bewegen // vi sich bewegen; (vehicle, ship) fahren; (go to another house) umziehen; to ~ sb to do sth jdn veranlassen, etw zu tun; to get a ~ on sich beeilen; **~ about** or **around** vi sich hin- und herbewegen; (travel) unterwegs sein; **~ along** vi weitergehen; (cars) weiterfahren; **~ away** vi weggehen; **~ back** vi zurückgehen; (to the rear) zurückwei-

chen; **~ forward** vi vorwärtsgehen, sich vorwärtsbewegen // vt vorschieben; (time) vorverlegen; **~ in** vi (to house) einziehen; (troops) einrücken; **~ on** vi weitergehen // vt weitergehen lassen; **~ out** vi (of house) ausziehen; (troops) abziehen; **~ over** vi zur Seite rücken; **~ up** vi aufsteigen; (in job) befördert werden // vt nach oben bewegen; (in job) befördern; **~ment** n Bewegung f.

movie ['muːvɪ] n Film m; to go to the **~s** ins Kino gehen; **~ camera** n Filmkamera f.

moving ['muːvɪŋ] a beweglich; (touching) ergreifend.

mow [məʊ], pt **mowed**, pp **mowed** or **mown** vt mähen; **~ down** vt (fig) niedermähen; **~er** n (machine) Mähmaschine f; (lawn~) Rasenmäher m.

MP n abbr of **Member of Parliament**.

m.p.h. abbr of **miles per hour**.

Mr, Mr. [mɪstə*] Herr m.

Mrs, Mrs. ['mɪsɪz] Frau f.

Ms, Ms. [mɪz] n (= Miss or Mrs) Frau f.

M.Sc. abbr of **Master of Science**.

much [mʌtʃ] a viel // ad sehr; viel // n viel, eine Menge f; how ~ is it? wieviel kostet das?; too ~ zuviel; it's not ~ es ist nicht viel; as ~ as sosehr, soviel; however ~ he tries sosehr er es auch versucht.

muck [mʌk] n (lit) Mist m; (fig) Schmutz m; **~ about** or **around** vi (col) herumalbern (with an +dat); **~ up** vt (col: ruin) vermasseln; (dirty) dreckig machen; **~y** a (dirty) dreckig.

mucus ['mjuːkəs] n Schleim m.

mud [mʌd] n Schlamm m.

muddle ['mʌdl] n Durcheinander nt // vt (also: ~ up) durcheinanderbringen; **~ through** vi sich durchwursteln.

muddy ['mʌdɪ] a schlammig.

mudguard ['mʌdgɑːd] n Schutzblech nt.

mud-slinging ['mʌdslɪŋɪŋ] n (col) Verleumdung f.

muff [mʌf] n Muff m // vt (chance) verpassen; (lines) verpatzen (col).

muffin ['mʌfɪn] n süße(s) Teilchen nt.

muffle ['mʌfl] vt (sound) dämpfen; (wrap up) einhüllen; **~d** a gedämpft.

muffler ['mʌflə*] n (US AUT) Schalldämpfer m.

mug [mʌg] n (cup) Becher m; (col: face) Visage f; (col: fool) Trottel m // vt überfallen und ausrauben; **~ging** n Überfall m.

muggy ['mʌgɪ] a (weather) schwül.

mule [mjuːl] n Maulesel m.

mull [mʌl]: **~ over** vt nachdenken über (+acc).

mulled [mʌld] a (wine) Glüh-.

multi- ['mʌltɪ] pref Multi-, multi-.

multicoloured, (US) **multicolored**

['mʌltı'kʌləd] *a* mehrfarbig.
multifarious [mʌltı'feəriəs] *a* mannigfaltig.
multi-level ['mʌltılevl] *a* (*US*) = **multistorey**.
multiple ['mʌltıpl] *n* Vielfache(s) *nt* // *a* mehrfach; (*many*) mehrere; ~ **sclerosis** *n* multiple Sklerose *f*.
multiply ['mʌltıplaı] *vt* multiplizieren (*by* mit) // *vi* (*BIOL*) sich vermehren.
multistorey ['mʌltı'stɔːrı] *a* (*Brit*: *building, car park*) mehrstöckig.
multitude ['mʌltıtjuːd] *n* Menge *f*.
mum [mʌm] *a:* to keep ~ den Mund halten (*about* über +*acc*) // *n* (*Brit col*) Mutti *f*.
mumble ['mʌmbl] *vti* murmeln // *n* Gemurmel *nt*.
mummy ['mʌmı] *n* (*dead body*) Mumie *f*; (*Brit col*) Mami *f*.
mumps [mʌmps] *n* Mumps *m*.
munch [mʌntʃ] *vti* mampfen.
mundane ['mʌn'deın] *a* banal.
municipal [mjuː'nısıpəl] *a* städtisch, Stadt-; ~**ity** [mjuːnısı'pælıtı] *n* Stadt *f* mit Selbstverwaltung.
mural ['mjuərəl] *n* Wandgemälde *nt*.
murder ['mɜːdə*] *n* Mord *m* // *vt* ermorden; ~**er** *n* Mörder *m*; ~**ous** *a* Mord-; (*fig*) mörderisch.
murky ['mɜːkı] *a* finster.
murmur ['mɜːmə*] *n* Murmeln *nt*; (*of water, wind*) Rauschen *nt* // *vti* murmeln.
muscle ['mʌsl] *n* Muskel *m*; ~ **in** *vi* mitmischen.
muscular ['mʌskjʊlə*] *a* Muskel-; (*strong*) muskulös.
muse [mjuːz] *vi* (nach)sinnen.
museum [mjuː'zıəm] *n* Museum *nt*.
mushroom ['mʌʃruːm] *n* Champignon *m*; Pilz *m* // *vi* (*fig*) emporschießen.
music ['mjuːzık] *n* Musik *f*; (*printed*) Noten *pl*; ~**al** *a* (*sound*) melodisch; (*person*) musikalisch // *n* (*show*) Musical *nt*; ~**al instrument** *n* Musikinstrument *nt*; ~**al hall** *n* (*Brit*) Varieté *nt*; ~**ian** [mjuː'zıʃən] *n* Musiker(in *f*) *m*.
musk [mʌsk] *n* Moschus *m*.
Muslim ['mʌzlım] *a* moslemisch // *n* Moslem *m*.
muslin ['mʌzlın] *n* Musselin *m*.
mussel ['mʌsl] *n* Miesmuschel *f*.
must [mʌst] *v aux* müssen; (*in negation*) dürfen // *n* Muß *nt*; **the film is a** ~ den Film muß man einfach gesehen haben.
mustard ['mʌstəd] *n* Senf *m*.
muster ['mʌstə*] *vt* (*MIL*) antreten lassen; (*courage*) zusammennehmen.
mustn't ['mʌsnt] = **must not**.
musty ['mʌstı] *a* muffig.
mute [mjuːt] *a* stumm // *n* (*person*) Stumme(r) *mf*; (*MUS*) Dämpfer *m*.
muted ['mjuːtıd] *a* gedämpft.
mutilate ['mjuːtıleıt] *vt* verstümmeln.
mutilation [mjʊtı'leıʃən] *n* Verstümmelung *f*.
mutiny ['mjuːtını] *n* Meuterei *f* // *vi* meutern.
mutter ['mʌtə*] *vti* murmeln.
mutton ['mʌtn] *n* Hammelfleisch *nt*.
mutual ['mjuːtjʊəl] *a* gegenseitig; beiderseitig; ~**ly** *ad* gegenseitig; für beide Seiten.
muzzle ['mʌzl] *n* (*of animal*) Schnauze *f*; (*for animal*) Maulkorb *m*; (*of gun*) Mündung *f* // *vt* einen Maulkorb anlegen (+*dat*).
my [maı] *a* mein; **this is** ~ **car** das ist mein Auto; **I've washed** ~ **hair** ich habe mir die Haare gewaschen.
myopic [maı'ɒpık] *a* kurzsichtig.
myriad ['mırıəd] *n*: **a** ~ **of** (*people, things*) unzählige.
myself [maı'self] *pron* mich (*acc*); mir (*dat*); (*emphatic*) selbst; *see also* **oneself**.
mysterious [mıs'tıərıəs] *a* geheimnisvoll.
mystery ['mıstərı] *n* (*secret*) Geheimnis *nt*; (*sth difficult*) Rätsel *nt*.
mystify ['mıstıfaı] *vt* ein Rätsel sein (+*dat*); verblüffen.
mystique [mıs'tiːk] *n* geheimnisvolle Natur *f*.
myth [mıθ] *n* Mythos *m*; (*fig*) Erfindung *f*; ~**ology** [mı'θɒlədʒı] *n* Mythologie *f*.

N

n/a *abbr* (= *not applicable*) nicht zutreffend.
nab [næb] *vt* (*col*) schnappen.
nag [næg] *n* (*horse*) Gaul *m*; (*person*) Nörgler(in *f*) *m* // *vti* herumnörgeln (*sb* an jdm); ~**ging** *a* (*doubt*) nagend // *n* Nörgelei *f*.
nail [neıl] *n* Nagel *m* // *vt* nageln; **to** ~ **sb down to doing sth** jdn darauf festnageln, etw zu tun; ~**brush** *n* Nagelbürste *f*; ~**file** *n* Nagelfeile *f*; ~ **polish** *n* Nagellack *m*; ~ **polish remover** *n* Nagellackentferner *m*; ~ **scissors** *npl* Nagelschere *f*; ~ **varnish** *n* (*Brit*) = ~ **polish**.
naive [naı'iːv] *a* naiv.
naked ['neıkıd] *a* nackt.
name [neım] *n* Name *m*; (*reputation*) Ruf *m* // *vt* nennen; (*sth new*) benennen; (*appoint*) ernennen; **by** ~ mit Namen; **I know him only by** ~ ich kenne ihn nur dem Namen nach; **maiden** ~ Mädchenname *m*; **what's your** ~? wie heißen Sie?; **in the** ~ **of** im Namen (+*gen*); (*for the sake of*) um (+*gen*) willen; ~**less** *a* namenlos; ~**ly** *ad* nämlich; ~**sake** *n* Namensvetter *m*.
nanny ['nænı] *n* Kindermädchen *nt*.
nap [næp] *n* (*sleep*) Nickerchen *nt*; (*on

cloth) Strich *m*; **to be caught ~ping** (*fig*) überrumpelt werden.

nape [neɪp] *n* Nacken *m*.

napkin ['næpkɪn] *n* (*at table*) Serviette *f*; (*Brit: for baby*) Windel *f*.

nappy ['næpɪ] *n* (*Brit: for baby*) Windel *f*; **~ liner** *n* Windeleinlage *f*; **~ rash** *n* wunde Stellen *pl*.

narcissus [naː'sɪsəs], *pl* **-si** [-saɪ] *n* (*BOT*) Narzisse *f*.

narcotic [naː'kɒtɪk] *a* betäubend // *n* Betäubungsmittel *nt*.

narrative ['nærətɪv] *n* Erzählung *f* // *a* erzählend.

narrator [nə'reɪtə*] *n* Erzähler(in *f*) *m*.

narrow ['nærəʊ] *a* eng, schmal; (*limited*) beschränkt // *vi* sich verengen; **to have a ~ escape** mit knapper Not davonkommen; **to ~ sth down to sth** etw auf etw (*acc*) einschränken; **~ly** *ad* (*miss*) knapp; (*escape*) mit knapper Not; **~-minded** *a* engstirnig.

nasty ['naːstɪ] *a* ekelhaft, fies; (*business, wound*) schlimm.

nation ['neɪʃən] *n* Nation *f*, Volk *nt*; **~al** ['næʃənl] *a* national, National-, Landes- // *n* Staatsangehörige(r) *mf*; **~al dress** *n* Tracht *f*; **N~al Health Service (NHS)** *n* (*Brit*) Staatliche(r) Gesundheitsdienst *m*; **N~al Insurance** *n* (*Brit*) Sozialversicherung *f*; **~alism** ['næʃnəlɪzəm] *n* Nationalismus *m*; **~alist** ['næʃnəlɪst] *n* Nationalist(in *f*) *m* // *a* nationalistisch; **~ality** [næʃə'nælɪtɪ] *n* Staatsangehörigkeit *f*; **~alize** ['næʃnəlaɪz] *vt* verstaatlichen; **~ally** ['næʃnəlɪ] *ad* national, auf Staatsebene; **~-wide** *a*, *ad* allgemein, landesweit.

native ['neɪtɪv] *n* (*born in*) Einheimische(r) *mf*; (*original inhabitant*) Eingeborene(r) *mf* // *a* (*coming from a certain place*) einheimisch; (*of the original inhabitants*) Eingeborenen-; (*belonging by birth*) heimatlich, Heimat-; (*inborn*) angeboren, natürlich; **a ~ of Germany** ein gebürtiger Deutscher; **a ~ speaker of French** ein französischer Muttersprachler; **~ language** *n* Muttersprache *f*.

Nativity [nə'tɪvɪtɪ] *n*: **the ~** Christi Geburt *no art*.

NATO ['neɪtəʊ] *n abbr* (= *North Atlantic Treaty Organization*) NATO *f*.

natter ['nætə*] (*Brit col*) *vi* quatschen // *n* Gequatsche *nt*.

natural ['nætʃrəl] *a* natürlich; Natur-; (*inborn*) (an)geboren; **~ gas** *n* Erdgas *nt*; **~ist** *n* Naturkundler(in *f*) *m*; **~ize** *vt* (*foreigner*) einbürgern; (*plant etc*) einführen; **~ly** *ad* natürlich.

nature ['neɪtʃə*] *n* Natur *f*; **by ~** von Natur (aus).

naught [nɔːt] *n* = **nought**.

naughty ['nɔːtɪ] *a* (*child*) unartig, ungezogen; (*action*) ungehörig.

nausea ['nɔːsɪə] *n* (*sickness*) Übelkeit *f*; (*disgust*) Ekel *m*; **~te** ['nɔːsɪeɪt] *vt* anekeln.

nautical ['nɔːtɪkəl] *a* nautisch; See-; (*expression*) seemännisch.

naval ['neɪvəl] *a* Marine-, Flotten-; **~ officer** *n* Marineoffizier *m*.

nave [neɪv] *n* Kirchen(haupt)schiff *nt*.

navel ['neɪvəl] *n* Nabel *m*.

navigate ['nævɪgeɪt] *vi* navigieren.

navigator ['nævɪgeɪtə*] *n* Steuermann *m*; (*AVIAT*) Navigator *m*; (*AUT*) Beifahrer(in *f*) *m*.

navvy ['nævɪ] *n* (*Brit*) Straßenarbeiter *m*.

navy ['neɪvɪ] *n* (Kriegs)marine *f*; **~(-blue)** *n* Marineblau *nt* // *a* marineblau.

NB *abbr* (= *nota bene*) NB.

near [nɪə*] *a* nah; *ad* in der Nähe // *prep* (*also*: **~ to**: *space*) in der Nähe (+*gen*); (: *time*) um (+*acc*) ... herum // *vt* sich nähern (+*dat*); **a ~ miss** knapp daneben; **~by** *a* nahe (gelegen) // *ad* in der Nähe; **~ly** *ad* fast; **I ~ly fell** ich wäre fast gefallen; **~side** *n* (*AUT*) Beifahrerseite *f* // *a* auf der Beifahrerseite.

neat *a*, **~ly** *ad* ['niːt, -lɪ] (*tidy*) ordentlich; (*solution*) sauber; (*pure*) pur.

nebulous ['nebjʊləs] *a* nebulös.

necessarily ['nesɪsərɪlɪ] *ad* unbedingt.

necessary ['nesɪsərɪ] *a* notwendig, nötig; **he did all that was ~** er erledigte alles, was nötig war.

necessitate [nɪ'sesɪteɪt] *vt* erforderlich machen.

necessity [nɪ'sesɪtɪ] *n* (*need*) Not *f*; (*compulsion*) Notwendigkeit *f*; **necessities** *pl* das Notwendigste.

neck [nek] *n* Hals *m* // *vi* (*col*) knutschen; **~ and ~** Kopf an Kopf.

necklace ['neklɪs] *n* Halskette *f*.

neckline ['neklaɪn] *n* Ausschnitt *m*.

necktie ['nektaɪ] *n* (*US*) Krawatte *f*.

née [neɪ] *a* geborene.

need [niːd] *n* Bedürfnis *nt* (*for* für); (*lack*) Mangel *m*; (*necessity*) Notwendigkeit *f*; (*poverty*) Not *f* // *vt* brauchen; **I ~ to do it** ich muß es tun; **you don't ~ to go** du brauchst nicht zu gehen.

needle ['niːdl] *n* Nadel *f* // *vt* (*fig: col*) ärgern.

needless ['niːdlɪs] *a* unnötig; **~ to say** natürlich.

needlework ['niːdlwɜːk] *n* Handarbeit *f*.

needn't ['niːdnt] = **need not**.

needy ['niːdɪ] *a* bedürftig.

negation [nɪ'geɪʃən] *n* Verneinung *f*.

negative ['negətɪv] *n* (*PHOT*) Negativ *nt* // *a* negativ; (*answer*) abschlägig.

neglect [nɪ'glekt] *vt* vernachlässigen // *n* Vernachlässigung *f*.

negligence ['neglɪdʒəns] *n* Nachlässigkeit *f*.

negligible ['neglɪdʒəbl] a unbedeutend, geringfügig.

negotiable [nɪ'gəʊʃɪəbl] a (cheque) übertragbar, einlösbar.

negotiate [nɪ'gəʊʃɪeɪt] vi verhandeln // vt (treaty) abschließen; (difficulty) überwinden; (corner) nehmen; **negotiation** [-'eɪʃən] n Verhandlung f; **negotiator** n Unterhändler m.

Negress ['niːgres] n Negerin f.

Negro ['niːgrəʊ] n Neger m // a Neger-.

neigh [neɪ] vi wiehern.

neighbour, (US) **neighbor** ['neɪbə*] n Nachbar(in f) m; ~**hood** n Nachbarschaft f; Umgebung f; ~**ing** a benachbart, angrenzend.

neither ['naɪðə*] a, pron keine(r, s) (von beiden) // cj: he can't do it, and ~ can I er kann es nicht und ich auch nicht // ad: ~ good nor bad weder gut noch schlecht.

nephew ['nefjuː] n Neffe m.

nerve [nɜːv] n Nerv m; (courage) Mut m; (impudence) Frechheit f; to have a fit of ~s in Panik geraten; ~**-racking** a nervenaufreibend.

nervous ['nɜːvəs] a (of the nerves) Nerven-; (timid) nervös, ängstlich; ~ **breakdown** n Nervenzusammenbruch m; ~**ness** n Nervosität f.

nest [nest] n Nest nt // vi nisten; ~ **egg** n (fig) Notgroschen m.

nestle ['nesl] vi sich kuscheln.

net [net] n Netz nt // a netto, Netto- // vt netto einnehmen; ~**ball** n Netzball m; ~ **curtain** n Store m.

Netherlands ['neðələndz] npl: the ~ die Niederlande pl.

nett [net] a = **net**.

netting ['netɪŋ] n Netz(werk) nt.

nettle ['netl] n Nessel f.

network ['netwɜːk] n Netz nt.

neuter ['njuːtə*] a (BIOL) geschlechtslos; (GRAM) sächlich // vt kastrieren.

neutral ['njuːtrəl] a neutral // n (AUT) Leerlauf m; ~**ity** [njuː'trælɪtɪ] n Neutralität f; ~**ize** vt (fig) ausgleichen.

never ['nevə*] ad nie(mals); I ~ went ich bin gar nicht gegangen; ~ in my life nie im Leben; ~**-ending** a endlos; ~**theless** [nevəðə'les] ad trotzdem, dennoch.

new [njuː] a neu; ~**born** a neugeboren; ~**comer** n Neuankömmling m; ~**fangled** a (pej) neumodisch; ~**found** a neuentdeckt; ~**ly** ad frisch, neu; ~**ly-weds** npl Frischvermählte pl; ~ **moon** n Neumond m.

news [njuːz] n Nachricht f; (RAD, TV) Nachrichten pl; a piece of ~ eine Nachricht; ~ **agency** n Nachrichtenagentur f; ~**agent** n (Brit) Zeitungshändler m; ~**caster** n Nachrichtensprecher(in f) m; ~ **dealer** n (US) = ~**agent**; ~ **flash** n Kurzmeldung f; ~**letter** n Rundschreiben nt; ~**paper** n Zeitung f; ~**print** n Zeitungspapier nt; ~**reader** n = ~**caster**; ~**reel** n Wochenschau f; ~**stand** n Zeitungsstand m.

newt [njuːt] n Wassermolch m.

New Year n Neujahr nt; ~'**s Day** n Neujahrstag m; ~'**s Eve** n Silvester(abend m) nt.

New York [-'jɔːk] n New York nt.

New Zealand [-'ziːlənd] n Neuseeland nt; ~**er** n Neuseeländer(in f) m.

next [nekst] a nächste(r, s) // ad (after) dann, darauf; (next time) das nächstemal; the ~ day am nächsten or folgenden Tag; ~ time das nächste Mal; ~ year nächstes Jahr; ~ **door** ad nebenan // a (neighbour, flat) von nebenan; ~ **of** **kin** n Familienangehörige(r) mf; ~ **to** prep neben; ~ **to nothing** so gut wie nichts.

NHS n abbr of **National Health Service**.

nib [nɪb] n Spitze f.

nibble ['nɪbl] vt knabbern an (+dat).

nice [naɪs] a (person) nett; (thing) schön; (subtle) fein; ~**-looking** a gutaussehend; ~**ly** ad gut, nett; **niceties** ['naɪsɪtɪz] npl Feinheiten pl.

nick [nɪk] n Einkerbung f // vt (col: steal) klauen; in the ~ of time gerade rechtzeitig.

nickel ['nɪkl] n Nickel nt; (US) Nickel m (5 cents).

nickname ['nɪkneɪm] n Spitzname m // vt taufen.

Nigeria [naɪ'dʒɪərɪə] n Nigeria nt.

niece [niːs] n Nichte f.

niggardly ['nɪgədlɪ] a geizig.

niggling ['nɪglɪŋ] a pedantisch; (doubt, worry) quälend; (detail) kleinlich.

night [naɪt] n Nacht f; (evening) Abend m; the ~ before last vorletzte Nacht; at or by ~ (after midnight) nachts; (before midnight) abends; ~**cap** n (drink) Schlummertrunk m; ~**club** n Nachtlokal nt; ~**dress** n Nachthemd nt; ~**fall** n Einbruch m der Nacht; ~ **gown** n = ~**dress**; ~**ie** n (col) Nachthemd nt.

nightingale ['naɪtɪŋgeɪl] n Nachtigall f.

nightly ['naɪtlɪ] a, ad jeden Abend; jede Nacht.

nightmare ['naɪtmɛə*] n Alptraum m.

night: ~ **porter** n Nachtportier m; ~ **school** n Abendschule f; ~ **shift** n Nachtschicht f; ~**time** n Nacht f.

nil [nɪl] n Null f.

Nile [naɪl] n: the ~ der Nil.

nimble ['nɪmbl] a beweglich.

nine [naɪn] num neun; ~**teen** num neunzehn; ~**ty** num neunzig.

ninth [naɪnθ] a neunte(r, s).

nip [nɪp] vt kneifen // n Kneifen nt.

nipple ['nɪpl] n Brustwarze f.

nippy ['nɪpɪ] a (col: person) flink; (Brit col: car) flott; (: cold) frisch.
nitrogen ['naɪtrədʒən] n Stickstoff m.
no [nəʊ] ◆ad (opposite of 'yes') nein; to answer ~ (to question) mit Nein antworten; (to request) nein sagen; ~ thank you nein, danke
◆a (not any) kein(e); I have ~ money/time ich habe kein Geld/keine Zeit; '~ smoking' 'Rauchen verboten'
◆n, pl ~es Nein nt; (~ vote) Neinstimme f.
nobility [nəʊ'bɪlɪtɪ] n Adel m.
noble ['nəʊbl] a (rank) adlig; (splendid) nobel, edel.
nobody ['nəʊbədɪ] pron niemand, keiner.
nocturnal [nɒk'tɜːnl] a (tour, visit) nächtlich; (animal) Nacht-.
nod [nɒd] vi nicken // vt nicken mit // n Nicken nt; ~ off vi einnicken.
noise [nɔɪz] n (sound) Geräusch nt; (unpleasant, loud) Lärm m.
noisy ['nɔɪzɪ] a laut; (crowd) lärmend.
nominal ['nɒmɪnl] a nominell.
nominate ['nɒmɪneɪt] vt (suggest) vorschlagen; (in election) aufstellen; (appoint) ernennen.
nomination [nɒmɪ'neɪʃən] n (election) Nominierung f; (appointment) Ernennung f.
nominee [nɒmɪ'niː] n Kandidat(in f) m.
non- [nɒn] pref Nicht-, un-; ~-**alcoholic** a alkoholfrei; ~-**aligned** a bündnisfrei.
nonchalant ['nɒnʃələnt] a lässig.
non-committal ['nɒnkə'mɪtl] a (reserved) zurückhaltend; (uncommitted) unverbindlich.
nondescript ['nɒndɪskrɪpt] a mittelmäßig.
none [nʌn] a, pron kein(e, er, es) // ad: ~ of you keiner von euch; I've ~ left ich habe keine(n) mehr; he's ~ the worse for it es hat ihm nicht geschadet.
nonentity [nɒ'nentɪtɪ] n Null f (col).
nonetheless ['nʌnðə'les] ad nichtsdestoweniger.
non: ~-**existent** a nicht vorhanden; ~-**fiction** n Sachbücher pl.
nonplussed ['nɒn'plʌst] a verdutzt.
nonsense ['nɒnsəns] n Unsinn m.
non: ~-**smoker** n Nichtraucher(in f) m; ~-**stick** a (pan, surface) Teflon- ®; ~-**stop** a Nonstop-.
noodles ['nuːdlz] npl Nudeln pl.
nook [nʊk] n Winkel m; ~s **and crannies** Ecken und Winkel.
noon [nuːn] n (12 Uhr) Mittag m.
no one ['nəʊwʌn] pron = **nobody**.
noose [nuːs] n Schlinge f.
nor [nɔː*] cj = **neither** // ad see **neither**.
normal ['nɔːməl] a normal; ~**ly** ad normal; (usually) normalerweise.
north [nɔːθ] n Norden m // a nördlich, Nord- // ad nördlich, nach or im Norden;

~-**east** n Nordosten m; ~**erly** ['nɔːðəlɪ] a nördlich; ~**ern** ['nɔːðən] a nördlich, Nord-; **N~ern Ireland** n Nordirland nt; **N~ Pole** n Nordpole m; **N~ Sea** n Nordsee f; ~**ward(s)** ad nach Norden; ~-**west** n Nordwesten m.
Norway ['nɔːweɪ] n Norwegen nt; **Norwegian** [-'wiːdʒən] a norwegisch // n Norweger(in f) m; (LING) Norwegisch nt.
nose [nəʊz] n Nase f // vi: to ~ **about** herumschnüffeln; ~**bleed** n Nasenbluten nt; ~-**dive** n Sturzflug m; ~**y** a = **nosy**.
nostril ['nɒstrɪl] n Nasenloch nt.
nosy ['nəʊzɪ] a (col) neugierig.
not [nɒt] ad nicht; he is ~ or **isn't here** er ist nicht hier; it's too late, **isn't it?** es ist zu spät, oder or nicht wahr?; ~ **yet/now** noch nicht/nicht jetzt; see also **all**, **only**.
notably ['nəʊtəblɪ] ad (especially) besonders; (noticeably) bemerkenswert.
notary ['nəʊtərɪ] n Notar(in f) m.
notch [nɒtʃ] n Kerbe f, Einschnitt m.
note [nəʊt] n (MUS) Note f, Ton m; (short letter) Nachricht f; (POL) Note f; (comment, attention) Notiz f; (of lecture etc) Aufzeichnung f; (bank~) Schein m; (fame) Ruf m // vt (observe) bemerken; (write down) notieren; ~**book** n Notizbuch nt; ~**d** a bekannt; ~**pad** n Notizblock m; ~**paper** n Briefpapier nt.
nothing ['nʌθɪŋ] n nichts; ~ **new/much** nichts Neues/nicht viel; **for** ~ umsonst.
notice ['nəʊtɪs] n (announcement) Bekanntmachung f; (warning) Ankündigung f; (dismissal) Kündigung f // vt bemerken; **to take** ~ **of** beachten; **at short** ~ kurzfristig; **until further** ~ bis auf weiteres; **to hand in one's** ~ kündigen; ~**able** a merklich; ~-**board** n Anschlagtafel f.
notify ['nəʊtɪfaɪ] vt benachrichtigen.
notion ['nəʊʃən] n Idee f.
notorious [nəʊ'tɔːrɪəs] a berüchtigt.
notwithstanding [nɒtwɪθ'stændɪŋ] ad trotzdem; ~ **this** ungeachtet dessen.
nought [nɔːt] n Null f.
noun [naʊn] n Substantiv nt.
nourish ['nʌrɪʃ] vt nähren; ~**ing** a nahrhaft; ~**ment** n Nahrung f.
novel ['nɒvəl] n Roman m // a neu(artig); ~**ist** n Schriftsteller(in f) m; ~**ty** n Neuheit f.
November [nəʊ'vembə*] n November m.
novice ['nɒvɪs] n Neuling m; (ECCL) Novize m.
now [naʊ] ad jetzt; **right** ~ jetzt, gerade; **by** ~ imzwischen; **just** ~ gerade; ~ **and then**, ~ **and again** ab und zu, manchmal; **from** ~ **on** von jetzt an; ~**adays** ad heutzutage.
nowhere ['nəʊweə*] ad nirgends.

nozzle ['nɒzl] n Düse f.

nubile ['njuːbaɪl] a (woman) gut entwickelt.

nuclear ['njuːklɪə*] a (energy etc) Atom-, Kern-.

nucleus ['njuːklɪəs], pl **~lei** [-lɪaɪ] n Kern m.

nude [njuːd] a nackt // n (ART) Akt m; **in the ~** nackt.

nudge [nʌdʒ] vt leicht anstoßen.

nudist ['njuːdɪst] n Nudist(in f) m.

nudity ['njuːdɪtɪ] n Nacktheit f.

nuisance ['njuːsns] n Ärgernis nt; **what a ~!** wie ärgerlich!

nuke [njuːk] (col) n Kernkraftwerk nt // vt atomar vernichten.

null [nʌl] a: **~ and void** null und nichtig.

numb [nʌm] a taub, gefühllos // vt betäuben.

number ['nʌmbə*] n Nummer f; (numeral also) Zahl f; (quantity) (An)zahl f // vt (give a number to) numerieren; (amount to) sein; **to be ~ed among** gezählt werden zu; **a ~ of** (several) einige; **they were ten in ~** sie waren zehn an der Zahl; **~ plate** n (Brit AUT) Nummernschild nt.

numeral ['njuːmərəl] n Ziffer f.

numerate ['njuːmərɪt] a rechenkundig.

numerical [njuːˈmerɪkəl] a (order) zahlenmäßig.

numerous ['njuːmərəs] a zahlreich.

nun [nʌn] n Nonne f.

nurse [nɜːs] n Krankenschwester f; (for children) Kindermädchen nt // vt (patient) pflegen; (doubt etc) hegen.

nursery ['nɜːsərɪ] n (for children) Kinderzimmer nt; (for plants) Gärtnerei f; (for trees) Baumschule f; **~ rhyme** n Kinderreim m; **~ school** n Kindergarten m; **~ slope** n (Brit SKI) Idiotenhügel m (col), Anfängerhügel m.

nursing ['nɜːsɪŋ] n (profession) Krankenpflege f; **~ home** n Privatklinik f.

nurture ['nɜːtʃə*] vt aufziehen.

nut [nʌt] n Nuß f; (screw) Schraubenmutter f; (col) Verrückte(r) mf; **~s** a (col: crazy) verrückt.

nutcrackers ['nʌtkrækəz] npl Nußknacker m.

nutmeg ['nʌtmeg] n Muskat(nuß f) m.

nutrient ['njuːtrɪənt] n Nährstoff m.

nutrition [njuːˈtrɪʃən] n Nahrung f.

nutritious [njuːˈtrɪʃəs] a nahrhaft.

nutshell ['nʌtʃel] n: **in a ~** in aller Kürze.

nylon ['naɪlɒn] n Nylon nt // a Nylon-.

O

oak [əʊk] n Eiche f // a Eichen(holz)-.

O.A.P. abbr of **old-age pensioner**.

oar [ɔː*] n Ruder nt.

oath [əʊθ] n (statement) Eid m, Schwur m; (swearword) Fluch m; **on** (Brit) **under ~** unter Eid.

oatmeal ['əʊtmiːl] n Haferschrot m.

oats [əʊts] npl Hafer m.

obedience [əˈbiːdɪəns] n Gehorsam m.

obedient [əˈbiːdɪənt] a gehorsam.

obesity [əʊˈbiːsɪtɪ] n Fettleibigkeit f.

obey [əˈbeɪ] vti gehorchen (+dat).

obituary [əˈbɪtjʊərɪ] n Nachruf m.

object ['ɒbdʒɪkt] n (thing) Gegenstand m, Objekt nt; (purpose) Ziel nt // [əbˈdʒekt] vi dagegen sein, Einwände haben (to gegen); (morally) Anstoß nehmen (to an +acc); **expense is no ~** Ausgaben spielen keine Rolle; **I ~!** ich protestiere!; **to ~ that** einwenden, daß; **~ion** [əbˈdʒekʃən] n (reason against) Einwand m, Einspruch m; (dislike) Abneigung f; **I have no ~ion to ...** ich habe nichts gegen ... einzuwenden; **~ionable** [əbˈdʒekʃnəbl] a nicht einwandfrei; (language) anstößig; **~ive** [əbˈdʒektɪv] n Ziel nt // a objektiv.

obligation [ɒblɪˈgeɪʃən] n Verpflichtung f; **without ~** unverbindlich.

obligatory [ɒˈblɪgətərɪ] a obligatorisch.

oblige [əˈblaɪdʒ] vt (compel) zwingen; (do a favour) einen Gefallen tun (+dat); **to be ~ed to sb for sth** jdm für etw verbunden sein.

obliging [əˈblaɪdʒɪŋ] a entgegenkommend.

oblique [əˈbliːk] a schräg, schief // n Schrägstrich m.

obliterate [əˈblɪtəreɪt] vt auslöschen.

oblivion [əˈblɪvɪən] n Vergessenheit f.

oblivious [əˈblɪvɪəs] a nicht bewußt (of gen).

oblong ['ɒblɒŋ] n Rechteck nt // a länglich.

obnoxious [əbˈnɒkʃəs] a widerlich.

obscene [əbˈsiːn] a obszön.

obscenity [əbˈsenɪtɪ] n Obszönität f; **obscenities** pl Zoten pl.

obscure [əbˈskjʊə*] a unklar; (indistinct) undeutlich; (unknown) unbekannt, obskur; (dark) düster // vt verdunkeln; (view) verbergen; (confuse) verwirren.

obscurity [əbˈskjʊərɪtɪ] n Unklarheit f; (darkness) Dunkelheit f.

obsequious [əbˈsiːkwɪəs] a servil.

observance [əbˈzɜːvəns] n Befolgung f.

observant [əbˈzɜːvənt] a aufmerksam.

observation [ɒbzəˈveɪʃən] n (noticing) Beobachtung f; (surveillance) Überwachung f; (remark) Bemerkung f.

observatory [əbˈzɜːvətrɪ] n Sternwarte f, Observatorium nt.

observe [əbˈzɜːv] vt (notice) bemerken; (watch) beobachten; (customs) einhalten; **~r** n Beobachter(in f) m.

obsess [əbˈses] vt verfolgen, quälen; **~ion** [əbˈseʃən] n Besessenheit f, Wahn m; **~ive** a krankhaft.

obsolescence [ɒbsə'lesns] *n* Veralten *nt*.

obsolete ['ɒbsəli:t] *a* überholt, veraltet.

obstacle ['ɒbstəkl] *n* Hindernis *nt*; ~ **race** *n* Hindernisrennen *nt*.

obstetrics [ɒb'stetrɪks] *n* Geburtshilfe *f*.

obstinate *a*, ~**ly** *ad* ['ɒbstɪnət, -lɪ] hartnäckig, stur.

obstruct [əb'strʌkt] *vt* versperren; (*pipe*) verstopfen; (*hinder*) hemmen; ~**ion** [əb'strʌkʃən] *n* Versperrung *f*; Verstopfung *f*; (*obstacle*) Hindernis *nt*.

obtain [əb'teɪn] *vt* erhalten, bekommen; (*result*) erzielen.

obtrusive [əb'tru:sɪv] *a* aufdringlich.

obvious ['ɒbvɪəs] *a* offenbar, offensichtlich; ~**ly** *ad* offensichtlich.

occasion [ə'keɪʒən] *n* Gelegenheit *f*; (*special event*) Ereignis *nt*; (*reason*) Anlaß *m* // *vt* veranlassen; ~**al** *a*, ~**ally** *ad* gelegentlich.

occupant ['ɒkjupənt] *n* Inhaber(in *f*) *m*; (*of house etc*) Bewohner(in *f*) *m*.

occupation [ɒkju'peɪʃən] *n* (*employment*) Tätigkeit *f*, Beruf *m*; (*pastime*) Beschäftigung *f*; (*of country*) Besetzung *f*, Okkupation *f*; ~**al hazard** *n* Berufsrisiko *nt*.

occupier ['ɒkjupaɪə*] *n* Bewohner(in *f*) *m*.

occupy ['ɒkjupaɪ] *vt* (*take possession of*) besetzen; (*seat*) belegen; (*live in*) bewohnen; (*position, office*) bekleiden; (*position in sb's life*) einnehmen; (*time*) beanspruchen; **to ~ o.s. with** *or* **by doing** sich mit etw beschäftigen.

occur [ə'kɜ:*] *vi* vorkommen; **to ~ to sb** jdm einfallen; ~**rence** *n* (*event*) Ereignis *nt*; (*appearing*) Auftreten *nt*.

ocean ['əuʃən] *n* Ozean *m*, Meer *nt*; ~**going** *a* Hochsee-.

o'clock [ə'klɒk] *ad:* **it is 5 ~** es ist 5 Uhr.

OCR *n abbr of* **optical character reader.**

octagonal [ɒk'tægənl] *a* achteckig.

October [ɒk'təubə*] *n* Oktober *m*.

octopus ['ɒktəpəs] *n* Krake *f*; (*small*) Tintenfisch *m*.

odd [ɒd] *a* (*strange*) sonderbar; (*not even*) ungerade; (*the other part missing*) einzeln; (*surplus*) übrig; **55 or so um die 60; at ~ times** ab und zu; **to be the ~ one out** (*person*) das fünfte Rad am Wagen sein; (*thing*) nicht dazugehören; ~**s and ends** *npl* Krimskrams *m*; ~**ity** *n* (*strangeness*) Merkwürdigkeit *f*; (*queer person*) seltsame(r) Kauz *m*; (*thing*) Kuriosität *f*; ~**-job man** *n* Mädchen *nt* für alles; ~ **jobs** *npl* gelegentlich anfallende Arbeiten; ~**ly** *ad* seltsam; ~**ment** *npl* Reste *pl*; ~**s** *pl* Chancen *pl*; (*betting*) Gewinnchancen *pl*; **it makes no ~s** spielt keine Rolle; **at ~s** uneinig.

odious ['əudɪəs] *a* verhaßt; (*action*) abscheulich.

odometer [əu'dɒmətə*] *n* (*esp US*) Tacho(meter) *m*.

odour, (*US*) **odor** ['əudə*] *n* Geruch *m*.

of [ɒv, əv] *prep* **1** von (+*dat*), *use of gen*; **the history ~** Germany die Geschichte Deutschlands; **a friend ~ ours** ein Freund von uns; **a boy ~ 10** ein 10-jähriger Junge; **that was kind ~ you** das war sehr freundlich von Ihnen
2 (*expressing quantity, amount, dates etc*): **a kilo ~ flour** ein Kilo Mehl; **how much ~ this do you need?** wieviel brauchen Sie (davon)?; **there were 3 ~ them** (*people*) sie waren zu dritt; (*objects*) es gab 3 (davon); **a cup ~ tea/vase ~ flowers** eine Tasse Tee/Vase mit Blumen; **the 5th ~ July** der 5. Juli
3 (*from, out of*) aus; **a bridge made ~ wood** eine Holzbrücke, eine Brücke aus Holz.

off [ɒf] *ad* (*absent*) weg, fort; (*switch*) aus(geschaltet), ab(geschaltet); (*Brit: food: bad*) schlecht; **to be ~** (*to leave*) gehen; **to be ~ sick** krank sein; **a day ~** ein freier Tag; **to have an ~ day** einen schlechten Tag haben; **he had his coat ~** er hatte seinen Mantel aus; **10% ~** (*COMM*) 10% Rabatt; **5 km ~ (the road)** 5 km (von der Straße) entfernt; **~ the coast** vor der Küste; **I'm ~ meat** (*no longer eat it*) ich esse kein Fleisch mehr; (*no longer like it*) ich mag kein Fleisch mehr; **on the ~ chance** auf gut Glück.

offal ['ɒfəl] *n* Innereien *pl*.

off-colour, (*US*) **off-color** ['ɒf'kʌlə*] *a* nicht wohl.

offence, (*US*) **offense** [ə'fens] *n* (*crime*) Vergehen *nt*, Straftat *f*; (*insult*) Beleidigung *f*; **to take ~ at** gekränkt sein wegen.

offend [ə'fend] *vt* beleidigen; ~**er** *n* Gesetzesübertreter *m*.

offensive [ə'fensɪv] *a* (*unpleasant*) übel, abstoßend; (*weapon*) Kampf-; (*remark*) verletzend // *n* Angriff *m*.

offer ['ɒfə*] *n* Angebot *f*; **on ~** zum Verkauf angeboten // *vt* anbieten; (*opinion*) äußern; (*resistance*) leisten; ~**ing** *n* Gabe *f*.

offhand ['ɒf'hænd] *a* lässig // *ad* ohne weiteres.

office ['ɒfɪs] *n* Büro *nt*; (*position*) Amt *nt*; **doctor's ~** (*US*) Praxis *f*; **to take ~** sein Amt antreten; (*POL*) die Regierung übernehmen; ~ **automation** *n* Büroautomatisierung *f*; ~ **block,** (*US*) ~ **building** *n* Büro(hoch)haus *nt*; ~ **hours** *npl* Dienstzeit *f*; (*US MED*) Sprechstunde *f*.

officer ['ɒfɪsə*] *n* (*MIL*) Offizier *m*; (*public ~*) Beamte(r) *m*.

official [ə'fɪʃəl] *a* offiziell, amtlich // *n* Beamte(r) *m*; ~**dom** *n* Beamtentum *nt*.

officiate [ə'fɪʃɪeɪt] *vi* amtieren.
officious [ə'fɪʃəs] *a* aufdringlich.
offing ['ɒfɪŋ] *n*: in the ~ in (Aus)sicht.
off-licence ['ɒflaɪsəns] *n* (*Brit: shop*) Wein- und Spirituosenhandlung *f*.
off-peak ['ɒfpiːk] *a* (*charges*) verbilligt.
off-season ['ɒfsiːzn] *a* außer Saison.
offset ['ɒfset] *vt* (*irreg: like* set) ausgleichen // *n* (*also:* ~ **printing**) Offset(druck) *m*.
offshoot ['ɒfʃuːt] *n* (*fig*) (*of organization*) Zweig *m*; (*of discussion etc*) Randergebnis *nt*.
offshore ['ɒf'ʃɔː*] *ad* in einiger Entfernung von der Küste // *a* küstennah, Küsten-.
offside ['ɒf'saɪd] *a* (*SPORT*) im Abseits // *ad* abseits // *n* (*AUT*) Fahrerseite *f*.
offspring ['ɒfsprɪŋ] *n* Nachkommenschaft *f*; (*one*) Sprößling *m*.
offstage ['ɒf'steɪdʒ] *ad* hinter den Kulissen.
off: ~-**the-cuff** *a* unvorbereitet, aus dem Stegreif; ~-**the-peg**, (*US*) ~-**the-rack** *ad* von der Stange; ~-**white** *a* naturweiß.
often ['ɒfən] *ad* oft.
ogle ['əʊgl] *vt* liebäugeln mit.
oh [əʊ] *interj* oh, ach.
oil [ɔɪl] *n* Öl *nt* // *vt* ölen; ~**can** *n* Ölkännchen *nt*; ~**field** *n* Ölfeld *nt*; ~ **filter** *n* (*AUT*) Ölfilter *m*; ~**fired** *a* Öl-; ~ **painting** *n* Ölgemälde *nt*; ~**rig** *n* Ölplattform *f*; ~**skins** *npl* Ölzeug *nt*; ~ **tanker** *n* (Öl)tanker *m*; ~ **well** *n* Ölquelle *f*; ~**y** *a* ölig; (*dirty*) ölbeschmiert.
ointment ['ɔɪntmənt] *n* Salbe *f*.
O.K., okay ['əʊ'keɪ] *interj* in Ordnung, O.K. // *a* in Ordnung // *vt* genehmigen.
old [əʊld] *a* alt; **how** ~ **are you?** wie alt bist du?; **he's 10 years old** er ist 10 Jahre alt; ~ **age** *n* Alter *nt*; ~-**age pensioner (O.A.P.)** *n* (*Brit*) Rentner(in *f*) *m*; ~-**fashioned** *a* altmodisch.
olive ['ɒlɪv] *n* (*fruit*) Olive *f*; (*colour*) Olive *nt* // *a* Oliven-; (*coloured*) olivenfarbig; ~ **oil** *n* Olivenöl *nt*.
Olympic [əʊ'lɪmpɪk] *a* olympisch; ~ **Games**, ~**s** *pl* Olympische Spiele *pl*.
omelet(te) ['ɒmlət] *n* Omelett *nt*.
ominous ['ɒmɪnəs] *a* bedrohlich.
omission [əʊ'mɪʃən] *n* Auslassung *f*; (*neglect*) Versäumnis *nt*.
omit [əʊ'mɪt] *vt* auslassen; (*fail to do*) versäumen.
on [ɒn] ◆*prep* **1** (*indicating position*) auf (+*dat*); (*with v of motion*) auf(+*acc*); (*on vertical surface, part of body*) an (+*dat*): it's ~ **the** table es ist auf dem Tisch; **she put the book** ~ **the** table sie legte das Buch auf den Tisch; ~ **the left** links
2 (*indicating means, method, condition etc*): ~ **foot** (*go, be*) zu Fuß; ~ **the**

train/plane (*go*) mit dem Zug/Flugzeug; (*be*) im Zug/Flugzeug; ~ **the telephone/television** am Telefon/im Fernsehen; **to be** ~ **drugs** Drogen nehmen; **to be** ~ **holiday/business** im Urlaub/auf Geschäftsreise sein
3 (*referring to time*): ~ **Friday** (am) Freitag; ~ **Fridays** freitags; ~ **June 20th** am 20. Juni; **a week** ~ **Friday** Freitag in einer Woche; ~ **arrival** he ... als er ankam, ... er ...
4 (*about, concerning*) über (+*acc*)
◆*ad see also* v + on **1** (*referring to dress*) an; **she put her boots/hat** ~ sie zog ihre Stiefel an/setzte ihren Hut auf
2 (*further, continuously*) weiter; **to walk** ~ weitergehen
◆*a* **1** (*functioning, in operation: machine, TV, light*) an; (: *tap*) aufgedreht; (: *brakes*) angezogen; **is the meeting still** ~? findet die Versammlung noch statt?; **there's a good film** ~ es läuft ein guter Film
2: **that's not** ~! (*col: of behaviour*) das liegt nicht drin!
once [wʌns] *ad* einmal // *cj* wenn ... einmal; ~ **he had left/it was done** nachdem er gegangen war/es fertig war; **at** ~ sofort; (*at the same time*) gleichzeitig; ~ **a week** einmal in der Woche; ~ **more** noch einmal; ~ **and for all** ein für allemal; ~ **upon a time** es war einmal.
oncoming ['ɒnkʌmɪŋ] *a* (*traffic*) Gegen-, entgegenkommend.
one [wʌn] ◆*num* eins; (*with noun, referring back to noun*) ein/eine/ein; **it is** ~ (o'**clock**) es ist eins, es ist ein Uhr; ~ **hundred and fifty** einhundertfünfzig
◆*a* **1** (*sole*) einzige(r, s); **the** ~ **book which** das einzige Buch, welches
2 (*same*) derselbe/dieselbe/dasselbe; **they came in the** ~ **car** sie kamen alle in dem einen Auto
3 (*indefinite*): ~ **day I discovered** ... eines Tages bemerkte ich ...
◆*pron* **1** eine(r, s); **do you have a red** ~? haben Sie einen roten/eine rote/ein rotes?; **this** ~ diese(r, s); **that** ~ der/die/das; **which** ~? welche(r, s)?; ~ **by** ~ einzeln
2: ~ **another** einander; **do you two ever see** ~ **another?** seht ihr beide euch manchmal?
3 (*impersonal*) man; ~ **never knows** man kann nie wissen; **to cut** ~'**s finger** sich in den Finger schneiden.
one: ~-**armed bandit** *n* einarmiger Bandit *m*; ~-**day excursion** *n* (*US: day return*) Tagesrückfahrkarte *f*; ~-**man** *a* Einmann-; ~-**man band** *n* Einmannkapell *f*; (*fig*) Einmannbetrieb *m*; ~-**off** *n* (*Brit col*) Einzelfall *m*.
oneself [wʌn'self] *pron* (*reflexive: after prep*) sich; (~ *personally*) sich selbst *or* selber; (*emphatic*) (sich) selbst; **to hurt**

~ sich verletzen.

one: ~**-sided** a (argument) einseitig; ~**-to-**~ a (relationship) eins-zu-eins; ~**-upmanship** n die Kunst, anderen um eine Nasenlänge voraus zu sein; ~**-way** a (street) Einbahn-.

ongoing ['ɒngəʊɪŋ] a momentan; (progressing) sich entwickelnd.

onion ['ʌnjən] n Zwiebel f.

onlooker ['ɒnlʊkə*] n Zuschauer(in f) m.

only ['əʊnlɪ] ad nur, bloß // a einzige(r, s) // cj nur, bloß; **an** ~ **child** ein Einzelkind; **not** ~ ... **but also** ... nicht nur ... sondern auch ...

onset ['ɒnset] n (beginning) Beginn m.

onslaught ['ɒnslɔːt] n Angriff m.

onto ['ɒntʊ] prep = **on to**.

onus ['əʊnəs] n Last f, Pflicht f.

onwards ['ɒnwədz] ad (place) voran, vorwärts; **from that day** ~ von dem Tag an; **from today** ~ ab heute.

ooze [uːz] vi sickern.

opaque [əʊ'peɪk] a undurchsichtig.

OPEC n abbr (= Organization of Petroleum-Exporting Countries) OPEC f.

open ['əʊpən] a offen; (public) öffentlich; (mind) aufgeschlossen // vt öffnen, aufmachen; (trial, motorway, account) eröffnen // vi (begin) anfangen; (shop) aufmachen; (door, flower) aufgehen; (play) Premiere haben; **in the** ~ (air) im Freien; ~ **on to** vi sich öffnen auf (+ acc); ~ **up** vt (route) erschließen; (shop, prospects) eröffnen // vi öffnen; ~**ing** n (hole) Öffnung f; (beginning) Anfang m; (good chance) Gelegenheit f; ~**ly** ad offen; (publicly) öffentlich; ~**-minded** a aufgeschlossen; ~**-necked** a offen; ~**-plan** a (office) Großraum-; (flat etc) offen angelegt.

opera ['ɒpərə] n Oper f; ~ **house** n Opernhaus nt.

operate ['ɒpəreɪt] vt (machine) bedienen; (brakes, light) betätigen // vi (machine) laufen, in Betrieb sein; (person) arbeiten; (MED): **to** ~ **on** operieren.

operatic [ɒpə'rætɪk] a Opern-.

operating ['ɒpəreɪtɪŋ]: ~ **table** n Operationstisch m; ~ **theatre** n Operationssaal m.

operation [ɒpə'reɪʃən] n (working) Betrieb m; (MED) Operation f; (undertaking) Unternehmen nt; (MIL) Einsatz m; **to be in** ~ (JUR) in Kraft sein; (machine) in Betrieb sein; **to have an** ~ (MED) operiert werden; ~**al** a einsatzbereit.

operative ['ɒpərətɪv] a wirksam; (MED) operativ.

operator ['ɒpəreɪtə*] n (of machine) Arbeiter m; (TEL) Telefonist(in f) m.

ophthalmic [ɒf'θælmɪk] a Augen-.

opinion [ə'pɪnjən] n Meinung f; **in my** ~

meiner Meinung nach; ~**ated** a starrsinnig; ~ **poll** n Meinungsumfrage f.

opponent [ə'pəʊnənt] n Gegner m.

opportunity [ɒpə'tjuːnɪtɪ] n Gelegenheit f, Möglichkeit f; **to take the** ~ **of doing** die Gelegenheit ergreifen, etw zu tun.

oppose [ə'pəʊz] vt entgegentreten (+dat); (argument, idea) ablehnen; (plan) bekämpfen; **to be** ~**d to sth** gegen etw sein; **as** ~**d to** im Gegensatz zu.

opposing [ə'pəʊzɪŋ] a gegnerisch; (points of view) entgegengesetzt.

opposite ['ɒpəzɪt] a (house) gegenüberliegend; (direction) entgegengesetzt // ad gegenüber // prep gegenüber // n Gegenteil nt.

opposition [ɒpə'zɪʃən] n (resistance) Widerstand m; (POL) Opposition f; (contrast) Gegensatz m.

oppress [ə'pres] vt unterdrücken; (heat etc) bedrücken; ~**ion** [ə'preʃən] n Unterdrückung f; ~**ive** a (authority, law) repressiv; (burden, thought) bedrückend; (heat) drückend.

opt [ɒpt] vi: **to** ~ **for** sich entscheiden für; **to** ~ **to do sth** sich entscheiden, etw zu tun; ~ **out of** vi sich drücken vor (+dat); (of society) ausflippen aus (+dat).

optical ['ɒptɪkəl] a optisch; ~ **character reader (OCR)** n optische(s) Lesegerät nt (OCR n f.)

optician [ɒp'tɪʃən] n Optiker m.

optimist ['ɒptɪmɪst] n Optimist m; ~**ic** ['ɒptɪ'mɪstɪk] a optimistisch.

optimum ['ɒptɪməm] a optimal.

option ['ɒpʃən] n Wahl f; (COMM) Option f; **to keep one's** ~**s open** sich alle Möglichkeiten offenhalten; ~**al** a freiwillig; (subject) wahlfrei; ~**al extras** n Extras auf Wunsch.

opulent ['ɒpjʊlənt] a sehr reich.

or [ɔː*] cj oder; **he could not read** ~ **write** er konnte weder lesen noch schreiben; ~ **else** sonst.

oral ['ɔːrəl] a mündlich // n (exam) mündliche Prüfung f.

orange ['ɒrɪndʒ] n (fruit) Apfelsine f, Orange f; (colour) Orange nt // a orange.

orator ['ɒrətə*] n Redner(in f) m.

orbit ['ɔːbɪt] n Umlaufbahn f.

orchard ['ɔːtʃəd] n Obstgarten m.

orchestra ['ɔːkɪstrə] n Orchester nt; (US: seating) Parkett nt.

orchid ['ɔːkɪd] n Orchidee f.

ordain [ɔː'deɪn] vt (ECCL) weihen; (decide) verfügen.

ordeal [ɔː'diːl] n Qual f.

order ['ɔːdə*] n (sequence) Reihenfolge f; (good arrangement) Ordnung f; (command) Befehl m; (JUR) Anordnung f; (peace) Ordnung f; (condition) Zustand m; (rank) Klasse f; (COMM) Bestellung f; (ECCL, honour) Orden m // vt (*also:* put in ~) ordnen; (*command*) befehlen (*sth dire acc, sb* jdm); (*COMM*) bestellen; **in** ~ in der Reihenfolge; **in** (**working**) ~ in gutem Zustand; **in** ~ **to do sth** um etw zu tun; **on** ~ (*COMM*) auf Bestellung; **to** ~ **sb to do sth** jdm befehlen, etw zu tun; **to** ~ **form** *n* Bestellschein *m*; **~ly** *n* (*MIL*) Sanitäter *m*; (*MED*) Pfleger *m* // *a* (*tidy*) ordentlich; (*well-behaved*) ruhig.

ordinary ['ɔːdnəns] *a* gewöhnlich; **out of the** ~ außergewöhnlich.

ordnance ['ɔːdnəns] *n* Artillerie *f*; **O~ Survey** *n* (*Brit*) amtlicher Kartographiedienst.

ore [ɔː*] *n* Erz *nt*.

organ ['ɔːgən] *n* (*MUS*) Orgel *f*; (*BIOL, fig*) Organ *nt*.

organization [ɔːgənaɪˈzeɪʃən] *n* Organisation *f*; (*make-up*) Struktur *f*.

organize ['ɔːgənaɪz] *vt* organisieren; **~r** *n* Organisator *m*, Veranstalter *m*.

oriental [ɔːrɪˈentəl] *a* orientalisch.

origin ['ɒrɪdʒɪn] *n* Ursprung *m*; (*of the world*) Anfang *m*, Entstehung *f*.

original [əˈrɪdʒɪnl] *a* (*first*) ursprünglich; (*painting*) original; (*idea*) originell // *n* Original *nt*; **~ly** *ad* ursprünglich; originell.

originate [əˈrɪdʒɪneɪt] *vi* entstehen // *vt* ins Leben rufen; **to** ~ **from** stammen aus.

ornament ['ɔːnəmənt] *n* Schmuck *m*; (*on mantelpiece*) Nippesfigur *f*; **~al** [ɔːnəˈmentl] *a* Zier-.

ornate [ɔːˈneɪt] *a* reich verziert.

orphan ['ɔːfən] *n* Waise *f*, Waisenkind *nt* // *vt*: **to be ~ed** Waise werden; **~age** *n* Waisenhaus *nt*.

orthodox ['ɔːθədɒks] *a* orthodox; **~y** *n* Orthodoxie *f*; (*fig*) Konventionalität *f*.

orthopaedic, (*US*) **orthopedic** [ɔːθəʊˈpiːdɪk] *a* orthopädisch.

ostensibly [ɒsˈtensəblɪ] *ad* vorgeblich, angeblich.

ostentatious [ɒstenˈteɪʃəs] *a* großtuerisch, protzig.

ostracize ['ɒstrəsaɪz] *vt* ausstoßen.

ostrich ['ɒstrɪtʃ] *n* Strauß *m*.

other ['ʌðə*] *a* andere(r, s) // *pron* andere(r, s) // *ad*: ~ **than** anders als; **the** ~ (**one**) der, die, das andere; **the** ~ **day** neulich; **~s** (~ *people*) andere; **~wise** *ad* (*in a different way*) anders; (*or else*) sonst.

ouch [aʊtʃ] *interj* aua.

ought [ɔːt] *v aux* sollen; **I** ~ **to do it** ich sollte es tun; **this** ~ **to have been corrected** das hätte korrigiert werden sollen.

ounce [aʊns] *n* Unze *f*.

our [aʊə*] *poss a* unser; *see also* **my**; **~s** *poss pron* unsere(r, s); *see also* **mine**; **~selves** *pron* uns (selbst); (*emphatic*) (wir) selbst; *see also* **oneself**.

oust [aʊst] *vt* verdrängen.

out [aʊt] *ad* hinaus/heraus; (*not indoors*) draußen; (*not alight*) aus; (*unconscious*) bewußtlos; (*results*) bekanntgegeben; **to eat/go** ~ auswärts essen/ausgehen; **to there** da draußen; **he is** ~ (*absent*) er ist nicht da; **he was** ~ **in his calculations** seine Berechnungen waren nicht richtig; ~ **loud** *ad* laut; ~ **of** *prep* aus; (*away from*) außerhalb (+*gen*); **to be** ~ **of milk** *etc* keine Milch *etc* mehr haben; ~ **of order** außer Betrieb; **~-and-~** *a* (*liar, theft etc*) ausgemacht.

outback ['aʊtbæk] *n* Hinterland *nt*.

outboard (motor) ['aʊtbɔːd ('məʊtə*)] *n* Außenbordmotor *m*.

outbreak ['aʊtbreɪk] *n* Ausbruch *m*.

outburst ['aʊtbɜːst] *n* Ausbruch *m*.

outcast ['aʊtkɑːst] *n* Ausgestoßene(r) *mf*.

outcome ['aʊtkʌm] *n* Ergebnis *nt*.

outcrop ['aʊtkrɒp] *n* (*of rock*) Felsnase *f*.

outcry ['aʊtkraɪ] *n* Protest *m*.

outdated [aʊtˈdeɪtɪd] *a* überholt.

outdo [aʊtˈduː] *vt* (*irreg: like* do) übertrumpfen.

outdoor ['aʊtdɔː*] *a* Außen-; (*SPORT*) im Freien; **~s** *ad* im Freien.

outer ['aʊtə*] *a* äußere(r, s); ~ **space** *n* Weltraum *m*.

outfit ['aʊtfɪt] *n* Kleidung *f*; **~ters** *n* (*Brit: for men's clothes*) Herrenausstatter *m*.

outgoing ['aʊtgəʊɪŋ] *a* (*character*) aufgeschlossen; **~s** *npl* (*Brit*) Ausgaben *pl*.

outgrow [aʊtˈgrəʊ] *vt* (*irreg: like* grow) (*clothes*) herauswachsen aus; (*habit*) ablegen.

outhouse ['aʊthaʊs] *n* Nebengebäude *nt*.

outing ['aʊtɪŋ] *n* Ausflug *m*.

outlandish [aʊtˈlændɪʃ] *a* eigenartig.

outlaw ['aʊtlɔː] *n* Geächtete(r) *m* // *vt* ächten; (*thing*) verbieten.

outlay ['aʊtleɪ] *n* Auslage *f*.

outlet ['aʊtlet] *n* Auslaß *m*, Abfluß *m*; (*also:* retail ~) Absatzmarkt *m*; (*US ELEC*) Steckdose *f*; (*for emotions*) Ventil *nt*.

outline ['aʊtlaɪn] *n* Umriß *m*.

outlive [aʊtˈlɪv] *vt* überleben.

outlook ['aʊtlʊk] *n* (*lit, fig*) Aussicht *f*; (*attitude*) Einstellung *f*.

outlying ['aʊtlaɪɪŋ] *a* entlegen; (*district*) Außen-.

outmoded [aʊtˈməʊdɪd] *a* veraltet.

outnumber [aʊtˈnʌmbə*] *vt* zahlenmäßig überlegen sein (+*dat*).

out: **~-of-date** *a* (*passport*) abgelaufen; (*clothes etc*) altmodisch; (*ideas etc*) überholt; **~-of-the-way** *a* abgelegen.

outpatient ['aʊtpeɪʃənt] *n* ambulante(r) Patient(in *f*) *m*.

outpost ['aʊtpəʊst] *n* (*MIL, fig*) Vorposten m.

output ['autput] n Leistung f, Produktion f; (*COMPUT*) Ausgabe f.

outrage ['autreidʒ] n (*cruel deed*) Ausschreitung f; (*indecency*) Skandal m // vt (*morals*) verstoßen gegen; (*person*) empören; **~ous** [aut'reidʒəs] a unerhört.

outright ['autrait] ad (*at once*) sofort; (*openly*) ohne Umschweife // a (*denial*) völlig; (*sale*) Total-; (*winner*) unbestritten.

outset ['autset] n Beginn m.

outside ['aut'said] n Außenseite f // a äußere(r, s), Außen-; (*chance*) gering // ad außen // prep außerhalb (+gen); at the ~ (*fig*) maximal; (*time*) spätestens; to go ~ nach draußen gehen; ~ **lane** n (*AUT*) äußere Spur f; **~-left** n (*FOOTBALL*) Linksaußen m; ~ **line** n (*TEL*) Amtsanschluß m; **~r** n Außenseiter(in f) m.

outsize ['autsaiz] a übergroß.

outskirts ['autskə:ts] npl Stadtrand m.

outspoken [aut'spaukən] a freimütig.

outstanding [aut'stændiŋ] a hervorragend; (*debts etc*) ausstehend.

outstay [aut'stei] vt: to ~ one's welcome länger bleiben als erwünscht.

outstretched ['autstretʃt] a ausgestreckt.

outstrip [aut'strip] vt übertreffen.

out-tray ['auttrei] n Ausgangskorb m.

outward ['autwəd] a äußere(r, s); (*journey*) Hin-; (*freight*) ausgehend // ad nach außen; **~ly** ad äußerlich.

outweigh [aut'wei] vt (*fig*) überwiegen.

outwit [aut'wit] vt überlisten.

oval ['əuvəl] a oval // n Oval nt.

ovary ['əuvəri] n Eierstock m.

ovation [əu'veiʃən] n Beifallssturm m.

oven ['ʌvn] n Backofen m; **~proof** a feuerfest.

over ['əuvə*] ad (*across*) hinüber/herüber; (*finished*) vorbei; (*left*) übrig; (*again*) wieder, noch einmal // prep über; // pref (*excessively*) übermäßig; ~ **here** hier(hin); ~ **there** dort(hin); **all** ~ (*everywhere*) überall; (*finished*) vorbei; ~ **and** ~ immer wieder; ~ **and above** darüber hinaus; to **ask sb** ~ jdn einladen; to **bend** ~ sich bücken.

overall ['əuvərɔ:l] n (*Brit*) Kittel m // a (*situation*) allgemein; (*length*) Gesamt- // ad insgesamt; **~s** pl Overall m.

overawe [əuvər'ɔ:] vt (*frighten*) einschüchtern; (*make impression*) überwältigen.

overbalance [əuvə'bæləns] vi Übergewicht bekommen.

overbearing [əuvə'beəriŋ] a aufdringlich.

overboard ['əuvəbɔ:d] ad über Bord.

overbook [əuvə'buk] vi überbuchen.

overcast ['əuvəka:st] a bedeckt.

overcharge ['əuvə'tʃɑ:dʒ] vt: to ~ sb von jdm zuviel verlangen.

overcoat ['əuvəkəut] n Mantel m.

overcome [əuvə'kʌm] vt (*irreg: like* come) überwinden.

overcrowded [əuvə'kraudid] a überfüllt.

overcrowding [əuvə'kraudiŋ] n Überfüllung f.

overdo [əuvə'du:] vt (*irreg: like* do) (*cook too much*) verkochen; (*exaggerate*) übertreiben.

overdose ['əuvədəus] n Überdosis f.

overdraft ['əuvədrɑ:ft] n (Konto)-überziehung f.

overdrawn ['əuvə'drɔ:n] a (*account*) überzogen.

overdue ['əuvə'dju:] a überfällig.

overestimate ['əuvər'estimeit] vt überschätzen.

overexcited ['əuvərik'saitid] a überreizt; (*children*) aufgeregt.

overflow [əuvə'fləu] vi überfließen // n ['əuvəfləu] (*excess*) Überschuß m; (*also:* ~ **pipe**) Überlaufrohr nt.

overgrown ['əuvə'grəun] a (*garden*) verwildert.

overhaul [əuvə'hɔ:l] vt (*car*) überholen; (*plans*) überprüfen // n ['əuvəhɔ:l] Überholung f.

overhead ['əuvəhed] a Hoch-; (*wire*) oberirdisch; (*lighting*) Decken- // ad [əuvə'hed] oben; **~s** pl, (*US*) ~ n allgemeine Unkosten pl.

overhear [əuvə'hiə*] vt (*irreg: like* hear) (mit an)hören.

overheat [əuvə'hi:t] vi (*engine*) heiß laufen.

overjoyed [əuvə'dʒɔid] a überglücklich.

overkill ['əuvəkil] n (*fig*) Rundumschlag m.

overland ['əuvəlænd] a Überland- // ad [əuvə'lænd] (*travel*) über Land.

overlap [əuvə'læp] vi sich überschneiden; (*objects*) sich teilweise decken // n ['əuvəlæp] Überschneidung f.

overleaf [əuvə'li:f] ad umseitig.

overload ['əuvə'ləud] vt überladen.

overlook [əuvə'luk] vt (*view from above*) überblicken; (*not notice*) übersehen; (*pardon*) hinwegsehen über (+acc).

overnight ['əuvə'nait] a (*journey*) Nacht- // ad über Nacht; ~ **stay** n Übernachtung f.

overpass ['əuvəpɑːs] n Überführung f.

overpower [əuvə'pauə*] vt überwältigen; **~ing** a überwältigend.

overrate [əuvə'reit] vt überschätzen.

override [əuvə'raid] vt (*irreg: like* ride) (*order, decision*) aufheben; (*objection*) übergehen.

overriding [əuvə'raidiŋ] a vorherrschend.

overrule [əuvə'ru:l] vt verwerfen.

overrun [,əuvə'rʌn] vt (irreg: like **run**) (country) einfallen in; (time limit) überziehen.

overseas ['əuvə'si:z] ad nach/in Übersee // a überseeisch, Übersee-.

overseer ['əuvəsɪə*] n Aufseher m.

overshadow [əuvə'ʃædəu] vt überschatten.

overshoot ['əuvə'ʃu:t] vt (irreg: like **shoot**) (runway) hinausschießen über (+acc).

oversight ['əuvəsaɪt] n (mistake) Versehen nt.

oversleep ['əuvə'sli:p] vi (irreg: like **sleep**) verschlafen.

overspill ['əuvəspɪl] n (Bevölkerungs)-überschuß m.

overstate ['əuvə'steɪt] vt übertreiben.

overstep [əuvə'step] vt: to ~ the mark zu weit gehen.

overt [əu'vɜ:t] a offen(kundig).

overtake [əuvə'teɪk] vti (irreg: like **take**) überholen.

overthrow [əuvə'θrəu] vt (irreg: like **throw**) (POL) stürzen.

overtime ['əuvətaɪm] n Überstunden pl.

overtone ['əuvətəun] n (fig) Note f.

overturn [əuvə'tɜ:n] vti umkippen.

overweight ['əuvə'weɪt] a zu dick.

overwhelm [əuvə'welm] vt überwältigen; ~ing a überwältigend.

overwork ['əuvə'wɜ:k] n Überarbeitung f // vt überlasten // vi sich überarbeiten.

overwrought ['əuvə'rɔ:t] a überreizt.

owe [əu] vt schulden; to ~ sth to sb (money) jdm etw schulden; (favour etc) jdm etw verdanken; **owing to** prep wegen (+gen).

owl [aul] n Eule f.

own [əun] vt besitzen // a eigen; a room of my ~ mein eigenes Zimmer; to get one's ~ back sich rächen; on one's ~ allein; ~ up vi zugeben (to sth etw acc); ~er n Besitzer(in f) m; ~ership n Besitz m.

ox [ɒks], pl ~en ['ɒksn] n Ochse m.

oxtail ['ɒksteɪl] n: ~ soup n Ochsenschwanzsuppe f.

oxygen ['ɒksɪdʒən] n Sauerstoff m; ~ mask n Sauerstoffmaske f; ~ tent n Sauerstoffzelt nt.

oyster ['ɔɪstə*] n Auster f.

oz. abbr of **ounce(s)**.

P

p [pi:] abbr of **penny, pence**.

P.A. n abbr of **personal assistant; public address system**.

p.a. abbr of **per annum**.

pa [pɑ:] n (col) Papa m.

pace [peɪs] n Schritt m; (speed) Tempo nt // vi schreiten; to keep ~ with Schritt halten mit; ~-maker n Schrittmacher

m.

pacific [pə'sɪfɪk] a pazifisch; // n: the P~ (Ocean) der Pazifik.

pacifist ['pæsɪfɪst] n Pazifist m.

pacify ['pæsɪfaɪ] vt befrieden; (calm) beruhigen.

pack [pæk] n (of goods) Packung f; (of hounds) Meute f; (of cards) Spiel nt; (gang) Bande f // vti (case) packen; (clothes) einpacken; to ~ sb off to jdn nach ... schicken; ~ it in! laß es gut sein!

package ['pækɪdʒ] n Paket nt; ~ tour n Pauschalreise.

packed lunch ['pækt-] n Lunchpaket nt.

packet ['pækɪt] n Päckchen nt.

packing ['pækɪŋ] n (action) Packen nt; (material) Verpackung f; ~ case n (Pack)kiste f.

pact [pækt] n Pakt m, Vertrag m.

pad [pæd] n (of paper) (Schreib)block m; (padding) Polster nt // vt polstern; ~ding n Polsterung f.

paddle ['pædl] n Paddel m; (US: for table tennis) Schläger m // vt (boat) paddeln // vi (in sea) planschen; ~ steamer n Raddampfer m.

paddling pool ['pædlɪŋ-] n (Brit) Planschbecken nt.

paddock ['pædək] n Koppel f.

paddy field ['pædɪ-] n Reisfeld nt.

padlock ['pædlɒk] n Vorhängeschloß nt // vt verschließen.

paediatrics, (US) **pediatrics** [pi:dɪ'ætrɪks] n Kinderheilkunde f.

pagan ['peɪgən] a heidnisch // n Heide m, Heidin f.

page [peɪdʒ] n Seite f; (person) Page m // vt (in hotel etc) ausrufen lassen.

pageant ['pædʒənt] n Festzug m; ~ry n Gepränge nt.

paid [peɪd] pt, pp of **pay** // a bezahlt; to put ~ to (Brit) zunichte machen.

pail [peɪl] n Eimer m.

pain [peɪn] n Schmerz m; to be in ~ Schmerzen haben; on ~ of death bei Todesstrafe; to take ~s to do sth sich (dat) Mühe geben, etw zu tun; ~ed a (expression) gequält; ~ful a (physically) schmerzhaft; (embarrassing) peinlich; (difficult) mühsam; ~fully ad (fig: very) schrecklich; ~killer n Schmerzmittel nt; ~less a schmerzlos; ~staking a gewissenhaft.

paint [peɪnt] n Farbe f // vt anstreichen; (picture) malen; to ~ the door blue die Tür blau streichen; ~brush n Pinsel m; ~er n Maler m; ~ing n Malerei f; (picture) Gemälde nt; ~work n Anstrich m; (of car) Lack m.

pair [peə*] n Paar nt; ~ of scissors n Schere f; ~ of trousers n Hose f.

pajamas [pə'dʒɑ:məz] npl (US) Schlafanzug m.

Pakistan [pɑ:kɪ'stɑ:n] n Pakistan nt; ~i

a pakistanisch // *n* Pakistani *mf*.
pal [pæl] *n* (*col*) Kumpel *m*.
palace ['pæləs] *n* Palast *m*, Schloß *nt*.
palatable ['pælətəbl] *a* schmackhaft.
palate ['pælɪt] *n* Gaumen *m*.
palatial [pə'leɪʃəl] *a* palastartig.
palaver [pə'lɑːvə*] *n* (*col*) Theater *nt*.
pale [peɪl] *a* blaß, bleich; **to be beyond the ~** die Grenzen überschreiten.
Palestine ['pælɪstaɪn] *n* Palästina *nt*; **Palestinian** [-'tɪnɪən] *a* palästinensisch // *n* Palästinenser(in *f*) *m*.
paling ['peɪlɪŋ] *n* (*stake*) Zaunpfahl *m*; (*fence*) Lattenzaum *m*.
pall [pɔːl] *n* (*of smoke*) (Rauch)wolke *f* // *vi* jeden Reiz verlieren, verblassen; **~bearer** *n* Sargträger *m*.
pallet ['pælɪt] *n* (*for goods*) Palette *f*.
pallid ['pælɪd] *a* blaß, bleich.
pallor ['pælə*] *n* Blässe *f*.
palm [pɑːm] *n* (*of hand*) Handfläche *f*; (*also: ~ tree*) Palme *f* // *vt*: **to ~ sth off on sb** jdm etw andrehen; **P~ Sunday** *n* Palmsonntag *m*.
palpable ['pælpəbl] *a* (*lit, fig*) greifbar.
palpitation [pælpɪ'teɪʃən] *n* Herzklopfen *nt*.
paltry ['pɔːltrɪ] *a* armselig.
pamper ['pæmpə*] *vt* verhätscheln.
pamphlet ['pæmflɪt] *n* Broschüre *f*.
pan [pæn] *n* Pfanne *f* // *vi* (*CINE*) schwenken.
panacea [pænə'sɪə] *n* (*fig*) Allheilmittel *nt*.
panache [pə'næʃ] *n* Schwung *m*.
pancake ['pænkeɪk] *n* Pfannkuchen *m*.
pancreas ['pæŋkrɪəs] *n* Bauchspeicheldrüse *f*.
panda ['pændə] *n* Panda *m*; **~ car** *n* (*Brit*) (Funk)streifenwagen *m*.
pandemonium [pændɪ'məʊnɪəm] *n* Hölle *f*; (*noise*) Höllenlärm *m*.
pander ['pændə*] *vi* sich richten (*to* nach).
pane [peɪn] *n* (Fenster)scheibe *f*.
panel ['pænl] *n* (*of wood*) Tafel *f*; (*TV*) Diskussionsrunde *f*; **~ling**, (*US*) **~ing** *n* Täfelung *f*.
pang [pæŋ] *n*: **~s of hunger** quälende(r) Hunger *m*; **~s of conscience** Gewissensbisse *pl*.
panic ['pænɪk] *n* Panik *f* // *vi* in Panik geraten; **don't ~** (nur) keine Panik; **~ky** *a* (*person*) überängstlich; **~-stricken** *a* von panischem Schrecken erfaßt; (*look*) panisch.
pansy ['pænzɪ] *n* (*flower*) Stiefmütterchen *nt*; (*col*) Schwule(r) *m*.
pant [pænt] *vi* keuchen; (*dog*) hecheln.
panties ['pæntɪz] *npl* (Damen)slip *m*.
pantihose ['pæntɪhəʊz] *n* (*US*) Strumpfhose *f*.
pantomime ['pæntəmaɪm] *n* (*Brit*) Märchenkomödie *f* um Weihnachten.
pantry ['pæntrɪ] *n* Vorratskammer *f*.

pants [pænts] *npl* (*Brit: woman's*) Schlüpfer *m*; (: *man's*) Unterhose *f*; (*US: trousers*) Hose *f*.
papal ['peɪpəl] *a* päpstlich.
paper ['peɪpə*] *n* Papier *nt*; (*newspaper*) Zeitung *f*; (*essay*) Referat *nt* // *a* Papier-, aus Papier // *vt* (*wall*) tapezieren; **~s** *pl* (*identity*) Ausweis(papiere *pl*) *m*; **~back** *n* Taschenbuch *nt*; **~ bag** *n* Tüte *f*; **~ clip** *n* Büroklammer *f*; **~ hankie** *n* Tempotaschentuch ® *nt*; **~weight** *n* Briefbeschwerer *m*; **~work** *n* Schreibarbeit *f*.
par [pɑː*] *n* (*COMM*) Nennwert *m*; (*GOLF*) Par *nt*; **on a ~ with** ebenbürtig (*+dat*).
parable ['pærəbl] *n* (*REL*) Gleichnis *nt*.
parachute ['pærəʃuːt] *n* Fallschirm *m* // *vi* (mit dem Fallschirm) abspringen.
parade [pə'reɪd] *n* Parade *f* // *vt* aufmarschieren lassen // *vi* paradieren, vorbeimarschieren.
paradise ['pærədaɪs] *n* Paradies *nt*.
paradox ['pærədɒks] *n* Paradox *nt*; **~ically** [pærə'dɒksɪkəlɪ] *ad* paradoxerweise.
paraffin ['pærəfɪn] *n* (*Brit*) Paraffin *nt*.
paragon ['pærəgən] *n* Muster *nt*.
paragraph ['pærəgrɑːf] *n* Absatz *m*.
parallel ['pærəlel] *a* parallel // *n* Parallele *f*.
paralysis [pə'rælɪsɪs] *n* Lähmung *f*.
paralyze ['pærəlaɪz] *vt* lähmen.
parameter [pə'ræmɪtə*] *n* Parameter *m*; **~s** *pl* Rahmen *m*.
paramount ['pærəmaunt] *a* höchste(r, s), oberste(r, s).
parapet ['pærəpɪt] *n* Brüstung *f*.
paraphernalia ['pærəfə'neɪlɪə] *n* Zubehör *nt*, Utensilien *pl*.
paraphrase ['pærəfreɪz] *vt* umschreiben.
paraplegic [pærə'pliːdʒɪk] *n* Querschnittsgelähmte(r) *mf*.
parasite ['pærəsaɪt] *n* (*lit, fig*) Schmarotzer *m*, Parasit *m*.
parasol ['pærəsɒl] *n* Sonnenschirm *m*.
paratrooper ['pærətruːpə*] *n* Fallschirmjäger *m*.
parcel ['pɑːsl] *n* Paket *nt* // *vt* (*also: ~ up*) einpacken.
parch [pɑːtʃ] *vt* (aus)dörren; **~ed** *a* ausgetrocknet; (*person*) am Verdursten.
parchment ['pɑːtʃmənt] *n* Pergament *nt*.
pardon ['pɑːdn] *n* Verzeihung *f* // *vt* (*JUR*) begnadigen; **~ me!, I beg your ~!** verzeihen Sie bitte!; **~ me?** (*US*), **(I beg your) ~?** wie bitte?
parent ['pɛərənt] *n* Elternteil *m*; **~s** *pl* Eltern *pl*; **~al** [pə'rentl] *a* elterlich, Eltern-.
parenthesis [pə'renθɪsɪs], *pl* **-theses** [-θɪsiːz] *n* Klammer *f*; (*sentence*) Parenthese *f*.
Paris ['pærɪs] *n* Paris *nt*.

parish ['pærɪʃ] n Gemeinde f.
parity ['pærɪtɪ] n (FIN) Umrechnungskurs m, Parität f.
park [pɑːk] n Park m // vti parken.
parking ['pɑːkɪŋ] n Parken nt; 'no ~' 'Parken verboten'; ~ **lot** n (US) Parkplatz m; ~ **meter** n Parkuhr f; ~ **ticket** n Strafzettel m.
parlance ['pɑːləns] n Sprachgebrauch m.
parliament ['pɑːləmənt] n Parlament nt; ~**ary** [pɑːlə'mentərɪ] a parlamentarisch, Parlaments-.
parlour, (US) **parlor** ['pɑːlə*] n Salon m, Wohnzimmer nt.
parochial [pə'rəʊkɪəl] a Gemeinde-; (narrow-minded) eng(stirnig).
parole [pə'rəʊl] n: on ~ (prisoner) auf Bewährung.
paroxysm ['pærəksɪzəm] n Anfall m.
parrot ['pærət] n Papagei m.
parry ['pærɪ] vt parieren, abwehren.
parsimonious [pɑːsɪ'məʊnɪəs] a knauserig.
parsley ['pɑːslɪ] n Petersilie m.
parsnip ['pɑːsnɪp] n Pastinake f.
parson ['pɑːsn] n Pfarrer m.
part [pɑːt] n (piece) Teil m; (THEAT) Rolle f; (of machine) Teil nt // ad = **partly** // vt trennen; (hair) scheiteln // vi (people) sich trennen; **to take ~ in** teilnehmen an (+dat); **to take sth in good ~** etw nicht übelnehmen; **to take sb's ~** sich auf jds Seite stellen; **for my ~** ich für meinen Teil; **for the most ~** meistens, größtenteils; **in ~ exchange** (Brit) in Zahlung; ~ **with** vt hergeben; (renounce) aufgeben; ~**ial** ['pɑːʃəl] a (incomplete) teilweise; (biased) parteiisch; **to be ~ial to** eine (besondere) Vorliebe haben für.
participant [pɑː'tɪsɪpənt] n Teilnehmer(in f) m.
participate [pɑː'tɪsɪpeɪt] vi teilnehmen (in an +dat).
participation [pɑːtɪsɪ'peɪʃən] n Teilnahme f; (sharing) Beteiligung f.
participle ['pɑːtɪsɪpl] n Partizip nt.
particle ['pɑːtɪkl] n Teilchen nt; (GRAM) Partikel m.
particular [pə'tɪkjʊlə*] a bestimmt; (exact) genau; (fussy) eigen; ~**s** pl (details) Einzelheiten pl; Personalien pl; **in ~** ad, ~**ly** ad besonders.
parting ['pɑːtɪŋ] n (separation) Abschied m; (Brit: of hair) Scheitel m // a Abschieds-.
partition [pɑː'tɪʃən] n (wall) Trennwand f; (division) Teilung f // vt aufteilen.
partly ['pɑːtlɪ] ad zum Teil, teilweise.
partner ['pɑːtnə*] n Partner m // vt der Partner sein von; ~**ship** n Partnerschaft f; (COMM) Teilhaberschaft f.
partridge ['pɑːtrɪdʒ] n Rebhuhn nt.
part-time ['pɑːt'taɪm] a Teilzeit- // ad stundenweise.

party ['pɑːtɪ] n (POL, JUR) Partei f; (group) Gesellschaft f; (celebration) Party f // a (dress) Party-; (politics) Partei-; ~ **line** n (TEL) Gemeinschaftsanschluß m.
pass [pɑːs] vt (on foot) vorbeigehen an (+dat); (driving) vorbeifahren an (+dat); (surpass) übersteigen; (hand on) weitergeben; (approve) genehmigen; (time) verbringen; (exam) bestehen // vi (go by) vorbeigehen; vorbeifahren; (years) vergehen; (be successful) bestehen // n (in mountains) Paß m; (permission) Passierschein m; (SPORT) Paß m; (in exam): **to get a ~** bestehen; **to ~ sth through sth** etw durch etw führen; **to make a ~ at sb** (col) bei jdm Annäherungsversuche machen; ~ **away** vi (euph) verscheiden; ~ **by** vi vorbeigehen; vorbeifahren; (years) vergehen; ~ **for** vi gehalten werden für; ~ **on** vt weitergeben; ~ **out** vi (faint) ohnmächtig werden; ~ **up** vt vorbeigehen lassen; ~**able** a (road) passierbar; (fairly good) passabel.
passage ['pæsɪdʒ] n (corridor) Gang m; (in book) (Text)stelle f; (voyage) Überfahrt f; ~**way** n Durchgang m.
passbook ['pɑːsbʊk] n Sparbuch nt.
passenger ['pæsɪndʒə*] n Passagier m; (on bus) Fahrgast m.
passer-by ['pɑːsə'baɪ] n Passant(in f) m.
passing ['pɑːsɪŋ] a (car) vorbeifahrend; (thought, affair) momentan; **in ~** en passant; ~ **place** n (AUT) Ausweichstelle f.
passion ['pæʃən] n Leidenschaft f; ~**ate** a leidenschaftlich.
Passover ['pɑːsəʊvə*] n Passahfest nt.
passport ['pɑːspɔːt] n (Reise)paß m; ~ **control** n Paßkontrolle f.
password ['pɑːswɜːd] n Parole f, Kennwort nt, Losung f.
past [pɑːst] prep (motion) an (+dat) .... vorbei; (position) hinter (+dat); (later than) nach // a (years) vergangen; (president etc) ehemalig // n Vergangenheit f; he's ~ **forty** er ist über vierzig; **for the ~ few/3 days** in den letzten paar/3 Tagen; **to run ~** vorbeilaufen.
pasta ['pæstə] n Teigwaren pl.
paste [peɪst] n (fish ~ etc) Paste f; (glue) Kleister m // vt kleben; (put ~ on) mit Kleister bestreichen.
pasteurized ['pæstəraɪzd] a pasteurisiert.
pastime ['pɑːstaɪm] n Zeitvertreib m.
pastor ['pɑːstə*] n Pfarrer m.
pastry ['peɪstrɪ] n Blätterteig m; (tarts etc) Stückchen pl.
pasture ['pɑːstʃə*] n Weide f.
pasty ['pæstɪ] n (Fleisch)pastete f // ['peɪstɪ] a bläßlich, käsig.
pat [pæt] n leichte(r) Schlag m, Klaps m

// vt tätscheln.

patch [pætʃ] n Fleck m // vt flicken; **(to go through) a** bad ~ eine Pechsträhne (haben); ~ **up** vt flicken; (quarrel) beilegen; ~**y** a (irregular) ungleichmäßig.

pâté ['pætei] n Pastete f.

patent ['peitənt] n Patent nt // vt patentieren lassen; (by authorities) patentieren // a offenkundig; ~ **leather** n Lackleder nt.

paternal [pə'tɜːnl] a väterlich.

paternity [pə'tɜːnɪtɪ] n Vaterschaft f.

path [pɑːθ] n Pfad m; Weg m; (of the sun) Bahn f.

pathetic [pə'θetɪk] a (very bad) kläglich.

pathology [pə'θɒlədʒɪ] n Pathologie f.

pathos ['peiθɒs] n Rührseligkeit f.

pathway ['pɑːθwei] n Weg m.

patience ['peiʃəns] n Geduld f; (Brit: CARDS) Patience f.

patient ['peiʃənt] n Patient(in f) m, Kranke(r) mf // a geduldig.

patio ['pætiəʊ] n Innenhof m; (outside) Terrasse f.

patriotic [pætrɪ'ɒtɪk] a patriotisch.

patrol [pə'trəʊl] n Patrouille f; (police) Streife f // vt patrouillieren in (+dat) // vi (police) die Runde machen; (MIL) patrouillieren; ~ **car** n Streifenwagen m; ~**man** n (US) (Streifen)polizist m.

patron ['peitrən] n (in shop) (Stamm)kunde m; (in hotel) (Stamm)gast m; (supporter) Förderer m; ~ **of the arts** Mäzen m; ~**age** ['pætrənɪdʒ] n Schirmherrschaft f; ~**ize** ['pætrənaɪz] vt (support) unterstützen; (shop) besuchen; (treat condescendingly) von oben herab behandeln; ~ **saint** n Schutzpatron(in f) m.

patter ['pætə*] n (sound: of feet) Trappeln nt; (: of rain) Prasseln nt; (sales talk) Gerede nt // vi (feet) trappeln; (rain) prasseln.

pattern ['pætən] n Muster nt; (sewing) Schnittmuster nt; (knitting) Strickanleitung f.

paunch [pɔːntʃ] n Wanst m.

pauper ['pɔːpə*] n Arme(r) mf.

pause [pɔːz] n Pause f // vi innehalten.

pave [peiv] vt pflastern; **to** ~ **the way for** den Weg bahnen für.

pavement ['peivmənt] n (Brit) Bürgersteig m.

pavilion [pə'vɪlɪən] n Pavillon m; (SPORT) Klubhaus nt.

paving ['peivɪŋ] n Straßenpflaster nt; ~ **stone** n Pflasterstein m.

paw [pɔː] n Pfote f; (of big cats) Tatze f, Pranke f // vt (scrape) scharren; (handle) betatschen.

pawn [pɔːn] n Pfand nt; (chess) Bauer m // vt verpfänden; ~**broker** n Pfandleiher m; ~**shop** n Pfandhaus nt.

pay [pei] n Bezahlung f, Lohn m // v (pt, pp **paid**) vt bezahlen // vi zahlen; (be profitable) sich bezahlt machen; **to** ~ **attention** achtgeben (to auf +acc); ~ **back** vt zurückzahlen; ~ **for** vt bezahlen; ~ **in** vt einzahlen; ~ **off** vt abzahlen // vi (scheme, decision) sich bezahlt machen; ~ **up** vi bezahlen; ~**able** a zahlbar, fällig; ~**ee** [pei'iː] n Zahlungsempfänger m; ~ **envelope** n (US) = ~ **packet**; ~**ment** n Bezahlung f; **advance** ~**ment** Vorauszahlung f; **monthly** ~**ment** monatliche Rate f; ~ **packet** n (Brit) Lohntüte f; ~ **phone** n Münzfernsprecher m; ~**roll** n Lohnliste f; ~ **slip** n Lohn-/Gehaltsstreifen m.

PC n abbr of **personal computer**.

p.c. abbr of **per cent**.

pea [piː] n Erbse f.

peace [piːs] n Friede(n) m; ~**able** a friedlich; ~**ful** a friedlich, ruhig; ~**keeping** a Friedens-.

peach [piːtʃ] n Pfirsich m.

peacock ['piːkɒk] n Pfau m.

peak [piːk] n Spitze f; (of mountain) Gipfel m; (fig) Höhepunkt m; (of cap) (Mützen)schirm m; ~ **period** n Stoßzeit f, Hauptzeit f.

peal [piːl] n (Glocken)läuten nt; ~**s of laughter** schallende(s) Gelächter nt.

peanut ['piːnʌt] n Erdnuß f; ~ **butter** n Erdnußbutter f.

pear [peə*] n Birne f.

pearl [pɜːl] n Perle f.

peasant ['pezənt] n Bauer m.

peat [piːt] n Torf m.

pebble ['pebl] n Kiesel m.

peck [pek] vti picken // n (with beak) Schnabelhieb m; (kiss) flüchtige(r) Kuß m; ~**ing order** n Hackordnung f; ~**ish** a (Brit col) ein bißchen hungrig.

peculiar [pɪ'kjuːlɪə*] a (odd) seltsam; ~ **to** charakteristisch für; ~**ity** [pɪkjuːlɪ'ærɪtɪ] n (singular quality) Besonderheit f; (strangeness) Eigenartigkeit f.

pedal ['pedl] n Pedal nt // vti (cycle) fahren, radfahren.

peddler ['pedlə*] n Hausierer(in f) m; (of drugs) Drogenhändler(in f) m.

pedestal ['pedɪstl] n Sockel m.

pedestrian [pɪ'destrɪən] n Fußgänger m // a Fußgänger-; (humdrum) langweilig; ~ **crossing** n (Brit) Fußgängerüberweg m.

pediatrics [piːdɪ'ætrɪks] n (US) = **paediatrics**.

pedigree ['pedɪgriː] n Stammbaum m // cpd (animal) reinrassig, Zucht-.

pedlar ['pedlə*] n = **peddler**.

pee [piː] vi (col) pissen, pinkeln.

peek [piːk] vi gucken.

peel [piːl] n Schale f // vt schälen // vi (paint etc) abblättern; (skin) sich schälen.

peep [pi:p] n (Brit: look) neugierige(r) Blick m; (sound) Piepsen nt // vi (Brit: look) gucken; ~ **out** vi herausgucken; ~**hole** n Guckloch nt.

peer [pɪə*] vi starren; (peep) gucken // n (nobleman) Peer m; (equal) Ebenbürtige(r) m; ~**age** n Peerswürde f.

peeved [pi:vd] a ärgerlich; (person) sauer.

peevish ['pi:vɪʃ] a verdrießlich.

peg [peg] n (stake) Pflock m; **clothes ~** n (Brit) Wäscheklammer f.

pelican ['pelɪkən] n Pelikan m; ~ **crossing** n (Brit AUT) Ampelüberweg m.

pellet ['pelɪt] n Kügelchen nt.

pelmet ['pelmɪt] n Blende f.

pelt [pelt] vt bewerfen // vi (rain) schütten // n Pelz m, Fell nt.

pelvis ['pelvɪs] n Becken nt.

pen [pen] n (fountain ~) Federhalter m; (ball-point ~) Kuli m; (for sheep) Pferch m.

penal ['pi:nl] a Straf-; ~**ize** vt (punish) bestrafen; (disadvantage) benachteiligen; ~**ty** ['penltɪ] n Strafe f; (FOOTBALL) Elfmeter m; ~**ty (kick)** n Elfmeter m.

penance ['penəns] n Buße f.

pence [pens] (Brit) pl of **penny**.

pencil ['pensl] n Bleistift m; ~ **case** n Federmäppchen nt; ~ **sharpener** n Bleistiftspitzer m.

pendant ['pendənt] n Anhänger m.

pending ['pendɪŋ] prep bis (zu) // a unentschieden, noch offen.

pendulum ['pendjuləm] n Pendel m.

penetrate ['penɪtreɪt] vt durchdringen; (enter into) eindringen in (+acc).

penetration [penɪ'treɪʃən] n Durchdringen nt; Eindringen nt.

penfriend ['penfrend] n (Brit) Brieffreund(in f) m.

penguin ['peŋgwɪn] n Pinguin m.

penicillin [penɪ'sɪlɪn] n Penizillin nt.

peninsula [pɪ'nɪnsjulə] n Halbinsel f.

penis ['pi:nɪs] n Penis m.

penitence ['penɪtəns] n Reue f.

penitent ['penɪtənt] a reuig.

penitentiary [penɪ'tenʃərɪ] n (US) Zuchthaus nt.

penknife ['pennaɪf] n Federmesser nt.

pen name ['penneɪm] n Pseudonym nt.

penniless ['penɪləs] a mittellos.

penny ['penɪ] n, pl **pennies** ['penɪz] or (Brit) **pence** [pens] Penny m; (US) Centstück nt.

penpal ['penpæl] n Brieffreund(in f) m.

pension ['penʃən] n Rente f; ~**er** n (Brit) Rentner(in f) m; ~ **fund** n Rentenfonds m.

pensive ['pensɪv] a nachdenklich.

Pentecost ['pentɪkɒst] n Pfingsten pl or nt.

penthouse ['penthaus] n Dachterrassenwohnung f.

pent-up ['pentʌp] a (feelings) angestaut.

penultimate [pɪ'nʌltɪmət] a vorletzte(r, s).

people ['pi:pl] n (nation) Volk nt // npl (persons) Leute pl; (inhabitants) Bevölkerung f // vt besiedeln; **several ~ came** mehrere Leute kamen; ~ **say that ...** man sagt, daß ...

pep [pep] n (col) Schwung m, Schmiß m; ~ **up** vt aufmöbeln.

pepper ['pepə*] n Pfeffer m; (vegetable) Paprika m // vt (pelt) bombardieren; ~**mint** n (plant) Pfefferminze f; (sweet) Pfefferminz nt.

peptalk ['peptɔ:k] n (col) Anstachelung f.

per [pɜ:*] prep pro; ~ **day/person** pro Tag/Person; ~ **annum** ad pro Jahr; ~ **capita** a (income) Pro-Kopf- // ad pro Kopf.

perceive [pə'si:v] vt (realize) wahrnehmen; (understand) verstehen.

per cent [pə'sent] n Prozent nt.

percentage [pə'sentɪdʒ] n Prozentsatz m.

perception [pə'sepʃən] n Wahrnehmung f; (insight) Einsicht f.

perceptive [pə'septɪv] a (person) aufmerksam; (analysis) tiefgehend.

perch [pɜ:tʃ] n Stange f; (fish) Flußbarsch m // vi sitzen, hocken.

percolator ['pɜ:kəleɪtə*] n Kaffeemaschine f.

percussion [pɜ:'kʌʃən] n (MUS) Schlagzeug nt.

peremptory [pə'remptərɪ] a schroff.

perennial [pə'renɪəl] a wiederkehrend; (everlasting) unvergänglich.

perfect ['pɜ:fɪkt] a vollkommen; (crime, solution) perfekt // n (GRAM) Perfekt nt // [pə'fekt] vt vervollkommnen; ~**ion** [pə'fekʃən] n Vollkommenheit f; ~**ionist** [pə'fekʃənɪst] n Perfektionist m; ~**ly** ad vollkommen, perfekt; (quite) ganz, einfach.

perforate ['pɜ:fəreɪt] vt durchlöchern.

perform [pə'fɔ:m] vt (carry out) durchor ausführen; (task) verrichten; (THEAT) spielen, geben // vi (THEAT) auftreten; ~**ance** n Durchführung f; (efficiency) Leistung f; (show) Vorstellung f; ~**er** n Künstler(in f) m; ~**ing** a (animal) dressiert.

perfume ['pɜ:fju:m] n Duft m; (lady's) Parfüm m.

perfunctory [pə'fʌŋktərɪ] a oberflächlich, mechanisch.

perhaps [pə'hæps] ad vielleicht.

peril ['perɪl] n Gefahr f.

perimeter [pə'rɪmɪtə*] n Peripherie f; (of circle etc) Umfang m.

period ['pɪərɪəd] n Periode f; (GRAM)

Punkt *m*; (*MED*) Periode *f* // *a* (*costume*) historisch; **~ic** [-'ɒdɪk] *a* periodisch; **~ical** [-'ɒdɪkəl] *n* Zeitschrift *f*; **~ically** [-'ɒdɪkəlɪ] *ad* periodisch.

peripheral [pə'rɪfərəl] *a* Rand-, peripher // *n* (*COMPUT*) Peripheriegerät *nt*.

perish ['perɪʃ] *vi* umkommen; (*fruit*) verderben; **~able** *a* (*fruit*) leicht verderblich.

perjury ['pɜːdʒərɪ] *n* Meineid *m*.

perk [pɜːk] *n* (*col: fringe benefit*) Vergünstigung *f*; **~ up** *vi* munter werden; **~y** *a* (*cheerful*) keck.

perm [pɜːm] *n* Dauerwelle *f*.

permanent ['pɜːmənənt] *a* dauernd, ständig.

permeate ['pɜːmɪeɪt] *vti* durchdringen.

permissible [pə'mɪsəbl] *a* zulässig.

permission [pə'mɪʃən] *n* Erlaubnis *f*.

permit ['pɜːmɪt] *n* Zulassung *f* // [pə'mɪt] *vt* erlauben, zulassen.

pernicious [pɜː'nɪʃəs] *a* schädlich.

perpendicular [pɜːpən'dɪkjʊlə*] *a* senkrecht.

perpetrate ['pɜːpɪtreɪt] *vt* begehen.

perpetual [pə'petjʊəl] *a* dauernd, ständig.

perpetuate [pə'petjʊeɪt] *vt* verewigen, bewahren.

perplex [pə'pleks] *vt* verblüffen.

persecute ['pɜːsɪkjuːt] *vt* verfolgen.

persecution [pɜːsɪ'kjuːʃən] *n* Verfolgung *f*.

perseverance [pɜːsɪ'vɪərəns] *n* Ausdauer *f*.

persevere [pɜːsɪ'vɪə*] *vi* durchhalten.

Persian ['pɜːʃən] *a* persisch // *n* Perser(in *f*) *m*; **the (~)** Gulf der Persische Golf.

persist [pə'sɪst] *vi* (*in belief etc*) bleiben (in bei); (*rain, smell*) andauern; (*continue*) nicht aufhören; **~ence** *n* Beharrlichkeit *f*; **~ent** *a* beharrlich; (*unending*) ständig.

person ['pɜːsn] *n* Person *f*; **in ~** persönlich; **~able** *a* gut aussehend; **~al** *a* persönlich; (*private*) privat; (*of body*) körperlich, Körper-; **~al assistant (P.A.)** *n* Assistent(in *f*) *m*; **~al computer (PC)** *n* Personalcomputer *m*; **~ality** [pɜːsə'nælɪtɪ] *n* Persönlichkeit *f*; **~ally** *ad* persönlich; **~ify** [pɜː'sɒnɪfaɪ] *vt* verkörpern.

personnel [pɜːsə'nel] *n* Personal *nt*.

Perspex ['pɜːspeks] *n ®* Plexiglas *nt ®*.

perspiration [pɜːspə'reɪʃən] *n* Transpiration *f*.

perspire [pəs'paɪə*] *vi* transpirieren.

persuade [pə'sweɪd] *vt* überreden; (*convince*) überzeugen.

persuasion [pə'sweɪʒən] *n* Überredung *f*; Überzeugung *f*.

persuasive [pə'sweɪsɪv] *a* überzeugend.

pert [pɜːt] *a* keck.

pertaining [pɜː'teɪnɪŋ]: **~ to** *a* betreffend (+*acc*).

pertinent ['pɜːtɪnənt] *a* relevant.

perturb [pə'tɜːb] *vt* beunruhigen.

peruse [pə'ruːz] *vt* lesen.

pervade [pɜː'veɪd] *vt* erfüllen.

perverse [pə'vɜːs] *a* pervers; (*obstinate*) eigensinnig.

pervert ['pɜːvɜːt] *n* perverse(r) Mensch *m* // [pə'vɜːt] *vt* verdrehen; (*morally*) verderben.

pessimist ['pesɪmɪst] *n* Pessimist *m*; **~ic** [pesɪ'mɪstɪk] *a* pessimistisch.

pest [pest] *n* (*insect*) Schädling *m*; (*fig: person*) Nervensäge *f*; (*: thing*) Plage *f*.

pester ['pestə*] *vt* plagen.

pesticide ['pestɪsaɪd] *n* Insektenvertilgungsmittel *nt*.

pet [pet] *n* (*animal*) Haustier *nt* // *vt* liebkosen, streicheln // *vi* (*col*) Petting machen.

petal ['petl] *n* Blütenblatt *nt*.

peter out ['piːtə-] *vi* allmählich zu Ende gehen.

petite [pə'tiːt] *a* zierlich.

petition [pə'tɪʃən] *n* Bittschrift *f*.

petrified ['petrɪfaɪd] *a* versteinert; (*person*) starr (vor Schreck).

petrify ['petrɪfaɪ] *vt* versteinern; (*person*) erstarren lassen.

petrol ['petrəl] (*Brit*) *n* Benzin *nt*, Kraftstoff *m*; **two-/four-star ~** ≈ Normal-/Superbenzin *nt*; **~ can** *n* Benzinkanister *m*.

petroleum [pɪ'trəʊlɪəm] *n* Petroleum *nt*.

petrol: ~pump *n* (*Brit: in car*) Benzinpumpe *f*; (*: at garage*) Zapfsäule *f*; **~ station** *n* (*Brit*) Tankstelle *f*; **~ tank** *n* (*Brit*) Benzintank *m*.

petty ['petɪ] *a* (*unimportant*) unbedeutend; (*mean*) kleinlich; **~ cash** *n* Portokasse *f*; **~ officer** *n* Maat *m*.

petulant ['petjʊlənt] *a* leicht reizbar.

pew [pjuː] *n* Kirchenbank *f*.

pewter ['pjuːtə*] *n* Zinn *nt*.

pharmacist ['fɑːməsɪst] *n* Pharmazeut *m*; (*druggist*) Apotheker *m*.

pharmacy ['fɑːməsɪ] *n* Pharmazie *f*; (*shop*) Apotheke *f*.

phase [feɪz] *n* Phase *f*; **~ out** *vt* langsam abbauen; (*model*) auslaufen lassen; (*person*) absetzen.

Ph.D. *abbr of* **Doctor of Philosophy**.

pheasant ['feznt] *n* Fasan *m*.

phenomenon [fɪ'nɒmɪnən], *pl* **-mena** [-mɪnə] *n* Phänomen *nt*.

philanthropist [fɪ'lænθrəpɪst] *n* Philanthrop *m*, Menschenfreund *m*.

Philippines ['fɪlɪpiːnz] *npl*: **the ~** die Philippinen *pl*.

philosopher [fɪ'lɒsəfə*] *n* Philosoph *m*.

philosophy [fɪ'lɒsəfɪ] *n* Philosophie *f*.

phlegm [flem] *n* (*MED*) Schleim *m*; (*calmness*) Gelassenheit *f*; **~atic** [fleg'mætɪk] *a* gelassen.

phone [fəʊn] n Telefon nt // vti telefonieren, anrufen; **to be on the ~** telephonieren; **~ back** vti zurückrufen; **~ up** vti anrufen; **~ book** n Telefonbuch nt; **~ box** or **booth** n Telefonzelle f; **~ call** n Telefonanruf m; **~-in** n (RADIO, TV) Phone-in nt.

phoney ['fəʊnɪ] a (col) unecht // n (person) Schwindler m; (thing) Fälschung; (pound note) Blüte f.

phonograph ['fəʊnəgrɑːf] n (US) Grammophon nt.

photo ['fəʊtəʊ] n Foto nt.

photocopier ['fəʊtəʊˈkɒpɪə*] n Kopiergerät nt.

photocopy ['fəʊtəʊkɒpɪ] n Fotokopie f // vt fotokopieren.

photogenic [fəʊtəʊˈdʒenɪk] a fotogen.

photograph ['fəʊtəgrɑːf] n Fotografie f, Aufnahme f // vt fotografieren; **~er** [fəˈtɒgrəfə*] n Fotograf m; **~ic** ['fəʊtəˈgræfɪk] a fotografisch; **~y** [fəˈtɒgrəfɪ] n Fotografie f.

phrase [freɪz] n Satz m; (expression) Ausdruck m // vt ausdrücken, formulieren; **~ book** n Sprachführer m.

physical ['fɪzɪkəl] a physikalisch; (bodily) körperlich, physisch; **~ education** n Turnen nt; **~ly** ad physikalisch.

physician [fɪˈzɪʃən] n Arzt m.

physics ['fɪzɪks] n Physik f.

physiotherapy [fɪzɪəʊˈθerəpɪ] n Heilgymnastik f, Physiotherapie f.

physique [fɪˈziːk] n Körperbau m.

pianist ['pɪənɪst] n Pianist(in f) m.

piano ['pjɑːnəʊ] n Klavier nt.

pick [pɪk] n (tool) Pickel m; (choice) Auswahl f // vt (fruit) pflücken; (choose) aussuchen; **take your ~** such dir etwas aus; **to ~ sb's pocket** jdn bestehlen; **~ off** vt (kill) abschießen; **~ on** vt (person) herumhacken auf (+dat); **~ out** vt auswählen; **~ up** vi (improve) sich erholen // vt (lift up) aufheben; (learn) (schnell) mitbekommen; (collect) abholen; (girl) (sich dat) anlachen; (AUT: passenger) mitnehmen; (speed) gewinnen an (+dat); **to ~ o.s. up** aufstehen.

picket ['pɪkɪt] n (striker) Streikposten m // vt (factory) (Streik)posten aufstellen vor (+dat) // vi (Streik)posten stehen.

pickle ['pɪkl] n (salty mixture) Pökel m; (col) Klemme f // vt (in Essig) einlegen, einpökeln.

pickpocket ['pɪkpɒkɪt] n Taschendieb m.

pickup ['pɪkʌp] n (Brit: on record player) Tonabnehmer m; (small truck) Lieferwagen m.

picnic ['pɪknɪk] n Picknick nt // vi picknicken.

pictorial [pɪkˈtɔːrɪəl] a in Bildern.

picture ['pɪktʃə*] n Bild nt // vt (visualize) sich (dat) vorstellen; **in the ~** (fig) im Bild; **the ~s** pl (Brit) das Kino; **~ book** n Bilderbuch nt.

picturesque [pɪktʃəˈresk] a malerisch.

pie [paɪ] n (meat) Pastete f; (fruit) Torte f.

piece [piːs] n Stück nt // vt: **to ~ together** zusammenstückeln; **~** sich (dat) zusammenreimen; **to take to ~s** in Einzelteile zerlegen; **~meal** ad stückweise, Stück für Stück; **~work** n Akkordarbeit f.

pie chart n Kreisdiagramm nt.

pier [pɪə*] n Pier m, Mole f.

pierce [pɪəs] vt durchstechen, durchbohren (also look); durchdringen (also fig).

piercing ['pɪəsɪŋ] a durchdringend.

piety ['paɪətɪ] n Frömmigkeit f.

pig [pɪg] n Schwein nt.

pigeon ['pɪdʒən] n Taube f; **~hole** n (compartment) Ablegefach nt.

piggy bank ['pɪgɪbæŋk] n Sparschwein nt.

pigheaded ['pɪgˈhedɪd] a dickköpfig.

piglet ['pɪglət] n Ferkel nt.

pigskin ['pɪgskɪn] n Schweinsleder nt.

pigsty ['pɪgstaɪ] n (lit, fig) Schweinestall m.

pigtail ['pɪgteɪl] n Zopf m.

pike [paɪk] n Pike f; (fish) Hecht m.

pilchard ['pɪltʃəd] n Sardine f.

pile [paɪl] n Haufen m; (of books, wood) Stapel m; (in ground) Pfahl m; (on carpet) Flausch m // vti (also: **~ up**) sich anhäufen.

piles [paɪlz] n Hämorrhoiden pl.

pile-up ['paɪlʌp] n (AUT) Massenzusammenstoß m.

pilfering ['pɪlfərɪŋ] n Diebstahl m.

pilgrim ['pɪlgrɪm] n Pilger(in f) m; **~age** n Wallfahrt f.

pill [pɪl] n Tablette f, Pille f; **the ~** die (Antibaby)pille.

pillage ['pɪlɪdʒ] vt plündern.

pillar ['pɪlə*] n Pfeiler m, Säule f (also fig); **~ box** n (Brit) Briefkasten m.

pillion ['pɪljən] n Soziussitz m.

pillory ['pɪlərɪ] vt (fig) anprangern.

pillow ['pɪləʊ] n Kissen nt; **~case** n Kissenbezug m.

pilot ['paɪlət] n Pilot m; (NAUT) Lotse m // a (scheme etc) Versuchs- // vt führen; (ship) lotsen; **~ light** n Zündflamme f.

pimp [pɪmp] n Zuhälter m.

pimple ['pɪmpl] n Pickel m.

pimply ['pɪmplɪ] a pick(e)lig.

pin [pɪn] n Nadel f; (for sewing) Stecknadel f; (TECH) Stift m, Bolzen m // vt stecken, heften (to an +acc); (keep in one position) pressen, drücken; **to ~ sth on sb** (fig) jdm etw anhängen; **~s and needles** n Kribbeln pl; **~ down** vt (fig: person) festnageln (to auf +acc).

pinafore ['pɪnəfɔː*] n Schürze f; ~ **dress** n Kleiderrock m.
pinball ['pɪnbɔːl] n Flipper m.
pincers ['pɪnsəz] npl Kneif- or Beißzange f; (MED) Pinzette f.
pinch [pɪntʃ] n Zwicken, Kneifen nt; (of salt) Prise f // vti zwicken, kneifen; (shoe) drücken // vt (col: steal) klauen; (arrest) schnappen; at a ~ notfalls, zur Not.
pincushion ['pɪnkuʃən] n Nadelkissen nt.
pine [paɪn] n (also: ~ tree) Kiefer f // vi: ~ **for** sich sehnen nach; ~ **away** vi sich zu Tode sehnen.
pineapple ['paɪnæpl] n Ananas f.
ping [pɪŋ] n Klingeln nt; ~**-pong** n Pingpong nt.
pink [pɪŋk] a rosa inv // n Rosa nt; (BOT) Nelke f.
pinnacle ['pɪnəkl] n Spitze f.
pinpoint ['pɪnpɔɪnt] vt festlegen.
pinstripe ['pɪnstraɪp] n Nadelstreifen m.
pint [paɪnt] n Pint nt; (Brit col: of beer) große(s) Bier nt.
pious ['paɪəs] a fromm.
pip [pɪp] n Kern m; (Brit: time signal on radio) Zeitzeichen nt.
pipe [paɪp] n (smoking) Pfeife f; (tube) Rohr nt; (in house) (Rohr)leitung f // vt (durch Rohre) leiten; (MUS) blasen; ~s pl (also: bag~s) Dudelsack m; ~ **down** vi (be quiet) die Luft anhalten; ~ **cleaner** n Pfeifenreiniger m; ~**-dream** n Luftschloß nt; ~**line** n (for oil) Pipeline f; ~**r** n Pfeifer m; (bagpipes) Dudelsackbläser m.
piping ['paɪpɪŋ] ad: ~ **hot** siedend heiß.
piquant ['piːkənt] a pikant.
pique [piːk] n gekränkte(r) Stolz m.
pirate ['paɪərɪt] n Pirat m, Seeräuber m; ~ **radio** n (Brit) Piratensender m.
Pisces ['paɪsiːz] n Fische pl.
piss [pɪs] vi (col) pissen; ~**ed** a (col: drunk) voll.
pistol ['pɪstl] n Pistole f.
piston ['pɪstən] n Kolben m.
pit [pɪt] n Grube f; (THEAT) Parterre nt; (orchestra ~) Orchestergraben m // vt (mark with scars) zerfressen; (compare: o.s.) messen (against mit); (: sb/sth) messen (against an +dat); the ~s pl (motor racing) die Boxen.
pitch [pɪtʃ] n Wurf m; (of trader) Stand m; (SPORT) (Spiel)feld nt; (MUS) Tonlage f; (substance) Pech nt // vt werfen; (set up) aufschlagen // vi (NAUT) rollen; **to** ~ **a tent** ein Zelt aufbauen; ~**-black** a pechschwarz; ~**ed battle** n offene Schlacht f.
pitcher ['pɪtʃə*] n Krug m.
pitchfork ['pɪtʃfɔːk] n Heugabel f.
piteous ['pɪtɪəs] a kläglich, erbärmlich.
pitfall ['pɪtfɔːl] n (fig) Falle f.
pith [pɪθ] n Mark nt.

pithy ['pɪθɪ] a prägnant.
pitiful ['pɪtɪful] a (deserving pity) bedauernswert; (contemptible) jämmerlich.
pitiless ['pɪtɪləs] a erbarmungslos.
pittance ['pɪtəns] n Hungerlohn m.
pity ['pɪtɪ] n (sympathy) Mitleid nt // vt Mitleid haben mit; **what a** ~! wie schade!
pivot ['pɪvət] n Drehpunkt m // vi sich drehen (on um).
pixie ['pɪksɪ] n Elf(e f) m.
pizza ['piːtsə] n Pizza f.
placard ['plækɑːd] n Plakat nt, Anschlag m.
placate [plə'keɪt] vt beschwichtigen.
place [pleɪs] n Platz m; (spot) Stelle f; (town etc) Ort m // vt setzen, stellen, legen; (order) aufgeben; (SPORT) plazieren; (identify) unterbringen; **to take** ~ stattfinden; **to be** ~**d third** (in race, exam) auf dem dritten Platz liegen; **out of** ~ nicht am rechten Platz; (fig: remark) unangebracht; **in the first** ~ erstens; **to change** ~s **with sb** mit jdm den Platz tauschen.
placid ['plæsɪd] a gelassen, ruhig.
plagiarism ['pleɪdʒɪərɪzəm] n Plagiat nt.
plague [pleɪg] n Pest f; (fig) Plage f // vt plagen.
plaice [pleɪs] n Scholle f.
plain [pleɪn] a (clear) klar, deutlich; (simple) einfach, schlicht; (not beautiful) alltäglich // n Ebene f; **in** ~ **clothes** (police) in Zivil(kleidung); ~ **chocolate** n Bitterschokolade f.
plaintiff ['pleɪntɪf] n Kläger m.
plaintive ['pleɪntɪv] a wehleidig.
plait [plæt] n Zopf m // vt flechten.
plan [plæn] n Plan m // vti planen; **according to** ~ planmäßig; **to** ~ **to do sth** vorhaben, etw zu tun.
plane [pleɪn] n Ebene f; (AVIAT) Flugzeug nt; (tool) Hobel m; (tree) Platane f.
planet ['plænɪt] n Planet m.
plank [plæŋk] n Brett nt.
planning ['plænɪŋ] n Planung f; **family** ~ Familienplanung f; ~ **permission** n Baugenehmigung f.
plant [plɑːnt] n Pflanze f; (TECH) (Maschinen)anlage f; (factory) Fabrik f, Werk nt // vt pflanzen; (set firmly) stellen.
plantation [plæn'teɪʃən] n Plantage f.
plaque [plæk] n Gedenktafel f; (on teeth) (Zahn)belag m.
plaster ['plɑːstə*] n Gips m; (in house) Verputz m; (Brit: also: sticking ~) Pflaster nt; (for fracture: also: ~ **of Paris**) Gipsverband m // vt gipsen; (hole) zugipsen; (ceiling) verputzen; (fig: with pictures etc) be- or verkleben; ~**ed** a (col) besoffen; ~**er** n Gipser m.

plastic ['plæstɪk] n Plastik nt or f // a (made of plastic) Plastik-; (ART) plastisch, bildend; ~ **bag** n Plastiktüte f.
plasticine ['plæstɪsi:n] n Plastilin nt.
plastic surgery n plastische Chirurgie f.
plate [pleɪt] n Teller m; (gold/silver) vergoldete(s)/versilberte(s) Tafelgeschirr nt; (flat sheet) Platte f; (in book) (Bild)tafel f.
plate glass n Tafelglas nt.
platform ['plætfɔ:m] n (at meeting) Plattform f, Podium nt; (RAIL) Bahnsteig m; (POL) Parteiprogramm nt; ~ **ticket** n Bahnsteigkarte f.
platinum ['plætɪnəm] n Platin nt.
platoon [plə'tu:n] n (MIL) Zug m.
platter ['plætə*] n Platte f.
play [pleɪ] n Spiel nt (also TECH); (THEAT) (Theater)stück nt // vti spielen; (another team) spielen gegen; to ~ **safe** auf Nummer sicher gehen; ~ **down** vt herunterspielen; ~ **up** vi (cause trouble) frech werden; (bad leg etc) weh tun // vt (person) plagen; to ~ **up to sb** jdm flattieren; ~**acting** n Schauspielerei f; ~**boy** n Playboy m; ~**er** n Spieler(in f) m; ~**ful** a spielerisch; ~**ground** n Spielplatz m; ~**group** n Kindergarten m; ~**ing card** n Spielkarte f; ~**ing field** n Sportplatz m; ~**mate** n Spielkamerad m; ~**-off** n (SPORT) Entscheidungsspiel nt; ~**pen** n Laufstall m; ~**school** n = ~**group**; ~**thing** n Spielzeug nt; ~**wright** n Theaterschriftsteller m.
plc abbr (= public limited company) AG.
plea [pli:] n Bitte f; (general appeal) Appell m; (JUR) Plädoyer nt.
plead [pli:d] vt (poverty*) zur Entschuldigung anführen; (JUR: sb's case) vertreten // vi (beg) dringend bitten (with sb jdn); (JUR) plädieren.
pleasant ['pleznt] a angenehm; ~**ness** n Angenehme(s) nt; (of person) Freundlichkeit f; ~**ries** npl (polite remarks) Nettigkeiten pl.
please [pli:z] vti (be agreeable to) gefallen (+dat); ~! bitte!; ~ **yourself!** wie du willst!; ~**d** a zufrieden; (glad) erfreut (with über +acc); ~**d to meet you** angenehm.
pleasing ['pli:zɪŋ] a erfreulich.
pleasure ['pleʒə*] n Freude f; (old: will) Wünsche pl // cpd Vergnügungs-; 'it's a ~' 'gern geschehen'.
pleat [pli:t] n Falte f.
plectrum ['plektrəm] n Plektron nt.
pledge [pledʒ] n Pfand nt; (promise) Versprechen nt // vt verpfänden; (promise) geloben, versprechen.
plentiful ['plentɪfʊl] a reichlich.
plenty ['plentɪ] n Fülle f, Überfluß m; ~ **of** eine Menge, viel.

pleurisy ['plʊərɪsɪ] n Rippenfellentzündung f.
pliable ['plaɪəbl] a biegsam; (person) beeinflußbar.
pliers ['plaɪəz] npl (Kneif)zange f.
plight [plaɪt] n (Not)lage f.
plimsolls ['plɪmsəlz] npl (Brit) Turnschuhe pl.
plod [plɒd] vi (work) sich abplagen; (walk) trotten; ~**der** n Arbeitstier nt.
plonk [plɒŋk] n (Brit col: wine) billige(r) Wein m // vt: to ~ **sth down** etw hinknallen.
plot [plɒt] n Komplott nt; (story) Handlung f; (of land) Grundstück nt // vt markieren; (curve) zeichnen; (movements) nachzeichnen // vi (plan secretly) sich verschwören; ~**ter** n (instrument) Plotter m.
plough, (US) **plow** [plaʊ] n Pflug m // vt pflügen; ~ **back** vt (COMM) wieder in das Geschäft stecken; ~ **through** vt (water) durchpflügen; (book) sich kämpfen durch.
ploy [plɔɪ] n Masche f.
pluck [plʌk] vt (fruit) pflücken; (guitar) zupfen; (goose) rupfen // n Mut m; to ~ **up courage** all seinen Mut zusammennehmen; ~**y** a beherzt.
plug [plʌg] n Stöpsel m; (ELEC) Stecker m; (col: publicity) Schleichwerbung f; (AUT) Zündkerze f // vt (zu)stopfen; (col: advertise) Reklame machen für; ~ **in** vt (ELEC) anschließen.
plum [plʌm] n Pflaume f, Zwetschge f // a (job etc) Bomben-.
plumage ['plu:mɪdʒ] n Gefieder nt.
plumb [plʌm] a senkrecht // n Lot nt // ad (exactly) genau // vt ausloten; (fig) sondieren.
plumber ['plʌmə*] n Klempner m, Installateur m.
plumbing ['plʌmɪŋ] n (craft) Installieren nt; (fittings) Leitungen pl.
plume [plu:m] n Feder f; (of smoke etc) Fahne f.
plummet ['plʌmɪt] vi (ab)stürzen.
plump [plʌmp] a rundlich, füllig // vt plumpsen lassen; to ~ **for** (col: choose) sich entscheiden für.
plunder ['plʌndə*] n Plünderung f; (loot) Beute f // vt plündern.
plunge [plʌndʒ] n Sturz m // vt stoßen // vi (sich) stürzen; to take the ~ den Sprung wagen.
plunging ['plʌndʒɪŋ] a (neckline) offenherzig.
pluperfect [plu:'pɜ:fɪkt] n Plusquamperfekt nt.
plural ['plʊərəl] n Plural m, Mehrzahl f.
plus [plʌs] n (also: ~ **sign**) Plus(zeichen) nt // prep plus, und; ten/twenty ~ mehr als zehn/zwanzig.
plush [plʌʃ] a (also ~**y**: col: luxurious) feudal.

ply [plaɪ] vt (trade) (be)treiben; (with questions) zusetzen (+dat); (ship, taxi) befahren // vi (ship, taxi) verkehren; **three-~** (wool) Dreifach-; **to ~ sb with drink** jdn zum Trinken animieren; **~wood** n Sperrholz nt.

P.M. abbr of **Prime Minister**.

p.m. ad abbr (= post meridiem) p.m.

pneumatic [njuːˈmætɪk] a pneumatisch; (TECH) Luft-; **~ drill** n Preßlufthammer m.

pneumonia [njuːˈməʊnɪə] n Lungenentzündung f.

poach [pəʊtʃ] vt (COOK) pochieren; (game) stehlen // vi (steal) wildern (for nach); **~ed** a (egg) verloren; **~er** n Wilddieb m; **~ing** n Wildern nt.

P.O. Box n abbr of **Post Office Box**.

pocket ['pɒkɪt] n Tasche f; (of resistance) (Widerstands)nest nt // vt einstecken; **to be out of ~** (Brit) kein Geld haben; **~book** n Taschenbuch nt; **~ knife** n Taschenmesser nt; **~ money** n Taschengeld nt.

pod [pɒd] n Hülse f; (of peas also) Schote f.

podgy ['pɒdʒɪ] a pummelig.

podiatrist [pɒˈdiːətrɪst] n (US) Fußpfleger(in f) m.

poem ['pəʊəm] n Gedicht nt.

poet ['pəʊɪt] n Dichter m, Poet m; **~ic** [pəʊˈetɪk] a poetisch, dichterisch; **~ laureate** n Hofdichter m; **~ry** n Poesie f; (poems) Gedichte pl.

poignant ['pɔɪnjənt] a (touching) ergreifend.

point [pɔɪnt] n Punkt m (also in discussion, scoring); (spot also) Stelle f; (sharpened tip) Spitze f; (moment) (Zeit)punkt m; (purpose) Zweck m; (idea) Argument nt; (decimal) Dezimalstelle f; (personal characteristic) Seite f // vt zeigen mit; (gun) richten // vi zeigen; **~s** pl (RAIL) Weichen pl; **to be on the ~ of doing sth** drauf und dran sein, etw zu tun; **to make a ~ of** Wert darauf legen; **to get the ~** verstehen, worum es geht; **to come to the ~** zur Sache kommen; **there's no ~ (in doing)** es hat keinen Sinn (etw zu tun); **~ out** vt hinweisen auf (+acc); **~ to** vt zeigen auf (+acc); **~-blank** ad (at close range) aus nächster Entfernung; (bluntly) unverblümt; **~ed** a, **~edly** ad spitz, scharf; (fig) gezielt; **~er** n Zeigestock m; (on dial) Zeiger m; **~less** a sinnlos; **~ of view** n Stand- or Gesichtspunkt m.

poise [pɔɪz] n Haltung f; (fig) Gelassenheit f.

poison ['pɔɪzn] n (lit, fig) Gift nt // vt vergiften; **~ing** n Vergiftung f; **~ous** a giftig, Gift-.

poke [pəʊk] vt stoßen; (put) stecken; (fire) schüren; (hole) bohren; **~ about** vi herumstochern; (nose around) herumwühlen.

poker ['pəʊkə*] n Schürhaken m; (CARDS) Poker nt; **~-faced** a undurchdringlich.

poky ['pəʊkɪ] a eng.

Poland ['pəʊlənd] n Polen nt.

polar ['pəʊlə*] a Polar-, polar; **~ bear** n Eisbär m; **~ize** vt polarisieren.

Pole [pəʊl] n Pole m, Polin f.

pole [pəʊl] n Stange f, Pfosten m; (flag~, telegraph ~ also) Mast m; (ELEC, GEOG) Pol m; (SPORT) (vaulting ~) Stab m; (ski ~) Stock m; **~ bean** n (US: runner bean) Stangenbohne f; **~ vault** n Stabhochsprung m.

police [pəˈliːs] n Polizei f // vt kontrollieren; **~ car** n Polizeiwagen m; **~man** n Polizist m; **~ state** n Polizeistaat m; **~ station** n (Polizei)revier nt, Wache f; **~woman** n Polizistin f.

policy ['pɒlɪsɪ] n Politik f; (insurance) (Versicherungs)police f.

polio ['pəʊlɪəʊ] n (spinale) Kinderlähmung f, Polio f.

Polish ['pəʊlɪʃ] a polnisch // n Polnisch nt.

polish ['pɒlɪʃ] n Politur f; (for floor) Wachs nt; (for shoes) Creme f; (nail ~) Lack m; (shine) Glanz m; (of furniture) Politur f; (fig) Schliff m // vt polieren; (shoes) putzen; (fig) den letzten Schliff geben (+dat); **~ off** vt (col: work) erledigen; (food) wegputzen; (drink) hinunterschütten; **~ed** a glänzend (also fig); (manners) verfeinert.

polite [pəˈlaɪt] a höflich; **~ness** n Höflichkeit f.

politic ['pɒlɪtɪk] a (prudent) diplomatisch; **~al** a, **~ally** ad [pəˈlɪtɪkəl, -ɪ] politisch; **~ian** [pɒlɪˈtɪʃən] n Politiker m; **~s** pl Politik f.

polka ['pɒlkə] n Polka f; **~ dot** n Tupfen m.

poll [pəʊl] n Abstimmung f; (in election) Wahl f; (votes cast) Wahlbeteiligung f; (opinion ~) Umfrage f // vt (votes) erhalten.

pollination [pɒlɪˈneɪʃən] n Befruchtung f.

polling ['pəʊlɪŋ]: **~ booth** n (Brit) Wahlkabine f; **~ day** n (Brit) Wahltag m; **~ station** n (Brit) Wahllokal nt.

pollute [pəˈluːt] vt verschmutzen, verunreinigen; **pollution** [pəˈluːʃən] n Verschmutzung f.

polo ['pəʊləʊ] n Polo nt; **~-neck** n Rollkragen(pullover) m.

polystyrene [pɒlɪˈstaɪriːn] n Styropor nt.

polytechnic [pɒlɪˈteknɪk] n technische Hochschule f.

polythene ['pɒlɪθiːn] n Plastik nt.

pomegranate ['pɒməgrænɪt] n Granatapfel m.

pommel ['pʌml] vt mit den Fäusten bearbeiten // n Sattelknopf m.

pompom ['pɒmpɒm] n, **pompon** ['pɒmpɒn] n Troddel f; Pompon m.

pompous ['pɒmpəs] a aufgeblasen; (language) geschwollen.

pond [pɒnd] n Teich m, Weiher m.

ponder ['pɒndə*] vt nachdenken über (+acc); ~ous a schwerfällig.

pong [pɒŋ] n (Brit col) Mief m.

pontiff ['pɒntɪf] n Pontifex m.

pontificate [pɒn'tɪfɪkeɪt] vi (fig) geschwollen reden.

pontoon [pɒn'tu:n] n Ponton m; (CARDS) 17-und-4 nt.

pony ['pəʊnɪ] n Pony m; ~tail n Pferdeschwanz m; ~ **trekking** n (Brit) Ponyreiten n.

poodle ['pu:dl] n Pudel m.

pool [pu:l] n (swimming ~) Schwimmbad nt; (private) Swimming pool m; (of spilt liquid, blood) Lache f; (fund) (gemeinsame) Kasse f; (billiards) Poolspiel n // vt (money etc) zusammenlegen; **typing** ~ Schreibzentrale f; (football) ~s Toto nt.

poor [puə*] a arm; (not good) schlecht; the ~ pl die Armen pl; ~ly ad schlecht; (dressed) ärmlich // a schlecht.

pop [pɒp] n Knall m; (music) Popmusik f; (drink) Limo(nade) f; (US col) Pa m // vt (put) stecken; (balloon) platzen lassen // vi knallen; ~ **in** vi kurz vorbeigehen; ~ **out** vi (person) kurz rausgehen; (thing) herausspringen; ~ **up** vi auftauchen; ~ **concert** n Popkonzert nt; ~**corn** n Puffmais m.

pope [pəʊp] n Papst m.

poplar ['pɒplə*] n Pappel f.

poppy ['pɒpɪ] n Mohn m.

Popsicle ['pɒpsɪkl] n ® (US: ice lolly) Eis nt am Stiel.

populace ['pɒpjʊlɪs] n Volk nt.

popular ['pɒpjʊlə*] a beliebt, populär; (of the people) volkstümlich; (widespread) allgemein; ~**ity** [pɒpjʊ'lærɪtɪ] n Beliebtheit f, Popularität f; ~**ize** vt popularisieren; ~**ly** ad allgemein, überall.

population [pɒpjʊ'leɪʃən] n Bevölkerung f; (of town) Einwohner pl.

populous ['pɒpjʊləs] a dicht besiedelt.

porcelain ['pɔ:slɪn] n Porzellan nt.

porch [pɔ:tʃ] n Vorbau m, Veranda f.

porcupine ['pɔ:kjʊpaɪn] n Stachelschwein nt.

pore [pɔ:*] n Pore f; ~ **over** vt brüten über (+dat).

pork [pɔ:k] n Schweinefleisch nt.

pornography [pɔ:'nɒgrəfɪ] n Pornographie f.

porous ['pɔ:rəs] a porös; (skin) porig.

porpoise ['pɔ:pəs] n Tümmler m.

porridge ['pɒrɪdʒ] n Haferbrei m.

port [pɔ:t] n Hafen m; (town) Hafenstadt

f; (NAUT: left side) Backbord nt; (wine) Portwein m; ~ **of call** Anlaufhafen m.

portable ['pɔ:təbl] a tragbar.

portent ['pɔ:tent] n schlimme(s) Vorzeichen nt.

porter ['pɔ:tə*] n Pförtner(in f) m; (for luggage) (Gepäck)träger m.

portfolio [pɔ:t'fəʊlɪəʊ] n (case) Mappe f; (POL) Geschäftsbereich m; (FIN) Portefeuille nt; (of artist) Kollektion f.

porthole ['pɔ:thəʊl] n Bullauge nt.

portion ['pɔ:ʃən] n Teil m, Stück nt; (of food) Portion f.

portly ['pɔ:tlɪ] a korpulent, beleibt.

portrait ['pɔ:trɪt] n Porträt nt.

portray [pɔ:'treɪ] vt darstellen; ~**al** n Darstellung f.

Portugal ['pɔ:tjʊgəl] n Portugal nt.

Portuguese [pɔ:tjʊ'gi:z] a portugiesisch // n, pl inv Portugiese m, Portugiesin f; (LING) Portugiesisch nt.

pose [pəʊz] n Stellung f, Pose f (also affectation) // vi posieren // vt stellen.

posh [pɒʃ] a (col) (piek)fein.

position [pə'zɪʃən] n Stellung f; (place) Lage f; (job) Stelle f; (attitude) Standpunkt m // vt aufstellen.

positive ['pɒzɪtɪv] a positiv; (convinced) sicher; (definite) eindeutig.

posse ['pɒsɪ] n (US) Aufgebot nt.

possess [pə'zes] vt besitzen; ~**ion** [pə'zeʃən] n Besitz m; ~**ive** a besitzergreifend, eigensüchtig.

possibility [pɒsə'bɪlɪtɪ] n Möglichkeit f.

possible ['pɒsəbl] a möglich; as big as ~ so groß wie möglich, möglichst groß.

possibly ['pɒsəblɪ] ad möglicherweise, vielleicht; I cannot ~ come ich kann unmöglich kommen.

post [pəʊst] n (Brit: letters, delivery) Post f; (pole) Pfosten m, Pfahl m; (place of duty) Posten m; (job) Stelle f // vt (notice) anschlagen; (Brit: letters) aufgeben; (Brit: appoint) versetzen; (soldiers) aufstellen; ~**age** n Postgebühr f, Porto nt; ~**al** a Post-; ~**al order** n Postanweisung f; ~**box** n (Brit) Briefkasten m; ~**card** n Postkarte f; ~**code** n (Brit) Postleitzahl f.

postdate [pəʊst'deɪt] vt (cheque) nachdatieren.

poster ['pəʊstə*] n Plakat nt, Poster nt.

poste restante ['pəʊst'restã:nt] n Aufbewahrungsstelle f für postlagernde Sendungen.

posterior [pɒs'tɪərɪə*] n (col) Hintern m.

posterity [pɒs'terɪtɪ] n Nachwelt f.

postgraduate ['pəʊst'grædjuɪt] n Weiterstudierende(r) mf.

postman ['pəʊstmən] n Briefträger m.

postmark ['pəʊstmɑ:k] n Poststempel m.

postmaster ['pəʊstmɑ:stə*] n Postmeister *m*.

post-mortem ['pəust'mɔːtəm] *n* Autopsie *f*.

post office ['pəustɒfɪs] *n* Postamt *nt*, Post *f* (*also organization*); **Post Office Box (P.O. Box)** *n* Postfach *nt* (Postf.).

postpone [pə'spəun] *vt* verschieben; ~**ment** *n* Verschiebung *f*.

postscript ['pəusskrɪpt] *n* Postskript *nt*; (*to affair*) Nachspiel *nt*.

postulate ['pɒstjuleɪt] *vt* voraussetzen; (*maintain*) behaupten.

posture ['pɒstʃə*] *n* Haltung *f* // *vi* posieren.

postwar ['pəust'wɔː*] *a* Nachkriegs-.

posy ['pəuzɪ] *n* Blumenstrauß *m*.

pot [pɒt] *n* Topf *m*; (*tea~*) Kanne *f*; (*col: marijuana*) Hasch *m* // *vt* (*plant*) eintopfen; **to go to ~** (*col: work, performance*) auf den Hund kommen.

potato [pə'teɪtəu] *pl* ~**es** *n* Kartoffel *f*; ~ **peeler** *n* Kartoffelschäler *m*.

potent ['pəutənt] *a* stark; (*argument*) zwingend.

potential [pəu'tenʃəl] *a* potentiell // *n* Potential *nt*; ~**ly** *ad* potentiell.

pothole ['pɒthəul] *n* (*Brit: underground*) Höhle *f*; (*in road*) Schlagloch *nt*.

potholing ['pɒthəulɪŋ] *n* (*Brit*): **to go ~** Höhlen erforschen.

potion ['pəuʃən] *n* Trank *m*.

potluck ['pɒt'lʌk] *n*: **to take ~ with** sth etw auf gut Glück nehmen.

potshot ['pɒtʃɒt] *n*: **to take a ~ at** sth auf etw (*acc*) ballern.

potted ['pɒtɪd] *a* (*food*) eingelegt, eingemacht; (*plant*) Topf-; (*fig: book, version*) konzentriert.

potter ['pɒtə*] *n* Töpfer *m* // *vi* herumhantieren; ~**y** *n* Töpferwaren *pl*; (*place*) Töpferei *f*.

potty ['pɒtɪ] *a* (*col*) verrückt // *n* Töpfchen *nt*.

pouch [pautʃ] *n* Beutel *m*.

pouf(fe) [puːf] *n* Sitzkissen *nt*.

poultry ['pəultrɪ] *n* Geflügel *nt*.

pounce [pauns] *vi* sich stürzen (*on* auf +*acc*) // *n* Sprung *m*, Satz *m*.

pound [paund] *n* (*FIN, weight*) Pfund *nt*; (*for cars, animals*) Auslösestelle *f*; (*for stray animals*) (Tier)asyl *nt* // *vt* (zer)stampfen // *vi* klopfen, hämmern; ~ **sterling** *n* Pfund Sterling *nt*.

pour [pɔː*] *vt* gießen, schütten // *vi* gießen; (*crowds etc*) strömen; ~ **away** *or* **off** *vt* abgießen; ~ **in** *vi* (*people*) hereinströmen; ~ **out** *vi* (*people*) herausströmen // *vt* (*drink*) einschenken; ~**ing** *a*: ~**ing rain** strömende(r) Regen *m*.

pout [paut] *vi* schmollen.

poverty ['pɒvətɪ] *n* Armut *f*; ~-**stricken** *a* verarmt, sehr arm.

powder ['paudə*] *n* Pulver *nt*; (*cosmetic*) Puder *m* // *vt* pulverisieren; **to ~ one's nose** sich (*dat*) die Nase

pudern; ~ **compact** *n* Puderdose *f*; ~**ed milk** *n* Milchpulver *nt*; ~ **room** *n* Damentoilette *f*; ~**y** *a* pulverig.

power [pauə*] *n* Macht *f* (*also POL*); (*ability*) Fähigkeit *f*; (*strength*) Stärke *f*; (*MATH*) Potenz *f*; (*ELEC*) Strom *m* // *vt* betreiben, antreiben; **to be in ~** (*POL etc*) an der Macht sein; ~ **cut**, (*US*) ~ **failure** *n* Stromausfall *m*; ~**ed** *a*: ~**ed by** betrieben mit; ~**ful** *a* (*person*) mächtig; (*engine, government*) stark; ~**less** *a* machtlos; ~ **point** *n* (*Brit*) elektrische(r) Anschluß *m*; ~ **station** *n* Elektrizitätswerk *nt*.

p.p. *abbr* (= *per procurationem*): ~ **J. Smith** i.A. J. Smith.

PR *abbr of* **public relations**.

practicable ['præktɪkəbl] *a* durchführbar.

practical *a*, ~**ly** *ad* ['præktɪkəl, -ɪ] praktisch; ~**ity** [-'kælɪtɪ] *n* (*of person*) praktische Veranlagung *f*; (*of situation etc*) Durchführbarkeit *f*; ~ **joke** *n* Streich *m*.

practice ['præktɪs] *n* Übung *f*; (*reality*) Praxis *f*; (*custom*) Brauch *m*; (*in business*) Usus *m*; (*doctor's, lawyer's*) Praxis *f* // *vti* (*US*) = **practise**; **in ~** (*in reality*) in der Praxis; **out of ~** außer Übung.

practise, (*US*) **practice** ['præktɪs] *vt* üben; (*profession*) ausüben // *vi* (sich) üben; (*doctor, lawyer*) praktizieren.

practising, (*US*) **practicing** ['præktɪsɪŋ] *a* praktizierend; (*Christian etc*) aktiv.

practitioner [præk'tɪʃənə*] *n* praktische(r) Arzt *m*.

pragmatic [præg'mætɪk] *a* pragmatisch.

prairie ['preərɪ] *n* Prärie *f*, Steppe *f*.

praise [preɪz] *n* Lob *nt* // *vt* loben; ~**worthy** *a* lobenswert.

pram [præm] *n* (*Brit*) Kinderwagen *m*.

prance [praːns] *vi* (*horse*) tänzeln; (*person*) stolzieren; (*gaily*) herumhüpfen.

prank [præŋk] *n* Streich *m*.

prattle ['prætl] *vi* schwatzen, plappern.

prawn [prɔːn] *n* Garnele *f*; Krabbe *f*.

pray [preɪ] *vi* beten; ~**er** [preə*] *n* Gebet *nt*.

preach [priːtʃ] *vi* predigen; ~**er** *n* Prediger *m*.

preamble [prɪ'æmbl] *n* Einleitung *f*.

precarious [prɪ'keərɪəs] *a* prekär, unsicher.

precaution [prɪ'kɔːʃən] *n* (Vorsichts)maßnahme *f*.

precede [prɪ'siːd] *vti* vorausgehen (+*dat*); ~**nce** ['presɪdəns] *n* Vorrang *m*; ~**nt** ['presɪdənt] *n* Präzedenzfall *m*.

preceding [prɪ'siːdɪŋ] *a* vorhergehend.

precept ['priːsept] *n* Gebot *nt*, Regel *f*.

precinct ['priːsɪŋkt] *n* (*US: district*) Bezirk *m*; (*round building*): ~**s** Gelände *nt*; (*area, environs*): ~**s** Umgebung *f*;

pedestrian ~ Fußgängerzone *f*; **shopping** ~ Geschäftsviertel *nt*.

precious ['preʃəs] *a* kostbar, wertvoll; (*affected*) preziös, geziert.

precipice ['presɪpɪs] *n* Abgrund *m*.

precipitate [prɪ'sɪpɪtɪt] *a* überstürzt, übereilt // *vt* [prɪ'sɪpɪteɪt] hinunterstürzen; (*events*) heraufbeschwören.

precise *a*, **~ly** *ad* [prɪ'saɪs, -lɪ] genau, präzis; **precision** [-'sɪʒən] *n* Präzision *f*.

preclude [prɪ'kluːd] *vt* ausschließen.

precocious [prɪ'kəʊʃəs] *a* frühreif.

preconceived ['priːkən'siːvd] *a* (*idea*) vorgefaßt.

precondition ['priːkən'dɪʃən] *n* Vorbedingung *f*, Voraussetzung *f*.

precursor [priː'kɜːsə*] *n* Vorläufer *m*.

predator ['predətə*] *n* Raubtier *nt*.

predecessor ['priːdɪsesə*] *n* Vorgänger *m*.

predestination [priːdestɪ'neɪʃən] *n* Vorherbestimmung *f*.

predicament [prɪ'dɪkəmənt] *n* mißliche Lage *f*.

predict [prɪ'dɪkt] *vt* voraussagen; **~able** *a* vorhersagbar; **~ion** [prɪ'dɪkʃən] *n* Voraussage *f*.

predominantly [prɪ'dɒmɪnəntlɪ] *ad* überwiegend, hauptsächlich.

predominate [prɪ'dɒmɪneɪt] *vi* vorherrschen; (*fig also*) überwiegen.

pre-eminent [priː'emɪnənt] *a* hervorragend, herausragend.

pre-empt [priː'empt] *vt* (*action, decision*) vorwegnehmen.

preen [priːn] *vt* putzen; **to** ~ **o.s.** (*person*) sich herausputzen.

prefab ['priːfæb] *n* Fertighaus *nt*.

prefabricated ['priːfæbrɪkeɪtɪd] *a* vorgefertigt, Fertig-.

preface ['prefɪs] *n* Vorwort *nt*.

prefect ['priːfekt] *n* Präfekt *m*; (*SCH*) Aufsichtsschüler(in *f*) *m*.

prefer [prɪ'fɜː*] *vt* vorziehen, lieber mögen; **to** ~ **to do sth etw lieber tun;** **~able** ['prefərəbl] *a* vorzuziehen(d) (*to dat*); **~ably** ['prefərəblɪ] *ad* vorzugsweise, am liebsten; **~ence** ['prefərəns] *n* Präferenz *f*, Vorzug *m*; **~ential** [prefə'renʃəl] *a* bevorzugt, Vorzugs-.

prefix ['priːfɪks] *n* Vorsilbe *f*, Präfix *nt*.

pregnancy ['pregnənsɪ] *n* Schwangerschaft *f*.

pregnant ['pregnənt] *a* schwanger.

prejudice ['predʒudɪs] *n* (*opinion*) Vorurteil *nt*; (*bias*) Voreingenommenheit *f*; (*harm*) Schaden *m* // *vt* beeinträchtigen; **~d** *a* (*person*) voreingenommen.

preliminary [prɪ'lɪmɪnərɪ] *a* einleitend, Vor-.

prelude ['preljuːd] *n* Vorspiel *nt*; (*fig also*) Auftakt *m*.

premarital ['priː'mærɪtl] *a* vorehelich.

premature ['premətʃʊə*] *a* vorzeitig, verfrüht; (*birth*) Früh-.

premeditated [priː'medɪteɪtɪd] *a* geplant; (*murder*) vorsätzlich.

premier ['premɪə*] *a* erste(r, s) // *n* Premier *m*.

première [premɪ'ɛə*] *n* Premiere *f*; Uraufführung *f*.

premise ['premɪs] *n* Voraussetzung *f*, Prämisse *f*; **~s** *pl* Räumlichkeiten *pl*; (*grounds*) Gelände *nt*; **on the ~s** im Hause.

premium ['priːmɪəm] *n* Prämie *f*; **to be at a ~** über pari stehen; ~ **bond** *n* (*Brit*) Prämienanleihe *f*.

premonition [premə'nɪʃən] *n* Vorahnung *f*.

preoccupation [priːɒkju'peɪʃən] *n* Sorge *f*.

preoccupied [priː'ɒkjupaɪd] *a* (*look*) geistesabwesend.

prep [prep] *n* (*SCH: study*) Hausaufgabe *f*; ~ **school** *n* = **preparatory school**.

prepaid ['priː'peɪd] *a* vorausbezahlt; (*letter*) frankiert.

preparation ['prepə'reɪʃən] *n* Vorbereitung *f*.

preparatory [prɪ'pærətərɪ] *a* Vor(bereitungs)-; ~ **school** *n* private Vorbereitungsschule für die Public School in Großbritannien oder die Hochschule in den USA.

prepare [prɪ'pɛə*] *vt* vorbereiten (*for* auf +*acc*) // *vi* sich vorbereiten; **to be ~d to ... bereit sein zu ...**

preponderance [prɪ'pɒndərəns] *n* Übergewicht *nt*.

preposition [prepə'zɪʃən] *n* Präposition *f*, Verhältniswort *nt*.

preposterous [prɪ'pɒstərəs] *a* absurd.

prerequisite ['priː'rekwɪzɪt] *n* (unerläßliche) Voraussetzung *f*.

prerogative [prɪ'rɒgətɪv] *n* Vorrecht *nt*.

Presbyterian [prezbɪ'tɪərɪən] *a* presbyterianisch // *n* Presbyterier(in *f*) *m*.

preschool ['priːskuːl] *a* Vorschul-.

prescribe [prɪs'kraɪb] *vt* vorschreiben; (*MED*) verschreiben.

prescription [prɪs'krɪpʃən] *n* (*MED*) Rezept *nt*.

presence ['prezns] *n* Gegenwart *f*; ~ **of mind** *n* Geistesgegenwart *f*.

present ['preznt] *a* (*here*) anwesend; (*current*) gegenwärtig // *n* Gegenwart *f*; (*gift*) Geschenk *nt* // *vt* [prɪ'zent] vorlegen; (*introduce*) vorstellen; (*show*) zeigen; (*give*): **to ~ sb with sth jdm etw überreichen; at ~ im Augenblick;** **~able** [prɪ'zentəbl] *a* präsentabel; **~ation** *n* Überreichung *f*, präsentabel; **~ation** *n* Überreichung *f*; **~-day** *a* heutig; **~er** *n* (*RADIO, TV*) Moderator(in *f*) *m*; **~ly** *ad* bald; (*at present*) im Augenblick.

preservation [prezə'veɪʃən] *n* Erhaltung *f*.

preservative [prɪ'zɜːvətɪv] n Konservierungsmittel nt.

preserve [prɪ'zɜːv] vt erhalten; (food) einmachen // n (jam) Eingemachte(s) nt; (hunting) Schutzgebiet nt.

preside [prɪ'zaɪd] vi den Vorsitz haben.

presidency ['prezɪdənsɪ] n (POL) Präsidentschaft f.

president ['prezɪdənt] n Präsident m; ~ial [prezɪ'denʃəl] a Präsidenten-; (election) Präsidentschafts-; (system) Präsidial-.

press [pres] n Presse f; (printing house) Druckerei f // vt drücken; (iron) bügeln; (urge) (be)drängen // vi (push) drücken; to be ~ed for time unter Zeitdruck stehen; to ~ for sth drängen auf etw (acc); ~ on vi vorwärtsdrängen; ~ agency n Presseagentur f; ~ conference n Pressekonferenz f; ~ing a dringend; ~-stud n (Brit) Druckknopf m; ~-up n (Brit) Liegestütz m.

pressure ['preʃə*] n Druck m; ~ cooker n Schnellkochtopf m; ~ gauge n Druckmesser m.

pressurized ['preʃəraɪzd] a Druck-.

prestigious [pres'tɪdʒəs] a Prestige-.

presumably [prɪ'zjuːməblɪ] ad vermutlich.

presume [prɪ'zjuːm] vti annehmen; to ~ to do sth sich erlauben, etw zu tun.

presumption [prɪ'zʌmpʃən] n Annahme f.

presumptuous [prɪ'zʌmptjʊəs] a anmaßend.

presuppose [priːsə'pəʊz] vt voraussetzen.

pretence, (US) **pretense** [prɪ'tens] n Vorgabe f, Vortäuschung f; (false claim) Vorwand m.

pretend [prɪ'tend] vt vorgeben, so tun als ob ... // vi so tun; to ~ to sth Anspruch erheben auf etw (acc).

pretense [prɪ'tens] n (US) = **pretence.**

pretension [prɪ'tenʃən] n Anspruch m; (impudent claim) Anmaßung f.

pretentious [prɪ'tenʃəs] a angeberisch.

pretext ['priːtekst] n Vorwand m.

pretty ['prɪtɪ] a hübsch // ad (col) ganz schön.

prevail [prɪ'veɪl] vi siegen (against, over über +acc); (custom) vorherrschen; to ~ (up)on sb to do sth jdn dazu bewegen, etw zu tun; ~ing a vorherrschend.

prevalent ['prevələnt] a vorherrschend.

prevent [prɪ'vent] vt (stop) verhindern, verhüten; to ~ sb from doing sth jdn (daran) hindern, etw zu tun; ~ative n Vorbeugungsmittel nt; ~ion [prɪ'venʃən] n Verhütung f, Schutz m (of gegen); ~ive a vorbeugend, Schutz-.

preview ['priːvjuː] n private Voraufführung f; (trailer) Vorschau f.

previous ['priːvɪəs] a früher, vorherig;

~ly ad früher.

prewar ['priː'wɔː*] a Vorkriegs-.

prey [preɪ] n Beute f; ~ on vt Jagd machen auf (+acc); it was ~ing on his mind es quälte sein Gewissen.

price [praɪs] n Preis m; (value) Wert m // vt (label) auszeichnen; ~less a (lit, fig) unbezahlbar; ~ list n Preisliste f.

prick [prɪk] n Stich m // vti stechen; to ~ up one's ears die Ohren spitzen.

prickle ['prɪkl] n Stachel m, Dorn m.

prickly ['prɪklɪ] a stachelig; (fig: person) reizbar; ~ heat n Hitzebläschen pl.

pride [praɪd] n Stolz m; (arrogance) Hochmut m // vt: to ~ o.s. on sth auf etw (acc) stolz sein.

priest [priːst] n Priester m; ~ess n Priesterin f; ~hood n Priesteramt nt.

prig [prɪg] n Selbstgefällige(r) mf.

prim [prɪm] a prüde.

primarily ['praɪmərɪlɪ] ad vorwiegend.

primary ['praɪmərɪ] a (main) Haupt-; (SCH) Grund-; ~ school n (Brit) Grundschule f.

prime [praɪm] a erste(r, s); (excellent) erstklassig // vt vorbereiten; (gun) laden; **in the ~ of life** in der Blüte der Jahre; **P~ Minister (P.M.)** n Premierminister m, Ministerpräsident m; ~r n Fibel f.

primeval [praɪ'miːvəl] a vorzeitlich; (forests) Ur-.

primitive ['prɪmɪtɪv] a primitiv.

primrose ['prɪmrəʊz] n (gelbe) Primel f.

primus (stove) ['praɪməs (stəʊv)] n ® (Brit) Primuskocher m.

prince [prɪns] n Prinz m; (ruler) Fürst m; **princess** [prɪn'ses] n Prinzessin f; Fürstin f.

principal ['prɪnsɪpəl] a Haupt- // n (SCH) (Schul)direktor m, Rektor m; (money) (Grund)kapital nt; ~ity [prɪnsɪ'pælɪtɪ] n Fürstentum nt.

principle ['prɪnsəpl] n Grundsatz m, Prinzip nt; **in** ~ im Prinzip; **on** ~ aus Prinzip, prinzipiell.

print [prɪnt] n Druck m; (made by feet, fingers) Abdruck m; (PHOT) Abzug m // vt drucken; (name) in Druckbuchstaben schreiben; (Photo) abziehen; **out of** ~ vergriffen; ~ed matter n Drucksache f; ~er n Drucker m; ~ing n Drucken nt; (of photos) Abziehen nt; ~out n (COMPUT) Ausdruck m.

prior ['praɪə*] a früher // n Prior m; ~ to sth vor etw (dat); ~ to going abroad, she had ... bevor sie ins Ausland ging, hatte sie ...

priority [praɪ'ɒrɪtɪ] n Vorrang m; Priorität f.

prise [praɪz] vt: to ~ open aufbrechen.

prison ['prɪzn] n Gefängnis nt // a Gefängnis-; (system etc) Strafvollzugs-; ~er n Gefangene(r) mf.

pristine ['pristi:n] *a* makellos.

privacy ['privəsi] *n* Ungestörtheit *f*, Ruhe *f*; Privatleben *nt*.

private ['praivit] *a* privat, Privat-; (*secret*) vertraulich, geheim // *n* einfache(r) Soldat *m*; '~' (*on envelope*) persönlich; **in ~** privat, unter vier Augen; **~ enterprise** *n* Privatunternehmen *nt*; **~ eye** *n* Privatdetektiv *m*; **~ly** *ad* privat; vertraulich, geheim; **~ property** *n* Privatbesitz *m*; **~ school** *n* Privatschule *f*; **privatize** *vt* privatisieren.

privet ['privit] *n* Liguster *m*.

privilege ['privilidʒ] *n* Privileg *nt*; **~d** *a* bevorzugt, privilegiert.

privy ['privi] *a* geheim, privat; **P~ Council** *n* Geheime(r) Staatsrat *m*.

prize [praiz] *n* Preis *m* // *a* (*example*) erstklassig; (*idiot*) Voll- // *vt* (hoch)schätzen; **~ giving** *n* Preisverteilung *f*; **~winner** *n* Preisträger(in *f*) *m*.

pro [prəʊ] *n* (*professional*) Profi *m*; **the ~s and cons** *pl* das Für und Wider.

probability [probə'biliti] *n* Wahrscheinlichkeit *f*.

probable *a*, **probably** *ad* ['probəbl, -bli] wahrscheinlich.

probation [prə'beiʃən] *n* Probe(zeit) *f*; (*JUR*) Bewährung *f*; **on ~** auf Probe; auf Bewährung.

probe [prəʊb] *n* Sonde *f*; (*enquiry*) Untersuchung *f* // *vti* erforschen.

problem ['probləm] *n* Problem *nt*; **~atic** [problɪ'mætik] *a* problematisch.

procedure [prə'si:dʒə*] *n* Verfahren *nt*.

proceed [prə'si:d] *vi* (*advance*) vorrücken; (*start*) anfangen; (*carry on*) fortfahren; (*set about*) vorgehen; **~ings** *pl* Verfahren *nt*; **~s** ['prəʊsi:dz] *pl* Erlös *m*.

process ['prəʊses] *n* Prozeß *m*; (*method*) Verfahren *nt* // *vt* bearbeiten; (*food*) verarbeiten; (*film*) entwickeln; **~ing** *n* (*PHOT*) Entwickeln *nt*.

procession [prə'seʃən] *n* Prozession *f*, Umzug *m*; **funeral ~** Trauerprozession *f*.

proclaim [prə'kleim] *vt* verkünden.

proclamation [proklə'meiʃən] *n* Verkündung *f*.

procrastinate [prəʊ'kræstineit] *vi* zaudern.

procreation [prəʊkri'eiʃən] *n* (Er)zeugung *f*.

procure [prə'kjʊə*] *vt* beschaffen.

prod [prod] *vt* stoßen // *n* Stoß *m*.

prodigal ['prodigəl] *a* verschwenderisch (*of* mit).

prodigious [prə'didʒəs] *a* gewaltig; (*wonderful*) wunderbar.

prodigy ['prodidʒi] *n* Wunder *nt*.

produce ['prodju:s] *n* (*AGR*) (Boden)produkte *pl*, (Natur)erzeugnis *nt* // *vt* [prə'dju:s] herstellen, produzieren; (*cause*) hervorrufen; (*farmer*) erzeugen; (*yield*) liefern, bringen; (*play*) inszenieren; **~r** *n* Erzeuger *m*, Hersteller *m*, Produzent *m* (*also CINE*).

product ['prodʌkt] *n* Produkt *nt*, Erzeugnis *nt*.

production [prə'dʌkʃən] *n* Produktion *f*, Herstellung *f*; (*thing*) Erzeugnis *nt*, Produkt *nt*; (*THEAT*) Inszenierung *f*; **~ line** *n* Fließband *nt*.

productive [prə'dʌktiv] *a* produktiv; (*fertile*) ertragreich, fruchtbar.

productivity [prodʌk'tiviti] *n* Produktivität *f*.

profess [prə'fes] *vt* bekennen; (*show*) zeigen; (*claim to be*) vorgeben.

profession [prə'feʃən] *n* Beruf *m*; (*declaration*) Bekenntnis *nt*; **~al** [prə'feʃənl] *n* Fachmann *m*; (*SPORT*) Berufsspieler(in *f*) *m* // *a* Berufs-; (*expert*) fachlich; (*player*) professionell.

professor [prə'fesə*] *n* Professor *m*.

proficiency [prə'fiʃənsi] *n* Können *nt*.

proficient [prə'fiʃənt] *a* fähig.

profile ['prəʊfail] *n* Profil *nt*; (*fig: report*) Kurzbiographie *f*.

profit ['profit] *n* Gewinn *m* // *vi* profitieren (*by, from* von); **~ability** [profitə'biliti] *n* Rentabilität *f*; **~able** *a* einträglich, rentabel.

profiteering [profi'tiəriŋ] *n* Profitmacherei *f*.

profound [prə'faʊnd] *a* tief.

profuse [prə'fju:s] *a* überreich; **~ly** *ad* überschwenglich; (*sweat*) reichlich.

profusion [prə'fju:ʒən] *n* Überfülle *f*, Überfluß *m* (*of* an +*dat*).

progeny ['prodʒini] *n* Nachkommenschaft *f*.

programme, (*US*) **program** ['prəʊgræm] *n* Programm *nt* // *vt* planen; (*computer*) programmieren.

programmer ['prəʊgræmə*] *n* Programmierer(in *f*) *m*.

programming, (*US*) **programing** ['prəʊgræmiŋ] *n* Programmieren *nt*.

progress ['prəʊgres] *n* Fortschritt *m* // *vi* [prə'gres] fortschreiten, weitergehen; **in ~** im Gang; **~ion** [prə'greʃən] *n* Folge *f*; **~ive** [prə'gresiv] *a* fortschrittlich, progressiv.

prohibit [prə'hibit] *vt* verbieten; **to ~ sb from doing sth** jdm untersagen, etw zu tun; **~ion** [prəʊi'biʃən] *n* Verbot *nt*; (*US*) Alkoholverbot *nt*, Prohibition *f*; **~ive** *a* (*price etc*) unerschwinglich.

project ['prodʒekt] *n* Projekt *nt* // *v* [prə'dʒekt] *vt* vorausplanen; (*film etc*) projizieren; (*personality, voice*) zum Tragen bringen // *vi* (*stick out*) hervorragen, (her)vorstehen.

projectile [prə'dʒektail] *n* Geschoß *nt*.

projection [prə'dʒekʃən] *n* Projektion *f*; (*sth prominent*) Vorsprung *m*.

projector [prə'dʒektə*] *n* Projektor *m*.

proletariat [prəʊlə'teəriət] *n* Proletariat

nt.

proliferate [prə'lıfəreıt] *vi* sich vermehren.

prolific [prə'lıfık] *a* fruchtbar; (*author etc*) produktiv.

prologue ['prəʊlɒg] *n* Prolog *m*; (*event*) Vorspiel *nt*.

prolong [prə'lɒŋ] *vt* verlängern.

prom [prɒm] *n abbr of* **promenade** *and* **promenade concert** // *n* (*US: college ball*) Studentenball *m*.

promenade [prɒmı'nɑ:d] *n* Promenade *f*; ~ **concert** *n* Promenadenkonzert *nt*.

prominence ['prɒmınəns] *n* (große) Bedeutung *f*.

prominent ['prɒmınənt] *a* bedeutend; (*politician*) prominent; (*easily seen*) herausragend, auffallend.

promiscuous [prə'mıskjʊəs] *a* lose.

promise ['prɒmıs] *n* Versprechen *nt*; (*hope*) Aussicht *f* (*of* auf + *acc*) // *vti* versprechen.

promising ['prɒmısıŋ] *a* vielversprechend.

promontory ['prɒməntrı] *n* Vorsprung *m*.

promote [prə'məʊt] *vt* befördern; (*help on*) fördern, unterstützen; ~**r** *n* (*in sport, entertainment*) Veranstalter *m*; (*for charity etc*) Organisator *m*.

promotion [prə'məʊʃən] *n* (*in rank*) Beförderung *f*; (*furtherance*) Förderung *f*; (*COMM*) Werbung *f* (*of* für).

prompt [prɒmpt] *a* prompt, schnell // *ad* (*punctually*) genau // *n* (*COMPUT*) Meldung *f* // *vt* veranlassen; (*THEAT*) soufflieren (+ *dat*); to ~ sb to do sth jdn dazu veranlassen, etw zu tun; ~**ly** *ad* sofort.

prone [prəʊn] *a* hingestreckt; to be ~ to sth zu etw neigen.

prong [prɒŋ] *n* Zinke *f*.

pronoun ['prəʊnaʊn] *n* Fürwort *nt*.

pronounce [prə'naʊns] *vt* aussprechen; (*JUR*) verkünden // *vi* (*give an opinion*) sich äußern (*on* zu); ~**d** *a* ausgesprochen; ~**ment** *n* Erklärung *f*.

pronunciation [prənʌnsı'eıʃən] *n* Aussprache *f*.

proof [pru:f] *n* Beweis *m*; (*PRINT*) Korrekturfahne *f*; (*of alcohol*) Alkoholgehalt *m* // *a* sicher.

prop [prɒp] *n* Stütze *f* (*also fig*); (*THEAT*) Requisit *nt* // *vt* (*also:* ~ up) (ab)stützen.

propaganda [prɒpə'gændə] *n* Propaganda *f*.

propagate ['prɒpəgeıt] *vt* fortpflanzen; (*news*) propagieren, verbreiten.

propel [prə'pel] *vt* (an)treiben; ~**ler** *n* Propeller *m*; ~**ling pencil** *n* Drehbleistift *m*.

propensity [prə'pensıtı] *n* Tendenz *f*.

proper ['prɒpə*] *a* richtig; (*seemly*) schicklich; ~**ly** *ad* richtig; ~ **noun** *n* Eigenname *m*.

property ['prɒpətı] *n* Eigentum *nt*; (*quality*) Eigenschaft *f*; (*land*) Grundbesitz *m*; ~ **owner** *n* Grundbesitzer *m*.

prophecy ['prɒfısı] *n* Prophezeiung *f*.

prophesy ['prɒfısaı] *vt* prophezeien.

prophet ['prɒfıt] *n* Prophet *m*.

proportion [prə'pɔ:ʃən] *n* Verhältnis *nt*; (*share*) Teil *m* // *vt* abstimmen (*to* auf + *acc*); ~**al** *a* proportional; ~**ate** *a* verhältnismäßig.

proposal [prə'pəʊzl] *n* Vorschlag *m*; (*of marriage*) Heiratsantrag *m*.

propose [prə'pəʊz] *vt* vorschlagen; (*toast*) ausbringen // *vi* (*offer marriage*) einen Heiratsantrag machen; to ~ to do sth beabsichtigen, etw zu tun.

proposition [prɒpə'zıʃən] *n* Angebot *nt*; (*statement*) Satz *m*.

proprietor [prə'praıətə*] *n* Besitzer *m*, Eigentümer *m*.

propriety [prə'praıətı] *n* Anstand *m*.

pro rata [prəʊ'rɑ:tə] *ad* anteilmäßig.

prose [prəʊz] *n* Prosa *f*.

prosecute ['prɒsıkju:t] *vt* (strafrechtlich) verfolgen.

prosecution [prɒsı'kju:ʃən] *n* (*JUR*) strafrechtliche Verfolgung *f*; (*party*) Anklage *f*.

prosecutor ['prɒsıkju:tə*] *n* Vertreter *m* der Anklage; **Public P~** *n* Staatsanwalt *m*.

prospect ['prɒspekt] *n* Aussicht *f* // *v* [prəs'pekt] *vt* auf Bodenschätze hin untersuchen // *vi* suchen (*for* nach); ~**ing** [prəs'pektıŋ] *n* (*for minerals*) Suche *f*; ~**ive** [prəs'pektıv] *a* möglich; ~**or** [prəs'pektə*] *n* (Gold)sucher *m*; ~**us** [prəs'pektəs] *n* (Werbe)prospekt *m*.

prosper ['prɒspə*] *vi* blühen, gedeihen; (*person*) erfolgreich sein; ~**ity** [prɒs'perıtı] *n* Wohlstand *m*; ~**ous** *a* wohlhabend, reich.

prostitute ['prɒstıtju:t] *n* Prostituierte *f*.

prostrate ['prɒstreıt] *a* ausgestreckt (liegend); ~ **with grief/exhaustion** von Schmerz/Erschöpfung übermannt.

protagonist [prəʊ'tægənıst] *n* Hauptperson *f*, Held *m*.

protect [prə'tekt] *vt* (be)schützen; ~**ion** [prə'tekʃən] *n* Schutz *m*; ~**ive** *a* Schutz-, (be)schützend.

protégé ['prɒteʒeı] *n* Schützling *m*.

protein ['prəʊti:n] *n* Protein *nt*, Eiweiß *nt*.

protest ['prəʊtest] *n* Protest *m* // *v* [prə'test] *vi* protestieren (*against* gegen) // *vt* (*affirm*) beteuern.

Protestant ['prɒtıstənt] *a* protestantisch // *n* Protestant(in *f*) *m*.

protracted [prə'træktıd] *a* sich hinziehend.

protrude [prə'tru:d] *vi* (her)vorstehen.

proud [praʊd] *a* stolz (*of* auf + *acc*).

prove [pru:v] *vt* beweisen // *vi*: **to ~ (to be) correct** sich als richtig erweisen; **to ~ o.s.** sich bewähren.
proverb ['prɒvɜ:b] *n* Sprichwort *nt*; **~ial** [prə'vɜ:bɪəl] *a* sprichwörtlich.
provide [prə'vaɪd] *vt* versehen; (*supply*) besorgen; **to ~ sb with sth** jdn mit etw versorgen; **~ for** *vt* sorgen für; (*emergency*) Vorkehrungen treffen für; **~d (that)** *cj* vorausgesetzt (, daß); **Providence** ['prɒvɪdəns] *n* die Vorsehung.
providing [prə'vaɪdɪŋ] *cj* vorausgesetzt (, daß).
province ['prɒvɪns] *n* Provinz *f*; (*division of work*) Bereich *m*.
provincial [prə'vɪnʃəl] *a* provinziell, Provinz-.
provision [prə'vɪʒən] *n* Vorkehrung *f*; (*condition*) Bestimmung *f*; **~s** *pl* (*food*) Vorräte *pl*, Proviant *m*; **~al** *a* provisorisch.
proviso [prə'vaɪzəʊ] *n* Bedingung *f*.
provoke [prə'vəʊk] *vt* provozieren; (*cause*) hervorrufen.
prow [praʊ] *n* Bug *m*.
prowess ['praʊes] *n* überragende(s) Können *nt*.
prowl [praʊl] *vi* herumstreichen; (*animal*) schleichen // *n*: **on the ~** umherstreifend; **~er** *n* Eindringling *m*.
proximity [prɒk'sɪmɪtɪ] *n* Nähe *f*.
proxy ['prɒksɪ] *n* (*Stell*)vertreter *m*; (*document*) Vollmacht *f*; **by ~** durch einen Stellvertreter.
prudence ['pru:dəns] *n* Umsicht *f*.
prudent ['pru:dənt] *a* klug, umsichtig.
prudish ['pru:dɪʃ] *a* prüde.
prune [pru:n] *n* Backpflaume *f* // *vt* ausputzen; (*fig*) zurechtstutzen.
pry [praɪ] *vi* seine Nase stecken (*into* in +*acc*).
PS *abbr* (= *postscript*) PS.
pseudo- ['sju:dəʊ] *pref* Pseudo-; **pseudonym** ['sju:dənɪm] *n* Pseudonym *nt*, Deckname *m*.
psychiatrist [saɪ'kaɪətrɪst] *n* Psychiater *m*.
psychic ['saɪkɪk] *a* (*also*: **~al**) übersinnlich; (*person*) paranormal begabt.
psychoanalyse, (*US*) **psychoanalyze** [saɪkəʊ'ænəlaɪz] *vt* psychoanalytisch behandeln.
psychoanalyst [saɪkəʊ'ænəlɪst] *n* Psychoanalytiker(in *f*) *m*.
psychological [saɪkə'lɒdʒɪkəl] *a* psychologisch.
psychologist [saɪ'kɒlədʒɪst] *n* Psychologe *m*, Psychologin *f*.
psychology [saɪ'kɒlədʒɪ] *n* Psychologie *f*.
PTO *abbr* (= *please turn over*).
pub [pʌb] *n abbr* (= *public house*) Kneipe *f*.
pubic ['pju:bɪk] *a* Scham-.
public ['pʌblɪk] *a* öffentlich // *n* (*also:*

general ~) Öffentlichkeit *f*; **in ~** in der Öffentlichkeit; **~ address system (P.A.)** *n* Lautsprecheranlage *f*; **~ly** *ad* öffentlich.
publican ['pʌblɪkən] *n* Wirt *m*.
publication [pʌblɪ'keɪʃən] *n* Veröffentlichung *f*.
public: **~ company** *n* Aktiengesellschaft *f*; **~ convenience** *n* (*Brit*) öffentliche Toiletten *pl*; **~ holiday** *n* gesetzliche(r) Feiertag *m*; **~ house** *n* (*Brit*) Lokal *nt*, Kneipe *f*.
publicity [pʌb'lɪsɪtɪ] *n* Publicity *f*, Werbung *f*.
publicize ['pʌblɪsaɪz] *vt* bekannt machen; (*advertise*) Publicity machen für.
public: **~ opinion** *n* öffentliche Meinung *f*; **~ relations (PR)** *pl* Public Relations *pl*; **~ school** *n* (*Brit*) Privatschule *f*; (*US*) staatliche Schule *f*; **~-spirited** *a* mit Gemeinschaftssinn; **~ transport** *n* öffentliche Verkehrsmittel *pl*.
publish ['pʌblɪʃ] *vt* veröffentlichen; (*event*) bekanntgeben; **~er** *n* Verleger *m*; **~ing** *n* (*business*) Verlagswesen *nt*.
puce [pju:s] *a* violettbraun.
pucker ['pʌkə*] *vt* (*face*) verziehen; (*lips*) kräuseln.
pudding ['pʊdɪŋ] *n* (*Brit*: *course*) Nachtisch *m*; Pudding *m*; **black ~** ≈ Blutwurst *f*.
puddle ['pʌdl] *n* Pfütze *f*.
puff [pʌf] *n* (*of wind etc*) Stoß *m*; (*cosmetic*) Puderquaste *f* // *vi* blasen, pusten; (*pipe*) paffen // *vi* keuchen, schnaufen; (*smoke*) paffen; **to ~ out smoke** Rauch ausstoßen; **~ed** *a* (*col*: *out of breath*) außer Puste.
puff pastry, (*US*) **puff paste** ['pʌf'peɪstrɪ, 'pʌf'peɪst] *n* Blätterteig *m*.
puffy ['pʌfɪ] *a* aufgedunsen.
pull [pʊl] *n* Ruck *m*; (*influence*) Beziehung *f* // *vt* ziehen; (*trigger*) abdrücken // *vi* ziehen; **to ~ sb's leg** jdn auf den Arm nehmen; **to ~ to pieces** (*lit*) in Stücke reißen; (*fig*) verreißen; **to ~ one's punches** sich zurückhalten; **to ~ one's weight** sich in die Riemen legen; **to ~ o.s. together** sich zusammenreißen; **~ apart** *vt* (*break*) zerreißen; (*dismantle*) auseinandernehmen; (*fighters*) trennen; **~ down** *vt* (*house*) abreißen; **~ in** *vi* hineinfahren; (*stop*) anhalten; (*RAIL*) einfahren; **~ off** *vt* (*deal etc*) abschließen; **~ out** *vi* (*car*) herausfahren; (*fig*: *partner*) aussteigen // *vt* herausziehen; **~ over** *vi* (*AUT*) an die Seite fahren; **~ round**, **~ through** *vi* durchkommen; **~ up** *vi* anhalten // *vt* (*uproot*) herausreißen; (*stop*) anhalten.
pulley ['pʊlɪ] *n* Rolle *f*, Flaschenzug *m*.
pullover ['pʊləʊvə*] *n* Pullover *m*.
pulp [pʌlp] *n* Brei *m*; (*of fruit*) Fruchtfleisch *nt*.

pulpit ['pʊlpɪt] n Kanzel f.
pulsate [pʌl'seɪt] vi pulsieren.
pulse [pʌls] n Puls m.
pummel ['pʌml] vt mit den Fäusten bearbeiten.
pump [pʌmp] n Pumpe f; (shoe) leichter (Tanz)schuh m // vt pumpen; ~ **up** vt (tyre) aufpumpen.
pumpkin ['pʌmpkɪn] n Kürbis m.
pun [pʌn] n Wortspiel nt.
punch [pʌntʃ] n (tool) Locher m; (blow) (Faust)schlag m; (drink) Punsch m, Bowle f // vt lochen; (strike) schlagen, boxen; ~**line** n Pointe f; ~-**up** n (Brit col) Keilerei f.
punctual ['pʌŋktjʊəl] a pünktlich.
punctuate ['pʌŋktjʊeɪt] vt mit Satzzeichen versehen; (fig) unterbrechen.
punctuation [pʌŋktjʊ'eɪʃən] n Zeichensetzung f, Interpunktion f.
puncture ['pʌŋktʃə*] n Loch nt; (AUT) Reifenpanne f // vt durchbohren.
pundit ['pʌndɪt] n Gelehrte(r) m.
pungent ['pʌndʒənt] a scharf.
punish ['pʌnɪʃ] vt bestrafen; (in boxing etc) übel zurichten; ~**ment** n Strafe f; (action) Bestrafung f.
punk [pʌŋk] n (also: ~ **rocker**) Punker(in f) m; (also: ~ **rock**) Punk m; (US col: hoodlum) Ganove m.
punt [pʌnt] n Stechkahn m.
punter ['pʌntə*] n (Brit: better) Wetter m.
puny ['pju:nɪ] a kümmerlich.
pup [pʌp] n = **puppy**.
pupil ['pju:pl] n Schüler(in f) m; (in eye) Pupille f.
puppet ['pʌpɪt] n Puppe f; Marionette f.
puppy ['pʌpɪ] n junge(r) Hund m.
purchase ['pɜ:tʃɪs] n Kauf m; (grip) Halt m // vt kaufen, erwerben; ~**r** n Käufer(in f) m.
pure [pjʊə*] a rein (also fig); ~**ly** ['pjʊəlɪ] ad rein.
purgatory ['pɜ:gətərɪ] n Fegefeuer nt.
purge [pɜ:dʒ] n Säuberung f (also POL); (medicine) Abführmittel nt // vt reinigen; (body) entschlacken.
purify ['pjʊərɪfaɪ] vt reinigen.
purity ['pjʊərɪtɪ] n Reinheit f.
purl [pɜ:l] n linke Masche f.
purple ['pɜ:pl] a violett; (face) dunkelrot.
purport [pɜ:'pɔ:t] vi vorgeben.
purpose ['pɜ:pəs] n Zweck m, Ziel nt; (of person) Absicht f; on ~ absichtlich; ~**ful** a zielbewußt, entschlossen.
purr [pɜ:*] n Schnurren nt // vi schnurren.
purse [pɜ:s] n Portemonnaie nt, Geldbeutel m // vt (lips) zusammenpressen, schürzen.
purser ['pɜ:sə*] n Zahlmeister m.
pursue [pə'sju:] vt verfolgen; (study) nachgehen (+dat); ~**r** n Verfolger m.

pursuit [pə'sju:t] n Verfolgung f; (occupation) Beschäftigung f.
purveyor [pɜ:'veɪə*] n Lieferant m.
pus [pʌs] n Eiter m.
push [pʊʃ] n Stoß m, Schub m; (MIL) Vorstoß m // vt stoßen, schieben; (button) drücken; (idea) durchsetzen // vi stoßen, schieben; ~ **aside** vt beiseiteschieben; ~ **off** vi (col) abschieben; ~ **on** vi weitermachen; ~ **through** vt durchdrücken; (policy) durchsetzen; ~ **up** vt (total) erhöhen; (prices) hochtreiben; ~**chair** n (Brit) (Kinder)sportwagen m; ~**over** n (col) Kinderspiel nt; ~-**up** n (US: press-up) Liegestütz m; ~**y** a (col) aufdringlich.
puss [pʊs], **pussy(-cat)** ['pʊsɪ(kæt)] n Mieze(katze) f.
put [pʊt], pt, pp **put** vt setzen, stellen, legen; (express) ausdrücken, sagen; (write) schreiben; ~ **about** vi (turn back) wenden // vt (spread) verbreiten; ~ **across** vt (explain) erklären; ~ **away** vt weglegen; (store) beiseitelegen; ~ **back** vt zurückstellen or -legen; ~ **by** vt zurücklegen, sparen; ~ **down** vt hinstellen or -legen; (rebellion) niederschlagen; (animal) einschläfern; (in writing) niederschreiben; ~ **forward** vt (idea) vorbringen; (clock) vorstellen; ~ **in** vt (application, complaint) einreichen; ~ **off** vt verschieben; (discourage) abbringen von; ~ **on** vt (clothes etc) anziehen; (light etc) anschalten, anmachen; (play etc) aufführen; (brake) anziehen; ~ **out** vt (hand etc) (her)ausstrecken; (news, rumour) verbreiten; (light etc) ausschalten, ausmachen; ~ **up** vt (tent) aufstellen; (building) errichten; (price) erhöhen; (person) unterbringen; to ~ **up with** sich abfinden mit.
putrid ['pju:trɪd] a faul.
putt [pʌt] n (golf) putten // n (golf) Putten nt; ~**ing green** n Rasenfläche f zum Putten.
putty ['pʌtɪ] n Kitt m; (fig) Wachs nt.
put-up ['pʊtʌp] a: ~ **job** abgekartete(s) Spiel nt.
puzzle ['pʌzl] n Rätsel nt; (toy) Geduldspiel nt // vt verwirren // vi sich den Kopf zerbrechen.
puzzling ['pʌzlɪŋ] a rätselhaft, verwirrend.
pyjamas [pɪ'dʒɑ:məz] npl (Brit) Schlafanzug m, Pyjama m.
pylon ['paɪlən] n Mast m.

Q

quack [kwæk] n Quaken nt; (doctor) Quacksalber m // vi quaken.
quad [kwɒd] abbr of **quadrangle**; **quadruplet**.

quadrangle ['kwɒdræŋgl] n (court) Hof m; (MATH) Viereck nt.

quadruple ['kwɒ'dru:pl] a vierfach // vi sich vervierfachen // vt vervierfachen.

quadruplets [kwɒ'dru:pləts] npl Vierlinge pl.

quagmire ['kwægmaɪə*] n Morast m.

quail [kweɪl] n (bird) Wachtel f // vi (vor Angst) zittern.

quaint [kweɪnt] a kurios; malerisch.

quake [kweɪk] vi beben, zittern // n abbr of **earthquake**.

Quaker ['kweɪkə*] n Quäker(in f) m.

qualification [kwɒlɪfɪ'keɪʃən] n Qualifikation f; (sth which limits) Einschränkung f.

qualified ['kwɒlɪfaɪd] a (competent) qualifiziert; (limited) bedingt.

qualify ['kwɒlɪfaɪ] vt (prepare) befähigen; (limit) einschränken // vi sich qualifizieren (for für); to ~ as a doctor/lawyer sein juristisches/medizinisches Staatsexamen machen.

quality ['kwɒlɪtɪ] n Qualität f; (characteristic) Eigenschaft f.

qualm [kwɑ:m] n Bedenken nt.

quandary ['kwɒndərɪ] n: to be in a ~ in Verlegenheit sein.

quantity ['kwɒntɪtɪ] n Menge f; ~ surveyor n Baukostenkalkulator m.

quarantine ['kwɒrənti:n] n Quarantäne f.

quarrel ['kwɒrəl] n Streit m // vi sich streiten; ~some a streitsüchtig.

quarry ['kwɒrɪ] n Steinbruch m; (animal) Wild nt; (fig) Opfer nt.

quart [kwɔ:t] n Quart nt.

quarter ['kwɔ:tə*] n Viertel nt; (of year) Quartal nt // vt (divide) vierteln; (MIL) einquartieren; ~s pl (esp MIL) Quartier nt; ~ of an hour n Viertelstunde f; ~ final n Viertelfinale nt; ~ly a vierteljährlich; ~master n Quartiermeister m.

quash [kwɒʃ] vt (verdict) aufheben.

quasi- ['kwɑ:zɪ] pref Quasi-.

quaver ['kweɪvə*] n (Brit MUS) Achtelnote f // vi (tremble) zittern.

quay [ki:] n Kai m.

queasy ['kwi:zɪ] a übel.

queen [kwi:n] n Königin f; ~ mother n Königinmutter f.

queer [kwɪə*] a seltsam // n (col: homosexual) Schwule(r) m.

quell [kwel] vt unterdrücken.

quench [kwentʃ] vt (thirst) löschen.

querulous ['kwerʊləs] a nörglerisch.

query ['kwɪərɪ] n (question) (An)frage f; (question mark) Fragezeichen nt // vt in Zweifel ziehen, in Frage stellen.

quest [kwest] n Suche f.

question ['kwestʃən] n Frage f // vt (ask) (be)fragen; (suspect) verhören; (doubt) in Frage stellen, bezweifeln; beyond ~ ohne Frage; out of the ~ ausgeschlossen; ~able a zweifelhaft; ~ mark n Fragezeichen nt.

questionnaire [kwestʃə'neə*] n Fragebogen m.

queue [kju:] n (Brit) Schlange f // vi (also: ~ up) Schlange stehen.

quibble ['kwɪbl] vi kleinlich sein.

quick [kwɪk] a schnell // n (of nail) Nagelhaut f; cut to the ~ (fig) tief getroffen; be ~! mach schnell!; ~en vt (hasten) beschleunigen // vi sich beschleunigen; ~ly a schnell; ~sand n Treibsand m; ~witted a schlagfertig.

quid [kwɪd] n (Brit col: £1) Pfund nt.

quiet ['kwaɪət] a (without noise) leise; (peaceful, calm) still, ruhig // n Stille f, Ruhe f // vt, vi (US) = ~en; keep ~! sei still!; ~en (also: ~en down) vi ruhig werden // vt beruhigen // vi sich beruhigen, ruhig; ~ly ad leise, ruhig; ~ness n Ruhe f, Stille f.

quilt [kwɪlt] n (continental ~) Steppdecke f.

quin [kwɪn] abbr of **quintuplet**.

quinine [kwɪ'ni:n] n Chinin nt.

quintuplets [kwɪn'tju:pləts] npl Fünflinge pl.

quip [kwɪp] n witzige Bemerkung f.

quirk [kwɜ:k] n (oddity) Eigenart f.

quit [kwɪt] pt, pp quit or quitted vt verlassen // vi aufhören.

quite [kwaɪt] ad (completely) ganz, völlig; (fairly) ziemlich; ~ a few of them ziemlich viele von ihnen; ~ (so)! richtig!

quits [kwɪts] a quitt; let's call it ~ lassen wir's gut sein.

quiver ['kwɪvə*] vi zittern // n (for arrows) Köcher m.

quiz [kwɪz] n (competition) Quiz nt // vt prüfen; ~zical a fragend.

quorum ['kwɔ:rəm] n beschlußfähige Anzahl f.

quota ['kwəʊtə] n Anteil m; (COMM) Quote f.

quotation [kwəʊ'teɪʃən] n Zitat nt; (price) Kostenvoranschlag m; ~ marks pl Anführungszeichen pl.

quote [kwəʊt] n see **quotation** // vi (from book) zitieren // vt (from book) zitieren; (price) angeben.

R

rabbi ['ræbaɪ] n Rabbiner m; (title) Rabbi m.

rabbit ['ræbɪt] n Kaninchen nt; ~ hole n Kaninchenbau m; ~ hutch n Kaninchenstall m.

rabble ['ræbl] n Pöbel m.

rabies ['reɪbi:z] n Tollwut f.

RAC n abbr (Brit) of Royal Automobile Club.

raccoon [rə'ku:n] n Waschbär m.

race [reɪs] n (species) Rasse f;

(*competition*) Rennen nt; (*on foot also*) Wettlauf m; (*rush*) Hetze f // vt um die Wette laufen mit; (*horses*) laufen lassen // vi (*run*) rennen; (*in contest*) am Rennen teilnehmen; **~ car** n (*US*) = **racing car**; **~ car driver** n (*US*) = **racing driver**; **~course** n (*for horses*) Rennbahn f; **~horse** n Rennpferd nt; **~track** n (*for cars etc*) Rennstrecke f.

racial ['reɪʃəl] a Rassen-; **~ist** a rassistisch // n Rassist m.

racing ['reɪsɪŋ] n Rennen nt; **~ car** n (*Brit*) Rennwagen m; **~ driver** n (*Brit*) Rennfahrer m.

racism ['reɪsɪzəm] n Rassismus m.

racist ['reɪsɪst] n Rassist m // a rassistisch.

rack [ræk] n Ständer m, Gestell nt // vt plagen; **to go to ~ and ruin** verfallen; **to ~ one's brains** sich (*dat*) den Kopf zerbrechen.

racket ['rækɪt] n (*din*) Krach m; (*scheme*) (Schwindel)geschäft nt; (*TENNIS*) (Tennis)schläger m.

racoon [rə'ku:n] n = **raccoon**.

racquet ['rækɪt] n = **racket** (*TENNIS*).

racy ['reɪsɪ] a gewagt; (*style*) spritzig.

radar ['reɪdɑ:*] n Radar nt or m.

radial ['reɪdɪəl] a (*also: US:* **~-ply**) radial.

radiance ['reɪdɪəns] n strahlende(r) Glanz m.

radiant ['reɪdɪənt] a strahlend; (*giving out rays*) Strahlungs-.

radiate ['reɪdɪeɪt] vti ausstrahlen; (*roads, lines*) strahlenförmig wegführen.

radiation [reɪdɪ'eɪʃən] n (Aus)strahlung f.

radiator ['reɪdɪeɪtə*] n (*for heating*) Heizkörper m; (*AUT*) Kühler m.

radical a, **~ly** ad ['rædɪkəl, -lɪ] radikal.

radii ['reɪdɪaɪ] npl of **radius**.

radio ['reɪdɪəu] n Rundfunk m, Radio nt; (*set*) Radio nt, Radioapparat m; **on the ~** im Radio.

radio... ['reɪdɪəu] pref Radio-; **~active** a radioaktiv; **~logy** [reɪdɪ'ɒlədʒɪ] n Strahlenkunde f.

radio station n Rundfunkstation f.

radiotherapy ['reɪdɪəu'θerəpɪ] n Röntgentherapie f.

radish ['rædɪʃ] n (*big*) Rettich m; (*small*) Radieschen nt.

radius ['reɪdɪəs], pl **radii** [-ɪaɪ] n Radius m; (*area*) Umkreis m.

RAF n abbr of **Royal Air Force**.

raffle ['ræfl] n Verlosung f, Tombola f // vt verlosen.

raft [rɑ:ft] n Floß nt.

rafter ['rɑ:ftə*] n Dachsparren m.

rag [ræg] n (*cloth*) Lumpen m, Lappen m; (*col: newspaper*) Käseblatt nt; (*Univ: for charity*) studentische Sammelaktion f // vt (*Brit*) auf den Arm nehmen; **~s** pl Lumpen pl; **~-and-**

bone man n (*Brit*) = **~man**; **~ doll** n Flickenpuppe f.

rage [reɪdʒ] n Wut f; (*fashion*) große Mode f // vi wüten, toben.

ragged ['rægɪd] a (*edge*) gezackt; (*clothes*) zerlumpt.

ragman ['ræg'mæn] n Lumpensammler m.

raid [reɪd] n Überfall m; (*MIL*) Angriff m; (*by police*) Razzia f // vt überfallen; **~er** n (*person*) (Bank)räuber m.

rail [reɪl] n Schiene f (*on stair*) Geländer nt; (*of ship*) Reling f; (*RAIL*) Schiene f; **~s** pl Geleise pl; **by ~** per Bahn; **~ing(s)** n(pl) Geländer nt; **~road** n (*US*), **~way** n (*Brit*) Eisenbahn f; **~way line** n (*Brit*) (Eisen)bahnlinie f; (*: track*) Gleis nt; **~wayman** n (*Brit*) Eisenbahner m; **~way station** n (*Brit*) Bahnhof m.

rain [reɪn] n Regen m // vti regnen; **in the ~** im Regen; **it's ~ing** es regnet; **~bow** n Regenbogen m; **~coat** n Regenmantel m; **~drop** n Regentropfen m; **~fall** n Niederschlag m; **~y** a (*region, season*) Regen-; (*day*) regnerisch, verregnet.

raise [reɪz] n (*esp US: increase*) (Gehalts)erhöhung f // vt (*lift*) (hoch)heben; (*increase*) erhöhen; (*question*) aufwerfen; (*doubts*) äußern; (*funds*) beschaffen; (*family*) großziehen; (*livestock*) züchten; **to ~ one's voice** die Stimme erheben.

raisin ['reɪzən] n Rosine f.

rake [reɪk] n Rechen m, Harke f; (*person*) Wüstling m // vt rechen, harken; (*with gun*) (mit Feuer) bestreichen; (*search*) (durch)suchen.

rakish ['reɪkɪʃ] a verwegen.

rally ['rælɪ] n (*POL etc*) Kundgebung f; (*AUT*) Rallye f // vt (*MIL*) sammeln // vi Kräfte sammeln; **~ round** vti (sich) scharen um; (*help*) zu Hilfe kommen (+*dat*).

RAM n abbr (= random access memory) RAM m.

ram [ræm] n Widder m; (*instrument*) Ramme f // vt (*strike*) rammen; (*stuff*) (hinein)stopfen.

ramble ['ræmbl] n Wanderung f // vi (*talk*) schwafeln; **~r** n Wanderer m.

rambling ['ræmblɪŋ] a (*speech*) weitschweifig; (*town*) ausgedehnt.

ramp [ræmp] n Rampe f; **on/off ~** (*US AUT*) Ein-/Ausfahrt f.

rampage [ræm'peɪdʒ] n: **to be on the ~** (*also ~ vi*) randalieren.

rampant ['ræmpənt] a wild wuchernd.

rampart ['ræmpɑ:t] n (*Schutz*)wall m.

ramshackle ['ræmʃækl] a baufällig.

ran [ræn] pt of **run**.

ranch [rɑ:ntʃ] n Ranch f.

rancid ['rænsɪd] a ranzig.

rancour, (*US*) **rancor** ['ræŋkə*] n Verbitterung f, Groll m.

random ['rændəm] a ziellos, wahllos // n: at ~ aufs Geratewohl; ~ **access** n (COMPUT) wahlfreie(r) Zugriff m.

randy ['rændɪ] a (Brit col) geil, scharf.

rang [ræŋ] pt of **ring**.

range [reɪndʒ] n Reihe f; (of mountains) Kette f; (COMM) Sortiment nt; (selection) (große) Auswahl f (of an +dat); (reach) (Reich)weite f; (of gun) Schußweite f; (for shooting practice) Schießplatz m; (stove) (großer) Herd m // vt (set in row) anordnen, aufstellen; (roam) durchstreifen // vi: to ~ over (wander) umherstreifen in (+dat); (extend) sich erstrecken auf (+acc); prices ranging from £5 to £10 Preise, die sich zwischen £5 und £10 bewegen; ~r n Förster m.

rank [ræŋk] n (row) Reihe f; (Brit: also: taxi ~) (Taxi)stand m; (MIL) Rang m; (social position) Stand m // vi (have ~) gehören (among zu) // a (strong-smelling) stinkend; (extreme) krass; the ~ and file (fig) die breite Masse.

rankle ['ræŋkl] vi nagen.

ransack ['rænsæk] vt (plunder) plündern; (search) durchwühlen.

ransom ['rænsəm] n Lösegeld nt; to hold sb to ~ jdn gegen Lösegeld festhalten.

rant [rænt] vi hochtrabend reden.

rap [ræp] n Schlag m // vt klopfen.

rape [reɪp] n Vergewaltigung f; (BOT) Raps m // vt vergewaltigen; ~ (seed) oil n Rapsöl nt.

rapid ['ræpɪd] a rasch, schnell; ~s npl Stromschnellen pl; ~ity [rə'pɪdɪtɪ] n Schnelligkeit f; ~ly ad schnell.

rapist ['reɪpɪst] n Vergewaltiger m.

rapport [ræ'pɔː*] n gute(s) Verhältnis nt.

rapture ['ræptʃə*] n Entzücken nt.

rapturous ['ræptʃərəs] a (applause) stürmisch; (expression) verzückt.

rare [rɛə*] a selten, rar; (underdone) nicht durchgebraten.

rarely ['rɛəlɪ] ad selten.

raring ['rɛərɪŋ] a: to be ~ to go (col) es kaum erwarten können, bis es losgeht.

rarity ['rɛərɪtɪ] n Seltenheit f.

rascal ['rɑːskəl] n Schuft m.

rash [ræʃ] a übereilt; (reckless) unbesonnen // n (Haut)ausschlag m.

rasher ['ræʃə*] n Speckscheibe f.

raspberry ['rɑːzbərɪ] n Himbeere f.

rasping ['rɑːspɪŋ] a (noise) kratzend; (voice) krächzend.

rat [ræt] n (animal) Ratte f; (person) Halunke m.

rate [reɪt] n (proportion) Rate f; (price) Tarif m; (speed) Tempo nt // vt (ein)schätzen; ~s pl (Brit) Grundsteuer f; to ~ as für etw halten; ~able value n (Brit) Einheitswert m (als Bemessungsgrundlage); ~payer n

rather ['rɑːðə*] ad (in preference) lieber, eher; (to some extent) ziemlich; I would or I'd ~ go ich würde lieber gehen.

ratify ['rætɪfaɪ] vt bestätigen; (POL) ratifizieren.

rating ['reɪtɪŋ] n Klasse f; (Brit: sailor) Matrose m.

ratio ['reɪʃɪəʊ] n Verhältnis nt; in the ~ of 100 to 1 im Verhältnis 100 zu 1.

ration ['ræʃən] n (usually pl) Ration f // vt rationieren.

rational a, ~ly ad ['ræʃənl, -nəlɪ] rational; ~e [ræʃə'nɑːl] n Grundprinzip nt; ~ize ['ræʃnəlaɪz] vt rationalisieren.

rat race ['rætreɪs] n Konkurrenzkampf m.

rattle ['rætl] n (sound) Rasseln nt; (toy) Rassel f // vi rasseln, klappern // vt rasseln mit; ~snake n Klapperschlange f.

raucous ['rɔːkəs] a heiser, rauh.

ravage ['rævɪdʒ] vt verheeren; ~s pl verheerende Wirkungen pl.

rave [reɪv] vi (talk wildly) phantasieren; (rage) toben.

raven ['reɪvn] n Rabe m.

ravenous ['rævənəs] a heißhungrig.

ravine [rə'viːn] n Schlucht f.

raving ['reɪvɪŋ] a: ~ lunatic völlig Wahnsinnige(r) mf.

ravishing ['rævɪʃɪŋ] a atemberaubend.

raw [rɔː] a roh; (tender) wund(gerieben); (inexperienced) unerfahren; to get a ~ deal (col) schlecht wegkommen; ~ material n Rohmaterial nt.

ray [reɪ] n (of light) Strahl m; ~ of hope Hoffnungsschimmer m.

raze [reɪz] vt dem Erdboden gleichmachen.

razor ['reɪzə*] n Rasierapparat m; ~ blade n Rasierklinge f.

Rd abbr of **road**.

re [riː] prep (COMM) betreffs (+ gen).

reach [riːtʃ] n Reichweite f; (of river) Strecke f // vt (arrive at) erreichen; (give) reichen // vi (try to get) langen (for nach); (stretch) sich erstrecken; within ~ (shops etc) in erreichbarer Weite or Entfernung; out of ~ außer Reichweite; ~ out vi die Hand ausstrecken; to ~ out for sth nach etw greifen.

react [riː'ækt] vi reagieren; ~ion [riː'ækʃən] n Reaktion f.

read [riːd], pt, pp **read** [red] vti lesen; (aloud) vorlesen; ~ out vt vorlesen; ~able a leserlich; (worth ~ing) lesenswert; ~er n (person) Leser(in f) m; (book) Lesebuch nt; ~ership n Leserschaft f.

readily ['redɪlɪ] ad (willingly) bereitwillig; (easily) prompt.

readiness ['redɪnəs] n (willingness) Bereitwilligkeit f; (being ready) Bereitschaft f; in ~ (prepared) bereit.

reading ['riːdɪŋ] n Lesen nt.

readjust ['riːə'dʒʌst] vt neu einstellen // vi (person): to ~ to sich wieder anpassen an (+acc).

ready ['redɪ] a (prepared, willing) bereit; // ad: ~-cooked vorgekocht // n: at the ~ bereit; ~-made a gebrauchsfertig, Fertig-; (clothes) Konfektions-; ~ money n Bargeld nt; ~ reckoner n Rechentabelle f; ~-to-wear a Konfektions-.

real [rɪəl] a wirklich; (actual) eigentlich; (not fake) echt; in ~ terms effektiv; ~ estate n Grundbesitz m; ~istic a, ~istically ad realistisch.

reality [riːˈælɪtɪ] n Wirklichkeit f, Realität f; in ~ in Wirklichkeit.

realization [rɪəlaɪ'zeɪʃən] n (understanding) Erkenntnis f; (fulfilment) Verwirklichung f.

realize ['rɪəlaɪz] vt (understand) begreifen; (make real) verwirklichen; (money) einbringen; I didn't ~ ... ich wußte nicht, ...

really ['rɪəlɪ] ad wirklich.

realm [relm] n Reich nt.

realtor ['rɪəltɔːʳ] n (US) Grundstücksmakler(in f) m.

reap [riːp] vt ernten.

reappear ['riːə'pɪəʳ] vi wieder erscheinen.

rear [rɪəʳ] a hintere(r, s), Rück- // n Rückseite f; (last part) Schluß m // vt (bring up) aufziehen // vi (horse) sich aufbäumen; ~guard n Nachhut f.

rearmament ['riːˈɑːməmənt] n Wiederaufrüstung f.

rearrange ['riːə'reɪndʒ] vt umordnen.

rear-view mirror ['rɪəvjuː-] n Rückspiegel m.

reason ['riːzn] n (cause) Grund m; (ability to think) Verstand m; // (sensible thoughts) Vernunft f // vi (think) denken; (use arguments) argumentieren; to ~ with sb mit jdm diskutieren; it stands to ~ that es ist logisch, daß; ~able a vernünftig; ~ably ad vernünftig; (fairly) ziemlich; ~ed a (argument) durchdacht; ~ing n Urteilen nt; (argumentation) Beweisführung f.

reassurance ['riːə'ʃuərəns] n Beruhigung f; (confirmation) Bestätigung f.

reassure ['riːə'ʃuəʳ] vt beruhigen; to ~ sb of sth jdm etw versichern.

reassuring ['riːə'ʃuərɪŋ] a beruhigend.

rebate ['riːbeɪt] n Rückzahlung f.

rebel ['rebl] n Rebell m; ~lion [rɪˈbeljən] n Rebellion f, Aufstand m.

rebirth ['riːˈbɜːθ] n Wiedergeburt f.

rebound [rɪˈbaund] vi zurückprallen // ['riːbaund] n Rückprall m.

rebuff [rɪˈbʌf] n Abfuhr f // vt abblitzen

lassen.

rebuild ['riːˈbɪld] vt irreg wiederaufbauen; (fig) wiederherstellen.

rebuke [rɪˈbjuːk] n Tadel m // vt tadeln, rügen.

rebut [rɪˈbʌt] vt widerlegen.

recalcitrant [rɪˈkælsɪtrənt] a widerspenstig.

recall [rɪˈkɔːl] vt (call back) zurückrufen; (remember) sich erinnern an (+acc) // n Rückruf m.

recant [rɪˈkænt] vi widerrufen.

recap ['riːkæp] vti wiederholen.

recapitulate [ˌriːkə'pɪtjuleɪt] vti = recap.

rec'd abbr (= received) Eing.

recede [rɪˈsiːd] vi zurückweichen.

receding [rɪˈsiːdɪŋ] a: ~ hair Stirnglatze f.

receipt [rɪˈsiːt] n (document) Quittung f; (receiving) Empfang m; ~s pl Einnahmen pl.

receive [rɪˈsiːv] vt erhalten; (visitors etc) empfangen; ~r n (TEL) Hörer m.

recent ['riːsnt] a vor kurzem (geschehen), neuerlich; (modern) neu; ~ly ad kürzlich, neulich.

receptacle [rɪˈseptəkl] n Behälter m.

reception [rɪˈsepʃən] n Empfang m; ~ desk n Empfang m; (in hotel) Rezeption f; ~ist n (in hotel) Empfangschef m/-dame f; (MED) Sprechstundenhilfe f.

receptive [rɪˈseptɪv] a aufnahmebereit.

recess [rɪˈses] n (break) Ferien pl; (hollow) Nische f; ~ion [rɪˈseʃən] n Rezession f.

recharge ['riːˈtʃɑːdʒ] vt (battery) aufladen.

recipe ['resɪpɪ] n Rezept nt.

recipient [rɪˈsɪpɪənt] n Empfänger m.

reciprocal [rɪˈsɪprəkəl] a gegenseitig; (mutual) wechselseitig.

recital [rɪˈsaɪtl] n Vortrag m.

recite [rɪˈsaɪt] vt vortragen, aufsagen.

reckless ['rekləs] a leichtsinnig; (driving) fahrlässig.

reckon ['rekən] vt (count) (be- or er)rechnen; (estimate) schätzen; (think): I ~ that ... ich nehme an, daß ...; ~ on vt rechnen mit; ~ing n (calculation) Rechnen nt.

reclaim [rɪˈkleɪm] vt (land) abgewinnen (from dat); (expenses) zurückverlangen.

reclamation [reklə'meɪʃən] n (of land) Gewinnung f.

recline [rɪˈklaɪn] vi sich zurücklehnen.

reclining [rɪˈklaɪnɪŋ] a Liege-.

recluse [rɪˈkluːs] n Einsiedler m.

recognition [rekəg'nɪʃən] n (recognizing) Erkennen nt; (acknowledgement) Anerkennung f; transformed beyond ~ völlig verändert.

recognizable ['rekəgnaɪzəbl] a erkennbar.

recognize ['rekəgnaɪz] vt erkennen; (POL, approve) anerkennen; to ~ as anerkennen als; to ~ by erkennen an (+dat).

recoil [rɪ'kɔɪl] vi (in horror) zurückschrecken; (rebound) zurückprallen; (person): to ~ from doing sth davor zurückschrecken, etw zu tun.

recollect [rekə'lekt] vt sich erinnern an (+acc); ~ion n Erinnerung f.

recommend [rekə'mend] vt empfehlen; ~ation n Empfehlung f.

recompense ['rekəmpens] n (compensation) Entschädigung f; (reward) Belohnung f // vt entschädigen; belohnen.

reconcile ['rekənsaɪl] vt (facts) vereinbaren; (people) versöhnen; to ~ o.s. to sth sich mit etw abfinden.

reconciliation [rekənsɪlɪ'eɪʃən] n Versöhnung f.

recondition ['riːkən'dɪʃən] vt (machine) generalüberholen.

reconnaissance [rɪ'kɒnɪsəns] n Aufklärung f.

reconnoitre, (US) **reconnoiter** [rekə'nɔɪtə*] vt erkunden // vi aufklären.

reconsider ['riːkən'sɪdə*] vti von neuem erwägen, (es) überdenken.

reconstruct ['riːkən'strʌkt] vt wiederaufbauen; (crime) rekonstruieren; ~ion ['riːkən'strʌkʃən] n Rekonstruktion f.

record ['rekɔːd] n Aufzeichnung f; (MUS) Schallplatte f; (best performance) Rekord m // a (time) Rekord- // vt [rɪ'kɔːd] aufzeichnen; (music etc) aufnehmen; in ~ time in Rekordzeit; off the ~ a vertraulich // ad im Vertrauen; ~ card n (in file) Karteikarte f; ~ed delivery [rɪ'kɔːdɪd-] n (Brit POST) Einschreiben nt; ~er [rɪ'kɔːdə*] n (TECH) Registriergerät nt; (MUS) Blockflöte f; ~ holder n (SPORT) Rekordinhaber m; ~ing [rɪ'kɔːdɪŋ] n (MUS) Aufnahme f; ~ player n Plattenspieler m.

recount ['riːkaʊnt] n Nachzählung f // vt (count again) nachzählen; [rɪ'kaʊnt] (tell) berichten.

recoup [rɪ'kuːp] vt: to ~ one's losses seinen Verlust wiedergutmachen.

recourse [rɪ'kɔːs] n: to have ~ to Zuflucht nehmen zu or bei.

recover [rɪ'kʌvə*] vt (get back) zurückerhalten; ['riː'kʌvə*] (quilt etc) neu überziehen // vi sich erholen; ~y n Wiedererlangung f; (of health) Erholung f.

recreate ['riːkrɪ'eɪt] vt wiederherstellen.

recreation [rekrɪ'eɪʃən] n Erholung f; ~al a Erholungs-.

recrimination [rɪkrɪmɪ'neɪʃən] n Gegenbeschuldigung f.

recruit [rɪ'kruːt] n Rekrut m // vt rekrutieren; ~ment n Rekrutierung f.

rectangle ['rektæŋgl] n Rechteck nt.

rectangular [rek'tæŋgjʊlə*] a rechteckig, rechtwinklig.

rectify ['rektɪfaɪ] vt berichtigen.

rector ['rektə*] n (REL) Pfarrer m; (SCH) Direktor(in f) m.

rectory ['rektərɪ] n Pfarrhaus nt.

recuperate [rɪ'kuːpəreɪt] vi sich erholen.

recur [rɪ'kɜː*] vi sich wiederholen; ~rence n Wiederholung f; ~rent a wiederkehrend.

red [red] n Rot nt; (POL) Rote(r) m // a rot; in the ~ in den roten Zahlen; ~ carpet treatment n Sonderbehandlung f, große(r) Bahnhof m; R~ Cross n Rote(s) Kreuz nt; ~currant n rote Johannisbeere f; ~den vti (sich) röten; (blush) erröten; ~dish a rötlich.

redeem [rɪ'diːm] vt (COMM) einlösen; (save) retten.

redeeming [rɪ'diːmɪŋ] a: ~ feature versöhnende(s) Moment nt.

redeploy ['riːdɪ'plɔɪ] vt (resources) umverteilen.

red-haired ['red'hɛəd] a rothaarig.

red-handed ['red'hændɪd] ad: to be caught ~ auf frischer Tat ertappt werden.

redhead ['redhed] n Rothaarige(r) mf.

red herring ['red'herɪŋ] n Ablenkungsmanöver nt.

red-hot ['red'hɒt] a rotglühend.

redirect ['riːdaɪ'rekt] vt umleiten.

red light ['red'laɪt] n: to go through a ~ (AUT) bei Rot über die Ampel fahren; **red-light district** n Strichviertel nt.

redo ['riː'duː] vt (irreg: like do) nochmals machen.

redolent ['redəʊlənt] a: ~ of riechend nach; (fig) erinnernd an (+acc).

redouble [riː'dʌbl] vt: to ~ one's efforts seine Anstrengungen verdoppeln.

redress [rɪ'dres] n Entschädigung f // vt wiedergutmachen.

Red Sea n: the ~ das Rote Meer.

redskin ['redskɪn] n Rothaut f.

red tape n Bürokratismus m.

reduce [rɪ'djuːs] vt (price) herabsetzen (to auf +acc); (speed, temperature) vermindern; (photo) verkleinern; '~ speed now' (AUT) ≈ 'langsam'; at a ~d price zum ermäßigten Preis.

reduction [rɪ'dʌkʃən] n Herabsetzung f; Verminderung f; Verkleinerung f; (of money) Nachlaß m.

redundancy [rɪ'dʌndənsɪ] n Überflüssigkeit f; (of workers) Entlassung f.

redundant [rɪ'dʌndənt] a überflüssig; (workers) ohne Arbeitsplatz; to be made ~ arbeitslos werden.

reed [riːd] n Schilf nt; (MUS) Rohrblatt nt.

reef [riːf] n Riff nt.

reek [riːk] vi stinken (of nach).

reel [ri:l] n Spule f, Rolle f // vt (also: ~ **in**) wickeln, spulen // vi (stagger) taumeln.

ref [ref] n abbr (col: = referee) Schiri m.

refectory [rɪ'fektərɪ] n (UNIV) Mensa f; (SCH) Speisesaal m; (ECCL) Refektorium nt.

refer [rɪ'fɜ:*] vt: to ~ sb to sb/sth jdn an jdn/etw verweisen // vi: to ~ to (to book) nachschlagen in (+dat); (mention) sich beziehen auf (+acc).

referee [refə'ri:] n Schiedsrichter m; (Brit: for job) Referenz f // vt schiedsrichtern.

reference ['refrəns] n (allusion) Anspielung f (to auf +acc); (for job) Referenz f; (in book) Verweis m; (number, code) Aktenzeichen nt; with ~ to in bezug auf (+acc); ~ **book** n Nachschlagewerk nt; ~ **number** n Aktenzeichen nt.

referendum [refə'rendəm], pl **-da** [-də] n Volksabstimmung f.

refill ['ri:'fɪl] vt nachfüllen // n ['ri:fɪl] (for pen) Ersatzmine f.

refine [rɪ'faɪn] vt (purify) raffinieren; ~**d** a kultiviert; ~**ment** n Kultiviertheit f.

reflect [rɪ'flekt] vt (light) reflektieren; (fig) (wider)spiegeln // vi (meditate) nachdenken (on über +acc); it ~s **badly/well on him** das stellt ihn in ein schlechtes/gutes Licht; ~**ion** n Reflexion f; (image) Spiegelbild nt; (thought) Überlegung f; on ~**ion** wenn man sich (dat) das recht überlegt.

reform [rɪ'fɔ:m] n Reform f // vt (person) bessern; ~**atory** n (US) Besserungsanstalt f.

refrain [rɪ'freɪn] vi unterlassen (from acc) // n Refrain m.

refresh [rɪ'freʃ] vt erfrischen; ~**er course** n (Brit) Wiederholungskurs m; ~**ing** a erfrischend; ~**ments** pl Erfrischungen pl.

refrigeration [rɪfrɪdʒə'reɪʃən] n Kühlung f.

refrigerator [rɪ'frɪdʒəreɪtə*] n Kühlschrank m.

refuel ['ri:'fjuəl] vti auftanken.

refuge ['refju:dʒ] n Zuflucht f; to take ~ in sich flüchten in (+acc).

refugee [refju'dʒi:] n Flüchtling m.

refund ['ri:fʌnd] n Rückvergütung f // vt [rɪ'fʌnd] zurückerstatten.

refurbish ['ri:'fɜ:bɪʃ] vt aufpolieren.

refusal [rɪ'fju:zəl] n (Ver)weigerung f; **first ~** n Vorkaufsrecht nt.

refuse ['refju:s] n Abfall m, Müll m // v [rɪ'fju:z] vt abschlagen // vi sich weigern; ~ **collection** n Müllabfuhr f.

refute [rɪ'fju:t] vt widerlegen.

regain [rɪ'geɪn] vt wiedergewinnen; (consciousness) wiedererlangen.

regal ['ri:gəl] a königlich.

regalia [rɪ'geɪlɪə] npl Insignien pl.

regard [rɪ'gɑ:d] n Achtung f // vt ansehen; **to send one's ~s to sb** jdn grüßen lassen; '**with kindest ~s**' mit freundlichen Grüßen; ~**ing, as ~s, with ~ to** bezüglich (+gen), in bezug auf (+acc); ~**less** a ohne Rücksicht (of auf +acc) // ad trotzdem.

regenerate [rɪ'dʒenəreɪt] vt erneuern.

régime [reɪ'ʒi:m] n Regime nt.

regiment ['redʒɪmənt] n Regiment nt // vt (fig) reglementieren; ~**al** [redʒɪ'mentl] a Regiments-.

region ['ri:dʒən] n Region f; **in the ~ of** (fig) so um; ~**al** a örtlich, regional.

register ['redʒɪstə*] n Register nt // vt (list) registrieren; (emotion) zeigen; (write down) eintragen // vi (at hotel) sich eintragen; (with police) sich melden (with bei); (make impression) wirken, ankommen; ~**ed** a (Brit: letter) Einschreibe-, eingeschrieben; ~**ed trademark** n eingetragene(s) Warenzeichen nt.

registrar [redʒɪs'trɑ:*] n Standesbeamte(r) m.

registration [redʒɪs'treɪʃən] n (act) Registrierung f; (number) polizeiliche(s) Kennzeichen nt.

registry office ['redʒɪstrɪ'ɒfɪs] n (Brit) Standesamt nt; **to get married in a ~** standesamtlich heiraten.

regret [rɪ'gret] n Bedauern nt // vt bedauern; ~**fully** ad mit Bedauern, ungern; ~**table** a bedauerlich.

regroup ['ri:gru:p] vt umgruppieren // vi sich umgruppieren.

regular ['regjʊlə*] a regelmäßig; (usual) üblich; (col) regelrecht // n (client etc) Stammkunde m; ~**ity** [regjʊ'lærɪtɪ] n Regelmäßigkeit f; ~**ly** ad regelmäßig.

regulate ['regjʊleɪt] vt regeln, regulieren.

regulation [regjʊ'leɪʃən] n (rule) Vorschrift f; (control) Regulierung f.

rehabilitation ['ri:həbɪlɪ'teɪʃən] n (of criminal) Resozialisierung f.

rehearsal [rɪ'hɜ:səl] n Probe f.

rehearse [rɪ'hɜ:s] vt proben.

reign [reɪn] n Herrschaft f // vi herrschen.

reimburse [ri:ɪm'bɜ:s] vt entschädigen, zurückzahlen (sb for sth jdm etw).

rein [reɪn] n Zügel m.

reincarnation ['ri:ɪnkɑ:'neɪʃən] n Wiedergeburt f.

reindeer ['reɪndɪə*] n Ren nt.

reinforce [ri:ɪn'fɔ:s] vt verstärken; ~**d concrete** n Stahlbeton m; ~**ment** n Verstärkung f; ~**ments** pl (MIL) Verstärkungstruppen pl.

reinstate ['ri:ɪn'steɪt] vt wiedereinsetzen.

reissue ['ri:'ɪʃu:] vt neu herausgeben.

reiterate [ri:'ɪtəreɪt] vt wiederholen.

reject ['ri:dʒekt] n (COMM) Aus-

schuß(artikel) *m* // [rɪ'dʒekt] *vt*
ablehnen; **~ion** [rɪ'dʒekʃən] *n*
Zurückweisung *f*.

rejoice [rɪ'dʒɔɪs] *vi*: to ~ **at** *or* **over** sich
freuen über.

rejuvenate [rɪ'dʒuːvɪneɪt] *vt* verjüngen.

rekindle ['riː'kɪndl] *vt* wieder anfachen.

relapse [rɪ'læps] *n* Rückfall *m*.

relate [rɪ'leɪt] *vt* (*tell*) erzählen;
(*connect*) verbinden // *vi* zusammenhän-
gen (to mit); (*form relationship*) eine
Beziehung aufbauen (to zu); **~d** *a* verwandt (to mit).

relating [rɪ'leɪtɪŋ] *prep*: ~ **to** bezüglich
(+*gen*).

relation [rɪ'leɪʃən] *n* Verwandte(r) *mf*;
(*connection*) Beziehung *f*; **~ship** *n* Verhältnis *nt*, Beziehung *f*.

relative ['relətɪv] *n* Verwandte(r) *mf* // *a*
relativ; **~ly** *ad* verhältnismäßig.

relax [rɪ'læks] *vi* (*slacken*) sich lockern;
(*muscles, person*) sich entspannen // *vt*
(*ease*) lockern, entspannen; **~ation**
[riːlæk'seɪʃən] *n* Entspannung *f*; **~ed** *a*
entspannt, locker; **~ing** *a* entspannend.

relay ['riːleɪ] *n* (SPORT) Staffel *f* // *vt*
(*message*) weiterleiten; (RAD, TV) übertragen.

release [rɪ'liːs] *n* (*freedom*) Entlassung
f; (TECH) Auslöser *m* // *vt* befreien;
(*prisoner*) entlassen; (*report, news*) ver-
lautbaren, bekanntgeben.

relegate ['relɪgeɪt] *vt* (SPORT): to be
~d absteigen.

relent [rɪ'lent] *vi* nachgeben; **~less** *a*,
~lessly *ad* unnachgiebig.

relevant ['relɪvənt] *a* wichtig, relevant;
~ **to** relevant für.

reliability [rɪlaɪə'bɪlɪtɪ] *n* Zuverlässigkeit
f.

reliable *a*, **reliably** *ad* [rɪ'laɪəbl, -blɪ]
zuverlässig; **to be reliably informed that
...** aus zuverlässiger Quelle wissen, daß
...

reliance [rɪ'laɪəns] *n* Abhängigkeit *f* (on
von).

relic ['relɪk] *n* (*from past*) Überbleibsel
nt; (REL) Reliquie *f*.

relief [rɪ'liːf] *n* Erleichterung *f*; (*help*)
Hilfe *f*; (*person*) Ablösung *f*.

relieve [rɪ'liːv] *vt* (*ease*) erleichtern;
(*bring help*) entlasten; (*person*) ablösen;
to ~ **sb of sth** jdm etw abnehmen; to ~
o.s. (*euph*) sich erleichtern (*euph*).

religion [rɪ'lɪdʒən] *n* Religion *f*.

religious [rɪ'lɪdʒəs] *a* religiös; **~ly** *ad*
religiös; (*conscientiously*) gewissenhaft.

relinquish [rɪ'lɪŋkwɪʃ] *vt* aufgeben.

relish ['relɪʃ] *n* Würze *f* // *vt* genießen; to
~ **doing** etw gern tun.

relocate ['riːləʊ'keɪt] *vt* verlegen // *vi*
umziehen.

reluctance [rɪ'lʌktəns] *n* Widerstreben
nt, Abneigung *f*.

reluctant [rɪ'lʌktənt] *a* widerwillig; **~ly**

ad ungern.

rely [rɪ'laɪ]: ~ **on** *vt* sich verlassen auf
(+*acc*).

remain [rɪ'meɪn] *vi* (*be left*) übrigbleiben; (*stay*) bleiben; **~der** *n* Rest
m; **~ing** *a* übrig(geblieben); **~s** *npl*
Überreste *pl*.

remand [rɪ'mɑːnd] *n*: **on** ~ in Untersu-
chungshaft // *vt*: to ~ **in custody** in
Untersuchungshaft schicken; ~ **home** *n*
(*Brit*) Untersuchungsgefängnis *nt* für
Jugendliche.

remark [rɪ'mɑːk] *n* Bemerkung *f* // *vt*
bemerken; **~able** *a*, **~ably** *ad*
bemerkenswert.

remarry ['riː'mærɪ] *vi* sich wieder ver-
heiraten.

remedial [rɪ'miːdɪəl] *a* Heil-; (*teaching*)
Hilfsschul-.

remedy ['remədɪ] *n* Mittel *nt* // *vt* (*pain*)
abhelfen (+*dat*); (*trouble*) in Ordnung
bringen.

remember [rɪ'membə*] *vt* sich erinnern
an (+*acc*).

remembrance [rɪ'membrəns] *n* Erinnerung *f*; (*official*) Gedenken *nt*.

remind [rɪ'maɪnd] *vt*: to ~ **sb to do sth**
jdn daran erinnern, etw zu tun; to ~ **sb
of sth** jdn an etw (acc) erinnern; **she ~s
me of her mother** sie erinnert mich an
ihre Mutter; **~er** *n* Mahnung *f*.

reminisce [remɪ'nɪs] *vi* in Erinnerungen
schwelgen.

reminiscent [remɪ'nɪsnt] *a*: be ~ **of sth**
an etw (acc) erinnern.

remiss [rɪ'mɪs] *a* nachlässig.

remission [rɪ'mɪʃən] *n* Nachlaß *m*; (*of
debt, sentence*) Erlaß *m*.

remit [rɪ'mɪt] *vt* (*money*) überweisen (to
an +*acc*); **~tance** *n* Geldanweisung *f*.

remnant ['remnənt] *n* Rest *m*; **~s** *pl*
(COMM) Einzelstücke *pl*.

remorse [rɪ'mɔːs] *n* Gewissensbisse *pl*;
~ful *a* reumütig; **~less** *a*, **~lessly** *ad*
unbarmherzig.

remote [rɪ'məʊt] *a* abgelegen; (*slight*)
gering; ~ **control** *n* Fernsteuerung *f*;
~ly *ad* entfernt.

remould ['riːməʊld] *n* (*Brit*)
runderneuerte(r) Reifen *m*.

removable [rɪ'muːvəbl] *a* entfernbar.

removal [rɪ'muːvəl] *n* Beseitigung *f*; (*of
furniture*) Umzug *m*; (*from office*) Entlassung *f*; ~ **van** *n* (*Brit*) Möbelwagen
m.

remove [rɪ'muːv] *vt* beseitigen, entfernen; **~rs** *npl* Möbelspedition *f*.

remuneration [rɪmjuːnə'reɪʃən] *n* Vergütung *f*, Honorar *nt*.

render ['rendə*] *vt* machen; (*translate*)
übersetzen; **~ing** *n* (MUS) Wiedergabe
f.

renew [rɪ'njuː] *vt* erneuern; (*contract,
licence*) verlängern; (*replace*) ersetzen;
~al *n* Erneuerung *f*; Verlängerung *f*.

renounce [rɪ'naʊns] vt (give up) verzichten auf (+acc); (disown) verstoßen.

renovate ['renəveɪt] vt renovieren; (building) restaurieren.

renown [rɪ'naʊn] n Ruf m; **~ed** a namhaft.

rent [rent] n Miete f; (for land) Pacht f // vt (hold as tenant) mieten; pachten; (let) vermieten; verpachten; (car etc) mieten; (firm) vermieten; **~al** n Miete f.

renunciation [rɪnʌnsɪ'eɪʃən] n Verzicht m (of auf +acc).

reorganize ['riː'ɔːgənaɪz] vt umgestalten, reorganisieren.

rep [rep] n abbr of **representative**; **repertory**.

repair [rɪ'pɛə*] n Reparatur f // vt reparieren; (damage) wiedergutmachen; **in good/bad ~** in gutem/schlechtem Zustand; **~ kit** n Werkzeugkasten m.

repartee [repɑː'tiː] n Witzeleien pl.

repatriate [riː'pætrɪeɪt] vt in die Heimat zurückschicken.

repay [rɪ'peɪ] vt (irreg: like pay) zurückzahlen; (reward) vergelten; **~ment** n Rückzahlung f; (fig) Vergeltung f.

repeal [rɪ'piːl] n Aufhebung f // vt aufheben.

repeat [rɪ'piːt] n (RAD, TV) Wiederholung(ssendung) f // vt wiederholen; **~edly** ad wiederholt.

repel [rɪ'pel] vt (drive back) zurückschlagen; (disgust) abstoßen; **~lent** a abstoßend // n: **insect ~lent** Insektenmittel nt.

repent [rɪ'pent] vti: to **~ (of)** bereuen; **~ance** n Reue f.

repercussion [riːpə'kʌʃən] n Auswirkung f; to have **~s** ein Nachspiel haben.

repertory ['repətərɪ] n Repertoire nt.

repetition [repə'tɪʃən] n Wiederholung f.

repetitive [rɪ'petɪtɪv] a sich wiederholend.

replace [rɪ'pleɪs] vt ersetzen; (put back) zurückstellen; **~ment** n Ersatz m.

replay ['riːpleɪ] n (of match) Wiederholungsspiel nt; (of tape, film) Wiederholung f.

replenish [rɪ'plenɪʃ] vt ergänzen.

replete [rɪ'pliːt] a (zum Platzen) voll.

replica ['replɪkə] n Kopie f.

reply [rɪ'plaɪ] n Antwort f // vi antworten; **~ coupon** n Antwortschein m.

report [rɪ'pɔːt] n Bericht m; (Brit SCH) Zeugnis nt // vt (tell) berichten; (give information against) melden; (to police) anzeigen // vi (make report) Bericht erstatten; (present o.s.): to **~ (to sb)** sich (bei jdm) melden; **~ card** n (US, Scot) Zeugnis nt; **~edly** ad wie verlautet; **~er** n Reporter m.

repose [rɪ'pəʊz] n: **in ~** (face, mouth) gelassen.

reprehensible [reprɪ'hensɪbl] a tadelnswert.

represent [reprɪ'zent] vt darstellen; (speak for) vertreten; **~ation** [-'teɪʃən] n Darstellung f; (being represented) Vertretung f; **~ations** pl (protest) Vorhaltungen pl; **~ative** n (person) Vertreter m; (US POL) Abgeordnete(r) mf // a repräsentativ.

repress [rɪ'pres] vt unterdrücken; **~ion** [rɪ'preʃən] n Unterdrückung f.

reprieve [rɪ'priːv] n (cancellation) Begnadigung f; (fig) Gnadenfrist f // vt (JUR) begnadigen.

reprimand ['reprɪmɑːnd] n Verweis m // vt einen Verweis erteilen (+dat).

reprint ['riːprɪnt] n Neudruck m // ['riː'prɪnt] vt wieder abdrucken.

reprisal [rɪ'praɪzəl] n Vergeltung f.

reproach [rɪ'prəʊtʃ] n Vorwurf m // vt Vorwürfe machen (+dat); to **~ sb with sth** jdm etw vorwerfen; **~ful** a vorwurfsvoll.

reproduce [riːprə'djuːs] vt reproduzieren // vi (have offspring) sich vermehren.

reproduction [riːprə'dʌkʃən] n (ART, PHOT) Reproduktion f; (breeding) Fortpflanzung f.

reproductive [riːprə'dʌktɪv] a reproduktiv; (breeding) Fortpflanzungs-.

reprove [rɪ'pruːv] vt: to **~ sb for sth** jdn für etw tadeln.

republic [rɪ'pʌblɪk] n Republik f.

repudiate [rɪ'pjuːdɪeɪt] vt zurückweisen.

repugnant [rɪ'pʌgnənt] a widerlich.

repulse [rɪ'pʌls] vt (drive back) zurückschlagen; (reject) abweisen.

repulsive [rɪ'pʌlsɪv] a abstoßend.

reputable ['repjʊtəbl] a angesehen.

reputation [repjʊ'teɪʃən] n Ruf m.

repute [rɪ'pjuːt] n hohe(s) Ansehen nt; **~d** a, **~dly** ad angeblich.

request [rɪ'kwest] n Bitte f // vt (thing) erbitten; to **~ sth of** or **from sb** jdn um etw bitten; (formally) jdn um etw ersuchen; **~ stop** n (Brit) Bedarfshaltestelle f.

require [rɪ'kwaɪə*] vt (need) brauchen; (demand) erfordern; **~ment** n (condition) Anforderung f; (need) Bedarf m.

requisite ['rekwɪzɪt] n Erfordernis nt // a erforderlich; **toilet ~s** (Brit) Toilettenartikel pl.

requisition [rekwɪ'zɪʃən] n Anforderung f // vt beschlagnahmen; to **~ (for sth)** (etw) anfordern.

resale ['riːseɪl] n Weiterverkauf m.

rescind [rɪ'sɪnd] vt aufheben.

rescue ['reskjuː] n Rettung f // vt retten; **~ from** vt befreien aus; **~ party** n Rettungsmannschaft f; **~r** n Retter m.

research [rɪ'sɜːtʃ] n Forschung f // vi forschen // vt erforschen; **~er** n Forscher *m*.

resemblance [rɪ'zembləns] *n* Ähnlichkeit *f*.

resemble [rɪ'zembl] *vt* ähneln (+*dat*).

resent [rɪ'zent] *vt* übelnehmen; ~**ful** *a* nachtragend, empfindlich; ~**ment** *n* Verstimmung *f*, Unwille *m*.

reservation [rezə'veɪʃən] *n* (*of seat*) Reservierung *f*; (*THEAT*) Vorbestellung *f*; (*doubt*) Vorbehalt *m*; (*land*) Reservat *nt*.

reserve [rɪ'zɜːv] *n* (*store*) Vorrat *m*, Reserve *f*; (*manner*) Zurückhaltung *f*; (*game* ~) Naturschutzgebiet *nt*; (*SPORT*) Ersatzspieler(in *f*) *m* // *vt* reservieren; (*judgement*) sich (*dat*) vorbehalten; ~**s** *pl* (*MIL*) Reserve *f*; **in** ~ in Reserve; ~**d** *a* reserviert.

reshape [riː'ʃeɪp] *vt* umformen.

reshuffle ['riː'ʃʌfl] *n*: **cabinet** ~ (*POL*) Kabinettsumbildung *f* // *vt* (*POL*) umbilden.

reside [rɪ'zaɪd] *vi* wohnen, ansässig sein.

residence ['rezɪdəns] *n* (*house*) Wohnsitz *m*; (*living*) Aufenthalt *m*.

resident ['rezɪdənt] *n* (*in house*) Bewohner *m*; (*in area*) Einwohner *m* // *a* wohnhaft, ansässig; ~**ial** [-'denʃəl] *a* Wohn-.

residue ['rezɪdjuː] *n* Rest *m*; (*CHEM*) Rückstand *m*; (*fig*) Bodensatz *m*.

resign [rɪ'zaɪn] *vt* (*office*) aufgeben, zurücktreten von // *vi* (*from office*) zurücktreten; (*employee*) kündigen; **to be** ~**ed to sth, to** ~ **o.s.** to sich mit etw abfinden; ~**ation** [rezɪg'neɪʃən] *n* (*from job*) Kündigung *f*; (*POL*) Rücktritt *m*; (*submission*) Resignation *f*; ~**ed** *a* resigniert.

resilience [rɪ'zɪlɪəns] *n* Spannkraft *f*; (*of person*) Unverwüstlichkeit *f*.

resilient [rɪ'zɪlɪənt] *a* unverwüstlich.

resin ['rezɪn] *n* Harz *nt*.

resist [rɪ'zɪst] *vt* widerstehen (+*dat*); ~**ance** *n* Widerstand *m*.

resolute *a*, ~**ly** *ad* ['rezəluːt, -lɪ] entschlossen, resolut.

resolution [rezə'luːʃən] *n* (*firmness*) Entschlossenheit *f*; (*intention*) Vorsatz *m*; (*decision*) Beschluß *m*.

resolve [rɪ'zɒlv] *n* Entschlossenheit *f* // *vt* (*decide*) beschließen // *vi* sich lösen; ~**d** *a* (*fest*) entschlossen.

resonant ['rezənənt] *a* voll.

resort [rɪ'zɔːt] *n* (*holiday place*) Erholungsort *m*; (*help*) Zuflucht *f* // *vi* Zuflucht nehmen (*to* zu); **as a last** ~ als letzter Ausweg.

resound [rɪ'zaʊnd] *vi*: **to** ~ (*with*) widerhallen von; ~**ing** *a* nachhallend; (*success*) groß.

resource [rɪ'sɔːs] *n* Findigkeit *f*; ~**s** *pl* (*financial*) Geldmittel *pl*; (*natural*) Bodenschätze *pl*; ~**ful** *a* findig.

respect [rɪs'pekt] *n* Respekt *m* // *vt* achten, respektieren; ~**s** *npl* Grüße *pl*; **with** ~ **to** in bezug auf (+*acc*), hinsichtlich (+*gen*); **in this** ~ in dieser Hinsicht; ~**ability** [rɪspektə'bɪlɪtɪ] *n* Anständigkeit *f*; ~**able** *a* (*decent*) anständig; (*fairly good*) leidlich; ~**ful** *a* höflich.

respective [rɪs'pektɪv] *a* jeweilig; ~**ly** *ad* beziehungsweise.

respiration [respɪ'reɪʃən] *n* Atmung *f*.

respite ['respaɪt] *n* Ruhepause *f*.

resplendent [rɪs'plendənt] *a* strahlend.

respond [rɪs'pɒnd] *vi* antworten; (*react*) reagieren (*to* auf +*acc*).

response [rɪs'pɒns] *n* Antwort *f*, Reaktion *f*; (*to advert etc*) Resonanz *f*.

responsibility [rɪspɒnsə'bɪlɪtɪ] *n* Verantwortung *f*.

responsible [rɪs'pɒnsəbl] *a* (*reliable*) verantwortungsvoll; verantwortlich (*for* für).

responsive [rɪs'pɒnsɪv] *a* empfänglich.

rest [rest] *n* Ruhe *f*; (*break*) Pause *f*; (*remainder*) Rest *m* // *vi* sich ausruhen; (*be supported*) (auf)liegen // *vt* (*lean*): **to** ~ **sth on/against** etw gegen etw (*acc*) lehnen; **the** ~ **of them** die übrigen; **it** ~**s with him to ...** es liegt bei ihm, zu ....

restaurant ['restərɔːŋ] *n* Restaurant *nt*; ~ **car** (*Brit*) Speisewagen *m*.

restful ['restful] *a* erholsam, ruhig.

rest home ['resthəʊm] *n* Erholungsheim *nt*.

restitution [restɪ'tjuːʃən] *n* Rückgabe *f*; **to make** ~ **to sb for sth** jdn für etw entschädigen.

restive ['restɪv] *a* unruhig.

restless ['restləs] *a* unruhig.

restore [rɪs'tɔː*] *vt* (*order*) wiederherstellen; (*customs*) wieder einführen; (*person to position*) wiedereinsetzen; (*give back*) zurückgeben; (*paintings*) restaurieren.

restrain [rɪs'treɪn] *vt* zurückhalten; (*curiosity etc*) beherrschen; (*person*): **to** ~ **sb from doing sth** jdn davon abhalten, etw zu tun; ~**ed** *a* (*style etc*) gedämpft, verhalten; ~**t** *n* (*self-control*) Zurückhaltung *f*.

restrict [rɪs'trɪkt] *vt* einschränken; ~**ion** [rɪs'trɪkʃən] *n* Einschränkung *f*; ~**ive** *a* einschränkend.

rest room ['restrʊm] *n* (*US*) Toilette *f*.

restructure ['riː'strʌktʃə*] *vt* umstrukturieren.

result [rɪ'zʌlt] *n* Resultat *nt*, Folge *f*; (*of exam, game*) Ergebnis *nt* // *vi* zur Folge haben (*in acc*); **as a** ~ **of** als Folge (+*gen*).

resume [rɪ'zjuːm] *vt* fortsetzen; (*occupy again*) wieder einnehmen // *vi* (*work etc*) wieder beginnen.

résumé ['reɪzjuːmeɪ] *n* Zusammenfassung *f*.

resumption [rɪ'zʌmpʃən] *n* Wiederaufnahme f.

resurgence [rɪ'sɜːdʒəns] n Wiedererwachen nt.

resurrection [rezə'rekʃən] n Auferstehung f.

resuscitate [rɪ'sʌsɪteɪt] vt wiederbeleben.

resuscitation [rɪsʌsɪ'teɪʃən] n Wiederbelebung f.

retail ['riːteɪl] n Einzelhandel m // a Einzelhandels- // v ['riː'teɪl] vt im Einzelhandel verkaufen // vi im Einzelhandel kosten; ~er n (servant) Einzelhändler m, Kleinhändler m; ~ **price** n Ladenpreis m.

retain [rɪ'teɪn] vt (keep) (zurück)-behalten; ~er n (servant) Gefolgsmann m; (fee) (Honorar)vorschuß m.

retaliate [rɪ'tælɪeɪt] vi: to ~ (against) zum Vergeltungsschlag (gegen +acc) ausholen.

retaliation [rɪtælɪ'eɪʃən] n Vergeltung f.

retarded [rɪ'tɑːdɪd] a zurückgeblieben.

retch [retʃ] vi würgen.

retentive [rɪ'tentɪv] a (memory) gut.

reticent ['retɪsənt] a schweigsam.

retina ['retɪnə] n Netzhaut f.

retinue ['retɪnjuː] n Gefolge nt.

retire [rɪ'taɪə*] vi (from work) in den Ruhestand treten; (withdraw) sich zurückziehen; (go to bed) schlafen gehen; ~d a (person) pensioniert, im Ruhestand; ~ment n Ruhestand m.

retiring [rɪ'taɪərɪŋ] a zurückhaltend.

retort [rɪ'tɔːt] n (reply) Erwiderung f; (SCI) Retorte f // vi (sharp) erwidern.

retrace [rɪ'treɪs] vt zurückverfolgen; to ~ one's steps denselben Weg zurückgehen.

retract [rɪ'trækt] vt (statement) zurücknehmen; (claws) einziehen // vi einen Rückzieher machen; ~able a (aerial) ausziehbar.

retrain [riː'treɪn] vt umschulen; ~ing n Umschulung f.

retread ['riːtred] n (tyre) Reifen m mit erneuerter Lauffläche.

retreat [rɪ'triːt] n Rückzug m; (place) Zufluchtsort m // vi sich zurückziehen.

retribution [retrɪ'bjuːʃən] n Strafe f.

retrieval [rɪ'triːvəl] n Wiedergewinnung f.

retrieve [rɪ'triːv] vt wiederbekommen; (rescue) retten; ~r n Apportierhund m.

retrograde ['retrəʊgreɪd] a (step) Rück-; (policy) rückschrittlich.

retrospect ['retrəʊspekt] n: in ~ im Rückblick; ~ive [retrəʊ'spektɪv] a (action) rückwirkend; (look) rückblickend.

return [rɪ'tɜːn] n Rückkehr f; (profits) Ertrag m (Brit: rail ticket etc) Rückfahrkarte f; (: plane) Rückflugkarte f // a (journey, match) Rück- // vi zurückkehren or -kommen // vt zurückgeben, zurücksenden; (pay back) zurückzahlen; (elect) wählen; (verdict) aussprechen; ~s npl (COMM) Gewinn m; (receipts) Einkünfte pl; in ~ dafür; by ~ of post postwendend; many happy ~s (of the day)! herzlichen Glückwunsch zum Geburtstag.

reunion [riː'juːnjən] n Wiedervereinigung f; (SCH etc) Treffen nt.

reunite ['riːjuː'naɪt] vt wiedervereinigen.

rev [rev] n abbr (= revolution: AUT) Drehzahl f // vti (also: ~ up) (den Motor) auf Touren bringen.

revamp ['riː'væmp] vt aufpolieren.

reveal [rɪ'viːl] vt enthüllen; ~ing a aufschlußreich.

reveille [rɪ'vælɪ] n Wecken nt.

revel ['revl] vi: to ~ in sth/in doing sth seine Freude an etw (dat) haben/daran haben, etw zu tun.

revelation [revə'leɪʃən] n Offenbarung f.

revelry ['revlrɪ] n Rummel m.

revenge [rɪ'vendʒ] n Rache f; to take ~ on sich rächen an (+dat).

revenue ['revənjuː] n Einnahmen pl.

reverberate [rɪ'vɜːbəreɪt] vi widerhallen.

revere [rɪ'vɪə*] vt (ver)ehren; **reverence** ['revərəns] n Ehrfurcht f.

Reverend ['revərənd] a: the ~ Robert Martin ≈ Pfarrer Robert Martin.

reverent ['revərənt] a ehrfurchtsvoll.

reverie ['revərɪ] n Träumerei f.

reversal [rɪ'vɜːsəl] n Umkehrung f.

reverse [rɪ'vɜːs] n Rückseite f; (AUT: gear) Rückwärtsgang m // a (order, direction) entgegengesetzt // vt umkehren // vi (Brit AUT) rückwärts fahren; ~-charge call n (Brit) R-Gespräch nt; **reversing lights** npl (AUT) Rückfahrscheinwerfer pl.

revert [rɪ'vɜːt] vi zurückkehren; to ~ to (to bad state) zurückfallen in (+acc).

review [rɪ'vjuː] n (MIL) Truppenschau f; (of book) Rezension f; (magazine) Zeitschrift f // vt Rückschau halten auf (+acc); (MIL) mustern; (book) rezensieren; (reexamine) von neuem untersuchen; ~er n (critic) Rezensent m.

revile [rɪ'vaɪl] vt verunglimpfen.

revise [rɪ'vaɪz] vt (book) überarbeiten; (reconsider) ändern, revidieren.

revision [rɪvɪʒən] n Prüfung f; (COMM) Revision f; (SCH) Wiederholung f.

revitalize ['riː'vaɪtəlaɪz] vt neu beleben.

revival [rɪ'vaɪvəl] n Wiederbelebung f; (REL) Erweckung f; (THEAT) Wiederaufnahme f.

revive [rɪ'vaɪv] vt wiederbeleben; (fig) wieder auffrischen // vi wiedererwachen; (fig) wieder aufleben.

revoke [rɪ'vəʊk] vt aufheben.

revolt [rɪ'vəʊlt] n Aufstand m, Revolte f // vi sich auflehnen // vt entsetzen; ~ing *a* widerlich.

revolution [revə'luːʃən] *n* (*turn*) Umdrehung *f*; (*POL*) Revolution *f*; ~ary *a* revolutionär // *n* Revolutionär *m*; ~ize *vt* revolutionieren.

revolve [rɪ'vɒlv] *vi* kreisen; (*on own axis*) sich drehen.

revulsion [rɪ'vʌlʃən] *n* Ekel *m*.

reward [rɪ'wɔːd] *n* Belohnung *f* // *vt* belohnen; ~ing *a* lohnend.

rewire ['riː'waɪə*] *vt* (*house*) neu verkabeln.

reword ['riː'wɜːd] *vt* anders formulieren.

rewrite ['riː'raɪt] (*irreg: like write*) *vt* umarbeiten, neu schreiben.

rheumatism ['ruːmətɪzəm] *n* Rheumatismus *m*, Rheuma *nt*.

Rhine [raɪn] *n*: the ~ der Rhein.

Rhone [rəʊn] *n*: the ~ die Rhone.

rhubarb ['ruːbaːb] *n* Rhabarber *m*.

rhyme [raɪm] *n* Reim *m*.

rhythm ['rɪðəm] *n* Rhythmus *m*.

rib [rɪb] *n* Rippe *f* // *vt* (*mock*) hänseln, aufziehen.

ribald ['rɪbəld] *a* saftig.

ribbon ['rɪbən] *n* Band *nt*; in ~s (*torn*) in Fetzen.

rice [raɪs] *n* Reis *m*; ~ pudding *n* Milchreis *m*.

rich [rɪtʃ] *a* reich; (*food*) reichhaltig; the ~ die Reichen *pl*; ~es *npl* Reichtum *m*; ~ly *ad* reich; (*deserve*) völlig; ~ness *n* Reichtum *m*; (*of food*) Reichhaltigkeit *f*.

rickets ['rɪkɪts] *n* Rachitis *f*.

rickety ['rɪkɪtɪ] *a* wack(e)lig.

ricochet ['rɪkəʃeɪ] *n* Abprallen *nt*; (*shot*) Querschläger *m* // *vi* abprallen.

rid [rɪd] *pt, pp* rid *vt* befreien (*of* von); to get ~ of loswerden.

ridden ['rɪdn] *pp of* ride.

riddle ['rɪdl] *n* Rätsel *nt* // *vt*: to be ~d with völlig durchlöchert sein von.

ride [raɪd] *n* (*in vehicle*) Fahrt *f*; (*on horse*) Ritt *m* // (*v: pt* rode, *pp* ridden) *vt* (*horse*) reiten; (*bicycle*) fahren // *vi* fahren, reiten; to take sb for a ~ mit jdm eine Fahrt *etc* machen; (*fig*) jdn aufs Glatteis führen; to ~ at anchor (*NAUT*) vor Anker liegen; ~r *n* Reiter *m*; (*addition*) Zusatz *m*.

ridge [rɪdʒ] *n* Kamm *m*; (*of roof*) First *m*.

ridicule ['rɪdɪkjuːl] *n* Spott *m* // *vt* lächerlich machen.

ridiculous *a*, ~ly *ad* [rɪ'dɪkjʊləs, -lɪ] lächerlich.

riding ['raɪdɪŋ] *n* Reiten *nt*; ~ school *n* Reitschule *f*.

rife [raɪf] *a* weit verbreitet; to be ~ grassieren; to be ~ with voll sein von.

riffraff ['rɪfræf] *n* Pöbel *m*.

rifle ['raɪfl] *n* Gewehr *nt* // *vt* berauben; ~ range *n* Schießstand *m*.

rift [rɪft] *n* Spalte *f*; (*fig*) Bruch *m*.

rig [rɪg] *n* (*outfit*) Takelung *f*; (*fig*) Aufmachung *f*; (*oil* ~) Bohrinsel *f* // *vt* (*election etc*) manipulieren; ~ out *vt* (*Brit*) ausstatten; ~ up *vt* zusammenbasteln; ~ging *n* Takelage *f*.

right [raɪt] *a* (*correct, just*) richtig, recht; (*right side*) rechte(r, s) // *n* Recht *nt*; (*not left, POL*) Rechte *f* // *ad* (*on the right*) rechts; (*to the right*) nach rechts; (*look, work*) richtig, recht; (*directly*) gerade; (*exactly*) genau // *vt* in Ordnung bringen, korrigieren // *interj* gut; ~ away sofort; to be ~ recht haben; ~ now in diesem Augenblick, eben; ~ in the middle genau in der Mitte; by ~s von Rechts wegen; on the ~ rechts; to be in the ~ im Recht sein; ~ angle *n* rechte(r) Winkel *m*; ~eous ['raɪtʃəs] *a* rechtschaffen; ~ful *a* rechtmäßig; ~-handed *a* rechtshändig; ~-hand man *n* rechte Hand *f*; ~-hand side *n* rechte Seite *f*; ~ly *ad* mit Recht; ~ of way *n* Vorfahrt *f*; ~-wing *n* rechte(r) Flügel *m*.

rigid ['rɪdʒɪd] *a* (*stiff*) starr, steif; (*strict*) streng; ~ity [rɪ'dʒɪdɪtɪ] *n* Starrheit *f*; Strenge *f*.

rigmarole ['rɪgmərəʊl] *n* Gewäsch *nt*.

rigorous ['rɪgərəs] *a* streng.

rigour, (*US*) **rigor** ['rɪgə*] *n* Strenge *f*, Härte *f*.

rile [raɪl] *vt* ärgern.

rim [rɪm] *n* (*edge*) Rand *m*; (*of wheel*) Felge *f*.

rind [raɪnd] *n* Rinde *f*.

ring [rɪŋ] *n* Ring *m*; (*of people*) Kreis *m*; (*arena*) Manege *f*; (*of telephone*) Klingeln *nt* // (*vi* (*pt* rang, *pp* rung) (*bell*) läuten; (*Brit: also:* ~ up) anrufen; ~ back *vti* zurückrufen; ~ off *vi* (*Brit*) aufhängen; ~ing *n* Klingeln *nt*; (*of large bell*) Läuten *nt*; (*in ears*) Klingen *nt*; ~ing tone *n* (*TEL*) Rufzeichen *nt*.

ringleader ['rɪŋliːdə*] *n* Anführer *m*, Rädelsführer *m*.

ringlets ['rɪŋlɪts] *npl* Ringellocken *pl*.

ring road ['rɪŋrəʊd] *n* (*Brit*) Umgehungsstraße *f*.

rink [rɪŋk] *n* (*ice* ~) Eisbahn *f*.

rinse [rɪns] *n* Spülen *nt* // *vt* spülen.

riot ['raɪət] *n* Aufruhr *m* // *vi* randalieren; to run ~ (*people*) randalieren; (*vegetation*) wuchern; ~er *n* Aufrührer *m*; ~ous *a*, ~ously *ad* aufrührerisch; (*noisy*) lärmend.

rip [rɪp] *n* Schlitz *m*, Riß *m* // *vti* (zer)reißen.

ripcord ['rɪpkɔːd] *n* Reißleine *f*.

ripe [raɪp] *a* reif; ~n *vti* reifen (lassen).

rip-off ['rɪpɒf] *n* (*col*): it's a ~! das ist Wucher!

ripple ['rɪpl] *n* kleine Welle *f* // *vt* kräuseln // *vi* sich kräuseln.

rise [raɪz] *n* (*slope*) Steigung *f*; (*esp in*

wages: Brit) Erhöhung *f*; (*growth*) Aufstieg *m* // *vi* (*pt* **rose**, *pp* **risen** ['rɪzn]) aufstehen; (*sun*) aufgehen; (*smoke*) aufsteigen; (*mountain*) sich erheben; (*ground*) ansteigen; (*prices*) steigen; (*in revolt*) sich erheben; **to give ~ to** Anlaß geben zu; **to ~ to the occasion** sich der Lage gewachsen zeigen; **rising** *a* (*increasing*: *tide, numbers, prices*) steigend; (*sun, moon*) aufgehend // *n* (*uprising*) Aufstand *m*.

risk [rɪsk] *n* Gefahr *f*, Risiko *nt* // *vt* (*venture*) wagen; (*chance loss of*) riskieren, aufs Spiel setzen; **to take** *or* **run the ~ of doing** das Risiko eingehen, zu tun; **at** *or* **in** Gefahr; **at one's own ~** auf eigene Gefahr; **~y** *a* riskant.

risqué ['riːskeɪ] *a* gewagt.

rissole ['rɪsəʊl] *n* Fleischklößchen *nt*.

rite [raɪt] *n* Ritus *m*; **last ~s** *pl* Letzte Ölung *f*.

ritual ['rɪtjʊəl] *n* Ritual *nt* // *a* ritual, Ritual-; (*fig*) rituell.

rival ['raɪvəl] *n* Rivale *m*, Konkurrent *m* // *a* rivalisierend // *vt* rivalisieren mit; (*COMM*) konkurrieren mit; **~ry** *n* Rivalität *f*; Konkurrenz *f*.

river ['rɪvə*] *n* Fluß *m*, Strom *m* // *cpd* (*port, traffic*) Fluß-; **up/down ~** flußaufwärts/-abwärts; **~bank** *n* Flußufer *nt*; **~bed** *n* Flußbett *nt*.

rivet ['rɪvɪt] *n* Niete *f* // *vt* (*fasten*) (ver)nieten.

Riviera [rɪvɪ'ɛərə] *n*: **the ~** die Riviera.

road [rəʊd] *n* Straße *f* // *cpd* Straßen-; **major/minor ~** Haupt-/Nebenstraße *f*; **~block** *n* Straßensperre *f*; **~hog** *n* Verkehrsrowdy *m*; **~map** *n* Straßenkarte *f*; **~ safety** *n* Verkehrssicherheit *f*; **~side** *n* Straßenrand *m* // *a* an der Landstraße (gelegen); **~ sign** *n* Straßenschild *nt*; **~ user** *n* Verkehrsteilnehmer *m*; **~way** *n* Fahrbahn *f*; **~ works** *pl* Straßenbauarbeiten *pl*; **~worthy** *a* verkehrssicher.

roam [rəʊm] *vi* (umher)streifen // *vt* durchstreifen.

roar [rɔː*] *n* Brüllen *nt*, Gebrüll *nt* // *vi* brüllen; **to ~ with laughter** brüllen vor Lachen; **to do a ~ing trade** im Riesengeschäft machen.

roast [rəʊst] *n* Braten *m* // *vt* braten, schmoren; **~ beef** *n* Roastbeef *nt*.

rob [rɒb] *vt* bestehlen, berauben; (*bank*) ausrauben; **to ~ sb of sth** jdm etw rauben; **~ber** *n* Räuber *m*; **~bery** *n* Raub *m*.

robe [rəʊb] *n* (*dress*) Gewand *nt*; (*US*) Hauskleid *nt*; (*judge's*) Robe *f*.

robin ['rɒbɪn] *n* Rotkehlchen *nt*.

robot ['rəʊbɒt] *n* Roboter *m*.

rock [rɒk] *n* Felsen *m*; (*Brit*: *sweet*) Zuckerstange *f* // *vti* wiegen, schaukeln; **on the ~s** (*drink*) mit Eis(würfeln); (*marriage*) gescheitert; (*ship*) auf-

gelaufen; **~ and roll** *n* Rock and Roll *m*; **~-bottom** *n* (*fig*) Tiefpunkt *m*; **~ery** *n* Steingarten *m*.

rocket ['rɒkɪt] *n* Rakete *f*.

rocking: **~chair** *n* Schaukelstuhl *m*; **~ horse** *n* Schaukelpferd *nt*.

rocky ['rɒkɪ] *a* felsig.

rod [rɒd] *n* (*bar*) Stange *f*; (*stick*) Rute *f*.

rode [rəʊd] *pt of* **ride**.

rodent ['rəʊdənt] *n* Nagetier *nt*.

roe [rəʊ] *n* (*deer*) Reh *nt*; (*of fish*) Rogen *m*; **hard/soft ~** Rogen *m*/Milch *f*.

rogue [rəʊg] *n* Schurke *m*.

role [rəʊl] *n* Rolle *f*.

roll [rəʊl] *n* Rolle *f*; (*bread*) Brötchen *nt*; (*list*) (Namens)liste *f*; (*of drum*) Wirbel *m* // *vt* (*turn*) rollen, (herum)wälzen; (*grass etc*) walzen // *vi* (*swing*) schlingern; (*sound*) (g)rollen; **~ about** *or* **around** *vi* herumkugeln; (*ship*) schlingern; (*dog etc*) sich wälzen; **~ by** *vi* (*time*) verfließen; **~ in** *vi* (*mail*) hereinkommen; **~ over** *vi* sich (herum)drehen; **~ up** *vi* (*arrive*) kommen, auftauchen // *vt* (*carpet*) aufrollen; **~ call** *n* Namensaufruf *m* ~**er** *n* Rolle *f*, Walze *f*; (*road* ~*er*) Straßenwalze *f*; ~**er coaster** *n* Achterbahn *f*; ~**er skates** *pl* Rollschuhe *pl*.

rolling ['rəʊlɪŋ] *a* (*landscape*) wellig; **~ pin** *n* Nudel- *or* Wellholz *nt*; **~ stock** *n* Wagenmaterial *nt*.

ROM *n abbr* (= **read only memory**) ROM *m*.

Roman [rəʊmən] *a* römisch // *n* Römer(in *f*) *m*; **~ Catholic** *a* römisch-katholisch // *n* Katholik(in *f*) *m*.

romance [rə'mæns] *n* Romanze *f*; (*story*) (Liebes)roman *m*.

Romania [rəʊ'meɪnɪə] *n* = **Rumania**.

Roman numeral *n* römische Ziffer.

romantic [rəʊ'mæntɪk] *a* romantisch; **~ism** [rəʊ'mæntɪsɪzəm] *n* Romantik *f*.

Rome [rəʊm] *n* Rom *nt*.

romp [rɒmp] *n* Tollen *nt* // *vi* (*also*: **~ about**) herumtollen.

rompers ['rɒmpəz] *npl* Spielanzug *m*.

roof [ruːf], *pl* **~s** *n* Dach *nt*; (*of mouth*) Gaumen *m* // *vt* überdachen, überdecken; **~ing** *n* Deckmaterial *nt*; **~ rack** *n* (*AUT*) Dachgepäckträger *m*.

rook [rʊk] *n* (*bird*) Saatkrähe *f*; (*chess*) Turm *m*.

room [rʊm] *n* Zimmer *nt*, Raum *m*; (*space*) Platz *m*; (*fig*) Spielraum *m*; **~s** *pl* Wohnung *f*; **'~s to let'**, (*US*) **'~s for rent'** 'Zimmer zu vermieten'; **single/ double ~** Einzel-/Doppelzimmer *nt*; **~ing house** *n* (*US*) Mietshaus *nt* (*mit möblierten Wohnungen*); **~-mate** *n* Mitbewohner(in *f*) *m*; **~ service** *n* Zimmerbedienung *f*; **~y** *a* geräumig.

roost [ruːst] *n* Hühnerstange *f* // *vi* auf der Stange hocken.

rooster ['ru:stə*] n Hahn m.
root [ru:t] n (lit, fig) Wurzel f // vi wurzeln; ~ **about** vi (fig) herumwühlen; ~ **for** vt Stimmung machen für; ~ **out** vt ausjäten; (fig) ausrotten.
rope [rəʊp] n Seil nt // vt (tie) festschnüren; **to know the** ~**s** sich auskennen; **to** ~ **sb in** jdn gewinnen; ~ **off** vt absperren; ~ **ladder** n Strickleiter f.
rosary ['rəʊzəri] n Rosenkranz m.
rose [rəʊz] pt of **rise** // n Rose f // a Rosen-, rosenrot.
rosé ['rəʊzeɪ] n Rosé m.
rosebud ['rəʊzbʌd] n Rosenknospe f.
rosebush ['rəʊzbʊʃ] n Rosenstock m.
rosemary ['rəʊzməri] n Rosmarin m.
rosette [rəʊ'zet] n Rosette f.
roster ['rɒstə*] n Dienstplan m.
rostrum ['rɒstrəm] n Rednerbühne f.
rosy ['rəʊzi] a rosig.
rot [rɒt] n Fäulnis f; (nonsense) Quatsch m // vi verfaulen (lassen).
rota ['rəʊtə] n Dienstliste f.
rotary ['rəʊtəri] a rotierend.
rotate [rəʊ'teɪt] vt rotieren lassen; (two or more things in order) turnusmäßig wechseln // vi rotieren.
rotating [rəʊ'teɪtɪŋ] a rotierend.
rotation [rəʊ'teɪʃən] n Umdrehung f.
rote [rəʊt] n: **by** ~ auswendig.
rotten ['rɒtn] a faul; (fig) schlecht, gemein; **to feel** ~ (ill) sich elend fühlen.
rotund [rəʊ'tʌnd] a rundlich.
rouble, (US) **ruble** ['ru:bl] n Rubel m.
rough [rʌf] a (not smooth) rauh; (path) uneben; (violent) roh, grob; (crossing) stürmisch; (without comforts) hart, unbequem; (unfinished, makeshift) grob; (approximate) ungefähr // n (Brit: person) Rowdy m, Rohling m; (GOLF): **in the** ~ im Rauh // vt: **to** ~ **it** primitiv leben; **to sleep** ~ im Freien schlafen; ~**age** n Ballaststoffe pl; ~**-and-ready** a provisorisch; (work) zusammengehauen; ~**cast** n Rauhputz nt; ~ **copy** n, ~ **draft** n Entwurf m; ~**en** vt aufrauhen; ~**ly** ad grob; (about) ungefähr; ~**ness** n Rauheit f; (of manner) Ungeschliffenheit f.
Roumania [ru:'meɪntə] n = **Rumania**.
round [raʊnd] a rund; (figures) aufgerundet // ad (in a circle) rundherum // prep um ... herum // n Runde f; (of ammunition) Magazin nt // vt (corner) biegen um; **all** ~ überall; **the long way** ~ der Umweg; **all the year** ~ das ganze Jahr über; **it's just** ~ **the corner** (fig) es ist gerade um die Ecke; **the clock** ad rund um die Uhr; **to go** ~ **to sb's** (house) jdn besuchen; **to go** ~ **the back** durch den Hintereingang gehen; **to go** ~ **a house** um ein Haus herumgehen; **enough to go** ~ genug für alle; **to go the** ~**s** (story) die Runde machen; **a** ~ **of applause** ein Beifall m; **a** ~ **of drinks/**

sandwiches eine Runde Drinks/ Sandwiches; ~ **off** vt abrunden; ~ **up** vt (end) abschließen; (figures) aufrunden; ~**about** n (Brit: traffic) Kreisverkehr m; (: merry-go-round) Karussell nt // a auf Umwegen; ~**ers** npl (game) ≃ Schlagball m; ~**ly** ad (fig) gründlich; ~**-shouldered** a mit abfallenden Schultern; ~ **trip** n Rundreise f; ~**up** n Zusammentreiben nt, Sammeln nt.
rouse [raʊz] vt (waken) (auf)wecken; (stir up) erregen.
rousing ['raʊzɪŋ] a (welcome) stürmisch; (speech) zündend.
route [ru:t] n Weg m, Route f; ~ **map** n (Brit: for journey) Streckenkarte f.
routine [ru:'ti:n] n Routine f // a Routine-.
roving ['rəʊvɪŋ] a (reporter) im Außendienst.
row [rəʊ] n (line) Reihe f // vti (boat) rudern; **in a** ~ (fig) hintereinander.
row [raʊ] n (noise) Lärm m; (dispute) Streit m // vi sich streiten.
rowboat ['rəʊbəʊt] n (US) Ruderboot nt.
rowdy ['raʊdi] a rüpelhaft // n (person) Rowdy m.
rowing ['rəʊɪŋ] n Rudern nt; (SPORT) Rudersport m; ~ **boat** n (Brit) Ruderboot nt.
royal ['rɔɪəl] a königlich, Königs-; ~ **Air Force (RAF)** n Königliche Luftwaffe f.
royalty ['rɔɪəltɪ] n (family) königliche Familie f; (for book) Tantieme f.
rpm abbr (= revs per minute) U/min.
R.S.V.P. abbr (= répondez s'il vous plaît) u.A.w.g.
Rt Hon. abbr (Brit: = Right Honourable) Abgeordnete(r) mf.
rub [rʌb] n (problem) Haken m // vt reiben; **to** ~ **sb up** or (US) ~ **sb the wrong way** jdn aufreizen; ~ **off** vi (lit, fig) abfärben (on auf +acc); ~ **out** vt herausreiben; (with eraser) ausradieren.
rubber ['rʌbə*] n Gummi m; (Brit) Radiergummi m; ~ **band** n Gummiband nt; ~ **plant** n Gummibaum m; ~**y** a gummiartig.
rubbish ['rʌbɪʃ] n (waste) Abfall m; (nonsense) Blödsinn m, Quatsch m; ~ **bin** n (Brit) Mülleimer m; ~ **dump** n Müllablageplatz m.
rubble ['rʌbl] n (Stein)schutt m.
ruby ['ru:bɪ] n Rubin m // a rubinrot.
rucksack ['rʌksæk] n Rucksack m.
ructions ['rʌkʃənz] npl Krach m.
rudder ['rʌdə*] n Steuerruder nt.
ruddy ['rʌdɪ] a (colour) rötlich; (col: bloody) verdammt.
rude [ru:d] a unverschämt; (shock) hart; (awakening) unsanft; (unrefined, rough) grob; ~**ness** n Unverschämtheit f; Grobheit f.

rudiment ['ru:dɪmənt] n Grundlage f.
rueful ['ru:ful] a reuevoll; (situation) beklagenswert.
ruffian ['rʌfɪən] n Rohling m.
ruffle ['rʌfl] vt kräuseln.
rug [rʌg] n Brücke f; (in bedroom) Bettvorleger m; (Brit: for knees) (Reise)decke f.
rugby ['rʌgbɪ] n (also: ~ football) Rugby nt.
rugged ['rʌgɪd] a (coastline) zerklüftet; (features) markig.
rugger ['rʌgə*] n (Brit col) Rugby nt.
ruin ['ru:ɪn] n Ruine f; (downfall) Ruin m // vt ruinieren; ~s pl Trümmer pl; ~ous a ruinierend.
rule [ru:l] n Regel f; (government) Regierung f; (for measuring) Lineal nt // vti (govern) herrschen über (+acc), regieren; (decide) anordnen, entscheiden; (make lines) linieren; as a ~ in der Regel; ~ out vt ausschließen; ~d a (paper) liniert; ~r n Lineal nt; Herrscher m.
ruling ['ru:lɪŋ] a (party) Regierungs-; (class) herrschend // n (JUR) Entscheid m.
rum [rʌm] n Rum m.
Rumania [ru:'meɪnɪə] n Rumänien nt; ~n a rumänisch // n Rumäne m, Rumänin f; (LING) Rumänisch nt.
rumble ['rʌmbl] n Rumpeln nt; (of thunder) Rollen nt // vi rumpeln; grollen.
rummage ['rʌmɪdʒ] vi durchstöbern.
rumour, (US) **rumor** ['ru:mə*] n Gerücht nt // vt: it is ~ed that man sagt or man munkelt, daß.
rump [rʌmp] n Hinterteil nt; ~ **steak** n Rumpsteak nt.
rumpus ['rʌmpəs] n Spektakel m.
run [rʌn] n Lauf m; (in car) (Spazier)fahrt f; (series) Serie f, Reihe f; (ski ~) (Ski)abfahrt f; (in stocking) Laufmasche f // v (pt ran, pp run) vt (cause to run) laufen lassen; (car, train, bus) fahren; (race, distance) laufen, rennen; (manage) leiten; (COMPUT) laufen lassen; (pass: hand, eye) gleiten lassen // vi laufen; (move quickly also) rennen; (bus, train) fahren; (flow) fließen, laufen; (colours) (ab)färben; there was a ~ on (meat, tickets) es gab einen Ansturm auf (+acc); on the ~ auf der Flucht; in the long ~ auf die Dauer; I'll ~ you to the station ich fahre dich zum Bahnhof; to ~ a risk ein Risiko eingehen; ~ **about** or **around** vi (children) umherspringen; ~ **across** vt (find) stoßen auf (+acc); ~ **away** vi weglaufen; ~ **down** vi (clock) stehenbleiben // vt (production, factory) allmählich auflösen; (with car) überfahren; (talk against) heruntermachen; to be ~ **down** erschöpft or abgespannt sein; ~ **in** vt (Brit: car) einfahren; ~ **into** vt (meet:

person) zufällig treffen; (: trouble) bekommen; (collide with) rennen/fahren gegen; ~ **off** vi fortlaufen; ~ **out** vi (person) hinausrennen; (liquid) auslaufen; (lease) ablaufen; (money) ausgehen; he ran out of money/petrol ihm ging das Geld/Benzin aus; ~ **over** vt (in accident) überfahren; ~ **through** vt (instructions) durchgehen; ~ **up** vt (debt, bill) machen; ~ **up against** vt (difficulties) stoßen auf (+acc); ~**away** a (horse) ausgebrochen; (person) flüchtig.
rung [rʌŋ] pp of **ring** // n Sprosse f.
runner ['rʌnə*] n Läufer(in f) m; (for sleigh) Kufe f; ~ **bean** n (Brit) Stangenbohne f; ~**-up** n Zweite(r) mf.
running ['rʌnɪŋ] n (of business) Leitung f; (of machine) Betrieb m // a (water) fließend; (commentary) laufend; to be in/out of the ~ for sth im/aus dem Rennen für etw sein; 3 days ~ 3 Tage lang or hintereinander.
runny ['rʌnɪ] a dünn.
run-of-the-mill ['rʌnəvðə'mɪl] a gewöhnlich, alltäglich.
run-up ['rʌnʌp] n: ~ **to** (election etc) Endphase vor (+dat).
runway ['rʌnweɪ] n Startbahn f.
rupee [ru:'pi:] n Rupie f.
rupture ['rʌptʃə*] n (MED) Bruch m // vt: to ~ **o.s.** sich (dat) einen Bruch zuziehen.
rural ['rʊərəl] a ländlich, Land-.
ruse [ru:z] n Kniff m, List f.
rush [rʌʃ] n Eile f, Hetze f; (FIN) starke Nachfrage f // vt (carry along) auf dem schnellsten Wege schaffen or transportieren; (attack) losstürmen auf (+acc); don't ~ **me** dräng mich nicht // vi (hurry) eilen, stürzen; ~ **hour** n Hauptverkehrszeit f.
rusk [rʌsk] n Zwieback m.
Russia ['rʌʃə] n Rußland nt; ~**n** a russisch // n Russe m, Russin f; (LING) Russisch nt.
rust [rʌst] n Rost m // vi rosten.
rustic ['rʌstɪk] a bäuerlich, ländlich.
rustle ['rʌsl] vi rauschen, rascheln // vt rascheln lassen; (cattle) stehlen.
rustproof ['rʌstpru:f] a rostfrei.
rusty ['rʌstɪ] a rostig.
rut [rʌt] n (in track) Radspur f; to be in a ~ im Trott stecken.
ruthless ['ru:θləs] a rücksichtslos.
rye [raɪ] n Roggen m; ~ **bread** n Roggenbrot nt.

S

sabbatical [sə'bætɪkəl] a: ~ **year** n Beurlaubungs- or Forschungsjahr nt.
sabotage ['sæbətɑ:ʒ] n Sabotage f // vt sabotieren.

saccharin(e) ['sækərın] n Saccharin nt.
sachet ['sæʃeɪ] n (of shampoo) Briefchen nt, Kissen nt.
sack [sæk] n Sack m // vt (col) hinauswerfen; (pillage) plündern; **to get the ~** rausfliegen; **~ing** n (material) Sackleinen nt; (col) Rausschmiß m.
sacred ['seɪkrɪd] a heilig.
sacrifice ['sækrɪfaɪs] n Opfer nt // vt (lit, fig) opfern.
sacrilege ['sækrɪlɪdʒ] n Schändung f.
sad [sæd] a traurig; **~den** vt traurig machen, betrüben.
saddle ['sædl] n Sattel m // vt (burden) aufhalsen (sb with sth jdm etw); **~bag** n Satteltasche f.
sadly ['sædlɪ] ad traurig; (unfortunately) leider; **she is ~ lacking (in)** ... ihr fehlt es leider ...
sadness ['sædnəs] n Traurigkeit f.
sae abbr (= stamped addressed envelope) adressierte(r) Rückumschlag m.
safe [seɪf] a (free from danger) sicher; (careful) vorsichtig // n Safe m; **~ and sound** gesund und wohl; **(just) to be on the ~ side** um ganz sicher zu gehen; **~-conduct** n freie(s) Geleit nt; **~-deposit** n (vault) Tresorraum m; (box) Banksafe m; **~guard** n Sicherung f // vt sichern, schützen; **~keeping** n sichere Verwahrung f; **~ly** ad sicher; (arrive) wohlbehalten.
safety ['seɪftɪ] n Sicherheit f; **~ belt** n Sicherheitsgurt m; **~ pin** n Sicherheitsnadel f; **~ valve** n Sicherheitsventil nt.
sag [sæg] vi (durch)sacken.
sage [seɪdʒ] n (herb) Salbei m; (man) Weise(r) m.
Sagittarius [sædʒɪˈtɛərɪəs] n Schütze m.
Sahara [səˈhɑːrə] n: **the ~ (Desert)** die (Wüste) Sahara.
said [sed] pt, pp of **say**.
sail [seɪl] n Segel nt; (trip) Fahrt f // vt segeln // vi segeln; (begin voyage: person) abfahren; (: ship) auslaufen; (fig: cloud etc) dahinsegeln; **to go for a ~** segeln gehen; **they ~ed into Copenhagen** sie liefen in Kopenhagen ein; **to ~ through** vti (fig) spielend schaffen; **~boat** n (US) Segelboot nt; **~ing** n Segeln nt; **~ing ship** n Segelschiff nt; **~or** n Matrose m, Seemann m.
saint [seɪnt] n Heilige(r) mf; **~ly** a heilig, fromm.
sake [seɪk] n: **for the ~ of** um (+gen) willen.
salad ['sæləd] n Salat m; **~ bowl** n Salatschüssel f; **~ cream** n (Brit) gewürzte Mayonnaise f; **~ dressing** n Salatsoße f.
salami [səˈlɑːmɪ] n Salami f.
salary ['sælərɪ] n Gehalt nt.
sale [seɪl] n Verkauf m; (reduced prices)

Schlußverkauf m; **'for ~'** zu verkaufen; **on ~** zu verkaufen; **~room** n Verkaufsraum m; **~s assistant**, (US) **~s clerk** n Verkäufer(in f) m; **salesman** n Verkäufer m; (representative) Vertreter m; **saleswoman** n Verkäuferin f.
salient ['seɪlɪənt] a bemerkenswert.
saliva [səˈlaɪvə] n Speichel m.
sallow ['sæləʊ] a fahl; (face) bleich.
salmon ['sæmən] n Lachs m.
saloon [səˈluːn] n (Brit AUT) Limousine f; (ship's lounge) Salon m.
salt [sɔːlt] n Salz nt // vt (cure) einsalzen; (flavour) salzen; **~ away** vt (col: money) auf die hohe Kante legen; **~cellar** n Salzfaß nt; **~ water** a Salzwasser-; **~y** a salzig.
salutary ['sæljʊtərɪ] a nützlich.
salute [səˈluːt] n (MIL) Gruß m; (with guns) Salutschüsse pl // vt (MIL) salutieren.
salvage ['sælvɪdʒ] n (from ship) Bergung f; (property) Rettung f // vt bergen; retten.
salvation [sælˈveɪʃən] n Rettung f; **S~ Army** n Heilsarmee f.
same [seɪm] a, pron (similar) gleiche(r, s); (identical) derselbe/dieselbe/dasselbe; **the ~ book as** das gleiche Buch wie; **at the ~ time** zur gleichen Zeit, gleichzeitig; (however) zugleich, andererseits; **all or just the ~** trotzdem; **the ~ to you!** gleichfalls.
sample ['sɑːmpl] n Probe f // vt probieren.
sanctify ['sæŋktɪfaɪ] vt weihen.
sanctimonious [sæŋktɪˈməʊnɪəs] a scheinheilig.
sanctity ['sæŋktɪtɪ] n Heiligkeit f; (fig) Unverletzlichkeit f.
sanctuary ['sæŋktjʊərɪ] n (for fugitive) Asyl nt; (refuge) Zufluchtsort m; (for animals) Schutzgebiet nt.
sand [sænd] n Sand m // vt (furniture) schmirgeln; **~s** pl Sand m.
sandal ['sændl] n Sandale f.
sand: **~box** n (US) = **~pit**; **~castle** n Sandburg f; **~ dune** n (Sand)düne f; **~paper** n Sandpapier nt; **~pit** n Sandkasten m; **~stone** n Sandstein m.
sandwich ['sænwɪdʒ] n Sandwich m or nt // vt (also: **~ in**) einklemmen; **~ed between** eingeklemmt zwischen; **cheese/ham ~** Käse-/Schinkenbrot; **~ board** n Reklametafel f; **~ course** n (Brit) Ausbildungsgang m mit abwechselnden Theorie- und Praxisteilen.
sandy ['sændɪ] a sandig; (hair) rotblond.
sane [seɪn] a geistig gesund or normal; (sensible) vernünftig, gescheit.
sang [sæŋ] pt of **sing**.
sanitary ['sænɪtərɪ] a hygienisch; **~ towel**, (US) **~ napkin** n (Monats)binde f.
sanitation [sænɪˈteɪʃən] n sanitäre Ein-

richtungen pl; ~ **department** n (US) Stadtreinigung f.

sanity ['sænɪtɪ] n geistige Gesundheit f; (good sense) Vernunft f.

sank [sæŋk] pt of **sink**.

Santa Claus [sæntə'klɔ:z] n Nikolaus m, Weihnachtsmann m.

sap [sæp] n (of plants) Saft m // vt (strength) schwächen.

sapling ['sæplɪŋ] n junge(r) Baum m.

sapphire ['sæfaɪə*] n Saphir m.

sarcastic [sɑ:'kæstɪk] a sarkastisch.

sardine [sɑ:'di:n] n Sardine f.

Sardinia [sɑ:'dɪnɪə] n Sardinien nt.

sardonic [sɑ:'dɒnɪk] a zynisch.

sash [sæʃ] n Schärpe f.

sat [sæt] pt, pp of **sit**.

Satan ['seɪtn] n Satan m.

satchel ['sætʃəl] n (SCH) Schulmappe f.

sated ['seɪtɪd] a (appetite, person) gesättigt.

satin ['sætɪn] n Satin m // a Satin-.

satisfaction [sætɪs'fækʃən] n Befriedigung f, Genugtuung f.

satisfactory [sætɪs'fæktərɪ] a zufriedenstellend, befriedigend.

satisfy ['sætɪsfaɪ] vt befriedigen, zufriedenstellen; (convince) überzeugen; (conditions) erfüllen; ~**ing** a befriedigend; (meal) sättigend.

saturate ['sætʃəreɪt] vt (durch)tränken.

saturation [sætʃə'reɪʃən] n Durchtränkung f; (CHEM, fig) Sättigung f.

Saturday ['sætədeɪ] n Samstag m, Sonnabend m.

sauce [sɔ:s] n Soße f, Sauce f; ~**pan** n Kasserolle f.

saucer ['sɔ:sə*] n Untertasse f.

saucy ['sɔ:sɪ] a frech, keck.

Saudi ['saudɪ]: ~ **Arabia** n Saudi-Arabien nt; ~ **(Arabian)** a saudiarabisch // n Saudiaraber(in f) m.

sauna ['sɔ:nə] n Sauna f.

saunter ['sɔ:ntə*] vi schlendern.

sausage ['sɒsɪdʒ] n Wurst f; ~ **roll** n Wurst f im Schlafrock, Wurstpastete f.

sauté ['səuteɪ] a Röst-.

savage ['sævɪdʒ] a wild // n Wilde(r) mf // vt (animals) zerfleischen; ~**ry** n Roheit f, Grausamkeit f.

save [seɪv] vt retten; (money, electricity etc) sparen; (strength etc) aufsparen; (COMPUT) speichern // vi (also: ~ up) sparen // n (SPORT) (Ball)abwehr f // prep, cj außer, ausgenommen.

saving ['seɪvɪŋ] a: the ~ **grace** of das Versöhnende an (+ dat) // n Sparen nt, Ersparnis f; ~**s** pl Ersparnisse pl; ~**s bank** n Sparkasse f; ~**s account** n Sparkonto nt.

saviour, (US) **savior** ['seɪvjə*] n (ECCL) Erlöser m.

savour, (US) **savor** ['seɪvə*] vt (taste) schmecken; (fig) genießen; ~**y** a pikant, würzig.

saw [sɔ:] pt of **see** // n (tool) Säge f // vti, pt **sawed**, pp **sawed** or **sawn** sägen; ~**dust** n Sägemehl nt; ~**mill** n Sägewerk nt; ~**n-off shotgun** n Gewehr nt mit abgesägtem Lauf.

say [seɪ] n: to have no/a ~ **in** sth (kein) Mitspracherecht bei etw haben; let him have his ~ laß ihn doch reden // vti, pt, pp **said** sagen; to ~ **yes/no** ja/nein sagen; that goes without ~**ing** das versteht sich von selbst; that is to ~ das heißt; ~**ing** n Sprichwort nt.

scab [skæb] n Schorf m; (pej) Streikbrecher m.

scaffold ['skæfəuld] n (for execution) Schafott nt; ~**ing** n (Bau)gerüst nt.

scald [skɔ:ld] n Verbrühung f // vt (burn) verbrühen; (clean) (ab)brühen.

scale [skeɪl] n (of fish) Schuppe f; (MUS) Tonleiter f; (on map, size) Maßstab m; (gradation) Skala f // vt (climb) erklimmen; ~**s** pl (balance) Waage f; **on a large** ~ (fig) im großen, in großem Umfang; ~ **of charges** Gebührenordnung f; ~ **down** vt verkleinern; ~ **model** n maßstabgetreue(s) Modell nt.

scallop ['skɒləp] n Kammuschel f.

scalp [skælp] n Kopfhaut f.

scamper ['skæmpə*] vi: ~ **away**, ~ **off** verschwinden.

scampi ['skæmpɪ] npl Scampi pl.

scan [skæn] vt (examine) genau prüfen; (quickly) überfliegen; (horizon) absuchen; (poetry) skandieren.

Scandinavia [skændɪ'neɪvɪə] n Skandinavien nt; ~**n** a skandinavisch // n Skandinavier(in f) m.

scant [skænt] a knapp; ~**ily** ad knapp, dürftig; ~**iness** n Knappheit f; ~**y** a knapp, unzureichend.

scapegoat ['skeɪpgəut] n Sündenbock m.

scar [skɑ:*] n Narbe f // vt durch Narben entstellen.

scarce ['skɛəs] a selten, rar; (goods) knapp; ~**ly** ad kaum.

scarcity ['skɛəsɪtɪ] n Mangel m.

scare ['skɛə*] n Schrecken m // vt erschrecken; to ~ **sb** stiff jdn zu Tode erschrecken; to be ~**d** Angst haben; **bomb** ~ Bombendrohung f; ~**crow** n Vogelscheuche f.

scarf [skɑ:f], pl **scarves** n Schal m; (head~) Kopftuch nt.

scarlet ['skɑ:lət] a scharlachrot // n Scharlachrot nt; ~ **fever** n Scharlach m.

scarves [skɑ:vz] pl of **scarf**.

scary ['skɛərɪ] a (col) schaurig.

scathing ['skeɪðɪŋ] a scharf, vernichtend.

scatter ['skætə*] vt (sprinkle) (ver)streuen; (disperse) zerstreuen // vi sich zerstreuen; ~**brained** a flatterhaft, schusselig.

scavenger ['skævɪndʒə*] n (animal) Aasfresser m.

scenario [sɪ'nɑːrɪəʊ] n (THEAT, CINE) Szenarium nt; (fig) Szenario nt.

scene [siːn] n (of happening) Ort m; (of play, incident) Szene f; (view) Anblick m; (argument) Szene f, Auftritt m; **~ry** ['siːnərɪ] n (THEAT) Bühnenbild nt; (landscape) Landschaft f.

scenic ['siːnɪk] a landschaftlich.

scent [sent] n Parfüm nt; (smell) Duft m // vt parfümieren.

schedule ['ʃedjuːl] n (list) Liste f; (plan) Programm nt; (of work) Zeitplan m // vt planen; **on ~** pünktlich; **to be ahead of/behind ~** dem Zeitplan voraus/im Rückstand sein; **~d flight** n (not charter) Linienflug m.

scheme [skiːm] n Schema nt; (dishonest) Intrige f; (plan of action) Plan m // vi intrigieren // vt planen.

scheming ['skiːmɪŋ] a intrigierend.

scholar ['skɒlə*] n Gelehrte(r) m; (holding scholarship) Stipendiat m; **~ly** a gelehrt; **~ship** n Gelehrsamkeit f; (grant) Stipendium nt.

school [skuːl] n Schule f; (UNIV) Fakultät f // vt schulen; (dog) trainieren; **~ age** n schulpflichtige(s) Alter nt; **~book** n Schulbuch nt; **~boy** n Schüler m; **~ children** npl Schüler pl, Schulkinder pl; **~days** pl (alte) Schulzeit f; **~girl** n Schülerin f; **~ing** n Schulung f, Ausbildung f; **~master** n Lehrer m; **~mistress** n Lehrerin f; **~teacher** n Lehrer(in f) m.

sciatica [saɪ'ætɪkə] n Ischias m or nt.

science ['saɪəns] n Wissenschaft f; (natural ~) Naturwissenschaft f.

scientific [saɪən'tɪfɪk] a wissenschaftlich; (natural sciences) naturwissenschaftlich.

scientist ['saɪəntɪst] n Wissenschaftler(in f) m.

scintillating ['sɪntɪleɪtɪŋ] a sprühend.

scissors ['sɪzəz] npl Schere f; **a pair of ~** eine Schere.

scoff [skɒf] vt (Brit col: eat) fressen // vi (mock) spotten (at über +acc).

scold [skəʊld] vt schimpfen.

scone [skɒn] n weiche(s) Teegebäck nt.

scoop [skuːp] n Schaufel f; (news) sensationelle Erstmeldung f // vt (also: ~ **out** or **up**) schaufeln.

scooter ['skuːtə*] n Motorroller m; (child's) Roller m.

scope [skəʊp] n Ausmaß nt; (opportunity) (Spiel)raum m.

scorch [skɔːtʃ] n Brandstelle f // vt versengen; **~ing** a brennend.

score [skɔː*] n (in game) Punktzahl f; (final ~) (Spiel)ergebnis nt; (MUS) Partitur f; (line) Kratzer m; (twenty) 20, 20 Stück // vt (goal) schießen; (points) machen; (mark) einritzen // vi (keep record) Punkte zählen; **on that ~** in dieser Hinsicht; **what's the ~?** wie steht's? **~ out** vt ausstreichen; **~board** n Anschreibetafel f; **~r** n Torschütze m; (recorder) (Auf)schreiber m.

scorn ['skɔːn] n Verachtung f // vt verhöhnen; **~ful** a verächtlich.

Scorpio ['skɔːpɪəʊ] n Skorpion m.

Scot [skɒt] n Schotte m, Schottin f.

scotch [skɒtʃ] vt (end) unterbinden; **S~** n Scotch m.

scot-free ['skɒt'friː] ad: **to get off ~** (unpunished) ungeschoren davonkommen.

Scotland ['skɒtlənd] n Schottland nt.

Scots [skɒts] a schottisch; **~man/ -woman** n Schotte m/Schottin f.

Scottish ['skɒtɪʃ] a schottisch.

scoundrel ['skaʊndrəl] n Schuft m.

scour ['skaʊə*] vt (search) absuchen; (clean) schrubben.

scourge [skɜːdʒ] n (whip) Geißel f; (plague) Qual f.

scout [skaʊt] n (MIL) Späher m; (also: boy ~) Pfadfinder m // vi: ~ **around** vi sich umsehen (for nach).

scowl [skaʊl] n finstere(r) Blick m // vi finster blicken.

scrabble ['skræbl] vi (claw) kratzen (at an + dat); (also: ~ **around**: search) (herum)tasten // n: **S~** ® Scrabble nt ®.

scraggy ['skrægɪ] a dürr, hager.

scram [skræm] vi (col) abhauen.

scramble ['skræmbl] n (climb) Kletterei f; (struggle) Kampf m // vi klettern; (fight) sich schlagen; **to ~ out/through** krabbeln ausdurch; **to ~ for sth** sich um etw raufen; **~d eggs** npl Rührei nt.

scrap [skræp] n (bit) Stückchen nt; (fight) Keilerei f; (also: ~ **iron**) Schrott m // vt verwerfen // vi (fight) streiten, sich prügeln; **~book** n Einklebealbum nt; **~ dealer** n Schrotthändler(in f) m; **~s** pl Reste pl; (waste) Abfall m.

scrape [skreɪp] n Kratzen nt; (trouble) Klemme f // vt kratzen; (car) zerkratzen; (clean) abkratzen // vi (make harsh noise) kratzen; **to ~ through** gerade noch durchkommen; **~r** n Kratzer m.

scrap heap ['skræphiːp] n Schrotthaufen m; **on the ~** (fig) beim alten Eisen.

scrap merchant ['skræpmɜːtʃənt] n (Brit) Altwarenhändler(in f) m.

scrappy ['skræpɪ] a zusammengestoppelt.

scratch [skrætʃ] n (wound) Kratzer m, Schramme f // a: ~ **team** zusammengewürfelte Mannschaft // vt kratzen; (car) zerkratzen // vi (sich) kratzen; **to start from ~** ganz von vorne anfangen; **to be up to ~** den Anforderungen entsprechen.

scrawl [skrɔːl] n Gekritzel nt // vti kritzeln.

scrawny ['skrɔːnɪ] a (person, neck) dürr.

scream [skriːm] n Schrei m // vi schreien.

scree [skriː] n Geröll(halde f) nt.

screech [skriːtʃ] n Schrei m // vi kreischen.

screen [skriːn] n (protective) Schutzschirm m; (film) Leinwand f; (TV) Bildschirm m // vt (shelter) (be)schirmen; (film) zeigen, vorführen; ~ing n (MED) Untersuchung f; ~play n Drehbuch nt.

screw [skruː] n Schraube f // vt (fasten) schrauben; (vulgar) bumsen; ~ up vt (paper etc) zerknüllen; (col: ruin) vermasseln (col); ~driver n Schraubenzieher m.

scribble ['skrɪbl] n Gekritzel nt // vt kritzeln.

script [skrɪpt] n (handwriting) Handschrift f; (for film) Drehbuch nt; (THEAT) Manuskript nt, Text m.

Scripture ['skrɪptʃə*] n Heilige Schrift f.

scroll [skrəʊl] n Schriftrolle f.

scrounge [skraʊndʒ] vt (col): to ~ sth off or from sb etw bei jdm abstauben // n: on the ~ beim Schnorren.

scrub [skrʌb] n (clean) Schrubben nt; (in countryside) Gestrüpp nt // vt (clean) schrubben; (reject) fallenlassen.

scruff [skrʌf] n: by the ~ of the neck am Genick.

scruffy ['skrʌfɪ] a unordentlich, vergammelt.

scrum(mage) ['skrʌm(ɪdʒ)] n Getümmel nt.

scruple ['skruːpl] n Skrupel m, Bedenken nt.

scrupulous ['skruːpjʊləs] a peinlich genau, gewissenhaft.

scrutinize ['skruːtɪnaɪz] vt genau prüfen.

scrutiny ['skruːtɪnɪ] n genaue Untersuchung f.

scuff [skʌf] vt (shoes) abstoßen.

scuffle ['skʌfl] n Handgemenge nt.

scullery ['skʌlərɪ] n Spülküche f.

sculptor ['skʌlptə*] n Bildhauer(in f) m.

sculpture ['skʌlptʃə*] n (ART) Bildhauerei f; (statue) Skulptur f.

scum [skʌm] n (lit, fig) Abschaum m.

scupper ['skʌpə*] vt (NAUT) versenken; (fig) zerstören.

scurrilous ['skʌrɪləs] a unflätig.

scurry ['skʌrɪ] vi huschen.

scuttle ['skʌtl] n (also: coal ~) Kohleneimer m // vt (ship) versenken // vi (scamper): to ~ away or off sich davonmachen.

scythe [saɪð] n Sense f.

SDP n abbr (Brit: = Social Democratic Party) Sozialdemokratische Partei f.

sea [siː] n Meer nt (also fig), See f // a Meeres-, See-; by ~ (travel) auf dem Seeweg; on the ~ (boat) auf dem Meer; (town) am Meer; to be all at ~ (fig) nicht durchblicken; out to or at ~ aufs Meer (hinaus); ~board n Küste f; ~ breeze n Seewind m; ~food n Meeresfrüchte pl; ~ front n Strandpromenade f; ~going a seetüchtig, Hochsee-; ~gull n Möwe f.

seal [siːl] n (animal) Robbe f, Seehund m; (stamp, impression) Siegel nt // vt versiegeln.

sea level ['siːlevl] n Meeresspiegel m.

sea lion ['siːlaɪən] n Seelöwe m.

seam [siːm] n Saum m; (edges joining) Naht f; (of coal) Flöz nt.

seaman ['siːmən] n Seemann m.

seamy ['siːmɪ] a (people, café) zwielichtig; (life) anrüchig.

seaplane ['siːpleɪn] n Wasserflugzeug nt.

seaport ['siːpɔːt] n Seehafen m.

search [sɜːtʃ] n Suche f (for nach) // vi suchen // vt (examine) durchsuchen; in ~ of auf der Suche nach; ~ for vt suchen nach; ~ through vt durchsuchen; ~ing a (look) forschend; ~light n Scheinwerfer m; ~ party n Suchmannschaft f; ~ warrant n Durchsuchungsbefehl m.

seashore ['siːʃɔː*] n Meeresküste f.

seasick ['siːsɪk] a seekrank; ~ness n Seekrankheit f.

seaside ['siːsaɪd] n Küste f; ~ resort n Badeort m.

season ['siːzn] n Jahreszeit f; (e.g. Christmas) Zeit f, Saison f // vt (flavour) würzen; ~al a Saison-; ~ed a (fig) erfahren; ~ing n Gewürz nt, Würze f; ~ ticket n (RAIL) Zeitkarte f; (THEAT) Abonnement nt.

seat [siːt] n Sitz m, Platz m; (in Parliament) Sitz m; (part of body) Gesäß nt; (part of garment) Hosenboden m // vt (place) setzen; (have space for) Sitzplätze bieten für; to be ~ed sitzen; ~ belt n Sicherheitsgurt m.

sea water ['siːwɔːtə*] n Meerwasser nt.

seaweed ['siːwiːd] n (See)tang m.

seaworthy ['siːwɜːðɪ] a seetüchtig.

sec. abbr (= second(s)) Sek.

secluded [sɪ'kluːdɪd] a abgelegen.

seclusion [sɪ'kluːʒən] n Zurückgezogenheit f.

second ['sekənd] a zweite(r, s) // ad (in ~ position) an zweiter Stelle // n Sekunde f; (person) Zweite(r) m; (COMM: imperfect) zweite Wahl f; (SPORT) Sekundant m; (AUT: also: ~ gear) zweiter Gang; (Brit SCOL: degree) mittlere Note bei Prüfungen // vt (support) unterstützen; ~ary a zweitrangig; ~ary school n höhere Schule f, Mittelschule f; ~-class a zweiter Klasse; ~-hand a aus zweiter Hand; (car etc) gebraucht; ~ hand n (on clock) Sekundenzeiger m; ~ly ad zweitens; ~ment [sɪ'kɒndmənt] n (Brit) Abordnung f; ~-

rate *a* mittelmäßig; **~ thoughts** *npl*: to have **~ thoughts** es sich (*dat*) anders überlegen; **on ~ thoughts** *or* (*US*) thought oder lieber (nicht).

secrecy ['siːkrəsɪ] *n* Geheimhaltung *f*.

secret ['siːkrət] *n* Geheimnis *nt* // *a* geheim, Geheim-; **in ~**, **~ly** *ad* geheim.

secretarial [sekrə'tɛərɪəl] *a* Sekretärinnen-.

secretary ['sekrətrɪ] *n* Sekretär(in *f*) *m*; (*government*) Minister *m*.

secretion [sɪ'kriːʃən] *n* Absonderung *f*.

secretive ['siːkrətɪv] *a* geheimtuerisch.

section ['sekʃən] *n* Teil *m*; (*department*) Abteilung *f*; (*of document*) Abschnitt *m*.

sector ['sektə*] *n* Sektor *m*.

secular ['sekjʊlə*] *a* weltlich, profan.

secure [sɪ'kjʊə*] *a* (*safe*) sicher; (*firmly fixed*) fest // *vt* (*make firm*) befestigen, sichern; (*obtain*) sichern.

security [sɪ'kjʊərɪtɪ] *n* Sicherheit *f*; (*pledge*) Pfand *nt*; (*document*) Wertpapier *nt*; (*national ~*) Staatssicherheit *f*.

sedan [sɪ'dæn] *n* (*US AUT*) Limousine *f*.

sedate [sɪ'deɪt] *a* gesetzt // *vt* (*MED*) ein Beruhigungsmittel geben (+*dat*).

sedation [sɪ'deɪʃən] *n* (*MED*) Einfluß *m* von Beruhigungsmitteln.

sedative ['sedətɪv] *n* Beruhigungsmittel *nt* // *a* beruhigend, einschläfernd.

sedentary ['sedntrɪ] *a* (*job*) sitzend.

sediment ['sedɪmənt] *n* (Boden)satz *m*.

sedition [sə'dɪʃən] *n* Aufwiegelung *f*.

seduce [sɪ'djuːs] *vt* verführen.

seduction [sɪ'dʌkʃən] *n* Verführung *f*.

seductive [sɪ'dʌktɪv] *a* verführerisch.

see [siː] *v* (*pt* **saw**, *pp* **seen**) *vt* sehen; (*understand*) (ein)sehen, erkennen; (*visit*) besuchen // *vi* (*be aware*) sehen; (*find out*) nachsehen // *n* (*ECCL*: *R.C.*) Bistum *nt*; (: *Protestant*) Kirchenkreis *m*; to **~** sb to the door jdn hinausbegleiten; to **~ that** (*ensure*) dafür sorgen, daß; to **~ about** sich kümmern um; **~ you soon!** bis bald!; to **~ sth through** etw durchfechten; to **~ through** sb/sth jdn/etw durchschauen; to **~ to it** dafür sorgen; to **~ sb off** jdn zum Zug *etc* begleiten.

seed [siːd] *n* Samen *m* // *vt* (*Tennis*) plazieren; to go to **~** (*plant*) schießen; (*fig*) herunterkommen; **~ling** *n* Setzling *m*; **~y** *a* (*café*) übel; (*person*) zweifelhaft.

seeing ['siːɪŋ] *cj*: **~ (that)** da.

seek [siːk], *pt*, *pp* **sought** *vt* suchen.

seem [siːm] *vi* scheinen; there **~s** to be ... es scheint, ...; **~ingly** *ad* anscheinend.

seen [siːn] *pp* of **see**.

seep [siːp] *vi* sickern.

seesaw ['siːsɔː] *n* Wippe *f*.

seethe [siːð] *vi*: to **~ with anger** vor Wut

kochen.

see-through ['siːθruː] *a* (*dress*) durchsichtig.

segment ['segmənt] *n* Teil *m*; (*of circle*) Ausschnitt *m*.

segregate ['segrɪgeɪt] *vt* trennen.

seize [siːz] *vt* (*grasp*) (er)greifen, packen; (*power*) ergreifen; (*take legally*) beschlagnahmen; **~ (up)on** *vt* sich stürzen auf (+*acc*); **~ up** *vi* (*TECH*) sich festfressen.

seizure ['siːʒə*] *n* (*illness*) Anfall *m*.

seldom ['seldəm] *ad* selten.

select [sɪ'lekt] *a* ausgewählt // *vt* auswählen; **~ion** [sɪ'lekʃən] *n* Auswahl *f*; **~ive** *a* (*person*) wählerisch.

self [self] *pron* selbst // *n*, *pl* **selves** Selbst *nt*, Ich *nt*; the **~** das Ich; **~-assured** *a* selbstbewußt; **~-catering** *a* (*Brit*) für Selbstversorger; **~-centred**, (*US*) **~-centered** *a* egozentrisch; **~-confidence** *n* Selbstvertrauen *nt*, Selbstbewußtsein *nt*; **~-conscious** *a* gehemmt, befangen; **~-contained** *a* (*complete*) (in sich) geschlossen; (*person*) verschlossen; (*Brit*: *flat*) separat; **~-control** *n* Selbstbeherrschung *f*; **~-defence**, (*US*) **~-defense** *n* Selbstverteidigung *f*; (*JUR*) Notwehr *f*; **~-discipline** *n* Selbstdisziplin *f*; **~-employed** *a* frei(schaffend); **~-evident** *a* offensichtlich; **~-governing** *a* selbstverwaltet; **~-indulgent** *a* zügellos; **~-interest** *n* Eigennutz *m*; **~-ish** *a* egoistisch, selbstsüchtig; **~ishness** *n* Egoismus *m*, Selbstsucht *f*; **~-lessly** *ad* selbstlos; **~-pity** *n* Selbstmitleid *nt*; **~-portrait** *n* Selbstbildnis *nt*; **~-possessed** *a* selbstbeherrscht; **~-preservation** *n* Selbsterhaltung *f*; **~-reliant** *a* unabhängig; **~-respect** *n* Selbstachtung *f*; **~-righteous** *a* selbstgerecht; **~-sacrifice** *n* Selbstaufopferung *f*; **~-satisfied** *a* selbstzufrieden; **~-service** *a* Selbstbedienungs-; **~-sufficient** *a* selbstgenügsam; **~-taught** *a* selbsterlernt; **a ~-taught person** ein Autodidakt.

sell [sel] *v* (*pt*, *pp* **sold**) *vt* verkaufen // *vi* verkaufen; (*goods*) sich verkaufen; to **~ at** *or* **for £10** für £10 verkaufen; **~ off** *vt* verkaufen; **~ out** *vi* alles verkaufen; **~-by date** *n* Verfalldatum *nt*; **~er** *n* Verkäufer *m*; **~ing price** *n* Verkaufspreis *m*.

Sellotape ['seləʊteɪp] *n* ® (*Brit*) Tesafilm *m* ®.

sellout ['selaʊt] *n* (*of tickets*): it was a **~** es war ausverkauft.

selves [selvz] *pl* of **self**.

semaphore ['seməfɔː*] *n* Winkzeichen *pl*.

semblance ['sembləns] *n* Anschein *m*.

semen ['siːmən] *n* Sperma *nt*.

semester [sɪ'mestə*] *n* (*US*) Semester

nt.

semi ['semɪ] n = ~**detached house**; ~**circle** n Halbkreis m; ~**colon** n Semikolon nt; ~**conductor** n Halbleiter m; ~**detached house** n (Brit) Doppelhaus nt; ~**final** n Halbfinale nt.

seminary ['semɪnərɪ] n (REL) Priesterseminar nt.

semiskilled ['semɪ'skɪld] a angelernt.

send [send] v (pt, pp **sent**) vt senden, schicken; (col: inspire) hinreißen; ~ **away** vt wegschicken; ~ **away for** vt anfordern; ~ **back** vt zurückschicken; ~ **for** vt holen lassen; ~ **off** vt (goods) abschicken; (Brit SPORT: player) vom Feld schicken; ~ **out** vt (invitation) aussenden; ~ **up** vt hinaufsenden; (Brit: parody) verulken; ~**er** n Absender m; ~**-off** n: a good ~**-off** eine Abschiedsparty.

senior ['siːnɪə*] a (older) älter; (higher rank) Ober- // n (older person) Ältere(r) m; (higher ranking) Rangälteste(r) m; ~ **citizen** n älterer Mitbürger(in f) m; ~**ity** [siːnɪ'ɒrɪtɪ] n (of age) höhere(s) Alter nt; (in rank) höhere(r) Dienstgrad m.

sensation [sen'seɪʃən] n Gefühl nt; (excitement) Sensation f, Aufsehen nt.

sense [sens] n Sinn m; (understanding) Verstand m, Vernunft f; (feeling) Gefühl nt // vt fühlen, spüren; ~ **of humour** Humor m; **to make** ~ Sinn ergeben; ~**less** a sinnlos; (unconscious) besinnungslos.

sensibility [sensɪ'bɪlɪtɪ] n Empfindsamkeit f; (feeling hurt) Empfindlichkeit f; **sensibilities** npl Zartgefühl nt.

sensible ['sensəbl] a vernünftig.

sensitive ['sensɪtɪv] a empfindlich (to gegen).

sensitivity [sensɪ'tɪvɪtɪ] n Empfindlichkeit f; (artistic) Feingefühl nt; (tact) Feinfühligkeit f.

sensual ['sensjuəl] a sinnlich.

sensuous ['sensjuəs] a sinnlich.

sent [sent] pt, pp of **send**.

sentence ['sentəns] n Satz m; (JUR) Strafe f; Urteil nt // vt: to ~ **sb to death**/ **to 5 years** jdn zum Tode/zu 5 Jahren verurteilen.

sentiment ['sentɪmənt] n Gefühl nt; (thought) Gedanke m; ~**al** [sentɪ'mentl] a sentimental; (of feelings rather than reason) gefühlsmäßig.

sentry ['sentrɪ] n (Schild)wache f.

separate ['seprət] a getrennt, separat // ['separeɪt] vt trennen // vi sich trennen; ~**ly** ad getrennt; ~**s** npl (clothes) Röcke, Pullover etc.

separation [sepə'reɪʃən] n Trennung f.

September [sep'tembə*] n September m.

septic ['septɪk] a vereitert, septisch; ~ **tank** n Klärbehälter m.

sequel ['siːkwəl] n Folge f.

sequence ['siːkwəns] n (Reihen)folge f.

sequin ['siːkwɪn] n Paillette f.

serene [sə'riːn] a heiter.

serenity [sɪ'renɪtɪ] n Heiterkeit f.

sergeant ['saːdʒənt] n Feldwebel m; (police) (Polizei)wachtmeister m.

serial ['sɪərɪəl] n Fortsetzungsroman m; (TV) Fernsehserie f // a (number) (fort)laufend; ~**ize** vt in Fortsetzungen veröffentlichen/senden.

series ['sɪəriz] n, pl inv Serie f, Reihe f.

serious ['sɪərɪəs] a ernst; (injury) schwer; ~**ly** ad ernst(haft); (hurt) schwer; ~**ness** n Ernst m, Ernsthaftigkeit f.

sermon ['sɜːmən] n Predigt f.

serrated [se'reɪtɪd] a gezackt.

servant ['sɜːvənt] n Diener(in f) m.

serve [sɜːv] vt dienen (+dat); (guest, customer) bedienen; (food) servieren; (writ) zustellen (on sb jdm) // vi dienen, nützen; (at table) servieren; (TENNIS) geben, aufschlagen; **it** ~**s him right** das geschieht ihm recht; **that'll** ~ **as a table** das geht als Tisch; ~ **out** or **up** vt (food) auftragen, servieren.

service ['sɜːvɪs] n (help) Dienst m; (trains etc) Verbindung f; (hotel) Service m, Bedienung f; (set of dishes) Service nt; (REL) Gottesdienst m; (car) Inspektion f; (for TVs etc) Kundendienst m; (TENNIS) Aufschlag m // vt (AUT, TECH) warten, überholen; **the S~s** pl (armed forces) die Streitkräfte pl; **to be of** ~ **to sb** jdm einen großen Dienst erweisen; ~**able** a brauchbar; ~ **area** n (on motorway) Raststätte f; ~ **charge** n (Brit) Bedienung f; ~**man** n (soldier etc) Soldat m; ~ **station** n (Groß)tankstelle f.

serviette [sɜːvɪ'et] n Serviette f.

servile ['sɜːvaɪl] a unterwürfig.

session ['seʃən] n Sitzung f; (POL) Sitzungsperiode f; **to be in** ~ tagen.

set [set] n (collection of things) Satz m, Set nt; (RAD, TV) Apparat m; (TENNIS) Satz m; (group of people) Kreis m; (CINE) Szene f; (THEAT) Bühnenbild n // a festgelegt; (ready) bereit // v (pt, pp **set**) vt (place) setzen, stellen, legen; (arrange) (an)ordnen; (table) decken; (time, price) festsetzen; (alarm, watch) stellen; (jewels) (ein)fassen; (task) stellen; (exam) ausarbeiten // vi (sun) untergehen; (become hard) fest werden; (bone) zusammenwachsen; **to be** ~ **on doing sth** etw unbedingt tun wollen; **to** ~ **to music** vertonen; **to** ~ **on fire** anstecken; **to** ~ **free** freilassen; **to** ~ **sth going** etw in Gang bringen; **to** ~ **sail** losfahren; ~ **about** vt (task) anpacken; ~ **aside** vt beiseitelegen; ~ **back** vt zurückwerfen; (in time): **to** ~ **back (by)** zurückwerfen (um); ~ **off** vi aufbrechen

// vt (explode) sprengen; (alarm) losgehen lassen; (show up small) hervorheben; **~ out** vi: **to ~ out to do sth** vorhaben, etw zu tun // vt (arrange) anlegen, arrangieren; (state) darlegen; **~ up** vt (organization) aufziehen; (record) aufstellen; (monument) erstellen; **~back** n Rückschlag m; **~ menu** n Tageskarte f.

settee [se'ti:] n Sofa nt.

setting ['setɪŋ] n Hintergrund m.

settle ['setl] vt beruhigen; (pay) begleichen, bezahlen; (agree) regeln // vi (also: **~ down**) sich einleben; (come to rest) sich niederlassen; (sink) sich setzen; (calm down) sich beruhigen; **to ~ for sth** sich mit etw zufriedengeben; **~ in** vi sich eingewöhnen; **to ~ on sth** sich für etw entscheiden; **to ~ up with sb** mit jdm abrechnen; **~ment** n Regelung f; (payment) Begleichung f; (colony) Siedlung f; **~r** n Siedler m.

setup ['setʌp] n (situation) Lage f.

seven ['sevn] num sieben; **~teen** num siebzehn; **~th** a siebte(r, s) // n Siebtel nt; **~ty** num siebzig.

sever ['sevə*] vt abtrennen.

several ['sevrəl] a mehrere, verschiedene // pron mehrere; **~ of us** einige von uns.

severance ['sevərəns] n: **~ pay** Abfindung f.

severe [sɪ'vɪə*] a (strict) streng; (serious) schwer; (climate) rauh.

severity [sɪ'verɪtɪ] n Strenge f; Schwere f; Ernst m.

sew [səu], pt **sewed**, pp **sewn** vti nähen; **~ up** vt zunähen.

sewage ['sju:ɪdʒ] n Abwässer pl.

sewer ['sjuə*] n (Abwasser)kanal m.

sewing ['səuɪŋ] n Näharbeit f; **~ machine** n Nähmaschine f.

sewn [səun] pp of **sew**.

sex [seks] n Sex m; (gender) Geschlecht nt; **to have ~ with sb** mit jdm Geschlechtsverkehr haben; **~ist** a sexistisch // n Sexist(in f) m.

sexual ['seksjuəl] a sexuell, geschlechtlich, Geschlechts-.

sexy ['seksɪ] a sexy.

shabby ['ʃæbɪ] a (lit, fig) schäbig.

shack [ʃæk] n Hütte f.

shackles ['ʃæklz] npl (lit, fig) Fesseln pl, Ketten pl.

shade [ʃeɪd] n Schatten m; (for lamp) Lampenschirm m; (colour) Farbton m // vt abschirmen; **in the ~** im Schatten; **a ~ smaller** ein bißchen kleiner.

shadow ['ʃædəu] n Schatten m // vt (follow) beschatten // a: **~ cabinet** n (Brit POL) Schattenkabinett nt; **~y** a schattig.

shady ['ʃeɪdɪ] a schattig; (fig) zwielichtig.

shaft [ʃɑ:ft] n (of spear etc) Schaft m;

(in mine) Schacht m; (TECH) Welle f; (of light) Strahl m.

shaggy ['ʃægɪ] a struppig.

shake [ʃeɪk] v (pt **shook**, pp **shaken**) vt schütteln, rütteln; (shock) erschüttern // vi (move) schwanken; (tremble) zittern, beben // n (jerk) Schütteln nt, Rütteln nt; **to ~ hands** die Hand geben (with dat); **to ~ one's head** den Kopf schütteln; **~ off** vt abschütteln; **~ up** vt (lit) aufschütteln; (fig) aufrütteln.

shaky ['ʃeɪkɪ] a zittrig; (weak) unsicher.

shall [ʃæl] v aux: **I ~ go** ich werde gehen.

shallow ['ʃæləu] a seicht.

sham [ʃæm] n Schein m // a unecht, falsch.

shambles ['ʃæmblz] n sing Durcheinander nt.

shame [ʃeɪm] n Scham f; (disgrace, pity) Schande f // vt beschämen; **it is a ~ that** es ist schade, daß; **it is a ~ to do ...** es ist eine Schande, ... zu tun; **what a ~!** wie schade!; **~faced** a beschämt; **~ful** a schändlich; **~less** a schamlos.

shampoo [ʃæm'pu:] n Shampoo(n) nt // vt (hair) waschen; **~ and set** n Waschen nt und Legen.

shamrock ['ʃæmrɒk] n Kleeblatt nt.

shandy ['ʃændɪ] n Bier nt mit Limonade.

shan't [ʃɑ:nt] = **shall not**.

shanty town ['ʃæntɪ-] n Elendsviertel nt.

shape [ʃeɪp] n Form f // vt formen, gestalten // vi (also: **~ up**) sich entwickeln; **to take ~** Gestalt annehmen; **-shaped** suff: **heart-shaped** herzförmig; **~less** a formlos; **~ly** a wohlproportioniert.

share [ʃeə*] n (An)teil m; (FIN) Aktie f // vt teilen; **to ~ out** (among or between) verteilen (unter or zwischen); **~holder** n Aktionär(in f) m.

shark [ʃɑ:k] n Hai(fisch) m; (swindler) Gauner m.

sharp [ʃɑ:p] a scharf; (pin) spitz; (person) clever; (MUS) erhöht // n (MUS) Kreuz nt // ad (MUS) zu hoch; **nine o'clock ~** Punkt neun; **~en** vt schärfen; (pencil) spitzen; **~ener** n (also: **pencil ~ener**) Anspitzer m; **~-eyed** a scharfsichtig; **~ly** ad (turn, stop) plötzlich; (stand out, contrast) deutlich; (criticize, retort) scharf.

shatter ['ʃætə*] vt zerschmettern; (fig) zerstören // vi zerspringen.

shave [ʃeɪv] n Rasur f // vt rasieren // vi sich rasieren; **to have a ~** sich rasieren (lassen); **~r** n (also: **electric shaver**) Rasierapparat m.

shaving ['ʃeɪvɪŋ] n (action) Rasieren nt; **~s** pl (of wood etc) Späne pl; **~ brush** n Rasierpinsel m; **~ cream** n Rasierkrem f.

shawl [ʃɔ:l] n Schal m, Umhang m.

she [ʃi:] pron sie // a weiblich; **~-bear** n

Bärenweibchen nt.

sheaf [ʃiːf], pl **sheaves** n Garbe f.

shear [ʃɪə*], pt **sheared**, pp **sheared** or **shorn** vt scheren; ~ **off** vi abbrechen; ~**s** pl Heckenschere f.

sheath [ʃiːθ] n Scheide f; (condom) Kondom m or nt.

sheaves [ʃiːvz] pl of **sheaf**.

shed [ʃed] n Schuppen m; (for animals) Stall m // vt, pt, pp **shed** (leaves etc) verlieren; (tears) vergießen.

she'd [ʃiːd] = **she had**; **she would**.

sheen [ʃiːn] n Glanz m.

sheep [ʃiːp] n Schaf nt; ~**dog** n Schäferhund m; ~**ish** a verlegen; ~**skin** n Schaffell nt.

sheer [ʃɪə*] a bloß, rein; (steep) steil; (transparent) (hauch)dünn // ad (directly) direkt.

sheet [ʃiːt] n Bettuch nt, Bettlaken nt; (of paper) Blatt nt; (of metal etc) Platte f; (of ice) Fläche f.

shelf [ʃelf], pl **shelves** n Bord nt, Regal nt.

she'll [ʃiːl] = **she will**; **she shall**.

shell [ʃel] n Schale f; (sea~) Muschel f; (explosive) Granate f // vt (peas) schälen; (fire on) beschießen.

shellfish ['ʃelfɪʃ] n Schalentier nt; (as food) Meeresfrüchte pl.

shelter ['ʃeltə*] n Schutz m; (air-raid ~) Bunker m // vt schützen, bedecken; (refugees) aufnehmen // vi sich unterstellen; ~**ed** a (life) behütet; (spot) geschützt.

shelve [ʃelv] vt aufschieben // vi abfallen.

shelves [ʃelvz] pl of **shelf**.

shepherd ['ʃepəd] n Schäfer m // vt treiben, führen; ~'**s pie** n Auflauf m aus Hackfleisch und Kartoffelbrei.

sherry ['ʃerɪ] n Sherry m.

she's [ʃiːz] = **she is**; **she has**.

Shetland ['ʃetlənd] n (also: **the** ~**s**, **the** ~ **Isles**) die Shetlandinseln pl.

shield [ʃiːld] n Schild m; (fig) Schirm m // vt (be)schirmen; (TECH) abschirmen.

shift [ʃɪft] n Verschiebung f; (work) Schicht f // vt (ver)rücken, verschieben; (arm) wegnehmen // vi sich verschieben; ~**less** a (person) träge; ~ **work** n Schichtarbeit f; ~**y** a verschlagen.

shilly-shally ['ʃɪlɪʃælɪ] vi zögern.

shin [ʃɪn] n Schienbein nt.

shine [ʃaɪn] n Glanz m, Schein m // v (pt, pp **shone**) vt polieren // vi scheinen; (fig) glänzen; **to** ~ **a torch on sb** jdn (mit einer Lampe) anleuchten.

shingle ['ʃɪŋgl] n Strandkies m; ~**s** pl (MED) Gürtelrose f.

shiny ['ʃaɪnɪ] a glänzend.

ship [ʃɪp] n Schiff nt // vt verschiffen; ~**building** n Schiffbau m; ~**ment** n Schiffsladung f; ~**per** n Verschiffer m; ~**ping** n (act) Verschiffung f; (ships)

Schiffahrt f; ~**shape** a in Ordnung; ~**wreck** n Schiffbruch m; (destroyed ship) Wrack nt // vt: **to be** ~**wrecked** Schiffbruch erleiden; ~**yard** n Werft f.

shire ['ʃaɪə*] n (Brit) Grafschaft f.

shirk [ʃɜːk] vt ausweichen (+dat).

shirt [ʃɜːt] n (Ober)hemd nt; **in** ~ **sleeves** in Hemdsärmeln; ~**y** a (col) mürrisch.

shit [ʃɪt] interj (col!) Scheiße f (!).

shiver ['ʃɪvə*] n Schauer m // vi frösteln, zittern.

shoal [ʃəʊl] n (Fisch)schwarm m.

shock [ʃɒk] n Erschütterung f; (mental) Schock m; (ELEC) Schlag m // vt erschüttern; (offend) schockieren; ~ **absorber** n Stoßdämpfer m; ~**ing** a unerhört.

shod [ʃɒd] pt, pp of **shoe** // a beschuht.

shoddy ['ʃɒdɪ] a schäbig.

shoe [ʃuː] n Schuh m; (of horse) Hufeisen nt // vt, pt, pp **shod** (horse) beschlagen; ~**brush** n Schuhbürste f; ~**horn** n Schuhlöffel m; ~**lace** n Schnürsenkel m; ~ **polish** n Schuhcreme f; ~ **shop** n Schuhgeschäft nt; ~**string** n (fig): **on a** ~**string** mit sehr wenig Geld.

shone [ʃɒn] pt, pp of **shine**.

shoo [ʃuː] interj sch!; (to dog etc) pfui!

shook [ʃʊk] pt of **shake**.

shoot [ʃuːt] n (branch) Schößling m // v (pt, pp **shot**) vt (gun) abfeuern; (goal, arrow) schießen; (kill) erschießen; (film) drehen // vi (gun, move quickly) schießen; ~ (**at**) schießen (auf) (+acc); ~ **down** vt abschießen; ~ **in/out** vi hinein-/hinausschießen; ~ **up** vi (fig) aus dem Boden schießen; ~**ing** n Schießerei f; ~**ing star** n Sternschnuppe f.

shop [ʃɒp] n (esp Brit) Geschäft nt, Laden m; (workshop) Werkstatt f // vi (also: **go** ~**ping**) einkaufen gehen; ~ **assistant** n (Brit) Verkäufer(in f) m; ~ **floor** n (Brit) Werkstatt f; ~**keeper** n Geschäftsinhaber m; ~**lifting** n Ladendiebstahl m; ~**per** n Käufer(in f) m; ~**ping** n Einkaufen nt, Einkauf m; ~**ping bag** n Einkaufstasche f; ~**ping centre**, (US) ~**ping center** n Einkaufszentrum nt; ~**soiled** a angeschmutzt; ~ **steward** n (Brit INDUSTRY) Betriebsrat m; ~ **window** n Schaufenster nt.

shore [ʃɔː*] n Ufer nt; (of sea) Strand m // vt: ~ **up** abstützen.

shorn [ʃɔːn] pp of **shear**.

short [ʃɔːt] a kurz; (person) klein; (curt) kurz angebunden; (measure) zu knapp // n (also: ~ **film**) Kurzfilm m // ad (suddenly) plötzlich // vi (ELEC) einen Kurzschluß haben; **to be** ~ **of sth** nicht genug von etw haben; **in** ~ kurz gesagt; ~ **of doing sth** ohne so weit zu

gehen, etw zu tun; **everything** ~ **of** ...
alles außer ...; **it is** ~ **for** das ist die
Kurzform von; **to cut** ~ abkürzen; **to fall**
~ **of sth** etw nicht erreichen; **to stop** ~
plötzlich anhalten; **to stop** ~ **of** haltmachen vor; ~**age** n Knappheit f, Mangel
m; ~**bread** n Mürbegebäck nt; ~-
change vt: to ~**change sb** jdm zuwenig
herausgeben; ~-**circuit** n Kurzschluß m
// vi einen Kurzschluß haben // vt kurz-
schließen; ~**coming** n Mangel m;
~(**crust) pastry** n (Brit) Mürbeteig m;
~ **cut** n Abkürzung f; ~**en** vt
(ab)kürzen; (clothes) kürzer machen;
~**fall** n Defizit nt; ~**hand** n (Brit)
Stenographie f; ~**hand typist** n (Brit)
Stenotypistin f; ~**list** n (Brit: for job)
engere Wahl f; ~**lived** a kurzlebig; ~**ly**
ad bald; ~**ness** n Kürze f; ~**s** npl
Shorts pl; ~-**sighted** a (Brit: lit, fig)
kurzsichtig; ~-**staffed** a: to be ~-
staffed zu wenig Personal haben; ~-
story n Kurzgeschichte f; ~-**tempered**
a leicht aufbrausend; ~-**term** a (effect)
kurzfristig; ~ **wave** n (RAD) Kurzwelle
f.
shot [ʃɒt] pt, pp of **shoot** // n (from
gun) Schuß m; (person) Schütze m;
(try) Versuch m; (injection) Spritze f;
(PHOT) Aufnahme f; **like a** ~ wie der
Blitz; ~**gun** n Schrotflinte f.
should [ʃʊd] v aux: **I** ~ **go now** ich
sollte jetzt gehen; **he** ~ **be there now er**
sollte eigentlich schon hier sein; **I** ~ **go**
if I were you ich würde gehen, wenn ich
du wäre; **I** ~ **like to** ich möchte gerne.
shoulder ['ʃəʊldə*] n Schulter f; (Brit:
of road): **hard** ~ Seitenstreifen m // vt
(rifle) schultern; (fig) auf sich nehmen;
~ **blade** n Schulterblatt nt; ~ **bag** n
Umhängetasche f; ~ **strap** n (MIL)
Schulterklappe; (of dress etc) Träger m.
shouldn't ['ʃʊdnt] = **should not**.
shout [ʃaʊt] n Schrei m; (call) Ruf m //
vt rufen // vi schreien; ~ **down** vt
niederbrüllen; ~**ing** n Geschrei nt.
shove [ʃʌv] n Schubs m, Stoß m // vt
schieben, stoßen, schubsen; (col: put):
to ~ **sth in(to) sth** etw in etw (acc) hin-
einschieben; ~ **off** vi (NAUT) abstoßen;
(fig col) abhauen.
shovel ['ʃʌvl] n Schaufel f // vt
schaufeln.
show [ʃəʊ] n (display) Schau f;
(exhibition) Ausstellung f; (CINE,
THEAT) Vorstellung f, Show f // v (pt
showed, pp **shown**) vt zeigen;
(kindness) erweisen // vi zu sehen sein;
to be on ~ (exhibits etc) ausgestellt
sein; **to** ~ **sb in** jdn hereinführen; **to** ~
sb out jdn hinausbegleiten; ~ **off** vi
(pej) angeben // vt (display) ausstellen;
~ **up** vi (stand out) sich abheben;
(arrive) erscheinen // vt aufzeigen;
(unmask) bloßstellen; ~ **business** n

Showbusineß nt; ~**down** n Kraftprobe f.
shower ['ʃaʊə*] n Schauer m; (of
stones) (Stein)hagel m; (~ bath) Dusche
f // vi duschen // vt: **to** ~ **sb with sth** jdn
mit etw überschütten; ~**proof** a
wasserabstoßend.
showing ['ʃəʊɪŋ] n Vorführung f.
show jumping ['ʃəʊdʒʌmpɪŋ] n
Turnierreiten nt.
shown [ʃəʊn] pp of **show**.
show-off ['ʃəʊɒf] n Angeber(in f) m.
showpiece ['ʃəʊpiːs] n Paradestück nt.
showroom ['ʃəʊrʊm] n Aus-
stellungsraum m.
shrank [ʃræŋk] pt of **shrink**.
shred [ʃred] n Fetzen m // vt zerfetzen;
(COOK) raspeln; ~**der** n (vegetable ~)
Gemüseschneider m; (document)
Reißwolf m.
shrewd [ʃruːd] a clever.
shriek [ʃriːk] n Schrei m // vti kreischen,
schreien.
shrimp [ʃrɪmp] n Krabbe f, Garnele f.
shrink [ʃrɪŋk] v (pt **shrank**, pp **shrunk**)
vi schrumpfen, eingehen // vt ein-
schrumpfen lassen; **to** ~ **from doing sth**
davor zurückschrecken, etw zu tun;
~**age** n Schrumpfung f; ~ **wrap** vt
einschweißen.
shrivel ['ʃrɪvl] vti (also: ~ up)
schrumpfen, schrumpeln.
shroud [ʃraʊd] n Leichentuch nt // vt:
~**ed in mystery** mit einem Geheimnis
umgeben.
Shrove Tuesday ['ʃrəʊv'tjuːzdeɪ] n
Fastnachtsdienstag m.
shrub [ʃrʌb] n Busch m, Strauch m;
~**bery** n Gebüsch nt.
shrug [ʃrʌg] n Achselzucken nt // vi: **to**
~ (**one's shoulders**) die Achseln zucken;
~ **off** vt auf die leichte Schulter
nehmen.
shrunk [ʃrʌŋk] pp of **shrink**.
shudder ['ʃʌdə*] n Schauder m // vi
schaudern.
shuffle ['ʃʌfl] n (CARDS) (Karten)-
mischen // vt (cards) mischen; **to** ~
(**one's feet**) schlurfen.
shun [ʃʌn] vt scheuen, (ver)meiden.
shunt [ʃʌnt] vt rangieren.
shut [ʃʌt] v (pt, pp **shut**) vt schließen,
zumachen // vi sich schließen (lassen);
~ **down** vti schließen; ~ **off** vt (supply) abdrehen; ~ **up** vi (keep quiet) den
Mund halten // vt (close) zuschließen;
~**ter** n Fensterladen m; (PHOT) Verschluß m.
shuttle ['ʃʌtl] n (plane, train etc)
Pendelflugzeug nt/-zug m etc; (space ~)
Raumtransporter m; (also: ~ **service**)
Pendelverkehr m.
shuttlecock ['ʃʌtlkɒk] n Federball m.
shy [ʃaɪ] a schüchtern; ~**ness** n
Schüchternheit f.
Siamese [saɪə'miːz] a: ~ **cat** n

Siamkatze f.
Siberia [saɪ'bɪərɪə] n Sibirien nt.
sibling ['sɪblɪŋ] n Geschwister nt.
Sicily ['sɪsɪlɪ] n Sizilien nt.
sick [sɪk] a krank; (joke) makaber; **I feel ~** mir ist schlecht; **I was ~** ich habe gebrochen; **to be ~ of sb/sth** jdn/etw satt haben; **~ bay** n (Schiffs)lazarett nt; **~en** vt (disgust) krankmachen // vi krank werden; **~ening** a (sight) widerlich; (annoying) zum Weinen.
sickle ['sɪkl] n Sichel f.
sick leave ['sɪkliːv] n: **to be on ~** krank geschrieben sein.
sickly ['sɪklɪ] a kränklich, blaß; (causing nausea) widerlich.
sickness ['sɪknəs] n Krankheit f; (vomiting) Übelkeit f, Erbrechen nt.
sick pay ['sɪkpeɪ] n Krankengeld nt.
side [saɪd] n Seite f // a (door, entrance) Seiten-, Neben- // vi: **to ~ with sb** jds Partei ergreifen; **by the ~ of** neben; **~ by ~** nebeneinander; **on all ~s** von allen Seiten; **to take ~s (with)** Partei nehmen (für); **~boards** (Brit), **~burns** pl Koteletten pl; **~car** n Beiwagen m; **~ drum** n (MUS) kleine Trommel; **~ effect** n Nebenwirkung f; **~light** n (AUT) Parkleuchte f; **~line** n (SPORT) Seitenlinie f; (fig: hobby) Nebenbeschäftigung f; **~long** a Seiten-; **~saddle** ad im Damensattel; **~ show** n Nebenausstellung f; **~step** vt (fig) ausweichen; **~ street** n Seitenstraße f; **~track** vt (fig) ablenken; **~walk** n (US) Bürgersteig m; **~ways** ad seitwärts.
siding ['saɪdɪŋ] n Nebengleis nt.
sidle ['saɪdl] vi: **to ~ up** sich heranmachen (to an +acc).
siege [siːdʒ] n Belagerung f.
sieve [sɪv] n Sieb nt // vt sieben.
sift [sɪft] vt sieben; (fig) sichten.
sigh [saɪ] n Seufzer m // vi seufzen.
sight [saɪt] n (power of seeing) Sehvermögen nt; (look) Blick m; (fact of seeing) Anblick m; (of gun) Visier nt // vt sichten; **in ~** in Sicht; **out of ~** außer Sicht; **~seeing** n Besuch m von Sehenswürdigkeiten; **to ‚go ~seeing** Sehenswürdigkeiten besichtigen.
sign [saɪn] n Zeichen nt; (notice, road ~ etc) Schild nt // vt unterschreiben; **to ~ sth over to sb** jdm etw überschreiben; **~ on** vi (MIL) sich verpflichten; (as unemployed) sich (arbeitslos) melden // vt (MIL) verpflichten; (employee) anstellen; **~ up** vi (MIL) sich verpflichten // vt verpflichten.
signal ['sɪgnl] n Signal nt // vt ein Zeichen geben (+dat); **~man** n (RAIL) Stellwerkswärter(in f) m.
signature ['sɪgnətʃə*] n Unterschrift f; **~ tune** n Erkennungsmelodie f.
signet ring ['sɪgnətrɪŋ] n Siegelring m.

significance [sɪg'nɪfɪkəns] n Bedeutung f.
significant [sɪg'nɪfɪkənt] a (meaning sth) bedeutsam; (important) bedeutend.
signify ['sɪgnɪfaɪ] vt bedeuten; (show) andeuten, zu verstehen geben.
sign language ['saɪnlæŋgwɪdʒ] n Zeichensprache f, Fingersprache f.
signpost ['saɪnpəʊst] n Wegweiser m.
silence ['saɪləns] n Stille f; (of person) Schweigen nt // vt zum Schweigen bringen; **~r** n (on gun) Schalldämpfer m; (Brit AUT) Auspufftopf m.
silent ['saɪlənt] a still; (person) schweigsam; **to remain ~** schweigen; **~ partner** n (COMM) stille(r) Teilhaber m.
silk [sɪlk] n Seide f // a seiden, Seiden-; **~y** a seidig.
silly ['sɪlɪ] a dumm, albern.
silt [sɪlt] n Schlamm m, Schlick m.
silver ['sɪlvə*] n Silber nt // a silbern, Silber-; **~ paper** n (Brit) Silberpapier nt; **~-plated** a versilbert; **~smith** n Silberschmied m; **~ware** n Silber nt; **~y** a silbern.
similar ['sɪmɪlə*] a ähnlich (to dat); **~ity** [sɪmɪ'lærɪtɪ] n Ähnlichkeit f; **~ly** ad in ähnlicher Weise.
simile ['sɪmɪlɪ] n Vergleich m.
simmer ['sɪmə*] vti sieden (lassen).
simpering ['sɪmpərɪŋ] a albern.
simple ['sɪmpl] a einfach; **~(-minded)** a einfältig; **~ton** n Einfaltspinsel m.
simplicity [sɪm'plɪsɪtɪ] n Einfachheit f; (of person) Einfältigkeit f.
simplify ['sɪmplɪfaɪ] vt vereinfachen.
simply ['sɪmplɪ] ad einfach.
simulate ['sɪmjʊleɪt] vt simulieren.
simultaneous [sɪməl'teɪnɪəs] a gleichzeitig.
sin [sɪn] n Sünde f // vi sündigen.
since [sɪns] ad seither // prep seit, seitdem // cj (time) seit; (because) da, weil; **~ then** seitdem.
sincere [sɪn'sɪə*] a aufrichtig; **yours ~ly** mit freundlichen Grüßen.
sincerity [sɪn'serɪtɪ] n Aufrichtigkeit f.
sinew ['sɪnjuː] n Sehne f.
sinful ['sɪnfʊl] a sündig, sündhaft.
sing [sɪŋ], pt **sang**, pp **sung** vti singen.
Singapore [sɪŋgə'pɔː*] n Singapur nt.
singe [sɪndʒ] vt versengen.
singer ['sɪŋə*] n Sänger(in f) m.
single ['sɪŋgl] a (one only) einzig; (bed, room) Einzel-, einzeln; (unmarried) ledig; (Brit: ticket) einfach; (having one part only) einzeln // n (Brit: also: ~ ticket) einfache Fahrkarte f; **~s** n (TENNIS) Einzel nt; **~ out** vt aussuchen, auswählen; **~ bed** n Einzelbett nt; **~-breasted** a einreihig; **in ~ file** hintereinander; **~-handed** a allein; **~-minded** a zielstrebig; **~ room** n Einzelzimmer nt.

singlet ['sɪŋglət] n Unterhemd nt.

singly ['sɪŋglɪ] ad einzeln, allein.

singular ['sɪŋgjulə*] a (GRAM) Singular-; (odd) merkwürdig, seltsam // n (GRAM) Einzahl f, Singular m.

sinister ['sɪnɪstə*] a (evil) böse; (ghostly) unheimlich.

sink [sɪŋk] n Spülbecken nt // v (pt sank, pp sunk) vt (ship) versenken // vi sinken; **to ~ sth into** (teeth, claws) etw schlagen in (+acc); **~ in** vi (news etc) eingehen (+dat).

sinner ['sɪnə*] n Sünder(in f) m.

sip [sɪp] n Schlückchen nt // vt nippen an (+dat).

siphon ['saɪfən] n Siphon(flasche f) m; **~ off** vt absaugen; (fig) abschöpfen.

sir [sɜ:*] n (respect) Herr m; (knight) Sir m; **S~ John Smith** Sir John Smith; **yes ~** ja(wohl, mein Herr).

siren ['saɪərən] n Sirene f.

sirloin ['sɜ:lɔɪn] n Lendenstück nt.

sissy ['sɪsɪ] n (col) Waschlappen m.

sister ['sɪstə*] n Schwester f; (Brit: nurse) Oberschwester f; (nun) Ordensschwester f; **~-in-law** n Schwägerin f.

sit [sɪt] v (pt, pp sat) vi sitzen; (hold session) tagen // vt (exam) machen; **~ down** vi sich hinsetzen; **~ in on** vt dabeisein bei; **~ up** vi (after lying) sich aufsetzen; (straight) sich gerade setzen; (at night) aufbleiben.

sitcom ['sɪtkɔm] n abbr (= situation comedy) Situationskomödie f.

site [saɪt] n Platz m; (also: building ~) Baustelle f // vt legen.

sitting ['sɪtɪŋ] n (meeting) Sitzung f; **~ room** n Wohnzimmer nt.

situated ['sɪtjueɪtɪd] a: **to be ~** liegen.

situation [sɪtju'eɪʃən] n Situation f, Lage f; (place) Lage f; (employment) Stelle f; **~s vacant** (Brit) Stellenangebote pl.

six [sɪks] num sechs; **~teen** num sechzehn; **~th** a sechste(r, s) // n Sechstel nt; **~ty** num sechzig.

size [saɪz] n Größe f; (of project) Umfang m; **~ up** vt (assess) abschätzen, einschätzen; **~able** a ziemlich groß, ansehnlich.

sizzle ['sɪzl] vi zischen; (COOK) brutzeln.

skate [skeɪt] n Schlittschuh m; (fish: pl inv) Rochen m // vi Schlittschuh laufen; **~r** n Schlittschuhläufer(in f) m.

skating ['skeɪtɪŋ] n Eislauf m; **to go ~** Eislaufen gehen; **~ rink** n Eisbahn f.

skeleton ['skelɪtn] n Skelett nt; (fig) Gerüst nt; **~ key** n Dietrich m; **~ staff** n Notbesetzung f.

sketch [sketʃ] n Skizze f; (THEAT) Sketch m // vt skizzieren; **~book** n Skizzenbuch nt; **~y** a skizzenhaft.

skewer ['skjuə*] n Fleischspieß m.

ski [ski:] n Ski m, Schi m // vi Ski or Schi laufen; **~ boot** n Skistiefel m.

skid [skɪd] n (AUT) Schleudern nt // vi rutschen; (AUT) schleudern.

skier ['ski:ə*] n Skiläufer(in f) m.

skiing ['ski:ɪŋ] n: **to go ~** Skilaufen gehen.

ski-jump ['ski:dʒʌmp] n Sprungschanze f // vi Ski springen.

skilful ['skɪlful] a geschickt.

ski-lift ['ski:lɪft] n Skilift m.

skill [skɪl] n Können nt; **~ed** a geschickt; (worker) Fach-, gelernt.

skim [skɪm] vt (liquid) abschöpfen; (glide over) gleiten über (+acc) // vi: **~ through** (book) überfliegen; **~med milk** n Magermilch f.

skimp [skɪmp] vt (do carelessly) oberflächlich tun; **~y** a (work) schlecht gemacht; (dress) knapp.

skin [skɪn] n Haut f; (peel) Schale f // vt abhäuten; schälen; **~-deep** a oberflächlich; **~ diving** n Schwimmtauchen nt; **~ny** a dünn; **~tight** a (dress etc) hauteng.

skip [skɪp] n Sprung m // vi hüpfen; (with rope) Seil springen // vt (pass over) übergehen.

ski: ~ pants npl Skihosen pl; **~ pole** n Skistock m.

skipper ['skɪpə*] n Kapitän m // vt führen.

skipping rope ['skɪpɪŋrəup] n (Brit) Hüpfseil nt.

skirmish ['skɜ:mɪʃ] n Scharmützel nt.

skirt [skɜ:t] n Rock m // vt herumgehen um; (fig) umgehen; **~ing board** n (Brit) Fußleiste f.

ski suit n Skianzug m.

skit [skɪt] n Parodie f.

skittle ['skɪtl] n Kegel m; **~s** n (game) Kegeln nt.

skive [skaɪv] vi (Brit col) schwänzen.

skulk [skʌlk] vi sich herumdrücken.

skull [skʌl] n Schädel m.

skunk [skʌŋk] n Stinktier nt.

sky [skaɪ] n Himmel m; **~light** n Oberlicht nt; **~scraper** n Wolkenkratzer m.

slab [slæb] n (of stone) Platte f.

slack [slæk] n (loose) locker; (business) flau; (careless) nachlässig, lasch // vi nachlässig sein // n: **to take up the ~** straffziehen; **~s** pl Hose(n pl) f; **~en** (also: **~en off**) vi locker werden; (become slower) nachlassen, stocken // vt (loosen) lockern.

slag [slæg] n Schlacke f; **~ heap** n Halde f.

slain [sleɪn] pp of **slay.**

slam [slæm] n Knall m // vt (door) zuschlagen; (throw down) knallen // vi zuschlagen.

slander ['slɑ:ndə*] n Verleumdung f // vt verleumden.

slant [slɑ:nt] n (lit) Schräge f; (fig) Tendenz f // vt schräg legen // vi schräg

liegen; **~ed, ~ing** a schräg.
slap [slæp] n Klaps m // vt einen Klaps geben (+dat) // ad (directly) geradewegs; **~dash** a salopp; **~stick** (comedy) Klamauk m; **~-up** a (Brit: meal) erstklassig, prima.
slash [slæʃ] n Schnittwunde f // vt (auf)schlitzen; (expenditure) radikal kürzen.
slat [slæt] n (of wood, plastic) Leiste f.
slate [sleɪt] n (stone) Schiefer m; (roofing) Dachziegel m // vt (criticize) verreißen.
slaughter ['slɔːtə*] n (of animals) Schlachten nt; (of people) Gemetzel nt // vt schlachten; (people) niedermetzeln; **~house** n Schlachthof m.
Slav [slɑːv] a slawisch.
slave [sleɪv] n Sklave m, Sklavin f // vi schuften, sich schinden; **~ry** n Sklaverei f; (work) Schinderei f.
slay [sleɪ], pt slew, pp slain vt ermorden.
sleazy ['sliːzɪ] a (place) schmierig.
sledge ['sledʒ] n Schlitten m; **~hammer** n Schmiedehammer m.
sleek [sliːk] a glatt; (shape) rassig.
sleep [sliːp] n Schlaf m // vi, pt, pp slept schlafen; to go to ~ einschlafen; **~ in** vi ausschlafen; (oversleep) verschlafen; **~er** (person) Schläfer m; (Brit RAIL) Schlafwagen m; (beam) Schwelle f; **~ing bag** n Schlafsack m; **~ing car** n Schlafwagen m; **~ing pill** n Schlaftablette f; **~less** a (night) schlaflos; **~walker** n Schlafwandler(in f) m; **~y** a schläfrig.
sleet [sliːt] n Schneeregen m.
sleeve [sliːv] n Ärmel m; (of record) Umschlag m; **~less** a ärmellos.
sleigh [sleɪ] n Pferdeschlitten m.
sleight [slaɪt] n: **~ of hand** Fingerfertigkeit f.
slender ['slendə*] a schlank; (fig) gering.
slept [slept] pt, pp of sleep.
slew [sluː] vi (veer) (herum)schwenken // pt of slay.
slice [slaɪs] n Scheibe f // vt in Scheiben schneiden.
slick [slɪk] a (clever) raffiniert, aalglatt // n Ölteppich m.
slide [slaɪd] n Rutschbahn f; (PHOT) Dia(positiv) nt; (Brit: for hair) (Haar)spange f // v (pt, pp slid) vt schieben // vi (slip) gleiten, rutschen; **~ rule** n Rechenschieber m.
sliding ['slaɪdɪŋ] a (door) Schiebe-; **~ scale** n gleitende Skala f.
slight [slaɪt] a zierlich; (trivial) geringfügig; (small) gering // n Kränkung f // vt (offend) kränken; **not in the ~est** nicht im geringsten; **~ly** ad etwas, ein bißchen.
slim [slɪm] a schlank; (book) dünn;

(chance) gering // vi eine Schlankheitskur machen.
slime [slaɪm] n Schleim m.
slimming ['slɪmɪŋ] n Schlankheitskur f.
slimy ['slaɪmɪ] a glitschig; (dirty) schlammig; (person) schmierig.
sling [slɪŋ] n Schlinge f; (weapon) Schleuder f // vt, pt, pp slung schleudern.
slip [slɪp] n (mistake) Flüchtigkeitsfehler m; (petticoat) Unterrock m; (of paper) Zettel m // vt (put) stecken, schieben // vi (lose balance) ausrutschen; (move) gleiten, rutschen; (decline) nachlassen; (move smoothly): to ~ into/out of (room etc) hinein-/hinausschlüpfen; to give sb the ~ jdm entwischen; ~ of the tongue Versprecher m; it ~ped my mind das ist mir entfallen; to ~ sth on/off etw über-/abstreifen; ~ away vi sich wegstehlen; ~ by vi (time) verstreichen; ~ in vt hineingleiten lassen // vi (errors) sich einschleichen; **~ped disc** n Bandscheibenschaden m.
slipper ['slɪpə*] n Hausschuh m.
slippery ['slɪpərɪ] a glatt.
slip: **~-road** n (Brit) Auffahrt f/Ausfahrt f; **~shod** a schlampig; **~-up** n Panne f; **~way** n Auslaufbahn f.
slit [slɪt] n Schlitz m // vt, pt, pp slit aufschlitzen.
slither ['slɪðə*] vi schlittern; (snake) sich schlängeln.
sliver ['slɪvə*] n (of glass, wood) Splitter m; (of cheese etc) Scheibchen nt.
slob [slɒb] n (col) Klotz m.
slog [slɒg] vi (work hard) schuften // n: it was a ~ es war eine Plackerei.
slogan ['sləʊgən] n Schlagwort nt; (COMM) Werbespruch m.
slop [slɒp] vi (also: ~ over) überschwappen // vt verschütten.
slope [sləʊp] n Neigung f; (of mountains) (Ab)hang m // vi: ~ down sich senken; ~ up ansteigen.
sloping ['sləʊpɪŋ] a schräg.
sloppy ['slɒpɪ] a schlampig.
slot [slɒt] n Schlitz m // vt: to ~ sth in etw einlegen; ~ machine n (Brit: vending machine) Automat m; (for gambling) Spielautomat m.
sloth [sləʊθ] n (laziness) Faulheit.
slouch [slaʊtʃ] vi: to ~ about (laze) herumhängen (col).
slovenly ['slʌvnlɪ] a schlampig; (speech) salopp.
slow [sləʊ] a langsam; to be ~ (clock) nachgehen; (stupid) begriffsstutzig sein // ad langsam; ~ down vi langsamer werden // vt verlangsamen; ~ up vi sich verlangsamen, sich verzögern // vt aufhalten, langsamer machen; '~' (road sign) 'Langsam'; **~ly** ad langsam; in ~ motion in Zeitlupe.
sludge [slʌdʒ] n Schlamm m.

slug [slʌg] n Nacktschnecke f; (col: bullet) Kugel f; **~gish** a träge; (COMM) schleppend.

sluice [slu:s] n Schleuse f.

slumber ['slʌmbə*] n Schlummer m.

slump [slʌmp] n Rückgang m // vi fallen, stürzen.

slung [slʌŋ] pt, pp of **sling**.

slur [slɜ:*] n Undeutlichkeit f; (insult) Verleumdung f // vt (words) verschlucken **~red** [slɜ:d] a (pronunciation) undeutlich.

slush [slʌʃ] n (snow) Schneematsch m; **~ fund** n Schmiergeldfonds m.

slut [slʌt] n Schlampe f.

sly [slaɪ] a schlau.

smack [smæk] n Klaps m // vt einen Klaps geben (+dat); **to ~ one's lips** schmatzen, sich (dat) die Lippen lecken; **~ of** vi riechen nach.

small [smɔ:l] a klein; **~ ads** npl (Brit) Kleinanzeigen pl; **in the ~ hours** in den frühen Morgenstunden; **~ change** n Kleingeld nt; **~ holder** n (Brit) Kleinbauer m; **~pox** n Pocken pl; **~ talk** n Geplauder nt.

smart [smɑ:t] a (fashionable) elegant, schick; (neat) adrett; (clever) clever; (quick) scharf // vi brennen, schmerzen; **~en up** vi sich in Schale werfen // vt herausputzen.

smash [smæʃ] n Zusammenstoß m; (TENNIS) Schmetterball m // vt (break) zerschmettern; (destroy) vernichten // vi (break) zersplittern, zerspringen; **~ing** a (col) toll.

smattering ['smætərɪŋ] n oberflächliche Kenntnis f.

smear [smɪə*] n Fleck m // vt beschmieren.

smell [smel] n Geruch m; (sense) Geruchssinn m // vti, pt, pp **smelt** or **smelled** riechen (of nach); **~y** a übelriechend.

smelt [smelt] vt (ore) schmelzen.

smile [smaɪl] n Lächeln nt // vi lächeln; **smiling** a lächelnd.

smirk [smɜ:k] n blöde(s) Grinsen nt.

smith [smɪθ] n Schmied m; **~y** ['smɪðɪ] n Schmiede f.

smock [smɒk] n Kittel m.

smoke [sməʊk] n Rauch m // vt rauchen; (food) räuchern // vi rauchen; **~d** a (bacon) geräuchert; (glass) Rauch-; **~r** n Raucher(in f) m; (RAIL) Raucherabteil nt; **~ screen** n Rauchwand f.

smoking ['sməʊkɪŋ] n: 'no ~' 'Rauchen verboten'.

smoky ['sməʊkɪ] a rauchig; (room) verraucht; (taste) geräuchert.

smolder ['sməʊldə*] vi (US) = **smoulder**.

smooth [smu:ð] a glatt // vt (also: ~ out) glätten, glattstreichen.

smother ['smʌðə*] vt ersticken.

smoulder, (US) **smolder** ['sməʊldə*] vi schwelen.

smudge [smʌdʒ] n Schmutzfleck m // vt beschmieren.

smug [smʌg] a selbstgefällig.

smuggle ['smʌgl] vt schmuggeln; **~r** n Schmuggler m.

smuggling ['smʌglɪŋ] n Schmuggel m.

smutty ['smʌtɪ] a schmutzig.

snack [snæk] n Imbiß m; **~ bar** n Imbißstube f.

snag [snæg] n Haken m.

snail [sneɪl] n Schnecke f.

snake [sneɪk] n Schlange f.

snap [snæp] n Schnappen nt; (photograph) Schnappschuß m // a (decision) schnell // vt (break) zerbrechen; (PHOT) knipsen // vi (break) brechen; (speak) anfauchen; **to ~ at** vt schnappen nach; **~ off** vt (break) abbrechen; **~ up** vt aufschnappen; **~py** a flott; **~shot** n Schnappschuß m.

snare [snɛə*] n Schlinge f // vt mit einer Schlinge fangen.

snarl [snɑ:l] n Zähnefletschen nt // vi (dog) knurren.

snatch [snætʃ] n (small amount) Bruchteil m // vt schnappen, packen.

sneak [sni:k] vi schleichen // n (col) Petze(r) mf.

sneakers ['sni:kəz] npl (US) Freizeitschuhe pl.

sneaky ['sni:kɪ] a raffiniert.

sneer [snɪə*] n Hohnlächeln nt // vi spötteln.

sneeze [sni:z] n Niesen nt // vi niesen.

sniff [snɪf] n Schnüffeln nt // vi schnieben; (smell) schnüffeln // vt schnuppern.

snigger ['snɪgə*] n Kichern nt // vi hämisch kichern.

snip [snɪp] n Schnippel m, Schnipsel m // vt schnippeln.

sniper ['snaɪpə*] n Heckenschütze m.

snippet ['snɪpɪt] n Schnipsel m; (of conversation) Fetzen m.

snivelling ['snɪvlɪŋ] a weinerlich.

snooker ['snu:kə*] n Snooker nt.

snoop [snu:p] vi: **to ~ about** herumschnüffeln.

snooty ['snu:tɪ] a (col) hochnäsig.

snooze [snu:z] n Nickerchen nt // vi ein Nickerchen machen, dösen.

snore [snɔ:*] vi schnarchen // n Schnarchen nt.

snorkel ['snɔ:kl] n Schnorchel m.

snort [snɔ:t] n Schnauben nt // vi schnauben.

snout [snaʊt] n Schnauze f.

snow [snəʊ] n Schnee m // vi schneien; **~ball** n Schneeball m // vi eskalieren; **~bound** a eingeschneit; **~drift** n Schneewehe f; **~drop** n Schneeglöckchen nt; **~fall** n Schneefall m; **~flake** n Schneeflocke f; **~man** n Schneemann *m*; **~plough,** (*US*) **~plow** *n* Schneepflug *m*; **~ shoe** *n* Schneeschuh *m*; **~storm** *n* Schneesturm *m*.

snub [snʌb] *vt* schroff abfertigen // *n* Verweis *m*; **~-nosed** *a* stupsnasig.

snuff [snʌf] *n* Schnupftabak *m*.

snug [snʌg] *a* gemütlich, behaglich.

snuggle ['snʌgl] *vi*: to ~ **up** to sb sich an jdn kuscheln.

so [səu] ♦ *ad* **1** (*thus*) so; (*likewise*) auch; ~ **saying** he walked away indem er das sagte, ging er; if ~ wenn ja; I **didn't do it — you did ~**! ich hab das nicht gemacht — hast du wohl! ~ **do I**, ~ **am I** *etc* ich auch; ~ **it is!** tatsächlich!; **I hope/think** ~ hoffentlich/ich glaube schon; ~ **far** bis jetzt
2 (*in comparisons etc: to such a degree*) so; ~ **quickly/big** (**that**) so schnell/groß, daß; **I'm** ~ **glad** to see you ich freue mich so, dich zu sehen
3: ~ **much** so viel // *ad* so sehr; ~ **many** *a* so viele
4 (*phrases*): **10 or** ~ etwa 10; ~ **long!** (*col: goodbye*) tschüs!
♦ *conj* **1** (*expressing purpose*): ~ **as to** um nicht; ~ (**that**) damit
2 (*expressing result*) also; ~ **I was right after all** ich hatte also doch recht; ~ **you see** ... wie du siehst ...

soak [səuk] *vt* durchnässen; (*leave in liquid*) weichen // *vi* (*ein*)weichen; ~ **in** *vi* einsickern; ~ **up** *vt* aufsaugen.

so-and-so ['səuənsəu] *n* (*somebody*) soundso *m*.

soap [səup] *n* Seife *f*; **~flakes** *pl* Seifenflocken *pl*; ~ **opera** *n* Familienserie *f* (*im Fernsehen, Radio*); ~ **powder** *n* Waschpulver *nt*; **~y** *a* seifig, Seifen-.

soar [sɔː*] *vi* aufsteigen; (*prices*) in die Höhe schnellen.

sob [sɒb] *n* Schluchzen *nt* // *vi* schluchzen.

sober ['səubə*] *a* (*lit, fig*) nüchtern; ~ **up** *vi* nüchtern werden.

so-called ['səu'kɔːld] *a* sogenannt.

soccer ['sɒkə*] *n* Fußball *m*.

sociable ['səuʃəbl] *a* gesellig.

social ['səuʃəl] *a* sozial; (*friendly, living with others*) gesellig // *n* gesellige(r) Abend *m*; ~ **club** *n* Verein *m* (*für Freizeitgestaltung*); **~ism** *n* Sozialismus *m*; **~ist** *n* Sozialist(in *f*) *m* // *a* sozialistisch; **~ize** *vi*: to ~ (**with**) gesellschaftlich verkehren (mit); **~ly** *ad* gesellschaftlich, privat; ~ **security** *n* Sozialversicherung *f*; ~ **work** *n* Sozialarbeit *f*; ~ **worker** *n* Sozialarbeiter(in *f*) *m*.

society [sə'saɪətɪ] *n* Gesellschaft *f*; (*fashionable world*) die große Welt.

sock [sɒk] *n* Socke *f*.

socket ['sɒkɪt] *n* (*ELEC*) Steckdose *f*; (*of eye*) Augenhöhle *f*; (*TECH*)

Rohransatz *m*.

sod [sɒd] *n* Rasenstück *nt*; (*col!*) Saukerl *m* (!).

soda ['səudə] *n* Soda *f*; (*also:* ~ **water**) Soda(wasser) *nt*; (*US: also:* ~ **pop**) Limonade *f*.

sodden ['sɒdn] *a* durchweicht.

sodium ['səudɪəm] *n* Natrium *nt*.

sofa ['səufə] *n* Sofa *nt*.

soft [sɒft] *a* weich; (*not loud*) leise; (*weak*) nachgiebig; ~ **drink** alkoholfreie(s) Getränk *nt*; **~en** ['sɒfn] *vt* weich machen; (*blow*) abschwächen, mildern // *vi* weich werden; **~ly** *ad* sanft; leise; **~ness** *n* Weichheit *f*; (*fig*) Sanftheit *f*.

software ['sɒftwɛə*] *n* (*COMPUT*) Software *f*.

soggy ['sɒgɪ] *a* (*ground*) sumpfig; (*bread*) aufgeweicht.

soil [sɔɪl] *n* Erde *f* // *vt* beschmutzen; **~ed** *a* beschmutzt.

solace ['sɒləs] *n* Trost *m*.

solar ['səulə*] *a* Sonnen-.

sold [səuld] *pt, pp* of **sell**; ~ **out** *a* (*COMM*) ausverkauft.

solder ['səuldə*] *vt* löten // *n* Lötmetall *nt*.

soldier ['səuldʒə*] *n* Soldat *m*.

sole [səul] *n* Sohle *f*; (*fish*) Seezunge *f* // *a* alleinig, Allein-; **~ly** *ad* ausschließlich; ~ **trader** *n* (*COMM*) Einzelunternehmen *nt*.

solemn ['sɒləm] *a* feierlich.

solicit [sə'lɪsɪt] *vt* (*request*) bitten um // *vi* (*prostitute*) Kunden anwerben.

solicitor [sə'lɪsɪtə*] *n* Rechtsanwalt *m*/ -anwältin *f*.

solid ['sɒlɪd] *a* (*hard*) fest; (*of same material*) massiv; (*not hollow*) massiv; (*without break*) voll, ganz; (*reliable, sensible*) solide // *n* Feste(s) *nt*.

solidarity [sɒlɪ'dærɪtɪ] *n* Solidarität *f*.

solidify [sə'lɪdɪfaɪ] *vi* fest werden.

solitary ['sɒlɪtərɪ] *a* einsam, einzeln; ~ **confinement** *n* Einzelhaft *f*.

solitude ['sɒlɪtjuːd] *n* Einsamkeit *f*.

soluble ['sɒljubl] *a* (*substance*) löslich; (*problem*) (auf)lösbar.

solution [sə'luːʃən] *n* (*lit, fig*) Lösung *f*; (*of mystery*) Erklärung *f*.

solve [sɒlv] *vt* (auf)lösen.

solvent ['sɒlvənt] *a* (*FIN*) zahlungsfähig // *n* (*CHEM*) Lösungsmittel *nt*.

sombre, (*US*) **somber** ['sɒmbə*] *a* düster.

some [sʌm] ♦ *a* **1** (*a certain amount or number of*) einige; (*a few*) ein paar; (*with singular nouns*) etwas; ~ **tea/ biscuits** etwas Tee/ein paar Plätzchen; **I've got** ~ **money, but not much** ich habe ein bißchen Geld, aber nicht viel
2 (*certain: in contrasts*) manche(r, s); ~ **people say that ...** manche Leute sagen, daß ...

3 (*unspecified*) irgendein(e); ~ **woman was asking for you** da hat eine Frau nach Ihnen gefragt; ~ **day** eines Tages; ~ **day next week** irgendwann nächste Woche

◆ *pron* **1** (*a certain number*) einige; **have you got** ~? Haben Sie welche?
2 (*a certain amount*) etwas; **I've read** ~ **of the book** ich habe das Buch teilweise gelesen

◆ *ad*: ~ **10 people** etwa 10 Leute.
somebody ['sʌmbədɪ] *pron*, **someone** ['sʌmwʌn] *pron* jemand; (*direct obj*) jemand(en); (*indirect obj*) jemandem.
somersault ['sʌməsɔːlt] *n* Salto *m* // *vi* einen Salto machen.
something ['sʌmθɪŋ] *pron* etwas.
sometime ['sʌmtaɪm] *ad* (irgend) einmal.
sometimes ['sʌmtaɪmz] *ad* manchmal.
somewhat ['sʌmwɒt] *ad* etwas.
somewhere ['sʌmwɛə*] *ad* irgendwo; (*to a place*) irgendwohin; ~ **else** irgendwo anders.
son [sʌn] *n* Sohn *m*.
sonar ['səʊnɑː*] *n* Echolot *nt*.
song [sɒŋ] *n* Lied *nt*.
sonic ['sɒnɪk] *a* Schall-; ~ **boom** *n* Überschallknall *m*.
son-in-law ['sʌnɪnlɔː] *n* Schwiegersohn *m*.
sonny ['sʌnɪ] *n* (col) Kleine(r) *m*.
soon [suːn] *ad* bald; ~ **afterwards** kurz danach; ~**er** *ad* (*time*) früher; (*for preference*) lieber; ~**er or later** früher oder später.
soot [sʊt] *n* Ruß *m*.
soothe [suːð] *vt* (*person*) beruhigen; (*pain*) lindern.
sophisticated [sə'fɪstɪkeɪtɪd] *a* (*person*) kultiviert; (*machinery*) hochentwickelt.
sophomore ['sɒfəmɔː*] *n* (*US*) College-Student *m* im 2. Jahr.
soporific [sɒpə'rɪfɪk] *a* einschläfernd.
sopping ['sɒpɪŋ] *a* patschnaß.
soppy ['sɒpɪ] *a* (col) schmalzig.
sorcerer ['sɔːsərə*] *n* Hexenmeister *m*.
sordid ['sɔːdɪd] *a* erbärmlich.
sore [sɔː*] *a* schmerzend; (*point*) wund // *n* Wunde *f*; ~**ly** *ad* (*tempted*) stark, sehr.
sorrow ['sɒrəʊ] *n* Kummer *m*, Leid *nt*; ~**ful** *a* sorgenvoll.
sorry ['sɒrɪ] *a* traurig, erbärmlich; ~! Entschuldigung!; **to feel** ~ **for sb** jdn bemitleiden; **I feel** ~ **for him** er tut mir leid.
sort [sɔːt] *n* Art *f*, Sorte *f* // *vt* (also: ~ **out**) (*papers*) sortieren, sichten; (*problems*) in Ordnung bringen; ~**ing office** *n* Sortierstelle *f*.
SOS *n* SOS *nt*.
so-so ['səʊ'səʊ] *ad* so(-so) la-la.
sought [sɔːt] *pt, pp of* **seek**.
soul [səʊl] *n* Seele *f*; (*music*) Soul *m*;

~-**destroying** *a* trostlos; ~**ful** *a* seelenvoll.
sound [saʊnd] *a* (*healthy*) gesund; (*safe*) sicher; (*sensible*) vernünftig; (*theory*) stichhaltig; (*thorough*) tüchtig, gehörig // *ad*: **to be** ~ **asleep** fest schlafen // *n* (*noise*) Geräusch *nt*, Laut *m*; (*GEOG*) Sund *m* // *vt* erschallen lassen; (*alarm*) (Alarm) schlagen; (*MED*) abhorchen // *vi* (*make a sound*) schallen, tönen; (*seem*) klingen; **to** ~ **like** sich anhören wie; ~ **out** *vt* (*opinion*) erforschen; (*person*) auf den Zahn fühlen (+*dat*); ~ **barrier** *n* Schallmauer *f*; ~ **effects** *npl* Toneffekte *pl*; ~**ing** *n* (*NAUT etc*) Lotung *f*; ~**ly** *ad* (*sleep*) fest; (*beat*) tüchtig; ~**proof** *a* (*room*) schalldicht; ~**track** *n* Tonstreifen *m*; (*music*) Filmmusik *f*.
soup [suːp] *n* Suppe *f*; **in the** ~ (col) in der Tinte; ~ **plate** *n* Suppenteller *m*; ~**spoon** *n* Suppenlöffel *m*.
sour ['saʊə*] *a* (lit, fig) sauer; **it's** ~ **grapes** (fig) die Trauben hängen zu hoch.
source [sɔːs] *n* (lit, fig) Quelle *f*.
south [saʊθ] *n* Süden *m* // *a* Süd-, südlich // *ad* nach Süden, südwärts; **S~ Africa** *n* Südafrika *nt*; **S~ African** *a* südafrikanisch // *n* Südafrikaner(in *f*) *m*; **S~ America** *n* Südamerika *nt*; **S~ American** *a* südamerikanisch // *n* Südamerikaner(in *f*) *m*; ~-**east** *n* Südosten *m*; ~**erly** ['sʌðəlɪ] *a* südlich; ~**ern** ['sʌðən] *a* südlich, Süd-; **S~ Pole** *n* Südpol *m*; ~**ward(s)** *ad* südwärts, nach Süden; ~-**west** *n* Südwesten *m*.
souvenir [suːvə'nɪə*] *n* Souvenir *nt*.
sovereign ['sɒvrɪn] *n* (*ruler*) Herrscher(in *f*) *m* // *a* (*independent*) souverän.
soviet ['səʊvɪət] *a* sowjetisch; **the S~ Union** die Sowjetunion.
sow [saʊ] *n* Sau *f* // *vt* [səʊ], *pt* **sowed**, *pp* **sown** [səʊn] (lit, fig) säen.
soy [sɔɪ] *n*: ~ **sauce** Sojasauce *f*.
soya bean ['sɔɪə'biːn] *n* Sojabohne *f*.
spa [spɑː] *n* (*place*) Kurort *m*.
space [speɪs] *n* Platz *m*, Raum *m*; (*universe*) Weltraum *m*, All *nt*; (*length of time*) Abstand *m* // *vt* (also: ~ **out**) verteilen; ~**craft**, ~ **ship** *n* Raumschiff *nt*; ~**man** *n* Raumfahrer *m*; **spacing** *n* Abstand *m*; (also: **spacing out**) Verteilung *f*.
spacious ['speɪʃəs] *a* geräumig, weit.
spade [speɪd] *n* Spaten *m*; ~**s** *n* (CARDS) Pik *nt*.
Spain [speɪn] *n* Spanien *nt*.
span [spæn] *n* Spanne *f*; (*of bridge etc*) Spannweite *f* // *vt* überspannen.
Spaniard ['spænjəd] *n* Spanier(in *f*) *m*.
Spanish ['spænɪʃ] *a* spanisch // *n* (LING) Spanisch *nt*; **the** ~ *npl* die Spanier.
spank [spæŋk] *vt* verhauen, versohlen.
spanner ['spænə*] *n* (*Brit*) Schrauben-

schlüssel m.
spar [spɑː] n (NAUT) Sparren m // vi
(BOXING) einen Sparring machen.
spare [speə*] a Ersatz- // n = ~ **part** //
vt (lives, feelings) verschonen; (trouble)
ersparen; **to** ~ (surplus) übrig; ~ **part**
n Ersatzteil nt; ~ **time** n Freizeit f; ~
wheel n (AUT) Reservereifen m.
sparing ['speəriŋ] a: **to be** ~ **with** geizen
mit; ~**ly** ad sparsam; (eat, spend etc)
in Maßen.
spark [spɑːk] n Funken m; ~**(ing) plug**
n Zündkerze f.
sparkle ['spɑːkl] n Funkeln nt; (gaiety)
Schwung m // vi funkeln.
sparkling ['spɑːkliŋ] a funkelnd; (wine)
Schaum-; (conversation) spritzig, geistreich.
sparrow ['spærəʊ] n Spatz m.
sparse [spɑːs] a spärlich.
spasm ['spæzəm] n (MED) Krampf m;
(fig) Anfall m; ~**odic** [spæz'mɒdɪk] a
(fig) sprunghaft.
spat [spæt] pt, pp of **spit**.
spate [speɪt] n (fig) Flut f, Schwall m;
in ~ (river) angeschwollen.
spatter ['spætə*] vt bespritzen, ver-
spritzen.
spatula ['spætjʊlə] n Spatel m.
spawn [spɔːn] vi laichen // n Laich m.
speak [spiːk] v (pt **spoke**, pp **spoken**)
vt sprechen, reden; (truth) sagen; (language) sprechen // vi sprechen (to mit or
zu); ~ **to sb** or **about sth** mit jdm
über etw (acc) sprechen; ~ **up!** sprich
lauter!; ~**er** n Sprecher(in f) m,
Redner(in f) m; (loud~er) Lautsprecher
m; (POL): **the S~er** der Vorsitzende
(Brit) des Parlaments or (US) des Kon-
gresses.
spear [spɪə*] n Speer m // vt aufspießen;
~**head** vt (attack etc) anführen.
spec [spek] n (col): **on** ~ auf gut Glück.
special ['speʃəl] a besondere(r, s); ~**ist**
n (TECH) Fachmann m; (MED)
Facharzt m, Fachärztin f; ~**ity**
[speʃɪ'ælɪtɪ] n Spezialität f; (study)
Spezialgebiet nt; ~**ize** vi sich
spezialisieren (in auf +acc); ~**ly** ad
besonders; (explicitly) extra.
species ['spiːʃiːz] n Art f.
specific [spə'sɪfɪk] a spezifisch; ~**ally**
ad spezifisch.
specification [spesɪfɪ'keɪʃən] n Angabe
f; (stipulation) Bedingung f; ~**s** pl
(TECH) technische Daten pl.
specify ['spesɪfaɪ] vt genau angeben.
specimen ['spesɪmɪn] n Probe f.
speck [spek] n Fleckchen nt.
speckled ['spekld] a gesprenkelt.
specs [speks] npl (col) Brille f.
spectacle ['spektəkl] n Schauspiel nt;
~**s** pl Brille f.
spectator [spek'teɪtə*] n Zuschauer(in
f) m.

spectre, (US) **specter** ['spektə*] n Geist
m, Gespenst nt.
speculate ['spekjʊleɪt] vi spekulieren.
speech [spiːtʃ] n Sprache f; (address)
Rede f; (manner of speaking)
Sprechweise f; ~**less** a sprachlos.
speed [spiːd] n Geschwindigkeit f;
(gear) Gang m // vi (pt, pp **sped**) zu schnell
fahren; **at full** or **top** ~ mit Höchstge-
schwindigkeit; ~ **up** vt beschleunigen //
vi schneller werden/fahren; ~**boat** n
Schnellboot nt; ~**ily** ad schleunigst;
~**ing** n zu schnelles Fahren; ~ **limit** n
Geschwindigkeitsbegrenzung f;
~**ometer** [spɪ'dɒmɪtə*] n Tachometer
m; ~**way** n (bike racing) Motor-
radrennstrecke f; ~**y** a schnell.
spell [spel] n (magic) Bann m; (period
of time) Zeitlang f // vt, pp **spelt**
(Brit) or **spelled** buchstabieren; (imply) bedeuten; **to cast a** ~ **on sb** jdn ver-
zaubern; ~**bound** a (wie) gebannt;
~**ing** n Rechtschreibung f.
spend [spend], pt, pp **spent** vt
(money) ausgeben; (time) verbringen;
~**thrift** n Verschwender(in f) m.
sperm [spɜːm] n (BIOL) Samenflüssig-
keit f.
spew [spjuː] vt (er)brechen.
sphere [sfɪə*] n (globe) Kugel f; (fig)
Sphäre f, Gebiet nt.
spherical ['sferɪkəl] a kugelförmig.
spice [spaɪs] n Gewürz nt // vt würzen.
spick-and-span ['spɪkən'spæn] a blitz-
blank.
spider ['spaɪdə*] n Spinne f.
spike [spaɪk] n Dorn m, Spitze f.
spill [spɪl] v (pt, pp **spilt** or
spilled) vt verschütten // vi sich
ergießen; ~ **over** vi überlaufen; (fig)
sich ausbreiten.
spin [spɪn] n (trip in car) Spazierfahrt f;
(AVIAT) (Ab)trudeln nt; (on ball) Drall
m // v (pt, pp **spun**) vt (thread)
spinnen; (like top) (herum)wirbeln // vi
sich drehen; ~ **out** vt in die Länge
ziehen.
spinach ['spɪnɪtʃ] n Spinat m.
spinal ['spaɪnl] a Rückgrat-; ~ **cord** n
Rückenmark nt.
spindly ['spɪndlɪ] a spindeldürr.
spin-dryer ['spɪn'draɪə*] n (Brit) Wä-
scheschleuder f.
spine [spaɪn] n Rückgrat nt; (thorn) Stachel m; ~**less** a (lit, fig) rückgratlos.
spinning ['spɪnɪŋ] n Spinnen nt; ~ **top**
n Kreisel m; ~ **wheel** n Spinnrad nt.
spin-off ['spɪnɒf] n Nebenprodukt nt.
spinster ['spɪnstə*] n unverheiratete
Frau f; (pej) alte Jungfer f.
spire [spaɪə*] n Turm m.
spirit ['spɪrɪt] n Geist m; (humour,
mood) Stimmung f; (courage) Mut m;
(verve) Elan m; (alcohol) Alkohol m;
~**s** pl Spirituosen pl; **in good** ~**s** gut auf-

gelegt; ~**ed** a beherzt; ~ **level** n Wasserwaage f.

spiritual ['spɪrɪtjʊəl] a geistig, seelisch; (REL) geistlich // n Spiritual nt.

spit [spɪt] n (for roasting) (Brat)spieß m; (saliva) Spucke f // vi, pt, pp **spat** spucken; (rain) sprühen; (make a sound) zischen; (cat) fauchen.

spite [spaɪt] n Gehässigkeit f // vt kränken; **in** ~ **of** trotz (+gen or dat); ~**ful** a gehässig.

spittle ['spɪtl] n Speichel m, Spucke f.

splash [splæʃ] n Spritzer m; (of colour) (Farb)fleck m // vt bespritzen // vi spritzen.

spleen [spli:n] n (ANAT) Milz f.

splendid ['splendɪd] a glänzend.

splendour, (US) **splendor** ['splendə*] n Pracht f.

splint [splɪnt] n Schiene f.

splinter ['splɪntə*] n Splitter m // vi (zer)splittern.

split [splɪt] n Spalte f; (fig) Spaltung f; (division) Trennung f // v (pt, pp **split**) vt spalten // vi (divide) reißen; ~ **up** vi sich trennen.

splutter ['splʌtə*] vi stottern.

spoil [spɔɪl], pt, pp **spoilt** or **spoiled** vt (ruin) verderben; (child) verwöhnen; ~**s** npl Beute f; ~**sport** n Spielverderber m.

spoke [spəʊk] pt of **speak** // n Speiche f.

spoken ['spəʊkn] pp of **speak**.

spokesman ['spəʊksmən] n Sprecher m.

spokeswoman ['spəʊkswʊmən] n Sprecherin f.

sponge [spʌndʒ] n Schwamm m // vt abwaschen // vi auf Kosten leben (on gen); ~ **bag** n (Brit) Kulturbeutel m; ~ **cake** n Rührkuchen m.

sponsor ['spɒnsə*] n Sponsor m // vt fördern; ~**ship** n Finanzierung f; (public) Schirmherrschaft f.

spontaneous [spɒn'teɪnɪəs] a spontan.

spooky ['spu:kɪ] a (col) gespenstisch.

spool [spu:l] n Spule f, Rolle f.

spoon [spu:n] n Löffel m; ~-**feed** vt irreg (lit) mit dem Löffel füttern; (fig) hochpäppeln; ~**ful** n Löffel(voll) m.

sport [spɔ:t] n Sport m; (person) feine(r) Kerl m; ~**ing** a (fair) sportlich, fair; **to give sb a** ~**ing chance** jdn eine faire Chance geben; ~**s car** n Sportwagen m; ~**s jacket**, (US) ~ **jacket** n Sportjackett nt; **sportsman** n Sportler m; **sportsmanship** n Sportlichkeit f; **sportswear** n Sportkleidung f; **sportswoman** n Sportlerin f; ~**y** a sportlich.

spot [spɒt] n Punkt m; (dirty) Fleck(en) m; (place) Stelle f; (MED) Pickel m // vt erspähen; (mistake) bemerken; **on the** ~ an Ort und Stelle; (at once) auf der Stelle; ~ **check** n Stichprobe f;

~**less** a fleckenlos; ~**light** n Scheinwerferlicht nt; (lamp) Scheinwerfer m; ~**ted** a gefleckt; ~**ty** a (face) pickelig.

spouse [spaʊz] n Gatte m/Gattin f.

spout [spaʊt] n (of pot) Tülle f; (jet) Wasserstrahl m // vi speien.

sprain [spreɪn] n Verrenkung f // vt verrenken.

sprang [spræŋ] pt of **spring**.

sprawl [sprɔ:l] vi sich strecken.

spray [spreɪ] n Spray nt; (off sea) Gischt f; (of flowers) Zweig m // vt besprühen, sprayen.

spread [spred] n (extent) Verbreitung f; (col: meal) Schmaus m; (for bread) Aufstrich m // v (pt, pp **spread**) vt ausbreiten; (scatter) verbreiten; (butter) streichen // vi sich ausbreiten; ~**-eagled** a: **to be** ~**-eagled** alle viere von sich strecken.

spree [spri:] n (shopping) Einkaufsbummel m; **to go on a** ~ einen draufmachen.

sprightly ['spraɪtlɪ] a munter, lebhaft.

spring [sprɪŋ] n (leap) Sprung m; (metal) Feder f; (season) Frühling m; (water) Quelle f // vi, pt **sprang**, pp **sprung** (leap) springen; ~ **up** vi (problem) auftauchen; ~**board** n Sprungbrett nt; ~**clean** n (also: ~**-cleaning**) n Frühjahrsputz m; ~**time** n Frühling m; ~**y** a federnd, elastisch.

sprinkle ['sprɪŋkl] vt (salt) streuen; (liquid) sprenkeln; **to** ~ **water on,** ~ **with water** mit Wasser besprengen.

sprinkler ['sprɪŋklə*] n (for lawn) Sprenger m; (for fire fighting) Sprinkler m.

sprite [spraɪt] n Elfe f; Kobold m.

sprout [spraʊt] vi sprießen; **(Brussels)** ~**s** npl Rosenkohl m.

spruce [spru:s] n Fichte f // a schmuck, adrett.

sprung [sprʌŋ] pp of **spring**.

spry [spraɪ] a flink, rege.

spun [spʌn] pt, pp of **spin**.

spur [spɜ:*] n Sporn m; (fig) Ansporn m // vt (also: ~ **on**) (fig) anspornen; **on the** ~ **of the moment** spontan.

spurious ['spjʊərɪəs] a falsch.

spurn [spɜ:n] vt verschmähen.

spurt [spɜ:t] n (jet) Strahl m; (acceleration) Spurt m // vi (liquid) schießen.

spy [spaɪ] n Spion(in f) m // vi spionieren // vt erspähen; ~**ing** n Spionage f.

sq. abbr of **square**.

squabble ['skwɒbl] n Zank m // vi sich zanken.

squad [skwɒd] n (MIL) Abteilung f; (police) Kommando nt.

squadron ['skwɒdrən] n (cavalry) Schwadron f; (NAUT) Geschwader nt; (air force) Staffel f.

squalid ['skwɒlɪd] a verkommen.
squall [skwɔːl] n Bö f, Windstoß m.
squalor ['skwɒlə*] n Verwahrlosung f.
squander ['skwɒndə*] vt verschwenden.
square [skweə*] n Quadrat nt; (open space) Platz m; (instrument) Winkel m; (col: person) Spießer m // a viereckig; (col: ideas, tastes) spießig // vt (arrange) ausmachen; (MATH) ins Quadrat erheben // vi (agree) übereinstimmen; **all** ~ quitt; **a** ~ **meal** eine ordentliche Mahlzeit; **2 metres** ~ 2 Meter im Quadrat; **1** ~ **metre** 1 Quadratmeter; ~**ly** ad fest, gerade.
squash [skwɒʃ] n (Brit: drink) Saft m // vt zerquetschen.
squat [skwɒt] a untersetzt // vi hocken; ~**ter** n Hausbesetzer m.
squawk [skwɔːk] vi kreischen.
squeak [skwiːk] vi quiek(s)en; (spring, door etc) quietschen.
squeal [skwiːl] vi schrill schreien.
squeamish ['skwiːmɪʃ] a empfindlich.
squeeze [skwiːz] n (POL) Geldknappheit f // vt pressen, drücken; (orange) auspressen; ~ **out** vt ausquetschen.
squelch [skweltʃ] vi platschen.
squid [skwɪd] n Tintenfisch m.
squiggle ['skwɪgl] n Schnörkel m.
squint [skwɪnt] vi schielen (at nach) // n: **to have a** ~ schielen.
squire ['skwaɪə*] n (Brit) Gutsherr m.
squirm [skwɜːm] vi sich winden.
squirrel ['skwɪrəl] n Eichhörnchen nt.
squirt [skwɜːt] vti spritzen.
Sr abbr (= senior) sen.
St abbr (= saint) hl., St.; (= street) Str.
stab [stæb] n (blow) Stich m; (col: try) Versuch m // vt erstechen.
stabilize ['steɪbəlaɪz] vt stabilisieren // vi sich stabilisieren.
stable ['steɪbl] a stabil // n Stall m.
stack [stæk] n Stapel m // vt stapeln.
stadium ['steɪdɪəm] n Stadion nt.
staff [stɑːf] n (stick, MIL) Stab m; (personnel) Personal nt; (Brit SCH) Lehrkräfte pl // vt (with people) besetzen.
stag [stæg] n Hirsch m.
stage [steɪdʒ] n Bühne f; (of journey) Etappe f; (degree) Stufe f; (point) Stadium nt // vt (put on) aufführen; (simulate) inszenieren; (demonstration) veranstalten; **in** ~**s** etappenweise; ~**coach** n Postkutsche f; ~ **door** n Bühneneingang m; ~ **manager** n Intendant m.
stagger ['stægə*] vi wanken, taumeln // vt (amaze) verblüffen; (hours) staffeln; ~**ing** a unglaublich.
stagnant ['stægnənt] a stagnierend; (water) stehend.
stagnate [stæg'neɪt] vi stagnieren.
stag party n Männerabend m (vom

Bräutigam vor der Hochzeit gegeben).
staid [steɪd] a gesetzt.
stain [steɪn] n Fleck m // vt beflecken; ~**ed glass window** buntes Glasfenster nt; ~**less** a (steel) rostfrei; ~ **remover** n Fleckentferner m.
stair [steə*] n (Treppen)stufe f; ~**case** n Treppenhaus nt, Treppe f; ~**s** pl Treppe f; ~**way** n Treppenaufgang m.
stake [steɪk] n (post) Pfahl m; (money) Einsatz m // vt (bet money) setzen; **to be at** ~ auf dem Spiel stehen.
stale [steɪl] a alt; (bread) altbacken.
stalemate ['steɪlmeɪt] n (CHESS) Patt nt; (fig) Stillstand m.
stalk [stɔːk] n Stengel m, Stiel m // vt (game) jagen; ~ **off** vi abstolzieren.
stall [stɔːl] n (in stable) Stand m, Box f; (in market) (Verkaufs)stand m // vt (AUT) (den Motor) abwürgen // vi (AUT) stehenbleiben; (avoid) Ausflüchte machen; ~**s** npl (Brit THEAT) Parkett nt.
stallion ['stæliən] n Zuchthengst m.
stalwart ['stɔːlwət] n treue(r) Anhänger m.
stamina ['stæmɪnə] n Durchhaltevermögen nt, Zähigkeit f.
stammer ['stæmə*] n Stottern nt // vti stottern, stammeln.
stamp [stæmp] n Briefmarke f; (for document) Stempel m // vi stampfen // vt (mark) stempeln; (mail) frankieren; (foot) stampfen mit; ~ **album** n Briefmarkenalbum nt; ~ **collecting** n Briefmarkensammeln nt.
stampede [stæm'piːd] n panische Flucht f.
stance [stæns] n Haltung f.
stand [stænd] n (for objects) Gestell nt; (seats) Tribüne f // v (pt, pp **stood**) vi stehen; (rise) aufstehen; (decision) feststehen // vt setzen, stellen; (endure) aushalten; (person) ausstehen; (nonsense) dulden; **to make a** ~ Widerstand leisten; **to** ~ **for parliament** (Brit) für das Parlament kandidieren; ~ **by** vi (be ready) bereitstehen // vt (opinion) treu bleiben (+dat); ~ **down** vi (withdraw) zurücktreten; ~ **for** vt (signify) stehen für; (permit, tolerate) hinnehmen; ~ **in for** vt einspringen für; ~ **out** vi (be prominent) hervorstechen; ~ **up** vi (rise) aufstehen; ~ **up for** vt sich einsetzen für; ~ **up to** vt: ~ **up to sth/sb** vt einer Sache gewachsen sein/sich jdm gegenüber behaupten.
standard ['stændəd] n (measure) Norm f; (flag) Fahne f // a (size etc) Normal-; ~**s** npl (morals) Maßstäbe pl; ~**ize** vt vereinheitlichen; ~ **lamp** n (Brit) Stehlampe f; ~ **of living** n Lebensstandard m.
stand-by ['stændbaɪ] n Reserve f; **to be on** ~ in Bereitschaft sein; ~ **ticket** n (AVIAT) Standby-Ticket nt.

stand-in ['stændɪn] n Ersatz m.
standing ['stændɪŋ] a (erect) stehend; (permanent) ständig; (invitation) offen // n (duration) Dauer f; (reputation) Ansehen nt; of many years' ~ langjährig; ~ **order** n (Brit: at bank) Dauerauftrag m; ~ **orders** pl (MIL) Vorschrift; ~ **room** n Stehplatz m.
stand-offish ['stænd'ɒfɪʃ] a zurückhaltend, sehr reserviert.
standpoint ['stændpɔɪnt] n Standpunkt m.
standstill ['stændstɪl] n: to be at a ~ stillstehen; to come to a ~ zum Stillstand kommen.
stank [stæŋk] pt of **stink**.
staple ['steɪpl] n (in paper) Heftklammer f; (article) Haupterzeugnis nt // a Grund-, Haupt- // vt (fest)klammern; ~r n Heftmaschine f.
star [stɑ:*] n Stern m; (person) Star m // vi die Hauptrolle spielen.
starboard ['stɑ:bəd] n Steuerbord nt.
starch [stɑ:tʃ] n Stärke f.
stardom ['stɑ:dəm] n Berühmtheit f.
stare [steə*] n starre(r) Blick m // vi starren (at auf +acc); ~ **at** vt anstarren.
starfish ['stɑ:fɪʃ] n Seestern m.
stark [stɑ:k] a öde // ad: ~ **naked** splitternackt.
starling ['stɑ:lɪŋ] n Star m.
starry ['stɑ:rɪ] a Sternen-; ~-**eyed** a (innocent) blauäugig.
start [stɑ:t] n Anfang m; (SPORT) Start m; (lead) Vorsprung m // vt in Gang setzen; (car) anlassen // vi anfangen; (car) anspringen; (on journey) aufbrechen; (SPORT) starten; (with fright) zusammenfahren; to ~ **doing** or **to do sth** anfangen, etw zu tun; ~ **off** vi anfangen; (begin moving) losgehen/-fahren; ~ **up** vi anfangen; (startled) auffahren // vt beginnen; (car) anlassen; ~**er** n (AUT) Anlasser m; (for race) Starter m; (Brit COOK) Vorspeise f; ~**ing point** n Ausgangspunkt m.
startle ['stɑ:tl] vt erschrecken.
startling ['stɑ:tlɪŋ] a erschreckend.
starvation [stɑ:'veɪʃən] n Verhungern nt.
starve [stɑ:v] vi verhungern // vt verhungern lassen; I'm **starving** ich sterbe vor Hunger.
state [steɪt] n (condition) Zustand m; (POL) Staat m // vt erklären; (facts) angeben; the S~s die Staaten; to be in a ~ durchdrehen; ~**ly** a würdevoll; ~**ment** n Aussage f; (POL) Erklärung f; **statesman** n Staatsmann m.
static ['stætɪk] n: ~ **electricity** n Reibungselektrizität f.
station ['steɪʃən] n (RAIL etc) Bahnhof m; (police etc) Wache f; (in society) Stand m // vt stationieren.
stationary ['steɪʃənərɪ] a stillstehend; (car) parkend.
stationer ['steɪʃənə*] n Schreibwarenhändler m; ~'**s** n (shop) Schreibwarengeschäft nt; ~**y** n Schreibwaren pl.
station master ['steɪʃənmɑ:stə*] n Bahnhofsvorsteher m.
station wagon ['steɪʃənwægən] n Kombiwagen m.
statistics [stə'tɪstɪks] n Statistik f.
statue ['stætju:] n Statue f.
stature ['stætʃə*] n Größe f.
status ['steɪtəs] n Status m.
statute ['stætju:t] n Gesetz nt.
statutory ['stætjʊtərɪ] a gesetzlich.
staunch [stɔ:ntʃ] a standhaft.
stave [steɪv]: ~ **off** vt (attack) abwehren; (threat) abwenden.
stay [steɪ] n Aufenthalt m // vi bleiben; (reside) wohnen; to ~ **put** an Ort und Stelle bleiben; to ~ **the night** übernachten; ~ **behind** vi zurückbleiben; ~ **in** vi (at home) zu Hause bleiben; ~ **on** vi (continue) länger bleiben; ~ **out** vi (of house) wegbleiben; ~ **up** vi (at night) aufbleiben; ~**ing power** n Durchhaltevermögen nt.
stead [sted] n: in sb's ~ an jds Stelle; to **stand sb in good** ~ jdm zugute kommen.
steadfast ['stedfəst] a standhaft, treu.
steadily ['stedɪlɪ] ad stetig, regelmäßig.
steady ['stedɪ] a (firm) fest, stabil; (regular) gleichmäßig; (reliable) beständig; (hand) ruhig; (job, boyfriend) fest // vt festigen; to ~ **o.s. on** or **against** sth sich stützen auf or gegen etw (acc).
steak [steɪk] n Steak nt; (fish) Filet nt.
steal [sti:l] v (pt **stole**, pp **stolen**) vti stehlen // vi sich stehlen.
stealth [stelθ] n Heimlichkeit f; ~**y** ['stelθɪ] a verstohlen, heimlich.
steam [sti:m] n Dampf m // vt (COOK) im Dampfbad erhitzen // vi dampfen; ~ **engine** n Dampfmaschine f; ~**er** n Dampfer m; ~**roller** n Dampfwalze f; ~**ship** n = ~**er**; ~**y** a dampfig.
steel [sti:l] n Stahl m // a Stahl-; (fig) stählern; ~**works** n Stahlwerke pl.
steep [sti:p] a steil; (price) gepfeffert // vt einweichen.
steeple ['sti:pl] n Kirchturm m; ~**chase** n Hindernisrennen nt.
steer [stɪə*] vti steuern; (car etc) lenken; ~**ing** n (AUT) Steuerung f; ~**ing wheel** n Steuer- or Lenkrad nt.
stellar ['stelə*] a Stern(en)-.
stem [stem] n Stiel m // vt aufhalten; ~ **from** vt abstammen von.
stench [stentʃ] n Gestank m.
stencil ['stensl] n Schablone f // vt (auf)drucken.
stenographer [ste'nɒgrəfə*] n (US) Stenograph(in f) m.

step [step] n Schritt m; (stair) Stufe f // vi treten, schreiten; **to take ~s** Schritte unternehmen; **~s** pl = **~ladder**; **in/out of ~ (with)** im/nicht im Gleichklang (mit); **~-daughter** n Stieftochter f; **~ down** vi (fig) abtreten; **~ off** vt aussteigen aus (+dat); **~ up** vt steigern; **~brother** n Stiefbruder m; **~father** n Stiefvater m; **~ladder** n Trittleiter f; **~mother** n Stiefmutter f; **~ping stone** n Stein m; (fig) Sprungbrett nt; **~sister** n Stiefschwester f; **~son** n Stiefsohn m.

stereo ['steriəu] n Stereoanlage f // a (also: **~phonic**) a stereophonisch.

stereotype ['stiəriətaip] n Prototyp m; (fig) Klischee nt // vt stereotypieren; (fig) stereotyp machen.

sterile ['sterail] a steril; (person) unfruchtbar.

sterling ['stɜ:lɪŋ] a (FIN) Sterling-; (character) gediegen // n (ECON) Pfund Sterling; **a pound ~** ein Pfund Sterling.

stern [stɜ:n] a streng // n Heck nt, Achterschiff nt.

stew [stju:] n Eintopf m // vti schmoren.

steward ['stju:əd] n Steward m; **~ess** n Stewardess f.

stick [stik] n Stock m; (of chalk etc) Stück nt // v (pt, pp **stuck**) vt (stab) stechen; (fix) stecken; (put) stellen; (gum) (an)kleben; (col: tolerate) vertragen // vi (stop) steckenbleiben; (get stuck) klemmen; (hold fast) kleben, haften; **~ out** vi (project) hervorstehen aus; **~ up** vi (project) in die Höhe stehen; **~ up for** vt (defend) eintreten für; **~er** n Aufkleber m; **~ing plaster** n Heftpflaster nt.

stickler ['stiklə*] n Pedant m (for in +acc).

stick-up ['stikʌp] n (col) (Raub)überfall m.

sticky ['stiki] a klebrig; (atmosphere) stickig.

stiff [stif] a steif; (difficult) hart; (paste) dick; (drink) stark; **~en** vt versteifen, (ver)stärken // vi sich versteifen; **~ness** n Steifheit f.

stifle ['staifl] vt unterdrücken.

stifling ['staiflɪŋ] a drückend.

stigma ['stigmə], pl (BOT, MED, REL) **~ta** [-tə], (fig) **~s** n Stigma nt.

stile [stail] n Steige f.

stiletto [sti'letəu] n (Brit: also: **~ heel**) Pfennigabsatz m.

still [stil] a still // ad (immer) noch; (anyhow) immerhin; **~born** a totgeboren; **~ life** n Stilleben nt.

stilt [stilt] n Stelze f.

stilted ['stiltid] a gestelzt.

stimulate ['stimjuleit] vt anregen, stimulieren.

stimulus ['stimjuləs], pl **-li** [-lai] n Anregung f, Reiz m.

sting [stiŋ] n Stich m; (organ) Stachel m // vti, pt, pp **stung** stechen; (on skin) brennen.

stingy ['stindʒi] a geizig, knauserig.

stink [stiŋk] n Gestank m // vi, pt **stank**, pp **stunk** stinken; **~ing** a (fig) widerlich.

stint [stint] n Pensum nt; (period) Betätigung f // vi knausern; **to do one's ~** seine Arbeit tun; (share) seinen Teil beitragen.

stipulate ['stipjuleit] vt festsetzen.

stir [stɜ:*] n Bewegung f; (COOK) Rühren nt; (sensation) Aufsehen nt // vt (um)rühren // vi sich rühren; **~ up** vt mob aufhetzen; (mixture) umrühren; (dust) aufwirbeln.

stirrup ['stirəp] n Steigbügel m.

stitch [stitʃ] n (with needle) Stich m; (MED) Faden m; (of knitting) Masche f; (pain) Stich m // vt nähen.

stoat [stəut] n Wiesel nt.

stock [stɔk] n Vorrat m; (COMM) (Waren)lager nt; (live~) Vieh nt; (COOK) Brühe f; (FIN) Grundkapital nt // a stets vorrätig; (standard) Normal- // vt (in shop) führen; **in/out of ~** vorrätig/nicht vorrätig; **to take ~ of** Inventur machen von; (fig) Bilanz ziehen aus; **~s** npl Aktien pl; **~s and shares** Effekten pl; **to ~ up with** Reserven anlegen von.

stockbroker ['stɔkbrəukə*] n Börsenmakler m.

stock cube n Brühwürfel m.

stock exchange n Börse f.

stocking ['stɔkɪŋ] n Strumpf m.

stockist ['stɔkɪst] n Händler m.

stock market ['stɔkmɑ:kɪt] n Börse f.

stock phrase n Standardsatz m.

stockpile ['stɔkpail] n Vorrat m // vt aufstapeln.

stocktaking ['stɔkteikɪŋ] n (Brit COMM) Inventur f, Bestandsaufnahme f.

stocky ['stɔki] a untersetzt.

stodgy ['stɔdʒi] a pampig; (fig) trocken.

stoke [stəuk] vt schüren.

stole [stəul] pt of **steal** // n Stola f.

stolen ['stəulən] pp of **steal**.

stolid ['stɔlid] a stur.

stomach ['stʌmək] n Bauch m, Magen m // vt vertragen; **~ache** n Magen- or Bauchschmerzen pl.

stone [stəun] n Stein m; (Brit: weight) Gewichtseinheit f = 6.35 kg // vt (olive) entkernen; (kill) steinigen; **~-cold** a eiskalt; **~-deaf** a stocktaub; **~work** n Mauerwerk nt.

stony ['stəuni] a steinig.

stood [stud] pt, pp of **stand**.

stool [stu:l] n Hocker m.

stoop [stu:p] vi sich bücken.

stop [stɔp] n Halt m; (bus~) Haltestelle f; (punctuation) Punkt m // vt anhalten; (bring to end) aufhören (mit), sein lassen // vi aufhören; (clock) stehenbleiben; (*remain*) bleiben; **to ~ doing sth** aufhören, etw zu tun; **~ dead** *vi* innehalten; **~ off** *vi* kurz haltmachen; **~ up** *vt* (*hole*) zustopfen, verstopfen; **~gap** *n* Notlösung *f*; **~lights** *npl* (*AUT*) Bremslichter *pl*; **~over** *n* (*on journey*) Zwischenaufenthalt *m*.

stoppage ['stɔpɪdʒ] *n* (An)halten *nt*; (*traffic*) Verkehrsstockung *f*; (*strike*) Arbeitseinstellung *f*.

stopper ['stɔpə*] *n* Propfen *m*, Stöpsel *m*.

stop press *n* letzte Meldung *f*.

stopwatch ['stɔpwɔtʃ] *n* Stoppuhr *f*.

storage *n* ['stɔːrɪdʒ] *n* Lagerung *f*; **~ heater** *n* (Nachtstrom)speicherofen *m*.

store [stɔː*] *n* Vorrat *m*; (*place*) Lager *nt*, Warenhaus *nt*; (*Brit: large shop*) Kaufhaus *nt*; (*US*) Laden *m*; **~s** *pl* Vorräte *pl* // *vt* lagern; **~ up** *vt* sich eindecken mit; **~room** *n* Lagerraum *m*, Vorratsraum *m*.

storey, (*US*) **story** ['stɔːrɪ] *n* Stock *m*.

stork [stɔːk] *n* Storch *m*.

storm [stɔːm] *n* (*lit, fig*) Sturm *m* // *vti* stürmen; **~y** *a* stürmisch.

story ['stɔːrɪ] *n* Geschichte *f*; (*lie*) Märchen *nt*; (*US*) = **storey**; **~book** *n* Geschichtenbuch *nt*; **~teller** *n* Geschichtenerzähler *m*.

stout [staʊt] *a* (*bold*) tapfer; (*too fat*) beleibt // *n* Starkbier *nt*; (*also*: **sweet ~**) ≃ Malzbier *nt*.

stove [stəʊv] *n* (Koch)herd *m*; (*for heating*) Ofen *m*.

stow [stəʊ] *vt* verstauen; **~away** *n* blinde(r) Passagier *m*.

straddle ['strædl] *vt* (*horse, fence*) rittlings sitzen auf (+*dat*); (*fig*) überbrücken.

straggle ['strægl] *vi* (*branches etc*) wuchern; (*people*) nachhinken; **~r** *n* Nachzügler *m*; **straggling, straggly** *a* (*hair*) zottig.

straight [streɪt] *a* gerade; (*honest*) offen, ehrlich; (*drink*) pur // *ad* (*direct*) direkt, geradewegs; **to put** *or* **get sth ~** etw in Ordnung bringen; **~away** *ad* sofort; **~ off** *ad* sofort; **~en** *vt* (*also*: **~en out**) (*lit*) gerade machen; (*fig*) klarstellen; **~-faced** *ad* ohne die Miene zu verziehen // *a*: **to be ~-faced** keine Miene verziehen; **~forward** *a* einfach, unkompliziert.

strain [streɪn] *n* Belastung *f*; (*streak, trace*) Zug *m*; (*of music*) Fetzen *m* // *vt* überanstrengen; (*stretch*) anspannen; (*muscle*) zerren; (*filter*) (durch)seihen // *vi* sich anstrengen; **~ed** *a* (*laugh*) gezwungen; (*relations*) gespannt; **~er** *n* Sieb *nt*.

strait [streɪt] *n* Straße *f*, Meerenge *f*; **~-jacket** *n* Zwangsjacke *f*; **~-laced** *a* engherzig, streng.

strand [strænd] *n* (*lit, fig*) Faden *m*; (*of*

---

hair) Strähne *f*; **~ed** (*lit, fig*) gestrandet.

strange [streɪndʒ] *a* fremd; (*unusual*) seltsam; **~r** *n* Fremde(r) *mf*.

strangle ['stræŋgl] *vt* erwürgen; **~hold** *n* (*fig*) Umklammerung *f*.

strap [stræp] *n* Riemen *m*; (*on clothes*) Träger *m* // *vt* (*fasten*) festschnallen.

strapping ['stræpɪŋ] *a* stramm.

strata ['strɑːtə] *pl of* **stratum**.

stratagem ['strætədʒəm] *n* (Kriegs)list *f*.

strategic [strə'tiːdʒɪk] *a* strategisch.

strategy ['strætədʒɪ] *n* (*fig*) Strategie *f*.

stratum ['strɑːtəm], *pl* **-ta** *n* Schicht *f*.

straw [strɔː] *n* Stroh *nt*; (*single stalk, drinking ~*) Strohhalm *m*; **that's the last ~!** das ist der Gipfel!

strawberry ['strɔːbərɪ] *n* Erdbeere *f*.

stray [streɪ] *a* (*animal*) verirrt; (*thought*) zufällig // *vi* herumstreunen.

streak ['striːk] *n* Streifen *m*; (*in character*) Einschlag *m*; (*in hair*) Strähne *f* // *vt* streifen // *vi* zucken; (*move quickly*) flitzen; **~ of bad luck** Pechsträhne *f*; **~y** *a* gestreift; (*bacon*) durchwachsen.

stream [striːm] *n* (*brook*) Bach *m*; (*fig*) Strom *m* // *vt* (*SCH*) in (Leistungs)gruppen einteilen // *vi* strömen; **to ~ in/out** (*people*) hinein-/hinausströmen.

streamer ['striːmə*] *n* (*pennon*) Wimpel *m*; (*of paper*) Luftschlange *f*.

streamlined ['striːmlaɪnd] *a* stromlinienförmig; (*effective*) rationell.

street [striːt] *n* Straße *f* // *a* Straßen-; **~car** *n* (*US*) Straßenbahn *f*; **~ lamp** *n* Straßenlaterne *f*; **~ plan** *n* Stadtplan *m*; **~wise** *a* (*col*): **to be ~wise** wissen, wo es lang geht.

strength [streŋθ] *n* Stärke *f* (*also fig*); Kraft *f*; **~en** *vt* (ver)stärken.

strenuous ['strenjʊəs] *a* anstrengend.

stress [stres] *n* Druck *m*; (*mental*) Streß *m*; (*GRAM*) Betonung *f* // *vt* betonen.

stretch [stretʃ] *n* Strecke *f* // *vt* ausdehnen, strecken // *vi* sich erstrecken; (*person*) sich strecken; **~ out** *vi* sich ausstrecken // *vt* ausstrecken.

stretcher ['stretʃə*] *n* Tragbahre *f*.

strewn [struːn] *a*: **~ with** übersät mit.

stricken ['strɪkən] *a* (*person*) ergriffen; (*city, country*) heimgesucht; **~ with** (*arthritis, disease*) leidend unter.

strict [strɪkt] *a* (*exact*) genau; (*severe*) streng; **~ly** *ad* streng, genau.

stride [straɪd] *n* lange(r) Schritt *m* // *vi*, *pt* **strode**, *pp* **stridden** ['strɪdn] schreiten.

strident ['straɪdənt] *a* schneidend, durchdringend.

strife [straɪf] *n* Streit *m*.

strike [straɪk] *n* Streik *m*; (*attack*) Schlag *m* // *v* (*pt, pp* **struck**) *vt* (*hit*) schlagen; (*collide*) stoßen gegen; (*come to mind*) einfallen (+*dat*); (*stand out*) auffallen (+*dat*); (*find*) finden // vi (*stop work*) streiken; (*attack*) zuschlagen; (*clock*) schlagen; on ~ (*workers*) im Streik; to ~ a match ein Streichholz anzünden; ~ **down** vt (*lay low*) niederschlagen; ~ **out** vt (*cross out*) ausstreichen; ~ **up** vt (*music*) anstimmen; (*friendship*) schließen; **~r** n Streikende(r) mf.

striking ['straɪkɪŋ] a auffallend.

string [strɪŋ] n Schnur f; (*row*) Reihe f; (*MUS*) Saite f // v (pt, pp **strung**) vt: to ~ **together** aneinanderreihen // vi: to ~ out (sich)verteilen; **the ~s** pl (*MUS*) die Streichinstrumente pl; to pull ~s (*fig*) Fäden ziehen; ~ **bean** n grüne Bohne f; **~(ed) instrument** n (*MUS*) Saiteninstrument nt.

stringent ['strɪndʒənt] a streng.

strip [strɪp] n Streifen m // vt (*uncover*) abstreifen, abziehen; (*clothes*) ausziehen; (*TECH*) auseinandernehmen // vi (*undress*) sich ausziehen; ~ **cartoon** n Bildserie f.

stripe [straɪp] n Streifen m; **~d** a gestreift.

strip lighting n Neonlicht nt.

stripper ['strɪpə*] n Stripteasetänzerin f.

strive [straɪv] vi, pt **strove**, pp **striven** ['strɪvn] streben (*for* nach).

strode [strəud] pt of **stride**.

stroke [strəuk] n Schlag m; (*swim, row*) Stoß m; (*TECH*) Hub m; (*MED*) Schlaganfall m; (*caress*) Streicheln nt // vt streicheln; at a ~ mit einem Schlag.

stroll [strəul] n Spaziergang m // vi schlendern; **~er** n (*US: pushchair*) Sportwagen m.

strong [strɒŋ] a stark; (*firm*) fest; they are 50 ~ sie sind 50 Mann stark; **~box** n Kassette f; **~hold** n Hochburg f; **~ly** ad stark; **~room** n Tresor m.

strove [strəuv] pt of **strive**.

struck [strʌk] pt, pp of **strike**.

structure ['strʌktʃə*] n Struktur f, Aufbau m; (*building*) Bau m.

struggle ['strʌgl] n Kampf m // vi (*fight*) kämpfen.

strum [strʌm] vt (*guitar*) klimpern auf (+*dat*).

strung [strʌŋ] pt, pp of **string**.

strut [strʌt] n Strebe f, Stütze f // vi stolzieren.

stub [stʌb] n Stummel m; (*of cigarette*) Kippe f // vt: to ~ one's toe sich (*dat*) den Zeh anstoßen; ~ **out** vt ausdrücken.

stubble ['stʌbl] n Stoppel f.

stubborn ['stʌbən] a hartnäckig.

stuck [stʌk] pt, pp of **stick** // a (*jammed*) klemmend; **~-up** a hochnäsig.

stud [stʌd] n (*button*) Kragenknopf m; (*place*) Gestüt nt // vt (*fig*): **~ded with** übersät mit.

student ['stju:dənt] n Student(in f) m; (*US also*) Schüler(in f) m // a Studenten-; ~ **driver** n (*US*) Fahrschüler(in f) m.

studio ['stju:dɪəu] n Studio nt; (*for artist*) Atelier nt; ~ **flat**, (*US*) ~ **apartment** n Appartement nt.

studious ['stju:dɪəs] a lernbegierig.

study ['stʌdɪ] n Studium nt; (*investigation also*) Untersuchung f; (*room*) Arbeitszimmer nt; (*essay etc*) Studie f // vt studieren; (*face*) erforschen; (*evidence*) prüfen // vi studieren.

stuff [stʌf] n Stoff m; (*col*) Zeug nt // vt stopfen, füllen; (*animal*) ausstopfen; **~ing** n Füllung f; **~y** a (*room*) schwül; (*person*) spießig.

stumble ['stʌmbl] vi stolpern; to ~ across (*fig*) stoßen auf (+*acc*).

stumbling block ['stʌmblɪŋblɒk] n Hindernis nt.

stump [stʌmp] n Stumpf m // vt umwerfen.

stun [stʌn] vt betäuben; (*shock*) niederschmettern.

stung [stʌŋ] pt, pp of **sting**.

stunk [stʌŋk] pt, pp of **stink**.

stunning ['stʌnɪŋ] a betäubend; (*news*) überwältigend, umwerfend.

stunt [stʌnt] n Kunststück nt, Trick m; **~ed** a verkümmert; **~man** n Stuntman m.

stupefy ['stju:pɪfaɪ] vt betäuben; (*by news*) bestürzen.

stupendous [stju'pendəs] a erstaunlich, enorm.

stupid ['stju:pɪd] a dumm; **~ity** [stju'pɪdɪtɪ] n Dummheit f.

stupor ['stju:pə*] n Betäubung f.

sturdy ['stɜ:dɪ] a kräftig, robust.

stutter ['stʌtə*] n Stottern nt // vi stottern.

sty [staɪ] n Schweinestall m.

stye [staɪ] n Gerstenkorn nt.

style [staɪl] n Stil m; (*fashion*) Mode f.

stylish ['staɪlɪʃ] a modisch.

stylist ['staɪlɪst] n (*hair* ~) Friseur m, Friseuse f.

stylus ['staɪləs] n (Grammophon)nadel f.

suave [swɑ:v] a zuvorkommend.

sub- [sʌb] *pref* Unter-.

subconscious ['sʌb'kɒnʃəs] a unterbewußt // n: the ~ das Unterbewußte.

subcontract ['sʌbkən'trækt] vt (*vertraglich*) untervermitteln.

subdivide ['sʌbdɪ'vaɪd] vt unterteilen.

subdue [səb'dju:] vt unterwerfen; **~d** a (*lighting*) gedämpft; (*person*) still.

subject ['sʌbdʒɪkt] n (*of kingdom*) Untertan m; (*citizen*) Staatsangehörige(r) mf; (*topic*) Thema nt; (*SCH*) Fach nt; (*GRAM*) Subjekt nt // vt [səb'dʒekt] (*subdue*) unterwerfen; (*expose*) aussetzen // a ['sʌbdʒɪkt]: to be

~ **to** unterworfen sein (+*dat*); (*exposed*) ausgesetzt sein (+*dat*); ~**ive** [səb'dʒɛktɪv] *a* subjektiv; ~ **matter** *n* Thema *nt*.

subjugate ['sʌbdʒugeɪt] *vt* unterjochen.

subjunctive [səb'dʒʌŋktɪv] *a* Konjunktiv- // *n* Konjunktiv *m*.

sublet ['sʌb'let] (*irreg*: *like* **let**) *vt* untervermieten.

sublime [sə'blaɪm] *a* erhaben.

submachine gun ['sʌbmə'ʃiːn-] *n* Maschinenpistole *f*.

submarine [sʌbmə'riːn] *n* Unterseeboot *nt*, U-Boot *nt*.

submerge [səb'mɜːdʒ] *vt* untertauchen; (*flood*) überschwemmen // *vi* untertauchen.

submission [səb'mɪʃən] *n* (*obedience*) Gehorsam *m*; (*claim*) Behauptung *f*; (*of plan*) Unterbreitung *f*.

submissive [səb'mɪsɪv] *a* demütig, unterwürfig (*pej*).

submit [səb'mɪt] *vt* behaupten; (*plan*) unterbreiten // *vi* (*give in*) sich ergeben.

subnormal ['sʌb'nɔːməl] *a* minderbegabt.

subordinate [sə'bɔːdɪnət] *a* untergeordnet // *n* Untergebene(r) *mf*.

subpoena [sə'piːnə] *n* Vorladung *f* // *vt* vorladen.

subscribe [səb'skraɪb] *vi* (*to view etc*) unterstützen; (*to newspaper*) abonnieren (*to acc*); ~**r** *n* (*to periodical*) Abonnent *m*; (*TEL*) Telefonteilnehmer *m*.

subscription [səb'skrɪpʃən] *n* Abonnement *nt*; (*money subscribed*) (Mitglieds)beitrag *m*.

subsequent ['sʌbsɪkwənt] *a* folgend, später; ~**ly** *ad* später.

subside [səb'saɪd] *vi* sich senken; **subsidence** [sʌb'saɪdəns] *n* Senkung *f*.

subsidiary [səb'sɪdɪərɪ] *a* Neben- // *n* (*company*) Tochtergesellschaft *f*.

subsidize ['sʌbsɪdaɪz] *vt* subventionieren.

subsidy ['sʌbsɪdɪ] *n* Subvention *f*.

subsistence [səb'sɪstəns] *n* Unterhalt *m*.

substance ['sʌbstəns] *n* Substanz *f*.

substantial [səb'stænʃəl] *a* (*strong*) fest, kräftig; (*important*) wesentlich; ~**ly** *ad* erheblich.

substantiate [səb'stænʃɪeɪt] *vt* begründen, belegen.

substitute ['sʌbstɪtjuːt] *n* Ersatz *m* // *vt* ersetzen.

substitution [sʌbstɪ'tjuːʃən] *n* Ersetzung *f*.

subterfuge ['sʌbtəfjuːdʒ] *n* Vorwand *m*; (*trick*) Trick *m*.

subterranean [sʌbtə'reɪnɪən] *a* unterirdisch.

subtitle ['sʌbtaɪtl] *n* Untertitel *m*.

subtle ['sʌtl] *a* fein; ~**ty** *n* Feinheit *f*.

subtotal [sʌb'təʊtl] *n* Zwischensumme *f*.

subtract [səb'trækt] *vt* abziehen; ~**ion** [səb'trækʃən] *n* Abziehen *nt*, Subtraktion *f*.

suburb ['sʌbɜːb] *n* Vorort *m*; **the** ~s die Außenbezirke; ~**an** [sə'bɜːbən] *a* Vorort(s)-, Stadtrand-; ~**ia** [sə'bɜːbɪə] *n* Vorstadt *f*.

subversive [səb'vɜːsɪv] *a* subversiv.

subway ['sʌbweɪ] *n* (*US*) U-Bahn *f*; (*Brit*) Unterführung *f*.

succeed [sək'siːd] *vi* gelingen (+*dat*), Erfolg haben // *vt* (nach)folgen (+*dat*); **he** ~**ed in doing it** es gelang ihm, es zu tun; ~**ing** *a* (nach)folgend.

success [sək'ses] *n* Erfolg *m*; ~**ful** *a*, ~**fully** *ad* erfolgreich; **to be** ~**ful** (**in doing sth**) Erfolg haben (bei etw).

succession [sək'seʃən] *n* (Aufeinander)folge *f*; (*to throne*) Nachfolge *f*.

successive *a* [sək'sesɪv] aufeinanderfolgend.

successor [sək'sesə*] *n* Nachfolger(in *f*) *m*.

succinct [sək'sɪŋkt] *a* knapp.

succulent ['sʌkjʊlənt] *a* saftig.

succumb [sə'kʌm] *vi* erliegen (*to dat*); (*yield*) nachgeben.

such [sʌtʃ] *a* solche(r, s); ~ **a book** so ein Buch; ~ **books** solche Bücher; ~ **courage** so ein Mut; ~ **a long trip** so eine lange Reise; ~ **a lot of** so viel(e); ~ **as** wie; **a noise** ~ **as to** ein derartiger Lärm, daß; **as** ~ an sich; ~**and**-~ **a time/town** die und die Zeit/Stadt.

suck [sʌk] *vt* saugen; (*ice cream etc*) lutschen; ~**er** *n* (*col*) Idiot *m*.

suction ['sʌkʃən] *n* Saugkraft *f*.

sudden ['sʌdn] *a* plötzlich; **all of a** ~ auf einmal; ~**ly** *ad* plötzlich.

suds [sʌdz] *npl* Seifenlauge *f*; (*lather*) Seifenschaum *m*.

sue [suː] *vt* verklagen.

suede [sweɪd] *n* Wildleder *nt*.

suet ['suɪt] *n* Nierenfett *nt*.

Suez ['suːɪz] *n*: **the** ~ **Canal** der Suezkanal *m*.

suffer ['sʌfə*] *vt* (er)leiden // *vi* leiden; ~**er** *n* Leidende(r) *mf*; ~**ing** *n* Leiden *nt*.

suffice [sə'faɪs] *vi* genügen.

sufficient *a*, ~**ly** *ad* [sə'fɪʃənt, -lɪ] ausreichend.

suffix ['sʌfɪks] *n* Nachsilbe *f*.

suffocate ['sʌfəkeɪt] *vti* ersticken.

suffocation [sʌfə'keɪʃən] *n* Ersticken *nt*.

suffrage ['sʌfrɪdʒ] *n* Wahlrecht *nt*.

sugar ['ʃʊgə*] *n* Zucker *m* // *vt* zuckern; ~ **beet** *n* Zuckerrübe *f*; ~ **cane** *n* Zuckerrohr *nt*; ~**y** *a* süß.

suggest [sə'dʒest] *vt* vorschlagen; (*show*) schließen lassen auf (+*acc*); ~**ion** [sə'dʒestʃən] *n* Vorschlag *m*; ~**ive** *a* anregend; (*indecent*) zweideutig.

suicide ['sʊɪsaɪd] *n* Selbstmord *m*; **to**

commit ~ Selbstmord begehen.

suit [suːt] n Anzug m; (CARDS) Farbe f // vt passen (+dat); (clothes) stehen (+dat); well ~ed (well matched: couple) gut zusammenpassend; ~**able** a geeignet, passend; ~**ably** ad passend, angemessen.

suitcase ['suːtkeɪs] n (Hand)koffer m.

suite [swiːt] n (of rooms) Zimmerflucht f; (of furniture) Einrichtung f; (MUS) Suite f.

suitor ['suːtə*] n (JUR) Kläger(in f) m.

sulfur ['sʌlfə*] n (US) = **sulphur**.

sulk [sʌlk] vi schmollen; ~**y** a schmollend.

sullen ['sʌlən] a mürrisch.

sulphur, (US) **sulfur** ['sʌlfə*] n Schwefel m.

sultry ['sʌltrɪ] a schwül.

sum [sʌm] n Summe f; (money also) Betrag m; (arithmetic) Rechenaufgabe f; ~ **up** vti zusammenfassen.

summarize ['sʌmərɑɪz] vt kurz zusammenfassen.

summary ['sʌmərɪ] n Zusammenfassung f // a (justice) kurzerhand erteilt.

summer ['sʌmə*] n Sommer m // a Sommer-; ~**house** n (in garden) Gartenhaus nt; ~**time** n Sommerzeit f.

summit ['sʌmɪt] n Gipfel m; ~ (**conference**) n Gipfelkonferenz f.

summon ['sʌmən] vt herbeirufen; (JUR) vorladen; (gather up) aufbringen; ~**s** n (JUR) Vorladung f // vt vorladen.

sump [sʌmp] n (Brit AUT) Ölwanne f.

sumptuous ['sʌmptjuəs] a prächtig.

sun [sʌn] n Sonne f; ~**bathe** vi sich sonnen; ~**burn** n Sonnenbrand m.

Sunday ['sʌndeɪ] n Sonntag m; ~ **school** n Sonntagsschule f.

sundial ['sʌndaɪəl] n Sonnenuhr f.

sundown ['sʌndaʊn] n Sonnenuntergang m.

sundry ['sʌndrɪ] a verschieden; all and ~ alle; **sundries** npl Verschiedene(s) nt.

sunflower ['sʌnflaʊə*] n Sonnenblume f.

sung [sʌŋ] pp of **sing**.

sunglasses ['sʌnglɑːsɪz] npl Sonnenbrille f.

sunk [sʌŋk] pp of **sink**.

sunlight ['sʌnlaɪt] n Sonnenlicht nt.

sunlit ['sʌnlɪt] a sonnenbeschienen.

sunny ['sʌnɪ] a sonnig.

sunrise ['sʌnraɪz] n Sonnenaufgang m.

sunset ['sʌnset] n Sonnenuntergang m.

sunshade ['sʌnʃeɪd] n Sonnenschirm m.

sunshine ['sʌnʃaɪn] n Sonnenschein m.

sunstroke ['sʌnstrəʊk] n Hitzschlag m.

suntan ['sʌntæn] n (Sonnen)bräune f; ~ **oil** n Sonnenöl m.

super ['suːpə*] a (col) prima, klasse; Super-, Über-.

superannuation ['suːpərænjʊ'eɪʃən] n Pension f.

superb [suː'pɜːb] a ausgezeichnet, hervorragend.

supercilious [suːpə'sɪlɪəs] a herablassend.

superficial [suːpə'fɪʃəl] a oberflächlich.

superfluous [sʊ'pɜːfluəs] a überflüssig.

superhuman [suːpə'hjuːmən] a (effort) übermenschlich.

superimpose ['suːpərɪm'pəʊz] vt übereinanderlegen.

superintendent [suːpərɪn'tendənt] n Polizeichef m.

superior [sʊ'pɪərɪə*] a überlegen; (better) besser // n Vorgesetzte(r) mf; ~**ity** [sʊpɪərɪ'ɒrɪtɪ] n Überlegenheit f.

superlative [su'pɜːlətɪv] a überragend.

superman ['suːpəmæn] n Übermensch m.

supermarket ['suːpəmɑːkɪt] n Supermarkt m.

supernatural [suːpə'nætʃərəl] a übernatürlich.

superpower ['suːpəpaʊə*] n Weltmacht f.

supersede [suːpə'siːd] vt ersetzen.

supersonic ['suːpə'sɒnɪk] n Überschall-.

superstition [suːpə'stɪʃən] n Aberglaube m.

superstitious [suːpə'stɪʃəs] a abergläubisch.

supervise ['suːpəvaɪz] vt beaufsichtigen, kontrollieren.

supervision [suːpə'vɪʒən] n Aufsicht f.

supervisor [suːpə'vaɪzə*] n Aufsichtsperson f; ~**y** a Aufsichts-.

supine ['suːpaɪn] a auf dem Rücken liegend.

supper ['sʌpə*] n Abendessen nt.

supplant [sə'plɑːnt] vt (person, thing) ersetzen.

supple ['sʌpl] a geschmeidig.

supplement ['sʌplɪmənt] n Ergänzung f; (in book) Nachtrag m // vt [sʌplɪ'ment] ergänzen; ~**ary** [sʌplɪ'mentərɪ] a ergänzend.

supplier [sə'plaɪə*] n Lieferant m.

supply [sə'plaɪ] vt liefern // n Vorrat m; (supplying) Lieferung f // a (teacher etc) Aushilfs-; **supplies** npl (food) Vorräte pl; (MIL) Nachschub m.

support [sə'pɔːt] n Unterstützung f; (TECH) Stütze f // vt (hold up) stützen, tragen; (provide for) ernähren; (be in favour of) unterstützen; ~**er** n Anhänger(in f) m.

suppose [sə'pəʊz] vti annehmen; to be ~**d** to do sth etw tun sollen; ~**dly** [sə'pəʊzɪdlɪ] ad angeblich.

supposing [sə'pəʊzɪŋ] cj angenommen.

supposition [sʌpə'zɪʃən] n Voraussetzung f.

suppress [sə'pres] vt unterdrücken; ~**ion** [sə'preʃən] n Unterdrückung f.

supremacy [sʊ'premǝsɪ] n Vorherrschaft f, Oberhoheit f.

supreme [sʊ'priːm] a oberste(r, s),

höchste(r, s).

surcharge ['sɜːtʃɑːdʒ] n Zuschlag m.

sure [ʃʊə*] a sicher, gewiß; ~! (of course) klar!; **to make ~ of sth/that** sich einer Sache vergewissern/vergewissern, daß; ~ **enough** (with past) tatsächlich; (with future) ganz bestimmt; **~-footed** a sicher (auf den Füßen); **~ly** ad (certainly) sicherlich, gewiß; **~ly it's wrong** das ist doch wohl falsch.

surety ['ʃʊərətɪ] n Sicherheit f; (person) Bürge m.

surf [sɜːf] n Brandung f.

surface ['sɜːfɪs] n Oberfläche f // vt (roadway) teeren // vi auftauchen; ~ **mail** n gewöhnliche Post f.

surfboard ['sɜːfbɔːd] n Wellenreiterbrett nt.

surfeit ['sɜːfɪt] n Übermaß nt.

surfing ['sɜːfɪŋ] n Wellenreiten nt.

surge [sɜːdʒ] n Woge f // vi wogen.

surgeon ['sɜːdʒən] n Chirurg(in f) m.

surgery ['sɜːdʒərɪ] n (Brit: place) Praxis f; (time) Sprechstunde f; (treatment) Operation f; **to undergo ~** operiert werden; ~ **hours** npl (Brit) Sprechstunden pl.

surgical ['sɜːdʒɪkəl] a chirurgisch; ~ **spirit** n (Brit) Wundbenzin nt.

surly ['sɜːlɪ] a verdrießlich, grob.

surmount [sɜːˈmaʊnt] vt überwinden.

surname ['sɜːneɪm] n Zuname m.

surpass [sɜːˈpɑːs] vt übertreffen.

surplus ['sɜːpləs] n Überschuß m // a überschüssig, Über(schuß)-.

surprise [səˈpraɪz] n Überraschung f // vt überraschen.

surprising [səˈpraɪzɪŋ] a überraschend; **~ly** ad überraschend(erweise).

surrender [səˈrendə*] n Kapitulation f // vi sich ergeben.

surreptitious [sʌrəpˈtɪʃəs] a verstohlen.

surrogate ['sʌrəgɪt] n Ersatz m; ~ **mother** n Leihmutter f.

surround [səˈraʊnd] vt umgeben; **~ing** a (countryside) umliegend // n: **~ings** pl Umgebung f; (environment) Umwelt f.

surveillance [sɜːˈveɪləns] n Überwachung f.

survey ['sɜːveɪ] n Übersicht f // [sɜːˈveɪ] vt überblicken; (land) vermessen; **~or** [səˈveɪə*] n Land(ver)messer(in f) m.

survival [səˈvaɪvəl] n Überleben nt.

survive [səˈvaɪv] vti überleben.

survivor [səˈvaɪvə*] n Überlebende(r) mf.

susceptible [səˈseptəbl] a empfindlich (to gegen); (to charms etc) empfänglich (to für).

suspect ['sʌspekt] n Verdächtige(r) mf // a verdächtig // vt [səsˈpekt] verdächtigen; (think) vermuten.

suspend [səsˈpend] vt verschieben; (from work) suspendieren; (hang up) aufhängen; (SPORT) sperren; **~ed sen-**

tence n (LAW) zur Bewährung ausgesetzte Strafe; **~er belt** n Strumpf(halter)gürtel m; **~ers** npl (Brit) Strumpfhalter m; (men's) Sokkenhalter m; (US) Hosenträger m.

suspense [səsˈpens] n Spannung f.

suspension [səsˈpenʃən] n (from work) Suspendierung f; (SPORT) Sperrung f; (AUT) Federung f; ~ **bridge** n Hängebrücke f.

suspicion [səsˈpɪʃən] n Mißtrauen nt; Verdacht m.

suspicious [səsˈpɪʃəs] a mißtrauisch; (causing suspicion) verdächtig.

sustain [səsˈteɪn] vt (maintain) aufrechterhalten; (confirm) bestätigen; (JUR) anerkennen; (injury) davontragen; **~ed** a (effort) anhaltend.

sustenance ['sʌstɪnəns] n Nahrung f.

swab [swɒb] n (MED) Tupfer m.

swagger ['swægə*] vi stolzieren.

swallow ['swɒləʊ] n (bird) Schwalbe f; (of food etc) Schluck m // vt (ver)schlucken; ~ **up** vt verschlingen.

swam [swæm] pt of **swim**.

swamp [swɒmp] n Sumpf m // vt überschwemmen.

swan [swɒn] n Schwan m.

swap [swɒp] n Tausch m // vt (ein)tauschen (for gegen).

swarm [swɔːm] n Schwarm m // vi wimmeln (with von).

swarthy ['swɔːðɪ] a dunkel, braun.

swastika ['swɒstɪkə] n Hakenkreuz nt.

swat [swɒt] vt totschlagen.

sway [sweɪ] vi (to schwanken; (branches) schaukeln, sich wiegen // vt schwenken; (influence) beeinflussen.

swear [swɛə*] vi, pt **swore**, pp **sworn** vi (promise) schwören; (curse) fluchen; **to ~ to sth** schwören auf etw (acc); **~word** n Fluch m.

sweat [swet] n Schweiß m // vi schwitzen.

sweater ['swetə*] n Pullover m.

sweatshirt ['swetʃɜːt] n Sweatshirt nt.

sweaty ['swetɪ] a verschwitzt.

swede [swiːd] n (Brit) Steckrübe f.

Swede [swiːd] n Schwede m, Schwedin f.

Sweden ['swiːdn] n Schweden nt.

Swedish ['swiːdɪʃ] a schwedisch // n (LING) Schwedisch nt.

sweep [swiːp] n (chimney ~) Schornsteinfeger m // v (pt, pp **swept**) vt fegen, kehren // vi (go quickly) rauschen; ~ **away** vt wegfegen; ~ **past** vi vorbeisausen; ~ **up** vt zusammenkehren; **~ing** a (gesture) schwungvoll; (statement) verallgemeinernd.

sweet [swiːt] n (course) Nachtisch m; (candy) Bonbon nt // a süß; **~corn** n Zuckermais m; **~en** vt süßen; (fig) versüßen; **~heart** n Liebste(r) mf; **~ness** n Süße f; ~ **pea** n Gartenwicke f.

swell [swel] n Seegang m // a (col) todschick // v (pt **swelled**, pp **swollen** or **swelled**) vt (numbers) vermehren // vi (also: ~ **up**) (an)schwellen; **~ing** n Schwellung f.

sweltering ['sweltərɪŋ] a drückend.

swept [swept] pt, pp of **sweep**.

swerve [swɜːv] vti ausscheren.

swift [swɪft] n Mauersegler m // a, **~ly** ad geschwind, schnell, rasch.

swig [swɪg] n Zug m.

swill [swɪl] n (for pigs) Schweinefutter nt // vt spülen.

swim [swɪm] n: to go for a ~ schwimmen gehen // v (pt **swam**, pp **swum**) vi schwimmen // vt (cross) (durch)schwimmen; **~mer** n Schwimmer(in f) m; **~ming** n Schwimmen nt; **~ming cap** n Badehaube f, Badekappe f; **~ming costume** n (Brit) Badeanzug m; **~ming pool** n Schwimmbecken nt; (private) Swimming-Pool m; **~suit** n Badeanzug m.

swindle ['swɪndl] n Schwindel m, Betrug m // vt betrügen.

swine [swaɪn] n (lit, fig) Schwein nt.

swing [swɪŋ] n (child's) Schaukel f; (swinging) Schwung m; (MUS) Swing m // v (pt, pp **swung**) vt schwingen // vi schwingen, schaukeln; (turn quickly) schwenken; in full ~ in vollem Gange; ~ **bridge** n Drehbrücke f; ~ **door**, (US) **~ing door** n Schwingtür f.

swingeing ['swɪndʒɪŋ] a (Brit) hart; (taxation, cuts) extrem.

swipe [swaɪp] n Hieb m // vt (col) (hit) hart schlagen; (steal) klauen.

swirl [swɜːl] vi wirbeln.

swish [swɪʃ] a (col: smart) schick // vi zischen; (grass, skirts) rascheln.

Swiss [swɪs] a Schweizer, schweizerisch // n Schweizer(in f) m; **the ~** die Schweizer pl.

switch [swɪtʃ] n (ELEC) Schalter m; (change) Wechsel m // vti (ELEC) schalten; (change) wechseln; ~ **off** vt ab- or ausschalten; ~ **on** vt an- or einschalten; **~board** n Zentrale f; (board) Schaltbrett nt.

Switzerland ['swɪtsələnd] n die Schweiz f.

swivel ['swɪvl] vti (also: ~ **round**) (sich) drehen.

swollen ['swəʊlən] pp of **swell**.

swoon [swuːn] vi (old) in Ohnmacht fallen.

swoop [swuːp] n Sturzflug m; (esp by police) Razzia f // vi (also: ~ **down**) stürzen.

swop [swɒp] = **swap**.

sword [sɔːd] n Schwert nt; **~fish** n Schwertfisch m.

swore [swɔː*] pt of **swear**.

sworn [swɔːn] pp of **swear**.

swot [swɒt] vti pauken.

swum [swʌm] pp of **swim**.

swung [swʌŋ] pt, pp of **swing**.

sycamore ['sɪkəmɔː*] n (US) Platane f; (Brit) Bergahorn m.

syllable ['sɪləbl] n Silbe f.

syllabus ['sɪləbəs] n Lehrplan m.

symbol ['sɪmbl] n Symbol nt; **~ic(al)** [sɪm'bɒlɪk(əl)] a symbolisch.

symmetry ['sɪmɪtrɪ] n Symmetrie f.

sympathetic [sɪmpə'θetɪk] a mitfühlend.

sympathize ['sɪmpəθaɪz] vi mitfühlen; **~r** n Mitfühlende(r) mf; (POL) Sympathisant(in f) m.

sympathy ['sɪmpəθɪ] n Mitleid nt, Mitgefühl nt; (condolence) Beileid nt; **with our deepest ~** mit tiefempfundenem Beileid.

symphony ['sɪmfənɪ] n Sinfonie f.

symposium [sɪm'pəʊzɪəm] n Tagung f.

symptom ['sɪmptəm] n Symptom nt; **~atic** [sɪmptə'mætɪk] a (fig) bezeichnend (of für).

synagogue ['sɪnəgɒg] n Synagoge f.

synchronize ['sɪŋkrənaɪz] vt synchronisieren // vi gleichzeitig sein or ablaufen.

syncopated ['sɪŋkəpeɪtɪd] a synkopiert.

syndicate ['sɪndɪkət] n Konsortium nt.

synonym ['sɪnənɪm] n Synonym nt.

synonymous [sɪ'nɒnɪməs] a: ~ (**with**) gleichbedeutend (mit).

synopsis [sɪ'nɒpsɪs] n Zusammenfassung f.

syphon ['saɪfən] = **siphon**.

Syria ['sɪrɪə] n Syrien nt.

syringe [sɪ'rɪndʒ] n Spritze f.

syrup ['sɪrəp] n Sirup m; (of sugar) Melasse f.

system ['sɪstəm] n System nt; **~atic** [sɪstə'mætɪk] a systematisch; ~ **disk** n (COMPUT) Systemdiskette f; **~s analyst** n Systemanalytiker(in f) m.

T

ta [tɑː] interj (Brit col) danke.

tab [tæb] n Aufhänger m; (name ~) Schild nt; to keep ~s on (fig) genau im Auge behalten.

table ['teɪbl] n Tisch m; (list) Tabelle f // vt (Parl: propose) vorlegen, einbringen; to lay or set the ~ den Tisch decken; ~ **of contents** n Inhaltsverzeichnis nt; ~ **lamp** n Tischlampe f.

tablecloth ['teɪblklɒθ] n Tischtuch nt.

table d'hôte ['tɑːbl'dəʊt] n Tagesmenü nt.

tablemat ['teɪblmæt] n Untersatz m.

tablespoon ['teɪblspuːn] n Eßlöffel m; **~ful** n Eßlöffel(voll) m.

tablet ['tæblət] n (MED) Tablette f; (for writing) Täfelchen nt.

table tennis ['teɪbltenɪs] n Tischtennis

nt.

table wine ['teɪblwaɪn] n Tafelwein m.

tabloid ['tæblɔɪd] n Zeitung f in kleinem Format; (pej) Boulevardzeitung.

tabulate ['tæbjuleɪt] vt tabellarisch ordnen.

tacit a, ~ly ad ['tæsɪt, -lɪ] stillschweigend.

taciturn ['tæsɪtəːn] a wortkarg.

tack [tæk] n (small nail) Stift m; (US: thumb~) Reißzwecke f; (stitch) Heftstich m; (NAUT) Lavieren nt; (course) Kurs m // vt (nail) nageln; (stitch) heften // vi aufkreuzen.

tackle ['tækl] n (for lifting) Flaschenzug m; (NAUT) Takelage f; (SPORT) Tackling nt // vt (deal with) anpacken, in Angriff nehmen; (person) festhalten; (player) angehen.

tacky ['tækɪ] a klebrig.

tact [tækt] n Takt m; ~ful a, ~fully ad taktvoll.

tactical ['tæktɪkəl] a taktisch.

tactics ['tæktɪks] npl Taktik f.

tactless a, ~ly ad ['tæktləs, -lɪ] taktlos.

tadpole ['tædpəʊl] n Kaulquappe f.

taffy ['tæfɪ] n (US) Sahnebonbon nt.

tag [tæg] n (label) Schild nt, Anhänger m; (maker's name) Etikett nt; (phrase) Floskel f; ~ along vi mitkommen.

tail [teɪl] n Schwanz m; (of list) Schluß m // vt folgen (+dat); ~ away, ~ off vi abfallen, schwinden; ~back n (Brit AUT) (Rück)stau m; ~ coat n Frack m; ~ end n Schluß m, Ende nt; ~gate n (AUT) Heckklappe f.

tailor ['teɪlə*] n Schneider m; ~ing n Schneidern nt; ~-made a (lit) maßgeschneidert; (fig) wie auf den Leib geschnitten (for sb jdm).

tailwind ['teɪlwɪnd] n Rückenwind m.

tainted ['teɪntɪd] a verdorben.

take [teɪk], pt **took**, pp **taken** vt nehmen; (trip, exam) machen; (capture: person) fassen; (: town) einnehmen; (carry to a place) bringen; (MATH: subtract) abziehen (from von); (extract, quotation) entnehmen (from dat); (get for o.s.) sich (dat) nehmen; (gain, obtain) bekommen; (FIN, COMM) einnehmen; (PHOT) machen; (put up with) hinnehmen; (respond to) aufnehmen; (interpret) auffassen; (assume) annehmen; (contain) Platz haben für; (GRAM) stehen mit; to ~ sth from sb jdm etw wegnehmen; ~ after vt ähnlich sein (+dat); ~ apart vt auseinandernehmen; ~ away vt (remove) wegnehmen; (carry off) wegbringen; ~ back vt (return) zurückbringen; (retract) zurücknehmen; ~ down vt (pull down) abreißen; (write down) aufschreiben; ~ in vt (deceive) hereinlegen; (understand) begreifen; (include) einschließen; ~ off vi (plane)

starten // vt (remove) wegnehmen; (clothing) ausziehen; (imitate) nachmachen; ~ on vt (undertake) übernehmen; (engage) einstellen; (opponent) antreten gegen; ~ out vt (girl, dog) ausführen; (extract) herausnehmen; (insurance) abschließen; (licence) sich (dat) geben lassen; (book) ausleihen; (remove) entfernen; to ~ sth out of sth (drawer, pocket etc) etw aus etw herausnehmen; ~ over vt übernehmen // vi ablösen (from acc); ~ to vt (like) mögen; (adopt as practice) sich (dat) angewöhnen; ~ up vt (raise) aufnehmen; (hem) kürzer machen; (occupy) in Anspruch nehmen; (engage in) sich befassen mit; ~away, (US) ~out a zum Mitnehmen; ~-home pay n Nettolohn m; ~off n (AVIAT) Start m; (imitation) Nachahmung f; ~over n (COMM) Übernahme f.

takings ['teɪkɪŋz] npl (COMM) Einnahmen pl.

talc [tælk] n (also: ~um powder) Talkumpuder m.

tale [teɪl] n Geschichte f, Erzählung f; to tell ~s (fig: lie) Geschichten erfinden.

talent ['tælənt] n Talent nt; ~ed a begabt.

talk [tɔːk] n (conversation) Gespräch nt; (rumour) Gerede nt; (speech) Vortrag m // vi sprechen, reden; ~s pl (POL etc) Gespräche pl; to ~ into doing sth jdn überreden, etw zu tun; to ~ sb out of doing sth jdm ausreden, etw zu tun; to ~ shop fachsimpeln; ~ about vi sprechen von (+dat) or über (+acc); ~ over vt besprechen; ~ative a gesprächig.

tall [tɔːl] a groß; (building) hoch; to be 1 m 80 ~ 1,80 m groß sein; ~boy n (Brit) Kommode f; ~ story n übertriebene Geschichte f.

tally ['tælɪ] n Abrechnung f // vi übereinstimmen (with mit).

talon ['tælən] n Kralle f.

tame [teɪm] a zahm; (fig) fade.

tamper ['tæmpə*]: ~ with vt herumpfuschen an (+dat).

tampon ['tæmpən] n Tampon m.

tan [tæn] n (on skin) (Sonnen)bräune f; (colour) Gelbbraun nt // a (colour) (gelb)braun // vt bräunen; (skins) gerben // vi braun werden.

tang [tæŋ] n Schärfe f.

tangent ['tændʒənt] n Tangente f; to go off at a ~ (fig) vom Thema abkommen.

tangerine [tændʒə'riːn] n Mandarine f.

tangible ['tændʒəbl] a greifbar.

tangle ['tæŋgl] n Durcheinander nt; (trouble) Schwierigkeiten pl; to get in(to) a ~ sich verheddern.

tank [tæŋk] n (container) Tank m, Behälter m; (MIL) Panzer m.

tanker ['tæŋkə*] n (ship) Tanker m; (vehicle) Tankwagen m.

tanned [tænd] a (skin) gebräunt.
tantalizing ['tæntəlaızıŋ] a verlockend; (annoying) quälend.
tantamount ['tæntəmaʊnt] a gleichbedeutend (to mit).
tantrum ['tæntrəm] n Wutanfall m.
tap [tæp] n Hahn m; (gentle blow) Klopfen nt // vt (strike) klopfen; (supply) anzapfen; (telephone) abhören; on ~ (fig: resources) zur Hand.
tap-dancing ['tæpdɑːnsıŋ] n Steppen nt.
tape [teıp] n Band nt; (magnetic) (Ton)band nt; (adhesive) Klebstreifen m // vt (record) aufnehmen; ~ **measure** n Maßband nt.
taper ['teıpə*] n (dünne) Wachskerze f // vi spitz zulaufen.
tape recorder n Tonbandgerät nt.
tapestry ['tæpıstrı] n Wandteppich m.
tar [tɑː*] n Teer m.
target ['tɑːgıt] n Ziel nt; (board) Zielscheibe f; ~ **practice** n Zielschießen nt.
tariff ['tærıf] n (duty paid) Zoll m; (list) Tarif m.
tarmac ['tɑːmæk] n (AVIAT) Rollfeld nt.
tarnish ['tɑːnıʃ] vt (lit) matt machen; (fig) beflecken.
tarpaulin [tɑːˈpɔːlın] n Plane f.
tarragon ['tærəgən] n Estragon m.
tart [tɑːt] n (Obst)torte f; (col) Nutte f // a scharf; ~ **up** vt (col) aufmachen (col); (person) aufstakeln (col).
tartan ['tɑːtən] n Schottenkaro nt // a mit Schottenkaro.
tartar ['tɑːtə*] n Zahnstein m; ~**(e) sauce** n Remouladensoße f.
task [tɑːsk] n Aufgabe f; **to take sb to** ~ sich (dat) jdn vornehmen; ~ **force** n Sondertrupp m.
tassel ['tæsəl] n Quaste f.
taste [teıst] n Geschmack m; (sense) Geschmackssinn m; (small quantity) Kostprobe f; (liking) Vorliebe f // vt schmecken; (try) probieren // vi schmecken (of nach); **you can** ~ **the garlic (in it)** man kann den Knoblauch herausschmecken; **can I have a** ~ **of this wine?** kann ich diesen Wein probieren?; **to have a** ~ **for sth** etw mögen; **in good/ bad** ~ geschmackvoll/geschmacklos; ~**ful** a, ~**fully** ad geschmackvoll; ~**less** a (insipid) fade; (in bad taste) geschmacklos; ~**lessly** ad geschmacklos.
tasty ['teıstı] a schmackhaft.
tatters ['tætəz] npl: **in** ~ in Fetzen.
tattoo [təˈtuː] n (MIL) Zapfenstreich m; (on skin) Tätowierung f // vt tätowieren.
tatty ['tætı] a (Brit col) schäbig.
taught [tɔːt] pt, pp of **teach**.
taunt [tɔːnt] n höhnische Bemerkung f // vt verhöhnen.
Taurus ['tɔːrəs] n Stier m.
taut [tɔːt] a straff.
tawdry ['tɔːdrı] a (bunt und) billig.

tawny ['tɔːnı] a gelbbraun.
tax [tæks] n Steuer f // vt besteuern; (strain) strapazieren; (strength) angreifen; ~**able** a (income) steuerpflichtig; ~**ation** [tækˈseıʃən] n Besteuerung f; ~ **avoidance** n Steuerumgehung f; ~ **collector** n Steuereinnehmer m; ~ **disc** n (Brit AUT) Kraftfahrzeugsteuerplakette f(, die an der Windschutzscheibe angebracht wird); ~ **evasion** n Steuerhinterziehung f; ~**free** a steuerfrei.
taxi ['tæksı] n Taxi nt // vi (plane) rollen; ~ **driver** n Taxifahrer m; ~ **rank** (Brit), ~ **stand** n Taxistand m.
taxpayer ['tækspeıə*] n Steuerzahler m.
tax relief n Steuerermäßigung f.
tax return n Steuererklärung f.
TB abbr (= tuberculosis) Tb f, Tbc f.
tea [tiː] n Tee m; (meal) (frühes) Abendessen nt; (meal) (frühes) Abendessen nt; ~ **bag** n Teebeutel m; ~ **break** n (Brit) Teepause f.
teach [tiːtʃ], pt, pp **taught** vti lehren; (SCH also) unterrichten; (show) beibringen (sb sth jdm etw); ~**er** n Lehrer(in f) m; ~**ing** n (teacher's work) Unterricht m; (doctrine) Lehre f.
tea cosy n Teewärmer m.
teacup ['tiːkʌp] n Teetasse f.
tea leaves ['tiːliːvz] npl Teeblätter pl.
team [tiːm] n (workers) Team nt; (SPORT) Mannschaft f; (animals) Gespann nt.
teapot ['tiːpɒt] n Teekanne f.
tear [tɛə*] n Riß m; [tıə*] Träne f // v [tɛə*] (pt **tore**, pp **torn**) vt zerreißen; (muscle) zerren // vi (zer)reißen; (rush) rasen; ~ **along** vi (rush) entlangrasen; ~ **up** vt (sheet of paper etc) zerreißen; ~**ful** ['tıəful] a weinend; (voice) weinerlich; ~ **gas** ['tıəgæs] n Tränengas nt.
tearoom ['tiːrʊm] n Teestube f.
tease [tiːz] n Hänsler m // vt necken.
tea set n Teeservice nt.
teaspoon ['tiːspuːn] n Teelöffel m.
teat [tiːt] n (of woman) Brustwarze f; (of animal) Zitze f; (of bottle) Sauger m.
tea time n (in the afternoon) Teestunde f; (mealtime) Abendessen nt.
tea towel n Küchenhandtuch nt.
technical ['teknıkəl] a technisch; (knowledge, terms) Fach-; ~**ity** [teknıˈkælıtı] n technische Einzelheit f; (JUR) Formsache f; ~**ly** ad technisch; (speak) spezialisiert; (fig) genau genommen.
technician [tekˈnıʃən] n Techniker m.
technique [tekˈniːk] n Technik f.
technological [teknəˈlɒdʒıkəl] a technologisch.
technology [tekˈnɒlədʒı] n Technologie f.
teddy (bear) ['tedı(bɛə*)] n Teddybär m.
tedious a, ~**ly** ad ['tiːdıəs, -lı] lang-

weilig, ermüdend.

tee [ti:] *n* (*GOLF*) Abschlagstelle *f*; (*object*) Tee *nt*.

teem [ti:m] *vi* (*swarm*) wimmeln (*with* von); it is ~ing (**with rain**) es gießt in Strömen.

teenage ['ti:neɪdʒ] *a* (*fashions etc*) Teenager-, jugendlich; ~**r** *n* Teenager *m*, Jugendliche(r) *mf*.

teens [ti:nz] *npl* Teenageralter *nt*; **to be in one's** ~ im Teenageralter sein.

tee-shirt ['ti:ʃɜ:t] *n* T-Shirt *nt*.

teeter ['ti:tə*] *vi* schwanken.

teeth [ti:θ] *npl of* **tooth**.

teethe [ti:ð] *vi* zahnen.

teething ['ti:ðɪŋ]: ~ **ring** *n* Beißring *m*; ~ **troubles** *npl* (*fig*) Kinderkrankheiten *pl*.

teetotal ['ti:'təʊtl] *a* abstinent.

telecommunications ['telɪkəmju:nɪ-'keɪʃənz] *npl* Fernmeldewesen *nt*.

telegram ['telɪgræm] *n* Telegramm *nt*.

telephone ['telɪfəʊn] *n* Telefon *nt*, Fernsprecher *m* // *vt* anrufen; (*message*) telefonisch mitteilen; ~ **booth**, (*Brit*) ~ **box** *n* Telefonzelle *f*; ~ **call** *n* Telefongespräch *nt*, Anruf *m*; ~ **directory** *n* Telefonbuch *nt*; ~ **number** *n* Telefonnummer *f*.

telephoto lens ['telɪfəʊtəʊ'lenz] *n* Teleobjektiv *nt*.

telescope ['telɪskəʊp] *n* Teleskop *nt*, Fernrohr *nt* // *vt* ineinanderschieben.

televise ['telɪvaɪz] *vt* durch das Fernsehen übertragen.

television ['telɪvɪʒən] *n* Fernsehen *nt*; ~ (**set**) *n* Fernsehapparat *m*, Fernseher *m*.

telex ['teleks] *n* Telex *nt* // *vt* per Telex schicken.

tell [tel], *pt, pp* **told** *vt* (*story*) erzählen; (*secret*) ausplaudern; (*say, make known*) sagen (*sth to sb* jdm etw); (*distinguish*) erkennen (*sb by sth* jdn an etw *dat*); (*be sure*) wissen // *vi* (*talk*) sprechen (*of* von); (*be sure*) wissen; (*divulge*) es verraten; (*have effect*) sich auswirken; (*distinguish*): **to** ~ **sth from** etw unterscheiden von; **to** ~ **sb to do sth** jdm sagen, daß er etw tun soll; **to** ~ **sb off** jdn ausschimpfen; ~**er** *n* Kassenbeamte(r) *mf*; ~**ing** *a* verräterisch; (*blow*) hart; ~**tale** *a* verräterisch.

telly ['telɪ] *n* (*Brit col*) *abbr of* **television**.

temerity [tɪ'merɪtɪ] *n* (Toll)kühnheit *f*.

temp [temp] *n abbr* (= *temporary*) *f* // *vi* Aushilfskraft *f* // *vi* als Aushilfskraft arbeiten.

temper ['tempə*] *n* (*disposition*) Temperament *nt*; (*anger*) Zorn *m* // *vt* (*tone down*) mildern; (*metal*) härten; **to be in a** (**bad**) ~ wütend sein; **to lose one's** ~ die Beherrschung verlieren.

temperament ['temprəmənt] *n* Temperament *nt*; ~**al** [tempərə'mentl] *a* (*moody*) launisch.

temperance ['tempərəns] *n* Mäßigung *f*; (*abstinence*) Enthaltsamkeit *f*.

temperate ['tempərət] *a* gemäßigt.

temperature ['temprɪtʃə*] *n* Temperatur *f*; (*Med: high* ~) Fieber *nt*; **to have** *or* **run a** ~ Fieber haben.

tempest ['tempɪst] *n* (wilder) Sturm *m*.

tempi ['tempi:] *npl of* **tempo**.

template ['templət] *n* Schablone *f*.

temple ['templ] *n* Tempel *m*; (*ANAT*) Schläfe *f*.

temporal ['tempərəl] *a* (*of time*) zeitlich; (*worldly*) irdisch, weltlich.

temporarily ['tempərərɪlɪ] *ad* zeitweilig, vorübergehend.

temporary ['tempərərɪ] *a* vorläufig; (*road, building*) provisorisch.

tempt [tempt] *vt* (*persuade*) verleiten; (*attract*) reizen, (ver)locken; **to** ~ **sb into doing sth** jdn dazu verleiten, etw zu tun; ~**ation** [temp'teɪʃən] *n* Versuchung *f*; ~**ing** *a* (*person*) verführerisch; (*object, situation*) verlockend.

ten [ten] *num* zehn.

tenable ['tenəbl] *a* haltbar.

tenacious *a*, ~**ly** *ad* [tə'neɪʃəs, -lɪ] zäh, hartnäckig.

tenacity [tə'næsɪtɪ] *n* Zähigkeit *f*, Hartnäckigkeit *f*.

tenancy ['tenənsɪ] *n* Mietverhältnis *nt*.

tenant ['tenənt] *n* Mieter *m*; (*of larger property*) Pächter *m*.

tend [tend] *vt* (*look after*) sich kümmern um // *vi* neigen (*to* zu); **to** ~ **to do sth** (*things*) etw gewöhnlich tun.

tendency ['tendənsɪ] *n* Tendenz *f*; (*of person also*) Neigung *f*.

tender ['tendə*] *a* zart; (*loving*) zärtlich // *n* (*COMM: offer*) Kostenanschlag *m* // *vt* (an)bieten; (*resignation*) einreichen; (*money*): **legal** ~ *n* gesetzliche(s) Zahlungsmittel *nt*; ~**ness** *n* Zartheit *f*; (*being loving*) Zärtlichkeit *f*.

tendon ['tendən] *n* Sehne *f*.

tenement ['tenəmənt] *n* Mietshaus *nt*.

tenet ['tenət] *n* Lehre *f*.

tennis ['tenɪs] *n* Tennis *nt*; ~ **ball** *n* Tennisball *m*; ~ **court** *n* Tennisplatz *m*; ~ **player** *n* Tennisspieler(in *f*) *m*; ~ **racket** *n* Tennisschläger *m*; ~ **shoes** *npl* Tennisschuhe *pl*.

tenpin bowling ['tenpɪn-] *n* Bowling *nt*.

tense [tens] *a* angespannt // *n* Zeitform *f*.

tension ['tenʃən] *n* Spannung *f*.

tent [tent] *n* Zelt *nt*.

tentacle ['tentəkl] *n* Fühler *m*; (*of sea animals*) Fangarm *m*.

tentative ['tentətɪv] *a* (*movement*) unsicher; (*offer*) Probe-; (*arrangement*) vorläufig; (*suggestion*) unverbindlich; ~**ly** *ad* versuchsweise; (*try, move*) vorsichtig.

tenterhooks ['tentəhʊks] npl: **to be on ~** auf die Folter gespannt sein.

tenth [tenθ] a zehnte(r, s).

tent peg n Hering m.

tent pole n Zeltstange f.

tenuous ['tenjʊəs] a schwach.

tenure ['tenjʊə*] n (of land) Besitz m; (of office) Amtszeit f.

tepid ['tepɪd] a lauwarm.

term [tɜːm] n (period of time) Zeit(raum m) f; (limit) Frist f; (SCH) Quartal nt; (UNIV) Trimester nt; (expression) Ausdruck m // vt (be)nennen; ~s pl (conditions) Bedingungen pl; **in the short/long ~** auf kurze/lange Sicht; **to be on good ~s with sb** gut mit jdm auskommen; **to come to ~s with** (person) sich einigen mit; (problem) sich abfinden mit.

terminal ['tɜːmɪnl] n (Brit: also: coach ~) Endstation f; (AVIAT) Terminal m; (COMPUT) Terminal nt or m // a Schluß-; (MED) unheilbar.

terminate ['tɜːmɪneɪt] vt beenden // vi enden, aufhören (in auf +dat).

terminus ['tɜːmɪnəs], pl **-mini** [-mɪnaɪ] n Endstation f.

terrace ['terəs] n (Brit: row of houses) Häuserreihe f; (in garden etc) Terrasse f; **the ~s** (Brit SPORT) die Ränge; ~**d** a (garden) terrassenförmig angelegt; (house) Reihen-.

terrible ['terəbl] a schrecklich, entsetzlich, fürchterlich.

terribly ['terəblɪ] ad fürchterlich.

terrific [tə'rɪfɪk] a unwahrscheinlich; ~! klasse!

terrify ['terɪfaɪ] vt erschrecken.

territorial [terɪ'tɔːrɪəl] a Gebiets-, territorial.

territory ['terɪtərɪ] n Gebiet nt.

terror ['terə*] n Schrecken m; (POL) Terror m; ~**ist** n Terrorist(in f) m; ~**ize** vt terrorisieren.

terse [tɜːs] a knapp, kurz, bündig.

test [test] n Probe f; (examination) Prüfung f; (PSYCH, TECH) Test m // vt prüfen; (PSYCH) testen.

testicle ['testɪkl] n Hoden m.

testify ['testɪfaɪ] vi aussagen; bezeugen (to acc); **to ~ to sth** etw bezeugen.

testimony ['testɪmənɪ] n (JUR) Zeugenaussage f; (fig) Zeugnis nt.

test match n (SPORT) Länderkampf m.

test tube n Reagenzglas nt.

testy ['testɪ] a gereizt; reizbar.

tetanus ['tetənəs] n Wundstarrkrampf m, Tetanus m.

tetchy ['tetʃɪ] a empfindlich.

tether ['teðə*] vt anbinden // n: **at the end of one's ~** völlig am Ende.

text [tekst] n Text m; (of document) Wortlaut m; ~**book** n Lehrbuch nt.

textiles ['tekstaɪlz] npl Textilien pl.

texture ['tekstʃə*] n Beschaffenheit f.

Thai [taɪ] a thailändisch // n Thailänder(in f) m; (LING) Thailändisch nt; ~**land** n Thailand nt.

Thames [temz] n: **the ~** die Themse.

than [ðæn] prep (in comparisons) als.

thank [θæŋk] vt danken (+dat); **you've him to ~ for your success** Sie haben Ihren Erfolg ihm zu verdanken; ~**ful** a dankbar; ~**less** a undankbar; ~**s** npl Dank m // interj danke; ~**s to** dank (+gen); ~ **you (very much)** danke (vielmals), danke schön; **T~sgiving (Day)** n (US) Thanksgiving Day m.

that [ðæt] ◆ a (demonstrative: pl **those**) der/die/das, jene(r, s); ~ **one** das da
◆ pron 1 (demonstrative: pl **those**) das; **who's/what's ~?** wer ist da/was ist das?; **is ~ you?** bist du das?; ~**'s what he said** genau das hat er gesagt; **what happened after ~?** was passierte danach?; ~ **is das heißt**
2 (relative: subject) der/die/das, die; (: direct obj) den/die/das, die; (: indirect obj) dem/der/dem, denen; **all (~) I have** alles, was ich habe
3 (relative: of time): **on the day (~)** an dem Tag, als; **the winter (~) he came** in dem Winter, in dem er kam
◆ cj daß; **he thought ~ I was ill** er dachte, daß ich krank sei or er dachte, ich sei krank
◆ ad (demonstrative) so; **I can't work ~ much** ich kann nicht soviel arbeiten

thatched [θætʃt] a strohgedeckt; (cottage) mit Strohdach.

thaw [θɔː] n Tauwetter nt // vi tauen; (frozen foods, fig: people) auftauen // vt (auf)tauen lassen.

the [ðiː, ðə] definite art 1 der/die/das; **to play ~ piano/violin** Klavier/Geige spielen; **I'm going to ~ butcher's/~ cinema** ich gehe zum Fleischer/ins Kino; **Elizabeth ~ First** Elisabeth die Erste
2 (+ adjective to form noun) das, die; ~ **rich and ~ poor** die Reichen und die Armen
3 (in comparisons): ~ **more he works ~ more he earns** je mehr er arbeitet, desto mehr verdient er.

theatre, (US) **theater** ['θɪətə*] n Theater nt; (for lectures etc) Saal m; (MED) Operationssaal m; ~**goer** n Theaterbesucher(in f) m.

theatrical [θɪ'ætrɪkəl] a Theater-; (career) Schauspieler-; (showy) theatralisch.

theft [θeft] n Diebstahl m.

their [ðɛə*] poss a ihr; ~**s** poss pron ihre(r, s); see also **my, mine.**

them [ðem, ðəm] pron (acc) sie; (dat) ihnen; see also **me.**

theme [θiːm] n Thema nt; (MUS) Motiv nt; ~ **song** n Titelmusik f.

themselves [ðəm'selvz] pl pron

(reflexive) sich (selbst); *(emphatic)* selbst; *see also* **oneself.**

then [ðen] *ad (at that time)* damals; *(next)* dann // *cj* also, folglich; *(furthermore)* ferner // *a* damalig; **the ~ president** der damalige Präsident; **from ~ on** von da an; **by ~** bis dahin.

theology [θɪ'ɒlədʒɪ] *n* Theologie *f.*

theoretical *a*, **~ly** *ad* [θɪə'retɪkəl, -ɪ] theoretisch.

theory ['θɪərɪ] *n* Theorie *f.*

therapist ['θerəpɪst] *a* Therapeut(in *f*) *m.*

therapy ['θerəpɪ] *n* Therapie *f.*

there [ðeə*] *ad* **1:** ~ **is,** ~ **are** es *or* da ist/sind; *(~ exists/exist also)* es gibt; ~ **are 3 of them** *(people, things)* es gibt drei davon; ~ **has been an accident** da war ein Unfall
2 *(referring to place)* da, dort; *(with v of movement)* dahin, dorthin; **put it in/on ~** leg es dahinein/dorthinauf
3: ~, ~ *(esp to child)* na, na.

thermometer [θə'mɒmɪtə*] *n* Thermometer *nt.*

Thermos ['θɜːmɒs] *n* ® Thermosflasche *f.*

thesaurus [θɪ'sɔːrəs] *n* Synonymwörterbuch *nt.*

these [ðiːz] *pl pron, a* diese.

thesis ['θiːsɪs] *n (for discussion)* These *f*; *(UNIV)* Dissertation *f*, Doktorarbeit *f.*

they [ðeɪ] *pl pron* sie; *(people in general)* man; ~ **say that ...** *(it is said that)* es wird gesagt, daß ...; **~'d** = **they had; they would;** **~'ll** = **they shall, they will; ~'re** = **they are; ~'ve** = **they have.**

thick [θɪk] *a* dick; *(forest)* dicht; *(liquid)* dickflüssig; *(slow, stupid)* dumm, schwer von Begriff // *n:* **in the ~ of** mitten in (+*dat*); **it's 20 cm ~** es ist 20 cm dick *or* stark; **~en** *vi (fog)* dichter werden // *vt (sauce etc)* verdicken; **~ness** *n (of object)* Dicke *f*; Dichte *f*; Dickflüssigkeit *f*; **~set** *a* untersetzt; **~skinned** *a* dickhäutig.

thief [θiːf], *pl* **thieves** [θiːvz] *n* Dieb(in *f*) *m.*

thieving ['θiːvɪŋ] *n* Stehlen *nt* // *a* diebisch.

thigh [θaɪ] *n* Oberschenkel *m.*

thimble ['θɪmbl] *n* Fingerhut *m.*

thin [θɪn] *a* dünn; *(person also)* mager; *(excuse)* schwach // *vt:* **to ~ (down)** *(sauce, paint)* verdünnen.

thing [θɪŋ] *n* Ding *nt*; *(affair)* Sache *f*; **my ~s** meine Sachen *pl*; **the best ~ would be to ...** das beste wäre, ...; **how are ~s?** wie geht's?

think [θɪŋk], *pt, pp* **thought** *vti* denken; **what did you ~ of them?** was halten Sie von ihnen?; **to ~ about sth/sb** nachdenken über etw/jdn; **I'll ~ about it** ich überlege es mir; **to ~ of doing sth**

vorhaben *or* beabsichtigen, etw zu tun; **I ~ so/not** ich glaube (schon)/glaube nicht; **to ~ well of sb** viel von jdm halten; **~ over** *vt* überdenken; **~ up** *vt* sich *(dat)* ausdenken; **~ tank** *n* Experten-gruppe *f.*

thinly ['θɪnlɪ] *ad* dünn; *(disguised)* kaum.

third [θɜːd] *a* dritte(r, s) // *n (person)* Dritte(r) *mf*; *(part)* Drittel *nt*; **~ly** *ad* drittens; **~ party insurance** *n (Brit)* Haftpflichtversicherung *f*; **~-rate** *a* minderwertig; **the T~ World** *n* die Dritte Welt *f.*

thirst [θɜːst] *n (lit, fig)* Durst *m*; **~y** *a (person)* durstig; *(work)* durstig machend; **to be ~y** Durst haben.

thirteen ['θɜː'tiːn] *num* dreizehn.

thirty ['θɜːtɪ] *num* dreißig.

this [ðɪs] ◆*a (demonstrative: pl* these) diese(r, s); ~ **evening** heute abend; ~ **one** diese(r, s) *(da)*
◆*pronoun (demonstrative: pl* these) dies, das; **who/what is ~?** wer/was ist das?; ~ **is where I live** hier wohne ich; ~ **is what he said** das hat er gesagt; ~ **is Mr Brown** *(in introductions/photo)* dies ist Mr Brown; *(on telephone)* hier ist Mr Brown
◆*ad (demonstrative):* ~ **high/long** etc so groß/lang etc.

thistle ['θɪsl] *n* Distel *f.*

thong [θɒŋ] *n (Leder)* riemen *m.*

thorn [θɔːn] *n* Dorn *m*; **~y** *a* dornig; *(problem)* schwierig.

thorough ['θʌrə] *a* gründlich; **~bred** *n* Vollblut *nt* // *a* reinrassig, Vollblut-; **~fare** *n* Straße *f*; **'no ~fare'** 'Durchfahrt verboten'; **~ly** *ad* gründlich; *(extremely)* äußerst.

those [ðəʊz] *pl pron* die (da), jene // *a* die, jene.

though [ðəʊ] *cj* obwohl // *ad* trotzdem.

thought [θɔːt] *pt, pp of* **think** // *n (idea)* Gedanke *m*; *(thinking)* Denken *nt*, Denkvermögen *nt*; *(thinking)* gedankenvoll, nachdenklich; *(kind)* rücksichtsvoll, aufmerksam; **~less** *a* gedankenlos, unbesonnen; *(unkind)* rücksichtslos.

thousand ['θaʊzənd] *num* tausend; **two ~** zweitausend; **~s of** Tausende (von); **~th** *a* tausendste(r, s).

thrash [θræʃ] *vt (lit)* verdreschen; *(fig)* (vernichtend) schlagen; ~ **about** *vi* um sich schlagen; ~ **out** *vt* ausdiskutieren.

thread [θred] *n* Faden *m*, Garn *nt*; *(on screw)* Gewinde *nt*; *(in story)* Faden *m* // *vt (needle)* einfädeln; **~bare** *a (lit, fig)* fadenscheinig.

threat [θret] *n* Drohung *f*; *(danger)* Gefahr *f*; **~en** *vt* bedrohen // *vi* drohen; **to ~en sb with sth** jdm etw androhen.

three [θriː] *num* drei; **~-dimensional** *a* dreidimensional; **~-piece** **suit** *n* dreiteilige(r) Anzug m; **~-piece suite** n dreiteilige Polstergarnitur f; **~-ply** a (wool) dreifach; (wood) dreischichtig; **~-wheeler** n Dreiradwagen m.

thresh [θreʃ] vti dreschen.

threshold [ˈθreʃhəʊld] n Schwelle f.

threw [θruː] pt of throw.

thrift [θrɪft] n Sparsamkeit f; **~y** a sparsam.

thrill [θrɪl] n Reiz m, Erregung f // to begeistern, packen; **to be ~ed** (with gift etc) sich unheimlich freuen über (+acc); **~er** n Krimi m; **~ing** a spannend; (news) aufregend.

thrive [θraɪv], pt **throve** [θrəʊv], pp **thrived** or **thriven** [ˈθrɪvn] vi gedeihen (on bei).

thriving [ˈθraɪvɪŋ] a blühend.

throat [θrəʊt] n Hals m, Kehle f; **to have a sore ~** Halsschmerzen haben.

throb [θrɒb] n Pochen nt // vi klopfen, pochen.

throes [θrəʊz] npl: **in the ~ of** mitten in (+dat).

throng [θrɒŋ] n (Menschen)schar f // vt sich drängen in (+dat).

throttle [ˈθrɒtl] n Gashebel m // vt erdrosseln.

through [θruː] prep durch; (time) während (+gen); (because of) aus, durch // ad durch // a (ticket, train) durchgehend; (finished) fertig; **to put sb ~** (TEL) jdn verbinden (to mit) to be ~ (TEL) eine Verbindung haben; (have finished) fertig sein; **'no ~ way'** (Brit) Sackgasse f; **~out** [θruːˈaʊt] prep (place) überall in (+dat); (time) während (+gen) // ad überall; die ganze Zeit.

throve [θrəʊv] pt of thrive.

throw [θrəʊ] n Wurf m // vt, pt **threw**, pp **thrown** werfen; **to ~ a party** eine Party geben; **~ away** vt wegwerfen; (waste) verschenken; (money) verschwenden; **~ off** vt abwerfen; (pursuer) abschütteln; **~ out** vt hinauswerfen; (rubbish) wegwerfen; (plan) verwerfen; **~ up** vti (vomit) speien; **~away** a Wegwerf-; **~-in** n Einwurf m.

thru [θruː] (US) = through.

thrush [θrʌʃ] n Drossel f.

thrust [θrʌst] n (TECH) Schubkraft f // vti, pt, pp **thrust** (push) stoßen.

thud [θʌd] n dumpfe(r) (Auf)schlag m.

thug [θʌg] n Schlägertyp m.

thumb [θʌm] n Daumen m // vt (book) durchblättern; **to ~ a lift** per Anhalter fahren (wollen); **~tack** n (US) Reißzwecke f.

thump [θʌmp] n (blow) Schlag m; (noise) Bums m // vi hämmern, pochen // vt schlagen auf (+acc).

thunder [ˈθʌndə*] n Donner m // vi donnern; (train etc) to ~ **past** vorbeidonnern // vt brüllen; **~bolt** n Blitz

nt; **~clap** n Donnerschlag m; **~storm** n Gewitter nt, Unwetter nt; **~y** a gewitterschwül.

Thursday [ˈθɜːzdeɪ] n Donnerstag m.

thus [ðʌs] ad (in this way) so; (therefore) somit, also, folglich.

thwart [θwɔːt] vt vereiteln, durchkreuzen; (person) hindern.

thyme [taɪm] n Thymian m.

thyroid [ˈθaɪrɔɪd] n Schilddrüse f.

tic [tɪk] n Tick m.

tick [tɪk] n (sound) Ticken nt; (mark) Häkchen nt // vi ticken // vt abhaken; **in a ~** (Brit col) sofort; **~ off** vt abhaken; (person) ausschimpfen; **~ over** vi (engine) im Leerlauf laufen; (fig) auf Sparflamme laufen.

ticket [ˈtɪkɪt] n (for travel) Fahrkarte f; (for entrance) (Eintritts)karte f; (price ~) Preisschild nt; (luggage ~) (Gepäck)schein m; (raffle ~) Los nt; (parking ~) Strafzettel m; (permission) Parkschein m; **~ collector** n Fahrkartenkontrolleur m; **~ office** n (RAIL etc) Fahrkartenschalter m; (THEAT etc) Kasse f.

tickle [ˈtɪkl] n Kitzeln nt // vt kitzeln; (amuse) amüsieren.

ticklish [ˈtɪklɪʃ] a (lit, fig) kitzlig.

tidal [ˈtaɪdl] a Flut-, Tide-; **~ wave** n Flutwelle f.

tidbit [ˈtɪdbɪt] n (US) Leckerbissen m.

tiddlywinks [ˈtɪdlɪwɪŋks] n Floh(hüpf)spiel nt.

tide [taɪd] n Gezeiten pl; **high/low ~** Flut f/Ebbe f.

tidy [ˈtaɪdɪ] a ordentlich // vt aufräumen, in Ordnung bringen.

tie [taɪ] n (Brit: necktie) Kravatte f, Schlips m; (sth connecting) Band nt; (SPORT) Unentschieden nt // vt (fasten, restrict) binden // vi (SPORT) unentschieden spielen; (in competition) punktgleich sein; **to ~ in a bow** zur Schleife binden; **to ~ a knot in sth** einen Knoten in etw (acc) machen; **~ down** vt (lit) festbinden; **to ~ sb down to** jdn binden an (+acc); **~ up** vt (dog) anbinden; (parcel) verschnüren; (boat) festmachen; (person) fesseln; **to be ~d up** (busy) beschäftigt sein.

tier [tɪə*] n Rang m; (of cake) Etage f.

tight [taɪt] a (close) eng, knapp; (schedule) gedrängt; (firm) fest; (control) streng; (stretched) stramm, (an)gespannt; (col) blau, stramm // ad (squeeze) fest; **~s** pl (Brit) Strumpfhose f; **~en** vt anziehen, anspannen; (restrictions) verschärfen // vi sich spannen; **~-fisted** a knauserig; **~ly** ad eng; fest; (stretched) straff; **~-rope** n Seil nt.

tile [taɪl] n (in roof) Dachziegel m; (on wall or floor) Fliese f; **~d** a (roof) gedeckt, Ziegel-; (floor, wall) mit Fliesen belegt.

till [tɪl] n Kasse f // vt bestellen // prep, cj = **until**.

tiller ['tɪlə*] n Ruderpinne f.

tilt [tɪlt] vt kippen, neigen // vi sich neigen.

timber ['tɪmbə*] n Holz nt; (trees) Baumbestand m.

time [taɪm] n Zeit f; (occasion) Mal nt; (rhythm) Takt m // vt zur rechten Zeit tun, zeitlich einrichten; (SPORT) stoppen; **in 2 weeks'** ~ in 2 Wochen; **a long** ~ lange; **for the** ~ **being** vorläufig; **4 at a** ~ zu jeweils 4; **from** ~ **to** ~ gelegentlich; **to have a good** ~ sich amüsieren; **in** ~ (soon enough) rechtzeitig; (after some time) mit der Zeit; (MUS) im Takt; **in no** ~ im Handumdrehen; **any** ~ jederzeit; **on** ~ pünktlich, rechtzeitig; **five** ~**s** 5 fünfmal 5; **what** ~ is it? wieviel Uhr ist es?, wie spät ist es?; ~ **bomb** n Zeitbombe f; ~**lag** n (in travel) Verzögerung f; (difference) Zeitunterschied m; ~**less** a (beauty) zeitlos; ~ **limit** n Frist f; ~**ly** a rechtzeitig; günstig; ~ **off** n freie Zeit f; **timer** n (~ switch: in kitchen) Schaltuhr f; ~ **scale** n Zeitspanne f; ~ **switch** n (Brit) Zeitschalter m; ~**table** n Fahrplan m; (SCH) Stundenplan m; ~ **zone** n Zeitzone f.

timid ['tɪmɪd] a ängstlich, schüchtern.

timing ['taɪmɪŋ] n Wahl f des richtigen Zeitpunkts, Timing nt; (AUT) Einstellung f.

timpani ['tɪmpənɪ] npl Kesselpauken pl.

tin [tɪn] n (metal) Blech nt; (container) Büchse f, Dose f; ~**foil** n Staniolpapier nt.

tinge [tɪndʒ] n (colour) Färbung f; (fig) Anflug m // vt färben; ~**d with** mit einer Spur von.

tingle ['tɪŋgl] n Prickeln nt // vi prickeln.

tinker ['tɪŋkə*] n Kesselflicker m; ~ **with** vt herumpfuschen an (+dat).

tinkle ['tɪŋkl] vi klingeln.

tinned [tɪnd] a (Bri: food) Dosen-, Büchsen-.

tin opener ['tɪnəʊpnə*] n (Brit) Dosen- or Büchsenöffner m.

tinsel ['tɪnsəl] n Rauschgold nt.

tint [tɪnt] n Farbton m; (slight colour) Anflug m; (hair) Tönung f; ~**ed** a getönt.

tiny ['taɪnɪ] a winzig.

tip [tɪp] n (pointed end) Spitze f; (money) Trinkgeld nt; (hint) Wink m, Tip m // vt (slant) kippen; (hat) antippen; (~ over) umkippen; (waiter) ein Trinkgeld geben (+dat); ~**-off** n Hinweis m, Tip m; ~**ped** a (Brit: cigarette) Filter-.

tipsy ['tɪpsɪ] a beschwipst.

tiptoe ['tɪptəʊ] n: **on** ~ auf Zehenspitzen.

tiptop ['tɪp'tɒp] a: **in** ~ **condition** tipptopp, erstklassig.

tire ['taɪə*] n (US) = **tyre** // vti ermüden, müde machen/werden; ~**d** a müde; **to be** ~**d of sth** etw satt haben; ~**less** a, ~**lessly** ad unermüdlich; ~**some** a lästig.

tiring ['taɪərɪŋ] a ermüdend.

tissue ['tɪʃuː] n Gewebe nt; (paper handkerchief) Papiertaschentuch nt; ~ **paper** n Seidenpapier nt.

tit [tɪt] n (bird) Meise f; ~**s** pl (col: breasts) Busen m; ~ **for tat** wie du mir, so ich dir.

titbit ['tɪtbɪt], (US) **tidbit** ['tɪdbɪt] n Leckerbissen m.

titillate ['tɪtɪleɪt] vt kitzeln.

titivate ['tɪtɪveɪt] vt schniegeln.

title ['taɪtl] n Titel m; ~ **deed** n Eigentumsurkunde f; ~ **role** n Hauptrolle f.

titter ['tɪtə*] vi kichern.

TM abbr (= trademark) Wz.

to [tuː, tə] ◆prep **1** (direction) zu, nach; **to go** ~ **France/school** nach Frankreich/zur Schule gehen; ~ **the left** nach links **2** (as far as) bis **3** (with expressions of time) vor; **a quarter** ~ 5 Viertel vor 5 **4** (for, of) für; **secretary** ~ **the director** Sekretärin des Direktors **5** (expressing indirect object): **to give sth** ~ **sb** jdm etw geben; **to talk** ~ **sb** mit jdm sprechen; **I sold it** ~ **a friend** ich habe es einem Freund verkauft **6** (in relation to) zu; **30 miles** ~ **the gallon** 30 Meilen pro Gallone **7** (purpose, result) zu; ~ **my surprise** zu meiner Überraschung ◆with v **1** (infinitive): ~ **go/eat** trinken/essen; **to want** ~ **do sth** etw tun wollen; **try/start** ~ **do sth** versuchen/anfangen, etw zu tun; **he has a lot** ~ **lose** er hat viel zu verlieren **2** (with v omitted): **I don't want** ~ ich will (es) nicht **3** (purpose, result) um; **I did it** ~ **help you** ich tat es, um dir zu helfen **4** (after adjective etc): **ready** ~ **use** gebrauchsfertig; **too old/young** ~ ... zu alt/jung, um ... ◆ad: **push/pull the door** ~ die Tür zuschieben/zuziehen.

toad [təʊd] n Kröte f; ~**stool** n Giftpilz m.

toast [təʊst] n (bread) Toast m; (drinking) Trinkspruch m // vt trinken auf (+acc); (bread) toasten; (warm) wärmen; ~**er** n Toaster m.

tobacco [tə'bækəʊ] n Tabak m; ~**nist** [tə'bækənɪst] n Tabakhändler m; ~**nist's (shop)** n Tabakladen m.

toboggan [tə'bɒgən] n (Rodel)schlitten m.

today [tə'deɪ] ad heute; (at the present time) heutzutage.

toddler ['tɒdlə*] n Kleinkind nt.

toddy ['tɒdɪ] n (Whisky)grog m.

to-do [tə'duː] n Theater nt.

toe [təu] n Zehe f; (of sock, shoe) Spitze f // vt: to ~ the line (fig) sich einfügen; ~**nail** n Zehennagel m.

toffee ['tɒfɪ] n Sahnebonbon nt; ~ **apple** n (Brit) kandierte(r) Apfel m.

together [tə'geðə*] ad zusammen; (at the same time) gleichzeitig; ~ **with** prep zusammen/gleichzeitig mit; ~**ness** n (company) Beisammensein nt.

toil [tɔɪl] n harte Arbeit f, Plackerei f // vi sich abmühen, sich plagen.

toilet ['tɔɪlət] n Toilette f // cpd Toiletten-; ~ **bag** n Waschbeutel m; ~ **paper** n Toilettenpapier nt; ~**ries** ['tɔɪlətrɪz] npl Toilettenartikel pl; ~ **roll** n Rolle f Toilettenpapier; ~ **water** n Toilettenwasser nt.

token ['təukən] n Zeichen nt; (gift ~) Gutschein m; **book/record** ~ (Brit) Bücher-/Plattengutschein m.

Tokyo ['təukjəu] n Tokio nt.

told [təuld] pt, pp of **tell**.

tolerable ['tɒlərəbl] a (bearable) erträglich; (fairly good) leidlich.

tolerate ['tɒləreɪt] vt dulden; (noise) ertragen.

toll [təul] n Gebühr f // vi (bell) läuten.

tomato [tə'mɑːtəu] n, pl ~**es** Tomate f.

tomb [tuːm] n Grab(mal) nt.

tomboy ['tɒmbɔɪ] n Wildfang m.

tombstone ['tuːmstəun] n Grabstein m.

tomcat ['tɒmkæt] n Kater m.

tomorrow [tə'mɒrəu] n Morgen nt // ad morgen; **the day after** ~ übermorgen; ~ **morning** morgen früh; **a week** ~ morgen in einer Woche.

ton [tʌn] n (Brit) Tonne f; (US: also: short ~) 907,18 kg; (metric ~) Tonne f; ~**s of** (col) eine Unmenge von.

tone [təun] n Ton m; ~ **down** vt (criticism, demands) mäßigen; (colours) abtonen; ~ **up** vt in Form bringen; ~**deaf** a ohne musikalisches Gehör.

tongs [tɒŋz] npl Zange f; (curling ~) Lockenstab m.

tongue [tʌŋ] n Zunge f; (language) Sprache f; **with** ~ **in cheek** scherzhaft; ~**tied** a stumm, sprachlos; ~**twister** n Zungenbrecher m.

tonic ['tɒnɪk] n (MED) Stärkungsmittel nt; (drink) Tonic nt.

tonight [tə'naɪt] ad heute abend.

tonsil ['tɒnsl] n Mandel f; ~**litis** [tɒnsɪ'laɪtɪs] n Mandelentzündung f.

too [tuː] ad zu; (also) auch; ~ **bad!** Pech!

took [tuk] pt of **take**.

tool [tuːl] n (lit, fig) Werkzeug nt; ~**box** n Werkzeugkasten m.

toot [tuːt] n Hupen nt // vi tuten; (AUT) hupen.

tooth [tuːθ] n, pl **teeth** Zahn m; ~**ache** n Zahnschmerzen pl, Zahnweh nt; ~**brush** n Zahnbürste f; ~**paste** n Zahnpasta f; ~**pick** n Zahnstocher m.

top [tɒp] n Spitze f; (of mountain) Gipfel m; (of tree) Wipfel m; (toy) Kreisel m; (~ gear) vierte(r) Gang m // a oberste(r, s) // vt (list) an erster Stelle stehen auf (+dat); **on** ~ **of** oben auf (+dat); **from** ~ **to bottom** von oben bis unten; ~ **up**, (US) ~ **off** vt auffüllen; ~ **floor** n oberste Stockwerk nt; ~ **hat** n Zylinder m; ~**heavy** a kopflastig.

topic ['tɒpɪk] n Thema nt, Gesprächsgegenstand m; ~**al** a aktuell.

topless ['tɒpləs] a (dress) oben ohne.

top-level ['tɒp'levl] a auf höchster Ebene.

topmost ['tɒpməust] a oberste(r, s).

topple ['tɒpl] vti stürzen, kippen.

top-secret ['tɒp'siːkrət] a streng geheim.

topsy-turvy ['tɒpsɪ'tɜːvɪ] ad durcheinander // a auf den Kopf gestellt.

torch [tɔːtʃ] n (Brit ELEC) Taschenlampe f; (with flame) Fackel f.

tore [tɔː*] pt of **tear**.

torment ['tɔːment] n Qual f // [tɔː'ment] vt (distress) quälen.

torn [tɔːn] pp of **tear** // a hin- und hergerissen.

torrent ['tɒrənt] n Sturzbach m; ~**ial** [tə'renʃəl] a wolkenbruchartig.

torrid ['tɒrɪd] a heiß.

tortoise ['tɔːtəs] n Schildkröte f; ~**shell** ['tɔːtəʃel] n Schildpatt m.

tortuous ['tɔːtjuəs] a gewunden.

torture ['tɔːtʃə*] n Folter f // vt foltern.

Tory ['tɔːrɪ] (Brit POL) n Tory m // a Tory-, konservativ.

toss [tɒs] vt schleudern; **to** ~ **a coin, to** ~ **up for sth** etw mit einer Münze entscheiden; **to** ~ **and turn** (in bed) sich hin und her werfen.

tot [tɒt] n (small quantity) bißchen nt; (small child) Knirps m.

total ['təutl] n Gesamtheit f; (money) Endsumme f // a Gesamt-, total // vt (add up) zusammenzählen; (amount to) sich belaufen auf.

totalitarian [təutælɪ'teəriən] a totalitär.

totally ['təutəlɪ] ad total.

totter ['tɒtə*] vi wanken, schwanken.

touch [tʌtʃ] n Berührung f; (sense of feeling) Tastsinn m // vt (feel) berühren; (come against) leicht anstoßen; (emotionally) rühren; **a** ~ **of** (fig) eine Spur von; **to get in** ~ **with sb** sich mit jdm in Verbindung setzen; **to lose** ~ (friends) Kontakt verlieren; ~ **on** vt (topic) berühren, erwähnen; ~ **up** vt (paint) auffrischen; ~**and-go** a riskant, knapp; ~**down** n Landen nt, Niedergehen nt; ~**ing** a rührend; ~**line** n Seitenlinie f; ~**y** a empfindlich, reizbar.

tough [tʌf] a zäh; (difficult) schwierig // n Schläger(typ) m; **~en** vt zäh machen; (make strong) abhärten.

toupée ['tuːpeɪ] n Toupet nt.

tour ['tuə*] n Tour f // vi umherreisen; (THEAT) auf Tour sein/gehen; **~ing** n Umherreisen nt; (THEAT) Tournee f.

tourism ['tuərɪzm] n Fremdenverkehr m, Tourismus m.

tourist ['tuərɪst] n Tourist(in f) // cpd (class) Touristen-; **~ office** n Verkehrsamt nt.

tournament ['tuənəmənt] n Turnier nt.

tousled ['tauzld] a zerzaust.

tout [taut] vi: to **~ for** auf Kundenfang gehen für // n: **ticket ~** Kundenschlepper(in f) m.

tow [təu] vt (ab)schleppen; **on** or (US) **in ~** (AUT) im Schlepp.

toward(s) [tə'wɔːd(z)] prep (with time) gegen; (in direction of) nach.

towel ['tauəl] n Handtuch nt; **~ling** n (fabric) Frottee nt or m; **~ rail**, (US) **~ rack** n Handtuchstange f.

tower ['tauə*] n Turm m; **~ block** n (Brit) Hochhaus nt; **~ing** a hochragend.

town [taun] n Stadt f; **to go to ~** (fig) sich ins Zeug legen; **~ centre** n Stadtzentrum nt; **~ clerk** n Stadtdirektor m; **~ council** n Stadtrat m; **~ hall** n Rathaus nt **~ plan** n Stadtplan m; **~ planning** n Stadtplanung f.

towrope ['təurəup] n Abschlepptau nt.

tow truck n (US: breakdown lorry) Abschleppwagen m.

toxic ['tɒksɪk] a giftig, Gift-.

toy [tɔɪ] n Spielzeug nt; **~ with** vt spielen mit; **~shop** n Spielwarengeschäft nt.

trace [treɪs] n Spur f // vt (follow a course) nachspüren (+dat); (find out) aufspüren; (copy) durchpausen; **tracing paper** n Pauspapier nt.

track [træk] n (mark) Spur f; (path) Weg m; (race-~) Rennbahn f; (RAIL) Gleis nt // vt verfolgen; to **keep ~ of sb** jdn im Auge behalten; **~ down** vt aufspüren; **~ suit** n Trainingsanzug m.

tract [trækt] n (of land) Gebiet nt; (booklet) Traktat nt.

traction ['trækʃən] n (power) Zugkraft f; (AUT: grip) Bodenhaftung f; (MED): **in ~** im Streckverband.

trade [treɪd] n (commerce) Handel m; (business) Geschäft nt, Gewerbe nt; (people) Geschäftsleute pl; (skilled manual work) Handwerk nt // vi handeln (in mit) // vt tauschen; **~ in** vt in Zahlung geben; **~ fair** n Messe nt; **~-in price** n Preis m, zu dem etw in Zahlung genommen wird; **~mark** n Warenzeichen nt; **~ name** n Handelsbezeichnung f; **~r** n Händler m; **tradesman** n (shopkeeper) Geschäftsmann m; (work-

man) Handwerker m; (delivery man) Lieferant m; **~ union** n Gewerkschaft f; **~ unionist** n Gewerkschaftler(in f) m.

trading ['treɪdɪŋ] n Handel m; **~ estate** n (Brit) Industriegelände nt.

tradition [trə'dɪʃən] n Tradition f; **~al** a traditionell, herkömmlich.

traffic ['træfɪk] n Verkehr m; (esp in drugs) Handel m (in mit) // vi: to **~ in** (esp drugs) handeln mit; **~ circle** n (US) Kreisverkehr m; **~ jam** n Verkehrsstauung f; **~ lights** npl Verkehrsampeln pl; **~ warden** n ≃ Verkehrspolizist m, Politesse f (ohne amtliche Befugnisse).

tragedy ['trædʒədɪ] n Tragödie f.

tragic ['trædʒɪk] a tragisch.

trail [treɪl] n (track) Spur f; (of smoke) Rauchfahne f; (of dust) Staubwolke f; (road) Pfad m, Weg m // vt (animal) verfolgen; (person) folgen (+dat); (drag) schleppen // vi (hang loosely) schleifen; (plants) sich ranken; (be behind) hinterherhinken; (SPORT) weit zurückliegen; (walk) zuckeln; **~ behind** vi zurückbleiben; **~er** n Anhänger m; (US: caravan) Wohnwagen m; (for film) Vorschau f; **~ truck** n (US) Sattelschlepper m.

train [treɪn] n Zug m; (of dress) Schleppe f; (series) Folge f // vt (teach: person) ausbilden; (: animal) abrichten; (: mind) schulen; (SPORT) trainieren; (aim) richten (on auf +acc) // vi (exercise) trainieren; (study) ausgebildet werden; **~ of thought** Gedankengang m; **~ed** a (eye) geschult; (person, voice) ausgebildet; **~ee** n Lehrling m; Praktikant(in f) m; **~er** n (SPORT) Trainer m; Ausbilder m; **~ing** n (for occupation) Ausbildung f; (SPORT) Training nt; **in ~ing** im Training; **~ing college** n Pädagogische Hochschule f, Lehrerseminar nt; **~ing shoes** npl Turnschuhe pl.

traipse [treɪps] vi latschen.

trait [treɪ(t)] n Zug m, Merkmal nt.

traitor ['treɪtə*] n Verräter m.

trajectory [trə'dʒektərɪ] n Flugbahn f.

tram(car) ['træm(kɑː*)] n Straßenbahn f.

tramp [træmp] n Landstreicher m // vi (walk heavily) stampfen, stapfen; (travel on foot) wandern.

trample ['træmpl] vt (nieder)trampeln // vi (herum)trampeln; to **~ (underfoot)** herumtrampeln auf (+dat).

tranquil ['træŋkwɪl] a ruhig, friedlich; **~ity** [træŋ'kwɪlɪtɪ] n Ruhe f; **~izer** n Beruhigungsmittel nt.

transact [træn'zækt] vt abwickeln; **~ion** n Abwicklung f; (piece of business) Geschäft nt, Transaktion f.

transcend [træn'send] vt übersteigen.

transcript ['trænskrɪpt] n Abschrift f, Kopie f; (JUR) Protokoll nt; **~ion** [træn'skrɪpʃən] n Transkription f; (product) Abschrift f.

transfer ['trænsfə*] n (transferring) Übertragung f; (of business) Umzug m; (being transferred) Versetzung f; (design) Abziehbild nt; (SPORT) Transfer m // [træns'fɜ:*] vt (business) verlegen; (person) versetzen; (prisoner) überführen; (drawing) übertragen; (money) überweisen; to ~ the charges (Brit TEL) ein R-Gespräch führen.

transform [træns'fɔ:m] vt umwandeln; **~ation** [trænsfə'meɪʃən] n Umwandlung f, Verwandlung f; **~er** n (ELEC) Transformator m.

transfusion [træns'fju:ʒən] n Blutübertragung f, Transfusion f.

transient ['trænzɪənt] a kurz(lebig).

transistor [træn'zɪstə*] n (ELEC) Transistor m; (radio) Transistorradio nt.

transit ['trænzɪt] n: **in ~** unterwegs.

transition [træn'zɪʃən] n Übergang m; **~al** a Übergangs-.

transitory ['trænzɪtərɪ] a vorübergehend.

translate [trænz'leɪt] vti übersetzen.

translation [trænz'leɪʃən] n Übersetzung f.

translator [trænz'leɪtə*] n Übersetzer(in f) m.

transmission [trænz'mɪʃən] n (of information) Übermittlung f; (ELEC, MED, TV) Übertragung f; (AUT) Getriebe nt.

transmit [trænz'mɪt] vt (message) übermitteln; (ELEC, MED, TV) übertragen; **~ter** n Sender m.

transparency [træns'pɛərənsɪ] n Durchsichtigkeit f; (Brit PHOT) Dia(positiv) nt.

transparent [træns'pærənt] a (lit) durchsichtig; (fig) offenkundig.

transpire [træns'paɪə*] vi (turn out) sich herausstellen; (happen) passieren.

transplant [træns'plɑ:nt] vt umpflanzen; (MED) verpflanzen; (fig: person) verpflanzen // ['trænsplɑ:nt] n (MED) Transplantation f; (organ) Transplantat nt.

transport ['trænspɔ:t] n Transport m, Beförderung f // vt [træns'pɔ:t] befördern; transportieren; **means of ~** Transportmittel nt; **~ation** [trænspɔ:'teɪʃən] n Transport m, Beförderung f; (means) Beförderungsmittel nt; (cost) Transportkosten pl; **~ café** n (Brit) Fernfahrerlokal nt.

transverse ['trænzvɜ:s] a Quer-; (position) horizontal; (engine) querliegend.

trap [træp] n Falle f; (carriage) zweirädrige(r) Einspänner m; (col: mouth) Klappe f // vt fangen; (person) in eine Falle locken; **~door** n Falltür f.

trappings ['træpɪŋz] npl Aufmachung f.

trash [træʃ] n (rubbish) Plunder m; (nonsense) Mist m; **~ can** n (US) Mülleimer m.

travel ['trævl] n Reisen nt // vi reisen // vt (distance) zurücklegen; (country) bereisen; **~ agency** n Reisebüro nt; **~ agent** n Reisebürokaufmann m; Reisebürokauffrau f; **~ler**, (US) **~er** n Reisende(r) m/f; (salesman) Handlungsreisende(r) m; **~ler's cheque**, (US) **~er's check** n Reisescheck m; **~ling**, (US) **~ing** n Reisen nt; **~ sickness** n Reisekrankheit f.

tray [treɪ] n (tea ~) Tablett nt; (receptacle) Schale f; (for mail) Ablage f.

treacherous ['tretʃərəs] a verräterisch; (road) tückisch.

treachery ['tretʃərɪ] n Verrat m.

treacle ['tri:kl] n Sirup m, Melasse f.

tread [tred] n Schritt m, Tritt m; (of stair) Stufe f; (on tyre) Profil nt // vi, pt **trod**, pp **trodden** treten; **~ on** vt treten auf (+acc).

treason ['tri:zn] n Verrat m.

treasure ['treʒə*] n Schatz m // vt schätzen.

treasurer ['treʒərə*] n Kassenverwalter m, Schatzmeister m.

treasury ['treʒərɪ] n (POL) Finanzministerium nt.

treat [tri:t] n besondere Freude f // vt (deal with) behandeln; to ~ sb to sth jdn zu etw einladen.

treatise ['tri:tɪz] n Abhandlung f.

treatment ['tri:tmənt] n Behandlung f.

treaty ['tri:tɪ] n Vertrag m.

treble ['trebl] a dreifach // vt verdreifachen; **~ clef** n Violinschlüssel m.

tree [tri:] n Baum m; **~ trunk** n Baumstamm m.

trellis ['trelɪs] n Gitter nt; (for gardening) Spalier m.

tremble ['trembl] vi zittern; (ground) beben.

trembling ['tremblɪŋ] n Zittern nt // a zitternd.

tremendous [trə'mendəs] a gewaltig, kolossal; (col: very good) prima.

tremor ['tremə*] n Zittern nt; (of earth) Beben nt.

trench [trentʃ] n Graben m; (MIL) Schützengraben m.

trend [trend] n Tendenz f; **~y** a (col) modisch.

trepidation [trepɪ'deɪʃən] n Beklommenheit f.

trespass ['trespəs] vi widerrechtlich betreten (on acc); **'no ~ing'** 'Betreten verboten.'

tress [tres] n Locke f.

trestle ['tresl] n Bock m; **~ table** n Klapptisch m.

trial ['traɪəl] n (JUR) Prozeß m; (test)

Versuch *m*, Probe *f*; *(hardship)* Prüfung *f*; **by ~ and error** durch Ausprobieren.

triangle ['traɪæŋgl] *n* Dreieck *nt*; *(MUS)* Triangel *f*.

triangular [traɪ'æŋgjʊlə*] *a* dreieckig.

tribal ['traɪbəl] *a* Stammes-.

tribe [traɪb] *n* Stamm *m*; **tribesman** *n* Stammesangehörige(r) *m*.

tribulation [trɪbjʊ'leɪʃən] *n* Not *f*, Mühsal *f*.

tribunal [traɪ'bju:nl] *n* Gericht *nt*; *(inquiry)* Untersuchungsausschuß *m*.

tributary ['trɪbjʊtərɪ] *n* Nebenfluß *m*.

tribute ['trɪbju:t] *n* *(admiration)* Zeichen *nt* der Hochachtung; **to pay ~ to** jdm/ einer Sache Tribut zollen.

trice [traɪs] *n*: **in a ~** im Nu.

trick [trɪk] *n* Trick *m*; *(CARDS)* Stich *m* // *vt* überlisten, beschwindeln; **to play a ~ on sb** jdm einen Streich spielen; **that should do the ~** daß müßte eigentlich klappen; **~ery** *n* Tricks *pl*.

trickle ['trɪkl] *n* Tröpfeln *nt*; *(small river)* Rinnsal *nt* // *vi* tröpfeln; *(seep)* sickern.

tricky ['trɪkɪ] *a* *(problem)* schwierig; *(situation)* kitzlig.

tricycle ['traɪsɪkl] *n* Dreirad *nt*.

trifle ['traɪfl] *n* Kleinigkeit *f*; *(COOK)* Trifle *m* // *ad*: **a ~** ein bißchen.

trifling ['traɪflɪŋ] *a* geringfügig.

trigger ['trɪgə*] *n* Drücker *m*; **~ off** *vt* auslösen.

trim [trɪm] *a* gepflegt; *(figure)* schlank // *n* (gute) Verfassung *f*; *(embellishment, on car)* Verzierung *f* // *vt* *(clip)* schneiden; *(trees)* stutzen; *(decorate)* besetzen; *(sails)* trimmen; **~mings** *npl* *(decorations)* Verzierung(en *pl*) *f*; *(extras)* Zubehör *nt*.

Trinity ['trɪnɪtɪ] *n*: **the ~** die Dreieinigkeit.

trinket ['trɪŋkɪt] *n* kleine(s) Schmuckstück *nt*.

trip [trɪp] *n* *(kurze)* Reise *f*; *(outing)* Ausflug *m*; *(stumble)* Stolpern *nt* // *vi* *(walk quickly)* trippeln; *(stumble)* stolpern; **on a ~** auf Reisen; **~ up** *vi* stolpern; *(fig also)* einen Fehler machen // *vt* zu Fall bringen; *(fig)* hereinlegen.

tripe [traɪp] *n* *(food)* Kutteln *pl*; *(rubbish)* Mist *m*.

triple ['trɪpl] *a* dreifach.

triplets ['trɪplɪts] *npl* Drillinge *pl*.

triplicate ['trɪplɪkət] *n*: **in ~** in dreifacher Ausfertigung.

tripod ['traɪpɒd] *n* *(PHOT)* Stativ *nt*.

trite [traɪt] *a* banal.

triumph ['traɪʌmf] *n* Triumph *m* // *vi* triumphieren; **to ~ (over)** triumphieren (über (+acc)) **~ant** [traɪ'ʌmfənt] *a* triumphierend.

trivia ['trɪvɪə] *npl* Trivialitäten *pl*.

trivial ['trɪvɪəl] *a* gering(fügig), trivial.

trod [trɒd], **trodden** ['trɒdn] *pt, pp* of **tread**.

trolley ['trɒlɪ] *n* Handwagen *m*; *(in shop)* Einkaufswagen; *(for luggage)* Kofferkuli *m*; *(table)* Teewagen *m*; **~ bus** *n* O(berleitungs)bus *m*.

troop [tru:p] *n* Schar *f*; *(MIL)* Trupp *m*; **~s** *pl* Truppen *pl*; **~ in/out** *vi* hinein-/ hinausströmen; **~er** *n* Kavallerist *m*; **~ing the colour** *n* *(ceremony)* Fahnenparade *f*.

tropic ['trɒpɪk] *n* Wendekreis *m*; **~al** *a* tropisch.

trot [trɒt] *n* Trott *m* // *vi* trotten; **on the ~** *(Brit fig: col)* in einer Tour.

trouble ['trʌbl] *n* *(problems)* Ärger *m*; *(worry)* Sorge *f*, *(in country, industry)* Unruhen *pl*; *(effort)* Mühe *f*; *(MED)*: **stomach ~** Magenbeschwerden *pl*; // *vt* *(disturb)* stören; **to ~ to do sth** sich bemühen, etw zu tun; **to be in ~** Probleme *or* Ärger haben; **~s** *pl* *(POL etc)* Unruhen *pl*; **to go to the ~ of doing sth** sich die Mühe machen, etw zu tun; **what's the ~?** was ist los?; *(to sick person)* wo fehlt's?; **~d** *a* *(person)* beunruhigt; *(country)* geplagt; **~-free** *a* sorglos; **~maker** *n* Unruhestifter *m*; **~shooter** *n* Vermittler *m*; **~some** *a* lästig, unangenehm; *(child)* schwierig.

trough [trɒf] *n* *(vessel)* Trog *m*; *(channel)* Rinne *f*, Kanal *m*; *(MET)* Tief *nt*.

trounce [traʊns] *vt* *(esp SPORT)* vernichtend schlagen.

trousers ['traʊzəz] *npl* Hose *f*.

trousseau ['tru:səʊ], *pl* **~x** *or* **~s** [-z] *n* Aussteuer *f*.

trout [traʊt] *n* Forelle *f*.

trowel ['traʊəl] *n* Kelle *f*.

truant ['tru:ənt] *n*: **to play ~** *(Brit)* (die Schule) schwänzen.

truce [tru:s] *n* Waffenstillstand *m*.

truck [trʌk] *n* Lastwagen *m*; *(RAIL)* offene(r) Güterwagen *m*; **~ driver** *n* Lastwagenfahrer *m*; **~ farm** *n* *(US)* Gemüsegärtnerei *f*.

truculent ['trʌkjʊlənt] *a* trotzig.

trudge [trʌdʒ] *vi* sich (mühselig) dahinschleppen.

true [tru:] *a* *(exact)* wahr; *(genuine)* echt; *(friend)* treu.

truly ['tru:lɪ] *ad* wirklich; **yours ~** Ihr sehr ergebener.

trump [trʌmp] *n* *(CARDS)* Trumpf *m*; **~ed-up** *a* erfunden.

trumpet ['trʌmpɪt] *n* Trompete *f*.

truncheon ['trʌntʃən] *n* Gummiknüppel *m*.

trundle ['trʌndl] *vt* schieben // *vi*: **~ along** entlangrollen.

trunk [trʌŋk] *n* *(of tree)* (Baum)stamm *m*; *(ANAT)* Rumpf *m*; *(box)* Truhe *f*, Überseekoffer *m*; *(of elephant)* Rüssel *m*; *(US AUT)* Kofferraum *m*; **~s** *pl* Badehose *f*; **~ (up)** *vt* fesseln.

truss 201 **turn**

truss [trʌs] n (MED) Bruchband nt.

trust [trʌst] n (confidence) Vertrauen nt; (for property etc) Treuhandvermögen nt // vt (rely on) vertrauen (+dat), sich verlassen auf (+acc); (hope) hoffen; (entrust): to ~ sth to sb jdm etw anvertrauen; ~**ed** a treu; ~**ee** [trʌs'ti:] n Vermögensverwalter m; ~**ful** a, ~**ing** a vertrauensvoll; ~**worthy** a vertrauenswürdig; (account) glaubwürdig; ~**y** a treu, zuverlässig.

truth [tru:θ], pl ~**s** [tru:ðz] n Wahrheit f; ~**ful** a ehrlich.

try [traɪ] n Versuch m; to have a ~ es versuchen // vt (attempt) versuchen; (test) (aus)probieren; (JUR: person) unter Anklage stellen; (: case) verhandeln; (courage, patience) auf die Probe stellen // vi (make effort) sich bemühen; to ~ to do sth versuchen, etw zu tun; ~ **on** vt (dress) anprobieren; (hat) aufprobieren; ~ **out** vt ausprobieren; ~**ing** a schwierig.

T-shirt ['ti:ʃɜ:t] n T-shirt nt.

T-square ['ti:skwɛə*] n Reißschiene f.

tub [tʌb] n Wanne f, Kübel m; (for margarine etc) Becher m.

tubby ['tʌbɪ] a rundlich.

tube [tju:b] n (pipe) Röhre f, Rohr nt; (for toothpaste etc) Tube f; (in London) U-Bahn f; (AUT: for tyre) Schlauch m.

tube station ['tju:bsteɪʃən] n (Brit) U-Bahnstation f.

tubing ['tju:bɪŋ] n Schlauch m; a piece of ~ ein (Stück) Schlauch.

tubular ['tju:bjulə*] a röhrenförmig.

TUC n abbr (Brit) of **Trades Union Congress.**

tuck [tʌk] n (fold) Falte f, Einschlag m // vt (put) stecken; (gather) fälteln, einschlagen; ~ **away** vt wegstecken; ~ **in** vt hineinstecken; (blanket etc) feststecken; (person) zudecken // vi (eat) hineinhauen, zulangen; ~ **up** vt (child) warm zudecken; ~ **shop** n Süßwarenladen m.

Tuesday ['tju:zdeɪ] n Dienstag m.

tuft [tʌft] n Büschel m.

tug [tʌg] n (jerk) Zerren nt, Ruck m; (NAUT) Schleppdampfer m // vti zerren, ziehen; (boat) schleppen; ~**-of-war** n Tauziehen nt.

tuition [tju:'ɪʃən] n (Brit) Unterricht m; (: private ~) Privatunterricht m; (US: school fees) Schulgeld nt.

tulip ['tju:lɪp] n Tulpe f.

tumble ['tʌmbl] n (fall) Sturz m // vi (fall) fallen, stürzen; ~ **to** vt kapieren; ~**down** a baufällig; ~ **dryer** n (Brit) Trockner m; **tumbler** n (glass) Trinkglas nt.

tummy ['tʌmɪ] n (col) Bauch m.

tuna ['tju:nə] n Thunfisch m.

tune [tju:n] n Melodie f // vt (put in tune) stimmen; (AUT) richtig einstellen; to

sing in ~/out of ~ richtig/falsch singen; to be out of ~ with nicht harmonieren mit; ~ **in** vi einstellen (to acc); ~ **up** vi (MUS) stimmen; **tuner** n (person) (Instrumenten)stimmer m; (part) Tuner m; **piano tuner** n Klavierstimmer(in f) m; ~**ful** a melodisch.

tunic ['tju:nɪk] n Waffenrock m; (loose garment) lange Bluse f.

tuning ['tju:nɪŋ] n (RAD, AUT) Einstellen nt; (MUS) Stimmen nt; ~ **fork** n Stimmgabel f.

Tunisia [tju:nɪzɪə] n Tunesien nt.

tunnel ['tʌnl] n Tunnel m, Unterführung f // vi einen Tunnel anlegen.

turbulent ['tɜ:bjulənt] a stürmisch.

tureen [tjʊ'ri:n] n Terrine f.

turf [tɜ:f] n Rasen m; (piece) Sode f // vt mit Grassoden belegen; ~ **out** vt (col) rauswerfen.

turgid ['tɜ:dʒɪd] a geschwollen.

Turk [tɜ:k] n Türke m, Türkin f.

turkey ['tɜ:kɪ] n Puter m, Truthahn m.

Turkey ['tɜ:kɪ] n Türkei f; **Turkish** a türkisch // n (LING) Türkisch nt.

turmoil ['tɜ:mɔɪl] n Aufruhr m, Tumult m.

turn [tɜ:n] n (rotation) (Um)drehung f; (performance) (Programm)nummer f; (MED) Schock m // vt (rotate) drehen; (change position of) umdrehen, wenden; (page) umblättern; (transform): to ~ sth into sth etw in etw (acc) verwandeln; (direct) zuwenden // vi (rotate) sich drehen; (change direction: in car) abbiegen; (: wind) drehen; (~ round) umdrehen, wenden; (become) werden; (leaves) sich verfärben; (milk) sauer werden; (weather) umschlagen; to do sb a good ~ jdm etw Gutes tun; it's your ~ du bist dran or an der Reihe; in ~, by ~s abwechseln; to take ~s sich abwechseln; it gave me quite a ~ das hat mich schön erschreckt; 'no left ~' (AUT) 'Linksabbiegen verboten'; ~ **away** vi sich abwenden; ~ **back** vt umdrehen; (person) zurückschicken; (clock) zurückstellen // vi umkehren; ~ **down** vt (refuse) ablehnen; (fold down) umschlagen; ~ **in** vi (go to bed) ins Bett gehen // vt (fold inwards) einwärts biegen; ~ **off** vi abbiegen // vt ausschalten; (tap) zudrehen; (machine, electricity) abstellen; ~ **on** vt (light) anschalten, einschalten; (tap) aufdrehen; (machine) anstellen; ~ **out** vi (prove to be) sich erweisen; (people) sich entwickeln; **how did the cake ~ out?** wie ist der Kuchen geworden? // vt (light) ausschalten; (gas) abstellen; (produce) produzieren; ~ **round** vi (person, vehicle) sich herumdrehen; (rotate) sich drehen; ~ **up** vi auftauchen; (happen) passieren, sich ereignen // vt (collar) hochklappen, hochstellen;

(nose) rümpfen; (increase: radio) lauter stellen; (: heat) höher drehen; ~ing n (in road) Abzweigung f; ~ing point n Wendepunkt m.

turnip ['tɜːnɪp] n Steckrübe f.

turnout ['tɜːnaʊt] n (Besucher)zahl f; (COMM) Produktion f.

turnover ['tɜːnəʊvə*] n Umsatz m; (of staff) Wechsel m.

turnpike ['tɜːnpaɪk] n (US) gebührenpflichtige Straße f.

turnstile ['tɜːnstaɪl] n Drehkreuz nt.

turntable ['tɜːnteɪbl] n (of record-player) Plattenteller m; (RAIL) Drehscheibe f.

turn-up ['tɜːnʌp] n (Brit: on trousers) Aufschlag m.

turpentine ['tɜːpəntaɪn] n Terpentin nt.

turquoise ['tɜːkwɔɪz] n (gem) Türkis m; (colour) Türkis nt // a türkisfarben.

turret ['tʌrɪt] n Turm m.

turtle ['tɜːtl] n Schildkröte f; ~ neck (sweater) n (Pullover m mit) Schildkrötkragen m.

tusk [tʌsk] n Stoßzahn m.

tussle ['tʌsl] n Balgerei f.

tutor ['tjuːtə*] n (teacher) Privatlehrer m; (college instructor) Tutor m; ~ial [tjuː'tɔːrɪəl] n (UNIV) Kolloquium nt, Seminarübung f.

tuxedo [tʌk'siːdəʊ] n (US) Smoking m.

TV ['tiː'viː] n abbr (= television) TV nt.

twang [twæŋ] n scharfe(r) Ton m; (of voice) Näseln nt.

tweezers ['twiːzəz] npl Pinzette f.

twelfth [twelfθ] a zwölfte(r, s).

twelve [twelv] num a zwölf; at ~ o'clock (midday) um 12 Uhr; (midnight) um Null Uhr.

twentieth ['twentɪɪθ] a zwanzigste(r, s).

twenty ['twentɪ] num a zwanzig.

twice [twaɪs] ad zweimal; ~ as much doppelt soviel.

twiddle ['twɪdl] vti: to ~ (with) sth an etw (dat) herumdrehen; to ~ one's thumbs (fig) Däumchen drehen.

twig [twɪg] n dünne(r) Zweig m // vt (col) kapieren, merken.

twilight ['twaɪlaɪt] n Zwielicht nt.

twin [twɪn] n Zwilling m // a Zwillings-; (very similar) Doppel- // vt (towns) zu Partnerstädten machen; ~-bedded room n Zimmer nt mit zwei Einzelbetten.

twine [twaɪn] n Bindfaden m // vi binden.

twinge [twɪndʒ] n stechende(r) Schmerz m, Stechen nt.

twinkle ['twɪŋkl] n Funkeln nt, Blitzen nt // vi funkeln.

twirl [twɜːl] n Wirbel m // vti (herum)wirbeln.

twist [twɪst] n (twisting), Drehung f; (bend) Kurve f // vt (turn) drehen; (make crooked) verbiegen; (distort) ver-

drehen // vi (wind) sich drehen; (curve) sich winden.

twit [twɪt] n (col) Idiot m.

twitch [twɪtʃ] n Zucken nt // vi zucken.

two [tuː] num zwei; to put ~ and ~ together seine Schlüsse ziehen; ~-door a zweitürig; ~-faced a falsch; ~fold a, ad zweifach, doppelt; to increase ~fold verdoppeln; ~-piece a zweiteilig; ~-piece (suit) n Zweiteiler m; ~-piece (swimsuit) n zweiteilige(r) Badeanzug m; ~-seater n (plane, car) Zweisitzer m; ~some n Paar nt; ~-way a (traffic) Gegen-.

tycoon [taɪ'kuːn] n: (business) ~ (Industrie)magnat m.

type [taɪp] n Typ m, Art f; (PRINT) Type f // vti maschineschreiben, tippen; ~-cast a (THEAT, TV) auf eine Rolle festgelegt; ~face n Schrift f; ~script n maschinegeschriebene(r) Text m; ~writer n Schreibmaschine f; ~written a maschinegeschrieben.

typhoid ['taɪfɔɪd] n Typhus m.

typical ['tɪpɪkəl] a, ~ly ad ['tɪpɪkəl, -klɪ] typisch (of für).

typify ['tɪpɪfaɪ] vt typisch sein für.

typing ['taɪpɪŋ] n Maschineschreiben nt.

typist ['taɪpɪst] n Maschinenschreiber(in f) m, Tippse f (col).

tyre, (US) **tire** [taɪə*] n Reifen m; ~ pressure n Reifendruck m.

U

U-bend ['juːbend] n (in pipe) U-Bogen m.

ubiquitous [juː'bɪkwɪtəs] adj überall zu findend; allgegenwärtig.

udder ['ʌdə*] n Euter nt.

UFO ['juːfəʊ] n abbr (= unidentified flying object) UFO nt.

ugh [ɜːh] interj hu.

ugliness ['ʌglɪnəs] n Häßlichkeit f.

ugly ['ʌglɪ] a häßlich; (bad) böse, schlimm.

U.K. n abbr of **United Kingdom**.

ulcer ['ʌlsə*] n Geschwür nt.

Ulster ['ʌlstə*] n Ulster nt.

ulterior [ʌl'tɪərɪə*] a: ~ motive n Hintergedanke m.

ultimate ['ʌltɪmət] a äußerste(r, s), allerletzte(r, s); ~ly ad schließlich, letzten Endes.

ultrasound ['ʌltrə'saʊnd] n (MED) Ultraschall m.

umbilical cord [ʌm'bɪlɪkl kɔːd] n Nabelschnur f.

umbrella [ʌm'brelə] n Schirm m.

umpire ['ʌmpaɪə*] n Schiedsrichter m // vti schiedsrichtern.

umpteen ['ʌmptiːn] num (col) zig; for the ~th time zum X-ten Mal.

UN, UNO n abbr = United Nations

(*Organization*)) UN *f*, UNO *f*.
unable ['ʌn'eɪbl] *a*: to be ~ to do sth
etw nicht tun können.
unaccompanied ['ʌnə'kʌmpənɪd] *a*
ohne Begleitung.
unaccountably ['ʌnə'kaʊntəblɪ] *ad*
unerklärlich.
unaccustomed ['ʌnə'kʌstəmd] *a* nicht
gewöhnt (*to* an +*acc*); (*unusual*) ungewohnt.
unanimous *a*, **~ly** *ad* [juː'nænɪməs, -lɪ]
einmütig; (*vote*) einstimmig.
unarmed [ʌn'ɑːmd] *a* unbewaffnet.
unashamed ['ʌnə'ʃeɪmd] *a* schamlos.
unassuming ['ʌnə'sjuːmɪŋ] *a* bescheiden.
unattached ['ʌnə'tætʃt] *a* ungebunden.
unattended ['ʌnə'tendɪd] *a* (*person*)
unbeaufsichtigt; (*thing*) unbewacht.
unauthorized ['ʌn'ɔːθəraɪzd] *a*
unbefugt.
unavoidable [ʌnə'vɔɪdəbl] *a*
unvermeidlich.
unaware ['ʌnə'wɛə*] *a*: to be ~ of sth
sich (*dat*) einer Sache nicht bewußt sein;
~s *ad* unversehens.
unbalanced [ʌn'bælənst] *a*
unausgeglichen; (*mentally*) gestört.
unbearable [ʌn'bɛərəbl] *a* unerträglich.
unbeatable ['ʌn'biːtəbl] *a* unschlagbar.
unbeknown(st) ['ʌnbɪ'nəʊn(st)] *ad*: ~
to me ohne mein Wissen.
unbelievable [ʌnbɪ'liːvəbl] *a* unglaublich.
unbend ['ʌn'bend] (*irreg: like* **bend**) *vt*
geradebiegen // *vi* aus sich herausgehen.
unbiased ['ʌn'baɪəst] *a* unparteiisch.
unbreakable ['ʌn'breɪkəbl] *a* unzer-
brechlich.
unbridled [ʌn'braɪdld] *a* ungezügelt.
unbroken ['ʌn'brəʊkən] *a* (*period*)
ununterbrochen; (*spirit*) ungebrochen;
(*record*) unübertroffen.
unburden [ʌn'bɜːdn] *vt*: ~ o.s. (jdm)
sein Herz ausschütten.
unbutton ['ʌn'bʌtn] *vt* aufknöpfen.
uncalled-for [ʌn'kɔːldfɔː*] *a* unnötig.
uncanny [ʌn'kænɪ] *a* unheimlich.
unceasing [ʌn'siːsɪŋ] *a* unaufhörlich.
unceremonious ['ʌnserɪ'məʊnɪəs] *a*
(*abrupt, rude*) brüsk; (*exit, departure*)
überstürzt.
uncertain [ʌn'sɜːtn] *a* unsicher;
(*doubtful*) ungewiß; (*unreliable*) unbeständig; (*vague*) undeutlich, vage; **~ty**
n Ungewißheit *f*.
unchanged ['ʌn'tʃeɪndʒd] *a*
unverändert.
unchecked ['ʌn'tʃekt] *a* ungeprüft; (*not
stopped: advance*) ungehindert.
uncivilized ['ʌn'sɪvɪlaɪzd] *a* unzivilisiert.
uncle ['ʌŋkl] *n* Onkel *m*.
uncomfortable [ʌn'kʌmfətəbl] *a*
unbequem, ungemütlich.
uncommon [ʌn'kɒmən] *a* ungewöhn-

lich; (*outstanding*) außergewöhnlich.
uncompromising [ʌn'kɒmprəmaɪzɪŋ]
a kompromißlos, unnachgiebig.
unconcerned [ʌnkən'sɜːnd] *a*
unbekümmert; (*indifferent*) gleichgültig.
unconditional ['ʌnkən'dɪʃənl] *a*
bedingungslos.
uncongenial ['ʌnkən'dʒiːnɪəl] *a*
unangenehm.
unconscious [ʌn'kɒnʃəs] *a* (*MED*)
bewußtlos; (*not meant*) unbeabsichtigt;
the ~ das Unbewußte; **~ly** *ad* unbewußt.
uncontrollable ['ʌnkən'trəʊləbl] *a*
unkontrollierbar, unbändig.
unconventional [ʌnkən'venʃənl] *a*
unkonventionell.
uncouth [ʌn'kuːθ] *a* grob.
uncover [ʌn'kʌvə*] *vt* aufdecken.
undecided ['ʌndɪ'saɪdɪd] *a* unschlüssig.
undeniable [ʌndɪ'naɪəbl] *a* unleugbar.
under ['ʌndə*] *prep* unter // *ad* darunter; ~ there da drunter; ~ repair in
Reparatur; **~-age** *a* minderjährig.
undercarriage ['ʌndəkærɪdʒ] *n* (*Brit
AVIAT*) Fahrgestell *nt*.
undercharge [ʌndə'tʃɑːdʒ] *vt* jdm zu
wenig berechnen.
underclothes ['ʌndəkləʊðz] *npl* Unterwäsche *f*.
undercoat ['ʌndəkəʊt] *n* (*paint*)
Grundierung *f*.
undercover ['ʌndəkʌvə*] *a* Geheim-.
undercurrent ['ʌndəkʌrənt] *n* Unter-
strömung *f*.
undercut ['ʌndəkʌt] *vt* (*irreg: like* **cut**)
unterbieten.
underdeveloped ['ʌndədɪ'veləpt] *a*
Entwicklungs-, unterentwickelt.
underdog ['ʌndədɒg] *n* Unterlegene(r)
mf.
underdone ['ʌndə'dʌn] *a* (*COOK*) nicht
gar, nicht durchgebraten.
underestimate ['ʌndər'estɪmeɪt] *vt*
unterschätzen.
underexposed ['ʌndərɪks'pəʊzd] *a*
unterbelichtet.
underfed ['ʌndə'fed] *a* unterernährt.
underfoot ['ʌndə'fut] *ad* am Boden.
undergo ['ʌndə'gəʊ] *vt* (*irreg: like* **go**)
(*experience*) durchmachen; (*operation,
test*) sich unterziehen (+*dat*).
undergraduate ['ʌndə'grædjʊət] *n*
Student(in *f*) *m*.
underground ['ʌndəgraʊnd] *n* U-Bahn *f*
// *a* Untergrund-.
undergrowth ['ʌndəgrəʊθ] *n* Gestrüpp
nt, Unterholz *nt*.
underhand(ed) ['ʌndə'hænd(ɪd)] *a* hin-
terhältig.
underlie [ʌndə'laɪ] *vt* (*irreg: like* **lie**)
(*form the basis of*) zugrundeliegen
(+*dat*).
underline [ʌndə'laɪn] *vt* unterstreichen;
(*emphasize*) betonen.
underling ['ʌndəlɪŋ] *n* Handlanger *m*.

undermine [ʌndə'maɪn] vt untergraben.
underneath ['ʌndə'niːθ] ad darunter // prep unter.
underpaid [ʌndə'peɪd] a unterbezahlt.
underpants ['ʌndəpænts] npl Unterhose f.
underpass ['ʌndəpɑːs] n (Brit) Unterführung f.
underprivileged ['ʌndə'prɪvɪlɪdʒd] a benachteiligt, unterpriviligiert.
underrate [ʌndə'reɪt] vt unterschätzen.
undershirt ['ʌndəʃɜːt] n (US) Unterhemd nt.
undershorts ['ʌndəʃɔːts] npl (US) Unterhose f.
underside ['ʌndəsaɪd] n Unterseite f.
underskirt ['ʌndəskɜːt] n (Brit) Unterrock m.
understand [ʌndə'stænd] vti (irreg: like stand) verstehen; I ~ that ... ich habe gehört, daß ...; am I to ~ that ...? soll das (etwa) heißen, daß ...?; what do you ~ by that? was verstehen Sie darunter?; it is understood that ... es wurde vereinbart, daß ...; to make o.s. understood sich verständlich machen; is that understood? ist das klar?; ~able a verständlich; ~ing n Verständnis nt // a verständnisvoll.
understood [ʌndə'stʊd] pt, pp of **understand** // a klar; (implied) angenommen.
understudy ['ʌndəstʌdɪ] n Ersatz-(schau)spieler(in f) m.
undertake [ʌndə'teɪk] (irreg: like take) vt unternehmen // vi: to ~ to do sth sich verpflichten, etw zu tun.
undertaker ['ʌndəteɪkə*] n Leichenbestatter m.
undertaking [ʌndə'teɪkɪŋ] n (enterprise) Unternehmen nt; (promise) Verpflichtung f.
undertone ['ʌndətəʊn] n: in an ~ mit gedämpfter Stimme.
underwater ['ʌndə'wɔːtə*] ad unter Wasser // a Unterwasser-.
underwear ['ʌndəwɛə*] n Unterwäsche f.
underworld ['ʌndəwɜːld] n (of crime) Unterwelt f.
underwriter ['ʌndəraɪtə*] n Assekurant m.
undesirable [ʌndɪ'zaɪərəbl] a unerwünscht.
undies ['ʌndɪz] npl (col) (Damen)-unterwäsche f.
undisputed ['ʌndɪs'pjuːtɪd] a unbestritten.
undo ['ʌn'duː] vt (irreg: like do) (unfasten) öffnen, aufmachen; (work) zunichte machen; ~ing n Verderben nt.
undoubted [ʌn'daʊtɪd] a unbezweifelt; ~ly ad zweifellos, ohne Zweifel.
undress ['ʌn'dres] vti (sich) ausziehen.
undue ['ʌn'djuː] a übermäßig.

undulating ['ʌndjʊleɪtɪŋ] a wellenförmig; (country) wellig.
unduly ['ʌn'djuːlɪ] ad übermäßig.
unearth ['ʌn'ɜːθ] vt (dig up) ausgraben; (discover) ans Licht bringen.
unearthly [ʌn'ɜːθlɪ] a (hour) nachtschlafen.
uneasy [ʌn'iːzɪ] a (worried) unruhig; (feeling) ungut.
uneconomic(al) ['ʌniːkə'nɒmɪk(əl)] a unwirtschaftlich.
uneducated ['ʌn'edjʊkeɪtɪd] a ungebildet.
unemployed [ʌnɪm'plɔɪd] a arbeitslos; the ~ die Arbeitslosen pl.
unemployment ['ʌnɪm'plɔɪmənt] n Arbeitslosigkeit f.
unending [ʌn'endɪŋ] a endlos.
unerring [ʌn'ɜːrɪŋ] a unfehlbar.
uneven [ʌn'iːvən] a (surface) uneben; (quality) ungleichmäßig.
unexpected a, ~ly ad [ʌnɪk'spektɪd,-lɪ] unerwartet.
unfailing [ʌn'feɪlɪŋ] a nie versagend.
unfair ['ʌn'fɛə*] a ungerecht, unfair.
unfaithful ['ʌn'feɪθfʊl] a untreu.
unfamiliar [ʌnfə'mɪlɪə*] a ungewohnt; (person, subject) unbekannt.
unfashionable [ʌn'fæʃnəbl] a unmodern; (area, hotel etc) nicht in Mode.
unfasten ['ʌn'fɑːsn] vt öffnen, aufmachen.
unfavourable, (US) **unfavorable** ['ʌn'feɪvərəbl] a ungünstig.
unfeeling [ʌn'fiːlɪŋ] a gefühllos, kalt.
unfinished ['ʌn'fɪnɪʃt] a unvollendet.
unfit ['ʌn'fɪt] a ungeeignet (for zu, für); (in bad health) nicht fit.
unfold [ʌn'fəʊld] vt entfalten; (paper) auseinanderfalten // vi (develop) sich entfalten.
unforeseen ['ʌnfɔː'siːn] a unvorhergesehen.
unforgettable [ʌnfə'getəbl] a unvergeßlich.
unforgivable [ʌnfə'gɪvəbl] a unverzeihlich.
unfortunate [ʌn'fɔːtʃnət] a unglücklich, bedauerlich; ~ly ad leider.
unfounded ['ʌn'faʊndəd] a unbegründet.
unfriendly ['ʌn'frendlɪ] a unfreundlich.
ungainly [ʌn'geɪnlɪ] a linkisch.
ungodly [ʌn'gɒdlɪ] a (hour) nachtschlafend; (row) heillos.
ungrateful [ʌn'greɪtfʊl] a undankbar.
unhappiness [ʌn'hæpɪnəs] n Unglück nt, Unglückseligkeit f.
unhappy [ʌn'hæpɪ] a unglücklich; ~ with (arrangements etc) unzufrieden mit.
unharmed ['ʌn'hɑːmd] a wohlbehalten, unversehrt.
unhealthy [ʌn'helθɪ] a ungesund.

unheard-of [ʌn'hɜ:dɒv] *a* unerhört.

unhook [ʌn'hʊk] *vt (from wall)* vom Haken nehmen; *(dress)* loshaken.

unhurt ['ʌn'hɜ:t] *a* unverletzt.

unidentified ['ʌnaɪ'dentɪfaɪd] *a* unbekannt, nicht identifiziert.

uniform ['ju:nɪfɔ:m] *n* Uniform *f* // *a* einheitlich; **~ity** [ju:nɪ'fɔ:mɪtɪ] *n* Einheitlichkeit *f*.

unify ['ju:nɪfaɪ] *vt* vereinigen.

unilateral ['ju:nɪ'lætərəl] *a* einseitig.

uninhabited [ʌnɪn'hæbɪtɪd] *a* unbewohnt.

unintentional ['ʌnɪn'tenʃənl] *a* unabsichtlich.

union ['ju:njən] *n (uniting)* Vereinigung *f*; *(alliance)* Bund *m*, Union *f*; *(trade ~)* Gewerkschaft *f*; **U~ Jack** *n* Union Jack *m*.

unique [ju:'ni:k] *a* einzig(artig).

unison ['ju:nɪzn] *n* Einstimmigkeit *f*; **in ~** einstimmig.

unit ['ju:nɪt] *n* Einheit *f*; **kitchen ~** Küchenelement *nt*.

unite [ju:'naɪt] *vt* vereinigen // *vi* sich vereinigen; **~d** *a* vereinigt; *(together)* vereint; **U~d Kingdom (U.K.)** *n* Vereinigtes Königreich; **U~d Nations (Organization) (UN, UNO)** *n* Vereinte Nationen *pl*; **U~d States (of America) (US, USA)** *n* Vereinigte Staaten *pl* (von Amerika) (US, USA *f*).

unit trust ['ju:nɪt'trʌst] *n (Brit)* Treuhandgesellschaft *f*.

unity ['ju:nɪtɪ] *n* Einheit *f*; *(agreement)* Einigkeit *f*.

universal [ju:nɪ'vɜ:səl] *a* allgemein.

universe ['ju:nɪvɜ:s] *n* (Welt) all *nt*.

university [ju:nɪ'vɜ:sɪtɪ] *n* Universität *f*.

unjust ['ʌn'dʒʌst] *a* ungerecht.

unkempt ['ʌn'kempt] *a* ungepflegt.

unkind [ʌn'kaɪnd] *a* unfreundlich.

unknown ['ʌn'nəʊn] *a* unbekannt *(to dat)*.

unlawful [ʌn'lɔ:fʊl] *a* illegal.

unleash ['ʌn'li:ʃ] *vt* entfesseln.

unless [ən'les] *cj* wenn nicht, es sei denn ...; **~ he comes** es sei denn, er kommt; **~ otherwise stated** sofern nicht anders angegeben.

unlike ['ʌn'laɪk] *a* unähnlich // *prep* im Gegensatz zu.

unlimited [ʌn'lɪmɪtɪd] *a* unbegrenzt.

unlisted [ʌn'lɪstɪd] *a (US)* nicht im Telefonbuch stehend.

unload ['ʌn'ləʊd] *vt* entladen.

unlock ['ʌn'lɒk] *vt* aufschließen.

unlucky ['ʌn'lʌkɪ] *a* unglücklich; *(person)* unglückselig; **to be ~** Pech haben.

unmarried ['ʌn'mærɪd] *a* unverheiratet, ledig.

unmask ['ʌn'mɑ:sk] *vt* entlarven.

unmistakable ['ʌnmɪs'teɪkəbl] *a* unverkennbar.

unmitigated [ʌn'mɪtɪgeɪtɪd] *a* ungemildert, ganz.

unnatural [ʌn'nætʃrəl] *a* unnatürlich.

unnecessary ['ʌn'nesəsərɪ] *a* unnötig.

unnoticed [ʌn'nəʊtɪst] *a*: **to go ~** unbemerkt bleiben.

UNO ['ju:nəʊ] *n abbr of* **United Nations Organization.**

unobtainable ['ʌnəb'teɪnəbl] *a*: **this number is ~** kein Anschluß unter dieser Nummer.

unobtrusive [ʌnəb'tru:sɪv] *a* unauffällig.

unofficial [ʌnə'fɪʃl] *a* inoffiziell.

unpack ['ʌn'pæk] *vti* auspacken.

unpalatable [ʌn'pælətəbl] *a (truth)* bitter.

unparalleled [ʌn'pærəleld] *a* beispiellos.

unpleasant [ʌn'pleznt] *a* unangenehm.

unplug ['ʌn'plʌg] *vt* den Stecker herausziehen von.

unprecedented [ʌn'presɪdəntɪd] *a* beispiellos.

unpredictable [ʌnprɪ'dɪktəbl] *a* unvorhersehbar; *(weather, person)* unberechenbar.

unprofessional [ʌnprə'feʃənl] *a* unprofessionell.

unqualified ['ʌn'kwɒlɪfaɪd] *a (success)* uneingeschränkt, voll; *(person)* unqualifiziert.

unquestionably [ʌn'kwestʃənəblɪ] *ad* fraglos.

unravel [ʌn'rævəl] *vt (disentangle)* auffasern, entwirren; *(solve)* lösen.

unreal ['ʌn'rɪəl] *a* unwirklich.

unrealistic [ʌnrɪə'lɪstɪk] *a* unrealistisch.

unreasonable [ʌn'ri:znəbl] *a* unvernünftig; *(demand)* übertrieben.

unrelated [ʌnrɪ'leɪtɪd] *a* ohne Beziehung; *(family)* nicht verwandt.

unrelenting ['ʌnrɪ'lentɪŋ] *a* unerbittlich.

unreliable [ʌnrɪ'laɪəbl] *a* unzuverlässig.

unremitting [ʌnrɪ'mɪtɪŋ] *a (efforts, attempts)* unermüdlich.

unreservedly [ʌnrɪzɜ:'vɪdlɪ] *ad* offen; *(believe, trust)* uneingeschränkt; *(cry)* rückhaltlos.

unrest [ʌn'rest] *n (discontent)* Unruhe *f*; *(fighting)* Unruhen *pl*.

unroll ['ʌn'rəʊl] *vt* aufrollen.

unruly [ʌn'ru:lɪ] *a (child)* undiszipliniert; schwer lenkbar.

unsafe ['ʌn'seɪf] *a* nicht sicher.

unsaid ['ʌn'sed] *a*: **to leave sth ~** etw ungesagt sein lassen.

unsatisfactory ['ʌnsætɪs'fæktərɪ] *a* unbefriedigend; unzulänglich.

unsavoury, *(US)* **unsavory** ['ʌn'seɪvərɪ] *a (fig)* widerwärtig.

unscathed [ʌn'skeɪðd] *a* unversehrt.

unscrew ['ʌn'skru:] *vt* aufschrauben.

unscrupulous [ʌn'skru:pjʊləs] *a* skrupellos.

unsettled ['ʌn'setld] *a (person)* rastlos;

(weather) wechselhaft.
unshaven [ʌn'ʃeɪvn] *a* unrasiert.
unsightly [ʌn'saɪtlɪ] *a* unansehnlich.
unskilled ['ʌn'skɪld] *a* ungelernt.
unspeakable [ʌn'spiːkəbl] *a* *(joy)* unsagbar; *(crime)* scheußlich.
unstable [ʌn'steɪbl] *a* instabil; *(mentally)* labil.
unsteady [ʌn'stedɪ] *a* unsicher; *(growth)* unregelmäßig.
unstuck [ʌn'stʌk] *a*: **to come ~** *(lit)* sich lösen; *(fig)* ins Wasser fallen.
unsuccessful ['ʌnsək'sesfʊl] *a* erfolglos.
unsuitable ['ʌn'suːtəbl] *a* unpassend.
unsuspecting ['ʌnsəs'pektɪŋ] *a* nichtsahnend.
unsympathetic ['ʌnsɪmpə'θetɪk] *a* gefühllos; *(response)* abweisend; *(unlikeable)* unsympathisch.
untapped ['ʌn'tæpt] *a* *(resources)* ungenützt.
unthinkable [ʌn'θɪŋkəbl] *a* unvorstellbar.
untidy [ʌn'taɪdɪ] *a* unordentlich.
untie ['ʌn'taɪ] *vt* aufschnüren.
until [ən'tɪl] *prep, cj* bis; **~ he comes** bis er kommt; **~ then** bis dann.
untimely [ʌn'taɪmlɪ] *a* *(death)* vorzeitig.
untold ['ʌn'təʊld] *a* unermeßlich.
untoward [ʌntə'wɔːd] *a* widrig.
unused ['ʌn'juːzd] *a* unbenutzt.
unusual [ʌn'juːʒʊəl] *a* ungewöhnlich.
unveil [ʌn'veɪl] *vt* enthüllen.
unwavering [ʌn'weɪvərɪŋ] *a* standhaft, unerschütterlich.
unwelcome [ʌn'welkəm] *a* *(at a bad time)* unwillkommen; *(unpleasant)* unerfreulich.
unwell ['ʌn'wel] *a*: **to feel** *or* **be ~** sich nicht wohl fühlen.
unwieldy [ʌn'wiːldɪ] *a* sperrig.
unwilling ['ʌn'wɪlɪŋ] *a*: **to be ~ to do sth** nicht bereit sein, etw zu tun; **~ly** *ad* widerwillig.
unwind ['ʌn'waɪnd] *(irreg: like wind)* *vt* *(lit)* abwickeln // *vi* *(relax)* sich entspannen.
unwise [ʌn'waɪz] *a* unklug.
unwitting [ʌn'wɪtɪŋ] *a* unwissentlich.
unworkable [ʌn'wɜːkəbl] *a* *(plan)* undurchführbar.
unworthy [ʌn'wɜːðɪ] *a* *(person)* nicht wert *(of gen)*.
unwrap ['ʌn'ræp] *vt* auspacken.
unwritten ['ʌn'rɪtn] *a* ungeschrieben.
up [ʌp] ◆ *prep*: **to be ~ sth** oben auf etw *(dat)* sein; **to go ~ sth** (auf) etw *(acc)* hinauf gehen; **go ~ that road** gehen Sie die Straße hinauf
◆ *ad* **1** *(upwards, higher)* oben; **put it a bit higher ~** stell es etwas weiter nach oben; **~ there** da oben, dort oben; **~ above** hoch oben
2: **to be ~** *(out of bed)* auf; *(prices, level)* gestiegen; *(building, tent)* stehen

3: **~ to** *(as far as)* bis; **~ to now** bis jetzt
4: **to be ~ to** *(depending on)*: **it's ~ to you** das hängt von dir ab; **it's not ~ to me to decide** die Entscheidung liegt nicht bei mir; *(equal to)*: **he's not ~ to it** *(job, task etc)* er ist dem nicht gewachsen; **his work is not ~ to the required standard** seine Arbeit entspricht nicht dem geforderten Niveau; *(col: be doing)*: **what is he ~ to?** *(showing disapproval, suspicion)* was führt er im Schilde?
◆ **~s and downs** *npl* *(in life, career)* Höhen und Tiefen *pl*.
upbringing ['ʌpbrɪŋɪŋ] *n* Erziehung *f*.
update [ʌp'deɪt] *vt* auf den neuesten Stand bringen.
upgrade [ʌp'greɪd] *vt* höher einstufen.
upheaval [ʌp'hiːvəl] *n* Umbruch *m*.
uphill ['ʌp'hɪl] *a* ansteigend; *(fig)* mühsam // *ad*: **to go ~** bergauf gehen/fahren.
uphold [ʌp'həʊld] *vt* *(irreg: like hold)* unterstützen.
upholstery [ʌp'həʊlstərɪ] *n* Polster *nt*; Polsterung *f*.
upkeep ['ʌpkiːp] *n* Instandhaltung *f*.
upon [ə'pɒn] *prep* auf.
upper ['ʌpə*] *n* *(on shoe)* Oberleder *nt* // *a* obere(r, s), höhere(r, s); **to have the ~ hand** die Oberhand haben; **~-class** *a* vornehm; **~most** *a* oberste(r, s), höchste(r, s); **what was ~most in my mind** was mich in erster Linie beschäftigte.
upright ['ʌpraɪt] *a* aufrecht.
uprising ['ʌp'raɪzɪŋ] *n* Aufstand *m*.
uproar ['ʌprɔː*] *n* Aufruhr *m*.
uproot [ʌp'ruːt] *vt* ausreißen.
upset ['ʌpset] *n* Aufregung *f* // *vt* [ʌp'set] *(irreg: like set)* *(overturn)* umwerfen; *(disturb)* aufregen, bestürzen; *(plans)* durcheinanderbringen // *a* [ʌp'set] *(person)* aufgeregt; *(stomach)* verdorben.
upshot ['ʌpʃɒt] *n* (End)ergebnis *nt*.
upside-down ['ʌpsaɪd'daʊn] *ad* verkehrt herum; *(fig)* drunter und drüber.
upstairs ['ʌp'steəz] *ad* oben; *(go)* nach oben // *a* *(room)* obere(r, s), Ober- // *n* obere(s) Stockwerk *nt*.
upstart ['ʌpstɑːt] *n* Emporkömmling *m*.
upstream ['ʌp'striːm] *ad* stromaufwärts.
uptake ['ʌpteɪk] *n*: **to be quick on the ~** schnell begreifen; **to be slow on the ~** schwer von Begriff sein.
uptight ['ʌp'taɪt] *a* *(col: nervous)* nervös; *(: inhibited)* verklemmt.
up-to-date ['ʌptə'deɪt] *a* *(clothes)* modisch, modern; *(information)* neueste(r, s); **to bring sth up to date** etw auf den neuesten Stand bringen.
upturn ['ʌptɜːn] *n* Aufschwung *m*.
upward ['ʌpwəd] *a* nach oben gerichtet; **~(s)** *ad* aufwärts.
uranium [juə'reɪnɪəm] *n* Uran *nt*.

urban ['ɜːbən] a städtisch, Stadt-.
urbane [ɜː'beɪn] a höflich.
urchin ['ɜːtʃɪn] n (boy) Schlingel m; (sea ~) Seeigel m.
urge [ɜːdʒ] n Drang m // vt: to ~ sb to do sth jdn (dazu) drängen, etw zu tun.
urgency ['ɜːdʒənsɪ] n Dringlichkeit f.
urgent ['ɜːdʒənt] a dringend.
urinal ['juərɪnl] n (MED) Urinflasche f; (public) Pissoir nt.
urinate ['juərɪneɪt] vi urinieren.
urine ['juərɪn] n Urin m, Harn m.
urn [ɜːn] n Urne f; (tea ~) Teemaschine f.
us [ʌs] pron uns; see also **me**.
US, USA n abbr of **United States (of America)**.
usage ['juːzɪdʒ] n Gebrauch m; (esp LING) Sprachgebrauch m.
use [juːs] n (employment) Gebrauch m; (point) Zweck m // vt [juːz] gebrauchen; in ~ in Gebrauch; out of ~ außer Gebrauch; to be of ~ nützlich sein; it's no ~ es hat keinen Zweck; what's the ~? was soll's?; ~d to [juːst] gewöhnt an (+acc); she ~d to live here sie hat früher mal hier gewohnt; ~ up [juːz] vt aufbrauchen, verbrauchen; ~d [juːzd] a (car) Gebraucht-; ~ful a nützlich; ~fulness n Nützlichkeit f; ~less a nutzlos, unnütz; ~r ['juːzə*] n Benutzer m; ~r-friendly a (computer) benutzerfreundlich.
usher ['ʌʃə*] n Platzanweiser m; ~ette [ʌʃə'ret] n Platzanweiserin f.
USSR n: the ~ die UdSSR.
usual ['juːʒuəl] a gewöhnlich, üblich; as ~ wie üblich; ~ly ad gewöhnlich.
usurp [juː'zɜːp] vt an sich reißen.
utensil [juː'tensl] n Gerät nt; kitchen ~s Küchengeräte pl.
utilitarian [juːtɪlɪ'teərɪən] a Nützlichkeits-.
utility [juː'tɪlɪtɪ] n (usefulness) Nützlichkeit f; (also public ~) öffentliche(r) Versorgungsbetrieb m; ~ room n Hauswirtschaftsraum m.
utilize ['juːtɪlaɪz] vt benützen.
utmost ['ʌtməʊst] a äußerste(r, s) // n: to do one's ~ sein möglichstes tun.
utter ['ʌtə*] a äußerste(r, s) höchste(r, s), völlig // vt äußern, aussprechen; ~ance n Äußerung f; ~ly ad äußerst, absolut, völlig.
U-turn ['juː'tɜːn] n (AUT) Kehrtwendung f.

V

v. abbr of **verse; versus; volt; vide**.
vacancy ['veɪkənsɪ] n (Brit: job) offene Stelle f; (room) freies Zimmer nt.
vacant ['veɪkənt] a leer; (unoccupied) frei; (house) leerstehend, unbewohnt;

(stupid) (gedanken)leer; ~ **lot** n (US) unbebaute(s) Grundstück nt.
vacate [və'keɪt] vt (seat) frei machen; (room) räumen.
vacation [və'keɪʃən] n Ferien pl, Urlaub m; ~**ist** n (US) Ferienreisende(r) mf.
vaccinate ['væksɪneɪt] vt impfen.
vaccine ['væksiːn] n Impfstoff m.
vacuum ['vækjʊm] n Vakuum nt; ~ **bottle** (US), ~ **flask** (Brit) n Thermosflasche f; ~ **cleaner** n Staubsauger m; ~-**packed** a vakuumversiegelt.
vagina [və'dʒaɪnə] n Scheide f.
vagrant ['veɪgrənt] n Landstreicher m.
vague [veɪg] a vage; (absent-minded) geistesabwesend; ~**ly** ad unbestimmt, vage.
vain [veɪn] a eitel; (attempt) vergeblich; in ~ vergebens, umsonst.
valentine ['væləntaɪn] n (also: ~ card) Valentinsgruß m.
valet ['væleɪ] n Kammerdiener m.
valiant a, ~**ly** ad ['væliənt, -lɪ] tapfer.
valid ['vælɪd] a gültig; (argument) stichhaltig; (objection) berechtigt; ~**ity** [və'lɪdɪtɪ] n Gültigkeit f.
valley ['vælɪ] n Tal nt.
valour, (US) **valor** ['vælə*] n Tapferkeit f.
valuable ['væljʊəbl] a wertvoll; (time) kostbar; ~s npl Wertsachen pl.
valuation [vælju'eɪʃən] n (FIN) Schätzung f; Beurteilung f.
value ['væljuː] n Wert m; (usefulness) Nutzen m // vt (prize) (hoch)schätzen, werthalten; (estimate) schätzen; ~ **added tax** (VAT) n (Brit) Mehrwertsteuer f (MwSt); ~**d** a (hoch)geschätzt.
valve [vælv] n Ventil nt; (BIOL) Klappe f; (RAD) Röhre f.
van [væn] n Lieferwagen m (Brit: RAIL) Waggon m.
vandalize ['vændəlaɪz] vt mutwillig beschädigen.
vanguard ['vængɑːd] n (fig) Spitze f.
vanilla [və'nɪlə] n Vanille f.
vanish ['vænɪʃ] vi verschwinden.
vanity ['vænɪtɪ] n Eitelkeit f; ~ **case** n Schminkkoffer m.
vantage ['vɑːntɪdʒ] n: ~ **point** gute(r) Aussichtspunkt m.
vapour, (US) **vapor** ['veɪpə*] n (mist) Dunst m; (gas) Dampf m.
variable ['veərɪəbl] a wechselhaft, veränderlich; (speed, height) regulierbar.
variance ['veərɪəns] n: to be at ~ (with) nicht übereinstimmen (mit).
variation [veərɪ'eɪʃən] n Variation f; (of temperature, prices) Schwankung f.
varicose ['værɪkəʊs] a: ~ **veins** npl Krampfadern pl.
varied ['veərɪd] a unterschiedlich; (life) abwechslungsreich.
variety [və'raɪətɪ] n (difference)

Abwechslung f; (varied collection) Vielfalt f; (COMM) Auswahl f; (sort) Sorte f, Art f; **~ show** n Varieté d.
various ['veərɪəs] a verschieden; (several) mehrere.
varnish ['vɑːnɪʃ] n Lack m; (on pottery) Glasur f // vt lackieren.
vary ['veərɪ] vt (alter) verändern; (give variety to) abwechslungsreicher gestalten // vi sich (ver)ändern; (prices) schwanken; (weather) unterschiedlich sein.
vase [vɑːz] n Vase f.
Vaseline ['væsɪliːn] n ® Vaseline f.
vast [vɑːst] a weit, groß, riesig.
VAT [væt] n abbr of **Value Added Tax.**
vat [væt] n große(s) Faß nt.
vault [vɔːlt] n (of roof) Gewölbe nt; (tomb) Gruft f; (in bank) Tresorraum m; (leap) Sprung m // vt (also: ~ over) überspringen.
vaunted ['vɔːntɪd] a: **much-~** vielgerühmt.
VCR n abbr of **video cassette recorder.**
VD n abbr of **venereal disease.**
VDU n abbr of **visual display unit.**
veal [viːl] n Kalbfleisch nt.
veer [vɪə*] vi sich drehen; (of car) ausscheren.
vegetable ['vedʒətəbl] n Gemüse nt // a Gemüse-; **~s** pl Gemüse nt.
vegetarian [vedʒɪ'tɛərɪən] n Vegetarier(in f) m // a vegetarisch.
vegetate ['vedʒɪteɪt] vi (dahin)-vegetieren.
vehemence ['viːɪməns] n Heftigkeit f.
vehement ['viːɪmənt] a heftig.
vehicle ['viːɪkl] n Fahrzeug nt; (fig) Mittel nt.
veil [veɪl] n (lit, fig) Schleier m // vt verschleiern.
vein [veɪn] n Ader f; (mood) Stimmung f.
velocity [vɪ'lɒsɪtɪ] n Geschwindigkeit f.
velvet ['velvɪt] n Samt m // a Samt-.
vendetta [ven'detə] n Fehde f; (in family) Blutrache f.
vending machine ['vendɪŋməʃiːn] n Automat m.
vendor ['vendɔː*] n Verkäufer m.
veneer [və'nɪə*] n (lit) Furnier(holz) nt; (fig) äußere(r) Anstrich m.
venereal [vɪ'nɪərɪəl] a: **~ disease (VD)** Geschlechtskrankheit f.
Venetian blind [vɪ'niːʃən-] n Jalousie f.
vengeance ['vendʒəns] n Rache f; **with a ~** gewaltig.
venison ['venɪsn] n Reh(fleisch) nt.
venom ['venəm] n Gift nt.
vent [vent] n Öffnung f; (in coat) Schlitz m; (fig) Ventil nt // vt (emotion) abreagieren.
ventilate ['ventɪleɪt] vt belüften.
ventilator ['ventɪleɪtə*] n Ventilator m.

ventriloquist [ven'trɪləkwɪst] n Bauchredner m.
venture ['ventʃə*] n Unternehmung f, Projekt nt // vt wagen; (life) aufs Spiel setzen // vi sich wagen.
venue ['venjuː] n Schauplatz m.
verb [vɜːb] n Zeitwort nt, Verb nt; **~al** a (spoken) mündlich; (translation) wörtlich; (of a verb) verbal, Verbal-; **~ally** ad mündlich; (as a verb) verbal.
verbatim [vɜː'beɪtɪm] ad Wort für Wort // a wortwörtlich.
verbose [vɜː'bəus] a wortreich.
verdict ['vɜːdɪkt] n Urteil nt.
verge [vɜːdʒ] n (Brit) Rand m; **'soft ~s'** (Brit AUT) 'Seitenstreifen nicht befahrbar'; **on the ~ of doing sth** im Begriff, etw zu tun // vi: **~ on** grenzen an (+acc).
verify ['verɪfaɪ] vt (über)prüfen; (confirm) bestätigen; (theory) beweisen.
veritable ['verɪtəbl] a wirklich, echt.
vermin ['vɜːmɪn] npl Ungeziefer nt.
vermouth ['vɜːməθ] n Wermut m.
vernacular [və'nækjulə*] n Landessprache f.
versatile ['vɜːsətaɪl] a vielseitig.
versatility [vɜːsə'tɪlɪtɪ] n Vielseitigkeit f.
verse [vɜːs] n (poetry) Poesie f; (stanza) Strophe f; (of Bible) Vers m; **in ~** in Versform.
versed [vɜːst] a: **(well-)~ in** bewandert in (+dat), beschlagen in (+dat).
version ['vɜːʃən] n Version f; (of car) Modell nt.
versus ['vɜːsəs] prep gegen.
vertebra ['vɜːtɪbrə] n, pl **~e** [-briː] (Rücken)wirbel m.
vertebrate ['vɜːtɪbrət] a (animal) Wirbel-.
vertical ['vɜːtɪkəl] a senkrecht.
vertigo ['vɜːtɪgəu] n Schwindel m.
verve [vɜːv] n Schwung m.
very ['verɪ] ad sehr // a (extreme) äußerste(r, s); **the ~ book which** genau das Buch, welches; **the ~ last** der/die/das allerletzte; **at the ~ least** allerwenigstens; **~ much** sehr.
vessel ['vesl] n (ship) Schiff nt; (container) Gefäß nt.
vest [vest] n (Brit) Unterhemd nt; (US: waistcoat) Weste f; **~ed interests** npl finanzielle Beteiligung f; (people) finanziell Beteiligte pl; (fig) persönliche(s) Interesse nt.
vestige ['vestɪdʒ] n Spur f.
vestry ['vestrɪ] n Sakristei f.
vet [vet] n abbr (= veterinary surgeon) Tierarzt m/-ärztin f // vt genau prüfen.
veterinary ['vetrɪnərɪ] a Veterinär-; **~ surgeon**, (US) **veterinarian** n Tierarzt m/-ärztin f.
veto ['viːtəu] n, pl **~es** Veto nt // vt sein Veto einlegen gegen.
vex [veks] vt ärgern; **~ed** a verärgert;

~ed question umstrittene Frage f.

VHF abbr (= very high frequency) UKW f.

via ['vaɪə] prep über (+acc).

viable ['vaɪəbl] a (plan) durchführbar; (company) rentabel.

vibrant ['vaɪbrənt] a (lively) lebhaft; (bright) leuchtend; (full of emotion: voice) bebend.

vibrate [vaɪ'breɪt] vi zittern, beben, (machine, string) vibrieren.

vibration [vaɪ'breɪʃən] n Schwingung f; (of machine) Vibrieren nt.

vicar ['vɪkə*] n Pfarrer m; **~age** n Pfarrhaus nt.

vicarious [vɪ'kɛərɪəs] a nachempfunden.

vice [vaɪs] n (evil) Laster nt; (TECH) Schraubstock m // pref: **~-chairman** n stellvertretende(r) Vorsitzende(r) m; **~-president** n Vizepräsident m.

vice squad n ≈ Sittenpolizei f.

vice versa ['vaɪsɪ'vɜːsə] ad umgekehrt.

vicinity [vɪ'sɪnɪtɪ] n Umgebung f; (closeness) Nähe f.

vicious ['vɪʃəs] a gemein, böse; ~ **circle** n Teufelskreis m.

victim ['vɪktɪm] n Opfer nt; **~ize** vt benachteiligen.

victor ['vɪktə*] n Sieger m.

Victorian [vɪk'tɔːrɪən] a viktorianisch; (fig) (sitten)streng.

victorious [vɪk'tɔːrɪəs] a siegreich.

victory ['vɪktərɪ] n Sieg m.

video ['vɪdɪəʊ] a Fernseh-, Bild- // n (~ film) Video nt; (also: ~ **cassette**) Videocassette f; (also: ~ **cassette recorder**) Videorekorder m; (also: ~ **tape** n Videoband nt.

vie [vaɪ] vi wetteifern.

Vienna [vɪ'enə] n Wien nt.

view [vjuː] n (sight) Sicht f, Blick m; (scene) Aussicht f; (opinion) Ansicht f; (intention) Absicht f // vt (situation) betrachten; (house) besichtigen; **to have sth in** ~ etw beabsichtigen; **on** ~ ausgestellt; **in** ~ **of** wegen (+gen), angesichts (+gen); **~er** n (viewfinder) Sucher m; (Phot: small projector) Gucki m; (TV) Fernsehzuschauer(in f) m; **~finder** n Sucher m; **~point** n Standpunkt m.

vigil ['vɪdʒɪl] n (Nacht)wache f; **~ance** n Wachsamkeit f; **~ant** a wachsam.

vigorous a, **~ly** ad ['vɪgərəs, -lɪ] kräftig; (protest) energisch, heftig.

vigour, (US) **vigor** ['vɪgə*] n Vitalität f; (of protest) Heftigkeit f.

vile [vaɪl] a (mean) gemein; (foul) abscheulich.

vilify ['vɪlɪfaɪ] vt verleumden.

villa ['vɪlə] n Villa f.

village ['vɪlɪdʒ] n Dorf nt; **~r** n Dorfbewohner(in f) m.

villain ['vɪlən] n Schurke m.

vindicate ['vɪndɪkeɪt] vt rechtfertigen.

vindictive [vɪn'dɪktɪv] a nachtragend,

rachsüchtig.

vine [vaɪn] n Rebstock m, Rebe f.

vinegar ['vɪnɪgə*] n Essig m.

vineyard ['vɪnjəd] n Weinberg m.

vintage ['vɪntɪdʒ] n (of wine) Jahrgang m; ~ **wine** n edle(r) Wein m.

viola [vɪ'əʊlə] n Bratsche f.

violate ['vaɪəleɪt] vt (law) übertreten; (rights, rule, neutrality) verletzen; (sanctity, woman) schänden.

violation [vaɪə'leɪʃən] n Verletzung f; Übertretung f.

violence ['vaɪələns] n (force) Heftigkeit f; (brutality) Gewalttätigkeit f.

violent a, **~ly** ad ['vaɪələnt, -lɪ] (strong) heftig; (brutal) brutal; (contrast) kraß; (death) gewaltsam.

violet ['vaɪələt] n Veilchen nt // a veilchenblau, violett.

violin [vaɪə'lɪn] n Geige f, Violine f; **~ist** n Geiger(in f) m.

VIP n abbr (= very important person) VIP m.

virgin ['vɜːdʒɪn] n Jungfrau f // a jungfräulich, unberührt; **the Blessed V~** die heilige Jungfrau Maria; **~ity** [vɜː'dʒɪnɪtɪ] n Unschuld f.

Virgo ['vɜːgəʊ] n Jungfrau f.

virile ['vɪraɪl] a männlich.

virility [vɪ'rɪlɪtɪ] n Männlichkeit f.

virtually ['vɜːtjʊəlɪ] ad praktisch, fast.

virtue ['vɜːtjuː] n (moral goodness) Tugend f; (good quality) Vorteil m, Vorzug m; **by** ~ **of** aufgrund (+gen).

virtuous ['vɜːtjʊəs] a tugendhaft.

virulent ['vɪrjʊlənt] a (poisonous) bösartig; (bitter) scharf, geharnischt.

virus ['vaɪərəs] n Virus m.

visa ['viːzə] n Visum nt.

vis-à-vis ['viːzəviː] prep gegenüber.

viscous ['vɪskəs] a zähflüssig.

visibility [vɪzɪ'bɪlɪtɪ] n (MET) Sicht(weite) f.

visible ['vɪzəbl] a sichtbar.

visibly ['vɪzəblɪ] ad sichtlich.

vision ['vɪʒən] n (ability) Sehvermögen nt; (foresight) Weitblick m; (in dream, image) Vision f.

visit ['vɪzɪt] n Besuch m // vt besuchen; (town, country) fahren nach; **~ing** a (professor) Gast-; **~ing card** n Visitenkarte f; **~ing hours** npl (in hospital etc) Besuchszeiten pl; **~or** n (in house) Besucher(in f) m; (in hotel) Gast m; **~or's book** n Gästebuch nt.

visor ['vaɪzə*] n Visier nt; (on cap) Schirm m; (AUT) Blende f.

vista ['vɪstə] n Aussicht f.

visual ['vɪzjʊəl] a Seh-, visuell; ~ **aid** n Anschauungsmaterial nt; ~ **display unit** (VDU) n Bildschirm(gerät nt) m; **~ize** vt sich (dat) vorstellen.

vital ['vaɪtl] a (important) unerläßlich; (necessary for life) Lebens-, lebenswichtig; (lively) vital; **~ity**

[vaɪ'tælɪtɪ] n Vitalität f; **~ly** ad: **~ly important** äußerst wichtig; **~ statistics** npl (fig) Maße pl.
vitamin ['vɪtəmɪn] n Vitamin nt.
vivacious [vɪ'veɪʃəs] a lebhaft.
vivid a, **~ly** ad ['vɪvɪd, -lɪ] (graphic) lebendig; (memory) lebhaft; (bright) leuchtend.
V-neck ['viː'nek] n V-Ausschnitt m.
vocabulary [vəʊ'kæbjʊlərɪ] n Wortschatz m, Vokabular nt.
vocal ['vəʊkəl] a Vokal-, Gesang-; (fig) lautstark; **~ cords** npl Stimmbänder pl.
vocation [vəʊ'keɪʃən] n (calling) Berufung f; **~al** a Berufs-.
vociferous a, **~ly** ad [vəʊ'sɪfərəs, -lɪ] lautstark.
vodka ['vɒdkə] n Wodka m.
vogue [vəʊg] n Mode f.
voice [vɔɪs] n (lit) Stimme f; (fig) Mitspracherecht nt // vt äußern.
void [vɔɪd] n Leere f // a (invalid) nichtig, ungültig; (empty): **~ of** ohne, bar (+gen); see **null**.
volatile ['vɒlətaɪl] a (gas) flüchtig; (person) impulsiv; (situation) brisant.
volcano [vɒl'keɪnəʊ] n Vulkan m.
volition [və'lɪʃən] n Wille m; **of one's own ~** aus freiem Willen.
volley ['vɒlɪ] n (of guns) Salve f; (of stones) Hagel m; (of words) Schwall m; (tennis) Flugball m; **~ball** n Volleyball m.
volt [vəʊlt] n Volt nt; **~age** n (Volt)spannung f.
voluble ['vɒljʊbl] a redselig.
volume ['vɒljuːm] n (book) Band m; (size) Umfang m; (space) Rauminhalt m; (of sound) Lautstärke f.
voluminous [və'luːmɪnəs] a üppig; (clothes) wallend; (correspondence, notes) umfangreich.
voluntary a, **voluntarily** ad ['vɒləntərɪ, -lɪ] freiwillig.
volunteer [vɒlən'tɪə*] n Freiwillige(r) mf // vi sich freiwillig melden; **to ~ to do sth** sich anbieten, etw zu tun.
voluptuous [və'lʌptjʊəs] a sinnlich.
vomit ['vɒmɪt] n Erbrochene(s) nt // vt spucken // vi sich übergeben.
vote [vəʊt] n Stimme f; (ballot) Abstimmung f; (result) Abstimmungsergebnis nt; (right to vote) Wahlrecht nt // vti wählen; **~ of thanks** n Dankesworte pl; **~r** n Wähler(in f) m.
voting ['vəʊtɪŋ] n Wahl f.
vouch [vaʊtʃ]: **~ for** vt bürgen für.
voucher ['vaʊtʃə*] n Gutschein m.
vow [vaʊ] n Versprechen nt; (REL) Gelübde nt // vt geloben.
vowel ['vaʊəl] n Vokal m.
voyage ['vɔɪɪdʒ] n Reise f.
vulgar ['vʌlgə*] a (rude) vulgär; (of common people) allgemein, Volks-; **~ity** [vʌl'gærɪtɪ] n Vulgarität f.

vulnerable ['vʌlnərəbl] a (easily injured) verwundbar; (sensitive) verletzlich.
vulture ['vʌltʃə*] n Geier m.

W

wad [wɒd] n (bundle) Bündel nt; (of paper) Stoß m; (of money) Packen m.
waddle ['wɒdl] vi watscheln.
wade [weɪd] vi: **to ~ through** waten durch.
wafer ['weɪfə*] n Waffel f; (ECCL) Hostie f; (COMPUT) Wafer f.
waffle ['wɒfl] n Waffel f; (col: empty talk) Geschwafel nt // vi (col) schwafeln.
waft [wɑːft] vti wehen.
wag [wæg] vt (tail) wedeln mit // vi (tail) wedeln.
wage [weɪdʒ] n (also: ~s) (Arbeits)lohn m // vt: **to ~ war** Krieg führen; **~ earner** n Lohnempfänger(in f) m; **~ packet** n Lohntüte f.
wager ['weɪdʒə*] n Wette f // vti wetten.
waggle ['wægl] vt (tail) wedeln mit // vi wedeln.
wag(g)on ['wægən] n (horse-drawn) Fuhrwerk nt; (US AUT) Wagen m; (Brit RAIL) Waggon m.
wail [weɪl] n Wehgeschrei nt // vi wehklagen, jammern.
waist [weɪst] n Taille f; **~coat** n (Brit) Weste f; **~line** n Taille f.
wait [weɪt] n Wartezeit f // vi warten; lie in **~ for sb** jdm auflauern; **I can't ~ to see him** ich kann's kaum erwarten, ihn zu sehen; **no ~ing** (Brit AUT) Halteverbot nt; **~ behind** vi zurückbleiben; **~ for** vt warten auf (+acc); **~ on** vt bedienen; **~er** n Kellner m; (as address) Herr Ober m; **~ing list** n Warteliste f; **~ing room** n (MED) Wartezimmer nt; (RAIL) Wartesaal m; **~ress** n Kellnerin f; (as address) Fräulein nt.
waive [weɪv] vt verzichten auf (+acc).
wake [weɪk] v (pt **woke** or **waked**, pp **woken** or **waked**) vt wecken // vi (also: ~ up) aufwachen; **to ~ up to** (fig) sich bewußt werden (+gen) // n (NAUT) Kielwasser nt; (for dead) Totenwache f.
waken ['weɪkən] vt aufwecken.
Wales [weɪlz] n Wales nt.
walk [wɔːk] n Spaziergang m; (way of walking) Gang m; (route) Weg m // vi gehen; (stroll) spazierengehen; (longer) wandern; **~s of life** Sphären pl; **a 10-minute ~** 10 Minuten zu Fuß; **to ~ out on sb** (col) jdn sitzenlassen; **~er** n Spaziergänger m; (hiker) Wanderer m; **~ie-talkie** n tragbare(s) Sprechfunkgerät nt; **~ing** nt // a Wander-; **~ing shoes** npl Wanderschuhe pl; **~ing stick** n

Spazierstock *m*; ~**out** *n* Streik *m*; ~**over** *n* (col) leichte(r) Sieg *m*; ~**way** *n* Fußweg *m*.

wall [wɔːl] *n* (inside) Wand *f*; (outside) Mauer *f*; ~**ed** *a* von Mauern umgeben.

wallet ['wɒlɪt] *n* Brieftasche *f*.

wallflower ['wɔːlflauə*] *n* Goldlack *m*; to be a ~ (fig) ein Mauerblümchen sein.

wallop ['wɒləp] *vt* (col) schlagen, verprügeln.

wallow ['wɒləu] *vi* sich wälzen.

wallpaper ['wɔːlpeɪpə*] *n* Tapete *f*.

wally ['wɒlɪ] *n* (col) Idiot *m*.

walnut ['wɔːlnʌt] *n* Walnuß *f*.

waltz [wɔːlts] *n* Walzer *m* // *vi* Walzer tanzen.

wan [wɒn] *a* bleich.

wand [wɒnd] *n* (also: magic ~) Zauberstab *m*.

wander ['wɒndə*] *vi* (roam) (herum)wandern; (fig) abschweifen.

wane [weɪn] *vi* abnehmen; (fig) schwinden.

wangle ['wæŋgl] *vt* (Brit col): to ~ sth etw richtig hindrehen.

want [wɒnt] *n* (lack) Mangel *m* (of an +dat); **for** ~ of aus Mangel an (+dat); mangels (+gen); ~**s** *pl* (needs) Bedürfnisse *pl* // *vt* (need) brauchen; (desire) wollen; (lack) nicht haben; to ~ to do sth etw tun wollen; to ~ sb to do sth wollen, daß jd etw tut; ~**ing** *a*: to be found ~**ing** sich als unzulänglich erweisen.

wanton ['wɒntən] *a* mutwillig, zügellos.

war [wɔː*] *n* Krieg *m*; to make ~ Krieg führen.

ward [wɔːd] *n* (in hospital) Station *f*; (child) Mündel *nt*; (of city) Bezirk *m*; ~ **off** *vt* abwenden, abwehren.

warden ['wɔːdən] *n* (guard) Wächter *m*, Aufseher *m*; (Brit: in youth hostel) Herbergsvater *m*; (UNIV) Heimleiter *m*; (Brit: also: traffic ~) ≈ Verkehrspolizist *m*, Politesse *f*.

warder ['wɔːdə*] *n* (Brit) Gefängniswärter *m*.

wardrobe ['wɔːdrəub] *n* Kleiderschrank *m*; (clothes) Garderobe *f*.

warehouse ['wɛəhaus] *n* Lagerhaus *nt*.

wares [wɛəz] *npl* Ware *f*.

warfare ['wɔːfɛə*] *n* Krieg *m*; Kriegsführung *f*.

warhead ['wɔːhed] *n* Sprengkopf *m*.

warily ['wɛərɪlɪ] *ad* vorsichtig.

warlike ['wɔːlaɪk] *a* kriegerisch.

warm [wɔːm] *a* warm; (welcome) herzlich; **I'm** ~ mir ist warm // *vti* wärmen; ~ **up** *vt* aufwärmen // *vi* warm werden; ~**-hearted** *a* warmherzig; ~**ly** *ad* warm; herzlich; **warmth** *n* Wärme *f*; Herzlichkeit *f*.

warn [wɔːn] *vt* warnen (of, against vor +dat); ~**ing** *n* Warnung *f*; **without** ~**ing** unerwartet; ~**ing light** *n* Warnlicht *nt*;

~**ing triangle** *n* (AUT) Warndreieck *nt*.

warp [wɔːp] *vt* verziehen; ~**ed** *a* (lit) wellig; (fig) pervers.

warrant ['wɒrənt] *n* Haftbefehl *m*.

warranty ['wɒrəntɪ] *n* Garantie *f*.

warren ['wɒrən] *n* Labyrinth *nt*.

warrior ['wɒrɪə*] *n* Krieger *m*.

Warsaw ['wɔːsɔː] *n* Warschau *nt*.

warship ['wɔːʃɪp] *n* Kriegsschiff *nt*.

wart [wɔːt] *n* Warze *f*.

wartime ['wɔːtaɪm] *n* Krieg *m*.

wary ['wɛərɪ] *a* mißtrauisch.

was [wɒz, wəz] *pt* of **be**.

wash [wɒʃ] *n* Wäsche *f* // *vt* waschen; (dishes) abwaschen // *vi* sich waschen; (do washing) waschen; to have a ~ sich waschen; ~ **away** *vt* abwaschen, wegspülen; ~ **off** *vt* abwaschen; ~ **up** *vi* (Brit) spülen; (US) sich waschen; ~**able**, *a* waschbar; ~**basin**, (US) ~**bowl** *n* Waschbecken *nt*; ~ **cloth** *n* (US: face cloth) Waschlappen *m*; ~**er** *n* (TECH) Dichtungsring *m*; (machine) Waschmaschine *f*; ~**ing** *n* Wäsche *f*; ~**ing machine** *n* Waschmaschine *f*; ~**ing powder** *n* (Brit) Waschpulver *nt*; ~**ing-up** *n* Abwasch *m*; ~**ing-up liquid** *n* Spülmittel *nt*; ~**-out** *n* (col: event) Reinfall *m*; (: person) Niete *f*; ~**room** *n* Waschraum *m*.

wasn't ['wɒznt] = **was not**.

wasp [wɒsp] *n* Wespe *f*.

wastage ['weɪstɪdʒ] *n* Verlust *m*; natural ~ Verschleiß *m*.

waste [weɪst] *n* (wasting) Verschwendung *f*; (what is wasted) Abfall *m*; ~**s** *pl* Einöde *f* // *a* (useless) überschüssig, Abfall- // *vt* (object) verschwenden; (time, life) vergeuden // *vi*: ~ **away** verfallen; to lay ~ verwüsten; ~ **disposal unit** *n* (Brit) Müllschlucker *m*; ~**ful** *a* verschwenderisch; (process) aufwendig; ~ **ground** *n* (Brit) unbebautes Grundstück *nt*; ~**land** *n* Ödland *nt*; ~**paper basket** *n* Papierkorb *m*; ~ **pipe** *n* Abflußrohr *nt*.

watch [wɒtʃ] *n* Wache *f*; (for time) Uhr *f* // *vt* ansehen; (observe) beobachten; (be careful of) aufpassen auf (+acc); (guard) bewachen // *vi* zusehen; to be on the ~ (for sth) (auf etw acc) aufpassen; to ~ TV fernsehen; to ~ sb doing sth jdm bei etw zuschauen; ~ **out** *vi* Ausschau halten; (be careful) aufpassen; ~ **out!** paß auf!; ~**dog** *n* (lit) Wachthund *m*; (fig) Wächter *m*; ~**ful** *a* wachsam; ~**maker** *n* Uhrmacher *m*; ~**man** *n* (also: night ~man) (Nacht)wächter *m*; ~**strap** *n* Uhrarmband *nt*.

water ['wɔːtə*] *n* Wasser *nt*; ~**s** *pl* Gewässer *nt* // *vt* (river) bewässern; (horses) tränken // *vi* (eye) tränen; ~ **down** *vt* verwässern; ~ **closet** *n* (Brit) (Wasser)klosett *nt*; ~**colour**, (US) ~**color** *n* (painting)

Aquarell nt; (paint) Wasserfarbe f; ~**cress** n (Brunnen)kresse f; ~**fall** n Wasserfall m; ~ **heater** n Heißwassergerät nt; ~**ing can** n Gießkanne f; ~ **level** n Wasserstand m; ~**lily** n Seerose f; ~**line** n Wasserlinie f; ~**logged** a (ground) voll Wasser; (wood) mit Wasser vollgesogen; ~**main** n Haupt(wasser)leitung f; ~**mark** n Wasserzeichen nt; (on wall) Wasserstandsmarke f; ~**melon** n Wassermelone f; ~ **polo** n Wasserball(spiel) nt; ~**proof** a wasserdicht; ~**shed** n Wasserscheide f; ~**skiing** n Wasserschilaufen nt; ~ **tank** n Wassertank m; ~**tight** a wasserdicht; ~ **way** n Wasserweg m; ~**works** npl Wasserwerk nt; ~**y** a wäss(e)rig.

wave [weɪv] n Welle f; (with hand) Winken nt // vt (move to and fro) schwenken; (hand, flag) winken mit; (hair) wellen // vi (person) winken; (flag) wehen; ~**length** n (lit, fig) Wellenlänge f.

waver ['weɪvə*] vi schwanken.

wavy ['weɪvɪ] a wellig.

wax [wæks] n Wachs nt; (sealing ~) Siegellack m; (in ear) Ohrenschmalz nt // vt (floor) (ein)wachsen // vi (moon) zunehmen; ~**works** npl Wachsfigurenkabinett nt.

way [weɪ] n Weg m; (method) Art und Weise f; (direction) Richtung f; (habit) Gewohnheit f; (distance) Entfernung f; (condition) Zustand m; which ~? — this ~ welche Richtung? — hier entlang; on the ~ (en route) unterwegs; to be in the ~ im Weg sein; to go out of one's ~ to do sth sich besonders anstrengen, um etw zu tun; to lose one's ~ sich verirren; give ~ (Brit AUT) Vorfahrt achten!; in a ~ in gewisser Weise; by the ~ übrigens; in some ~s in gewisser Hinsicht; '~ in' (Brit) 'Eingang'; '~ out' (Brit) 'Ausgang'.

waylay [weɪ'leɪ] vt (irreg: like lay) auflauern (+dat).

wayward ['weɪwəd] a eigensinnig.

W.C. ['dʌblju'si:] n (Brit) WC nt.

we [wi:] pl pron wir.

weak [wi:k] a schwach; ~**en** vt schwächen // vi schwächer werden; ~**ling** n Schwächling m; ~**ly** ad schwach; ~**ness** n Schwäche f.

wealth [welθ] n Reichtum m; (abundance) Fülle f; ~**y** a reich.

wean [wi:n] vt entwöhnen.

weapon ['wepən] n Waffe f.

wear [weə*] n (clothing): sports/baby ~ Sport-/Babykleidung f; (use) Verschleiß m // v (pt **wore**, pp **worn**) vt (have on) tragen; (smile etc) haben; (use) abnutzen // vi (last) halten; (become old) (sich) verschleißen; evening ~ Abendkleidung f; ~ and tear Verschleiß

m; ~ **away** vt verbrauchen // vi schwinden; ~ **down** vt (people) zermürben; ~ **off** vi sich verlieren; ~ **out** vt verschleißen; (person) erschöpfen.

weary ['wɪərɪ] a müde // vt ermüden // vi überdrüssig werden (of gen).

weather ['weðə*] n Wetter nt // vt verwittern lassen; (resist) überstehen; under the ~ (fig: ill) angeschlagen (col); ~**-beaten** a verwittert; ~**cock** n Wetterhahn m; ~ **forecast** n Wettervorhersage f; ~ **vane** m Wetterfahne f.

weave [wi:v], pt **wove**, pp **woven** vt weben; ~r n Weber(in f) m; **weaving** n (craft) Webkunst f.

web [web] n Netz nt; (membrane) Schwimmhaut f.

wed [wed], pt, pp **wedded** vt heiraten // n: the newly-~s die Frischvermählten.

we'd [wi:d] = **we had**; **we would**.

wedding ['wedɪŋ] n Hochzeit f; silver/golden ~ (Brit), silver/golden ~ anniversary Silberhochzeit f/Goldene Hochzeit; ~ **day** n Hochzeitstag m; ~ **dress** n Hochzeitskleid nt; ~ **present** n Hochzeitsgeschenk nt; ~ **ring** n Trau- or Ehering m.

wedge [wedʒ] n Keil m; (of cheese etc) Stück nt // vt (fasten) festklemmen; (pack tightly) einkeilen.

wedlock ['wedlɒk] n Ehe f.

Wednesday ['wenzdeɪ] n Mittwoch m.

wee [wi:] a (esp Scot) klein, winzig.

weed [wi:d] n Unkraut nt // vt jäten; ~**killer** n Unkrautvertilgungsmittel nt; ~**y** a (person) schmächtig.

week [wi:k] n Woche f; a ~ today/on Friday heute/Freitag in einer Woche; ~**day** n Wochentag m; ~**end** n Wochenende nt; ~**ly** a, ad wöchentlich; (wages, magazine) Wochen-.

weep [wi:p], pt, pp **wept** vi weinen; ~**ing willow** n Trauerweide f.

weigh [weɪ] vti wiegen; to ~ anchor den Anker lichten; ~ **down** vt niederdrücken; ~ **up** vt abschätzen.

weight [weɪt] n Gewicht nt; to lose/put on ~ abnehmen/zunehmen; ~**ing** n (allowance) Zulage f; ~**lifter** n Gewichtheber m; ~**y** a (heavy) gewichtig; (important) schwerwiegend.

weir [wɪə*] n (Stau)wehr nt.

weird [wɪəd] a seltsam.

welcome ['welkəm] n Willkommen nt, Empfang m // vt begrüßen; thank you — you're ~! danke — nichts zu danken.

weld [weld] n Schweißnaht f // vt schweißen; ~**ing** n Schweißen nt.

welfare ['welfeə*] n Wohl nt; (social) Fürsorge f; ~ **state** n Wohlfahrtsstaat m; ~ **work** n Fürsorge f.

well [wel] n Brunnen m; (oil ~) Quelle f // a (in good health) gesund // ad gut //

interj nun, na schön; **I'm ~** es geht mir gut; **as ~** auch; **as ~ as** sowohl als auch; **~ done!** gut gemacht!; **get ~ soon!** gute Besserung; **to do ~** *(person)* gut zurechtkommen; *(business)* gut gehen; **~ up** *vi* emporsteigen; *(fig)* aufsteigen.

we'll [wi:l] = **we will, we shall**.

well-behaved ['welbɪ'heɪvd] *a* wohlerzogen.

well-being ['welbi:ɪŋ] *n* Wohl *nt*.

well-built ['wel'bɪlt] *a* kräftig gebaut.

well-deserved ['weldɪ'zɜ:vd] *a* wohlverdient.

well-dressed ['wel'drest] *a* gut gekleidet.

well-heeled ['wel'hi:ld] *a* *(col: wealthy)* gut gepolstert.

wellingtons ['welɪŋtənz] *npl* *(also:* **wellington boots)** Gummistiefel *pl.*

well-known ['wel'nəʊn] *a* bekannt.

well-mannered ['wel'mænəd] *a* wohlerzogen.

well-meaning ['wel'mi:nɪŋ] *a* *(person)* wohlmeinend; *(action)* gutgemeint.

well-off ['wel'ɒf] *a* gut situiert.

well-read ['wel'red] *a* *(sehr)* belesen.

well-to-do ['weltə'du:] *a* wohlhabend.

well-wisher ['welwɪʃə*] *n* Gönner *m*.

Welsh [welʃ] *a* walisisch; **the ~** *npl* die Waliser; **~man/woman** *n* Waliser *m*/ Waliserin *f*; **~ rarebit** *n* überbackene Käseschmitte *pl.*

went [went] *pt of* **go**.

wept [wept] *pt, pp of* **weep**.

were [wɜ:*] *pt pl of* **be**.

we're [wɪə*] = **we are**.

weren't [wɜ:nt] = **were not**.

west [west] *n* Westen *m* // *a* West-, westlich // *ad* westwärts, nach Westen; **the W~** *n* der Westen; **the W~ Country** *n* *(Brit)* der Südwesten Englands; **~erly** *a* westlich; **~ern** *a* westlich, West- // *n* *(CINE)* Western *m*; **W~ Germany** *n* Westdeutschland *nt*, Bundesrepublik Deutschland *f*; **W~ Indian** *a* westindisch // *n* Westindier(in *f*) *m*; **W~ Indies** *npl* Westindische Inseln *pl*; **~ward(s)** *ad* westwärts.

wet [wet] *a* naß // *vt*: **to get ~** naß werden; **'~ paint'** 'frisch gestrichen'; **~ blanket** *n* *(fig)* Triefel *m*; **~ suit** *n* Taucheranzug *m*.

we've [wi:v] = **we have**.

whack [wæk] *n* Schlag *m* // *vt* schlagen.

whale [weɪl] *n* Wal *m*.

wharf [wɔ:f] *n* Kai *m*.

what [wɒt] ◆ *a* 1 *(in direct/indirect questions)* welche(r, s), was für ein(e); **~ size is it?** welche Größe ist das?
2 *(in exclamations)* was für ein(e); **~ a mess!** was für ein Durcheinander!
◆ *pron (interrogative/relative)* was; **~ are you doing?** was machst du gerade?; **~ are you talking about?** wovon reden

Sie?; **~ is it called?** wie heißt das?; **~ about ...?** wie wär's mit ...?; **I saw ~ you did** ich habe gesehen, was du gemacht hast
◆ *interj (disbelieving)* wie, was; **~, no coffee!** wie, kein Kaffee?; **I've crashed the car — ~!** ich hatte einen Autounfall — was!

wheat [wi:t] *n* Weizen *m*; **~ germ** *n* Weizenkeim *m*.

wheedle ['wi:dl] *vt*: **to ~ sb into doing sth** jdn dazu überreden, etw zu tun; **to ~ sth out of sb** jdm etw abluchsen.

wheel [wi:l] *n* Rad *nt*; *(steering ~)* Lenkrad *nt*; *(disc)* Scheibe *f* // *vt* schieben; **~barrow** *n* Schubkarren *m*; **~chair** *n* Rollstuhl *m*; **~ clamp** *n* *(AUT)* Radblockierung *f* *(von der Polizei an falschparkenden Autos angebracht.*

wheeze [wi:z] *vi* keuchen.

when [wen] ◆ *ad* wenn
◆ *cj* 1 *(at, during, after the time that)* wenn; *(with past reference)* als; **she was reading ~ I came in** sie las, als ich herkam; **be careful ~ you cross the road** seien Sie vorsichtig, wenn Sie über die Straße gehen
2 *(on, at which)* als; **on the day ~ I met him** am dem Tag, an dem ich ihn traf.
3 *(whereas)* wo ... doch.

where [wɛə*] *ad (place)* wo; *(direction)* wohin; **~ from** woher; **~abouts** ['wɛərə'baʊts] *ad* wo // *n* Aufenthaltsort *m*; **nobody knows his ~abouts** niemand weiß, wo er ist; **~as** [wɛər'æz] *cj* während, wo ... doch; **whereby** *pron* woran, wodurch, womit, wovon; **whereupon** *cj* worauf, wonach; *(at beginning of sentence)* daraufhin.

wherever [wɛər'evə*] *ad* wo (immer).

wherewithal ['wɛəwɪðɔ:l] *n* nötige (Geld)mittel *pl.*

whet [wet] *vt (appetite)* anregen.

whether ['weðə*] *cj* ob; **I don't know ~ to accept or not** ich weiß nicht, ob ich es annehmen soll oder nicht; **~ you go or not** ob du gehst oder nicht.

which [wɪtʃ] ◆ *a* 1 *(interrogative: direct, indirect)* welche(r, s); **~ one?** welche(r, s)?
2: **in ~ case** in diesem Fall; **by ~ time** zu dieser Zeit
◆ *pron* 1 *(interrogative)* welche(r, s); *(of people also)* wer
2 *(relative)* der/die/das; *(referring to clause)* was; **the apple ~ you ate/~ is on the table** der Apfel, den du gegessen hast/der auf dem Tisch liegt; **he said he saw her, ~ is true** er sagte, er habe sie gesehen, was auch stimmt.

whiff [wɪf] *n* Hauch *m*.

while [waɪl] *n* Weile *f* // *cj* während; **for a ~** eine Zeitlang; **~ away** *vt (time)* sich *(dat)* vertreiben.

whim [wɪm] *n* Laune *f*.

whimper ['wɪmpə*] n Wimmern nt // vi wimmern.

whimsical ['wɪmzɪkəl] a launisch.

whine [waɪn] n Gewinsel nt, Gejammer nt // vi heulen, winseln.

whip [wɪp] n Peitsche f; (POL) Fraktionsführer m // vt (beat) peitschen; (snatch) reißen; n ~**ped cream** n Schlagsahne; ~**-round** n (Brit col) Geldsammlung f.

whirl [wɜːl] n Wirbel m // vti (her-um)wirbeln; ~**pool** n Wirbel m; ~**wind** n Wirbelwind m.

whirr [wɜː*] vi schwirren, surren.

whisk [wɪsk] n Schneebesen m // vt (cream etc) schlagen; **to** ~ **sb away** or **off** mit jdm davon sausen.

whisker ['wɪskə*] n (of animal) Barthaare pl; ~**s** pl (of man) Backenbart m.

whisky, (US, Ireland) **whiskey** ['wɪskɪ] n Whisky m.

whisper ['wɪspə*] n Flüstern nt // vti flüstern.

whistle ['wɪsl] n Pfiff m; (instrument) Pfeife f // vti pfeifen.

white [waɪt] n Weiß nt; (of egg) Eiweiß nt // a weiß; ~ **coffee** n (Brit) Kaffee m mit Milch; ~**-collar worker** n Angestellte(r) m; ~ **elephant** n (fig) Fehlinvestition f; ~ **lie** n Notlüge f; ~**ness** n Weiß nt; ~ **paper** n (POL) Weißbuch nt; ~**wash** n (paint) Tünche f; (fig) Ehrenrettung f // vt weißen, tünchen; (fig) reinwaschen.

whiting ['waɪtɪŋ] n Weißfisch m.

Whitsun ['wɪtsn] n Pfingsten nt.

whittle ['wɪtl] vt: **to** ~ **away** or **down** stutzen, verringern.

whizz [wɪz] vi: **to** ~ **past** or **by** vorbeizischen, vorbeischwirren; ~ **kid** n (col) Kanone f.

who [huː] pron **1** (interrogative) wer; (acc) wen; (dat) wem; ~ **is it?**, ~**'s there?** wer ist da?
2 (relative) der/die/das; **the man/woman** ~ **spoke to me** der Mann/die Frau, der/die mit mir sprach.

whole [həʊl] a ganz // n Ganze(s) nt; **the** ~ **of the town** die ganze Stadt; **on the** ~, **as a** ~ im großen und ganzen; ~**hearted** a rückhaltlos; ~**heartedly** ad von ganzem Herzen; ~**meal** n (bread, flour) Vollkorn-; ~**sale** n Großhandel m // a (trade) Großhandels-; (destruction) Massen-; ~**saler** n Großhändler m; ~**some** a bekömmlich, gesund; ~**wheat** a = ~**meal**.

wholly ['həʊlɪ] ad ganz, völlig.

whom [huːm] pron **1** (interrogative: acc) wen; (: dat) wem; ~ **did you see?** wen haben Sie gesehen?; **to** ~ **did you give it to?** wem haben Sie es gegeben?
2 (relative: acc) den/die/das; (: dat) dem/der/dem; **the man** ~ **I saw/to** ~ **I**

spoke der Mann, den ich sah/mit dem ich sprach.

whooping cough ['huːpɪŋkɒf] n Keuchhusten m.

whore ['hɔː*] n Hure f.

whose [huːz] a (poss: interrog) wessen; ~ **book is this?**, ~ **is this book?** wessen Buch ist das?; (: rel) dessen; (after f and pl) deren // pron wessen; ~ **is this?** wem gehört das?

why [waɪ] ad warum, weshalb ◆cj warum, weshalb; **that's not** ~ **I'm here** ich bin nicht deswegen hier; **that's the reason** ~ deshalb ◆interj (expressing surprise, shock, annoyance) na so was; (explaining) also dann; ~, **it's you!** na so was, du bist es!

wick [wɪk] n Docht m.

wicked ['wɪkɪd] a böse.

wicker ['wɪkə*] n (also: ~**work**) Korbgeflecht nt.

wicket ['wɪkɪt] n Tor nt, Dreistab m.

wide [waɪd] a breit; (plain) weit; (in firing) daneben // ad: **open** ~ weit offen; **to shoot** ~ daneben schießen; ~**-angle lens** n Weitwinkelobjektiv nt; ~**-awake** a hellwach; ~**ly** ad weit; (known) allgemein; ~**n** vt erweitern; ~**-open** a weit geöffnet; ~**spread** a weitverbreitet.

widow ['wɪdəʊ] n Witwe f; ~**ed** a verwitwet; ~**er** n Witwer m.

width [wɪdθ] n Breite f, Weite f.

wield [wiːld] vt schwingen, handhaben.

wife [waɪf] n (Ehe)frau f, Gattin f.

wig [wɪg] n Perücke f.

wiggle ['wɪgl] n Wackeln nt // vt wackeln mit // vi wackeln.

wild [waɪld] a wild; (violent) heftig; (plan, idea) verrückt; **the** ~**s** die Wildnis; ~**erness** ['wɪldənəs] n Wildnis f, Wüste f; ~**-goose chase** n (fig) fruchtlose(s) Unternehmen nt; ~**life** n Tierwelt f; ~**ly** ad wild, ungestüm; (exaggerated) irrsinnig.

wilful ['wɪlfʊl] a (intended) vorsätzlich; (obstinate) eigensinnig.

will [wɪl] ◆ v aux **1** (forming future tense) werden; **I** ~ **finish it tomorrow** ich mache es morgen zu Ende
2 (in conjectures, predictions): **he** ~ or **he'll be there by now** er dürfte jetzt da sein; **that** ~ **be the postman** das wird der Postbote sein
3 (in commands, requests, offers): ~ **you be quiet!** sei endlich still!; ~ **you help me?** hilfst du mir?; ~ **you have a cup of tea?** Trinken Sie eine Tasse Tee?; **I won't put up with it!** das lasse ich mir nicht gefallen!
◆vt wollen; ~**ing** a gewillt, bereit; ~**ingly** ad bereitwillig, gern; ~**ingness** n (Bereit)willigkeit f.

willow ['wɪləʊ] n Weide f.

willpower ['wɪlpaʊə*] n Willenskraft f.

willy-nilly ['wɪlɪ'nɪlɪ] *ad* einfach so.
wilt [wɪlt] *vi* (ver)welken.
wily ['waɪlɪ] *a* gerissen.
win [wɪn] *n* Sieg *m* // *vti, pt, pp* **won** gewinnen; **to ~ sb over** *or* (*Brit*) **round** jdn gewinnen, jdn dazu bringen.
wince [wɪns] *n* Zusammenzucken *nt* // *vi* zusammenzucken.
winch [wɪntʃ] *n* Winde *f.*
wind [waɪnd] *v* (*pt, pp* **wound**) *vt* (*rope*) winden; (*bandage*) wickeln // *vi* (*turn*) sich winden; **~ up** *vt* (*clock*) aufziehen; (*debate*) (ab)schließen.
wind [wɪnd] *n* Wind *m*; (*MED*) Blähungen *pl*; **~fall** *n* unverhoffte(r) Glücksfall *m.*
winding ['waɪndɪŋ] *a* (*road*) gewunden.
wind instrument ['wɪndɪnstrumənt] *n* Blasinstrument *nt.*
windmill ['wɪndmɪl] *n* Windmühle *f.*
window ['wɪndəʊ] *n* Fenster *nt*; **~ box** *n* Blumenkasten *m*; **~ cleaner** *n* Fensterputzer *m*; **~ envelope** *n* Fensterbriefumschlag *m*; **~ ledge** *n* Fenstersims *m*; **~ pane** *n* Fensterscheibe *f*; **~sill** *n* Fensterbank *f.*
windpipe ['wɪndpaɪp] *n* Luftröhre *f.*
windscreen ['wɪndskriːn], (*US*) **windshield** ['wɪndʃiːld] *n* Windschutzscheibe *f*; **~ washer** *n* Scheibenwaschanlage *f*; **~ wiper** *n* Scheibenwischer *m.*
windswept ['wɪndswept] *a* vom Wind gepeitscht; (*person*) zerzaust.
windy ['wɪndɪ] *a* windig.
wine [waɪn] *n* Wein *m*; **~ cellar** *n* Weinkeller *m*; **~glass** *n* Weinglas *nt*; **~ list** *n* Weinkarte *f*; **~ merchant** *n* Weinhändler *m*; **~ tasting** *n* Weinprobe *f*; **~ waiter** *n* Weinkellner *m.*
wing [wɪŋ] *n* Flügel *m*; (*MIL*) Gruppe *f*; **~s** *pl* (*THEAT*) Seitenkulisse *f*; **~er** *n* (*SPORT*) Flügelstürmer *m.*
wink [wɪŋk] *n* Zwinkern *nt* // *vi* zwinkern, blinzeln.
winner ['wɪnə*] *n* Gewinner *m*; (*SPORT*) Sieger *m.*
winning ['wɪnɪŋ] *a* (*team*) siegreich, Sieger-; (*goal*) entscheidend // *n:* **~s** *pl* Gewinn *m*; **~ post** *n* Ziel *nt.*
winter ['wɪntə*] *n* Winter *m* // *a* (*clothes*) Winter- // *vi* überwintern; **~ sports** *npl* Wintersport *m.*
wintry ['wɪntrɪ] *a* Winter-, winterlich.
wipe [waɪp] *n:* **to give sth a ~** etw (ab)wischen; **~ off** *vt* abwischen; **~ out** *vt* (*debt*) löschen; (*destroy*) auslöschen; **~ up** *vt* aufwischen.
wire [waɪə*] *n* Draht *m*; (*telegram*) Telegramm *nt* // *vt* telegrafieren (*sb* jdm, *sth* etw).
wireless ['waɪəlɪs] *n* (*Brit*) Radio(apparat *m*) *nt.*
wiring ['waɪərɪŋ] *n* elektrische Leitungen *pl.*
wiry ['waɪərɪ] *a* drahtig.

wisdom ['wɪzdəm] *n* Weisheit *f*; (*of decision*) Klugheit *f*; **~ tooth** *n* Weisheitszahn *m.*
wise [waɪz] *a* klug, weise.
...wise [waɪz] *suff:* time~ zeitlich gesehen.
wisecrack ['waɪzkræk] *n* Witzelei *f.*
wish [wɪʃ] *n* Wunsch *m* // *vt* wünschen; **best ~es** (*on birthday etc*) alles Gute; **with best ~es** herzliche Grüße; **to ~ sb goodbye** jdn verabschieden; **he ~ed me well** er wünschte mir Glück; **to ~ to do sth** etw tun wollen; **~ for** *vt* sich (*dat*) wünschen; **~ful thinking** *n* Wunschdenken *nt.*
wishy-washy ['wɪʃɪ'wɒʃɪ] *a* (*col: colour*) verwaschen; (*: ideas, argument*) verschwommen.
wisp [wɪsp] *n* (Haar)strähne *f*; (*of smoke*) Wölkchen *nt.*
wistful ['wɪstful] *a* sehnsüchtig.
wit [wɪt] *n* (*also:* **~s**) Verstand *m no pl*; (*amusing ideas*) Witz *m*; (*person*) Witzbold *m.*
witch [wɪtʃ] *n* Hexe *f*; **~craft** *n* Hexerei *f.*
with [wɪð, wɪθ] *prep* **1** (*accompanying, in the company of*) mit; **we stayed ~ friends** wir übernachteten bei Freunden; **I'll be ~ you in a minute** einen Augenblick, ich bin sofort da; **I'm not ~ you** (*I don't understand*) das verstehe ich nicht; **to be ~ it** (*col: up-to-date*) auf dem laufenden sein; (*: alert*) (voll) da sein (*col*)
2 (*descriptive, indicating manner etc*) mit; **the man ~ the grey hat** der Mann mit dem grauen Hut; **red ~ anger** rot vor Wut.
withdraw [wɪð'drɔ:] (*irreg: like draw*) *vt* zurückziehen; (*money*) abheben; (*remark*) zurücknehmen // *vi* sich zurückziehen; **~al** *n* Zurückziehung *f*; Abheben *nt*; Zurücknahme *f*; **~n** *a* (*person*) verschlossen.
wither ['wɪðə*] *vi* (ver)welken.
withhold [wɪθ'həʊld] *vt* (*irreg: like hold*) vorenthalten (*from sb* jdm).
within [wɪð'ɪn] *prep* innerhalb (*+gen*) // *ad:* **~ reach** in Reichweite; **~ sight of** in Sichtweite von; **~ the week** innerhalb dieser Woche.
without [wɪð'aʊt] *prep* ohne.
withstand [wɪθ'stænd] *vt* (*irreg: like stand*) widerstehen (*+dat*).
witness ['wɪtnəs] *n* Zeuge *m*, Zeugin *f* // *vt* (*see*) sehen, miterleben; (*sign document*) beglaubigen; **~ box**, (*US*) **~ stand** *n* Zeugenstand *m.*
witticism ['wɪtɪsɪzəm] *n* witzige Bemerkung *f.*
witty ['wɪtɪ] *a* witzig, geistreich.
wives [waɪvz] *pl of* **wife.**
wizard ['wɪzəd] *n* Zauberer *m.*
wk *abbr of* **week.**

wobble ['wɒbl] *vi* wackeln.
woe [wəʊ] *n* Kummer *m*.
woke [wəʊk], **woken** ['wəʊkən] *pt, pp* of **wake**.
woman ['wʊmən] *n, pl* **women** Frau *f*; ~ **doctor** *n* Ärztin *f*; **women's lib** *n* (col) Frauenrechtsbewegung *f*; ~**ly** *a* weiblich.
womb [wuːm] *n* Gebärmutter *f*.
women ['wɪmɪn] *pl* of **woman**.
wonder ['wʌndə*] *n* (marvel) Wunder *nt*; (surprise) Staunen *nt*, Verwunderung *f* // *vi* sich wundern // *vt*: **I** ~ **whether** ... ich frage mich, ob ...; **it's no** ~ **that** es ist kein Wunder, daß; **to** ~ **at** sich wundern über (+acc); **to** ~ **about** sich Gedanken machen über (+acc); ~**ful** *a* wunderbar, herrlich; ~**fully** *ad* wunderbar.
won't [wəʊnt] = **will not**.
wood [wʊd] *n* Holz *nt*; (forest) Wald *m*; ~ **carving** *n* Holzschnitzerei *f*; ~**ed** *a* bewaldet; ~**en** *a* (lit, fig) hölzern; ~**pecker** *n* Specht *m*; ~**wind** *n* Blasinstrumente *pl*; ~**work** *n* Holzwerk *nt*; (craft) Holzarbeiten *pl*; ~**worm** *n* Holzwurm *m*.
wool [wʊl] *n* Wolle *f*; **to pull the** ~ **over sb's eyes** (fig) jdm Sand in die Augen streuen; ~**len**, (US) ~**en** *a* Woll-; ~**lens** *npl* Wollsachen *pl*; ~**ly**, (US) ~**y** *a* wollig; (fig) schwammig.
word [wɜːd] *n* Wort *nt*; (news) Bescheid *m* // *vt* formulieren; **in other** ~**s** anders gesagt; **to break/keep one's** ~ sein Wort brechen/halten; ~ **processing** *n* Textverarbeitung *f*; ~ **processor** *n* Textverarbeitungsgerät *nt*; ~**ing** *n* Wortlaut *m*.
work [wɜːk] *n* Arbeit *f*; (ART, LITER) Werk *nt* // *vi* arbeiten; (machine) funktionieren; (medicine) wirken; (succeed) klappen; **to be out of** ~ arbeitslos sein; ~**s** *n sing* (Brit: factory) Fabrik *f*, Werk *nt*; *pl* (of watch) Werk *nt*; ~ **loose** *vi* sich lockern; ~ **on** *vi* weiterarbeiten // *vt* (be engaged in) arbeiten an (+dat); (influence) bearbeiten; ~ **out** *vi* (sum) aufgehen; (plan) klappen // *vt* (problem) lösen; (plan) ausarbeiten; **it** ~**s out at £100** das gibt *or* macht £100; ~ **up** *vt*: **to get** ~**ed up** sich aufregen; ~**able** *a* (soil) bearbeitbar; (plan) ausführbar; **workaholic** *n* Arbeitssüchtige(r) *mf*; ~**er** *n* Arbeiter(in *f*) *m*; ~**force** *n* Arbeiterschaft *f*; ~**ing class** *n* Arbeiterklasse *f*; ~**ing-class** *a* Arbeiter-; **in** ~**ing order** in betriebsfähigem Zustand; ~**man** *n* Arbeiter *m*; ~**manship** *n* Arbeit *f*, Ausführung *f*; ~**sheet** *n* Arbeitsblatt *nt*; ~**shop** *n* Werkstatt *f*; ~ **station** *n* Arbeitsplatz *m*; ~**-to-rule** *n* (Brit) Dienst *m* nach Vorschrift.
world [wɜːld] *n* Welt *f*; **to think the** ~ **of**

sb große Stücke auf jdn halten; ~**ly** *a* weltlich, irdisch; ~**-wide** *a* weltweit.
worm [wɜːm] *n* Wurm *m*.
worn [wɔːn] *pp* of **wear** // *a* (clothes) abgetragen; ~**-out** *a* (object) abgenutzt; (person) völlig erschöpft.
worried ['wʌrɪd] *a* besorgt, beunruhigt.
worry ['wʌrɪ] *n* Sorge *f* // *vt* beunruhigen // *vi* (feel uneasy) sich sorgen, sich (dat) Gedanken machen; ~**ing** *a* beunruhigend.
worse [wɜːs] *a comp of* **bad** schlechter, schlimmer // *ad comp of* **badly** schlimmer, ärger // *n* Schlimmere(s) *nt*, Schlechtere(s) *nt*; **a change for the** ~ eine Verschlechterung; ~**n** *vt* verschlimmern // *vi* sich verschlechtern; ~ **off** *a* (fig) schlechter dran.
worship ['wɜːʃɪp] *n* Verehrung *f* // *vt* anbeten; **Your W**~ (Brit: to mayor) Herr/Frau Bürgermeister; (: to judge) Euer Ehren.
worst [wɜːst] *a superl of* **bad** schlimmste(r, s), schlechteste(r, s) // *ad superl of* **badly** am schlimmsten, am ärgsten // *n* Schlimmste(s) *nt*, Ärgste(s) *nt*; **at** ~ schlimmstenfalls.
worsted ['wʊstɪd] *n* Kammgarn *nt*.
worth [wɜːθ] *n* Wert *m* // *a* wert; **it's** ~ it es lohnt sich; **to be** ~ **one's while** (to do) die Mühe wert sein (, etw zu tun); ~**less** *a* wertlos; (person) nichtsnutzig; ~**while** *a* lohnend, die Mühe wert.
worthy ['wɜːðɪ] *a* wert (of gen), würdig (of gen).
would [wʊd] *v aux* **1** (conditional tense): **if you asked him he** ~ **do it** wenn du ihn fragtest, würde er es tun; **if you had asked him he** ~ **have done it** wenn du ihn gefragt hättest, hätte er es getan
2 (in offers, invitations, requests): ~ **you like a biscuit?** möchten Sie ein Plätzchen?; ~ **you ask him to come in?** würden Sie ihn bitte hineinbitten?
3 (in indirect speech): **I said I** ~ **do it** ich sagte, ich würde es tun
4 (emphatic): **it WOULD have to snow today!** es mußte ja ausgerechnet heute schneien!
5 (insistence): **she** ~**n't behave** sie wollte sich partout nicht anständig benehmen
6 (conjecture): **it** ~ **have been midnight** es ungefähr Mitternacht gewesen sein; **it** ~ **seem so** es sieht wohl so aus
7 (indicating habit): **he** ~ **go there on Mondays** er ging jeden Montag dorthin.
wouldn't ['wʊdnt] = **would not**.
wound [waʊnd] *pt, pp* of **wind** // *n* [wuːnd] (lit, fig) Wunde *f* // *vt* [wuːnd] verwunden, verletzen (also fig).
wove [wəʊv], **woven** ['wəʊvən] *pt, pp* of **weave**.
wrangle ['ræŋgl] *n* Streit *m* // *vi* sich zanken.

wrap [ræp] n (stole) Schal m // vt (also: ~ **up**) einwickeln; ~ **up** vt (deal) abschließen; **~per** n Umschlag m, Schutzhülle f; **~ping paper** n Einwickelpapier nt.
wrath [rɒθ] n Zorn m.
wreak [riːk] vt (havoc) anrichten; (vengeance) üben.
wreath [riːθ] n Kranz m.
wreck [rek] n (ship) Wrack nt; (sth ruined) Ruine f // vt zerstören; **~age** n Trümmer pl.
wren [ren] n Zaunkönig m.
wrench [rentʃ] n (spanner) Schraubenschlüssel m; (twist) Ruck m // vt reißen, zerren; **to ~ sth from sb** jdm etw entreißen or entwinden.
wrestle ['resl] vi: **to ~ (with sb)** mit jdm ringen; **wrestler** n Ringer(in f) m; **wrestling** n Ringen nt.
wretched ['retʃid] a (hovel) elend; (col) verflixt; **I feel ~** mir ist elend.
wriggle ['rɪgl] n Schlängeln nt // vi sich winden.
wring [rɪŋ], pt, pp **wrung** vt wringen.
wrinkle ['rɪŋkl] n Falte f, Runzel f // vt runzeln // vi sich runzeln; (material) knittern.
wrist [rɪst] n Handgelenk nt; **~watch** n Armbanduhr f.
writ [rɪt] n gerichtliche(r) Befehl m.
write [raɪt], pt **wrote**, pp **written** vti schreiben; ~ **down** vt aufschreiben; ~ **off** vt (dismiss) abschreiben; ~ **out** vt (essay) abschreiben; (cheque) ausstellen; ~ **up** vt schreiben; **~-off** n: **it is a ~-off** das kann man abschreiben; **~r** n Schriftsteller m.
writhe [raɪð] vi sich winden.
writing ['raɪtɪŋ] n (act) Schreiben nt; (hand~) (Hand)schrift f; **in ~** schriftlich; **~ paper** n Schreibpapier nt.
written ['rɪtn] pp of **write**.
wrong [rɒŋ] a (incorrect) falsch; (morally) unrecht; **he was ~ in doing that** es war nicht recht von ihm, das zu tun; **you are ~ about that, you've got it ~** da hast du unrecht; **be in the ~** im Unrecht sein; **what's ~ with your leg?** was ist mit deinem Bein los?; **to go ~** (plan) schiefgehen; (person) einen Fehler machen // n Unrecht nt // vt Unrecht tun (+dat); **~ful** a unrechtmäßig; **~ly** ad falsch; (accuse) zu Unrecht.
wrote [rəʊt] pt of **write**.
wrought [rɔːt] a: ~ **iron** n Schmiedeeisen nt.
wrung [rʌŋ] pt, pp of **wring**.
wry [raɪ] a ironisch.
wt. abbr of **weight**.

X

Xmas ['eksməs] n abbr of **Christmas**.
X-ray ['eks'reɪ] n Röntgenaufnahme f // vt röntgen; **~s** npl Rontgenstrahlen pl.

Y

yacht [jɒt] n Jacht f; **~ing** n (Sport)segeln nt; **~sman** n Sportsegler m.
Yank [jæŋk], **Yankee** ['jæŋkɪ] n (col) Ami m.
yap [jæp] vi (dog) kläffen.
yard [jɑːd] n Hof m; (measure) (englische) Elle f, Yard nt, 0,91 m; **~stick** n (fig) Maßstab m.
yarn [jɑːn] n (thread) Garn nt; (story) (Seemanns)garn nt.
yawn [jɔːn] n Gähnen nt // vi gähnen; **~ing** a (gap) gähnend.
yd. abbr of **yard(s)**.
yeah [jeə] ad (col) ja.
year [jɪə*] n Jahr nt; **be 8 ~s old** acht Jahre alt sein; **an eight-~-old child** ein achtjähriges Kind; **~ly** a, ad jährlich.
yearn [jɜːn] vi sich sehnen (for nach); **~ing** n Verlangen nt, Sehnsucht f.
yeast [jiːst] n Hefe f.
yell [jel] n gellende(r) Schrei m // vi laut schreien.
yellow ['jeləʊ] a gelb // n Gelb nt.
yelp [jelp] n Gekläff nt // vi kläffen.
yeoman ['jəʊmən] n: **Y~ of the Guard** Leibgardist m.
yes [jes] ad ja // n Ja nt, Jawort nt; **to say/answer ~** ja sagen/mit Ja antworten.
yesterday ['jestədeɪ] ad gestern // n Gestern nt; ~ **morning/evening** gestern morgen/abend; **all day ~** gestern den ganzen Tag; **the day before ~** vorgestern.
yet [jet] ad noch; (in question) schon; (up to now) bis jetzt; **it is not finished ~** es ist noch nicht fertig; **the best ~** das bisher beste; **as ~** bis jetzt; (in past) bis dahin // cj doch, dennoch.
yew [juː] n Eibe f.
yield [jiːld] n Ertrag m // vt (result, crop) hervorbringen; (interest, profit) abwerfen; (concede) abtreten // vi nachgeben; (MIL) sich ergeben, '~' (US AUT) 'Vorfahrt gewähren'.
YMCA n abbr (= Young Men's Christian Association) CVJM m.
yoga ['jəʊgə] n Joga m.
yog(h)ourt, **yog(h)urt** ['jɒgət] n Joghurt m.
yoke [jəʊk] n (lit, fig) Joch nt.
yolk [jəʊk] n Eidotter m, Eigelb nt.
yonder ['jɒndə*] ad dort drüben, da drüben // a jene(r, s) dort.

you [ju:] *pron* **1** (*subject, in comparisons: German familiar form: sing*) du; (: *pl*) ihr; (*in letters also*) Du, Ihr; (: *German polite form*) Sie; ~ **Germans** ihr Deutschen; **she's younger than** ~ sie ist jünger als du/Sie **2** (*direct object, after prep + acc: German familiar form: sing*) dich; (: *pl*) euch; (*in letters also*) Dich, Euch; (: *German polite form*) Sie; **I know** ~ ich kenne dich/euch/Sie. **3** (*indirect object, after prep + dat: German familiar form: sing*) dir; (: *pl*) euch (*in letters also*) Dir, Euch; (: *German polite form*) Ihnen; **I gave it to** ~ ich gab es dir/euch/Ihnen **4** (*impersonal: one: subject*) man; (: *direct object*) einen; (: *indirect object*) einem; **fresh air does** ~ **good** frische Luft tut gut.

you'd [ju:d] = **you had; you would.**

you'll [ju:l] = **you will, you shall.**

young [jʌŋ] *a* jung // *npl* die Jungen; ~**ish** *a* ziemlich jung; ~**ster** *n* Junge *m*, junge(r) Bursche *m*/junge(s) Mädchen *nt*.

your [jɔ:*] *poss a* (*familiar: sing*) dein; (: *pl*) euer, eure *pl*; (*polite*) Ihr; *see also* **my.**

you're ['juə*] = **you are.**

yours [jɔ:z] *poss pron* (*familiar: sing*) deine(r, s); (: *pl*) eure(r, s); (*polite*) Ihre(r, s); ~ **sincerely/faithfully** mit freundlichen Grüßen; *see also* **mine.**

yourself [jɔ:'self] *pron* (*emphatic*) selbst; (*familiar: sing*) (*acc*) dich (selbst); (*dat*) dir (selbst); (: *pl*) euch (selbst); (*polite*) sich (selbst); *see also* **oneself.**

youth [ju:θ] *n* Jugend *f*; (*young man*) junge(r) Mann *m*; ~**s** *pl* Jugendliche *pl*; ~ **club** *n* Jugendzentrum *nt*; ~**ful** *a* jugendlich; ~ **hostel** *n* Jugendherberge *f*.

you've [ju:v] = **you have.**

YTS *n abbr* (*Brit: = Youth Training Scheme*) staatliches Förderprogramm für arbeitslose Jugendliche.

Yugoslav ['ju:gəu'slɑ:v] *a* jugoslawisch // *n* Jugoslawe *m*, Jugoslawin *f*.

Yugoslavia ['ju:gəu'slɑ:vɪə] *n* Jugoslawien *nt*.

YWCA *n abbr* (= *Young Women's Christian Association*) CVJF *m*.

Z

zap [zæp] *vt* (*COMPUT*) löschen.

zeal [zi:l] *n* Eifer *m*; ~**ous** ['zeləs] *a* eifrig.

zebra ['zi:brə] *n* Zebra *nt*; ~ **crossing** ['zi:brə'krɒsɪŋ] *n* (*Brit*) Zebrastreifen *m*.

zero ['zɪərəu] *n* Null *f*; (*on scale*) Nullpunkt *m*.

zest [zest] *n* Begeisterung *f*.

zigzag ['zɪgzæg] *n* Zickzack *m*.

zip [zɪp] *n* (*also:* ~ **fastener,** (*US*) ~**per**) Reißverschluß *m* // *vt* (*also:* ~ **up**) den Reißverschluß zumachen (+*gen*); ~ **code** *n* (*US*) Postleitzahl *f*.

zodiac ['zəudɪæk] *n* Tierkreis *m*.

zombie ['zɒmbɪ] *n*: **like a** ~ (*fig*) wie im Tran.

zoo [zu:] *n* Zoo *m*.

zoology [zəu'ɒlədʒɪ] *n* Zoologie *f*.

zoom [zu:m] *vi*: **to** ~ **past** vorbeisausen; ~ **lens** *n* Zoomobjektiv *nt*.

zucchini [zu:'ki:nɪ] *npl* (*US: courgettes*) Zucchini *f*.

GERMAN IRREGULAR VERBS

*with 'sein'

infinitive	present indicative (2nd, 3rd sing.)	preterite	past participle
aufschrecken*	schrickst auf, schrickt auf	schrak or schreckte auf	aufgeschreckt
ausbedingen	bedingst aus, bedingt aus	bedang or bedingte aus	ausbedungen
backen	bäckst, bäckt	backte or buk	gebacken
befehlen	befiehlst, befiehlt	befahl	befohlen
beginnen	beginnst, beginnt	begann	begonnen
beißen	beißt, beißt	biß	gebissen
bergen	birgst, birgt	barg	geborgen
bersten*	birst, birst	barst	geborsten
bescheißen*	bescheißt, bescheißt	beschiß	beschissen
bewegen	bewegst, bewegt	bewog	bewogen
biegen	biegst, biegt	bog	gebogen
bieten	bietest, bietet	bot	geboten
binden	bindest, bindet	band	gebunden
bitten	bittest, bittet	bat	gebeten
blasen	bläst, bläst	blies	geblasen
bleiben*	bleibst, bleibt	blieb	geblieben
braten	brätst, brät	briet	gebraten
brechen*	brichst, bricht	brach	gebrochen
brennen	brennst, brennt	brannte	gebrannt
bringen	bringst, bringt	brachte	gebracht
denken	denkst, denkt	dachte	gedacht
dreschen	drisch(e)st, drischt	drasch	gedroschen
dringen*	dringst, dringt	drang	gedrungen
dürfen	darfst, darf	durfte	gedurft
empfehlen	empfiehlst, empfiehlt	empfahl	empfohlen
erbleichen*	erbleichst, erbleicht	erbleichte	erblichen
erlöschen*	erlischt, erlischt	erlosch	erloschen
erschrecken*	erschrickst, erschrickt	erschrak	erschrocken
essen	ißt, ißt	aß	gegessen
fahren*	fährst, fährt	fuhr	gefahren
fallen*	fällst, fällt	fiel	gefallen
fangen	fängst, fängt	fing	gefangen
fechten	fichtst, ficht	focht	gefochten
finden	findest, findet	fand	gefunden
flechten	flichtst, flicht	flocht	geflochten
fliegen*	fliegst, fliegt	flog	geflogen
fliehen*	fliehst, flieht	floh	geflohen
fließen*	fließt, fließt	floß	geflossen
fressen	frißt, frißt	fraß	gefressen
frieren	frierst, friert	fror	gefroren
gären*	gärst, gärt	gor	gegoren
gebären	gebierst, gebiert	gebar	geboren
geben	gibst, gibt	gab	gegeben
gedeihen*	gedeihst, gedeiht	gedieh	gediehen
gehen*	gehst, geht	ging	gegangen
gelingen*	——, gelingt	gelang	gelungen
gelten	giltst, gilt	galt	gegolten
genesen*	gene(se)st, genest	genas	genesen
genießen	genießt, genießt	genoß	genossen
geraten*	gerätst, gerät	geriet	geraten
geschehen*	——, geschieht	geschah	geschehen

infinitive	present indicative (2nd, 3rd sing.)	preterite	past participle
gewinnen	gewinnst, gewinnt	gewann	gewonnen
gießen	gießt, gießt	goß	gegossen
gleichen	gleichst, gleicht	glich	geglichen
gleiten*	gleitest, gleitet	glitt	geglitten
glimmen	glimmst, glimmt	glomm	geglommen
graben	gräbst, gräbt	grub	gegraben
greifen	greifst, greift	griff	gegriffen
haben	hast, hat	hatte	gehabt
halten	hältst, hält	hielt	gehalten
hängen	hängst, hängt	hing	gehangen
hauen	haust, haut	haute	gehauen
heben	hebst, hebt	hob	gehoben
heißen	heißt, heißt	hieß	geheißen
helfen	hilfst, hilft	half	geholfen
kennen	kennst, kennt	kannte	gekannt
klimmen*	klimmst, klimmt	klomm	geklommen
klingen	klingst, klingt	klang	geklungen
kneifen	kneifst, kneift	kniff	gekniffen
kommen*	kommst, kommt	kam	gekommen
können	kannst, kann	konnte	gekonnt
kriechen*	kriechst, kriecht	kroch	gekrochen
laden	lädst, lädt	lud	geladen
lassen	läßt, läßt	ließ	gelassen
laufen*	läufst, läuft	lief	gelaufen
leiden	leidest, leidet	litt	gelitten
leihen	leihst, leiht	lieh	geliehen
lesen	liest, liest	las	gelesen
liegen*	liegst, liegt	lag	gelegen
lügen	lügst, lügt	log	gelogen
mahlen	mahlst, mahlt	mahlte	gemahlen
meiden	meidest, meidet	mied	gemieden
melken	melkst, melkt	melkte	gemolken
messen	mißt, mißt	maß	gemessen
mißlingen*	——, mißlingt	mißlang	mißlungen
mögen	magst, mag	mochte	gemocht
müssen	mußt, muß	mußte	gemußt
nehmen	nimmst, nimmt	nahm	genommen
nennen	nennst, nennt	nannte	genannt
pfeifen	pfeifst, pfeift	pfiff	gepfiffen
preisen	preist, preist	pries	gepriesen
quellen*	quillst, quillt	quoll	gequollen
raten	rätst, rät	riet	geraten
reiben	reibst, reibt	rieb	gerieben
reißen*	reißt, reißt	riß	gerissen
reiten*	reitest, reitet	ritt	geritten
rennen*	rennst, rennt	rannte	gerannt
riechen	riechst, riecht	roch	gerochen
ringen	ringst, ringt	rang	gerungen
rinnen*	rinnst, rinnt	rann	geronnen
rufen	rufst, ruft	rief	gerufen
salzen	salzt, salzt	salzte	gesalzen
saufen	säufst, säuft	soff	gesoffen
saugen	saugst, saugt	sog	gesogen
schaffen	schaffst, schafft	schuf	geschaffen
scheiden	scheidest, scheidet	schied	geschieden
scheinen	scheinst, scheint	schien	geschienen
schelten	schiltst, schilt	schalt	gescholten

infinitive	present indicative (2nd, 3rd sing.)	preterite	past participle
scheren	scherst, schert	schor	geschoren
schieben	schiebst, schiebt	schob	geschoben
schießen	schießt, schießt	schoß	geschossen
schinden	schindest, schindet	schindete	geschunden
schlafen	schläfst, schläft	schlief	geschlafen
schlagen	schlägst, schlägt	schlug	geschlagen
schleichen*	schleichst, schleicht	schlich	geschlichen
schleifen	schleifst, schleift	schliff	geschliffen
schließen	schließt, schließt	schloß	geschlossen
schlingen	schlingst, schlingt	schlang	geschlungen
schmeißen	schmeißt, schmeißt	schmiß	geschmissen
schmelzen*	schmilzt, schmilzt	schmolz	geschmolzen
schneiden	schneidest, schneidet	schnitt	geschnitten
schreiben	schreibst, schreibt	schrieb	geschrieben
schreien	schreist, schreit	schrie	geschrie(e)n
schreiten	schreitest, schreitet	schritt	geschritten
schweigen	schweigst, schweigt	schwieg	geschwiegen
schwellen*	schwillst, schwillt	schwoll	geschwollen
schwimmen*	schwimmst, schwimmt	schwamm	geschwommen
schwinden*	schwindest, schwindet	schwand	geschwunden
schwingen	schwingst, schwingt	schwang	geschwungen
schwören	schwörst, schwört	schwor	geschworen
sehen	siehst, sieht	sah	gesehen
sein*	bist, ist	war	gewesen
senden	sendest, sendet	sandte	gesandt
singen	singst, singt	sang	gesungen
sinken*	sinkst, sinkt	sank	gesunken
sinnen	sinnst, sinnt	sann	gesonnen
sitzen*	sitzt, sitzt	saß	gesessen
sollen	sollst, soll	sollte	gesollt
speien	speist, speit	spie	gespie(e)n
spinnen	spinnst, spinnt	spann	gesponnen
sprechen	sprichst, spricht	sprach	gesprochen
sprießen*	sprießt, sprießt	sproß	gesprossen
springen*	springst, springt	sprang	gesprungen
stechen	stichst, sticht	stach	gestochen
stecken	steckst, steckt	steckte or stak	gesteckt
stehen	stehst, steht	stand	gestanden
stehlen	stiehlst, stiehlt	stahl	gestohlen
steigen*	steigst, steigt	stieg	gestiegen
sterben*	stirbst, stirbt	starb	gestorben
stinken	stinkst, stinkt	stank	gestunken
stoßen	stößt, stößt	stieß	gestoßen
streichen	streichst, streicht	strich	gestrichen
streiten*	streitest, streitet	stritt	gestritten
tragen	trägst, trägt	trug	getragen
treffen	triffst, trifft	traf	getroffen
treiben*	treibst, treibt	trieb	getrieben
treten*	trittst, tritt	trat	getreten
trinken	trinkst, trinkt	trank	getrunken
trügen	trügst, trügt	trog	getrogen
tun	tust, tut	tat	getan
verderben	verdirbst, verdirbt	verdarb	verdorben
verdrießen	verdrießt, verdrießt	verdroß	verdrossen
vergessen	vergißt, vergißt	vergaß	vergessen
verlieren	verlierst, verliert	verlor	verloren

infinitive	present indicative (2nd, 3rd sing.)	preterite	past participle
verschleißen	verschleißt, verschleißt	verschliß	verschlissen
wachsen*	wächst, wächst	wuchs	gewachsen
wägen	wägst, wägt	wog	gewogen
waschen	wäschst, wäscht	wusch	gewaschen
weben	webst, webt	webte or wob	gewoben
weichen*	weichst, weicht	wich	gewichen
weisen	weist, weist	wies	gewiesen
wenden	wendest, wendet	wandte	gewandt
werben	wirbst, wirbt	warb	geworben
werden*	wirst, wird	wurde	geworden
werfen*	wirfst, wirft	warf	geworfen
wiegen	wiegst, wiegt	wog	gewogen
winden	windest, windet	wand	gewunden
wissen	weißt, weiß	wußte	gewußt
wollen	willst, will	wollte	gewollt
wringen	wringst, wringt	wrang	gewrungen
zeihen	zeihst, zeiht	zieh	geziehen
ziehen*	ziehst, zieht	zog	gezogen
zwingen	zwingst, zwingt	zwang	gezwungen

UNREGELMÄSSIGE ENGLISCHE VERBEN

present	pt	pp	present	pt	pp
arise	arose	arisen	**fling**	flung	flung
awake	awoke	awaked	**fly (flies)**	flew	flown
be (am, is,	was, were	been	**forbid**	forbade	forbidden
are; being)			**forecast**	forecast	forecast
bear	bore	born(e)	**forego**	forewent	foregone
beat	beat	beaten	**foresee**	foresaw	foreseen
become	became	become	**foretell**	foretold	foretold
begin	began	begun	**forget**	forgot	forgotten
behold	beheld	beheld	**forgive**	forgave	forgiven
bend	bent	bent	**forsake**	forsook	forsaken
beseech	besought	besought	**freeze**	froze	frozen
beset	beset	beset	**get**	got	got, (US) gotten
bet	bet, betted	bet, betted	**give**	gave	given
bid	bid, bade	bid, bidden	**go (goes)**	went	gone
bind	bound	bound	**grind**	ground	ground
bite	bit	bitten	**grow**	grew	grown
bleed	bled	bled	**hang**	hung,	hung, hanged
blow	blew	blown		hanged	
break	broke	broken	**have (has;**	had	had
breed	bred	bred	**having)**		
bring	brought	brought	**hear**	heard	heard
build	built	built	**hide**	hid	hidden
burn	burnt,	burnt, burned	**hit**	hit	hit
	burned		**hold**	held	held
burst	burst	burst	**hurt**	hurt	hurt
buy	bought	bought	**keep**	kept	kept
can	could	(been able)	**kneel**	knelt,	knelt, kneeled
cast	cast	cast		kneeled	
catch	caught	caught	**know**	knew	known
choose	chose	chosen	**lay**	laid	laid
cling	clung	clung	**lead**	led	led
come	came	come	**lean**	leant,	leant, leaned
cost	cost	cost		leaned	
creep	crept	crept	**leap**	leapt,	leapt, leaped
cut	cut	cut		leaped	
deal	dealt	dealt	**learn**	learnt,	learnt, learned
dig	dug	dug		learned	
do (3rd	did	done	**leave**	left	left
person:			**lend**	lent	lent
he/she/it			**let**	let	let
does)			**lie (lying)**	lay	lain
draw	drew	drawn	**light**	lit, lighted	lit, lighted
dream	dreamed,	dreamed,	**lose**	lost	lost
	dreamt	dreamt	**make**	made	made
drink	drank	drunk	**may**	might	—
drive	drove	driven	**mean**	meant	meant
dwell	dwelt	dwelt	**meet**	met	met
eat	ate	eaten	**mistake**	mistook	mistaken
fall	fell	fallen	**mow**	mowed	mown, mowed
feed	fed	fed	**must**	(had to)	(had to)
feel	felt	felt	**pay**	paid	paid
fight	fought	fought	**put**	put	put
find	found	found	**quit**	quit, quitted	quit, quitted
flee	fled	fled	**read**	read	read

present	pt	pp	present	pt	pp
rid	rid	rid	split	split	split
ride	rode	ridden	spoil	spoiled, spoilt	spoiled, spoilt
ring	rang	rung			
rise	rose	risen	spread	spread	spread
run	ran	run	spring	sprang	sprung
saw	sawed	sawn	stand	stood	stood
say	said	said	steal	stole	stolen
see	saw	seen	stick	stuck	stuck
seek	sought	sought	sting	stung	stung
sell	sold	sold	stink	stank	stunk
send	sent	sent	stride	strode	stridden
set	set	set	strike	struck	struck, stricken
shake	shook	shaken	strive	strove	striven
shall	should	—	swear	swore	sworn
shear	sheared	shorn, sheared	sweep	swept	swept
shed	shed	shed	swell	swelled	swollen, swelled
shine	shone	shone	swim	swam	swum
shoot	shot	shot	swing	swung	swung
show	showed	shown	take	took	taken
shrink	shrank	shrunk	teach	taught	taught
shut	shut	shut	tear	tore	torn
sing	sang	sung	tell	told	told
sink	sank	sunk	think	thought	thought
sit	sat	sat	throw	threw	thrown
slay	slew	slain	thrust	thrust	thrust
sleep	slept	slept	tread	trod	trodden
slide	slid	slid	wake	woke, waked	woken, waked
sling	slung	slung			
slit	slit	slit	waylay	waylaid	waylaid
smell	smelt, smelled	smelt, smelled	wear	wore	worn
			weave	wove, weaved	woven, weaved
sow	sowed	sown, sowed			
speak	spoke	spoken	wed	wedded, wed	wedded, wed
speed	sped, speeded	sped, speeded			
			weep	wept	wept
spell	spelt, spelled	spelt, spelled	win	won	won
			wind	wound	wound
spend	spent	spent	withdraw	withdrew	withdrawn
spill	spilt, spilled	spilt, spilled	withhold	withheld	withheld
			withstand	withstood	withstood
spin	spun	spun	wring	wrung	wrung
spit	spat	spat	write	wrote	written

NUMMER

NUMBERS

ein(s)	1	one	
zwei	2	two	
drei	3	three	
vier	4	four	
fünf	5	five	
sechs	6	six	
sieben	7	seven	
acht	8	eight	
neun	9	nine	
zehn	10	ten	
elf	11	eleven	
zwölf	12	twelve	
dreizehn	13	thirteen	
vierzehn	14	fourteen	
fünfzehn	15	fifteen	
sechzehn	16	sixteen	
siebzehn	17	seventeen	
achtzehn	18	eighteen	
neunzehn	19	nineteen	
zwanzig	20	twenty	
einundzwanzig	21	twenty-one	
zweiundzwanzig	22	twenty-two	
dreißig	30	thirty	
vierzig	40	forty	
fünfzig	50	fifty	
sechzig	60	sixty	
siebzig	70	seventy	
achtzig	80	eighty	
neunzig	90	ninety	
hundert	100	a hundred	
hunderteins	101	a hundred and one	
zweihundert	200	two hundred	
zweihunderteins	201	two hundred and one	
dreihundert	300	three hundred	
dreihunderteins	301	three hundred and one	
tausend	1000	a thousand	
tausend (und) eins	1001	a thousand and one	
fünftausend	5000	five thousand	
eine Million	1000000	a million	
erste(r,s)	1.	first	1st
zweite(r,s)	2.	second	2nd
dritte(r,s)	3.	third	3rd
vierte(r,s)	4.	fourth	4th
fünfte(r,s)	5.	fifth	5th
sechste(r,s)	6.	sixth	6th
siebte(r,s)	7.	seventh	7th
achte(r,s)	8.	eighth	8th
neunte(r,s)	9.	ninth	9th
zehnte(r,s)	10.	tenth	10th

elfte(r,s)	11.	eleventh	11th
zwölfte(r,s)	12.	twelfth	12th
dreizehnte(r,s)	13.	thirteenth	13th
vierzehnte(r,s)	14.	fourteenth	14th
fünfzehnte(r,s)	15.	fifteenth	15th
sechzehnte(r,s)	16.	sixteenth	16th
siebzehnte(r,s)	17.	seventeenth	17th
achtzehnte(r,s)	18.	eighteenth	18th
neunzehnte(r,s)	19.	nineteenth	19th
zwanzigste(r,s)	20.	twentieth	20th
einundzwanzigste(r,s)	21.	twenty-first	21st
dreißigste(r,s)	30.	thirtieth	30th
hundertste(r,s)	100.	hundredth	100th
hunderterste(r,s)	101.	hundred-and-first	101st
tausendste(r,s)	1000.	thousandth	1000th

Bruche usw.

Fractions etc.

ein Halb	½	a half	
ein Drittel	⅓	a third	
ein Viertel	¼	a quarter	
ein Fünftel	⅕	a fifth	
null Komma fünf	0,5	(nought) point five	0.5
drei Komma vier	3,4	three point four	3.4
sechs Komma acht neun	6,89	six point eight nine	6.89
zehn Prozent	10%	ten per cent	
hundert Prozent	100%	a hundred per cent	

Beispiele

Examples

er wohnt in Nummer 10
es steht in Kapitel 7
auf Seite 7
er wohnt im 7. Stock
er wurde 7.
im Maßstab eins zu
   zwanzigtausend

he lives at number 10
it's in chapter 7
on page 7
he lives on the 7th floor
he came in 7th
scale one to twenty thousand